THE
MAKING
OF THE
ANCIENT
GREEK
ECONOMY

THE
MAKING
OF THE
ANCIENT
GREEK
ECONOMY

INSTITUTIONS, MARKETS,
AND GROWTH IN THE
CITY-STATES

ALAIN BRESSON

Translated by Steven Rendall

PRINCETON UNIVERSITY PRESS
PRINCETON AND OXFORD

PRESS.PRINCETON.EDU

Ouvrage publié avec le concours du Ministère français chargé de la Culture—Centre national du
Livre.

This book is published with support from the French Ministry for Culture—National Book Center.

Jacket art courtesy of *Historic Ornaments and Designs CD-Rom and Book*, ©2003 by
Dover Publications, Inc.

Library of Congress Cataloging-in-Publication Data
Bresson, Alain.

[L'économie de la Grèce des cités. English]
The making of the ancient Greek economy : institutions, markets, and growth in the city-states /
Alain Bresson ; translated by Steven Rendall. — Expanded and updated English edition.
pages cm
Originally published in 2 vols.: Paris : Armand Colin, c2007 and c2008.
Includes bibliographical references and index.
ISBN 978-0-691-14470-2 (hardback : alkaline paper) — ISBN 978-1-4008-5245-1
(e-book)   1. Greece—Economic conditions—To 146 B.C.   2. Urban economics.   3. Cities and
towns, Ancient—Greece.   I. Rendall, Steven, translator.   II. Title.
HC37.B7413 2015
330.938—dc23
2015017835

British Library Cataloging-in-Publication Data is available

This book was originally published in France, Armand Colin, Publishers

This book has been composed in Adobe Jenson Pro

Printed on acid-free paper. ∞

Printed in the United States of America

1 3 5 7 9 10 8 6 4 2

CONTENTS

EXPANDED CONTENTS   VII
LIST OF FIGURES   XV
LIST OF TABLES   XVII
INTRODUCTION   XXI

I   The Economy of Ancient Greece: A Conceptual Framework   1

Structures and Production

II   People in Their Environment   31
III   Energy, Economy, and Transport Cost   71
IV   The *Polis* and the Economy   96
V   Agricultural Production   118
VI   The Economy of the Agricultural World   142
VII   Nonagricultural Production, Capital, and Innovation   175
VIII   The Logic of Growth   199

Market and Trade

IX   The Institutions of the Domestic Market   225
X   Money and Credit   260
XI   City-States, Taxes, and Trade   286
XII   The *Emporion* and the Markets   306
XIII   International Trade Networks   339
XIV   Strategies of International Trade   381
XV   The Greek Cities and the Market   415

APPENDIX: WEIGHTS, MEASURES, AND CURRENCY UNITS   439
ABBREVIATIONS   443
NOTES   449
SOURCES   531
BIBLIOGRAPHY   535
INDEX   603

EXPANDED
CONTENTS

I

THE ECONOMY OF ANCIENT GREECE: A CONCEPTUAL FRAMEWORK   *1*

The Universe of Economic Theory   2

  Primitivism or Modernism?   2
  The German Historical School of Political Economy   4
  Classical and Neoclassical Economists   5
  Economics and Scientific Discourse   7
  Moses I. Finley and Max Weber   8
  Institutional Analysis and Karl Polanyi   11
  The Economy of Antiquity after Moses Finley   13

New Institutional Economics and the Economy of Antiquity   15

  Homo economicus *Facing His Critics*   16
  New Institutional Economics (NIE) and the Transaction Costs Theory   19
  Constrained Choices, Limited Rationality, and Economic Performance   22
  The Genesis and Evolution of Institutions   25

STRUCTURES AND PRODUCTION

II

PEOPLE IN THEIR ENVIRONMENT   *31*

The Ecological Framework   *31*
  The Constraints Imposed by Topography and Soils   *32*

Topography	33
The Climatic Constraint	35
The Variability of the Climate and Vegetation	39
The Demographic Model of Ancient Greece	41
Fertility	42
Mortality	43
Demographic Structures and the Potential for Expansion	49
Sex Ratio Imbalance, Birth Control, and Infanticide	51
The Dynamics of Population	54
Numbers	54
Population Trends	56
The Ecological Environment and Population	64
The Variability of Climate	64
Demographic Crises and Famine	66

III

ENERGY, ECONOMY, AND TRANSPORT COST 71

The Logic of Energy	72
Sources of Heat	72
The Cost of Energy and the Fate of the Steam Engine	75
Wind, Connectivity, and Transport Costs	79
Roads and Overland Transport	81
Maritime Transport and Ships	84
Maritime Transport and Ports	84
Techniques of Navigation and Ports	88
Attempts to Dig Canals and Build Portage Routes	91

IV

THE *POLIS* AND THE ECONOMY 96

From the Bronze Age Crisis to the Archaic Revival	97
Tax Rates, the Market, and the Status of Land in Ancient Greece	102
Tax Rates	102
The City and the Economy	105
Royal Land and Civic Land	110

V

AGRICULTURAL PRODUCTION   *118*

The Mediterranean Trilogy   119

   Grain   119
   Grapes   122
   Olives   127

Complementary Products   129

Animal Husbandry   132

   The Debate on "Pastoralism"   132
   Constraints in Animal Husbandry   133
   Regional Types   135
   Rangeland Ecology and Management   138

VI

THE ECONOMY OF THE
AGRICULTURAL WORLD   *142*

The Structures of Real Property   142

   The Distribution of Property   142
   The Size of the Estates   149
   Access to Land and Farming Systems   152

Permanence, Risk, and Changes   157

   Uncertainty, Risk, and the Choice of Products   157
   Tradition and Innovation in Agriculture and in Animal Husbandry   161
   The Increase in the Area Cultivated   164
   Economic Choices and Yield Increases   166
   Changes in Agriculture and the Market   170

VII

NONAGRICULTURAL PRODUCTION,
CAPITAL, AND INNOVATION   *175*

Fish Production and Consumption   175

   Fish in the Ancient Greek World: A Reassessment   176
   Salt and Salting   180

The Greek Cities and Their Coastal Waters   181
Fish Trade and Fish Consumption   184

Artisanal Trades   187

The Diversity of Trades   187
The Case of Textile Manufacturing   190

Capital and Technological Innovation   194

VIII

THE LOGIC OF GROWTH   199

Self-Consumption and Growth   199

Self-Consumption and the Market   199
The Question of Growth   203

The Problem of the "Failure of Ancient Civilization"   206

Innovation   208

The Pace and Spread of Innovation   208
Supply, Demand, and the Time of Innovation   211

Modernity or Phases of Progress?   219

MARKET AND TRADE

IX

THE INSTITUTIONS OF THE
DOMESTIC MARKET   225

Private Property   225

Private Property and Trade   225
Law Relating to Transactions   230

The World of the Agora   234

The Agora as a Legal Space   234
The Agora in the City-State, Local Agoras, and Temporary Markets   236
Buying and Selling in the Agora   238

Legal Constraints on the Agora   239

The Supervision of Transactions   239
Supervision of Contracts and Production   244
The Authority of the Agoranomoi   246

Informational Asymmetry and Guarantee of Sales   250

Legal Constraints and Informational Asymmetry   250
Informational Asymmetry in the Agora and the City's Response   252

Price Control Policies   254

Market Supply and Price Control   255
The Option of Fixed Prices   257

X

MONEY AND CREDIT   260

Money and Trade in the World of the Greek City-States   261

Precious Metals and Monetary Instruments   261
The Rise of Coinage   264
Having or Not Having Coined Money   265
Money as an Institution   271
Minting and the Use of Money   274
Coined Money and Economic Growth   276

Credit   278

Forms of Credit in Ancient Greece   278
Maritime Loans   280

XI

CITY-STATES, TAXES, AND TRADE   286

Supervision of Foreign Trade   286

Supervision of Trade and Customs Duties   286
Monitoring and Privileges   288

The Sea, Taxes, and the Market   293

Taxes, Transit Fees, and the "Race to the Sea"   293
Tax and Trade   297

Economic Information and Security of Trade   299

Circulation of Information and the Uncertainty of Economic Decisions   299
The Security of International Trade   302

XII

THE *EMPORION* AND THE MARKETS   306

The *Emporion*   306
   The City's Supervision of Foreign Trade   307
   The Deigma   309
   The Rules of the Emporion   313
Commercial Courts   317
   The City-States' Principles of Justice   317
   Trials Concerning Large-Scale Trade   322
Supplying the Market and Prices   325
   The Policy of Price Control   325
   Grain Purchase Funds and the Regulation of Sales   332

XIII

INTERNATIONAL TRADE NETWORKS   339

Trade and the International Division of Labor   339
   Conceptions of Ancient Political Theorists   339
   Ancient Questionings   341
   The Theory of International Trade   343
   The International Division of Labor and Gains in Productivity   345
   Center and Periphery: The Model   348
Trade Flows   351
   Consumption, Production, and Prices   351
   Metals   352
   Textiles   353
Markets in Networks and Systems of Exchange   358
   Trade Networks and Niches   358
   Hermione's Trade   361
   Regional Supply and Long-Distance Trade   364
   Networks and "Free Riders"   368
   International Trade Networks   374
   Actors in Trade and Redistribution Centers   376

XIV

STRATEGIES OF INTERNATIONAL TRADE *381*

The Logic of Trade 382

Mutual Trade and Nondirectional Trade 382
Grain Buyers 384

Control over Grain Trade 393

Trade Prohibitions and Grain Supplies 393
The Grain Supply: Free Sale, Forced Sale, and Civic Taxes 395
The Grain Supply: The Royal Contributions 399

The Grain Policy of Athens and the Aegean Cities' Food Supply 402

The Prohibition of Exports and the Logic of Trade 402
Importers and Suppliers of Grain 409

XV

THE GREEK CITIES AND THE MARKET *415*

Cities, Markets, and Prices 416

Center and Periphery: Historical Development 416
Predation, Economic Space, and Political Space 418
Prices and Market Integration 422

Markets: Supply, Demand, and Nash Equilibrium 427

In Perspective: The Medieval and Early Modern European Markets 427
Uncertainty, Risk Management, and the "Imperfect Market" 429
Institutional Constraints and Nash Equilibrium 434

FIGURES

Figure 1.1	Map of Greece.	xviii–xix
Figure 2.1.	Relief map of Greece.	34
Figure 2.2.	Temperature and precipitation in Athens and Ioannina (Epeiros).	36
Figure 2.3.	Map of precipitation.	37
Figure 2.4.	Diagram of precipitation (between Elis in the west and the Keramic Gulf in the east).	38
Figure 10.1.	Main cities that coined silver ca. 500 BCE.	265
Figure 12.1.	Indexed prices of wood and pigs in Delos, 274–169 BCE.	327
Figure 12.2.	Prices of olive oil and of the rents of the farm of Phytalia, 290–179 BCE.	328
Figure 13.1.	Distribution of tiles stamped *Tumnia* (third century BCE).	366
Figure 14.1.	Map of grain imports from Cyrene in the early 320s BCE.	412
Figure 14.2.	Distribution of grain imports from Cyrene in the early 320s BCE.	413
Figure 15.1.	The production of Attic tetradrachms from 164/3 to 90/89 BCE (number of dies per period of five years).	426
Figure 15.2.	The production of Attic tetradrachms from 164/3 to 90/89 BCE (moving average of the production of dies on a three-year basis).	427

TABLES

Table 2.1.   Temperature (°C) and precipitation (mm) in Athens.   36
Table 2.2.   Temperature (°C) and precipitation (mm) in Ioannina
             (Epeiros).   36
Table 2.3.   Number of sites by region.   59
Table 2.4.   Probability of precipitation in Athens, Melos, and Thera.   65
Table 2.5.   Index of the growth of trees in 1873–1874 in Keskin District
             (in percentage of annual growth).   66
Table 3.1.   Cargo capacity of the largest ships attested by shipwrecks.   87
Table 6.1.   Distribution of landholdings in Attika.   144
Table 6.2.   Distribution of estate types in Attic boundary stones.   156
Table 10.1. Ratio of value among metals during the Classical period.   262
Table 13.1. Comparative productivity before and after specialization
             (in hours worked).   344
Table 13.2. Comparative transport costs.   365
Table 13.3. Deliveries of Attic ceramics in Etruria.   372
Table 14.1. Grain production in Attika and its external possessions:
             gross.   406
Table 14.2. Grain production in Attika and its external possessions:
             percentage.   407
Table 14.3. Ancient and modern grain production in Attika.   408
Table 14.4. Estimate of sources of grain of Athens in the mid-fourth
             century BCE.   411

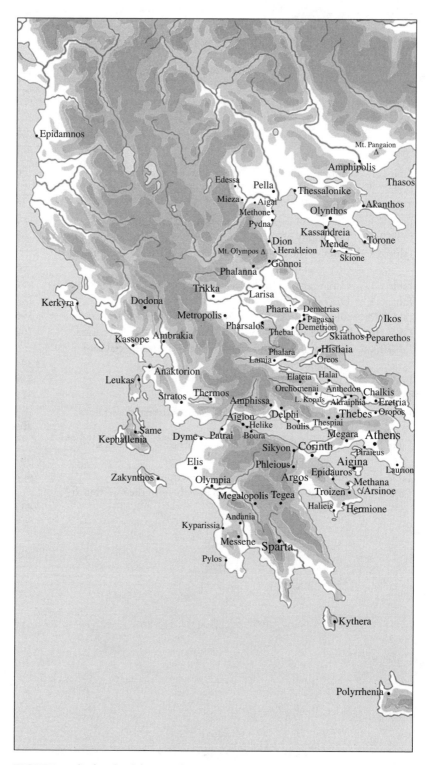

FIGURE 1.1 (Left and right). Map of Greece

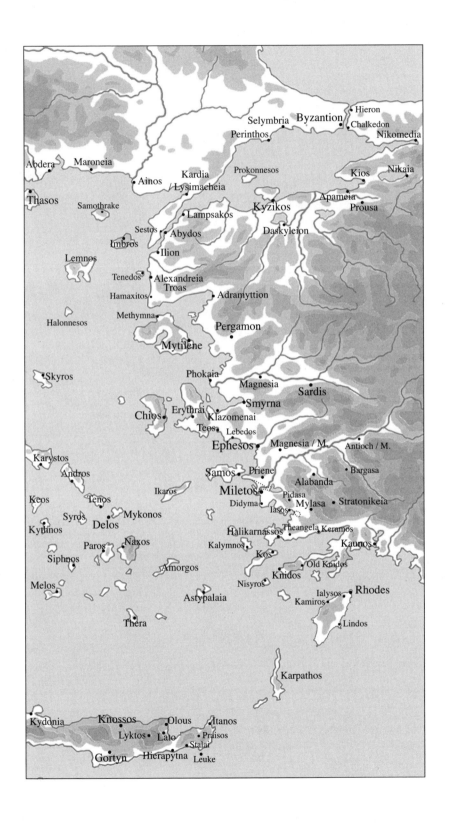

INTRODUCTION

This book has a hero: not Achilles or Pericles, but the exceptional economic growth that took place in the ancient Greek world in the Archaic, Classical, and Hellenistic periods. But why this focus on growth? Is there any legitimacy in studying growth in a traditional society? And what if the worlds of the past were worlds of no-growth—and even showed no interest in growth? Wouldn't this emphasis on growth correspond to a form of obsession characteristic of our modern world, where it is the be-all and end-all of every economic policy? And ultimately, was there any economic growth at all in the ancient Greek world?

The unfortunately still common cliché that there was no "interest in growth" in the ancient world and other societies of the past, and thus that for this reason it would be illegitimate to apply the concept of growth to these periods, is doubly misleading. First, it is not correct to imagine that in the past people were unable to observe phases of prosperity or wealth shrinkage, and that they could not have aimed at increasing their individual or collective riches. Second, and above all, growth is an abstract construct, and thus it stands to reason that before the recent development of economic analysis it was impossible to reason in terms of growth.

But in turn this leads us to an even more fundamental objection, which is that of the legitimacy of applying modern concepts (in this case, economic concepts) to societies of the past. Here again the answer is easy. Growth is an objective process in the sense that it can be independently measured. How many people were there? What was their standard of living? Did the population and the standard of living increase, stagnate, or decline? Were the evolutions of population level and standard of living parallel or did they move in opposite directions? Insofar as growth can be objectively measured—although this is an especially difficult task for societies where archives have disappeared and only proxies can be used—it is perfectly legitimate to analyze growth and processes of growth for any society of the past. In any case, the difficulty of measurement cannot be a pretext for refusing to face up to growth as the central issue of economic history.

The focus on growth as the goal of economic-historical analysis is thus central to this book. At the outset, it should be observed that, in economic terms, growth can be positive, negative, or null (which invalidates the argument of the alleged "obsession with growth" on the part of economists and economic historians). Periods of negative growth—that is to say, in more ordinary terms, periods of decline or brutal collapse of the quantity of goods available—are of course also part of the investigation. Therefore, saying that the Greek world enjoyed a period of economic growth in the Archaic, Classical, and Hellenistic periods is in fact a shortcut for saying that it had "positive economic growth." Above all, thinking in terms of growth also entails thinking in terms of factors of growth: labor, capital, and technology. By adopting this perspective, the economic historian benefits from the wide array of tools, concepts, and hypotheses that have been made available by what is conventionally called economic science, from the works of the founding fathers (Smith, Ricardo, Marx, Keynes) to the most recent research, hypotheses—and controversies.

Bringing to light and analyzing the exceptional (positive) growth experienced in the ancient Greek world is the first task of this book. In doing so, it directly contradicts the previous orthodoxy, which, while granting that there was some limited demographic growth, described ancient Greece as a no-growth society. Domestic self-sufficiency, a negligible foreign trade except in luxury goods for the elite, a lack of economic initiative and technological stagnation, and finally an absence of per capita economic growth are supposed to have been the main characteristics of the ancient Greek economy. This book shows quite the opposite: that complete domestic self-sufficiency is a pure myth; that foreign trade was fundamental and concerned not only luxury goods but, at an unprecedented level, basic consumer goods for the mass of the population; that in the long term technological innovation was remarkable and could result in a reallocation of the workforce; that there was per capita growth, at a level unprecedented before the early modern period. This does not (in any way whatsoever) make the ancient Greek economy a "modern" economy. But cataloguing what it lacked or "missed" as compared to a modern society would be nonsensical. Instead, we should emphasize that Greece experienced a process of growth that found no parallel in other cultures of that time. "Wealthy Hellas," as Josiah Ober has put it, is thus an appropriate definition for Greece in this period.[1]

But measuring growth is only one side of the economic historian's task. The other side consists in investigating the institutional developments that made it possible to reach a certain level of labor supply, capital accumulation, and technological knowledge. Rendering the complexity of these evolutions is the key to making sense of the process of growth. This is why, for Greece, this book is also about the ecological milieu and the natural resources that were available, or not available; about demography and the specific demographic and social structures that conditioned the labor supply; about patterns of consumption; and no less about the global political and legal framework than about the specific institutions organizing economic life. Of course, social constructs and antagonisms are also a significant part of the picture. Showing how growth was perfectly possible "in a traditional society," as Philip Hoffman has already proved in the case of early modern France, is a fundamental aspect of this research.[2]

At the end of the nineteenth century or in the first half of the twentieth century, many books aimed at providing general syntheses on the economy of the Greek world.[3] However, for good or less good reasons, they were severely criticized for their lack of conceptualization. The following generation of historians took a different stand. The only possible method for analyzing ancient economic history was seemingly to take a structural and sociopolitical standpoint. The excellent book by Michael M. Austin and Pierre Vidal-Naquet, *The Economic and Social History of Ancient Greece* (1977), which set its stamp on several generations of students and scholars, remains emblematic of this way of seeing things.

Times have changed, and so has the outlook for studies in this area. First, it must be emphasized that our knowledge has greatly increased in recent years. Archeologists, epigraphists, papyrologists, and numismatists have pursued their work. All too often the result is of benefit only to small groups of specialists. This book seeks to introduce as much new evidence as possible (especially from archaeology) into economic debate. This new information often helps to blow up old orthodoxies. At the same time, aided by changes brought about by the study of sources, there has been a conceptual revolution. Today, despite some lingering resistance here and there, analyzing the economic growth, technological progress, population increase, and money supply of the ancient world are no longer the taboo subjects they were until recently. It is now increasingly acknowledged that the economy of the ancient Greek world is a topic worthy of attention for its own sake, which of course, does not mean, as we noted earlier, that the economic should be dissociated and separated from the social, political, or even religious constructs. Besides, this holds for all societies, and not only for those too easily qualified as "preindustrial" or "precapitalist," as if our world provided the standard for measuring everything else. However that may be, it is increasingly clear that just as there is, for example, a logic peculiar to politics and religion that justifies studying them using a specific methodology, there is also a logic of the economy that fully merits a specific approach. In this perspective, ancient economic history is no longer an exception. Analyzing the economy of ancient Greece in terms of growth, and thus in specifically economic terms, is also a way of reintegrating its study into the general field of economic history.

This book differs in part from the classic works on ancient history. Naturally, the analysis constantly relies on sources (unless otherwise noted, the translations of the ancient texts are my own). But this book also reserves an important role for overall hypotheses. It aims at presenting the foundations on which our knowledge of the economy of ancient Greece is currently constructed, takes stock of a few major historiographical debates, and provides an introduction to methods of study that combine traditional tools for analyzing sources in ancient history with contemporary perspectives on economic research. Readers will profit more from it if they have some sense of the economic approach in general, but they do not need to have a technical knowledge of this domain. They should also know that they will not find here a purely descriptive economic history of ancient Greece, with minute regional and chronological developments. This study makes no claim to be exhaustive—limits of length would in any case render that impossible—or to provide a *sum* of the current state of our knowledge in this domain. Its goal is rather to provide a thematic analysis of the economic structures of the ancient Greek world.

This book focuses on the period from the last century of the Archaic period (the sixth century BCE) to the end of the Hellenistic period (in fact, the end of the first century BCE), which saw the maximal economic expansion (and the beginning of the decline) of the Greek world. However, the starting point of the investigation lies at the end of the second millennium BCE, with the collapse of the Bronze Age societies. In this period, Greece experienced the creation of a new form of political organization, the *polis*, or city-state, which proved fundamental for the later phase of economic expansion. The geographical frame of reference is Aegean Greece and the western coast of Asia Minor, but the relevant context sometimes extends to the whole of the Mediterranean.[4] Indeed, in that they play such an important role in the economic development of the Hellenic world as a whole, the peripheral regions of the Mediterranean colonized by the Greeks cannot be ignored, even though they are not analyzed for their own sakes. The same goes for the kingdoms that resulted from Alexander's conquests.

Because of the debates to which the economy of the world of antiquity in general has given rise, the work begins with a chapter on historiography and method. The first part of the book is devoted to structures and production. It presents the factors determining the basis of the economy of the Greece of the city-states and production data. The ecological framework of Greece is probably vaguely familiar to most readers, but its real economic implications are less well-known. As for the demographic structures of ancient Greece, this book argues that in terms of labor supply, they gave its economy forms of flexibility unknown to many other societies of the past. In terms of energy, the ancient Greek world benefited from an indefinitely renewable source of energy: wind. But it could use that resource for maritime transport only because it also developed shipbuilding technology to an unprecedented level. The question of the "failure of the Greek steam engine" is given an answer that sharply differs from the usual one, which attributes this failure to the lack of interest in technology that was long supposed to be characteristic of the ancient Greek world. An analysis of the city-state in ancient Greece shows that it was a major factor in economic development, insofar as it provided the basic framework for the appropriation of the land and also of the workforce (in the form of slaves). The main sectors of production are analyzed in detail: agriculture, of course (with animal husbandry and fishing), but also craftsmanship, with special attention to textiles. It was long a commonplace that the ancient world experienced no technological innovation. On the contrary, in accord with the most recent research on the topic, this book insists on innovation—political innovation, but also technological innovation—as one of the key sources of growth in ancient Greece.

The second part of this book takes up the question of trade and markets. What was the "nature of the economy" of ancient Greece? Was it a "market economy" or not? The debate on the economy of the Greece of the city-states is often couched in these terms. This book takes a pragmatic approach to answering this question.

Private property (including the workforce) was guaranteed by the existence of the city-state, which provided its foundation. The main trait of the system was that all citizens and free people in general were allowed to dispose of the great majority of what they produced as they saw fit. That was an important difference with respect to the kingdoms of the Near East, where tribute in kind remained a fundamental source of income for states and where the proportion of the economic activity that states could channel to their benefits was larger than in Greece. In the Greek city-states, free men controlled their units of production. They could trade with their counterparts in the framework of their city-state or, under certain conditions that were defined collectively, with partners outside their city of origin. For this reason, in the Greek world commercial exchange (not tribute in kind) played a decisive role in the circulation of goods. New institutions played a major role in these transformations. Coinage, which began around 650 BCE and developed very rapidly at the end of the Archaic period, provided a powerful accelerator for transactions. New laws and administrative procedures were developed, organized around the two sites for trade: the agora for internal commerce, and the *emporion* for foreign trade. Up to now, the attention of economic historians has been focused on the city-state. The goal of this book is to shift the attention toward the economic logic of the "society of the city-states." Interactions between various regions and interregional networks covering the whole Mediterranean are crucial to making sense of the growth of the Greek world for the supply of foodstuff, raw material, and labor. Finally, drawing on game theory, the book investigates the limits of growth in the ancient Greek world.

Every book has a history. This one is transcontinental. The first version was published in French. This American edition is fundamentally an English version of the first edition, and for this I owe an immense gratitude to Steven Rendall, who has not only provided a wonderful translation but also made many useful suggestions. But in addition, although the core of the argument has not been changed, many modifications have been introduced into the original text wherever it has seemed necessary. These modifications may affect a few words or a few sentences. Sometimes, however, whole paragraphs have been written anew. This was done to correct inaccuracies or on several topics to introduce the inevitable modifications of my own views over the years. No less importantly, I have also had to take into account the considerable developments in research that have taken place since 2007. This has raised a dilemma. It soon proved impossible, and would not have made sense, to systematically incorporate all this new literature. I decided to make use only of new research that could be directly connected to the text as it stood. The opposite decision would have meant writing another book, or perhaps several others. As such, however, the list of literature quoted in the notes is already 50 percent longer than in the original edition. The list of references remains more multilingual than in similar English or American publications. But, in accordance with the new audience of the book, this edition has many more English titles than the original text. For the reasons mentioned earlier, it also goes without saying that this edition completely replaces the first one.

Much of what is published here was first presented to my graduate students at the University of Bordeaux 3, to my students at the University of Chicago in spring 2005, and again to my students in Chicago after January 2008 during the updating and revision process. They constantly asked pertinent and challenging questions and also obliged me to modify a number of my views or reformulate them in order to make them more easily comprehensible. I would like to express my deep thanks to Maurice Sartre, who urged me to undertake this adventure, and to the friends and colleagues who have provided references or made useful suggestions—in particular, Pascal Arnaud, Jean-Pierre Bost, Marie-Françoise Boussac, Patrice Brun, François de Callataÿ, Laurence Cavalier, Véronique Chankowski, Pierre Debord, Claude Domergue, Panagiotis Doukellis, Gérald Finkielsztejn, Christophe Flament, Jérôme France, Vincent Gabrielsen, Yvon Garlan, Edward Harris, Bruno Helly, Thomas Keith, François Kirbihler, Denis Knœpfler, Barbara Kowalzig, Elio Lo Cascio, John Ma, Joseph Manning, Alexandre Marcinkowski, Emanuel Mayer, Lina Mendoni, Stephen Mitchell, Claudia Moatti, Christel Müller, Josiah Ober, Graham Oliver, Christophe Pébarthe, Karl Gunnar Persson, Olivier Picard, Nathalie Prévost, Selini Psoma, Gary Reger, Pierre Rouillard, Richard Saller, and Ronald Stroud. The list might be longer, and I apologize in advance to colleagues and friends whose names do not appear here. But I cannot fail to mention my Chicago colleagues, especially Clifford Ando, Jonathan Hall, Cameron Hawkins, Brian Muhs, David Schloen, François Velde, and Glen Weyl, for the stimulating conversations I have had with them in recent years on economic topics. In Bordeaux, Nathalie Pexoto helped with the maps and Stéphanie Vincent made available all her competence in dealing with graphics. I thank both of them, as well as the librarians of the Institut Ausonius and the Bibliothèque Universitaire in Bordeaux, and those of the Sorbonne, the Institut Louis Gernet, and the École Normale Supérieure in Paris. On the American side, I owe an immense debt of gratitude to the Regenstein Library in Chicago and especially to its Classics librarian Catherine Mardikes. I also thank the Princeton University Press team and Rob Tempio for their help with the final form given to the manuscript. I am very grateful to the University of Chicago and to Martha Roth, the dean of the Humanities Division, who has allowed me to use my research credit to help defray the cost of the translation of this book. This book is published with support from the French Ministry for Culture—National Book Center. Finally, I would like to express my special gratitude to the "Cestas clan," Michèle, François, Julie, and Frédéric, for their invaluable help and unflagging support during the period when I was preparing and writing this book, both in its original version and its new English edition.

Chicago
October 1, 2014

THE

MAKING

OF THE

ANCIENT

GREEK

ECONOMY

I

THE ECONOMY OF ANCIENT GREECE: A CONCEPTUAL FRAMEWORK

Can a book on the economy of ancient Greece be written? Forty years ago, in a famous work with the paradoxical title *The Ancient Economy*, Moses I. Finley answered this question in the negative.[1] For Finley, it was an illusion to think that such a project could be carried out, not because of the insufficiency of our information, but simply because, in his view, the project made no sense at all. What should we take that to mean? Of course, Finley did not doubt that it was possible to present basic data on production, trade, and finance. But he thought it was illusory to look for an economic logic that would organize these facts, because there wasn't any. His chief target was the existence of a "political economy" on the part of states. But the criticism was still more radical. The determinants structuring the facts of production or trade were social, political, or religious in nature, but certainly not economic in the sense of having a logic of organization peculiar to them. To be sure, before and after the proclamation of this edict, many books and articles were published that claimed, each in its own way, to deal with the ancient economy. But the basic question remains. Finley's methodological challenge must be taken seriously, and to do so we must first define unambiguously what we mean by the "economy of ancient Greece." It is clear that one has to give great attention to the empirical data supplied by the sources, which are to historical economics what laboratory experiments are to the exact sciences. But a conceptual and methodological clarification is indispensable as the basis for a project whose coherence must be justified before any further development is undertaken. In this way, we can at least protect ourselves against dangers that a "naïve" analysis would not allow us to avoid. On a subject as perilous as the economy of ancient Greece, attempting to dispense with a preliminary conceptual analysis would be like trying to negotiate a mountain path at night without a flashlight: the result would be only too predictable. Here we will try first to draw up a synthetic balance sheet on the complex relationship the study of ancient societies has entertained with what is generally called the science of economics, before making new proposals from the point of view of new institutional economics.

THE UNIVERSE OF ECONOMIC THEORY

Primitivism or Modernism?

The story is well-known, or at least it has often been told.[2] It has its source in the controversy that arose between two illustrious German masters at the end of the nineteenth century and the beginning of the twentieth century and that has repeatedly popped up again ever since. In 1893, the economist Karl Bücher (1847–1930), a professor at the University of Leipzig, published a book titled *Die Entstehung der Volkswirtschaft*, viz. "The Genesis of Political Economy," translated into English under the title *Industrial Evolution*.[3] In this book, he set forth a view of the ancient economy that came to be called "primitivist." The answer came two years later, in 1895. Eduard Meyer (1855–1930), then a professor at the University of Halle and a specialist in Greek antiquity, delivered before an assembly of German historians a speech titled "Economic Development in Antiquity," in which he vehemently refuted Bücher's recently published views."[4] Meyer reaffirmed his opinions in various articles and books that he published later.[5] He is with good reason considered to be the leader of the so-called modernists.

For Bücher, the ancient economy had fundamentally remained at a not very advanced stage of development.[6] It was characterized by domestic production and was intended to meet the immediate needs of the family, whether it involved agricultural production or craft production. Mercantile exchange played only a limited role, and conversely, the processes of transferring goods were characterized by gifts, rapine, or war. Capital, in the sense of an element of production, was almost nonexistent, and money, piled up in houses, had no function other than that of a reserve, a means of insurance. The division of labor could apparently be quite extensive, but it remained purely technical and had no foundation in the structure of capital, since the latter had no reality.

Meyer saw things in a totally opposite way.[7] First, he was aware of the evolution that the Greek world had undergone between the Homeric and the Hellenistic periods, to the point that he did not hesitate to compare the former to the early Middle Ages, the Archaic period to the end of the Middle Ages, and the Classical period to the dawn of modern times. For him, there was no doubt that the economy of ancient Greece had all the characteristics of a developed economy. It was all about mercantile exchange, money, the division of labor, an industrial type of production, and even competing states seeking to conquer export markets—whence conflicts such as the Peloponnesian War.

Bücher or Meyer? It is impossible to decide between these two adversaries. Even though we may now too easily smile at their errors, each of them had arguments to defend his point of view. But on the methodological level, and in order to avoid finding ourselves in the dead ends mentioned earlier, we must ask why these two scholars were able to occupy such opposed positions. How could the observation of the same reality end up producing two such contrary images of the ancient economy? Without entering into the detail of their theories, we can observe that each of the two adversaries selected only the observed features that he could bring to bear in the service of his model, leaving the rest aside. Thus, the two scholars were not in fact describing the same reality. With different motives, they were both seeking to issue a value judgment on Greek society in relation to a society that served as their standard: European society of their time. It was in the light of the degree of proximity to this perfect model and of the traits selected that ancient Greek society could be judged either completely "primitive" or, on the contrary, completely "evolved." The two adversaries shared the same evolutionary conception, in the version that posits "necessary stages" in historical evolution and that was characteristic of German scholarship and science in that period, though Meyer had in addition an underlying cyclical conception of time.

From the "Bücher-Meyer" controversy, we can draw the lesson that we cannot claim to "classify" societies and make value judgments regarding the more or less "primitive" or "evolved" character of the ancient economy in relation to our own. But we should also ask the fundamental question concerning the apparent ambivalence of the economy of ancient Greece, which paradoxically could support both Bücher's "primitivist" judgment and Meyer's "modernist" view. However, if commerce, money, and even craft production were in fact present, the economy of ancient Greece was certainly not an "industrial" economy. Although agriculture was the main productive sector, and though in the countryside self-consumption of what was produced was still the rule, it was not a "primitive" economy either (if only because all home production was not home consumed). There is an ambivalence here that we still have trouble accounting for. This "twofold" character of Greek society, which is judged to be "primitive" or "modern" depending on the sector of activity, the region, or the period, is still often considered to be a strange and inexplicable characteristic of the economy of ancient Greece. Thus agriculture is supposed to be the example of archaic routine, while banking and "wheeling and dealing" are supposed to be innovative aspects. The end of the fifth century is said to mark the beginning of a "modern" development, while earlier Greece is supposed to have remained "primitive." Naturally, with judgments of this kind, we do not choose between Bücher and Meyer. But then we are content to let a "primitivist" and a "modernist" view coexist, usually by according a larger role to the former and attributing to the aspects considered "modern" only the status of an exceptional island in the midst of a primitive ocean. The economy of the Greek city-states is thus alleged to resemble a kind of patchwork. It is this dichotomous model, juxtaposing two types of economy that have almost no connection with each other, that has to be revised.

The German Historical School of Political Economy

New historical analyses connected with the Bücher-Meyer debate, and more generally with the social sciences in Wilhelmine Germany, have stressed how much the views adopted by the two schools were overdetermined by the opposing ideological positions they were defending. Meyer thought he had rediscovered in the world of Classical Greece the antagonisms between the great powers that were characteristic of Europe in his time. Bücher adhered to the so-called German Historical School of Political Economy ("Historische Schule der Nationalökonomie"), some of whose famous representatives at the time were Friedrich List (1789–1846), Johann Karl Rodbertus (1805–1875), and especially Gustav von Schmoller (1838–1917).[8] At the end of the nineteenth century, Germany was undergoing a crucial transformation. It was emerging from an Old Regime society, becoming unified politically and economically, and industrializing at a rapid pace. At the same time, it was trying to catch up with and if possible advance beyond the British economy, whose credo was free trade, an ideology that seemed to have paved the way for Britain's success and its domination over Europe. On the contrary, the economists of the "German School" urged the state to intervene to ensure the German nation's economic development and resolve the "social question," which was in line with Bismarck's views. In this battle, Bücher provided arguments for those who wanted to show the historical contingency of economic categories. This is a problem that goes far beyond the Bücher-Meyer controversy.

For Schmoller and the adepts of the Historical School, the economy did not exist as such. The method used by adherents to this theory was based on the interpretation of observations (and hence on the constitution of statistical series) and not on hypothetical-deductive models. For them, the economy was merely the product of an institutional arrangement that itself resulted from a power relationship among social groups. Supply and demand, which some people sought to conceptualize as realities that could be autonomously modeled, were only illusions, "compact expressions of an order of magnitude in which the wills of human groups will confront each other; the causes determining these orders of magnitude are partly natural, but mainly they are connections and power relationships between people, human thoughts and actions."[9] The German Historical School of Political Economy, therefore, did not deny the "class struggle": it fully recognized the latter's existence. However, unlike Marx, it did not prophesy that this struggle would be resolved by revolution. On the contrary, it maintained that the state had to act in such a way—for instance, through intervention in matters of social welfare—as to prevent this struggle from becoming overt confrontation. For Schmoller and his disciples, economic institutions were arrangements whose origin was purely social and rooted in the affirmation of the "values" peculiar to each society. The same could be said of the market, which was thus in no way the expression of a natural form of exchange. According to Schmoller, "the political economy is thus an integral part of social life; while its development is rooted in nature and technology, its true principle is society's shaping of economic processes."[10] Belief in the stability of economic institutions is no more than another illusion founded on the mistaken belief in an atemporal "abstract man" capable in all times and places of making rational economic choices. By describing a "primitive" society without a market and radically different from European society, Bücher brought an important contribution to the German Historical School of Political Economy and its effort to demonstrate the historical nature of economic categories. The ancient world, with which every educated person was then so familiar, thus provided a model opposed to that of a society dominated by a free-market economy.

Classical and Neoclassical Economists

Supporters of the Historical School were opposed to theorists of free-market economics, those who are now seen as constituting the "classical school." The latter's founders and most famous representatives were the Scotsman Adam Smith (1723–1790), the author of the famous essay titled *An Inquiry into the Nature and Causes of the Wealth of Nations* (1776), and the Englishman David Ricardo (1772–1823), author of the no less famous *On the Principles of Political Economy and Taxation* (1817).[11] In opposition to the Old Regime's regulatory supervision of economic processes, they praised individual freedom and the unfettered operation of the market, which in their view could satisfy demand far better than any regulation. Adam Smith's thought has often been seen as summed up in his famous notion of the market's "invisible hand"; the latter was supposed by its very nature to serve the common interest. Ricardo worked out a theory of value based on labor and not on utility that had a direct influence on Marx. In defending free trade, Ricardo also developed famous theories of international commerce.

The Historical School completely dominated the German intellectual horizon, but it was fundamentally challenged by the "Austrian school." Carl Menger (1840–1921) was one of the founders and one of the most typical representatives of this school, which also later included Ludwig von Mises (1881–1973) and Friedrich Hayek (1899–1992).[12] Menger's fundamental contribution was the notion of "marginalism." Whereas classical economists defined value by labor and, following the Aristotelian tradition, tried to establish a distinction between use value and exchange value, Menger defined the value of a good by the utility of its last unit consumed or produced.[13] Thus we see a radical epistemological break that is at the heart of all contemporary economic theory. For the Austrian school, which is the starting point of the so-called neoclassical school, economics is a science. Its analytical models have nothing to do with historical categories—and this gave rise to the debate with the German Historical School known as the "Methodenstreit," or "dispute on methods." Economics is the science of the consequences of choices made by free individuals operating in a market where they can exercise their judgment. The individual will never fail to pursue his (or her) own interest. The *homo economicus* of classical or neoclassical theory is a rational actor. As a result, his choice is predictable. If that is so, then economics is based on the principle of the predictability of results, which was then considered to be the fundamental criterion of the scientific character of a discipline. In the framework of the Austrian school, the discourse of economics must therefore be fundamentally deductive—and that is why, although the founders of the school did not make use of mathematical models, their followers soon did. Alongside the Austrian school, or in its wake, several schools of economics have emerged, but they all share the same premises, those of "methodological individualism"—that is, of a theory that takes individual choice as its point of reference.

These schools have produced the body of knowledge that is now taught in universities as "economics," and that is also described as a "mainstream" theory. Microeconomics has been constituted as a science of the management of business firms. It assumes that the head of the firm desires to maximize profits. How much capital should be invested to achieve this goal? What is the optimal level of production for the firm? How should stocks be managed? At what level should the price of a good or service be set? Microeconomics answers these questions (which come down to a single one: how can profits be maximized?) using differential calculus and integral calculus. Macroeconomics, on the other hand, develops models that are supposed to make it possible to achieve maximal efficiency in the interaction of production factors on the scale of a society as a whole. One of the most elaborate models is that of the general equilibrium proposed by Léon Walras (1834–1910), a professor at the University of Lausanne, and his successor Vilfredo Pareto (1848–1923). For Walras, a market economy tends toward an equilibrium between supply and demand, mediated by prices.[14] His model gave rise to countless debates and controversies. In any case, it is based on a model of "pure and perfect competition." The actor/decision-maker of neoclassical economics operates in a market where he has access to complete information regarding prices and products, and the choices he makes are not burdened by obstacles of any kind.

We see that, in its own way, the model of "pure and perfect competition" corresponding to the plenitude of *homo economicus* is an abstract type, even if it can have a heuristic value: it does not actually exist anywhere, even in the contemporary world. In reality, information on prices and products is far from being always available, and furthermore we know that there are all sorts of legal, cultural, and material obstacles that deform the model of pure and perfect competition to a greater or lesser degree. Economists have not been satisfied merely to note this fact. They have also worked out a whole series of mathematical approaches that model more complex situations of imperfect competition, such as those in which a monopoly is held by the seller (monopoly proper) or by the buyer (monopsony). The application to economics of models borrowed from game theory is a good example of this. Game theory is interested in the interaction of agents' decisions: what will X choose in relation to what he (or she) thinks Y's choice will be (and reciprocally for Y, with a mirroring effect that complicates the choices)? We should also mention here the theory of "rational anticipations," which analyzes economic behavior with regard to choices about general political economy and shows how they are diverted by agents, and the analysis of "informational asymmetry" between buyer and seller. We will see the importance of these ideas later on.

Economics and Scientific Discourse

Economic theory cannot be reduced to the model of "general equilibrium" or "pure and perfect competition," even if these constitute its distant horizon. Besides, we have to point out a residual ambiguity in the discourse of economics: it is inherently descriptive because it seeks to explain reality, whether by analyzing "pure and perfect competition" or the more concrete forms of "imperfect markets," but since it is supposed to describe the conditions for growth and optimal profits, it is also used to propose solutions for what *should* be the case. Thus it also has a normative and performative aspect. Consequently, the discourse of economics does not limit itself to proposing technical solutions; it also makes proposals that have a vast institutional, social, and political impact. Consider the example of state intervention in the economy. For some mainstream economists (those who adhere directly to the views of the founders of the neoclassical school and the Austrian school), any state intervention distorts market forces and is ultimately counterproductive because it leads to equilibriums that are much lower than those that free competition could have produced. For other economists—for example, Keynesians—who do not challenge the market as a system allowing the highest levels of production to be attained for the satisfaction of needs, state intervention can be temporarily useful in dealing with "failures" of the market.

The tradition of the Historical School, which saw the scientific aspect of economics as consisting solely in its mode of documentation and otherwise considered it as merely the result of social and political struggles, found it easier to practice a "committed discourse." In the same vein, but with a different orientation, "anti-globalization" economists (those who oppose current forms of globalization) who adopt the Marxist point of view and seek to destroy the capitalist system also refuse to grant any scientific character to the tradition of classical, neoclassical, or neo-institutional economics. They reduce the latter to a mere discourse of authority that benefits the "powerful of this world," to use the usual phrase. In an extreme form, this way of seeing things shaped the Leninist tradition, according to which the categories of economics were no longer to be a subject to be studied, but rather were to be "transformed."

We see to what extent economics, which claims to be scientific, nonetheless finds itself at the heart of debates that involve the realm of action. It would therefore be naïve to think that the stakes involved in the study of an economy, even if it is that of ancient Greece, are "neutral." Does that mean that in the study of an economy, any scientific discourse is doomed in advance? If so, we would have to reject all the social sciences—studies on political sociology or the sociology of religion, for example—that have just as many, and perhaps more, possible implications for the realm of action. We will not follow that line of thought. The sole validity that a scientific discourse can claim is that of its internal coherence and its ability to describe reality. The ideological uses to which the results of this research may be put are of another order and do not concern us here.

Moses I. Finley and Max Weber

Whether the discourse of economics regarding contemporary societies can claim to be scientific is already a debatable question. *A fortiori*, we can see how its application to the economy of societies that preceded the emergence of capitalism could be debated. In the case of these societies, we are confronted by an additional problem. In describing them, is it legitimate to use categories that were developed to account for our contemporary society of market capitalism? If in these earlier societies the market was not the dominant economic form, or if there was not any market at all, how could economic theory be applied to them? Thus, to take only the example of growth, a veritable obsession of the capitalist system, how could mainstream economics be of any use if past societies did not consider growth an ideal? That is the source of the implicit or explicit distinction frequently drawn as soon as we are dealing with the economy of Classical antiquity (or that of any other ancient society): developed "by and for" contemporary capitalist societies, the neoclassical theory would seem to have at best a limited application to the world that gave rise to it. Thus even those who grant its validity for the analysis of the contemporary economy consider it inappropriate for use in analyzing past societies. That was obviously Finley's position. *A fortiori*, those who deny the discourse of neoclassical economics any pertinence for the analysis of contemporary society refuse to regard it as having any interest for the analysis of societies that preceded capitalism.

Besides, Finley was not a theoretician. For the most part, he adopted the positions of Max Weber (1864–1920) and also to some extent those of Karl Polanyi (1886–1964). To do them justice, we have once again to return to the previously mentioned debates in German universities around the turn of the previous century. We have seen that the Historical School of Economics long exercised a massive domination over German thinkers. The emergence of the Austrian school, and then the challenges provoked by World War I and the failure of the German imperial model, resulted in the Historical School being swept off the stage a few years later by the revolutionary shift to an economics that was henceforth essentially mathematical. The last representative of the old school, but one who paradoxically was able to move beyond its bases, was Max Weber, a professor of economics at the University of Freiburg im Breisgau and later at Heidelberg.[15] In Germany, Weber's works made him the founder of a new discipline, sociology, at the same time that in France Émile Durkheim was performing a similar role, though on different foundations.

If Weber's initial inspiration was the same as that of the Historical School, his methods were different. For the evolutionism that sought to explain a given social form as a "survival" of earlier forms, and for the theory of "successive stages" in the history of humanity that had been current up to that time, Weber substituted an analysis in terms of "ideal types" that sought to reconstruct a stylized portrait of a society on the basis of what he considered its most significant characteristics. These characteristics are coherent with each other. They constitute what we would now call "invariants," which are a society's specific signature. Moreover, Weber paid special attention to intentionality, to the motivations of actors' behavior and to their awareness of it. This was in fact the very foundation of his sociology.

Max Weber maintained that societies' degree of rationality was a crucial criterion in classifying them. He worked out his ideas on the basis of an analysis of individual rationality, a logic of action that was characteristic of the method of "methodological individualism." He defined what he meant by "rationality" this way: "Action is instrumentally rational (*zweckrational*) when the end, the means, and the secondary results are all rationally taken into account and weighed. This involves rational consideration of alternative means to the end, of the relations of the end to the secondary consequences, and finally of the relative importance of different possible ends."[16] Weber explained this general definition by applying it to the various goals of action. Thus he distinguished two forms of rationality of action, rationality in relation to the objective (or instrumental rationality, which makes the end and the means coherent) and rationality in relation to values (which makes the objective and the meaning coherent). Concerning the latter, Weber stated: "Examples of pure value-rational orientation would be the actions of persons who, regardless of possible cost to themselves, act to put into practice their convictions of what seems to them to be required by duty, honour, the pursuit of beauty, a religious call, personal loyalty, or the importance of some 'cause' no matter in what it consists. In our terminology, value-rational action always involves 'commands' or 'demands' which, in the actor's opinion, are binding on him."[17] Thus Weber distinguished between an immediate rationality of action (to achieve a goal, whatever it might be, one has to move through a series of specific stages; this might be described as "first-order rationality") and a rationality that selects a goal in relation to a system of values ("second-order rationality").

As for economic rationality, Weber drew a distinction between two types: a "material rationality" seeking to supply a group in relation to ethical, religious, political, or social criteria, and a "formal rationality" based on calculation making it possible to measure the use made of the available resources. Whereas contemporary capitalist society is considered to be the only one that has a formal rationality, all past societies are said to have had only diverse forms of material rationality. Thus we supposedly have a decisive criterion for differentiating between developed capitalist society and the societies of the past. For this reason, it would be futile to look in these societies for anything other than a process of immediate supply. Their economies were therefore nonexistent, since they were governed by principles other than those of rational management.

One should emphasize Weber's insistence on the provisional character of this distinction, which seemed to him difficult to establish.[18] Reflection on economic rationality was itself situated in the context of a wider reflection on the rationality of social activity. Weber applied his method to various societies, including those of Classical antiquity, but he certainly accorded the most attention to capitalist society and its genesis, which in any case served for him as a standard for assessing other societies. The thesis of *The Protestant Ethic and the Rise of Capitalism* (first published in 1904–1905, with a new edition by Weber himself in 1920) was that the source of capitalism's development was to be sought in a particular code of ethics: the Calvinist property-owner did not seek to enjoy the use of his profits, because his morality forbade him to do so.[19] Weber insisted on the very special ethics of capitalist man, who was of a new kind: reserved, orderly, and obsessed by the idea of measuring, accounting, and by the quest for profits that in reality brought him no immediate advantage. He accumulated to accumulate, in a process whose reason is not found in itself, because the motivation is entirely external to the act.[20] The thesis was brilliant and new because it underscored the unintentional character of the capitalist revolution. For Weber, the incarnation of this new kind of man was the Protestant bourgeois of northern Europe. In fact, the essence of Weber's thesis is questionable, if only because it pays little attention to the Italian, Flemish, and (pre- and post-Reformation) Dutch antecedents of the "development of capitalism" in England in the seventeenth and eighteenth centuries, and in northern Germany in the nineteenth century. Furthermore, Weber should not have tried to account for this development experimentally by observing the economic behavior of various religious components of the populations in the Germany of his time, for in the sketchy form in which they are presented his analyses are far from being convincing.[21] Weber's last works offered analytical lines of thought that were much more fully worked out. Besides, it should be clear that if puritanism admittedly played a significant role in the development of capitalism, it did so only insofar as it exploded the traditional attitudes of group modes of thinking and replaced them by personal and critical ones.

However that may be, this thesis remains very typical of Weber's method. Moreover, it was in a similar way that Weber himself, and then authors drawing on him, dealt with the development (or rather, in their view, the lack of development) of the world of Classical antiquity. Concerning precisely the world of antiquity, Weber expresses himself in the clearest manner in the famous *Agrarverhältnisse im Altertum*, a text that was published in three successive editions in 1897, 1898, and 1909 and appeared in English as *The Agrarian Sociology of Ancient Civilizations* (1976).[22] This is the work of Weber's that has had the greatest influence on the conceptualization of the ancient economy down to our own time. It is also a work full of paradox, where on the one hand Weber acknowledged the dynamism of the ancient economy and its achievement, and on the other he fell into the trap of the binary comparison between antiquity and the modern era. According to Weber, it is because Greece and Rome lacked an appropriate ideology that they did not undergo the "transition to industrial capitalism." The ideology of landowners in antiquity, who were absentee owners and took no interest in developing their farms, is supposed to have kept agriculture at a deplorably low technological level.[23] In this respect, the tone of Weber's descriptions resembles that of Bücher. Although he was well aware of Meyer's theories, Weber could attribute to the techniques of handling capital in antiquity only a role that was very primitive in comparison to that of the early modern or even the medieval world. For Weber, the citizen of the ancient city did not at all seek to develop an "enterprise." The system of accounting then in use was primitive.[24] The citizen himself was not a *homo economicus* but rather a *homo politicus*. He was inclined to enjoy the use of the revenues from the lands that his city had conquered through war. Thus we note almost no technological progress.[25] Hence the economy of antiquity, in the sense of an activity consciously oriented toward profit, can only be regarded as nonexistent. As for social antagonisms, in antiquity they had to do with questions of status: the modest peasant did not want to be enslaved by the landlord, the slave wanted to be free. All that had nothing to do with the claims made in the medieval period by journeymen against masters or by artisans against capitalists, which were the forerunners of modern antagonisms between owners and workers.[26]

Thus, for those who follow Max Weber, in antiquity the economy had no independent existence. We have to note, paradoxically, that Weber's definition of "economy" does not differ from that of classical or neoclassical economists. It consists in acknowledging that the existence of an economy involves the rational management of the scarcity of goods. Can this definition be applied to the world of antiquity? Weber's response was that only the economy of the modern, capitalist West could be considered rational. In all other societies, the economy was supposedly governed by institutional rules alien to economic rationality. For Weber, the fact that the institutions that preceded those of contemporary capitalism were not economically rational made it futile to pursue any strictly "economic" study of "precapitalist" societies. In his view, instead of an impossible "economics of precapitalist societies," the goal should be a sociology, which alone might be capable of explaining behavior relative to the management of goods. For Bücher, the economy of antiquity had not moved beyond the stage of managing the *oikos* and consumption of self-produced goods. Weber was able to recognize that Bücher's statements were excessive. But he nonetheless insisted that the absence of rational management gave an irreducibly primitive character to the ancient economy. The task he implicitly assigned to the historian of the ancient world was thus to demonstrate the irrational, "noneconomic" character of the "ancient economy." It was to show that this "economy," understood as the production and administration of material goods, lacked an internal, economic rationality. In a certain way, Johannes Hasebroek's works on commerce and traders in the Greek world were fully within this tradition.[27]

Institutional Analysis and Karl Polanyi

Another school of thought deserving special attention for the study of the ancient economy is that of institutionalism, represented by a group of American scholars to which one may add the Hungarian-born Karl Polanyi.[28] At the very moment when, with World War I and then World War II, the Historical School was disappearing from the German intellectual horizon, and where with Max Weber's sociology had just been founded and had bright prospects, new theorists, Americans this time were taking over the work of conceptual reflection. One must emphasize that the earliest of these were directly and explicitly linked with the German Historical School of Political Economy. Thus at the end of the nineteenth and the beginning of the twentieth centuries, there developed in the United States a school of thought known as "institutionalist," represented by thinkers like Thorstein Veblen (1857–1929) and John Commons (1862–1945), who assigned an essential role to social institutions (in the broadest sense of the term). Veblen, the great destroyer of the utilitarian and calculating vision of neoclassical economics, is known chiefly for his *Theory of the Leisure Class*, a work in which he criticized the appropriation of the social surplus by a class of idle people.[29] His analysis of institutional development through a process of adaptation is not without interest, but remains vague, and his sociology, which lapses into racism, quickly shows its limitations. In his *Institutional Economics* of 1934, Commons focused his attention on transactions, which he regarded as pacified and institutionalized conflicts (here we see the connection with the German Historical School). Specifically, he studied the way in which property and law structured American capitalism.[30] Because of their common inspiration, it is not unusual to see Weber and especially Polanyi ranked among the institutionalists.

Along with Weber, Karl Polanyi incontestably exercised the greatest influence on the way the economies of the societies that preceded capitalism, and especially those of antiquity, were understood. Like Weber, Polanyi wondered about the singularity of the "Western path" that led to the Industrial Revolution and the triumph of the capitalist system. For both men, capitalism is only one culture among others—but their assessments of it are diametrically opposed. For the bourgeois university professor Weber, capitalism was undeniably the most fully realized form of civilization. For the socialist thinker Polanyi, capitalism was only a transitory historical form whose birth and development could be described and that would, he thought, soon die and be replaced by a socialist system: that was the drift of his book *The Great Transformation*, published in 1944.[31]

Three main ideas structured Polanyi's reasoning. The first was that in all societies (except one: capitalist society), the economy normally serves solely to satisfy what he called "human needs": food, clothing, shelter, and an environment that allows one to live decently in accord with the living standards of the time. In this sense, what he called "the substantive economy" was necessarily radically opposed to the role taken by the economy within a market society like that of capitalism. The second idea, which is a corollary of the first, was that capitalist society was the only one in the history of mankind in which the economy existed as a separate entity, with its own autonomous institutions. Earlier, the economy was embedded in the social, the political, or the religious, and it was those institutions that performed—incidentally, as it were—the economic functions. Thus we find here, formulated in a different way,

Weber's thesis about the objectification of economic relationships in capitalist society. Finally, the third idea was that in past societies, social action did not take into account the profit-maximizing point of view and was not governed by the law of self-interest, but could have quite different motivations: exit *homo economicus*, with his rational choices that are supposed to maximize utility. Thus, according to Polanyi, prices are purely conventional and do not correspond to the interplay of a supply and a demand. Precapitalist economies were "substantive" economies dedicated to satisfying people's needs. They could not, therefore, be the subject of "formal" studies like those of contemporary market societies.

Polanyi was a scrupulous, open-minded man with a great talent for identifying fundamental problems (which may be the most difficult task in intellectual inquiry). The undeniable success of his theory is also due to his ability to provide simple, easily understandable solutions in terms of the dichotomy between capitalism and all the other societies that preceded it. But whether this is the right way to analyze the economy of past societies is far from certain.[32]

The Economy of Antiquity after Moses Finley

To summarize: the neoclassical school's basic presupposition was the universality of actors' behaviors, which could be restrained only by institutions opposed to their choices. Institutionalist thinkers (in the broad sense, including Weber and Polanyi) substituted for this way of seeing things the pure historicity of economic categories. For them, past societies thus had an economy "in itself," essentially oriented toward providing subsistence for the people, but not an economy "for itself"—that is, a system of rules consciously manipulated and endowed with a logic peculiar to it, a logic of growth. This is what is said to justify the absence of a "science of economics" in worlds that could not conceptualize a reality that was alien to them. Thus, efforts to reconstitute a logical system that did not exist would be futile. The current reformulation of the debate between "formalists," who are supposed to acknowledge the existence of the ancient economy as a separate, autonomous sphere, but less sophisticated than it is today, and "substantivists," for whom the ancient economy has no reality other than the concern about food supplies and is otherwise completely under the control of other authorities—political, religious, and so on—reproduces, if not totally at least largely, the old cleavages between modernists and primitivists.[33]

It was Weber's theses, and only partly and more critically those of Polanyi, that Finley popularized and set forth in his book *The Ancient Economy* (1973, with a new augmented edition in 1985), explicitly and repeatedly acknowledging his debt to Weber.[34] Finley's title is ironic, since he maintains that the illusory quest for an organized system whose goal is the maximization of profits should be replaced by a sociology of landowners, their ideology, and their form of consumption (ostentatious and economically useless), and thus by a sociology of the multiple factors obstructing growth in a society whose motivations were alien to rational management and the maximization of profit.

Beyond the respective contents of each of these theses, it is their fundamental inspiration that must be challenged. The world of antiquity (or of any other society anterior to capitalism) is never studied in and of itself. It is conceived as "defective" and is the object of a "negative reasoning." It is only the negative counterpart of the capitalist world. Like the negative confessions made by the deceased arriving in the kingdom of the dead in Pharaonic Egypt ("I have not committed an injustice, I have not stolen . . ."), Weber and Finley encourage their readers to identify all the "lacks" in the ancient economy by comparison with the contemporary economy. To be sure, the list is long. But this analysis of "defects," which is only a projection onto the ancient economy of the capitalist world's analytical scheme, is also the surest way not to understand the ancient economy in a positive way and to fail to recognize its possible internal coherence. A still more serious problem is that this view encourages us to interpret the sources—archaeological or textual—systematically in a primitivist sense. To be sure, the tradition of Weber and Finley differs from Bücher's primitivism. But, for the methodological reasons already mentioned, it inevitably led to taking positions similar to those of the primitivists. It was naturally characterized by a refusal to describe the ancient economy as an integrated system and also by the minimization of quantities or the systematic refusal to quantify, even on the rare occasions when ancient documentation allows us to do so.

Nevertheless, the notion of "embedding" and its corollary, "disembedding," led Polanyi to make a strange discovery. If all the societies of the past had substantive economies organized either on the basis of reciprocity or on that of redistribution, it would be logically impossible to find, before our own time, a market that set a price determining the nature and volume of production. However, among the very diverse societies on which Polanyi concentrated his efforts, there is one that interested him particularly, given his classical training: that of ancient Greece.[35] Polanyi thus was surprised to observe a phenomenon that was unexpected in his theory: the constitution of a market system undergoing fluctuations in prices for products made for mass consumption and extending over vast geographical areas. Certainly, Polanyi was wrong to locate the "disembedding" (to adopt his vocabulary provisionally) of Greek society at the beginning of the Hellenistic period, around 330–300 BCE.[36] In reality, great changes in the society and economy of ancient Greece had already been under way since at least the end of the Archaic period and were situated in a line of development that began with the Greek Dark Ages (from the twelfth to the ninth century). Thus it is the logic of "embedding" and "disembedding" itself that must be challenged. The debate between Polanyi and Finley was rooted in their common conception of a stage theory of history, itself a heritage of the German Historical School. As such, this debate clearly could lead only to Byzantine discussions on the "proportions of modernity" in this or that society. Nonetheless, it remains true that Polanyi perceived a crucial fact amply confirmed by all the sources: that of variations in price (which of course invalidated his theory of "fixed prices" in the societies of the past). In addition, here one need mention only that in his *Poroi* (4.6), written in 355/4 BCE, Xenophon emphasizes as an obvious fact that not only did prices vary but also that it was price fluctuations that determined the choice of the objects to be produced.[37]

In fact, this observation could not be a simple exception to Polanyi's conceptual system. It was a breach that would inevitably lead sooner or later to questioning the whole theory—but it is significant that Polanyi did not try to substitute dogma for observation. He had clearly seen that the mutations that had occurred in Greece, and which he described as "disembedding," were fundamental and could not be reduced to a few marginal developments or at best supposed to be "forerunners" (how could they have been that?) of transformations that took place two millennia later in modern Europe. In this sense, his break with Finley, precisely over the question of the "disembedding" of the economy of ancient Greece, is not merely anecdotal: it is essential for understanding the position at which Polanyi had arrived toward the end of his life. Finley was surely right to point out the factual errors in Polanyi's essay, but more than that, he had correctly perceived that Polanyi's challenge to "disembedding" threatened the very foundations of the conception Finley himself was defending. We should not follow Finley in attempting to paper over the difficulties introduced by Polanyi's observations. On the contrary, this conceptual "breach" opened up by the case of ancient Greece must be enlarged and exploited. Above all, it invites us to reopen in a new light the fundamental debate about the relationship between economies and institutions.

Today, one must move beyond this characteristic neoprimitivist rhetoric, in which any quantitative observation is generally accompanied by a formula such as "less than has been alleged" (read: "less than modernists have claimed"), as if this unacknowledged neoprimitivism could serve as a conceptual horizon. Moreover, it has been shown that the great Russian scholar Mikhail I. Rostovtzeff (1870–1952), the author of a monumental *Economic and Social History of the Hellenistic World* published in Oxford in 1941 and often seen as the archetype of modernist scholarship, was much closer to Finley on many points than is generally admitted.[38] Today it is possible to give new content to the economic analysis of a society. To do so, we must incorporate the contributions of the great masters of the past. But we must also take into account the considerable conceptual advances that have been made since Weber and Polanyi in the domain of economics and the other social sciences. The economic history of ancient societies is taking on a new orientation that has been vigorously illustrated by recent studies.[39] It is this conceptual horizon that needs to be considered next.

NEW INSTITUTIONAL ECONOMICS AND
THE ECONOMY OF ANTIQUITY

Max Weber's pages on the economy of antiquity were part of an overall reflection, a vast theory of social processes. Similarly, an alternative theory of the ancient economy can be proposed only within a broader conceptual horizon. That is the only way to move beyond the dichotomy between "economic" capitalist societies and societies defined as "precapitalist" and thus "without economies." First, we will recall the contradictions to which traditional approaches (including Weber's) have led in the theory of the relationship between economies and institutions and in the theory of social development. Then it will be shown that we can now move beyond the contradiction in Weber's view by proposing a new analysis of economic rationality. Finally, on this basis, it will be shown that the issue at stake is to define a new model of the genesis of institutions and their transformation.[40]

Homo economicus *Facing His Critics*

On the macroeconomic as well as on the microeconomic level (even if these distinctions did not exist in their time), the approach adopted by classical economists—whether Adam Smith, Malthus, or Ricardo—did not take the specificities of social forms into account. On the macroeconomic level, Smith's England and Portugal, which traded cloth for wine, were pure abstractions. We find the same mode of reasoning in Malthus and Ricardo. For Malthus, the limited nature of human resources (arable land) periodically conflicted with the level of population, the latter always tending to grow—whence, periodically, crises of adaptation to bring the population back down to the level it should not have exceeded. The abstract character of these theories was what gave them their power and novelty. In fact, today it is banal to reason in terms of aggregates—that is, in numerical values synthesizing data of the same type. We find the same kind of reasoning in microeconomics. The classical economists' economic agent, the *homo economicus*, always chooses what is in his own self-interest. In this sense, his behavior can be considered rational, hence predictable. *Homo economicus* moves in the universe of the pure and perfect market. He is fully informed regarding the choices offered him. There is no connection between his successive choices. The latter are not restricted by any political, social, or cultural obstacle.

Of course, no one has ever claimed that reality conformed to these abstract models. Moreover, we have to avoid any naïve condemnation. Abstraction is the precondition for any scientific reasoning. However, the gap between the model and reality sometimes seems so great that it may seem to invalidate the model itself, or at least invite us to limit its application. In fact, no contemporary market society corresponds to the definition of the "pure and perfect" market. A fortiori, is it not dangerous to apply the model of the *homo economicus*, developed to analyze market situations, to societies "without markets," or even to those in which the market did not play the same role as it does today? History shows a multitude of societies with political and religious forms of organization that seem incapable of being reduced to the model of the *homo economicus*. Kinship structures, temple or sanctuary, empire, city-state, or manor—these organizational forms, which we will henceforth call "institutions," take on such importance for the societies concerned that it is impossible to see how they could be bracketed in the analysis of their economies. Furthermore, these institutions never remain stable. Slowly or rapidly, they are constantly transforming themselves in what seems to be a strange disorder.

Marxism tried to account for this apparent chaos. For Marx, institutions are mere products of the class struggle, which is itself determined by the "level of productive forces." The watermill is supposed to have generated feudalism and the steam engine modern capitalism. Here we are in the logic of a "two-stroke engine," a causal system in which institutional development finds its source directly in the logic of productive forces, understood in the material sense of the term. For Marx, in the final analysis technological progress was the motor of history. The schema was based on an evolutionist logic that assigned to technological progress, to productive forces, and to increasingly extensive mastery over nature the role of vectors ineluctably determining social evolution. The possible correspondence between a certain level of productive force and a given institutional organization is one thing (for the watermill, the rule posited was, however, very unfortunate).[41] But, as has long been recognized, it is quite another thing to establish a clear causal link between the two factors. In fact, one can just as well maintain that capitalism is necessary for the invention of the steam engine as the inverse, so that one explanation cancels out the other.

Weber inverted the paradigm (whence, for a long time, the desire to make his teaching an antidote to Marx). For him, the institution gave life to the economic system, not the other way around. One might say that in this conception, there is no steam engine without the Puritan bourgeoisie. Of course, as has already been observed, the somewhat simplistic reasoning presented in *The Protestant Ethic* was later replaced by more complex analyses.[42] But the fundamental inspiration remained the same, and it was no accident that Weber was particularly interested in describing the religious and political forms of ancient Judaism and the worlds of India and China. It seemed to him that these cultural analyses might define the social (and economic) forms of these societies. The objectification of economic relationships in a separate sphere, which is characteristic of contemporary Western society, then appears as simply a specific cultural construction, only one among many, even if, as a man of his time, Max Weber could not help judging other cultural constructions by the standard of those of the Western European culture. Besides, at the end of his preface to *The Protestant Ethic*—a text particularly interesting for its sketchiness in contrast to the more fully worked-out studies published after 1910—Weber himself could not resist raising the question of the origin of the specific forms of institutions. With the greatest prudence, it is true, and as if regretfully, he put forward the idea that hereditary factors probably played a role, but that for the time being this role could not be measured adequately.[43] The content of his answer to the question, overdetermined by the ideology of a particular period and social milieu, matters little here. Weber explained that for the moment, the quest for factors connected with the milieu seemed to him the only one possible. But what counts is that he was aware of the problem raised by the determinants of institutions.

Thus it is piquant that Weber's analysis also led to this contradiction: how can the "foundation be founded," whether it is an "infrastructure" or a "superstructure"? Marshall Sahlins has proposed a radical solution. For him, any form of interaction between humans and their environment belongs to the "symbolic order," whose arbitrary aspect is connected with the fact that it is a product, by definition changing, of human will. There is no "pure constraint" by nature: "The material forces taken by themselves are lifeless. Their specific motions and determinate consequences can be stipulated only by progressively compounding them with the coordinates of the cultural order." [44] The filter of the symbolic order renders futile any attempt to find a logic of any kind in institutional arrangements, and in any case obliges us to deny a determining character to material factors: "We have seen that nothing in the way of their capacity to satisfy a material (biological) requirement can explain why pants are produced for men and skirts for women, or why dogs are inedible but the hindquarters of the steer are supremely satisfying of the need to eat. No more are the relations of production—the division of categories and capacities of the population." [45] The infrastructure-superstructure dialectic Marx considered so important and the vision of a goal-oriented history are thus erased in favor of the paradigm of a history dominated by the arbitrariness of cultural constructions. If we push this logic all the way, not only does history no longer have any ultimate goal (a proposition that would be easy to endorse), but it also has no logic: it is nothing but disorder and chaos, making us think of Macbeth's dark meditation on life: "A tale told by an idiot, full of sound and fury, signifying nothing" (M. Act 5, sc. 5).

The interest of this analysis is that it forces us to revisit Weber's distinction between two levels of rationality: material rationality, that of immediate action, and rationality in value, corresponding to ethical, aesthetic, moral, or religious imperatives. On the one hand, as Sahlins has shown, there is no "immediate" action, outside an institutional context: on this point, his analyses are rigorous and convincing. On the other hand, the arbitrary nature of cultural characteristics should not mask the reality of the way the oppositions highlighted by Sahlins's work. The markers that differentiate between genders vary from one society to another, but what remains constant is the fact of distinction itself, for example between genders or among social levels. In this respect, Pierre Bourdieu's works on the arbitrariness of "cultural tastes" provide a response to what seems to be the nonsense of a forest of contradictory signs. A dominant social stratum abandons one element of distinction in favor of another as soon as it is widely disseminated. What counts is not the signified of the element of distinction, but rather its signifier as a social marker: "the (sociologically well-founded) illusion of 'natural distinction' is ultimately based on the power of the dominant to impose, by their very existence, a definition of excellence that, being nothing other than their own way of existing, is bound to appear simultaneously as distinctive and different, and therefore both arbitrary (since it is one among others) and perfectly necessary, absolute and natural." [46] If that is so, then we have to look into the criteria of distinction between genders or among social levels, which, beyond the arbitrariness of signs, present astonishing forms of regularity.

New Institutional Economics (NIE) and the Transaction Costs Theory

Thus in the end we are brought back to a fundamental question: how can the genesis and evolution of institutions be explained? This is the question that has interested the thinkers who for that reason are called "institutionalists," above all Veblen and Commons, or more recently, the adherents of the school known as New Institutional Economics (NIE), the first of whom were Ronald H. Coase, Oliver E. Williamson, and, in a more historical perspective, Douglass C. North.[47] Classical economists focused all their attention on production and consumption. With New Institutional Economics, institutions cease to be a simple variable of adjustment, a peripheral or marginal element. On the contrary, in both their functioning and their historical genesis, they are at the center of the neo-institutional way of thinking. We see how interesting this thought can be for historians. Neo-institutional theorists seek to analyze the institutions that condition and determine the performance of an economic system. Unlike neoclassical economists, they fully recognize the importance of these institutions. The notion that one can do without them, as if the perfect market could do away with all institutions, and thus all rules, is for them a contradiction in terms: the law of self-interest, pushed all the way, would make society a jungle in which all organized social life would be impossible. Neoclassical economics focused on choice to establish the relationship between ends and scarce means with alternative uses. NIE substitutes a science of contract in lieu of a science of choice.[48]

Williamson, and then Coase and North, take as their point of departure interaction among individuals, defined as "transaction." Transactions, which as a set are nothing more than what is ordinarily called social life, presuppose exchanges of information. By definition, this information can never be complete or totally reliable. Social life is thus the domain of uncertainty. An institution has as its goal precisely to reduce to a tolerable level the uncertainty of transactions, so that the future is no longer a domain of unpredictable chaos, but rather one of reasonable forecasting.[49] Two examples, marriage and business contracts, will suffice to illustrate this view. Marriage is an institution that makes it possible to guarantee a stable personal life and filiation. A business contract makes it possible to have a reasonable assurance that a good will be delivered and paid for.[50] In addition, each of these institutions is part of a larger whole. Marriage and a business contract both presuppose the existence of a minimum of stability, guaranteed by a higher-level institution: the state, in whatever form. Thus the state organizes courts of law where business conflicts will be decided, and it is clear that these contracts take on meaning only in a universe in which, if one of the partners fails to meet his contractual obligations, the other can hope to obtain redress in court. But the state apparatus has a cost. More generally, all transactions have a cost. The neo-institutional economy is thus often defined as "the economy of transaction costs."

Douglass North tried to define more precisely the notion of an institution.[51] Institutions include all the forms of constraint used by humans to regulate their mutual relationships. Institutions are in fact both formal and informal: legal rules, simple conventions, codes of conduct—all of these can fall under the rubric of "institutions." Institutions can be created, like the Constitution of the United States, or they can evolve over time, like British Common Law. Institutional constraints include both the forbidden and the permitted. They are comparable to the rules of playing a game. An essential part of the functioning of institutions is the cost of identifying violations and carrying out sanctions. North introduces in addition a distinction between institutions and organizations. Like institutions, organizations provide structure for human relations. The cost of this institutional framework is not limited to the framework itself but also includes that of the organizations that have developed as a result of the framework. Thus North distinguishes between rules (institutions) and actors (organizations). Rules are the rules of the game. But the objective of the team (the organization) is to win the game through a combination of competences, strategies, and coordinations, by fair means and sometimes by foul. Modeling the strategies and competences of a team is a process different from that of modeling the creation, evolution and consequences of rules. Organizations include political bodies (political parties, city councils, regulatory agencies, and so on), economic bodies (firms, unions, farms, cooperatives), social bodies (churches, clubs, athletic associations), and educative bodies (schools, universities). These are groups that have been formed to attain specific objectives. Here the accent is put on the interaction between institutions and organizations.

Defining institutions as constraints that humans impose on each other creates a definition complementary to the approach of the theory of choices that is the foundation of classical economics. Institutions affect the performance of the economy through their effect on the costs of exchange and production. Like the technology used, they determine the costs of transaction and transformation (production) that together constitute the total cost. Before Coase and Williamson, the analysis of transaction costs in the economic domain had been neglected. Neoclassical microeconomics was interested in production and consumption, not in transaction costs. North shifted the focus to the latter—for example, in a world in which legal rules prevail, to the analysis of the cost of contracts and the settlement of legal conflicts (attorney's fees, court costs). He even shows that in complex societies like those of our own time, the branches that are directly involved in guaranteeing that transactions proceed correctly (legal services, financial supervision, insurance, and so on) tend to become the primary sector of activity. Here we are at the antipodes of societies that preceded the Industrial Revolution, in which the great majority of the population was occupied in producing food. In North's work, in addition to the sector that is directly connected with what we now call the "economic sector," the existence of organizations ensuring the predictability of future transactions is thus itself the object of an economic analysis. Providing for the maintenance of property rights has a cost—for instance, the cost of the police, the army, and the legal system, which are the organizations that guarantee these rights. Beyond these, the interaction of all forms of social life can be analyzed in terms of cost. Education has a cost, as does the upbringing of children. Thus, to give one among many possible examples, the rise or fall of the standard of living generally has direct effects on demography that may vary radically depending on the period and the environment.

In North's view, the diverse parameters of social life can be analyzed in terms of cost. He has been accused of proposing a kind of "cliometric imperialism" that, while distinguishing itself from neoclassicism, nonetheless applies to social life as a whole analytical categories that the neoclassical economists restricted to the sphere of the production and consumption of material goods. Moreover, New Institutional Economics (which, to simplify matters, we will consider here as a unified whole) sets out to analyze in economic terms the genesis of institutions. This is not in itself a totally new project, but it is the first time that it has been developed systematically. We also see the difference from Weberism: the latter made institutions "things in themselves" existing independently of the economy, which they take charge of and overdetermine. As we have seen, that is why for Weber the "economy" of the societies that preceded capitalism could only be nonexistent, a set of *membra disjecta* without internal coherence. It is true that the theory of institutional evolution worked out in North's first works is open to legitimate criticism. Analyzing the forms of European expansion in the Middle Ages and the modern period, North showed that this expansion took place in the framework of a genuine transformation of the institutional environment: the replacement of the regulatory systems of the Middle Ages by a system guaranteeing all property rights and doing away with any communitarian restrictions on them.[52]

But above all, North stressed that it was the comparative efficiency of the new institutions that had caused the old ones to disappear. In short, whereas according to Gresham's law "bad money drives out good," here the opposite is the case: good institutions drive out bad. If that had been the case, we would have had the key to the development of societies. While pursuing his analyses in terms of transaction costs, North himself quickly stressed the limits of this way of thinking. The conscious, voluntary replacement of less efficient economic institutions with others that perform better is possible only in the framework of societies that seek economic performance. The counterexamples of the maintenance of underperforming institutions (if we adhere to North's definition cited earlier) are so numerous that they invalidate *a priori* the idea that we could apply the neoclassical rule of comparative efficiency to forms of institutional change, and consequently to the performance of economic systems. North himself was thus vulnerable to the criticism that he wanted to attribute institutional change to a single cause to be sought in the effect of a constraint of rarity. He tried to escape this logical trap by presenting a series of analyses showing the complexity of the historical forms of economic development and institutional change. In 1981, for example, North showed that when a state is in the hands of a group that uses it for its own benefit, this can block any development. Concern for the common interest was certainly not characteristic of the groups that traditionally monopolized state power for their own ends, as the "second North" conceded. His more recent analyses, particularly regarding the economic development of modern Europe, also show his effort to counter this criticism.[53]

Constrained Choices, Limited Rationality, and Economic Performance

The special interest of North's work is thus that it does away with the airtight barrier between political or religious institutions and economic paradigms. If institutions, which structure the economy, are themselves a function of constraints of rarity through the costs they impose, if institutional change can have rarity as one of its structuring constraints, then the two-stroke engine of an infrastructure for which the superstructure takes responsibility in societies before capitalism loses all plausibility. However, while North was interested in the logic of the transformation of institutions, we still have to establish an overall model of the different types of social institutions and their interconnections. Today, the challenge is to move analyses of isolated phenomena (kinship, political institutions, and so on) to a general model of the interconnections among institutions and, in the same way, a general model of institutional evolution. Thus, meeting this challenge also means proposing a single analytical model of the place and role of the economy in societies as different as those of hunter-gatherers, an empire, the Classical Mediterranean world, the European Middle Ages, or contemporary globalized capitalism.

From this point of view, we should emphasize first that institutions are not gratuitous constructions. They have to manage concrete situations in which they must play their role of limiting uncertainty. The system of rules and social norms has its own logic, which is historically constituted, and these norms are "polished" over time to become perfectly effective in the context of the society concerned. This logic is a function of the constraints of the world in which they are situated. The goal of this system of rules and norms is to guarantee the reproduction of this social organization. Actors' behavior is modeled on these rules. This is the case in particular for institutions providing for the management of material goods. As soon as we begin to study the logic of a system of production or exchange in a precapitalist society, we see that we are very far from being in an "irrational" world—in fact, the contrary is true. Production processes, whether in the area of agriculture or that of craftsmanship, usually show a perfect adaptation to the milieu and to technological constraints. If that had not been so, no production or trade would have been possible, and the society in question would have collapsed. In dealing with the constraint of rarity, the corresponding institutions function in an organized and rational way. They are structured on the basis of what we will call an "internal rationality." They are, of course, more or less "efficient," depending on the particular case—that is, depending on natural resources, the technological level, or other institutional constraints, they guarantee a more or less elevated level of the production of material goods. But in no way can they be relegated to a form of the logic of chaos and of irrational behavior.

The analyst's task is therefore not to make value judgments, to establish a borderline separating "economically rational societies" from "economically irrational societies." The task is first to describe the logic of an institutional system and if possible to demonstrate in a comparative way its degree of efficiency. Thus we see that we have to provide a definition of economics different from the one that was initially given. *Homo economicus*, an individual whose choices are perfectly free, who is perfectly informed, and who exercises his free will as if he were the only one to do so, is no longer appropriate. An economic actor has to confront a multitude of constraints, those of the natural environment, of the technological level, and of institutions. His information is imperfect and his rationality is by definition limited. Thus economics can be defined as the theory of choices within constraints applied to the management of goods.

As for economic performance, the internal rationality of an institutional system can either favor individual maximizing behaviors (everything depends on the circumstances and stakes involved for its own reproduction) or discourage them. All societies, from hunter-gatherer societies to contemporary society, are subject to the law of rarity and costs. Behaviors that maximize utility and avoid risks are potentially found in all times and places. They must be related to the potentially rational character of individuals in achieving their objectives, even though institutions may be as far removed from "rational" and "productive" as possible. Whatever the technological environment, a peasant who sees himself systematically deprived of a large part of what he produces will have no interest in producing more, in improving his farming. In short, the propensity to maximize, which exists in every system, and without which there would be no production of goods and services at all, is a function of the incentives provided by rules for reproducing the social system. This allows us to explain the differential between stagnant societies and those that are undergoing rapid change. Thus we avoid the dichotomy between maximizing capitalist societies and nonmaximizing precapitalist societies. The modification of the rules brought about by the evolution of the system also allows us to explain the fact that a single culture may undergo a series of phases of expansion, stagnation, or regression.

Let us add that, far from neglecting mastery over material goods (commercial exchange being only one form of transfer among others), we could say, paradoxically, that traditional societies are completely obsessed with it. It is this mastery that also conditions the behavior of individuals (immediate survival is always at stake for the shepherd or farmer) and groups (a community will use all its advantages in its relations with other communities, a state will demand all the tributes that are due it, and so on). Mastery over material goods can lead to fierce violence in interindividual or group-to-group relations (although of course this is not the only source of such violence). The same goes for the symbolic level: the group's life and reproduction are guaranteed by the deities, whether in the form of the sun god of the Egyptians or the Incas, the Mesopotamian or Syrian gods, the Jewish god, and so forth: the gods are above all the protectors of the cosmic order, vegetation, and the simple reproduction of beings in their very existence. But the logic of organizations, in which the means becomes an end, leads to processes of accumulation for accumulation's sake that naturally have nothing to do with a "concern about growth in productivity," but neither do they have anything to do with a so-called substantive economy imagined to "satisfy people's needs." The expenditures made for the gods in monumental constructions or religious festivals are "nonrational on the economic level" only if we forget that it was the gods who were believed to reproduce the social order and the existence of the system itself. Thus we see here a loop in which the effect (the symbolic construction) is taken for the cause, but in which the institutional logic makes the expenditure perfectly rational in the eyes of the actors.

It is thus correct to say that a society had no economy and lived for politics or religion if we consider only that society's discourse on itself; but put forth in a universal way, the proposition makes no sense, because the religious or political discourse is itself only the symbolic form of the system of reproduction. It goes without saying that this symbolic form is directly and inseparably connected with organizations that guarantee that it will be put into practice: a peasant who does not pay his taxes on time will be beaten by tax collectors, as is shown by numerous representations on Egyptian tomb-walls. This kind of situation is found in all traditional societies. That is why the claim, in the tradition of Weber or Finley, that in Classical antiquity *homo politicus* put the economy in the service of politics is a contradiction in terms: *qua* state, the ancient city is only a form of organization in the system of reproduction, and it cannot be separated from the economic system. To put the point concretely: through both their private activities and their participation in the life of the city, citizens had a sense of their economic interests, and constantly imputing "irrational" behaviors to them grossly contradicts the information in our sources.

The institutional and organizational subsystem responsible for the material reproduction of a society is thus governed by what we have called "internal rationality." This is a logic that has its own coherence. On a scale of the maximization of the use of means—that is, the management of rarity, which is the definition given by classical and neoclassical economics—we see systems that will maximize to a greater or lesser degree the means available to them. Moreover, the analysis must be conducted in two ways: through observation at a given time, after which the analysis makes it possible to measure the greater or lesser adaptation to the environment, and through observation over time, after which the analysis will take into account performance in transforming the means, that is, the developments in productivity. In other words, we also have to analyze the "external rationality" of a system.

It can be maintained that the internal rationality of a system will be "judged" by its external rationality, understood as the assessment of how a given society makes use of its material resources. An organizational system that does not guarantee a sufficient level of utilization of the material factors available to it will end up collapsing if in order to reproduce itself as a system (which has nothing to do, at least not directly, with the people's standard of living) it consumes more resources than it produces. That is the "iron law" of social organizations. Social organizations could almost be seen as business enterprises in the "jungle of the market," where some finally go bankrupt (except, naturally, that the goal of social organizations is not to make a profit). Even without being impacted by the consequences of a defeat against a foreign enemy, the material basis of a tribal society or an empire can collapse. The reason is that its system of material reproduction cannot perform its role anymore. Beyond a certain point, the use of resources not only no longer allows reproduction of this society, but even leads to its destruction. And without this material basis, the system is doomed.[54]

From this point of view, how should we analyze the place of capitalist societies? They will be defined as societies within which the internal rationality of the system tends to merge with external rationality. Capitalism is a system in which the rules of social organization tend explicitly to operate in such a way that external rationality can be exercised with a minimum of constraints (which does not imply an absence of social rules, but rather the existence of rules integrated into a system allowing the maximization of the production of goods). In this society, the propensity to maximize is at its greatest, and individual maximizing behaviors are magnified. In any case, we see that capitalist society is no longer the ultimate reference point, as it is in Max Weber, but only a society in which "internal rationality" and "external rationality" are closer than they are in others.

The Genesis and Evolution of Institutions

The theory of choices within constraints also allows us to understand the genesis of institutions. How should the genesis of the institutional forms that constitute social life be explained? How can we explain the existence of kinship rules, the state, the different forms of religious belief, and, more generally, institutions, of which the history of human societies offers an infinitely varied picture? The genesis of institutions can be analyzed by reference to constraints connected with the structure of interindividual relationships. These constraints are brought out by game theory, often associated in particular with the mathematician John Nash.

Game theory seeks to analyze and model in mathematical terms the decisions made by different actors, each of whom has his or her own strategy (which may be antagonistic to those of other actors), in dealing with a given situation. Inasmuch as in real life collectivities and individuals are constantly required to make choices, social life as a whole constitutes an immense field to which game theory can be applied. This field includes all the forms of social life, and the management of material goods—the economy, in the ordinary sense of the term—is only one of them.

A well-known case of the application of game theory is the famous "prisoner's dilemma." The police arrest two persons suspected of committing a crime but do not have enough evidence to convict either of them. The investigators offer each of them—separately—a deal. If one of them confesses and the other doesn't, the one who confessed (implicating his accomplice) will be set free, and the one who didn't confess will be sentenced to ten years in prison. If both of them confess, they will each be sentenced to five years in prison. If neither of them confesses, each will be sentenced to only six months in prison. We see that the two actors' strategies are by definition antagonistic. Logically, each of them has an interest in confessing, because he is threatened by the other's decision. But in that case, each of them will be sentenced to five years in prison (thus a total of ten years), whereas if neither of them confesses, the total time in prison will be only one year. This type of situation is called a non-zero-sum game, because the sum of the gains varies depending on the decisions made by the actors and is less than or more than zero, in contrast with zero-sum games, in which the sums of the gains and losses sum to zero (the advantages of some players being exactly balanced by the losses of the others). The model of the prisoner's dilemma is only a simplified example of the situations analyzed by game theory, which is also interested more broadly in situations in which the actors are led to make a series of choices (and not a single choice, as in the simplified case of the prisoner's dilemma). Game theory shows that after a series of choices made by a multitude of actors, one arrives at a situation of equilibrium in which choices can no longer be changed.

This is why game theory is now of crucial importance for understanding social life in general and the genesis of institutions in particular. Institutions are no longer "inexplicable"; they are no longer the prerogative of this or that particular "race," as was commonly thought in the nineteenth century. They correspond to situations of equilibrium, taking into account the constraints of a system at a given moment, and emphasizing, naturally, that the institutional past of a society is one of the system's constraints.[55] Thus we can also understand why different societies that may be entirely foreign to one another can produce similar institutional forms, a point that was already noted by Karl Polanyi.[56]

Thus institutions are on the one hand the result of individual choices, which explains why they are susceptible to transformation, whether slowly and inconspicuously or brutally, depending on the case. On the other hand, in individual choices institutions play the role of a system of constraints. In addition to their role in the functioning of a society, the most prominent characteristic of institutions is to produce rules and organizations that guarantee their own survival. To limit uncertainty, which is their primary role, institutions have to provide a guarantee of their own permanence, which ensures that later on the rules they have defined will still be valid.

The institutions of a given society can be classified in four main sectors[57]: the political (the state or other forms of collective authority), the symbolic (religion and other worldviews), the reproduction of persons (kinship and demography), and the production of material goods (economics). Together, they form a system with a specific structure, and each of these sectors has only a relative autonomy. Beyond their declared function, they also guarantee the reproduction of the dominant groups that embody them and to the advantage of which they have been constituted. So far as economic institutions are concerned, the logic of material reproduction varies considerably from one institutional system to another. Thus institutions can have an internal logic of reproduction involving, for example, the constant renewal of their material base (whence expanding societies, of which capitalist society is an example, though not the only possible one), or their strict, identical reproduction (whence static societies, stagnating for millennia).

In theory, the institutional system is intended to reproduce itself unchanged. In practice, because it is confronted by constraints not only of an external order (the confrontation with other societies) but also, and just as much, of an internal order (through an endogenous transformation of the social equilibrium), sooner or later we see a blockage of the process of reproduction involving, for example, the emergence within the system of social groups that challenge the old order—that is, the old dominant groups and their institutional systems—and these new groups may eventually succeed in imposing new institutional configurations.

Opposing a "rationality" of the capitalist world to an "irrationality" of other societies merely reflects an evolutionist prejudice. It is possible and legitimate to analyze the economy of societies anterior to capitalism, and particularly the ancient economy, which was not the primitive and irrational world portrayed by Max Weber and Moses Finley. The specific economic institutions of the ancient world, whose study cannot be separated from that of other institutions (politics, religion, kinship), were not in any way "irrational." They simply responded to constraints that were different from those of our own world. Institutionalist and neo-institutionalist thinkers have shown that institutions functioned to reduce uncertainty. At the same time, they have shown that these institutions themselves had a cost. Furthermore, they have raised the question of the genesis of institutions, which cannot be separated from their economic function. In place of a model of the systematic replacement of "less successful" institutions by "more successful" ones, we should, however, substitute a multifactorial model in which the diverse institutional systems that guarantee the reproduction of (1) the supervision of people (politics); (2) the symbolic image-repertory (religion); (3) the human fabric (kinship); and (4) material life (the economy) are constantly reverberating off each other. So far as material life is concerned, the "internal rationality" of the system of reproduction (its institutional logic) is subject to a reality principle. Its performance in matters concerning the use of the natural resources put at its disposal is defined here as its "external rationality": a society cannot consume more than it produces, on pain of death. The inspiration provided by "neo-institutional economics" allows us to move beyond the old debates between primitivists and modernists or substantivists and formalists. It is from this perspective that the study of the ancient economy will be envisaged here.[58]

STRUCTURES
AND
PRODUCTION

II

PEOPLE IN THEIR ENVIRONMENT

As Karl Popper famously pointed out, "To say that a species now living is adapted to its environment is, in fact, almost tautological. Indeed, the terms 'adaptation' and 'selection' are used in such a way that one can say that, if the species were not adapted, it would have been eliminated by natural selection."[1] This is hardly surprising, since adaptation is the primary condition for a species' existence. The same remark can be applied to the particular "species" constituted by human societies. By definition, they are all "adapted to their environments," but it is the forms of adaptation that distinguish them from one another. In relation to the technological level and the dynamics peculiar to it, a society takes advantage of the possibilities its natural environment offers. But the constraints this environment imposes on it also guide its development. In a way, a society becomes itself an element of the ecology of a region. It is the interrelations among these multiple factors as they react to one another that have to be taken into account, precisely on the model of ecological studies. Among these factors, energy plays a paramount role because of its implications for economic development. Particular attention will be given to this factor in the next chapter.

In the development of the environment, the number of people is an essential parameter. In the same way, the dynamics of population is both a determinant and a resultant of economic development. The demographic history of Greece from the Archaic to the Hellenistic period shows this in an eloquent way.

THE ECOLOGICAL FRAMEWORK

Greece famously falls into the category of Mediterranean countries. In a rare coincidence, two books published in two successive years have explored the milieu of the Mediterranean area. In their systematic ecological analysis of Mediterranean Europe, published in 2001, Alfred T. Grove and Oliver Rackham noticed that fragmentation can be considered one of the region's distinctive features.[2] Peregrine Horden and Nicholas Purcell, meanwhile, produced in 2000 a global study of the

31

Mediterranean region as a whole in a social and economic perspective, considering that its hallmark was "connectivity," defined as a forced collaboration between non-self-sufficient microregions.[3] Fragmentation and an exceptional biodiversity in a collection of niches also appear prominently in the "super longue durée" history of the Mediterranean provided by Cyprian Broodbank.[4] Thus, with good cause, these three studies insisted (to varying degrees) on the fragmentation of the Mediterranean milieu as one of its most fundamental characteristics. Not only is Greece no exception to this rule, but it also provides perhaps its best possible example.

The Constraints Imposed by Topography and Soils

Greece's topography results from the collision of two tectonic plates, the European plate and the Asiatic plate.[5] The zone of subduction constituted by the Aegean Sea corresponds to the contact between the two plates. This is a first factor of instability. In addition, the pressure of the African plate makes itself felt to the south. The African plate is moving north and tends to slide underneath the European and Asiatic plates. One of the consequences of this is the existence of a vast tectonic underwater trench that arcs around Greece on the south and reaches depths of more than 5,000 meters. That is why Greece and Asia Minor are extensively fractured and very seismically active areas. Thus the zone of the Gulf of Corinth is repeatedly ravaged by earthquakes. In Asia Minor, the fragmentation of the topography corresponds to fault lines. The depression of the Propontis (the Sea of Marmara) in the north, the great axis formed by the valley of the Maeander in the center, or, farther to the south, the Keramic Gulf (Gulf of Gökova), all correspond to tectonic troughs. The Aegean islands are raised fault blocks in a system fractured like piano keys. The same reasons explain the presence of several volcanic islands in the Aegean. From Methana, in Argolis, to Nisyros, off the coast of Asia Minor, there is a volcanic arc that passes through Melos and Thera. This very specific tectonic configuration has a series of crucial consequences for the geographical conformation of the Aegean area and hence for its economic life.

First, the fragmentation of the topography and the presence of a series of subducted cells mean that even in mainland Greece, the sea is never very far away. No point in the territory of the modern Greek Republic is more than ninety kilometers from the sea. Obviously, there are regional variations: a region like Thessaly, separated from the sea by the mountain ridge of Magnesia, was not as oriented toward maritime activities as was the Attic peninsula. But no region of Greece was so far from the sea that it could escape the latter's influence. On the economic level, given the type of organization that was established in the Greece of the first millennium BCE, this is a major fact that favored, if not the unity, at least the homogeneity of the various polities' economic organization, as well as the intense interaction of the various regions.

Second, the frequency of earthquakes in the Aegean area, some of which could be particularly destructive, was not without economic consequences.[6] It is easy to understand why Poseidon, who was the god of the sea but also the god of earthquakes, was revered throughout Greece. Some of these earthquakes had far-reaching historical consequences. The one that struck Sparta in 464 BCE caused a significant number of casualties among the young *eirenes* (the equivalent of the Athenian *ephebes*), who were killed when their gymnasium collapsed, and it led to a major revolt of the helots.[7] In 373 BCE, the Achaian city of Helike, located east of Aigion on the south coast of the Gulf of Corinth, was swallowed up by the sea in a single night as a result of the slippage of a fault block (Boura, its little neighbor, was destroyed by the earthquake).[8] The major Rhodes earthquake that occurred between 229 and 226 BCE was very devastating, but it also resulted in a strong show of solidarity on the part of the great powers of the time.[9] At frequent but unpredictable intervals, these societies confronted the risk of serious human losses and the repeated destruction of their infrastructure, both rural (less spectacular but with serious economic consequences) and urban.[10]

To be sure, no traditional technology can survive major earthquakes. But in addition, despite the desire to make structures earthquake-proof that is shown by many construction details, the architectural techniques of antiquity were on the whole poorly adapted to resist seismic activity. In construction using large stone blocks, the latter were connected by cramp irons that could limit their movement in the event of a weak earthquake. But temples and public buildings using the technique of the column, usually made of drums set atop one another, were likely to be sheared off in the event of strong seismic shocks parallel to the ground, although this also gave some flexibility in case of minor earthquakes. Buildings using the technique of the arch and vault, with the distribution of forces that it makes possible, resist earthquakes better. Introduced in the Hellenistic period, this technique was largely used in Roman times but was not fully developed until the medieval period.

However, beyond isolated events whose local consequences can be very important, the question must be asked what overall impact these phenomena might have had on economic development. Incontestably, seismic activity was a factor that must have slowed development, since in some regions massive investments had to be made periodically simply in order to regain the previous level of equipment. Nonetheless, if we consider the whole of the Greek world over the long term, earthquakes and tsunamis certainly had no more than a marginal impact on the economic development of Greece.

Topography

The topography of Greece is a young one, the result of a geological movement accompanied by folding that dates from the Tertiary Period. Mountains are found everywhere. With a few rare exceptions, such as the subduction basins of Thessaly and Boiotia, Greece has plains of only limited extent. While the sea is always nearby, this is also true for zones of mountains or high hills. That is the basis for the opposition between *ager*, the cultivated area, and *saltus*, the wild, peripheral area, which is characteristic of all Mediterranean countries, but is particularly accentuated in Greece.

The fundamental orientation of the topography is determined by a line of upheaval and folding that runs from northwest to southeast. This essential axis can be clearly seen on a map, with the axis of the Pindos mountain range in northern Greece, and is also found in the orientations of the island of Euboia (east of Attika), of the peninsulas of the southern Peloponnese, and of the Kykladic island chains (figure 2.1). Northern Greece is characterized by the presence of a major mountain range, the Pindos, accompanied farther east by another line of uplands that includes the highest peak in Greece, Mount Olympos (2,980 meters). The two slopes of the Pindos differ sharply, and despite their strong interrelationships the two zones are sufficiently distinct for their history and economic life to have developed in opposite directions: Macedon has always looked more to the Aegean than toward Epeiros, while Epeiros has always looked more toward Adriatic horizons than toward Macedon. Farther south, in central Greece and the Peloponnese, such

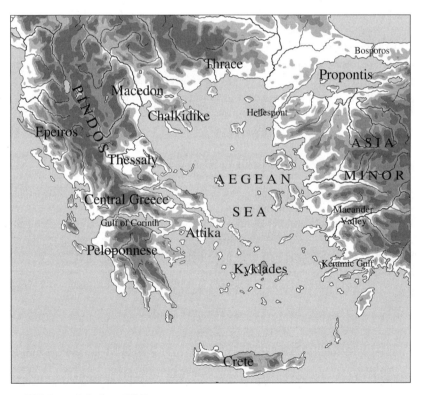

FIGURE 2.1. Relief map of Greece.

a strong opposition between slopes tends to disappear, because the topography does not constitute a barrier of the same magnitude.

The soils correspond to the topography. There are few or no soils that have been accumulated as a result of winds. For the most part, the soils are of the karst type.[11] In the higher areas, there are only very poor soils, or even bare rock: these areas are not arable and can be used only for forest plantations or pastures. On the plains, the soils are essentially clays formed by the decomposition of limestone. This differentiation between upland zones and plain zones also has major hydraulic consequences. In the limestone-rich areas of the uplands, water is rapidly absorbed, and these zones suffer from chronic droughts. But in the clayey soils of the basins, water accumulates and forms marshy areas if there is no easy outlet to the sea. That was the case for Boiotia, the center of which was occupied by Lake Kopais, whose level oscillated with the blocking or unblocking of the *katavothres*, the natural outlets that passed through the karst.[12] This was also the case in Thessaly, which was inadequately drained by the Enipeus and Peneios rivers. Though they are less extensive (as for example in Euboia with Lake Ptechai, well known for the projects undertaken to drain it), marshy areas are found nearly everywhere. Although they were not without economic usefulness, they reduced the surface area available for agriculture.[13]

Depending on their degree of evolution and on their thickness, the natural soils might be of little agricultural value or, on the contrary, very fertile. It would therefore be a mistake to think that Greek soils were uniformly poor. Red and black clays may locally produce soils permitting good harvests—usually, however, over limited areas. Pockets of excellent soil in doline sinks may be found in the middle of hilly areas that have virtually no soil or vegetation. The micro-local fragmentation of arable land is thus a special constraint on agriculture, because it can mean that it takes a long time to get from one parcel of arable land to another. The coastal plains of Asia Minor offered larger areas for cultivation on alluvial soils, where there was also frequently a drainage problem. Finally, on the island of Lemnos, there were volcanic soils of exceptional fertility, but only over limited areas.

The Climatic Constraint

As explained later, the climate in Greece in antiquity was not exactly the same as that of today. However, it was also a Mediterranean climate, which justifies basic structural comparisons with the climate of today.[14] One might begin by quoting many authors on "a sunlit and picturesque country," where "the mountains clearly outline their contours against the intense azure of the sky." To be sure, this description is correct, at least for the summer. But things are not so simple. Greece has a Mediterranean climate, and thus it is marked by violent contrasts. There is a clear difference between winter and summer, both in temperature and in rainfall (tables 2.1 and 2.2; figure 2.2). It rarely freezes in Athens. In January, the average temperature does not fall below 10°C. But in summer, it can rise to 40°C, and the average for the warmest month is 28°C. Rainfall is heavy from October to March, but light

TABLE 2.1. Temperature (°C) and Precipitation (mm) in Athens

	J	F	M	A	M	JU	JY	A	S	O	N	D
Temp.	10.3	10.6	12.3	15.9	20.7	25.2	28	27.8	24.2	19.5	15.4	12
Prec.	43.2	40.9	39.7	26	15.2	5.6	5.2	7	9.6	47.8	55.4	64.1

TABLE 2.2. Temperature (°C) and Precipitation (mm) in Ioannina (Epeiros)

	J	F	M	A	M	JU	JY	A	S	O	N	D
Temp.	4.7	6.1	8.8	12.4	17.4	21.9	24.8	24.3	20.1	14.9	9.7	5.9
Prec.	124.2	111.6	95.4	78	69.3	43.5	32	31.2	54	99.5	167.9	174.9

during the rest of the year. The long dry period in summer, about four months long, eliminates species that cannot endure it. For the ancient Greeks, the dead season was summer. With certain qualifications, this description could be applied to the whole of Aegean Greece.

However, an important corrective factor should be mentioned. The Pindos mountain range, which, as we have seen, extends into central Greece and as far as the Peloponnese, produces an orographic lift. Epeiros, upper Macedon, the central Peloponnese, and in general all the mountainous regions have very low temperatures in the winter that sometimes fall as low as −20°C. Snow covers all the higher areas, including in Crete. Average January temperatures in Ioannina, in Epeiros, are much lower than in Athens, and summers there are less warm. Above all, the summer drought is absent. In winter, rainfall is abundant. In Ioannina, we are in a humid Greece where dryness is not a problem (figure 2.3).[15]

The map shows a dissymmetry between western Greece, which is wet and has an annual rainfall above 800 millimeters, and Aegean Greece, where, especially in

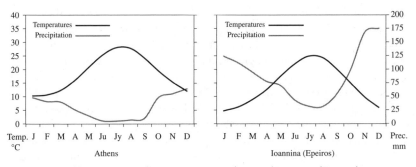

FIGURE 2.2. Temperature and precipitation in Athens and Ioannina (Epeiros).

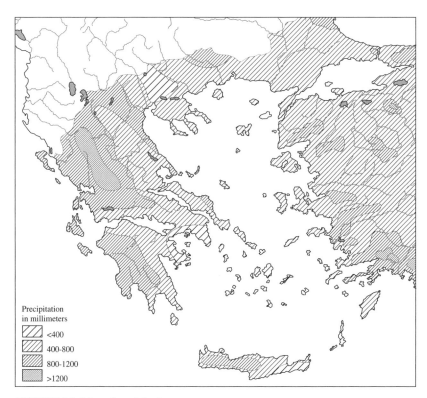

FIGURE 2.3. Map of precipitation.

Attika and the islands, the average annual rainfall can be less than 400 millimeters. Athens receives on average only 360 millimeters of rain per year, but Ioannina receives 1,082 millimeters. This dissymmetry can be seen in figure 2.3 and in figure 2.4, which presents a diagram of precipitation along an axis stretching from Elis in the west to the Keramic Gulf in the east. The hydraulic deficit is thus not general. It concerns only the area around the Aegean basin. However, inasmuch as it was in this zone that the largest and most populous, and (at least in the Classical period) most economically advanced cities were found, this hydraulic deficit took on a special importance. Because the climatic constraint was very severe, it forced people to find ways of coping with it, and that is an essential factor for understanding the mode of development of the cities in these regions. The end of the Classical period and the beginning of the Hellenistic period saw a partial revenge of "humid Greece" (Macedon, Epeiros, and Aitolia).

The system of winds is characterized by an opposition between summer and winter. From May to September, the winds on the Aegean Sea blow from north to south. They are strong, regular, dry winds caused by the high-pressure systems that build up in the Balkans during the summer.[16] Starting at the end of September, the

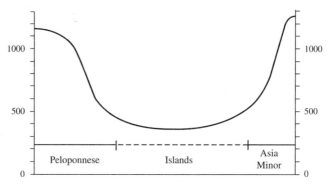

FIGURE 2.4. Diagram of precipitation (between Elis in the west and the Keramic Gulf in the east).

winds turn around, blowing out of the south because of high pressures in Africa and low pressures in the Balkans, and they bring rain.

In the driest part of Greece, the vegetation is typical of Mediterranean countries. Its natural form is forest (live oak, cork oak, pine, fir on the uplands), which may deteriorate into scrubland. Tall groves of cypress, oak, and even pine were rather rare in Aegean Greece. Most tree species provided little more than firewood, and few logs suitable for use in constructing roofs or ships. Northern and western Greece, as well as the more elevated parts of Asia Minor (Troas, Mysia, inner Karia), could, however, provide this material in abundance.

There were no doubt extensive forests at the dawn of the Neolithic Age and still around 2000 BCE, at the end of the Early Bronze Age. But by the Classical period, Greece was suffering from severe deforestation, and lacked wood for naval construction and heating. This is not a cliché. Deforestation was fundamentally linked to the demographic burden that Greece had to bear at that time. In a famous passage of the *Critias* (110d–111e), the one where he develops the myth of Atlantis, Plato rhetorically contrasts the Attika of the past with that of his own time. In earlier times, he says, Attika was covered with forests and the soil was rich. But in the course of time and after many catastrophic deluges, the earth had slipped into the sea, leaving only the soil's carcass.[17] Now the soil of Attika was poor, the forest had disappeared, and the proud Athenians, who had once defeated the inhabitants of Atlantis, had lost their former virtue. We see all the philosopher's ulterior motives. But there is still the picture of an Attika with poor soils and a meager vegetative cover. Nearly everywhere in Greece, the conjunction of karst, steep slopes, and localized but extremely violent floods can lead to soil erosion, which can be limited (certainly not wholly checked) only by a careful human management of the landscape.[18] Greece in the Classical and Hellenistic period was a heavily populated region where wood was in very high demand for timber and fuel and where goat-raising did a great deal to prevent trees from growing back. This must have markedly contributed to the progressive deterioration of the environment.[19]

The Variability of the Climate and Vegetation

Ancient perceptions lead us to raise the fundamental question of climate and its consequences for paleo-environments. Up to this point, this question has been ignored, as if one could simply assume that the climate of Classical and Hellenistic Greece was identical with the contemporary climate. However, the old dogma of the invariability of climates in the historical period has now been definitively exploded. The rapid variations being undergone by the climate today have accentuated our sensitivity to and interest in this question. In France, Emmanuel Le Roy Ladurie has been a pioneer in collecting data that allow us to identify climatic variations during the medieval and early modern periods.[20] We can now distinguish the phases of cooling and warming that have taken place over the past millennium. We can also gauge their historical consequences, or at least attempt to estimate the impact of these phases. Europe underwent a period of warming during the "Medieval Climate Optimum" (also known as "Medieval Climate Anomaly," or MCA) that started around 900 CE and lasted until about 1200 CE. This was succeeded by what is generally called the "Little Ice Age (LIA)," which began in the fourteenth century and ended in the middle of the nineteenth, and which first peaked at the turn of the seventeenth century, then at the turn of the eighteenth century, and then peaked again at the turn of the nineteenth century. The advance of glaciers observed at that time is one of numerous manifestations of this phenomenon.

Unfortunately, for the history of ancient Greece we do not have written sources comparable to the personal diaries or the monastic archives in western Europe or Japan of the medieval and early modern periods, although some indications given by ancient writers point to a climate that was both colder and wetter than today.[21] Nor do we have paintings showing significant landscapes, like the paintings of Alpine glaciers that have been so brilliantly used by Le Roy Ladurie. However, we should not underestimate the indications provided by ancient writers. The study of ancient climates is currently based on proxies like sedimentation, tree rings, ice cores, or sea levels. Each of these proxies both brings valuable information and has its own specific difficulties of interpretation. Recent studies have begun to provide detailed evidence for long-term climate evolutions, themselves linked to cycles of solar activity.[22] Although most of them are interested more in the climate evolution over the last two millennia, for the first time studies on long-term evolution that include the first millennium BCE have recently been made available. Even if these results still need to be fully confirmed and refined, they provide interesting indications on the climate evolution for the period from ca. 600 BCE to the Common Era. The conclusions, it must be remembered, have to be adapted to the regions in question. The explanatory schema concerns the Mediterranean area and is not a universal key. For example, cycles of "warming/dryness" and "cooling/heavier rainfall" are not characteristic of northern Europe, where, because of different air circulation patterns, temperature variations do not have the same effect. During the period of global warming of the MCA, not only temperatures were higher in northern

Europe, but precipitations increased, the reverse being true for southern Europe. The reverse took place during LIA, where precipitation decreased in northern Europe, but increased in southern Europe.

Several convergent series of observations show that late antiquity and the beginning of the Byzantine period were marked by very heavy alluvial deposits, and hence by a sharp increase in precipitation, which was itself connected with a decrease in temperatures.[23] The cooling phase was particularly intense after 500 CE. It was at this time, for instance, that the site of the sanctuary at Olympia was partly destroyed and covered with heavy layers of fluvial alluvium (gravel).[24] Then came the warming that corresponded to the previously mentioned Medieval Climate Optimum. In the same way, based on these studies of alluvial deposits it has been possible for the first time to propose a plausible (if not yet certain) schema of climatic evolution in Classical, Hellenistic, and Roman Greece.

If on the whole, as observed earlier, antiquity was certainly somewhat cooler and wetter than today, the Greek Classical age seems to have been marked by a brief but very strong cooling phase that started around 500 BCE and extended into the fourth century, a sort of Little Ice Age.[25] The Hellenistic period and Early Imperial period appear to have been comparatively warmer. These provisional conclusions, also based on soil studies carried out in Sicily (Selinous) and in central and northern Italy, have to be qualified and confirmed by other analyses made in the Mediterranean area, particularly in Greece.[26] However, we should keep in mind that a reversal of the climatic situation could have played a significant role in the economic development of a region. It is clear that for Mainland Greece and the islands, a decrease in temperature and an increase in precipitation are particularly favorable for the driest areas, like Attika, the Eastern Peloponnese, and the Kyklades, where they would make larger harvests possible. In regions where rainfall was abundant, like northern and western Greece, an excess of rain could only be harmful, rotting seeds and thus reducing harvests. The reverse is true when the climate becomes warmer and drier, as was the case in the Hellenistic period and in the first two centuries of the Imperial period. The driest areas are negatively impacted, while the wettest regions benefit from new warmer and drier conditions.

In less technologically advanced societies, which involved much greater direct interaction with the natural environment than is the case for modern societies, climate could certainly have had an influence on economic development, including both long-term tendencies and short-term contexts. One thinks, for instance, of the series of poor harvests at the end of the eighteenth century that contributed to the instability that led to the French Revolution. That said, even if the climate and its evolution play the role of a constraint, they should not be made a causal factor, let alone the only causal factor. It was in the depths of the LIA, and for reasons that went far back and had nothing to do with climate, that England laid the foundations of the economic revolution that later gave it a decisive advantage over the rest of Europe. In the economic and political evolution of Greece in the fourth century BCE and in the Hellenistic period, coinciding factors, such as the decline of Athens, certainly played an essential role. The dynamism of northern and western Greece might, however, have been favored by what was for them more clement climatic conditions. As in the case of medieval and early modern Europe, the role of climate must thus be kept in perspective, but not denied or forgotten.

THE DEMOGRAPHIC MODEL OF ANCIENT GREECE

The standard methods of historical demography have been worked out by studies based on parish registers and other records of vital statistics that have been regularly kept and preserved in early modern and contemporary European societies. But, as in the case of other societies of the past whose archives have been lost, the study of the demography of ancient Greece has to be carried out on different bases. We have to fall back on two kinds of investigation. If we adhere to the traditional method, we must interpret textual sources that provide information of a demographic type. However, because they are not part of regularly kept registries, these sources raise problems of evaluation and interpretation. For a long time, studies of ancient demography focused on the question of numbers. Karl J. Beloch's works on the population of the Greek world in Classical antiquity and those of Arnold W. Gomme on the population of Athens long ago demonstrated the interest of this approach.[27] But in the absence of coherent registries, these works could not take up the basic question of the fundamental demographic parameters of the world of the Greek city-states. So far as texts are concerned, new information is limited to the publication of new inscriptions. But the fundamental biases inherent in the filter imposed by the nature of the evidence and the absence of a large body of demographic information recorded over time remain untouched.

Recently, the study of the demography of antiquity has taken a different direction. Using "model life tables" compiled on the basis of information provided by contemporary populations, attempts have been made to reconstitute the demographic history of a region or country. This is what Mogens H. Hansen and Walter Scheidel have done for fourth-century Athens and Roman Egypt, respectively.[28] The results of archaeological surveys of the territory of the city-states constitute an important addition to the documents available to us and complement earlier points of view. Today, the study of ancient demography is an autonomous field endowed with a considerable bibliography.[29]

Before taking up the question of the size of the population and its evolution, we must first define the demographic model of the world of the Greek city-states.[30] We must also prove (truth be told) that a specific model exists. One may in fact legitimately wonder whether the demographic structures of the world of the Greek city-states when compared with other preindustrial societies, were not in reality perfectly commonplace.[31] Like all societies of the preindustrial period, Greece is said to have been crushed by an excess of mortality. During the most auspicious periods, a low rate of economic growth is supposed to have made possible, over the very long term, slow demographic growth. In turn, reversals of the economic trend are supposed to have provoked a gradual decline in population. But this way of seeing things has to be challenged. To be sure, economic growth rates were much lower than the "records" achieved in our own time, and the rates of decline might be much more rapid than those we have experienced. Nonetheless, in the history of the populations of past societies, the demography of ancient Greece was truly unique. This is the model we have to try to reconstruct. Since the development of a population is connected with its characteristics in matters of fertility and mortality, we must first seek to define these parameters.

Fertility

The fertility rate is a function of two basic variables. The first is the length of the period of reproductive capacity, balanced by the average rate of survival to the age of reproduction.[32] The length of the period of reproduction is calculated by the difference between the average age at which the period of fertility following the menarche begins and the average age at which the period of sterility preceding menopause begins. The period of reproduction can also depend directly on adult female longevity if the average age of death for adult females is lower than the age of sterility preceding menopause, as is the case in many societies. In such circumstances, it is the age of death that determines the length of the period of reproduction. Naturally, these parameters are a function of nutritional and hygienic conditions. For instance, better nutrition can lead to puberty at an earlier age. The second variable, the interval between live births, depends on the length of gestation, the percentage of the population that is sterile, and the fetal death rate.

But fertility also depends on cultural factors, which are of two kinds: on the one hand, those that are the result of social practices that have in themselves no demographic goal, and on the other, those that have an explicit demographic goal.[33] In the first category, we can put the age of marriage, the incidence of separation or divorce, the absence of a husband, the death of a spouse and remarriage, polygamy, postnatal sexual abstinence, abstinence during certain seasons or ceremonies, and temporary or permanent celibacy among certain parts of the population. In the second category, we can put contraceptive practices, abortion, and infanticide. One remark on this last point is necessary here. If we consider infanticide a kind of "late abortion," it is clear that it causes fertility to decline. However, it has been shown that the high number of deaths among infants, whether natural or the result of infanticidal practices, was a factor that tended to increase potential fertility, because the mother was thereby freed of the heavy obligations and fatigue resulting from the presence of an infant: in reality, she was more available for reproduction.

What was the situation in ancient Greece? With rare exceptions such as the age of marriage, the data available for Classical and Hellenistic Greece on the variables that have to be taken into consideration in constructing a demographic model are qualitative, not quantitative, in nature. This does not mean that they are of no interest, however. On the whole, we can assume that menstruation began on average at the age of fourteen.[34] According to the Gortyn code (fifth century BCE), girls could marry starting at the age of twelve.[35] However, as implied by Ephorus, if the bride was too young to be taken to the conjugal bed by her husband, the latter had to wait until his wife was able to play her role.[36] The agreement of the Gortyn inscription and the literary source confirms that the consummation of a marriage would in fact be early, but probably not before around the age of fifteen. In Thasos around 350 BCE, the age of marriage set by the city-state was fourteen.[37] In Marseilles, according to Lucian (*Toxaris or Friendship* 24), Menekrates' daughter was still unmarried at the age of eighteen because she was particularly unattractive.[38] Generally speaking, the isolated scraps of data given by the sources indicate that the age of marriage for women seems to have been around fifteen, while that for men was about thirty, but varied more widely.[39]

Divorce was relatively frequent, and so was the death of a spouse and subsequent remarriage.[40] Men were frequently absent, whether for military campaigns, commercial travel, or other reasons. Polygamy seems to have existed only in very exceptional cases, such as at Athens after the Peloponnesian War, where it was practiced in order to fill the gap left by the heavy losses during the last years of the conflict.[41] We can thus conclude that in general Athenians were monogamous. Whereas a not negligible proportion of men remained unmarried, women had to be married by fifteen or shortly thereafter. This picture, which describes the situation in Athens during the Classical and Hellenistic periods, would certainly be valid, more or less, for most of the cities of the Greek world from early to late antiquity.

Concerning these various parameters, it is true that variations that might *prima facie* seem slight can have very important consequences: a change in any one of the parameters in one direction or another can lead to very different fertility rates, and induce either a decline or a rapid increase in population, assuming that the other variables have not changed. It is precisely the need to assess these phenomena that compels us to construct a demographic model peculiar to ancient Greece.

Mortality

We have seen that the idea most widely held today is that ancient peoples could hardly have had a rate of mortality lower than that of the populations of preindustrial Europe.[42] The burden of proof is on those who seek to challenge this point of view. But the reasons given to explain the decline in mortality that started in 1750 deserve closer examination: the spread in the Old World of plants from the New World; growing immunity to infectious diseases; improvements in hygiene, the environment, and living conditions; increasingly useful medical knowledge. However, can the "preindustrial world" really be considered an undifferentiated whole? If we were to accept that premise, the specificity of each period, society, or region would be negated. Any study would be *a priori* pointless, because we would already know the outcome. In reality, all we can say is that the mortality rates in non- and preindustrial societies were on the whole significantly *higher* than those we experience. But we cannot conclude from this that mortality rates in ancient Greece were consequently *identical* with those of medieval and early modern Europe.

Moreover, within a single country and period—for example, France in the seventeenth and eighteenth centuries—there were significant differences between one region and another. In the eighteenth century, in villages in damp and insalubrious areas like Sologne and Dombes, more than 30 percent of the children died before reaching their first birthdays.[43] In both cases, stagnant water and persistent fog, along with a lack of hygiene, suffice to explain the terrible death rate. In the town of Saint-Trivier-en-Dombes, for instance, everything led to an elevated mortality rate: its location on a poorly drained plain; numerous ponds; a multitude of pools and bogs; the absence of springs, which forced the inhabitants to resort to wells; and the contamination of these poorly constructed wells (edges at ground level, seepage coming from pits for slurry or manure). But in Crulai and many rural parishes in northern France in the seventeenth and eighteenth centuries that were not exactly models of hygiene, the mortality rate of infants less than one year old fell below 25 percent.[44] In eighteenth-century Bigorre (in southwestern France), the mortality rate for the same age category even fell as low as 15 percent. Such major disparities, which were related above all to the conditions of cleanliness and general hygiene, have to make us think. To be sure, for a country like France in the eighteenth century, we can, in theory at least, obtain averages, but they mask the reality, which is the difference from one region to another, and even from one micro-region to another, from the countryside to the city, and, within a single city, between poor neighborhoods and wealthy ones.[45] If we refer to "early modern Europe," what figure should we give? The average, supposing that it could be established? Or higher figures? Or lower ones? Instead of trying desperately to make a quantified comparison, we should reserve judgment regarding the role of the factors in mortality that this excursion through the demography of preindustrial Europe establishes.

Thus we must return to the arguments about the factors lowering mortality that were mentioned earlier, while leaving aside, of course, the one that relates to plants imported from the New World, and, for different reasons, the one concerning immunity to infectious diseases, since the latter is only a consequence of other factors. Can we say that hygienic conditions in the countryside or cities of ancient Greece, from the Classical to the Hellenistic periods, were comparable to those of Europe in the Middle Ages or at the beginning of the modern period—that is, on the whole, just as mediocre? Nothing is less certain. As early as the fourth century BCE, ancient Greek city planning was very far advanced.[46] When possible—that is, when a city was to be founded or refounded—the site was carefully chosen, taking into account first of all climatic conditions. Drawing on a tradition that goes back to the physician and hygienist Hippocrates and to Aristotle, and whose "intermediaries could only be the architects who built the Hellenistic cities," the Roman architect Vitruvius recommended choosing a site where the temperature remained moderate and that was far from swamps, in order to avoid miasmas and fogs.[47] The reflections of physicians, architects, and philosophers on the "type of men" produced by this or that orientation of the city may make us smile.[48] But the fact remains that so far as they could, the city planners of ancient Greece sought to protect inhabitants from diseases. Thus they chose locations away from valley floors, as in the case of Priene, in order to avoid the problems connected with proximity to stagnant water.[49]

If we believe the account given by Heracleides Criticus, the author of a treatise *On the Cities of Greece* written in the first quarter of the third century BCE, Athens was a mediocre town: "Poorly supplied with water, the city is arid. Because it is so old, it is poorly laid out. Most of the houses are simple, few are comfortable."[50] This not very optimistic but surely realistic picture gives us an idea of cities of the ancient type. Argos must have been much the same.[51] But many Greek cities, and in any case all the new cities founded from the fifth century on (including Piraeus, the port of Athens), benefited from city planning of the "Hippodamian" type. A strictly orthogonal grid layout allowed an optimal amount of sunlight to enter the city and made it easier to keep the streets clean. Administrative, commercial, and polluting craft activities were concentrated in special quarters, and this also had hygienic advantages.[52] Other craft activities might be practiced throughout the city and inside homes. If necessary, polluting activities had special facilities, such as basins with running water for the markets where meat and fish were sold in Corinth and Priene.[53] In the largest cities, trash removal seems to have been the rule: Aristotle describes the refuse service in Athens.[54] But this was also the case in more modest cities such as Paros or Thasos.[55] A constant concern for cleanliness is illustrated in Pergamon by the famous regulation of the *astunomoi*: this document shows the minuteness with which a city could care for its general hygiene.[56] As early as the fifth century, cities like Akragas were beginning to build sewer systems.[57] According to Diodorus (11.25.3), after the battle of Himera (480), Carthaginian prisoners were used to dig underground sewers to drain water from the city. It is true that the pipes were not always underground. Built in the fourth century, Priene's facilities reflect a hesitation between the two systems. But three centuries later, Strabo (14.1.37) mentions as an exception among the cities of his time the case of Smyrna, which had no underground sewer system, and he immediately refers to risk of pollution. By the fourth century, even old cities like Athens had underground sewer systems. The same is true of great centers like Ephesos, Delos, and Rhodes, and also of more modest cities like Thasos.[58]

Above all, the water supply was the object of vigilant care.[59] Aristotle emphasized that the salubrity of the water was an absolute imperative for the health of the inhabitants, and recommended that when there was a lack of springs, a double system of distribution should be built, with one network for drinking water and another for household use.[60] We find this principle applied in the little town of Pellene in Achaia.[61] In the Archaic period, several cities had already built aqueducts, some of which brought water from very far away.[62] Naturally, one should also think of the works of tyrants like Periandros in Corinth, Theagenes in Megara, Peisistratos in Athens, and Polykrates in Samos, where the engineer Eupalinos of Megara built his famous tunnel.[63] Hellenistic Rhodes had an excellent freshwater conveyance system.[64] But it is important to emphasize that even small cities, such as Bargasa in the Harpasos Valley in Asia Minor, also had water supply systems that were carefully buried (both for security and hygienic reasons) and well maintained.[65] Finally, public fountains were numerous in the cities of the Classical and Hellenistic periods. Any pollution of these fountains by humans or animals was subject to very severe laws.[66] However, recourse to cisterns was necessary as a precaution, primarily in order to be able to hold out in case of a siege, but probably just as often, despite an increasingly efficient system of aqueducts, for protection against excessively long droughts in summer. In any case, a regulation like that in Pergamon, requiring owners of cisterns to guarantee their cleanliness and watertightness, also shows the city's vigilance.

Generally speaking, the cities of ancient Greece displayed coherent urban planning and had fairly extensive facilities. This was true at the domestic level as well as the public level: the average free man possessed a house that was usually not very spacious, except in the wealthiest neighborhoods, but always with a tiled roof that provided shelter from the rain: Massalia, where the houses had roofs made of clay mixed with straw, was an exception worthy of note.[67] This detail is more important than it at first seems if we remember that until the end of the seventeenth century, houses in many parts of Europe had thatched roofs that offered less protection against humidity and were a source of miasmas. The houses in Olynthos provide a precious clue here. To be sure, Olynthos was a "modern" city (with a Hippodamian layout) and rich, but nothing indicates that it was exceptional. Its destruction by Philip of Macedon in 348 allows us to discover what this "Pompeii of the North" was like. Excavations of houses there have revealed a very harmonious disposition of rooms and a general structure well-adapted to the climate.[68] The north wings of houses were higher to reduce the force of the wind, and the main façades faced south. Interior colonnades provided protection from the heat of summer. Beyond the case of Olynthos, excavations reveal ever more well-built individual houses in various parts of Greece—for example in the Troad.[69]

It is clear, of course, that there was a social hierarchy. Not everyone enjoyed good lodging. The size of houses and their degree of comfort were a function of the means at the disposal of their owners or renters. Many humble people lived in apartment buildings, called *sunoikiai* by our sources, where the space was divided among several occupants.[70] In Delos, despite the existence of large houses (but that were occupied by several households), a large part of the population apparently lived in one- or two-room accommodations, which, if they were on ground floor and opened on a street, could also function as shops or workshops, and which were thus the equivalent of the Roman *tabernae*.[71] In Greek towns, there were also homeless people, who tried to find shelter for instance under the porticos of sanctuaries. We can glimpse this in a famous inscription at the Heraion of Samos, from the second half of the third century: in this sanctuary, we see soldiers, "unemployed men" (*apergoi*), and suppliants (probably including fugitive slaves) trying to traffic alongside people authorized to operate shops conceded by the sanctuary, and also obviously trying to live there.[72] Even within the most imposing houses belonging to the middle or upper class of free men, there was a great difference between the wretched corner reserved for the slave and the master's more comfortable rooms.

Even so, on the whole the achievement is impressive if we compare it to what we see in European cities at the end of the Middle Ages and the beginning of the early modern age. The comparison is not trivial. We have to look to sixteenth- and seventeenth-century Holland to find an urban organization and a private living standard of comparable quality for the mass of the population (in fact, Holland certainly outdid Greece in this regard).

Hygiene is an important factor in reducing mortality in and of itself. We know that even before better food and medical science was able to make a significant contribution in this regard, it was the improvement of hygiene, thanks to general administrative measures and an elevation of the cultural level, that allowed the eighteenth century to achieve the first significant decrease in mortality in the history of Western Europe. But the most ordinary citizen of the Greek cities could certainly have taught Louis XIV of France and his court something about hygiene. In Olynthos, at least a third of the houses that have been excavated had a bathroom equipped with a small "wooden-shoe bathtub."[73] It is likely that in most cities, the proportion of households with such facilities was lower.[74] But even if they did not usually have bathtubs, the Greeks clearly cared a great deal about their personal hygiene, as is abundantly shown by textual sources, vase paintings, and archaeological evidence. For laundry or dishwashing or to make their ablutions at home, Greeks normally used a basin.[75] However, in the fifth century and even more widely in the fourth century BCE, public baths with hot water and bathtubs began to be built, on the model of facilities in gymnasiums, where it was possible to bathe very conveniently for a modest sum.[76] Furthermore, the practice of physical exercise, at least for free, male persons (and even for female citizens in Sparta), could not fail to help fortify health.

When considering factors capable of reducing mortality, we must not forget climatic conditions, which during much of the year were generally more favorable than those in Western Europe. Naturally, there are very noticeable regional differences in Greece. The mountainous regions are very cold in winter, while the interior basins like Boiotia are torrid in summer. Nonetheless, many regions have a moderate climate. Herodotus (1.142.1) is no doubt somewhat ethnocentric but also correct in praising the climate of Ionia, where numerous large urban centers were located: excessive humidity, cold, and heat are in fact all unknown there. Thus, on the one hand, it was possible to save on heating costs, and on the other, infections contracted because of the cold and humidity, which were commonplace but could have serious consequences for infants and young children, were, if not avoided, at least mitigated. To be sure, as Hippocrates already knew,[77] the summer heat could lead to other health problems that were often fatal to newborns (enterocolitis and other digestive infections).[78] Nevertheless, the climatic balance sheet is much more favorable than that of western Europe.

As for the role of medical science in reducing mortality in modern Europe, we know that this became a major factor only belatedly, in the course of the nineteenth century. It was at that time that medicine became truly a science, and, moreover, that its benefits were no longer reserved for a tiny minority of privileged people. So far as ancient medicine is concerned, we must not have any illusions about its scientific level.[79] The real progress made through observation during the Hellenistic period was quickly blocked by social taboos surrounding dissection, and people soon returned to the theory of humors. However, we cannot ignore the services that medicine rendered in practice through a few measures based on common sense. Some physicians clearly seem to have been experienced in matters of childbirth, even if maieutics was in general the prerogative of midwives. It is also certain that doctors could be of significant help in dealing with fractures and, up to a point, in treating wounds. Moreover, medical practitioners were not rare. The institution of "public doctors" allowed cities to acquire the services of a physician in return for compensation and a place where he could treat patients.[80] This does not mean that medical care was free of cost, because doctors continued to receive payments from private individuals. But in the event of a crisis (an epidemic or a military conflict that led, for example, to a siege of the city), having access to a doctor whose services were, under those circumstances, certainly no longer paid for individually, constituted a precious advantage. It may also have been the case that doctors did not refuse to help those who could not pay for treatment.[81] On the whole, we cannot claim that medicine, *qua* science, was a significant direct factor in the decline of mortality. But in association with city planners and administrative officials in the cities, doctors made an important contribution to the decrease in mortality through their role as hygienists and "health officers."[82] The numerous votes for decrees expressing thanks for the activities of one or another doctor tend to confirm the impression that their activities were recognized and appreciated.[83]

It is remarkable that as a whole, Archaic, Classical, and Hellenistic Greece did not experience demographic disasters comparable to those that struck medieval Europe. Cholera seems to have been unknown, as were, it seems, syphilis and smallpox. But most other common diseases were present. Tuberculosis was widespread. Leprosy is well attested in the Hellenistic period—it has been maintained that it might have come into Greece only with the return of Alexander's army, but this is far from certain.[84] The "plague" of Athens in 430–429 and 426, which was certainly not plague but rather typhus, does not represent a normal situation.[85] In fact, the epidemic became so virulent—a third of the population of Athens may have died—only because the whole rural population, fleeing Peloponnesian raids, had crowded into the city without adequate hygiene. It is true that many other diseases claimed their share of victims, like malaria in wet areas, tuberculosis, and diphtheria. A Hippocratic treatise describes with considerable precision an epidemic of diphtheria in Perinthos at the end of the fifth century BCE.[86]

In general, although plants from the New World were not yet available, food supplies must not have been too scanty; the age of puberty for girls was distinctly lower than that in early modern Europe (fourteen as opposed to seventeen or eighteen), and we know the role played by nutrition in this variable. In addition, it is certain that one's exposure to the risk of malnutrition varied depending upon one's social level, status, and gender; in difficult times, the poor could no longer feed themselves appropriately, and slaves and female children were deliberately less well nourished.[87]

In conclusion, we must first of all emphasize that the goal is not to draw an idyllic hygienic picture of antiquity. Certainly, as compared to what we now experience in developed countries, mortality was very high. Everyone was well aware that many babies died in their first week. "Fevers" were not unknown. The rules of hygiene were not always respected (Greek society would be exceptional if they had been).[88] Similarly, the use of cisterns in situations where no source of potable water was available must have been the cause of many problems if all the necessary precautions were not taken. In case of a serious disease, medical treatment was of no avail. The list of factors affecting the mortality rate could certainly be much longer. But in the end, and with the indispensable reservations connected with chronological, climatic, and economic differences, nothing indicates that mortality in ancient Greece should be equated with the highest levels found in early modern Europe. On the contrary, everything suggests that average or even low figures should be adopted. If we want to construct a demographic model of ancient Greece, we have to introduce an important corrective to the model of a very elevated mortality rate that has been accepted up to this point.

Demographic Structures and the Potential for Expansion

There is in addition a major difference from the demography of early modern Europe. The age of marriage for women in ancient Greece, which, as previously stated, was usually around fifteen (or a little after), contrasts with the late marriage practiced in France and England in the seventeenth and eighteenth centuries. Thus in northern France between 1650 and 1750, women married, on average, at the age of twenty-six or twenty-seven, depending on the region.[89] Whereas the rate of celibacy was very low (a few percentage points), couples had on average five or six children, again with regional variations.[90] In England, the mean age at first marriage for women oscillated between 26.0 and 26.5 between 1600 and 1749, with a peak between 1650 and 1699.[91] Additionally, in England the proportion of unmarried people was significantly high, peaking above 25 percent in the years 1686–1691.[92] It was observed long ago that late marriage and celibacy were the most effective means of birth control in preindustrial societies. In late eighteenth-century England, the lowering of age at first marriage immediately translated into higher fertility rates.[93] But in ancient Greece, with a period of fertility ten years longer than in late seventeenth-century England, we can very roughly estimate the potential fertility, in the absence of contraception or factors such as the departure of the spouse, at an average of about ten children per adult married woman.

This figure seems scandalously high, but less so if we compare it, for example, with the fertility actually observed at the beginning of the twentieth century among the Hutterites, an American-Canadian Anabaptist sect that did not practice birth control.[94] Among the Hutterites (who admittedly lived in an environment assuring them both good health and good nutrition), on average a woman married at the age of twenty and had 10.6 to 10.9 children. Taking into account a higher general mortality, but also an earlier age of marriage, average figures for the potential fertility in ancient Greece are likely to have been ten children per adult married woman. An often-overlooked passage in Plato's *Laws* bears on this very question.[95] In the concrete and practical version of the perfect city presented in this work (the *Republic* offering the ideal version), Plato suggests that the fertility of couples be very strictly controlled. In cases where births are numerous and in the common situation in which the city does not need to replenish its population, the period of procreation should be limited to ten years. Beyond that limit, couples who did not want to live chastely would be ostracized and dishonored. Thus Plato clearly envisaged limiting the period of fertility as a way of controlling births: that is what we should take from this passage, even if the "practical" measures that Plato is proposing are in reality utterly utopian. Plato thinks a ten-year period of fertility per couple suffices to maintain the population at the same level. Plato was not, of course, a demographer. The figure of ten years is offered without previous analysis and *a priori* it cannot be considered as indicating the period of fertility that would suffice to renew the population. Nonetheless, what Plato saw every day in the cities showed him that a period of fertility much shorter than the one that obtained in reality would make it possible to reach a stable level of population, at least when the city did not have to make up for losses due to epidemics or wars.

In reality, then, early marriage for women, an average adult female life span that we have every reason to think went beyond the age of menopause, and a general mortality rate (or mortality profile), especially among infants, much like that of "early modern Europe" produced the necessary conditions for a permanent demographic explosion. This must surely have been the essential characteristic of ancient Greek demography. Otherwise, how could we explain the ability to catch up after being seriously depleted by wars that was shown by so many cities, and that obviously allowed them to recoup their losses rapidly? Why were philosophers of the Classical period like Plato and Aristotle haunted, not by a lack, but rather by an excess of population?[96] Let us assume that the theoretical figure of a minimum of ten children per couple accurately represents the potential fertility. It will then suffice to reflect on the conclusions Pierre Chaunu draws regarding fertility in seventeenth-century France: "A little more than six [children], and the population will rapidly grow; a little less than five, and it is stagnant or even declining."[97] That was at a time of late marriage and high mortality as a result of poor hygiene. Scheidel thinks that on average only one child in two arrived at adulthood, which, as compared with the early modern age, accurately represents a very high level of loss. And we have to add that this concerns only children whose parents had decided to raise them. But even with this mortality rate (probably too high for Greece) and in relation to parallels taken from the early modern age, we see that all the conditions for rapid demographic expansion were in fact met in antiquity. In reality, there is every reason to think that theorists like Plato and Aristotle were well aware that the demographic structures of ancient Greece had an explosive potential that was capable of destroying the social order of the cities. We should recall that with a birthrate of 36 per thousand, a mortality rate of 30 per thousand, and an annual growth of 6 per thousand, a population grows by a factor of 1.8 in a single century. But even if we cannot determine the precise figures—which will in any case have varied depending on the place and time—it is in these terms that the debate should be framed. Freeing up this energy in a Mediterranean world that was still "empty" allowed the expansion of the Archaic Greek world as a whole, and gave to certain cities that enjoyed a favorable political and economic situation the means to play a major role and increase their advantages—and here we think naturally of Athens in the fifth century BCE. But if their economic opportunities were stagnant, this kind of demographic growth was intolerable unless the state was somehow still able to organize a massive emigration. Otherwise, regulation of demographic processes was considered indispensable, whether it was left to the initiative of the families or directed in an authoritarian manner by the state.

It is, therefore, the idea that the populations of the world of the Greek city-states could not have experienced growth, that they were virtually doomed to a *perpetuum immobile*, that we must challenge on a fundamental level. Donald Engels admitted the existence of phases of growth only for small groups and for a limited time, a position that is also untenable.[98] But the colonization movement in the Archaic period, and especially the demographic expansion of these colonies, would be incomprehensible without demographic growth. The existence of phases of rapid demographic expansion in fifth-century Athens can no longer be in doubt. Other examples could be provided. Thus everything leads us to reject the schema of a permanent balance between birth and death rates, or of phases of extremely slow expansion. The reality was different. The potential for expansion was great, and it was economic and social opportunities, not biological factors alone, that determined the phases of expansion, stagnation, or retreat of the city-states' populations.

Sex Ratio Imbalance, Birth Control, and Infanticide

Except in the case of a severe demographic accident produced by a war or epidemic, battling the excess of births was thus a priority. According to Aristotle (*Politics* 2.7.5), in Crete homosexuality was encouraged by cities as a way of limiting births. He also implied (*Politics* 7.14.10) that in his view voluntary birth control should be preferred to infanticide by exposure, but that if couples insisted on having too many children, the city should require abortion at an early stage. Voluntary sexual abstinence, contraceptive practices, and abortions are well attested, particularly in medical literature.[99] But in addition we have to return to the question of exposing infants and infanticide in ancient Greece. Of course, exposing an infant was in theory not necessarily a death sentence—foundlings might be rescued and raised as slaves—but statistically speaking, the vast majority of exposed infants surely perished. The question of precisely how widespread the practice of exposure was has been a veritable apple of discord. The starting point for all this research is the articles by Gustave Glotz, *Expositio* (1892) and *Infanticidium* (1900), in Daremberg and Saglio's *Dictionnaire des Antiquités*. Glotz concluded that infanticide by exposure was hugely common in antiquity, including at Athens during the Classical period. Since then, two opposing schools of thought have arisen on this subject. The first accepted and extended Glotz's conclusions: some prominent members of this camp are Archibald Cameron (1932), Rudolf Tolles (1941), and William W. Tarn (1952: 100–101). The other school, which includes Larue Van Hook (1920) and Hendrik Bolkestein (1922), strongly opposes Glotz's views. Since the 1970s, the debate has been revived by the works of Mark Golden (1981 and 1990: 86–88), William V. Harris (1982 and 1994), and Sarah B. Pomeroy (1983, 1997), all of whom accept the idea that exposure and infanticide may have been common practices.[100] The idea has been followed up by Emil Eyben (1982–1983) and Cynthia Patterson (1985). The opposing view has been represented by Louis R. F. Germain (1975); Donald Engels (1980), who wanted to show the impossibility of infanticide in a society with a fragile demographic balance; Robert Sallares (1991); and Wayne Ingalls (2002).[101] This brief chronological outline gives some idea of the vigor of the debate.[102]

We have no lack of literary, papyrological, and epigraphic sources that inform us about infanticide in ancient Greece. But it is one thing to note the frequency of reference to a phenomenon, and another to draw a quantitative evaluation from it. The authors who contest the prevalence of infanticide maintain that in the absence of a statistical assessment, the references to this phenomenon, even though numerous, prove nothing. Taking his starting point from this reasoning—with which, moreover, we can initially only agree—Van Hook was able to argue that the frequent appearance of the theme of the exposed infant in the authors of New Comedy, and, after them, in Plautus and Terence, was only a convenient dramatic device unrelated to social realities, and that the same judgment should be applied to myths, in which the *topos* of the exposed infant is so frequent. In short, we could compare the theme of the abandonment of the child to that of criminality in contemporary societies. The latter constitutes a very real problem, to be sure. Newspapers constantly report all sorts of violence. The crime novel and films about the underworld have become classic genres. But would we be justified in inferring that criminality plays a significant role as a factor in the mortality of European societies (this would be different in other parts of the world)? Clearly not, and we see the caution with which this kind of problem must be approached. Yet the salience of these criticisms should not blind us to the fact that few of those who downplay the significance of infanticide have been able to give a compelling defense of their position. Only Engels has attempted to do so.

Nonetheless, we must first note that in some cases ancient authors made judgments that went far beyond a simple reference in fiction to the theme of the abandonment of children. This is the case for the passage in Polybius (36.17.5–9) that explicitly designates the exposure of children as one of the causes of the depopulation of Greece in the second century BCE.[103] But it is also the case—even if it is in a stage play—for a formula like that of the comic poet Poseidippus (*Hermaphrodite*, fr. 11 Kock = 12 Kassel-Austin, ca. 300 BCE): "A son, everyone raises him, even if he is poor; a daughter, people expose her, even if they are rich," with the valuable reference to the sex of most of the children exposed. In light of sources like these or Aristotle's explicit testimony, we can safely conclude that the mass of scattered testimony of all kinds that we have for so many cities and all periods illustrates a widespread phenomenon, and the claim that the exposure of children was only a simple literary conceit thus becomes completely untenable. In addition, if, as we have seen, the demographic structures of the world of the Greek city-states were defined by very early marriage for females and a mortality that is moderate for a preindustrial society, then it is certain that the exposure of children and infanticide were not exceptional, but corresponded to a statistically significant phenomenon. The practice chiefly concerned girls, because it could be assumed that military losses or departures to far-off places would solve the problem of male overpopulation.

Thus it is also clear that in the Greek cities, there was often a major gender imbalance in favor of males, a fact to which our information on the sex ratio among the Cretans of Miletos in the late third century and the contrast between the sex ratio of Greek settlers and the native population in third-century BCE Egypt testifies eloquently.[104] In the case of the Cretans at Miletos, the sex ratio among minors was somewhere between 3:1 and 4:1 in favor of males. Among Greeks in the Fayum villages, one can observe a sex ratio of 1.3–1.4 in favor of males, as compared to 0.9–1.1 in Egyptian families. A factor correcting the raw figures (at least for Miletos) is the early marriage of girls. This also affects our picture of the adult population, due to the presence in the household of unmarried older males (which in itself, however, also reflects the unbalanced sex ratio at marriage age). Despite these inevitable corrections (which are, in fact, more pertinent to the case of Miletos than to that of Egypt), there should be no doubt that these figures actually reflect a cultural practice of infanticide of which girls were the most frequent victims.[105] In the fourth century BCE, Theopompus observed as a notable fact that the Etruscans reared all their children, and Aristotle made a similar observation concerning the Egyptians.[106] In the first century BCE, both Diodorus and Strabo made the same remark about native Egyptians.[107] This proves that the Greeks themselves were fully aware that in this matter their practices differed sharply from those of their neighbors.

There is no reason to doubt that Greek parents normally loved their children. They took good care of them: free children received a formal education and played with toys or with domestic animals, although in the poorer families they also had to work at an early age, this being especially true for young girls. Similarly, it is clear that parents felt keenly the loss of those children who met with the (all too frequent) misfortune of an untimely death.[108] But this applied only to the children whom they had decided to raise. If the Greek cities of the Classical period were remarkably generous in accepting military losses—and those of Athens reached exceptionally high levels in the course of the fifth century—it was only because they knew they had a considerable potential for demographic recovery that would allow them quickly to make up their losses if necessary. A simple temporary decrease in the practices of contraception, abortion, and infanticide would make it possible to increase the number of births again. Conversely, if the economic situation turned around, it then became necessary to intensify these practices. These seem to have been the characteristic patterns of behavior that shaped the demographic model of ancient Greece, and they were both entirely original and merciless. This was the Greek way of trying to avoid the Malthusian trap.

THE DYNAMICS OF POPULATION

"The strength of the commonwealth consists in men," Jean Bodin famously said.[109] The formula can be interpreted in many ways. If it is applied to a society that bases most of its wealth on agricultural production and that has an essentially stable technological level, it means that without numerous producers, it is impossible to obtain the quantities that will make the state rich and powerful. If it is a question of a market society, an increase in the population will play a positive role because it will help stimulate production. Inversely, we must not forget that a population that is too numerous for each individual to be able to find a means of subsistence is not only a curse but an economic burden. Against Jean Bodin, we can cite Thomas R. Malthus and his theory, according to which the earth's productive capacity has an upper limit, whereas the population has no internal limit to its growth.[110] Thus, no matter how we approach the question, it is clear that population constitutes an economic determinant of the greatest importance. The overarching question is how to establish the role of the demographic factor in the history of the world of the Greek city-states, which leads us to envisage the demographic question from several different angles.

Numbers

The study of ancient Greek demography poses a problem of method. In the total absence of statistics, we can at first base ourselves only on impressions and estimates. Archaic Greece sent colonists to all the shores of the Mediterranean. Classical Greece, victorious in every domain, was capable of opposing the Persians and then, with the Macedonians, of conquering the immensity of Asia, sending groups of colonists to regions that up to that point had never heard of the Greeks. In 1886, Beloch had already assembled all the data then available and tried to propose quantitative estimates for the population of Greece, region by region. He also took into account the agricultural potential and comparisons with the population of modern Greece.

Beloch's figures are certainly not absurd. He had an admirable knowledge of the ancient sources and always chose the most reasonable hypotheses. For him, Attika was the most populous region of Greece in absolute numbers, with 250,000 inhabitants for a single city in 431 BCE, ca. 205,000–210,000 in 323 BCE , and a density of respectively 90 and 80 inhabitants per square kilometer. With 230,000 inhabitants, Lakonia and Messenia combined had in the Classical period almost as great a population as Attika, but with a density of only 28.6 inhabitants per square kilometer. Macedon and Chalkidike together had 400,000–500,000 inhabitants, but with a still lower density of 12.5–15.6 inhabitants per square kilometer.[111] In this way, for mainland Greece (including Macedon) Beloch arrived at a total population of three million people in 115,000 square kilometers, with a density of 26 inhabitants per square kilometer.[112] Thus in terms of numbers, the population of mainland Greece in the Classical age would have reached a level at least equal to its population in the nineteenth century. To this figure, we should probably add a million for the Greeks of Western Asia Minor, at least a million more for the Greek colonies in the west, as well as another quarter-million for the Greek population of Cyrenaica and about 400,000 (?) for the Greek cities on the Black Sea. Thus we can reasonably assume that on the eve of Alexander's conquest, the total Greek-speaking population of the Mediterranean region, including both Greece proper and its colonies, was about 5.5 to 6 million. These figures correspond to the minimum that can be envisaged for the Classical period, but they are of a reasonable order. Mogens H. Hansen has recently proposed higher figures: between 7.6 million and 10 million Greek-speakers in total, of whom 4.5 million to 6 million inhabited Greece proper. [113]

These figures are based on extrapolations from the estimated urban populations. However, as observed by Simon Price, two considerations highlight the need for caution.[114] The first is that urban densities can vary considerably from one side to the other. The second is that the model of a population concentrated behind the walls of the main city center is certainly not a model that might be considered universal. If (as he himself underscores) Beloch proposed figures that are minimums and if Hansen's figures are maximums (they are probably well above the target), the two series of numbers provide nonetheless a range for what the population level of ancient Greece must actually have been.

A few comparisons will help us assess the population data given for Greece. The population of Roman Egypt has been studied in detail by Walter Scheidel. Comparing it with the population of Egypt in the modern period, he concluded that the population of Roman Egypt must have been between 5 and 7 million, with a quarter of the inhabitants living in cities such as Alexandria and about fifty regional capitals. [115] However, all indications are that Roman Egypt underwent rather significant demographic growth. In this case, if we want to retain similar proportions we would have to say with Joseph G. Manning that the overall population of Ptolemaic Egypt was approximately 3.5 to 4.5 million.[116] According to Makis Aperghis, Alexander's kingdom, with its European possessions, Egypt, and the valley of the Indus, had a population of 25 to 30 million, and the Seleukid kingdom (from Asia Minor to Central Asia) had a population of between 15 and 20 million.[117] Regarding Roman Italy, there is vigorous debate about how to interpret a key document, Augustus's census, which mentions 4,063,000 citizens.[118] Did this include only adult male citizens, as in the previous censuses (which give much lower figures), or did it now count both citizens and their families? Depending on which interpretation we choose, we can arrive at either a low figure, around 5.5 to 7.5 million (so Beloch and Peter A. Brunt), or double that amount (so Elio Lo Cascio and Paolo Malanima).[119] A new detailed investigation by Saskia Hin has interestingly proposed a "middle count." The free population of Italy would have been almost 5 million in 225 BCE (to which should be added an undetermined number of slaves) and 6.7 million in 14 BCE, viz. with ca. 1.5 million slaves a total around 8.2 million for the population of Italy in 28 BCE.[120] The demographic edge in favor of Italy would remarkably help in making sense of the triumph of Rome in the Mediterranean arena in the third to first centuries BCE.

Population Trends

Beloch's figures, amended and updated by Jean-Nicolas Corvisier and Wiesław Suder, are thus plausible.[121] But it is equally clear that they are based very largely on estimates, on the idea that can be formed by consulting the literary sources, more than on positive data. Furthermore, they do not inform us about the evolution of population, except in relation to the testimony given by ancient authors. These impressions have been gradually clarified by observations provided by archaeology. From this point of view, information about demography has not been a primary objective, but only a by-product. Studies on the population density of rural and urban sites were initially carried out in an empirical manner: it was possible to bring together the results of the various excavations and field research that had been conducted. Then, with archaeological surveys, investigation entered a systematic phase. The goal of such surveys is to rediscover the ways in which rural areas were occupied. To accomplish this, teams of observers walk an area in parallel lines, noting all the traces humans have left on the surface, from the most humble ceramic sherd to a major site whose remains are still visible on the landscape. The distance between the lines of observers varies: five meters, ten meters, or more, depending on the team's means and manpower. Over the years, efforts of this kind have become increasingly numerous in Greece proper. Thus since the early 1970s onward, researchers have begun to publish a series of surveys dealing with Messenia, Lakonia, the islands of Melos and Keos, Boiotia, southern Argolis, the region around Phaistos, the plain of Mesara in Southern Crete, and so forth.[122] In Asia Minor, the eastern part of Lykia has been systematically investigated through the efforts of Frank Kolb and his team in the Kyaneai region.[123] The territory of the kingdom of the Bosporos has also been the object of large-scale investigations.[124] Synthetic studies such as Susan Alcock's famous *Graecia Capta* have allowed us to draw conclusions from these decades of work.[125] The outcome of thirty years of surveys has much to teach us. But the time has also come to take up a certain distance from some of the conclusions drawn.[126] Without being hypercritical, we should reexamine the methods and results. Rather than rejecting *en bloc* the results of the surveys, as some have been tempted to do, we should try to propose new ways of interpreting the data, even if the latter sometimes seem contradictory.

First, a basic criticism has been made of the method used by archaeological surveys. Inasmuch as surveys by definition observe only the visible remains on the surface, researchers deprive themselves of the possibility of assessing the real importance of a site, which may be very imperfectly manifested by surface remains. The nature and size of a rural establishment—a simple shepherd's hut or a permanent home of a certain size—are difficult to determine. But if we want to draw demographic conclusions, this is a bit of information of great importance, since the population may be either dispersed or grouped together. In short, an "empty" or "nearly empty" countryside does not *a priori* indicate a low demographic density if the population is highly concentrated in an urban center or in a few large farms. Because the way in which the land is occupied is a parameter difficult to determine by surveys, demographic conclusions drawn from them may be vitiated. In other words, we have to be wary of raw numbers. A famous case of this is the number of tombs found in Attika in the Archaic period, which reached an apex at the end of the eighth century BCE: it might seem that we can conclude that the population tripled in one century. But according to Ian Morris, it would be better to assume that we are dealing with a cultural change in which new strata of the population gained access to a mode of burial that had previously been reserved for an elite: we should not necessarily see in this proof that the population had increased.[127]

Another reservation regarding surveys has to do with the disparities between the methods used by different teams, even regarding the dating of archaeological material. Thus ceramics for everyday use, to cite just one example, are not easy to date. Survey results are also often dependent upon the time period in which each of them was carried out (the more recent the survey, the more accumulated experience its members can draw on, and the more accurate their results are likely to be), the extent of the surface that has been covered, and the means that could be drawn upon (which has a direct effect on how close the surveyors are to each other). Moreover, the periodization used is not always the same from one survey to another.

Although certain aspects of this criticism are not without interest, they too have to be kept in perspective. The disparities between surveys can sometimes make comparisons difficult, but they do not make them impossible. Above all, even if the surface manifests the deep remains only imperfectly—or rather, irregularly—we cannot therefore conclude that the method has no value. First, it would by definition be impossible to excavate all the sites where people have lived; in this domain, the requirement of exhaustiveness leads to nihilism, and this would constitute a serious epistemological regression. Second, the Mediterranean landscape is far more likely to preserve remains than is that of Atlantic zones, because in general the formation of soils is less rapid around the Mediterranean, except in areas of intense alluvial deposits. Sometimes the remains of ancient walls or other traces of habitation are still clearly visible. If not, soils that are not very deep do not prevent cultivation from bringing remains of human occupation back to the surface, most often in the form of ceramics. Generally speaking, valley floors in the Mediterranean area thus tend be covered by several meters of accumulated sediments that make observation of remains on the surface a matter of chance. Correctives therefore need to be made regarding the zone of observation. Yet even when these caveats are taken into account, surface remains still usually seem to provide valuable testimony about past occupation. If we try to synthesize the results in the form of a table, adding synthetic observations (not produced by systematic surveys) regarding Attika, we obtain interesting results (table 2.3).[128]

Setting aside Melos and Pylos, the data uniformly indicate an increase in the number of sites during the Archaic period. In addition, when it is possible to make specific observations on the occupied sites, we also see that we are dealing in every case with an increase in their size between the Geometric and the Classical periods. If we then combine these results with other archaeological or textual data, there can be no doubt, despite all the objections that have been made, that the augmentation of the number of sites corresponds to an actual augmentation of the population. This augmentation was significant not only in the Archaic period, but continued in the Classical period as well. In the fifth and fourth centuries, we are dealing with a "full" Greece. Obviously, this holds true for Attika, where in the fourth century occupation of the territory was maximal and where even marginal, not very productive soils were put to use, as in the farms of the deme of Atene, near Sounion.[129] But it also holds true for Keos, Lakonia, Argolis, Boiotia, and Central Greece (Lokris and Phokis). The result is not surprising, certainly, but it is very significant that the increase that we could assume had taken place can be confirmed by quantitative data.

We can now apply similar methods to address the much-debated question of demographic change in Hellenistic and Roman Greece. Starting at the end of the Classical period, did Greece experience a vast demographic decline that began slowly in the third century, and then accelerated in the second and first centuries, the low point being situated at the height of the Roman period? If so, why? Taking as a basis the cases of Phokis, Melos, southern Argolis, and Corinth (which does not appear in table 2.3), Alcock has shown that there was a considerable decrease in the density of the sites.[130] Should we infer a decrease in population? Alcock's interpretation remains very prudent, taking into account the parameter of the form of occupation of the countryside mentioned earlier.[131] The formation of large rural estates and the concentration of the habitat do not necessarily indicate a decline in population, at least not in proportions as great as those suggested by the numbers. In the case of Keos, for example, we see that the population would have to have decreased by 80 percent,

TABLE 2.3. Number of Sites by Region

	KEOS	MELOS	LASITHI	MESARA	ACHAIA	S. ARGOLIS	PYLOS	LAKONIA	BOIOTIA	E. PHOKIS	W. LOKRIS	ATTIKA
Geom.	—	39	4	13	—	16	10	13	17	5	7	26
Arch.	78	39	22	13	5	27	10	39	46	7	12	50
Class.	159	28	7	26	15	79	13	87	74	16	16	70
Hell.	97	15	7	52	20	32	27	—	58	13	15	—
Imp.	29	51	28	—	10	22	60	—	39	11	11	—

Source: Data excerpted from the more exhaustive array in Corvisier 2004, 27, corrected for the southern Argolid by the data of Jameson et al. 1994, 229.

which is very unlikely. Thus surveys do not provide a direct answer to the questions of demography that have been raised. They may, however, give us the elements we need to construct an answer. Should we conclude that the burden of Roman domination, with an accentuation of social inequality and massive taxes levied for Rome's benefit, was the main factor in the economic downturn, and led to a decrease in population? But in that case, insofar as Roman's control over Greece was effective from the last half of the second century, how can we explain the fact that in several regions the number of sites began to diminish at the beginning of the third century?[132] Or must we go so far as to hold that the reorganization of rural space in the Hellenistic period was not marked by any overall decline in population?

An answer to these questions can be constructed only in the framework of an overall assessment of the significance of the increase in population during the preceding period, with in particular increases in the maxima during the Classical period. We would like to be able to separate observation and interpretation more distinctly, but the sources at our disposal do not allow us to do so. Taking into account all the available sources, it is, however, possible to formulate a general hypothesis that has a good chance of corresponding to reality. What we must first examine are the conditions of growth during the Archaic age and of the maximum during the Classical age. We have seen that over a long period of time, there was a steadily increasing density of occupation of an ever greater rural space, since even marginal lands were cultivated. At this time, Greece undeniably increased in prosperity, as is attested, for example, by the average surface area of houses, which grew by a factor of five or six between 800 and 300 BCE.[133] This prosperity was based on control over long-distance Mediterranean trading networks that made it possible to import the grain and other products that Greece regularly needed, from the end of the Archaic age onward, to provide for the subsistence of its population.[134] A new cycle of prosperity began at the end of the sixth century and continued until the end of the fourth century. This prosperity was connected with the emergence of coined money and particularly, at least in the south Aegean area, with the extraction of silver from the mines of Laurion. It is this new cycle of prosperity that explains the maxima of population not only in Athens but also in the whole of the Aegean, in which virtually every city or settlement was connected directly or indirectly with Athens. Athens had by then become the driving force for growth. One of the consequences of the establishment of these far-reaching supply networks was the possibility of importing grain in quantities sufficient to allow a level of population that was much higher than could have been attained on the basis of consuming foodstuffs produced in a strictly regional framework. From the point of view of population distribution and the types of economic activity pursued, this high level of imports also made it possible for a much higher percentage of the population to live in an urban environment than would have been feasible in a society living exclusively on what could be produced in its own territory.

The resounding victory at Salamis, in which Athens played such a crucial role, proclaimed the emergence of Athens as a major power, which had been an established fact since the end of the sixth century and the victory over the Boiotians in

506. In the Classical period, Athens was a huge city, almost a genuine "nation."[135] In this respect, Herodotus's catalogue (9.28–30) of the heavy infantry mobilized at Plataiai in 479 provides a good illustration of the disproportion between the cities. For Athens, its wealth in men—that is, "male citizens"—was one of the sources of its power. Whereas most cities had only a few hundred or a few thousand citizens (fewer than 10,000 in any case), Athens may have had more than 40,000 citizens in the fifth century and perhaps at least 30,000 in the fourth century.[136] On the basis of this power, it was also able to accept numerous metics and buy many slaves. Moreover, the Greeks were aware that *poluanthropia*, "an abundance of men," was a fundamental power factor for a city.[137] Athens's defeat at Amorgos in 322 marked the beginning of a downward spiral that was characterized by the Macedonian occupation of the fortress of Mounychia in Piraeus, which put the city under *de facto* Macedonian control, and was punctuated by more catastrophic episodes like the siege of 295 and the Chremonidean War (268–262).[138] The cessation (or quasi cessation) of silver mining in Laurion at the end of the fourth century made it no longer possible to maintain a high level of grain imports. Athens was not all that was broken by the Macedonian conquest. The latter also put an end to the cycle of prosperity that had begun in the sixth century, in which cities like Corinth and Aigina had at first played a major dynamic role before being forced to play second fiddle to Athens. By establishing long-distance commercial networks, these cities were, of course, pursuing their own interests. But at the same time, they played a major role in inciting overall prosperity. As is shown by the circulation of its coins, a city like Keos, for instance, looked directly to Athens.[139] Athenian prosperity was thus a driving force in the wider economic life of the Aegean.

It was this cycle of prosperity that was interrupted by the Macedonian victory, not so much by the defeat at Chaeronea as by the new balance of power that was established afterward. The reorganization of society on a more conservative basis began in the early Hellenistic period, but it greatly accelerated when Rome took direct control at the end of the second century and in the course of the first century. It is legitimate to think that from then on, the decrease in population was not an artificial construct, a mirage created by the conditions under which it was investigated (in this case, the method of counting sites during surveys). This decrease is one of the major facts of demographic development that it no longer seems possible to deny.

In a famous passage, Polybius (36.17.5–11) describes the actual demographic conditions that obtained in his time. He contrasts the difficulties associated with climatic risks (which could cause poor harvests) and epidemics, two factors that do not depend on human will, with the causes of depopulation prevalent in his own day:[140]

> In our own time the whole of Greece has been subject to childlessness and a general decrease of the population, owing to which cities have become deserted and the land has ceased to yield fruit, although there have neither been continuous wars nor epidemics. If, then, any one had advised us to send and ask the gods about this, and find out what we ought to say or do, to increase

in number and make our cities more populous, would it not seem absurd, the cause of the evil being evident and the remedy being in our own hands? For as men had fallen into such a state of pretentiousness, avarice, and indolence that they did not wish to marry, or if they married to rear the children born to them, or at most as a rule but one or two of them, so as to leave these in affluence and bring them up to waste their substance, the evil rapidly and insensibly grew. For in cases where of one or two children the one was carried off by war and the other by sickness, it is evident that the houses must have been left unoccupied, and as in the case of swarms of bees, so by small degrees cities became resourceless and feeble. About this it was of no use at all to ask the gods to suggest a means of deliverance from such an evil. For any ordinary man will tell you that the most effectual cure had to be men's own action, in either striving after other objects, or if not, in passing laws making it compulsory to rear children who are born. Neither prophets nor magic were here of any service, and the same holds good for all particulars.

Thus Polybius describes a depopulated Greece in which land is abandoned, the birth rate is low, and people refuse to raise children. Let us note that he is describing a real phenomenon, and not simply crafting an ideologically driven fantasy. What is, however, ideological and characteristic of ancient thought is that he explains this phenomenon by the taste for pleasure, and thus by individual factors of a moral nature. But his view anticipates that of Strabo, who emphasizes the depopulation that took place in the Peloponnese and in western and central Greece.[141] We find the same scourge of depopulation in Dio Chrysostom's *Euboean Discourse* (7.34), written in the first century CE. A notable of a Euboian city complains that two-thirds of the city's territory has been abandoned as a result of the prevalent depopulation. He himself is incapable, for lack of labor, of cultivating a large portion of his land, not only in the mountains, but also on the plain. He even claims that he is prepared to pay a tenant in order to see his lands maintained! Similarly, at the end of the first century and at the beginning of the second century CE, Plutarch deplores the fact that the Greece of his time has experienced a sharp decline in population: according to him, it could scarcely mobilize 3,000 soldiers, the number that little Megara had provided at the Battle of Plataiai.[142] Despite likely exaggerations, these repeated observations, for which we find no equivalent in the Classical period, should not be rejected—they describe the actual demographic situation of Greece in the late Hellenistic and Roman periods.[143]

It is as if today there were a reluctance to admit that the evolution of a population, and, more generally, of a society as a whole, might not be linear—whence the temptation to construct alternative schemas that enable us to reject in spite of everything, "the inadmissible decline" in population undergone by Greece in the late Hellenistic and Roman periods. This takes us back to the problem mentioned earlier of the autonomy of the demographic factor. We have to acknowledge that if on the one hand population was a specific factor in economic development, on the other hand it should also be understood as a dependent variable. This was even more true of the slave population, which was not supposed to reproduce itself, but rather to work as hard as possible for the master—which of course does not mean that there was not a certain percentage of reproduction nonetheless. We can even say that there were rapid increases or decreases in this slave population as a function of economic necessities, even if it remains difficult for us to reach absolute figures, for the slaves no less than for the free population.[144] In the event of a reversal in the economic situation, a decline in population was a solution that made it possible to find a new equilibrium at a lower level.[145] That is exactly what happened in continental Greece and in the Kyklades during the Hellenistic period and the early Imperial period, before there was a new reversal—only in the West—in late antiquity, which is also fully corroborated by archaeological surveys.

What is more, surveys and other observations show that the population decline during the Hellenistic period was not uniform. It concerned chiefly mainland Greece—Athens, central Greece, the Kyklades, and part of the northern Peloponnese. Crete, Lakonia, and Messenia (Pylos) underwent a different development. These regions had not been integrated into the cycle of Athenian prosperity. The Hellenistic and early Imperial periods offered them new opportunities. It will also be interesting to examine the results of new surveys in western Asia Minor when they have been completed. In Lykia, in any case, the Hellenistic period was certainly one of growth.[146] This is also suggested by the prosperity of Rhodes and the very clear impression given by its countryside, where there is a great density of Hellenistic sites, even if no regular survey has yet been conducted on the island. It was only at the end of the first century that Rhodes entered an unmistakable negative cycle.[147] The Hellenistic decline in population was therefore neither uniform nor universal.

In regions that did not undergo this decline, there were only two solutions to the problem of excessive demographic pressure. The first was emigration, which must have reached previously unparalleled levels. With Alexander's conquest, the Eastern world was henceforth open to the Greeks. They could seek their fortunes there all the more easily because the "demand for Greeks" was very strong in the kingdoms that emerged from the conquest. Soldiers, administrators, and simple colonists or traders were more than welcome in kingdoms in which, until the Roman takeover, Hellenism held political and ideological power, but where the Greeks were everywhere very much in the minority. The flow of people leaving Greece to take up residence in the new kingdoms is impossible to quantify. But the literary and epigraphic evidence attesting to these departures is extensive (and, naturally, is not restricted to the regions of mainland Greece). Immediately after the defeat at Amorgos, thousands of Athenians left their fatherland to settle as colonists in Thrace.[148] In 205, the city of Antioch in Persis could stress its "friendship" and "family relationship" with Magnesia on the Maeander, which three generations before had sent it great numbers of colonists "distinguished by their value." [149] Thus the emigrants were not recruited among marginal groups but among citizens conscious of the duties they would have to fulfill in their new homeland. We can easily imagine that the call for colonists from old

Greece, and indeed the urgent, explicit demand for them in the cities of western Asia Minor subject to royal control, was one characteristic of kingdoms' policies for, at the very least, the entire first part of the Hellenistic age. We see collective migrations in an Aegean context as well. Miletos accepted emigrants coming from Crete in the third century, and Ilion also received new citizens.[150]

We must therefore reject any attempt to characterize ancient populations as either static or growing only slowly. Quite the contrary: the malleability of the population of ancient Greece is striking. In this way, we can explain the contrasting trends of the Hellenistic period. Thus some regions, such as western Asia Minor, experienced further expansion. Due to continuous emigration and intensification of practices such as birth control or exposure of children, some other regions, such as Athens and Boiotia, experienced a temporary or prolonged decline in the level of their population.

THE ECOLOGICAL ENVIRONMENT AND POPULATION

The Variability of Climate

Finally, it is necessary to address the relationship between the ecological environment and population. As we have seen, it appears that after a cold, wet period stretching from the end of the Archaic age to the fourth century, a period of relative warming began. For the agriculture of the driest regions of the Aegean world, this was a negative economic factor. However, one must avoid construing this as a direct causal factor in the demographic "reversal of the situation" that occurred in the fourth century. To the extent that the people's food supply depended in large measure on grain imported from other parts of the Mediterranean world, a possible warming of the climate could at most have been a secondary factor in demographic change, not a decisive one. Furthermore, it is possible that a warming climate in the Hellenistic period favored an increase in the population of Macedon and northern and western Greece in general, finally giving it a prominence on the Greek scene that it had not previously had. It is also quite possible that Macedon's success in the fourth century was due in large part to demographic expansion.[151] But this is still only a hypothesis, and will have to be validated by further empirical studies.

The Greeks considered their country very privileged. For Herodotus (3.106.1), Greece had the best of climates. According to him, other countries were all marked by excesses: they were either too hot or too cold. Nor is he entirely off the mark: the climate of Greece does indeed avoid all the "excesses" found in the countries south of the Mediterranean, where, apart from a few exceptions, the more intense sunshine and insufficient rainfall have resulted in deserts. Similarly, Greece does not have the very low temperatures that are found in the countries that the Greeks believed belonged to the "Hyperboreans"—that is, the areas north of the Black Sea. But above all, it is clear that Herodotus is offering us a textbook case of ethnocentrism, insofar as this analysis serves in addition as a foundation for the cultural anthropology that he develops in the following paragraphs.[152] Beyond the criticism of this ethnocentrism, however, the question of the particular constraints that the Greek climate imposed on its economy must be raised.

Even so, it is not enough simply to criticize Herodotus's ethnocentrism; we must address the question his comments raise about the particular constraints that Greece's climate imposed on its economy. In Greece, virtually the whole range of plants known at that time could be grown, especially since the changing topography provided for a great regional variety. Another advantage was that, except in the mountainous regions of Pindos, home heating could be limited or absent. In this regard, Aegean Greece east of Pindos, the islands, and the coastal cities of Asia Minor enjoyed a significant comparative advantage.

However, averages mask one of the peculiar characteristics of the Greek climate: its great annual and regional variations. It is a climate that has a high coefficient of variability. The problem is particularly acute in areas where precipitation is at the lower limits required for agriculture. Below 250 millimeters of annual rainfall, even the barley harvest is compromised. On average, in the Aegean world one year out of three has insufficient rainfall. This high variability may occur even in the same micro-region. Thus on the island of Thera, two adjacent valleys may have very different amounts of precipitation.[153]

In a single region, annual rainfall can vary by 100 percent or even more. If a given year is too dry, production drops to almost nothing. Thus on Naxos, rainfall was 172 millimeters in 1898 and 542 millimeters in 1928. In Pobia, in Crete, it was 823 millimeters in 1954, but only 318 millimeters in 1958.[154] Furthermore, we must emphasize that the sources show that it is impossible to distinguish cycles of wet or dry years. The differences between years defy any prediction. Relying upon information from modern Greece, Thomas W. Gallant has collected significant data regarding the probability of precipitation in Athens and the islands in modern times (table 2.4).[155]

Thus we see that in Athens and on Thera, a situation of acute hydraulic deficit occurs almost one year out of three, and that in Athens an absolutely catastrophic situation (less than 200 millimeters) can occur six times in a century.

TABLE 2.4. Probability of Precipitation in Athens, Melos, and Thera

	< 400 MM		< 350 MM		< 300 MM		< 200 MM	
	A	B	A	B	A	B	A	B
Athens	71	50	35	12	28	8	6	0.3
Melos	56	31	25	6	11	1	0.6	0.1
Thera	85	72	48	23	34	12	3	1

A = Probability of rainfall lower than the level of reference.
B = Probability of rainfall lower than the level of reference for two consecutive years.

Demographic Crises and Famine

Did ancient Greece experience genuine famines, such as are attested in the archives of the medieval and early modern European world or in those of the Chinese world? Peter Garnsey is certainly correct to respond in the negative, which naturally does not mean that Greece did not have to cope with frequent and serious shortages.[156] Classical and Hellenistic sources are largely silent on this point, except when discussing sieges and wars. We must first determine what a drought or a famine might mean for a population. In modern times, the case of the famine that struck the Turkish district of Keskin, east of Ankara, in 1873–1874 gives us some idea of the ravages caused by a drought followed by a famine.[157] The traces of this drought have been observed in the effects it had on the growth of trees at eight sites in the region concerned (table 2.5).

These figures give us an idea of the magnitude of the hydraulic deficit in comparison with the average rainfall. The consequences for the population were tragic: 81 percent of the cattle and 97 percent of the sheep died. Out of a population of 52,000 inhabitants, 7,000 emigrated and 20,000 died. In the provinces of Kastamonu, Ankara, and Kayseri, 150,000 people died and 100,000 head of livestock, or 40 percent of the herds, perished. During the winter of 1873–1874, 100,000 additional persons died of hunger and disease.

It happens that for a region of Asia Minor situated a little farther to the south, Pisidia, ancient documentation has provided a famous document about a grain shortage. This is the edict of L. Antistius Rusticus, which dates from 92 or 93 CE, during the reign of Domitian.[158] Promulgated at the request of the magistrates and decurions of Antioch in Pisidia, the edict mentions the severity of the winter, which has compromised the supply of grain. In fact, in contrast with neighboring areas, modern geographic observations have shown that in the center of Asia Minor tem-

TABLE 2.5. Index of the Growth of Trees in 1873–1874 in Keskin District (in Percentage of Average Annual Growth)

VILLAGE	1873	1874	VILLAGE	1873	1874
Mihalıçcık	25.2	20.8	Güdül	74.4	69.6
Çeltikçi	23.0	54.2	Kızılcahamam	70.9	70.0
Çamlıtepe	46.7	87.8	Bağlum	59.4	94.4
Hamidiyeköy	54.6	85.7	Yarakın	69.1	95.1
Yozgat	66.1	67.7	Çatacık	84.6	87.1
Ovacık	66.3	73.9			

peratures below −10°C are common in the winter, and droughts are also common in the summer, but reach exceptional levels only rarely (as in the case of the drought in the Keskin district mentioned earlier). On the other hand, the coastal regions of Asia Minor, from the lower valley of the Maeander to the gulf of Issos, today experience temperatures below −10°C only once a century, and a hydraulic deficit about once every twenty years. For the region of the Hellespont, the Bosporos, and the Pontic coast, temperatures below −10°C occur only once every ten years, and droughts never.[159] Western Asia Minor (Lydia, Bithynia) has values between those of the interior and those of the coast. So far as Asia Minor is concerned, some regions are thus more vulnerable than others.

The geographical fragmentation and the great variability from one region to the next are thus major givens. All the regions of Greece and Asia Minor could be struck by grain shortages, but it is clear that so far as production *stricto sensu* is concerned, the interior of Asia Minor was far more fragile than the coastal regions, which were likely to be struck more rarely. In other words, the famine of 1873–1874 in the Keskin district, which was caused by drought, and the (admittedly much less serious) famine in 92 or 93 CE in Antioch in Pisidia, which was caused by very low winter temperatures, are characteristic of the interior of Asia Minor. As for continental Greece and the Greek islands, it is clear that it was the Aegean slope and the islands, above all, that must have been forced to cope with difficult situations that could become tragic if repeated.

This is the situation that Herodotus describes (4.151.1) with regard to the island of Thera in the seventh century BCE. The people of Thera had ignored the Delphic oracle's injunction telling them to found a colony in Libya. They paid heavily for this negligence: "For the following seven years, not a drop of rain fell on Thera. As a result, all the trees on the island dried up, with the exception of one." When consulted, the Delphic oracle could only repeat its ancient injunction. Once an initial settlement was established on an island close to the coast, "the Therans decided to send to Libya men from each of the seven districts of their city, designating by lot one brother out of two" (ibid., 4.153). Since the early stages of colonization proved to be difficult, the colonists wanted to return to their native island. They were not allowed to do so: "The Therans threw stones at them, prevented them from landing and forced them to go away again." A fourth-century BCE inscription in Cyrene, which contains a decree of isopoly between Cyrene and Thera, also records the oath that the founders supposedly took before their departure and gives a somewhat different version of the circumstances of this emigration.[160] In all likelihood, the oath is not authentic, at least in the form preserved in the inscription. However, it is not a simple plagiarism of Herodotus, either, and probably corresponds to an independent tradition from the end of the Archaic period and the Classical period. This text is thus all the more interesting because, whatever the authenticity of the tradition, it shows how a city represented to itself the constraint imposed on its members. The city of Thera is thus supposed to have stipulated the following: "Under equal and similar conditions, one son per household will depart; a catalogue of all the adult men in all the districts will be drawn up (?); and every free Theran who wants to can depart (?)" (ll. 28–30).[161] The text then provides that if it turns out that at the end of five years the colony is a failure, and if the Therans are unable to help the colonists, "let them be able to leave this territory in confidence and come back to Thera to recover their property, and let them be citizens" (ll. 35–37). By contrast, the penalties would be very heavy for anyone who refused to sail for the colony: "Anyone who refuses to sail even though the city has designated him for departure will be liable to the death-penalty and his property will be confiscated by the city. Anyone who gives him asylum or conceals him, even a father with his son or a brother with his brother, will be subject to the same punishment as the one who refused to sail" (ll. 37–40).

Behind both the legendary façade of the oracle's command in Herodotus and the legal phraseology of the founders' oath in the inscription at Cyrene, we can divine the violence that a community could visit on its members in order to cope with an extreme situation. Forced departure was the last resort. In most cases, the solution that consisted in the individual's leaving voluntarily remained always open, and it is very clear that after Alexander, the conquest of the East and the creation of a multitude of new Greek cities offered the permanent possibility of departure, at least for the most adventurous.

All things considered, apart from periods of war (and especially times of siege, when people in the cities were reduced to starvation), Classical and Hellenistic Greece does not seem to have experienced famines accompanied by large numbers of deaths comparable to those that have been previously mentioned or to the great famine of Edessa in northern Syria in 499–500 CE, caused by an invasion of locusts that destroyed virtually all the harvests over a vast area.[162] On the one hand, as we have seen, only one area within the Aegean domain is highly likely to be struck by extreme calamities, while the remaining areas experience them only rarely. On the other hand, these regions are very close to the sea, and hence they can be resupplied, provided that the community has adequate financial resources. At the other end of the spectrum, the geographical isolation of Anatolia is an aggravating factor and explains the violence of phenomena like the famine of 1873–1874, which preceded the construction of the trans-Anatolian railway.

Additionally, the existence of numerous and heavily populated cities, precisely in the driest part of the Aegean world—first, naturally, Athens, but also island cities such as Chios, Samos, or Rhodes—was a risk factor that increased dependence on external sources of supply. When we learn that in Athens, the price of grain often varied by 300 percent (or even more) in the same year, we have to imagine the consequences for feeding the population. The supply networks Athens built up and the measures taken by city authorities were intended to cope with precisely these difficulties. It seems that these authorities usually succeeded in limiting the consequences of grain shortages.[163] But it would be overstating the case to maintain that Greek cities, even during the Classical or Hellenistic periods, never experienced extreme situations that led to genuine deaths by starvation. We do not know of any situation in Greece as difficult as the one in Rome in 440 BCE mentioned by Livy

(4.12.11), where food shortages led to a wave of suicides among the plebeians, but that probably has to do only with the limitation of our sources.[164] In fact, we do not have annals for any of the cities of the Greek world comparable to the ones that Livy and Dionysius of Halicarnassus left us for Rome. But for our present purposes, the fact that Rome was not a Greek city matters little.

So far as problems of food supply were concerned, at least, the moderately sized city that was early Rome did not differ much from the Greek cities of the same period. The problems they had to cope with and the solutions they found were the same. If we must make a broad assessment, it seems that during the period that concerns us, Greece never experienced massive and generalized famines affecting vast areas or killing hundreds of thousands of people, of the sort that has been attested for ancient China or Japan, or even for medieval and early modern Europe. If such famines had occurred, our sources would necessarily mention the fact, and they do not. Sporadic famines, in this or that city, affecting the most deprived social classes, like the ones that can be observed at times in Rome, must certainly have occurred. However, as the case of Rome in 440–439 demonstrates, particularly intense food crises often resulted from inefficient trade networks. Consequently, so far as chronological development is concerned, it is probable that the greater efficiency of trade networks in the Classical and Hellenistic periods made famines less intense than they had been in the Archaic period.

If, then, we can confidently assert that Classical and Hellenistic Greece did not experience great, devastating famines, we must nonetheless take into account the health and social consequences of the frequent grain shortages. Striking the lower classes very hard, even for a short time, they must have retarded the growth of children and caused rickets, various kinds of bone deficiencies, and finally abnormally high death rates. It is no accident that the vocabulary of ancient Greece designates the wealthy as "the fat." An advantageous external appearance, which was a certain criterion of social differentiation, was connected primarily with a prepossessing physique, which itself depended on the quality of nutrition, and also with clothing. Finally, it is clear that, as we still see today, there must have been a differential by sex (in may cities, girls were undernourished compared with boys), not to mention status, slaves being systematically less well nourished during shortages.[165]

To conclude, the ecological framework of the core of the Greek world (mainland Greece and Western Asia Minor) presents characteristics that can be rather easily defined. The topography of the zone is a young one. The country is fragmented into a series of subregions, and the sea is never very distant. The characteristics of the Mediterranean climate are nuanced by the presence of high reliefs, which give an alpine character to the climate of the zone of the Pindos ridge, central Peloponnese, and parts of northern Greece. Soils are mostly of karstic origin, from rich clay layers in the plains to barren rock on many hills or mountain summits. Unpredictability of the climate, with marked differences from one year to the other, inevitably heavily impacts traditional agriculture. Climate risk and its management thus represented a major challenge for ancient Greek peasants.

As for the demographic model of the ancient Greek world, it possessed an exceptional potential of rapid growth. Mortality was moderate due to relatively good hygiene and food supply conditions. Fecundity was very high due to an early age at marriage for girls, between fifteen and eighteen. This created all the conditions of a rapid demographic expansion if the economic context was good or if emigration was possible. This also explains why Greek cities were so generous with their military losses. Besides, if conditions were less favorable, exposure of children was the norm and homosexuality could be encouraged to prevent too many births.

If precise figures for ancient Greek populations are not easy to reach, it remains clear that ancient Greece reached a historic high that was not matched before the end of the nineteenth or even the beginning of the twentieth century. The Archaic and then the Classical period saw a sharp and general population increase. The situation of the Hellenistic period is more contrasted. In Asia Minor, the process of demographic growth was not stopped. But in Mainland Greece began a demographic decline that was slight in the early Hellenistic period, but at least in some regions more marked in the late Hellenistic period.

III

ENERGY, ECONOMY, AND TRANSPORT COST

Reduced to its simplest form, the production of material goods consists in a process of transforming the environment by bringing into it a certain quantity of energy. Every society is thus confronted by the challenge of energy. The way it uses energy is a function of its technological level. For millennia, human societies were able to use energy only directly, without transforming it. Since the discovery of the laws of thermodynamics, we know that energy can take two forms, heat and movement. In the industrial era, the great power of modern economies has been their ability to draw on technologies that can transform heat into movement and vice versa. Ancient societies, like all preindustrial societies, did not have access to this kind of transformation of energy. For reasons that will be examined later, Hero of Alexandria's famous "steam engine" remained only a prototype without any practical use. The ancient Greek scientists had no theoretical notion of the laws of thermodynamics, although interestingly Hero's steam engine was a first step in proving that heat can be transformed into mechanical energy.

Nonetheless, the energy they had at their disposal was one of the fundamental factors in the economic development of ancient societies. Whether in the form of heat or movement, the energy used must be analyzed in relation to three questions: Can it be stored? Is it renewable? How much does it cost? In many respects, the innovations introduced between the Classical and the Hellenistic periods determined most of the ways of using energy during the two following millennia. However, the dynamics of the economy of the world of the Greek city-states was based more on the introduction of new technologies allowing a better utilization of existing sources of energy than it was on the introduction of radically new ones, with the exception of the rotary mill and of the watermill.[1] The specificity of the economic development of the world of the Greek city-states consisted in the fact that it was the transportation sector, more than the production sector, that benefited from the new input of energy. Ultimately, that is why trade, commerce, and the market were at the heart of economic growth. Nevertheless, the impact of these transformations on the production sector should not be underestimated either.

THE LOGIC OF ENERGY

In the societies that emerged from the "Neolithic Revolution" (to use the traditional expression), energy in the form of movement consisted chiefly of human and animal muscle power and wind power. In the form of heat, energy was represented by solar warming and the use of fuels, almost exclusively wood. This picture does not fundamentally change in Greece, though there were important innovations on certain points.

Sources of Heat

So far as sources of heat are concerned, the primary source of energy available to the Greeks was the sun. Radiant energy from the sun is an indispensable factor in the growth of plants. It also contributed to comfort by limiting to a minimum the need to heat houses. As already observed, in Olynthos, houses systematically faced south and had no openings on their north sides.[2] The "pastas" type house, with a double portico on a closed courtyard like at the Vari-farm in Attika, made it possible to cut the wind and retain heat during the winter.[3] Except in the mountains, people probably relied mainly on the sun to stay warm, even in winter. The absence of primary rocks means that there are no coal deposits in the Mediterranean area. We find only rare references to the mining of lignite in Greece. Theophrastus (On Stones 16) mentions that "coal" (anthrakes) was mined in Elis, on the road leading to Olympia. He notes that blacksmiths used it. This must have been lignite rather than bituminous coal, but its use was very limited. For all practical purposes, wood was the only fuel available.

In ancient Greece, as in all preindustrial societies, wood was used in two ways: as a construction material and as a source of heat.[4] These uses inevitably competed with each other, and the result was that different kinds of wood were used for different purposes. Tree trunks were reserved primarily for construction, while firewood consisted chiefly of smaller branches and twigs taken not only from trees but also and perhaps especially from bushes and thickets, which were more commonly available. These two ways of using wood led to entirely different modes of production and trade. Wood (and its derivative, pitch, which was used in naval construction and also to make ceramic vessels waterproof) was in great demand and was a very valuable product.

Wood was the only fuel that could be used for cooking, and this was no doubt the main way it was used domestically. Except in mountainous areas where wood was abundant, people had poor or inadequate heating. Houses seem not to have had fireplaces. When it was particularly cold, people had to make do with heat from portable charcoal stoves. The most deprived gathered around stoves at the village baths because they could not heat their homes.[5] Although this resulted in discomfort during the winter months (and had certainly serious health consequences, for instance a higher mortality rate, especially among children), it also made it possible to use less firewood. Wood was expensive, and the poorest people could not afford to consume much of it. Its high cost was a function of very high demand. Wood was the only fuel available for use in crafts such as ceramic making and dying, while metallurgical production and the mining industry required large quantities of charcoal to process a ton of ore. Huge amounts of wood were necessary. Thus for example in Laurion, in southern Attika, where charcoal was used to smelt galena and to separate lead from silver, perhaps 10,000 tons of wood for charcoal were needed per ton of silver.[6]

To be used as fuel, wood thus had to be collected and sold primarily in areas of maquis shrubland. Small branches that burned easily were used; their form was unimportant. A legal speech from the fourth century refers to the revenues a wealthy Athenian, Phainippos, received from the woods on his estate. Daily, his six asses brought firewood to the agora, which his adversary in the suit claimed earned him 12 drachms a day.[7] This was the source of wood used for charcoal making, an important activity in rural areas that must have occupied many landless peasants. We should imagine long lines of asses or carts coming into the city daily from the countryside in order to supply the large urban markets, as we see for example in an anecdote reported by Aeneas Tacticus (*Poliorcetics* 29.8, first half of the fourth century), in which the leader of a conspiracy enters a city by hiding in a load of brush.

Wood is a renewable source of energy if it is not overused. The outlying areas on the edges of the city (*eschatiai*) must have been drawn upon very heavily, but their use must also have encountered limits. If we examine the contemporary Mediterranean landscape in both Greece and Turkey, we may be tempted to conclude that the shrubland is inexhaustible—but that would be a mistake. If we observe the same landscapes in photos taken by archeologists at the beginning of the twentieth century, we see a radical difference. The land is bare—"clean," as it were—the numerous herds of goats cleared it of vegetation and at the same time prevented the growth of bushes and thickets that could provide the small-caliber wood used for heating.[8] This resulted in a contradiction that surely meant that the large urban markets could not derive their wood supply solely from their immediate surroundings. Deforestation was certainly not the rule for the whole of the Greek world (and for antiquity in general). But in the most urban and developed zone, where the population and the demand was very high, it seems pointless to deny the phenomenon.[9]

Wood was therefore a valuable commodity. How valuable, we can see in a religious regulation like the one for the sanctuary of Apollo Erithaseos, west of Acharnai, in northwest of Attika (end of the fourth century).[10] It forbids taking "logs, loppings, dry stick, or fallen leaves" outside the sanctuary. Infractions are to be punished by a fine of fifty drachms for a free man, and fifty lashes for a slave. The regulation may have had a religious aspect—using Apollo's sacred wood might have been forbidden—but it could also have been instituted with another end in view: reserving for the sanctuary alone the income from sales of the wood. It is intriguing that this regulation comes from a region known for its charcoal production (Aristophanes' Acharnians are supposed to be primarily charcoal burners). We can guess that the local people had their eyes on this wood, which was "their own" because Apollo Erithaseos was their god; but the collectivity wanted to prevent it being diverted to the benefit of individuals. Similarly, land-leasing agreements of the end of the third century from Amos, a Rhodian mainland deme near Physkos (today Marmaris), regulate the use of wood: a person leasing agricultural land is allowed to cut only so much wood on the land as he requires to make stakes, and if he cuts more than that, he has to leave it there.[11]

In the Hellenistic and Imperial periods, the benefactor of the gymnasium had to supply not only oil for the athletes, but also firewood to heat the baths that provided the necessary relaxation after exercise and also ensured hygiene, which was at that time considered not a luxury but an indispensable element of a citizen's life (the phenomenon is even better attested during the Roman period because of the larger number of extant sources). In regions where wood was rare or even nonexistent, as in the interior of Asia Minor or in Egypt, cow pie or straw was used to heat baths.[12] In Greece, people did not go that far, but regional differences in the extent of forests made transport of wood from one area to another indispensable. Southern Greece, which had few forests or had seriously depleted their ability to reproduce themselves naturally, imported construction timber from Macedon or northwest Asia Minor. But urban areas or craft production sites had to import their firewood from closer sources. Some Aegean islands were more densely populated than others, and the payment in silver that one could receive for firewood must have led many island dwellers to cut all the wood they could in the marginal areas of their islands. As mentioned, the Laurion mines were heavy consumers of firewood and charcoal, and there is little likelihood that local production sufficed to meet this demand. Firewood and charcoal must have been brought in mainly from the Kyklades or from Euboia rather than from more distant regions. In any case, the proximity of the sea made importing wood easier and thus less expensive.[13]

Charcoal (*anthrax*) was very heavily used.[14] This fuel has numerous advantages. Per unit of weight, it produces significantly more heat than dry wood: the ratio is 1.65 to 1.[15] To produce the same quantity of energy, transporting charcoal rather than wood thus represented proportionate savings. In addition, used in a home or domestic workshop, it has the advantage of producing fewer fumes and much more constant heat than wood does. Finally, charcoal not only makes it possible to produce much higher temperatures, which are indispensable for certain operations, especially in metallurgy, but it also allows the specific additions of carbon that are necessary for making steel. Until the technique of smelting using coke was mastered in the eighteenth century, charcoal remained the fundamental fuel of the metallurgical industry.

The disadvantage of charcoal, however, is that producing it involves an energy loss, since the fuel wood to charcoal conversion efficiency is 5 to 1 by weight on an oven-dry wood basis, and commonly 7 to 1 (a little below 15 percent) on a common wet wood basis (the rest is used as fuel or is lost through unwanted complete carbonization).[16] Nevertheless, charcoal was produced in massive quantities. The wood was burned not in pits but in elevated kilns of the kind Theophrastus briefly describes.[17] In the Greek world, kilns were scattered all over the countryside, and smoke constantly rose from them: it took several weeks to complete the carbonization phase through slow, reductive combustion, and twice as much time to cool the kiln. This activity nonetheless had the advantage of providing resources in marginal areas. Charcoal analysis from Pompeii between the third century BCE and 79 CE shows that beechwood remained the largest source of fuel for charcoal production (ca. 80 percent in the third to second century BCE to ca. 60 percent in the first century CE), with small wood or macchia playing only a minimal role.[18] The charcoal-burners of Acharnai were citizens. However, slaves were commonly assigned this task, as in the slave Syriskos seen in Menander's play Men at Arbitration (Epitrepontes 257 and 407–8), who belongs to a great landowner. An inscription from Teos in Ionia from the second half of the fourth century reports the annexation of a small inland community whose name is no longer known: in this mountain area, slaves produced wood and charcoal, which they carried to market on the backs of asses.[19]

Unlike wood used in construction, which was sold by measured volume, firewood was sold by weight, and charcoal by unit volume. In the Eudemian Ethics (7.4.4), Aristotle also uses a comparison with weighed wood: "So in cases of small degrees of superiority disputes naturally occur (for a small amount is not of importance in some matters, as in weighing wood, though in gold plate it is)."[20] An illustration is also provided by a Delian law on wood and coal that alludes to the weights for weighing wood and the measures used for charcoal.[21]

The Cost of Energy and the Fate of the Steam Engine

During the Hellenistic period, the price of firewood in Delos varied between 4 obols and at least 1 drachm, 4 obols the talent (about 26 kilograms, or a dozen logs), which was very high in comparison to other commodities.[22] In Athens around 330 BCE, the daily pay for an unskilled worker (taking into account the fact that there was in reality no fixed salary and that prices and salaries varied over time) was about 1 drachm, 3 obols.[23] Charcoal was even more expensive because of what was involved in producing it, but it made it possible to achieve the high temperatures that were required for casting and working metals. In Delos, a "basket" of charcoal cost 9 drachms, 3 obols (or, to transpose this figure into fourth-century Athens, the equivalent of more than six days' labor by an unskilled worker).[24] Energy was very expensive, and it is clear that this was a factor limiting economic development—for instance, the development of large-scale steel production, which was in any case held back by the amount of wood available. It is interesting to note that the first phase of the growth of the British steel industry in the eighteenth century was made possible not so much by the use of coke (because this technology had not yet been mastered) as by the fact that coal came into general use for heating homes, making more wood and charcoal available for steel production. When toward the middle of the century, coke began to be used for smelting, the limit of the use of charcoal had not yet been reached.[25]

We might think that the Greek world of the *polis* simply had to find alternative solutions. That is in fact what it tried to do. In this respect, the steam engine is a fine opportunity to carry out a counterfactual experiment. A small steam engine was built by Hero of Alexandria (an engineer of the first century CE who had absorbed the whole Hellenistic tradition, in particular from the great Ctesibius, who lived in the third century BCE). The *Pneumatics*, his most famous work,[26] begins with a theoretical introduction on the properties of air, the void, and the behavior of liquids under the influence of the force of gravity, and then goes on to describe a very long series of practical applications, all of which demonstrate Hero's ingenuity in this domain. The book is a veritable festival of technological achievements using air and liquids. In it, we find a multitude of famous mechanisms such as birds that sing when water is poured into a vase (*Pneumatics* 1.15), a fire engine (1.28), a hydraulic organ (1.42), and a machine for automatically opening the doors of a temple (1.38). Among these mechanisms, we also find the description of a steam turbine (2.11). The principle is simple. The steam passes into a sphere that turns on an axle. The steam emerging from small tubes with right-angle bends on each side of the sphere make it turn. The sphere can be made to rotate very rapidly. If the ancient Greeks knew the principle of the steam engine (and especially since it was Hero's description that provided the starting point for the engineers and mechanics of the Renaissance), don't we have to see their failure to make use of it as proof that they were not interested in economic issues, and particularly in the development of new sources of energy?

In reality, there were two obstacles to the practical use of the machine. The first of these was technical in nature. Aage G. Drachmann and John G. Landels have shown the weaknesses of Hero's machine.[27] Drachmann pointed out an engineering problem: the ancient engineers had no steel tubing or any metal screws for assembling the machine. The metal's lack of strength would in fact have considerably reduced the possibility of making a machine that was not constantly in need of repair. Then there is the question of the connection between the moving part (the sphere) and the fixed part (the tubes carrying the steam). The second, no less difficult problem would have been how to use the rotary force produced. To make the energy usable, this force would have had to be transferred to an axle turning much less rapidly but developing much greater power. A system of gears would be required, but Hero certainly knew how to use gears. Such a machine could attain as much as 1,500 rpm. But in that case, given the quality of the gear systems available at that time, the losses in energy would have been considerable. Landels therefore concludes that Hero's machine would have produced an output equivalent to about 1 percent of the input of energy, which would have disqualified it in advance for any practical application because of its prohibitive cost in relation to simple human labor.

As Landels notes, the crucial difference between Hero's steam engine and the one invented by Thomas Newcomen, an early eighteenth-century British engineer, is the latter's association of a boiler, intake valves, a piston, and a cylinder. Hero did not go that far, and in this sense he did not invent the machine that ended up revolutionizing the use of energy in the modern world. However, the perfecting of the "true steam engine" by Newcomen and Watt raises the problem of the social and economic conditions under which it appeared.[28] There is in fact a paradox here that we must immediately note and that did not escape Landels. Why didn't Hero or one of his Alexandrian predecessors become the Newcomen of antiquity? Since Ctesibius, all the necessary technical elements had been separately available. The camshaft, which makes it possible to transform rotary movement into an alternating, discontinuous rectilinear movement, was known to Hero.[29] It was used to operate pestles and sawmills in the Imperial period.[30] The discovery of the Hierapolis sawmill relief proves that the technology of the connecting rod, which can transform an alternating, discontinuous movement into a continuous circular movement and vice versa, was developed in antiquity—contrary to what was still thought a few years ago.[31] Not only was there no conceptual barrier to such a development, but the basic technologies necessary to develop a steam engine of the Newcomen type were known to Hellenistic and Roman engineers. In addition, a multitude of other applications shows that the Hellenistic tradition inherited by Hero was capable of combining many different techniques in very original ways. It has been argued that general orientation of the Greeks' scientific inspiration was little inclined toward the study of movement.[32] But Hero's engine suggests that exceptions were possible. Hero's "autokinetic sphere" seems in fact to have been an experimental tool successfully proving, against Aristotle, the possibility of autonomous movement.[33] Thus there should be no doubt that something else was lacking: an economic motive and conditions favorable to development, rather than the sheer impossibility of devising such an engine.

Neither should we imagine that the taste for "gadgets" shown by a man like Hero was an obstacle to the practical and "industrial" use of the techniques he describes.[34] On the contrary, the production of all kinds of gadgets for the European elite of the modern era has made an important contribution to technological development by forcing designers and craftspeople to meet increasingly precise standards—for instance, in polishing lenses intended for use in opera glasses.[35] This tradition was one of the sources of the precision machining required for building a Newcomen steam engine. Similarly, the steam engine benefited from the advances made in boiler-making in breweries. In antiquity, improvement of machining techniques would have been favored by the availability of large quantities of metal, which would itself have required access to greater quantities of energy.

But what matters most here is the economic conditions for using steam engines. In the decade 1551–1560, England was already producing 210,000 tons of coal.

The increase over the following century was considerable: by 1700, coal production had risen to about 3.5 million tons.[36] Coal mining, which had already been pursued in the Middle Ages (and even already in antiquity), took off in the sixteenth century. It is striking to see that the rise in coal mining accompanied a rise in population. Coal was then used primarily for domestic heating, and not for metallurgical production, which began only later on. Nonetheless, this increase had a profound impact on the English economy. Despite the pollution it caused, it had the advantage of providing, at a relatively low cost compared with wood, levels of heating, and thus of comfort and hygiene, incomparably superior to those of earlier times. In addition, by offering a substitute for other fuels, the use of coal freed up large tracts of land and a considerable quantity of labor, which then became available for other uses. Per capita, even before the invention of the steam engine, the quantity of both energy and iron at the disposal of an Englishman around 1700 was far greater than that available to his continental counterpart. However, the English mines raised a serious problem. Because they were very deep, they were particularly liable to be flooded by water. The available technologies for dealing with this problem remained very expensive. This was the terrain on which the Newcomen steam engine appeared. It was intended to meet a specific demand—pumping water out of mines—and it did so effectively. The high cost of installing a large engine, and especially its relatively low efficiency, presupposed its use where coal was available at low cost. It was also preferable that the engine be used near the place where coal was produced, to minimize the cost of transport, which remained high unless it was by waterway. For almost a century, the Newcomen steam engine (and at first even Watt's engine, starting in 1763) was used chiefly to pump water out of coal mines and, to a lesser extent, out of tin mines in Cornwall.[37] It was some time before the steam engine was put to other uses (for instance, in the textile industry). But the engine worked marvelously in mines and made very deep shafts possible, thus overcoming an obstacle that traditional mining would inevitably have met.[38]

The improvement of the steam engine—that is, the technical process that leads from invention to innovation, to adopt Joseph A. Schumpeter's distinction—could take place only in a context in which using it presented a genuine advantage. That required a low-cost fuel with a high-energy content: coal. Edward A. Wrigley rightly emphasizes the role of chance here. Coal allowed England to make a true transition into the industrial era, whereas Holland, which had better institutional conditions and the hardest-working people in the world, ultimately gave up its pioneering role.[39] The ecology of the Mediterranean world happened to lack fossil fuels. The only fuel ancient Greece had was wood, which was rare and expensive. A talent of wood (ca. 26 kilograms) would not have sufficed to produce enough pressure to even start operating a Newcomen steam engine. Because of the costs involved, there was no chance that the development of the steam engine might be envisaged in antiquity. Even when compared with human muscle-power, a steam engine of the type described by Hero (assuming that it could have been adapted for practical use) would simply have had no advantage.

A particularly interesting case of ancient technological imagination is found in an anonymous work of the fourth century CE. The author of the treaty *On Matters of War* (*De rebus bellicis* 17.1–3) imagined a warship with paddlewheels that would have made it superior to all enemy ships.[40] The wheels would have been driven by oxen turning a wheel connected with the paddlewheels by a system of gears. But the actual use of such a ship would have required a source of energy other than animal power. This has been seen as the symbol of the limits of ancient technology.[41] Couldn't Hero's steam engine have been used to leap two millennia ahead and invent the steamship of the early nineteenth century? In reality, Hero's engine and Newcomen's were separated by nothing less than the 3.5 million tons of coal that were mined annually in England at the beginning of the eighteenth century.

Wind, Connectivity, and Transport Costs

Therefore, the steam engine could not provide more energy for the world of the Greek city-states. Nonetheless, crucial innovations were made in the transformation of movement, with applications of great importance in milling technology and in the use of hydraulic power to turn the mills.[42] In aggregate terms, they did not significantly increase the quantity of available energy. But they had an important impact on long-term or short-term economic development.

However, at least for transport by sea, ancient Greece had a source of energy that made movement both cost-free and inexhaustible: wind. It lowered maritime transport costs for heavy materials over great distances. The reason for the difference in cost between overland transport and maritime transport by sea is simple. The resistance to movement by water is weak and therefore requires much less energy. It is this permanent supply of free energy provided by wind that constitutes the true "secret hero" of the growth of the economy in the ancient Mediterranean world, and particularly in the world of the Greek city-states. Our contemporary capitalist market is still based primarily on the transformation of fossil energy and on organization into firms. In contrast, the market in the world of the Greek city-states was based on the direct use of the wind and on the *polis*. It was therefore connected with the development of a particular ecological environment. By radically lowering transport costs, wind energy enabled people to initiate trade cycles between production areas so distant from each other that transportation of goods by land would never have been possible. Moreover, transportation cycles were much shorter. Time was already money.

The question of "connectivity" is central to the recent study by Peregrine Horden and Nicholas Purcell, which has been rightly called a fundamental work on the long-term history of the Mediterranean, though this does not mean that its theses have been universally accepted.[43] Although it would be totally unfair to reduce his work to this aspect (for he was also perfectly aware of the diversity of the Mediterranean and of the role of regional trade), Fernand Braudel focused on the great navigation routes that connected the major cities of the Mediterranean, and on longue distance quite as much on *longue durée*.[44] On the contrary, Horden and Purcell emphasize the extreme fragmentation of the Mediterranean world on both the local and the micro-local levels. Climatic instability was so great that each region or micro-region—a plain, a valley—was sometimes forced to cope with extreme shortages of basic food resources, forcing it to rely temporarily on external resources for subsistence. In other words, nature forced Mediterranean countries to communicate with each other. Horden and Purcell call this forced inclination to communication "connectivity."[45]

However, we still need to agree about the level of this connectivity, which obviously has not remained the same from antiquity to the present day. How high was it in the ancient world? Are we dealing with an economy whose scope of action was very limited and founded on a generalized autarky (in the modern sense of a self-sufficient economy severely limiting interaction with the outside world), at whatever level we examine (family farms or larger estates, cities, regions)? Was this a static economy in which trade played a limited and auxiliary role, only providing a substitute when an environmental catastrophe occurred? This schema was long dominant and still has its supporters. Or are we dealing on the contrary with an economy in which connectivity was not only general but included all forms of trade from the most modest at the micro-local level to the most distant across the Mediterranean? In this case, it would have a market dynamics in an analytical schema totally opposed to the preceding one. That is what is at stake in this debate, and in this book as well. The analysis of transport costs in ancient Greece is a precondition that determines the rest of this study.

The rule of transport costs is that the unit of transport cost is inversely proportional to the unit value per unit of weight and volume (to simplify, we will combine the two aspects). In other words, if the unit value of a given quantity decreases, the cost of transport increases proportionately. This rule obviously applies no matter what the means of transportation. The latter is a parameter that plays the role of a coefficient in the preceding equation.[46]

This rule can be easily demonstrated by an example. If gold is being transported, the cost of physical transport per unit of weight and volume will be negligible. If heavy materials are being transported, the cost per unit of weight increases very quickly with a decrease in unit value. Accounts in Delos show that in 279 BCE, for a load of tiles shipped from the neighboring island of Syros (thus by sea), the freight charges added 25.5 percent to the cost of the cargo.[47] In 277, it rose to 250 percent of the purchase price for a load of bricks, which had a comparatively lower value than tiles per unit weight. The freight cost for heavy materials was so high that the administrators of the sanctuary tried to decrease this cost directly by regulating it.

The scale of the relationship between the cost of maritime transport and overland transport remains to be determined. Clearly, the cost of overland transport was much higher. A relationship of 1 to 40 has been proposed, based on prices mentioned in Diocletian's *Edict on Maximum Prices* in the late Roman Empire.[48] This ratio was determined on very theoretical bases, and cannot be considered universally and absolutely valid.[49] However, we can conclude that in any event the cost of overland transport was "tens of times higher" than that of maritime transport. But we must add one corrective: the usual idea of ancient roads—always poor, and impassable for carts as soon as the terrain ceased to be flat—is certainly a carica-ture, as Hans Lohmann has shown for Classical Athens and Stephen Mitchell for the roads of Roman Anatolia.[50] It is true that in the previous period the road net-work was not as good, far from it. However, for transport over short distances (within cities) or medium distances, on certain very precise routes (though one cannot speak of road networks such as are found in the Roman period), the existence of roads is undeniable. Oliver Rackham had already drawn attention to the fact that in ancient Greece roads and transport were more important than is generally thought, the distinction between roads that were suitable for vehicles and those that were not going back to Homer.[51]

ROADS AND OVERLAND TRANSPORT

When roads were available, overland transport used carts drawn by oxen, the "heavy-duty motor" of transport in antiquity, to use Georges Raepsaet's expres-sion.[52] Long trains of oxen were used to transport huge tree trunks or large blocks of marble. The existence of this kind of very heavy transport, in which as many as thirty pair of oxen moved loads weighing as much as six or seven tons, has been clearly demonstrated by Alison Burford. But we also see that the cost was very high, and that such transport was limited to a few dozen kilometers at most.[53] At the same time, on roads, but also on rough terrain and for much lighter loads, mules and asses were used; they could go everywhere.

The image of a Greece without roads would be quite wrong. Archeology and inscriptions provide convergent evidence to the contrary. The excavations con-ducted in Mesogaia, in Attika, have revealed for the Classical period a dense net-work of carefully laid out, well-marked roads that could be traveled not only by asses and mules, but also by carts.[54] It is clear that we are always dependent on field research or excavations, but in the islands, a city like Kamiros, in the island of Rhodes, had a good road network (even in mountain areas) already in the Helle-nistic period.[55] In 187 BCE, the small town of Pidasa, in western Asia Minor, wanted to be connected with the sea by a road that could be used by vehicles, and had it written into the treaty unifying the town with Miletos.[56] In Crete, the treaty of 109/8–108/7 BCE between Lato and Olous proves that there were roads that can be called major thoroughfares and were traveled by foreigners.[57] Roads traveled by Greek traders linked coastal cities (thus Maroneia and Pistiros on the Thracian coast) but also led into the heart of Thrace to the *emporion* that had been set up there by the Odrysian kings.[58]

But we must also stress the limits of overland transport. It is true that heavy loads might be carried as far as several hundred kilometers. The proof of this is provided by the situation in the nineteenth century, when grain produced in the interior of Anatolia might be exported to the coast, or from one province to another, but at very high cost. When transported from Çankırı (ancient Gangra) to Kastamonu (the Byzantine Kastamon, west of Pompeiopolis, today Taşköprü) by a 132-kilometer route crossing the Ilgaz mountains in Paphlagonia, the price of wheat doubled.[59] Wheat from Sivas (ancient Sebasteia), which lay inland, might be transported to the port of Samsun (ancient Amisos) over a distance of 346 kilometers. But on arrival, the price had quadrupled. "Under such conditions," the French geographer Vital Cuinet observed, "no commodity is transportable if it is not absolutely necessary, of superior quality, not subject to spoilage, and above all very cheap at its production site." However, that did not prevent goods from being transported—for instance, half the grain produced in the province of Angora (Ankara, ancient Ankyra) was exported.[60] But as a rule, as Cuinet emphasizes, these costs had a negative effect: in the vilayet of Sivas, of 300,000 tons of wheat, only 25,000 tons of the best quality durum wheat were exported. It was only the excellent quality of Sivas wheat that justified transporting it.[61] Besides, two-thirds of the fruit production (which had a higher commercial value) was exported to Constantinople. Still, compared with those of other provinces, the roads in the region were exceptionally good. But the conditions of transport remained poor. Carts carrying a maximum load of one ton each took a week to transport goods from Sivas to Samsun (thus at a rate of about fifty kilometers per day). If dromedaries (which were known in the Middle East in the period discussed in this book, but not used as a means of transport in Greece and Western Asia Minor) were used, each one carrying 250 kilograms, it took ten to twelve days.[62] A mule took eight or nine days, but carried still less than a dromedary.[63] So far as transport capacities are concerned, these figures correspond to Raepsaet's tabulations of the comparative efficiency of different pack animals (230 and 150–180 kilos for the dromedary and the mule, respectively; an ass or a mule could carry that load at a rate of about 24 kilometers a day).[64]

Thus we see that in the nineteenth century the absolute limit of overland commerce in heavy goods seems to have been about 300 kilometers. At significantly longer distances, overland transport of heavy goods was simply out of the question, not only because it was too expensive, but also for other reasons. First, a network of stations for changing animals would have had to be established. Then, in Antiquity before the Roman Imperial period institutional and political instability would have made journeys of this kind very risky. What was possible in exceptional cases—for instance, with the Roman *cursus publicus* first organized in the early Imperial period for the transmission of official information only—was simply inconceivable for mass transport of ordinary products for ordinary customers.[65] We know that in the nineteenth century, it was possible to organize genuine long-distance railway networks only when businesses organized as companies were established, and it is difficult to see how these could have developed under the technical conditions of transport in antiquity.[66] Furthermore, the time factor operated against overland transport: for long-distance transport, very slow means of overland transport (for example, by oxcart) would take too long. In other words, there was a physical limit to overland transport of heavy goods, which was limited to a maximum of a few hundred kilometers in the most favorable cases, and at very high basic costs.

The case of the grain produced in Philomelion, in Phrygia, offers proof of this.[67] In 70 BCE, Cicero (*Verrines* 2.3.191–92) used this city as an example in a legal speech denouncing the behavior of Verres, who had been governor of Sicily. During the Republican period, provincial governors commonly had grain delivered for their personal use (*frumentum aestimatum* or *cellae nomine*), though it was in fact customarily replaced by a cash payment. Some took advantage of this to receive grain at the highest price in the province (thus a much higher sum in money), a dishonorable but not illegal practice. Cicero—who must have known the situation well because in 75 BCE he had held the office of *quaestor* (magistrate in charge of financial administration) in Lilybaion in Sicily—claimed that although wheat prices were the same everywhere in Sicily, Verres had abused his authority by having grain delivered to him at 12 sesterces the *modius*, whereas nowhere in the province did the price exceed 2 to 3 sesterces. In this connection, Cicero mentions, *a contrario*, provinces where the price of grain varied greatly depending on the region. For the province of Asia, he takes the example of Philomelion, a city about 400 kilometers from Ephesos as the crow flies, or at least 450 kilometers by road. It was the easternmost point in the province, and despite Manius Aquilius's policy of road-building there is no doubt that the constraints on transport in late Hellenistic Asia Minor were similar to those in the later Ottoman Turkey.[68]

If we hypothetically apply the coefficient mentioned earlier for transport from Sivas to Samsun, the price of grain would have quintupled between Philomelion and Ephesos. To make such transport possible, Philomelion would have had to have grain that was both of exceptional quality and ridiculously cheap. Cicero notes that in order to pay their taxes, the people of Philomelion did not even consider going to buy grain in Ephesos in order to supply it on site (which others did, however), but preferred to pay a compensatory sum of money. Cicero claims, for the purposes of his argument, that prices were the same everywhere in Sicily. Hence governors could not make the profits they made elsewhere by requiring that their wheat be the highest-priced in the province—since wheat could be bought at the place of delivery at the same price as in their own cities. Cicero's anecdote probably stretches the truth: it is more than likely that prices were nonetheless somewhat higher in the port cities of Sicily. In any case, even though this was not Cicero's objective, the anecdote shows that even in Sicily there would have been an advantage in saving transport costs from the interior to the coast. However, we must recall that in a country like Sicily the cost of transport over short distances had a relatively modest effect on the price paid. In fact, it took only one day to transport grain from Enna, which was about fifty kilometers from the coast (this is Cicero's example). But for very long distances, even for a product like grain overland transport was out of the question.

Thus we come back to our initial problem, cost relationships as a function of values per unit of weight and volume. Jacques Le Goff calculated that in the Middle Ages, the percentage of the final cost represented by maritime transport was 2 percent for wool and silk, 15 percent for grains, and 33 percent for alum.[69] It is possible that the scale was more or less the same for overland transport. We have to take into consideration that in trade conducted exclusively overland, preference was given to high-value products that cost little to transport. That is why textiles—in the Hellenistic period, for instance, those of Hierapolis in Phrygia or other cities in the interior of Asia Minor—or even metallurgical products such as worked iron from Kibyra, might find buyers in distant places.[70] Painted vases might also be transported far into the interior, and that explains why Attic ceramics were found at Gordion at the end of the sixth or the beginning of the fifth century.[71] The presence of amphoras of Thasian wine on the site of the big *emporion* discovered in inland Thrace near the modern city of Vetren can be understood in the same way:[72] this wine was a high-priced good worth transporting.[73] Besides, finding a large number of amphoras far from maritime or inland waterway routes is uncommon. We have only to examine the wide diffusion of Hellenistic Rhodian amphoras over the Mediterranean world to see that the great majority of them were found at coastal sites, sometimes in the inland but at a few dozen kilometers from the sea, as for example at Pergamon or on the sites of Judaea-Samaria. They are rarely found in sites more distant from the Mediterranean, like Failaka on the Persian Gulf, where they had been transported, however, by way of the Euphrates after transiting by land on the isthmus between the Orontes and the Euphrates. All the same, the Rhodian amphoras of Vieille-Toulouse in southern Gaul had necessarily been brought there by land, but only after the long voyage to Agde or Narbonne by sea.[74] Few Rhodian amphoras are found in the interior of Asia Minor. For instance, there are comparatively few Rhodian (as well as Knidian and Koan) amphoras in Kelainai—Apameia Kibotos, in inland Phrygia.[75] It was other products that were involved in long-distance trading by overland transport.

MARITIME TRANSPORT AND SHIPS

Maritime Transport and Ports

In 111 CE, Pliny the Younger was the administrator of the province of Pontos and Bithynia, and he wrote regularly to the Emperor Trajan to keep him informed and to submit projects to him. this is how he described the situation in the great city of Nikomedia:[76]

> Within the territory of Nikomedia there is a very large lake; marble, grain, wood, and all kinds of other products are transported over it by boat, without much effort or cost. But from that point on they have to be transported to the coastal area by wagon, at a much higher cost and with great effort.

Then Pliny mentions the project of digging a canal to join Nikomedia's lake with the sea. Trajan's response was not hostile, but it was reserved. Nonetheless, Pliny's comparison between maritime transport and overland transport is eloquent. The lake was 17 kilometers long from east to west. The isthmus between the lake and Propontis (the sea of Marmara) was only 16 kilometers across, but crossing it was difficult and costly. When people had a choice, they always moved heavy goods by water. That was particularly true for marble and wood. To transport marble from Latmos to Didyma and its large temple of Apollo, the blocks were loaded at the port of Ioniapolis and unloaded at Panormos, as close as possible to Didyma, and carried from there to their destination.[77] More generally, this holds for all heavy goods. Wood was, of course, floated down the rivers of northern Greece and Asia Minor, which were large enough to make this kind of transport possible.[78]

In general, but especially for heavy goods, the possibility of using maritime transport was a decisive factor in the development of economic activity. Marble quarries that were close to the sea were given priority, like those on Paros or in Nikomedia (whose lake minimized overland transport to the sea). Some of these, like those at Aliki, south of Thasos, were actually on the seacoast, and this made it possible to load the marble directly onto the boats, avoiding any overland transport.[79]

The true royal road was thus maritime. But transport by sea presupposes mastery of an elaborate technology and professional experience. The Mediterranean, with its annex, the Pontos Euxeinos (Black Sea), is a very fragmented body of water.[80] There are, of course, major wind patterns. Thus as we have seen, the Aegean has two opposite systems: between May and the end of September, the winds blow out of the north; from the end of September to April, they blow out of the south. One peculiarity of the Aegean is that in July winds that the ancient Greeks called "Etesian" (*etesiai*, "annual") blow; in modern Greek they are called *meltemi* (from the Turkish word for "breeze"). The north winds grow stronger and blow constantly and very hard, sometimes giving rise to violent storms. Despite these patterns, unlike the trade winds in the Atlantic or the monsoon in the Indian Ocean, the characteristic feature of the winds on the Mediterranean is their instability. Because of the proximity of continental areas and their reliefs, the wind frequently changes in direction, locally sometimes several times a day. Navigating on the Mediterranean thus presupposes a good knowledge of the local winds and the traps they sometimes lay for sailors, especially since the coast and the risk of shipwreck are never very far away.

Even if, except during unusual storms, the Mediterranean does not have the heavy swells of the open ocean and the high waves that accompany them, sailing on it can still be described as difficult. Strong ships that can stand up to the short but shattering waves and can be quickly maneuvered to deal with the winds' frequent changes in direction are thus necessary for safe sailing on the Mediterranean. Ancient naval construction technology and quality of the ships' rigging do not have a very good reputation. They are often contrasted with those of the builders of caravels, the ships that made it possible to cross the Atlantic, despite their small dimensions. The details of naval construction are certainly not unimportant. It is clear that in the late Middle Ages ships were stronger and more maneuverable. A multitude of small technical innovations that had been introduced over the preceding millennium and a half gave them qualities that ancient ships lacked. Clinker construction is only one of many such innovations. Overall, techniques of assembly and of constructing ribs became much more effective.

Once again, however, it would be a mistake to assume that in antiquity no progress was made in this regard. Ships of the Archaic period were "stitched together," like some of those found during excavations in the port of Marseilles.[81] This technique, which consisted in assembling the various parts of the ribs and the planking by ligatures, was still known to Aeschylus, and we have archeological proof that it continued to be used into the early fifth century. Starting at that time, it was gradually abandoned in favor of the technique of tenons pegged into mortises, which made the ship much stronger and limited distortions of the hull (and thus leaks) when it was subjected to the wind. This made also the maintenance of the ship much easier and cheaper. Other improvements were implemented. As early as the Classical period, ships had a keel and wineglass hull section that reduced leeway. In the Hellenistic period, metal pins were used to provide a better connection between the hull and the keel. The Hellenistic period saw the introduction of bilge pumps and sounding weights.[82] Large iron or lead anchors replaced stone models and allowed a better hooking into the seabed.[83]

Indeed, already at the end of the Archaic period we find ships being built that are both stronger and larger, capable of carrying several hundred, and soon several thousand, amphoras. However, shipwrecks indicate that even in the late Classical or Hellenistic period, most ships were under 20 meters in length and did not have a cargo capacity beyond 50 tons.[84] For this reason, the famous ship found off Kyrenia, north of Cyprus, must have been a typical ship of the period. Dated to the end of the fourth century, it was around fifteen meters long and carried over 400 amphoras, chiefly from Rhodes and Samos.[85] This was admittedly a small ship. Besides, speeches in Attic courts and inscriptions show that by the fourth century, the Greeks also had larger ships capable of transporting at least 3,000 amphoras or 3,000 *medimnoi* of grain. This seems to have been a very common load for long-distance transport in both the Classical and the Hellenistic periods.[86] On the basis of about 30 kilograms per *medimnos* (and not 40, as was previously thought), 3,000 *medimnoi* represented a load of about 90 tons.[87] Thus the load capacity of bigger ships in the Aegean world of the Classical and Hellenistic periods was greatly superior to that of the preceding period, and this presupposes a significant improvement in techniques of naval construction. A regulation of the port of Thasos dated to the third century alludes to two categories of ships, those that have a capacity of no less than 3,000 talents (78 tons) and those that have a capacity of no less than 5,000 talents (130 tons).[88] The Thasian law shows that we would be wrong to think that only "Kyrenia-type" ships were involved, even if de facto most vessels entering the harbors must have been of that kind. Smaller ships were best suited for the needs of a redistributive trade in a short- and medium-distance horizon. For the long-distance shipping of large quantities of wine or oil amphoras, or for bringing grain from Egypt, Sicily, or Pontos, in view of the distance covered and the capital that had to be invested, it made sense to choose a larger ship to ensure profitability.

Evidence from shipwrecks conclusively proves an increase in the capacity of the ships in the Mediterranean world (table 3.1).[89] It does not matter whether the ships were Phoenician, Etruscan, or Greek, as maritime technologies migrated easily from one cultural context to the other. Although the late Bronze Age Uluburun ship probably already had a tonnage of ca. 20 tons (and was built with mortise-and-tenon technology), in the mid-seventh century the largest ships we know of could transport ca. 12 tons of cargo.[90] By the end of the sixth century, their capacity had grown to ca. 27–30 tons. As early as the end of the fourth century, the figure was over 100 tons. Around 100 BCE, it was over 250 tons. Two exceptional wrecks with even bigger cargoes are attested in the course of the first century BCE, and they remain by far the biggest vessels attested by ancient shipwrecks (although literary sources in the Imperial period offer proof of the existence of other ships of that size).[91]

If we limit the comparison to the end of the second century and the Mahdia wreck, this was an increase of the cargo capacity from one to twenty over six and a half centuries. Again, these ships were certainly only those of the largest size in their time. But it is inevitable to conclude that the average cargo capacity of the ships increased in the same time span, although of course in more modest proportions. Even if it were only by a factor in the order of one to five to one to ten, the increase would remain spectacular. Sturdier ships meant also somewhat decreasing the risk of loss at sea (although of course not eliminating it). The huge increase observed in the quantities transported by sea in the Classical and Hellenistic periods would not have been possible without these technological achievements and the increase in the capacity of ships. The limit of the size increase of ships was more economical than technological.

TABLE 3.1. Cargo Capacity of the Largest Ships Attested by Shipwrecks

WRECK	SHIP	DATE BCE	CARGO ORIGIN	CARGO WEIGHT TONS
Off Ashkelon	Phoenician	ca. 750	Phoenician	12
Grand Ribaud F	Etruscan or Greek	500–475	Etruscan	28–35
Alonnisos	Greek	420–400	Greek, North Aegean	140
Mahdia	Roman	110–90	Roman	230–250
Albenga	Roman	90–80	Roman	500–600
La Madrague de Giens	Roman	75–60	Roman	375–400

In addition, the construction of oversize ships showed its limits. A giant ship like the *Syracusan* that was built by Archimedes for Hieron II of Syracuse possibly around 240 BCE was a spectacular achievement that led to no further developments. The description of this ship and its cargo capacity transmitted by Athenaeus (5 206d–209e) does not permit us to establish with exactitude either the ship's capacity (around 4,000 tons?) or its size (it must, however, have been between 65 and 75 meters long).[92] In any event, this ship, which was designed to be a luxury passenger liner, a warship, and a cargo boat (and which in fact transported grain, wool, and salt fish) made only a single voyage. Because he could find no harbors capable of receiving it, Hieron sent it to Alexandria, after which it sat at the dock. Its gigantic size thus showed that there was an upper limit to the size of ships if their operation was to be profitable. It remains worth stressing however that Archimedes and his team managed to overcome a long series of technical difficulties, ranging from the conception of the ship to its launching. The ship was seaworthy and was able to cross the Mediterranean. This success proves that the question of the hydrostatic equilibrium of a very large ship had been correctly asked and answered, in both theory (the calculation of the centers of gravity) and practice (plans for the geometry of the hull).[93]

Finally, it should be observed that ancient ships' navigational qualities should not be underestimated. They used a large square sail on a central mast as their chief source of propulsion.[94] In the Hellenistic period, a second sail placed forward, on an inclined mast, probably helped stabilize the ship's course. The lateen sail was not known, but the use of brails to give the sail a triangular shape probably largely compensated for this lack.[95] Thus even if these ships were built to sail running before the wind, they could also (although imperfectly) beat to windward.[96] To be sure, they could not turn into the wind and they had to lower their speed to come about, but in this they did not differ from the large sailing ships of the early modern era. Lateral rudders were not as effective as stern rudders, but they did make it possible to guide the ships easily in calm weather.[97] Problems arose in stormy weather, when there seems to have been no solution other than to lower the sails and even the mast, drop out anchors (there were several on each ship), and then go with the wind, hoping the coast was not too close.

Techniques of Navigation and Ports

Navigational techniques were based almost entirely on the experience accumulated by preceding generations.[98] There were no nautical charts. At best, documents resembling medieval "portolans" might be used; these described the coasts, currents, treacherous winds in a particular region, or hidden reefs. But we should not imagine that the ancient Greeks or Romans had anything like our nautical charts (which are themselves no substitute for direct experience). The compass, a Chinese invention that arrived in Europe only in the Middle Ages, was unknown in antiquity. The astrolabe or its equivalent remained a scientific curiosity, and the only way to determine latitude was the rise of the stars—a very imprecise method that could be used only at night and when the sky was clear. There was no way of determining longitude. Must we conclude from this that ancient navigation was fundamentally mediocre? In reality, it was only at the end of the eighteenth century, with the introduction of portable clocks that worked on rolling seas and then of the chronometer, that it became possible to determine a ship's longitude.[99] In all, the most important disadvantage of ancient navigational techniques as compared with those of the Middle Ages was certainly the lack of the compass.

Given these conditions, did ancient seafarers venture onto the high seas or did they limit themselves to sailing along the coast, for fear of getting lost, so to speak?[100] Horden and Purcell put special emphasis on coastal shipping, and challenge Braudel's notion of major nautical routes. However, the sources attesting to voyages on the high seas are so numerous that we can hardly doubt that they took place. Furthermore, for the reasons previously explained, sailing along the coast was not without dangers. But the difficulty of locating one's position in latitude and longitude meant that a ship captain never knew exactly where he was going to end up. For example, for a crossing between Crete and Cyrene, one might arrive to the east or to the west of the desired destination; then the port of Cyrene had to be reached by sailing along the coast. Because of commercial constraints, after sailing from one zone to another, merchants went from port to port selling the goods they had brought with them. Finally, we must emphasize that given the configuration of the Mediterranean, many of the long-distance routes passed along the coasts, but were still like high-seas sailing because ships went several days without landing.[101] Thus coastal shipping cannot be regarded as a universal rule. In fact, ancient seaborne commerce relied on a small number of segmented routes associating crossing with coasting.[102] Great mercantile profits were connected with trade between different zones, which ancient navigational techniques made fully possible.

The length of a voyage depended on wind and sea conditions. If they were good, a voyage could be made in the time forecast; ancient sources show that in fact there were estimated "standard" times for a given itinerary in a given season. It goes without saying that these estimated times were dependent on the winds: if they were bad, no forecast was possible. Ships' speeds therefore varied greatly.[103] During the summer, with good weather and taking into account the direction of the prevailing winds, it took five days to sail from Byzantion to Rhodes (nine and a half from the Kimmerian Bosporos). However, sailing in the opposite direction, which was less favorable, it took ten days to get from Rhodes to Byzantion. One could sail from Rhodes to Egypt in three or four days with favorable winds, but it took ten days to get from the Levantine coast (Caesarea) to Rhodes, and thus about twelve days to sail there from Egypt. Nonetheless, several round-trips between Rhodes and Egypt, for example, could be made in a single year.

The wrecks of ancient trading ships that have been found (usually located by the cargoes of amphoras that cover the remains of the ribs and planking) show that maritime tragedies were not rare.[104] The economic question is what the percentage of shipwrecks was and what economic effect they had. If, based on Venetian insurance rates in the Middle Ages, we suppose the rate of loss to have been 3 to 5 percent, we see that the toll was very heavy but not unbearable.[105]

Cities' investments in port facilities, in proportion to their resources, show that they did not lack interest in commerce. For many of them, supplies brought in by sea were a vital necessity, and they had to have facilities that could receive trading ships loaded with grain. But since they had to export as well as import, their harbor facilities also allowed them to receive the traders who exported their products and imported the indispensable goods. The necessity of defending the harbors against enemy attacks also presupposed appropriate defense systems, which required major investments. Although many small cities probably did not always have anchorages in protected bays (for example, island cities), large cities built carefully equipped ports.

In the Classical period, Athens abandoned the use of Phaleron Bay in favor of the natural coves at Piraeus.[106] The commercial port was set up in the vast Kantharos basin, which provided excellent shelter for ships. Naturally, at Athens and elsewhere the opportunities offered by the coastal relief were used; doing so greatly reduced the necessary investments. But, with a first program launched by Themistokles in the 490s, the whole area was also carefully fortified.[107] The Kantharos port was surrounded by porticos that provided traders the facilities they expected, and were at the same time an impressive setting for all the sailors arriving in the city. The ports of Rhodes, probably four in number, were also built for the most part with a view to the particularities of the relief and the prevailing winds.[108] Whereas at Thasos ships were arranged by size, at Rhodes they were arranged by where they came from.[109] Knidos built its two ports with care—one was for warships and the two of them were linked by a channel.[110]

The construction of artificial ports, which underwent a huge development in Roman times, began in the Hellenistic period: we know at least the case of the port of Amathous, in Cyprus, built on a coast that offered no natural shelter.[111] This expensive facility is typical of the lavish expenditure and investment of the high Hellenistic period. Moreover, the port of Amathous was certainly chiefly military, and was used (if at all) only for a short time. The creation of a port *ex nihilo* was thus justified only if the natural environment did not make it possible to minimize costs, and it should perhaps be seen as evidence of overinvestment. In any event, it provides no proof of a particular economic rationality.

The internal equipment of ports probably seldom included docks. At Delos, no doubt because of the conditions under which excavation was conducted in the nineteenth century, the topography of the ancient port remains largely unknown.[112] We know that a jetty was built, because its existence is proven by the accounts of the administrators of the sanctuary (*hieropoioi*). In Rhodes, the ancient military port (present-day Mandraki) was enclosed by a large jetty. But even at Delos, it is not certain that stone docks were built in the port. The latter required significant investments and must have been the exception, and were found only in ports that had large resources. Wooden jetties must have allowed ships to unload conveniently, unless rowboats were used without the ship being in direct contact with the jetty. Monuments built in prominent locations, like the temple of Poseidon at Sounion at the southern tip of Attika, could be used as beacons indicating dangers on nautical routes. The existence of lighthouses has been hypothesized as early as the late Archaic period for Thasos, and for the Hellenistic period at Delos, although, at least for Thasos, the function of the buildings interpreted as lighthouses has been put in doubt.[113] The example of the big lighthouse of Alexandria does not seem to have been followed in Greece itself or in western Asia Minor (at least, we have no information on this point).[114] Lighthouses seem to have become more common only in the Imperial period.

One would like to know the general cost of shipping. But we have very few sources on this point for the world of the Greek city-states. Demosthenes' speech *Against Timotheus* (49.29) shows us that in 373 or 372 BCE the shipping cost (*naulon*) for transporting wood from Macedon to Athens was about 1,750 drachms. We do not know how much wood was involved. But if, as is likely, it was a whole shipload, the figure nonetheless gives us an idea of shipping costs. They were certainly high in relation to the value of the goods, and might, for example in the case of grain, lead to increases of 50 to 100 percent over the purchase price if the distance to be traveled was long. But comparing them with price increases resulting from overland transport would not even make sense.

Attempts to Dig Canals and Build Portage Routes

Given the interest of shipping by water, breaks in waterways caused by isthmuses led to projects for digging canals. When he mentions the possibility of digging a canal to join Nikomedia's lake to the sea, Pliny explains that in the same region a basin that had already been dug might testify to a similar project undertaken by one of the "former kings," that is, a king of Bithynia, between 279 and 74 BCE:

> In the same region, I myself have found a canal dug by a king, but it is not known whether it was made to drain the surrounding land or to connect the river with the lake; in fact, it was not completed. It is not known whether this resulted from the king's death or from the loss of hope that the work could be finished.[115]

This report is precious because it reveals the existence of a Hellenistic king's attempt to dig a canal for a directly economic purpose. However, we must examine the topography of the region more carefully. There was not one interruption of the waterway, but two: one between the Sangarios River and the lake, and another between the lake and the sea. Pliny's description, which is in fact quite muddled, does not allow us to form a clear opinion on the question. Moreover, it is very rhetorical: the emperor Trajan will succeed where the earlier kings necessarily failed. The distance between the latter is less than two kilometers and the difference in elevation small, especially considering that at that time the course of the Sangarios lay farther to the west than it does today. The canal must have corresponded to the course of the little Melas River, which *a fortiori* allowed an easy junction.[116] If the Hellenistic canal was really a canal situated east (and not west) of the lake, was it in fact left uncompleted? Or had it, in Pliny's time, silted up because of a lack of maintenance, as would be normal in such a case, especially for a river as full of alluvium as the Sangarios? We know that regular maintenance was necessary on the canal dug between the Nile and the Red Sea, passing by way of the Great Bitter Lake.[117] It seems, however, less probable that the Bithynian kings really dreamed of linking the lake with the sea. The interpretation of the sections of canal found west of the lake, toward the sea, should thus be revised.

In fact, digging such long canals raised major technical problems that exceeded the Greek cities' engineering abilities, and even those of the Hellenistic kingdoms. Before the era of explosives and steam engines, only the use of massive amounts of human energy might have made such operations possible. Before the modern period, only two major canals were dug in the Western world: the one connecting the Nile and the Red Sea by way of the Great Bitter Lake, constructed in the time of Necho, and the one dug by Xerxes across the Athos isthmus in 480 BCE. According to Herodotus (2.158.5), 120,000 Egyptians died during the digging of the canal between the Nile and the Red Sea. Whatever the value of the anecdote, it shows an awareness that large bodies of men had to be assembled to complete such projects.[118] The canal across the Athos isthmus, which allowed Persian warships to cross safely, had no economic use, and this tour de force, by which the Persian king also showed his power, could be realized only thanks to the huge labor force provided by the largest invading army in antiquity.[119] Moreover, its length was not more than 2.2 kilometers, and the land was almost flat, thus offering exceptionally favorable conditions.[120] Other attempts or projects in later periods ended in failure because of the technical problems (such as the crumbling of the banks) encountered and the difficulty of assembling a large labor force. This was probably the case (although whether the enterprise succeeded or failed is still a matter of debate) for the *Fossa Carolina*, Charlemagne's 793 attempt to dig a canal between the Rezat and the Altmühl rivers, which would have joined the Rhine basin with that of the Danube.[121] In 1591, the famous Sinan Pasha considered using 30,000 workers to dig a canal across the isthmus separating Nikomedia's lake from the sea.[122] Even though it is only 16 kilometers across, the isthmus reaches an altitude of 40 meters, which would have implied earthmoving on a very large scale.

In the cases mentioned, completed, or begun and then interrupted, or perhaps only planned, we see that bringing together the necessary workforce was based either on direct coercion or on putting part of an army to work. Nothing of the sort could be envisaged in the framework of the Greek *polis*, where citizen labor was both too precious and too expensive, and slave labor still too expensive to be used in such a way. Interestingly, according to Herodotus (3.39.4), the tyrant Polykrates used Lesbian prisoners of war to build the moat surrounding the fortification of the town of Samos.[123] To cross isthmuses, the only practical solution was a system of portage routes, generally constructed of wood smeared with grease in order to make it easier to slide loads. Across the Corinth isthmus, which was 6 kilometers wide, reached an altitude of 80 meters, and consisted of hard limestone, it was impossible to dig a canal: a projected canal desired by Nero was hardly begun, and in any case would have had no chance of being completed. The realistic solution, which goes back to the Archaic period and is rightly or wrongly attributed to Periandros, tyrant of Corinth between about 625 and 585 BCE, consisted in constructing a paved portage route, known as the *diolkos*, that made it possible to drag loads across the isthmus.[124] Archeologists have been able to investigate a section of this route several hundred meters long; the rest was destroyed by the construction of the Corinth canal at the end of the nineteenth century. Part of the portage route was winding, taking the most favorable path, and as a whole it must have been about 8 kilometers long. Grooves were cut into the stone to keep carts from going off course and to maximize the power of the ox-trains that drew them. The first literary mention of the *diolkos* is found in Thucydides, who says that in 428 BCE the Lakedaimonians used it to move their warships from the Gulf of Corinth to the Saronic Gulf.[125]

Until the thirteenth century CE, the date of its last known use, we have a series of testimonies that show that small and medium-sized fleets of warships could be pulled across the isthmus. However, no text alludes to an economic use of the *diolkos*. Must we conclude, as is usually done, that the nature of our historical sources—which, as we know, systematically give priority to the political and military aspects—masks the economic use of this route? From the outset, Corinth's prosperity was indubitably based on its commerce by overland or maritime routes, as Thucydides emphasizes (1.13.5). Individuals must have profited from it as intermediaries. As for the Corinthian state, it must also have derived fiscal benefits from taxes on merchandise passing through its territory, whether the latter involved goods transported overland between central Greece and the Peloponnese, or goods that had arrived by sea in the twin ports of Lechaion, on the Gulf of Corinth, and Kenchreai, on the Saronic Gulf.[126] Should we therefore conclude that trading ships loaded with goods were also put on trolleys and pulled across the isthmus, which would have had the advantage of allowing them to avoid rounding the proverbially dangerous Cape Malea at the southern tip of the Peloponnese?

That would have been impossible, however, for a simple technical reason. The rounded shape of trading ships made them difficult to lift onto a trolley. To do so, the Greeks would have needed very powerful cranes with a capacity of dozens of tons, and sometimes considerably more than 100 tons for the largest ships fully loaded. Even if this had been managed, at the slightest bump and without the counterpressure of the water, there would be a danger of the cargo shifting and breaking through the ships' planking. Moreover, if at Eleusis it took more than thirty pairs of oxen to move five-ton blocks of stone, how many oxen would have been required to move loads ten or twenty times heavier, and up a steep slope to boot? However, one objection immediately comes to mind: if it was possible to move warships, at least small and middle-sized ones, over the *diolkos*, why couldn't the same have been done with merchant ships? The answer to this question is two-fold. Even if a trireme might weigh as much as thirty tons or more, it is clear that it was hauled empty, which on the one hand indicated an upper weight limit, and on the other avoided the problem of the hull's fragility mentioned earlier in connection with merchant ships. But above all, warships had their own haulage forces: their rowers, who as a group had enough power to haul the boat over the *diolkos*.[127] This was obviously not the case for a large merchant sailing ship's crew, which numbered about ten at most (only four for a Kyrenia-type ship). These constraints lead us to a clear conclusion: fully loaded merchant ships could not have been hauled across the isthmus of Corinth using the *diolkos*.

Must we therefore conclude that the *diolkos* had no economic utility and was used only for military purposes? That would again be a mistake. Its military use may even have been only occasional—and that is why each time the "exploit" attracted the attention of historians and chroniclers, at least when large fleets were involved—whereas its economic use was regular. In exceptional cases, small commercial boats must have been moved across the isthmus empty. But the *diolkos* must have been used mainly by heavy carts by which goods were transported across the isthmus from one port to the other, where they were loaded onto other boats. This must have been the Corinthians' true vocation, especially for goods that could be easily offloaded and then reloaded. Most of the vessels at the disposition of traders who had had their goods transported across the isthmus and wanted to continue on their way must also have been owned by Corinthians. This would explain the two ports' prosperity. Besides, the costs connected with offloading, hauling over the isthmus, and transit duties must have been so high for the transportation of heavy goods from western waters (particularly from Sicily, Magna Graecia, or the Adriatic and the coasts of western Greece) that traders generally preferred to round the perilous Cape Malea south of the Peloponnese. There is no doubt that this was the route taken, for example, by the ships loaded with grain coming from southern Italy or Sicily that supplied Athens in the fifth and fourth centuries. The grain arrived on the same ships on which it had been initially loaded. That was the case, for instance, for the ship mentioned in the Demosthenic speech *Against Zeno-themis*; nothing indicates that it had crossed by the *diolkos*.[128]

Thus the *diolkos* had a genuine economic use, but it was limited. Corinth had been the political and economic center of Archaic Greece. Everyone went there for supplies. The *diolkos* must have been heavily used and the interplay between the two ports must have made it possible to ignore the costs of transport over the isthmus. But with the rise of Athens in the late sixth century and the development of its central role, an essential part of this trade, that involving heavy goods and particularly grain and products transported in amphoras, no longer passed through Corinth. However, with the new equilibria of Hellenistic Greece, and in particular the decline of Athens, Corinth prospered again. It is striking to see that it was only after Corinth was destroyed by Mummius in 146 BCE that Delos rose to prominence, as is explicitly indicated by Strabo and confirmed by the coins minted by the Athenians that fed the activity of this new Aegean and Mediterranean *emporion*.[129]

We can make an initial assessment of the contribution of technological innovation to the mastering of energy in the world of the Greek city-states.[130] It seems that no major breakthrough took place at first. The sun, wind, and wood remained the almost exclusive providers of energy during the whole period. The Greek engineers were perfectly able to conceive, as a scientific experiment, a small steam engine. But this machine could find no industrial application the way Newcomen's steam engine famously did. However, the main reason for this difference may be not a lack of interest in innovation or industrial application but a lack of fossil fuels in the Mediterranean area. Because of the high cost of wood, there was no incentive to develop a steam engine. On the other hand, many technological innovations were introduced in maritime technology. For example, innovations in shipbuilding made it possible to build vessels that were larger, safer, and cheaper (at least to maintain). The exceptional development of maritime transport from the Archaic to the Hellenistic period is in large part based on these technological improvements. In the debate between Walter Scheidel and Andrew Wilson concerning the contribution of innovation in maritime trade to the growth of the Greek world, Scheidel privileged institutional innovations, whereas Wilson, though following the same line of reasoning, suggested a more balanced relationship between institutional and technological factors.[131] Actually, one should even go one step further. Institutional and technological innovations went hand in hand. It should be clear that both institutional and technological innovations (not the former only) were a fundamental factor in the process of growth in the Mediterranean area from the Archaic to the Hellenistic period.

IV

THE *POLIS* AND THE ECONOMY

The constraints of ecology, of population dynamics, and of energy had by themselves an autonomous weight in the logic of development of the ancient Greek economy. But these constraints also resonated with a fundamentally new institutional framework, that of the city-states, which slowly emerged from the Iron Age and became the standard political structure in Greece in the Archaic and Classical periods. The reasons why the new political system came into being are only beginning to be explored. But it is clear that it was this new political structure that drove the specific logic of growth that can be observed in the Greek world before its absorption by Rome. Since the fourth millennium, kingdoms and palatial systems had been the dominant forms of political, social, and economic organizations. Their logic was based on the extraction of a massive tribute in kind (although starting at an early date, and increasingly in the first millennium BCE, they also began to make use of precious metals as a privileged good playing the role of money). This tribute enabled them to finance numerous armies and to build huge structures (temples or palaces). Their long-lasting success is corroborated by what we can observe in terms of population or measurable economic growth in general. Clearly, these kingdoms or palatial systems were not monolithic, and they certainly allowed some forms of social and economic flexibility, and thus of "private" transactions. But the weight of the state (and temples) remained the dominant characteristic of these societies.

The success and triumph of the city-state is all the more perplexing. How is it possible that a multitude of micro-political structures was able not only to crystallize into a stable political, social, and economic structure but was able also, at least for a while, to become the dominant political structure in the Mediterranean world? And how is it that this new structure drove an unprecedented economic growth in the same region? The Greek city-states were able to defeat the huge Achaemenid Persian Empire during the Persian Wars (490–479 BCE). And even if it was not a Greek city but a kingdom, that of Macedon, that destroyed the Persian Empire in 331 BCE, this development was still based on the dynamics launched by

96

the Greek cities in the previous centuries, and so much so that the new Hellenistic kingdoms could not do without the institutional framework of the city-state, and that they themselves created a large number of new *poleis*.

A short historical overview of the development that took place in Greece from the end of the Bronze Age will set the scene for the analysis. Then attention will focus on the fundamental question of tribute and of its replacement by comparatively modest levels of communal taxes and private rents in the framework of the Greek cities as a key factor in the process of growth. Finally, a comparison will be made with the status of royal land in late Classical Macedon and in the Hellenistic kingdom, which despite some limitations also provided a stable institutional framework for economic development.

FROM THE BRONZE AGE CRISIS TO THE ARCHAIC REVIVAL

This book deals with a period of six centuries. It opens with the last century of the Archaic period, at the beginning of the sixth century BCE. But the history of the economy of ancient Greece did not begin at that point. To account for the economic and social process that allowed Greece to achieve such an impressive level of development at this juncture in its history, we have to go back six centuries earlier. In the second millennium BCE, the Mediterranean basin and especially (but not only) its eastern part, was the stage of a spectacular growth. Greece was only part of this brilliant history.[1] Around 1200 BCE, the territory of mainland Greece, the islands of the South Aegean, and Crete, along with a few enclaves along the southwest coast of Asia Minor, was now mainly occupied by a Greek speaking population. The Greeks had established a series of regional kingdoms like among others those of Knossos in Crete, Pylos, Mykenai, and Tiryns in the Peloponnese, and Athens. Relying on Homer, who in the *Iliad* makes the king of Mykenai the leader of the Achaeans besieging Troy, modern scholarship has given the name "Mycenaeans" to these Greeks of the second millennium BCE.[2] They were powerful political and economic units ruled by dynasts that our sources call *wanakes*. The Mycenaeans were heirs to the splendid Minoan civilization. Tablets written in a syllabic script that the Mycenaeans borrowed from their Minoan predecessors are a major source of information about these kingdoms. However, the Mycenaeans lent a strong military and warlike coloring to the earlier culture.

The tablets written in Linear B are exceptionally valuable, because they give us an idea of these kingdoms' structure. They show us a sophisticated system of taxation or fees, paid exclusively in kind: bronze, hides, clothing, linen, livestock. The archives of the kingdom of Pylos, which more or less coincided with the future Messenia, show that it was divided into two regions, conventionally referred to by current scholarship as the Hither and the Further Provinces, each composed of a series of districts, which themselves included several villages. The archives also provide evidence of careful accounting, with estimates of revenues, records of occasional deficits with regard to predicted revenues, which were supposed to be made up the following year, and also tax exemptions.[3]

Concerning these taxes and fees, the concept of a system of "redistribution" of staple goods that has long prevailed (as if the royal palace undertook to equitably distribute them to everyone) has given way to a totally different approach. The commodities brought in through the palace economy no doubt provided a living for the king, his soldiers and his entourage and probably for some of the urban areas surrounding the palace. They were also used as payments for the workers in the service of the palace, but also they were used (as raw material and as payment to the workers) to produce high-value prestige goods that would be used to maintain the loyalty of elites beyond the palace itself.[4] They were also consumed in big festivals that enhanced the symbolic prestige of the palace.[5] As for taxes and fees, they may well have been part of either a system of taxes on "private" lands or "rents" or a system of "fees" for lands temporarily granted to an individual or a vocational group, the concession being, however, always revocable. The difference between "private" lands and "granted lands" does not find easily a modern equivalent. Thus in this respect as well, the Mycenaean system might seem to have direct parallels with the Mesopotamian system.[6] But if by their very nature the tablets shed light only on the Mycenaean palace economy, they should not be extrapolated to Mycenaean society and the economy as a whole. In Pylos, the "palatial" and the "private" spheres certainly overlapped and the palace was not in control of the whole economic activity.[7] The centralized nature of the kingdom of Knossos, the most important of the Mycenaean kingdoms, has recently been put in doubt. If the palatial elites controlled long-distance trade both in prestigious and indispensable goods (especially metals), there existed other forms of regional economic integration. Thus it becomes increasingly clear that ordinary households were integrated into regional networks of the circulation of goods (for instance, ceramics, from what we can observe) that were not directly under the control of the palace. Also, the discovery of weights and measures both in palatial and nonpalatial contexts inevitably suggests the existence of some local forms of institutionalized exchange.[8]

That said, it remains that these kingdoms had considerable economic and political scope. In Knossos, no doubt the most powerful of the Mycenaean kingdoms, the royal flocks could be as large as 100,000 head, while in Pylos they might reach 10,000 head.[9] As many as 15,000 persons may have lived in Knossos, and 5,000 to 10,000 in mainland urban areas. These kingdoms maintained relations with other regions of the Mediterranean, which were of vital importance to them because it was only through long-distance trade that the Mycenaeans could procure copper and tin, two metals that were required to make bronze and that the Aegean world lacked. Tin probably came from Luristan and perhaps also from the distant west, from islands located somewhere off the western coast of Europe (and which the Greeks of the first millennium BCE were to call the Kassiterides, after the Greek word for tin, *kassiteros*). On the other hand, most of the copper came from Cyprus. Shipwrecks like those found near Uluburun (ca. 1325 BCE) and Cape Gelidonya (ca. 1200 BCE), both in southwest Asia Minor, or Point Iria in the Argolic Gulf (ca. 1200 BCE) provide excellent testimony to the nature of the Mycenaean world's trade with Cyprus and the East.[10] With its ten tons of copper ingots (usually in the characteristic shape of oxhides) and a ton of tin ingots (of unknown provenance), its 149 amphoras of the Syrian-Palestinian or Ugaritic type, its 350 kilograms of Egyptian blue glass ingots, its textiles, its luxury items (ivory, ebony), and various other goods (weapons, a trumpet, and so on), the Uluburun shipwreck testifies to the intensity of the ties with Cyprus, the Near East, and Egypt. The Point Iria shipwreck contained Cypriot vases (including several *pithoi*), Cretan vases, and a third kind of vase whose provenance is unknown but is of Mycenaean origin (perhaps from Pylos), and it shows the interconnections within the Mycenaean world.[11]

This prosperous palace civilization, well integrated into Mediterranean networks but also warlike, suddenly disappeared at the beginning of the twelfth century BCE. Between 1250 and 1150, and seemingly more precisely in the period 1190–1170, the Mycenaean kingdoms were wiped off the map. The origins of this crisis are still poorly understood. Internal factors may have been involved, but it is hard to imagine how they could have led to a general and abrupt collapse. All kinds of triggering factors have been envisaged to make sense of the collapse: epidemics, earthquakes, drought, conflicts between Mycenean kingdoms, invasion by the northern neighbors, or diverse combinations of these factors. But none of these explanations is convincing, and perhaps all the more so as it remains puzzling that several other states of the eastern Mediterranean collapsed at the same time. An attractive new explanation suggests that the collapse of the kingdoms was only the consequence of the growth, as the palatial economies and their elites found themselves unable to control the efflorescence that they had made possible.[12] Conventionally, the collapse of the late Bronze Age kingdoms is explained by the invasion of the "Sea Peoples." Indeed, it still seems quite possible that a migration starting from an ill-defined part of the western Mediterranean (southern Italy, Sardinia?) grew steadily larger in the course of time with the successive ruination of the states it assailed. Being left no other choice, the victims in turn joined the wave of invasion, triggering a general collapse. But in the framework of this "revisionist explanation," it appears that the migration was only the most acute symptom of a deeper phenomenon of disintegration of the system. The Near East and the Hittite and Ugaritic kingdoms were swept away by the invasion, which also struck most of the southern Levant. Only Pharaoh Merenptah's Egypt was strong enough to repel it in a great battle that took place at the gates of Egypt.[13]

Mykenai was devastated, and the period that began with the fall of the Mycenaean kingdoms thus appears to deserve the traditional label of Greek "Dark Ages," a designation that obviously matches the "Middle Ages" of Western Europe.[14] As the Dark Ages now seem to have been less "Dark" than previously envisaged (and despite the fact that the Middle Ages also seem brighter, though the designation has not changed), the consensus is now to call this period the "early Iron Age." Conventionally, the early Iron Age is seen as lasting from ca. 1150 BCE to ca. 800 BCE or ca. 700 BCE (the new expansion of the eighth century marking in any case a break between two periods). The kingdoms disappeared, taking with them the Linear B script (which survived in a modified form only in Cyprus, where many Mycenaeans had taken refuge). The great architecture, painting, and refined ceramics also disappeared, together with long-distance trade. A major decrease in population took place, though it is difficult to determine exactly how great it was—in many places, the population seems to have fallen by a factor of four or five, sometimes more. The size of the sites occupied declined sharply. A Mycenaean culture that had been highly unified despite its political divisions was replaced by a world based on an extreme micro-regional fragmentation. The Mycenaean kingdom of Knossos covered 50 to 70 percent of Crete, or between 4,000 to 6,000 square kilometers. Although Knossos, along with Gortyn, remained one the two most powerful Cretan states of the first millennium, it never regained this power, and Crete was, according to Homer, the island of "one hundred cities," which despite the exaggeration describes well the extreme political fragmentation of the island.[15] Other Mycenaean states also covered much larger areas than their successors of the Iron Age.[16] A technological regression obviously took place. The ceramics of the early Iron Age suggest that potters had mediocre technical skills. It is clear that a genuine apocalypse occurred during this period, and there is no doubt that it was experienced as such by contemporaries.

But on the other hand, this period was also that of genuinely new experimentation.[17] Starting at the turn of the eleventh and the tenth centuries, a kind of recovery began, though at first it was slow. We have no written documents from that time, and thus archaeological evidence is our main source of knowledge about life during the period. Nevertheless, although the question of how they were written is still a matter of lively debate, the Homeric poems might give us some insight into society at the end of the early Iron Age or the beginning of the Archaic period (depending on the date at which Homer is set and how the Archaic period is defined).[18] First, this period of regression paradoxically also witnessed, between 1200 and 1000 BCE, the introduction of a new technology, iron metallurgy. Casting iron required a higher temperature (1540°C) than casting copper (1100°C) and tin.[19] This technology was imported from the Caucasus and eastern Anatolia, not suddenly, but through a slow and gradual process that began in the Eastern Mediterranean at the end of the Bronze Age. In addition to making it possible to manufacture weapons and tools that were sharper and less fragile than bronze, iron also had the great advantage that it could be found in more places. Iron ore deposits were more common than copper or tin deposits, which were very localized, as we have seen. Thus iron production did not depend on long-distance trade. The fragmentation of the Early Iron Age, which resulted in a shortage of tin, may have accelerated the emergence of iron technology. The perfection of the technique of adding carbon at high temperatures, followed by abrupt cooling (tempering), possibly a Cypriot invention, may have been the decisive factor that caused iron to be preferred to bronze.[20] The technique of tempering was known to Homer, who uses it in a comparison:

"And as when a smith dips a great axe or an adze in cold water amid loud hissing to temper it—for therefrom comes the strength of iron—even so did his eye hiss" (*Odyssey* 9.391–93).[21] In any case, iron technology and the autonomy it provided was well adapted to the period's cultural and political fragmentation.

We find a recovery first in certain regions—for instance, on the site of Lefkandi, in Euboia.[22] The Euboians' activity had already been manifested in their efforts in the north, where they colonized the region that was later called Chalkidike after the name of the city of Chalkis, Eretria's neighbor, which was itself probably descended from Lefkandi. Crete, where inland upland sites provided a refuge against aggressions from the outside, was also a region in which the regression was less marked than elsewhere, and which recovered a certain dynamism more quickly than others. The reestablishment of contacts with the Eastern Mediterranean from the late eleventh century onward certainly had an energizing effect on the modest societies of the early Iron Age. Phoenician merchants were the first to start operating along the coasts of the Aegean. Then Greek adventurers, first the Euboians, began traveling in the reverse direction, toward the Levant.

When the characteristics of this recovery (or what we think we can guess about them by reading the Homeric poems and studying archaeological evidence) begin to emerge, we see a society different from that of the preceding period, although this does not mean that there was a total break. The primary characteristic of Greek society in the first millennium BCE is political fragmentation, which certainly already existed during the preceding period; Mycenaean culture did not produce a great, unified kingdom. However, as observed earlier, the size of several Mycenaean states on which we have information was somewhat larger than the corresponding states of the later period.[23] In the first millennium, the fragmentation seems more extreme. The second characteristic is a hierarchical relationship between an elite of *basileis* (a word that could be translated as "kings") that held power and the mass of the people. On this level, too, we might say that there was a continuity with the preceding period, which was also characterized by a high degree of social inequality. But the third characteristic, which is in some sense negative, is that the palace economy, with its organization of centralized taxation, was not reconstituted. While in the second millennium the political and economic structure of Greek society was in every respect very similar to that of the great Eastern kingdoms, in the first millennium it took on a different appearance. The *basileis* of the Homeric world already had to deal with a popular assembly that consisted of warriors. Even if that assembly had, strictly speaking, no political power, it was nonetheless a factor of inertia that had to be reckoned with.

In the Archaic period, and particularly thanks to the "eighth-century revolution," Greek society acquired clearer and genuinely new features. For reasons that still remain unclear (a cooler climate episode?), eighth-century Greece experienced a first phase of significant growth.[24] The first and certainly major aspect was a strong demographic growth. As if both phenomena went hand in hand, the population growth was accompanied by a new prosperity, manifested in many new and larger buildings. The population growth also helps explain the first wave of colonization toward the west, in Sicily and Southern Italy. One might imagine that the palace economy and system of control would be gradually restored: in the contemporary East, this system was thriving more than ever, especially in Mesopotamia and still, to a certain extent, in Egypt. In Greece, on the contrary, this did not happen. The authority of the kings was diminished or abolished and gave way to a less inegalitarian system. The aristocracy seized power, but it had to deal with a peasantry that gradually asserted its social importance—initially simply because of its military role, and even if this world was very far from any kind of "democratic power" in the sense that can be observed later in the Classical period. This was a world of competition between leading aristocrats, but with new cultic forms that integrated the commoners. Whether or not there was a radical "hoplite revolution," the Greece of the Archaic period appears to have been a very original civilization that implemented unprecedented social solutions. Even when leading aristocrats managed to monopolize the political power to their benefit, as was the case with the tyrants of the seventh and sixth century in major cities like Corinth, Megara, Sikyon, Athens, or Samos, they never managed to establish systems of control similar to those of the Eastern kingdoms.[25] For a while, the tyrants managed to concentrate in their hands substantial amounts of riches that allowed them to pay soldiers or guards at their exclusive service, to undertake policies of public works, and to live a luxurious life. But there was nothing comparable to the situation prevailing in the Eastern kingdoms. The council, the magistrates, and the citizens' assemblies were not suppressed. And when the concentration of power in the hands of one man only was no longer tolerable, the tyrannies were all abolished, nowhere leading to a form of institution similar to that of the Eastern kings or dynasts.

TAX RATES, THE MARKET, AND THE STATUS
OF LAND IN ANCIENT GREECE

Tax Rates

Greece in the Archaic period differs from other contemporary societies of a comparable economic level, such as Egypt or the tributaries of Mesopotamia and the surrounding regions, in that it was a community based on reciprocal trade. But it would be false to say that these other areas had no markets. We now know, in increasing detail, that the Eastern world had local markets, at least in the cities, where a series of everyday consumer goods necessary to feed the inhabitants were traded—in Babylon, for instance. Moreover, thanks to the documentation provided by tablets, we are able to follow the daily fluctuations of the prices of common consumer goods, which sometimes varied in the course of a single day.[26] The Mesopotamian world, like the Egyptian world, had written contracts and relatively sophisticated banking operations. Similarly, temples might hire workers—for example, farmhands or in some cases more specialized workers—and pay them, in kind or silver, in accord with a contract. At the end of the Greek Archaic period, in the sixth century, Mesopotamia experienced an unprecedented phase of relative prosperity and growth.[27] In many respects, Greek society was not fundamentally different from the eastern Mediterranean world.

In what, then, did the very real difference between the Greek world and that of Mesopotamia or Egypt consist? The paradox is that it has nothing to do with the fundamental economic potential of the two areas. It is clear that yields from irrigated fields in Mesopotamia or Egypt were far above those from nonirrigated land in the Greek world. The question is what role was played by the allocation of goods through the intermediary of the market. In Egypt and Mesopotamia, genuinely "autonomous" or "private" actors, operating on their own initiative or as agents of temples or members of the elite, could also exchange goods through markets. While the role of weighed silver as money has long been acknowledged for Mesopotamia, specialists now also admit that the situation was not fundamentally different in Egypt.[28] But in Egypt and in Mesopotamia, there existed a completely different system of allocation that was tributary in nature and benefited the state (going far beyond supplying the royal palace *stricto sensu*) and the temples. During the Achaemenid period, the king seems to have levied two forms of taxes: the *tagē*, which aimed at satisfying directly the needs of the king and his army, was paid mainly in kind, while the *phoros* was mainly paid in silver.[29] The temples, which owned vast estates and had numerous flocks, might also make direct use of a labor force that was under their control, and only if the latter was lacking did they resort to outside labor. Thus the question is not that of the basic agricultural wealth of the East in relation to that of Greece. It has to do with the share of the surplus produced by the peasant masses that fell into the hands of the king and the temples and which the peasants could therefore no longer directly sell.

Can we estimate the share that was taken away from the tribute-paying peasant masses? The data from Eastern kingdoms before the Hellenistic period do not seem to allow us to determine the proportion with certitude. Besides, the actual amount left in the hands of the peasant must have constantly varied, depending on the time and place, and from one year to the next: given the sums demanded, some of which at least were fixed, a good harvest might leave a peasant with a considerable surplus, whereas a bad harvest forced him to go heavily into debt to pay his tribute. On the other hand, if we assume (provisionally) that in Egypt and the East the Hellenistic kingdoms adopted the earlier systems of taxation, we arrive at figures that suggest what the burden of these tributes might have been. The Hellenistic kings also benefited from taxes paid both in money and in kind. The customs duties or *phoroi* levied on cities and also on subjugated peoples provided the kings with monetary revenues. But they also received vast resources in kind that were levied on the king's land.

This was the case with the Ptolemies. In addition to the deliveries of grain, the Ptolemaic rulers enjoyed a series of monopolies on vegetable oil, linen, salt, and beer. A list of all the necessary tools for producing these commodities was drawn up, and they were put under seal except during the period in which their use was authorized, in order to prevent them from being used illegally. The same went for the production of papyrus. According to St. Jerome (*In Daniel* 11.5), Ptolemy received 14,800 silver talents from Egypt alone, and in addition 1.5 million *artabai* of wheat (1 Ptolemaic *artaba* = 39.4 liters), or roughly 45,500 metric tons.[30] For a good part, the 14,800 silver talents probably should be understood as the product of the in-kind contributions made by the peasants and transformed into money by the banking system. The 1.5 million *artabai* may correspond to the quantity of grain the king reserved to sell by himself, probably largely by export. As for the proportions, the native peasants seem to have paid (in kind) up to 50 percent of their cereal crops, one-sixth of the production of their vineyards or orchards (whereas Greek cleruchs paid only 10 percent of their harvest), and craftsmen, depending on the case, contributed between a third and a quarter of what they produced.[31] If peasants had to hand over up to 50 percent of their cereal production and a significant portion of their other productions, to deliver all the products that were imposed on them by the monopolies, and also to do forced labor for the crown, then the proportion of their production activity that was levied by the state must have been in the range of 50 percent.

The Seleukids seem to have imposed similar levies. Thus in 152 a letter from Demetrios I (I Maccabees 10.29–30 and 42) lists the sources that the king is prepared to give up if the Jews support him against the usurper Alexander Balas: exemption from the poll tax, the salt tax, the obligation to provide gold crowns, and a renunciation of the "third part" of the harvests in the fields and the "half" of the fruit orchard harvests to which he was entitled. If we extrapolate these proportions to the whole of the Hellenistic kingdoms and if we consider that contributions of between a third and a half of the produce were levied on the rural masses, we see that beyond what was necessary for their immediate survival and that of their families, peasants must have had only small surpluses they could actually sell. Here we touch on an essential question, whose assessment we will leave to specialists on the Eastern kingdoms: that of the way in which local markets were supplied, in which dignitaries, the temples, and the king might play a much more important role. The bulk of the surplus that could be sold in large-scale trade was in the hands of the king. In other words, the development of a market system was limited by the system of royal levies that concentrated most of the rural world's surplus production.

There remained a fundamental difference between the world of the kingdoms and what was the civic world in the Greek manner. We know that it would be a mistake to believe that the cities did not have direct taxation.[32] Except for the cities that were exploiting an empire, as in the case of fifth-century Athens, there must frequently have been a system of direct taxation of agricultural production. In Athens at the time of Peisistratos, if we set aside indirect taxes, the tax was, according to Aristotle (*Constitution of Athens/Ath. Pol.* 16.4), a *dekatē*, a one-tenth tax on the products of farms belonging to citizens.[33] Under the sons of Peisistratos according to Thucydides (6.54.5), it was an *eikostē*, a tax of one-twentieth (5 percent). In accord with a law of 374/3 BCE, Athens levied a *dōdekatē*, that is, a tax in kind of one-twelfth or 8.33 percent, on the grain produced in its external possessions, the islands of Imbros, Lemnos, and Skyros.[34] In the third century, the authorities on Samos certainly levied an *eikostē*—that is, a tax of one-twentieth or 5 percent—on the continental territory of Anaia.[35] (We should not overlook the fact that like Anaia, Imbros, Lemnos, and Skyros were wealthy territories, and this might have justified a relatively high tax—which makes it all the more interesting that these were territories that were the possessions of citizens. Anaia was under the direct control of citizens of Samos,[36] while the three islands in the north Aegean under the control of Athens were occupied by *klērouchoi*, viz. military "land-lot-holders."[37]) These two tax rates were high. In Iasos, around 200, there was a *dōdekatē* on wine.[38] The other tax rates that have come down to us are never more than a *dōdekatē*, a tax of 8.33 percent. As Ronald S. Stroud points out, Demosthenes (14.27) emphasizes that an *eisphora* (a direct wealth tax) at the rate of one-twelfth would be intolerable for Athenians.[39] Lending rates of more than 8.33 percent seem to have been generally regarded as usurious.[40] Similarly, in Athens the land rent never exceeded a rate of about 8 percent.[41]

Naturally, it was inevitable that certain taxes would be concurrent, but usually they did not affect the same individuals engaged in the same activities. An Athenian peasant of the sixth century had to pay a direct tax of 5 or 10 percent, and if, for example, he bought a slave, he had to pay a specific tax on that operation. Nonetheless, the basic tax rates on the amount of goods produced remained relatively modest.

In contrast to Athens and the developed cities of the Greek world in general, there was one city where the tax rate was much higher: Sparta. The figures for the income of the Spartans reported by Plutarch in his *Life of Lycurgus* (8.4) are in absolute numbers and cannot be used to determine the rate of the rent helots had to pay on their overall production. More interesting is a statement by Tyrtaeus, a poet traditionally supposed to have lived in the late seventh century BCE. It is all the more significant because it is a truly Spartan source and goes back to the early phase of the history of the city. Tyrtaeus indicates that the Messenians, "just like asses worn out by heavy burdens, bringing to their masters out of grievous necessity half of all the produce that the land brings forth."[42]

The City and the Economy

The authenticity of this passage, like that of Tyrtaeus's work as a whole, was once strongly challenged, but it has now been firmly established, although the debate on the date of Tyrtaeus goes on.[43] However, it has recently been interpreted in contradictory ways. For Mischa Meier, since after the first Messenian War the population of Messenia had still not been reduced to the status of helots, though Messenia was reduced to the status of a dependency of Sparta, there can be no question of claiming that the text describes the true situation of the Messenians. According to Meier, it served only as a general warning to Spartans regarding the fate that awaited them in the event they were defeated.[44] Although he published his analysis without having been able to examine Meier's objections, Stephen Hodkinson pronounced unequivocally in favor of the authenticity of the passage. His analysis tries to combine Tyrtaeus's testimony with that of Plutarch, who wrote apropos of the helots (*Inst. Lac.* no. 41 = *Moralia* 239e): "The helots worked the land for the benefit of their Spartan masters, paying them the rent [*apophora*] levied in the past. A curse was instituted against anyone who wanted to make them pay more, so that they might serve with joy because they were making a profit and so that the Spartans themselves did not try to get more out of them." Hodkinson concludes, reasonably, that (1) the rent consisted in a set portion of the crop (50 percent), with a system of sharecropping, and was not a system of fixed tribute; (2) the notion that Messenia was not enslaved but merely dependent is only a later Messenian legend, and therefore that this passage does indeed refer to Messenian helots.[45] Finally, Edmond Lévy thinks that the amount of this rent applied only to the Messenians who had just been conquered, and not to all helots.[46] But it might also be thought that the Messenians had just been reduced to the common lot of all helots present and future. In fact, we may consider it established that all helots, Lakonians as well as Messenians, paid a quota of 50 percent of their harvests, which constituted a very burdensome dependency but one that nonetheless had an advantage over a system of fixed tribute.

This happiness in slavery was, of course, wholly relative. The Messenians, like the helots of Lakonia, were in a state of *douleia*, bondage, which explains why they revolted against their masters every time they got a chance to do so. The Greeks of other cities found their situation "cruel and bitter," as the fourth-century BCE historian Theopompus put it clearly.[47] With regard to the levies, the situation of the helots was thus comparable to that of the peoples of Mesopotamia or Egypt, on whom their masters imposed levies of the same level. By contrast, it helps us understand the situation of Greeks living in the cities, who had no masters other than themselves, and who imposed on themselves only modest taxes proportional to their revenues.

In a city like Athens, the suppression of the *hektēmoroi* system in the course of Solon's reforms in 594/3 BCE was a crucial change. The *hektēmoroi* system was a rent of one-sixth, or 16.66 percent. It was thus a heavy charge, double the later maximum rate of the ground rent during the Classical and Hellenistic periods. An inevitable consequence of these high rent rates was an accumulation of unpaid debts, which in turn meant that those who became dependent might be sold, along with their families, into bondage. In Mesopotamia, a number of documents show that parents who did not have enough food might sell their own children into slavery.[48] With Solon and the suppression of enslavement for debt, and certainly with comparable reforms in cities that resembled Athens (but not in Sparta, of course), the city was definitively transformed into a community whose members were not necessarily all property-owners (and that is the significance of Solon's measures urging every man to teach his son a trade), but were nonetheless masters of themselves and what they produced, and could never fall into slavery.[49] Consequently, they were also likely to trade their products among themselves. That is exactly how Plato defines the *polis* in the *Republic* (369d–371b).[50] Each member of the community has different needs, and this fact is the origin of the division of labor: to make a *polis*, you need a farmer, a mason, a weaver, a cobbler, a carpenter, a smith, and so on. Then the members of the community trade among themselves the fruits of their labor in order to provide food, lodging, and clothing, and everything else required for a good life.

The basic presupposition of the market is precisely the existence of a large community whose members make their own decisions and control the fruit of their labor, and for that reason are prepared to enter into trade relationships with other members of the community because of the diversity and complementarity of their occupations. This helps us understand the difference between Greece and the East, a stubbornly persistent question in debates between specialists on the Greek world and specialists on Eastern kingdoms. The point is certainly not to return to a meaningless dichotomy between a Greek world that is supposed to have been a "market economy" and Eastern kingdoms living under the regime of "Oriental despotism," a concept that is now totally discredited. As mentioned earlier, the Eastern kingdoms did not ignore the market. They had cities and villages, populations of farmers and shepherds, as well as vast and rich agricultural areas. But there was nothing remotely analogous to the specific social relationship that united the members of the Greek *polis*.

In Mesopotamia or Egypt, most of what was not consumed by producers was stored in the granaries of the temples or palaces until it was recirculated, usually in the form of rations. One portion of what was produced was sold, whether it came from the producers themselves (having escaped the tributary levies) or from the temples or the state. Indeed, selling a portion of what had been collected in kind from the countryside seems to have been a permanent concern for the satraps of the Persian Empire, and later for the Hellenistic kingdoms. However, what was bought and sold by the temples or the state did not give rise to generalized trade, but only to a more elaborate form, mediated by a monetary equivalent (usually silver, but not always), of the command economy.

In Greece, most of the social product that was not consumed by the producer's family passed through direct trade relationships among members of the community in the public marketplace that in ancient Greece was incarnated by the institution of the agora.[51] The proportion of the social product levied by the state in the form of taxes was small. Every taxpayer finds his taxes too high, and many documents show us that in Greece as well tax evasion, and even social and political conflict connected with the burden of taxation, was not unknown: in *Politics*, Aristotle gives several very telling examples of this.[52] Nonetheless, compared with Eastern tributary kingdoms, taxes were low. The Greek *polis* did not have the sumptuous palaces and colossal funerary monuments found in Mesopotamia or Egypt. Not only did the Greek cities avoid this kind of expense, but one of their secrets was precisely to have set up a state organization that was both very efficient (in comparison with Eastern states) and cheap.[53]

A *contrario*, the case of Sparta is very instructive. To be sure, like other cities, Sparta had an agora, a local market, as both Herodotus (1.153, implicitly) and Xenophon (*Hellenica* 3.3.5–7, explicitly) tell us. But fundamentally it was a city that had developed only a very limited market economy, both internally and externally. We also know that this city did not mint coins until the third century.[54] Besides, in all likelihood, these coins were intended more for paying mercenary soldiers in the Peloponnese than for domestic circulation in Sparta itself.[55] The correlation between the existence of a proportionally large contingent of actors with negotiable surpluses that were produced on site or acquired through trade was obviously a crucial factor in the development of minted currency. The latter did not appear in systems based on in-kind transfers (Egypt, the Mesopotamian kingdoms, and the Achaemenid kingdom) or, after it appeared, it played only a secondary, supporting role in regions that were in contact with a monetary economy of the civic type.

A network of small- and medium-sized property-owners with saleable surpluses must be considered a key element in the development of the market of the ancient Greek city-state. These surpluses sold on the market made it possible to feed a whole population of nonagricultural producers, giving rise to a thorough division of labor. The basic source for this claim is the previously mentioned passage in Plato's *Republic* (370a–371b).[56] Plato emphasizes that no one can be self-sufficient and that trade is indispensable. It is striking—and this has not be sufficiently stressed—that for Plato, the foundation of the *polis* is the division of labor. This division of labor and specialization make it possible to increase not only the quantity but also the quality and the "facility" to produce the needed goods: "more things [*pleiō*] are produced, and better and more easily" (370c)—that is, at a lower price. Finley, making use solely of the discussion of the division of labor in Xenophon's *Cyropaedia* (8.2.5) and ignoring that in Plato's *Republic*, is thus proved wrong when he concludes that the (again according to him) rare references in ancient authors to the division of labor regularly concern improvement of quality, never of quantity (for Finley, increase in quantity could be conceived only in a Smithian perspective foreign to the "ancient mind").[57] Plato adds (371b) that trade in these products will, of course, take place by means of buying and selling. Thus we see a general increase in the value of the goods produced and in overall wealth. In the process, a new category of consumers was also created that was a fundamental characteristic of the world of the city-states. In terms of distribution of income, the societies of the city-states were also far less inegalitarian than those of Mesopotamia or Egypt, and their Gini coefficient was significantly lower. This "virtuous circle" did not have the development observed in modern industrial societies, but it was sufficient to give to ancient Greek society a profile that sharply differed from that of the world of the kingdoms of the eastern Mediterranean.

In the societies that preceded the contemporary period, military spending was always the largest element in state expenditures.[58] Given war's role in shaping the world of the Greek cities, there is no doubt that this was true for them as well. The institution of the armed citizen or hoplite made it possible to avoid inflating the state's expenses. The absence of a standing army was the key to this system. In the traditional model of hoplite warfare, the army was mobilized only when necessary. Furthermore, the citizen paid for his own military equipment and even part of his food while he was on a campaign. Only expenses connected with long campaigns and with building fortifications remained a major cost for the state. Thus the fixed costs involved in maintaining a standing army were eliminated. Summer campaigns did not result in major social costs because little farm work was done during the summer. Moreover, a victory and the pillaging and ransoms that accompanied it might be a genuine source of profit. It is true that, starting in the sixth century, naval warfare introduced new constraints. It established a hierarchy between cities that had the means to maintain navies and those that did not. Most cities could not maintain navies, but at the same time they did not have to finance them. Thus we can conclude that the hoplite model remained valid until the Peloponnesian War. Even in the fourth century and the Hellenistic period—that is, during a time when recourse to mercenaries and also the increasing cost of fortifications might lead to far greater expenses—it did not disappear altogether: up until the Roman occupation, the Greek cities continued to constitute citizen-armies that provided the first line of defense against the threat of pirates or overly aggressive neighbors.[59] In any case, in the Archaic and Classical periods, cities' military expenses were very limited in comparison to those of Eastern states.

Both the Greeks and the peoples of the East were probably well aware of the difference between their two systems. The sixth-century poet Phocylides of Miletos (who as a Greek from Asia Minor knew what he was talking about) put it clearly: "A *polis* on a barren rock, small, but settled in an orderly fashion, is greater than senseless Nineveh" (until its destruction in 612 BCE, Nineveh had been the capital of the Assyrian kingdom, which dominated and terrorized the whole eastern Mediterranean region in the seventh century BCE).[60] Aristotle, who so much appreciated the "mean" and the "middle" as a definition for the ideal city and citizen, praised Phocylides for stating: "Much advantage is theirs who are midmost, and midmost in a city would I be."[61] This was also a way of contrasting the *polis* system to that of the Eastern kingdoms, where a hyperconcentration of wealth and power in the hands of a very few prevailed. It is no accident that the Greeks thought that only the *polis* system allowed men to live in freedom: the first criterion of this freedom was the absence of economic dependency and control over what one produced, and thus tax levies that were very low compared to those prevalent in the tributary economies of the East. During the Hellenistic period, new Greek kingdoms established on the territories of the former Achaemenid kingdom gave this opposition between the *polis* and the native *chōra* a genuinely institutional form.

Thus we see that the primary factor in the development of the market was the freedom of peasants and craftsmen to dispose of their surpluses as they saw fit. We see the outlines of this around 700 BCE in Hesiod's poem *Works and Days*, despite the presence of *basileis*, "kings (at that time, noblemen ruling the city), whom the poet calls "gift-eaters" (ibid., 38–39). Division of labor soon led to an urban-type development. The movement was at first slow in the western part of mainland Greece, the traditional Greece of Thucydides. But it was much more rapid in Aegean Greece. By the end of the Archaic period, steadily increasing grain imports made possible a more advanced division of labor and the establishment of a specialized agriculture based on slave labor and production for the market. This appeared first on the west coast of Asia Minor, in particular on the island of Chios, and then in other centers that adopted the same methods. We might say that the world of the *polis* during the Archaic period launched an autonomous and cumulative process: the growth of an economy in which the market was the principal institution for the transfer of the social product. From the seventh century on, this market took on an elaborate monetized form with the introduction of coinage.[62]

The Greek cities had a very advanced system of the division of labor in craftwork, due to the fact that a larger part of their populations did not have to produce their own food, as they did elsewhere. There was also a division of labor in agricultural production on the international level. Finally, a famous text by Xenophon (*Poroi* 4.6) proves that it was the movement of prices that determined production.[63] We are thus clearly dealing with a society in which the market was not an inarticulate phantom but a coherent whole. That does not mean that every good that was produced passed through the market, far from it. What is at stake is the portion of what was produced that was not consumed by the producers or subject to levies. This portion provided the basis on which the market of the Greek cities was constructed.

The point of departure for the growth of the market in ancient Greece was thus fundamentally institutional: the comparatively large body of free people of the city-states controlled the fruit of their labor, and the equality before the law of all members of the *demos* was gradually established. The institution of the ancient market developed in the framework of the *polis*. It is not identical with the image of the market in nation-states elaborated by economists of the eighteenth century and later times, which in any case is no more "natural." But the fact that the market institutions of ancient Greece were not those of contemporary industrial capitalism does not mean that its market was a kind of formless, negligible appendix to a society of "household production and consumption," "reciprocity," or "redistribution," as old orthodoxies claimed.

ROYAL LAND AND CIVIC LAND

The difference in status between what the Greeks called "civic land" (*gē* or *chōra politikē*) and "royal land" (*gē* or *chōra basilikē*) is of capital importance for understanding the very status of property and land ownership within the framework of the city. This holds true for the Hellenistic period, which saw the creation of large kingdoms controlled by Macedonian-Greek elite, but which maintained a difference between the land of the king and that of the cities. But no less significantly it holds true for the Classical period. While it is ever clearer that the matrix of the institutions of the Hellenistic kingdoms is to be found in those of the Macedonian kingdom, it had not been clear so far that the status of the land in Hellenistic kingdoms finds direct precedents in the Macedonian kingdom before Alexander's conquest.

The relationship between "civic land" and "royal land" is complex, and the very definition of "royal land" raises questions.[64] Here is offered only a brief clarification and a few remarks relating particularly to Aegean Greece. A series of texts in which we see the status of land put in question must be reexamined. In an area that was part of royal territory, high taxes were levied in kind and in money. Its inhabitants were not allowed to manage their own finances in an autonomous way, first because most of what they produced was appropriated by the royal authority. In contrast, the cities had in theory a system of self-taxation at low rates, and could manage their own expenses. In practice, however, cities that were under royal authority also had to pay a *suntaxis* or a *phoros*, and they were subject to direct or indirect supervision by royal magistrates. But it would be a great mistake to think that for this reason the distinction between the city and royal land disappeared, even in the case of new kingdoms. The difference was clear to everyone and was based in particular on a very significant difference in the level of taxation.

When he arrived in Asia in 334 BCE, Alexander defined the status of the city of Priene by carefully distinguishing between the territories that would belong to the city and those that would be subject to his authority—that is, those that would be part of the royal territory. The indigenous peasants living in villages near to Priene but on royal land would pay tribute to him.[65] That is also why, in the second century (between ca. 188 and 159/8 BCE, more probably at the end of this interval), the Attalid king Eumenes II was still reluctant to grant the status of city to the community of Toriaion/Tyriaion of Kabalis in Phrygia Paroreia.[66] In his first letter, although he finally agrees to accord the civic status requested by the inhabitants of Toriaion, he emphasizes the sacrifice that this requires of him (ll. 17–19): "For my own part, I have observed that your requests concern subjects that are of considerable importance to me, connected as they are with many matters of greater consequence." This is a rhetorical clause that allows Eumenes II to mention the power delegated to him by Rome, and especially to emphasize that insofar as the concession was definitive, it represented a major sacrifice for the royal treasury. It is no accident that in his second letter (ll. 39–44), which includes a new concession and discusses finances, the king grants (at least provisionally) the tax revenue from the market to pay for the gymnasium's oil, before another source of revenue, a tithe on an estate or land, replaces it (ll. 45–47). If the kings were rich, it was first because they had considerable revenues, levied on the peasant masses at very high rates, and we can easily understand why they were loath to make any concession likely to reduce these revenues. This surely explains why even those who received personal land grants in the royal land wanted them to be part of a Greek city's territory. Three cases, all from Seleukid Asia Minor, allow us to illustrate this situation.

The first is that of the grant made by King Antiochos I to Aristodikides of Assos between about 277 and 261 BCE. Aristodikides received 5,500 *plethra* of land, or around 495 hectares (or perhaps only 3,500 *plethra* or around 315 hectares).[67] But above all, he was given an opportunity to annex (*prosorizein*) these lands to the city of his choice, provided that it was "in the king's alliance." Naturally, Antiochos did not want to see the produce from his grant fall under the authority of a city that was either completely independent—which might have implied hostile choices with regard to him and in any case a complete loss of tax revenues, since even cities "in the alliance" paid tribute to the king in the form of a *phoros* or a *suntaxis*—or, *a fortiori*, was allied with another king.

The second case concerns the honors the city of Priene granted to the Seleukid official Larichos around 275–270 BCE, or a little after. Larichos had benefited from three successive decrees made by the city. The second (decree B, ll. 20–27) stipulated that Larichos was to have "the exemption [*ateleia*] of all the flocks and all the persons at his disposal, both on his own domains [*en te tois idiois ktēmasi*] and in the city [*kai en tēi polei*]" (ll. 24–26). Philippe Gauthier interprets the passage this way: Larichos had received from Antiochos an estate near the city of Priene, and also the right to annex it to the civic land of Priene. [68]

The third case is that of Antiochos II's sale of domains near Kyzikos and Zeleia to his repudiated wife, Laodike, in 254/3 BCE). Laodike also received the privilege of annexing these domains to the city of her choice.[69]

The interest of such an annexation was twofold. On the one hand, the holder of the property thereby became its definitive owner. On the other hand, he enjoyed a far more favorable tax rate, since taxes on civic land were much lower. If land was not annexed in this way, even if it was "given" by a king it remained part of the "royal territory." A set of Macedonian inscriptions from the end of the fourth century and the beginning of the third century provides conclusive proof of this and helps to define the status of the land within the royal territory.

In 348 BCE, Philip of Macedon destroyed the Chalkidian League, which was the chief threat on the very frontiers of his kingdom, and which prevented the latter's expansion to the east. The city of Olynthos, the capital of the League, was left in ruins, as was Stageira, Aristotle's birthplace, which had unwisely killed the governor Philip had appointed for it. The wealthy lands around Olynthos passed under the control of the Macedonian crown. In other words, they became "royal land" (*chōra basilikē*), even if the term is not used in the two extant documents that mention royal grants in the Olynthos sector. The first grant, to a man named Perdikkas, was made by Kassandros, who controlled Macedon from 319 to his death in 298 BCE.[70] This document has the peculiarity of showing that three of the domains in question had either previously been granted to his grandfather and father two generations earlier by King Philip (that is, at the latest in 336 BCE) or bought from a third party, but who himself had been granted the land by King Alexander.[71] The second grant, to a certain Limnaios, was made by Lysimachos, who ruled Macedon from 285 to 281 BCE, but the document can be dated precisely to 285/4 BCE.[72] The formula of donation directly echoes that of the first document, but it does not mention earlier grants. The text of these two grants was displayed in the city of Kassandreia and mentions the eponymous priest of the city.

These donations concern large domains that were granted to members of the Macedonian kings' immediate entourages. The size of the lands given Perdikkas is not mentioned, probably because it was a repetition of the grant. But the lands granted Limnaios totaled 2,480 *plethra*, or 223 hectares.[73] Koinos, Perdikkas's father, was the homonymous companion of Alexander.[74] As for the second grant, one of Limnaios's neighbors was none other than Agathokles, Lysimachos's own son, who had himself just received from his father a domain in the same region. It is this reference to Agathokles that allows us to date the document to 285/4 BCE, the first year of the Macedonian reign of Lysimachos, since the latter had Agathokles killed in 284.[75] Another neighbor, Bithys, was a close associate of Lysimachos.[76] It is thus clear that these people belong to the aristocratic Macedonian elite.

In 316 BCE, Kassandros decided to build a new city bearing his name, Kassandreia, and according to Diodorus, it was endowed with a "vast territory."[77] It was located at the site of the former Potidaia. The new city obviously included the Chalkidian League's former territories south of Anthemous and Stageira—Sinos, Spartolos, Olynthos, Sermylia, and Strepsa. In the first phase of its existence, Kassandreia did not have the character of a Macedonian city. In many respects, it was instead a resuscitation of Olynthos. It was only under Antigonos II Gonatas that it was transformed into a Macedonian city, thus adopting the Macedonian calendar. It has been maintained that it was the foundation of Kassandreia that led to the registration of domains that had formerly been part of its territory and the point at stake in these documents would have been the passage from the status of "royal land" to that of civic land.[78]

But these grants cannot be seen as being made in order to register these lands in the newly founded city of Kassandreia, for two reasons. First, in that case, the registration should have occurred in 316 or shortly thereafter, on Kassandros's accession to power, and not at least ten years later, in or after 306. It is therefore clear that the public display of the grants in Kassandreia was a simple matter of publicity, undertaken so that local administrators knew what to expect with regard to the holder's rights. If what was at stake in Kassandros's grant was not the registration of lands within the framework of the city of Kassandreia, what was it then? From our modern point of view, there seems to be a contradiction between the gift of a land "in ownership and as a patrimony" (*en ktēsei kai em patrikois*) and the successive grants by different kings. Indeed, the grant includes a right of possession, alienation, and sale. That this was not a fiction if proved by the fact that Perdikkas had bought a domain that had been given to his former holder by King Alexander. But this would seem to presuppose that gifts of land made by former kings could not be renewed, when in fact they were.

The key to making sense of the text is the status of the land granted by the king: Polemokrates, the first beneficiary of the grant, received the land as a *klērouchos*, a land-lot-holder (*eklērouchese*). One must recognize here the status of the future *klērouchoi*, or Greek military colonists, of the Hellenistic kingdoms, for which we have a fairly abundant documentation for Ptolemaic Egypt, and also for some regions of Syria or the Persian Gulf. This also means that the cleruch status of the Hellenistic kingdoms had a Macedonian matrix.[79] A *klērouchos* had a a sort of contract with the king. He was to serve in the army and pay specific taxes on the land he had received from the king.[80] The compensation was that he could hold a land that *de jure* never ceased to belong to the king.[81] If he did not perform his military duties or did not pay his taxes, the king could immediately deprive him of his land.[82] The system gave the holder of the land great freedom. He could use it as he saw fit—sell it, or bequeath it to his son. But if there was no direct male heir, the property was to revert to the king, and not to any city, no matter which one.[83] The crucial point is that at the death of every *klērouchos*, the royal administration intervened to check the succession (in Egypt, it was only from the second half of the second century onward that cleruchic land began to be transmitted like normal land, even in absence of direct male offspring).[84] It also had to intervene if there was some legal dispute concerning the *klēros*, which might well justify Kassandros's new donation to Perdikkas.[85] This is certainly also what justifies the "new donation" in the wording of the Macedonian inscription for Perdikkas or the inquiry into succession in view of "registration" (*epigraphēnai*) in the name of the new holder in the case of the Ptolemaic documents. If Perdikkas's land had been his "full property" and if the king had lost any right over it, the donation would not make sense.

The Macedonian legal procedure of the "grant in ownership and as patrimony" to the *klērouchos* was to preserve the king's superior rights.[86] It is clear as well that the need to check the transmission of the land in every new generation meant that the beneficiaries of such gifts had to serve the reigning king loyally. A "lot" (*klēros*) assigned by a sovereign "as a gift" (*en dōreai*) could apparently always be revoked if the precision "as a patrimony" was not mentioned in the donation.[87] The "grant as patrimony" implied a possible hereditary transmission, although that did not mean that the king's superior rights evaporated, and the holders of properties that were provisionally granted held them by delegation. Aristotle (*Rhetoric* 1.5.7) defines ownership (*ta oikeia*) as the owner's power to alienate his possession by gift or sale. Besides, while being fully private, in the framework of the city property was also in some sense common, as Aristotle himself makes clear in *Politics* (2.2.4): the city-state combines "the advantage of property being common and the advantage of its being private."[88] Elaborating on this definition, one can say that the cleruchs on royal land were the owners of their estates, although this never suppressed the king's property right as supreme user of the land. The rule applies perfectly to the Macedonian donations.[89] With the two donations alluded to before in the region of Kassandreia, it is clearly no question of the domains becoming part of Kassandreia's civic land. This is definitely proved wrong in the case of the first donation by the new gift made by the king. If the domains had belonged to the city, not only the Argead kings would not have been able to give them, but Kassandros would of course not have been able to give then a second time.

By the same token, the role of the city of Kassandreia should be reexamined. In this case, the Macedonian kings who preceded Kassandros had granted large domains in the zone of what was to become the territory of the new city. But when he renews the grant to Perdikkas in conformity with the procedure of a "grant as patrimony," Kassandros makes not the slightest reference to the new city, which is only the place where the document is displayed. The king is acting as a sovereign power. This is even more the case for Lysimachos in 285/4 BCE. At that time, Kassandreia had already existed for more than thirty years. We might thus think that the city would have had at least a right to have a say in what happened on its own territory. However, Lysimachos once again does whatever he sees fit on his royal territory: he makes a "grant as patrimony" (*dedōke em patrikois*, ll. 3–5), like those a series of earlier rulers had no doubt made to members of their families and their friends—without referring to the city or the civic land of Kassandreia.

Kassandros's and Lysimachos's grants involved domains located in the immediate neighborhood of Kassandreia. This proximity may seem sufficient to justify the public display of the decrees in the city. But if that was so, it was above all because at that time Kassandreia functioned as one of the capitals of the kingdom of Kassandros, who saw himself as the ruler of a kingdom larger than the Macedonian state. If Kassandros gave his name to this city, it was precisely so that it could play this role. In 309 BCE, Lysimachos had founded Lysimacheia (on the site of the former Kardia, at the northern tip of the Thracian Chersonese) with the same intention.[90] This allows us better to understand the fiscal privileges Kassandros conferred, in the same year that he made the land grant to Perdikkas, on a man who was probably a citizen of Kassandreia, as is suggested by the mention of the district to which he belonged. This man, who bore the name of Chairephanes, may very well be the same person as a rich contractor known through an inscription in Eretria dated a little after 318.[91] But the import and export privileges for his personal usage granted him obviously held not only for Kassandreia, but for the whole kingdom. The display of these privileges in Kassandreia was significant precisely because it played the role of a capital city. We have documents showing that fiscal privileges were granted by the Macedonian monarchy at a much earlier date (such as an exemption granted as the time of Amyntas III, king of Macedon from 393 to 370 BCE[92]), and they cannot be reduced to the area of a city.

In any case, so far as property rights are concerned, nothing indicates that, by comparison with property within the civic framework, holding land with a status of *klērouchos* was a synonym for negligence or absence of investment, on the pretext that the right of possession was precarious. The status of *klērouchia* ensured the stability of the rights of the landholders and preserved the superior interests of the

king (who expected the cleruch to perform military service and pay the royal tribute, the *phoros*).[93] This justified the exceptional investments made in their properties
by Macedonian aristocrats at the end of the fourth century or the beginning of the
third century. This was true for the lands *en dōreai* apparently even if the hereditary
transmission was not guaranteed. The papyrological evidence relating to the activity of Zenon, Apollonios's administrator in the Fayum, and the archaeological documents relating to the great Macedonian estates lead to the same conclusion.[94]
Although the geographical context, the social environment, and the type of agriculture are very different, and although the status of the land may have varied (being
seemingly either a land *en dōreai* or a *klērouchia*), we should set the archaeological
and the papyrological documentation side by side, and Zenon's archives will help
us understand what ambitions the holder of a domain in Macedon or in the Troad
might have had. Far from producing inertia, the desire to maximize profits as
quickly as possible is always present. This was all the more true when the possibility of familial inheritance was guaranteed; it was a supplementary incitement to
make long-term investments.

New research should now be undertaken to reanalyze and redefine the status of
the cleruchies, and especially those of Athens, in the framework of the Greek cities.
It is now clear that, despite what was previously thought, the Athenian cleruchs of
the fourth century could alienate their lands.[95] The specific rights of the Athenian
cleruchs as well as their duties (military service and certainly also the payment of
specific taxes in kind) are thus strangely similar to those of the Macedonian
cleruchs. Only the owner of the land is different, a city in the former case, a king in
the latter. It is tempting to consider that the institutional definition of the cleruchy
was the same in the framework of the city and in that of a kingdom. Again future
research should clarify this point.

Greece emerged from the early Iron Age with an original institutional system,
that of the city-state. Instead of coming back to a system based on tribute and on a
centralization of the economic resources, these city-states explored a new direction.
They innovated in creating a system based on cooperation and horizontal circulation of goods and information. Of course, the process took several hundred years,
but by around 600 BCE some central features of the system that crystallized one
century later already appear clearly. Its main characteristic was that the state with-
held comparatively low taxes. Thus individuals could sell on the market a significant part of their surplus. Private property of land—which was a privilege of citizens only, at least in the Classical period—was at the root of the system. In the
territory of the kingdoms (and most importantly already the Macedonian kingdom
of the Classical period), property rights were defined differently. The pockets of
territory of the cities enjoyed the privileges previously defined, especially that of
paying low taxes. On the royal land, the land-lot-holders (*klērouchoi*) would receive
from the kings lands that they could possess, alienate, sell, and transmit to their
sons. But the rule held true only provided they acknowledged full loyalty to the

king and served in his army. If they had no male heir, the land came back to the king, which proves that the latter's superior property was never abolished. The rights of the *klērouchoi* and other beneficiaries of donations were however sufficiently well established to allow them to devote full attention to their domains and make all the investments that they required.

V

AGRICULTURAL PRODUCTION

An inscription from the second half of the fourth century preserves the authentic text, already known to ancient authors, of the oath young Athenians took after they entered the *ephēbeia*, the equivalent of our military service.[1] They promised to defend sacred things and their fatherland, to obey their officers, and to see to it that the laws were respected. They then called upon "Aglauros, Hestia, Enyo, Enyalios, Ares, Athena Areia, Zeus, Thallo, Auxo, Hegemone, Herakles, the boundary markers of their homeland, the wheat, the barley, the grapevines, the olive trees, and the fig trees" to witness their oath. Enyo, Enyalios, Ares, and Athena were gods of war, which is very understandable in this context. Zeus, "the father of the gods and of men" was the supreme guarantor of the order of things. Herakles was the tutelary divinity of young ephebes. But the other divine entities are directly connected with vegetation. Aglauros, who in Athens was also Ares' wife, was connected through her sisters Herse ("dew") and Pandrosos ("rain") with the growth of plants. Thallo, one of the Horai, evoked the growth of plants in the spring. Auxo (another Hora) evoked vegetal growth, and was, along with Hegemone, one of the Graces, who were nature divinities.

The ephebes were supposed to defend the boundary markers of their territory, the city's *chōra*. It was the produce of this territory that enabled the city to exist and persevere in its being: whence the reference to wheat, barley, grapevines, olive trees, and fig trees, which provided most of people's food supply in ancient Greece. There is no doubt that throughout Greece, from the Archaic period to Hellenistic period, the concerns of leaders and common citizens were the same as those we find reflected institutionally in the oath taken by the Athenian ephebes. Agriculture was by far the ancient world's most important wealth-creating sector, and it is therefore important to define its enduring characteristics in the Greek city-states. At the same time, we must beware of a static, atemporal view of agriculture and the farmers' world. On the contrary, by inquiring into the growth of production we need to draw attention to its evolutions and mutations and to the consequences of these changes.

Our sources regarding agricultural life in ancient Greece are diverse in nature. The written sources are now supplemented by a wealth of archaeological data, linked to the new interest in the countryside of the Greek cities and their rural landscapes. As for written sources, the literary ones come first, starting with Hesiod's *Works and Days*, which offers a representation of the peasant world around 700 BCE. Theophrastus's *Enquiry into Plants (Historia Plantarum)* and *On Plant Physiology (De causis plantarum)* and Xenophon's *Economics* also provide much information on agriculture in the Classical period. In other literary works from Aeschylus and Herodotus to later authors, we also find a great deal of useful information about farm life. We must take care not to forget the authors who are (for convenience's sake) known as the "Roman agronomists," Cato, Varro, and Columella. The latter drew (especially) on the Greek and Punic agronomists, whose works have now been lost. Columella's *On Farming (De re rustica* 1.1.7–11) cites thirty-four authors of whom only the names remain.[2] We can also add the *Geoponica*, written in Greek in the tenth century and based on the homonymous work by Cassianus Bassus in the sixth century CE, a compilation of extracts from ancient agronomists. With these, we can also compare a large category of inscriptions that register land leases. Entered into by cities and individuals, sanctuaries, demes, or other basic city groups, these leases constitute a mine of information on the cultural practices and organization of rural life. These inscriptions intersect directly with the information given by Theophrastus and thus confirm the value of the latter for our study of Greek agriculture. As for the archaeological sources, many vase paintings of the Archaic and Classical periods, sometimes also reliefs, murals, or mosaics from the later periods (but there exist few of these before the Imperial period), vividly illustrate scenes of the rural life. In addition, in the last decades excavations of farms (and other sites like rural amphora kilns) have yielded direct evidence regarding technology and production choices, which make a major contribution to a new understanding of ancient Greek agriculture. Provided that it is used with care to build hypotheses about the past, ethno-archaeological information, like that to be found in Paul Halstead's most inspiring *Two Oxen Ahead*, also proves to be very helpful.[3] Taken as a whole, this information allows us to go beyond the clichés of crass backwardness and routine traditionally attached to Greek agriculture.

THE MEDITERRANEAN TRILOGY

Grain

Ancient Greek agriculture consisted in what is generally called "the Mediterranean trilogy"—grain, olives, and grapes (at least where possible), along with livestock raising, especially sheep and goats. Consuming grain, wine, and cooked meat from sacrifices was a definition of culture.[4] In Homer, a civilized man—as opposed to a savage—is defined as a *sitophagos*, an "eater of grain."[5] In this series, there is thus a first element: grain. As in all the societies that emerged from the Neolithic period, grain constituted the essential element in the Greek food supply, and probably provided on average at least 70 percent of the needed calories. People might experience a temporary lack of this or that other food that served as a nutritional complement, but they could not survive without grain. Compared to livestock raising, per unit of arable land growing cereals makes it possible to feed a population four times larger. The orientation of agricultural production in the Mycenaean world and in the early first millennium BCE remains controversial, but there should be no doubt that even in the early Iron Age Greece did not turn into an exclusively pastoralist society.[6]

The Greeks used the general term *sitos* to refer to cereals, which in practice meant wheat (*puros*) or barley (*krithē*). Wheat was the aristocratic cereal par excellence. The Greeks planted "naked wheat," an evolved variety whose grain could be easily separated from the hulls when threshed.[7] Until the Greeks arrived, the Egyptians used only *Triticum turgidum* of the *dicoccum* variety, which required more labor to arrive at the same result.[8] The wheat planted in ancient Greece was a variety of hard wheat, *Triticum durum*, used as a winter crop (it was planted in the autumn and spent the winter underground). Although *Triticum durum* is better adapted to producing what is now called pasta, their wheat flour enabled the Greeks to make bread of relatively good quality. Wheat bread, which was easier to digest, provided more calories for a given volume. Barley flour out of grilled grain was eaten either in the form of a baked or unbaked rough bread or gruel (*maza*). Millet (*kenchros*), a cereal that provides few calories and was usually eaten as boiled grains (like rice), seems to have been rarely cultivated. Rye was unknown.

The choice to cultivate this or that cereal grain depended first on environmental conditions. Wheat requires soils rich in nitrogen and phosphorus, and ideally at least 600 millimeters of rain per year, even if a mediocre crop can be raised where annual rainfall is only 300 to 400 millimeters. Its growth is favored by cold winter temperatures, which promote the growth of secondary stems that will bear ears of wheat in the spring. Barley can be raised on poorer soils, with annual rainfalls as low as 250 to 300 millimeters. Furthermore, where rainfall is minimal, barley produces larger harvests than does wheat. Millet can grow on very poor soils, with levels of rainfall even lower than those required for barley, but the quantities produced per unit of surface are very small: if in addition we take into consideration the low level of calories it provides, we understand why millet was grown only in the most arid areas. Thus wheat and barley constituted the basis of Greek cereal culture, but in proportions that were a direct function of rainfall. Generally, in all of eastern mainland Greece, the cities near the Aegean and the islands, where rainfall was light, barley was by far the most widely grown cereal grain. On the other hand, in western and northern Greece, where there was more rain, and naturally also in the distant colonial lands on the Black Sea, wheat played a larger role, and in some places the largest. This geographical division between zones of production is in itself a significant factor: it implies that the people of the great urbanized regions of Aegean Greece could not produce the wheat they wanted to eat, and that for the most part they had to import it. We see that tastes and eating habits evolved over time. Wheat bread, which in the Archaic period was probably eaten only by the wealthy, gradually spread to broader strata of the population. Because of imports of wheat from the northern Black Sea regions, which produced a variety of wheat best adapted to making bread (*Triticum compactum*), in fifth- and sixth-century Athens wheat bread made from imported grain began to seriously compete with *maza* as the basic foodstuff, and it did so even more in the cities of the Hellenistic world, at least for relatively well-off free people.[9] On the other hand, barley still remained the basic food for the lower classes and for slaves.

Growing grain was the foundation of agricultural production, no matter what the region concerned. Even in regions that specialized in other products intended for sale, cereals were grown, because this made it possible to minimize the cost of buying grain. The basic cycle of cereal production covered two years.[10] In March of the first year, the earth was plowed to turn it over. This eliminated weeds.[11] This plowing could not be done earlier, because the soil would be too wet to work, nor could it be done later, because the soil would be too dry and too hard. On this already plowed soil, a second plowing was possible in July. In November, after the land was plowed a third time, the seed was sown. The grain was harvested in May or June. Then the land lay fallow until the following March. The goal of these successive plowings was first to preserve the humidity of the soil by preventing the formation of a crust on the surface that would, by capillary action, bring the water to the surface in summer and thus dry out the earth.[12] Moreover, the successive plowings made the soil friable, which promoted the growth of the grain, and also eradicated weeds that might have competed with the grain. The length of the fallow period was justified first of all by the inadequacy of manures. To be sure, agriculture and stock raising went hand in hand. But insofar as most of the land available was devoted to growing cereals, flocks were insufficient in number to produce the quantities of manure that would have made it possible to eliminate the fallow period. At the same time, plowing before sowing created "bare fallow land" that could not be used for grazing, which was another disadvantage. We see that there was an internal constraint blocking progress, and it had to do with the universality of cereal growing, a point to which we will have to return.

The techniques of cereal growing in ancient Greece may seem to have been unchanging. The world of the third century BCE described in Theocritus's *Thalusia*—the title alludes to the harvest festival on Kos (and in other Dorian lands)—seems to be the same as that of Hesiod four centuries earlier. The poorest peasants might work the soil by hand, since they could not afford an ox. But in this case, the surface cultivated was at most two or three hectares, which if planted in cereals provided at best a life of poverty and hard work. Then it was more desirable to rent a pair of oxen to do the heavy labor. With two oxen to pull the plow, up to five hectares could easily be cultivated if one had enough land left to pasture the oxen (for example, on city's or deme's land).[13] A cereal farm of five to eight hectares could provide a family with a decent living. Tools seem to have developed little. In Greece, the plow was still an iron-shod ard plow that opened the soil without turning it, and did not allow deep cultivation. Harrowing, which closes the furrows after sowing and burying the seed, and which thus produces larger crops, appears—at least in our sources—only in the first century CE.[14] Before that time, children did this work by stamping down the furrows. Harvesting was always done with a sickle. We see the same traditionalism in the way grain was processed. Threshing was done in an area usually located immediately adjacent to the farmhouse (or other agricultural buildings). Animals were made to stamp the ground, thereby separating the grain from the husks. Finally, there was the process of winnowing, which consisted in separating the wheat from the chaff by throwing the mixture of grain and chaff into the air so that the wind would carry away the chaff. For this work, a large workforce was required at certain times of the year.[15] In general, if we believe Hesiod, around 700 BCE a standard peasant family already owned several slaves who helped do the heavy labor.[16] But the family as a whole, including the children, worked during the harvest, the threshing, and the winnowing.

Grapes

After grain, the second element of the Mediterranean trilogy is wine grapes. Greek viticulture goes back to the second millennium BCE at least. It is no exaggeration to say that except in the highest and coldest areas, the Greeks practiced viticulture everywhere they went in the Mediterranean. The goal of viticulture was to produce wine and its by-product, vinegar, and secondarily raisins or table grapes. The consumption of wine was a pleasure enjoyed at all social levels, but it was above all an indispensable part of the diet. Cereal flours supplied mainly reserve carbohydrates (starch is a carbohydrate that is assimilated slowly) and proteins. Wine provides not only a caloric complement (alcohol and quickly assimilated sugars) but also a variety of vitamins. A great deal of wine was consumed. As in traditional Mediterranean societies until recent times, it seems that an adult male's average daily wine consumption was between a half-liter and a liter a day.[17] Cato (*On Agriculture* 57) recommended a yearly allocation of ten quadrantals of wine (about 260 liters) for a slave forced to work in chains. If we take into account the fact that slaves' rations were certainly decreased during the winter, when they were not employed full time, we see that during the work period their wine ration must have been about one liter per day. Similarly, soldiers were given large quantities of wine. The city of Chios thanked one of its citizens who, during the War of Antiochos, had subsidized the maintenance of the Roman soldiers stationed on the island and gave them an amphora of wine.[18] That is why we also find large numbers of amphoras at garrison sites—for example, the camp at Koroni, in Attika, which was briefly occupied by soldiers from Ptolemy's expeditionary corps at the time of the Chremonidean War (268–262 BCE).[19]

To meet these increased needs, wine had to be made in large quantities.[20] Since wine could be produced almost everywhere (except in mountainous regions), it is certain that unlike what we see in the area of grain production, most needs were met by local producers. Roman agronomists were quite capable of distinguishing high-quality grape varieties that produced small quantities from those that yielded mediocre wine but in large quantities. They had also noticed that land on the plain was more productive than land in the hills. To meet its own needs, the peasant world could of course draw on an abundant production of mediocre wine. It could also supply urban markets with low-quality wine. We can be sure that in areas near cities, in Aegean Greece and in the colonies, large quantities of low-priced everyday wine were produced for consumption by the lower classes. That is why these consumers, who usually drank only this everyday wine, were so eager to receive the free wine distributed during festivals, as we can tell from several decrees issued during the Hellenistic period thanking benefactors for providing it. In sum, Greek viticulture sought to produce either poor-quality wines sold at relatively low prices but in large quantities, the whole operation taking place within a limited area to hold down transportation costs, or more expensive medium- to high-quality wines sold in a wide-ranging sales network.

The viticultural cycle differed from that of cereal production.[21] After planting the vines, one had to wait several years before they began to produce. Pliny (*Natural History* 17.35 [182]) recommended allowing seven years after taking cuttings— that is, four or five years after the new vines were planted—before beginning to harvest them. It is true that Columella (*On Farming* 3.3.9) claimed to have reduced this period to two years, but we do not know whether he was subsequently able to maintain the productivity of his vineyard. This was a constraint that, in addition to the heavy initial investment represented by planting the vines themselves, assumed the existence of other sources of revenue on which one could draw while waiting for the vines to begin producing. In other words, viticulture assumed that one had access to capital. If this capital was not inherited, it could be gradually accumulated, starting from nothing or almost nothing, even by a poor peasant. Luck (no vine diseases) and hard work were required. Once the vine was planted, production followed an annual rhythm. We see, however, that viticulture was not immediately accessible to everyone.

The establishment of a new vineyard represented a major investment. Leases from Amos, in the Rhodian Peraia, allow us to determine the agronomists' main recommendations.[22] Trenches 0.75 meter deep had to be dug, leaving plowed intermediary strips 1.80 meters wide between the rows. These leases also called for different modes of planting depending on whether the vineyard was in the plain or on rocky land. In addition, they also demanded that 1,000 vines be planted per *mina* (100 drachms) of rent, for a density of probably 4,100 to 7,000 vines per hectare, depending on whether the land was rocky (where the plants were more closely set) or in the plain. The Amos leases also provided for stakes. These stakes, which are attested almost everywhere (on Kerkyra or in Attika), were expensive.[23] In addition, one had to have vinification and storage facilities. Finally, since a large workforce was needed to maintain the vineyard, in Greek society this heavy labor was usually done by slaves. In compensation for these large investments, a vineyard could produce financial yields considerably greater than those to be derived from growing cereals. That is the significance of the questions asked by the Latin agronomists, particularly Columella, when they are dealing with vineyards. Should one plant grapevines, and if so, under what circumstances? We note here that the treatises written by the "agronomists" do not correspond to what we would now call agronomy. They should be compared instead to guides addressed to wealthy investors. They reason in terms of opportunity costs to determine the best investment. They compare investments in vines that produce large or small crops. Hence it is futile to reproach the Latin agronomists for their inadequate technical description of agricultural practices. In reality, their goal was to provide investors with advice regarding the best way to place their capital and then how to manage the type of crop chosen as profitably as possible. The technical observations they offer are intended chiefly to help investors make an initial choice, and then, once the investment is made, to limit the uncertainty by telling them how to manage it. It is in this conceptual framework that we should read the advice given by the Latin agronomists regarding wine growing.

There were, then, two main types of wine: everyday wines and high-quality wines. In the Greek sources, the former remain largely anonymous, except in the numerous allusions to the production, sale, and consumption of wine in the papyri of Ptolemaic and Roman Egypt, which may give us an idea of everyday use that for the most part eludes us in the framework of Aegean Greece. In contrast, high-quality wines are well known through literary sources and the amphoras showing that these wines were exported to foreign markets. This is odd, since most of the wine consumed was ordinary wine. Three cases will suffice to illustrate this local production.

In Sparta, wine was one of the things the citizen was supposed to bring to the *sussition*, the collective banquet that one had to attend on pain of being excluded from the community. According to Plutarch, every Spartan had to provide eight *choes* of wine every month. The standard of reference is probably the Lakonian-Aiginetan standard, which explains why Dicearchus mentions eleven to twelve *choes*, the equivalent in Attic measures of the eight Lakonian *choes*.[24] Thus the equivalent of an Attic *metrētēs*—about forty liters—had to be provided monthly, or about five hectoliters per year. Many anecdotes confirm that in Sparta as well, wine was part of everyday life, that it was drunk daily, and *a fortiori* on holidays. Not only do the literary sources stress the low levels of Spartan imports, especially of luxury products, of which high-quality wines were an integral part, but the lack of sherds of imported amphoras confirms that these wines were not consumed in Sparta. The wine that was consumed in Sparta was therefore produced locally.

Athens is not considered to be a city that produced wine with a particularly high reputation. But we have a series of documents that show that viticulture was practiced there on a large scale. The festival of *Anthestēria* (which was moreover celebrated by all Ionians) took place in the month of *Antesthēriōn* (February–March). It honored Dionysos and was a new-wine festival, its three days bearing evocative names:[25] *Pithoigia* ("opening of the jars"), *Choes* ("jugs"), and *Chutroi* ("pots," "kettles"). There is thus no doubt that this was a festival celebrating the wine produced locally in Athens. The festivals of Dionysos in other cities had the same meaning. Athenaeus (14 654a) mentions a grape variety, *nikostrateios*, as peculiar to Attika. In Aristophanes, we already find a multitude of allusions to wine production.[26] On the steles listing the goods seized in connection with the Hermokopids scandal in 415 BCE, we find mentioned among Panaitios's possessions 104 amphoras and seven *choes* of "pure Attic wine" (an amphora was both a container and a measure of capacity in a given standard, here corresponding to a *metrētēs*), or a little more than 41 hectoliters.[27] In addition to 1,000 *medimnoi* of grain, a rich Athenian like Phainippos (Pseudo-Demosthenes *Against Phaenippus* 42.20) was supposed to produce (before 330 BCE) more than 800 *metrētai* of wine, or more than 315 hectoliters. Attic land leases frequently mention viticultural production.[28] This wine produced in large quantities by a large landowner like Phainippos, or in more modest quantities by a humble Attic peasant, was not celebrated by ancient authors. At least during the Classical and Hellenistic periods, this Athenian wine (like most of Attika's agricultural products) was not exported, and thus has left no trace in the form of amphoras. However, there is no doubt that the larger part of the wine consumed in Attika was of local origin.

The situation in Athens may be found in most of the cities where the climate made wine growing possible. We have to take into account a vast production of "anonymous" wine—that is, wine with no particular reputation, or only a modest one, but which we constantly find mentioned in written sources (allusions to locally produced wine) or archaeological artifacts (wine presses, *pithoi* for storing the wine, and so on). Thus, though the evidence is tenuous, wine was produced even on the two little islands of Delos and Rheneia, though of course in much smaller volume.[29] This wine could have been consumed only by the local people. Here we find the tradition of wines that are designated in Zenon's papyri as "local" (*enchōrios*), the ones that remain anonymous, and do not travel.[30]

On the other hand, some wines were exported to nearby or distant areas. Homer already distinguishes certain wines. Already in the seventh century, Athens as well as several cities of Western Asia Minor and neighboring islands exported their wines (and no doubt their olive oil).[31] In absolute terms, wine exports were not a novelty that appeared only at the end of the Archaic period or during the Classical age. What was new was that these exports began to become more widespread and to undergo a marked ascension that was further amplified during the Hellenistic period. By the end of the Archaic period (when Athens had stopped its exports), more cities were already exporting wine. We can see this in the written sources, but still more in the amphoras. The latter's forms generally developed in the same way. Greek amphoras were pot-bellied and spherical at the end of the Archaic period and during the Classical age, and still did not show any significant modifications related to the conditions under which they were transported.[32] During the Hellenistic period, however, their shapes grew more elongated. It is likely that this tendency reflects experience and the practice of stacking amphoras in the holds of ships. It had been realized that if the amphoras were stacked in front of each other, the load was more stable and there was less danger that it might cause the ship to capsize (or even break its planking) by shifting in high seas. This could be prevented with elongated amphoras that could more easily be stacked alternately. Within the great families of shapes that had a regional base, some cities (among others, Rhodes and Knidos in the Hellenistic period) nonetheless had a shape of amphora that was peculiar to them.[33] If some of these types of amphoras are well known, especially those used by the large cities, many corresponding to smaller cities have not yet been attributed. Even if, despite the great progress that has been made, there still remains much to do in the domain of what is generally called "amphorology," we can already see certain major tendencies emerging.

The geography of exporting zones developed over time. At the end of the Archaic period and during the Classical age, wine from northern Greece was highly prized. Thracian wines, for example those from Maroneia, Thasos, and the Chalkidian cities (Mende, Akanthos) were well known everywhere, and had been since the Homeric period.[34] On the coast of Asia Minor, the wines from Lesbos and especially Chios were also very famous. An island like Peparethos (modern Skopelos), north of Euboia, also enjoyed a great reputation and its wines were exported.[35] Choices were made on the basis of the kind of wine, white for wines from Mende, red for wines from Thasos or Chios.[36] In the Hellenistic period, a new geography emerges. The export of luxury wines continues. But other wines intended for a broader clientele (which does not nullify earlier comments on mass consumption being supplied by local wines), for a "middle class" or for specific categories of buyers such as mercenaries, were sold on the most diverse markets. This was the case for wine from Rhodes, which acquired its market share in the third century and further expanded it in the second century.[37] It was still more the case for wines from Knidos and Kos in the last half of the second century and in the first century. These wines were often "salted" (*epithalassioi*) to facilitate their preservation and transport—not necessarily to the detriment of their quality, for this might also have enhanced the taste.[38]

The transition to quality wine production that was intended for distant consumers thus presupposed a radical choice in favor of a speculative form of agriculture that worked for a market and provided a product whose quality would be recognized. This economic transformation, which was fundamental for an agricultural production that only occasionally supplied foreign markets, was first made by the city of Chios at the end of the Archaic period. According to Theopompus, the inhabitants of Chios were the first to buy slaves in large numbers, and these slaves were not Greeks but barbarians.[39] Theopompus also notes that the inhabitants of Chios were the first to produce red wine, and that they learned the technique of planting the vines directly from Oinopion, Dionysos's son.[40] In the Classical age, coins from Chios, in silver or bronze, bore on their obverse the images of a sphinx, an amphora, and grapes.[41] Thucydides (8.40.2) mentions that on Chios, slaves were more numerous than anywhere else except for Sparta: when in 412 BCE Athenian troops came to Chios to put down a revolt by the inhabitants, the latter's slaves fled to the Athenians. This was particularly disastrous for the inhabitants of Chios, because these slaves knew the island well and were consequently able to advise the Athenians. It is clear that Thucydides is alluding here to the relationship between the free and the unfree population.[42] In other words, the transition to a large-scale, speculative viticulture also presupposed a transition to a system based on large-scale slavery, with all the consequences that that implied. Other large-scale slave revolts took place on Chios in the first half of the third century.[43]

Kerkyra (modern Corfu) was another island where viticulture underwent a special development. In his account of the civil war that broke out in the city of Kerkyra in 427 BCE, Thucydides mentions that among the mutual accusations made by the democrats and the oligarchs, the democratic leader Peithias reproached the five wealthiest oligarchs for having cut wood on sacred lands belonging to Zeus and Alkinoos in order to make stakes for wine growing. They were fined one *statēr* per stake. Although Thucydides (3.70.4–5) does not tell us the number of these stakes, there must have been many of them, as we might expect for objects of this kind and as the rest of Thucydides' account also suggests. He adds that the enormity of the sum to be paid left these rich oligarchs no choice but to try to start a revolution. The inevitable result was a true civil war between the oligarchs and the democrats. The two parties immediately tried to win the support of the slaves by sending emissaries into the countryside, but most of the slaves joined the democrats' camp (ibid., 3.73). The merchandise stored in the buildings around the agora, which the retreating oligarchs burned down during these ruthless battles—Thucydides (3.74.2, with 72.3) says that they did not spare their own properties any more than they did those of their adversaries—gives an idea of the city's wealth and the commercial orientation of its economy. A passage in a treatise traditionally attributed to Aristotle mentions that in the lands far to the north of Greece there was a market where merchants coming from Pontos brought products from Lesbos, Chios, and Thasos, whereas merchants coming from the Adriatic brought amphoras from Kerkyra.[44] The latter are now well identified: they are of a type defined as "Corinthian B." They had in fact earlier been attributed to Corinth, but we now know that these amphoras were produced in several places, particularly in Kerkyra and perhaps not in Corinth at all. These amphoras were widely exported and they are found throughout the Mediterranean world—for instance, in Euhesperides, in Cyrenaica, where they constitute the most numerous category of amphoras imported during the fourth and third centuries.[45]

Olives

The olive tree is the third typically Mediterranean plant.[46] Olives were eaten partly in the form of fruits (after suitable preparation), but above all they were transformed into oil, which both constituted a basic food and could be used in other ways, such as to anoint the body before participating in athletic activities at the gymnasium or stadium, or for lighting.[47] However, it is clear that the alimentary function was primordial. Olive oil provides lipids that are indispensable for human nutrition (they are almost completely absent from cereals and completely absent from wine), especially for growth. In a society in which little meat and dairy products were consumed, olive oil's nutritional contribution was thus essential. The olive is a characteristic Mediterranean tree. There are two varieties, one wild (the oleaster, widespread in the Mediterranean world) and one cultivated (*Olea europaea L. Sativa*); only the latter was important for mass production.[48] However, the oleaster nonetheless continued to have an interest in the Greek world because it alone provided the fine oil necessary for perfume bases.[49]

The olive is a tree that needs well-drained soil. It grows on both rich and poor soils. To flower, it needs period of low temperatures, but it can survive droughts, even long ones. Thus it can live in areas of low annual rainfall (but only down to 200 millimeters). It can withstand temperatures as low as −13°C, provided they are not too prolonged. Thus, the olive cannot grow above a certain altitude, though what that altitude is cannot be determined on an a priori basis because everything depends on the local climate: in general, we might say that in the Mediterranean world the upper limit for the olive varies between 600 and 1,000 meters, depending on the region.[50] We see that on the plains and hills of the Mediterranean area, the olive is the cultivated tree par excellence. It could be planted in stony areas where no other crop could have been grown. It goes without saying, however, that olive trees planted in areas with rich, well-drained soils and fairly heavy rainfall produced much more than those that were grown in areas with poor soils and semi-arid climates.

The olive tree was propagated primarily by taking cuttings. It had to be grafted to increase its production. Whether it was planted in a field, on a plain, or on a terraced hillside, the soil had to be deeply cultivated and planting holes had to be dug. The trees were then planted in rows, the distance between the rows varying depending on the richness of the soil and the kind of production chosen. It was common to plant cereal grains in the space between the trees. Thus the Greeks practiced what is known in modern Italy as *coltura promiscua* (mixed cultivation).[51] But on rocky hillsides, they might also dig cavities and construct low walls to hold the earth around each cavity, and then add soil and vegetable matter before planting the tree. In this way, without having a genuine field, and at the cost of considerable work, it was possible to grow olive trees even in areas where there was no plant cover (similar practices can still be commonly observed today in Greece and Turkey). The olive tree does not produce a crop for the first five or six years after it is planted. It takes about thirty years for it to come into full production, and the tree may live as long as several hundred years (but the productivity of an old tree may decrease considerably). Once it has begun to produce, and if conditions are good, the tree produces only every other year, as Columella observed (*On Farming* 5.8.2). Varro (*On Agriculture* 1.55.3) believed (wrongly) that this was caused by bad harvesting. It remains that poor weather conditions and diseases (frequent in olive trees, which in this respect are fragile) must have made production irregular. In any case, our sources mention both exceptionally good harvests and very meager ones. We see that like grapevines, the olive tree involved a long-term investment. An olive grove constituted a form of capital that could be handed down from generation to generation.[52]

When growing olives in an open field, it was necessary to plow at least once a year, in the spring, in order to ensure that rain would penetrate the soil and to eliminate weeds. If they had it, the growers put animal manure or olive marc around the foot of the trees. The trees also had to be pruned to keep their branches from growing too high and to clear out branches that were dead or had ceased to produce fruit. It is not certain, however, that in antiquity this pruning was done under optimal conditions. The work took at least a month, in the spring. The harvest took place between autumn and the beginning of winter. In early autumn, olives that were still green might be collected. They were to be eaten as fruit, after having been fermented in brine. Later in the season, until January, ripe (black) olives were collected. Green olives were collected by hand, in order to avoid damaging the fruit, while black olives were usually picked either by hand (if the branches could be reached) or by shaking or striking the branches: the fruit was then picked up off the ground (today olives are made to drop onto a cloth spread under the tree, and it is likely that this was also done in antiquity).[53] On a small farm, this work involved the whole family. Larger groves that had hundreds or thousands of trees required outside labor. Aristophanes (*Wasps* 712) mentions these paid workers who collected olives. Cato (*On Agriculture* 144–46) even recommended selling the crop on the trees and leaving the harvesting to a contractor who had a large workforce.

COMPLEMENTARY PRODUCTS

Cereals, grapes, and olives constituted the heart of agricultural production in ancient Greece. However, the role of other products was not negligible. Among shrubby plants, the fig, another characteristically Mediterranean tree, comes right after grapes and olives. The fig tree is also well adapted to the Mediterranean climate. It can also get along in poor soils, but it needs more water. Its fruits (one or two harvests, depending on the variety) are gathered in the fall (after a first harvest in July for two-crop varieties). Fig trees were grown in warm, humid areas all over Greece, but certain cities or regions had made them a specialty, like Kamiros in the island of Rhodes and its neigbors Idyma or Kaunos in Karia.[54] Dried, the fruits kept well. Figs are rich in sugar, vitamins, and mineral nutrients. They were frequently fed to slaves, and even to soldiers if necessary: that is how King Philip V, stuck in Karia during the winter of 201 BCE, was able to feed his troops.[55] The tree begins producing five or six years after planting. It can survive with limited care. The Amos land leases enjoined lessees to plant fig trees, which shows that they were, in addition to being long-lived and less fragile than olive trees, also valued as capital.[56] Walnut trees were also planted on appropriate soils.

Even if the range of plants cultivated was narrower than it is today, all kinds of vegetables were grown—turnips, peas, cabbage, beets, chicory, garlic, onions, and mustard were all part of the ordinary diet.[57] The seizure of property in connection with the Hermokopids scandal in 415 BCE shows that in addition to cereals, wine, and vinegar, the people involved produced on their lands almonds, coriander, sesame, figs, lentils, and vetches (*orobos*, a variety of lentil with low nutritive value that was eaten by the poorest classes).[58] These were chiefly local products grown on family farms dispersed over the territory and also in the gardens around the cities, which could then make use of urban organic waste as manure. At Athens, the gardener of foreign origin, whom a source happens to make known to us (he was included in the list of the foreigners who were granted citizenship in 401/0 because they had taken part in the battle of Mounychia during the civil war against the oligarchs), must have been part of a group of market gardeners who came to the agora on every open day to sell their products directly.[59] But we should not conclude that these products were intended to supply only a local market. As in the case of wine, there were regional specializations, and some products had a particular quality that brought higher prices on the market. This was true, for instance, of vegetables from Phleious, a city in the northern Peloponnese, whose products were prized outside its own boundaries. This is emphasized by Apuleius (*Apology* 24), a Latin author of the second century CE who was clearly drawing on a source from the Classical period, because he compares Phleious's vegetables with wine from Thasos: "Wine-sellers and vegetable-sellers have the right to promote their products by drawing attention to the excellence of the soil that produced them, as is the case, for example, for wine from Thasos or vegetables from Phleious. In fact, for these products of the soil, the fertility of the region favors an improvement in flavor, just as do rainfall, clement winds, the warmth of the sun, and rich soil."

Near the cities, roses and other flowers were planted in order to supply urban markets. For example, near the colonial city of Cyrene the roses produced were of such high quality that they were also used to make famed perfumes.[60] A variety of wild or semicultivated plants could also be found in the markets—for example, oregano, which was used in cooking and as a medicine. Honey production, and its by-product, beeswax, was also a way of using the margins of agricultural lands, the hilly areas around the main cropland, where agricultural activity was more difficult.[61] Honey was all the more important because it was the only available source of sugar. In the Hellenistic period, cane sugar was known to travelers who had visited India. But this curious discovery, mentioned by Diodorus (19.94.10), was never developed in ancient Greece. Literary texts and inscriptions indicate that honey was produced in Greece from the Archaic period to the Hellenistic period. Solon (Plutarch *Solon* 23.6) had already ordered that a new hive must be set up no closer than 300 feet from an already existing hive. Solon did not make this law without a reason. The honey from Attika was among the most famous in Greece, along with the honey from Theangela in Karia and the honey from Rhodes. It just happens that these three places where honey was produced are associated in the customs declaration for products imported by ship into Pelousion in 259 CE.[62] Many archaeological remains allow us to locate ancient hives. They were often made of pottery, frequently cylindrical, and arranged horizontally or vertically. Many of them have been found in Attika and more recently during excavations at Isthmia (Hellenistic period).[63] Columella devotes most of Book IX of his *On Farming* to apiculture. Most of the sources he cites and the documentation he uses are clearly Greek or Carthaginian. It is remarkable that in addition to offering advice regarding the varieties of flowers from which bees should glean pollen in order to make high-quality honey, the arrangement of the hives, and the care they must be given, he also shows a concern to maximize production. Thus he goes on (9.14.18–19):[64]

> [Celsus] says that only in a few places are conditions so favorable as to provide different foods for the bees in winter and summer, and that, therefore, in places where suitable flowers are lacking after the season of spring, the swarms ought not to be left without being moved, but, when the spring foods are consumed, they should be transferred to places which can offer the bees a more liberal diet from the late-flowering blossoms of thyme, marjoram and savory. This, he says, is the practice both in the regions of Achaia, where the bees are transferred to pastures in Attika, and in Euboia, and also in the islands of the Kyklades, when they are transferred from other islands to Skyros, and likewise in Sicily, when they are moved from the other parts of the island to Hybla.[65]

Aulus Cornelius Celsus, Columella's source and his contemporary, was a Roman physician and naturalist who lived at the end of the first century BCE and the beginning of the first century CE. The "Achaia" to which he refers is naturally the Roman province of the same name, which corresponded roughly to southern Greece (to the south of Thessaly). It is striking to note that Celsus and Columella propose as a model for their Roman audience Greek beekeepers who did not hesitate to move their hives over rather long distances, transferring them for instance from Euboia and the Kyklades to the island of Skyros, which was farther north and more mountainous and humid, and whose vegetative cycle differed from that of its southern neighbors. According to Dioscorides (2.10), the best honey came precisely from Attika, the Kyklades, and Euboia.[66] On mule-back or in boats, the hives were moved about so that the harvest would be more abundant and better in quality.

Unlike that of wine or olive oil, the production of honey required only a small investment of capital. Therefore, it could be engaged in by members of the lower social strata, who did not have access to large amounts of capital. Thus although these activities could of course be pursued on some middle-sized or large farms, it seems that less well-off people could also earn a living by them, even if they had to rent gardens to start their activities.

ANIMAL HUSBANDRY

The Debate on "Pastoralism"

The world of the Cretan palace economies had very large flocks. The palace at Knossos controlled a flock of perhaps up to 100,000 sheep.[67] Later, Homer's description of Greece suggests a world in which animal husbandry occupied a much larger place than it did in later periods. He frequently mentions flocks, and his characters often consume meat and milk. But assessing the economic role of animal husbandry in terms of raw figures or quantities is not sufficient. The parallel between the Cretan palaces and the world of Homer is already quite telling. The former exploited large flocks of sheep for their wool. The latter apparently gave their preference to cattle for meat. The different forms of animal husbandry corresponded to different economics systems and organizational strategies.

The recent debate on "pastoralism" in the Early Iron Age should be envisaged in the light of this general interpretive framework. Anthony Snodgrass famously proposed that the "Dark Ages" witnessed an extension of animal husbandry, followed by a return to an economy more centered on agriculture.[68] This view has been challenged, considering especially that the prism of the Homeric poems, which are centered on the life of heroes, deformed an unaltered reality in which the role of animal husbandry had not changed since the Bronze Age, and which was not to change later on.[69] In Homer, the embellishment of the life of the heroes of the past may have made of the exceptional (eating meat) the usual. The archaeology of the sites of the Early Iron Age shows clearly that the cultivation of grain (or other plants) was still the main activity.[70]

This reevaluation forces us to reject the model of an Early Iron Age world exclusively devoted to animal husbandry, as if it were a pastoralist society. In a pastoralist society, all the life of the community is centered on livestock-raising and grain production is marginal or absent. Homer's people were "eaters of bread," and the *Odyssey* reveals the tensions existing with the shepherds and other marginal populations.[71] But—and this was in fact Snodgrass's argument—this does not mean that in the economy of the Early Iron Age animal husbandry did not play a more significant role than was the case later. Besides, an increase in livestock raising does not mean a drastic abandonment of grain growing. Even the economy of Crete in the Classical and Hellenistic periods—where, at that time, pastoralism played a more significant role than in Attika or the Aegean islands—was far from being exclusively devoted to animal husbandry. As for the valuation of cattle in Homer, it is also revealing of a situation where the relative share of animal husbandry, and especially of cattle raising, in individual patrimonies (and thus in social values in general) was more significant than it was later.[72]

Recent bone studies from northern and western Greece help to define longue durée evolutions in the orientations of animal husbandry. In the site of Kastanas, in Macedon, cattle were the main source of meat in the Early and Middle Bronze

Age. Sheep, goats, and pigs became equally important in the Late Bronze Age. But cattle regained its position in the Early Iron Age.[73] In sites in Thesprotia (southern Epeiros), bone studies reveal that cattle were also dominant in the Early Iron Age, while in the late Classical and Hellenistic period a shift to more diverse sources of meat can be observed, with especially a sharp increase in the consumption of pig meat. In the Thesprotian town of Kassope, located not far from the sea, the frequency of cattle bones drops between the third and the first century BCE, while that of pig, wild game (red deer), and bird bones (and seafood) rises.[74] These differences in meat consumption over time can best be explained in a context where phases of population increases both required a diversification of the sources of meat and led to a reduction of the area devoted to cattle grazing.

The reasons for the reorganization of animal husbandry can fundamentally be linked to the quantity of animal food available and to the use made of the animal products. If indeed the Early Iron Age was characterized by low demographic densities (and we have every reason to think so), the areas available for pasture must have been comparatively larger.[75] In these circumstances, it is hard to see why the society of the Early Iron Age would not have made use of this new possibility to increase the flocks, especially the cattle flocks, which does not mean that these people became exclusively pastoralists. A similar development famously took place all over medieval Europe after the Black Death.[76] The overall population increase in the periods following the Early Iron Age played the role of a constraint favoring a reduction in cattle raising in the most developed parts of the Greek world, accompanied by an increase of pig raising. Pigs can be fed on poor pasture in the forests, or without resorting to pasture if the animals are fed in the pigsty on grain and turnip. All aspects being taken into account, raising pigs considerably reduces the aggregate agricultural area devoted to animal husbandry. Thus it seems clear that in the post–Early Iron Age period, livestock raising saw its relative share decrease, while the decline in cattle raising was accompanied by an increase in pig raising, especially in the regions around the Aegean, as the environment was less favorable to cattle and as demographic pressure and urban demand for meat was at it peak.

Constraints in Animal Husbandry

For the most part, animal husbandry was directly associated with three main types of products. The first was constituted by foodstuffs, milk (cows, sheep, and goats) and meat (the same animals and also fowl). The second type consisted of various raw materials, chiefly leather and wool. Finally, except for human muscle-power, livestock provided the only source of energy easily adaptable for transportation and other uses such as threshing. A by-product of livestock raising was manure, which was all the more important because it constituted the main source of nitrogen fertilizer. In passing, we can also mention other kinds of services, such as raising dogs; some of the latter were indispensible for tending the flocks, while others were raised solely for the pleasure of hunting or as guard dogs (which might find a military use). Horses were also bred for use in war, racing, or ceremonial contexts. Raising poultry was common, but birds were also raised as pets.[77] Then as now, maximum use was normally made of the animal. Thus a draft ox would end up at the butcher and his hide would be tanned. It is clear that the kind of flock or herd always corresponded to a strategy for using it. The choice of the kind of stock to be raised was normally determined by a main goal, which was itself first a function of the pasturelands available. Thus oxen and horses required large amounts of grass. Sheep could get along with less luxuriant pastures, but whether it was on the plain or in the mountains, the terrain had to be relatively open. Goats, which gave the most milk and reproduced somewhat more rapidly, could be left to run free on very steep terrains.

However, strategy did not necessarily imply specialization, a question that has been heavily debated over the last decades.[78] As for agriculture, a humble peasant's strategy might have consisted in wanting to have "a little of everything"—that is, to have a brace of oxen to pull the plow, a few goats and ewes for milk or wool to be spun and woven by the household's women and girls, a few pigs and chickens, and a few beehives. But the constraints associated with stock raising are heavy. If one had more than a few animals, caring for them required an attention and an investment in work that quickly proved incompatible with agriculture in the strict sense. It also required particular kinds of knowledge and expertise that made it difficult to be competent in all areas. Thus a flock of a few dozen ewes or even goats demanded the permanent attention of a shepherd who saw to it that the flock did not stray and who milked the animals daily and made cheese, the only known way of transforming and thus preserving dairy products. This implies that large flocks presupposed a kind of specialized labor, which in turn forces us to ask not only what their place was in the agricultural system and the way land was organized, but also how they fit into a sales network, since in this case production would far exceed the needs of a single family. Thus examining the place of livestock raising in ancient Greece comes down to the question of choices of specialization—whether such choices were made, and if they were, how to define them. However, we should keep in mind that specialization does not necessarily imply exclusivity, whether we are concerned with stock-raising *stricto sensu* or with the place of stock raising in the cycle of agricultural production as a whole.

The first constraint weighing on stock raising was the amount of fodder available. The second, which may at first seem less obvious, is the quantity of water, whose consumption is a function of the animal's weight and the temperature. At temperatures higher than 30°C, a bovine weighing 200 kilograms consumes more than thirty liters of water a day, a horse more than fifty liters a day. Sheep and goats can get along with smaller quantities of water, between five and six liters a day, and a pig requires less than ten liters a day. In the driest areas, especially in the islands, a significant reserve of cistern water was necessary to maintain a single ox during the long dry period in summer (a supply for four months—that is, at least 3,600 liters). This means that in these regions, only oxen used as draft animals could be kept year round. On the other hand, calves could be easily raised during the winter and sold for slaughter in the spring: this explains both the small numbers of oxen in the Greek islands in the modern period and the fact that some islands, like Andros, exported oxen.[79] These seasonal rhythms also certainly explain the striking frequency of young and even very young animals (of all species) among the stock slaughtered for meat, as is shown for example by the statistics for animal slaughter in Delos: between the fourth and the first century BCE, between 42 and 50 percent of the animals were slaughtered before they were a year old, and the other half before the age of three.[80]

Thus rainfall was everywhere a specific constraint on stock raising. But this should not be seen in a narrowly deterministic way, as if the map of stock raising directly reflected that of rainfall. Other constraints might be involved, such as competition with agriculture or forestry, which were themselves connected with more or less intense exploitation of the land, the existence of markets for agricultural products, and, not least, the forms of political organization, which could have a significant impact on the kinds of livestock people chose to raise. Thus we can take into account here the three main regional types of stock raising described by Christophe Chandezon.[81] Naturally, we must not try to establish airtight distinctions among them, but we need to outline the main tendencies.

Regional Types

The first great regional type is that of the southern Aegean, including Attika, the Kyklades, and southern Ionia. Stock raising was pursued everywhere in this area, but usually in direct complementarity with agriculture. Except for a few local exceptions (there are some even in the Kyklades), oxen were rarely raised, and flocks of sheep and goats were prevalent. This did not exclude specialization, quite the contrary: Miletos specialized in "covered sheep"—that is, sheep that were covered with a blanket to protect their wool. This made the wool easier to pull out (the sheep were not shorn) and kept it cleaner, producing a fine wool that brought a high price.[82] We can suppose that the proximity of large cities such as Athens also provided very attractive markets for cheese and meat. A good illustration of what an average landowner's strategy might have been is offered by a document dating from 414 BCE that concerns the sale of goods belonging to Panaitios, one of those who profaned the Eleusinian Mysteries:[83]

[Goods] belonging to Panaitios. [. . .] 104 amphoras seven *choes* of pure Attic wine. (Sales tax of) 3 dr. [for a value of] 260 dr., [for] [. . .] beehives on the estate located at Isthmos.

[Sales tax of] 1 dr. 1 ob. [for a value of] 100 dr., [for] two draft oxen at [. . .].

[Sales tax of] 1 dr. 1 ob. [for a value of] 70 dr., [for] two oxen.

[Amounts lost for] four cows and [. . .] calves.

[Amounts lost for] 84 ewes and their lambs.

[Sales tax of] 7 dr. 2 ob. [for a value of] 710 dr., [for] 67 goats and their kids.

It is not certain that all these activities were pursued in the same place. But we can clearly discern a strategy of diversification, since some activities were devoted to producing wine: even if a little more than 41 hectoliters is not a high level of production, it still goes well beyond any form of self-consumption. The presence of a brace of draft oxen probably indicates cereal production, even if the crop was not seized by the city. The presence of two other oxen and four cows with their calves shows an interest in cattle raising, though a very limited one: the long dry periods in summer explain why this kind of stock raising was not more extensive in an area like Attika. That said, despite the small size of the herds, selling cattle for sacrifices could have been very lucrative. The two flocks of 84 ewes with their lambs and 67 goats with their kids are far more numerous. The goats could graze on hills with little grass. The sheep could be raised in conjunction with cereal farming (the sheep grazed on the stubble after the harvest on half of the farm's land[84]). The two flocks of sheep and goats presuppose the existence of a shepherd for each of them. We know that shepherds were usually (but not always) slaves who were specialized in a particular kind of stock raising. We can thus clearly discern here forms of special-ization, raising sheep and goats being prevalent but not excluding other activities, since Panaitios also had vineyards, and probably especially cultivated lands. In the islands, stock raising was necessarily limited because of the prevalence of terrace agriculture. Small animals were dominant. Locally, however, because of more favor-able conditions and especially where animals were kept in stables, cattle raising was not unknown.[85]

The second great regional type covered a wide band extending from Thessaly to Crete and passing by way of central Greece and the Peloponnese, to which we must add the northeast fringes of Asia Minor starting in northern Ionia. In this area, the more humid mountainous zones were generally reserved for flocks of sheep and goats. These *eschatiai* were usually public lands; they belonged to the cities and were therefore available for animal husbandry. Control over low-lying lands and mountain areas made it possible to take the flocks to higher altitudes in the sum-mer, where they could graze on denser grass when the plains were burned by the summer drought. A good example of these large flocks that required vast migration lands is offered by the agreement between the city of Orchomenos and a citizen of Elateia concluded around 230–210 BCE:[86]

Under the archonship of Thynarchos in Orchomenos, in the month of Alal-komenios, and under that of Menoitas son of Archelaos in Elateia, in the first month, an agreement between Eubolos of Elateia and the city of the Orchomenians: given that Eubolos has recovered from the city all he lent it by virtue of the conventions made under the archonship of Thynarchos, in the month of Theilouthios, and that he is no longer owed anything by the city, but considers that it has completely paid its debt, and that those who held the conventions have returned them to the city, let the city grant in addition to Eubolos a period of pasture rights of a duration of four years for two hundred twenty cattle or horses and for a thousand sheep or goats; that this period begins with the year after that of the archonship of Thynarchos in Orchomenos; that each year Eubolos declares in writing to the treasurer and the commissioner for pastures the marks of the sheep, goats, cows, and mares, the possible number of unmarked animals, and how many there are in all; that he does not declare more than what is written in the concession; and if someone reclaims Eubolos's right of pasturage [*ennomion*], the city of the Orchomenians will have to pay Eubolos forty silver minas every year with an interest of three drachms per mina and by month, and that the city of the Orchomenians may be called upon by Eubolos [——].

Eubolos was a man wealthy enough to be able to grant loans to the city of Orchomenos. The size of his flocks is a gauge of his wealth. The agreement mentions 220 cattle or horses and a thousand sheep or goats, which for four years he receives the right to graze for free on the common land of the city of Orchomenos. The precision of the first figure must correspond to data provided by Eubolos himself. In addition, the agreement emphasizes that beyond the numbers mentioned, the right of pasture would no longer be free, which presupposes that the flocks belonging to this important man might have been still larger. Elateia was about twenty kilometers northwest of Orchomenos, and the two cities could easily have been in communication because they were both located in the valley of the Kephisos, a river that flowed into Lake Kopais.

The third regional type was characteristic of the vast migratory areas of western Greece: Akarnania, Aitolia, Epeiros, Upper Macedon, and thus in general the slopes and highlands of the Pindos. In this region, where the system of the *polis* was not well established, political structures of the *ethnos* type were prevalent, corresponding to confederations of cities and villages (as in Aitolia) or to principalities governed by kings (Epeiros and Upper Macedon). The kings themselves might own large flocks: according to Plutarch (*Pyrrhus* 5.5), the steward in charge of the flocks belonging to King Neoptolemos of the Molossians (a tribe in Epeiros) was part of his immediate entourage. The areas controlled by each of these states were all much larger than those controlled by the cities on the Aegean slope, but they were also less populated. Archaeological investigation has revealed sites occupied by these semi-nomadic shepherds whose life can be imagined by means of anthropological parallels.[87] Studies on Sarakatsani and Vlach shepherds in northern Greece during the first half of the twentieth century have shown that there were groups entirely devoted to animal husbandry that had specific structures of solidarity based on kinship and that traded their products with farmers living in the low valleys and the hills.[88] In antiquity, these flocks were used chiefly to produce cheese and especially wool, as is attested by ancient authors.[89] Although their history is rather poorly documented for the Classical and Hellenistic periods, we can be sure that through the intermediary of cities like Kerkyra and Epidamnos, their products might also be found in the markets of the great cities on the Aegean slope of Greece.[90]

These regional types are fundamentally based on climate zones. Besides, one should also take into account differences based on specific institutional developments and constraints. For instance, Athens was not a good area for livestock raising, but it had a significant market for meat, especially for sacrificial meat. In Sparta, the elite was fond of racehorses and of meat, while in Thessaly the aristocratic regime was directly connected to both horse and cattle raising as a source of wealth, prestige and power.[91]

Rangeland Ecology and Management

Should the migration of flocks be considered a form of transhumance? The question was vigorously debated before a realistic view based on a better definition of transhumance was suggested by Christophe Chandezon.[92] If we reserve the term "transhumance" for the great transhumance (which involves the migration of large numbers of animals over long distances), then it is unsuitable to describe ancient Greece. In modern Europe, in the case of the Castilian *mesta* or the Neapolitan *dogana*, or again the annual migrations of flocks of sheep from the banks of the Garonne River to the Pyrenees through the Landes of Gascony, we are dealing with transfers of flocks over several hundred kilometers. In these cases, the sheep were raised for their wool, not their meat (flocks that migrate over long distances produce poorer quality meat). These movements of flocks, which might involve as many as several hundred thousand animals, were thus connected with a great manorial property and with the existence of a large-scale wool industry. They also presupposed the existence of a territorial state that imposed its authority on a vast area, as did Castile in the Iberian Peninsula or Naples in southern Italy. However, it should be stressed that in the long term, the *grande transhumance* is the exception in the Mediterranean world, not the rule (even if great migrations of flocks may also have taken place in Roman Italy of the imperial period).[93] Therefore one cannot maintain that this was necessarily a mode of operation that was more fully realized, more rational than others, as if it represented the "culmination of the pastoral economy." The notion might even obscure our study of the pastoral economy more than it illuminates it. If on the other hand one adopts a truly comparative approach, one can see that, beyond specific features that are not needed to rehearse here, the notion of transhumance invites to enquire into the institutions that govern pastoral life.

In the world of the Greek city-states, access to pastures in the borderlands (usually in mountainous areas) usually presupposed the existence of public lands reserved, unless a special concession had been made, for citizens alone. These were pasturelands belonging directly to the city, but we must emphasize that the demes or sanctuaries might also own pasturelands, just as they might own cultivated lands. Even if this principle is accepted, our information regarding the mode of access to these public lands remains murky. However, a few points emerge clearly. Our sources use the term *epinomia* in referring to the right of access to the cities' common lands.[94] This privilege allowing citizens to graze their flocks on these lands might be granted, on an individual or collective basis, to foreigners: many epigraphic documents from diverse parts of the Greek world (but all of them corresponding to the second type of animal husbandry defined earlier) testify to this fact. On the other hand, it is more difficult to determine whether this right of access was free of cost: in some cases, at least, it is certain that a fee (*ennomion*) was charged (see the text from Orchomenos quoted earlier), whereas in others access seems to have been free.[95] But pastures in the mountains or in borderlands posed institutional difficulties. First, there might be an antagonism between shepherds and farmers. A text from the end of the third century BCE from a very small island in the Kyklades, Herakleia, near Naxos, testifies to this:[96]

> [oath] by Herakles and all the other gods who hold the island under their sway, if his oath is respected, everything goes well, but if he betrays it, the contrary of these advantages; if anyone, resorting to violence to introduce or graze goats on the island in violation of this decree and this oath, kills someone who tries to keep him from doing so, let the victim's family and the whole island community bring him to justice; let everyone pay his share of all expenses connected with the trial; let the *hieropoios* Epistrophides have this decree engraved on a stone stele and placed in the Metroion; let the expenses relating to the stele and the engraving be paid by the public treasury; let these prescriptions permit the safeguarding and salvation of all the Herakleians as well as other residents of the island.

The constraints peculiar to this kind of activity, such as the lack of fodder in certain areas, and temptations such as using the pasturelands of a nearby city in order to keep one's own available for use at the end of the summer, had led since time immemorial to conflicts between shepherds of two neighboring cities.[97] In Homer, we already find Nestor, the son of the king of Pylos, raiding the flocks of his Eleian neighbors (*Iliad* 11.671–89): the incidents degenerated into a genuine war. Frontier incidents and disputes over pasture rights on this or that land, public or sacred, persist throughout Greek history, until the end of the Hellenistic period. They should not be considered an outlandish relic of a distant, "Homeric" past. They testify to the continuing role of animal husbandry as a major source of wealth and prestige in many cities, especially (but not only) in southern and western Greece.[98] As a result of disputes over transhumance routes on Parnassos and the thefts of flocks that had resulted from them, Phokians and Lokrians several times ended up going to war.[99] In the last half of the second century BCE, a prolonged dispute between the two Cretan cities of Hierapytna and Itanos provides another illustration.[100] But encounters between shepherds from different cities did not all lead to conflicts. The key scene in Sophocles *Oedipus the King* (vv. 1132–40) is the one in which two slave shepherds, one from Thebes, the other from Corinth, meet. The latter reminds the former, who pretends not to remember, of the circumstances under which he had handed the infant Oedipus over to him. When Oedipus questions him, the Corinthian answers:[101]

> No wonder he doesn't know me, master.
> But let me refresh his memory for him.
> I'm sure he recalls old times we had
> on the slopes of Mount Kithairon;
> he and I grazing our flocks, he with two
> and I with one—we both struck up together,
> three whole seasons, six months at a stretch
> from spring to the rising of Arktouros in the fall,
> then with winter coming on I'd drive my herds
> to my own pens, and back he'd go with his
> to Laios's folds. Now that's how it was,
> wasn't it—yes or no?

Kithairon was the mountain separating Attika from Boiotia, but it also separated the latter from Megaris. In the heroic times in which this scene is supposed to take place, Corinth may have still controlled what later became the city of Megara and thus it is conceivable that the shepherds from the two cities met on the flanks of this mountain. Sharing the same hard life, it is logical that they would have spent time together the better to endure their isolation. The existence of "territories common" to two cities is thus easily justified, which does not mean that these territories on the borders held in common did not also raise problems.[102] Thus a Rhodian inscription from the end of the third century mentions the *koina chōra*, the territory common to Kamiros and Lindos, concerning which disputes had arisen. Kamiros and Lindos were then part of the state of Rhodes, and it was the court in Rhodes that must have settled the dispute.[103] If the two cities had been independent, it would have been necessary to call in a third state to arbitrate the case. However, we should note that the necessity of sharing resources led the Greeks to find institutional solutions that went beyond the excessively narrow framework of the city.

Thus in Hellenistic Crete, despite incessant conflicts, a series of agreements between cities attests to the concern to find an institutional solution for better use of the lands over which herds passed, especially since in Crete these flocks certainly constituted a larger part of people's patrimonies than they did in cities oriented more toward agriculture. As Angelos Chaniotis has pointed out, we thus have a series of treaties of *isopoliteia* (mutual citizenship rights) that guaranteed reciprocal use of pasturelands depending on the season.[104] These agreements were usually made with neighboring cities, but could *de facto* concern whole regions. Thus on the south side of Crete, in the early third century Hierapytna made an agreement with Priansos, more than forty kilometers to the west, for the common use of pasturelands in Mount Aigion (we must assume that smaller cities lying between the two had been reduced in one way or another to dependent communities). Then, in the first half of the second century, Hierapytna made a pastureland agreement with Praisos, the same distance away but toward the northeast, in the direction of the Dikte mountains. Praisos was itself involved in a rivalry over territory and pastureland with Itanos, at the extreme northeast extremity of the island. We have to conclude that the agreement with Praisos did not suffice to satisfy Hierapytna's ambitions. After having absorbed small communities like Larisa and Oleros, extended its boundaries as far as Minoa, on the north coast of the island, and also absorbed Stalai to the east, in 145 BCE or just afterward Hierapytna destroyed Praisos for good, seized considerable territory in eastern Crete, and took control of the island of Leuke. This led to a conflict between Hierapytna and Itanos, settled only in 112 or 111 BCE after two visits from another Roman commission and an arbitration entrusted to the city of Magnesia on the Maeander: the text of the arbitration shows that what was at stake in the conflict over territory was precisely control over pasturelands on Mount Dikte and the island of Leuke.[105]

It is usually thought that agriculture represented 80 percent of the value produced in ancient Greece, while craftwork and financial and commercial activities together accounted for only 20 percent.[106] This figure cannot be verified, and it probably significantly understates the nonagricultural activities. Nevertheless it remains true that the "Mediterranean trilogy," with its ancillary products and in association with animal husbandry, constituted the bulk of the production of goods in the world of the Greek city-states. However, the view of ancient Greek agriculture and its landscape as an "eternal Mediterranean changeless world" doomed to immobility is proved wrong. Examining the conditions of access to land and its social constraints, along with the question of yields, fully confirms this.

VI

THE ECONOMY OF THE AGRICULTURAL WORLD

The description of agricultural products in the preceding chapter has already shown that Greek agriculture was not static and immutable, but that despite appearances to the contrary, over time this world underwent profound transformations. We must now address the social and technical conditions that both structured the Greek agricultural economy's permanent features and presided over the changes it experienced. This implies examining the structures of real property as well as the system of access to the land. It also supposes to tackle the crucial questions of risk management in an unpredictable environment and of agricultural yields. Were ancient Greek farms autarkic (in the modern sense of the word) and disconnected from the market? Was the form of risk-management of the Greek peasants really only a source of routine and did it block all possible growth? A close examination reveals complex realities that do not fit with the traditional paradigm.

THE STRUCTURES OF REAL PROPERTY

The Distribution of Property

No document from any period provides a complete land registry for a city's property. It is not that no such registers existed; everything indicates that the contrary is true. Like so many others, this kind of document, which was essential to the life of the city but was only rarely engraved on stone, has not been preserved, or only in a very fragmentary state.[1] The image we can form of real property in Greece therefore cannot be very precise, *a fortiori* city by city. Moreover, it is clear that for all sorts of reasons—areas available, types of exploitation (according more or less importance to animal husbandry, grain, or viticulture)—the situation was not the same everywhere, and that for a single region it might change considerably over time. The figures given later must therefore be considered estimates, though they may very well provide a plausible image of reality.

142

Generally less populated and heir to a more aristocratic tradition, western and northern Greece probably had a more inegalitarian system of real property than the Greece of the southern and Aegean city-states, with their more limited *chōrai* and their (on the whole) more egalitarian institutions. The properties held in the cities in Asia Minor were certainly also larger than those on the islands. The question, naturally, is how to make these figures more precise. If we limit ourselves to the framework of the city-state, we must remain aware that unlike later on, during the Roman period, large estates could hardly have consisted (with a few exceptions) of several thousand hectares, simply because in many cases they would then have been larger than the city's total arable land. Very large estates existing here and there must have consisted at most of a few hundred hectares.

As for other properties, we can offer only estimates of their size. In Athens, after 403 BCE (hence after the considerable population decreases due to the Peloponnesian War, and setting aside debates over the level of Attika's population in the fourth century), on the basis of statistical estimates provided by Alison Burford Cooper, we can try to produce a synthetic table of real estate holdings. In Burford Cooper's schema, Athens would have had a little more than 25,000 citizens (25,200 being used as a basis for calculation). However Burford Cooper's figures are somewhat lower than those currently accepted, viz. a population level of ca. 30,000 for the second half of the fourth century BCE.[2] In that case, the number of landless citizens would inevitably reach 10,000. For an arable land area of 750,000 *plethra* (67,500 hectares, or 675 square kilometers out of the 2,000 square kilometers of Attika's total area, or 33 percent), we would have a distribution as shown in table 6.1.[3] The percentages corresponding to both population estimates are mentioned in columns 6 and 7.

These data are based on estimates, of course, but on realistic ones. The 9,200 owners of estates of 4.5 hectares and over may correspond to the 9,000 hoplites who fought at Marathon. We also know that at the end of the fourth century, 12,000 citizens owned at least 30 *plethra* (2.7 hectares) of land and 9,000 owned more than that. We have to understand that the fact that someone did not own land did not necessarily mean that he was a farmworker living in poverty in the countryside. Many citizens who owned no land, or very little, earned their livings in other ways. We see, after all, that 85 percent of the land was held by a good third of the citizen population. If the metics and the many slaves who worked in the mines or various other crafts are taken into account, then it is clear that in the case of Attika, agriculture, even in the fourth century, was not the main sector of activity for a majority of the population. Another specificity of the Athenian case was that the distribution of real property seems to have been less inegalitarian than elsewhere. The farm buildings that have been excavated indicate middle-sized farms, and these may have been characteristic of Attika in the fourth century. The farmhouse at Dema, which was constructed in the fifth century on a site immediately adjacent to the future Dema defensive wall northwest of Athens, and which was occupied only for a short time, was large for Attika, consisting of a rectangular building 21 meters by 15 meters.[4]

TABLE 6.1. Distribution of Landholdings in Attika

NUMBER OF PROPERTIES PER CATEGORY	AVERAGE AREA HELD (IN PLETHRA)	AVERAGE AREA HELD (IN HECTARES)	TOTAL PROPERTIES BY CATEGORY (IN PLETHRA)	TOTAL PROPERTIES BY CATEGORY (IN HECTARES)	PERCENTAGE OF THE CITIZEN POPULATION (25,200)	PERCENTAGE OF THE CITIZEN POPULATION (30,200)	PERCENTAGE OF PROPERTIES HELD
5,000/10,000	0	0	0	0	20	33	0
11,000	10	0.9	110,000	9,900	43.5	36.5	15
8,000	50	4.5	400,000	36,000	31.5	26.5	53
1,200	200	18.2	240,000	21,600	5	4	32

The farmhouse at Vari, an isolated settlement in the deme of Anagyrous (on the coast south of Athens) was more modest: also rectangular, it was 17.7 meters by 13.7 meters.[5] The farmhouses in the deme of Atene (near Sounion) are more or less of similar shape and size.[6] In the classical city-state, a whole group of owners of small and middle-sized properties formed the backbone of the city. Ian Morris considers that the Gini coefficient for landholding in fourth-century Athens was inferior to all but two recent Mediterranean communities studied by anthropologists and to all the ancient Roman communities.[7]

In third-century BCE Thessaly, the city of Pharsalos granted in perpetuity estates of 60 *plethra* (5.4 hectares) to young men who had fought for the city, which proves that even at that date, it was still thought that one could live honorably off that much land, even if naturally there must also have been larger estates.[8] In the cities of Keos, the island closest to Attika, where the average size of estates seems to have been smaller than in Attika, the hierarchy of farm buildings nonetheless suggests the existence of a social hierarchy in the possession of land or access to it.[9] Before the Battle of Leuktra, the Lakedaimonian state, which combined Messenia with Lakonia, covered some 8,500 square kilometers. From this, we have to deduct the territory of the cities of the *perioikoi*. According to estimates that have been put forward, the area under the direct control of the Spartans might have been 135,000 hectares of arable land.[10] According to Herodotus (7.234.2), at the beginning of the fifth century Sparta had 8,000 citizens, all of whom by definition were property owners; 6,500 citizen households owned land (taking into account sons who had not yet inherited land from their fathers); ordinary property owners may have had estates of about 18 hectares, while wealthier ones may have had about 44 hectares. The average size of the properties was thus significantly larger than in Athens.

Land ownership was far less unequally distributed in the Greek city-states than it was in the societies of the Eastern Mediterranean world: that was one of the bases of the city-state. But there was nonetheless a certain inequality. The few examples of the size of estates that we know about, although they are anecdotal, give us some idea of what was considered a small or large estate in classical Greece. As usual, most of our evidence concerns Athens. In the legal speech *On the Estate of Dikaiogenes* (Isaeus 5.22), ca. 389 BCE, an estate of 60 *plethra* (5.4 hectares) is mentioned as of modest value (in fact, this land was only a small part of the late Dikaiogenes' property, the legacy having gone through several versions). In the second quarter of the fifth century BCE, the city of Athens apparently gave Lysimachos, the son of Aristeides, an estate in Euboia consisting of 100 *plethra* of planted land (with vineyards and olive groves) and 100 *plethra* of uncultivated land, for a total of 18 hectares.[11] This estate corresponds more or less to the estimated size (180 *plethra* or 16 hectares) of the "farm of Timesios" in the mining sector of southern Attika, which is identified by several inscriptions on the site.[12] In the late fifth century, Alkibiades' estate in the deme of Erchia was not quite 300 *plethra*, or 27 hectares.[13] The property of the politician Aristophanes, acquired by him shortly after 394 and confiscated by the Athenian state in 389, also amounted to 300 *plethra* (27 hectares).[14]

The size of the estate owned by Phainippos, a great Athenian landlord, has been interpreted in contradictory ways. We have some information about this estate thanks to *Against Phaenippus* (42), a legal speech in the Demosthenes corpus that seems to have been written before 330 BCE, so far as we can tell, and in any case during a period of high prices. The estate was located in the deme of Kytheros (42.5). Unfortunately, the location of the deme of Kytheros is unknown (it might have been located in the coastal territory of Attika, the *Paralia*, but this location is not certain).[15] An interesting parallel is however provided by the deme of Erchia, in the rich territory of the Mesogaia, where Alkibiades had his property, and which was also the deme of elite people like Isocrates and Xenophon.[16] Thus it is worth comparing the latter's description of this estate (*Economics* 11.15–18), where people rode horses to train for warfare—not, in theory, to get around—with the malicious allusions in the Demosthenic speech to the attitude of Phainippos, who was alleged to have sold his warhorse (42.24). Auguste Jardé thought the estate comprised 300 to 390 hectares, while Finley thought it comprised between 280 and 400 hectares.[17] On the other hand, according to Geoffrey de Ste. Croix it covered only 40 hectares.[18] His interpretation has been widely criticized, but this low figure is the one that now seems to be used in all the analyses of land ownership in Attika that determine our notion of what constituted a large estate in the city of Athens.[19] The property is known to us through a legal speach for an "exchange of property" (*antidosis*), a procedure peculiar to Attic law that made it possible to sue someone who was considered to be wealthier and on whom the city had nevertheless not imposed the obligation of paying for a "liturgy" (a public service that was supposed to be paid for by people owning substantial property). If the court decided in favor of the plaintiff, an exchange of properties was made, naturally on the condition that the new holder of the property considered to be larger paid for the liturgy in question.[20] According to certain interpretations, only the liturgical obligation was exchanged, not the properties, but this view contradicts what we read in *Against Phaenippus* (42.19), where the exchange of properties is explicitly provided for. The plaintiff certainly had an interest in showing that his adversary's property was very large, but his description could not be completely unrealistic, because if he won his case and the value of the new property turned out to be very inferior to what he said it was, he had engineered his own loss.[21]

Thus the description of Phainippos's wealth may embellish things, but cannot be unrelated to reality. His property is mentioned in Pseudo-Demosthenes' speech (*Against Phaenippus* 42.5) in terms of its circumference: more than forty *stadia*, or more than seven kilometers. The statement is vague. A surface area expressed in terms of *plethra* would have made it possible to know the actual extent of the estate. We can suppose that the estate was all of one piece, but as de Ste. Croix points out, nothing indicates that its boundaries described a regular figure—it would in fact be astonishing if they did. But it may also be that a simple statement in terms of surface area would have been very insufficient to describe the value of the estate, which depended on the way it was used. The figure of "more than forty stadia," as vague as it is, nonetheless gives us a valuable clue. Let us adopt it as a first hypothesis. If the estate was square, its area would have been more than 315 hectares, which is the maximum size that can be attributed to it. That is what justifies the high estimates that have been proposed. But the production figures advanced by the plaintiff allow us to form a more precise idea of Phainippos's estate, at least such as it was seen by his adversary. According to the latter, the estate produced 1,000 *medimnoi* of barley (*Against Phaenippus* 42.20) or, at 27 kilograms the *medimnos*, a total of 27,000 kilograms. On the basis of an average productivity in Attika of 700 kilograms per hectare (a generous figure), we can thus conclude that this production required 38.6 hectares—that is, about forty hectares.[22] Naturally, however, production had to take place on the basis of a system of biennial crop rotation, which shows that Phainippos's estate had about 80 hectares devoted to growing grain.

Phainippos's estate also produced at least 800 *metrētai* of wine, or about 315 hectoliters. On the basis of an average productivity of 30 hectoliters per hectare, his vineyard must have covered about 10 hectares.[23] Between the barley and the grapevines, Phainippos's estate thus could not have had less than 90 hectares of cultivated land. But this kind of operation also needed several pairs of oxen—at least four of them for 40 hectares in barley. The need to spread manure on both the land planted in grapevines (which requires a great deal of fertilizer) and the land planted in grain presupposes the presence of a flock of sheep. As we have seen, the parallel with other farms in Attika that we know about shows that this was a common situation. The estate thus also must have had less fertile lands for grazing livestock. Phainippos's adversary also claimed (42.24) that he raised horses. We know (42.7) that the estate had areas of fallow land and shrubland, probably in the hilly parts, since—still according to his adversary—every day he sent six asses loaded with firewood to the agora, and this firewood brought in 12 drachms a day. To the 90 hectares of cultivated land we must thus add an indeterminable area of pasture for the horses, grazing lands for a flock of sheep, and a shrubland area from which firewood could regularly be taken. Hence it seems reasonable to add to the cultivated land at least 20 to 30 hectares. What could be described as Phainippos's "virtual estate" therefore consisted of at least 110 to 120 hectares.

What was the real extent of Phainippos's estate? It is difficult to say precisely. De Ste. Croix pointed out letters of credit in the amount of 1 talent 4,000 drachms. The securities taken in the case of a loan of this kind were at least twice the value of the loan.[24] Thus the property was worth at least 3 talents 2,000 drachms—but not much more, according to de Ste. Croix. While recognizing the futility of any calculation of the price of land by unit of area, for we cannot know the current rates and the precise value of Phainippos's property, de Ste. Croix proposes the figure of 40 hectares. He was certainly right to emphasize the rhetorical character of the plaintiff's statements. But even though they were made under oath, should we believe Phainippos's own claim that the volume of his harvests was not even a tenth of the amount alleged by his adversary (42.24)? The latter formally accused Phainippos of having broken the seals put on his estate in order to remove produce (see 42.1–9 and 19).

Finally, de Ste. Croix's figure of 40 hectares is not based on any positive evidence but only on a "reasonable estimate." It is merely one of the possible figures. In describing Phainippos's "virtual" property, which as we have seen cannot have consisted of less than 110 to 120 hectares, the plaintiff was clearly engaging in exaggeration. But how great an exaggeration? That is what it seems impossible to determine.

This conclusion may seem disappointing, but we must add two observations. According to Phainippos's adversary, the latter controlled not a single *oikos* (patrimonial property), but two: that of his father and that of his adoptive father (42.21). In theory, this kind of double inheritance was illegal. But if this may be why Phainippos was able to have such a vast estate (for in the contrary case we might wonder how he had managed up to that point to escape paying for more expensive liturgies). The second observation is that although we cannot prejudge the actual size of Phainippos's estate, the plaintiff would not have been able to claim such high production figures before the court unless they had some plausibility, which supposes that other landowners really had properties as large as Phainippos's "virtual estate," and perhaps even larger. Although he does not name a specific figure, Aristotle (*Constitution of Athens* 27.3) mentions that in the fifth century Cimon, the famous political leader, had a "fortune comparable to that of a tyrant" (*ousia turrhanikē*). Cimon's land was not fenced, and he let all the members of his deme, Lakiades, pick his fruit.[25] Such a property makes us think of a latifundian estate rather than a property of only a few dozen hectares. Even if they were very much in the minority, large estates thus existed, even in Attika. In the Boiotian city of Thespiai in the third century, we know of an estate of 540 *plethra*—that is, supposing that the *plethron* had the same value as at Athens, an area of a little more than 50 hectares.[26] We have also seen the extent of Eubolos of Elateia's flocks, more than 220 cattle or horses and more than 1,000 sheep:[27] even if he was obviously looking for cheap grazing lands on the territory of neighboring cities, it seems that his own estate must have consisted of more than 200 hectares of grazing lands.

This information relating to three different cities, Athens, Thespiai, and Elateia forces us to remain circumspect regarding the size of estates in the Classical period and the early Hellenistic period. It is true that the existence of small and middle-sized properties was a basic social fact. But at the same time, it should be emphasized that there was also a limited social stratum of very wealthy landlords who had estates consisting of at least fifty hectares, and sometimes of considerably more than one hundred hectares. This analysis obliges us to return to the case of Sparta. Let us suppose that around 480 BCE Sparta had about 8,000 citizens. With a body of citizens that was at least five times smaller at the beginning of the fourth century, assuming that less wealthy landowners still had estates of around eighteen hectares, the average size of the estates of the wealthiest Spartans must necessarily have been around two hundred hectares. To be sure, after the Battle of Leuktra, Sparta lost Messenia and everyone who owned land in Messenia was to that extent impoverished. But the new decrease in the number of citizens and the intensification of the inequality of land ownership among Spartans forces us to see that in the third century, what was at stake in revolutionary struggles was the dividing-up not of middle-sized estates of a few dozen hectares but rather of estates of several hundred hectares in the case of the richest Spartans (or perhaps even several thousands of hectares in the case of the elite of the elite). With the ulterior motive of reestablishing Sparta's military power and reconstituting a class of landowning peasants, the objective of the social struggles was thus to destroy the latifundian system that has been set up in order to return to much more modest properties of ten to twenty hectares, or thirty to forty hectares at most—which had not existed in Sparta since the beginning of the Classical period.

The Size of the Estates

Can we discern a development in the size of properties? It does seem that in the long term, there was a tendency toward growth. But this is not an obvious fact, a "natural evolution," as it were. It is a fact of a completely historical nature. Not that it should be believed, as it was for a long time, that in Athens the Peloponnesian War was followed by a "generalized impoverishment"—this old claim, which has no foundation in the sources, was famously debunked by Finley.[28] The fact is that in the democratic city-state, or at least in the run-of-the-mill city-states of the Classical period (not all of which were democratic), land ownership was relatively widely distributed (which does not mean that it was egalitarian, as we have seen in the case of Athens). In the Hellenistic period, however, there was a definite tendency toward a concentration of land ownership in fewer hands. The reasons for this are first of all political. In his campaigns in Asia Minor, Alexander presented himself as the restorer of democracy. In the same way, the Hellenistic kings might have believed that they were defending the freedom of the city-states. The reality was otherwise. Hellenistic democracy, although it provided a form of popular participation, came to be more synonymous with a "regime that functioned in accord with law, without personal tyrannical power" than with a democracy considered to be "extreme" like the Athenian democracy. The Macedonian victory and the establishment of direct or indirect monarchical domination over the world of the city-states was also a victory for wealthy landowners.

A clear case of this is provided by Athens, where in 322 BCE, under the rule of Phokion, civil rights were limited to property owners who had a fortune of at least 2,000 drachms. As a result, the number of active citizens dropped from 21,000 to 9,000.[29] Many citizens were sent to Thrace as colonists.[30] In 317, under the rule of Demetrios of Phaleron, the amount was reduced to 1,000 drachms.[31] As for real property, whereas archaeological surveys reveal a "saturated" Attika in the fourth century, the situation was certainly different in the following period. We find a decrease in the number of sites, but a considerable augmentation of the size of farm buildings, which moreover henceforth included several buildings and possibly a large enclosed courtyard. Thus in Mesogaia, the rich plain located east of Attika (beyond the Hymettos mountain range), excavations have revealed one of these large Hellenistic farm complexes, including a wine-press.[32] At the end of the century, in 217 BCE, King Philip V of Macedon complained that the territory of the city of Larisa in Thessaly was poorly developed and that twice he had to demand that new citizens be registered so that the land was not left fallow.[33] Maybe he was acting for strategic reasons, because he preferred to see his lands producing grain rather than used for grazing flocks belonging to great landowners. As an explanation for this, we may suppose (as a plausible hypothesis, not a certainty) that in Larisa there had been a tendency to constitute large estates, even though this left part of the territory fallow.

The kings made land grants of considerable proportions to members of their families and their friends. These grants were not made in southern Greece, where the interventions of the kings who were Alexander's heirs still remained indirect. In northern Greece, in contrast, where they had complete control, the kings of Macedon were able to manipulate territories as they wished. As already mentioned, several donations of the early Hellenistic period allow us to gain a better appreciation of the size of large estates in this period.[34] In 285/4 BCE, near the new city of Kassandreia, Lysimachos granted properties with a total surface of 2,480 *plethra* (223 hectares), including 360 *plethra* (32.4 hectares) southwest of the former city of Olynthos, 1,200 *plethra* (108 hectares) near Sermylia, and 900 *plethra* (81 hectares) near Strepsa "planted in trees." Antiochos I made various gifts to his "friend" (a member of his court and close advisor) Aristodikides of Assos, probably between 277 and 261 BCE. Aristodikides received several properties in the Troad with a total area of 5,500 *plethra* of land, or around 495 hectares (or perhaps only 3,500 *plethra*, or around 315 hectares).[35] At the same time, another friend of the king, Athenaios, received an estate of 1,500 *plethra* (135 hectares) in the same region.[36] To be sure, these were estates taken from the royal lands, not from the *chōra* of Greek city-states, and they were supposed to be cultivated by *laoi*, peasants collectively bound to the land. But even in the Troad, hence in a region of the Aegean coast where many Greek or Hellenized cities had been established, we see that the king's power weighed heavily on both the land and the civic system.

First, the kings subjected the region to profound manipulations: thus around 310 BCE, Antigonos I Monophthalmos founded a new city on the coast, which was refounded by Lysimachos a decade later under the name of Alexandria Troas. The city included a large part of the central Troad and later underwent several amputations and enlargements.[37] In the dossier relating to the donations made to Aristodikides, Antiochos's first letter shows that Aristodikides received the right to annex the first land he received to the city of his choice, and that he had chosen the city of Ilion. Thus, voluntarily or involuntarily—it was under the Seleukids' complete control—Ilion found its civic territory considerably expanded. But above all, it henceforth had within its territory a great landowner who himself swung considerable weight. The case of Aristodikides can be compared with that of the lands Antiochos II sold in 254/3 to Queen Laodike, the village of Pannos and the *laoi* peasants that lived there.[38] This estate was on the borders of the cities of Zeleia and Kyzikos, on the Hellespont (at a later date, Kyzikos was to absorb Zeleia).[39] Laodike received the right to attach all or part of the estate to the city of her choice. This new situation could not fail to have political and economic consequences of the first order. It is likely that great landowners could hope in one way or other to free themselves from the restraints imposed on ordinary citizens by laws regarding imports and exports, *a fortiori* because they were backed by the king's full authority.

Recent excavations in Macedon have revealed large farm complexes from the end of the fourth century and the Hellenistic period.[40] These farm complexes were very imposing. Three of them deserve particular attention.

The first is on the site of modern Komboloi, on the territory of ancient Leibethra, immediately east of Olympos and quite near the coast.[41] Various remains suggest the presence of isolated buildings from the middle of the fourth century. But a large farm complex was constructed on the same site in the second half of the fourth century. It consisted of two main buildings: one large, square structure 28.5 meters on a side, and immediately adjacent to it on the west, a vast cellar measuring 19.5 by 19.5 meters. The whole complex thus covered almost 1,200 square meters (courtyards included). The cellar, with its *pithoi* found on the site, proves that the farm was mainly involved in wine-growing. In addition to numerous sherds of black-varnished drinking vases, excavation revealed a number of iron tools (shovels, two-pronged hoes, shears, billhooks, sickles, and so on) that show that the farm was well-equipped. The site also produced about 220 ancient coins, most of them apparently from the end of the fourth century and the beginning of the third century BCE (Philip II, Alexander III, Kassandros, Demetrios Poliorketes, and also coins from cities in Macedon, Thessaly, and Akarnania). The farm seems to have been destroyed in the early third century, probably during the Keltic invasion, and only partly restored afterward, the last traces of occupation dating from the second century.

Still to the east of Olympos, on the site of modern Tria Platania, on the territory of ancient Herakleion, another farm complex has the same profile.[42] It was even more impressive, with its vast rectangular building of 55 by 42.5 meters, an internal courtyard with a central tower in the middle, and a total area (including the internal courtyard) of almost 2,400 square meters. During the first phase of its occupation, there was also a cellar with sixteen *pithoi* or pits for *pithoi*. The farm also had a pottery kiln. The coins (106, most of them bronze, but also some silver ones dating from the time of Philip and Alexander) go as far as the reign of Philip V (the time of the site's destruction), but they are concentrated in the early Hellenistic period (48 bronze coins issued by Kassandros prior or posterior to his accession to the throne). The archaeological material resembles that found in Komboloi. Also constructed in the second half of the fourth century and probably destroyed during the Keltic invasion, the farm was, however, partially reoccupied, and converted to olive oil production.

Finally, southwest of Amphipolis, along the coast in the direction of Chalkidike, near ancient Pennana and on the site of modern Liotopi Routscheli, excavations have revealed the existence of a large complex located on the slopes of Mount Kerdyllion.[43] After an initial phase of occupation during which it resembled the farm at Vari in Attika, it was considerably enlarged and took the form of a large, square tower, while three adjacent courtyards enclosed by additional buildings and by walls completed the complex. The chronology of the site can be determined by means of the coins found there, which range from the reign of Philip II to the end of the reign of Antigonos Gonatas (239 BCE) or shortly thereafter. A great deal of pottery was found on the site, but it does not allow us to determine the main agricultural activity pursued there. On the other hand, in the first phase of its occupation, a large ironworks was operated on the site, with three furnaces and a workshop for making tools. The ore must have come from nearby Mount Kerdyllion.

These large Macedonian farms reveal a manorial type of production totally different from what is found in Attika at the same period, and they can only have been owned by members of the Macedonian power elite. They allow us to give a concrete meaning to the gifts of estates made by the kings.[44] That the two farms located at the foot of Mount Olympos made wine for export is all the more clear because there was nearby, in Herakleion, a workshop for making amphoras directly related to the type of amphoras that came from Mende. This workshop was active from the end of the fifth century to the second half of the fourth century.[45] The presence of numerous coins also shows that the farms participated in monetized commercial networks. Thus the size of these farms and what they did makes them very different from the farms of southern Attika in the Classical period, which seem very mediocre in comparison. It is also significant that these massive investments date from the period when the Macedonians had considerable sources of revenue after subjugating Thrace and Greece and seizing the Persian king's enormous reserves of precious metals. The many hoards of gold staters and silver tetradrachms buried in this period testify of an exceptional abundance of precious coinage.[46] It is no less revelatory that after the catastrophic invasion of the Kelts in 279, resources were not available to restore several of these estates, because the means that had been available earlier were available no longer.

When the Greek world came under Roman control, large estates were increasingly established in Greece proper. Sulla gave Archelaos, King Mithridates' friend and general, an estate of 10,000 *plethra*, or 900 hectares, which had certainly been confiscated after the Battle of Orchomenos in late 86 BCE (Plutarch *Sylla* 23.2).[47] Of more than anecdotal value, gifts of this size reveal another change with regard the preceding period. Beyond such land grants, Rome's seizure of control over the Aegean Greek world at the end of the second century and the beginning of the first century BCE was the origin of a new trend toward the concentration of land ownership that directly prefigures that of the new Greece dominated by Rome during the imperial period.[48]

Access to Land and Farming Systems

Access to land must be distinguished from working it. Private landowners could either work their land themselves or have it worked by someone else. It was a choice left to them. But as a rule, in the framework of the Greek city-state land held collectively (land belonging to the city, a sanctuary, a deme, a phratry, or various kinds of associations) was never worked directly by the owners (that is, using salaried workers or slaves), differing in this from the system prevalent not only in the East Mediterranean but in pre-Greek Asia Minor. Such lands were systematically leased out, at least if it was decided that they should be cultivated. This qualification is justified by the religious implications of the ban to put certain lands under cultivation, as in the case of the sacred land (*orgas*) belonging to two goddesses in Eleusis, or of that in Delphi, whose cultivation by the Phokians served as a pretext for the Third Holy War.[49] It is through leases made by collective entities like sanctuaries and demes, and often engraved on stone, that we are informed about the legal form of these contracts.[50] They either provide laconic hints or reveal genuine contracts for working the land, as is the case in Attika or the deme of Amos (in the Rhodian Peraia).[51] The lease was always payable in money, never in kind. The size of the properties leased out might vary considerably, as we see through the leases from Thespiai in Boiotia.[52] The cost of the leases ranges from 6 drachms (no doubt for a simple garden) to 1,450 drachms (for a large property). However, with that exception, the leases run from 6 to 375 drachms, most of them being between 50 and 100 drachms, which thus corresponds to modest-sized properties, though some lessees rented several pieces of land. Unfortunately, we cannot determine how representative the documents we possess are. *A fortiori*, we cannot know in the case of individual farms how much of the land was owned and how much leased, why, or where. However, given the modest size of most of the lands leased, we have to conclude that they were merely supplementary.

In ancient Greece, there were in general two ways of acceding to land ownership: either by inheritance, which must have constituted most patrimonies, or by purchase, including in Sparta, even if procedures there were probably less transparent than in Athens. Inheritance usually being egalitarian between male siblings (see the following for the gender imbalance), the result was a fragmentation of land ownership. Even in colonial cities, where archaeology reveals allotments that were apparently initially egalitarian, there is no doubt that over time these *klēroi* were subjected to repeated divisions.[53] The fragmentation of parcels was obviously the rule. Thus owning ten hectares normally did not mean that one had a contiguous estate of that size, but four, five, or even more parcels, depending on the family's history and the number of children in successive generations.

With regard to purchase and sale of lands, one conception has long been dominant: because land must have been a good that was transmitted exclusively by inheritance, there could not have been a real estate market.

However, our documentation increasingly contradicts that hypothesis, and the mobility was obviously much greater than previously supposed. New documents show that in all regions lands changed hands, sometimes for considerable sums. In Hellenistic Macedon, for instance in Mieza of Bottiaia, a single individual bought four different lands totaling at least 32 hectares at a price of more than four talents.[54] The same thing occurred in Athens as in Macedon or Chalkedon, in Tenos as in Thessaly, and even in Sparta.[55] In the case of Sparta, in fact, there is no reason to doubt the existence of Epitadeus's law reported by Plutarch (*Agis* 5.1–4), which authorized land cessions.[56] Even if in Plutarch the story is embellished to give it a moralizing quality, the case is nonetheless a good example of institutional development. To be sure, for lack of sufficient data we cannot establish the price curves for land, or, *a fortiori*, compare prices in different regions.[57] Not only were the purchase and sale of lands common, but they might lead to speculative operations. The father of Xenophon's Ischomachos (*Economics* 20.22–29) got rich by purchasing lands that were fallow or in poor condition, hence at a low price, and then, once the land had been made suitable for cultivation, reselling them at a much higher price (he says "many times more dearly," but this should probably not be taken literally). Xenophon adds that some people did the same thing with houses. He compares this quest for profit with that of merchants who go wherever profit is to be found. Thus all the evidence shows that there was a genuine real estate market in ancient Greece.

This question is connected with that of the distribution of property along gender lines. As for property owned by women, there is not a single model but several. In Athens, women were not allowed to own land, if not *de jure* at least *de facto*. This is the well-known model requiring that at the time of her marriage an Athenian woman receive a dowry in the form of movable property (money, jewels, blankets, and other valuable objects), but apart from exceptional cases, not land.[58] But in Sparta, at least until the revolutionary changes at the end of the third century, women had broad access to land ownership. Aristotle mentions that in his time— that is, in the second half of the fourth century—women owned two-fifths of the land. Regarding the situation prevalent a century later, Plutarch tells us that women owned most of the land in the city.[59] In fact, large estates, and above all property held by women, was the chief issue in the revolutionary tensions of the third century. The goal was to make Sparta a "normal city," where women would own only a small share of the land. In reality, the tensions aroused by the inequality of wealth thus coincided with tensions between the genders, all the bitterness being concentrated on women. It is possible that with the accession of Nabis and after the acute tensions of the preceding decades, the question of the social role of women found its "solution" in Sparta. In Gortyn, women were entitled to a third of their parents' property, not including flocks and houses in the city.[60] In Larisa in Thessaly, a land register from ca. 200 shows lands corresponding to an area of about four square kilometers. Women—10 out of 42 landowners, or 24 percent—owned 735.5 *plethra* out of a total of 2,274.9, or 26.6 percent.[61] On the island of Tenos at the end of the fourth century or at the beginning of the fifth century, in a register of land transactions covering a century and a half, women are involved in 37 out of a total of 80 transactions (46 percent).[62] On Tenos, dowries could consist in land as well as in money, which marks a clear difference from Athens. But on Tenos as elsewhere, the question is how to determine women's real autonomy, since they always appear, at least formally, under the authority of a tutor (*kurios*).[63]

As for the land-tenure structures, the world of the cities of Aegean Greece between the end of the Archaic period and the end of the Hellenistic period is not a uniform whole. To provide for their families, owners of small farms needed to have another activity. They had to hire out as agricultural workers or live from their craftwork. In the same way, the situation of the peasant working his own land on the Hesiodic model differs from that of the wealthier landowner, and even more from that of the great landlord. The uniform image of peasants consuming what they produced is not entirely wrong, although consuming what one produced did not mean a complete break with the market. The fact that they left to do business in town, or to serve the city, suggests that they had at least one worker—usually a slave (as already observed, Hesiod's peasant had several), necessarily bought at the market—who helped them in their work. The situation of the great landlords must have been different again. For many of the latter, political obligations and their own activities (finance, mining) meant that not only did they not engage in farming themselves, but of course necessarily left it to stewards to run their farms. Pericles had a meticulous treasurer who managed the finances of his household and thus freed him from all the accounting tasks.[64] He probably also had good stewards on his estates. An anecdote about the scientist and politician Archytas, a contemporary of Plato, shows that not everyone was so lucky: "Coming home from the war (he was at that time a *stratēgos*) and finding his land lying fallow, Archytas of Taras [Taranto] summoned his steward and told him 'You would regret this if I were not too angry.'"[65] The proportion of workers who were subject to a form of forced labor was necessarily much greater: Spartan helots, and other dependents with the same status in Crete, slave-chattels in the cities of a type resembling Athens, and dependent *laoi* in Asia Minor.

The strategies of land exploitation were also a function of the kind of residence. An interesting debate has recently developed regarding the form of the settlement. Security constraints and parallels in modern Mediterranean Europe (especially in southern Italy) might suggest a grouped settlement, excluding settlement in the form of isolated farms. On a territory of about 2,400 square kilometers, Athens had 139 demes, most of which were scattered over the territory, only a small number of them being in the cities of Athens and Piraeus. Naturally, it is therefore not a matter of imagining a grouped settlement exclusively in cities. The point at issue is whether settlement was grouped in villages supposed to have been four or five kilometers apart all over the territory.[66] To this problem, we must add that there even existed a hierarchy among grouped settlements: aside from Eleusis and the communities clustered around it, there were also large villages such as Dekeleia, Acharnai, Marathon, Rhamnous, and Sounion. But we still do not know about dozens of other villages and hamlets on the territory. According to Nicholas Jones's statistics, out of 266 boundary stones found in Attika (Classical and early Hellenistic period), 186 indicate mortgaged lands of the *chōrion* type (rural property, fields) or the *oikia/oikēma* type (construction, building), terms that may appear alone or in conjunction (table 6.2).[67]

TABLE 6.2. Distribution of Estate Types in Attic Boundary Stones

KIND OF MENTION	CHŌRION ALONE	OIKIA / OIKĒMA ALONE	CHŌRION + OIKIA / OIKĒMA
Gross number	66	62	58
Percentage	35.5	33.5	31

Naturally, the term *oikēma* might seem applicable to an isolated farm building on the land that did not serve as a residence, or even a temporary residence, as has been thought. According to Jones, the fact that all the boundary stones of the second type (*oikia* or *oikēma* alone) come from cities (Athens, Piraeus) or (a few) from large villages—essentially those mentioned earlier—suggests that village settlements did not exist. In addition to the testimony of a few literary sources, the excavations of farms conducted in Attika confirm, as we have seen, the existence of genuine farmhouses in the countryside. Should we go so far as to conclude that most of the Attic demes had no true center in the form of a village? This might be a conclusion that would require confirmation, since the existence of village sites has been proven in the demes of Halai Aixonidai (on the coast south of Phaleron), Anagyrous (Vari, slightly east of the preceding deme), and Thorikos.[68] Generally speaking, it is better to refer to the existence of a mixed settlement pattern that might vary depending on the period and the subregion, even within Attika.

In the case of other cities—for example, Rhodes—references to isolated farms in literary sources leaves no doubt that they existed. Thus in 305/4 BCE, during the famous siege of Rhodes, Demetrios Poliorketes pillaged the farms (*epauleis*) on the territory of Ialysos.[69] Letters by Pseudo-Aeschines (9.1–2 and 12.11–12) mention the territory of Amos, in the Rhodian Peraia. These letters were not written by Aeschines. But tradition informs us that Demosthenes' famous adversary had retired to Rhodes, and it was tempting to attribute a correspondence to him. The interest of this document is that the author, obviously a Rhodian, was well acquainted with the places he was writing about. The letters give a vivid description of the rural landscape around Amos, with olive trees, numerous vineyards, sowed fields (grain or legumes?) and fine pastures. The buildings are in ruins, but "Aeschines" is preparing to rebuild them. He hopes to settle there with his family, two of his friends, and seven *therapōntes*, no doubt slave servants. The existence of the village of Amos thus did not exclude dispersed settlement in the form of large farmhouses built in the middle of estates. In the continental territories controlled by Rhodes north of the Keramic Gulf, which were part of what is conventionally known as "subject Peraia," we find a network of small towns, a few houses, and possibly a tower (with agricultural facilities such as oil presses), but also isolated, fortified farmhouses.[70] In other words, we must not reduce the form of rural occupation to a single type. In this case, we must also take into account development over time. The old form of settlement (Karian—but chronology is at least as pertinent a factor as "ethnic group") seems to have been a group of houses on an elevated site. Then, starting in the fourth century and the Hellenistic period, we see rural settlement becoming more dense, with the emergence of hamlets and fortified farmhouses.

In neighboring Lykia, the systematic survey of Kyaneai has proved that the model of an agro-town, with a population mainly concentrated in the city center, is not valid.[71] In Roman times, the city center concentrated perhaps no more than 15 percent of the total population. The vast majority of the population lived in the 6 villages, 71 hamlets, and 215 farms on the territory. In Roman times, more secure conditions may have increased the high number of isolated farms. But per se this was not a new phenomenon. The estimates for the total population are in a range of 3,775–6,200.[72] But these numbers are far above the 1,640 inhabitants of the same area in 1985. They also reveal a systematic exploitation of a territory where soils were relatively poor and unattractive.

Thus the problem of development in rural areas does not have to do solely with technical data. To be sure, the interest of a dispersed settlement pattern is clear. It made it possible to avoid having to travel too far to reach the fields. But, and perhaps especially, in the context of a slave economy the system had the advantage of allowing closer supervision of the workforce, which literally lived under the eye of the master or his steward. In this way, it was possible to demand the maximum from the workers and at the same time avoid theft, fraud, and even sabotage (very understandable for a workforce laboring under constraint and without any reward other than that of its own survival). Farms with towers were the symbol of these productive units that marked the rural landscape. They are not specific to a particular period or region. In the Hellenistic period, they sometimes reached considerable heights, fifteen meters or more.[73] They were frequently part of heavily fortified complexes that testify to the ambient insecurity but also to the owners' wealth. It is tempting to adopt the recent hypothesis according to which the towers are supposed also to have served to keep under surveillance and confine the numerous slaves working on the estates.[74] In any case, the towers show the density of rural settlement, whose regional variants also illustrate the diversity of strategies for making use of the land.[75]

PERMANENCE, RISK, AND CHANGES

Uncertainty, Risk, and the Choice of Products

Every agricultural product involves a specific risk. For animal husbandry, it may be epidemic diseases, which can, in the absence of vaccination, wipe out an immense herd in a few days. The Greeks attributed these to Apollo, as they did epidemics that struck humans.[76] They could not be fought in any way and had to simply run their natural course. Even bees could get diseases, for which Columella (9.3.4 and 9.13.1–14) proposes remedies whose efficacy seems not to have been guaranteed.

In the case of vineyards, there was in addition a risk of frost or hail. But the processes of vinification could also run serious risks.[77] By experience, it had been learned that fermentation led to rising temperatures that could prematurely halt the increase in alcohol content and also made it more likely that the wine would spoil (as a result of the proliferation of bacteria that transformed the wine into vinegar). This risk was partly avoided by burying the storage jars (*pithoi*), by picking overly ripe grapes to facilitate an increase in alcohol content, and finally by regularly cleaning the jars. But our sources show that a large part, or even most, of the grape harvest might be lost.[78]

The essential characteristic of Greek agriculture was that it had to cope with a very uncertain climate.[79] Of course, climatic variability also exists in oceanic systems, and other factors besides rainfall can influence production: an excess of rainfall in the spring or in early summer can make the crops rot, and excessive cold can destroy the seed sowed for winter cereal crops. However, rainfall is much more aleatory in the Mediterranean system. In addition, in the arid part of Greece (that is, the Aegean slope, the islands, and part of the coast of Asia Minor), rainfall can be so low that it causes cereal production to decrease dramatically. The risk of excess rainfall or cold does not exist in Greece, except for certain mountain regions (on the other hand, it was a real problem for the colonies on the north coast of the Euxine). While Mediterranean agriculture is not the only one that has to deal with climatic fluctuations, in relation to the Atlantic system the true difference is that the level of production is characterized by much greater variation.

For example, in Athens there is a 28 percent chance (or almost one in three) that the level of precipitation will be too low to permit a wheat harvest. Here we encounter a level of uncertainty so high that it discouraged the production of wheat. Moreover, we must emphasize that even a level of precipitation between 300 and 400 millimeters was far from being optimal. This explains why Attika produced far more barley than any other cereal.[80] Only in the northern parts of Attika, where rainfall was significantly higher, could farmers afford to raise wheat. We must also stress that it is not only the overall rainfall that matters here, but also its distribution. To ensure that grain will grow, one needs rains both in the fall and in the spring. If the total annual rainfall comes in one season, for example in autumn or early winter, and if the spring is completely dry, the seeds may not sprout well and the harvest will be very small. More generally, these are the diverse factors that explain why the yields of the main agricultural products in the Mediterranean area fluctuate between 30 and 50 percent, depending on the year.

This extreme variability and the total unpredictability of the climate are fundamental to the strategies that seek to limit uncertainty.[81] They operate at two levels: at the individual level and at the collective level. Insofar as they have a direct impact on production, it is the individual strategies that will be examined here, collective strategies involving, on the other hand, all the regulations regarding the cities' external trade. In addition, we have to keep in mind that although they had to cope with the same situation, a peasant living off his land and a great landlord for whom land was an investment could not adopt the same strategies. Once we have registered that qualification (whose importance we will see later), it is not an exaggeration to say that such strategies have been developed by all the peasants of the traditional Mediterranean world, especially by Greek peasants, and more by those in the Aegean area than by those in western Greece, which is on average much more humid.

The peasants' primary objective was to ensure a minimum subsistence level harvest, whatever it might be, and to prepare for the possibility of a bad harvest the following year. To do that, the basic strategy consisted in providing for a systematic diversification of the crops so as not to be dependent on a single product. This supposed also that the peasants had to make the best possible use of the labor force available in order to cope with risk. What we know of the strategies of modern Greek peasants confronted by the same environment provides, at least for the question of risk management, the best possible parallel for the situation of ancient Greek agriculture.[82] Thus polyculture did not result from the blindness of a peasantry incapable of specializing in order to minimize its costs—on the contrary, it was a rational strategy for limiting uncertainty. *Coltura promiscua* (to use this modern Italian term), in which cereals were grown between the rows of olive trees, is a good example of this. "Produce a little of everything"—that is, in addition to growing grain, producing oil, wine, and also vegetables, while at the same time keeping a few head of livestock and some fowl, or possibly a few beehives, was a reasonable strategy. For example, in case autumn rains were insufficient to obtain a good cereal harvest, one could hope to find a compensation in the vegetable crop, thanks to more satisfactory spring rains. At worst, one would always have a little wine, oil, or honey to trade. Diversification was also achieved by cultivating fields in various parts of the territory. In this respect, it was in the peasant's interest not to have all his land in the same area. A property that was very fragmented as a result of divisions connected with inheritances as well of as the circulation of land connected with dowries—if not in Athens, at least in many other regions—must have often provided this insurance against the risk involved in having all one's lands in the same area.

The other strategy for countering uncertainty consisted in accumulating supplies in order to survive the predictable bad years. *Ariston hudōr*, "water is the most precious good," said Pindar (*Olympian* 1.1), even if he probably understood this in a more abstract sense. Water management was a way of dealing with the risk of shortage and also of intensifying production. In this respect, however, we should remember that a large proportion of the Greek cities (in western and northern Greece and in northern Asia Minor) did not suffer from droughts, but instead, locally, from excess water: the fundamental question was then that of drainage.[83] In "arid" Aegean Greece, both peasants and city-dwellers (and even public collectivities) had to build up reserves. Runoff from roofs was collected in cisterns: water was a commodity too precious to waste.[84] It might also be the object of a specific law designed to ensure that everyone would have water. According to Plutarch (*Solon* 23.5), a peasant without a well was supposed to have the right to draw every day from his neighbor's well a quantity of water limited to 12 *choes* (ca. 40 liters).

This water could then be used for human consumption and for a few head of live-stock, but it could not in any case be used for irrigation. Water collected in cisterns might also be used to irrigate fields, as in Delos, where a system of gravity-fed irrigation made it possible to grow crops on terraces that were intended to supply the city.[85] However, except for gardens, it is clear that most Greek agriculture relied solely on rainfall, which in Aegean Greece meant "dry farming."[86] A significant part of the harvest might also be preserved and held in reserve for the following year. Some products, such as figs, can be preserved by drying them. But others that keep less well were nonetheless sometimes stored up too. The peasants of modern Greece deliberately practiced overproduction in order to store the excess, and thanks to Pseudo-Aristotle, we have proof that the same could be done in ancient Greece, as is shown by an anecdote that relates to Selymbria and seems to date from 360 BCE.[87] But since storage conditions were not ideal, the grain from the preceding year was very likely to be partially spoiled by insects or mold: this grain thus did not have the same quality as the grain produced the same year. If it was not eaten the second year, it could ordinarily be used to feed animals, but we know of at least one case in which it was sold.[88] Thus the only part of the harvest that could be put on the market was what was left after providing for annual consumption, seed grain, and reserves for the following year. But we must emphasize that for a great landlord oriented toward sale from the outset, this kind of strategy of accumulation over two years could have played only a marginal role, to feed his slaves, since he sold most of what he produced on the market.

In any case, it is clear that these strategies were not without drawbacks. The strategy of diversification turned its back on specialization in one or two products with which one might have hoped for better yields, whereas the strategy consisting in "producing a little of everything" involved growing crops that produced low yields (for example, olives in a more elevated region) and thus presupposed a decrease in the overall productivity of labor. The fragmentation of land entailed having to travel long distances from one parcel to another, resulting in a loss of time that some-times, in relation to the investment in labor, must have been disproportionately high. Finally, the strategy of overproducing and storing to survive a possible poor harvest also implied a loss of sales. We cannot suppose that owners of small and middle-sized farms did not have as their goal to maximize, or even partially special-ize, production: that was indeed a goal, but it was subordinate to the main goal of minimizing the immediate risk of famine that would imperil the survival of the family group itself.

Such strategies for protecting oneself against climatic uncertainty—to which in the context of ancient Greece we must add a great political uncertainty—were not always successful. If there was a catastrophic cereal harvest and one did not have, or had no longer, a reserve from the preceding year, one could try to sow seeds in the spring (if one still had seeds) or rely on gardening. People did not fail to pray and sacrifice to Zeus Ombrios ("of the showers") or to Zeus Hyetios ("of the rain"), di-vinities whose worship is attested in a series of places, among others in the city of Kamiros, where it was said laconically that one must make a sacrifice to Zeus Hyetios "when necessary"—that is, naturally, in the event of drought.[89] If a man got desperate, he could sell or slaughter his animals, or borrow from some great landlord, and end up selling his property and trying to make his way elsewhere, which would inevitably entail the dislocation of the family group. In the Archaic period, in Athens before Solon, it was no doubt common, as it was in the East, to sell one's own children into slavery, or even to sell oneself.[90] But after Solon's reforms (594/3 BCE), such solutions were no longer acceptable in Attika, and in fact elsewhere in Greece. The overall increase in wealth in Greece certainly played a role and especially the fact that communities as such could seek temporary solutions by borrowing or importing.[91]

Tradition and Innovation in Agriculture and in Animal Husbandry

Was Greek agriculture a world "outside time," and an inefficient world of routine to boot? Did it remain unchanged over the centuries, from the time of Hesiod down to the Roman takeover and well beyond, until the end of antiquity? The answer is no, but it does not suffice to invert the paradigm to arrive at a satisfactory response. It is above all the notion of routine that has to be examined. Like any other activity in a traditional society, working the land was not based on theoretical, scientific knowledge learned in books. It was based first on an immemorial knowledge, a multitude of experiences accumulated over the generations and learned through slow, gradual apprenticeship, usually from childhood on. This technical knowledge (concerning how to plow, plant, or guide a flock) set a calendar for every task as if it could not be otherwise. Experience showed that if for one reason or another one did not conform to this calendar, he was exposing himself to serious consequences and losing his harvest. That is the meaning of the advice the poet-peasant Hesiod gave to his brother Perses in *Works and Days* around 700 BCE. This general knowledge was accompanied by more detailed knowledge concerning the characteristics of a property, which told farmers for example that a given land needed to be turned over more often or that another was not good for growing wheat. The very nature of this totally empirical knowledge, in which practices were not explained, did not favor rapid innovation. It favored slow, almost imperceptible improvements that in the course of time were nonetheless likely to have a significant impact on productivity. This empirical knowledge has by definition a routine aspect, but that does not in any way mean that it is "outside time," and *a fortiori* that it was inefficacious. It is the pace of change and the potential slowness of technical innovations that we have to look into. The technologies of the ancient Greek world are initially comparable to those of any traditional society, but it is their degree of malleability that needs to be investigated— for instance, in certain segments of production where techniques were deficient and where, even without innovations involving the implementation of abstract knowledge, improvements could have been made. This was the case, for example, of harrowing, which was apparently introduced quite late.[92]

However, even practices derived from traditional knowledge can increase productivity in the very long term. Consider the technique of setting aside seed for the following year. In traditional agriculture, peasants select the finest ears of wheat or barley for use as seed. The traditionalism inherent in empirical technical knowledge thus does not necessarily prevent an increase in yields. This increase is in a way inscribed in the long-term history of agriculture. Such changes are observable over a period of at least four or five thousand years. On the other hand, it is also clear that Greek agriculture did not tend toward very rapid changes such as the agricultural world has recently experienced, when yields have multiplied by four or five in a single century.

The question is whether Greece tended toward change at a very slow pace corresponding to a millennial rhythm that amounted almost to stagnation, or whether it tended toward development at a slow pace that nonetheless led to clearly perceptible changes over a period of a thousand years, or even a few hundred years. Moreover, we need to ask whether in ancient Greece there were particular institutional reasons that encouraged the activation of this change, or whether on the contrary institutional conditions inclined Greek agriculture to become a world of stagnation and relative immobility. Although basic agricultural tools underwent only slow changes, this was not the case for the processing of agricultural products, which experienced spectacular gains in productivity.[93] Therefore, we have to draw up a differentiated balance sheet for innovation in the agricultural world.

So far as the productivity of the species cultivated and of its herds of livestock are concerned, Greece seems to have been inclined toward slow but clearly perceptible change not only over a chronological period on the order of a millennium, but also over shorter periods on the order of a few hundred years. We have seen that in the case of wheat, Greek peasants planted the variety called *Triticum durum*, hard wheat, whereas at the same period, Egyptian peasants always used the variety *Triticum turgidum* of the *dicoccum* variety, which required more work and yielded less.[94] In Egypt, the general adoption of hard wheat was not immediate. On the other hand, the Greeks did not hesitate to adopt foreign plants, like *poa mēdikē*, alfalfa, which was brought in by the Persians. For grapevine stocks, they had a wide choice and did not hesitate to bring in varieties adapted to this or that product. Zenon's papyri show how many different varieties were available: he had a nursery with ten varieties of grapevines (including two top-quality varieties from Thrace, Mende, and Maroneia; one from Cilicia; and one from Phoenicia).[95] For vegetables as well, the best seeds were imported from far away in order to improve products.

In the domain of livestock, we can observe very clear progress. By selecting the best reproducers, livestock underwent considerable improvement. For sheep, we see in Tiryns at the end of the Bronze Age a height at the withers of 50 centimeters; in Delos, in the sixth century BCE, the height was 62.5 centimeters, and finally reached 67 centimeters in the first century BCE.[96] During the same period, the size of hogs and oxen increased by similar proportions at the two sites. Thus we find a tendency to slow but very clear growth in the size of the livestock. One would like to be able to see other changes—for example, in the quantity of wool produced by sheep or the quantity of milk produced by ewes and goats. But there is no reason why important gains would not have been made in these areas as well. Agronomic literature was fully aware of these developments, and Columella (7.2.4) emphasized that "experience has taught us to create new breeds." Moreover, he never ceases to refer to the selection of the best reproducers to improve livestock, as well as for race horses (3.9.5). This scientific literature, which must to a large extent merely synthesize traditional experience, may also have had a direct influence on great landlords insofar as precisely by its encyclopedic, interregional character, it offered a range of choices and suggested approaches that an isolated individual would not have thought of.

The pace of the changes observed, in particular in the domain of animal husbandry, invites us to inquire into their institutional conditions. The factors were of two kinds. The first was no doubt individual farmers' desire to maximize their revenues. Unlike what can be observed not only in the kingdoms of the eastern Mediterranean area, but also in Greece itself in cities founded on exploiting a class of dependents, peasants in most Greek cities of the Classical world and even in the Hellenistic period were free landowners who controlled most of what they produced.[97] As a result, there was a strong incentive to produce more and better quality goods, because the fruit of their labor was directly perceptible in an increase in revenue. In systems in which any increase in production is systematically skimmed off by a ruling power that in any case leaves the peasants only the minimum necessary to survive, any incentive to increase productivity disappears; there is little motivation to select seeds or cross-breed livestock to obtain finer animals. In the ancient world, at least as long as the city-state endured, there was thus a strong individual incentive to increase yields.

Noneconomic institutional reasons also encouraged the improvement of livestock. According to Xenophon (*Hellenica* 6.4.29), for the festival of the *Puthia*, Jason of Pherai "had proclaimed by a herald that the Thessalian city that raised the finest ox to lead the herd intended for the god would win a golden crown as its prize" (370 BCE). Around 120 BCE, the city of Bargylia entrusted to *boutrophoi* the raising of oxen for sacrifice that were then to be examined by a commission to determine their order in the procession for the festival of Artemis Kindyas.[98] The spirit was not that of the agricultural competitions in nineteenth-century Europe, whose explicit goal was to improve productivity in the framework of an ideology of economic and social progress. Yet Xenophon (*Hieron* 9.7–8) envisaged the creation of such competitions, which at least proves that there was no obstacle to imagining their existence: "Agriculture itself, most useful of all occupations, but just the one in which the spirit of competition [*philonikia*] is conspicuous by its absence, would make great progress if prizes were offered for the farm or the village that can show the best cultivation, and many good results would follow for those citizens who threw themselves vigorously into this occupation. For apart from the consequent increase in the revenues . . . ."[99] It does not seem however that such competitions were actually organized. But even if the competition took place within an institution that was religious in character, the agonistic spirit of Greek society was reflected in an improvement in livestock. Besides, the desire to have the finest animals for sacrifice, thus arousing the envy of the community, did not exclude a desire to increase one's revenues by selling one's animals at the best price. This was precisely what Xenophon envisaged as a consequence of the improvement of farms.

The Increase in the Area Cultivated

In discussing the question of the increase in yields, we must paradoxically begin with the development of new lands. These were not only lands that after being cleared would have been suitable for cultivation, but also new lands that had been, as it were, won from nature, which required a particular technical knowledge and a major investment in labor and possibly in capital. Two kinds of areas might be the object of these efforts to "create agricultural land."

These were first of all lands developed on hills and mountains. To increase cultivated area, one way is to create from scratch new fields on sloping ground. According to Isocrates (*Panegyric* 4.132, ca. 380 BCE), islanders "cultivated the mountains," which implies that they built terraces on them. Clear archaeological traces of ancient terraces can be found in the fossilized landscape of Delos.[100] The ancient landscape of Keos was probably not very different from what it still is, with long terraced strips winding along the slopes of the island. Aerial views of the countryside of Keos (modern Kea) perfectly convey the meaning of Isocrates' statement.[101] At Kyaneai in Lykia, a survey has revealed a similar type of terraced landscape, which (were further proof needed) shows that terraces were not a solution used solely in the islands.[102] More broadly, these terraces clearly prove the will to make maximal use of a city's territory, and when not enough good land in a plain was available, to supplement it with fields created by the hard labor of generations of peasants.

The other area that might be won for cultivation was lakes and marshy zones. Mediterranean agriculture has to cope not only with a lack of water during long summer droughts but also with the problem of accumulations of water and stagnant waters in inland basins or on littoral plains, where the declivity is insufficient to evacuate the water naturally. Many of the wettest regions in Greece have these difficulties (the Peloponnese, central Greece, northern Greece especially, and the northern part of Asia Minor). The most striking but not unique case is that of central Boiotia, a vast karstic basin without a natural outlet to the sea, where water from the winter rains accumulated. The center of the basin was occupied by Lake Kopais, whose level rose and fell according to the season. But the lake's level also changed in a more aleatory way depending on the obstruction or unblocking of the *katavothres*, the natural outlets that ran through the karst. Since the nineteenth century, this region has been entirely drained. In antiquity, major projects were undertaken to limit flooding.

The first of these took place at the end of the Mycenaean period, and doubtless there were others later on. In the time of Alexander, an engineer named Krates of Chalkis tried to unblock the *katavothres*, which made the water level rise when they were obstructed and threatened to flood several cities around the lake. The work could not be completed because of a revolt by the Boiotians, but several cities had already been drained, including apparently Orchomenos. Our only source, Strabo (9.2.18), is not very explicit. If the ancients never had the means to construct a large drainage canal (which would necessarily have been partly underground) to carry water from Lake Kopais to the sea, their techniques of water evacuation were nonetheless sufficiently developed to obtain tangible results by digging drainage wells to allow the water to flow out, or by constructing dikes to protect certain areas in the event that the water level rose. However, the uncertain institutional context (constant wars, in this case probably the revolt of Thebes in 335 BCE) prevented the work from advancing continuously, and at the same time the division of the cities also made it impossible to mobilize the resources needed to carry out a project like the total drainage of Lake Kopais. At almost the same period, perhaps shortly after 318 BCE, Eretria decided to drain Lake Ptechai, which was probably in the central part of the city's territory.[103] Eretria made a contract with a certain Chairephanes, who was to be responsible for all the work. In return, he was to have the right to rent the drained territory for ten years at the (high) rate of three talents a year. In short, the city took no risk: if the project failed, it lost nothing because it had invested no funds in it. The city merely favored the operation by granting various exemptions from import taxes on the material that had to be brought in. To launch into such a project, the renter, Chairephanes, must have felt sure that he could complete it. He must also have had enough capital to be able to invest considerable sums in the venture. Finally, the revenues to be drawn from the use of the land must have been high enough not only to allow him to pay an annual rent of three talents for ten years and cover his initial investment, but also to provide a significant profit, without which all these efforts would have been futile. The amount of the rent, 18,000 drachms, was itself higher than that of all the tenant farms of Delian Apollo, which brought in 11,500 drachms in 250 BCE.[104] The lands that were to be improved must have amounted to a minimum of a hundred hectares. It seems logical to think that at least ten talents, and perhaps much more, were invested in the operation.

We might wonder whether Chairephanes, who is otherwise unknown, was the citizen of Kassandreia to whom around 300 King Kassandros granted a series of tax exemptions similar to those that had been granted by the Eretrians.[105] If he was acting on his own, he might well have been a companion of Alexander or one of the Diadochi who had grown rich during the campaigns in the East, as one might suspect for a Plataian who around the same time (319/8 BCE) lent a large sum—several talents, since the remission of debt alone amounted to 2,100 drachms—to the little city of Pladasa in Karia.[106] Chairephanes was less likely to have been an engineer than a rich notable who belonged to the Macedonian king's entourage and who was looking for something to invest in. At that time, there was a lot of money to be invested and put to use, perhaps even in projects that were technically risky (but not politically risky, since even if it was officially free, at that time Eretria seems not to have been able to refuse anything to Macedon and its notables and officials who were active in the region). Unfortunately, we do not know if the project was completed. In any case, it is striking that the declared goal of the project was to gain new lands, just as had been done on the shores of Lake Kopais.[107] Other projects of the same kind and aiming at gaining new land were undertaken in Larisa, in Thessaly, and in Philippoi, in Thrace.[108]

Thus it is clear that far from being crushed by the implacable wheel of traditionalism, Greek agriculture, in any case in its most dynamic sectors, sought innovation. A common way of increasing yields was to import breeds of animals and varieties of plants that were more productive or had some particular quality. It is above all in private archives and in the treatises of the agronomists that we find proof of a conscious, organized effort to improve products. On the *dōrea* (estate) of Apollonios, Ptolemy II's royal treasurer (middle of the third century), we can see a genuine will to agricultural change. Zenon of Kaunos, right-hand man of Apollonios since 261 BCE and the steward of his *dōrea* in the Fayum between 258 and 246, undertook to increase production and improve yields. Most of what the *dōrea* produced was, of course, intended for sale. The first step was to develop new lands by draining marshlands or irrigating lands near the desert. The estate was divided into identical units in which the efficiency of the drainage canals or irrigation would be maximal. Similarly, Zenon carefully chose the plant varieties he decided to put in, bringing them from nurseries set up near Memphis.[109] He imported sheep of a Milesian breed that would allow him to produce fine wool that would sell at a high price.[110]

Economic Choices and Yield Increases

The question is whether Zenon was typical or exceptional. Was his attitude entirely marginal? Or was it, on the contrary, representative of Greek attitudes at the time? We know that Zenon's correspondence was preserved by mere chance. There is absolutely no reason to think that Zenon was exceptional in any way. We would, moreover, have to determine why he was exceptional, what would have caused an anonymous Greco-Karian have a particular, unique genius in matters of agronomy. It is more coherent to maintain that managing Apollonios's estate gave Zenon an opportunity. He could put into practice on a large scale and with almost complete freedom principles that were common to everyone in his milieu who was in his situation, wherever they lived in the Hellenized world of the third century BCE, which stretched from Marseilles and Iberia to the borders of India. It is also more interesting to note that here the innovation was made by the steward of a vast estate, a number of which existed in Greece proper, in Macedon, and on the coast of Asia Minor, but less frequently than in the colonial world.

The true question is thus through whom innovation came about. It is probable that innovation had a differential character. The most ambitious innovations must have been connected with financial resources and especially with great landlords. The latter had monetary capital that made it possible for them to make the necessary advances. They could afford to wait several years to see their investments bear fruit, which a small farmer could not do. They could take the risk of possible failure, which would result in a financial loss but would not endanger their standing as members of the elite. Moreover, for estates in areas in contact with the barbarian world (in colonial regions like Egypt and Syria, but also in the immediate interior of Asia Minor and Thrace) their political position often also gave them a power of coercion over a workforce that could be used for large projects. In passing, we see that Zenon's case (like that of the much later Heroninos in the third century CE[111]) suffices to disprove Max Weber's view, adopted by Finley, according to which landlords' absenteeism led to careless management of great estates.[112] The publication of new cases like Zenon's (which was not known to Weber, but which was to Finley) suggests a radically different conclusion. Today, a basic rule of good management is to distinguish between financial management (buying or selling an enterprise), commercial management, and technical management: each domain requires specific kinds of knowledge. This was well understood by a great landlord who relied on his steward (*oikonomos* in Greece, *vilicus* in Rome). That is why all he needed was the general knowledge provided by the writings of the "agronomists," as we saw earlier.

Should we then conclude that inversely, owners of smaller amounts of land were necessarily forced to adhere to routine? Facing a high number of threats, from natural disasters to personal health difficulties or devastations of war, the Greek peasant seems to have had good reasons to be strongly conservative.[113] For the poorest among them, who were barely able to survive, and for reasons the inverse of those that were mentioned earlier regarding great landlords, it is probable that they were, even if the pressure of poverty must have led them to take advantage of every opportunity to sell their surplus products on the market (fowl, pigs, and so on). But we must also take into account a series of slow improvements made by selecting seeds and cross-breeding animals, which must have been practiced by most of the middle-level peasants. It is in any case beyond doubt that actors, each at his own level, had a certain freedom of choice. For example, Columella's writings, which were addressed to great landlords, show that the various vinestocks available in Italy were compared with one another. Columella's description invited the reader to make his choice in relation to his objectives: high quality or high yield. At a more modest level (but not necessarily that of poor peasants), the tablets from Dodona give us an idea of the range of choices a Greek peasant might have (the references are to Lhôte's edition).[114]

—"Should I devote myself to working the land" (165, no. 75, ca. 400–375 BCE).

—"Is it preferable for Agelochos, who came from Hergetion, to devote himself to working the land?" (165–68, no. 75, ca. 340–30? BCE).[115] Hergetion was a small city in the interior of Sicily, probably in the Iblei Mountains, about sixty kilometers from Syracuse.

—"(Question) regarding the fruit of Demeter and Dionysos" (170–72, no. 78, fourth century BCE).
This seems to mean that the question concerning the *karpos*, the "fruit of the earth," the "harvest," referred to the "fruit of Demeter," that is, grain, and the "fruit of Dionysos," that is, the grape harvest.[116] Was it a matter of choosing between growing grain and growing grapes?

—"Kleotas asks Zeus and Diona whether it is advantageous and profitable for him to devote himself to raising sheep" (173–75, no. 80, first half of the fourth century BCE).

—"God. Good fortune. The person seeking advice asks whether, by devoting himself to raising ducks, he can succeed and know success for the present and the future" (177–79, no. 82, beginning of the fourth century BCE).

The fundamental question about Greek agriculture remains that of its level of productivity. In this domain, the level of productivity in our own world does not have to be the standard of comparison, or if it is, only as a distant horizon; instead, the standard should be the level of productivity of the societies contemporary with Classical and Hellenistic Greece, and their ability to evolve. It is true that starting in the middle of the sixteenth century and accelerating over time major changes occurred in England, accompanied by a significant increase in agricultural yields. For example, the productivity per worker employed in agriculture more than doubled between 1600 and 1700, an increase unprecedented in earlier history.[117] The agricultural revolution spread to the continent in the nineteenth century. Following England, Western Europe (France, Germany, northern Italy) also experienced major increases in yields.

In comparison, the agriculture of ancient Greece (and Mediterranean agriculture in general) seems to have been doomed to have only low yields. According to Columella (3.3.4)—but it matters that this passage is a rhetorical construction—on most lands Italian agriculture had seed/production yields on the order of 1 to 4 (four grains harvested for every one planted). Greek agriculture is said to have done not much better, with yields on the order of 1 to 6 or 1 to 7. It is the whole logic of traditional Mediterranean agriculture (and thus of Greek agriculture) that has to be held responsible. Low agricultural yields are connected with the system of letting land lie fallow—and moreover, without any plant cover—every other year, which in some sense symbolizes this archaism. Land was cultivated only one year out of two, which had the advantage of not exhausting it. Repeated plowings were able to eliminate weeds that might otherwise have competed with cereal crops. Thus they made it possible to store up, so to speak, two years' rainfall for the grain harvest. But in that way, the soil did not benefit from the renewal connected with growing forage plants such as alfalfa or vetch. In addition, and especially, it limited animal husbandry to the strict minimum, since the animals found nothing to eat on the bare fallow earth during the year that it was not cultivated. As a result, the quantity of manure available remained insufficient.[118] However, only a major addition of the manure connected with large-scale livestock raising could have raised the soil's productivity.[119] In other words, if Greek farmers had established a system similar to the one that prevailed in England with the "Norfolk revolution," ancient Greece would also have been able to increase its yields significantly. Modern experiments made in Cyprus using either artificial or traditional fertilizers (manure) show immediate, considerable increases in yields. It is clear that the key to a possible agricultural revolution lay in systematically associating animal husbandry with agriculture in order to obtain quantities of manure sufficient to allow agriculture, and perhaps even the Greek economy in general, to take off. In early twentieth-century Greece before the introduction of fertilizers (or even systematic use of animal dung), yields per hectare were 5.1 and 6.2 quintals per hectare, respectively, for wheat and barley. In comparison already before World War I, the countries of Western Europe had yields 100 percent to 500 percent higher (between 10 to 25 quintal per hectare) according to the country. We have good reason to believe that ancient Greek yields in volume were of the order of those of Greece in the early twentieth century (although with finally a grain with a lower weight).[120] It would seem that here we really have definitive proof of the archaism of Greek agriculture, and its "cause" seems to be purely ideological: a lack of interest—clearly inexplicable—in agricultural progress.

In its simplicity, this schema seems to have great explanatory force. The reality is more complex. First, while it is correct that increasing the quantity of fertilizer normally has very positive effects on yields, in the driest areas it does not always produce the expected results, and may even cause a decrease in yields.[121] Second, other variables have to be taken into account, such as how far the land was from the owner's place of residence and the travel time required to get to it in a system of very fragmented land ownership in hilly terrain where the danger to personal security increased with the distance from one's residence (which was usually fortified in some way or another). These factors meant that the choice to engage in an intensive agriculture that went so far as almost to be gardening tended to be reserved for areas closest to the central residence.[122] However, we must emphasize that several documents show that a system of rotation was introduced, at least in part—for example, a lease from the region of Rhamnous, in Attika, from 339/8 BCE, which recommends planting legumes on half of land that was not planted in wheat or barley, hence on one-quarter of the land, and leaving only one-quarter fallow.[123]

Finally, and especially, the English agricultural revolution cannot be dissociated from its general economic and social consequences. It was accompanied by a radical reorientation in favor of pastures that yielded animal products sold in the great urban markets, which were rapidly expanding. In the same way, it also allowed an increase in yields on lands that were still devoted to growing grain. But it was wagered that most of the grain would henceforth be imported, which assumed that England controlled the seas (which was in fact the case). Moreover, in England the enclosure movement was accompanied by a massive expulsion of small tenant farmers and the constitution of large estates that could apply the new principles of agriculture.

In other words, economic data cannot be isolated from general social and institutional conditions. Interestingly, in modern Greece the two-year fallow period was a "luxury" that the poorest among the peasants could not afford (although of course failing to leave land fallow quickly impacted its yields).[124] So far as social conditions are concerned, large estates were not unknown in the city-state system. But in any case, this system was based on a collectivity of peasants owning small and middle-sized properties. Only their forcible eviction would have made it possible to carry out a large-scale transformation of the agricultural system. As for the institutional environment, the general insecurity, which was both political and climatic (with much greater variations in precipitation than in oceanic climates), led to priority being systematically given to the short term and to cereal production, since it was known that in the event of shortages, the vertiginous rise in prices would make it possible to realize very substantial profits. All these reasons combined to limit the transformations of agriculture, and hence an increase in production. It was not, strictly speaking, the concept that was lacking, since crop rotation was practiced, but not systematized: it was the general institutional conditions and the social power relationships that were not favorable to this transformation, or at least to a radical transformation, because the Hellenistic period nonetheless underwent a kind of transformation in this direction.

Changes in Agriculture and the Market

The world of rural ancient Greece thus leaves a contrasting impression. We have seen that cereal growing evolved very little, except for the slow but ultimately very real improvement in seeds. Animal husbandry underwent a clearer evolution with the partial introduction of forage crops, but for the reasons previously mentioned, this change was not decisive. Viticulture also experienced a slow but real evolution in vine stocks and techniques of cultivation, but this did not result in a drastic improvement in yields. So far as agricultural implements are concerned, it was probably during the Roman period in the West that the most important innovations were made, such as the harrow, the wheel plow and the moldboard plow in the Po valley, the scythe in Gaul, and even the combine harvester in northern Gaul—but these new techniques did not move beyond the regional context that gave rise to them.[125] They came into general use only much later, and at first only in western Europe, during the medieval and modern periods. In any case, whatever the social level of the producers, it is clear that the incentive to produce more and to improve quality was the profit that each property owner might hope to derive from his land, and that the medium that made it possible to realize this hope was the market. This rule held for the most modest producer as well as for the great landlord. Varro (*On Agriculture* 3.16.10–11) reports the case of two brothers in Italy who managed to produce enough honey to bring in 10,000 sesterces (about 2,500 drachms) a year. He adds that they "waited for the right time to sell and were never in a hurry to sell at any price." In other words, they knew how to play the market and not dispose of their merchandise by lowering the price too much if they thought it was not sufficiently remunerative. In this they were acting no differently from a great landowner like the Athenian Phainippos (Pseudo-Demosthenes *Against Phaenippus* 42.20 and 42.31), who knew how to take advantage of market conditions. His adversary claimed that Phainippos sold his barley at 18 drachms the *metrētēs* and his wine at 12 drachms the *metrētēs*—at least three times the usual market prices. In fact, the higher prices were probably not inflated by Phainippos's adversary but maximum prices attained for a short time in one year or another. The plaintiff could mention them to make it seem that Phainippos always sold at these prices, which was not, of course, the case. But in any case the accusation was plausible because everyone knew that producers might be tempted to use this tactic. Besides, there is no reason to doubt that Phainippos's estate was indeed quite profitable.[126]

Fluctuations in prices explain the considerable profits that producers might make when supplies of a certain product decreased. But putting a very prized product on the market was also a guaranteed way to make a good profit. In Athens the ordinary price of local wine was four or five drachms the *metrētēs*, and it was probably only when exceptional shortages occurred that it rose to twelve drachms.[127] The price of fine wines was much higher. According to Plutarch (*On Tranquility of Mind* 470 f), in the time of Socrates wine from Chios, which was with the wine from Thasos one of the best Greek wines, was sold at the very high price of "one mina" (100 drachms; the unit of volume is not mentioned, but it must have been the *metrētēs*). In this case, either the price is exaggerated ("a mina" could mean simply "very expensive") or this was an exceptional wine that for some reason unknown to us had become especially desirable. It is very difficult to deduce clues to wine prices from graffiti found on vases, because they are usually hard to read, and moreover the relation between quantities and prices is even more difficult to determine.[128] Other, incontestable clues suggest prices that are more realistic, but still high. This is the case with the customs declarations at Pelousion regarding goods imported into Egypt and intended for Alexandria in May–June 259 BCE. Wine from Chios was estimated at 18 drachms the amphora, and wine from Thasos at 20 drachms the amphora.[129] To be sure, these are prices on entry into Egypt (and thus included higher transportation costs than would be involved in shipping the wine to an Aegean destination), and moreover at the beginning of the Hellenistic period.

However, at that time, after the inflation of the late fourth century BCE, prices had already begun to decline considerably, and it is therefore not absurd to compare them with prices during the Classical period.[130] In addition, we must remember that amphoras from Chios and Thasos held considerably less wine than the Attic amphora. At the end of the fifth century BCE, amphoras from Chios held about 23 liters (only 20 at the beginning of the century), which amounted to only 60 percent of the volume of the Attic amphora.[131] Assuming (and this would have to be verified) that the capacity of amphoras from Chios remained unchanged at the beginning of the Hellenistic period, and comparing the price of an amphora of Attic wine at 4 drachms for 39.3 liters with an amphora of wine from Chios at 18 drachms for 23 liters, the price ratio is in the range of 1 to 8 per unit volume.

Analogous remarks can be made regarding wines of middling quality, like those from Rhodes, Kos, and Knidos, which began to flood the markets in the middle of the Hellenistic period. According to the accounts of the *Posideia* festival organized in Delos, between 190 and 180 BCE twelve amphoras of wine from Knidos cost 52 drachms, or 4 drachms 2 obols per amphora. Thirty-five amphoras of wine from Kos cost 115 drachms 5 obols, or about 3 drachms 2 obols per amphora.[132] If we assume that these amphoras had a capacity of about 20 liters, we observe a level of prices about twice that of Attic wine, and about four or five times less than that of the fine wines from Chios and Thasos. However that may be, even with prices that were only double those of "ordinary wine" it was entirely worthwhile to produce and sell these wines. Of course, from the final price we have to deduct the cost of transport over a long distance and middlemen's profit margins. If we estimate the cost of freight at one drachm per amphora (for a standard cargo of 3,000 amphoras during the Hellenistic period), even with the margins taken by various middlemen, starting in the Classical period there was a strong incentive to develop wine production, and it grew even stronger during the Hellenistic period.[133] For producers, the market thus represented a reliable way of increasing their revenues, or at least trying to do so. As for the quantities involved, they were sufficient to show that while some of the wine was consumed by producers, on middle-sized and large estates, at least, the basic outlet for what was produced could only be the market. If we take the example of winegrowing, given the levels of production there can be no question of the wine being consumed solely by the producers. This is the case for the production figures we have for two vineyards in Attika—104 and 800 *metrētai*.[134] Production figures from a large winegrowing region like Thasos show that a given producer might far surpass this amount. On an estate on Thasos, steles connected the Hermokopid scandal dating from 414 BCE record the seizure of 590 amphoras and 3 *choes* (certainly in Attic measures so that they would be comprehensible in an Athenian document; since the amphora contained a *metrētēs* it was possible to refer to either amphoras or *metrētai*), or 232 hectoliters.[135] On another estate on Thasos, 93 *pithoi* (storage jars) were seized. If the content of each *pithos* is estimated at ca. 10 hectoliters or about 25 Attic amphoras, the 93 *pithoi* are the equivalent of 930 hectoliters or 2,325 *metrētai*, corresponding to an area of about thirty hectares.[136] It is clear that this wine was intended for the market, as is abundantly shown by the exports of amphoras from Thasos. The geography of the amphora workshops on Thasos, which were always located near the coast in order to limit handling and make it easier to load the ships, shows how interested Thasians were in these exports.[137] Vineyards might be located farther inland, the wine being carried down to the sea in goatskins loaded on mules.

A case showing the particular interest of access to the sea is provided by the treaty of *sumpoliteia* (joint citizenship or constitution) between Miletos and Pidasa, probably dating from 187 BCE.[138] The treaty authorized Pidasans who owned land in the neighboring city of Euromos to export under certain conditions as much as 1,000 *metrētai* of their wine to Miletos. The amount of this limitation can be understood only as an upper limit for each exporter—and not for all the exporters taken together, which would have been completely unmanageable: if ten producers had hastened to export 100 *metrētai* apiece, what about the eleventh? Finally, leases from Mylasa and Euromos repeatedly refer to lands planted with grapevines. Viticulture was thus one of Euromos's main sources of wealth. This was mass production.[139] The limit imposed by the treaty between Miletos and Pidasa was therefore per producer. Its goal was to prevent tax breaks from benefitting very large producers, who had genuine fortunes in vineyards and did not particularly need help. In addition, we should note that there is no reason to think that the *metrētēs* of Miletos had a capacity as high as that of Athens, which means not that vineyards were small, but that the figure of 1,000 *metrētai* was more easily attained than one might think. In Attika, an area of 13 hectares would have been required to produce 1,000 *metrētai*. If the *metrētēs* in Miletos was smaller than the Attic *metrētai*, the 1,000 *metrētai* may have represented about 10 hectares, supposing that one had not chosen much more productive plants, as Columella recommended for everyday wine. When we reflect that Euromos had several dozen square kilometers—that is, several thousand hectares—of good agricultural land, the total portion owned by Pidasans, even it was as much as a few dozen or even a hundred hectares in all, could not have been more than a small percentage of the whole.

Like the wine from Attika, the wine from Euromos and Mylasa is not particularly mentioned in literature as being among the fine wines, nor is it prominent in the amphoric remains connected with wine exported to distant markets. It must have long been consumed regionally. But the Pidasans wanted to export it, and thus to have easy access to the sea. That is why they were certainly at the origin of the request for the construction of a road suitable for vehicles linking their territory with the port of Ioniapolis, which would give them easy access to the Milesian market, especially for their wines. The impressive network of paved roads revealed by archaeological research in the region of Mount Latmos and Ioniapolis gives us an idea of the investments that were made in the Hellenistic period to facilitate contact between the hinterland and the coast.[140]

Thus we see once again that we must avoid clichés regarding the "immobility of agriculture." The variability of the constraints imposed by nature and also by the market explains developments that partially diverge, depending on the sector. Besides, the image of the family farm producing exclusively for the needs of the household and selling only its occasional surplus must be radically abandoned. Market strategies were part of the horizon of every Greek farmer, although of course at various levels. Even small-holder farmers could not ignore them. Although not their only source of income, agriculture was a major source of cash for the wealthy.[141]

VII

NONAGRICULTURAL PRODUCTION, CAPITAL, AND INNOVATION

Agriculture was thus the main production sector. However, it would be inexact to reduce productive activity to agriculture alone. It is clear that other sectors were made possible by the ecology of the Mediterranean milieu—for example, fishing, whose importance in the food supply must not be underestimated. But many artisanal activities also developed, partly because they provided indispensable services, and partly because they were themselves made feasible by the level of productivity in other sectors. In turn, through productivity they were able to attain, they made it possible to produce and put on the market large quantities of goods that helped raise the general standard of living. In Classical and Hellenistic Greece, houses grew larger and were better equipped, and the quantity of goods available increased considerably over a period of a few centuries. Thus in addition to describing the activities pursued, one must also examine the logic of production and the question of innovation.

FISH PRODUCTION AND CONSUMPTION

Fernand Braudel wrote a classical account of the importance of fish, especially herring, for the peoples of northern Europe.[1] Along the shores of the Baltic, the North Sea, and the northwest Atlantic an intensive fishing industry grew up that provided a large part of the food supply (though it is impossible to say exactly how large) not only for coastal cities but also for people living far inland. Braudel noted that in comparison, the Mediterranean was poor in fishing resources. This difference is commonly explained by several factors: the absence of large rivers allowing a mixture of waters (except in the Black Sea, where fish are abundant at the mouths of large rivers) or major currents bringing deep waters to the surface, excessive warmth, and high salinity.[2] Fishing could therefore provide only a small part of the food supply. So far as ancient Greece is concerned, this view of matters was further emphasized by Thomas W. Gallant,[3] for whom the Greeks developed fishing techniques only to a very limited extent. According to him, most fishing was done from the shore, by throwing out nets or by using fishing lines, a method that could produce only very small yields: at most a kilogram per fisherman per day. In general, he says, it was not until the Roman period that the technique of fishing with nets from boats was introduced. The modern *comparanda* (data from the region of the Adriatic Sea) should lead us to think that fishing played a negligible role in the food supply. Socially, fishing could not have been a full-time activity; it was something done by peasants, for whom it provided only supplementary revenues. Because of these primitive techniques and its minor social interest, fishing is thus supposed to have been completely unimportant in Greece's food supply. In any event, Gallant maintains, the ancient world never had enough salt to preserve large quantities of fish.

Fish in the Ancient Greek World: A Reassessment

Gallant's view is not without interest, especially when he stresses the seasonal character of fishing in many regions. Often fishing was in fact an activity supplementary to agriculture. But whether fishing made a negligible contribution to the food supply is another question. In reality, Gallant's thesis seems to be based on a misunderstanding. He calculates that on the basis of 300 triremes in Athens in 431 BCE (and then implicitly extrapolating from the number of men by trireme, viz. ca. 200), if fish had represented one-third of the annual food supply, 21,576.4 metric tons of it would have been required, more than the total production of fish in Greece in 1938, along with 7,845.9 metric tons of salt to preserve it, a quantity he considers absurdly high. However, this way of reasoning is inappropriate. The figure of "300 triremes in 431" is meaningless: in itself, it is grossly overestimated. But above all what is at issue here is the total population of Greece of the time. Moreover, it is impossible to imagine that the average caloric contribution made by fish amounted to one-third. That is not the point; the question is whether in Greece people could achieve an intake of animal proteins on the order of 15 to 20 percent of the total caloric intake by combining, in various proportions according to the region, fish, meat, and dairy products (though the latter were comparatively rare and expensive). As for salt, a figure of 8,000 tons (or in fact well above that amount) could certainly be reached by the ancient cities around the Aegean. The great salt evaporation ponds in nineteenth-century Asia Minor each produced around 1,500 to 2,000 tons a year, and there is no reason why their production should have been well below this level in antiquity. And to these should be added many other local salt ponds.[4] Besides, one has to take into account imports from other regions, particularly from the Black Sea. The existence of "salt-transporting ships" to which Plutarch alludes (even if the allusion does not refer to a specific time, as John K.

Davies points out) obviously speaks in favor of large-scale salt transportation.[5] Thus the ancient Aegean world was certainly not short of salt.

A different view was proposed by John Bintliff, and Gallant's thesis has more recently been rejected by Tønnes Bekker-Nielsen,[6] who shows, using contemporary anthropological parallels, that even fishing done from the coast could reach a reasonable level of productivity. In addition, there is every indication that fishing at sea was already known well before the Roman period, as is shown, for example, by Xenophon's testimony (*Hellenica* 5.1.23) regarding the Lakedaimonian Teleutias's seizure at sea, in 387 BCE, of "numerous fishing boats" along the southern coast of Attika, between Piraeus and Sounion. In short, fishing was an ordinary activity, and it is only the aleatory nature of our discoveries that explains the lack of representations of it dating from the Classical and Hellenistic periods (almost all the figurative mosaics showing boats come from the Roman period). So far as fishing with nets from boats goes, one should note that in the Christian Gospels it appears to be a common activity, and it is hard to believe that it was then a recent innovation.[7] Finally, even fishing with lines can be very productive if multiple hooks are used. One might add that this technique is still frequently practiced by professional fishermen: it is well adapted to fishing for large, high-quality fish intended to be put on display and sold at elevated prices. Bekker-Nielsen's analyses are broadly confirmed by a whole series of sources that allow us to form a more precise idea of the modes of fishing employed in ancient Greece.

As for fishing at sea, one can distinguish four main types that do not correspond to large, easily defined geographical areas, even though in a given region one type may be more prominent than another. First, it is undeniable that there was small-scale coastal fishing, practiced virtually everywhere by peasants as a complement to their main activity and intended to meet the needs of local populations on the basis of self-consumption or limited trade. That fishing with lines was practiced is shown by the discovery of fishhooks along the coast of Argolis,[8] and the same kind of fishing can be found in the Kyklades.[9] But this was not the only fishing practiced in Greece. There was also professional fishing intended to supply the great urban markets with fresh fish. The agoras of Athens and Piraeus were regularly supplied by fishermen who worked at night (as is suggested by the episode reported by Xenophon that was mentioned earlier) to avoid the heat of the sun, ensure the quality of the fish, and get the fish to the market as soon as it opened, early in the morning. Many anecdotes reported by the comic poets show that eating fresh fish was common in Athens.[10] Fishermen seem to have attracted public hostility by trying to sell their products at excessive prices and not hesitating to use tricks such as repeatedly sprinkling the fish with water (in theory forbidden) to make them look better. Paintings like the one found on an Italiote vase from the fourth century BCE showing a very large fish displayed in a fishmonger's stall confirm the existence of this market.[11]

A third type of fishing was practiced where there were large seasonal runs of fish in well-defined areas. This was the case for the migrating tuna that crossed the

Bosporos in the spring to reach the Black Sea, and left again in the autumn for the warmer waters of the western Mediterranean. As a result, the narrow straits around Byzantion were particularly favorable for tuna-fishing. Ancient authors gave precise descriptions of this activity that evince a very good knowledge of the phenomenon.[12] They also insist on the superabundance of the catch: the tuna migrated in large schools and it was easy to trap them in *madragues*, a series of funnels that guided the fish to the place where the nets could be most easily pulled in. Hence tuna-fishing was particularly prosperous in Byzantion: the city was called "the tuna metropolis" or "the mother of young tuna"—nicknames that require no commentary.[13]

However, many other cities benefited from the tunas' passage, because they migrated along the Greek coast. In the third century BCE, Halieis, in Argolis, dedicated to Poseidon the first tuna caught each year.[14] Fishing for tuna was also practiced on all the Aegean islands, from Eretria to Samos, from Lemnos to Naxos, and from Thera to Melos.[15] According to Pausanias (10.9.3–4), in Kerkyra exceptional schools of tuna were observed by a cowherd, and this detail perfectly reflects the local population's need to avoid missing their seasonal passage. The city could also benefit from "miraculous catches" that brought in considerable profits celebrated by tradition:

> At the entrance to the sacred domain [of Delphi] we find first a bronze bull, the work of Theopropos of Aigina. It was dedicated by the people of Kerkyra. It is said that in Kerkyra a bull left the rest of the herd of cattle that was grazing in a pasture and went to bellow at the seaside. Since this happened every day, the cowherd went down to the shore and saw a prodigious number of tuna. He immediately alerted the people in the city. The latter tried to catch the tuna, but without success. So they sent *theōroi* [sacred ambassadors] to Delphi. The oracle's reply was that they must sacrifice this bull to Poseidon. As soon as they had carried out this sacrifice, they were able to catch the fish. The dedication at Delphi and the one at Olympia represent a tenth of their catch.

The reference to the famous sculptor Theopropos of Aigina situates this episode around 480 BCE. The catch was sold and brought in so much money for the city, either through a monopoly on fishing or through taxes, that it was able to make these dedications in Delphi and Olympia. In modern Greece, the observation of the tuna migration was done from high watchtowers.[16] Another series of ancient documents, ranging from Aristophanes (*Knights* 313) to Oppian (*Halieutics* 3.637–41) in the Imperial period, show that this was already a common practice throughout the ancient Greek world.[17] Since the schools of tuna came no closer than 100 to 200 meters from the coast, they must have been caught from boats (which once again refutes the hypothesis that fishing was done only from the shore).[18]

A fourth type of fishing, similar to the preceding one but not involving large seasonal migrations, was fishing in estuaries, inlets, or bays that were easily accessible for this activity. In the area of the Hellespont and Bosporos, not only tuna but all kinds of fish were caught.[19] Thus Byzantion was famous for its mackerel and its swordfish, while Parion was famous for another particular variety of mackerel.[20] Strabo (14.2.21) writes about Iasos in Karia: "The city has a port and it draws most of its resources from the sea; indeed it has an abundance of fish but its territory is rather poor." Fishing must have been practiced in the interior gulf east of Iasos known as the "Little Sea."[21] Thus one can mention the case of Kaunos, near the mouth of the Kalbis (the river that provided access to the sea from the lake of Köyceğiz). and its marshy areas that promoted fish's reproduction. In a classic study, Louis Robert demonstrated the interest of the *dalyan* (the current Turkish name for these fishing dams) installed opposite ancient Kaunos, in a village named precisely Dalyan. In the modern period, mullet eggs (botargo) and salted fish in general were exported from Dalyan to Rhodes.[22] There must also have been an active fishing industry in ancient Kaunos, since the salt indispensable for preserving fish was also produced there. According to Gallant, the *madrague* fishing technique was not used, but this statement is entirely contradicted by the sources.[23]

Finally, it should be pointed out that in addition to fish, all kinds of shellfish were also harvested (in particular oysters, a luxury food), cuttlefish, crustaceans (crawfish, crabs, lobsters), and other edible animals: according to Athenaeus (7 318f), octopus from Thasos had no peer other than that from Karia, and that is only one of numerous examples of the "regional reputation" enjoyed by one product or another. In Delos, from the Archaic period to the first century BC, marine fauna is always abundantly represented in the archaeological material found in urban milieu, with a high proportion (varying according to the period) of mollusk remains.[24] These "local foods" should not be neglected in determining human caloric intake.

The fish consumed came not only from the sea but also from freshwater lakes. Byzantion, once again, controlled a whole series of such lakes, on both its European and its Asiatic territories, all of them full of fish that enjoyed a high reputation.[25] In Athens, Aristophanes' peasants, like Dikaiopolis in the *Acharnians* (880–94), are fond of eels imported from Boiotia, where the marshes along the shores were full of fish. Generally, numerous documents from all over Greece show that swampy areas were not at all considered to be without economic utility.[26] Thus toward the end of the fifth century or the beginning of the fourth century, a subgroup of the citizens of Erythrai, in Asia Minor, the *chiliastus* (a civic subunit, supposedly a "group of 1,000") of the Peproioi, had magistrates called "supervisors of the marshes."[27] Among the real property leased on Chios in the second half of the fourth century, we find a marsh and a lake.[28] Fish might also be raised in a pond, as is shown by a question asked of the oracle at Dodona: "If I buy the little pond near the Damatrion, will I do something good . . . ?"[29] A pond could be used as a source of fertilizing mud, and also to raise fish or perhaps ducks.

The essential problem raised by food supplies is that of their preservation. The technique of distillation was unknown in antiquity, so alcohol was not one of the possible methods of preservation (and even if it had been, it could not have been used on a large scale because its cost is comparatively high). Vinegar might be used to preserve certain products, but it was expensive and significantly affected the taste. Drying preserved foods for a few months. Because wood was usually a rare and expensive fuel, even on the north coast of the Black Sea, which was very good for fishing but was a treeless steppe (the wooded steppe was far inland), it is not surprising that the technique of smoking fish, which was so important in medieval and modern Europe, seems to have remained marginal in the Greek world.[30] The main way of preserving foods was clearly salting, widely practiced for fish and also for meat.[31] *Taricheiai*, or salted foods, were usually transported in amphoras, and sometimes also in baskets. The *garon* (the Roman *garum*), a fish sauce made with salted and macerated fish intestines that resembled the modern Indochinese *nuoc mam*, was also known from the fifth century on, but it seems to have been less frequently consumed then than it was during the Roman period.[32]

Thus it was necessary to have large quantities of salt, which was also both a required component of human and animal food, and a necessary adjuvant of metal production.[33] This explains why salt production was frequently monopolized by the state, in the world of the city-states as well as in "royal economies," for example that of the Seleukids.[34] Producing salt was a lucrative activity, because all the regions that produced fish needed it. It was usually produced by using evaporation ponds. Not far from Byzantion and the Black Sea, the salt ponds of Tragasai, on the territory of Hamaxitos in the southern Troad, supplied large quantities of salt, and modern parallels show that it was a salt of good quality.[35] In this case, the salt was produced thanks to an exceptional conjunction: geothermal springs that were extremely hot (nearly 100°C) and whose water was very salty (more than seawater), with summer winds and sun that aided evaporation. Finally, the proximity of the sea made this salt particularly attractive. With a low production cost, the profits on the production of salt must have been particularly high. In the nineteenth-century, there were two major salt-producing areas on the west coast of Turkey, Tuzla (Hamaxitos) and Mandalya, that is, the region of the Gulf of Bargylia, whose shallow waters made it particularly suitable for this activity.[36] It is very possible that the same was true in antiquity. Several other regions also produced salt. The region of Priene and the mouth of the Maeander had active saltpans, which were still operated in the Byzantine and early Ottoman period.[37] The region of the Little Sea, East of Iasos, which was certainly much larger than it is today, might also have had some.[38] In Kaunos, the area around Köyceğiz Lake must have been particularly suitable for salt ponds. According to Pliny, salt from Kaunos was famous for its use in treating eye diseases, but especially salt production was farmed out, which shows that it was produced in large quantities.[39]

However, European Greece also produced salt. There are no archaeological remains of salt ponds, because they were not permanent and consisted of just a few earthen dikes. On the other hand, written sources, sometimes consisting merely of ancient or Byzantine toponymy, clearly reveal their existence: thus the toponym Halike (Aliki), found on Thasos and in Argolis.[40] Attika had its deme of Halai (literally, "saltpans"), and the documents concerning the Salaminian *genos* show that it had an estate located on the seacoast that included a salt pond, as is shown by the description given of it.[41] A contractor operating a salt pond appears in the agreement made in the second century between Arsinoe-Methana and Troizen, on the east coast of Argolis.[42] Thus salt must have been produced in abundance almost everywhere along the coasts of the Greek peninsula and of Asia Minor. The production of salted foods consumed large quantities of salt. It was a product that was easy to transport and kept well. Hence it must have been a source of significant profits for coastal areas.

The Greek Cities and Their Coastal Waters

In a passage of the *Laws* (824bc, quoted later) that is crucial for the analysis of the legal framework applicable to fishing, and especially coastal fishing, Plato states that fishermen should be allowed to fish everywhere, except in harbors, sacred rivers, marshes and lakes. The text has been so far understood as indicating that Plato was supporting the view that the sea was "in open access" to everyone. Starting from this common assumption, opinions have diverged. According to Jacques Dumont, our evidence would contradict Plato.[43] In fact, the Greeks would have developed a legal framework that would anticipate our own principle of territorial waters. Quite the opposite, Gianfranco Purpura and Ephraim Lytle have independently argued that both Plato and our ancient evidence would prove that the concept of territorial waters did not exist in antiquity.[44] In the Roman Empire, the legal framework pertaining to fishing would have been no different. Indeed, the *Corpus iuris civilis* seems to vindicate this view, as it stipulates repeatedly that the sea was common to everyone (*mare commune omnium*), that the fish was a *res nullius*, a property of him who had caught it, and that no one was allowed to prohibit fishing along the coast.[45] Thus from Plato to the *Digest*, there would exist a transcultural and transhistorical consensus that the sea was common to everyone and could not be appropriated, even in coastal waters.

However, the context of Plato's development makes it clear that the meaning of the passage is the opposite of what has been assumed so far. What Plato actually states is the following: "Let no one hinder the fowler in wasteland and mountains, but the one who meets him in tilled fields and in sacred fields, let him expel him; similarly, the fisherman shall be permitted to fish in all waters except in harbors, sacred rivers, marshes and lakes." The text should not be read in the perspective of the seventeenth-century debate between Hugo Grotius, who published his *Mare Liberum* in 1609, and John Selden, who answered him with his *Mare Clausum* in

1636. What was at stake in early Modern Europe was the right to sail, trade, and fish in huge tracts of the high seas.[46] Nothing of the kind can to be found in the *Laws*. Plato's point was not to investigate the question of the appropriation of the sea in general or to discuss a point of international law. The passage quoted earlier comes as a sort of addendum to a long development on the education and behavior of citizens (*politai*).[47] As for hunting, only that of big animals was considered worthy of true citizens (or more precisely, "really free men"), the elite members of the community.[48] Fowling and fishing were not. Obviously, Plato thought these activities were to be performed by the members of the lower classes or by slaves (like herdsmen, fishermen could be slaves, as is clear in Alciphron's *Letters of Fishermen*). For this reason, they had to be strictly regulated. But of course, Plato nowhere even imagines that the fowler and the fisherman might be foreigners. For instance, in Athens it would be unthinkable to have Megarians or Boiotians freely roaming Attika to catch birds. Beyond obvious security reasons, the Athenians insisted on reserving their resources for themselves. Even within the border of a city such as Athens or Rhodes, public or sacred lands belonging to a deme, or other local subdivision were normally leased only to members of that subdivision.[49] Plato's fowler, and the fisherman as well, are people of the city, not foreigners. The meaning of the text is thus that in principle the right to fish will be granted to anyone (provided he belongs to the city), and of course it refers to fishing in coastal waters, from or along the coast.

Thus in fact the passage of Plato's *Laws* proves exactly the opposite of what has been concluded so far (supposing that Plato was wrong or that he had no concept of coastal waters). It shows that the coast and the waters along the coast were under the authority of the city and that only the local people could access them. The parallel between, on the one hand, wasteland and mountains and, on the other hand, the "all waters" except harbors, sacred rivers, marshes, and lakes (viz. inevitably coastal waters) implies that both were under the jurisdiction of the city; otherwise the comparison would not make sense. Beyond, on the high sea, the city had no authority. It was a zone where fishermen of all cities could practice their activities (and of course meet, peacefully or not).[50] The implementation of the modern rules concerning "territorial waters" supposes the existence of nautical charts and of measurements of distance from the coast based on coordinates in latitude and longitude.[51] Nothing of the kind existed in the ancient Greek world. The Greek cities reasoned in terms of exploitation of their coastal domains. The immediate coastal waters are all the more of vital importance in the Mediterranean sea in general as this is the zone where the main catches are made in terms of fish (which uses the rocky coast to hide and reproduce), shellfish (including the murex shells), crustaceans, and sponge. This is especially true in Greece, where the continental shelf has a limited extension and where the continental slope is most often close to the shore and has a strong gradient. These coastal waters were an integral part of the sources of revenue (*poroi*) of the city. For this reason only, it would have been unthinkable to leave them open to foreigners, not to mention the risks of smuggling or piracy if ships from foreign cities had been allowed to moor everywhere along the shore and exploit as they wished the coastal waters. This is why for instance in his examination of the sources of revenue of Attika, Xenophon could explain that "the sea around the territory is most fruitful."[52] In the various versions of the legend telling the story of the gold tripod lost at sea and found by fishermen, the principle is always the same: the local fishermen from either Miletos, Kos, or Athens have the right to fish in their own waters—for instance, in the "Koan sea" or "in the sea of the Athenians." [53] This gives them a legal right to their catch, which they can sell or bring to their own city.

It should even be stressed that in its general definition the *Corpus Iuris Civilis* is in full agreement with Plato: everyone should be allowed to fish along the coast. The question at stake is to determine who this "everyone" was. In the time of Plato, it meant that in principle all the citizens of a city were allowed to fish along the coast of their city. More specifically, this meant that local property owners could not bar access of the coastal waters to fishermen: this is exactly also what we find in the *Digest*.[54] It would remain to be determined by a specific analysis if really in the Imperial period, when Rome had established its authority over the whole Mediterranean, any fisherman from any local city or region could fish anywhere on the coast of the Empire.[55] But even if it were the case, the possible trans-Mediterranean logic of imperial Rome can certainly not be transposed back into the Greek Archaic, Classical or Hellenistic periods, with its multitude of city-states jealous of their individual sovereignty and fiercely competing with each other.

If the principle was that in a city the coastal waters were open to the common exploitation of its citizens, the fact that the city had a right of supervision of the coast meant also that it might also decide to sell some right of exploitation and derive certain revenues from it, just as it did from public domains on land. In the second century the two cities of Arsinoe-Methana and Troizen exploited in common tuna traps (*thunneia*) on their coasts, exactly in a territory that was common to both cities, and exploited in common by them.[56] If fishermen from any other city at all had been able to fish along the coasts of these cities, this leasing would have made no sense. Thus one can understand how, according to Pseudo-Aristotle (*Economics* 2.2.3), the city of Byzantion, which needed money, was able to sell permits for maritime fishing (exactly: the "fishing right of the sea")—given the importance of fishing in Byzantion, this was a very important measure—and also to sell salt (which was connected with fishing). A decree issued by Iasos probably in 323 BCE congratulates two of its notables, Gorgos and Minnion, who had obtained from Alexander the Great the restitution of the Little Sea, that is, certainly exclusive fishing rights on the interior gulf located east of Iasos; the exclusive right to fish must have represented a considerable increase of the sources of private revenue for its citizens and indirectly, by way of taxes on fish sales, of the public revenue for the city.[57]

Documents concerning cities located in eastern Crete also illustrate the exploitation of coastal waters by these communities. In an early third-century treaty, the inland city of Praisos granted to its neighboring coastal subject community of

Stalai to keep "its territory, city, sea and islands."[58] In the second century, after the withdrawal of Ptolemaic forces from Itanos, this city and Hierapytna were in conflict among others about the small island of Leuke. War began in 144 BCE. The dispute provoked two interventions of Rome, which assigned the quarrel to an arbitration of Magnesia on the Maeander. In 112 or 111, the court granted the island to Itanos, because of its ancestral rights on the territory. Leuke was a rich sponge and murex fishing center and was probably one of the islands exploited by Stalai in the previously mentioned settlement imposed by Praisos.[59] In the first century BCE, the city of Kos sold the right to collect the tax on "public watchtowers" from which one could observe the migration of fish, just as there was also a tax on the sale of salt fish, and another on fishmongers (who were thus distinguished from sellers of salt fish).[60]

Indeed, in ancient Greece the principle prevailed that the sea was common to all. This did not contradict the other principle that the exploitation of coastal waters was the privilege of each city, provided it could efficiently control its coasts. The debate on the existence or not of "territorial waters," which supposes the existence of nautical charts and of precise measurements of distance from the coast, is ill-founded.[61] The ancient Greek city-states did not reason in these terms. They had a patrimonial logic in which their coastal waters were part of the domain on which their citizens had an exclusive right. A powerful state, with a dense population and local forces able to intervene on its coasts, could enforce this right. A weak, thinly populated city with very long coasts could not, which certainly left wide tracks of wild coast open to exploitation of fishermen of various origins. But the principles remained the same everywhere.

Fish Trade and Fish Consumption

Thus so far as fishing is concerned, one can adopt Braudel's comparison mentioned at the outset, but his conclusions have to be considerably amended. It is quite true that there is a real difference between the medieval and modern world of northern Europe and that of ancient Greece. The fishermen of northern Europe very quickly took to the high seas, voyaging ever farther, even to the shores of Newfoundland, in search of herring and cod, which they salted at sea and brought back in large quantities to the markets of European cities. The conditions in ancient Greece were quite different. Most of the fishing took place in coastal waters, drawing on the local fishing resources. This coastal fishing remained within the domain of the city-state and was practiced for the benefit of its members as well as of the city's treasury. The Mediterranean is certainly less rich in fish than the Atlantic, but it nonetheless offers a wide variety of species. But above all, it has a fish that is particularly abundant and is of great nutritive value: tuna. This fish was the "leading product" of Greek fishing, even if it represented only a minority of the catches. Its migrations from the Black Sea to Sicily offered multiple opportunities to catch it and profit from it. Fishing techniques were not "primitive," and they were obviously capable of producing high yields. For all that, however, it seems that they never led to overfishing that would have prevented the tuna from reproducing. The population of the Greek peninsula, of Sicily, and of Italy was less than that of medieval northern Europe, which moreover experienced an unprecedented economic expansion starting at the end of the Middle Ages. In other words, the tuna resources, to which should be added a number of secondary fish, could easily have played a role in feeding the people of ancient Greece comparable to that of herring for the people of northern Europe in the medieval and modern periods. It is true that the social status of fishermen was mediocre, that their life was difficult and even dangerous. The question Phaikylos asked the god of Dodona in the fourth century constitutes the counterpoint to this: "God. For Good fortune. Does the god tell Phaikylos to practice the trade of his ancestors, namely fishing, and does the god indicate that in this way Phaikylos will succeed?"[62]

From the inferior status of fishermen, society's scorn for their trade, and the endless accusations of fraud made against them, it has been wrongly concluded that fish played only a secondary role in the food supply.[63] One can guess that in most cities, fresh fish played a rather minor role. The fine catches were consumed by the wealthy. An excessive predilection for fish eating, *opsophagia*, was regarded as an extravagance of the well-to-do people.[64] Ordinary fish (small fry, anchovies, sardines) might be part of the diet of more modest people in port cities. The tariff of Akraiphia, which sets a maximum price for a very long list of sea fishes (and for a short list of freshwater fishes from Lake Kopais), shows the concern to limit price fluctuations for a product that must have been considered essential for feeding the people of this Boiotian city.[65] The revenue from the 10 percent tax on fish sales in Delos in the first half of the third century helps us estimate the local level of production and consumption. At Delos, it seems that an average per capita annual consumption of fresh seafood in a range of 18–36 kilograms must be accepted.[66] Akragas went even further. According to Diodorus (11.25.4), the city had Carthaginian prisoners taken in the Battle of Himera in 480 dig a fishpond that enabled the city to provide a large quantity of food. Fresh sea fish could be sold in inland cities, provided they were not too far from the sea, as is proved by the case of Akraiphia in Boiotia. However, in every season and even far inland, salt fish (locally produced or imported) was everywhere available. Strabo (7.6.2) implicitly refers to large *taricheiai* factories in Byzantion. In his description of the enormous ship built by Hieron of Syracuse in the second half of the third century, Athenaeus (5 209a) notes that 60,000 *medimnoi* of grain (1,800 metric tons) were loaded on it, along with 10,000 jars of salted Sicilian fish, 20,000 talents of wool (520 metric tons), and other freight weighing an additional 20,000 talents. It is clear that only once in all antiquity were such quantities of goods loaded on a single ship. But it is striking that after grain, Sicily's first export would be *taricheiai*.

Tuna was and still is caught in large quantities off Sicily, and there is no doubt that it was the fish that had been processed to be transported in this way. In fifth-century Athens, the comic poet Hermippus praised salt fish from Pontos.[67] On the other hand, in the fourth century, in his pseudo-epic poem *Hedupatheia* ("Life of Luxury"), the poet Archestratus praised tuna from Sicily or Byzantion as better than the specialities of Pontos.[68] In the fifth-century "Punic Amphora Building" in Corinth, Punic amphoras for *taricheiai* from the Iberian peninsula were found.[69] Even if they might have contained salt meat, a Carthaginian specialty, they could also have contained tuna, because the western endpoint of the tuna migration was near Cadiz. Throughout antiquity, salt fish from this region was famous. In addition to imports of salt fish from western Greece (Corfu), Sicily, and even the Punic West, the Greek cities could benefit from massive imports from the Hellespont-Bosporos, Kyzikos (it is no accident that tuna still figures on the electrum coins of that city), or Byzantion, among other places, and also from the great fishing grounds farther north at the mouths of the rivers flowing into the Black Sea: the Istros (Danube), the Hypanis (Bug), the Borysthenes (Dnieper), and the Tanais (Don), where another large fish, the sturgeon, was caught in considerable quantities.[70]

These exports may have been still further increased during the Roman period, but all the evidence suggests that major exports were already taking place earlier. Thus Polybius (4.38.4–5) could state that the Euxine still provided honey, beeswax, and fish, whereas its grain exports were (at least at his time) irregular. It is true that exports of fish from Pontos pose the problem of the containers in which they were shipped, insofar as amphoras coming from Pontos (Sinope or Herakleia) are rather rarely found on the Aegean, and may moreover have contained wine or oil.[71] It has been proposed that amphoras sent to the Black Sea filled with wine or oil produced in the Aegean region were reused for exporting fish.[72] Amphoras from Sinope containing the remains of cut-up fish were found in the Varna shipwreck (Classical or early Hellenistic period), proving that one must not always equate amphoras with wine or oil. These Sinopean amphoras might originally have been filled with fish in Sinope itself. Another shipwreck, the one at Tektaş Burnu from the third quarter of the fifth century, contained at least a dozen amphoras from Mende, nine of them full of resin, the tenth (along with a pseudo-Samian amphora) full of cut-up (and thus necessarily salted) meat.[73] This also raises the question of the possible reuse of amphoras, because wine is the product one expects to find in amphoras from this city. But even in this case, one cannot be certain that these amphoras were reused (one could be sure only if the remains of a previous content could be detected). Whatever one may think of the hypothesis that the amphoras were reused, one has to admit, with the two authors cited earlier, that most of the fish coming from the Black Sea was transported in baskets or boxes that have left no archaeological traces.

To conclude on the question of the importance of fish and other products of the sea, the idea that they played only a negligible role in the Greeks' food supply must therefore be rejected.[74] On the sites where it has been possible to carry out detailed studies of common pottery, the importance of cooking fish is striking. Among the fourth- and third-century BCE household "cooking utensils" found in Olbia in Provence (near Hyères in southeastern France), the *lapas*, a stockpot for cooking fish, constituted 50 percent of the pots.[75] These proportions cannot be generalized without precautions, because Olbia is a rather small site. Nonetheless, it is obvious that fish represented an important part of the food supply, particularly for people living near the sea. Bekker-Nielsen's thesis that fish was in reality the "fourth major food" along with grain, wine, and oil is correct.[76] Whereas meat consumption was limited, the consumption of fish, usually dried, provided animal proteins that were absolutely essential for slaves and the ordinary free people. In Pseudo-Demosthenes' *Against Lacritus* (35.31–32 and 34), a landowner from Theodosia, on the Kimmerian Bosporos (Crimea) brings salt fish from Pantikapeion to feed agricultural workers. Similarly, salt fish was a basic food for sailors and soldiers. As the proverb said, "if you don't have meat, you have to like salt fish."[77]

ARTISANAL TRADES

In terms of value, the sector of artisanal trades was largely dominated by agriculture, but once again that does not mean that it should be regarded as a primitive sector. The distinctive character of artisanal production was usually that it was geographically diffuse, not only in the countryside, but also in cities. Even for mass production, there were normally no vast workshops, production not taking place in factory-like structures. Nonetheless, there were exceptions. One has to look into these structures of production and understand the kinds of constraints, both in terms of technology and capital, to which this way of organizing artisanal work responded.[78]

The Diversity of Trades

The dialogue between Socrates and Adeimantos in the *Republic* (2 369d–370c) offers a good introduction to the question:[79]

> Tell me, then, said I, how our city will suffice for the provision of all these things. Will there not be a farmer for one, and a builder, and then again a weaver? And shall we add thereto a cobbler and some other purveyor for the needs of the body?—Certainly.—The indispensable minimum of a city, then, would consist of four or five men.—Apparently.—What of this, then? Shall each of these contribute his work for the common use of all? I mean, shall the farmer, who is one, provide food for four and spend fourfold time and toil on the production of food and share it with the others, or shall he take no thought for them and provide a fourth portion of the food for himself alone in a quarter of the time and employ the other three-quarters, the one in the provision of a house, the other of a garment, the other of shoes, and not have the bother of associating with other people, but, himself for himself, mind his own affairs?—And Adeimantos said, But, perhaps, Socrates, the former way is easier.—It would not, by Zeus be at all strange, said I,

for now that you have mentioned it, it occurs to me myself that, to begin with, our several natures are not all alike but different. One man is naturally fitted for one task, and another for another. Don't you think so?—I do.— Again, would one man do better working at many tasks or at one?—One at one, he said.—And, furthermore, this, I fancy is obvious—that if one lets slip the right season, the favorable moment in any task, the work is spoiled.— Obvious.—That I take it, is because the business will not wait upon the leisure of the workman, but the workman must attend to it as his main affair, and not as a bywork.—He must indeed.—The result then, is that more things are produced, and better and more easily when one man performs one task according to his nature, at the right moment, and at leisure from other occupations.—By all means.

This text shows that people were well aware of the significance of the division of labor. The reasoning is simple. The diversity of needs makes it impossible to perform all tasks oneself. Anyone who tried to do so would be wasting his time, because no one can be a specialist in everything. The division of labor solves all these problems at once by making it possible to increase quantity, improve quality, and save time: thus it is a source of productivity.[80] The vocabulary of artisanal trades in Athens illustrates their great variety and specialization. An inventory of the names of trades in Athens produced a list of 170 different activities (admittedly including commercial and "service" activities): from the flute maker to the potter, from the nut seller to the jar maker, there was a great diversity that corresponds in some degree to Plato's program.[81] Naturally, many of these activities were in reality very similar, but it remains significant that the need was felt to distinguish among them.

Trades were usually practiced by a single artisan, possibly assisted by one or two apprentices or slaves. This was true of all the activities involved in small-scale production or services—shoemaking, for instance. Working in isolation, the producer was in direct contact with the customer. If mass production was envisaged larger workforces could be required for activities such as pottery workshops, where diverse tasks had to be performed. One needed unskilled workers to wash the clay, specialists in producing ceramics on the potting wheel, specialists in painting on vases (if painted vases were being made), and specialists in firing pottery in kilns, so that there must have been at least six or seven persons working in the same workshop. One case might *a priori* seem more problematic: that of large construction projects. Here one had to collect a far more numerous workforce. However, it can be observed that here, too, the work was generally divided up among different enterprises. One or two large enterprises were not set up to take responsibility for a whole part of the project, such as providing the columns, or sculpting all the sculptured parts. On the contrary, the tasks specified in the estimate made by the architect in charge of the project were divided up among a multitude of small enterprises, most of which undertook a small part of the project: the fluting on a column was assigned to one artisan, and that on the next column to a different artisan.[82]

This atomization of tasks presupposed that the architect saw to it that the specifications accepted by the enterprise were rigorously met. However, this way of proceeding had at least two advantages: it permitted very strict quality control and kept costs low by making artisans compete with each other for contracts.

In any case, the construction accounts of sanctuaries in the Classical and Hellenistic periods (at Epidauros, Delphi, Eleusis, the Parthenon, Delos) show that the mode of remuneration was a function of the type of activity involved. Those who provided more specialized work were paid by the piece, whereas unskilled workers were paid by the day.[83] The distinction between horizontal and vertical specialization, which under another name (as Edward Harris has pointed out) was perceived by Max Weber, allows us to solve this enigma.[84] The great diversity of trades corresponded to the great diversity of needs. We can call this "horizontal specialization." On the other hand, these activities had a common denominator: they required little vertical specialization. The latter can be defined as the sum of the activities required to arrive at the final product. By comparison with a modern industrial system, the production line was short, that is, a limited number of operations separated the raw material from the finished product. Production required only a fairly modest set of tools. Relatively speaking, the role of capital in the value of the product was proportionally small in relation to that of labor. Thus it did not justify concentration in a single workshop or a single team gathered around complex and expensive equipment. The only case where bringing workers together in the same place could be justified was the one in which, by dividing up the tasks, one could specialize actions in the framework of what might be called "mass production." That was certainly what was done in weapons workshops, cutleries, and bed factories, of which we can form an idea from the speeches connected with Lysias's weapons factory (*Against Eratosthenes* 12.8) or with the workshops mentioned by Demosthenes (*Against Aphobus I* 27.9–11). The knife factory owned by Demosthenes' father had 32 or 33 slaves, and his furniture factory had 20. Besides, rationalization in the organization of production was not unknown. A good case is provided by two ceramic workshops that were active between the fourth century and the second century BCE and were located in the Mesogaia (the eastern part of Attika).[85] Interestingly, the workshops transformed and developed over time. In one of the workshops, the initial two small circular kilns (diameter 1.20–1.50 meters) were supplemented by a larger square one (side 2.50 meters). They were then replaced by a larger rectangular one (3.5 by 5.0 meters), and finally by a very large piriform-shaped kiln (diameter 6.5 meters, length 8.50 meters). These workshops produced tiles, water spouts, and beehives that were in use in the whole surrounding plain.

As for the spatial distribution of the workshops, ceramic production provides an excellent test case, because it leaves the best archaeological traces. In reality, it varied according to the types of production and also changed over time. The proximity of water, of a source of raw material (such as clay for ceramics workshops), and also of potential clients, such as visitors to a sanctuary (who for instance might buy the productions of the coroplasts' workshops) were the main factors determining the location of the workshops. Some were operated in the countryside—for instance, because of the proximity of a mine supplying metal workshops, of a clay pit, or of a waterway or road. This was precisely the case of the two previously mentioned eastern Attika ceramic workshops.[86] It was also the case of the amphora workshops, normally located in the vicinity of farms, and usually also very close to the local ports from which the cargoes would be shipped. The cases of the islands of Thasos and Rhodes provide excellent examples of peripheral (that is, coastal) locations meeting both requirements.[87]

In the towns, a concentration in the same neighborhood of workers plying a given trade was not the rule for all trades.[88] At Eretria in Euboia, as at Sicilian Naxos in the Archaic and Classical periods, there is no clear sign of a geographical concentration of workshops.[89] But in the sixth- and fifth-century Athens, pottery production was concentrated in the Ceramic quarter (northwest of the center), viz. in the "Inner Ceramic" (within the walls of the city) and "Outer Ceramic," outside the walls, which was also a necropolis zone. This location was not justified by reasons directly connected with the logic of production but by reasons of public hygiene or the logic of sales, because buyers could easily find a certain category of products.[90] In the fourth century, probably under the pressure of private funerary construction, the workshops moved to the area behind the southern hills, between the long walls.[91] In sixth- and fifth-century Selinous, a huge "industrial district" extending (within the fortification circuit) along the eastern part of the walls has been identified.[92] At Hellenistic Lokroi Epizephyrioi, many ceramics kilns have been identified in blocks near the large street (*plateia*) parallel to the southern walls, while others were situated outside the walls, and a metal workshop has been found right in front of the wall, southeast of the town.[93] An interesting case is provided by the many workshops located in the western outskirts of Alexandria, on the narrow tract of land separating the sea from Lake Mareotis, which were already active in the Hellenistic period. There were large amphora workshops that were connected with the prosperous local farms, but were also involved in various other productions.[94]

The Case of Textile Manufacturing

Textile manufacturing allows us to raise in a greater detail the question of how enterprises were structured and how unskilled labor was used. It also invites us to evaluate the importance of this sector in the economic life of a region. Wool especially but also flax (for fine fabrics) and hemp (for crude fabrics) were the main products processed. Silk was worked only in certain particular regions, especially on Kos.[95] Most of the production operations were performed by women. They cleaned and washed the wool or carded the flax.[96] Spinning was done on a spindle. Weaving was normally done on large, vertical wooden looms. The archaeological trace of these trades is constituted by the numerous loom weights that were used to stretch the threads, and which thus permit us, in the absence of any other evidence, to identify the presence of a loom. Then wool fabrics had to be milled to make them dense and soft: a mixture of urine (which contains ammonia) and earth was used. This activity was carried out by men, in workshops located in specific neighborhoods, because of the odor involved. It might remain to dye the fabrics—in the Hellenistic period, the demand for purple fabrics rose in proportion to the increase in the number of people able to afford them—and perhaps make clothes from them. Athenian sources, both literary and epigraphic, allow us to form a fairly good idea of the structure of production. Most of the diverse phases of the activity mentioned earlier are found represented by the names of specific trades.

Indeed, textiles were traditionally household productions intended to meet the needs of the family. The Homeric model of Penelope weaving all day with her servants was still fully valid. Every young girl or adult woman, of whatever status (free or slave), was typically supposed to be trained in this activity. In Xenophon's *Economics* (7.6), this is explicitly what Ischomachos expects from his young wife. But even home production could find its way to the market. This is definitely proved by the case of Olynthos, where loom weights are found in many houses, but where some houses concentrated a large quantity of them. This means that in these houses textile production far outstripped any possible household consumption.[97] While never eliminating household production (at least in a rural context) specialization and production in dedicated workshops were thus introduced as early at the Classical period and developed even more over the following centuries.

One source of particular interest is in Athens the lists drawn up after "trials for defection" (*dikē apostasiou*).[98] The law allowed a former master to take legal action against a manumitted slave who did not remain with him or went to work for another man. If the manumitted slave was found guilty, he reverted into slavery. If he won his case, he received complete freedom. In the latter case, he had to consecrate a commemorative phial worth 100 drachms. That is why there exists, for the period 330–322 BCE, a long list of consecrations made by emancipated slaves. One may wonder whether the lawsuit was not a pure legal fiction to keep a record of the slave emancipation. For the time being however, it seems that our documentation does not allow us to vindicate this (very attractive) hypothesis. Most of these trial cases concern women, who are called *talasiourgoi*, "wool spinners" or "wool workers." The "liberation" of women from labor as a result of new techniques of grinding grain and their substitution effect made this kind of investment both possible and profitable.[99] Hence such situations involving emancipated female slaves were frequent. These inscriptions confirm what is indicated by literary sources. It was common for anyone who had capital to invest in trade production. In *Against Timarchus* (1.97), Aeschines mentions Timarchos's fortune: real estate, and also a workshop with nine or ten slaves and their overseer employed in leather-working, one workwoman set up separately to make "Amorgos fabrics" (*amorgina*) that she sold on the market herself, and an embroidery worker. Thus people bought slaves in the same way that today they buy machines, which reminds us of the famous remark in Aristotle's *Politics* (1.2.5): "If shuttles could weave all by themselves and *plektra* play the *kithara* by themselves, then foremen would have no need of attendants and masters no need of slaves." Usually, then, slaves were bought to toil in small work-shops or even in individual workshops. In the city, the structure of production might be fragmented. The owner continued to control the process of production because it was he who provided the raw material. After the Peloponnesian War, there was a serious economic crisis in Athens, and many women had lost their husbands. The widows, with their children, had to take refuge with relatives. The latter thus found themselves with numerous mouths to feed. In a scene in Xeno-phon's *Memorabilia* (2.7.2–12), Socrates advises Aristarchos, who has fourteen mouths to feed, to put the women of his household to work so that they can pro-vide revenues for this expanded family: instead of the "barbarian" women who were usually forced to do the work, the situation required free women to take it on. Socrates provides the examples of four wealthy Athenians who made their fortunes respectively from swine and cattle raising, from baking, from cloak making, and from mantle making. Xenophon's comparisons show how common it was to set up textile workshops with slaves who had been bought (this was the first example provided by Socrates). Convinced by Socrates, Aristarchos decides to borrow the start-up capital (*aphormē*) that will allow him to buy wool and put to work the women of his households, both slaves and free persons.[100]

Thus the importance of textile production should be reevaluated. Far from con-forming to Vincent J. Rosivach's schema, which essentially accepted only produc-tion within the household to satisfy immediate needs, textiles were a sector con-cerning which it is no exaggeration to say that despite its fragmented production structure, it provided genuine mass production.[101] First, we have to return to the important point about the production of the raw material. It has been observed that livestock raising was omnipresent in Greece. For mainland Greece however, using the livestock raising zones identified by Chandezon, it can be observed that if its place was more limited in the arid part of Greece on the shores of the Aegean, in the two zones farther to the west it was much more developed. This was also the case in inland Asia Minor, where livestock raising was much very extensive and might even become the main agricultural activity.[102] Now, this involved chiefly rais-ing sheep for wool production. Thus we are dealing with production in large quan-tities. The question has to be raised as to how and by whom this wool was pro-cessed. It has been observed that even overland, the cost of transport became virtually negligible for a product of great value like textiles. Thus the question is not whether the wool mass-produced in the pastureland zones of western Greece or Asia Minor was consumed by the great urban centers located on the edge of the Aegean: that is certain, and it provides a particularly interesting example of the economic integration of vast regions, with some producing wool, others receiving the textile products and necessarily, in one form or another, sending back other products in exchange. The question is where the processing was performed. Was it done on site, or was the wool transported in raw form to be processed in large workshop-cities that added considerable value to it?

An amusing contrast is made in Theocritus's *Idyll* 15, where Gorgo complains that her husband has bought her a poor piece of cloth, while her friend Praxinoa has cloth worth two *minae* (200 drachms). The story is interesting because the characters, who belong to the middle stratum of citizens, one of modest condition, the other well-off, have bought cloth and used it to make their clothing. However, tunics and mantles could be bought ready-made in the markets, as several anecdotes demonstrate.[103] The story also invites us to think that in matters of textiles, one has to distinguish luxury products made for wealthy customers who appreciated cloth made of fine wool, flax, or silk, from consumer products mass-produced for an ordinary clientele.

We have proof that wool could be transported. The mention of the transport of several bales of wool in *Against Lacritus* (35.34) is anecdotal. But Aeneas Tacticus (29.4–6) describes ships carrying baskets of crude wool as nothing out of the ordinary. Hieron II's *Syracusan* was loaded not only with grain and salt fish but also with 20,000 talents, or 520 metric tons, of wool.[104] Thus it is clear that transport of wool in crude form was common. The inevitable conclusion is that large quantities of wool were easily transported by ship to large cities on the Aegean that specialized in textile production. Thanks to traders from Aigina, Megara must have found it easy to procure the raw material, as did Athens, where textiles seem to have been a veritable "household industry." The city of Megara was known especially for its inexpensive wool tunics (*exōmides*).[105] Corinth was famous for its fine wool cloth.[106] The many documents concerning textile activity in Athens invite to admit that the city was a large textile production center. As for Asia Minor, textile production there had developed early on, with specialties in luxury fabrics from Miletos. However, in the Archaic and Classical periods all of Ionia and the region of Kos already produced these goods in large quantities. What seems to have been a real novelty in the late Hellenistic period, a phenomenon that became established and grew during the Imperial period, was the development of a large-scale textile trade in the cities of the Anatolian hinterland, cities that henceforth entered into trade with the Greek world: Thyateira, Saittai in the valley of the Hermos, Hypaipa, Philadelphia, Hierapolis, and Laodikeia in the Maeander Basin all became major textile centers.[107] There, wool produced in the region could be used (sheep raising was very developed in this area) and the finished products exported. In that way, to the extent to which textiles were products of great value per unit of weight, one could compensate for the disadvantage of being located far inland and enter into the great cycle of Mediterranean commerce.[108]

In passing, it is clear that the old concept of "consumer city," no matter how it is understood, should henceforth be considered obsolete. The cities in general, and in particular the great metropolises of the Classical period, were production sites par excellence, for metallurgical products in general, for ceramics (decorated or utilitarian), for luxury industries like perfumes, which had the advantage of combining very great value and very small volume,[109] and for leather, but above all for textiles, the sector that employed the most labor and which must have produced by far the most profit. At least for the world of the Greek city-states, the image of the "parasite city" living off the countryside and not giving anything back to it should be totally abandoned. It suffices to observe the equipment of the farms in Macedon to understand how wrong that idea can be.[110] Urban products that supplied the countryside also entered into distant commercial circuits and helped pay for imports of basic products, in particular grain and oil. It is the whole equation of Athenian import and export commerce that has to be reinterpreted in this perspective. How were the massive purchases of cereal grains made by Athens in the Classical period financed? To be sure, it was by exporting silver (in the form of coins) from the mines of Laurion, but also, for the remainder, by exporting artisanal products, among others ceramics and textiles.

CAPITAL AND TECHNOLOGICAL INNOVATION

A speech that Thucydides (1.71.2–3) puts in the mouth of the Corinthian delegate to the Spartan assembly in the autumn of 432 starkly raises the question of innovation. The Corinthian enlightens the Spartans as to their responsibilities and the stakes in the conflict with the Athenians. Above all, he shows that the Athenians are formidable adversaries, because they are constantly making new conquests and do not draw back before any new idea. He emphasizes at length that on this level, the contrast with the Spartans is as complete as might be. Then he adds:

> Even if you were the neighbors of a city like your own, you would find it difficult to prevail. But as I have shown, your institutions are outmoded compared with theirs. It is the same as in arts and crafts [technē]: new solutions inevitably prevail. For a city at peace, immutable systems are best. But if one is faced with numerous needs, one is forced to introduce numerous improvements. That is why the Athenians, with their varied experience, have been far more innovative than you have.

Thus the best comparison Thucydides can make to illustrate his remarks on the confrontation between two institutional systems is that of competition in technology. It was notorious that in the world of the trades, one won out over one's rivals—one sold more—if one had innovated. Of course, we have to assess the innovations.[111] Ordinarily—not always, as will become clear—it was not a matter of creating products to be used for radically new and unprecedented purposes, as might be the case today. It was more a matter of improvements of detail: offering a product better adapted to its function, or with an updated appearance. It remains that this is nonetheless an important point, because it means that there was a genuine incentive to innovate: that of seizing a larger market share.

A series of innovations were thus introduced in textiles. For an increasingly numerous wealthy clientele, the technique (already known for a long time) of dyeing with the color purple, using the murex, a shellfish mass-produced for this purpose, was developed. These luxury fabrics could moreover be interwoven with golden threads. Aristotle (later followed by Pliny) even preserved the name of a weaver-woman, Pamphila, who was traditionally said to have invented the technique of spinning wild silk, which became a specialty of the region of Kos.[112] Even if the date is debated, the invention thus went back to at least the fourth century. Silks were highly prized products and very expensive.[113] In certain cases, there was a genuine process of invention, and not merely the adoption of procedures already known elsewhere (as in the case of the murex and purple dye, which were already known to the Phoenicians).

The most spectacular progress was made in the area of processing agricultural products. Making flour requires crushing and grinding the grains; making oil from olives requires that they be crushed and then pressed; and other grains (mustard, ricin, sesame) also have to be crushed and pressed. The first phase of winemaking involves pressing the must. In these three domains, Greece contributed decisive innovations that gradually spread to the surrounding civilizations and remained the technological basis for these products for two millennia. Until the Classical period, Greece seems not to have developed a technology different from the one that is found at the same period in the world of the Eastern Mediterranean. In the Bronze Age and down to the Archaic period, large, flat stone mortars with rollers were used to crush olives. For grains, saddle querns were the normal device, and it was women's work to prepare the flour. Later, decisive changes were made.

Several new types of crushers for grain appeared.[114] At first, these were "hopper-rubbers" (also called "Olynthos mills"), known from the fifth century on—reciprocating crushers consisting of a stone fitted with an arm that moved it back and forth in a stone trough. The flour flowed out through an orifice in the lower part.[115] These small, relatively "portable" crushers were very convenient for domestic use, but they were still labor-intensive and could be operated only by a human being. The introduction of the rotary mill represented a groundbreaking innovation. The rotary crusher, which was already known in the western Mediterranean in the early Classical period and was obviously non-Greek in origin, was introduced and widely adopted in the Aegean world only in the course of the Hellenistic period.[116] It varied in size (large ones had considerable milling power for each mill). In its more elaborate design, the rotary mill consisted of a moving part shaped like a double funnel, the *catillus* (in the Roman vocabulary), which turned on a conical fixed part, the *meta*, with the flour emerging on the edge of the latter. These two types of rotary mills could be operated by humans, but even better by animals, either oxen or asses. These devices could make excellent flour while saving human labor if draft animals were available.

For crushing olives, the most spectacular invention was what is usually called a *trapetum* (a Latin word derived from the Greek that means "turning machine"). The *trapetum* was present on sites dating from the Hellenistic period, but since these sites had been occupied since the Classical period, it is difficult to determine the exact date of its initial appearance. However, unless they were brought there at a later date, fragments found in Olynthos, which was destroyed by Philip in 348 and partially reoccupied by 316 at the latest, suggest that the *trapetum* may already have been in use in the fourth century.[117] Besides, examples of *trapetum* found in archaeological contexts dating from the end of the fourth century make it clear that it was already in use in this period.[118] The *trapetum* consists of a large stone trough with a pivot in the center on which two hemispheric millstones are made to turn, gradually crushing the olives. Preferably, the millstones are turned by animal power.

Here one must inquire into the process of invention and innovation. The crucial element in three of these facilities is the introduction of rotary movement. But beyond the concept itself, there is the matter of its realization. Tools perfectly adapted to their function had to be "machined" in stone in order to be truly productive. Thus the *trapetum* and the *meta/catillus* presupposed the mutual adaptation of two complex parts, each of which had to be perfectly adjusted to the other. The fabrication of these "machines" implied thorough precision in the shaping of these curved surfaces. This required exact measurements and great skill in cutting the stone. The experience gained from large architectural projects (making stone columns, sculpting statuary) must have been put to use in producing these machines. To make the millstones last as long as possible, they were usually cut from very hard materials, preferably basalt, and if this was not available, then in hard limestone. Layers of basalt, particularly those found on the volcanic islands of Nisyros (in the southeast Aegean) and Pantelleria (off Sicily) gave rise to an active trade in the millstones that came from these regions. Thus the millstones from Nisyros were used all over the Aegean and as far as Cyprus or the western Mediterranean (they played an indispensable role as ships' ballast, becoming commercial objects again when they were unloaded). In briefly describing Nisyros, Strabo (10.5.16) does not fail to mention that the island is defined by its basalt, which was extensively exported to neighboring regions. The considerable weight of basalt millstones, their inertia, and their hardness made these mills incomparably more efficient than the devices inherited from the Bronze Age.

The new technologies considerably reduced the time women had to devote to grinding operations, or even totally freed them from that work. It has been calculated that with the saddle quern, about three hours per day were needed to grind enough flour for a household, viz. ca. 2 kilograms.[119] As observed by Halstead, this meant a total of 130 man-days per year (on the basis of a nine-hour workday throughout the year). This is more than the total of the labor required for tilling/sowing, reaping, threshing, dehusking, and final cleaning of the same quantity of grain (126 man-days).[120] This work could be invested in other domains—for example, in childcare, which led to better hygiene and health and made it possible to give children a better bringing-up. Women were also able to produce textiles at home, an activity that allowed them to increase the family's revenues. Thus it is clear that such innovations were important not only directly, by saving time and improving quality, but also indirectly, through their major economic implications. These inventions spread only gradually to other parts of the Mediterranean world.

For pressing either olives or grapes, the press with a lever and a counterweight of large blocks of stone, which was well known in the East, was long used in Greece. It is attested nearly everywhere, and especially in one of the capitals of oil production, the city of Klazomenai.[121] However, there was an important innovation in this domain as well, the screw press. The screw was invented by Hellenistic engineers connected with the school of mathematics in Alexandria. It was undoubtedly not only a purely technical feat but also the result of scientific thought.[122] This invention was to have an immense future. In antiquity, the screw was made of wood only. But its application to oil and wine presses made it possible to obtain an efficiency superior to that of traditional presses. However, the new technology was not easy to implement, because the design of the screw had to be perfect and because its manufacturing process was complex and relatively expensive. Thus only the most advanced "entrepreneurs" could have it, and the new technology never completely replaced the old counterweight systems, which were cruder and less efficient, but easier to construct and operate.

The innovation that crowned all the others was the watermill, which made it possible to economize the energy used to turn the millstones. An epigram attributed by the *Greek Anthology* (9.418 = 82 G-P) to Antipater, without giving further details, presents this invention in a poetic form. Two poets bore that name, Antipater of Sidon, who lived at the end of the second century and beginning of the first century BCE, and Antipater of Thessalonike, who lived in the Augustan period. The consensus is now in favor of the second Antipater, although no certainty can be reached.[123] The text is especially interesting as it describes an elaborate and more efficient model of "overshot" watermill, the rotation being initiated by the water falling into buckets at the top of the wheel (in an "undershot" mill, the wheel is rotated by the flow of water striking the paddles at the bottom of the wheel). Deo is Demeter's alternative name, and the nymphs are water divinities:

Do not put your hand to the millstone, you women grinders, slumber on, even if the cocks' crowing announces the dawn. For Deo has assigned the nymphs to do the labor of your hands. And they, spurting to the top of the wheel, turn the axle that thanks to the curved spokes, moves the heavy, hollow millstones from Nisyros. Once again we enjoy the life of the first age, if we learn to feast on Deo's fruits without labor.

Archaeological evidence shows that the watermill also took off strongly in the West, especially in Gaul, at the end of the first century BCE. It is striking that the epigram insists directly on the fundamental point mentioned earlier: economizing work by women. The invention was Greek, but its adoption by Roman entrepreneurs is easily understood. Water is scarce all over the Aegean part of the Greek world, but not in western Greece or Asia Minor. In describing the palace of Mithridates in Pontos, Strabo (12.3.30) notes that it included a watermill. Thus it is certain that this device was invented before the first century BCE, and it is even possible that it goes back to the third century.[124] The exceptionally rapid adoption of the watermill in the Roman West can be explained by the fact that, there, much more capital had become available.

The watermill was introduced too late in the history of the Greece of the city-states to profoundly alter trends in its economic development. It is nonetheless clear that it was the culmination of a process of invention that was directly connected with the history of the Greek world. In a declaration that sounds astonishingly modern, the Roman engineer Vitruvius (9. Pr. 1–3), who lived in the first century BCE and early first century CE, did not conceal his admiration for the Greek philosophers and scientists of the past, those "benefactors of humanity" who, in his view, were far more worthy of praise than the winners of athletic competitions.

VIII

THE LOGIC OF GROWTH

At this point, it is possible to draw some initial conclusions regarding the logic of growth in the world of the Greek city-states. After having lain fallow for several decades, the study of the ancient economy is now a flourishing field. Much remains to be discovered, and new syntheses remain to be written. However, it appears that the age of late Archaic, Classical, and Hellenistic Greece can be defined as a moment of transitory equilibrium. Its history has to be resituated in the wider context of a process of growth starting in the Early Iron Age and accelerating during the Archaic period, of the relationships with the royal economies established in the East by the Greco-Macedonians, and also of the economic development of the Mediterranean empire finally unified by Rome. Even if it has to be provisional, a sketch may be drawn to serve as a basis for future research.

SELF-CONSUMPTION AND GROWTH

Self-Consumption and the Market

For many scholars, self-consumption remains the most serious obstacle, if not to the recognition that a market existed in ancient Greece (which is now no longer contested), at least to acceptance of the fact that the market was able to play a role of some importance in the general economy. Some scholars regard it as no more than a very secondary way of allocating goods. The essential way, they maintain, was domestic allocation in the framework of the family, which took the form of self-consumption. It is supposed to have been supplemented by trade in goods and services within family, neighborhood, local, or other proximate networks, outside the market, and, of course, not monetized. The story of Philemon and Baucis told by Ovid depicts a family of peasants living in the Golden Age dear to ancient writers.[1] Two beggars knock at the door of all the houses in a village in Phrygia. No one will take them in. They finally knock at the door of a poor shack belonging to an elderly couple, Philemon and Baucis, good people who agree to let them in. The hosts set the table, bring out a ham to satisfy their guests' hunger, and then make a feast with the products of the household. The beggars turn out to be none other than Zeus and Hermes in disguise. They reveal their identities and grant Philemon and Baucis exceptionally long lives before transforming them for eternity into two intertwining trees. But the gods punish everyone in the country by sending a flood that washes away all the houses and their inhabitants. With Philemon and Baucis, one thinks of Aristophanes' Acharnians, who, forced to take refuge in Athens during the Peloponnesian War, bitterly miss their village, where people don't even know what the word "buy" means.[2] How could it be doubted that there was a world peculiar to rural people that was based on the *oikos*, on the authority of the father and the family, and that was maintained even as it was transformed during the Classical and Hellenistic periods?[3] Neither is there any reason to doubt the existence of practices of mutual aid and nonmonetary exchange. If as everyone agrees in the Greece of the city-states (Athens being no doubt a special case), the majority of people always lived off the land, wouldn't self-consumption—and not the market—have been the paradigm of economic organization? We can see how Karl Bücher could nostalgically rediscover in the barrels of sauerkraut and pickled pork of his childhood the life in the Golden Age praised by Aristophanes' peasants.[4]

But can we limit ourselves to these observations? In addressing the question of self-consumption, value judgments should be avoided. Self-consumption and rural life were not virtuous "choices" but were primarily plain necessities. First, if one was running a grain farm that was not very productive, but in a period when grain prices were high and fluctuated greatly, he would have to have a singular lack of foresight to sell all his wheat and barley and then go buy it back on the market, possibly at higher prices, and in any case paying the cost of transport to and from the market. What was good for Pericles at his social level—having his intendant sell his whole crop and then buying what he needed on the market—made no sense for a humble peasant.[5] Such a peasant could hope to get through hard times with poor harvests by suspending his sales of grain on the market for a year in order to feed his family.

But it is the very idea of self-consumption that must be more precisely defined. In fact, even a great landlord had an interest in feeding his slaves with grain or wine produced on his farm, even if the estate clearly did not operate on the basis of self-consumption, because most of what it produced was sold. One should restrict the concept of self-consumption to productive units most of whose products were consumed by the producers. On the one hand, there were middle-sized property holders who lived on their own production while also selling on the market. In the event of an adverse economic situation, their reserves in grain and money allowed them to maintain their farms a few years despite the circumstances, or switch to another activity. On the other hand, there were farms with low productivity whose operators lived under precarious conditions on marginal lands (the *eschatiai*). The latter could survive only by seizing opportunities, by selling a few sacks of grain when the price on the urban market was exceptionally high. In order to get a supplementary income, they also had to hire themselves out, at the highest possible wages, to the owners of middle-sized and large estates in the region. A prolonged crisis in the urban system was disastrous for these peasants who, without reserves of grain or money that allowed them get through bad years, had no maneuvering room.

Fundamentally, the main reason for the system of self-consumption was the level of agricultural productivity. If we hypothesize a (generous) average productivity in Greece of 7 to 1 for barley, and production on the basis of family farms of 5 hectares working practically throughout the year mainly at this activity, it is clear that the number of people who could be fed per worker employed in agriculture was low. Even if we concede that, all other things being equal, ancient Greek agriculture was more productive than that of other traditional societies, the proportion of the non-agricultural population that could be fed by the grain put on the market probably could not have been more than 25 percent. In other words, the majority of the grain produced necessarily went to feed those who produced it. If out of seven grains produced, one had to be saved for seed and four were eaten by the producers (and their families), only two (or less than 30 percent) remained available for sale on the market. For the producer, half of that amount went to pay various taxes (in any case, outside Athens it was probably common to pay a tenth of the harvests, and in addition various taxes on sales or goods). The other half, or 15 percent (20 percent at a maximum) represented the revenue available to the peasant.

However, this 15 percent played a vital role. With this amount, the peasant had to buy everything he needed in the way of tools for farming (iron tools, in any case), for the household (pottery). He also had to make larger investments if he wanted to construct a new house in the event that two brothers shared property, and also replace the slave whose help was indispensable for heavy tasks and for the continuity of agricultural work when the master had to be absent (particularly because of his activity as a citizen). For such a peasant, the market price of the grain sold was therefore a key factor. If it was high, lands that were not very profitable might be put under cultivation, because with even a small surplus it was possible to obtain monetary resources that would allow the farm to be maintained. If the situation soured—for whatever reason—these little farms were doomed.

Let us describe the model in detail and assume that a farm surviving on its own products and growing grain needed to sell on average 30 percent of what it produced, and was able to provide completely for the subsistence of the family with the 70 percent that remained. In the event that prices collapsed—for example, as a result of a political catastrophe—the large city next door would not be able to absorb his products or if it could, only at very low prices. On the other hand, the price of goods that the farmer had to buy did not necessarily decrease in the same proportion, because the factors influencing their prices might not be determined by the local situation. The basic economic question is that of the average production cost: one had to pay for slaves, for oxen, for amphoras (if it was possible to develop a complementary wine or oil production), and inevitably from time to time for tools. Below a certain level of profitability, that is, if the price of grain and other foodstuffs sold on the market did not make it possible to buy these products, the farm was doomed. It could continue on the basis of complete self-sufficiency so long as its means of production did not need to be replaced. If it was necessary always to sell more to purchase equipment, clothing, or indispensable supplemental foods, an ongoing "scissors crisis" set in. It then became impossible to maintain the "self-sufficient farm," even if purchases were still further reduced. In his excellent critique of the notion of a "natural" surplus, Harry W. Pearson pointed out the fallacious idea of the "net product" as conceived by the Physiocrats:[6]

> The mysterious power of producing a surplus which the Physiocrats attributed to Nature was nothing more than the market measurement of the difference between production cost and selling price. If, through the normal operation of market forces the price of grain should fall to the level of the labor, the *produit net* would disappear.

This is exactly what occurred in Athens at the beginning of the Hellenistic period. With the decrease in population, the very marked decline in the attractive power of the city of Athens, and the slowing of monetary circulation, the maintenance of farms on the less fertile marginal lands could no longer be justified. Probably after an initial phase of going into debt, the farm was sold to some great landlord at a ridiculous price or simply abandoned. That is the explanation for the disappearance of the farms in the deme of Atene, in southern Attika, in the early third century. The closure of the mines in Laurion deprived these farms of an outlet that justified their existence. There had been a large number of slaves working in the mines who had to be fed, and a circulation of capital that made attractive prices possible.[7] Once the mines had closed, the farms were doomed. Even the farm at Vari, which seems to have specialized in bee-keeping, disappeared at the same time, probably at the end of the fourth century.[8] On the other hand, in the territory of Mesogaia, which was much richer, and where a concentration of property can also be discerned, agricultural activity was apparently continued without difficulty.[9]

In other words, the least profitable farms and those on which self-consumption was the most practiced were those whose existence was the most fragile. So long as Athens remained rich and powerful (that is, until the Battle of Amorgos in 322 BCE), so long as money continued to flow into it in abundance, so long as its population remained large (which led to strong demand for grain), and so long as grain prices stayed high and passed through periods of accelerated increase because of interruptions in supply connected with extrinsic causes, since in general Attic agriculture must have fed only one inhabitant in four, it was possible to maintain numerous farms that operated essentially on the basis of self-consumption. This was the most significant phase of agricultural expansion Attika experienced until the end of the nineteenth century. If an economic downturn occurred, these farms would immediately be swept away. It is clear that if Greek farms had really operated on the basis of self-consumption, they would have been unaffected by economic fluctuations. However, the reverse proves to be true. The depression that began in central and insular Greece in the early third century accelerated in the second and first centuries BCE. In this second phase, large farms were able to survive, but even middle-sized ones must have encountered great difficulties, and archaeological surveys suggest that many of them disappeared as well. Outside the great estates, there remained here and there a few marginalized farmers stubbornly resisting civic life, marrying among themselves, and living almost totally on the basis of self-consumption, as one can imagine them through the *Euboean Discourse* Dio Chrysostom composed in the early Imperial period. To be sure, one has to take into account the role of romantic fiction and commonplaces about the city-country opposition.[10] But in Dio Chrysostom's description there must also be traits borrowed from the real world, if only the vision of an empty, depopulated countryside that would have been unthinkable in the Classical period.

The ahistorical, Rousseauistic schema of the farm existing in the mode of self-consumption must therefore be abandoned. For instance, the transformation Athenian agriculture underwent between the fourth and the third centuries BCE would be inexplicable in terms of this schema. In reality, even farms on which 80 percent of what was produced was consumed were not only also connected with the market, but paradoxically they were still more dependent on it because they were barely surviving.

Besides, even in a single *polis* different people could have different strategies. For instance, at Olynthos in the first half of the fourth century (as already mentioned, the town was destroyed in 348 BCE) the houses in the southern district, in the so-called Villa Section, had large storage facilities (possibly for home consumption) and seem not to have engaged in household industry, thus apparently suggesting that their owners pursued a strategy of greater independence from the market. On the contrary, the houses on the North Hill, close to the agora, had much smaller storage facilities (allowing households to store food for a few weeks only, not a whole year, as could the houses of the Villa Section). Besides, they reveal an active artisanal production that inevitably aimed not only at meeting the needs of a family, as is proved, for example, by the presence of shops. The owners of these houses were thus much more linked to the market. This does not mean that their owners did not own lands in the countryside (unfortunately our sources do not allow us to know). But they may well have decided to sell their crops and engage in other activities, just as did Pericles, who sold his whole crop at once after the harvest.[11] Archaeology alone cannot provide all the answers, but is sufficient to suggest the existence of different strategies and the omnipresence of the market, even when self-consumption is also well attested.

The Question of Growth

The ancient economy may be considered "primitive" because according to our criteria, the volumes produced remained small, the technological level remained low, and productivity was weak. Despite a few achievements that were indeed significant but very localized, the scientific level remained too low to have a decisive impact on technological innovation. As for the key question of control over energy, the only innovation that was to have an important future was the water mill. It is the sum of these factors that made agriculture remain vulnerable to variations in rainfall from one year to another, for example, and kept the quantities of iron and steel available per capita low. If we judge by these criteria, the ancient economy was certainly not a "developed economy" (this notion remaining relative, of course). But this would be a rash judgment. What has to be brought out above all is not the difference from our level of development, but only the relative advances that were made and the transformations that they entailed.

If that point of view is adopted, one must draw a quite different conclusion, and one can no longer claim that the economy of the Greece of the city-states was characterized by stagnation and immobility, experiencing growth only in the form of the extension of the area cultivated, without increasing yields and without innovation: in short, that it was an immobile world, despite its political ups and downs, which seem all the more trivial. It is the impressive demographic, political, economic, and cultural growth of the Greek world of the city-states in the Archaic and Classical periods that must be underscored, as perfectly shown by Josiah Ober in his programmatic "Wealthy Hellas."[12] Although the area under Greek control was extended even before Alexander's conquest, the population was already growing far faster than the surface under cultivation. As for the growth in people's wealth, which is directly measurable by the size of their houses and by their equipment, it was considerable. When a chance event allows us a snapshot of the wealth of an ancient city—as in the case of the destruction of Olynthos in 348 BCE by the troops of Philip II, or that of the destruction of Pompeii in 79 CE by an eruption of Vesuvius—we can gauge the wealth that had been accumulated in these places—even if the city of Olynthos was thoroughly pillaged by the victors before being razed. The claim that the extent of the area under Greek control increased without any growth in productivity contradicts the empirical evidence too much to be acceptable. So far as technology and productivity are concerned, if an analytical comparison is made between the situation prevalent at the end of the Archaic period and the one found at the end of the first century CE, there is no revolution, but there are very considerable changes.

In the domain of agricultural production, with the improvement in seeds, the introduction of new species like alfalfa, and the considerable improvement of livestock, there was significant progress. In the area of the processing of agricultural products, decisive innovations were made. In many respects, in the rural Mediterranean world the technologies of antiquity provided until the nineteenth century the basis for rural equipment, and more generally what might be called the "technology of everyday life." As for transport by sea, the size of ships during the late Hellenistic and Imperial periods was considerably larger than in the Archaic period, which in one way or another presupposes that in the interim there was a multitude of innovations in the details of naval construction.[13] In the realm of construction techniques, Hellenistic architects introduced the vault, which was to have such a brilliant future. Advances in geography and mathematics culminated in a mathematical representation of the world: the notion of coordinates expressed in terms of latitude and longitude, which is so familiar to us, is also an invention of the Hellenistic period that anticipates Ptolemy's map (second century CE) and his systematic indication of geographical coordinates for the sites that he mentions.[14] The mathematization of the world did not have to wait for the modern period.

It is true that in the final analysis the rates of real growth may seem disappointing. Richard Saller has compared the rate of growth of Holland between 1520 and 1820, about 0.2 percent a year, that of the United Kingdom between 1820 and 1890, 1.2 percent per year, and that of the United States between 1890 and 1970, 2.2 percent a year, with the estimated growth of Rome between about 200 BCE and the beginning of the common era, 0.1 percent a year.[15] With such a low rate of growth, overall production increased less than 25 percent over two centuries. This would be a very slow growth. But does that correspond to what happened in Archaic and Classical Greece? In other terms, what was Greece's rate of growth during that period? Before examining the data in detail, one must note that average figures over the long term can be deceptive. For example, Holland had its Golden Age between 1550 and 1675. Holland's growth rate during this period was about 0.6 to 0.7 percent per year. The economic situation then changed for the worse, and the country fell into stagnation—indeed, phases of recession marked by declines in foreign trade and in real salaries.[16]

If the parameter chosen by Ian Morris—namely, the size of houses—is accepted, it appears that in ancient Greece the latter increased by a factor of 5 or 6 between 750 and 350 BCE.[17] To be sure, this figure could be challenged. It nonetheless constitutes an interesting clue, even if it has to be used with caution. However, it should also be emphasized that everything we know about the upheaval that Greece underwent at this period, from the improvement in the general level of living conditions to the radical change in the level of education, leads us to accept a proportion on this order. Let us therefore adopt this figure. On the basis of a factor of 5 over four centuries, there would be an average growth rate of about 0.4 percent per year. This rate is certainly lower than that of modern economies. It nonetheless makes the economic growth of the Greece of the city-states not very different from that of Holland in its most flourishing age, the one that caused it to be called "the first modern economy."[18] In that case, the economic growth of the world of the Greek city-states should be seen in a different light. Above all, compared with the growth experienced by so many preindustrial societies that can be called stagnant (that is, those with rates of growth below 0.1 percent), the economy of the Greece of the city-states shows an original profile of rapid growth (that is, rapid not with respect to the growth rates with which we have become familiar, but with respect to those of the numerous other cultures with which Greek society was in contact). Thus it was not "modern." Its rate of growth did not hover around 1 to 2 percent a year. But if it was capable of maintaining a growth rate of around 0.4 percent per year over four centuries, it is clear that it presents a profile unparalleled before the Dutch paradigm two millennia later. This growth corresponded to both a strong demographic growth and a per capita growth that itself might have been around 0.1 percent a year.[19] This figure may seem shockingly high. But if both technological and institutional innovations are combined, it seems inevitable that a high figure, around 0.1 percent, rather than a low one (say, 0.01 percent per year) should be accepted. Thus it becomes understandable that starting with a situation of negative growth at the end of the Bronze Age and probably very slow growth during the Early Iron Age, in the space of 400 years, between about 700 BCE and 300 BCE, the Greek cities managed to become the dominant culture in the Mediterranean.

THE PROBLEM OF THE "FAILURE OF ANCIENT CIVILIZATION"

How, then, does it happen that so many negative judgments have been made regarding the economy of the Greek world of the Classical and Hellenistic periods? There is still a basic reason, a common reproach, as it were: it did not manage to achieve the "capitalist revolution" or the "industrial revolution" (no matter which term is used, even if in reality the two phenomena are not strictly identical).

There are several ways of viewing this "failure." The most famous is Weber's sociological thesis, which was largely adopted by Finley. According to this thesis, the elites showed no interest in the economy. At most, landowners were eager for profit and wanted monetary revenues in the short term. But insofar as they did not invest in the productive sector, or took no interest in "economics" in order to devote themselves entirely to politics (or to their personal pleasures), they are supposed to have constituted a parasite class that would have completely blocked any "economic take-off" before it got started. The productive sector, essentially consisting in agriculture, would thus have remained a derelict, routine world, a chaotic realm doomed to stagnation. The same picture is supposed to hold for large estates, where the landlords' absenteeism is supposed to have had serious effects on production. As for middle-sized or small properties, a still gloomier picture would have to be drawn, because of the absence of initiative on the part of their owners. Thus it is supposed that a change in "the ideology of the elites" would have sufficed to make an economic takeoff possible. But unfortunately that spark was not forthcoming, and the ancient economy is supposed to have remained in its state of mediocrity. In its simple form, this narrative seems obviously right. Antiquity in general is supposed to have experienced only an extensive, not an intensive growth: production increases in the agricultural sector should therefore be attributed exclusively to increases in population and the area under cultivation, never to a process of intensification. Negligence with regard to production and technological stagnation would thus be the fundamental characteristics of the ancient economy.

On one point at least, one can only agree with this view: the ancient world did not undergo an "industrial revolution." But Weber's interpretive schema proposed cannot be adopted. The basis of his reasoning was that the ancient world could have known only a stagnant, immobile economy without innovation, undergoing a quantitative rise only through the extension of the surface under cultivation. This schema is at the origin of a specific form of primitivism that was that of a tradition inaugurated by Weber. As already observed, this view contradicts the available empirical evidence. Thus one must engage in a kind of counterfactual exercise in order to provide the elements of an answer to the question as to why, unlike seventeenth- and eighteenth-century Europe, the ancient world did not make the great leap into modernity. Put another way, why couldn't Europe simply dispense with the Middle Ages?

To start with, it must be observed that the geographical and chronological context of the Greece of the city-states from the end of the Archaic period to the Hellenistic period is poorly adapted to provide an exhaustive answer to this question. It is clear that the dynamics of the ancient Mediterranean economy found its culmination in the Roman Empire. The unification of the Mediterranean world under a single state constitutes the endpoint of a social, political, and economic evolution that began simultaneously in the two peninsulas of Greece and Italy at the end of the Greek Dark Ages and the beginning of the Archaic period. For a long time, it was the Greeks who led this development. Alexander's conquest allowed Hellenism to spread throughout the Eastern world. At the end of the third century BCE, after Rome's defeat of Carthage and its seizure of control over the Occidental world, it might have seemed that in the Mediterranean area there was an equilibrium between the Hellenized East and the West under the control of Rome. But it was at just at this time that this equilibrium started to break down, to the advantage of Rome. At the beginning of the fourth century BCE, Rome began its great process of expansion; within two centuries it had subjected all Italy and defeated Carthage. The fragmentation of the Greek political world made it easy for Rome to gain control over the Eastern Mediterranean. After Rome's victories over Antigonid Macedon (197 BCE) and the Seleukid kingdom (189 BCE), no force could any longer oppose it, even if the direct submission of the last great Hellenistic kingdom, that of the Ptolemies, did not come until 30 BCE.

What needs to be understood here is the process through which, despite the unification of the Mediterranean world under the aegis of Rome, a leap forward in economic life did not take place, and why, on the contrary, after a century and a half of undeniable prosperity, the system entered a phase of decline and then increasingly rapid recession. The final result of this process was a political collapse which, at the beginning of the fifth century CE, totally swept away the western part of the Empire, and then, in the early seventh century, and despite the Byzantine recovery of the fifth and sixth centuries, large portions of its Eastern part. In Weber's view, the ultimate failure of ancient civilization condemned its whole past. One might add that this failure seems all stranger in that one might have imagined that, through a kind of "virtuous circle," the *Pax Romana* would have offered better conditions for continuous progress. The benefits of this peace should have been considerable, since in theory returns on investment would have been secure and the general prosperity would have promoted inventions and gains in productivity. Thus production and trade should have been able to develop unhindered. However, that is not what happened. That is why some might even be tempted to go beyond the obvious and conclude that the early Roman Empire was also a period of stagnation. But it was not. It was the time when watermills were widely installed to turn millstones, both in the countryside and in the city. It was also a time that saw a multitude of innovations tending to increase productivity in agriculture and mining and to improve maritime transport.[20] Hence the slowdown, which was marked by an economic and demographic decline that began in the second half of the second century CE, seems still more difficult to explain.

Apart from exogenous shocks such as the epidemics that struck the empire in the second century CE, the history of the forms taken by the final crisis that led to the fall of the Roman Empire is above all a history of the crisis in the state.[21] This is not the place to discuss that crisis in detail. But its roots were much deeper, and in a certain sense they were already present in the social and economic system of the Hellenistic world. The crux of the problem is how to determine why the "virtuous circle" did not win out. The solution is found in the relative pace of the processes at work. For an economy to go through a period of growth, two sets of conditions have to be fulfilled. On the micro-economic level, economic growth is directly connected with technological innovations, with reorganizations of the productive apparatus, and with the creation of more efficient institutions. On the macro-economic level, it presupposes that supply and demand can grow at the same pace, constantly finding new balances at a higher level. It is the specific features of the ancient economy related to these two levels of analysis that have to be highlighted.

INNOVATION

The Pace and Spread of Innovation

On the micro-economic level, the emphasis will be on technological innovation, because the reorganizations of the productive apparatus and the institutional innovations have already been discussed at length. It has already been observed that a series of important innovations, in particular (but not only) in the processing of agricultural products, were introduced during the Hellenistic period. The focus should now be on their overall impact and the speed with which they spread.

The incentive to innovate lay in the potential increase in profits and the reduction of production costs. This is a fundamental characteristic of innovation. In the short term, it was less expensive to install a watermill than to buy and maintain animals to turn millstones. The figures we have for the later Roman Empire can surely be transposed, *mutatis mutandis*, to the situation a few centuries earlier; then the cost of the millstone and the mechanism would be equivalent to the cost of a mill moved by an ass, to or an agricultural worker's salary for twenty-four days.[22] Even if the cost of the rest of the installation, which necessarily depended on local conditions, is added, a water mill was quickly amortized. The replacement of labor by capital posed no problem if it produced immediate profits. As a result, the watermill was widely adopted at the end of the Hellenistic period and the beginning of the Imperial period. This occurred, no doubt, in response to market pressures. The invention of the watermill was revolutionary: for the first time, a complementary source of power became available that was free and limited only by the presence or absence of a waterfall.

Nonetheless, the limits of this innovation must also be examined. On the macro-economic level, the watermill's contribution of power to the overall economic system remained minimal; most economic activity remained dependent on traditional sources of power (including wind as the propulsive force for ships). In this respect, the impact of the watermill cannot be compared to that of the steam engine two millennia later. In barely a century, the steam engine revolutionized most sectors of economic life, especially industrial production and transport, before the internal combustion engine made possible a radical transformation of agriculture as well.[23] At first, the watermill remained too sectorial to have a decisive impact that would make a complete reorganization of production necessary. Another characteristic of a technological innovation like the watermill was that it made it possible to reduce the cost of an element of the production cycle, but not to offer products providing a new service that could have given the innovation a crucial advantage. A region might very well continue to use an old technology without this having a fundamental effect on its production costs. In addition, the cost of transport (which was far higher than production costs) and climatic variations (which could completely cancel any technological advantage) largely evened out the final costs. Thus even if a technological innovation made it possible to reduce the cost of production in a specific area, this saving might be offset in a given region by ecological or social conditions that made general production costs much lower in another one. One should also add that general information, including technological information (as opposed to specific information, for example, a king's death), spread slowly, because certain basic innovations—first, paper, and then printing—had not yet been introduced. Thus despite the fact that innovations important and even decisive for the future were made, the overall speed with which they were introduced was slow.

Finally, even the immediate impact of an innovation on the production cycle (for example, the impact of the water mill on the production of foodstuffs) remained limited. This can be compared with the quality of a signal in an information transmission chain: even if one of the quality of one of the elements in the chain is significantly improved, the final quality of the signal will be determined by that of the weakest element in the chain. An increase in productivity connected with a single element of the production cycle would certainly permit a decrease in the cost of that element, but this would not significantly affect overall productivity. Ultimately there would be no significant increase in demand, and only a minimal portion of the labor force would be freed up for employment elsewhere. An economic "take-off" presupposes an increase in the productivity of agriculture that makes it possible to feed a larger urban population, and at the same time innovations in the artisanal or proto-industrial world that can absorb this labor force.

Improving one element in the cycle of production would thus make it possible to reduce the cost of that element, but would have no decisive transformative effect on the cycle as a whole. For such a transformative effect to take place, technological revolutions have to occur over the whole productive cycle not only for a given product, and also for other products. The migration of an innovation from one sector to another was not easy, because the traditional production cycle had its own logic. Since the interest of an innovation was limited to a specific sector and usually had only a minimal effect on the final cost, it did not become a permanent constraint on production. Innovations did migrate from one production cycle to another, and technologies did spread geographically, but only after a relatively long lapse of time, which does not for all that mean that the process was blocked. The geographical diffusion of an innovation from one region to another was not stimulated by the existence of a market where products of various kinds would be in competition. That ancient markets were less integrated than modern capitalist markets is a truism. As such, this observation would go nowhere. The issue is how to explain both the innovations (which per se cannot be accounted for in the framework of the old orthodoxies) and their relative slowness to spread.[24]

On the one hand, as already observed, the gains in productivity connected with innovation in a given region might be entirely or partly cancelled out by imports of products coming from regions where the ecological or social conditions of production were far more favorable, even though their technologies remained more traditional. For instance, an abundant workforce in a region, and thus the low cost of labor, might offset the benefits of a cost-cutting innovation made in another region. On the other hand, in a logic that is the opposite of the preceding one, the high cost of land transport could cancel out the benefits of innovation in a given region. Lower production costs would be offset by transportation costs that remained prohibitively high, and that in turn provided no direct incentive to adopt a new technology. Thus the wheat produced in northern Gaul with the new harvester would be a little cheaper than wheat harvested in other regions with a sickle, but it could not be supplied at a reasonable price on the Roman market. This also explains the relative slowness with which innovations spread, not because regional markets were disconnected from one another, but because of the kind of competition that prevailed in them and between them, which differed from that of a modern capitalist market. As a result, technological innovations long remained confined to given production or regional sectors and did not form a system of innovation.

However, one must immediately introduce some important qualifications. If a localized innovation was made in one area of production—for example, milling techniques—it might nonetheless have very favorable effects on other sectors. Thus the new grinding techniques introduced in the Classical period freed up female workers, considerable numbers of whom were thus made available for work in textile production, ultimately resulting in an increase in the productivity of women's labor and a distinct increase in overall prosperity. Similarly, it had been thought that the use of hydraulic power remained limited exclusively to milling, whereas it might also have been used for other tasks such as sawing or hammering metal, as it was on a large scale during the medieval and early modern periods.[25] Some delay in the migration of this technology to other sectors of production may have been connected with the latter's inadequate capitalization and the fact that the use of water power was not considered immediately profitable, as it had been in the case of milling.[26] Nevertheless, this migration did take place already in the Roman Empire.[27] It is now clear that waterpower was already used in the sawmills of Asia Minor and the eastern Mediterranean area by the Imperial period, from the third century CE onward.[28] At the end of the fourth century CE, Ausonius mentioned as something well known that along one of the Moselle's tributaries, watermills were used both to mill grain and "to draw the saw's strident blade across the tender blocks of marble, producing a sound constantly heard on both banks of the river."[29] It seems also very likely that water power was used in metallurgy.[30]

The relative slowness and minimal integration of innovation into an economic system thus do not signify its complete absence. The notion of the slow pace of innovation must be put in perspective. Innovation and its spread were slow in relation to our norms. But in the world of that time, their pace was also unprecedented. After the collapse that followed the fall of the Roman Empire, such a rapid pace of innovation cannot be observed again until the later Middle Ages. It has only been quite recently, in the last two or three centuries, that innovation has gradually become an integral part of economic development. Despite many undeniable medieval and of course early modern advances, Mediterranean Europe's technology up to and including the eighteenth and nineteenth centuries, and even that of northern Europe from the sixteenth to the eighteenth centuries, continued to be based on the technologies introduced in antiquity. This is most obvious in the case of energy, the watermill remaining a crucial source of energy until it began to be replaced by the steam engine three centuries ago.

Supply, Demand, and the Time of Innovation

The forms of innovation are associated with specific forms of supply and demand. Innovation made it possible to reduce costs in a segment of the production cycle, but not, in most cases, to put new products on the market. One can cite the case of Attic vases, which became prevalent between the sixth and the fourth centuries, probably because of particular commercial circuits that lent Athens priority, but certainly also because of the superiority of their glaze, which was brilliant, lustrous, and hard: the secrets of its fabrication were long jealously guarded and were the key to a long-lasting success. But this was a difference in quality, not a difference in the service rendered by the product. In the ancient market, competition was not based on the elasticity of supply but on variations in price or quality for an essentially static supply. By itself, supply could not create new demand, and it thus remained dependent on the earlier level of demand. Under these conditions, the propensity for innovation was lower than in a capitalist market, since it was linked only to a decrease in the costs or an increase in the quality of existing products. That is what distinguishes it from the capitalist production cycle, in which enterprises that are initially directly dependent on the credit market, and later on the price of their product on the market, have constantly to innovate and introduce new products simply in order to survive. There was very real innovation in the ancient world. It made it possible to realize larger profits, but it was not economically vital in the short term because land was still the essential productive force. Moreover, because of the relative slowness of technological progress, these profits could not usually be reinvested in innovation to make new profits. There is here a classic circular process at work that explains perfectly why the "miracle" of the transition to capitalism could not take place.

Finally, innovation remained limited not only to one segment of the production cycle and possibly to a single geographical sector but also to a single social group. It benefited above all the great landlords, but did not by itself permit the accumulation of sufficient capital to allow one social class to become dominant as a result of the profits connected with innovation. In Rome and Asia Minor in the Imperial period, the emergence of a stratum of well-off artisans can be discerned.[31] But unlike what can be observed in the fragmented world of the medieval Italian cities, in the Roman world it was unthinkable that these artisans might compete with the magnates of the land, the super-rich who possessed very large estates, sometimes in several provinces.[32] In its technological development, then, ancient civilization was in no way an immobile society. Besides, it is clear that so far as supply is concerned, it would have taken far more time than it had for innovations that remained isolated and scattered to form a system, and also for new inventions to emerge and have a decisive impact on the overall economic process. Ancient civilization entered into a process of decline and economic recession before there could be a coalescence and before new, integrated technological systems could be constituted.

This is the heart of the problem of the ancient economy. Beyond the study of contingencies—which is necessary, but is outside our topic here because it would require examining the process of the disaggregation of the imperial state and of Roman society—there is the fundamental question of the relationship between time and innovation in ancient societies. It can be maintained that it is because the market, despite its imperfections, functioned too well that innovation did not have time to transform in depth an economic system whose tendency to concentrate land ownership led directly to its destruction. The market provided a context favorable to innovation. At the same time, it created the conditions not only for its own disappearance, but also for that of the whole of ancient civilization.

First, it should be pointed out this market economy was very profitable, although it was not based on the use of fossil fuels. To make use of capital, the most profitable short-term investment—but also the riskiest—was to exploit the possibilities offered by trade between different regions. If one was willing to accept a somewhat lower level of profitability, but one that was also less risky, it was legitimate to invest in an efficient agriculture producing for the market. Far from being "unproductive, poorly managed, and routine," far from being economic "black holes," the great estates of the Hellenistic period that produced oil and especially wine were highly profitable. That was, moreover, why this sector emerged so strongly in the Hellenistic period, a phenomenon that continued and became more accentuated under the early Roman Empire. Investment was concentrated in this sector, and it was possible to make large profits. This was the sector where there was enough capital to innovate and lower costs. And it was on these highly profitable estates that it was possible to concentrate large slave labor forces, because it was on them that the slave system's profitability was maximal. The other sectors, such as artisanal work, were less profitable and attracted less investment, and that explains why progress in these sectors was slower, though not nonexistent, as is shown by the use of waterpower in sawmills during the Imperial period.

In any event, a highly profitable agricultural and commercial sector emerged during the Hellenistic and Imperial periods, and it was not hostile to innovation. Profits in this sector were considerable, as was the accumulation of capital. Moreover, during the financial crises of the late Republic, people in Rome who had capital were looking for sectors where they could invest it.[33] As for investing in innovation themselves, developing institutions and organizations that might have helped innovation, that was another matter, because what interested investors was the short-term profitability of their investments.

As for supply, a neo-Keynesian approach has proposed a new version of Weber's thesis concerning the incapacity of the elites, who are supposed to have neither understood nor acknowledged that by paying higher salaries they would have *ipso facto* created a market that would then have been able to absorb the products of an urban proto-industry.[34] In the absence of such an incentive, the latter is supposed to have been unable to develop and to create the bases for capitalist development. As a description, this schema is on the whole correct: there was in fact no broad market capable of stimulating the production of a proto-industry—or rather this market existed, but it was too small to play a major role as an incentive. However, it would be difficult to make use of a Fordian schema here (in the 1920s, Henry Ford calculated that his workers would be his first customers). In fact, it would presuppose that there was already a large stratum of salaried workers employed in industry (or rather in artisanal work, under the conditions of the ancient world). This explanation in terms of demand assumes that there is already a vast category of buyers, and that it would have sufficed to raise their income in order to "prime the pump" of development.

Formulated in this way, the explanation cannot be accepted, because the whole point is precisely that there was no large stratum of salaried workers whose income it would have sufficed to raise. However, the focus on demand as a market stimulus—because that is what is involved here—remains very interesting. First of all, one must emphasize that antiquity was not unaware of "growth through demand," at least if one recognizes the limits of what can be done with this concept. For example, Plutarch made the unambiguous observation that through his public works policy, Pericles distributed salaries that provided a living for a large category of artists and artisans.[35] There is no reason to think that Plutarch's remark is an anachronism on his part. It has nothing to do with the ideology of "bread and games" that was prevalent in his time, in the second half of the first century and the beginning of the second century CE. On the contrary, it corresponds perfectly to what we know about the politics of Athenian democracy. It is true that this was not, strictly speaking, an economic policy intended to increase "supply" or "demand," but rather a social welfare policy intended to support a part of the population by means of public projects. More generally, however, it is without dispute that the Athenian state's massive distribution of monetary liquidities stimulated demand and thus supply, not only in Athens but in all of the west Aegean. In the world of the city-states, at least in the largest ones, the state itself was a major economic actor by its expenses for war, public buildings and public festivals.[36] The countryside benefited from the distribution of liquidities coming from the city.

However, it is acknowledged that in other contexts—for example, in Holland in the early modern period—increasing wealth in the countryside was a powerful stimulus to economic development: a prosperous countryside promoted the development of urban artisans providing buyers for their products.[37] In this respect, the contrast with the ancient world is clear. The increasing development of the great estates using slave labor during the Hellenistic period was not a factor that permitted the development of a major stratum of prosperous consumers. The same was true for the gap between rich and poor, which steadily increased during the same period and became extreme in the course of time during the Roman Empire.[38] In other words, the market allowed the emergence of a stratum of very wealthy property owners. But at the same time, it impoverished broad strata of the rural and urban population that since the end of the Hellenistic period had been dependent on a narrow stratum of notables. This phenomenon became still more accentuated during the Imperial period and ended up creating monstrous social gaps unprecedented in the preceding periods.

At the end of the Hellenistic period, the egalitarian legal system of the Classical city-state was already being damaged by widening social gaps. In the course of the first century BCE, the Roman rulers reduced *de jure* the people's power in the cities of the Hellenistic East by institutionalizing political systems where real political power was in the hands of the wealthy. The erosion of the civic framework continued and increased during the Imperial period, to the point that differences in social status ended up being written into law in the form of the distinction between *honestiores* and *humiliores*. At the end of the Imperial period, a handful of great landowners controlled immense estates scattered over several provinces. A mass of slaves and impoverished peasants excluded from the political sphere could no longer constitute a sufficient market even for the great estates owned by the elite, whose products were henceforth frequently bought by the state for the army or for public distributions. In other words, the system was increasingly dependent on the state. Paradoxically, the very wealthy elites of the late Empire found it more and more difficult to put their capital to work. Because the Mediterranean economy unified by Rome could not find new balances at a higher level through permanent innovation (as modern capitalism does, defying all predictions of its imminent demise—those of Marx or Polanyi, for example), it found itself threatened by its own success. In addition, innovation had not become a component fully integrated into the process of production. Land remained the basic productive force, and this constituted a limitation on growth, since arable areas are finite. In an economy of the capitalist type, in which innovation itself is the main productive factor, growth is *a priori* "infinite" (provided it does not destroy its ecological framework, which is now its specific challenge). In the ancient world, there were real innovations, but they emerged too slowly in relation to the speed with which the market was destroying the social conditions of its own existence. Thus this economy was not able to avoid a dramatic decline—in short, to avoid the Middle Ages, to adopt the formulation mentioned earlier.

When the state itself entered into a crisis, it was the whole system that collapsed. The Mediterranean of the Archaic and Classical periods, fractured into a multitude of micro-states, was less vulnerable to ecological, political, and economic shocks that might occur. The reason for this apparent paradox is that it was not dependent on a centralized system. Thus despite the major role it played on the Greek scene at that time, the catastrophe that struck Ionia in 494 BCE with the repression of the revolt against Persia did not destroy the world of the Hellenic cities.

On the other hand, Imperial Rome was a world that had moved far beyond the framework of the Greek cities on the Classical model. Thus, by contrast, it is easy to understand why in those cities foreigners were not allowed to own land.[39] This was a measure intended to prevent the constitution of immense fortunes, such as occurred in the last years of the Roman Republic and *a fortiori* during the Imperial period. That was the premonitory meaning of Aristotle's remarks: the acquisition of unlimited wealth was incompatible with the civic framework and threatened to do no less than destroy it. The city-state was based on a mutual exchange of services, linked to a feeling and bond that the Greeks called *charis*, the grace of the donor and the gratitude of the receiver (the Greek uses the same word for the two mindsets). Exchange of mutually profitable services was the basis of Aristotle's argument in Book Five of the *Nicomachean Ethics*, which is devoted to justice in the city.[40] Charis, the beautiful goddess, also symbolized the gratitude members of the city-state felt to each other. It is no accident that, in addition to Hermes and Peitho, the divinities of commerce and persuasion, Aphrodite, the graceful goddess par excellence, was also revered in the agoras, and was sometimes explicitly linked to the Charites.[41]

By contrast this is why, according to Aristotle, Dionysios of Syracuse prohibited the activity of a speculator who had gotten rich by buying up all the available iron and then having a monopoly on its resale.[42] It was not that this monopoly made prices rise; on the contrary, the price of iron remained the same, no doubt thanks to the economies of scale the monopoly made possible. But in a short time, the speculator had also accumulated the equivalent of a hundred talents, so that he threatened the power of Dionysios himself. The anecdote must therefore be put back in the particular context of a city dominated by a tyrant. But steps intended to prevent the concentration of wealth might also be taken in the framework of a democratic city-state like Athens in the fourth century—for example, in the case of the grain trade, in which a series of regulations set quotas on purchases. In the framework of the city-state, differences in wealth were supposed to remain "reasonable."

The principle that land should be reserved for citizens alone was naturally a way of keeping the land for oneself. But inversely, the same principle also provided a way of limiting wealth. Without explicit permission, it was impossible to buy land in other city-states, not because one's own city prohibited it, but because like one's own, the other city-states did not allow it. The closure of the city-state, the fact that one could buy land only in one's own city, was thus a way of keeping people from amassing huge fortunes. The tendency to get rich by buying land abroad was permanent, and was in no way a novelty in the Classical or Hellenistic periods. What mattered was the level of resistance to this tendency put up by the city's institutions. In the Classical period, in the framework of the *archē* of the fifth century, wealthy Athenians had already hastened to purchase land in the tributary cities, as is shown by steles recording the seizure of property connected with the episode of the Hermokopids.[43] The fall of Athens in 404 BCE marked the end of this process. That is why the Athenians, when in 377 BCE they reconstituted a league that was in theory supposed to be egalitarian, promised their allies that they would give up the estates that they might happen to possess publicly or privately on the territories of their new allies and not acquire new ones.[44] This was a very important clause that occupies a large place in the decree founding the confederation, immediately after the clauses relating to political autonomy. It shows on this point that people still had bitter memories of the fifth-century Athenian Empire. But it also shows that even after the end of their *archē*, the Athenians were still able to acquire property outside their own territory. During the Hellenistic period, it seems that it began to be common to own land outside one's city of origin. Just as the Athenians had done in the framework of their empire, the Rhodians made use of their political influence and of their private wealth to acquire land in the cities of Asia Minor.[45] But even without any special political influence, it became more and more common to acquire lands in other cities.[46] At first, this involved neighboring cities, and to that extent the phenomenon can be understood, since it was only a matter of finding ways of coping with the excessively narrow framework of civic life. But gradually, with the erosion of the civic framework, the circle grew and it was no longer a question only of owning land in neighboring cities but also in more distant cities. Rome's takeover in the Hellenistic East allowed the social elite gradually to free itself from the civic framework, which became hardly more than a municipal framework in the modern sense of the term. The Greek elites rushed into the breach opened up by the Roman *negotiatores*, who were profiting from the new balance of power favorable to Rome to acquire land or lend money at very high rates. In this connection, it is worthwhile to compare briefly Athens's empire with that of Rome. The failure of the Athenian *archē* of the fifth century interrupted the generalized purchase of land abroad, and thus the unlimited enrichment of the elites.

Here one can rely on Thucydides's judgment. Following a series of blatant errors in political and economic management, Athens, too eager to extend its empire, lost a war that it "should not have lost." The basic reason—the origin of these "errors," which were in reality inevitable—should probably be sought in political institutions poorly adapted to the new role of an imperial city; but that would be another question. Had it won the Peloponnesian War, Athens would have sooner or later found itself in a position to unify the Mediterranean to its advantage. It was Rome, a very different city, with and economy based on land exploitation rather than on international trade, and inclined to absorb rather than to exclude, like every Greek city-state, that was able carry out the inevitable unification of the whole of the Mediterranean.[47]

That is the paradox of the ancient economy. The civic framework and the "society of the city-states" made possible an exceptional development that was based on a real inter-regional division of labor and exploited to the full all the ecological potential of the Mediterranean world. The rise of this civilization was founded on the civic framework, which tended to be fundamentally egalitarian. It was this civic framework that made it possible to raise the level of the population's education. Most free young boys went to school, and it must be assumed that the larger part of the free male population (to which should be added some girls and women) knew how to read and write, as early as the Classical period in the most urbanized city-states.[48] Beyond the many testimonies that prove the widespread usage of writing as early as the late Archaic period, our sources specify the existence of schools. In Athens, there clearly existed civic legislation relating to schools.[49] According to Herodotus (6.27.2), in the island of Chios a little before 494 BCE a roof fell on the children of a school, and out of 120 of them only one survived. Some slaves must also have had been able to read and write, although obviously in more modest numbers. It is now clear that even at Sparta, reading and writing were common practice among the group of the "peers" (*homoioi*), the members of the ruling class of the population, and as well as in the more privileged groups of the lower strata of the population.[50] Although we are not able to give figures for the percentage of the population that was able to read and write, it remains certain that the Classical and Hellenistic Greek cities were not a world of "limited literacy." It is now clear that the daily life of Classical Greek democracies, starting with Athens, constantly resorted to written material. The rendering of accounts of magistrates, the recording of the archives of the council, the management of public finance and the functioning of the courts were all based on written documents.[51]

Schools were even more widespread in the Hellenistic period.[52] Polybius (31.31.1–3) could condemn the lack of dignity of the Rhodians who had accepted the (huge) gift of 280,000 *medimnoi* of grain aimed at creating a fund the interest on which would pay the teachers of their children. In cash, at 5 drachms the *medimnos*, the grain represented 233 talents 2/3, viz. with a 10 percent interest rate, a little more than 23 talents of yearly income. For various cities like Teos, Miletos, and Delphi, our sources testify to the existence of school foundations.[53] This educational level of the population is per se a major asset for economic growth. It gives access to a level of general culture that is crucial for the way people can understand and master the world in which they live. In a more technical sense for the economy of the Greek city-states, their level of education enabled property-owners and managers active in farming, in craftsmanship and in trading to systematically rely on written documents. This in itself was crucial for the quality of accounting and for the circulation of economic information in general.

Another fundamental characteristic of the world of the Greek city-states was the privilege of untrammeled and agonistic debate enjoyed by their free population. This habit of debate created in turn the possibility of a free debate among intellectuals and artists. The "disenchantment of the world" started by the Milesian philosophers of the sixth century BCE paved the way for the fundamental technological inventions of the Hellenistic period. The "piston and the screw," or more generally the "mathematization of the world," represented by the description of every point on the globe in the form of mathematical coordinates, are products of this abstract thought.

The flipside of the freedom of citizens—was mass slavery and the extreme exploitation of nonfree people. In the economic domain, the civic framework had allowed not only a great expansion of the quantities produced but also gains in productivity through the interregional division of labor, through the massive exploitation of a slave labor force in the most profitable sectors, such as the great estates that specialized in products for the market, and through technological innovations.

With the triumph of Rome at the end of the Hellenistic period, the progressive dissolution of the civic framework and the introduction of strictly hierarchical relationships in social and political life put an end to the possibility of scientific knowledge. "Enlightenment" and a new culture that systematically associated science with technology and was oriented toward progress have been advocated by Joel Mokyr as the decisive factor in the development of modern capitalism and the industrial revolution.[54] In fact, ancient Greece saw the beginning of an "enlightened" culture. This is the "forgotten revolution" referred to by Lucio Russo.[55] Freedom of debate and the existence of a "competitive critical community" played a primary role in this development.[56] There was a link between democracy and knowledge, in the broader sense of the word.[57] A fundamental invention like that of the screw was the direct result of a scientific and mathematical approach to the world. In the form of Archimedes' screw it famously found a direct application for presses and also for pumping water out of mines .[58] But at some point, the process of scientific research was interrupted. The period of progress during the Archaic, Classical, and Hellenistic periods was followed by a phase of decline under the Roman Empire. In sheer numbers, the statistics of known Greek and Roman scientists shows a growth in number until the reign of Augustus, followed by a continuous decline until the fourth and fifth centuries CE.[59] At the end of the process, scientists and scholars were harassed or massacred by the new authorities. The tragic death of Hypatia of Alexandria, a philosopher and mathematician, in 415 CE is symbolic of this new atmosphere.[60] By its increasing denial of scientific research and knowledge, the ancient world deprived itself of a fundamental source of innovation. The only source of growth that then remained was empirical innovation, which never stopped, but which by itself could not lead to the systematized achievements of the Enlightenment.

MODERNITY OR PHASES OF PROGRESS?

Thus one must not use the Weberian concept of modernity without caution. It remains luminous and indispensable for describing the various states of development in Europe from antiquity to the contemporary period. But it must be emphasized that by itself, it does not explain the phenomenon it points to. The transition to modernity was a kind of construction, a process. It is this process that has to be accounted for. Therefore, it cannot be reduced to merely the "invention" of a superior class or group or religious community: otherwise, one risks making it impossible to analyze the phenomenon that is to be explained.

Moreover, the notion of "modernity" is by definition determined by the position of the observer. Making the transition to modernity a radical leap, contrasting a "before" and an "after" in the history of societies, and thus focusing attention on the factors and forms of transformation of that period alone, means at the same time determining the interpretation of the phenomenon. Instead of a sudden and to some extent unexpected change, one must propose a different schema. First, even the English Industrial Revolution of the late eighteenth century could develop only on the basis of experience previously gained in Italy, Flanders, and Holland at the end of the Middle Ages and at the beginning of the modern period.[61] Above all, one must analyze the transition to modernity not as a sudden leap, which becomes almost incomprehensible, but rather as the endpoint of a long process that began in the early second millennium BCE. It is, in fact, the third phase in the expansion of the Western world (in the broad sense of the term).

The first phase of expansion was that of the Bronze Age societies. The mastery of bronze symbolizes the transformations that took place at that time. In Crete and Greece, it was accompanied by great economic prosperity. This was the age of the palaces and of comparatively high population growth. This was true all over the Mediterranean, and in particular in the western Mediterranean. This first phase of expansion was followed by a period of collapse and regression, that of the Greek Dark Ages. In Greece, it saw the destruction of the palaces, the end of long-distance trade networks, and a very significant decline in population. A new phase of expansion and "regeneration" began with the Archaic period, that of Iron Age civilizations.[62] This growth cycle, which in Greece and Italy corresponds to the age of the city-states, lasted until the second century CE. The disintegration of this system took several centuries, but in the East, by the beginning of the seventh century CE (two centuries earlier in the West), a deep phase of regression began. It lasted until the economic recovery starting in the West after 1000 CE, which finally led to modernity many centuries later. Very long-term history thus shows that progress is in no way continuous, and that a long-term process of expansion does not prevent crises and temporary regressions of great scope. During these phases of regression, a multitude of knowledge and technologies that has been accumulated may disappear, but at the same time, there is a kind of selection: a core is preserved that makes it possible to lay the foundations for a renaissance a few centuries later. Thus Archaic Greece lost the Linear B system of writing, and more generally all the social forms connected with the palace civilization. But it did not forget the technology involved in making bronze. The Middle Ages lost almost all of antiquity's construction techniques, but the watermill, glass, and the vault were not forgotten. These losses of memory correspond to the collapse of a social system, but at the same time they allow new developments in radically new directions.

The point is not to claim that a temporary return to "barbarism" is a good thing, because value judgments of that kind have no justification. Besides, one should observe that for societies a collapse through internal contradictions is not in itself an exceptional event, and that there is nothing unique about the process of disintegration undergone by the ancient world. The same observations could be made regarding the history of the Native American empires. Even in the history of the Greek world, the collapse in late antiquity had a precedent a millennium and a half earlier. The "transition to modernity" is thus better interpreted as the (provisional) endpoint of an economic and cultural development that began almost four millennia before. In the European realm, this process had three successive waves and two intermediate phases of regression. In any event, the transition to modernity was possible only because by the sixteenth century European society had not only developed (or rediscovered) most of the technologies of antiquity, but also, in certain key sectors, moved beyond them. For example, the watermill, a capital invention of the Hellenistic period, remained the main source of power until the end of the eighteenth century. To this, one could add the screw press and all the other inventions of the Hellenistic period. On the other hand, turning to maritime technology, for instance, the difference with the ancient world is clear: in the technique of ship construction, rigging, and the introduction of the compass, decisive advances were made in late medieval and early modern Europe that enabled sailors to set out to conquer the world, whereas their predecessors had remained limited to the Mediterranean and its associated waters, the waters near the Atlantic coast of western

Europe and North Africa, and the Indian Ocean by way of the Red Sea. Finally, in the quality and quantity of their finished products, the techniques of metallurgy at the beginning of the early modern age were far more advanced than those of the ancient world.

If one adds to this paper-making (a technique of Chinese origin), which was an indispensable precondition for the development of the printing press, gunpowder (also of Chinese origin), the techniques of polishing glass to make magnifying lenses, and a level of mathematical knowledge incomparably superior to that of antiquity, without neglecting the massive use of coal for domestic heating in certain regions, it is clear how much the "English revolution" of the seventeenth and eighteenth centuries had been broadly prepared by a whole series of factors that had given Europe in general a technological level much higher than the one attained in the Mediterranean world a millennium and a half earlier. If one now adds social factors, particularly the extent to which a social class distinct from the aristocracy was able gradually to benefit from the new economic boom and to establish itself first economically and then politically, one can understand why the ancient world could not make the "leap into capitalism and modernity" that some people are astonished it did not make. Neither in its technological level—even though this was much higher than that Greece and Italy had attained a millennium earlier—nor in its social structure was the Mediterranean world of the late Hellenistic period and the early Imperial period ready to make the leap that western Europe was able to achieve between the sixteenth and the eighteenth centuries.

The history of the economy of the Greece of the city-states is thus part of the long history of the western world, in the broad sense of the term. After the period of empires—those of Mesopotamia and Egypt—the Mediterranean world offered a new field of possibilities because of its potential for connectivity. The Greeks and Phoenicians were the first to benefit from this. A larger population, a greater distance from bureaucratic kingdoms, and especially the egalitarian model of their city-states allowed the Greeks to seize a decisive advantage and to spread their model over the whole of the Mediterranean. Unified under the aegis of a monarchical power, the Greeks even succeeded in liquidating, in less than five years, the immense Persian Empire. This temporary unification anticipated the other, more stable one that Rome imposed on the whole of the Mediterranean world. But far from representing the "triumph of the city-state," the Roman unification completed the dissolution of the egalitarian legal framework that had been the basis of the Greek city-state's success.

The final collapse of the ancient system should not lead us to make a negative *a posteriori* judgment on the economy of the Greece of the city-states. Thanks to the flexibility of its institutional system, in the Classical and Hellenistic periods Greece established an exceptionally dynamic and prosperous economy that exploited to the maximum the possibilities offered by its environment. By keeping its internal and external markets separate, it managed to maintain for several centuries an equilibrium that began to break down only in the late Hellenistic period. These successes should not make us forget the cruel exploitation of slaves, which was one of the pillars of the system. But despite its crucial role, slavery, which was the counterpart of the citizens' liberty, cannot alone and by itself explain the dynamism of the Greek economy in the age of the city-state. This dynamism was also founded on the initiative of free men, citizens or resident foreigners, on their high level of education, and on technical innovations, some of which were, for the first time in history, the result of scientific research and not simply of practical experience. The governmental structure of the city-states, which was really the citizens' "common property," did not impose a crushing tax burden. Consequently, "economic actors" retained control over most of what they produced, and this encouraged them to improve its quality and increase its quantity.

Initiative, inventiveness, the quest for the most profitable institutional solution, and at the same time the limitless exploitation of slaves: such were the driving forces in the economy of the Greek city-states, which at their best were able to make maximum use of the available resources to transform, for a few centuries, an environment that was rather unpromising but had the best potential for connectivity into the most prosperous area of the Mediterranean world. Freedom, both individual and collective, was expressed by the ability to bear arms: citizens were warriors, and the city-state was frequently at war. As a result, the world of the city-states was perpetually unstable. But this instability was inextricably connected with freedom and prosperity. The defeat at the hands of the Macedonians led to a first challenge to the city-state system. Since it was indispensable for the Hellenistic kings, because consubstantial with Hellenism, the city-state system was maintained, though under supervision. The fatal blow was struck by the *Pax Romana*, which at first seemed to provide stability and prosperity, but which in the long run, by undermining the civic system, sapped the foundations of what had been the driving force of the economy of Greece since the end of the Dark Ages. It was no longer law that ruled, *nomos despotēs*, but a distant, omnipotent master—*despotēs hēmōn*, "our master," people said in referring to the emperor in the late Empire. The city-state was then definitively dead.

MARKET
AND
TRADE

IX

THE INSTITUTIONS OF
THE DOMESTIC MARKET

The city-state was both a living community and a collective state. Freedom, a privilege of the citizen, did not mean that there were no rules. On the contrary, freedom could not be achieved outside a system of laws that guaranteed that it could be exercised. For the citizen, one aspect of this freedom consisted in being able to trade with his peers if he wanted to. He could do so in the marketplace, the agora (or agoras, as in the case of large cities like Athens and Rhodes, which had several). The agora was a space in which trade was regulated by the city-state's institutions, represented by one or several magistrates. It was their task to see to it that trade relationships among citizens were based on the principles of equity and justice. Seen from that point of view, transactions in the agora were not solely private, but also fully involved in the life of the collectivity. That is why the city-state had to supervise food supplies and the prices of the products offered for sale. An inadequate food supply or excessively high prices could have a destructive effect on the community. As the regulator and arbiter of trade, the city-state could thus also become an actor in matters of exchange.

PRIVATE PROPERTY

Private Property and Trade

A definition of the ownership of goods is a precondition for any transaction. The form of property varies from one society to another. Here, we must distinguish the form of property that prevailed in Greece from those of other contemporary societies. In the states of the eastern Mediterranean before the Persian conquest and in the Persian Empire itself, property rights were not defined in a uniform way. At the apex of the social pyramid, the sovereign usually had a superior right to own not only land, but also everyone and everything in the kingdom. Peasant communities

225

living on royal land had to pay very high tributes to their sovereigns. Even though in practice private property also existed in both Egypt and Mesopotamia, it did not have at all the character it had in the world of the Greek city-states. However, the recent attention to the *laoi* (dependent peasants) in the kingdom of Macedon during the early third century shows that labor was used in similar ways on both sides of the Aegean.[1] Within the world of the city-states, there could also be major differences between those that preserved a traditional model based on exploiting dependent peasants, as in Crete or Sparta, and those that were urbanized and open to trade, where a form of unlimited ownership prevailed. We will be interested here chiefly in city-states of the latter type, whose model was widely adopted during the Classical period, and especially during the Hellenistic period.

Private ownership of goods was the very foundation of civil society. Aristotle strongly emphasizes this point.[2] The institution of private property meant that one had the right to dispose freely of one's goods and what they produced. It therefore included the possibility of buying and selling freely productive goods (land), useful goods (such as furniture and houses), or products intended for sale (agricultural or craft products). In addition, it presupposed the right to transfer property to one's heirs. This was the foundation of the citizen's freedom: he was master of his property, as he was master of himself. On the other hand, as Greek sources expressly note, in the Persian world there was only one free man, the king: even the greatest dignitaries of the realm were his slaves and he had at least the legal right to make use of them and their persons as he saw fit. However, the citizen's right to hold private property, from which that of metics derived, was itself founded on the city's appropriation of a defined territory that it could defend by arms and on which it could enforce its laws. That is why land could be owned only by the citizens. Therefore, the concept of property included a relationship to violence exercised by the civic community: the military conquest of new territories was legitimate, right being based on might. In the colonial cities the Greeks established on lands occupied by barbarian (non-Greek) peoples, this meant that the natives' land was expropriated and handed over to Greek colonists. In the same way, the collective power relationship was also the foundation of people's enslavement: ownership of goods included the ownership of persons.

This is an essential difference with respect to private property as it is defined in modern societies. Labor became a transmissible form of capital. As already stated, after Solon (594 BCE), the distinction between free men and slaves in Athens became radical: a free man could not be enslaved, nor could he sell his wife or children.[3] This defined a demarcation between citizens (and thus free men in general) and slaves.[4] The former could buy and sell all kinds of goods, whereas the latter were defined exclusively as chattels that could be bought and sold. In other city-states, the dichotomy between free people and slaves also became a fundamental characteristic of the social structure. Slaves could be enfranchised by their masters, although in fact most of the time they apparently rebought their own freedom, as is proved by a considerable body of slave manumission documents. Most of the manumissions took the form of a fictive sale and consecration of the slave to the god. The solemnity of the acts of manumission is in itself a proof of the fundamental character of the legal distinction between slavery and freedom. However, frequently a clause known as *paramonē* implied that the freed man had to continue working for his former master under certain conditions, on pain of being reenslaved if he did not fulfill his obligations.[5] Slaves could ask the gods by way of an oracle whether their masters would enfranchise them, which testifies how strongly slaves could desire to be enfranchised.[6] The promise of freedom was certainly an incentive for the slaves not to run away, and thus for the masters a powerful way maintaining control over their slaves.

The city-state guaranteed property rights and public order in general. It was up to the magistrates to see to it that these rights were respected. The details of their powers and titles varied depending on the domain for which they were responsible and also on the city-state involved. In the *Politics* (6.5.3–4), Aristotle explains what tasks might be assigned to urban policemen (*astunomoi*), to rural constables (*agronomoi*), and to forest wardens (*hulōroi*). We know that in the countryside property owners had to have their fields guarded during harvests, as they still did until recently in Mediterranean Europe. Wooden watchtowers were used for this surveillance.[7] Offenders might be handed over to magistrates. In a general way, magistrates were supposed to prevent or arbitrate property disputes, and to see to it that boundary stones were not moved. Thus on Chios there were "boundary-stone guards" (*horophulakes*).[8] Various kinds of centralized or decentralized cadastral land registration in public archives also made it possible to guarantee the permanence of property. It now appears that in the Hellenistic period, this registration was more the rule than the exception.[9] Moreover, the registration of private contracts must have already been frequent during the Classical period, because Aristotle describes it as commonplace (*Politics* 6.5.4).

Within the civic framework, the property owner's identity was of little importance. Property might be owned by an abstract entity (a god), a civic or akin to civic subdivision (for example, a deme or a phratry), or an individual (usually a citizen). Unless they enjoyed a particular privilege, metics—that is, resident aliens—were not allowed to own civic land. Some lands were under a special taboo, and it was forbidden to cultivate them. In some respects, and this was true throughout Greece, domains belonging to a god were treated no differently from those held by an ordinary individual: they were leased out.[10] In Delphi, for instance, certain lands could not be cultivated (*hiera chōra*), while others were leased out under contract.[11] Formally, these contracts probably did not differ much from private lease contracts (paradoxically, because of the nature of our sources, the latter are less well known). Similarly, sanctuaries' reserves of precious metals might be lent to individuals, even if, obviously, this was not a general rule.[12] The revenues derived from properties belonging to the god were used to maintain the buildings or to pay the costs of worship, in particular those connected with festivals and sacrifices, which directly benefited members of the civic community owning the sanctuary.

Private property was never seriously put in question. Plato's utopian vision in the *Republic* of a society in which private property has been abolished in favor of a strict division of labor among social classes, on the model of a beehive, existed only as a speculation. As for Sparta, the idea that it had a form of collective property, with the state redistributing land allotments to each new generation, is no more than a myth of modern historiography.[13] A challenge, not to private property, but to the current distribution of property, could come only from social protest. In the city-state, an excessively unequal distribution of wealth might in fact lead to a challenge to the established order. From Archaic to Hellenistic times, two demands were always made when crises arose: the cancellation of debts and a redistribution of land.[14] To some extent, the latter demand corresponded to a desire to return to a mythical original state in which all citizens were equal. In reality, many cities underwent revolutionary phases that were sometimes accompanied by extreme violence.[15] But basically, the goal was only to replace the current property owners with other property owners, not to put property itself in question.

The other way of challenging property might proceed from slaves. Despite the threats of severe corporal punishment to be meted out to fugitive slaves when caught, it was not unusual for slaves to run away. In a snapshot of what seems to have been quite common, Plato (*Protagoras* 310c) describes one of Socrates's friends chasing his runaway slave who had fled to Oinoe, a deme (and a fortress) on the border between Attika and Boiotia. The reader was probably invited to assume that the slave was seeking to cross to Boiotia (and perhaps was arrested at the border). Papyri from Egypt reveal that slave-owners sent out real search bulletins listing the fugitives' physical characteristics.[16] To recuperate slaves who tried to escape abroad, city-states made agreements for the reciprocal exchange of fugitive slaves. At the beginning of the second century BCE, the treaty between the two neighboring cities of Miletos and Magnesia (which had previously been at war) has a clause on the reciprocal return of the slaves who had taken refuge in the other city.[17] In any case, it was in order to protect against the possibility that slaves might escape that the first insurance scheme was invented. In Babylon, after the Macedonian conquest, the Rhodian Antimenes offered soldiers compensation, in return for a premium, in the event that a slave ran away.[18] As for slave revolts, several of them were of considerable scope. On the one hand, slaves might take advantage of a war context to defect to the opposing camp, hoping in that way to win their freedom. That happened in the case of the slave revolts on Kerkyra in 427 BCE, when slaves defected to the camp of the democrats and the Athenians, and on Chios in 412, when they defected to the camp of the Athenians.[19] But it also happened when 20,000 Athenian slaves fled to Dekeleia during the Peloponnesian War.[20] However, in cases where there were large concentrations of slaves, revolts might break out independently, without connection to a war fought locally, as at Delos in 133 BCE, and then again at the end of the second century.[21] Nothing suggests that there was ever any thought of "doing away with slavery." During the great slave revolt in Sicily around 130, the leader of the rebels, Eunous, proclaimed himself king, adopting the name Antiochos. He took revenge on his former masters, to be sure, but he did not seek to abolish slavery.[22]

We can therefore conclude that in the framework of the kind of collective appropriation constituted by the city-state, citizens (and, through them, metics—though the latter could not own land) were free to use their property as they wished. Each citizen's ambition was supposed to become self-sufficient, *autarkēs*. But this ambition did not mean that the citizen should be closed to others and reject exchange (the modern definition of "autarky"). On the contrary, Aristotle emphasizes that everyone inevitably needs others to satisfy the needs of a life worthy of the name. The peasant, who could not engage in all the categories of agricultural production, also needed to call upon masons, cobblers, and smiths. Aristotle considered it obvious that the division of labor was the foundation of the city-state.[23] For him, *autarkeia*—that is, self-sufficiency—could be realized only in and through collective life. To be sure, in his view the possibility of engaging in equitable trade did not suffice to define self-sufficiency, but was nonetheless an indispensable precondition for it.[24]

In addition, as Aristotle also insists (and here we can assume that he was reflecting, as he often did, the common opinion on the question), the use of property implied a certain number of duties. As a member of a collectivity that provided the foundation for individual appropriation, the property-owning citizen was not supposed to use his wealth solely for personal ends. Once he had satisfied his own needs, he was also supposed to put his wealth in the service of the collectivity. Since the latter in fact provided the basis for satisfying his own needs, in using his private property the citizen was supposed to be generous toward the city-state and his fellow citizens, because his self-interest rightly understood resided in the maintenance of the civic collectivity. If he had the necessary means, he should therefore not evade the collective responsibilities—called "liturgies"—that were imposed on him. These might include, for example, financing festivals (*chorēgiai*) or outfitting warships (*triērarchiai*, trierarchies).[25] Similarly, the citizen was expected to make voluntary contributions to subscription campaigns to pay for public projects (for instance, the purchase of grain or the construction of fortifications).[26] On the other hand, the exchange of goods among citizens (indeed, all exchange that took place on the city's territory, regardless of the parties involved) was supposed to adhere strictly to the principle of equity. Disputes between sellers and buyers, or more broadly between parties to a contract (for example, contracts between employers and employees), could lead to serious problems. To maintain order and equity in transactions was thus also to ensure the continuity of the civic collectivity.

In the area of social and political life, Aristotle offered his readers a treatise on morals, an ethics that was to guide them in their conduct as citizens, both public and private. According to him, the key to all these domains was remaining moderate. One must not enrich oneself too much. King Midas died of his greed, because everything he touched was transformed into gold.[27] Neither should one make excessive expenditures that might lead to the loss of one's patrimony, which would conflict with the goal of maintaining the civic collectivity. The model Aristotle rec-ommended was a system of moderate distribution that would make it possible to attenuate social tensions and guarantee the city-state's permanence. But the reality might be very different. The tension between the civic, egalitarian ideal and the enrichment of a minority was always one of the main factors in the development of Greek civil societies.

Law Relating to Transactions

So far as law is concerned, we must first emphasize that each Greek city-state had its own legal code, even under the Roman Empire. Thus we can say that there was never a "Greek law," but only a multitude of city-states.[28] In the course of a history extending over a millennium (from the Archaic period to the end of the third cen-tury CE), there were numerous political developments, and thus also juridical de-velopments. There is no doubt that in the Classical period, to take only one exam-ple, the laws in Sparta and Gortyn were very different from those in Athens (for instance, in the area of family law). However, we can nonetheless say that beyond this genuine diversity, the basic principles of law were essentially the same in the city-states that were the most urbanized and most open to trade.

That is why a Greek never felt out of place in a city other than his own, because in it he found a legal environment that was familiar to him and into which he could quickly integrate himself by making a few adaptations. To account for the differ-ences noted among city-states (even if this question is not dealt with here), it would be better to raise the question of the law in the Greek city-states in terms of varia-tions and permutations within the framework of an overall structure that limited the field of the possible. If each of the Greek city-states had each been a monad sharing no common trait with the others, Aristotle would never have undertaken to write the *Politics*. Moreover, the specificity of Roman law is connected only with the fact that it was the law of a particular city which, having become a worldwide state, ended up imposing its law on the whole of its empire—a process that took several centuries. We must furthermore emphasize that what is conventionally called Roman law is in fact a composite of legislative texts along with commentaries by legal advisers and jurisprudence (a repertory of decisions handed down by mag-istrates, especially under the Empire), the sum total of which was put together only very late, in the time of Justinian, who caused to be written, not only the code that bears his name, but also the *Digest* and the *Institutes*.[29] The image of Roman law that was forged in medieval and early modern Europe thus did not really corre-spond to the reality of Roman Republican law. So far as the practice of the law is concerned, the specificity of the Greek city-state caused the body politic as a whole (the citizens) to be seen not only as the principle that governed the state (the *polis*), but as constituting the state apparatus, which could not be distinguished from the citizens themselves. As a result, legal practices differed from those seen in Roman law as it was established starting under the later Republic and in the early Imperial period. In the Greek city-states, the tribunal was simply the people (or its representative) gathered to declare the law. According to Plato (*Laws* 715d), the judge was to be a slave to the law.[30] Aristotle (*Politics* 3.11.3–9) also insisted on the necessity of the rule of law and the superiority of the laws to the desires of the individual judges.[31] In Greece, the decisions of the judges were not bound by a jurisprudence with a value independent of the law's authority.[32]

However, the specificity of the Greek city-states' law and legal practices might appear to have introduced an uncertainty in the matter of property rights. We must not assume that property was unstable and that the tribunals' decisions were arbitrary. A view that is still largely dominant maintains that in Greece, in comparison with the situation that prevailed in Rome or modern Europe, property was poorly defined. This point deserves attention. In Greece, property was connected with belonging to a civic community and with the latter's existence, which constituted its foundation. Three characteristics suffice to illustrate this point. First, only citizens had the right to own land. Second, there might be specific constraints on property, as is shown in Athens by a law that in theory prohibited rooting out olive trees.[33] Third, again in Athens, a procedure like that of *antidosis*—that is, the exchange of patrimonies in the case of a suit between two citizens regarding the amount of the taxes they were to pay (the accuser being able to demand to exchange of his property for that of his adversary, whom he deemed to be wealthier, even though the latter paid a lower tax)—is entirely specific to world of the city-states.[34] In addition, the city-state's eminent domain was manifested by various limitations such as the city's right to make use of the land's subsurface. In Athens, for instance, the owner of the land did not have the right to run a mine; only the city-state could accord this right (it was called a "sale," but in fact it was only a long-term concession) in exchange for a fee to be paid periodically. This differs radically from the principle of English common law, *cujus est solum ejus est usque ad coelum et ad inferos*, "Ownership of the land reaches from the heavens to the underworld."[35]

Beyond these limitations, however, in Greece the owner was free to use his property as he saw fit. Aristotle (*Rhetoric* 1.5.7) defined property this way: "Ownership [may be defined] as the right of alienation or not, by which I mean giving the property away or selling it."[36] Transactions, and more generally all kinds of contracts, were subject to specific laws that protected buyers and sellers and were intended to settle property disputes. Regarding precisely the law of sale and more broadly the law of obligations, the prevailing opinion today claims that they were seriously defective in comparison to Roman law. We owe this view to Fritz Pringsheim, who set forth his thesis in a landmark study, *The Greek Law of Sale* (1950). For him, there are necessarily three kinds of law relating to contracts. Historically, the first kind was the formal contract, in which specific words uttered by the parties commit them and make the contract binding: the type is the Roman *stipulatio*. The second kind is the real contract, in which a contract becomes valid (and thus can become the object of litigation) only if the delivery has been made and if the price has been paid. The third kind is the consensual contract, in which a simple, direct agreement between the parties makes the contract binding (and thus can become the object of litigation).

Now, according to Pringsheim, the Greek world, unlike Rome, never reached the stage of consensual contracts, and therefore continued to have a primitive kind of law of sale and obligations. In particular, he maintains that the Greeks were unable to distinguish between possession and ownership. Faced with the practical obstacles connected with the primitive nature of their law, the Greeks are supposed to have been forced to develop all sorts of legal fictions to get around them, which we would see especially in the law of Ptolemaic Egypt. Even during the Imperial period, when they were dominated by Rome, the Greeks are supposed to have retained their traditional kinds of law. One of the main concrete results is supposed to have been that the Greek world did not know the system of sale on credit, since what defines this kind of sale is that the buyer is temporarily the possessor of a good that he had not yet completely paid for.

Pringsheim's point of departure—namely, that the law of the city-states did not recognize the binding nature of agreements freely contracted between private parties—nonetheless collides with a superabundance of explicit testimony to the contrary.[37] In *Rhetoric* (1.15.9 and 21–22), Aristotle describes the principles of contract law this way:

> Again, it is necessary to see whether the law is contradictory to another approved law or to itself; for instance, one law enacts that all contracts should be binding [*kuria*], while another forbids making contracts contrary to the law . . . and it is not the contracts that make the law binding [*kurion*], but it is the laws that give force to legal contracts. And in a general sense the law itself is a kind of contract, so that whoever disobeys or subverts a contract [makes it *akuron*], subverts the laws. Further, most ordinary and all voluntary transactions are carried out according to contract; so that if you destroy the authority of contracts, the mutual intercourse of men is destroyed.[38]

Of course, as one might expect in what is a sort of manual for trial lawyers, Aristotle goes on to develop the contrary argument, by opposing natural law to positive law (the principle of justice is superior even to the law itself). But the principles of positive law remain. Demosthenes and Dinarchus both repeatedly emphasize that agreements (*homologiai*) freely consented to are binding (*kuriai*). Finally, the lexicographer Pollux (8.31) mentions a "law on the violation of contracts." Considering that this was a late testimony, Pringsheim denied it any value, but his argument is very weak given the testimony of Aristotle, Demosthenes, and Dinarchus.[39]

Beyond general principles, what did the law of sale and contracts consist in? The seller might receive only part of the purchase price on delivery, the rest to be paid at some later date (the seller advances credit). Or the buyer might make a deposit to secure an option on goods to be delivered later (the seller advances part of the purchase price). Forward selling is only a particular kind of advance made by the buyer: the good has not yet been produced and its market price can only be estimated, but the two parties nonetheless agree on a delivery, the conditions, date, and price being set by the contract. For both parties, forward selling involves a risk. The seller has the advantage of being paid in advance the whole or (more commonly) a part of the sum agreed upon, but he also commits himself to deliver the product on the date set, no matter what the circumstances, and this can prove dangerous if he is not able to meet this obligation. The buyer has the advantage of being sure that he will receive the product at the specified date, but he is also taking a risk because market conditions might have changed in the interim, with the result that the current price for the product in question turns out to be lower than the one he has agreed to pay, so that he is risking a major financial loss. It is this second aspect, the advance on the part of the buyer, that we will take up first.

From the outset, it should be emphasized that sales involving deposits made against the future delivery of the product existed at least from the first half of the fifth century BCE. Dated between 480 and 460 BCE and written on a lead sheet, the record of a transaction from a small commercial port on the southern coast of France where Greeks, Etruscans, and Iberians engaged in trade already mentions a sale with an advance deposit (*arrhabōn*) and a guarantee (*enguētērion*).[40] There is no testimony relating to deposits in Attic documentation, but that is probably connected with the kind of sources we have for that city.[41] On the other hand, we find the system of sale with advance deposit in Ptolemaic Egypt, where it was in common use. Take, for example, a petition sent to King Ptolemy IV by a wool merchant who had bought fleeces to be delivered later. Having paid a 13.2 percent advance deposit (76 drachms out of an agreed total price of 575 drachms, 1 obol, and 4 *chalkoi*) for 118 fleeces, the wool merchant claims that he has bought them and that the royal authority should force the unscrupulous seller, who sheared the sheep and kept the wool for himself, to deliver the product as agreed.[42] Here we have a clear case where owner and possessor are distinct. Moreover, that is why in this type of contract litigation regarding delivery occurs, the seller not being able to deliver the goods (probably the most frequent case) or the buyer no longer wanting to receive the goods and pay the remaining balance.

In the second case, we thus have an example of forward selling—that is, a sale in which the obligations of the parties, the buyer and the seller, are to be met after the purchase date. This contract explicitly mentions that the product was *bought*, even though only part of the price was paid. An even more explicit case is that of a Thasian law of the end of the fifth century BCE regarding wine trading, in which two clauses concern forward selling. [43] The law provides that must or wine not yet made cannot be sold before the month of Plynterion, which probably corresponds to late June and early July in our calendar. Obviously, the city of Thasos wanted to avoid any disputes over forward sales made too much in advance: such sales had to wait until a reasonable estimate of the quantity and quality of the harvest could be made, that is, until early summer (for a grape harvest in September). In all likelihood, the law became necessary after too many suits that involved forward sales made too early in the year were filed. The second clause concerning forward sales provides that when wine is bought in jars (*pithoi*)—that is, once the grapes are harvested and the wine put in jars—the sale will be considered "complete" (*kuria*) as soon as the buyer's seals have been put on the jars (even though the wine is still in the winemaker's cellar). A sale is thus considered "complete" when the parties have agreed upon the product and the price. It is then legally binding. Once the buyer has put his seal on the *pithoi*, he is considered the owner of the wine. From that moment on, he is the one who runs the risk that the wine will deteriorate. Wine is fragile, especially under the conditions of vinification obtaining in antiquity, and can spoil very quickly. It is also the buyer who runs the risk of loss in the event that the *pithos* is broken or begins to leak.

We find the same clauses in Roman law, as is shown by chapter 18.6 of the *Digest*, *De periculo et commodo rei venditae* ("Risk and benefit of the thing sold"), which gives special attention to the example of wine. The Latin expression *signare dolium*, "seal a jar," appears with the same legal value as in the Thasian law: "If a jar has been sealed by the buyer, Trebatius states that it is considered to have been delivered."[44] Once again, the distinction between fact (possession) and law (ownership) is perfectly clear in Greek law, as it is in Roman law. Thus it makes no sense to contrast them in order to assert the "inferiority" of Greek law. Greek law recognized forward sales so well that, as in Thasos, it could even regulate them (regarding the date of forward sales). It is obvious that these contracts between individuals could give rise to litigation, as is shown by the abundant papyrological documentation from the Ptolemaic period, which does not testify to a peculiar law fundamentally distinct from the law of the Greek city-states, but rather to a direct extension of the latter. Only the loss of the corresponding documentation prevents us from knowing the details of sales procedures (and the litigation connected with them) in the law of the Greek city-states.

THE WORLD OF THE AGORA

The Agora as a Legal Space

In 545 BCE, when King Cyrus of Persia was about to attack the Greek cities on the Ionian coast, the Spartans informed him that they considered themselves the protectors of those cities. According to Herodotus (1.152–3), Cyrus still knew nothing about the Spartans. When he learned who they were, he said: "I never yet feared men who set apart a place in the middle of their city where they perjure themselves and deceive each other" (1.153.1).[45] Herodotus explains that Cyrus was referring to the agora. Even if Cyrus's attitude can be analyzed in the framework of Achaemenid ideology, according to which the king is the master of the Truth and his enemies are merely liars, which makes the anecdote more plausible, the latter is naturally only one of the mirror-stories a people attributes to others the better to define itself.[46] In this respect, the Persians in Montesquieu's *Persian Letters* are true descendants of Herodotus's Cyrus. In any case, the anecdote about the marketplace seems to have been a *topos* in ancient Greece, since it is found in a similar form in remarks that tradition attributes to one of the Seven Sages of Greece, the famous Anacharsis, who, as a friend of Solon, is supposed to have lived in the early sixth century BCE. According to Diogenes Laertius (1.105), the Skythian Anacharsis is supposed to have said that "the agora is a special place where people deceive one another and acquire more than that to which they have a right." The same Anacharsis is supposed to have been surprised to learn "how it happened that the Greeks were able to proscribe lying and at the same time lie blatantly when engaging in retail trade" (ibid., 1.104).

The views attributed to Anacharsis do not hold solely for the Archaic period. They are not characteristic of a particular period in the history of the Greek world or of a single social class (in any case certainly not of the aristocracy alone). It is true that aristocratic ideology influenced all periods of the history of Greece and Rome: thus we find in Cicero, who is following his Greek masters, the same idea of the market as a space of mendacity.[47] But hostility to the merchants of the agora emanated from all social strata, and perhaps even more from the lower classes, who frequented them on a daily basis. The aristocratic elite scorned petty traders, but in everyday life it dealt less often with the small merchants of the agora, for wealthier people sent their slaves to make purchases for them in the agora.[48] It is true that a good reputation is the best guarantee of success for a trader. In a society where kinship and friendship bonds were still paramount, maintaining one's reputation, including one's reputation in trade, was certainly also a strong incentive against cheating.[49] But in big cities, increasing anonymity, especially for retail trade where both suppliers and clients are many, could lead to other behaviors. There, it can hardly be doubted that the market was the place where it was tempting to try to make the greatest possible profit—using dishonest methods, if need be. But it would be a mistake to conclude that the city-state's institutions allowed lying and deception to reign in the agora. The city's institutions were there precisely to force buyers and sellers to be honest, *nolens volens*. In Athens, a law mentioned by Demosthenes explicitly prohibited fraudulent practices in the agora: "A law prescribes that it is forbidden to deceive in the agora."[50] Hyperides also mentions this law in the same terms.[51] The ability to deceive in the agora has to do with a situation called "informational asymmetry," the seller having information regarding the objects for sale that he does not divulge, sometimes even going so far as to disguise his products so that the buyer is deceived concerning their quality. The city-state's legislative apparatus was there to remedy this situation.[52]

Did all exchanges of products take place in the agora? In the case of some products, allusions to the determination of the place and duration of the market suggest this. A fourth-century BCE law concerning wool from Erythrai forbids its sale anywhere other than the place defined by the city-state and after "the middle of the day."[53] The same is suggested by the various references to the sectors of the agora (see later), to the sale sites—as in the Delian law regarding wood and charcoal—or more generally, to the location of the market and its duration—as in the law concerning the *panēguris* (religious festival) in Andania (in Messenia), dating from 91 BCE or 23 CE.[54] The city-state's interest in levying taxes on sales naturally led it to concentrate commerce in the agora.

But does that mean that all sales had to take place in the agora, and that all contracts had to be made there? That would be an extreme view. To be sure, the streets of the Greek city-state were not systematically lined with shops. But it was in no way forbidden to buy things from craftsmen in the specialized neighborhoods where they had set up shop, like the cobblers whom we see on a black-figure Attic amphora from the end of the sixth century tailoring shoes for a wealthy female client.[55] Besides, some poor-quality goods could be sold in some specific locations, different from the agora. According to Aristophanes, salted goods (*tarichos*) were sold at the gates of the city, a location that is specifically opposed to the agora and clearly defined as a place where third-quality goods were sold.[56] It was in this place, where prostitutes used to operate (the connection between salted goods and salacious activities was clear to everyone), that the Athenian politician Cleon would be condemned to sell his asses' and dogs' meat sausages.[57] Furthermore, important transactions, such as the purchase of a house or shop, or making a commercial contract, might take place in private homes. We must therefore conclude that the regulation of commerce must have been constraining (prohibiting sales outside periods and places determined by the city-state) only for a limited number of products such as grain and foodstuffs in general, products being sold by middlemen, and products that were particularly important for the economy of the city-state in question, like the wool from Erythrai (both wholesale and retail). For other "products"— slaves, for example—even if most of the purchases must have been made in the agora, we nonetheless have several examples of sales made outside the framework of the agora *stricto sensu*.

The Agora in the City-State, Local Agoras, and Temporary Markets

The agora itself was divided into sectors, each corresponding to a particular product, as clearly explained by Xenophon, or to this or that category of workers for hire.[58] Starting at the end of the Hellenistic period, and especially during the Imperial period, the agoras were increasingly surrounded by colonnaded porticos. Excavations of the agora in Pella (in Macedon), a city that was destroyed by an earthquake at the beginning of the first century BCE, give a good idea of how agoras might have been arranged at that time. It was a vast area surrounded by porticos, the interior spaces being divided by thin walls that defined two spaces, one in front of the other, that could serve as shops or workshops. The wealth of archaeological material found on the site (silver and bronze coins, amphora handles, various metal objects, ivory styli for writing, and so on) testify to the intense activity that went on there.[59] In Magnesia on the Maeander in the early Imperial period, it was the spaces between the columns (which varied in number) that were assigned to different categories of trade. Generally speaking, in the agoras of large cities, there were sectors reserved for butchers, fishmongers, grain merchants, clothing merchants, and sellers of ceramics, iron or bronze tools, ornaments, birds, and so on. Thus the customer wasted no time in running all over the agora to find the things he needed. Similarly, this arrangement made it easier for the *agoranomoi* and other market officials to supervise the transactions taking place. For auction sales, special constructions and equipment were used, such as the "circles" (*kukloi*), one of which has been found in Delos.[60]

The image of the agora as a marketplace in the center of the city is justified. However, it must be connected with other official places of exchange that were also institutionalized. For a large city-state like Classical Athens, which had two cities, Athens and Piraeus, there was not a single large agora, but two, one in each city, each supervised by five *agoranomoi*. But in Athens, there were also local agoras in the demes. Some of them are attested in our sources (even if it is clear that not all of the 139 demes had their own agoras), and several have even left significant archaeological traces.[61] Thus the deme of Rhamnous decided to finance expenditures for the new sacrifice in honor of King Antigonos by using revenues from the *agorastikon*—that is, from the taxes levied on the deme's agora.[62] These markets had an obvious interest for the local inhabitants, who could not procure their supplies in the main agoras of Athens or Piraeus, which were too far away for most rural Athenians. But a religious association like the *genos* of the Salaminians had its own agora at a specific location, "in the Koile."[63] The situation in Rhodes was like that in Athens; apart from the *agoranomoi* of the city of Rhodes, there was at least one *agoranomos*, and hence an agora, in Lindos, one of the towns on the island.[64] Agoras on the borders are also attested by our sources, which shows that it was possible to trade with foreign merchants on the periphery of the city-state.[65]

The religious festivals known as *panēgureis* were also an opportunity to trade.[66] These festivals attracted large numbers of visitors, and thus took on an economic aspect, since it was necessary to feed and house the pilgrims, to entertain them, and more generally to provide them with everything they needed for worship—for example, animals to be sacrificed. Thus they became genuine markets. Merchants could use the sanctuary, installing a temporary agora in it. During the *panēguris* that took place in the sanctuary of Artemis Amarysia in Eretria, the merchants had the explicit right to sell "inside the sanctuary."[67] They were supervised by the *agoranomoi*, magistrates of the city where the festival took place, or magistrates specially appointed for the occasion. In certain cases, at least, the nature of some of the products exchanged and the periodicity of the *panēguris* are not in doubt. Thus although it cannot be stated as a general rule, in some cases at least, the goal was not simply to provide for visitors to the festival, and a genuine fair was held alongside it. The celebration of the festival of Artemis Amarysia in Eretria or the *Aktia* at Anaktorion in Akarnania involved genuine fairs. At the *Aktia*, as proved by a document of 216 BCE reorganizing the *panēguris*, slaves were sold (and taxes levied on their sales), and thus it was not merely a matter of providing for the pilgrims.[68]

Like ordinary agoras, the *panēgureis* were governed by strict regulations. They were subject to the authority of the *agoranomoi* or panegyriarchs. Some of these *panēgureis* were even a blend of the agora and a temporary *emporion* (because not only local but also foreign merchants participated in them). As for magistrates, taxes, or tax exemptions, we find a picture similar to that found in the agoras or the *emporia*, depending on the case. In rural areas, *panēgureis* might play the role of periodic markets. But the international character of some of these *panēgureis* shows that they went far beyond the bounds of a simple rural market.

Buying and Selling in the Agora

Why did sellers flock to the agora? The latter provided a place where sellers could easily find customers.[69] Concretely, this means that the seller's costs were reduced to the cost of transporting his goods to market and to the payment of the market tax (*epōnion*).[70] For a relatively small entrance fee, he gained access to a potential clientele that was no longer aleatory and that minimized the costs of making himself known—what we would now call advertising costs. In addition, there was the advantage of being able to acquire information that allowed him to adjust his prices in relation to those of other sellers. Finally, the city-state guaranteed the maintenance of order, thus ensuring that the seller could defend his property rights against all pressure, in the event that buyers found the price of foodstuffs too high. What was the advantage for the buyer? In the agora, the buyer could easily find the products he wanted at the best price. The cost of information about the prices was minimized, because by moving around the agora, the buyer could rapidly (and thus at minimal cost) obtain information regarding the price of the products he wanted—all the more easily because, as we have seen, traders selling the same or similar products were grouped together in sectors within the agora. Furthermore, those who bought at the agora could benefit from the additional goods offered for sale by foreign merchants (who could also use the agora). To get comparable information without an agora, the buyer would have had to spend several days going around to all the producers in the villages or on farms located in the city-state's territory.

The agora, the *emporion*, and the *panēgureis* offered considerable advantages for trading partners because they made it possible to minimize transaction costs. These specialized sites of exchange thus provided a valuable service. But it came at a price: the city had to pay the costs of setting up the agora, the salaries of the magistrates and staff entrusted with keeping order, and for maintenance and cleaning, as is shown by a law from Piraeus concerning the agora's cleanliness.[71] Thus the city-state usually levied a tax on all sales, the *epōnion*, and (according to the sacred law of Andania, which prohibits it) a fee for a place in the agora.[72] Given the service it was rendering and the resulting costs, the city-state was justified in taking a share of the profit on the sales operated in the city. The practice was in accord with the principle that revenues (*prosodoi*) could be earned not only by private individuals but also by the collectivity.

We can therefore conclude that the institution of the agora was a way of lowering the cost of information for both buyer and seller. Moreover, the city-state's institutional role was to minimize the informational asymmetry connected with the relationship between buyer and seller. In this way, the city-state minimized the cost of commercial transactions, thus providing a powerful incentive for trade. Through its very existence, the institution of the agora was a positive factor in economic development, because it encouraged producers to produce more since they had a better chance of finding a buyer at a minimal cost. For the citizen consumer, the benefit was proportional to the decrease in the cost of transactions.

LEGAL CONSTRAINTS ON THE AGORA

The Supervision of Transactions

Special magistrates, the *agoranomoi*, were responsible for overseeing the regularity of the transactions carried out in the market.[73] For Athens, we are fairly well informed regarding their number and their powers, thanks to Aristotle's *Constitution of Athens* (51.1–3):[74]

> Also market-controllers [*agoranomoi*] are elected by lot, five for Piraeus and five for the city. To these the laws assign the superintendence of all merchandise, to prevent the sale of adulterated and spurious articles. Also ten controllers of measures [*metronomoi*] are appointed by lot, five for the city and five for Piraeus, who superintend all measures and weights, in order that sellers may use just ones. Also there used to be ten grain-wardens elected by lot [*sitophulakes*], five for Piraeus and five for the city, but now there are twenty for the city and fifteen for Piraeus. Their duties are first to see that unground grain in the market is on sale at a fair price, and next that millers sell barley-meal at a price corresponding with that of barley, and baker women loaves at a price corresponding with that of wheat, and weighing the amount fixed by the officials—for the law orders that these shall fix the weights.

A text from Erythrai (*I.Erythrai* 15) dating from ca. 360–300 BCE gives us an idea of the regulation of the sale of a particular product, in this case wool, which was one of the city's chief exports:[75]

> And let the sellers weigh the wool that each of them sells, and let them do the weighing without treachery; if one of them cheats, let him pay twenty drachms [per talent?]; let the *agoranomoi* carry out the execution of the fine; let [the sellers] sell until noon; if it rains, let them not present their wool; let them not sell wool from the one-year-old sheep; let the merchant or retail trader not sell wool or gratings of fleece in any circumstance from a place other than the [wool market]; if he sells elsewhere, let him be deprived of his

wool and made to pay a fine of twenty drachms, and let everything be sold at auction by the *prutaneis* or let the sale be carried out [by the public scale?].

Among the regulations for the Mysteries at Andania were those to be followed in the market connected with the festival:[76]

> Let the *hieroi* ["sacred men"] determine a place where all transactions will take place. Let the city's *agoranomos* take care that sellers sell products that have not been adulterated and are of authentic quality, and that they use weights and measures in conformity with public measures; let him set neither sale price nor times, and let no one require sellers to pay a fee for a place; those of the sellers who will not conform to this regulation, let him have them whipped if they are slaves; if they are free, let him make them pay a fine of twenty drachms, and let the sentence be carried out by the *hieroi*.

These three texts show that the market magistrates' primary task was to prevent fraud by seeing to it that the seller did not deceive the buyer regarding the quality or the quantity of the products offered for sale. However, in some cities and for some products, specialized magistrates replaced the *agoranomoi*. This was the case in particular for the *sitophulakes* in Athens, in Rhodes, and in Priene: these magistrates were responsible for supervising trade in grain.[77] We must first emphasize that the work of *agoranomoi* (and other magistrates in charge of the market) was based on a specific legal framework. In Athens and Miletos, there was a *nomos agoranomikos*, a "market law," and this must have also been the case in most cities.[78] The *agoranomoi* (in small cities there was just one) exercised their office in the agora. This public space was delimited by boundary stones. The area that fell within their purview, at least for retail sales, was therefore well defined. In Aristophanes' *Acharnians* (719), Dikaiopolis begins by delimiting the space of his agora by setting boundary stones. Archaeological investigation has discovered such boundary stones in Athens.[79] The agora opened and closed at set hours. An anecdote reported by Plutarch (*Table Talk* 4.4 = *Moralia* 668a) taunted those who listened eagerly for the sound of the agora's bell and rushed off to the fishmongers as soon as the market opened. In Erythrai, the wool market was open only until noon.[80] However, the *agoranomoi*'s powers went beyond regulating retail sales, and this is an aspect to which we will return. In the agora, in any case, they usually had an office, the *agoranomion*. There they were supposed to keep the tools peculiar to the exercise of their responsibilities (scales, weights and measures, standards, possibly archives). It was in front of the *agoranomion*, among other places, that the regulations concerning prices and sales might be posted.[81] To make their proclamations, they probably used a kind of podium, possibly made of stone, like the platform used by heralds.

So far as the quality of products is concerned and as already mentioned, according to Aristotle the *agoranomoi* were supposed to see to it that the products sold were "authentic in quality and not adulterated." We frequently find almost the same formula in later periods. The prescription found on the temporary agora of the *panēguris* in Andania has no other goal: products sold must "not have been adulterated" and must be of "authentic quality." That is the meaning of the formula still found in Egypt in the Imperial period, according to which wheat sold or delivered as a fee must be "from the same year's harvest, free of any adulteration, not doctored and not mixed with barley."[82] In other words, wheat must not be sold mixed with old grain (that is, from the preceding year), or damaged (by mold or vermin), or mixed with a cereal grain of an inferior quality, like barley. Similarly, flour must not be mixed with bran, and wine must not be watered. The already mentioned end of the fifth century BCE law from Thasos (a major wine-producing city) refers to a law forbidding the watering of wine.[83] Under the technical conditions obtaining in antiquity, when the alcohol content could not be tested, enforcing this rule must not have been easy.[84] Generally speaking, tests of quality were thus on the whole a matter of empirical estimates made by the *agoranomoi* rather than exact measurements. Fishmongers and other sellers of fresh foodstuffs were particularly suspect, because their products spoiled very quickly. In Athens, a law prohibited wetting fish to make it look fresher.[85] But other merchants were also capable of cheating. For example, Aristophanes refers to wool-sellers who wetted their wool.[86] The most credulous buyers were taken in by crude tricks. Dioscorides (2.80.6) reports how a Roman merchant fooled his customers who were crazy about crocodile feces, which they used as a cosmetic: he sold them the feces of starlings that had been fed on rice.[87]

As for the quantities sold, the magistrates' task consisted in ensuring that the sellers used weights and measures certified by the city-state. Each city-state had its own measuring system. The original weights and measures—that is, the standards— were carefully preserved in sanctuaries.[88] On the basis of these originals, and under the supervision of the *agoranomoi*, weights and measures were made and given to the sellers. That is why we have such a vast collection of weights bearing the signature of one or several *agoranomoi*. Perfectly calibrated, these weights and measures usually bore the city-state's symbol, such as the owl for Athens. Thus they were easily identifiable. As Aristotle notes, in wealthy cities with large populations like Athens, specialized magistrates, the *metronomoi*, were responsible for supervising weights and measures. But in most cities, this office did not exist, and the *agoranomoi* performed this function. In fact, in the Hellenistic period (as well as later in the Imperial period), many weights bear the signature of the *agoranomos*, or of the board of *agoranomoi*, who were in charge of their fabrication, and often paid for it.[89] Dishonest merchants might be tempted to use weights from other cities, which looked much the same but weighed less than the legal weight. They might also be tempted to use counterfeit weights. Local merchants were probably expected to keep the weights and measures that had been given them, and to have them regularly checked by the *agoranomoi*. As for foreign merchants—who might also have access to the agora, as is shown by Aristophanes (*Acharnians* 720–22), they may have been expected to return the weights and measures when they left. In any case, the magistrates thus had to see to it that the merchants did not cheat buyers by meddling with the weights or scales and selling less than what was declared: this obligation is made explicit in the law from Erythrai concerning the sale of wool. In the particular case of wool, the same law prohibited its sale on rainy days, because then the wet wool would weigh more than its normal weight and the customer would be cheated. The higher the unit value of the product, the more tempting it was to cheat. Sellers of Tyrian purple dye, a very valuable substance, were tempted to rig their scales.[90]

The textual and archaeological documentation regarding "commercial equipment" is richest on Delos. This equipment included first a balance-beam scale with two pans, scale chains, graduated metal beams for steelyards, and weights made of stone or metal.[91] One of the most characteristic objects of the agora was the *sēkōma*. Limiting ourselves to the documentation preceding the Imperial period, we find a multitude of these, from the Black Sea to the Peloponnese, from the West (Sicily) to Asia Minor and the Levant (Maresha).[92] The *sēkōma* is a stone table with circular cavities in the top that corresponded to a given volume and had openings in the bottom. A single table thus had a series of cavities for different volumes. For dry products like grain, or for liquids like wine or oil, the use of *sēkōmata* guaranteed the buyer a certain volume (he was sure not to be cheated), and at the same time the device had the advantage for the seller that it saved him time in measuring.[93] It was characteristically a way of decreasing transaction costs, but for the magistrates it was also a way of monitoring quantities. Precisely, magistrates frequently dedicated standard weights and *sēkōmata* to the local divinity.

Thus on Delos, *sēkōmata* were dedicated by the *agoranomoi* or, after the island became an Athenian possession in 167 BCE, by the Athenian *epimelētēs*.[94] *Sēkōmata* seem to have been particularly numerous in the island.[95] Sometimes an inscription on the *sēkōma* indicates the commodity that it was to measure, such as "*sēkōma* of a half *medimnos* of grain."[96] The size of the *sēkōmata* varies: some are suitable for measuring large quantities, while others are for middle-sized or small volumes, like a Delian *sēkōma* with four cavities of 0.6, 0.3, 0.15, and 0.06 liters.[97] The unit value of the product weighed was no doubt inversely proportional to the capacity, but the large number of *sēkōmata* and the variety of the capacities measured clearly shows that they were in general use for liquids and semi-liquids. As for scales, the law of Delos regarding wood and charcoal and other documents of the same kind show that there were several types. Even heavy goods could be sold according to their weight, as was the case on Delos for firewood and similar items. Charcoal seems to have been sold according to its volume, using specific measures, but checkweighed for control.[98] For weighing precious metals, small precision scales might be used.[99]

Finally, by requiring the use of a particular currency, the state provided an additional guarantee for transactions. This was its own coinage if the city in question had a mint, as all the large cities did (with the exception of Sparta until the third century BCE). For the smaller cities that had no coinage, or only a coinage for small-value transactions (bronze coins but not silver coins), this was the foreign coinage to which they gave legal tender. The use of a single, incontestable currency in transactions in the agora avoided the disputes to which the common way of measuring value and carrying on trade constituted by money might itself have given rise. Thus it is logical that the state did everything it could to see to it that the currencies that were used in the markets were not counterfeits and, if necessary, sought to remove the latter from circulation.[100]

Moreover, beyond the agora *stricto sensu*, the city ensured that a whole range of finished products was in accord with a preestablished model. That is why we find in the Athens agora, for example, a standard (in marble) that gave the dimensions that tiles were supposed to have. In addition to tiles, bricks and even weights for looms or fishing nets were also standardized products.[101] Similarly, containers like amphoras (which might differ in capacity: full unit, half-unit, and so on) were also calibrated products. The amphoras produced in a city had to conform to a single model and to be of the same capacity (or capacities, if they were several sizes of amphoras). Under the production conditions obtaining at the time, this concern for standardization is remarkable. It was indispensable that the amphoras have, within a reasonable margin of error, a specified capacity: if their capacity was insufficient, the buyer would be deceived, because products were bought by the amphora. The important point is that the person who filled an amphora with wine be able to put the specified amount in it.[102] This standardization provided a guarantee for the buyer. At some periods and in some cities, just like tiles, bricks, and weights, amphoras might bear a stamp.

The stamp itself was certainly linked to a fiscal process, corresponding probably to a tax on amphora production. In some cases, such as the amphoras of Akanthos, the stamps also officially stated their capacity.[103] This certainly does not prove that the stamp "certified" the quantity, but it proves the existence of a possible concern for quantity on behalf of the city. Above all, there is no doubt that the cities regulated the size of the amphoras, whether or not they were stamped.[104] The format, the symbol (which was often the same as the one found on the city's coins), and possibly the text of the seal (the names of priests or magistrates, and so on) changed from one city to the next. In some cases, the magistrate was not only an eponym who dated the stamp and the product but was also connected with the supervision of the city's activities. In the Hellenistic period, amphora stamps in Sinope bore the name of an *astunomos*, that is, of the magistrate responsible for maintaining order in the city. In Knidos at the beginning of the second century they bore the names of the phrourarchs—that is, the commanders of the fortresses guarding the territory (who were thus also responsible for safeguarding the production sites on their territory). In the late Hellenistic period and in the Imperial period, it became almost the rule that the names of the magistrates that figured on small objects (especially the weights) bearing the city's stamp were those of one or several *agoranomoi*.

Supervision of Contracts and Production

The agora was not only a public area devoted to small-scale commerce. It was also the place where purchase and sales contracts were made. As Aristotle indicates in the *Politics* (6.5.2), these were both small contracts and large contracts for financing foreign trade:[105]

> So first, provision for essential needs passes through the agora, where there must be a magistracy entrusted with supervising commercial contracts [*sumbolaia*] and maintaining good order. In nearly all cities, people have to buy some products and sell others to meet mutual needs, and this is the most direct way of attaining the self-sufficiency [*autarkeia*] for which people decide to gather together in a single political community.

Aristotle was alluding to contracts in general, including those that might have international scope, which guaranteed the collectivity's self-sufficiency, and were therefore of vital importance to the city.

However, it goes without saying that these were all contracts made in the agora under the supervision of the magistrates. The agora was in fact a place where many contracts were made. Thus in the novel *Chaereas and Callirhoe* (1.14.3 and 2.1.6), after paying a deposit, the robber Theron promises to conclude the sales contract in the agora.[106] Was the place where the contract was made important in itself? Was it explicitly mentioned in the contract? Was the contract registered in a particular way by the magistrates, thus giving it a specific guarantee, even if it was later deposited with individuals? The question is worth asking, at least in cities like Athens in the Classical period, where the law did not require private contracts to be deposited in the archives, as was later the case during the Hellenistic period.

We know that in Athens and certainly in most cities, every contract freely consented to was in principle *ipso facto* binding on both parties. A dispute that arose in Athens around 330 BCE, that reported by Hyperides' *Against Athenogenes*, is a good illustration of this. Having fallen passionately in love with a young slave, a customer who wanted to buy him bought at the same time a perfumery. The purchase contract was made in a private house (3.8). But in his haste and imprudence, the buyer also agreed to assume the perfumery's unspecified debts, which amounted, as it turned out, to the very considerable sum of 5 talents: more than enough to completely ruin the buyer, who was unable to raise such a large sum. Whereas the purchase took place in a private house, the stormy meeting between the seller and the buyer, who considered himself cheated, took place in the agora (3.12). The seller (3.13) took refuge in the principle that every contract freely consented to is binding on those who made it. The plaintiff (3.14), on the contrary, tried to restrict the principle to agreements made in good faith and to show that the deal fell under the law that prohibited deceit in the market. Moreover (3.15), he invoked in his favor a law that protected the buyer by requiring the seller to take back a slave who turns out after the purchase to be suffering from an illness that was hidden by the seller, or at least came to light only after the purchase.

A contract (*sumbolaion*) or contractual commitment (*sunallagma*) could take several forms. A written contract (*sungraphē*) was only a particular form of contract.[107] In general, it was the *agoranomos* who was responsible for *sumbolaia*, including, for example, labor contracts.[108] We can gauge the importance of the question by a decree issued on Paros in the first half of the second century BCE that shows what the role of the *agoranomoi* was with respect to labor contracts. The *agoranomos* is praised for preventing labor conflicts:[109]

> Regarding those who work for a salary and those who employ them, he saw to it that neither of the two parties was cheated, ensuring that the employees did not strike but went to work, and that the employers paid their workers the salary due them, in accordance with the law, and without the case being brought before a judge.

The praise for the *agoranomos* has a general implication: if a conflict occurred, he intervened successfully. The conflict obviously had to do with salary questions, though we cannot say more precisely what was at issue. Confronted by a conflict between employers and employees, the *agoranomos* played the role of a conciliator.

In the cities, the law generally prohibited strikes. But employees were apparently prepared to violate the law to deal with a situation they considered unjust. As for the employers, they were taking the risk of seeing the project in question halted. By succeeding in conciliating the parties, the *agoranomos* avoided a trial, with all the delays and problems that it might cause. The Paros Hellenistic decree has surprising counterparts in the Imperial documentation and anthropological parallels that help us understand how hiring took place. In Magnesia on the Maeander, probably in the time of Hadrian (117–138 CE), there was south of the agora a place (*topos*) designated for masonry workers (*huperetai oikodomoi*).[110] This was surely the agreed-upon place where employers came to negotiate with masons (*oikodomoi*) who were looking for work. A parallel can be found in the contemporary world—for instance, in the cities of Sicily, where until the 1950s employers came in the morning to the public square to find farmhands and other kinds of laborers they needed.[111] The Paros decree also finds a counterpart in an inscription from Miletos from the end of the second or beginning of the third century CE. Here we see masons (*oikodomoi*) gathered around a *technitēs* (the word is partially restored)—that is, a master mason playing the role of foreman—asking the oracle of Apollo whether they should continue work on a project in the Miletos theater or seek another job.[112] A tempting hypothesis is to consider that the death of the foreman (mentioned in the text) was the source of this question: the oracle answered that they should finish their task.

A sixth-century CE text from Sardis shows a surprising correspondence with the other documents on this subject:[113] the point is to see to it that the work is not interrupted—apparently a very frequent event to which the text from Miletos bears witness (the masons' question, after the death of the foreman, may have involved whether or not they would be paid). The condition for the continuation of work was that the salaries would be paid. But the parallel with the Paros decree goes further: this text mentions that a strike, or an interruption of the work, was forbidden by law. That was precisely the goal of the *homologia* or *stipulatio* of Sardis: it involved a formal commitment on the part of the masons that they would not leave their work. A constant in the laws of the cities thus seems to have been the prohibition on work stoppages. Obviously, in the fifth century BCE there was already in the Athenian corpus a law prohibiting strikes. Alkibiades appealed to this law when he wanted to sue the painter Agatharchos for having ceased working on a project, whereas in fact Alkibiades had sequestered him in his house to force him to work, and the painter had succeeded in escaping.[114]

The Authority of the Agoranomoi

Like other magistrates, the *agoranomos* was invested with an authority that he was supposed to exercise within the framework of the law. The symbol of this authority was the whip: it was not that he was permitted to inflict punishments by whipping (moreover, only slaves could be whipped). But in the event of a dispute, if order had to be maintained in the case of a disturbance, the whip was the symbol and the instrument of his power. The "Skythian archers" (policemen) in Athens also carried whips, as did the explicitly named *mastigophoroi* (whip-bearers) in the games.[115] The anger of Jesus, who "drove the money-changers out of the temple" with a whip, has always posed a problem for theologians. Clearly, it has a religious meaning. But the scene does not refer to an act of violence. Jesus' attitude is modeled on that of an *agoranomos*—that is, someone who has a legitimate authority. The whip in Jesus' hand in John's version is another indication showing that the Gospel narrative is based on the image of the *agoranomos*.[116] Even if the *agoranomos* exercised his office within the framework of the law, he still had a large measure of personal discretion. This was the case in particular for the quality of products. Thus the *agoranomos* must have acted in an arbitrary manner more often than is generally thought: the (imaginary) case reported by Apuleius, in which an *agoranomos* tramples on fish that have just been bought by a customer, claiming that the price was too high (whereas in fact the *agoranomos's* real objective is simply a gratuitous assertion of his authority) is an excellent illustration of this.[117]

The *agoranomoi* had the power to sanction anyone who violated the laws relating to the agora. In the imaginary city in Plato's *Laws* (764b), the *agoranomoi* could use their own authority to sentence slaves and foreigners to be whipped. Similarly, they could also impose a fine of a hundred drachms on their compatriots, and the fine could be raised to two hundred drachms if they declared it in concert with the *astunomoi* (who were responsible for maintaining order in the city). These provisions reflect Plato's authoritarian ideas, and probably also the legal practices of conservative cities. However, in cities that had a moderate or a democratic system (which became the standard system during the Hellenistic period), the *agoranomoi*'s power, like that of other magistrates, was basically limited to gathering evidence for a trial before a court. Aristotle (*Politics* 4.11.5) notes (to deplore it) that in democracies magistrates made no decisions but merely prepared for decisions: in legal matters, this means that they were supposed to prepare the case before bringing it before a competent court, but not to make a judgment themselves. In the list of the eight tribunals he gives in *Politics*, Aristotle mentions fifth "a court dealing with important private contracts" (4.13.1). But eighth and last, he adds: "In addition to these courts, there is one that deals with small contracts, for amounts of one drachm or a little more. A judgment is necessary in these affairs as well, but without bringing in a large number of judges" (4.13.2).[118] In general, in the law of the cities the number of judges was a function of the significance of the case, which itself corresponded to the estimated amount of the penalty, declared in writing by the plaintiff at the time of filing the suit.[119] Moreover, we must distinguish the magistrates' power to impose fines on offenders caught *in flagrante delicto* from the power they might still have to act as judges in cases that involved a fine up to a certain amount, beyond which they had to transfer the case to another jurisdiction.[120] On this point as on so many others, the law of the cities was not identical everywhere, even though once again we find features that are widely shared among the different bodies of law.

In Athens, *agoranomoi* and *sitophulakes* (for grain) were the principal magistrates ensuring that the legal rules regarding the agora were respected. However, we do not know exactly what their jurisdictional power was, for the *Constitution of Athens* (52.1–53.2) does not give details of their competence on this point. On the other hand, a little farther on (52.2–3), the same source shows the role of the magistracy of the introducers (*eisagōgeis*):[121]

> They also elect by lot five men as introducers [*eisagōgeis*], who introduce the cases to be tried within a month, each official those of two tribes. These cases include prosecutions for nonpayment of dowry due, actions for the recovery of loans borrowed at one drachm interest [per month, that is, a loan at 12 percent interest], and of capital borrowed from one party by another wishing to do business in the market; and also actions about outrage, friendly-society business, partnerships, slaves, draft animals, naval command, and bank cases. These officials, therefore, bring into court and decide these suits within a month.

It is thus clear that the introducers were responsible for a whole series of suits having to do with activities directly connected with transactions and, directly or indirectly, with activities in the agora. *A priori*, we can assume that the introducers had to introduce all the cases before a court. However, the *Constitution of Athens* goes on (52.3–53.2):[122]

But the receivers [*apodektai*] decide suits brought by tax-farmers or against them, having power [*kurioi*] to deal summarily with suits up to ten drachms but bringing the others into the jury-court within a month. They also elect by lot the Forty, four from each tribe, who are the court before which the other suits are brought; formerly they were thirty and went on circuit trying cases in each deme, but since the oligarchy of the Thirty their number has been raised to forty. They have summary jurisdiction in claims not exceeding ten drachmas, but suits above that value they pass on to the arbitrators.

Thus in this case, it is clear that magistrates had the power to judge directly cases involving sums as large as ten drachms. Here it is not a matter of affairs directly connected with the agora or with trade, even though the Forty, who played the role of judges in demes, must often have had to make decisions in cases involving commercial or financial transactions.

The fact that some magistrates could deal with certain cases directly only if they involved no more than ten drachms is confirmed by the Athenian law of 375/4 BCE regarding the use of Attic currency.[123] In the event that this law was violated, the magistrates—*sitophulakes* for the grain markets of Athens and Piraeus, *sullogeis* of the people for the market in Athens and for the city as a whole, *epimelētai* for the *emporion* in Piraeus—were competent (*kurioi*) to deal with cases (*diagignōskein*) involving up to ten drachms. Beyond that amount, the magistrates had to ask the *thesmotētai*, who were in charge of civil justice in Athens, to convoke a tribunal and make it available to the magistrates so that a trial could be held. The *Constitution of Athens* does not mention a jurisdictional limit for *sitophulakes*, *sullogeis* of the people, and *epimelētai*. But the law of 375/4 BCE on the supervision of currency leads us to ask whether magistrates other than the ones it mentions explicitly were not also dependent on the same jurisdictional principle: were *sitophulakes*, *sullogeis* of the people and the *epimelētai* of the *emporion* competent to judge cases involving up to ten drachms only for infractions concerning currency? Wouldn't it be more logical to maintain that on the contrary, it was because they were competent up to ten drachms that the law specified that in the case of currency, the same rule was to be applied? But then what about the *agoranomoi*? Can't we assume that they were subject to the same rule? Lacking a source, no conclusion can be drawn, but it is clear that the question has to be asked.

Similar procedures can be observed or presumed in other cities. The previously mentioned Paros decree for the *agoranomos* Killos honors him for having kept a dispute between employers and salaried workers from going to court (l. 20): thus there is reason to believe that *agoranomoi* on Paros were expected to bring before a court the legal cases they had prepared. The also previously mentioned mid-Hellenistic Delian law on wood and charcoal (ll. 14–31) shows that the *agoranomos* was supposed to register complaints against people suspected of violating the law and to bring them before the court of the Thirty-One within a month after the accusation was made.[124] If the accused was convicted, the *agoranomoi* were supposed to carry out the sentence within ten days.[125] It should be emphasized that the same law seems to set a single fine of fifty drachms. As often happens, the amount of the fine was not proportional to the offense, but a fixed amount. We can assume that the threat of relatively high fixed fines had a dissuasive role: in this case, for many retailers, the threat of having to pay a fine of fifty drachms was supposed to dissuade them from cheating (which corresponds perfectly to the atmosphere in which this ad hoc law was approved, during a period of allegedly abusive price hikes in certain very specific categories of goods). At Andania in Messenia, in the event that regulations regarding sales in the market, water supplies or the functioning of the baths were violated, the decree on the organization of the *panēguris* of the Mysteries prescribed punishment by whipping (the number of strokes was not specified) for slaves and a fine of twenty drachms for free men, noting in the three cases that the judgment (*krima*) was to be pronounced before the *hieroi*, the commissioners assigned to organize the festival.[126] As in the Delian law, there is a set fine and the *agoranomoi* put the case before a court. At Delphi, the amphictionic law regarding the use of Attic tetradrachms from the end of the second century might seem to be a return to Plato.[127] It shows that in cities that belonged to this religious confederation, "magistrates" (the term is general, because the name of the magistrates varied from one city to another) and *agoranomoi* had a duty to levy a fine of two hundred drachms on those who did not use the Attic tetradrachm at its official rate. However, though laconic, the decree does not oblige us to conclude that the magistrates had the power to levy this very high fine without going through a court.

The *agoranomoi* of Melitaia appear to represent an exception to the principle that magistrates were limited to preparing cases for court.[128] Melitaia and Peraia were two (small) neighboring cities of Achaia Phthiotis in southern Thessaly. Peraia had entered into "joint citizenship" or "constitution" (*sumpoliteia*) with Melitaia, but retained a certain autonomy. Following disputes between the two communities, the Aitolian confederation arbitrated between them (213/2 BCE). This arbitration provided that the *agoranomoi* of Melitaia would come to Peraia every four months to judge suits among Peraians that were submitted by the local *agoranomoi* (the period of four months probably being connected with the *agoranomoi*'s terms of office). The *agoranomoi* from Melitaia would thus act as did the Athenian itinerant judges. The knowledge they had gained as *agoranomoi* was supposed to provide them with the technical competence to judge matters relating to the agora, whereas their distance from the affairs of Peraia was supposed to ensure their impartiality.

We see, therefore, that the competence of the *agoranomoi* of Melitaia did not constitute a true exception. On the contrary, we can state it as a principle that in the Classical and Hellenistic periods, when the amount of the fine that might be levied on offenders exceeded a certain level, the trial was held not before the magistrates but before a court. The latter played the role of a third party and the number of its members (in proportion to the case) was supposed to provide the best guarantee of impartiality (by preventing influence and corruption). This intent to separate magistracy from the exercise of justice gave answerable parties, including in principle the humblest merchants or customers in the agora, a guarantee against arbitrariness, at least so long as a formal equality among free men continued to exist in the civic world. In the world of the agora, the law of the city was supposed to prevail for the benefit of all. The magistrates were expected to see to it that merchants did not cheat and did not violate the agora's regulations, which protected buyers' interests. If merchants were convicted of violating these regulations, they could be fined (or whipped, if they were slaves). In addition, the goods they had for sale might be confiscated and auctioned off by the city. In Athens, after Pericles' decree prohibiting the importation of products from Megara, merchandise accused of being from Megara was immediately sold at auction.[129] Also in Athens, merchants who did not respect the law requiring them to accept coins approved by public currency supervisors were to have their merchandise confiscated the same day.[130] In Erythrai, wool sellers who violated the rules of sale saw their merchandise sold at auction.[131] In Delos, in the second half of the third century BCE, the law on wood and charcoal mentions (l. 6) merchandise sold at public auction—certainly merchandise that had been seized for import violations or fraudulent sales in the market.[132]

But the law also protected sellers against buyers. In his *Characters* ("The Shameless Man," 9.4), Theophrastus shows how some customers might go to great lengths to escape paying: "When he goes shopping, he reminds the butcher of any favor he has done him, then stands by the scales and throws in preferably some meat, or otherwise a bone for the soup, and if he gets it, good, otherwise he grabs some tripe from the table with a laugh as he goes away." We see why the same Theophrastus, in his treatise *On the Laws*, emphasized that the role of the *agoranomoi* was to prevent deception not only on the part of sellers but also on the part of buyers.[133] An amusing scene imagined by Aristophanes (*Wasps* 1388–1414) shows how a simple baker woman (who was also a citizen; she gives the names of her mother and father) could file a complaint with the *agoranomoi*. A drunkard (Philocleon) had bumped into her stall and knocked down her loaves of bread (and other merchandise) representing a total value of two drachms and two obols, which led to a trial for the perpetrator.[134] In the democratic city, justice was in principle meted out equally to all.

INFORMATIONAL ASYMMETRY AND GUARANTEE OF SALES

Legal Constraints and Informational Asymmetry

The principle of commercial trade is that a given good with a certain value must be exchanged for a good of equivalent value. This kind of exchange thus presupposes the existence of both a value common to goods so that they can be recognized as appropriate for exchange, and a system for measuring value that is recognized by the parties involved in the exchange. In the framework of an analysis of commercial trade, it will suffice here to keep in mind that, as Aristotle explicitly emphasized, it is the principle of utility that is applied, utility measured in monetary terms.[135] Once the buyer and the seller have agreed upon the value of the goods to be exchanged and upon the way of measuring that value, it remains to move on to the practical phase of the exchange. How can the buyer be sure that a good will in fact have the expected value? How can he know that it will be delivered in the agreed-upon quantity? And how can the seller be sure that he will be paid in proportion to what he has delivered? These are a few of the many uncertainties inherent in commercial trade. The theory of trade has occupied many contemporary economists. We have seen that the goal of market institutions was precisely to limit the uncertainty inherent in transactions in general, and especially in commercial trade.[136] If we accept the premise that there can be no regular trade without institutions, then we have to conclude that the market is not a "natural" form that is somehow the normal or original state of the way in which societies function. On the contrary, the market is necessarily a social construction. The institutions that manage it have not always existed: they themselves have a complex history that is directly linked with other forms of social structuring in the society in question.

The theory of commercial trade may be considered a subset of information theory. In the framework of commercial trade, just as the material character of exchange has a cost (that of the physical transportation of the commodity traded), the procedure of exchange also has a cost. This cost is that of the acquisition and management of the information used in the exchange. Where can one buy a certain commodity? At what price? On what conditions? This information constitutes the precondition for any exchange. However, before the exchange, information regarding goods is unequally distributed. The informational asymmetry between trading partners can be defined as the difference in the quality and quantity of information that the seller and the potential buyer have, respectively, concerning the product offered for sale. The buyer has an advantage over the seller, in that he knows (in theory) what he is selling, but he may not want to divulge this information to his potential customer. In this case, at the moment that the purchase is concluded, there is a situation of informational asymmetry between the two partners to the exchange. The first author to have formalized this idea was Kenneth Arrow, discussing the relationship between the physician and his patient, with all the consequences that can be drawn concerning the quality of the diagnosis and the safety of the patient.[137] But the classic example of the analysis of the situation of informational asymmetry is the one proposed by George Akerlof concerning the used car market in his article "The Market for Lemons."[138] In this market, the buyer is totally dependent on the information the seller is willing to provide: only the seller knows the car's history, how it has been driven and maintained, and whether it has been involved in accidents. But the tendency is to maintain that the market price of used cars is fundamentally the same depending on a few basic parameters, of which the age of the car is the most important. As a result, if all cars are sold at the same price, someone who cannot prove that his car is of good quality and therefore cannot ask a high price will not be inclined to sell it. According to a principle analogous to Gresham's law, which holds that bad money drives out good, we can say that bad cars drive out good cars. Consequently, the average price of used cars will decrease. Thus we have a case of "adverse selection" in which the market does not by itself perform the function of correcting imperfections related to the unequal distribution of information between buyers and sellers.[139]

Generalizing this kind of situation, Akerlof showed how only institutional measures (written explicitly into contracts and laws) can decrease the uncertainty connected with situations of informational asymmetry.[140] This is the case for the seller's guarantee of his product for a certain period of time defined in advance, the state's certification that the product meets a given norm, or the existence of a brand and the reputation connected with it. The example of the used car market thus shows that if it is not counteracted by institutional measures, informational asymmetry can threaten the very existence of a market. It can be shown that the Greek cities had already taken fully into account the potential consequences of informational asymmetry between buyer and seller and made an appropriate response to them.

Informational Asymmetry in the Agora and the City's Response

If the buyer and the seller thus both had an interest in resorting to the agora to minimize their costs of acquiring information regarding prices, the buyer had an additional interest: the guarantee of honest trade. The first guarantee provided by the city's magistrates was that of the seller's ownership. An illustration of this is provided by an anecdote in Plautus's *The Persian* (*Persa*), which is an adaptation of a Greek original from the fourth century BCE. In Athens, the slave merchant Dordalos allows himself to be seduced by the prospect of an additional business deal. He buys at very low cost, but without having witnesses who can guarantee the slave's origin, a young girl who the seller claims was kidnapped in Arabia, but who is in reality an Athenian citizen; as the seller explicitly reminds him (v. 589), the sale thus takes place at his own risk. Once he has paid the price, it appears that he has been cheated, but he cannot protest on pain of severe punishment for having tried to reduce an Athenian citizen to slavery.[141]

Plautus's legal vocabulary is that of Roman society, with a particular reference to the principle of the *mancipium*, the legal category of property in the Roman world.[142] However, it is clear that the principle could not have been different in Classical Athens, since the scene constitutes the mainspring of the play and cannot have been added by Plautus. Therefore we can say with confidence that in the Greek original of *The Persian*, the sale could not be guaranteed without the presence of witnesses. A sale that was not made in the agora (as we have seen, this was perfectly possible and legal) thus had to be accompanied by specific guarantees. In the agora, magistrates were responsible for supervising the origin of products and guaranteeing ownership. As for the reputation of a product from a specific origin or from a particular commercial house, it is enough to say here that this was already commonplace in antiquity (even if *stricto sensu*, the notion of a brand, which is connected with the existence of companies, did not yet exist).[143] As already observed, the amphora stamps (when there were stamps, which is far from being a rule) correspond to a process of taxation.[144] It remains that the very shape of the amphora, which was ordinarily peculiar to a region or even to a city, made it relatively easy to determine the origin of its contents (even if this did not prevent fraud involving the containers as well as their contents). Then on a distant market, the stamp, when there was one, gave a supplementary indication regarding the origin of the amphora. More generally, as we have seen, the city had established an arsenal of measures to guarantee the quality and quantity of the product sold.

Among these measures, there is however one that illustrates still better this concern to provide a guarantee for the buyer in the event that there was a specific informational asymmetry connected with the very nature of the product sold, as in the case of the used car market analyzed by Akerlof. Attempted fraud in selling grain, oil, or wine was subject to immediate denunciation by the *agoranomos*—for example if the grain or oil, though spoiled, was sold at the price of a fresh product, if the wine had been watered, or if a cheap wine was sold at the price of an expensive one: that is the sense of the anecdote reported by Apuleius already mentioned. To be sure, there was at that time no method for "scientifically" measuring quality, and the *agoranomos* had to rely on his sense of observation and his taste (for instance, in determining whether wine had been watered, because the other methods of testing for this that are mentioned in ancient sources are either far-fetched or unreliable).[145] Therefore a certain arbitrariness might enter into the steps taken by the *agoranomoi*. It is no accident that merchants made dedications to "their" *agoranomoi*, praising their sense of fairness and impartiality.[146] Some *agoranomoi* must have abused their power; that was a risk inherent in the system. But the absence of supervision, and thus of a guarantee, would have been far more prejudicial for buyers, and also, in the end, for the sellers as well.

A case in which informational asymmetry was still greater and which corresponds directly to the situation Akerlof described is that of the sale of livestock and slaves. Cynically, Cato (*On Agriculture* 2.7) advised selling everything that might represent a loss in value of one's property: "Sell worn-out oxen, blemished cattle, blemished sheep, wool, hides, an old wagon, old tools, an old slave, a sickly slave, and whatever else is superfluous."[147] Plutarch, in his *Life of Cato* (4.4 and 5.1–6), did not conceal the disgust that such behavior elicited in him. However, while it may not have been universal, this kind of behavior must nonetheless have been frequent, because Cato was able to recommend it overtly. Cato does not say whether the master was supposed to provide reliable information regarding the true age of his livestock and the health of his old slaves. Apparently he left that up to the seller. In other words, sick slaves, for example, might be put up for sale. So how could the buyer know whether the animal or the slave did not have some hidden defect, known but deliberately concealed, that would appear only later on? The law protected the buyer.[148] In the *Laws* (916ac), Plato proposes a redhibition period of one year for a slave with epilepsy and six months for slaves with other illnesses. In other words, if some defect could be proved, the sale would be annulled and the slave would be returned to the previous owner. Hyperides (*Against Athenogenes* 3.15) also emphasizes that it is the seller's duty to mention any defect when selling a slave, and that if he does not, bringing suit against him is justified.

Epigraphic texts confirm the existence of laws of this type. For instance, there is a law from Abdera, dating from slightly before 350 BCE, in which, even though the text is mutilated, we can see that for a slave the redhibition period was one year for the "sacred illness" (epilepsy), ten months for dysentery, and three months for other illnesses (we do not know which ones).[149] There were analogous clauses for oxen, horses, and mules, but the specification of the redhibition period has been lost. A law from Knossos dating from the third century lists the conditions of redhibition for oxen (draft or plow animals).[150] It provides that if the buyer wishes, he may, on his own initiative (and thus without suspecting fraud) return a bovine within five days of the purchase, on the condition that he pay one triobol per day. On the other hand, if it appears that he has been sold an untrained ox—which assumes that he had in principle been sold an ox ready for work—he can give it back without paying the daily triobol required when the redhibition is purely at the initiative of the buyer. Therefore, we can say that if the buyer had not noticed any defect within the stipulated period, the sale could no longer be challenged.

Thus it can be concluded that the cities took fully into account the uncertainty associated with the situation of trade and sought to reduce it by institutional measures. Thanks to the city's institutions and the activity of its magistrates, the buyer benefited from a guarantee of information about the products offered on the market. The informational asymmetry connected with the individual relationship between buyer and seller was minimized, because the buyer had access to certified information guaranteed by the city's institutional action. In addition, for some transactions in which there could be no *ex ante* guarantee, the clause providing for return within a certain period of time defined by law provided the necessary guarantee *ex post*. The city thus tried to ensure the transparency of transactions. By limiting uncertainty regarding purchases, it reduced their cost and thus increased the volume and velocity of transactions, which was doubly beneficial: to the trading partners, for the additional benefits they could obtain, and to the public collectivity through the additional tax revenues it could count on.

PRICE CONTROL POLICIES

Finally, the city's authorities had to see to it that the market was supplied and, so far as possible, that the price of commodities on sale remained affordable for customers. To realize this goal, several options were available: trying to negotiate affordable prices with importers or using public intervention funds to stabilize prices, especially for grain.[151] The most common policy was, however, to supervise prices.

Market Supply and Price Control

While the city supervised quality and ensured the standardization of the quantities of products sold in the agora, it also monitored prices. On the one hand, it sought to prevent profiteering, which in the context of the Greek city involved asking prices that were "in conformity with fairness." Once again, this involves nothing less than ensuring the honesty of transactions, this time by acting on prices. On the other hand, the city tried to see to it that prices did not suddenly shoot up. Although, as we will see, these two actions were closely related, the first concerned essentially retail sales, whereas the second concerned mainly imported products (especially grain).

The city's retail price controls were based on the principle that the retailer's profit margin should not be excessive. This can be seen in Lysias's speech *Against the grain dealers* (22.8), from 386 BCE. Athenian law prohibited retailers from taking a margin of more than one obol, which undoubtedly meant one obol per drachm (and not per *medimnos* of grain).[152] The margin could thus not exceed 16.66 percent of the purchase price. The *P.Teb.* 703, l. 176 (end of the third century BCE) mentions a similar rule in Ptolemaic Egypt. Among the instructions the *dioikētēs*, the superintendant of finances in the Ptolemaic kingdom, gave to the *oikonomoi* of the nomes when they took office was the following: "See to it that the products offered for sale are not sold at prices higher than those set by the regulation; as for products that do not have fixed prices (*hestēkuia timē*), for which the sellers can set the price they want, do not supervise them superficially, either, but after having determined the reasonable profit on the merchandise sold, force them . . . to sell it."[153] The regulation, which was *a priori* valid for all of Egypt, thus distinguished between products whose prices were set by the authorities and those whose prices were not fixed but "free" (but which in reality were controlled, because the "reasonable margin" was set by the nome's *oikonomos*). For the retailer, fraud thus consisted in increasing his margins beyond the authorized limits, whether from the outset, or by making a profit on stockpile sales.

These practices are denounced by an anonymous orator in Lysias's speech *Against the grain dealers*. These merchants bought grain from major foreign traders (*emporoi*), metics, or citizens who supplied the city with imported grain. They were supposed to retail it, respecting the margin that was set by the city. The orator accuses them in violent terms (22.14) of benefiting from all the increases in profits related to the circumstances: according to him, they were prepared to use every bit of bad news, every rumor to inflate their prices. Far from respecting the limit of one obol per drachm of the purchase price, they did not hesitate to make profits on the stockpile at their disposal, which was strictly forbidden by the law. The orator finds the proof that this was the case in the fact that their prices might change several times a day (22.12). In addition to the limit on the profit margin, the law sought to prevent speculation on stockpile by prohibiting hoarding and strictly forbidding grain merchants, on pain of death, to "buy cumulatively" (*sunōneisthai*) more than fifty "loads" (*phormoi*) at a time.[154] The Delian law on the sale of wood and charcoal punished offenders with a rather heavy fine of fifty drachms.[155] But in Athens, for a product as vital to the population as grain, the law prescribed nothing less than death, and that was in fact the penalty that the plaintiff asked the court to impose on the defendants in Lysias's case.

However, the grain merchants' defense and the prosecution's argument (22.5–6) reveal in addition the practice of negotiating the price of grain. In their defense, the grain merchants argued that since the price of imported grain was rising, they had in fact exceeded the limit of fifty "loads," but that they did so at the request of the magistrates—which the latter naturally denied. Whether or not the magistrates had suggested that the authorized limit be exceeded, we must still ask why they might have done so. The answer is clear: by purchasing larger quantities, the buyers could obtain a better price. Anytos, one of the three magistrates who were in charge of supervising the grain merchants' activity, acknowledged that he had advised the grain merchants. We should note that Anytos was also one of the city's main political figures at the beginning of the fourth century BCE. This fact makes the advice he gave the grain merchants (22.8) all the more important. To fight the rise in prices, Anytos advised the merchants to form a common front in dealing with the importers. For a multitude of competing buyers, he suggested substituting a virtual single buyer, the grain merchants agreeing in advance on a price. In that way, by partially reversing the power relationship in their favor, the buyers would be able to obtain a better price.

The virtual substitution of a single purchaser for the multitude of local buyers provided the basis for the institution of the "official price" (*kathestēkuia timē*), which we find in Athens in the last third of the fourth century and in the first half of the third century BCE. Our sources show that at that time, the magistrates negotiated with the importers an "official price" for grain.[156] Naturally, this price varied considerably depending on the relationship between supply and demand. The magistrates did not simply set an arbitrarily low price, which would have been meaningless because it would not have been respected or, had it been enforced, would have had only the effect of driving importers away from the Athens market. Instead, they negotiated with the importers, an agreement with one of the latter leading the others to adopt—at least temporarily—a benchmark price. The principle was exactly the same one we see at work in 386 BCE, when Anytos advised the grain merchants to substitute a single purchaser for the multitude of actors. The fact that the city was itself a major buyer helped it to negotiate the grain prices with the importers. The difference with the situation in 386 is that in the second half of the fourth century the practice of negotiating through a single purchaser had been institutionalized by the city, which itself undertook the negotiations.

Moreover, this practice of having the magistrates themselves negotiate the price of imported grain was not in any way exceptional. A series of Hellenistic decrees shows that the *agoranomoi* obtained discounts from grain importers. Their form was perhaps not as institutionalized as that of the "official price" on the Attic market (though we must emphasize that for these cities the literary sources that provide a large part of the Attic documentation on the question are lacking), but the principle was the same.[157]

The Option of Fixed Prices

However, many inscriptions show that the *agoranomoi*, or the city, could in fact set prices. The documentation comes from the Hellenistic and the early Imperial periods. In Delphi, in the third century BCE, we find a list of prices for various fish.[158] In Akraiphia in Boiotia, at the end of the third century BCE, a list of prices for both salt- and freshwater fish was inscribed by the *agōnarchoi* (the Boiotian name for *agoranomoi*) at the city's command.[159] In Oinoanda in Lykia, in 124–125 CE, the clause in the regulations for the festival of the *Dēmostheneia* concerning the agora of the *panēguris* gave the three panegyriarchs "the power to post a list of prices for the supplies for sale." The panegyriarchs also had to monitor the latter's quality and see to their distribution.[160] A letter from Hadrian to Pergamon concerning public bankers mentions "the *agoranomoi*'s assessment of the small fish sold by weight."[161] A series of inscriptions from Ephesos in the second and third centuries CE shows the concern to set the price of bread during the main festivals (along with the fairs that they attracted) and probably also when there were shortages.[162] The regulations for the Mysteries at Andania enjoined the *agoranomoi* to monitor the weight and quality of products, but forbade them to set prices.[163]

In the Piraeus agora, between 33–34 and 18–17 BCE, the *agoranomos* Aischylos erected a regulation setting prices for tripe. A few years later, the stele was taken down and a new regulation was inscribed, in which the prices were slightly lower than those in the preceding regulation.[164] The prices of these products were therefore fixed.[165]

TEXT I

Under the archon Pammenes, Aischylos, son of Aischylos, of the deme Hermos, who held the office of *agoranomos*, dedicated the "stones" and the scales-stand.

By order of the assembly, according to the law.

Pork: two feet, 7 ch.; belly, 1 ob. 7 ch.; womb, per mina, 2 ob. 6. ch; liver, per mina, at the price of meat; lungs, the mina, half this price; head bone, a third of this price; brains, [—].

Goat or sheep: four feet, 4 ch.; brains, 3 ch.; head, 1 ob. 3 ch.; womb, per mina, [—]; liver, per mina, at the price of meat; teats, per mina, at the price of meat; lungs, per mina, half this price.

Beef: foot, [—]; liver and spleen, per mina, at the price of meat; lungs, per mina, half this price; brains, [—].

All the intestines, per mina [—] and at a quarter of the price (?) [—].

Pork: two feet, [—] ch.; belly, 1 ob. 4 ch.; womb, per mina, 2 ob. 4 ch.; liver, per mina, at the price of meat; lungs, per mina, half this price; head bone, a third of this price; brains, 3 ch.

Goat: 4 feet, 3 ch.; head, 1 ob. 2 ch.; brains [—]; womb, per mina, 1 ob. 6 ch.; teats, per mina, at the price of meat; liver, per mina, at the price of meat; lungs, per mina, half this price.

Beef: foot, 1 ob.; liver and spleen, at the price of meat; lungs, half this price; brains, 3 ch.

All the intestines, per mina [—] and at a quarter of this price (?).

We have seen that in the *Constitution of Athens* (51.1), Aristotle mentioned the geographical distribution of the magistrates responsible for regulating trade and supplies for the city-state's cities: "*Agoranomoi* are also chosen by lot, five for Piraeus and five for the city." This distribution of the magistrates is confirmed by other sources.[166] We should note, however, that at the time of this text and also later, during the Imperial period, Athens had no more than two *agoranomoi*, one for the town of Athens proper and one for Piraeus. Aischylos was therefore the *agoranomos* in charge of Piraeus. Strictly speaking, it was not he who had set the prices, but rather probably "the assembly," *hoi kuklōi*—that is, the people of Athens gathered in assembly at the theater at Athens or at Piraeus, as the law gave them the power to do (whence the phrase "according to the law").[167] The price of tripe in the agora of Piraeus was thus set by a public authority, of which the *agoranomos* was only the executor. This reminds us of the way in which the price of grain from the islands was supposed to be set, according to the Athenian law of 374/3—that is, by an assembly of the citizens of the city-state.[168]

Thus there were a series of situations in which the public authority was led to intervene to set prices. We note that it did so for products regarding which it was in a strong position, because they were either locally produced or could not be stored: for instance, tripe and fish. But the prices of products that were consumed by the mass of the people were also controlled. Price increases affected more seriously the poorest strata of the population, which did not have the means to deal with them. The point of setting prices during festivals is thus perfectly clear. The same thing was done in early modern Europe (and even until the nineteenth century). In many French cities, the price of fish was taxed during Lent, because that was when it was consumed the most.[169] Under the Old Regime, the French corporations, particularly the butchers, worked under a system of price controls. The Le Chapelier law of 1791 that abolished the "corporations" (that is, the guilds) in France nonetheless reserved for the public authorities the power to tax the price of meat. As late as 1855, a proposal to set the price of meat was based on the following principle: "Fix the price of the meat that workers eat, and let the wealthy pay for the choice cuts, as they pay for special bread."[170] The same principle seems to have prevailed in the markets of the world of the Greek city-states.

In the agora—that is, in the world of small trade (even though large contracts might also be made there)—the city offered users of the market a stable legal universe that allowed business to be done in a predictable way and thus reduced transaction costs.[171] In the event of a dispute between buyer and seller or between a seller and a magistrate, a court's judgment provided in principle the guarantee of an adversary procedure that would allow the accused to defend his arguments. This does not mean that everything was perfect there, or that magistrates were never arbitrary. But the agora was defined as a world where justice was supposed to prevail. In the democratic city-states, at least, everyone was in theory equal before the law, whatever the social standing or wealth of the parties involved. Therein lay the institution's true originality. The Roman aedile, the *sāhib al-sūq* and the *muhtasib* of the Islamic world performed functions similar to that of the *agoranomos*: keeping order in the market, checking weights and measures, and seeing to it that the products sold conformed to the prescribed model and were of the requisite quality.[172] The similarities betweeen market legislation in ancient Greek cities and that in the towns of medieval and early modern Europe are also striking.[173] But the Greek *agoranomoi*, at least in the democratic city-states, were themselves under the collectivity's control. The *agoranomoi*'s exercise of their authority was strictly supervised by the collectivity, whose interests it was supposed to serve. Thus the *agoranomoi* made the market a law-governed space, not a place where the arbitrary will of an aristocracy or a monarch held all the real power.

Finally, we note that the Greek city-states' interest in the quality of products and the honesty of trade is not proof of an absence of economic thought, as if the latter began only when, starting with Smith and Ricardo, the classical economists developed a theoretical distinction between exchange value and use value (all the more as their views were originally based on Aristotle). The quality of products and the honesty of trade are constitutive elements of institutionalized trade. It was on the basis of that observation that the conception of rational expectations could be defined. Information relating to the quality of products is not a datum external to trade: it has a direct influence on the conduct of transactions. By making the agora a law-governed space, the city-states also made a major contribution to the general economic upswing.

X

MONEY AND CREDIT

In an exchange network limited to the family or the immediate neighborhood, money does not have to be used. Information regarding partners is optimal and reciprocity is guaranteed by a system of values transcending trade. Goods and services are not quantified with precision because what one receives in return is not strictly equivalent in quality and quantity to what one initially provided. Thus the reciprocity inherent in trade does not have to be formally guaranteed by an organization external to the trading partners. Similarly, there is no need for an intermediary to guarantee an exchange that is to take place at a later time.

We have just described, *ex negativo*, what are customarily called the three functions of money: to provide a measure of value, a medium of exchange, and a store of value. In a complex society tending toward anonymity, only a third element external to the trading partners can make it possible to quantify the goods and services exchanged and to guarantee the indispensable reciprocity of trade. A system of supervision by a third party in the form of a bureaucracy is one of the two possible ways of guaranteeing this reciprocity. The other way consists in resorting to an autonomous instrument recognized by both parties as having the same value: that is what we call money. Whether every society has used money is the subject of a classical debate in economic anthropology. We can answer this question in the affirmative, because debt, which is intrinsically linked to money, is a universal phenomenon. But the forms taken by "money" in various societies should be carefully differentiated.

In the "general history of money," the Greek world invented something that was to remain a landmark in the Western tradition for more than two millennia: the use of a metal disk of a standard weight as a monetary instrument, this disk having an intrinsic or a fiduciary value and bearing the mark of the state, which conferred on it the privilege of being accepted by everyone. The key element in producing these metal coins was that of their minting. That is why we usually call the monetary instrument of ancient Greece "minted" or "coined" money. The latter made the Greek world the first society that had a monetary instrument that combined in a

260

single element, with unprecedented precision and convenience, the three functions of money previously mentioned. The monetary history of Greece at the end of the Archaic period and during the Classical period was the history of the generalization of minted coins, along with that of the noteworthy innovations that made this possible. The monetary history of the Hellenistic period was the heir to this earlier history. Money (that is, minted coins, as defined earlier) came into constant use in all economic processes. An ancillary question is how much coined money was in circulation and what the evolution of the money supply was.

But although coined money constituted both the daily and the ultimate point of reference in monetary matters, we must also pay special attention to credit. In a stable institutional environment, the possession of a monetary instrument made possible drawing rights on the present and the future. But someone who does not have this instrument of exchange may also receive, conditionally, immediate drawing rights—in that case, he has access to credit. But in view of what has been said about the role in ancient Greece of coins struck in precious metal, one should inquire into the connection between credit and money, as well as into the possibility that credit might have an autonomous role as a monetary instrument.

MONEY AND TRADE IN THE WORLD OF THE GREEK CITY-STATES

Precious Metals and Monetary Instruments

The monetary use of precious metals was not peculiar to Greek society.[1] As early as the third millennium BCE, silver or electrum began to play the role of a privileged merchandise and a value reserve in Egypt and the kingdoms of the Near East. In the second millennium, and increasingly in the first half of the first millennium, silver was used not only as a reserve and a measure of value, but also as an instrument of payment. Because of their inalterability, their divisibility, and their high intrinsic value connected with the great difficulty of procuring them, gold, electrum and, especially in the Near East, silver, thus took on the role of money. Whether archaeological or textual, the evidence from the Mesopotamian states and from the Levant shows that silver was increasingly used as a monetary instrument in the first millennium BCE. Chunks of silver (the so-called *Hacksilber*) are found in more than twenty hoards in the Levant in the Iron Age period, which does not mean, however, that the speed of circulation was as great as that of coined silver.[2] The expansion of the Babylonian and Mesopotamian economy in the sixth century is also clearly linked to the increasing role of silver as money metal in transactions.[3]

In this respect, the Greek world was not in any way a precursor. The use of precious metals as monetary instruments was introduced there only after a significant delay. Mycenaean tablets from the second millennium reveal a society that delivered products in kind, and at least so far as we can tell from the present evidence, this did not permit the monetary use of precious metals. The "Homeric world" did not assign any particular monetary privilege to precious metals. It calculated value in numbers of oxen or other objects and no good or merchandise had a monopoly on the monetary function. During the Early Iron Age and the early Archaic period, bronze and iron certainly played a role as reserves and as measures of value. This is shown by the offerings of bronze tripods and iron spits in sanctuaries of that period. The system of calculating weight and money during the Classical and Hellenistic periods still bears the mark of this, since its basic unit is the drachm (*drachmē* means "handful") and its subunit is the obol (*obelos* means "spit": a drachm was equivalent to a "handful of six spits"). But increasing bronze and especially iron production, and the qualities that made gold and silver more appropriate for monetary use, led to the emergence of the latter (in Greece, chiefly silver, de facto) as the privileged monetary metals. If we combine prices in the fifth and fourth centuries (which is plausible given what we know about the general development of prices during this period), we can form an idea of the relationships of value among the various metals during the Classical period (table 10.1).[4] This will allow us to understand better the notion of "precious metal."

This table shows why during the Classical period, iron had only a use value. The price relationship between iron and silver, on the order of 1 to 500, is a concrete manifestation of this. Iron came into common use as a result of the proliferation of production centers, so that everyone was henceforth able to gain access to this metal through trade among cities. We must, however, not conclude that there is a direct relationship between the scale of value for metals and the overall production numbers for the various metals. A brief excursus on iron production will lead us to a few subjects for reflection.

TABLE 10.1. Ratio of Value among Metals during the Classical Period

METAL	RATIO	VALUE PER TALENT	COMMENTARY
Gold	21,201	60,000 dr.	Ratio 1:10 after ca. 350; higher earlier
Silver	2,120	6,000 dr.	—
Tin	82.3	233 dr.	Athens, fifth century
Bronze	21.3	60 dr. 1.5 ob.	Worked, Athens mid-fourth century
Copper	12.4	35 dr. 1 ob.	Athens, fifth century
Iron	4.4	12 dr. 3 ob.	Wholesale worked metal, Delphi, mid-fourth century
Lead	1	2 dr. 5 ob.	Epidauros

Notes: Base 1 = lead. Reminder: bronze is a copper-tin alloy. See the data collected by Treister 1995, 248–50. The figures in column 2 should of course be taken *cum grano salis*: beyond the illusion of a false precision, the point is to get an estimate of the ratio.

All other things being equal, iron and bronze continued to be produced in modest quantities by our standards. Moreover, *comparanda* drawn from early modern Europe will allow us to gauge the magnitude of ancient production. In the sixteenth century, England, which was then one of the most advanced countries in Europe, produced only a few thousand metric tons of cast iron.[5] After a period of steady growth in the second half of the sixteenth century and the beginning of the seventeenth century, iron production rose to more than 10,000 tons, reaching 18,500 tons around 1620, 23,000 tons around 1770, around 100,000 tons at the end of the century, but exploding quickly to several hundred thousands after 1800, once technological changes (smelting with coke) had produced their full effects. It is true that to domestic British production we must add imports, which varied depending on the period, but which in the eighteenth century far exceeded domestic production.

As for the ancient Aegean world, it had a number of iron ore deposits.[6] However, in most of Aegean Greece, inadequate forestation and thus inadequate fuel supplies limited metallurgical production. During the Classical and Hellenistic periods, an annual production of cast iron in the Aegean basin of about 1,500 metric tons, perhaps supplemented by imports on the order of 500 to 1,000 tons per year, appears to be the maximum we can envisage. (In comparison, we might recall that the weight of the metal in the Eiffel Tower is about 7,300 tons.) During the Imperial period, a major iron-smelting site like the upper basin of the Dure in southern Gaul, produced about 250 tons per year.[7] Much higher annual production figures have been suggested for the rich deposit in Populonia, in Etruria: 2,000 tons per year on the basis of two million tons of slag produced over a period of four hundred years.[8] But if the production period was longer than has been supposed, the annual production figure could be significantly lower. In any case, Aegean Greece did not have iron deposits as rich as those of Etruria and on the island of Elba.

On the other hand, if we add up the silver produced in Laurion and in the mines of northern Greece and Thrace, various factors suggest an average production of silver in the Aegean basin on the order of 1,000 to 1,500 talents (26 to 39 metric tons) during the Classical period.[9] Of course, these figures provide no more than crude approximations. However, on the basis of a minimal silver production of about 1,000 talents or about 26 tons, an iron supply of about 2,600 tons (certainly a very optimistic figure, as we have seen), the value relationship between silver and iron in the Aegean area would seem to have been on the order of 1 to 100. However, it appears to have been about 1 to 500. Rather than increasing the estimate for iron production or lowering that for silver production, we have to see that the demand for silver, both on the domestic and international market, was greatly increased by the specific nature of monetary demand. All our sources show that individuals and sanctuaries stored up significant quantities of precious metals.[10] Systematically subtracting part of silver production from the amount that was in circulation (which was not done for iron) must have contributed to silver's higher value. Well-attested and constant exports of silver toward the eastern Mediterranean must also have helped increase the value of silver in the Greek world. Again, we hardly need to add that these figures are only rough estimates. In any event, the production of silver or iron must have constantly varied. But these estimates at least allow us to explain why iron was not the precious metal that it had been a few centuries earlier, and why silver (and gold) henceforth played their specific role.

The Rise of Coinage

The system of minted money was established between 650 and 625 BCE in the crucible of civilizations represented by the Greek coastal city-states and the kingdom of Lydia. Gold and silver were abundant in the Lydian kingdom. Coins were first made of an artificial alloy of gold and silver that the Greeks called "electrum." The ratio between the two metals was manipulated in various ways that show the highly elaborate nature of the decisions made by the monetary authorities of the city-states and the Lydian monarchy.[11] In its initial phase, coinage in Asia Minor thus corresponded distinctively to a form of monometallism.[12] However, before the middle of the sixth century, gold and silver were minted separately under the Lydian king Croesus, who issued coins that our sources call "croesids." This system was adopted by the Persians after they conquered western Asia Minor in 546 BCE. From that time on, electrum coins existed only residually. Only rare exceptions to this rule are found, mainly coins struck by the city of Kyzikos, which continued to mint a large number of electrum coins down to the second half of the fourth century, and whose currency was dominant in the area of the Bosporos and Pontos, and those minted jointly by the two cities of Phokaia and Mytilene.[13]

Following the tradition established by the Lydian king Croesus (with his Croeseids of both gold and silver), the Persian king distinguished himself by minting the two metals. Later, King Darius modified the standards to strike the gold "darics" named after himself, and the silver "shekels" (the *sigloi* of the Greeks). By contrast but on the basis of these experiments, the cities of mainland Greece began to mint coins themselves, but silver coins only. Exceptions to this rule are rare. As far as we now know, silver coins were first minted west of the Aegean around or after 550 BCE, in Aigina, Athens, and Corinth (the exact chronology of the introduction of coinage in the three cities is still uncertain). Between 540 and 480 BCE, silver coins began to be issued in a multitude of other city-states, as far as Massalia (Marseilles) in the far west and Pantikapaion on the northern coast of the Black Sea (figure 10.1). Apart from coins minted by the Persian monarchy, minting was initially associated with the Greek city-state only, since at least at the end of the Archaic period and at the very beginning of the Classical period neither the Phoenician cities of the Levant, Carthage, nor the Etruscan cities struck precious metal (the Phoenician cities, Tyre and Sidon, and cities of Philistia began to strike coins perhaps around 450 BCE only).[14] The coins issued by the cities of Karia and Lykia do not constitute an exception to this rule.[15] These cities were not only closely connected with the Greeks. They were also city-states whose social system was probably not very different from that of the Greeks, although indeed they were commonly under

FIGURE 10.1. Main cities that coined silver ca. 500 BCE (from Kim 2001, p. 10).

the control of local "big men," dynasts or tyrants. In two fourth-century epigraphic texts, these cities call themselves *poleis*, "city-states."[16] Mylasa, Kaunos, and Xanthos could vote decrees just as Greek cities did.[17]

Having or Not Having Coined Money

At the outset, therefore, and for several centuries, coinage was specific to the Greeks. Thus we must inquire not into the origin and function of coinage (a complex question that cannot be dealt with in this work), but rather into the equivalence between the economic and social system on the one hand and the monetary system and the circulation of value on the other.

To explain the existence of coinage, we must of course first mention the technical considerations: to mint a precious metal, one must obviously have the metal. Thus we could conclude that peoples like the Etruscans, the Phoenicians, and their Punic cousins, who had no silver mines on their territory, were thereby discouraged from imitating the Greeks. While it is true that the Greeks had fairly abundant resources in silver, these were very unequally distributed. The mines of the island of Siphnos were exhausted before the end of the Archaic period, and in the Classical period, most of the silver produced must have come from the mines of Laurion and from northern Greece, Thrace (particularly from the famous district of Mount Pangaion), Troad, and possibly also, to a small extent, from mines situated in Illyria or even in Iberia. Thus the great majority of cities procured through trade the metal they needed for coinage, and this alone suffices to prove the connection between

trade and metal coinage. Although the world of Etruscan and Roman Italy continued to use bronze as commodity money, this was not the case in the Near East,
where silver had played that role since at least the end of the second millennium.

It is therefore certain that although having a stock of metal was a necessary
condition for coinage, it was not a sufficient condition. Clear proof of this is provided by the Achaemenid kingdom. Over the centuries, the Achaemenid kings accumulated huge quantities of precious metals, which in the second half of the
fourth century amounted to a colossal total of 180,000 talents (in equivalent silver).[18] Nonetheless, except for coins minted in the western part of the kingdom,
where the Achaemenid kingdom was in contact with the Greek Mediterranean, to
finance military expeditions, it did not issue large numbers of gold or silver coins.
Those that were struck represented only a small proportion of the enormous reserves of precious metals at its disposal. These coins were in no way capable of
providing for an internal monetary circulation in the various regions of the kingdom. This is not a simple technological fact. The tributary structure of the Persian
Empire, which was itself heir to the ancient tradition of the Mesopotamian kingdoms, was based on a principle radically different from that of the circulation of
goods among equals.[19] The state levied tributes not only in the form of precious
metal, but also in that of forced labor or deliveries in kind: grain, livestock (war
horses, cattle, or sheep), products such as wood and bitumen, and so on. The goods
provided by the state, which were piled up in royal storehouses, were then usually
redistributed in kind, on written order of the king or his administration, or in cash,
in the form of weighed silver. Even if the state, the temples, and rich individuals
gave priority to recovering amounts due in the form of precious metal, weighed
silver was only one means of circulation of value among others.[20] This difference is
also illustrated by the contrast between the economy of Babylon and Mesopotamia, in which weighed silver began to play an increasingly growing role in transactions from the sixth century onward, and that of Persis—the heart of the Achaemenid empire—which was a sophisticated economy, but based on transfers that at
least in our sources are exclusively in kind.[21]

This tributary system, which was so effective in carrying out major works or
assembling large armies, had long since demonstrated its superiority over the traditional system of tribal chiefdoms. It had allowed the kingdoms of the Eastern Mediterranean world to extend their dominion over ever-vaster regions until the Persian Empire finally reached from India to Egypt and the Aegean. Through time and
through the successive expansion zones of the kingdoms of Egypt, and then especially Assyria and Babylon, and finally Persia, there is a steady logic that shows the
dynamics of this system. The king of Persia could legitimately believe himself destined to rule the world until he encountered an adversary he could not conquer,
first in the Massagetans[22] and the Skythians[23] (in reality, only because they took
advantage of the wide open spaces and could not be cornered), and then, especially,
the Greeks (the sole sedentary group to succeed in resisting him). Even if locally
(weighed) silver could commonly be used as money by temples, satraps or "private

individuals," as far as the central Achaemenid state was concerned, precious metals became the king's private property. The king's enormous reserves permitted him to establish a political power relationship incommensurable solely with those who might have proven to be rivals, because his own financial reserves were virtually limitless.

In the Persian world, silver and gold thus entered the central royal treasury as a tribute, but for the most part they did not emerge from it again. They were essentially destined to be removed from circulation, and hence to become sterile. They did not serve as a means of social communication. The revenues and expenditures of the state, on the one hand, and those of private individuals on the other, were fundamentally heterogeneous. The state played ordinarily no role in trade between individuals, which thus remained mainly private. Of course, the compartmentalized form of the instrument of trade did not prevent fluctuations in price determined by the rules of the market.[24] We should note that living without coinage did not mean "living apart from the economy," or even "living apart from the economy of exchange." In Persepolis, at the turn of the sixth and fifth centuries BCE, the Persepolis Fortification Tablets testify to an economy of a region (southern Persis) where deliveries of goods and supplies of rations were accounted for exclusively in kind. Coming from the same site, the Persepolis Treasury Tablets (first half of the fifth century BCE) show a more sophisticated system of accounting in silver.[25] The various ways of transferring value (small-scale commerce, large-scale commerce, tributes paid to the king and the latter's expenditures) were not structurally integrated.[26]

Thus there were three important practical differences between Classical and Hellenistic Greece, on the one hand, and the "eastern Mediterranean world" (in an inclusive definition, that is, from Egypt to Iran) on the other. The first of these is that in the markets of Egypt, the Levant, and Mesopotamia, silver was not the sole means of payment. Even in Babylon, the largest city in Mesopotamia until Alexander's conquest, other commodities such as barley, dates, wool, or sometimes gold might serve in this role.[27] The second difference is that throughout the eastern Mediterranean world, it was traditional always to weigh silver to obtain the appropriate quantity for a given exchange, since preweighed silver in the form of minted coins was not available. The third difference had to do with distrust regarding the metal that circulated. In the world of weighed silver, each payment was open to challenge because it was purely private and did not benefit from the immediate sanction of public authority: hence there were frequent disputes about the quality of the silver used in transactions.[28] Indeed, in sixth-century pre- and post-Achaemenid Babylon, the mentions of *ginnu* ("certified") silver show clearly that public authority (acting in the name of the King) could intervene to guarantee the quality of the silver used in transactions.[29] But this was not a universal practice. In the absence of a general state guarantee, which would have been provided by the central Achaemenid state or its satraps, it remained impossible to trust the quality of the precious metal. Thus Greek coins that circulated in the Achaemenid Empire were often treated no differently than local *Hacksilber* and they frequently have a chisel cut. Their users had no reason to believe that in some distant Greek city the state guaranteed the coin's value. And thus in the large Asyut hoard in Middle Egypt, most of whose coins were minted before 475 BCE and which may have been closed around 460 BCE, many of the coins had been chiseled, showing that people had no confidence in the value of a coin, which was treated as bullion.[30]

Thus there was a radical difference between the Achaemenid world and that of the Greek city-states, all of which, even the largest, were ridiculously small in comparison to the immense Persian Empire. That is, in a way, the paradox of Marathon. But despite the sentimental image, there is a reality: that of a society based on principles profoundly different from those of the tributary system, a society whose principle Herodotus formulated in a remark he attributes to Cyrus:[31] the world of the Greek city-states was a world whose center was the agora. This public square was a place of exchange among equals in which, in the operation of exchange itself (of course not in society at large), inequalities of birth or fortune were of little or no importance. This relationship of formal equality before the law held for economic exchange because it was also based on at least the theoretical formal equality of the members of the *dēmos*. It was this formal legal equality, of which the political equality in the democratic city-state was only the most radical manifestation, that made possible the development of the general equivalent constituted by the coinage of precious metals. The Greek *polis* was not a reality separate from the body of citizens, situated at a higher, inaccessible hierarchical level, but rather the common possession of the citizens who were members of it.[32] Exchange constituted the very definition of political speech in the assembly (and in the theater, at least in the fifth century). In Greece, precious metals were a value that circulated, just like words. Sitta von Reden has shown that for Herodotus, exchange was the structuring principle of society.[33] Herodotus judged the world through the category of exchange because it was consubstantial with the system of the polis. In Persian society, which was stratified with the king at its summit, a hierarchical circulation of wealth (the levying of tributes or the distribution of rations) left little room for exchange among equals, because social relationships were fundamentally asymmetrical. The king, the master of Truth, held a monopoly on political speech, just as he reserved most of the precious metal for himself.[34] Here we are at the antipodes of a society based on communication among equal partners.[35] The transition to coinage was in a way the outcome and best instrument of this generalized system of exchange.

Of course, in the reserves held by states and by sanctuaries, there was a kind of public accumulation that constituted the indispensable reserves that could be issued in the form of coins or the ultimate reserves that were drawn upon only when absolutely necessary.[36] But in a way, this process of accumulation was part of circulation. In any case, once issued, coins played the role of a general equivalent, serving both as a measure and reserve of value and as an instrument of exchange. In the world of the Greek city-states, only silver coins minted by the city-state and foreign coins it accepted as legal tender could be used. This monopoly may seem odd or even superfluous. Why wouldn't a given quantity of weighed silver have the same value as an equivalent weight in coined metal? What was the difference between the Greece of the city-states, where trade was carried on using silver coins, and the markets of the Babylon under the Achaemenids (or even in large measure under the Seleukids), where trade was carried on by weighing out silver?

The fundamental point is that the coined silver used in transactions among citizens had passed at least once—when it was minted—through the hands of the state, which had put its stamp on it. In addition to factors that are certainly not negligible but remain marginal for our subject here (the privilege of coined metal over weighed metal, the difference between real weight when issued and theoretical weight, the profit taken by the state issuing the money, the wear of coins), what is most important to note is that the state guaranteed its coins. The quality and quantity of the metal were certified by the state's stamp. Thus the transparency of any transaction was assured: normally, except in cases where coins had to be reminted, coins were counted, not weighed.[37] Not to mention the practical convenience of using coins of a standard weight, exchange among individuals was thus both guaranteed by the state and at the same time completely freed from the latter's intervention.

In Greece, mercantile trade was not carried on in a hermetically sealed cell, alongside other modes of transferring value such as tributes. Beyond a few exchanges among private individuals in a family context or in a neighborhood trade network, mercantile trade was the general and unique principle of the circulation of value, and most payments were traditionally made in cash. Depending on the region, the transition between payments in kind or other forms of values took place at various dates between the second half of the Archaic period and the beginning of the Classical period. While in Asia Minor, payments in coined electrum were introduced as early as the second half of the seventh century, on mainland Greece or among the western Greeks the transition from the world of payments in kind or weighed silver to that of payments in coined money began only one century later, in the second half of the sixth century and the first half of the fifth century in the most advanced states. Thus, around 500 BCE, the recruitment contract for the secretary-archivist Spensithios in the little city of Datalla, in central Crete, still specifies that compensation is to be paid in various goods.[38] Similarly, the contract for a public physician in Cyprus around 470 BCE mentions that he will receive either a talent of silver or a piece of land in payment for his services.[39] But later, silver coins became the universal mode of payment in all the urbanized cities open to trade. By the fourth century at the latest, most payments were made in coined money. Thus in inscriptions from the fourth century, even ground rents, as they appear in the numerous extant land leases, are always calculated in monetary terms. The source of the system of coining precious metals is to be sought in the universal character of coins as a means of payment. They were used for all income and expenditures, whether those of the state (levies and taxes on the one hand, payment for services or expenditures for equipment for the use of the community on the other) or those of private individuals (purchases on the domestic market, in the agora, payment of ground rents or salaries, acquisitions on the foreign market, in the *emporion*). It was of course through the payments made by the state that coinage was pumped into circulation. The specific relationship entertained between the state and economic activity—this was not a command economy and the state paid for the services it needed—is thus crucial for the existence of coinage as a privileged means of payment in Ancient Greece. That was the key to the Greek city-states' system of coined money.[40]

In their fundamentally egalitarian legal context (it is not necessary to take into account here the avatars of the history of the city-states, in the course of episodes of tyranny and revolutions), coined money was the symbolic form of the circulation of value, which both manifested the formal equality among legally equal trading partners and guaranteed the cohesion of the civic community. The difference from the Persian world's tributary system is thus revealed. In the Greek city-state trade, even if it was still carried on at the free initiative of the partners, always bore the stamp of the state by the simple fact that coined money was used.

The proof *a contrario* of the connection between coined money and market exchange can be found not only in the Achaemenid Empire but also in the Greek world. Like the Cretan cities, Sparta had inherited from the early Archaic period strongly stratified political and social structures. But the contrasts were sharper among the Lakedaimonians than elsewhere. At the apex of the social pyramid, a group of citizens of the city of Sparta proper, or "peers" (*homoioi*), exploited a dependent peasantry, the helots, forcing them to hand over half of what they produced. The citizens of Sparta were not supposed to be engaged in any activity related to production. The city of Sparta itself controlled a series of peripheral cities inhabited by second-class citizens, the so-called *perioikoi*. Agricultural production was thus carried out by helots or *perioikoi*, domestic trade probably being handled mainly by the *perioikoi* and other categories of people of inferior status. Although the city-state of Lakedaimon cannot have been completely ignorant of foreign trade, it did all it could to limit it. Sparta had the reputation of being a closed city that regularly "expelled foreigners" (these expulsions were called *xenēlasiai*).[41] Furthermore, the wealth of Lakonia and the neighboring regions in the realms of agriculture and iron ore explains why foreign trade could be far less important there than elsewhere. Sparta began to coin money only in the second quarter of the third century BCE, almost three centuries after Athens (and for limited usage only).[42] This was, of course, no accident: on the contrary, it was a fundamental characteristic of the system. There was no room for a transparent instrument of exchange in this hierarchized, inegalitarian city-state, which was also as little open to foreign trade as possible. Furthermore, we have proof that at the beginning of the fourth century BCE, Spartan leaders deliberately refused to introduce silver coinage, even though after their resounding victory over Athens in the Peloponnesian War they had the means to do so.[43] They said that they preferred to retain the old system of using iron bars. In fact, the point was chiefly to prevent transparent ways of circulating value and to give priority to credit based on land and to documents acknowledging debts.

By putting money into legal circulation, the state provided an additional guarantee for transactions. The use of a single and unchallengeable currency in transactions in the agora or the *emporion* forestalled the disputes to which money, as the common instrument of measuring values and of exchange, might itself have given rise. But this required more than a mere declaration of principle. The necessary steps to ensure that the principle was applied had to be taken. The repression of counterfeit coins—counterfeiting was punishable by death—shows the importance attached guaranteeing money.[44] But transactions also had to be conducted using this money. That is certainly already the meaning of an archaic law of Eretria from the sixth century BCE, even if the text is very mutilated.[45] A law of Olbia from the fourth century required the exclusive use of the city's currency, though it allowed metal coined by other cities to come in and go out freely.[46]

In most of the cities that minted coins, excavations have shown a significant predominance of the city's coins, which is logical, of course, but also allows us to assume that legislation existed (and certainly differed from one city to another) to ensure that the money was actually used. Thus in the hoards found on Rhodian territory, we find only coins from Rhodes, whereas during excavations on the island a small proportion of bronze coins from other cities has been found.[47] However, the definition of which coins were legal tender sometimes posed a problem. This was the case in Athens during the first decades of the fourth century. The city's coinage had been so abundant in the fifth century that it had become a sort of *de facto* standard. As a result, it had also been imitated by a number of other states, perhaps especially just after the defeat of 404 (when Athens briefly stopped issuing coins). These coins, which circulated internationally, ended up by returning to the Athenian market, mixed with "genuine Attic coins." The city had to legislate, and the decree it issued in 375/4 BCE illustrates the ways in which coins were monitored.[48] There was already an inspector responsible for verifying coins, who officiated in the agora in Athens. The law provided for a second inspector in Piraeus to check the coins used by ship-owners and wholesale traders. Counterfeit coins, for example those that were made of bronze with a thin layer of silver on the surface, were to be chiseled and withdrawn from circulation. Foreign coins bearing Athenian types were returned to the traders, evidently so that they could make free use of them, but without sellers being under any obligation to accept them. On the other hand, coins recognized as authentically Attic could not be refused, on pain of having the merchandise offered for sale confiscated.[49] Using the coins that were legal tender on the market was not an option: it was an obligation. This was a crucial difference with trade exchange based on weighed silver. Through the provisions of the law, we can guess the modalities of supervision. There was no systematic examination of coins in either the agora or the *emporion*. If a seller had doubts about the coins given him in payment for his merchandise, he could go with his customer to consult an inspector, who would examine the coins in question.

Athenian law thus tolerated, without designating them as legal tender, a certain number of foreign coins that did not meet Athenian norms, provided that they were of genuine quality. Furthermore, we can understand why Athens proceeded in this way. If it had taken no steps, it would have undermined confidence in its own money, and even encouraged traffickers to come to Athens to pass their inferior coins or counterfeits. Conversely, had it been too strict and authorized only its own money, it would have risked paralyzing trade, because it was difficult to distinguish foreign coins from authentic Attic coins, the latter often being of mediocre quality. By obliging people to accept coins recognized as authentically Attic, it nonetheless maintained the latter's privileged status.

Moreover, depending on their monetary policy, the city-states made one series of coins legal tender and denied that status to another series. A law of Gortyn from the third century BCE made new bronze obols legal tender but silver obols were no longer legal tender; those who did not observe the law were fined.[50] Users were obviously wary of the new coins—whence this law's prohibition on demanding a premium when bronze coins were used. This was more than a simple matter of style. We know, for example, that in Ptolemaic Egypt an official premium had to be paid when using bronze coins. Furthermore, if a city-state wanted to revalue its money (and profit from the operation), a simple way of doing so consisted in announcing that all its coins had to be turned in. The coins were then struck with a countermark that gave them a new value, and which had to be present for these coins to be legal tender in the city-state. The latter retained some of the coins (the number of countermarked coins returned to the owners was lower than that of the unmarked coins they had handed in) and thus made a kind of profit.

Beyond the details of these procedures, we note that as a rule, if a city-state coined money—and almost all the large ones did, with the exception of Sparta until the third century BCE—it was made legal tender on its territory. Most of the cities that did not mint money—that is, most of the smaller ones—had to accept foreign coins as legal tender. However, almost from the outset, certain currencies went into international use, making the situation more complex. This first occurred with the "turtles" from Aigina (these coins bore the image of a sea turtle on their obverse) at the end of the Archaic period and the beginning of the Classical period. These coins have been found from Sicily (the Selinous hoard) and Illyria (the hoard of Hollm) to Egypt.[51] The spread of the Aiginetan standard over a large part of the southern Aegean shows that on this basis a genuine monetary zone was established.

Then came the famous "owls" of Athens (so called because these coins bore the image of Athena's head on the obverse and on the reverse that of an owl). This coin was very widely distributed in the fifth century BCE, at the time of the Athenian Empire, partly because owls were issued in considerable quantities, and partly because Athens finally forbade minting other coins within its empire. After a period of contraction at the beginning of the fourth century, these coins underwent a further phase of internationalization as a result of renewed activity at the mines in

Laurion after 350 BCE and the pivotal commercial role played by Piraeus. In the Hellenistic period, this phenomenon was further accentuated and took on an institutional form. Royal Macedonian coinages, gold staters of Philip, silver tetradrachms and gold staters of Alexander, all of them on the Attic standard, became the genuinely international currencies of the Hellenistic world.

This was particularly true of the silver Alexander tetradrachms, which bore on their obverse an image of Herakles wearing a lion's scalp that was in fact a representation of Alexander, and on their reverse side an image of Zeus sitting in majesty on his throne. These coins were struck during Alexander's lifetime, but after his death in 323 BCE they were struck in still larger quantities by his first successors, until around 290. Starting around 240 BCE, some cities in the Levant began to strike what are called "posthumous Alexanders." In turn, coastal cities in southern and western Asia Minor minted Alexanders until about 160 BCE. Only an additional indication (for example, a meander for Magnesia on the Maeander or a rose for Rhodes) made it possible to determine the provenance of these coins.[52] Moreover, the minting of posthumous Alexanders, undertaken by a multitude of cities, surely responded to a desire to compensate for the shortage of royal coins. As we have seen, the minting of Alexanders was interrupted at the beginning of the third century BCE, and by the middle of that century, the number of them had considerably diminished as they wore out or were lost, exported to barbarian countries, recast in the form of dishware or jewel, or used to mint other coins. Moreover, all these coins (old lifetime Alexanders and posthumous Alexanders) were disseminated in a vast international circulation.[53] Even if a certain number of local standards and coins still persisted, there is no doubt that international trade was considerably facilitated by these Alexander coins that transcended the traditional borders of the city-states. Thus there existed a genuine international currency on which everyone agreed because it had every possible advantage for trade: the same standard and the same form, no matter who issued it.

The picture changes starting about 160 BCE. Some cities in western Asia Minor struck, still on the Attic standard and down to about 140, "wreathed" coinages (so called because there was the image of a wreath on the reverse). These coins circulated side by side and, one way or another (and although the reason why they were minted remains much debated), met the needs of international trade between Asia Minor and the Levant.[54] In mainland Greece, against the background of the established decrease or simple cessation of most of the minting of silver, Attic coins were almost the only ones that remained. Starting in 164/3 BCE, it seems Athens even introduced a new coin that was somewhat lighter than the earlier one and also bore the image of a wreath on its reverse (whence the name of this coin, *stephanēphoros*). The great success of this coin is connected with Athens's supervision of Delian commerce.[55] At some time during the last fifteen years of the second century, Athens also succeeded in persuading the amphictiony of Delphi, the "religious confederation" that governed the sanctuary, to issue a decree obliging "all Greeks" to accept the Attic tetradrachms as legal tender.[56] Here, "all Greeks" meant all the cities of mainland Greece south of the province of Macedon (probably including the western Kyklades). This inaugurated a new phase in the internationalization of Attic currency. Between the end of the second century and the catastrophic war against Rome waged from 88 to 86 BCE, *stephanēphoroi* coins played *de facto*, and for many cities also *de jure*, the role of an international currency from the Roman province of Macedon to Crete.

Minting and the Use of Money

The attention city-states gave to the use of minted money raises the question of how this money was used. This question leads us to ask in turn why a state decided to mint money or not. Paradoxically, many studies have shown that by minting money states were not necessarily seeking to provide for regular monetary circulation. What led many states to mint money was chiefly the need to finance their own expenditures. For the kingdoms, the first budget item was expenditures for financing war. This is demonstrated by the kingdom of Mithridates VI of Pontos, where the highpoint of minting corresponded in each case to the wars were being waged or prepared by this king.[57] There is every reason for thinking that the same was true for the city-states, which also frequently had to finance heavy war expenses. Furthermore, this was not a situation peculiar to antiquity; the states of modern Europe and even of the contemporary world vastly increased the money supply in wartime. Another important budget item was construction, when new cities were being founded or after natural disasters such as earthquakes that led to major urban building projects. The case of the city of Rhodes offers a good example of the relationship between coin production and wars or phases of construction or reconstruction.[58]

However, although the increase in the money supply was very logically connected with periods of war or construction, we cannot conclude that state expenditures were the "cause" of coinage. To corroborate this, we have only to note that in the eastern Mediterranean the states that preceded the Persian Empire had always financed considerable war expenditures without ever having introduced coinage. Instead, we should say that state expenditures were the main way in which coins were introduced into a circulation that they thereby helped create and maintain. The minting of Alexanders by Alexander himself or by his first successors, using precious metals pillaged from the Persian treasuries, fall completely into the category of financing war expenses (we must, naturally, include in these the salaries paid mercenaries). At the same time, these massive mintings directly supplied a very widespread circulation of coined money. In addition, if we consider the case of a few city-states that minted large quantities of coins, as Athens did at the end of the Archaic period and in the Classical period, we see that the key factor in these issues is to be sought in the monetization of the resources produced by the mines of Laurion. On the one hand, the state received directly the rent on the mining concessions. On the other, it could mint for individuals the products from their mines. For the owners of the mines, it was essential to convert the silver taken from the mines into coins. If only in order to continue to work the mines, the coins thus minted had to be reinjected into monetary circulation. In other words, the pace of monetary issues was basically governed by constraints other than the desire to encourage monetary circulation. It is this mediation, in which we see clearly that expenditures for war could not be considered as being the direct "cause" of minting, that accounts for the connection between minting money and monetary circulation.

However, nothing allows us to conclude that there was no interest in fueling money supply, because a collectivity necessarily directly experienced the difficulty of providing enough coined metal. But issuing coins in precious metals was expensive; metal had to be collected, secured, and finally minted. Since a high-quality currency was very likely to be exported to foreign markets, we can understand why to pay its external expenses, the average small city preferred to rely on the great currencies circulating on the international markets rather than mint money by itself. That is also why the policy of "closed currency systems" was widely adopted; this policy made it possible to take advantage of an unfavorable exchange rate for imported currencies with respect to the local currency, which was struck on a lower weight-standard, in order to retain the coins the city-state had put into circulation.[59] These closed-currency system policies may remind us of those urged by mercantilists in the modern period, who maintained that the state's interest was to acquire as much money as it could.[60] For individuals who held them, these coins represented the most convenient way of preserving their wealth or acquiring new property on the market. In this respect, we must ask how much these coins were worth. The most valuable coins, especially gold coins (whose value in relation to silver was 13.3:1 in the fifth century, 10:1 after about 350 BCE) and large silver coins such as tetradrachms, were used for all major purchases: land, houses, luxury goods. They were also used to pay mercenaries, and constituted the medium of large-scale commerce as well. Finally, they were the privileged instrument used by the elite of the city-states for all payment operations, both public and private. Taken as a whole, they represented most of the value of the coins minted. But given that these had a very high intrinsic value, should we therefore conclude that the world of everyday trade, that of the agora, remained outside a monetarized system, as was long thought? That would contradict the previously stated principle of the homogeneity and unity of the monetary instrument. In fact, we now know that from the end of the Archaic period and the beginning of the Classical period, Athens as well as city-states in Asia Minor and Sicily issued not only large monetary units but also very small ones, going as far as the obol or a fraction of an obol.[61] The problem raised by these fractions is that they necessarily weighed very little, less than 0.20 gram, or even 0.10 gram for the smallest of them. They were also as small as a few millimeters in diameter. That is why they were neglected for such a long time. On the one hand, they did not interest collectors; on the other, no one knew how to find them: metal detectors now make it possible to identify them, even buried deep in the earth.

Thus the monetization of everyday trade in the agora began at the end of the Archaic period and in the early Classical period. However, the system had disadvantages as well as advantages. It was not very user-friendly. Small coins could easily be lost and they must not have always been easy to identify. For the city-state, minting these small coins was expensive.[62] The result was that while some cities regularly minted fractional coinage, others did not. The true innovation came from Magna Graecia. Shortly after 450 BCE, a system of fractional bronze coins began to be established in southern Italy and then in Sicily.[63] It replaced silver coins for denominations of low value. Why did the Italiot cities have this priority? The absence of silver mines in Italy and the tradition of bronze coins in the Etruscan and Italic cities might well have played a role in this. The first cities to mint such coins were Thourioi and Rhegion. Before the end of the century, their example was followed by Poseidonia, Velia, Metaponton, Kroton, and Kaulonia, as well as by the cities of Sicily. From the west, the movement rapidly spread to the Aegean, and before the end of the fifth century, a certain number of city-states had begun to mint bronze. Then, during the first half of the fourth century, coined bronze was adopted everywhere and established itself as the normal currency for trade in the agora. Bronze coins had a fiduciary value, because the value of the metal they contained always remained significantly lower than their legal exchange value. As a result, even if the aggregate value of the bronze coins remained comparatively small, the issuer nonetheless made a profit by minting. In addition, there was the profit derived from exchanging these coins against foreign currencies.[64] Thus introducing and maintaining bronze coins was within the reach of most city-states, even the smallest.[65] In fact, beginning in the fourth century we find masses of these small bronze coins, especially, of course, in the agora sectors of the various city-states.[66]

In this movement, Athens was not a precursor, not introducing bronze coins until well into the fourth century. It is very possible that the preference for silver played a braking role in a city-state whose supply of this metal was guaranteed by the mines of Laurion. It is also possible that the experience with emergency currencies after the Peloponnesian War—bronze coins plated with silver, "genuine counterfeits," so to speak—may have left bad memories. In his play *The Assemblywomen* (815–22), Aristophanes mentions the demonetarization of this "bad bronze" at the beginning of the fourth century.

Coined Money and Economic Growth

Economists have long debated the notion of the "veil of money": does money play only the role of a pure "seismograph" of economic activity, or does it have an impact of its own, positive or negative, on that activity? The first point of view is that of classical economics, while the second is especially associated with the Keynesian tradition. So far as contemporary economic thought is concerned, one should emphasize Milton Friedman's and John Maynard Keynes's theories regarding monetary policy. Thus Friedman's principle of the necessity of maintaining a balance between the amount of money in circulation and the level of economic activity presupposes that a disequilibrium (for example, resulting from inflation or deflation) would have a negative impact on the level of economic activity. Keynes, on the other hand, wanted a moderate increase in the amount of money, assuming that money could itself increase activity.

The economy of the Greece of the city-states was certainly very far from the contemporary world's economy based on credit-money. However, given the conditions of precious metal merchandise-money in antiquity, it is worthwhile to ask whether money by itself had an impact on economic development. For this purpose, the best example is Athens, and beyond it the system of trade that grew up around that city during the Classical period. At the end of the Archaic period and the beginning of the Classical period, Athens underwent a lightning-fast development from a city that was important, to be sure, but not of the first rank, to become the leading city in the Greek world, in various ways and for almost two centuries.

A classic explanation of Athens's dominance emphasizes the political factor. Clisthenes's reform in 508/7 BCE made Athens the first city-state to establish an egalitarian system that would rapidly become the first democracy in the world of the Greek city-states. But in addition to the political aspect, from the end of the Archaic to the end of the Classical period Athens was also the city-state that minted the most coins. Athens enjoyed the advantage of having the silver deposits in Laurion at its disposal. These mines had been in operation in the Mycenaean period. We know very little about mining during the Archaic period, but it is possible that there was a small amount of activity in Laurion. With Aigina and Corinth, Athens was one of the first city-states to issue silver coins, the famous *Wappenmünzen*, or "heraldic coins." These coins were not struck on a single type, but on several (whence their name, for in the nineteenth century it was thought that they had been issued by great families that wanted to sign their money with their coats of arms—a theory that has now been abandoned).[67]

The date when this coinage began remains uncertain: after 540 BCE at the earliest, or perhaps after 530 BCE, is the most likely. Physical analysis has shown that these coins did not use metal from Laurion but rather silver that came from elsewhere (northern Greece?). At the end of the century, around 515 BCE perhaps, a new coin was introduced that bore an image of the head of Athena on the obverse and that of an owl on the reverse.[68] These types were to remain virtually unchanged until the introduction of the *stephanēphoroi* in the second century. From the outset, these coins were minted using silver from Laurion. This was, of course, a major change. According to tradition, the Athenians found a new vein of silver that was particularly rich and allowed a rapid increase in monetary production. To reach this new vein, it was necessary to dig deeply and pierce through a particularly hard layer of rock before reaching the strata from which the silver could be extracted. It was the production of this metal that made it possible to finance the construction of the triremes that won the Battle of Salamis in 480 BCE.

Naturally, mining did not begin immediately before the battle. It was the result of a development that had begun more than three decades earlier, between 520 and

510 BCE.[69] The Athenians had to make investments (in slaves, in structures, in importing fuel) and also take risks, because all the pits did not turn out to be equally productive. Thus a conscious desire to make profits was required both collectively, on the part of the city-state that sold the temporary mining concessions, and individually, on the part of investors. A quantitative analysis allows us to gauge the impact of the rise of Laurion on coinage. Based on the chronology of issues drawn up by Chester G. Starr in 1970, the annual average production rose from about 11.5 talents for the first *Wappenmünzen* to 19 talents for the second series, then to about 155 talents for the owls issued between 510 and 475 and about 470 talents for those issued between 474 and 449. As Christophe Flament has shown, Starr's assumptions have to be reexamined.[70] If, as Flament suggests, this development took place over a shorter period of time than envisaged by Starr, the growth would be even more spectacular. Basing himself on an analysis of the costs of mining, Flament estimates that after 450 BCE, and then again between 350 and 340 BCE, annual silver production in Laurion must have exceeded 1,000 talents.[71] Even if these figures are debatable, they nonetheless give us an idea of the rapidity of the increase in monetary production after the transition to owls. They also allow us to gauge the dynamism of Athens at the end of the Archaic period and the beginning of the Classical period. It is no accident that alluding to Laurion, the chorus in Aeschylus's *Persians* (238) says that the source of the Athenians' wealth was the possession of a "source of silver, the treasure of their soil." Athens took great care of its production of silver, which was basic not only to its political but also to its economic dynamism, since coined silver was one of its main products for export.[72]

To return now to the question asked at the outset regarding the impact of coined money on economic development, we can say that, being naturally connected with the whole of the city-state's institutional system and with the vast commercial network that was then being established, and of which it was the center, the growth of Attic coinage triggered a process of production and trade, and thus economic growth, in a large part of the Mediterranean world.[73]

CREDIT

Ancient Greece thus created a monetary system that was both flexible and coherent, and integrated all aspects of trade. It remains to be determined how credit operated.

Forms of Credit in Ancient Greece

Lending is a practice very frequently attested in Greece. Literary sources and inscriptions, among others those on the numerous mortgage stones (especially in Attika) guaranteeing loans, prove that it existed.[74] When someone needed money, where did he go? Today, we would expect him to go to a bank. And in fact, apart from their activities in currency exchange and holding deposits, banks made loans, at least to members of the social elite.[75] But there were several other sources of financing that seem to have been much more frequently used by ordinary borrowers. To get a small loan, one went first to relatives and friends to obtain a loan that was usually interest-free. An *eranos* ("friendship group"[76]) often undertook to make these loans. Our sources show how frequent such loans were in the Greek world, particularly in Athens.[77] Why were such favors done? Solidarity was strong within the family, which was a lively, very supportive social unit, and it was also strong within the friendship group. In addition, we should note that loans raised a serious question: their repayment. Within the framework of a network of family members or friends, the lenders had in theory the best possible information regarding the borrower's reliability. Moreover, the solidarity of the network also exercised social pressure to ensure that the sum borrowed would be repaid.

What were the advantages of this arrangement for the borrower and the lender? So far as the borrower is concerned, the absence of interest was obviously a considerable advantage. The multiplicity of lenders also made it possible to accumulate a larger sum. This characteristic also had advantages for the lender, because it allowed him to limit his risks. Moreover, the lender could count on the solidarity of the network of friends if someday he needed help himself. That said, the lender making a friendly loan could also ask for guarantees, such as a lien on the borrower's property. Finally, in the event that the loan was not repaid, he could legitimately file a legal suit against the borrower, exactly as in the case of a loan at interest, knowing that the jury would be disinclined to excuse the beneficiary of a friendly loan who failed to repay it. We note that this kind of group, which might now be described as a "rotating savings and credit association," can still frequently be observed today in Asian and African countries, and among nationals of those countries living abroad. In itself, it is thus in no way peculiar to antiquity. The advantage of this kind of loan was all the more significant in antiquity, when the ordinary interest rate exacted by high-profile money-lenders was between 10 and 12 percent a year.

Borrowers could also go to sanctuaries, which might lend them part of their store of precious metal in the form of a loan at interest. Thus in the fifth century, the sanctuary of the goddess Nemesis in Rhamnous, in northeast Attika, made loans at interest. Our sources show that between 450 and 440 BCE, this sanctuary granted loans in the amount of 200 or 300 drachms. Over a period of four years, it lent between 8 and 10 talents, a considerable sum.[78] Loans of 200 or 300 drachms were certainly not very large, but they were nonetheless roughly equivalent to a worker's annual income.

One could also hope to obtain a loan from his deme, his phratry, or another organized social group.[79] As a last resort, one might borrow from a private individual, but at high rates of interest. In his *Letters* (1.13), Alciphron, who wrote during the Imperial period but situated his characters in a conventional late Classical Greece, provides interesting testimony on this subject. Since fish are abundant and his nets are damaged, a fisherman borrows from a usurer, mortgaging his boat as security. On the appointed day, the usurer demands repayment of principal and interest, an obligation that the fisherman is unable to meet. To free himself from his loan, and swearing that he will never fall into the same trap again, he has to sell his wife's gold necklace to the banker Pasion. Beyond the anecdote, we should note that such loans were completely ordinary.

Why did people resort to loans? That is one of the points on which historians disagree. For some, following Moses Finley, these loans were exclusively "consumer" loans intended to finance operations such as the marriage of a daughter, a *chorēgia*, or a trierarchy. We know that one could, paradoxically, be rich and still lack short-term liquidities: whence the recourse to a loan. The existence of such motivations is not in doubt. But the question is whether this kind of motivation was the only one. Did people borrow for other reasons—for example, to acquire land, to improve their farms or their equipment, or to buy slaves and put them to work on their land or in a mine? The answer is clearly that they did. We have already seen that in the *Constitution of Athens*, Aristotle mentions among the city-state's magistrates the "introducers" (*eis-agōgeis*), one of whose responsibilities was to present before a court matters that concerned "borrowing start-up capital [*aphormē*] to conduct business in the agora." But more generally all the evidence suggests that there was no borderline or firewall between a traditional economy based on land and dominated by an elite concerned solely with its own status, and an economy oriented toward profits and, in Athens, toward mining in particular, but also toward other activities, such as textiles.[80] This is clearly proven by the already mentioned anecdote of the advice given by Socrates to his friend Aristarchos, who had fourteen mouths to feed at home after the Peloponnesian War. *Pace* Raymond Bogaert, the anecdote does not prove a reluctance to borrow money for productive investment.[81] Quite the opposite: it proves how common it was. First, the discussion between Socrates and Aristarchos is not focused on borrowing or not borrowing, but on the need to put free women from normally wealthy families to work, just as if they were slaves. When Aristarchos is convinced by Socrates to put his women to work, he immediately decides for himself to borrow the start-up capital (*aphormē*) that will allow him to buy wool to start a business, no doubt just as everyone did when it came to putting slaves to work. While initially, before deciding to put the women of his household to work, Aristarchos stated it was difficult to find money lenders—for a nonproductive loan, this was quite understandable; lenders would not easily lend knowing that a borrower will not be able to reimburse a loan—he does not seem to doubt that he will immediately find a loan for a productive investment. Beyond the case of Athens, the "hunger for money" we find in the Greece of the city-states and the desire to find sources of loans at any price, through foundations or possibly by making use of the sanctuaries' reserves, as in Delos, show that credit was very widespread and constituted a key element in economic activity.[82]

Maritime Loans

To finance large-scale commercial operations, it was necessary to resort to other circuits. Here only a minority of enterprising people could obtain the indispensable financing.[83] Banks could provide loans. But borrowers often also approached wealthy private individuals who were known to invest part of their resources in commercial loans.

Such loans were often sought to finance maritime ventures. The risk was great, the amounts involved were large, and the rates of interest were high, justified by the risks inherent in this kind of commercial voyages. Profits (and sometimes losses) could be considerable. The Demosthenic speech *Against Lacritus* (35.10–14) preserves a commercial contract made in Athens for a voyage to the Bosporan kingdom, one of the commercial voyages that were fundamental for supplying Athens. This text is an exceptional source that long remained the only one of its kind. Until the publication in 1985 of a papyrus bearing a maritime contract from the Roman period for a voyage from Alexandria to India and back, the document transmitted to us by the speech *Against Lacritus* was the only complete commercial contract extant for all of antiquity.[84] It is not that this kind of document was rare, but insofar as it was a private document, a contract had no chance of being inscribed on stone. Thus outside Egypt, all the public and private archives of the Greek city-states have been lost. That is why a kind of document as ordinary as a commercial contract is known to us only through a few rare testimonies. Moreover, nothing indicates a priori that the contract in *Against Lacritus* was unusual or exceptional, on the contrary. The speech is part of the Demosthenes corpus. Its authenticity has been debated: is it or is it not a work by Demosthenes? The answer is probably that it is not, but this point is unimportant for the study of the form of the contract, since it was not composed by Demosthenes but rather by the parties to the litigation. The question of its date is more important, even though it too, remains uncertain: around 340 BCE or a little later? However that may be, it dates from a time when at Athens business was going well and when the city served as a transit point for trade. The lender, Chrysippos, was suing the merchant Phormion and his associates, whom he accused of not respecting the clauses of the commercial contract to which they had agreed.

> Androkles from the deme of Sphettos and Nausikrates from Karystos lent Artemon and Apollodoros from Phaselis 3,000 silver drachms for a voyage from Athens to Mende or Skione, and from there to Bosporos, and then, if it pleased them, as far as Borysthenes by sailing along the coast at the left, with a return to Athens. The interest is 225 per 1,000 and, if they sail only after the rising of the Guardian of the Bear star [Arktouros] to go from Pontos to Hieron, 800 per 1,000. The loan is guaranteed by 3,000 amphoras of wine from Mende, to be loaded in Mende or Skione, on a ship with twenty oars commanded by Hyblesios, the said security reserved free and clear, without being subject to any debt present or future. The merchandise bought in Pontos, along with the product of the sale, will be brought back to Athens on the same ship. If they arrive safe and sound in Athens, the borrowers will pay the lenders the capital and interest within twenty days after their arrival, without any deduction other than what has had to

be jettisoned by common agreement among the passengers and any ransom paid to the enemy, all other losses to be borne by the borrowers. The security reserved will be made available to the creditors free and clear of any right of seizure, until the capital and interest have been paid in conformity with the contract. If the payment is not made within the agreed time, the creditors will have the right to mortgage the security reserved and to sell it at the going rate. If the price is insufficient to reimburse the creditors for the sum that they are supposed to receive in accord with the terms of the contract, their right of seizure will be extended to all the other property of Artemon and Apollodoros, both terrestrial and maritime, wherever it might be, as if there had been a court judgment against them and the deadline has passed, the said right belonging to both creditors. If they do not pursue their voyage to the end, they will stop in the Hellespont ten days after the rising of the Dog Star [Sirius] and will unload the merchandise in a place where the Athenians cannot be the object of reprisals; they will return from there to Athens and will pay the interest specified in the contract the preceding year. In the event that the ship on which the cargo will be transported is wrecked, if it is possible to save the merchandise that is affected by the loan, the part saved will belong to the creditors undivided. With regard to all these points, the present agreement supersedes any contrary rule.

Witnesses: Phormion, from the deme of Piraeus, Kephisodotos from Boiotia, Heliodoros from the deme of Pithos.

Testimony: Archenomides, son of Archedamas, from the deme of Anagyrous, testifies that a contract has been deposited with him by Androkles, from the deme of Sphettos, Nausikrates from Karystos, Artemon and Apollodoros from Phaselis, and that he still holds this document.

—Read also the testimony of those present.

Testimony: Theodotos, a a foreigner with equal tax rights [*isotelēs*], Charinos, son of Epichares, from the deme of Leukonoe, Phormion, son of Ktesiphon, from the deme of Piraeus, Kephisodotos, Boiotian, Heliodoros, from the deme of Pithos, testify that they were present when Androkles loaned Apollodoros and Artemon 3,000 silver drachms, and that they know that the document was deposited with Archenomides, from the deme of Anagyrous.

Even though this document is a *unicum* for the Greece of the city-states, what we can learn from other sources suggests that a contract of this kind was perfectly ordinary in fourth-century Athens. We see first of all that it is a written contract, and not a purely oral agreement. Naturally, oral procedures continued to play an important role in Athenian law. Moreover, witnesses are required, summoned before the court by the parties to the suit after the declaration of the contract, so that it can be considered valid.

The subject of the contract is a loan, in this case, a loan of 3,000 silver drachms for a commercial voyage whose itinerary and calendar are largely determined in advance. The borrower is therefore not free to use the money as he sees fit, but only as stipulated by the contract. As for the itinerary, in this case it is a voyage to the Kimmerian Bosporos, with an obligatory return to Athens. For obvious reasons, this kind of contract for a round-trip voyage (*amphoteroplous*) seems to have been particularly common: it gave lenders a better chance of getting their money back. However, there were also contracts for one-way voyages. The voyage had to take place during the season of good weather, before the rise of the of Arktouros in the autumn. If the voyage was longer or riskier, with a return after the beginning of the season of bad weather, the interest rate would be higher.

The interest rate was 22.5 percent for a voyage during the season of good weather, and 30 percent for a longer voyage. These were interest rates common at the time. For one-way voyages (*heteroplous*), the interest rate was lower (10–12 percent). The contract also provided for the case in which the captain had to jettison all or part of his cargo in order to save the ship. We see that in that event, the lenders shared in the loss and could not reclaim the corresponding money. The same was true for ransom paid to the enemy, and also, implicitly, for shipwreck, though there was a clause providing that the lenders would have priority in selling the goods that might be saved. We find such provisions in the law of the Hellenistic period, and also in Roman law, Byzantine law, and even contemporary law. In all other cases, on the other hand, the borrowers were completely responsible, and their responsibility extended to all their property.

We may find the mortgage clause curious. In fact, the property that serves as security for the loan is none other than a cargo of wine amphoras that is supposed to be purchased during the voyage, not real property that is already in the hands of the borrowers and that they own.[85] However, as is shown by many other documents, including the mortgage boundary-stones that were so numerous in fourth-century Athens, in that city the practice of mortgaging was governed by rules that are familiar to us: for example, a borrower mortgaged his land or his house in order to obtain a loan. If this was not the case in this maritime contract, that is first of all because foreigners and metics did not own real property in Athens (unless they had a special privilege), so that in their case the usual practices of mortgaging were not applicable: whence the procedure of the "reserved security" (*hupothēkē*) that was constituted by merchandise to be bought, which was the only kind possible. In the event of default, this "reserved security" was supposed to serve as a source of revenue to compensate the lender.[86] The loan was for 3,000 drachms and the mortgage for 3,000 amphoras: these are obviously connected (if we assume that an amphora was worth two drachms, the value of the mortgage was double that of the amount loaned).

The contract distinguished *emporoi* (merchants) from *nauklēroi* (ship-owners, who were often both owners and captains of the ship). It happened that *nauklēroi* were also *emporoi*, but usually the two activities were distinct. Here, the merchants Artemon and Apollodoros are carefully distinguished from the owner of the ship, Hyblesios.

The parties to the contract were of diverse origins. One of the lenders, Androkles from the deme of Sphettos, was an Athenian, while the other, Nausikrates, was a foreigner from the neighboring city-state of Karystos, whose history was closely linked with that of Athens. The borrowers, Artemon and Apollodoros, were both foreigners from Phaselis, a city on the southern coast of Asia Minor. We note that we find the same diversity among the witnesses to the contract: two Athenians, Phormion, from the deme of Piraeus, and Heliodoros, from the deme of Pithos, and a Boiotian foreigner, Kephisodotos, while two other witnesses were present, Theodotos, an *isotelēs*, that is, a foreigner who was treated as a citizen for tax purposes, and Charinos, a citizen of the deme of Leukonoe. What is most striking is that no distinction is made among them: in business matters, nationality was not a factor. We must not forget that it was precisely around 340 that Athens established the system of the *dikai emporikai*, which instituted a legal system specific to commercial affairs in which the nationality of the parties did not matter.[87]

The key question is how people from Phaselis came to make a contract in Athens for a voyage to the Bosporos and back. The answer is simple: Athens was a rich city and it imported massive amounts of grain to meet the needs of its population. The origin of the actors involved was of little importance: all that counted was that there be a commercial venture to be undertaken and profits to be made for merchants of all origins. Athens was also a city in which capital was abundant and it was easy to find money to be borrowed. We see that in this case the money was lent by an Athenian and a foreigner, probably a metic who had settled in Athens. For lenders, such a loan was an advantageous investment. In a short time (three to four months if everything went well) it could bring in a profit ranging from 22.5 to 30 percent, whereas ordinary loans were made at annual interest rates of about 10 to 12 percent. On the other hand, it was also a riskier investment (and that is what justified the higher interest rate): the proof of this is the situation of the parties to the suit here, who cannot recover the funds they have lent.

For the borrower, the rate of interest was certainly high. But this kind of maritime contract had a considerable advantage. In the event of shipwreck, the sum borrowed did not have to be repaid. We can therefore conclude that in addition to the profit corresponding to the risk taken by the lender, the elevated interest rate was justified on both sides by the cost of the insurance that was thus provided. In addition, on the basis of the profits that could be made in this kind of venture, such a loan made it possible to use leverage to full effect, and thus to maximize gains in relation to the capital invested.[88]

At the same time, this contrast no doubt provides an excellent view of the commercial actors and main commercial routes in the Greek world of the fourth century. Thus from the fifth century onward, people from Phaselis seem to have been among the most active (if not the most active) foreign traders operating in Athens. It is no accident that the oldest extant legal agreement in Athens was made with Phaselis.[89] If we believe the plaintiff, people from Phaselis did not have a good reputation in Athens, probably simply because of their role in trade. Phaselis was a city of middling size, but its merchants ranged over the seas in all directions, earn-ing their livings or their fortunes by serving as intermediaries. People from Phaselis took maximum advantage of the possibilities offered by the financial market in Athens.

Thus an original monetary system, that of coined money, and credit institutions that were both flexible and solidly guaranteed by law gave the world of the Greek city-states a stable and effective financial instrument. Within the limits of a world in which land was still an essential production factor, credit, even if it could not become an autonomous monetary element, played a fundamental role in economic life. By sharply decreasing transaction costs and by enabling capital concentration, the joint development of coined money and credit made a significant contribution to the growth of trade and to economic growth in general.

XI

CITY-STATES, TAXES, AND TRADE

Taxes on trade and commerce were one of ancient states' principal sources of revenue. Documents concerning tax exemptions are often our best sources of information about this subject, and we must therefore give them special attention. In any case, traders were constantly seeking privileges that would allow them to avoid taxes. Maritime shipping being the quickest and least expensive way to move goods, access to the sea was indispensable. The highest amount of taxes was levied in the ports. Cities situated on the coastline benefited from an economic rent related to their location, and they did not fail to exploit it. On the other hand, inland cities did everything they could to overcome their disadvantage, if necessary by opening an access to the sea.

SUPERVISION OF FOREIGN TRADE

Supervision of Trade and Customs Duties

Greek city-states were both living communities and genuine states exercising their prerogatives of sovereignty over entry into and exit from both their territory and the nearby waters. Although citizens had the right to import and export what they wanted, they had to respect the laws that defined this right and could limit it. As for foreigners, the city-state's territory was not an open space to which they could have had a right of access.

As a general rule, entrance to the territory was monitored, and everywhere the principle was the same.[1] Only with the city's permission could foreigners enter its territory—not just for a lengthy period, but even for a stay of a few days, as was the case for traders. Both persons and goods were monitored. However, the detail of the permissions granted varied. Conservative city-states such as Sparta restricted access to their territory as much as they could, even if they did not forbid it. According to Thucydides (1.144.2), Pericles mocked the Lakedaimonians' attitude when they enjoined the Athenians to abrogate a decree excluding Megarians from

286

the markets of Athens and allied cities, even though they themselves were expelling from their territory citizens of Athens and other cities of the Athenian empire. In many city-states, such as Athens and the trading cities in general, access for foreigners was a simple formality (though this did not prevent monitoring). But if for one reason or another the city decided to restrict access by foreigners or a certain category of foreigners, it could do so at will. There were three reasons for such monitoring: first, the desire to maintain the civic community, which entailed identifying new arrivals so that if they were foreigners they could be given a particular status distinct from that of citizens; second, the necessity of coping with the numerous problems of insecurity that could be connected with the presence of foreigners who might help enemies to invade the city; and finally, the financial interest, since taxes on trade were often a city-state's primary source of revenue. We have many documents from the most diverse city-states that grant an "import and export license" (*eisagōgē kai exagōgē*), often in combination with a tax exemption (*ateleia*) which, moreover, frequently appears by itself. It is also through the question of the privileges granted to certain foreigners, or to categories of foreigners, that we can account for the legal modalities governing foreign trade.

Two texts relating to travel through the territory of a city-state show irrefutably that entry and exit from a city-state's territory were not free for either persons or goods. In a satirical scene in the *Birds* (187–93), Aristophanes imagines the establishment of a toll on goods in transit. He puts the following advice to the birds in the mouth of Pisthetairos:[2]

> Between them and the earth is air, no? So look: just as we must ask the Boiotians for a visa [*diodos*] whenever we want to visit Delphi, in the same way, whenever humans sacrifice to the gods, you won't let the aroma of the thigh bones pass through unless the gods pay you tribute.

Thus just as the Athenians had to ask the Boiotians for permission to cross Boiotia to get to Delphi, so the gods would have to ask the birds to allow the smoke rising toward heaven to pass through their air, and, of course, they would have to pay a tax. Access to the territory of a city-state was thus not a right, except for its own citizens. One had to request permission to enter another city-state, for oneself and for the goods one was transporting. Much later (in the first century CE), in his speech *To the Nicomedians on Concord with the Nicaeans*, Dio Chrysostom described a similar situation. He advocated harmony within and between cities, and thus between Nikomedia and Nikaia, two cities in the region of the eastern Hellespont that were neighbors and rivals. But dissension between cities could arise from conflicts connected with the transit of persons and goods. Thus Dio referred to the case of landlocked cities. During the imperial period, Nikomedia's location along the coast of Bithynia still allowed it to benefit from an economic rent with regard to the cities of the interior, which wanted access to the sea.[3] We can see why Dio (38.32) advised the people of Nikomedia, who enjoyed a favorable situation on the coast, to adopt an open attitude with regard to the cities of the interior like Nikaia: in that way—this reflects the eternal agonistic spirit of the ancient Greeks—they could surpass their Nikaian rivals in Hellenic public opinion:

> You are able to offer the cities more numerous and greater benefits than they [the people of Nikaia] can, chiefly and especially because of the sea, by which all goods are transported and made available to the cities, either by means of a privilege (which must be publicly granted by the city, not privately by certain citizens),[4] by smuggling, or by constantly renewed requests. You never reject the requests that are made of you. But having to make a request is onerous in itself. If you allow these peoples (from whom you receive every day requests for products that are absolutely necessary for them), to receive all these goods, is it not likely that you will appear to them greater benefactors? And at the same time you will increase concord, which will spread everywhere.

Dio Chrysostom's wish was not utopian. Several documents show that the importation and exportation of goods could be the object of a general agreement between two cities that made it possible to avoid having to make individual requests on each occasion. For example, we can cite the agreements between Miletos and Sardis (mutual rights of entry and exit for people and goods), or the agreement between Magnesia on the Maeander and Phokaia (the Phokaians' right to export to and import from Magnesia) in the late fourth century or perhaps the early third century BCE.[5] A series of Cretan bilateral conventions dating from the Hellenistic period shows that this kind of general concession was not rare.[6] Thus we come back to precisely the recommendations that Dio formulated in the early imperial period, no doubt because administrative difficulties and the financial cost of taxes on trade poisoned relations between cities.

Monitoring and Privileges

However, as a general rule—that is, in the absence of such bilateral conventions—the request for admission that had to be made by foreigners at the entrance to a city was an opportunity to check identity and to make a preliminary examination of the nature of the goods being transported. Obtaining authorization "to get in and to get out" probably required the payment of a small standard tax, which must be clearly distinguished from custom duties or transit taxes (if merchandise in transit was involved), assessed *ad valorem*, and of a substantial amount. Numerous decrees reveal that various cities granted foreigners, as a privilege, an "arrival permit" (*aphixis, eisaphixis*) or a "permit to enter and leave the port" (*eisplous kai ekplous*) that might be associated with a "import and export license" and a "tax exemption." In addition, in some cases these rights appear linked to a privilege of exemption from customs duties. The granting of a right of entry or a right of importation and exportation was thus accompanied, on the part of the city that granted it, by a guarantee of security, expressed in a clause of inviolability and neutrality (*asulei kai aspondei*) or security (*asphaleia*), that seems to have been of special importance. In this way the city committed itself to protecting the foreigner from practices of the "right of seizure" (*sulān*) that could be applied to all foreign goods in transit, and also from any unjustified violence.[7] Attacks on the person of foreign citizens might in fact take place, as is shown by the case of the death sentences demanded by Ephesos against residents of Sardis who had attacked Ephesian religious envoys (*theōroi*) in that city.[8] The security clause could thus involve real responsibilities.

A decree from Kos for a Tyrian, which can be dated to the fourth or third century BCE, provides a good example of the privileges that a city might grant:[9]

> It was resolved by the council and the people. Diagoras, son of Kleuchios made the following proposal: whereas Theron, son of Boudastratos, of Tyre, has shown himself to be a good man with regard to the people of Kos and, on every occasion, never ceases to render services to them, may it please the council to eulogize him and make him a public host [*proxenos*] of the city of Kos, along with his descendants; let them have a permit to enter and leave the port in time of peace and time of war with the privilege of inviolability and neutrality for them and for their goods; let the "sellers" [*pōlētai*] in charge of farming out public contracts auction the inscription of the decree granting the status of public host on a stele and the erection of the latter in the sanctuary of the Twelve Gods.

In this case, we see the city granting a series of privileges to this foreigner, but not tax exemption. However, such exemptions were also frequently made. An example is found in a decree from Stratos of Akarnania dating from about 400 BCE:[10]

> It was resolved by the city of Stratos to confer on Lysias, son of Kallias of Megara, and to Aristion, son of Lysias, and to Kallipos, son of Lysias, the status of public host, *pronomia* and *propraxia*, for them and their descendants. Sureties: Grottos, Bryson, Teisandros; in addition tax exemption [*ateleia*]. Spintharos, son of Sitylos, of Phoitiai, presided over the council.[11]

These two documents immediately raise an essential question. We can grant that privileges such as the right to import or export and a tax exemption (*de facto*, usually an exemption from paying customs duties, but in some cases it must be understood in a broader sense) were conferred on foreigners. But in that case, what about citizens? What were their rights? Could it be that they themselves did not have these rights, and were thus systematically disadvantaged with respect to foreigners? It would be very odd if that were the case, since as already mentioned, a large number of decrees from every part of the Greek world, throughout both the Classical and the Hellenistic periods, granted rights of this kind.

On the basis of the inscriptions of Eretria, Denis Knœpfler has shown that the goal of these diverse privileges was in fact to bring foreigners and citizens closer together.[12] Although some decrees from Eretria refer only to the tax exemption, others add the qualification "like other Eretrians."[13] Decrees issued in Ilion during the Hellenistic period indicate that privileged foreigners would benefit from the tax exemption "enjoyed by citizens" or "enjoyed by Ilians."[14] Two third-century BCE decrees from Delphi accord metic foreigners exemption "from all the taxes from which other citizens are exempt."[15] The rights granted to privileged foreigners thus define the rights of the citizen. Ordinarily, export and import privileges and a limited and precisely defined exemption from custom duties were only for citizens. In the framework of the city's laws, which might prohibit this or that import or export, the members of the civic community thus had a right to import and export as they saw fit, without having to make a special request or pay a special duty, whereas, a priori, foreigners were required to do so: that is what justifies the transit taxes mentioned earlier. Fourth-century BCE decrees from Iasos confirm that by conferring this or that privilege on a foreigner cities were giving him what was ordinarily the right of the citizen.[16] Thus we read:[17]

> To [—], son of Artaos, from Chalketor, who is a benefactor of the Iasians, the Iasians have granted inviolability, a place of honor, tax equality [*isoteleia*] as an Iasian, as well as an import and export license in wartime and in peacetime, like an Iasian.

Some Athenian decrees, and in any case Boiotian decrees from the Hellenistic period in which "tax equality" and "tax exemption" seem to appear alternatively, also tended to bring these privileged foreigners closer to the citizens.[18] The privileges relating to foreign trade or taxes must be connected with other privileges that foreigners might obtain, such as the right to own land and a house (*enktēsis*), which was the citizen's privilege par excellence, or judicial privileges, which were also usually enjoyed only by citizens. Citizens had a right to enter and leave the port or to import or export without needing to request special authorization: we have seen that this was a constitutive element of the citizen's freedom, though of course the laws had to be respected. We thus see why the local authorities had to check the identity of a transient arriving in the city or leaving it, in order to determine whether he was a citizen or a foreigner, and also what his home port was and under what kind of commercial contract he was making his trip, because at first sight his rights were not the same. Given in addition the necessity of monitoring the entrance of slaves into the territory (because they were chattels subject to a specific tax) as well as their exit (because their exporters had to pay the tax associated with exportation and to prevent slaves from fleeing the territory), we see that people's mobility was consubstantial with the city's sovereignty in economic matters (which does not mean that it was the latter's only dimension, as we have already seen).

As for exemption from import or export taxes, the decrees are usually very laconic on this point, so that it is not easy to determine the nature of the exemption granted. However, pending the results of more extensive studies of the question, nothing forces us to conclude that in general these were privileges of a commercial nature. In most cities, in fact, citizens seem to have paid customs duties, in particular the famous tax of a fiftieth (*pentēkostē*), just like foreigners. On the other hand, citizens had the privilege of importing and exporting tax-free a certain quantity of goods for their personal use and that of their households. Several decrees specify that these privileges concerned exclusively the beneficiary's personal use, "for his use," or "for his household" (*es ton idion oikon*).

In general, the volume or value of the goods that one could import and export tax-exempt "for personal use" must have been defined in the city's laws for a specific period and amount. In that way, it was supposed to be possible to avoid disputes. A decree of Abdera for the Roman citizen Marcus Vallius of the second century BCE thus provides the indication that he will have "an export and import permit for his own usage and not for large-scale trade," as well as "an export permit for his own usage every year up to one hundred *medimnoi*."[19] Indeed, the volume, value and real destination of the goods imported and exported was inevitably a matter of concern.

In Crete, during the second half of the second century BCE, the agreement between Lato and Olous provided that "there is a right of exportation for the Latian on leaving Olous and for the Olontian in Lato, tax exempt if by land, and if by sea, then paying duties in conformity with the laws of the respective cities, and swearing that the goods concerned are for personal use."[20] The clause on swearing an oath is interesting, because it shows that the distinction between personal use and commercial use was still not easy to make. A privilege of exemption conferred by King Kassandros of Macedon and displayed in Kassandreia around 306–298 BCE also provides a good example of the possible specific character of these limitations:[21]

> Under Kydias, in the month of Athenaion, King Kassandros granted Chairephanes, son of Aischylos, [of the subdivision] of the Hippotadai, an exemption on all goods, to him and to his descendants, for importation and exportation, for purchase and for sale, except those that are intended for large-scale trade.

In that case, the privilege of import and export covered goods that could be sold for retail, but that could not be the object of large-scale trade—in other words, goods that could be sold in the agora but not at the *emporion*, which inevitably implied a limitation in volume or value. Although most of the decrees of tax exemption that we have concern exemptions for personal use, and not for commercial use, there are some cases in which the tax exemption had greater scope: for example, in this decree from Ilion around 300 BCE:[22]

> To Teisandros, Aischines, Charops, and Nikasidikos, son of Aristoxenos, from Tenedos, public hosts and benefactors, to them and to their descendants, the Ilians have granted a complete tax exemption and anyone who purchases on their behalf or sells them something, let it be tax-exempt; if someone demands that they pay a tax [that is, contrary to this decree], let him pay ten times as much to the public hosts; let them also have the privilege of inviolability in peacetime and in wartime, and the right to own land and houses anywhere they wish, tax exempt; let them also be Ilians and let them be registered in a tribe, if they wish; and if they suffer damages on the part of a foreigner, let them be allowed to exercise a right of seizure, taking as their basis the territory of Ilion, and let the community of the Ilians help them in this; let them be invited to occupy a place of honor in the Panathenaic festivals, proclaiming their name and that of their father, they and their descendants; let them also have food at the prytaneion; let anyone who tries to abrogate any of these provisions be cursed.

The clauses of this decree thus concern fiscal privileges with commercial value, but they remain exceptional, in proportion to the exceptional nature of the services rendered to Ilion by the brothers from Tenedos. With regard to the latter, the people of Ilion were thus in fact fiscally disadvantaged, though it is true that the members of the Tenedos family could also become citizens and thus be privileged among the privileged, and not merely foreigners in a better fiscal position than citizens.

But how about when fiscal advantages were granted not to an individual but to a group, to whole categories of foreigners? In addition to the privileges granted on an individual basis and limited to the beneficiary's personal use, fiscal privileges for commercial activity were undoubtedly also granted. Thus in Delos, the law concerning wood and charcoal provided for the existence of a category of the tax-exempt (*ateleis*).[23] This category was sufficiently vast for the decree not only to mention it but also to specify that, in every other respect, those exempted were expected to obey all the rules relating to trading in wood and charcoal. In addition, some states might grant collective exemptions to large categories of merchants. For instance, the rulers of the principality of Bosporos accorded particularly advantageous conditions to traders who were delivering grain to Athens, because they benefited from a total exemption from customs duties (*ateleia*), a privilege whose value was stressed by Demosthenes in 355/4 BCE.[24] We know that at the same period, other categories of foreigners might enjoy similar, though less significant advantages—for instance, in the Bosporan kingdom as well, those who exported grain to Mytilene enjoyed partial exemption.[25] This should even lead to the question whether in some cases trade tax-privileges were not extended to the local citizens, to make sure that they did not find themselves oddly disadvantaged with respect to foreign merchants.

THE SEA, TAXES, AND THE MARKET

Taxes, Transit Fees, and the "Race to the Sea"

Extant customs documents reveal the meticulous formulation of taxes on trade. A customs papyrus from 475 BCE enumerating the Greek (in practice, exclusively from Phaselis) and Phoenician ships in an Egyptian port gives us a precious glimpse of this trade and shows the variety of the products imported (mainly, but not only, wood, wine, iron, bronze, wool) and exported (natron, and other undefined goods), even though it certainly does not reflect the full range of the diverse goods exchanged.[26] It corresponds to a period of war during which, among Greek merchants, only those from Phaselis were allowed into the empire's ports, because their city had remained loyal to the Achaemenids. Phoenician vessels were subject to an *ad valorem* tax of 10 percent, paid in kind, so that we have details of the products imported. The system of taxation for ships coming from Phaselis was different. First, there was a heavy tax payable in gold and silver, and then a far smaller tax payable in wine, oil, wood, and ceramics. In the Hellenistic period, a papyrus from Pelousion dating from 259 BCE shows the amounts of the taxes levied and their high level (half, a third, or a quarter of the value of the products, along with various small additional taxes).[27]

As already mentioned, the cost of transport by sea was far less than that of transport by land, and having direct access to the sea was a considerable advantage. This was true for both individuals and cities because of the customs duties that they could levy on the loading or unloading of products to be traded. It is easy to show that from the Archaic to the Imperial period, the most developed, most prosperous, and most dynamic cities were always those that were on the coast or near it. Even at the local level, it was this attraction to the sea and maritime trade that explains the descent toward the "corrupting sea," to use Horden and Purcell's evocative expression. Starting in the Classical period, and *a fortiori* during the Hellenistic period, a series of moves from the interior toward the coast can be observed.

In the early fifth century, Athens built a maritime port, Piraeus, and although after the Persian wars the site of the city of Athens itself was not transferred to Piraeus, the latter underwent a remarkable increase in size and importance, to the point that the sources sometimes refer to the "cities" of Attika—that is, Athens and Piraeus.[28] The foundation of the city of Rhodes in 408/7 BCE, at the northern extremity of the island of the same name, placed that city precisely on the privileged axis of circulation along the coast of Asia. The unequal development of the cities of Lesbos is also very significant. Of the seven original cities, it was Mytilene and Methymna, the ones that were situated on the coast and also on the navigation channel that ran along Asian coast, that surpassed the others.[29] Probably in 353/2 BCE, the landlocked city of Mylasa bought a coastal tract of land from the city of Kindye, which gave it an access to the sea or enlarged the one it had before.[30] Even in Crete, a region that was particularly conservative, the phenomenon of the descent to the sea began in the Hellenistic period.[31] In the early second century BCE, little Pidasa, near Miletos, wanted to be connected with the sea by a road that would allow it to export its products.[32]

Consequently, access to the sea could itself be a source of conflict. If in the area of the Keramic Gulf, in the late third century or the early fourth century, a city of the interior like Pisye seized the coastal city of Pladasa, or a part of it, that was clearly because in that way it gained access to a port that would allow it to avoid paying transit taxes. It is true that in this case the movement toward the sea was futile, because Pisye had hardly gained access to the Keramic Gulf before it was absorbed in turn by Rhodes.[33] In the same region, but in the second century, the great inland city of Stratonikeia probably tried to absorb the coastal city of Keramos by joint citizenship or constitution (*sumpoliteia*). In this case, the attempt at absorption had the same ulterior motive: gaining access to the sea.[34] Once again, this movement led nowhere, certainly because of the influence of Rhodes, which was keen to keep its control over this zone. Several additional examples could be given.

Along with taxes on agricultural products, and probably sometimes even more than these, taxes on trade were a primary "revenue source" (*poros*) for cities. This fact has to be justified. Today, in various ways, depending on the country, value-added taxes and taxes on profits constitute the primary sources of government revenues. These taxes are based on accounts that businesses provide to public authorities and that are deemed reliable. This system is characteristic of a developed capitalist economy founded on a system of credit in which every aspect of a business's life is subject to exhaustive and uniform accounting procedures. Nothing of the kind existed in antiquity, because, while credit was central to launch a business, daily operations were not themselves based on credit. Accounts were assumed to be reliable in judicial disputes, as we can see in certain banking matters in the fourth century BCE and also in the Imperial period.[35] On the other hand, they could not be used as a basis for taxes. Taxes on agricultural products were based on declarations made by those subject to the tax, or by tax collectors who were present on the threshing floors or in the wine cellars, or else in relation to the number of livestock or the number of beehives. Since commercial profit could not be taxed by examining private accounts, the simplest way of taxing "invisible" economic activity was to levy commercial taxes: taxes in the agora on retail commerce and, especially, customs duties on goods entering or leaving the territory.[36] At the customs house, nothing escaped the officials' inspection, provided that they were vigilant and not corrupt.

Examples that prove the crucial role of taxes on trade in the income of the cities or kingdoms are many. In the late fifth century BCE, probably in 413, Athens even replaced tributes by a 5 percent tax on trade.[37] The relative amount of customs duties varied with the wealth of the territories. Banned from Athens in the late

360s BCE, the Athenian political exile Kallistratos reorganized the finances of the kingdom of Macedon (under Perdikkas III or Philip II), making it possible to double the revenues from port taxes, which were raised from 20 to 40 talents.[38] In his speech *Against Aristocrates* (23.110), Demosthenes could indirectly refer to the fact that the revenues from the Thracian Chersonese (no doubt mainly agricultural revenues) amounted to no more than 30 talents, whereas the revenues that the Odrysian king Kersobleptes could draw from commercial ports (*emporia*) on the coast amounted to more than 200 talents. The opposition is a rhetorical construction, because the Chersonese is a small size territory, whereas the *emporia*—whose identity is not specified—were none other than Greek cities.[39] Nonetheless, the figures Demosthenes gives show the importance of custom duties in state revenues. To cope with the financial difficulties resulting from his defeat by Rome, the Macedonian king Philip V did not resort to an exceptional tax levy. He preferred to increase receipts drawn from customs duties and leases on royal land and mines.[40] The Rhodian state drew a million drachms (almost 167 talents) from customs duties levied in its port, before the creation of the free port of Delos in 166 BCE caused the amount to fall to 150,000 drachms (25 talents).[41] It is true that before 166 the Rhodian state also received from Stratonikeia and from Kaunos a combined tribute of 120 talents.[42] But the latter city was a port some of whose revenue came from taxes on trade with the hinterland.[43] The kingdom of Pergamon (and later the Roman province of Asia, whose fiscal system was modeled on that of the Attalids), surrounded western Asia Minor with a long chain of customs offices: a list of these is provided by the so-called *monumentum Ephesenum*, the stele bearing the regulations concerning taxation of the Roman province of Asia.[44]

A contrario, being exempted from customs duties thus represented a considerable advantage. When Rome began to take over the eastern Mediterranean, the treaty it concluded with Ambrakia in 187 BCE imposed from the outset exemption from customs duties for Romans and Latins.[45] In view of the later "conquering" attitude of the Romans and Italians in the East, it is logical to think that the measure was applied in the same way everywhere. If that was the case, "distorted competition" represented a significant comparative advantage for the Romans and Italians. This also allows us to better understand the jealousies that this privilege must have aroused and thus (when combined with the tax collectors' exactions) the reasons why during the crisis of 88 BCE there was such an explosion of hatred against the Romans and Italians who had settled in Asia Minor. The amusing scene in the *Birds* in which Pisthetairos considers making the gods pay a transit fee on the smoke from sacrifices was not a pure invention: the usual reflex of an omnipotent state was to raise taxes on trade. We have seen that Pisthetairos himself made the parallel with the transit fee the Boiotians levied on Athenians going to Delphi. The levying of transit fees on persons or merchandise moving through a territory was not limited to large cities. It finds an interesting parallel in a second-century document from northern Thessaly. Two cities, Kondaia (west of Gonnoi, on the left bank of the Peneios) and another, unnamed city that may have been Gyrton (whose location is still unknown) rather than Gonnoi, were engaged in a border dispute. The legal proceeding to resolve the conflict was based on a series of testimonies, including one by a shepherd from a third city, Askyris (in the mountains north of Kondaia):[46]

> Testimony of Ladikos, son of Harmodios, of Askyris, in favor of the Kondaians; I know this territory, which I personally showed to the judges from the summit of the Nyseion down the slope on our side of the mountain as far as the gorge that the Kondaians showed the judges, and I have always heard it said by our elders that our border with the Kondaians was at this place, and I myself, because I have long grazed my flocks in this territory, know that the Kondaians cause a transit fee [*paragōgion*] to be levied there.

The gorge mentioned by the shepherd from Askyris was an unavoidable point of passage. Hence it was there that Kondaia had established a customs office to levy a fee on merchandise entering or leaving the territory. These customs offices set up at inevitable points of passage—gorges, bridges, the mouths of rivers, and of course also ports—marked the Mediterranean landscape until very recently.[47]

Thus to the extent to which access to the international market, to the "commercial highway" constituted by the sea, was a vital need, coastal cities could exploit their natural advantage to the maximum. In economic terms, we find here a typical case of "distorted competition." The notion of an economic rent based on location that allows one to make others pay a fee to use a collective medium is the active version of the notion of "free riding" in which one benefits at no cost from services paid for by others. Cities thus exploited their coastal location by establishing customs duties not only on merchandise entering or leaving their territory, but also on persons who were in transit. That was, moreover, the sense of Dio Chrysostom's recommendation to the Nikomedians. He advised them to offer people from the hinterland advantageous options and to spare them the constant humiliations that other cities did not hesitate to inflict on the cities of their hinterlands. Dio himself was a native of the neighboring city of Prousa. This city had to deal with the maritime city of Apameia in Bithynia, which exploited its location to subject the people of Prousa to every possible hassle.[48] Three cases will suffice to illustrate the importance of access to the sea.

Relating the origins of the Peloponnesian War, Thucydides (1.120.2) reports that addressing the assembly of the Peloponnesian allies, the Corinthians had emphasized that every city was concerned by the war with Athens. They underscored the threat that Athenian imperialism represented not only for the maritime cities, which were already well acquainted with the Athenians' practices, but also for the inland cities. The Corinthians thus warned the people from the interior of the Peloponnese: "They must realize that if they do not defend the people of the lowlands, they will find it more difficult to sell their fresh products and, inversely, to receive in exchange what the sea provides for the continent." The people on the coast and those of the hinterland may or may not have been bound together in a happy solidarity, but the Corinthians' remarks remain interesting. It has been rightly suggested that they were thinking of the Arcadians.[49] But we must certainly also mention the people of Phleious, who were so near Corinth, and who were also dependent on foreign trade. So far as the "fresh products" mentioned by Thucydides are concerned, we must recall that Phleious produced grain and wine.[50] But it appears to have been particularly famous for its vegetables, which were exported far and wide in the same way as Thasos exported wine.[51] For the Corinthians, the lesson was clear: if the Peloponnesians of the interior let the lowlands people succumb to the Athenians, they would themselves inevitably fall victim to the Athenians' exorbitant demands. The second example is that of Kyme in Aeolis. The case of this city has a remarkable trait that shows how the finances of the coastal cities must have been greatly enriched by transit fees. In Kyme, an inscription from the time of Philetairos shows this in an unquestionable way: fees on grain in transit (*diagōgimos sitos*) were supposed to provide the money necessary to pay for the shields that the city urgently needed.[52] It was these transit fees on indispensable products that must have provoked the anger of the cities of the hinterland, as Dio Chrysostom emphasized.

A city nonetheless had the right to levy transit fees on its own territory. But this was not true if these fees were levied on a maritime channel. Around 220 BCE, the Byzantines decided to levy transit fees (*diagōgia*) on ships crossing the Bosporos strait, first at the entrance into Pontos, and then again on leaving, which considerably increased the cost of maritime trade and was injurious to commercial interests.[53] Levying transit fees on the waters of a maritime channel was not within the accepted norms, and that explains why, under pressure from the Rhodians, whom the merchants had asked to intervene on their behalf, the Byzantines had to quickly abandon this demand.[54]

Tax and Trade

The fundamental economic question is whether the multitude of transit fees had an impact on the level of economic activity, and if it did, whether this impact was negative or positive. On the one hand, it is evident that the large number of taxes represented a considerable hindrance to the general development of overland commerce. First, the latter was already burdened by prohibitive transport costs for heavy goods. Having to pay successive transit fees to reach the sea, landlocked cities far inland obviously had a major handicap with respect to those that were located along the coast. Excessive taxation discouraged trade. On the other hand, according to Keith Hopkins's model of "tax and trade," it can be maintained that these taxes might have had the paradoxical effect of encouraging production, by forcing those who were thus taxed to produce more, whether they wanted to or not.[55] That said, we should have no illusions regarding this model: if in the end the revenues derived from these taxes were not used effectively, their overall economic impact could only be negative.

Securing a direct access to the sea, if necessary by resorting to war, might make sense for cities that were in the immediate hinterland. It was out of the question for cities that were farther inland. In Kaunos, as proved by a long document, in the time of Hadrian a fund that had been established by generous benefactors, Menophanes and Menestratos, to allow merchants to escape some of the fees levied on merchandise in transit shows how aware of the problem people could be.[56] Of course, as Louis Robert saw, Kaunos was above all a city oriented toward the sea, and moreover the corpus of the inscriptions of Kaunos demonstrates the preponderantly maritime character of this city's foreign relations.[57] At the same time, literary sources show us that Kaunos had significant relationships with the distant and inland city of Kibyra, certainly via the Indos valley. Over the centuries, Kaunos's will to control Kalynda clearly corresponded to a desire to close the valley of the Indos and to ensure that all the markets of the upper Indos were wholly under its control. The conflict with Rhodes in 164 BCE, reported by Polybius, had no other goal.[58] But if each city through whose territory goods were transported levied customs duties on them, it is clear that such a procedure made overland commerce particularly burdensome: not only was the basic cost of transportation much higher than by sea, but in addition the multiple taxes significantly increased the cost of the product when it arrived at its destination.

The way in which Christian Marek reconstructs the great Kaunos tax document and connects it with the famous document from Myra also shows this very well.[59] A brief summary of its main conclusions will suffice to prove its significance for the history of taxation not only under the Roman empire, but also during earlier periods. First, the Kaunos document is from the age of Hadrian—that is, from the same period as a similar document from Myra. At that time, Kaunos was an integral part of the Lykian League. The documents from Kaunos and Myra can thus be seen as governed by the same system. In both cases, we are dealing with documents regulating the levying of the *portorium*, the *tessarakostē* being nothing other than the *quadragesima* that we find in other provinces of the empire, that is, a tax of 2.5 percent. But in the Lykian League, the right to levy this tax had been granted to the League itself. The system was thus fundamentally different from the one prevailing in Asia. In Lykia, a single customs law (*dēmosionikos nomos*) governed the system of import-export taxes. On the other hand, it was the cities that were entrusted with collecting it. The principle was that the cities received the taxes on imports, while the League received all the taxes on exports. Any re-exportation of a product that had not been sold in Kaunos, whether it had come in by land or by sea, could thus be taxed twice: on importation and on exportation (for a total tax of 5 percent). Contrary to what has been assumed, there was therefore no Lykian customs union: transfers from one city to another were subject to tax as they would be in any other city. In Kaunos, however, thanks to the fund established by Menophanes and Menestratos, which compensated the city's loss of profit, a series of imports were exempted from customs duties. Similarly, thanks to this same fund, products imported by sea and not sold could be re-exported after a period of twenty days without paying an additional tax, provided that they had been adequately declared.

This system worked in Kaunos only because of the fund established by Menophanes and Menestratos, and it was not in use elsewhere. As for the exemption during the festival time (*panēguris*), naturally we think of the similar exemptions in Kyzikos.[60] It is unfortunate that the mutilation of the fourth-century BCE inscription from Xanthos (from the period of Pixodaros) mentioning privileges granted Xanthos, Tlos, Pinara, and "[Kanda]ÿda" (probably the future Kadyanda), and also mentioning Kaunos, regarding a *dekatē tēs empo[rias]*, possibly a 10 percent commercial tax, prevents us from completely understanding the goal of the privilege (exemption? or rather the attribution of a tax?).[61] But in every period, the question of taxes and privileges is central for analyzing the forms of commerce.

In the system we have just described—assuming that the cities did not have generous benefactors like Menophanes and Menestratos, and that they did not themselves have the generosity that Dio Chrysostom urged on Nikomedia—after passing through the territory of five different cities—if no special privilege had been negotiated—the cost of the product would be increased by 25 percent (and even then we have to assume that the tax was on the base value of the product, and not on its increased value after passing from one city to another). This is why one must assume that transit fees were normally lower than regular customs duties; otherwise, the situation would have been unbearable for inland cities.

ECONOMIC INFORMATION AND SECURITY OF TRADE

Circulation of Information and the Uncertainty of Economic Decisions

For merchants, benefiting from a tax exemption thus constituted a precious advantage. But being informed about economic conditions prevailing in the ports where they were likely to go was no less important.[62] Economic information, in the narrow sense (information about quantities available, prices, and so on) or in the broad sense (information about the internal politics of cities or about international tensions) was multiform. It involved first of all informal sources, information passed on by word of mouth. In this sense, information might be spread not only by travelers, and certainly by merchants who circulated a great deal, but also by members of social categories that needed to move about: ambassadors, grain commissioners sent abroad, craftsmen moving from one project to another, *theōroi* visiting sanctuaries, or artists coming to organize a festival. In various ways, all these travelers needed all kinds of information, depending on the type of travel involved, and thus they might in turn be vectors of information. For instance, in 396 BCE a Syracusan—therefore someone "neutral"—who was in Phoenicia and who happened to witness a vast mobilization of the Phoenician fleet in the service of Persia, hurried off to the Peloponnese to tell his Lakedaimonian friends, who were at war with the Great King, about the imminent danger.[63] However, merchants were primarily interested in information regarding quantities and prices. Thus in his *Economics* (20.27–28), Xenophon presents information relative to quantities and prices:

> Thus these merchants are so eager for grain that when they learn that there is a great deal of it somewhere, they hasten to the spot, crossing the Aegean, the Black Sea, and the Sicilian Sea. Then, after having loaded as much of it as they can on their ships, they board the same vessels themselves and cross the sea. And when they need money, they do not unload the grain just anywhere, but take it and deliver it where they have learned that the price of grain is highest and where people want it most.

Whether they are buying or selling, information is what leads people to move about. In this case, economic information is also a good that one might keep to oneself. This was true of the network of informers that Kleomenes of Naukratis put together. In 332 BCE, Alexander named him governor of Egypt, a province rich in grain. In the early 320s, he set up a network of informers in the Aegean that allowed him to send grain where it would bring the highest prices.[64] In his treatise *On Duties* (*De officiis* 3.12 [50–53] and 15 [63]), using an example that he had certainly borrowed from his Rhodian teachers (themselves probably inspired by the lessons of the Rhodian philosopher Panaitios), Cicero mentioned what might be called the merchant's dilemma: a merchant is bringing wheat from Alexandria to Rhodes at a time when in this city the price of wheat is very high because of a shortage; along the way, he meets other ships loaded with wheat that are headed for Rhodes; being the first to arrive in Rhodes, will he tell the Rhodians about these other ships, or will he keep quiet and sell his wheat as dearly as he can?[65] Cicero reports the Stoic masters' divergent opinions: Diogenes of Babylon thought that the merchant had only to abide by the law and that in this case it was not illegitimate to take the profit available to him, whereas his disciple Antipater considered it immoral not to reveal the information. After a long discussion, Cicero finished by citing another Stoic philosopher, Hekaton of Rhodes, who pointed out that getting rich was in itself useful to one's family and one's city, and implicitly concluded that in the end, there was no obligation to reveal the information.

Hieron ("Sacred Place," "Sanctuary"), located on the Asiatic coast at the entrance to the Black Sea north of Byzantion, was the place where merchant ships gathered before entering or leaving.[66] That is what Menippus of Pergamon, an author of the first century CE, says explicitly, identifying this sanctuary as dedicated to Apollo Ourios and adding:[67] "This fort is the point of departure for navigators who are heading for Pontos." The place appears as a point of reference in navigational itineraries, as in Pseudo-Skylax (67.8 and 92.1), and also in contracts like that of the Demosthenic speech *Against Lacritus* (35.10). The proof of this is that it was there that Philip II was able to take by surprise a fleet loaded with grain that was being sent to Athens.[68] But Hieron also clearly served as a hub where economic information was exchanged.

Since navigators of all origins and backgrounds, whether entering Pontos or leaving it, met there, Hieron served as a place where information regarding prices, trade conditions, and political insecurity circulated informally. If, as we see in *Against Lacritus*, navigational contracts might specify the route to be followed and the date of the voyage, they also left a rather large margin of discretion, so that the navigators, ship's captains (*nauklēroi*), and merchants (*emporoi*), could adapt their voyage to the circumstances. The information gleaned in a place like Hieron certainly played an essential role in the decisions that the actors had to make.

But Hieron served as a site for communicating institutional information as well. It is there that was found, engraved on a stele, a law from Pontic Olbia, on the northwestern coast of the Black Sea.[69] This law, which dates from the fourth century BCE, informed merchants about the conditions governing the importation of currencies, the modalities of buying and selling, and trade in Olbia. These conditions were very favorable because coined gold and silver could be freely imported and exported, and could also be freely exchanged, provided that the exchange took place on the stone of the *ekklēsiastērion*, the place where the assembly met.

Only the exchange rate of the Cyzicene, a large electrum coin in use in the region, was established by the law. Thus all merchants entering Pontos were informed in advance of the conditions prevailing in Olbia, and they could make their choices accordingly. By publishing this law in Hieron, the citizens of Olbia also showed their desire for transparency of information. Not only the law of Olbia, but also decrees relating to the privileges received by the Athenians from the dynasts of Bosporos, along with those that the Athenians had accorded them in return, were also displayed there, engraved on stone. This point appears very clearly in Demosthenes' speech *Against Leptines* (20.35–37), from 355/4 BCE: "For you should not believe that the steles that stand there are anything other than the contracts of privileges that you have received or that you have granted." If they canceled the tax privileges accorded to the rulers of Bosporos, Demosthenes suggested, the Athenians would shame themselves before all "international opinion" and Hieron, the place where the steles were displayed, would act as a sounding board for their infamy: the steles erected by the dynasts of Bosporos would testify, *a contrario*, to the baseness of the Athenians. Beyond the specific context of *Against Leptines*, it is easy to understand why for the two partners it was important that their mutual concessions be displayed in Hieron. For navigators and merchants, it was an inducement to go there to carry out contracts for the transport of goods to Athens, since the tax exemption was guaranteed. Reciprocally, a few Bosporan navigators might also have an interest in coming to Athens to benefit from the symmetrical conditions favoring them.[70] The stele in the *emporion* of inland Thrace (shortly after 359 BCE) that enumerates the privileges guaranteed by the Thracian king Kotys and one of his successors to Greek merchants in Thrace was of exactly the same nature.[71]

The Security of International Trade

Security is the primary factor of economic development, since it provides a context in which rational predictions can be made. This principle holds in particular for international trade.

The city-state was a "legally constituted state," and it therefore had to undertake to provide security for people and property on its territory, including for foreign traders. In any event, even if violent acts were committed by individuals, it was the city that was held responsible, and it was up to the city to ensure that victims were compensated. These acts included blatant aggressions against foreigners, in which case the city had to provide compensation. Thus the Dolopes of the island of Skyros were convicted by the "international" tribunal of the amphictions of Delphi because some of them had jailed and robbed Thessalian merchants who had made a stopover on their territory. In consequence the city of the Dolopes required the offenders to pay damages.[72] An inscription from Ephesos dating from the end of the fourth or the beginning of the third century shows that the Ephesians had demanded, and obtained, a death sentence for forty-six citizens of Sardis who had attacked an Ephesian religious delegation on Sardian territory.[73] The exorbitant nature of the punishment is explained by the religious character of the attack. However, it may be thought that for offenses of a civil nature, the procedures were of the same order, but normally did not resort to such extreme sanctions. Pseudo-Aristotle's *On Marvellous Things Heard* (85) reveals that security on an "international road" could be the subject of a kind of common pact binding the residents: "A road that begins in Italy goes as far as the land of the Kelts, to the country of the Kelto-Ligurians and the Iberians, a road that is called the 'Heraklean Way.' If a Greek or a foreigner traveled along it, the inhabitants of the region saw to it that they were not harmed. The possible penalty for harming them had to be paid by those on whose territory the offense was committed." In eastern Crete, the treaty between Lato and Olous concluded in 109/8–108/7 BCE provided for very heavy penalties, but in the form of fines, for those who violated the security of the roads:[74] "Let the roads used by foreigners be sacred; if anyone commits an illegal act on these roads, he must pay six times the amount of the fine if he loses his case." Similarly, in the early fourth century BCE, the Thracian kings guaranteed that merchants coming to the *emporion* of inland Thrace would pay taxes only once, which amounted to guaranteeing them that they would not be subject to exactions in the form of unauthorized transit fees imposed along the way.[75] "Making the roads sacred" and the exceptionally high fines must have discouraged attacks on merchants traveling along the itineraries they took—that is, on the main routes leading to cities and ports. In a region like Crete, where pirates were still active even at a late date, and where violence continued to be endemic, even among neighboring cities, such legislation sought to limit robbery of merchants.

Besides, piracy was economically ambiguous. One the one hand, it was a provider of goods for the market, especially slaves—commonly free men (barbarians, but also Greeks) reduced to slavery by the use of violence. On the other hand, it represented a threat to trade routes, and merchants and travelers had to be protected against pirates.[76] A decree from the western Asia Minor city of Teos dating from the second half of the third century BCE shows the exorbitant cost that an attack by pirates might entail.[77] Pirates seized the city and took the residents hostage. To regain its freedom, and to free the hostages, Teos had to require all inhabitants, both citizens and foreigners, to hand over in their coined gold and silver (it seems), their valuable crockery, and even their scarlet robes and the gold braid on women's dresses in order to ransom themselves. All this theoretically took the form of a loan to the city at the rate of 10 percent. In short, the pirates seized everything valuable that they could carry away. In addition to its human cost, an attack by pirates thus had a very high financial cost.

The suppression of piracy and secure sea travel were thus preconditions for regular commercial trade. In the Classical period, Athens served as the guardian of maritime security. After the Persian wars, Cimon began a campaign against Skyros, an island located at the mouth of the Euboian Channel, on the commercial route leading to Thrace and Pontos. This was a direct result of the attack on Thessalian merchants, of the subsequent conviction of the Dolopes of Skyros by the court of the amphictions and of its follow-up, which gave way to the Athenian intervention.[78] Merchants could not be left exposed to such a threat, although of course the capture of the island directly benefited the Athenians. Throughout its fifth-century empire, Athens policed the Aegean seas. Leaving from Athens or other naval bases on the Aegean, and operating almost everywhere, Athenian ships clearly provided decades of peace in the Aegean.[79] The tribute paid by the cities, which was in most cases modest, was in a way the price to be paid for security. Most of the tribute must have gone to pay for the fleet of warships. At a rate of one drachm per man-day, it cost 350 talents to maintain a fleet of thirty-five triremes with crews of 200 men apiece for ten months.[80] If to this we add the costs of building and maintaining the ships, we are not far from the "460 talents" of the tribute before 431. Most of the time, there were probably not that many ships mobilized over such a long period. But at other times, the mobilizations were more extensive. The tribute supported many Athenians (and foreigners) who rowed the triremes, but as such it did not enrich the city of Athens. In other words, paying tribute to Athens was well worth it for the security provided at no additional cost. Even if, like any tribute rendered to a foreign power, paying it must have seemed unbearable, it probably constituted a much smaller contribution than the one the tributary cities would have had to make, had they been able to do so, to maintain a fleet capable of providing that security. Many people must have been fully aware of this, and it is likely that this is why Athens had many supporters in the cities of the empire.

With the fall of Athens in 404 BCE, a period of great instability began. Henceforth, even if Athens fairly quickly resumed an important role in the Aegean, it no longer had the means to police the seas as it had done during the preceding century. If the Athenians launched naval expeditions, it was first and foremost to protect their own maritime routes, and the consequences for other cities were, so to speak, only a collateral outcome. From the mid-fourth century on, Athens thus had to battle the piracy practiced by the cities on the coast south of Rome as far as Campania, which the Greeks always called "Tyrrhenian"—that is, "Etruscan" (whether or not they were actually Etruscan). It was explicitly in order to defend their supply routes that the Athenians conducted expeditions against these pirates and even considered establishing a relay post somewhere west of the Peloponnese in order to carry out campaigns against them more expeditiously.[81] One way to ensure security for merchant vessels in a context of growing insecurity was to provide escorts for them. Thus on several occasions in the course of the fourth century, a convoy of ships was escorted by an Athenian fleet. This was particularly the case for ships coming from Pontos, a grain-shipping route that was vital for Athens.[82]

In defense of Athenian generals who were short of funds and had to increase the contributions made by the cities in order to support their troops, Demosthenes explained, in his speech of 341 BCE *On the Affairs of the Chersonese* (8.25), the interest of this policy, even for the cities that had to make the contributions:

> The generals who have only one or two ships levy only a comparatively small contribution; those who have more levy a larger one. But whether it is small or large, those who pay this sum are not paying it for nothing, they are not so mad as that. By purchasing for merchants who are sailing from their ports the right not to suffer harm, not to have their cargoes seized, and to see their own ships escorted, they say that they are making "generous gifts" that is the name given these "exactions" [that are attributed to our generals].

When we consider that Demosthenes earlier (8.24) took Chios and Erythrai as examples of cities making such contributions, and thus cities that were primarily involved in foreign trade, we can fully grasp the meaning of this remark. Alongside the ships that were to go to Athens or to its allies and that were seized in Hieron, at the northern entrance to the Bosporos strait, in 340 BCE, there were also ships going to nonbelligerent cities, probably about fifty of them.[83] However, even though it must have suffered the effects of the new Macedonian domination, the Athenian fleet remained a significant force until its irremediable defeat at Amorgos in 322 BCE, which, far more than Chaironeia, sounded the death knell of Athenian power.

During the Hellenistic period, even before the siege to which it was subjected by Demetrios Poliorketes, Rhodes took over its role. It was probably in the context of these conflicts with the Tyrrhenians (well attested by Rhodian inscriptions of the period) and their diplomatic consequences that Rhodes made its first contacts with Rome, as Polybius expressly indicates.[84] It is possible that the payment of 5,000 drachms that the Delians made in 298 "for protection from the Tyrrhenians" was intended to help pay for a (Rhodian?) fleet to fight these pirates, or in any case to finance an operation of that kind.[85] In the third century, it was the Aitolians, then at the end of the third century and in the second century the Cretans, and finally, at the end of the second century and the beginning of the third century, the Kilikians, who represented the chief threat. The Rhodians were never able to police the seas as effectively as the Athenians had in the fifth century; Athens had a much larger fleet (as many as two hundred vessels when necessary) and a genuine empire.[86] Except for the exceptional mobilization during the war against Antiochos, the Rhodian fleet consisted of only about thirty vessels. But the Rhodians had light, fast ships that were well suited to fighting pirates, and their experience as sailors made them dangerous adversaries.[87] Finally, if a power infringed on the freedom of maritime communications, the Rhodians did not hesitate to intervene. That was what happened around 220 BCE, when Byzantion, trying to meet the Kelts' demands, decided to levy a fee on the Bosporos strait, first on entering Pontos, and then on leaving it as well, which considerably increased the cost of maritime trade and was hard on merchants. Polybius indicates that the sea people "came to see the Rhodians, who controlled the seas," to ask them to intervene. It was the Rhodians who led a small maritime expeditionary force (ten vessels in all, six Rhodian and four allied) and finally forced the Byzantines to lift their blockade.[88]

Thus it is clear that the ease of levying taxes on commerce, and in particular on maritime commerce, made them one of the main sources of revenue for Greek city-states. At the same time, the comparison with the medieval and modern worlds, for example with the situation that prevailed in the Netherlands in the early modern period, shows that internal tariffs could also operate to slow the development of trade, and thus hinder economic growth as such.[89] It is no accident that a place like Delos underwent such rapid growth during the late Hellenistic period: the absence of taxes there surely made a large contribution to this growth. However, one must also point out that the tax burden was to some extent compensated by the transparency of institutional information and maritime security.

XII

THE *EMPORION* AND
THE MARKETS

The city-state formed a self-contained, delimited entity, which does not mean that it was a space closed to foreign trade. The *emporion* was precisely the institutional structure that made communication with outside areas possible and provided it with a legal framework. However, the city did not limit itself to a passive role in matters of trade. Not only was it capable of intervening directly in the negotiation of prices in the *emporion*, but it could also act as a purchaser, thus becoming itself an actor in the market. In this way, the city had an influence on prices. Naturally, this was chiefly part of a policy of supplying the domestic market, but the city also supervised its exports, which were necessary for the life of the city as a whole. Finally, it did not hesitate to intervene directly in trade by constituting funds for this purpose, especially regarding grain.

THE EMPORION

We take as our point of departure a twofold definition of the *emporion*. In a broad sense, the *emporion* was a "trading port" or "the port area," and thus also the "business area." But in the space of a city, the *emporion* was also and primarily a particular legal space, geographically delimited, and marked out by boundary stones.[1] Thus in Piraeus, a boundary stone has been found that bears the inscription "boundary stone of the *emporion* and the street."[2] Pseudo-Demosthenes (35.28) refers for Athens to the "limits of the *emporion*," outside which it was not legal to carry on trade, and in this speech the litigant accuses his adversary of having unloaded his cargo in the "thieves' harbor" in order to avoid respecting his obligations and to be able to commit fraud more easily.

The significance of this episode can perhaps be illustrated by another in Chariton of Aphrodisias's novel *Chaereas and Callirhoe*, which recounts the romantic love affair of the hero and heroine, set in a conventional fifth century BCE (1.11.4.–

2.1.9). This work was likely written in the mid-first century CE.[3] However, the scenes described represent basic legal realities that had not changed since the Classical period. The beautiful Kallirhoe has been kidnapped in Syracuse by a brigand called Theron, who takes her not to Athens—where, we are told, the supervision is too strict—but to Miletos. There he arranges to sell his prey at the highest possible price. He does not moor his boat in the city's harbor, but outside the city, and tells his customers that he has done so in order to avoid the customs officials—and they find nothing wrong in this. Theron passes himself off as a Sybarite (an origin that is supposed to be plausible, since he comes from the West). He lures the buyer by taking a talent as a deposit and promising to meet him later in the agora to complete the contract. In fact he immediately absconds—but leaves Kallirhoe behind. The buyer is doubly injured: he has given a talent as a deposit for nothing and finds himself the possessor of property that was brought into the territory illegally and for which he cannot provide a valid sales contract.

This episode shows a contrario both the constraints and the advantages of the emporion. It was a space of transparency in transactions. It was governed by the city's laws and in it one had to pay taxes, in particular customs duties. On the other hand, it provided the benefit of a legal guarantee for the transactions made in it.

The City's Supervision of Foreign Trade

The space of the emporion was governed by specific laws enforced by specialized magistrates who were often called, at least in great trading cities like Athens, Delos, Miletos, Rhodes and Amphipolis, "overseers of the port" (epimelētai of the emporion). Thus we see a complete parallel with the agora, which was also a space delimited by boundary stones and governed by a set of specific laws (the nomos agoranomikos) and supervised by special magistrates (the agoranomoi). Whereas for the exchange of goods, the agora was reserved for retail trade, the emporion was for wholesale trade. It was there that traders of every nationality gathered to meet a city's wholesale buyers (either citizens or metic residents, indifferently) or other merchants. An emporion was in fact the lungs of the city, the place that allowed it to carry on its foreign trade, but it was also a space where arrangements for forwarding merchandise could be made.

In this respect, one of the key points in the jurisdiction of the emporion was the question of the loading and unloading of cargoes. To analyze this issue, one must start from the conditions under which a ship could anchor in a port. When a ship remained at the dock, its owner had to pay port taxes, probably corresponding to the space that the ship occupied (thus to its tonnage) and the length of its stay there. We do not know much about these taxes, but their existence is beyond doubt. Thus in Delos, in the third century BCE, there were several taxes of this kind: limēn ("port," certainly an anchorage fee), stropheia (apparently a fee on usage of a capstan), and hairesia (perhaps a fee linked to the usage of a space reserved to load and unload).[4] In the port at Sounion, in the fifth century, a tax of seven obols per thousand talents of cargo weight was levied.[5] We have seen that it can be assumed that taxes whose amount was a function of the ship's tonnage might have been the source of the regulation in the port at Thasos.[6] The amount of these taxes seems not to have been very high (which does not mean that they were negligible if the ship remained in port for several weeks).[7]

However, far higher taxes might be levied in the form of customs duties. In general, this was a tax of one-fiftieth (*pentēkostē*), payable on entering and leaving the port with merchandise. Does this mean that the tax was levied on the cargo as soon as the ship entered the port? In fact, it was only when the merchandise had been unloaded (or before it was loaded) that the tax had to be paid. A regulation from Kyparissia (in Messenia, dating from the fourth or the third century BCE) provides proof of this:[8]

> God. Whoever imports into Kyparissia's territory must, when he unloads the cargo, submit a written declaration to the receiver of the fiftieth [*pentēkostolo-gos*] and pay the fiftieth [*pentēkostē*] before he takes anything into the city, or sells it, on pain of paying ten times the usual duty if he does not. Whatever one exports by sea, one shall submit for it to the receivers of the fiftieth a written declaration and pay the fiftieth, and then load the return cargo, after having summoned the receiver of the fiftieth. It is forbidden to load before this is done; whoever violates this rule shall pay ten times the fiftieth, in ac-cord with the general regulation. To whomever who makes an underestima-tion, the receiver of the fiftieth shall confiscate [his cargo] for the amount of the claimed sum, in accord with the general regulation.

In a Greek city's port, the police magistrates could board a ship to check its cargo—for example, to see if the ship was transporting men or weapons that might be used to seize the city. But this monitoring did not involve the levying of a cus-toms duty. It was for the *pentēkostologoi*, who levied the one-fiftieth tax, to receive the estimate of the merchandise when it was unloaded or loaded: that was the key moment in the procedures for handling merchandise in the *emporion*. So long as merchandise was not unloaded, it could leave the port again without the city hav-ing had to levy a customs duty. On the other hand, once the merchandise was un-loaded, it had to be immediately declared and its owner had to pay the tax on it.

For the Greek world, we have no figures regarding the loading or unloading of a ship. For the Roman world, however, there are reliefs and mosaics that help us picture these scenes of loading and unloading—for instance, on the relief of the *Tabularii* at the Port of Trajan in Ostia, from the end of the second or the begin-ning of the third century CE, we see bearers (the equivalent of our longshoremen) unloading a cargo of amphoras from a ship, while on the dock a supervisor scrupu-lously notes down the merchandise unloaded. In a fresco of the same period repre-senting a ship being loaded with grain, the *Isis Giminiana*, we see a supervisor (?) carrying what looks like a rope bearing a series of sticks that might have served to count the trips made by the bearers (who would themselves have been paid in proportion to the quantity loaded).[9] These sticks might have been tally sticks, with notches cut in the wood for counting the steps in a process. The use of these sticks in systems of accounting and monitoring during the Middle Ages, in particular a set of tally sticks represented in a scene of commercial activity depicted in a stained-glass window in the Cathedral of Tournai, seems to support this hypothesis.[10] Given the close correspondences between the practices of the world of the western Mediterranean and those of the eastern Mediterranean, the Greek world might well have used the same system, or at least an analogous one. In any event, the monitor or supervisor thus had not only to determine the quantity of merchandise loaded or unloaded, but also to check its quality. In the case of amphoras, for instance, the declared price might vary considerably depending on the quality of the wine.[11] The *pentēkostologoi* or other magistrates of the port were not able to check every cargo in detail. That is shown by an episode recounted by Aeneas Tacticus, in which the crates of merchandise bore the monitor's seal only after they had been declared and, in theory, checked. However, despite this monitoring, weapons hidden among various kinds of merchandise might be introduced into a city.[12] Thus it is clear that only part of the cargo was subjected to exhaustive examination. On the other hand, the penalties for making a false customs declaration were heavy, as is shown by the law of Kyparissia.

The Deigma

When we move beyond retail sales in the narrow sense, we find that the usual practice was to sell on the basis of samples. In his *Life of Demosthenes* (23.4), Plutarch tells how Demosthenes showed that handing over to Macedon the leaders of the anti-Macedonian party in Athens would amount to selling the Athenian people as a whole. He was thinking of the practice of selling on the basis of samples: "As we see corn-masters sell their whole stock by a few grains of wheat that they carry about with them in a dish."[13] Euripides' *Cyclops* alludes indirectly to a practice of sampling, even if the word is not used: Odysseus wants to buy bread, and having no gold, he offers Silenus some of the wine that he has in the hold of his ship. At first, he offers him a taste (*geuma*), and Silenus replies: "A reasonable offer; for of a truth a taste invites the purchase."[14]

Other texts prove that a genuine institution grew up around the system of sales on the basis of samples. This can be seen in the principle formulated by Aeneas Tacticus, which called for placing under surveillance any imported weapons that might be found in the agora or in shops in the city, except those displayed as sample (*deigma*).[15] These texts also show that by extension the word *deigma* designated the place in the *emporion* where this system was practiced. Thus, the lexicographer Pollux, citing Hyperides, refers to "the sectors of the port, the *deigma*, the jetty, the *emporion*, and, as Hyperides says, the loading dock where cargoes are loaded; as it were, the *deigma* gets its name from providing samples of merchandise [*agōgima*] to buyers, according to Hyperides in the speeches *On Salt Fish*."[16] This might lead us to think that the *deigma* was distinct from the *emporion*. But Harpocration's entry (quoting two sources of the fourth century BCE) dissipates the ambiguity:[17] "*Deigma*, mainly what is shown of each of the products sold, as well as the place with this name in the *emporion* of Athens where samples were brought. It is in fact the habit in Athens to name places after what they contain. Demosthenes in *In the Matter of a Period of Service as Trierarch* and Lysias."

By extension, the *deigma* was thus the place where business was transacted. Regarding Athens, Xenophon tells us that the *deigma* fell victim to the raid made on Piraeus by the Spartan Teleutias in 388 BCE and that "some (of the attackers) leaped ashore to raid the *deigma*, seized some merchants and shipowners and forced them to embark onto their ships."[18] In the speech *Against Lacritus*, as in other sources, the *deigma* appears as the place where business was normally transacted.[19] It is not clear whether the *deigma* was a particular building or not: for some scholars, it was a simple open place or agora, in accord with the designation of the *deigma* as a *topos* in some ancient sources, so that the *deigma* in Athens would have been merely the agora, of which Pausanias says that it was near the port;[20] for others, it was a regular building, a portico constructed for the specific purpose of providing space for merchants and businessmen.[21] An inscription from Piraeus from the mid-Augustan era mentions the "*deigma* built by Magnus": Magnus is supposedly Pompey the Great, who is said to have reconstructed the *deigma* after its destruction by Sulla.[22] A letter of emperor Hadrian aiming at controlling fish prices at Eleusis and at Athens was supposed to be displayed at the Piraeus in front of the *deigma*, presumably where it was found.[23]

Moreover, the system of the *deigma* was not limited to Athens. It is true that the existence of a *deigma* in Delos remains uncertain. The institution is not attested in the literary or epigraphic sources. It has been proposed that a small *stoa* that can now be seen behind the portico of Philip (built later) and parallel to it served as a *deigma*.[24] Until the construction of the portico of Philip at the end of the third century, this portico had in fact direct access to the port.[25] However, in Pontic Olbia an inscription from the Hellenistic period mentions a gate of the *deigma*.[26] Diodorus mentions the *deigma* in Rhodes in the context of the flood in 316, and tells us that the whole sector of the *deigma* and the *Dionysion*, the sanctuary of Dionysos, was flooded.[27] Diodorus's account makes it clear that the *deigma* was in the lower part of the town, adjacent to the port. Finally, Polybius notes that after the earthquake of ca. 229–226 BCE, Hieron II of Syracuse had a statue of the people of Rhodes crowned by the Syracusan people erected "in" or "on the *deigma*."[28] The references to Olbia and Rhodes, confirmed by what we can guess about Piraeus, allow us to assume that the *deigma* was a very precise area of the *emporion*, and had a portico-type building where transactions took place.[29]

How can we imagine the functioning of the system of sales on the basis of samples? This difficult topic has been the object of much debate. However, decisive progress has recently been made and it is now possible to propose a new and integrated hypothesis for the role of the *deigma* and for the organization of trade procedures and taxation. Our documentation shows that the unloading or loading of goods on a ship was the key to the payment of the tax. It was at that moment that it was possible to determine what quantity was officially imported, or exported, and for what value.

To begin with, let us consider the unloading of goods. It was the official owner of the unloaded good who had to make the declaration and to pay the tax. The crucial point is the identity of the importer (*eisagōn*). He was commonly the merchant who had accompanied the cargo and who hoped to find clients after he had unloaded his goods. But there are indications that he could also be a local client, most of the time a wholesaler, who had bought a cargo on the basis of a sample presented to him at the *deigma*.[30] The *deigma* was thus the place where supply met demand, where negotiations were conducted and where a price equilibrium was found. For a foreign trader, finding a local wholesaler at the *deigma* was the ideal scheme. He thus minimized his time of presence in the port, and did not face the risk of having to deal with unsold goods. Indeed, one of the main issues involved in customs registration in Kaunos in the early second century CE was the management of these unsold goods, products that had been unloaded but had found no buyers: thanks to funds provided by generous benefactors, merchants could avoid paying a tax at the reloading of their products.[31]

Sample sales were no less significant for exports and loading of goods, and this for various reasons. The cities in general sought to control their foreign trade, going so far as to limit the point of contact with foreign traders to a single port, other ports being reserved for local traffic. The kingdom of Bosporos had only one *emporion*, at Pantikapeion, until the conquest of Theodosia made it possible to open another *emporion* in that port.[32] What precisely was the situation in large cities that had local ports? This point raises the problem of the relation between the *emporion* and the territory's products. Was the *emporion* merely a convenient framework in which merchants preferred to buy their supplies, rather than buying them in small local ports, it being understood that they could nonetheless trade freely in the latter? Or were they, on the contrary, obliged to buy through the city's *emporion*? Ultimately, was there only a single port open to foreign trade in cities like Athens, Rhodes, or even Thasos? Consider the case of Rhodes, whose civic territory extended to a series of islands and areas along the coast of Asia. If we adopt the hypothesis that local ports were closed to foreigners, we have to imagine that every year several tens of thousands of amphoras and other containers coming not only from the island of Rhodes, but also from the continental territories (the Peraia), the Rhodian islands of Chalke, Karpathos, Nisyros and Telos, had to pass through the port of Rhodes before they could be exported. We know that this kind of transportation (necessarily by sea) would have involved a loss of time and money, because loading ships was a delicate task and entailed significant costs (it is no chance that a papyrus of the Roman period underscores that if a tax-officer exacts the unloading of a ship for control and that no fraud can be proved he has to pay the cost of unloading to the merchant).[33] But in the contrary case, why would merchants have gone to the *emporion*?

When Isocrates wanted to give his audience an example of the speeches he had written, he explained: "I could not read them all *in toto*, because the time we have is short; but as one would for the fruits of a harvest, I shall try to present you with a sample [*deigma*] of each one."[34] Isocrates' remark is interesting not only because it defines the notion of a sample, but also because it establishes a parallel with samples of the *karpos*, the "fruits of the earth." The term usually designated a territory's harvest. Pollux's *agōgima* mentioned earlier were "merchandise," not *eisagōgima*, "imported products" (or, for that matter, *exagōgima*, "exported products"). If we turn to somewhat later documents, we see that in Ptolemaic Egypt as well, samples of the harvest were sent from the nomes to the capital.[35] There was even a specialized magistrate, a *deigmatokatagōgos*, whose responsibility was to oversee the transfer of these samples to Alexandria.[36] Zenon's papyri, which date from the third century, show in addition that in private practice it was common to buy at a distance on the basis of small, sealed samples that circulated separately from the merchandise. The buyer made a deposit and paid the balance on delivery.[37] Thus there is every reason to think that the role of trading center of the *deigma* was not only to present samples of imported products but also to offer both local and foreign merchants a broad range of the country's products, so that their choices could be made as rapidly and as well as possible. It is in this sense that we can say that the *deigma* was truly the crossroads of a city's trade. Otherwise, we would have to suppose that a foreign merchant who wanted to buy supplies of wine or Rhodian honey had to visit all the small ports in the territory in order to find the product he was looking for. For another large wine exporter like Thasos, the problem is the same, and it seems difficult to imagine that the loading of wine amphoras for export was centered in the port of Thasos.[38] In this sense, the *deigma* was in fact the heart of the *emporion*, the place where the most important transactions took place, and this explains why in Rhodes, as in Athens during the Classical period, it was full of brokers, moneychangers, bankers, and other intermediaries.

It thus seems very likely that purchasing in the *deigma* and the *emporion* facilitated the tasks of merchants who had traveled long distances and did not want to lose time visiting small local ports to find the products they wanted. Was it also a legal obligation? Given the other constraints that we know cities put on trade, this offers a plausible schema. For the time being, we have no document that allows us to provide proof of that hypothesis. What remains out of the question however is to imagine that foreign merchants had free access to all a city's secondary ports or moorings: had that been the case, it would have been impossible effectively to control foreign trade or to levy any tax on it. One should suggest instead that the *deigma*'s main function was to allow contracts to be made under the best conditions. Then the actual delivery of products must have taken place in a certain number of relay ports, duly supervised as well, but where all that remained to be done was to load the products on presentation of the proper documents and payment of the balance due on the price of the merchandise.[39]

If this hypothesis is correct, we can say that the *deigma* was the key institution in trade, not only for imports but also for exports. Standardizing prices in the *emporion* and in the agora seems to have been a major concern for cities. The *deigma* must have allowed this standardization, which would have been impossible to achieve if merchants had been able to negotiate separately with individual producers in local ports. At the same time, loading in local ports the cargoes that had been purchased in the city-state's central *emporion* allowed the system to retain all the indispensable flexibility and limited transaction costs, since it was not necessary to load and unload the merchandise twice.

The Rules of the Emporion

In cities where the magistrates supervising commerce made a sharp distinction between foreign trade and domestic trade (in many cases, it was the *agoranomoi* who oversaw both the agora and the *emporion*), it was *epimelētai*, "inspectors," who were responsible for maintaining order in the *emporion*. Aristotle (*Constitution of Athens* 51.4) describes the responsibility the Athenians gave to the *epimelētai* of the *emporion*: "They choose by lot ten *epimelētai* of the *emporion*. These are ordered to oversee the markets and to force the merchants to transport to the city two-thirds of the grain coming by sea and unloaded at the grain market (*sitikon emporion*)." That the markets were supervised can be taken for granted. We can assume that these magistrates were responsible for seeing to it that fights did not break out among sailors and that disputes among traders did not degenerate into violent acts. But their role also had several other facets. One of these appears in the currency law dating from 375/4 BCE.[40] The magistrates of the *emporion* were to station in Piraeus, near the stele of Poseidon, the public slave entrusted with verifying currency for shipowners and traders, and they were responsible for receiving complaints in this connection.

The role of the magistrates of the *emporion*, like those of the agora, was thus to ensure the transparency of transactions, and that is why the *emporion* could be defined as a legal space (*nomimon*). That is the meaning of Isocrates' advice (2.22 *To Nicocles*) to "offer all foreigners a city in which they are safe and a legal framework for contracts" (*polin . . . pros ta sumbolaia nomimon*).[41] In the *emporion* as in the agora, the power of the city's laws was given material form on the steles on which were displayed the texts of the laws governing commerce: thus the previously mentioned Attic coinage law regarding currency monitoring was to be displayed not only in the city agora (that is the one that has been found, along with the law on grain from the islands) but also in Piraeus, "near the stele of Poseidon." The order desired by the city was also expressed in the emphasis on sectors specialized by product. Just as there were in the cities' agoras distinct sectors for each type of product, and in the port specific basins or sectors to which ships were assigned by type or provenance, in the *emporion* there might also exist sectors for a specific kind of product, as is shown by Aristotle's text.[42]

For example, in Piraeus a sector was reserved for grain, and in Delos there was clearly also a sector reserved for trading in wood and charcoal.[43] This separation of activities must have been the one of the responsibilities of magistrates of the *emporion*.

Each *emporion* had its own rules, depending on the city's needs and objectives. In Athens, the buying and selling of grain was carried on separately from that of other products. Both wholesale and retail grain transactions were supervised by specialized magistrates, the *sitophulakes*, or "grain wardens."[44] The latter supervised the activity of the "grain port" (*sitikon emporion*). As previously mentioned, according to Aristotle it was the responsibility of the magistrates of the *emporion* to force the importers to have two-thirds of the grain imported into the city-state brought into the agora of the "city," obviously at the importer's expense. This clause does not mean, as was long thought, that the remaining third could be re-exported. On the contrary, as proved by Philippe Gauthier, it was a matter of seeing to it that two-thirds of the imports were taken to the agora of the city of Athens itself, the final third remaining available for the agora of Piraeus.[45] The cost of land transport between Piraeus and Athens, over a distance of about seven or eight kilometers, was paid by the importers, which was a way of keeping down the final price by trimming the importers' profit margin. In all likelihood, this transport was made in wagons.[46] Given that the grain merchants were still in control of the grain and that they had to deliver it to the agoras in proportions fixed by the law, it is thus certain that the tax at the unloading of the grain was paid by the importers (and not by the middlemen, who intervened only later in the process). The *epimelētai* thus provided a genuine internal regulation of supplies, and did not play a purely passive role with regard to grain imports.

Aristotle indicates that the law obliged importers to take their grain to the two agoras of Athens and Piraeus. However, this does not mean that negotiations between importers and Athenian wholesalers took place at the entrance to these agoras. Instead, they were conducted in the *emporion*, or more precisely in the grain market (*sitikon emporion*).[47] Otherwise, what would the function of this market have been? Could it have been merely a transit point for grain? It is not for nothing that the Attic law of 375/4 BCE specifies that the *sitophulakes* were supposed to register complaints concerning currencies in the sector for which they were responsible, and this proves that it was in fact a place where financial transactions were made.[48] Thus it is certain that the *sitophulakes* dealt with sales of grain and flour at both the agora and the *emporion*.[49] That is why they had records of the quantities imported from abroad, as Demosthenes' *Against Leptines* (20.32) emphasizes: they were obviously present in the *emporion* and it was they who supervised the activity of the *sitikon emporion*. Once the grain had been bought in the *emporion*, and thus at a uniform price—that was the city's whole objective—there remained the question of delivery. After the purchase had been negotiated, Athenian law obliged the importers to pay the cost of delivery as far as the entrance to the agoras.

In the grain market, the importers thus had to find several buyers, because each of them could buy no more than 50 "loads" (*phormoi*), as Lysias stresses (*Against the grain dealers* 22.5–6).[50] The distribution of the quantities between Athens and Piraeus also assumes that, before gaining access to the grain market, the importer had to declare what quantity he was going to put on sale. And this in turn supposes that this quantity had been unloaded and that the associated tax had been paid, as mentioned earlier: the system took care to prevent the merchant from speculating and selling his grain little by little, unloading it gradually in proportion to the buyers and prices that he had found. He had to agree to declare at the same time to the *sitophulakes* both the quantity he was going to sell and the price he was going to ask. By thus ensuring this quantitative division between the two agoras, and by forcing importers to sell to middlemen in the two cities, the city-state prevented the largest part of the grain from being accumulated in the nearest agora, that of Piraeus. Otherwise, whatever the legislation prohibiting large-scale purchases (each middleman being able to buy no more than fifty *phormoi*), there would inevitably have been a process of resale in order to supply the agora in Athens, and thus middlemen's profits between the importer and final client. Like the Delian law on the sale of wood and charcoal, this was exactly what the Athenian law sought to prevent (without, however, going so far as the Delian law's requirement that all intermediaries be abolished, because then the importer would himself have had to be a retailer[51]). In addition, the system generally ensured a uniform price in the city-state's two main agoras, which was also a way of rendering processes of resale and speculation pointless, in this case even for individuals, and controls easier.

Thus we can also see why it was the same magistrates, the *sitophulakes*, who supervised the system of grains sales from start to finish, in order to keep the price of the product from rising between the point of unloading and the point of sale. The retailer's profit margin was tolerated, but a maximum profit was set by the city.[52] Beyond the case of Athens, we therefore understand why a series of decrees by other cities thanked importers for allowing themselves to be persuaded by local magistrates to sell at a price lower than the prevailing one. It was the responsibility of these magistrates to register the price of products at the time that they were unloaded. Lysias's speech *Against the grain dealers* (22.8), which dates from 386 BCE, proves that Athenian buyers could negotiate prices with importers. The prosecutor (who was a member of the council) reminds the court that at the magistrates' suggestion, the Athenian grain merchants (*sitopōlai*) had decided to form a buying cartel against the importers. More broadly, however, the price negotiations were conducted in the presence of the magistrates, who could influence them.

Another important regulation that prevailed at the Athens *emporion* was the constraint put on those who made maritime loans. An Athenian law, which is known to us by three different sources but especially by a legal speech (Pseudo-Demosthenes' *Against Lacritus* 35.50–51), strictly regulated these loans.[53] In this case, the litigant had made a loan to merchants from Phaselis, represented here by Lakritos, the brother of the borrower and his heir. The loan was for a round-trip voyage to Pontos, and even if the contract does not expressly say so, the ship must have been supposed to take on a load of grain there. But the intended cargo never arrived in Piraeus, and suspicion could have fallen on the moneylender, who thus had to plead his good faith before the Athenian tribunal:

> It is not only in these matters, judges, that I have been injured by this Lakritos. In addition to being robbed of my money, I could have been, as a result of his actions, thrown into the greatest danger, had I not had the written contract made with these people, which shows that I provided them money for a voyage to Pontos and back to Athens. You know, judges, how severe the law is, if an Athenian transports grain elsewhere than to Athens or loans money for a voyage to a port [emporion] other than that of Athens, how heavy and hard the penalties are in that case. But read them the law, so that they might be informed about it more precisely. —Law— "It is illegal for any Athenian or metic residing in Athens, or for those of whom they are the masters, to loan money for a ship whose purpose is not to import to Athens grain or the other products specifically mentioned. Anyone who lends in contravention of these measures will be indicted before the overseers of the port [epimelētai emporiou], in accord with the same measures as those relating to the ship and to the grain, and will not be able to file suit to regain the money lent for a voyage that does not have Athens as its destination, and in this case let no magistrate prepare a case for trial.

Thus Athenian law made it illegal in Athens, on pain of death, to loan money for shipping certain goods, and first of all grain, to a destination other than Athens. We have every reason to think that these goods also included oil, other basic food products, and probably further merchandise that might be considered strategic, such as metals, canvas, and rigging. It is clear that what was involved here was a supply system whose purpose was to serve the interests of a community. The city was a full economic agent, not external to mercantile operations, but also an actor, framing the rules of trade to its benefit. Just as a city reserved to itself the use of its land, forbidding foreigners to buy real estate on its territory, so it reserved the use of its capital for its own benefit.

Thus in Thasos it was forbidden for "Thasian ships to import foreign wine into the waters between Athos and Pacheia," a vast area of the northern Aegean.[54] The main goal of this prohibition was apparently to protect Thasian wine from imports of wine from other sources. The penalties imposed on importers who violated this prohibition were the same as those imposed on those who, by outright fraud, watered the wine they sold. We can legitimately assume that it was a question of guaranteeing potential customers that they were buying authentic Thasian wine, that is, high-quality wine. The period when this law was enacted (probably late fifth century BCE) was also close to that when Thasos began to put a stamp on its amphoras (ca. 390 BCE), which might have reflected a desire to authenticate them as being of Thasian origin.[55] One may wonder whether, by forbidding "Thasian ships" to import foreign wine, the law did not open an opportunity for foreign merchants, but nothing indicates that foreign ships had an "importation right" for foreign wine. In fact, recent research has proved the existence of imports of foreign amphoras to Thasos (even if the large majority of them are clearly from the Hellenistic period).[56] This raises the question of the duration of the period during which the law was in effect. Moreover, if we examine the Thasian law from another point of view, we see that it also forced the island's merchants to limit their activity to exporting local wine and importing other products such as grain. The law thus strongly directed these merchants' activity.

COMMERCIAL COURTS

The City-States' Principles of Justice

Transactions often end up in court, and good institutions guarantee fair justice, something that is all the more difficult in international matters because the parties to the dispute commonly belong to various and geographically distant communities that sometimes have no particular affinity. That was the meaning of Isocrates' remarks cited earlier: the city had to see to it that litigation regarding transactions could be resolved in the courts. It seems, however, that not all Greek cities were able to provide economic and juridical security for transactions. Heracleides' depiction of the judicial system in Thebes in Boiotia in the third century is not very edifying. This city looks more like a thieves' lair than a city that cares about justice:[57]

> The Thebans are insolent, violent, and arrogant. They behave with violence indiscriminately towards foreigners and their fellow citizens, and they pay no attention to justice. In conflicts relating to contractual commitments [*sunallagmata*], they do not use verbal arguments but violence, resorting to insults and blows, and thus bring into the judicial arena the violent behavior with regard to each other that is that of athletes in gymnastic competitions. That is why among them it takes at least thirty years to arrive at a judgment. Anyone who refers to this situation before the people and does not immediately leave Boiotia but remains there a short time, is waylaid at night by those who do not want the trial to take place, and is killed. In fact, among them, murder is committed on the first pretext that comes along.

Like the Lestrygonians in the *Odyssey*, the Boiotians did not receive foreigners well. Their courts dragged out trials regarding business matters, and those who were summoned to appear before the courts did not hesitate to resort to violence, even going so far as to physically eliminate their adversaries in order to make sure that the trial would not take place. The picture is all the less reassuring because Polybius (20.6.1) provides a similar portrait of the Boiotian system of justice at the beginning of the second century. He describes a complete interruption of trials that lasted a quarter of a century, the magistrates themselves always finding a pretext to prevent them from proceeding. There might well be some literary exaggeration in the description (although it is hard to believe that the account is a pure fiction).[58] But even if this were pure invention, it would reveal what was considered as an abnormal situation in terms of law and justice.

The older form of international law in the world of the city-states consisted in exercising a right to reprisals (*sulān*).[59] The principle was simple: if someone considered himself to have been harmed by a foreigner whom he could not or could no longer reach because the latter had left the city's territory, he could hold each of the offender's fellow citizens responsible for the harm he had suffered. From the end of the Archaic period at least, in the world of the city-states one could no longer exercise this right on one's own initiative. It had to be officially recognized by one's own city. Then it became legitimate to seize any of the goods being transported on behalf of the adverse city-state. This procedure, which went back to the Homeric age, was still in use in the Classical and Hellenistic periods. We can see its importance in the contract involved in *Against Lacritus*, where it is explicitly provided that the ship leaving Athens for a round-trip voyage to Pontos was not to stop in a port where a right of reprisal against the Athenians was likely to be exercised. Also in the fourth century, the city of Cyrene had to compensate a number of individuals belonging to cities in the northern Peloponnese, along with Athens, Delphi and Melos, for the rights of reprisals that these cities were entitled to exercise. In order to do so, it paid out considerable sums, amounting to 159 talents in all. We might wonder how it happened that Cyrene ended up in this situation. Was it a matter of paying back loans made for political reasons?[60] The map of the cities that were compensated corresponds largely to that of the Peloponnesian cities that imported grain (Athens and the northern Peloponnese), as we know from the "cereal stele" of the early 320 BCE.[61] Besides one of the persons compensated by the city of Cyrene was a "drug merchant"—could he have been involved in transactions with Cyrene to buy *silphion*?[62] That is merely a supposition, not a certainty. In any case, the episode illustrates the Cyreneans' desire to free their trade routes from this sword of Damocles that would otherwise have continued to hang over them.

One of the basic questions of international trade was its mode of financial payment. Should one depend on the civil authorities to guarantee payments? According to the treaty between the two Cretan cities of Lato and Olous, "in Olous, a Latian dealing with an Olountian must buy, sell, borrow and transact every other kind of business by way of the register of debts, in conformity with the laws in force in the two cities, and an Olountian dealing with a Latian in Lato must do the same."[63] This text offers the best parallel to the famous treaties regulating trade between Rome and Carthage. According to Polybius, three treaties had been made, one in 508/7 BCE (according to the traditional chronology), that is, the first year of the Republic; the second probably in 348; and the third on the occasion of the war against Pyrrhos in 279.[64] It provided in particular that in Carthage mutual trade would take place through the intermediary of a herald. The first treaty stipulated that:[65]

> Concerning those who come to carry on commerce, let no transaction be made in the absence of a herald or a secretary. Concerning merchandise that has been purchased in the presence of the latter, let the public guarantee be applied for the seller for what is bought in Libya and Sardinia. If a Roman goes into the part of Sicily governed by the Carthaginians, let all relations with the Roman be on the basis of equality.

The public guarantee (in Latin, *fides publica*) was given to commercial partners. We have to assume that the herald kept a record of the operations. If there was a conflict between the parties, his archives might allow him to attest to the good faith of one of the two parties. Thus it was a question of providing a legal guarantee for international trade, but also of providing the legal stability this trade required. Thus we cannot contrast a Greek legal practice to a Roman one, since some Greek cities, like those of Crete mentioned earlier, were able to set up procedures that were both juridical and commercial and entirely similar to the one that is illustrated in the western Mediterranean by the treaty between Rome and Carthage. The difference between them has probably to do chiefly with the great development of silver currency, which, along with the flexibility it provided, also early on encouraged Greek cities to explore other ways of providing legal guarantees for trade.[66]

A more elaborate form of law was that of judicial agreements (*sumbolai, sumbola*). These had as their goal to safeguard individual rights in the other city.[67] Having diverse forms and modalities, their primary goal was often to shelter their beneficiaries from the exercise of the right of reprisal. Among other things, they might also regulate the way trials were to take place in the case of a legal conflict. One of the oldest that has come down to us is the agreement between Athens and Phaselis in the fifth century, and which is known to us through an inscription found in Athens:[68]

> It pleased the council and the people: the Akamantis tribe exercised the prytany; [—]nasippos was secretary, Neo[k—]ledes was *epistatēs*, Leon proposed: that the decree for the Phaselitans be recorded [in the archives]; if a contract is made [in Athens], the trials take place in Athens before the polemarch, as for the Chiotes, and nowhere else; so far as concerns other trials that take place by virtue of the agreements made with the Phaselitans, the trials are conducted in line with the agreements made with the Phaselitans; — if another magistrate agrees to commence legal proceedings against a Phaselitan, if the latter is convicted, let the conviction be without legal value; if someone contravenes the provisions of this decree, let him pay ten thousand drachms to the treasury of Athena; let the secretary of the council

transcribe this decree on a stone stele and have it placed on the acropolis at the expense of the Phaselitans.

Even if its interpretation still raises several questions, the agreement between Athens and Phaselis is a good example of the judicial agreement between cities. First, it should be emphasized that this document does not constitute the principal text of the agreement. Clearly, the allusion to agreements already made between Athens and Phaselis shows that this was only a supplement, but one that made additions that were certainly very important, at least in the view of one of the contracting parties.[69] The two partners to the agreement were not second-rate cities. In the Classical period, Athens was obviously the greatest market in the Mediterranean world, the one that attracted all the merchants who wanted to sell a large cargo rapidly and at a good price. Like Aigina, Phaselis was one of the cities in which commerce was a vital activity. It lived off international trade. From the first half of the sixth century on, Phaselis was a first-rate commercial city, since it was one of the founding cities of the Hellenion of Naukratis in Egypt.[70] During the Classical period and the Hellenistic period, Phaselitan merchants were present in all the markets and carried out commercial operations far away from their city. They were very active in the Athens marketplace during the Classical period, and in Rhodes during the Hellenistic period. The context was that of the Athenian empire, and it was long thought that the clauses of this agreement corresponded in some way or another to a form of legal imperialism on the part of Athens. In reality, nothing allows us to maintain this point of view. On the other hand, it is clear that the advantages granted the Phaselitans by Athens offered them an excellent compensation for the loss of their Eastern Mediterranean markets. Until the Eurymedon campaign, Phaselis was the only Greek city that remained loyal to Persia. The Eurymedon campaign forced it to join the Athenian empire, and Phaselis's Chiot friends had played a key role in this change in alliance. Thus the Phaselitans had to be compensated for the cost of switching side and entering the Athenian empire.[71] An initial judicial agreement, whose details are unknown to us, had been previously made. This agreement was elaborated by another document, which is the one we have.

The key point is that trials relating to a contract made in Athens were prepared in Athens by the polemarch. It seems that disputes involving foreigners were usually judged by port magistrates such as the *nautodikai*, "judges of maritime affairs," whose competence remained in fact very ill-defined, or by the *epimelētai* of the *emporion*.[72] In that case, everything depended on the decision of a single magistrate. The case against the other party was not prepared, and the risk of partiality was high. On the other hand, access to the city's tribunal made possible a genuine preliminary inquiry of the case and guaranteed a judgment made by a large number of jurors who were in theory impartial (because they could not receive bribes). In Athens, the polemarch was responsible for preparing for trial cases concerning metics or resident aliens. When people from Chios (and then also to Phaselitans) were granted access to the polemarch, they were also granted access to the city's tribunal, as if they were metics. However, we see that this clause did not hold for all Phaselitans but only for contracts made in Athens and involving at least one Phaselitan. Thus it was clearly an agreement with economic significance that was well adapted to the commercial role the Phaselitans played. The agreement was not bilateral, even formally: no provision was made for Athenian merchants who might be "temporarily in Phaselis." The point was clearly to facilitate Phaselitans' business dealings in Athens. Moreover, it was also the Athenians' interest rightly understood, since through their energy and activity the Phaselitans made a major contribution to the life of the *emporion* and, more broadly, to supplying the city with food. A guarantee against arbitrary power was granted to Phaselitans because no magistrate other than the polemarch was to launch a procedure relating to a contract made in Athens.[73]

Legal agreements between cities are usually general in character, but questions relating to litigation of a commercial and financial order easily find their place there among other clauses. This is the case for the agreement made during the last decades of the fourth century between Miletos and the city of Olbia, on the Black Sea.[74] It is situated in the specific context of the traditional relations between the two cities: Miletos was in fact Olbia's mother city (*mētropolis*). This was a veritable treaty of "equal citizenship" (*isopoliteia*): a citizen of Olbia who took up residence in Miletos could immediately become a citizen of Miletos and vice versa. A person who wanted only to live temporarily in the other city nonetheless benefited from a tax exemption (*ateleia*), which should probably be understood as the usual tax exemption enjoyed by the citizen in his city (that is, an exemption on goods for his personal use).[75] But in ll. 14–17, the law also provided that "if a Milesian holds a contract [*sumbolaion*] made in Olbia, within a period of five days he shall have access, as plaintiff and as defendant, to the people's tribunal." We see that the crucial point is where the contract is made, which determines whether or not a complaint is acceptable.

It is true that in the agreement between Olbia and Miletos, as in the agreement between Athens and Phaselis, the word *sumbolaion* is usually translated as "business dispute," which seems capable of leading to the opening of a judicial procedure. Even if this meaning is sometimes attested, the more common and ordinary meaning is "contract." In addition, Attic legal speeches show very clearly that the formula *sumbolaion gignetai* refers to the making of a contract.[76] The law of the city-states did not take as its foundation the common observation of a factual situation, as if the trial necessarily took place where the alleged "legal conflict" broke out. Quite the contrary, the primary criterion that might enable a trial was the place "where the contract was made." Here we have a fundamental principle of the law of the Greek city-states, and even of Roman law: the trial took place not "where the conflict occurred" but "where the contract was made" (*actio sequitur forum contractus*, and not *actio sequitur forum rei*).[77] Thus a *sumbolaion Athēnēsi* is a contract made in Athens, which had to be judged in Athens. As a general rule, it was only at the place where a contract had been made that the magistrates could receive a complaint.

Thus in Isocrates' *Trapeziticus* (17.52), Satyros, the dynast of the kingdom of Bosporos, refuses to render a judgment regarding the acceptability of the complaint concerning a contract because the contract was made in Athens.[78] In the Demosthenic speech *Against Zenothemis* (32.9) the magistrates of Kephallenia refuse to take up a complaint because, coming from Syracuse, the ship was in fact making a round-trip voyage to Athens. When Dionysius of Halicarnassus mentions that Rome had made an agreement with the Latins providing for the trial to take place among the people where *to sumbolaion ginētai*, we must interpret this as meaning among the people "where the contract was made."[79] Moreover, there is nothing surprising about this: to decide between the parties, the judges had to base themselves on a legal foundation, and this was provided by the contract. From the Archaic period down to the end of the Classical period, the value of the contract, whatever form it took (written or oral), was guaranteed by the witnesses who could attest to its validity: thus in the Gortyn code, around 450 BCE, regarding a contract for exportation, the judges made their decision on the basis of the testimony of the witnesses, whose number varied depending on the importance of the case.[80] Later, and in Athens definitely, a written contract (*sungraphē*) was de rigueur for loans of a certain amount and even required for maritime trade, even though its validity could still be guaranteed only by witnesses.[81]

In the Hellenistic period, the development of the system of public archives of the kind that we see functioning on Paros certainly increased the value of the written contract.[82] But in every case, it was necessary and indispensable to have the elements of the contract in order to have a basis for judgment. The right to open judicial proceedings at the place where the contract had been made was thus a dominant principle of international law as it had gradually been established since the Archaic period, and as in any case we see it functioning in the clearest way in the Classical period and at the beginning of the Hellenistic period.[83]

Trials Concerning Large-Scale Trade

However, at least in Athens, another principle could lead to beginning a judicial procedure in the framework of "commercial suits" (*dikai emporikai*), which as their name shows in the Greek concerned only large-scale trade.[84] This new category of trials seems to have been officially established starting in the middle of the fourth century. Several sources refer to an Athenian system of "commercial suits." Aristotle, in his *Constitution of Athens* (59.5) alludes to this only briefly. But Pseudo-Demosthenes' speech *Against Zenothemis* (32.1) points out that "the law allows suits to be brought by shipowners and traders involving contracts [*sumbolaia*] for large-scale trade made in or for the market in Athens and suits that have the form of a written contract [*sungraphē*]." This passage alone has already led to a debate. Should it be interpreted as distinguishing two categories of suits that fall under this procedure, or as referring to two conditions that have to be fulfilled in order for the suit to be included among "trials concerning large-scale trade"? In fact, it rapidly becomes clear that if any written contract could provide grounds for a trial of this kind, then virtually all trials concerning business, including the humblest and those that had nothing to do with large-scale trade, would fall into this category, and thus the specificity and interest of this procedure would completely disappear.[85] Hence only the second interpretation is acceptable.

Pseudo-Demosthenes' *Against Apaturius* (33.23) also explains that "traders can file suit monthly from [the month of] Boedromion to [the month of] Mounichion, so that they can obtain justice without delay and go back to sea." In other words, commercial trials had to take place during the winter, more or less between September and April. However, following the argument made by the great Italian jurist Ugo Enrico Paoli, scholars have generally adopted the inverse thesis, assuming that summer was the season most propitious for this kind of trial, insofar as it was the season when traders were able to travel, and also the one in which they might need their cases to be immediately decided.[86] But as Edward E. Cohen has shown, this thesis does violence to Demosthenes' text and is also not very realistic:[87] it was after the sailing season, when in theory all the ships (or most of them) were in port, that the year's activity could be assessed. Thus, for example, how could the suit filed against Lakritos have been filed during the summer, when the maritime contract provided that the voyage could take place as late as the autumn?[88] In the summer, sailors and merchants were busy at sea. It was in the winter that they had time for possible trials and that the whole community of merchants, citizens, and metics, like the defendants in *Against Lacritus*, would have gathered in the ports. Thus we have to stick to Demosthenes' text and not question the principle that "trials concerning large-scale trade" took place in the winter.

Finally, there is a third text, that of the lexicographer Pollux (8.101), which emphasizes another specific trait of these trials that was already mentioned in the previously cited passage in *Against Apaturius*: legal suits concerning trade are monthly [*emmēnoi*]. There has been a debate about this point as well, between those who think that trials began monthly and those who think that this clause means that such cases had to be resolved within one month. A literal reading of these texts forces us to conclude that such trials began each month. However, the suggestion that the system allowed cases to be rapidly resolved suggests that the monthly beginning of trials had another advantage; otherwise trials would have been able drag on. If a new cycle of trials began each month, we can presume that the preceding series was concluded, so that the clause providing for the monthly beginning of trials can also quite plausibly be seen as implying that judgments had to be rendered within one month.[89]

The novelty of these "commercial suits" was that they provided the same legal recourse (that is, the privilege of having access to the city's law courts) to foreign traders, whether resident or nonresident, as was enjoyed by Athenian citizens, whether or not their cities had a specific agreement with Athens. In other words, in the very precise area of maritime commerce and in view of the constraints, the privileges of citizenship were erased in favor of a legal conception that, in the framework of well-defined limits, took into account only the kind of activity and not the status of the individuals involved. The *dikai emporikai* thus did not eliminate the interest of agreements, including bilateral judicial agreements between cities, simply because the scope of such agreements went far beyond commercial litigation alone. Under the conditions concerned—namely, those of the written contract and specific clauses to which we will return—whatever one's nationality or residence, one could obtain quick and impartial justice in the Athenian courts.

There remains, however, the first and foremost condition for access to commercial legal suits: the contract had to have been made in Athens—that was the commonly accepted clause—or for shipment to Athens. Therein consisted, perhaps, the novelty of the system of the *dikai emporikai*, even if it only made old practices official. Even if a contract had been made elsewhere than Athens, it was still possible to bring suit provided that the commercial contract specifically designated the city as the destination of the voyage. We see that by making it possible to file suits of this kind, Athens opened a door for litigation, since the site of the trial was no longer defined ipso facto by the place where the contract was made but might also be defined concurrently in two different cities. If Athens acted in this way, it was because it knew it could do so. Traders (or lenders) involved in a commercial voyage whose destination was Athens might wish to have the convenience of finding a court there, and it was also in Athens that possible seizures of the cargo could be carried out. In addition and above all, Athens's position in the fourth century as a hub for international commerce made it in any case unavoidable. Finally, the good reputation of its courts and of its currency must have inspired confidence and made possible the application of a principle that might seem to infringe upon the traditional sovereignty of the city-states.[90]

Thus it is not to yield to the sirens of evolutionism or to a kind of "institutionalist fatalism" to conclude that over time, the institutions of international trade were shaped to take into account the mutual interests of various parties. As a result, outside the city-state one was not in a jungle but in a universe in which common legal principles were recognized and accepted. However, one of the peculiarities of the system was still that the new rules ("commercial suits") did not eliminate the old ones (international agreements, suits on the basis of the place where the contract was made). If this was the case, it was simply because a world like that of the world of the city-states including more than one thousand partners during the Classical period, and even more in the Hellenistic period, could not operate in unison and be everywhere governed by the same laws.[91] Some city-states were more economically advanced than others. There were also traditional affinities between certain cities, and rivalries that were just as traditional set some cities against each other. The play of interests might also vary. But this complex legal universe also had common legal principles, which explains why such intense commercial trading was able to develop in the world of the Greek city-states. The apocalyptic picture that Heracleides and Polybius give of the judicial system in Boiotia, even it was somewhat exaggerated, is meaningful only because it was the exception, not the rule.

The city-states did not remain passive when confronted by price variations. Naturally, it was first of all the prices of imported products that had to be monitored, because excessive increases were likely to lead to serious social problems. The city-state was a state of a particular type. The collectivity was both subject and object, and the citizens themselves were sovereign in it.[92] Thus it is not surprising that just as they were interested in the sale of their products abroad, or saw to it that a competing city-state did not develop on their doorstep, they paid special attention to the prices they paid for the basic commodities.[93]

The Policy of Price Control

As observed earlier, climatic and political instability were the rule in the world of the Greek city-states. Thus it might happen that in a given year, the grain or oil harvest that was being counted upon fell far short. Or this calamity might befall its usual trading partner. Or both cities could both be struck by shortages at the same time, for reasons that were completely independent of each other. The direct economic consequence of such events was the risk of chaotic changes in prices: very low in a year in which everything went well for everyone, and unbearably high the following year if everything went badly. The leaders of the city-states sought to limit these erratic fluctuations. In the *emporion*, the city's magistrates might intervene, like those in Ephesos around 300 BCE, to persuade foreign merchants to sell at a lower price:

> It has pleased the council and the people. Dion, son of Diopeithes, has proposed that: whereas Agathokles, son of Hagemon, a Rhodian, while he was importing into our city fourteen thousand *hektai* of wheat and found grain being sold in the agora at more than six drachms, was convinced by the *agoranomos* to do our people a favor by selling all his grain at a price lower than that at which grain was being sold in the agora, may it please the council and the people to grant equal and full citizenship to Agathokles and to his descendants; let the *essēnes* [priests of Artemis] place him by lot in a tribe and a *chiliastys* ["group of one thousand," that is, subdivision of a tribe], and let the *neōpoiai* ["temple builders," that is, temple administrators] register [these privileges] for him in the sanctuary of Artemis, where they inscribe other titles of citizenship, so that everyone will know that the people takes care to thank those who grant it benefits. Drawn by lot are the tribe Bembine, the *chiliastys* Aigoteus.

It can be observed that the city did not hesitate to grant major privileges to a foreign merchant who agreed to lower his prices in this way. Here, the city of Ephesos grants him the highest possible reward, since he receives Ephesian citizenship. The importance of the privilege was proportionate to the gift made by Agathokles, who imported 14,000 *hektai* of wheat, the equivalent of 2,330 *medimnoi*, or the cargo of a ship of average tonnage (if we accept a standard of around 3,000 talents).[94] If, as is likely, Agathokles did not come to reside in Ephesos, the privilege would have remained purely honorific.

On the other hand, we can assume that henceforth, as an Ephesian citizen, Agathokles would benefit from the privilege of personal tax exemption that accompanied citizenship.[95] In any case, these advantages were among the series of honorific privileges that Xenophon proposed to grant foreign merchants; a place of honor in the theater, invitation by the city, and other marks of honor.[96] An important point is that the grain sold was intended for the "people," and was sold at a price lower than that of the agora. There is thus a good chance that this grain was sold directly at wholesale price to the citizens of Ephesos, in a system that shortened the sale process by bypassing the retailers.[97] It remains that by agreeing to sell his grain below the price that had been established at the agora of Ephesos, and especially by importing such a large quantity of it, Agathokles put pressure on prices and forced a decrease in the price in the agora as well.

This system in which the magistrates intervened to lower prices was very common, and decrees from many other cities testify to this. First, it is clear that in a city-state, at a given moment, there was no price anarchy, in the sense that there would have existed several different price sets, disconnected one from another. Far from it, market mechanisms as well as interventions of the cities concurred to establish one basic price for commodities at a given time. This of course did not exclude the existence of a basic difference between wholesale and retail prices as well as between prices of goods reserved to citizens and prices on the free market; of slight differences for retail prices; and of price variations over time. It remains clear that there existed a common knowledge on the order of prices of various commodities. In a dialogue in Aristophanes' *Acharnians* (v. 758–59) that despite its humorous character has tragic undertones, Dikaiopolis asks the Megarian about the price of grain in his city: "Anyway, what's new in Megara? How is the price of grain?" The Megarian replies: "Among us it is held in very high esteem, as high as the gods." Naturally, this is a play on words that means that prices are extremely high, as a result of the blockade put into effect by the Athenians. In Athens, as already observed, we have a series of literary and epigraphic documents that show that the institutionalization of prices went so far as the establishment of an "official price" (*kathestēkuia timē*; this price was the standard market price).[98] This price was not fixed. A fixed price would have made no sense since ultimately it was the law of supply and demand that determined price levels. But the role of the magistrates was to see to it that the price remained moderate, by persuading importers (especially large-scale importers) to sell at a price below the market price in order to allow a decrease of the "official price," which served as a standard for purchases in general. Fundamentally, the goal was to avoid extreme fluctuations in prices that led to fear and turmoil. Increases and decreases were therefore supposed to take place in gradual stages. Above all, in Athens, as in Ephesos and elsewhere, the goal of the magistrates' interventions was to take the place of purchases by wholesalers who, because they were competing with one another, would end up buying grain at a higher price. In Athens, in 386 BCE, grain wholesalers defended themselves against the accusation of selling at artificially inflated prices, stressing that they had formed a cartel in their transactions with importers as a way of getting lower prices, a method the magistrate and politician Anytos had advised them to use.[99] By substituting themselves for individual buyers in the negotiation with importers to establish a standard price, the magistrates drove prices down: in economic terms, a market in which there is only one buyer is called a monopsony. A monopsony undoubtedly makes it possible to lower prices, but has the disadvantage of decreasing the total quantity of what is exchanged.[100]

City-states thus sought to intervene to control commodity prices. If necessary, they might enact a law allowing intervention for this purpose. That occurred in Delos in the second half of the third century. There we find the best illustration of how a city might react to price increases. In this case, the increase concerned the prices of wood and charcoal. During the second half of the third century there was an accelerated increase in the prices of these commodities, as we can see on a graph of the development of prices in Delos at that period (figures 12.1 and 12.2).

Some scholars have supposed that unlike medieval cities that kept records of price trends, ancient cities were incapable of forming an idea of changes in the prices of products for sale on their markets.[101] However, we know that on the contrary, most cities, at least during the Hellenistic period, carefully maintained their

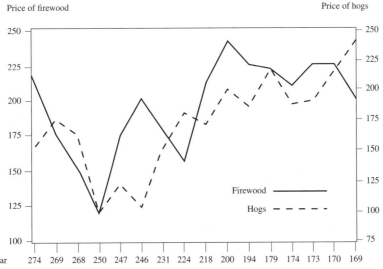

FIGURE 12.1. Indexed prices of wood and pigs in Delos, 274–169 BCE (from Reger 1994, fig. 5.4, p. 179).

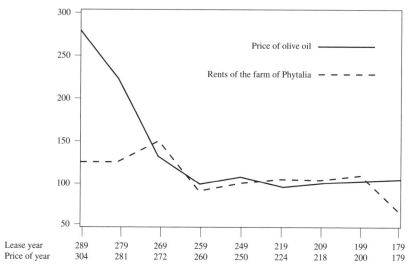

| Lease year | 289 | 279 | 269 | 259 | 249 | 219 | 209 | 199 | 179 |
| Price of year | 304 | 281 | 272 | 260 | 250 | 224 | 218 | 200 | 179 |

FIGURE 12.2. Prices of olive oil and of the rents of the farm of Phytalia, 290–179 BCE (from Reger 1994, fig. 6.7, p. 208).

archives and thus had basic information on this subject. In addition, in a city like Delos, the general interest (represented in this case by the interest of the sanctuary of Apollo, which was a large buyer) coincided with the individual interest. We have seen that prices for wood and charcoal were high.[102] These were indispensable commodities for cooking (including the preparation of sacrificial meat), and marginally for heating houses. But we must not forget that there was a significant artisanal activity on the island, which also required fuel, and especially charcoal for metallurgy. Pliny emphasizes that the bronzes from Delos were famous, which without any doubt reflects the Delian craftsmen's reputation for producing luxury furniture, with a specialty in bed- and couch-making.[103] Thus statuettes, vases, and even statues must have been produced on the island, and might easily find buyers among the local or transitory clientele. In a house in the theater area of the ancient city, bronze scoria have been excavated.[104] Farms in the countryside (on Delos or Rheneia) also needed fuel, as did a few producers of ceramics.[105] The production of perfumes made use of heating processes as well.[106] Above all, outside the theater area, a house in the Stadium area has a long furnace with four interconnected hearths and a opening making it possible to control the draft. It has been suggested that this was associated with a workshop where "dyestuffs" were boiled or (a less probable hypothesis) with a popular restaurant.[107] Whatever this particular setup was, the craft of making purple and other dyestuffs required energy.[108]

Of course, the peak of this activity was reached after 166 BCE. Moreover, it would be desirable to be able to more accurately date the archaeological remains of craft activity. But we must not neglect the possibility that workshops devoted to the same activities might have succeeded each other on the same site. However that may be, as early as the second half of the third century we see a clear increase in Delian activity that justifies the tension regarding the prices of wood and charcoal, like that we see regarding hog prices. The development of wood and charcoal prices contrasts with that of grain and oil prices, which tended to remain stable after a sharp drop at the beginning of the third century.[109]

It was certainly in order to cope with this rise in prices that the Delians decided to enact a specific law concerning trade in wood and charcoal. The text of the law is not dated, but various criteria allow independent dating between ca. 275–225, and rather in the earlier part of the interval. In any case the inscription corresponds to a period when in contrast with oil and grain prices for the products involved rose sharply. This increase in prices is well known in all its aspects and provides excellent testimony to the possible reaction of a Greek city-state when faced with a specific crisis. Of course, the law aimed at curbing the price increase:[110]

(1) The charcoal, logs, and wood that are sold measured by the weights for the wood—it is forbidden to sell them if they have been bought in Delos. (2) It is also forbidden to sell any of this merchandise after having bought them when they were on board a ship and after having made the [import] declaration in one's name. (3) It is forbidden to sell, after having been declared the purchaser [without immediately taking it away], merchandise sold at public auction, as well as wood, logs, and charcoal for a third party. (4) Let only importers in person be allowed to sell and let them not be allowed to sell at a price either above the one that they have declared in writing to the one-fiftieth tax collectors, or below it. (5) Let importers also make a written declaration to the *agoranomoi*, before the sale, of the same price that they have declared to the collectors of the one-fiftieth tax.

Anyone who sells without respecting these prescriptions shall be subject to a fine of fifty drachms, and every citizen shall have the right to accuse him before the *agoranomoi*. Let the *agoranomoi* refer these accusations to the Thirty-one within the month during which they were made. Let the accuser deposit the salary of the tribunal. If the accused is found guilty, let him pay the salary back to the accuser and pay him two-thirds of the prescribed fine, and the last third to the public treasury, and let the *agoranomoi* make him pay it within ten days following the judgment, without being liable to suit on this account. If they are unable to do this, let them excuse themselves on oath and deliver the accused and his goods to the accuser, and after they have inscribed the decision on the tablet on which they inscribe other writings, let them transmit [the sentence] to the council in the public archives.

(6) Let the beneficiaries of an exemption from customs duties [*ateleis*] who import wood, logs, or charcoal, merchandise that is sold measured by the weight for the wood, make, before the sale, a declaration to the *agoranomoi* of the price at which they will sell, and let it not be allowed to sell at a

price higher or lower than the one they have declared. If certain individuals do not act in conformity with these prescriptions, the *agoranomoi* shall not deliver to them either the scales or the measures for charcoal, and, let them pay to the city, as a fee for renting the space where they have unloaded their wood, logs, and charcoal, one drachm per day until they have removed their merchandise, and let the *agoranomoi* make them pay without being liable to suit on this account.

The underlying causes of this rise in the price of wood and charcoal were probably connected with the "overheating" of the local economy in a regional environment that did not respond quickly enough, or at all, to the increase in demand on Delos and in fact in the whole region (if we think of the boom of the cities of the Eastern Aegean in this period).[111] The Delians had typically no means of intervening in the production of wood and charcoal, since these products were entirely imported. On the other hand, they could intervene in matters that were under their control, namely commercial circuits. In principle, the goal of the Delian law, like that of the Athenian grain laws, was to shorten commercial circuits. It prohibited sale through intermediaries, and thus profits made by the latter, which could only increase the final price. To eliminate any possibility of getting around this law, it prohibited re-sales from local wholesalers who bought the cargoes while they were still on the ship, before they were unloaded, which would have been a way of evading the law (this is the meaning of clause 2, which has long been disputed).[112]

The table of monthly variations in the price of wood between 272 or 271 and 170 BCE shows that in some years, the price might be relatively stable, as in 179 (the price remained stable for ten months) or undergo frequent increases or decreases, as in 250 (when it remained stable for only two months in a row).[113] The price variations might be modest (on the order of 2 percent) or very large (as much as 38 percent). When the rise exceeded 20 or 30 percent, it might be tempting to make profits on stockpiles. It was this maneuver that the law explicitly prohibited, just as it also prohibited reselling even merchandise sold at auction.

The law also called for two declarations of prices, first to the customs officials (*pentēkostologoi*) and again to the *agoranomoi* in the agora when the merchandise was sold (in the case of products that would not be re-exported). If the two declarations were not identical, a fine was levied. What seems curious about this is that the second declared price not only could not be higher than the first but also could not be lower. The fundamental concern was not fiscal: if the second declared price had been lower than the first, the city would have received less tax, of course, but all the buyers, including the sanctuary and the city, would have benefited because the decrease in the final sale price would have amply compensated for the lost taxes. Instead, the law's goal was to prevent speculative behavior, which would have been the case if the importer had first declared the highest possible price, and then lowered it for sales in the agora if the price he had declared proved to be too high. Finally, the law allowed of no exceptions, and even those who were exempted from taxes had to meet the same requirements as others or have their goods confiscated. We have seen that this category of the tax-exempt included not only privileged foreigners but also possibly the Delian citizens, which made it a sufficiently large category to deserve special attention.

The law displays a remarkable knowledge of market behaviors. It anticipates all kinds of speculative behavior and attempts to control price increases. It tries to prevent any form of speculation. Did it really make it possible to counter price increases? That is difficult to establish. In any case, the true reasons for price increases were external to Delos, and the city could thus intervene only on the margins. But the law nonetheless certainly made it possible to limit increases by suppressing speculative profits. It provides an excellent illustration of what was meant in antiquity by the quest for a "fair price."

Thus everything indicates that we are dealing with a general desire to control prices for wood and charcoal as well as for grain and oil. To remain in the island area near Delos, we could also mention Paros's decree for Killos, son of Demetrios, who, as an *agoranomos*, saw to it "that the people lives in prosperity and abundance, buying bread and flour at the best price and of the best quality."[114] Similar formulas are found, for example, in the decrees for the *agoranomoi* of Astypalaia.[115] A concern for low prices is also found in an inscription from Andros for the Athenian benefactor Antidotos.[116] There is thus no lack of examples in the Kyklades. On Delos itself, a city decree for a Byzantine merchant shows that the Delians also wanted to spend as little as possible for their grain.[117] That is why it is a priori hard to see why things would have been different in the case of charcoal and wood.

In passing, an expression used by Aristotle and the two decrees from Astypalaia show precisely in what state of mind a city might take steps of the kind we see in the Delian law on charcoal and wood. In this way we can also give a definition of what Aristotle understood by what is usually called "fair price." In the *Constitution of Athens* (51.3), he indicates that the task of the Athenian *sitophulakes* was to see to it "that grain be sold in an equitable manner [*dikaiōs*] in the agora," a formula similar to what we find in the two previously mentioned decrees form Astypalaia, where the *agoranomos* is thanked for having seen to the affairs of the agora in such a way that "the goods are sold there at the best price and in the most equitable manner" (*hōs euōnotata kai dikaiotata*). What then is a "fair price" established "in accord with justice"? The decrees show that the notion is distinct from that of "cheap" (and even from "normal price"), even if the two notions often go hand-in-hand: the fair price is a price that has been established without the seller having been able to make a speculative profit. An unjustified profit is one that corresponds not to a real action but to pure profit-taking without providing an additional service between the moment when the price is first registered and the moment of the actual sale to the final consumer. On the other hand, processing or especially transporting goods to a distant market completely justify profit. If the season is far advanced and thus dangerous, or if war is prevalent, it is normal that a merchant who takes the risk of going to sea should sell his products at a particularly high price:

even if consumers consider that price too high for their means, under those conditions the increase is still justified and will not be considered as "unfair." Andocides could claim that he took the risk of making a commercial voyage at a perilous time of year (which was also implicitly for him a way to justify the profits he had made in the shipping activity).[118] But increasing from one day to the next the prices of stockpiled goods was considered "unfair" or "unjust."

Grain Purchase Funds and the Regulation of Sales

It was logical for cities to try to protect themselves against fluctuations in supply, given the instability of the conditions affecting the latter. In all traditional societies, at least those that are heavily dependent on the products of their own territories, the cycle of annual price increases is a function of the date of the harvest. As a rule, prices fall after the harvest, and all the more if it was abundant. Then they slowly rise in the course of the year, but become critical during the "crossover" period before the arrival of the following harvest, because the previous year's stocks are exhausted. If the outlook for the next harvest is poor, prices rise sharply. Only cities that have an international grain market can partially avoid this strictly seasonal cycle. That was the case for Amsterdam in the early modern period. But it seems that it was also the case in Delos in the third century BCE, because it depended almost entirely on external trade networks in which prices were not subject solely to seasonal constraints.[119]

To cope with this chronic instability and the risks of an interruption in supply, states became direct actors in the market. But they might also intervene more indirectly by buying grain themselves. Thus a number of cities in medieval and early modern Europe maintained permanent public granaries. They bought grain on the market when prices were low and kept it in reserve in order to influence prices in the course of the year and to ensure that the city would be supplied during the crossover period, even if this economic system had disadvantages as well as advantages.[120] The situation was no different for the many ancient Greek cities that already made use of this system.

We have seen how in ancient Greece magistrates tried to directly influence prices on importation.[121] An inscription from Oropos dating from the early second century BCE records a purchase made directly by the city for later resale by the city itself.[122]

> Agathokles was a magistrate of the Boiotian confederation, Theokydes a priest of Amphiaraos, in the month of Homoloïos, decree of proxeny: Kittos son of Ariston proposed: whereas Dionysios son of Ariston and Heliodoros son of Mousaios show their devotion by bringing in grain at the request of the polemarchs and selling it to the city at a suitable price, so that the city might show that it offers such people appropriate thanks, let it please the council and the people that Dionysios son of Ariston, Tyrian, and He-

liodoros son of Mousiaos, Sidonian, be public hosts and benefactors of the city of Oropos, that they have the right to own lands and houses, enjoy equality in taxation and the certainty that their goods will not be seized, and be able to benefit from personal security on land and at sea, in peace time and in war time. . . .

Here we find the same system of putting pressure on merchants to get them to sell their cargo at the lowest price, but in this case, and in a similar system in the case of the Ephesian decree for the Rhodian Agathokles, the city is buying grain directly in order to build up a reserve for intervention in the market. A city might also be led to buy oil directly from foreign merchants: this can be seen in an inscription from Athens dating from the early second century BCE.[123] Oil was indispensable for activities in the gymnasium. But purchases of grain to build up reserves for intervention in the market must have been the most frequent.

In this way, although cities did not hesitate to intervene to control prices, they might also intervene directly in trade. In modes that were analogous (but not strictly identical) to those prevailing in medieval and early modern Europe, in ancient Greece there were public granaries filled with grain belonging to the city itself. In general, it does not seem that a portion of the harvests was requisitioned; this was done only in exceptional circumstances, as in the case of Klazomenai, or in extreme famines.[124] Cities ordinarily used a system that was more flexible and financially more advantageous, that of a fund (in cash) reserved for grain purchases, which, based on the Greek name for grain (*sitos*) was often called *sitōnikon* or *sitōnika*. The city entrusted public grain purchases to commissioners called "grain buyers" (*sitōnai*). For some cities, the goal was clearly to build up a safety reserve enabling them to intervene rapidly in the event of a sudden shortage, while for others the goal seems to have been to set up a system of ongoing regulation. It also seems that the tendency during the Hellenistic period was toward the generalization of permanent funds. In any case, we know of such funds almost everywhere in the Greek world, from the West—Thourioi in Italy and Tauromenion in Sicily—to the islands and Asia Minor—Delos, Samos, Teos and Lebedos, Miletos, Iasos—and, no less, in continental Greece itself—Delphi, Thespiai, or Koroneia, not to mention Athens, since the existence of such a purchasing fund is clearly proven by documents mentioning the existence of public grain purchases and the office of *sitōnēs*, or "grain buyer."[125]

From the end of the Classical period at least, Athens had a fund for managing grain prices. Demosthenes donated a talent "for the purchase of grain."[126] In 328/7 BCE, the wealthy merchant Herakleides of Salamis donated a talent of silver for the same purpose.[127] Also in the 320s, the Demosthenic speech *Against Phormio* (34.39) refers to a gift made by two other rich merchants, Chrysippos and his brother, a talent "for the purchase of grain in the name of the people," a clear indication that there was a fund intended to build up a grain reserve with grain bought in the Athens *emporion*. The office of *sitōnēs* is attested in Athens in the fourth century, since Demosthenes himself held this office in 338/7 BCE.[128] A series of sources from the early Hellenistic period confirms the existence at this time of a fund for grain purchases in Athens.[129] The office of *sitōnēs* did not in itself imply travel outside the city. The *sitōnai* could fill the public granary with grain bought on the local market if supplies were sufficient. Thus during the Hellenistic period the *sitōnai* of Delos, who were elected annually to manage a public grain reserve, did not have to travel abroad: they bought their grain in the Delos *emporion*.[130] On the other hand, if the situation became critical the *sitōnai* did not hesitate to try their luck on foreign markets.[131]

The management of these funds might vary: either the money was used for direct grain purchases, the income resulting from sales then being paid back into the fund, or it was loaned at interest, and then it was only the interest on the loans that was used to buy grain (this was, in theory, a way of preserving the capital). However, there had to be initial seed money. This could proceed from generous donors, as we have seen in Athens. It could also be given by a king, who might make a donation in cash or in kind (a certain quantity of grain, the income from its sale serving to constitute a purchasing fund): that was the case in Delphi, where Eumenes II of Pergamon made, at the Delphians' request, a gift of three and half talents for the city's grain fund, and in Delos, which received grain from the Numidian king Masinissa.[132] It might also proceed from the treasury of a sanctuary, as in Delos. It might involve a levy on the city's ordinary funds, as was the case in Teos-Lebedos, the new city that emerged from the forced synoecism imposed by Antigonos, which was authorized to levy 1,400 staters of gold (the equivalent of 28,000 silver drachms) for its grain purchase fund. It might also involve taking out a loan, in the classic form or in the form of a public subscription to be paid back.[133] Or a city might resort to the system of public subscription (in the form of a loan, as we have just seen, but also in the form of donations) which, through the efforts of a large number of donors, was able to obtain the same result.[134]

Finally, in order to obtain grain, some cities drew specific revenues from taxes in kind. This was the case in the island city of Samos in the third century, which we know made free distributions thanks to a one-twentieth tax collected on the continental territory of Anaia. In fact, these free distributions were coupled with a sophisticated financial system that also made it possible to draw income from this grain.[135] This was also the case in fourth-century Athens, which levied a one-twelfth tax in kind on its external island possessions, Imbros, Lemnos, and Skyros. The grain was then sold at a price set by the popular assembly.[136]

In this respect, the city of Thespiai in Boiotia offers a good example of the diversity of sources for financing a grain fund. Around 220–210 BCE, there was a system of two grain-purchase funds. The first, endowed by a royal donation, was managed by two *sitōnai* and a treasurer. The second was a religious fund also managed by two *sitōnai* and treasurer. Three *sitopōlai* or "grain sellers," assisted by a treasurer, were responsible for selling to the public the grain bought by the *sitōnai*.[137] In this case, it is noteworthy that the terms *sitōnēs*, "grain buyer," and *sitopōlēs*, "grain seller," corresponded exactly to their functions. In the early second century, it seems, a third fund was added (or replaced the earlier ones if their funds were exhausted?):[138] it was financed by public subscription, some subscribers paying fifty drachms, others one hundred drachms. In Delos, we can follow the development of the system over almost a century and a half, starting at the end of the fourth century BCE. We see that in the middle of the third century the sanctuary was able to make loans to the city for the purchase of grain. Later, there was an autonomous fund, distinct from the sanctuary's treasury and from the public treasury.[139]

The remaining question concerns these funds' ability to intervene in a significant manner in the people's food supply. A city like Delos had a richly endowed fund (about 55,000 drachms in 192 and 179 BCE) for a small population (probably around 1,200 citizens). According to Léopold Migeotte's calculations, if three-quarters of this sum was used to buy barley, 1,200 citizens could have been fed for three-quarters of the year.[140] That is a considerable proportion, even if we must not forget the citizens' families, slaves, and resident aliens. But Delos certainly represents a genuine exception. It was a center for grain redistribution and as such, except under truly extraordinary circumstances, was not in danger of shortages. The modest quantity of grain (500 *medimnoi*) sold at favorable price and at the city's request by the merchant Dionysios of Byzantion, around 250 BCE, does not reflect the situation of a city always on the brink of famine, but rather probably the Delians' desire, in this domain as in others, to make maximum use of the opportunities for profit that were made available to them.[141]

In most other cities, it seems that "public grain" (*sitos dēmosios*) could have served only to influence prices or to provide additional supplies, the great majority of the people's food supply remaining dependent on the private market. This should not lead us to underestimate the role of public granaries. Even if public grain probably never represented the majority of the food supply, it nevertheless played a crucial role in the life of populations. It brought immediate relief in times of sudden grain shortages or famines. This is why for most cities, maintaining a public granary must have been considered a first-rank priority. In any case, this grain was not distributed free of charge but sold. Since it was the city that set the sales price, we might have expected that to put pressure on prices it would in any case sell the grain at a price far below the rate on the open market. But—and this is a crucial point—the cost constraints that weighed on grain purchases meant that at best the city could sell at cost, or slightly below cost, the grain it had bought from merchants who frequented its port or that had been bought on foreign markets by agents sent abroad for that purpose. If the city had sold far below the cost price, it would have dried up the fund's revenues and compromised its future.

Then we must also imagine the social tensions that might affect sales that involved the collectivity. Again, it is Livy (2.34.7–8) who provides the best information on social tensions connected with food supplies. In Rome, in 491 BCE, the question of the price of grain was a veritable apple of discord between the plebeians and the senate:

Then under the consulate of M. Minucius and A. Sempronius [491 BCE], a large quantity of grain arrived from Sicily and the senate discussed the price at which it would be provided to the people. Many thought that the time had come to put pressure on the people and to recover the rights that had been extorted from the senators by secession and violence.

Rome was not a Greek-speaking state, but it faced the same challenge as the Greek cities, although it faced them with a characteristically conservative attitude. We also see in Livy (4.12.6–11) that, if supplies were inadequate, alternative solutions had to be found and the internal market regulated. In 440 BCE, Rome was struck by another famine, and draconian steps to requisition grain had to be taken:

The tranquility of this political situation was followed by the year in which Proculus Geganius Macerinus and L. Menenius Lanatus were consuls, and that was marked by all kinds of disasters and dangers: seditions, famine, and the yoke of royalty was close to being accepted because of the attraction of the generous gifts that were made. All that was lacking was a foreign war, and if the situation had been thereby further aggravated, the help of all the gods would scarcely have sufficed to resist. The misfortunes began with the famine, either because the year had been a bad one for the harvests, or because the attraction of public meetings and the city led people to stop cultivating the fields: both versions are reported. The senators accused the plebeians of laziness, and the plebeians accused the consuls of fraud and negligence. Finally, the misfortunes led the plebeians, without the senate opposing them, to name L. Minucius commissioner for supply; but he turned out to be more successful in safeguarding freedom than in managing his task, although finally a decrease in the price of supplies ended up winning him recognition and glory, which were, moreover, not unmerited. After having sent a multitude of purchasing commissions by land and by sea to the surrounding peoples, in vain except for a small amount of grain from Etruria that had no influence on supplies, he turned to the management of the shortage. He forced people to declare their grain and to sell any that exceeded needs for one month, decreased the amount of food given daily to slaves, and brought grain merchants before the court and exposed them to the people's anger. But this ruthless inquisitorial stance worsened the shortage more than it relieved it, so that many plebeians, having lost hope, covered their heads and threw themselves into the Tiber rather than drag out their lives in misery.

In the event of a shortage, when supplies did not arrive it was necessary to take steps to requisition them. In the Imperial period, more precisely in 92 or 93 CE—that is, more than five centuries after the famine in Rome—a very hard winter caused a famine that struck the city of Antioch in Pisidia in Asia Minor.[142] The governor of Cappadocia-Galatia, Antistius Rusticus, held sway over a very large province that included the Roman colony of Antioch in Pisidia. At the request of local authorities, he issued an edict, probably in June, that sought to regulate grain sales:

> Lucius Antistius Rusticus, propraetorian legate of Emperor Caesar Domitianus Augustus Germanicus, proclaims:
> —Seeing that the *duumuiri* and the decurions[143] of the very splendid colony of Antioch have written to me that following the hard winter the price of grain has risen sharply, and that they have asked me to see to it that the common people might be in the position to buy,
> —With good fortune: that all those who are colonists or residents in the colony of Antioch declare to the *duumuiri* of the colony of Antioch, within the space of thirty days starting from the promulgation of this edict, the quantity of grain that each of them has and where, and the quantity of this grain he deducts for seed and to feed his family for the year, and let him make all the rest of the grain available to the colony of Antioch's buyers. I set the date of the sale the first day of the calends of next August. Anyone who shall disobey should know that everything he has acquired in contravention of my edict will be confiscated, an eighth part to be given to informers as their reward;
> —As I am assured that before this long, hard winter the price of grain in the colony was eight or nine asses the *modius* and that it would be very unjust that anyone profit from the famine of his fellow citizens, I forbid the sale of grain at a price above one *denarius* the *modius*.

Thus, in strict parallel with the steps taken in Rome in 440 BCE or in Selymbria around 360 BCE, Antistius Rusticus had grain requisitioned on the basis of a declaration made by the producers.[144] Each family could keep seed grain for the following year's crop and to feed itself for one year. All the rest had to be put on the market in a forced sale that was to take place on the first day of the calends of August. It was the "buyers" (*emptores*, that is, the public buyers, the exact equivalent of the *sitōnai* previously mentioned for the world of the Greek cities) of the colony of Antioch who were to buy the grain.[145] As for the maximum price mentioned at the end of the edict, this was in any event the sale price on the date of the forced sale. The producers could not count on receiving a price higher than one *denarius* the *modius* (the equivalent of 6 Attic drachms the *medimnos*). Grain was normally sold at eight or nine *as* the *modius*. Since the *denarius* was worth sixteen asses, the maximum price was thus set at double the standard price, which must already have assured producers a revenue that allowed them to limit the loss of profit represented by the shortfall of grain to be delivered. The decree does not say whether in order to avoid speculative buying, quotas per family were to be set, but it is likely that they were.

How frequent were such requisitions? First, we must avoid artificially opposing a "Greek tradition" to a more coercive "Roman tradition" that often went so far as to requisition the whole harvest. Instead, we are confronted by a whole range of measures ranging from the simple "insurance fund" that a city that was normally well-off nonetheless constituted in order to insure the comfort of its inhabitants (as Delos did in the third century BCE), through permanent arrangements in cities in which shortages were chronic (as in Teos), to extraordinary measures taken by cities that had to cope with a crisis of exceptional proportions. The seriousness of the crisis, the size of the community, the possibilities that remained open on the foreign markets, and, not least, domestic power relationships, determined which steps were taken. In 440 BCE, Rome resorted to such measures only when it became clear that there was no possibility of importing grain. In the case of Antioch in Pisidia in 92 or 93 CE, we have to note that given its location far inland, the city could not count on imports to meet domestic demand: that is why it had to totally replace the free market by the public sale of local grain that had been requisitioned.[146] Were such requisitions really effective? If we believe what Livy says about the famine of 440 BCE, they were not, since in their despair the most impoverished people committed suicide by jumping into the Tiber. Historical parallels amply show that requisition inevitably resulted in harvests being squirreled away and a decrease in the quantities actually put on the market. That may also be what happened in Antioch in Pisidia.

Thus the city-states established powerful means of intervening in the markets, the framework for which was constituted by the *emporion*, its magistrates, and its specific laws. The city-states did not hesitate to try to control fluctuations of the foreign market price. Of course, they did not have all the basic data. On the other hand, so far as they could they tried to prevent unjustified, speculative profits, profits that irritated the masses so much and that might lead them to explode in anger. To prevent merchants from profiting from competition between buyers, the city-states did not hesitate to take the place of buyers in order to establish a form of monopsony or even bought grain themselves for their public granaries. Furthermore, everything shows that the authorities of the city-states had an excellent knowledge of market mechanisms. Finally, in order to reduce the effects of tensions in the foreign market, the city-states did not hesitate to act as buyers and to constitute intervention funds that could influence prices on the domestic market. Confronted by the networks of international trade of which they were themselves parts, the city-states were thus in no way passive with regard to the market.

XIII

INTERNATIONAL
TRADE NETWORKS

Although there is no doubt that Greek city-states were heavily involved in foreign trade, there remains to determine how they intervened in the processes of exchange. Did they act under the constraint of natural contingencies in order to compensate for permanent or temporary deficiencies? In that case, the description that can be given of the differences in production between geographic regions and the associated trade flows could not, strictly speaking, be a matter of an international division of labor, but only of a trade of necessity subject solely to natural constraints. Or did intercity trade also proceed, beyond the constraints of their natural resources, from choices of production and deliberate, organized exchange to exploit natural advantages? Had that been the case, natural advantages would not have been a crushing constraint, but on the contrary simply means in the service of sophisticated trade policies. Then we could maintain that in Greece there was a genuine international division of labor. The second option is the right one, as we will show by first taking up this notion directly, and then by analyzing the particular form of trade flows and networks of exchange in the world of the Greek city-states.

TRADE AND THE INTERNATIONAL DIVISION OF LABOR

Conceptions of Ancient Political Theorists

No ancient "political theorist" seems to have imagined that a city-state could get along without foreign trade. The unknown author of the *Constitution of the Athenians* (2.11–13), which was written around 420 BCE and which tradition wrongly attributed to Xenophon, shows how important control over the seas was for the Athenians. He emphasizes the unequal distribution of natural resources:

[The Athenians] are the only ones among the Greeks and Barbarians who can have wealth. If a city is rich in wood suitable for naval construction, where would it sell it if it did not obtain the agreement of the power that dominates the sea? And if a city is rich is iron or in copper or in flax, where will it sell them if it does not obtain the agreement of the power that dominates the sea? However, it is with these materials that I construct my warships, one providing me with wood, another with bronze, another with flax, and still another with wax. Moreover, our enemies will no longer be able to transport their products abroad, or at least they will not be able to do it by sea. But I, without doing anything, obtain all these products of the earth thanks to the sea, whereas no city has two of these products. For the same city does not have both wood and flax, but where there is an abundance of flax, the country is flat and treeless. Similarly, there are not both bronze and iron in the same city, nor two or three others of these products in the same city, but there is one product here and another there.

We find the same idea in Isocrates (*Panegyric* 4.42), who expresses it clearly: "There is no people that has a territory that can be self-sufficient [*autarkēs*], each one lacking some products and having an excess of others." From the observation that natural resources were unequally distributed derived the idea that foreign trade ought to make it possible to compensate for this natural inequality: whence also the very widespread idea that the goal of trade is to export surpluses and import things that are lacking. Thus in a passage in the *Politics* (1.3.13) on the origins of money, Aristotle remarks:[1]

For when they had come to supply themselves more from abroad by importing things in which they were deficient and exporting those of which they had a surplus, the employment of money necessarily came to be devised.

In the same vein, when he notes the advantages for the Byzantines connected with the situation of their city, Polybius (4.38.9) emphasizes that "they can export the totality of their excess production, and as for what they lack, they can import it directly and advantageously, without difficulty and without risk."[2]

This kind of reasoning is characteristic of societies in which, insofar as environmental conditions and technologies of production do not make it possible to achieve a level of production regularly exceeding the population's needs, security interests took precedence over all others. Strictly speaking, that would mean that the Greek city-states' foreign trade had no goal other than to balance out surpluses or deficits connected with natural conditions. In the initial phase of the analysis, that logic may in fact seem generally prevalent. On the one hand, there was an international division of labor that was initially a function of the presence of resources that existed only in certain regions, or of natural potentialities that made a particular kind of production advantageous. On the other hand, supervisory policies or restrictions on trade were established to ensure the security of supply.[3]

So far as unequal distribution of natural resources is concerned, it is easy to find examples. Copper, tin, marble, and even iron were not equally distributed. As for agricultural products, the regions with the heaviest rainfall and the richest soil had yields of wheat and even barley that were significantly higher than those in the dry parts of Greece—the islands and the Aegean coast. On the other hand, the latter could produce wine, olive oil, figs, and honey better in quality than those of the regions with more rainfall, and products that could not be grown, or only with difficulty, in the higher-altitude regions and especially in the colder regions north of the Black Sea (consider, for instance, the heaps of stones that had to be accumulated in the vineyards of Tauric Chersonesos to prevent the vine stocks from freezing[4]).

In a world where technological capital was still relatively small and where production remained largely dependent on location, natural advantages and their unequal distribution was thus an essential factor in international trade. If we take into account both ancient authors' considerations and the distribution of natural advantages, we might thus conclude, with most ancient thinkers, that international trade as such played only the simple role of evening out the opportunities available to regions. In other words, beyond a strict logic of supply, foreign trade did not play the role of creating wealth in economic development.

In any case, this kind of analysis is not the prerogative of ancient political theorists. Mercantilists saw things the same way. Their theses, which were dominant in early modern Europe, were in this respect very close to those of the ancients. The way Antoine de Montchrestien sees foreign trade is very significant. In his *Traicté de l'œconomie politique* published in 1615, he maintains that the essence of trade consists in "the exportation of things we have in excess and the importation of things we lack."[5] He observes that up to a certain point, it is logical for England to export to France the lead that the latter lacks, and for France to sell England wine in turn.[6] It is noteworthy that in these passages at least Montchrestien does not cite any ancient author in support of his view.[7] He seems to base these ideas on his own judgment, unless he is repeating something that was commonly said at the time. This makes the parallel between Montchrestien's observations and those of ancient authors all the more interesting. Here we are, so to speak, at the most basic level of economic conceptualization, which nonetheless suggests that despite the intervening change in scale, the structural conditions governing foreign trade in the world of the Greek city-states and in that of the territorial states of early modern Europe have a number of features in common.

Ancient Questionings

In antiquity, as at the dawn of the modern period, the theory of importing to meet deficiencies and exporting surpluses thus undeniably constitutes a basic element of the ideology of international trade, and it guided the policies cities adopted. If we had to account for international trade exclusively in these terms, we would be forced to say not only that no goods were imported that were in fact produced locally in sufficient quantities, but even that no goods were imported that *could* be locally produced in sufficient quantities. The theory of trade in terms of "lack versus surplus" presupposes that each of the trading partners exploits its natural potential to the fullest. Another characteristic of this theory is that it analyzes trade from a discrete, punctual point of view, taking as its reference point commercial exchange at a given moment in time.

The fundamental characteristics of the economy of antiquity, in particular a modest level of productivity that only grew slowly over time, meant that in fact each city tended to exploit to the maximum its natural potentialities in order to be an actor in international trade. The basic rule of international trade has always been the exportation of products whose value is roughly equivalent to that of imports. Besides, the notion of a trade balance is so much an integral element of the theory of trade on the basis of "lack versus surplus" that it usually remains implicit in the writings of the ancients. Thus when he points out that goods exported pay for imports, Plato is merely making this presupposition explicit.[8] Power relationships in the ancient world normally appear directly, not attenuated or deferred, as is now the case for changes in exchange rates:[9] if a city lacked grain and had no exportable goods or precious metals of equivalent value, its residents had to face the hard reality of famine. As Plutarch says in his *Life of Solon* (22.1), "traders at sea import nothing to those that could give them nothing in exchange."[10] Borrowing could be no more than a temporary expedient that also quickly reached its limits.[11]

However, some ancient political theorists clearly discerned the insufficiency of these analyses in terms of "lack" and "surplus." A city's development, in terms not only of demographic fluctuations but also of wealth, presupposed a corresponding development in the conditions of foreign trade. Aristotle pointed out that an increase in the volume of trade had led to the introduction of money.[12] He thus saw that lacks and surpluses were not absolutes but conditions that might change over time. For example, if we consider a "lack of foodstuffs," we can certainly observe that even if all its agricultural land was occupied, and taking into account existing technologies, a given city's agricultural production might not be able to feed its population. But the size of a population is not a mechanical result but rather the outcome of a complex social process. Population growth is governed in part by endogenous factors connected with the way kinship is organized: whatever the individual or collective behaviors with regard to children might have been, including the most extreme ones, it must have frequently happened that within a few decades a city found itself with an excess of mouths to feed.

Several ancient political theorists were aware of these changes in population, even if they expressed their point of view in normative terms (a population should not increase beyond what is reasonable).[13] The ways in which cities might cope with the existence of a certain percentage of poor and indigent people obviously varied greatly: they imposed repressive measures or forced departures, or else on the contrary encouraged the development of a craft activity (thereby accepting a larger population, on condition that the poorest could provide for their subsistence by working). There was, of course, an absolute limit to demographic growth that was set by the quantity of food available, but the ways in which civil societies took into account the poorest strata of their populations could also lead to very different population levels. Purely quantitative analyses cannot account for the complexity of these processes.

Besides, ancient political theorists also frequently condemned expenditures on luxuries, and thus imports of luxury products, which were considered useless and leading to a deplorable exit of money from the city. Conversely, they wanted to ban the export of products necessary to the city. For imports, this is what Plato does in the *Laws* (847c), quoting frankincense and purple and other dyes among the products of which the import should be banned: the city should satisfy of her own luxury productions only. The similitude with the mercantilist program of the early modern period is very clear. But although this was not Plato's intention he also implicitly pointed to the social and relative character of needs. For the popular strata, basic foodstuffs were the primary budget item, whereas the wealthy classes were drawn to fine wines, precious fabrics, jewels, and luxury objects in general.

But the most penetrating view, which breaks with a static model of imports and exports, is Plato's observation in the *Republic* (370e–371a) according to which surpluses exist only because they have been deliberately produced to finance imports:[14]

> — But further, said I, it is practically impossible to establish the city in a region where it will not need imports. — It is. — There will be a further need, then, of those who will bring in from some other city what it requires. — There will. — And again, if our servitor goes forth empty-handed, not taking with him any of the things needed by those from whom they procure what they themselves require, he will come back with empty hands, will he not? — I think so. — Then their home production must not merely suffice for themselves but in quality and quantity meet the needs of those of whom they have need. — It must. — So our city will require more farmers and other craftsmen. — Yes, more.

For Plato, surpluses are thus in no way natural. They are the product of an awareness of the necessary balance between imports and exports. We find here the elements of another logic of foreign trade that we must now examine from the point of view of contemporary theories.

The Theory of International Trade

The turning point in the theory of international trade comes in the second half of the eighteenth century. We owe it to Adam Smith and especially to David Ricardo.[15] For Smith, economic progress presupposed a specialization of activities.[16] According to his famous example of a pin factory, ten workers laboring exclusively at this task could produce 48,000 pins a day. Thus the unit cost of a pin (and thus its sale price) could be considerably reduced. Similarly, on the international level, Smith maintained that a specialization of production by country in relation to natural advantages would lead to a general increase in productivity. He reasoned in terms of "absolute advantages": each country specialized in the product for which it had a productivity superior to that of other countries. David Ricardo extended Smith's ideas, but introduced a new notion into the theory of international trade, that of comparative advantage. In his *Principles of Political Economy and Taxation*, Ricardo showed that a country has an interest in specializing in the products for which its productivity is highest.[17] It is supposed that the only factor of production that counts is labor, and that transaction costs (in particular transportation costs) are nil. Ricardo demonstrates that even if a country has lower productivity in all domains, it is still in its interest to engage in trade. The classical example he gives is commercial relations between two countries, England and Portugal, which are able to exchange their two products, cloth and wine.

Let us suppose that England has a lower productivity in both sectors, since in England it takes 100 hours of labor to produce one unit of cloth and 120 hours to produce one unit of wine, whereas in Portugal the figures are 90 hours and 80 hours, respectively. If both countries specialize in what they are comparatively able to do best, England will be able to produce two units of cloth in 200 hours, and Portugal will be able to produce two units of wine in 160 hours, for a total of 360 hours for both products (instead of 390 if the two countries had not specialized): the thirty hours thus gained by trade can be devoted to producing more or to producing other goods (table 13.1).

The theory of comparative advantages (whereas Adam Smith took into consideration only absolute advantages) allows us to show that international trade is not a zero-sum game, as the mercantilists thought, but rather a positive-sum game. The international division of labor connected with international trade makes it possible to increase overall production, to the benefit of all. The theory of comparative advantages shows that trade is profitable in all cases, including those in which—like that of England in Ricardo's example—the country has a lower productivity for all the products that it can offer.[18]

TABLE 13.1. Comparative Productivity before and after Specialization (in Hours Worked)

	CLOTH	WINE	TOTAL		CLOTH	WINE	TOTAL
Portugal	90	80	170	Portugal	0	160	160
England	100	120	220	England	200	0	200
Total	190	200	390	Total	200	160	360

Production before specialization   Production after specialization

It is true that Ricardo's theory assumes a situation of pure and perfect competition that is never fully realized. It abstracts from power relationships among states and from the social problems that may arise. Its presupposition, which Ricardo moreover makes explicit, is the stability of capital in the country of origin (as we know, this is now put in question by the mobility of capital). Reduction to trade between two partners is, naturally, an abstract model, and it is recognized as such by Ricardo, who stresses that the reality of international trade is far more complex. His theory of comparative advantages has given rise to many new analyses and variants. However, since it was proposed, it has never been seriously challenged, and it constitutes a powerful tool for analyzing international trade. Ricardian concepts have been reworked for contemporary international trade in the framework of what is known as the "Heckscher, Ohlin, and Samuelson model" (HOS model), developed by three economists who sought to show how the capital-labor relationship in the production of a commodity affects the rate of productivity for this commodity and thus specialization by country. A high intensity of capital gives certain countries an advantage in the production of goods involving sophisticated technology: capital is abundant and cheap, labor is rare and expensive. The same principle works in reverse for countries where capital is rare and expensive, but labor is abundant and cheap.[19]

The International Division of Labor and Gains in Productivity

It may seem that here we are far away from the world of ancient Greece. Should we maintain that the only result of international trade was to make available products that were not available and to export surpluses? Should we conclude that trade was only a zero-sum game? That way of seeing things would be altogether inadequate. Although the ancient economy was one in which land remained the principal factor of production and in which absolute advantages played a primordial role, it is possible to show that Ricardo's theses allow us to throw new light on the role of international trade in the world of the Greece of the city-states.

How can the perspective of contemporary economics help us? If, as we have seen, in antiquity the usual economic analysis (and the dominant ideology that flowed from it) remained focused on exporting surpluses and importing what was lacking, can we reasonably seek to apply a contemporary theoretical framework to an ancient reality without exposing ourselves to the criticism that we are trying to impose a contemporary fact on an ancient economy that we know differed from our own in important ways? Several replies can be made to this potential criticism. First, just because an analytical instrument did not exist at a certain time does not mean that one has to forego using it; otherwise, we would have to give up any attempt at scientific study. Economic analysis allows us to account for a number of phenomena observed in ancient Greece that cannot be explained using only the theoretical tools available at the time. However, one must not neglect the question of the form taken by discourse on foreign trade in the Greece of the city-states.

Second, as already observed, the dominant ideology of the time did not prevent some thinkers from going further in their reflections. Thus it is noteworthy that Plato introduced time as one of the variables in his analysis of foreign trade. That is precisely what Ricardo did much later in his theory of comparative advantages: the increase in the two partners' production, which is a result of gains in productivity, can be measured only after a certain period of time has elapsed. And this temporal dimension must be taken into account in analyzing foreign trade in the Greece of the city-states, even if the dominant ideology of the age did not do so.

In reality, not only did the cities of the Greek Aegean world in the classical and Hellenistic periods live on trade, but their development was possible only because of parallel developments in a series of peripheral regions. The process started in the mid-eighth century (even though the volume of goods trade was still modest), being attested in two sites as distant one from the other as Pithekoussai in the Bay of Naples in the West and Methone in the Thermaic Gulf in the northern Aegean.[20] In the seventh century, it is now attested also by more wrecks of this period.[21] In the course of the sixth century, the process accelerated and established itself on a larger scale.[22] By the end of the Archaic period, the main trading routes as well as the main mechanisms of trade were already clearly emerging. In the Classical and Hellenistic periods, international trade gained further momentum and decisively fueled economic growth. From the Archaic to the Hellenistic period, trade actors and partners changed, and the amphoras, as objects of trade, give us a sense of this evolution.[23] But the main point to underscore is that the development of the "core of the Greek world" (the Aegean world) at the end of the Archaic period and during the Classical period was made possible only by the massive imports of raw materials from the periphery. Similarly, the development of the periphery was made possible only by the steadily increasing demand from the Aegean world. The supplies made available by one party gradually increased in function of the other's demand and vice versa. The static notion of surplus and lack is incapable of describing this dynamics.

However, we must go still further and, as Ricardo's ideas encourage us to do, erase the conceptual borderline between absolute advantages and comparative advantages. It is not that the idea of absolute advantage corresponds to no reality, because it is fundamental to the difference in productivity between regions. But it suffices to see that absolute advantage is only a modality of comparative advantage. In other words, it does not matter whether the partners have freely decided to specialize or were forced to do so by necessity, or whether they were initially in a situation of productivity of the "absolute advantage" type or one of the "comparative advantage" type. What counts is ultimately that the major differences in productivity between regions that can be observed in the Greece of the city-states and the unification of these different regions by the international market led to particularly large gains in productivity.[24]

Concretely, this means that if the cities of the Aegean world had had to produce all the grain they needed for levels of population as elevated as theirs were, they would have had to put into cultivation all the available lands, including the least fertile ones, with a marginal and rapidly decreasing productivity. In any case, it is clear that by relying on their own production, they could not have achieved the population level they had reached by the Classical period, and that is a crucial point in the economic history of these regions. But so far as gains in productivity are concerned, it is of little importance that without imports they would not have been capable of attaining these levels of production. On the contrary, the productivity differential was an advantage all the more considerable. These cities benefited from imports of grain and other foodstuffs produced with a far higher productivity than their own. These foodstuffs came to them at a comparatively low price. In this way, the cities of the Aegean world benefited from considerable savings in labor. They were able to use them by specializing in other production sectors in which they could in turn achieve a maximal level of productivity. As Willem M. Jongman stressed, specializing in wine and oil made it possible to produce about five times more calories per hectare than with grain.[25] This fundamental reorientation of their economies supposed also reorganizing production structures and resorting massively to slave labor. In the cities of Asia Minor, the case of Chios being famous, the process was already well under way at the end of the Archaic period.[26]

It was through this vast international division of labor and the gains in productivity connected with it that the Greek world was able to attain the level of development we see in the Classical period. Although out of concern for their security all the city-states tried to attain a minimal level of grain production, each of them specialized in a limited number of products, trying to achieve a quality that would allow it to establish an indisputable reputation. In accord with Ricardo's system, international trade in the Greece of the city-states, which connected the Aegean world with Egypt, Cyrenaica, the Black Sea, Cyprus, Italy, Sicily and beyond can be defined as a system of distributed production. It is in this sense that despite the geographical distance and the fragmentation into a multitude of cities that could authorize or prohibit imports and exports, all the territories concerned formed one and the same market for the products in question, in the form of the interconnection of diverse market areas. This does not mean that the whole production of the cities involved was put on the market (whether domestic or, *a fortiori*, foreign), or that prices were the same everywhere—on the contrary, since it was price differentials that generated trade flows between regions. Interestingly, the best example of long-distance transfers of commodities on the basis of a price difference is that of silver. From the Archaic to the Hellenistic period, as proved by the coin hoards, silver was massively transferred from the Aegean (where it was produced and was relatively cheap) to Egypt and the eastern Mediterranean (where there were no silver mines). The only and perfectly logical exception is the few decades following Alexander's conquest and seizure of the huge Persian treasures in 333–331 BCE, when flows were reversed. The paradox is that while each of the cities tended to organize its external trade strictly on the basis of its own interest, they nonetheless lived in a close economic interdependency that favored their mutual development.

Center and Periphery: The Model

Thus we can say that the world of the late Archaic and Classical periods functioned on the basis of a center-periphery relationship, the center being constituted above all by the cities of the Aegean area, and the periphery by the regions defined earlier. On the other hand, the Hellenistic world became multipolar, mainland Greece and the Aegean islands being henceforth only one of the centers of development, and at a level substantially lower than in the preceding period. Starting at the end of the second century, a new center was established in the west that reduced the Aegean cities and other regions of the eastern basin of the Mediterranean to relay zones for goods going to Rome and Italy. At that time, the large estates newly set up in Italy, Sicily, and Africa were supplied with large numbers of slaves coming from various regions, particularly those who had passed through Delos.

The center-periphery model of the late Archaic period and the Classical period raises the question of the terms of trade between the two regions. It seems clear that in large measure the periphery provided raw materials, grain, hides, wood, metal ingots and slaves, whereas the center provided more processed products. The latter included artisanal products such as fabrics and clothing (ordinary or luxurious), carpets, dyes, ceramics, weapons, precious vases, tools, furniture, cobblers' products, and also, of course, high-quality wines and oil, or again books, musical instruments, perfumes and the small perfume vases that accompanied them, cosmetics, mirrors, and even bronze statues, all exported in every direction, depending on the local demand.[27] Shipwrecks show that these goods were transported by sea to distant markets.[28] Whether they were craft or agricultural products or "works of art," they required an expert workforce that had a long tradition of technical expertise: thus in the case of ceramics, where the technical and aesthetic quality of Attic products was supreme for three centuries, from the first half of the sixth century to the end of the fourth century.

Depending on the product, the workforce employed might be small or very numerous. The first category included, for example, the production of perfumes, an activity that produced little in volume but had a high unit value. It is no accident that a large distribution center like Delos in the late Hellenistic period was a place where perfumes were produced: sales at the best price were thereby assured. The vineyards, on the other hand, employed large numbers of workers. In addition, relative to the prevailing conditions of production, these products had the peculiarity of requiring heavy capital investment. It is clear that it was the central areas, those that benefited from the largest accumulation of capital, that were able to invest in the kinds of production mentioned earlier. These were products with a high unit price per volume. The sales margin on quality wines was considerable, as already observed.[29] The same could be true for costly textiles and, more generally, for all products providing pleasure and luxury products that might be exported by the large Aegean cities.[30] The high value of the products exported by the center made it possible to buy raw materials cheaply, especially grain, which were necessary to supply the people of the cities, whom their lands would never have been able to feed.[31]

However, we must avoid seeing in this model in which the center exploited an increasingly impoverished periphery. In the case of the Greece of the late Archaic and Classical periods, expansionary phases were truly "win-win," because the rise of the periphery leaves no doubt regarding the profits that were made. It is thus logical, on the other hand, that the reversal of the situation in the early Hellenistic period was also marked by serious problems in certain peripheral regions such as the Black Sea, even if some endogenous factors, such as the pressure of new barbarian tribes, might also have played a role in this.[32] At the same time, one must also inquire into the nature of this "periphery," which was for the most part composed of cities or principalities belonging to the Hellenic community. The latter had their own "periphery," and it was there that true exploitation might take place, particularly by buying slaves from the barbarian tribes or kingdoms with which they were in contact. Besides, the various regions of the "periphery" kept a distinct cultural identity.[33]

One should also avoid seeing in the notions of "center" and "periphery" monolithic entities, as if the "periphery" sent to the "center" only raw materials and received only processed products in return. The terms "center" and "periphery" refer instead to two main poles of exchange with two dominants in the products, but without exclusivity, in function of the opportunities but also of local know-how, without overlooking the fact that a large part of the periphery corresponded either to peoples with ancient cultures, like Egypt and Phoenicia, or to Greek colonial cities. Thus in the fifth century, Egypt was a country that mainly supplied Aegean cities with raw materials such as grain, natron and alum, but it also provided them with linen, rope, and papyrus, all products that could easily fall into the category of processed and valuable products. As for Egypt's imports, they consisted in wine, oil, ceramics, wool, iron, bronze, copper, tin, and wood, some of which could be considered raw materials, and other luxury products.[34]

In addition, within each region there were complex networks, and between the two poles, there could also be a multitude of intermediary zones that took advantage of the establishment of these trade flows to prosper in their own turn.[35] Thus we are dealing with a single system, which does not mean that there were not regional autonomies and changes in the overall configuration, such as the passage from a world centered on the Aegean to a multicentered world in the Hellenistic period, before the return to a world centered on Rome and Italy at the end of the Hellenistic period and at the beginning of the Imperial period. Finally, against a background of trade between partners who enjoyed absolute advantages, one must also observe kinds of international trade that do not fit into this framework. One doesn't carry coals to Newcastle, as the British say. But wine was imported to Athens, which also produced it. This shows that we have to move beyond the simple observation of imports and exports on the basis of an exchange of different products and take more complex phenomena into account. The question calls for a twofold answer.

First, it has to do with the structure of consumption, which is itself a function of the social structure of the distribution of wealth. In the aggregate, a city's "lack" might be defined as its overall external demand. However, depending on the social level, this lack did not always have the same meaning: in value, the popular strata's demand bore essentially on vital necessities, while that of the elites bore on luxury products that were out of reach for the poorest people. The definition of needs is thus not an absolute given. The political model of Greek societies, which tended to be egalitarian, did not prevent a very high inequality of incomes. The aristocracies of the Archaic period and the wealthy elites of the Classical period and especially the Hellenistic period had incomes that gave them access to forms of consumption that were unknown to the masses. This social differentiation structured in turn imports of all products that could not be found in one's city. The vain person mocked by Theophrastus was par excellence an importer of exotic, rare, and precious products who flaunted his membership in the elite of wealth, if not of taste.[36]

Nonetheless, beyond the importation of exotic curiosities (even if they were high-priced), importing from distant producers massive amounts of products that were already produced locally raised problems of a different magnitude. A patent case of this in the second and first centuries BCE is provided by exports of oil and wine from Italy, Sicily, and Africa, which were sent in large quantities to the eastern Mediterranean—in the Aegean, to Delos and Ephesos, or in the Levant, for instance to Maresha.[37] In the Levant, Maresa/Maresha consumed an impressive number of amphoras from Italy and Africa. There must have been, at the point of arrival, consumers free to buy these products, since there was obviously no obligation to buy them and nothing indicates that they were consumed only by an emigrant Italian clientele. The presence of large urban markets, in the case of Delos or Ephesos, might have justified these imports, which were added to local or regional products. But despite transportation costs, on arrival the product must have remained competitive with local products, or even offered at a lower price. We have to consider that the large slave-worked farms of southern Italy, Sicily, and Africa in the late Republican period produced wine and oil at a price lower than that of more traditional farms in the Aegean or the Levant.

One must not, of course, draw a general rule from this, but one seems again forced to conclude that it was differences in production prices between various geographical areas that justified long-distance trade. This time, however, natural advantages were not involved, as it had been the case for the "wine for grain" trade between the Aegean and the Bosporan Kingdom in the Classical period. The difference in the production cost between the two regions was connected with three factors. First, it had to do with a different organization of the structures of production, because the large wine or oil producing estates in Italy, Sicily, and Africa made economies of scale possible. Second, it also had to do with the conditions of over-exploitation of a slave labor force whose abundance at that time ensured a particularly low purchase price—in other words, thanks to massive imports of slaves, labor was cheap on the farms of Italy, Sicily and Africa. Last, it had to do with a general rearrangement of trade networks oriented toward Rome and Italy, which created a trade flow from which exports of these products benefited.

TRADE FLOWS

Consumption, Production, and Prices

The system of surpluses and lacks presupposes that products from a single origin were transported directly to a place where they would be wholly consumed. There is no doubt that this model held for many, probably even most cases of commercial exchange. This was the model that governed trade in foodstuffs and that thus prevailed in trade between the Black Sea and the cities of the Aegean, first of all Athens, which was a major grain importer. In the 340s BCE, the plaintiff in *Against Lacritus* (35.35) accused his adversaries of not having respected a contract that obliged them to return to Athens with a cargo bought in Pontos. The accused claimed that their ship had been wrecked while they were on their way back to Athens with a cargo of wine and other products. The plaintiff tried to show the absurdity of this claim:

> Just see how impudent these people are. You, members of the jury, think if you know in some way, or if you have ever heard of people who imported wine from Pontos commercially, particularly wine from Kos. On the contrary, wine is imported to Pontos from our regions, from Peparethos, Thasos, Mende, and a whole series of other cities; it is other products that are imported here from Pontos.

In the Hellenistic period, the terms of trade had remained the same, but general political and economic uncertainties had made the Black Sea a less secure area for grain imports, as Polybius indicates (4.38.4–5):

> For needs indispensable for life, it is undeniably the regions of Pontos that provide, both in very large quantities and with the best quality, our livestock and most of our slaves; as for what is superfluous, they provide us with honey, wax, and salted meats. For their part, they receive from our regions our surplus oil and wines of all kinds. As for grain, the relationships can be reversed: sometimes, in the event of a good harvest, they are the providers, and sometimes they are the importers of grain coming from our area.

The whole series of products mentioned consists of raw materials or ones that have undergone simple processing on the production site, as in the case of salted meats. Thus we have a model that corresponds to the system of "surpluses" and "lacks," in accord with the schema mentioned earlier.

But this system of trade in raw materials intended for immediate consumption does not exhaust the diversity and complexity of trade networks. We must also take into account the fact that trade played a role in constituting regions of integrated production based on the importation of basic products before re-exporting them, possibly to a distant destination. Most artisanal products had to make use of imported materials. Being processed in specialized workshops, finished products could then be re-exported to a variety of destinations. Thus, even the production of fine ceramics might require imported products: in Attika, vase painters used ochre of a fine orange color, the best of which was imported from the island of Keos.

An interesting case is provided by perfume making. Perfume was definitely a luxury product, and employed few workers, but it could bring in very high profits. Women (and not only courtesans) and men as well frequently used perfumes.[38] The perfume vases that have been found in large numbers on Classical and Hellenistic sites show the clientele's taste for these products. In addition, Attic vase paintings very often represent *alabastra* (small ovoid perfume vases), which shows that perfumes were in general use at least by the middle and upper classes.[39] The production of perfumes required various ingredients. Some of these might be of local origin (oil, flowers, honey, salt). But others came from more or less distant sources: *aspalathos* (a plant that has still not been well identified) came from Nisyros, Rhodes, and Syria; *sturax* from the region of Selge, in Pisidia; *schoinos* and *kalamos* grew in Lebanon; the *kupros* flower (which yields henna) came from Africa, Arabia, Persia, and northwest India; myrrh, cardamom, and cinnamon came from around the Indian Ocean. The price of perfume was based first of all on that of the products that went into its fabrication. The simple *murrhon rhodinon*, the most common perfume, based on rose petals with few exotic components, was sold at four drachms the *kotulē* in Delos in 269 BCE and 4.5 drachms in 250.[40] This provides us with a precious clue regarding the price range for this product. But other perfumes were much more expensive. According to Dioscorides, the formula for the perfume known as *kupros* or *kuprinon* included, among other ingredients, *kalamos*, *kupros* (henna), myrrh, and cardamom.[41] In addition, this was a perfume whose preparation was difficult and took a long time. The result was that in Athens, in the middle of the third century, it sold, according to the Cynic philosopher Teles, at one *mina* per *kotulē*, or about twenty to twenty-five times the price of Delian "rose myrrh" at the same period.[42] Thus it is clear that the final price was a direct function of the complexity and size of the trade network that governed the product's fabrication. Metals and textiles provide two cases that illustrate the variety and complexity of systems of trade.

Metals

Even if the delivery of finished products was not excluded, dealing in metals seems usually to have taken the form of transporting ingots. Then the metal was worked where it was delivered. However, as Pseudo-Xenophon emphasizes, metal deposits were not regularly distributed in every region. Thus in order to procure metal, international trade was absolutely necessary. But distances to the production centers varied:[43] longest for copper (most of which came from Cyprus and eastern Asia Minor) and tin (which came from the distant Kassiterides [literally, "Tin Islands"], and also probably from the Luristan, in the Zagros Mountains), and shorter for iron, because there were more deposits of this metal.[44]

In Greece itself, there were iron deposits in Macedon, in Chalkidike, and in Thasos, in the Parnon ridge in eastern Lakonia, in eastern Boiotia and in Euboia, in several Kyklades and as far as Kos and Lesbos, and finally in central and western Crete.[45] Many of these deposits were worked in antiquity.[46] Northern Asia Minor also produced iron. A commonplace in ancient sources has it that the country inhabited by the Chalybes, east of Amisos and the Iris River, in the hinterland of Themiskyra, Kotyora, and Pharnakeia (Kerasous), was particularly rich in this metal, but beyond the commonplace, the geographer Strabo (12.3.19) confirms that this was in fact the case. However, there were other mines closer to the Straits. This is shown by an allusion to them made by Apollonius of Rhodes (*Argonautica* 2.141, see 792–95) and confirmed by modern mining, which has discovered traces of ancient mines in the hinterland of Herakleia Pontika, between the Sangarios and Hypios Rivers (the latter being about thirty miles to the east of the former). Thus we see that Bithynia also produced iron and that two tribes, the Bebrykes (to the west; they were replaced by the Thracian tribe of the Bithynians) and the Mariandynians (to the east), "who were always fighting over the iron-producing land," had both claimed the area in ancient times.[47] To the west, Etruria was rich in metals, in particular with the iron ore from the island of Elba, which was worked in Populonia.[48] Finally, in Languedoc, the iron ore of the Montagne Noire might also find its way to the Mediterranean and the Greek city-states network. Thus as regards iron, the cities of mainland Greece and the Aegean islands, having mines (and more or less sufficient quantities of charcoal), could be autonomous. Other cities—that is, the majority—had to import iron, the distance from the sources of supply being variable, relatively close if the metal came the Aegean region, more distant if it had to be imported from the Black Sea or the iron mines in the West.

Because of their high value and weight per unit volume (which meant that they occupied little space in the hulls of ships), trade in metals must have been particularly profitable. International trade was thus one of the vectors of the relatively widespread use of iron.

Textiles

The various operations required for textile production relied on a trade network that made it possible to acquire the indispensable materials, which might come from very diverse sources.[49] Preparation of linen and wool involved the use of materials like (respectively) natron and alum, some or all of which were imported.[50] The raw material, flax (or linen) or wool, was also an object of trade, and so was also the dyestuff.

One should first mention the uses of natron.[51] Natron is sodium bicarbonate, closely related to salt (sodium chloride). One of its most well-known artisanal uses was in glassmaking. Pliny (*Natural History* 31.46 [110]) also mentions that it was used in dyes, in particular for purple, and this has been confirmed by modern experiments.[52] But one should underscore above all its bleaching properties for linen. It was already used for this purpose in Pharaonic Egypt.[53] Mixed with water, natron yields a basic solution (pH > 8) that is well suited to this use. Natron may still be employed for this purpose by the textile industry. There is little doubt that natron was also used for bleaching linen in Greece proper. It does not come as a surprise to observe that the Greeks in Egypt made use of natron for bleaching linen, as proved by a papyrus of 250 BCE.[54] Much later, the French scholars accompanying Bonaparte's expedition to Egypt did not fail to note both the usage of natron by local linen bleachers and the massive export of this product toward Europe.[55] For the Greek city-states, the main provider of natron was also certainly Egypt, as proved by the customs papyrus of 475 BCE.[56]

As for alum, an aluminum and potassium sulfate, it was a vital ingredient for wool dyeing.[57] After an initial treatment involving intensive washing, wool was dipped in a bath based on alum, along with ferrous compounds and possibly also vinegar. This operation ("mordanting") made it possible to set dyes used on fabrics.[58] Recent research has identified amphoras from the Imperial period that might have been used chiefly to transport alum: particularly amphoras from the Lipari islands and the island of Melos. The production of Liparian amphoras "for alum" began in the early first century BCE.[59] Our information about earlier periods is vaguer. We know that alum was used in the Aegean world as early as the second millennium BCE. Sources from the Roman period (literary or archaeological, or both) show that in the eastern Mediterranean basin, alum from the Lipari islands, from Melos, Macedon, Miletos, Hierapolis in Phrygia, and Pontos was known, and to this list Egypt must be added.[60] The question is whether these deposits were also mined in earlier periods. Diogenes Laertius (5.42) attributes to Theophrastus a treatise *On Salt, Natron and Alum*, which has unfortunately been lost. A religious law dating from ca. 350–250 BCE and coming from Thebai at Mykale (north of Priene, and thus north of Miletos) notes that a priest received as part of his income the tax revenues from alum, which would tend to confirm testimonies from the Imperial period referring to the existence of alum in Miletos.[61] During the siege of Piraeus by Sulla in 87/6 BCE, King Mithridates made heavy use of alum to fireproof a siege engine.[62] There is no doubt that it was used in the Classical and Hellenistic periods (and probably earlier as well). In the case of Melos and the Lipari islands, it may not have been transported in amphoras, which would explain the difference from what we can be observed in the following period.

Finally, there was the raw material, that is, flax and wool and flax. Flax was a specialty of regions with rainy plains. Thus it was not found everywhere, as Pseudo-Xenophon pointed out.[63] In Greece itself, high-quality flax was produced in Elis, in the Peloponnese.[64] Apart from production in the western part of Asia Minor, our sources show that the main providers of flax were (above all) Egypt and also the regions to the east of the Black Sea. Herodotus (2.105) and Pollux (5.26) praised the flax from Kolchis, at the foot of the Caucasus, in present-day Georgia. Strabo (11.2.17) emphasizes that this region exported its linen fabrics. Xenophon (*On Hunting* 2.4) recommends flax nets from Carthage or the Phasis (the main river in Kolchis). In the Pontos region as well, Amastris put the image of the flax flower on his coins, which shows that this plant was also widely cultivated on the Paphlagonian coast, where the rainfall was as heavy as it was in Kolchis.[65] Wool was produced almost everywhere, but especially in western Greece and in Asia Minor. Although wool was often transported raw or semi-processed (there is proof that dyed wools might have been transported), it is linen rather than flax that seems usually (although not always) to have been exported as a raw material, which did not exclude a further elaboration of this linen in another location.[66]

For textiles, imports of raw materials from long distances was thus perfectly common. In this respect, the Greek world did not differ from Egypt or Babylonia. The already mentioned customs document from Egypt from 475 BCE shows imports of wool from Phoenicia and massive exports of natron on Greek ships.[67] It is all the more worth stressing that the places where natron was produced were located in the delta, one of them being the area called today Wadi El Natrun, ancient Sketis, which is located just 25 kilometers west of Naukratis. Pliny stresses that there were two large natron beds in Egypt, one near Naukratis, the other near Memphis, the second one being however of inferior quality.[68] On the basis of the information on exports on Greek ships provided by the customs document of 475 BCE, it is tempting to conclude that in addition to the proximity of Sais (then the capital of Egypt), that of a natron-producing region might well have been one of the main reasons why the Greeks initially settled at Naukratis rather than on a different arm of the Nile. Mesopotamian documents from the seventh and sixth centuries BCE already testify to trade in alum and natron from Egypt, wool dyed with purple, and fibers (wool or flax).[69] It is worthwhile to try to define the supply network for cities known for textile activities in the Classical period, for instance in the northern Peloponnese, Corinth, Megara, or Hermione. Later, during the Imperial period, this role was taken over by the Roman colony of Patras. In the latter city, according to Pausanias (7.21.14), there were twice as many women as men, and they produced high-quality linen from flax grown in the neighboring region of Elis. The predominance of women can be explained only by the presence of a well-developed textile industry.[70] Corinth was, as already observed, one of the main centers producing valuable fabrics. Embroidery could be done by the cities' expert women workers.

The wool must have come chiefly from not only the Peloponnese but from western Greece, and that is probably one of the reasons why the Corinthians jealously protected their western trade routes, over which they received the wool they needed for their textile production.[71] Megara's position was similar to that of Corinth. It also had two ports, Pagai on the Gulf of Corinth and Nisaia on the Saronic Gulf.

Even though it is not possible to determine exactly what kind of activity led him to go there, the fact that the Megarian Kallias received, along with his sons, the title of *proxenos* in Stratos in Akarnania around 400 BCE testifies to the interest of Megarians in western Greece.[72] In the early third century, the Megarians themselves chose a *proxenos* in the coastal Akarnanian city of Astakos.[73] As for traders from Aigina, the Hollm hoard, found on the border between Illyria and Macedon, shows that they were also present in this area.[74] The price of wool varied depending on its quality, and where it came from must have been an important factor. Pliny the Elder (*Natural History* 8.73 [190]) indicates that in his time (that is, around the middle of the first century CE), no wool (thus even the fine wools from southern Italy or Miletos) cost more than 100 sesterces a pound (the equivalent of 25 drachms for 324 grams).

But wool also had to be dyed in order to satisfy a wealthy and demanding clientele, and also to compete successfully in a market in which the quality of products was the decisive criterion. In this respect, Pliny shows clearly that there were fashions for purple clothes, just like there were for other luxury goods like perfumes.[75] Producers had to innovate constantly and establish the reputations of products the sale of which was not assured in advance, at least at the expected price.[76] The price of dyeing was an important part of the final cost of the fabric sold. Ancient dyes were mainly based on vegetal or animal products. Among the vegetal products were crocus flowers, from which saffron (*krokos*) was drawn for yellow tones. The crocus is a rare and delicate flower. It takes 150,000 flowers to produce a kilogram of saffron, which gives us some idea of the inevitably high price of this product. In the *Georgics* (1.56), Virgil praises the quality of the crocuses grown on Mount Tmolos, a high mountain in Lydia, between Sardis and the plain of Caÿstros. Dyes based on animal products were mainly made from a kind of sea snail called murex, which was used to make purple. The dyestuff was extracted from a tiny gland in the murex, and since this had to be done one by one, the time it took could not be reduced. Moreover, the price varied in relation to the quality of the dye and fashions.

Thus Pliny (*Natural History* 9.63 [137]), quoting Cornelius Nepos, mentions the price of a few dyes that were fashionable in Italy in the second half of the first century CE: "In my youth, violet purple was in fashion, and was sold at a price of a hundred *denarii* [= 100 drachms] per pound, and then shortly afterward Tarantine red, followed by Tyrian 'double-dip,' which could not be bought even for 1,000 *denarii* per pound." Although he emphasizes the variations in price related to the productivity of the areas from which it came, Pliny himself (*Natural History* 9.64 [138]) notes that in his time no one should purchase dye based on "marine" purple at more than 50 *denarii* per hundred pounds, or dye based on whelks at more than 100 *denarii* for the same weight. But it took large quantities of dyestuffs to dye a fabric, whether it was wool or silk. It is true that the question is subject to debate, and that some specialized studies suggest that a single murex gland could dye a gram of wool (even if other, more recent experiments lead us to conclude that the figure is more like three murex glands per gram).[77] In fact, the figure must have varied depending on the quality of the pigment. Even on the minimal basis of one murex per gram, it can be conclude that dyeing a ton of wool required a minimum of a million murex glands. But the best quality required, as Pliny indicated, two (or even three) dippings, that is, for a deluxe fabric weighing one kilogram, 2,000 to 3,000, or 6,000 to 9,000 murex glands, according to the estimate adopted.

Depending on the dye, and thus also on the quality and the color chosen, ordinary or luxurious, the price could vary considerably.[78] The great textile-producing cities thus had to acquire dyestuffs and import them. In addition to the products of their own territories, Megara and especially Corinth had to be able to count on products from the Gulf of Corinth. Describing the cities of Phokis in the second century CE, Pausanias (10.37.3) mentions that in the little town of Boulis, west of Delphi and thus across from Lechaion, Corinth's western port, "more than half the people of the place gather shellfish from which purple-colored dye is made." In view of the reputation of Corinthian textiles in the Classical period, it is very tempting to conclude that what held true for Roman Corinth had already been true of Corinth before it was sacked in 146.[79] Murex production must have made it possible to procure exportable resources. That is why this resource was exploited almost everywhere, on the coasts of the Gulf of Corinth, the southern Peloponnese, Euboia, Thessaly, Lakonia (and Kythera), on the islands (such as Delos), and on the coasts of Asia Minor, for instance in Miletos and the little city of Aperlai in Lykia, where the remains of hundreds of thousands of shells have been found, and no less in the colonial worlds, for instance in Taras and Euhesperides (present-day Benghazi).[80] Naturally, in centers famous for their high-quality textiles, such as Miletos and Taras for wool, producers must have preferred to use a local purple (Taras's purple was famous). Euhesperides produced murex, and was obviously also an active weaving center, as is shown by the numerous loom weights found on the site. But if local production of purple was insufficient, then the dye certainly had to be imported.

If we assess the supply networks for textile production in the cities of the northern Peloponnese and their distribution, we see that in large measure they were long-distance networks, natron coming from Egypt, and alum from several places on the Aegean or farther away (Lipari or Egypt), while dyestuffs might be local in origin (but not always strictly local) or come from distant sources (if, for example, we are speaking of saffron from Asia Minor). Wool itself might come from regional sources or more distant ones (western Greece or even Sicily or Italy), and linen fabrics might be imported from western Peloponnese (from the region of Elis, which, receiving heavy rainfall, was suitable for growing flax[81]), the Black Sea, or especially Egypt, which was the principal producer.

Finally, one must recall that the labor force might be composed of free female citizens or metics of modest status, but also of slaves imported from distant markets. These complex supply networks for raw materials and the possible long-distance distribution of the products show that simple notions of "lacks" and "surpluses" related to natural givens are insufficient to describe these productions and exchanges, which were far more a function of both a system of the technical division of labor and a system of capital and markets (to sell the products). In order to force Megara to submit to his authority, shortly before or in 432 BCE Pericles caused to be approved the famous decree which, by depriving this city of access to the markets of Athens and its empire, condemned the Megarians to death if they did not submit to Athens's will.[82] This was certainly not the cause of the Peloponnesian War, but it was its *casus belli*. The decree thus perfectly illustrates Megara's dependency on foreign markets.

MARKETS IN NETWORKS AND SYSTEMS OF EXCHANGE

Trade Networks and Niches

Faced with the absolute necessity of finding exportable resources to finance indispensable purchases abroad, if only the grain that might be needed in the event of a poor harvest, even if it had a territory sufficiently rich to feed its population in ordinary times, every city tried to get as much as it could out of its environment, or created a specialty if it really had no natural advantage. If it had land that was rich and suitable for producing grain, wine, or olive oil, or if it had wood or mines for silver, iron, or copper, the choice of its specialization was obvious. The same was true if, as in Paros, Thasos, Prokonnesos, or Nikomedia (at the end of the Hellenistic period and the beginning of the Imperial period), the city had marble that could be sold at a good price, like the famous marble from the Pentelikon near Athens. Moreover, specialization did not imply exclusivity: Cyrene was rich in grain, oil, and wine, but also produced large quantities of *silphion*, a plant with medicinal uses, but which was also used in cooking, and could be found nowhere other than in Cyrene's hinterland.[83] Others had to occupy a niche that was as specific as possible in order to provide foreign markets with products that would easily find buyers. Theangela was famous for its honey.[84] In the warm waters of the southern Aegean, or, farther on, for the cities of southern Asia Minor, Magna Graecia, Sicily, and Cyrenaica, murex production could occupy and feed a large population. Coastal cities could work maritime salt beds, like those in the area of Aliki of Lemnos or the Gulf of Kalloni in Mytilene.[85] Keos produced its ochre (*miltos*), which was used in painting, especially warships, and was thus considered a strategic material; it was also used to fight infestations of larvae and wood rot fungi in trees and vines.[86] In addition to its agricultural products, Sinope sold a first quality ochre, actually coming from Kappadokia, before the trade route was diverted to Ephesos.[87] During the Hellenistic period, Kythnos sold its cheeses as far away as Egypt.[88] Siphnos provided its alum and its "stone of Siphnos," which Pliny tells us could be cut and turned to make kitchen utensils, because when it was heated in oil it turned black and hardened.[89] But specialties could also be artisanal. Sikyon sold its *sikuōnia*, special leather shoes.[90] Taras sold its *tarantina*, and the island of Amorgos its *amorgina*, two varieties of fine and transparent fabrics (the production was then apparently imitated in other cities), just as Megara specialized in *exōmides*, inexpensive woolen coats.[91] The list could be greatly extended.

For cities that clearly had no environmental niche to take advantage of or any well-defined artisanal specialty, there remained transportation activities. Thus, as Aristotle stresses (*Politics* 4.4.1), the people of Tenedos, whose island was situated at the entrance to the Bosporos strait in an area where dangerous winds made navigation very difficult, had specialized as ferrymen (*porthmeis*), not only transporting products from one shore of the Hellespont to the other, but certainly also forwarding products for sailors in a hurry or who did not want to continue on to the Black Sea.[92] Thus, in the early third century BCE, Heracleides Criticus gives a vivid description of the little Boiotian city of Anthedon, situated on the Euboian Channel. The people of this city, too, earned their living by providing ferry services, but they also engaged in naval construction, fishing for fish and sponges, collecting murex. The most elderly gathered *phukos*—that is, seaweed with tinctorial properties producing a red pigment that could be used as a second-quality dyestuff or in cosmetics, or applied themselves to fishing from the coast:[93]

> The city is not of large size. It is situated directly on the Euboian Sea. It has an agora entirely planted in trees, which is surrounded by double porticos. It is rich in wine and fish, but it lacks grain, because its territory is infertile. Its inhabitants are almost all fishermen. They earn their livings by their hooks and by fish, or else by purple and sponges, and when they get old, staying on the shore, at [collecting] *phukos* or at [exploiting] fishermen's shacks. They have a ruddy complexion and they are all thin. The ends of their fingernails are damaged by work at sea. Most of them are trained ferrymen or are shipbuilders. They not only do not cultivate the land, but do not have any, as they say they are the descendants of Glaukos the sailor, who is supposed to have been a fisherman.

It is fascinating that Heracleides' description finds correspondence in the modern anthropological description of the fishing village of Trikeri, at the tip of the Magnesia peninsula. There, the same exclusive orientation of the men toward activities connected with the sea (in modern Trikeri, it is women who own the land) can be observed.[94] The environmental constants under very different technological conditions justify identical specializations. Along the same lines, one should especially emphasize that according to Ephorus, quoted by Strabo, it was because of the poverty of their island that the inhabitants of Aigina turned to maritime trade: they nonetheless succeeded in making their island the main commercial city of the Greek world at the end of the Archaic period and the beginning of the Classical period, and one of the most prosperous, if not the richest.[95]

However, since there were usually competitors in the same niche, a brand image had to be created for the product and a reputation established that made it possible to succeed on foreign markets. Even wealthy cities wanted to have a "specialty." Selge, in Pisidia, which nonetheless had many other resources, was proud to be the city of the *sturax*, a plant whose resin went into the composition of very powerful perfumes. The city frequently represented the *sturax* on its silver and bronze coins in the late Hellenistic period (second to first centuries), and returned to this theme on its Imperial period coins.[96] Specialties might be regional, even becoming a generic name for products that were later copied elsewhere, like the goat-hair fabrics from Phrygia, a technique that was perfected in Cilicia, whence the name "Cilicians" (*cilices*). These fabrics might be exported to distant lands.[97] Each city thus tried to have a specific niche that allowed it to be identified on the international market, and to sell products that would in turn allow it to import indispensable commodities. It is thus beyond dispute that products had regional reputations, and it was these reputations that made them valuable. However, it is also true that there was no "trademark," and that not all *tarantina* came from Taras (Taranto), all *amorgina* from Amorgos, or even all "cheese of Kythnos" from the island that gave it its name.[98] Nonetheless, when the import came from another city, the provenance of each product was carefully checked. The documents that accompanied the trader and the ship captain (receipts for the tax paid on leaving the port where the merchandise was loaded, passes for the persons leaving the port) were easy to verify. Containers like amphoras revealed at least the region where they came from, sometimes the city where they had been produced.[99] One thing is certain: the customs documents identified the origin of at least a good series of containers. For example a customs document from Pelousion in Egypt from 259 BCE mentions "wine amphoras from Chios," "wine amphoras from Chios" (not "wine amphoras of Chian wine"), and "(wine) amphoras of Thasos."[100] This proves that the customs officers in such a distant port were perfectly able to identify the city of origin of at least a certain number of frequently traded containers. Additional information like amphora stamps, when they existed (even though they were not designed for that purpose), could provide the additional proof of origin of a certain type of amphora:[101] this was the case for the Rhodian amphoras, which starting during the third century until at least the turn of the second and first century BCE, not only had a characteristic shape but also bore characteristic stamps allowing to corroborate their origin. Classical and early Hellenistic specific amphora stamps allowed to easily separate Thasian amphoras from other amphoras of the same region that shared with them a similar shape. Indeed the previously mentioned customs document from Pelousion proves the care with which the provenance of the imported goods could be noted. To the extent to which the amounts of the tax were a function of the product's value, which was based on its origin, it was possible to distinguish products of original quality from possible poor imitations.

Naturally, production processes continued to be based for the most part on technologies that were more work-intensive than capital-intensive, implying more an increase in the number of workers than technological innovations and major investments of capital (for example, the introduction of machines, but with the ambiguity that slaves were also a capital).[102] This is obvious in the case of textiles and associated activities, including gathering murex and weaving wool, flax, or silk. It remains that the possibility of feeding murex producers or textile workers—free women working with their daughters in the framework of the *oikos* in cities and villages, or slave women also working in the framework of the *oikos* or in urban workshops—relied on innovations connected with new techniques of milling grain and on grain imports from highly productive regions.[103] In turn, the latter justified the existence of this artisanal work by providing it with an outlet.

Hermione's Trade

The little city of Hermione, in southern Argolis, furnishes an excellent example of the kind of case in which archaeological sources join with written sources to cast light on part of the network that supplied the city, on the one hand, and on the scope of its products' distribution on the other hand.[104] Like all other Greek cities, Hermione cultivated its agricultural territory intensively. An arbitration by judges who had come from Miletos and Rhodes shows us that in the Hellenistic period Hermione contended with Epidauros for a grazing land for goats until a judgment (end of the third century?) made the disputed area a territory shared by the two cities.[105] But although it obviously had to import supplementary grain, Hermione was also a grain producer, of course, as an exploration of its territory has shown.[106] That is why Hermione put the image of Demeter Chthonia on the obverse of its coins, and on their reverse side the image of an ear of wheat.[107] It also produced oil, because the remains of several oil mills have been discovered on the city's territory. In all, in southern Argolis (including Halieis, Hermione's neighbor) between 25 and 28 oil mills have been excavated.[108] Even though it never developed into a monoculture, in the Classical period olive oil seems to have provided a significant part of the area's considerable export revenue.[109] Although the local clay appears to have been of poor quality, *pithoi* and amphoras must also have been produced. In the late Imperial period, when the economy was undergoing a clear revival after the depression of the Hellenistic and early Imperial periods, along the coast there were workshops producing bricks, tiles, and amphoras. For example, on one coastal production site a cargo of amphoras ready for loading has been found.[110]

The wreck of a ship dating from the Classical period or the early Hellenistic period that was transporting a cargo of Lakonian tiles has been discovered near the island of Petrokaravo, close to Spetsai (ancient Pityoussa), across from Halieis. Thus one may wonder whether this ship was really going to sell its merchandise in Halieis, as has been thought, or whether she was not sailing from that port.[111] Whatever the truth may be in this particular case, the exportation of tiles might have been an additional resource for Hermione and Halieis in the Classical and Hellenistic periods.

Moreover, the city itself produced dyestuffs, since considerable quantities of murex shells have been found on the peninsula south of the city.[112] An anecdote reported by Alciphron (*Letters* 3.10) indicates the reputation enjoyed by this city's purple. The anecdote concerns a parasite and thief (in Athens, since it is generally thought that the scenes reported by Alciphron are supposed to take place in Athens). Brought into a banquet hall to amuse the guests, he plans to take advantage of the general drunkenness to make off with the silver drinking cups. But since these have been prudently put away, he leaves with the tablecloth, saying to another parasite: "See how magnificent it is, fine Egyptian cloth dyed with purple from Hermione, marvelously light and of the greatest value. If I can sell it without getting caught, I will take you to the innkeeper Pithaknion and I will stuff you with food."[113] The anecdote is interesting because it shows that textiles might be imported from far away—in this case, fine cloth from Egypt, which was dyed and finished (possibly) in Hermione. Nor is it too much to think that Hermione must also have been able to import woolens from inland Peloponnese to finish and export them.

Regarding precisely dyestuffs from Hermione, Plutarch (*Alex.* 36.1–2) reports that when Alexander took Susa in 331 BCE, he found forty thousand talents of coined silver and many other valuables, including five thousand talents of "purple from Hermione." Stored there over a period of a hundred and ninety years (that is, since 521 BCE, the date of Darius's accession), this purple is supposed to have remained perfect in quality, the secret of the exceptionally long preservation of dyes being for purple dye to be prepared with honey, and for white dye to be prepared with "white" olive oil.[114] The text raises various problems of interpretation. The Greek word *porphura* can mean both "purple dye" and "purple cloth." As a result, since in any case it does not seem possible that it referred to the weight of the textiles, it is often thought that Plutarch was alluding to 5,000 silver talents' worth of purple cloth.[115] In fact, the Greek "5,000 talents of purple" does not authorize (at least not directly) such a translation and interpretation. Furthermore, in Babylonia, the tablet of Uruk YOS 6 168, from 550 BCE, has several entries for dyestuff.[116] Strabo (15.3.21) underlines that to accumulate them in Susa, the Achaemenid kings demanded silver from tributary peoples living close to the sea and "colors (*chrōmata*), drugs, horsehair, and wool" from those living inland, along with any other product in which they specialized. Colors in the form of pigments were very sought-after, and they might come from very far away. They must have been used not for dyes but for paints, but the principle remains the same.[117]

Hellenistic documentation from Delos confirms that purple was sold by weight.[118] Finally, it can observed that Plutarch concludes the passage by adding that the kings of Persia also stored water from the Nile and the Danube to show the extent of their power: all this confirms the importance of liquids, and thus of dyes. The hypothesis that dyes were exported directly to Susa, which is the one most in agreement with the Greek text, is thus the only acceptable one. The 5,000 "talents" must have corresponded to 5,000 amphoras, since an amphora might well have a capacity of about 26 liters (viz. a weight of ca. 26 kilograms, or one talent). The period of one hundred and ninety years does not mean that the dyestuff was purchased in 521 BCE, but rather accumulated over a long period (like cash reserves), supposedly starting at that date. The important point is that if we believe this anecdote, purple dye from Hermione was prized and exported as far as the court of the king of Persia, certainly to the great benefit of the people of Hermione. Did all the dyes accumulated in Susa come from Hermione? That is another question, which will probably never be answered. On the other hand, the clue is valuable, and shows that even in the distant Persian capital, the reputation of purple from Hermione was well established.

Thus in addition to fabrics dyed with purple, the people of Hermione also exported dyes. The accounts of the sanctuary of Delos show that purple was sold for silver by weight. Two minas of purple were sold for two minas of silver.[119] That may explain why in the enumeration of the treasures of Susa, the 5,000 talent-weights of purple, probably evaluated at 5,000 silver talents (or a sum of that order) appeared on the list of treasures just after the 40,000 silver talents. For Hermione, producing purple was thus an important source of revenue for its foreign trade balance, which made it possible to feed a comparatively large labor force (even if the producers themselves did not get rich on it). Judging by the three triremes sent to the Battle of Salamis and the 300 hoplites present at Plataiai in 479 BCE, it is possible to estimate the population of the city at between 5,000 and 7,500.[120] Since the murex sea snails were edible, the population must also have found in them a valuable additional source of protein. It has already been observed that Hermione's neighbors showed an interest in fishing grounds.[121]

Finally, Hermione appears on the famous list of grain exports from Cyrene to Greece, for an amount of 8,000 *medimnoi*.[122] There is no reason to think that these imports were exceptional.[123] One should also point out that in the fourth century, Hermione also appears alongside the cities of the Kyklades that borrowed from Delos, which shows that it was in need of cash and capital.[124] Thus it is possible to legitimately postulate the schema of a small city whose population was greater than the opportunities offered by its territory could sustain. Thanks to its exports not only of olive oil but also of dyes or dyed textiles, which were fabricated locally or bought from other partners for dyeing and finishing in Hermione, as Alciphron's anecdote suggests, Hermione was able to pay for its grain imports. The modest but real prosperity of Hermione, like that of its neighbor Halieis, at this time is undeniable. In Halieis, the depositories (*koprōnes*) of the fourth century reveal exceptionally high percentages of ceramics imported from Attika, Argos, and Corinth: 31.3 percent in one house, 42.4 percent in another.[125] This does not mean that by themselves these imports represented a particularly high value. But they prove that the city was fully connected to international trade networks.

At this period, Hermione minted its own coins in small quantities, issued between about 365 and 325 BCE. These were minted in silver (triobols and obols) and in bronze (*trichalkoi, dichalkoi,* and *chalkoi*), and were clearly intended for circulation within the city, even if a few silver coins are found in small numbers in the hoards of the northwestern Peloponnese. Besides, other communities in southern Argolis suffered severely from the Hellenistic recession in the Aegean world, to the point of disappearing, as did Halieis, whose territory was absorbed by Hermione. But although it was weakened, Hermione succeeded in maintaining itself as an independent city, as is shown by testimonies relating to its immediate territorial environment. Between 229 and 146 BCE, it again issued new silver and bronze coins of the Achaian Confederation bearing the ethnic of Hermione, which shows that it was able to maintain a certain level of prosperity.[126]

Regional Supply and Long-Distance Trade

Transport costs, which are a function of the unit value of the product and the distance, constitute a constraint that structures trade networks. Observation shows that even today, in most cases, the intensity of trade relations is a function of distance: for economies of the same size trade partners are distributed on a gradient corresponding to the distance between them.[127] This was the case *a fortiori* in an economy like that of ancient Greece, because transport costs were relatively much higher than they are now, and there were considerable differences in the value of the goods transported (table 13.2).

These figures help us represent the value relationships among various cargoes by comparing the prices by cubic meter (in fact, one should also take into account the weight of the various cargoes, which inevitably also impacted the traders' decisions—for instance, tiles were much heavier than grain per unit volume, which discouraged long-distance transport even more). One should note that the data are established on the basis of the price on arrival for foodstuffs or for tiles, but for ceramic vases, in most cases the prices are those in Athens—that is, at the point of departure (that is why, for grain we also give in line 4 the estimated prices at the point of departure). In any case, these figures allow us to compare the relative value of cargoes. They show the interest there may have been in transporting oil and wine over long distances, rather than tiles (and *a fortiori* bricks, whose value was much lower). We can also derive from this a "gradient" of the trading distance that is inversely proportional to the value of the goods (and hence to transport costs). Thus regarding building materials imported to Delphi, Epidauros, Eleusis, or Delos for sanctuaries, we are dealing with regional supplies.[128] Marble and large cypress beams (for roof structures) might be imported from more distant sources: according to Hermippus, at the end of the fifth century BCE "beautiful Crete [sent to Athens] cypress for the gods."[129] But small quantities were involved, and in any case the unit cost was high. Importing tiles and bricks was already more difficult, because they are, obviously, things that can be produced almost anywhere. But the availability of high-quality clay, more abundant and therefore less expensive wood, and a particular kind of know-how could make the difference and justify imports. In Delos, the sanctuary's accounts show that bricks and tiles might be imported from neighboring islands.[130] The discovery in the Saronic Gulf near southern Argolis of at least one wreck from the Classical or early Hellenistic period of a ship carrying Lakonian tiles confirms that such things were frequently transported.[131] In a case that is of special interest because the tiles are stamped, it is even possible to demonstrate the existence of a genuine regional network. Tiles bearing the stamp *Tumnia*, which very probably came from the deme of Tymnos in the Rhodian Peraia, were distributed in a regional environment: they have been found in the

TABLE 13.2. Comparative Transport Costs

PRICE/ CHOUS	OIL 17 AMPH., EACH 7 CHOES	PRICE/ CHOUS	OIL 14 AMPH., EACH 7 CHOES	PRICE/ CHOUS	WINE 17 AMPH.	PRICE/ CHOUS	WINE 14 AMPH.	PRICE/ MED-IMNOS	WHEAT	PRICE/ MED-IMNOS	BARLEY	PRICE/ THICK-NESS	CORIN-THIAN TILES	PRICE BY TYPE	VASES
4,6	547	4,6	451	1:2	238	1:2	196	16	305	6	114	1:1	89	1	67
3	357	3	294	2:1	119	2:1	98	6	114	5	95	1:0.8	74	2	42
1	119	1	98	3:0.4	50	3:0.4	41	5	95	3	57	2:1	44	3	28
								2	38	1	19	2:5	37		

Source: After Gill 1991, 46, modified for the grain values.

Notes: Right columns: comparative prices per cubic meter of cargo.
The prices indicated (in drachms) correspond to prices seen in Greece in the fourth century. They must, of course, be taken *cum grano salis*. But they allow us to form an idea of price relationships. The variations correspond to differences in quality or the mode of packaging. To simplify the interpretation of the table, prices in *oboloi* are reduced to fractions of a drachm: 0.4 dr. = 2.5 *oboloi*.

- For wine, type 1 = wine from Chios at 2 dr. per *chous*; type 2 = Thasos at 1 dr. per *chous*; type 3 = Attic at 2.5 *oboloi* per *chous*.
- For tiles, type 1 = tiles 3 cm thick; type 2 = tiles 6 cm thick
- For ceramic vases, type 1 = red-figured *hudriai* at 3 dr. apiece; type 2 = a set of vases including six bell-shaped craters; type 3 = a set of red-figured, bell-shaped craters, *lēkythoi*, or amphoras from Nola.

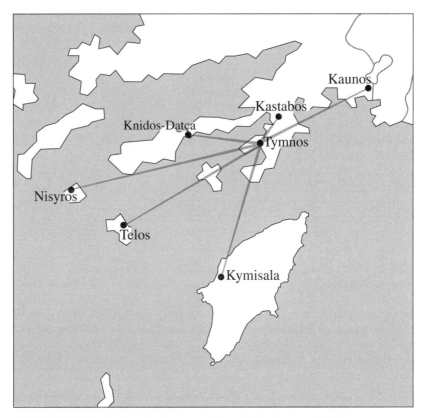

FIGURE 13.1. Distribution of tiles stamped *Tumnia* (third century BCE).

sanctuary of Kastabos (north of Tymnos), to the east in Kaunos; to the west in Knidos (Datça), and on the islands of Nisyros, Telos, and Rhodes (deme of Kymisala).[132] Availability and competitive prices, even when transportation costs were included, was the key to this kind of regional commerce in heavy products that met specific needs (figure 13.1).

Over greater distances—that is, if one wanted to move into another regional network—it was no longer profitable to transport these heavy materials, whose value per unit volume was low: their prices would not have been competitive with products from the region concerned. In Delos, precisely for tiles transported from the nearby island of Syros (about 30 kilometers away), the transport cost added 25.5 percent to the cost of the cargo.[133] On the other hand, products whose value per unit volume was high were transported over long distances. The ingredients of perfumes might come from the "Red Sea" (what we call the Indian Ocean). In the third century BCE, "Kythnos cheese" might well have been transported as far as Egypt, since at that time it sold for 90 drachms per talent.[134] Naturally, grain, wood, or iron might also be transported over long distances, even though their unit value was comparatively low, because transporting them was usually still justified, provided that prices at the destination remained sufficiently high. However, this was not always the case. According to Livy (30.38.5), at the end of the Second Punic War, grain deliveries from Sardinia caused the price in Rome to fall so low that merchants let ship captains keep the grain to pay the freight.

Thus it is clear that the notion of "regional network" has to be used with caution, since the distances covered by the goods traded were a function of their unit value. Every major importing city, whether Athens in the Classical period, or Delos or Rhodes in the Hellenistic period, was at the center of complex networks whose structure, whether for imports or for exports, was closely related to transportation costs. This does not mean that the latter were the only parameter structuring trade: traditional preferences or political and commercial agreements were also factors in selecting trading partners and in establishing these networks. But the rule of costs nonetheless applied in every case.[135]

That is why each geographical basin of the Mediterranean tended to constitute a particular trade area: the Greek far west around Marseilles, Magna Graecia, and Sicily (each of the latter two areas having its own autonomy within this larger whole), the Aegean, the Black Sea, or the area formed in the Classical period and *a fortiori* in the Hellenistic period by the southern coasts of Asia Minor, Cyprus, the coasts of the Levant, and Egypt. Though they provide a very imperfect index of commercial circulation, coin hoards show this amply.[136] In each of the areas mentioned earlier, the coins of the area in question are broadly predominant. In the west, coins from Marseilles are not often found around the city, but they nonetheless constituted the vast majority of the coins circulating in that area in every period. The same can be said, although to a lesser extent, about the area of Magna Graecia and Sicily. Thus even a large mixed hoard like the Taranto hoard *IGCH* 1874 is for the most part composed of coins from that area, along with a few coins from Northern Greece, Aigina, Athens, Corinth, and the Kyklades. The Selinous hoard from the end of the last decade of the sixth century—in which, out of 165 coins, 81 came from Aigina, 39, from Corinth, and one from Abdera, the rest coming from Italy and Sicily (including 35 from Selinous itself)—constitutes a true exception and shows the importance of the great trading cities of Aigina and Corinth in the period.[137] Similarly, in every period the Aegean was a region in which most of the trade was conducted on the basis of proximity. On the Black Sea, a major portion of the trade was between cities in the region: thus most of the amphoras from Herakleia and Sinope were sold in Pontos.[138] Much the same was true for the eastern Mediterranean area. Many testimonies ranging from the Archaic to the Hellenistic period show the existence of this eastern commercial *koinē*. A papyrus that happens to contain a fragment of an entry register from an Egyptian port (Alexandria?) of the second century CE (after 117 CE) shows that this tendency persisted in the Imperial period. Out of twelve provenances, nine are ports in the eastern Mediterranean, along with one mention of Ostia for a very large ship that was going to take back grain to what was then the capital of the Mediterranean world, and two ports whose identity has not been clearly established.[139]

However, this strong tendency to regional trade, which was a function of transportation costs and did not extend beyond a limited geographical basin, obviously did not exclude trade among regions, over long distances, for products whose price in a port in another region remained attractive, despite the addition of transportation costs. With a few exceptions, heavy products of low value per unit volume were thus not transported over long distances. The exceptions have to do with the fact that a ship making a round-trip sometimes had to make one leg without being able to load a cargo of great value. But since a ship had to be loaded in order to be seaworthy, it might be filled with a cargo that did not have much commercial value. Consider the case, which is however very particular because it concerns voyages made on behalf of the state, of the annonary ships of the Imperial period, which were supposed to come back from Carthage (and other African ports) loaded with grain, but for the outgoing voyage were loaded with bricks. One can suppose that this was done for lack of a more profitable cargo, although the loading of bricks made specifically for the construction of baths and cisterns suggests that the bricks were not chosen at random.[140] As for the Classical and Hellenistic periods, we may suspect that millstones from Nisyros might have been transported as ballast, and then replaced by a cargo of commercial value if an opportunity arose to sell them, because they were nonetheless sought-after products.[141] That is why millstones from Nisyros were taken to Cyprus, as is shown by the 29 millstones found in the Kyrenia shipwreck from the end of the fourth century, and even to the far west, as is shown by the El Sec shipwreck from the middle of the fourth century BCE: the location of this wreck in the Balearics suggests that the ship, which was carrying the millstones, along with Greek Aegean, Greek-Italic, and Punic amphoras and Attic ceramics, was en route to the Iberian peninsula.[142]

Networks and "Free Riders"

The system of surpluses and lacks leads us to conceive international trade in terms of a difference in potential between two poles: one city has wine, the other grain. The difference in potential (or tension) between them is manifested in the existence of a mutual trade flow. Thus in the Classical period, the Aegean sent its wine to the Bosporan kingdom and received grain in return. However, onto this base, which constituted the backbone of the system, so to speak, were grafted a multitude of activities that took advantage of it to insinuate themselves into the established flow. Similarly, a series of regions or cities located on the axis of circulation took advantage of it to develop themselves.

This was the case during the Classical period for a whole series of cities located on the route between Athens and Pontos, beginning with those on the Euboian Channel.[143] Starting from Athens, ships did not usually try to make a direct crossing to the north (which, moreover, would have had to be made against the prevailing wind). In particular, they did not sail around Euboia, because the north side of the island is very inhospitable and battered by the wind. The *Mediterranean Pilot* strongly discourages sailors from venturing near this rocky coast, which has no havens.[144] When during the summer of 480 BCE, Xerxes attempted to round Euboia in a bold maneuver to encircle the Greek fleet, many of the ships involved in this perilous enterprise were struck during the night by a storm in the "Hollows of Euboia" and were all lost, as Herodotus mentions (8.13).

It was in these same Hollows of Euboia that the hero of Dio Chrysostom's *Euboean Discourse* (7.2) was shipwrecked.[145] Taking up the theme of the return of the Achaeans to their homeland after the conquest of Troy, Euripides (*Helen* 766–67 and 1126–31) makes Cape Kaphereus (north of Karystos, on the north coast of Euboia) an accursed place. It was there that Nauplios, the mythical king of Euboia, had used a navigation lamp to attract ships coming back from Troy, in order to avenge his son Palamedes, who had been unjustly condemned by the Achaeans. We may wonder whether the legend reflected actual practices of the people living on the north side of the island.

In fact, sites on the north side of Euboia were of no importance, in contrast to a series of sites on the Euboian Channel, on the island, and on the continent. It is there, on the southern coast of the island, that the great civic centers of Histiaia, Chalkis, Eretria, and Karystos were located, each of which dominated several minor sites. On the continent, there was also a series of cities and secondary sites, from Lamia in Malis in the north to Oropos in the south. For example, in Lokris and in Boiotia, Halai, Larymna, Anthedon, Aulis, and Delion, all show the density of this occupation. Destroyed during the Persian Wars, Halai was rebuilt starting in the late fourth century and reached the apex of its prosperity in the Hellenistic period, its development probably corresponding to the rise of Macedon, to the control that the latter exercised over Euboia, and to the concomitant rise of the ports of Demetrias and Histiaia.[146] In all likelihood, Halai engaged in the same activities as its neighbor Anthedon, ferrying and fishing.[147] The attraction of a navigational axis, with the opportunities that it offered, was a powerful vector of development. On the axis of circulation that ran along the coast of Asia and on which ships were also protected from the high winds on the open sea, an entirely similar phenomenon can be observed. For instance on the island of Lesbos, the difference in development of cities situated on the maritime route and the others is striking. Methymna and Mytilene, on the channel along the coast of Asia, became the island's two most important cities. On the west coast, however, Antissa and Eresos remained secondary cities, and the cities in the center of the island, Arisbe and Pyrrha, collapsed altogether.[148]

As for the relations between Athens and the Bosporan Kingdom, it is possible to observe the implications of the establishment of a mutual trade flow between these two poles. The prosperity of Mende (on the Pallene peninsula of Chalkidike), which lay on the maritime route between Athens and the Bosporan Kingdom, is a good example. The contract in *Against Lacritus* shows that in the fourth century a ship could leave Athens almost empty. With the 3,000 drachms that he has been lent, the trader is supposed to buy wine in Chalkidike, Mende, or Skione (on the Pallene peninsula), and then head for Pontos. Athens thus paid for its grain with its silver: but on the way, this silver was transformed into wine.[149] The development of vineyards in northern Greece during the Classical period, those in the northern Sporades (Peparethos, Ikos), Chalkidike (Mende, Skione, Akanthos), or Thasos, was thus probably due in large measure to its role as an intermediary between Athens and Pontos.[150]

Mende produced a highly prized, smooth, dry wine.[151] The city's amphoras, which were triangular in form, were easily recognizable. There are many shipwrecks from the Classical period that contain amphoras from Mende. The wreck of Porticello on the straits of Sicily shows that these amphoras could also travel the western route (there is even one in the El Sec wreck in Majorca), but they are found above all in the Aegean.[152] Several spectacular wrecks from the fifth century have been found in the northern Sporades, north of Euboia. A first one comes from the little island of Kyra Panagia. It can be dated (roughly) to the mid-fifth century and contained Mendean amphoras. A second one comes from the island of Alonnisos (ancient Ikos), a little farther west. This large wreck can be dated to the end of the fifth century and contained more than 4,000 amphoras from Mende and Peparethos (the western neighbor of Ikos).[153]

On average, Mende paid Athens the comparatively high tribute of 8 talents. The city's prosperity can also be observed in its coinage, with its fine series of tetradrachms from the fifth century representing on their obverse perhaps a drunken Hephaistos (rather than Dionysos?) sitting on an ass and holding a *kantharos*, and on their reverse a vine stock.[154] Its neighbor Torone (on the Sithonia peninsula of Chalkidike) put on its coins the image of an amphora or an *oinochoē*, depending on the denomination. Peparethos was also very prosperous in this period. Dionysos, the god of wine, grapes and a *kantharos* (as wine drinking vessel) figure prominently on its various coin series. It paid 3 talents to the Athenian empire when the islands of Ikos and Skiathos paid respectively only 1,500 and 1,000 drachms, viz. twelve and eighteen times less.[155] It is clear that for these regions, Athenian silver and navigational contracts from Athens represented, on the one hand, a considerable influx of capital that helped develop vineyards, and on the other hand ensured that the cities of Pontos would continue to have an interest in their products.

In the Hellenistic period, references to Mende's wine become rarer, and seem to disappear from our sources after the second century BCE. However, wine was still produced, and exported, from the territory of the city in the third and second centuries BCE. The Mendean origin of the amphora type of the so-called Parmeniskos Group is now certain.[156] To be sure, after being compelled to submit to Olynthos in the early fourth century, in 316 BCE Mende's inhabitants were forced to move to the new city of Kassandreia.[157] It should be observed that the city of Torone, on the neighboring Sithonia peninsula, also underwent a marked decline starting in the late fourth century, as is shown by the archaeology of the site.[158] However, Kassandros would have liked to maintain a profitable export, and that is why, according to Athenaeus (11 784c), he asked the great sculptor Lysippus to create a new kind of container (*keramion*) for Kassandreia, which exported Mende wine. Athenaeus says that Lysippus created an original container by taking features from each of many existing types of amphoras. The amphoras of the Parmeniskos Group might correspond to the type created by Lysippus, although this attractive hypothesis still lacks formal proof. Thus it is certain that in Chalkidike, just like in Thasos or in the Sporades wine continued to be produced after the Classical period. [159] In the first part of the Hellenistic period, Macedon, Thrace, and the Black Sea could still represent attractive markets. But increasingly new trading routes and new exporting cities tended to replace the networks of the Classical period. In the Imperial period the (uncertain) testimony of Alciphron (*Letters of Parasites* 3.2.2), does not in any way mean that this wine was still held in high esteem: this is an archaizing text that actually refers to a situation of the Classical period.[160]

For Athens, the regression began in the late fourth century and was confirmed in the first decades of the third century with Macedon's direct or indirect control over Athens. The decay of mining in Laurion, an activity that had been the motor driving trade with Pontos, was a crucial aspect of this decline. In the Hellenistic period, people in northern Pontos drank locally produced wine (such as that from Chersonesos), wine produced in Chalkidike or in other Back Sea regions (such as wine from Sinope, which was widely exported in Pontic regions). They now also massively imported wine from the south east Aegean area, from Rhodes, Kos, and Knidos. Previously secondary trade circuits, which ran along the coast of Asia and had Rhodes as their pivot, gained new importance. They caused the old networks centered on Athens to be forgotten and led to the decline of several cities that were not able to find another way of integrating themselves into international circuits that would have replaced the failing "Athenian network." Thus in a trade flow, we see a hierarchy among the partners, with elements that are, strictly speaking, the driving forces of the system, whereas others, although they participate fully in it, occupy only a secondary place because they are not autonomous partners.

What holds for partners also holds for the goods exchanged. On a ship, certain commodities constituted the principal cargo, while others were secondary. These were cargoes that were transported only by taking advantage of the existence of a trade flow that was external to them. In a certain way, these cargoes can be compared to "free riders." The economic concept of "free riders" designates persons or groups who benefit from a public good without paying part of the corresponding cost.[161] It can be said, with David W. J. Gill, that the ceramics produced by Athens constitute an exemplary case of a good that was widely distributed abroad not because it was an indispensable commodity, but because it benefited from an established trade flow.[162]

The exportation of decorated Attic ceramics began in the eighth and seventh centuries BCE. But between the sixth century and the end of the fourth, the phenomenon took on a new magnitude. Starting in the sixth century, with the perfecting of a black glaze of exceptional quality, Attic ceramics reached their period of technical maturity. At first, Attic painters adopted the tradition that consisted in representing figures in black against a red background ("black-figure technique"), and then reversed the method of decoration at the end of the sixth century ("red-figure technique"). Until the end of the fourth century, these vases were widely exported in all directions, from the west to Cyprus and the Levant, and from the Black Sea to Cyrene. In addition to fine decorated ceramics, undecorated black-glazed ceramics can also be found on numerous sites, which shows that they were also widely exported.

The success of Attic ceramics is thus connected with their technical quality. "Competitors" in Corinth and in Asia Minor were eliminated by the second half of the sixth century.[163] If there is no doubt that we should see in this a market phenomenon involving a product that became dominant because of its quality, this was nonetheless not the main reason for the crushing dominance of Attic ceramics. Technical quality is a necessary but not sufficient condition for explaining the success of this product over two and half centuries. The first condition of its success seems to have been based on another model: that of the concern of traders leaving from Athens or passing through Athens to load a cargo to maximize the profitability of their voyage. Before the silver mines of the Laurion took off, the first growth in the distribution of Attic ceramics can be explained by the Athenians' mad desire to export everything they could in order to pay for their imports. But compared to the following period, the quantities were still small (table 13.3).[164]

From the last quarter of the sixth century on, Athens's chief export by far was silver from Laurion. All our sources converge to show that it was with the silver mined in Laurion that Athens paid for its grain imports.[165] Deliveries of Attic ceramics in Etruria reflected this rise of Athens, which was henceforth an obligatory stopping point for sailors. Beyond the particular case of Etruria, from the end of the sixth century and for the next two hundred years, the exportation of ceramics fol-

TABLE 13.3. Deliveries of Attic Ceramics in Etruria

DATES BCE	625–600	600–575	575–550	550–525	525–500	500–475	475–450	450–425	425–400
Numbers	1	17	99	443	1470	983	629	228	41
Percentage	0.04	0.68	3.96	17.72	58.8	39.32	25.16	9.12	1.64

Source: After Gill 1991, 47.

Notes: On the other hand, it is not possible to agree with Gill 1994, 102, in his estimates of the quantity of ceramics that arrived in Etruria or other sites, as if archaeological discoveries corresponded to the quantities that objectively arrived at their destination: although we can rely on discoveries in estimating the chronological development of these arrivals, we cannot in any way maintain that these discoveries directly reflect the volume of the quantities that arrived—as if all the sites had been excavated, and in addition excavated exhaustively. Obviously, there is every chance that they represent only a tiny portion of the quantities that actually arrived, in a proportion that must be estimated using entirely different methods.

lowed the rhythm of silver exports. Athenian citizens or metics, along with foreign-ers passing through the city, exported or came to get silver coins that would later be accepted everywhere. That was what provided an opportunity to export ceramics produced in Athens (the diminution and then the collapse of Attic ceramics exports to Etruria in the second half of the sixth century might have to do both with Etruria's own internal situation in that period and with difficulties in Athens during the Pelo-ponnesian War—in general, the west imported far more Attic ceramics in the fourth century, whether to sites in the Iberian peninsula or to Alalia-Aléria in Corsica[166]).

To be sure, beyond painted ceramics Athens still had a number of valuable prod-ucts to export, such as marble, textiles, honey, and probably a long list of various products such as weapons and luxury items. However, none of these commodities could provide the majority of a cargo to fill a ship. In the amusing bargaining be-tween the Athenian Dikaiopolis and the Boiotian in Aristophanes' *Acharnians* (898–905), it is ceramics that appear as the Athenian product par excellence:

> Dikaiopolis: So, what prices do you say? Or do you intend to take away an-other kind of merchandise from here in exchange? — The Boiotian: What is found in Athens and what we don't have in Boiotia. — Dikaiopolis: Take as purchases anchovies from Phaleron or ceramic vases. — The Boiotian: An-chovies or vases? But we have those there. I want what we don't have at home and is found here in large quantities. — Dikaiopolis: Ah! I see: export a syco-phant, after having wrapped him up like a ceramic.

In all likelihood ceramic vases, which were produced in great numbers, constituted, in volume, the largest export from Piraeus for goods produced in Athens. But even if Athens produced them in large quantities, these vases could in no way provide a cargo volume (and value) comparable to that of oil, wine, or wood, which were truly "mass products." Other Athenian-produced commodities (those in the list previ-ously mentioned) certainly represented in value, if not in volume, a more profitable export. Besides one should add that, as stressed by Xenophon (*Poroi* 3.2: "In Athens it is possible to export in return most of the goods that people are in need of"), the Piraeus was also a port of re-export, which attracted traders from all cities.[167]

Thus we have fundamentally a model in which traders found in Athens capital in the form of a loan that could be used either to buy right away a cargo for an outgoing voyage, or be directly exported to buy elsewhere a product that would easily find buyers on a foreign market, such as wine from the Sporades or Chalki-dike. Exporting a return cargo bought in a port normally brought in a larger finan-cial profit than simply exporting local silver coinage. But in the *Poroi* (3.1–2), Xeno-phon emphasizes that traders who could not find a cargo could always sail from Athens with Attic silver money, which given its reputation (based on its purity and weight accuracy) could be sold with profit everywhere—so that we have here a clear case where a currency is treated as a commodity. Athens thus had a lack of exportable goods, and only silver provided a sizable value, allowing it to pay for its huge imports. Exporting ceramics was only a way of maximizing a voyage; ceramics were not a basic product that would justify by themselves making a stop in Athens. It was silver, as a source of capital and a commodity to export, that was at the origin of the prosperity of this city in the late Archaic and Classical period.

This does not in any way mean that the exportation of ceramics was not a valuable source of revenue for export traders. The prices on the vases, a few *oboloi* or at most one to three drachms, were usually the sales price in Athens. They tell us nothing about the sales prices among distant customers, whether Greeks or Barbarians, who might be fascinated by the "world of images" offered by Attic ceramics, and who in any case often esteemed these products enough to have themselves buried with them, along with jewels, weapons, and other valuable objects.[168] On the other hand, for traders to be able to make significant profits, purchase prices in Athens must have been low. We encounter here the same logic as for grain, and that is why it is necessary to be cautious in interpreting the price of products (see the table earlier) when their price was high (grain in Athens) and when it was low (ceramics in Athens). One should compare the price per unit volume of grain in the Bosporan Kingdom with that of ceramics in Athens: in this case, we see that the unit volume of ceramics at the point of departure had a far superior value to that of grain—barley, but also wheat—at the point of departure. That is why along with a series of other products that left hardly any archaeological traces (except in unusual cases, such as shipwrecks), it must have always been very profitable for a trader to take along a few crates of ceramics decorated with figures. If it is asked whether ceramics represented merely an almost unprofitable way of filling up space in a ship's hull in order to provide ballast, it is possible to definitely reply that it did not.[169] For this way of seeing things, one must substitute an analysis in terms of "free riders," which seems to account better for the facts.

International Trade Networks

On the other hand, if one calculates in aggregate terms, it is clear that even though at their height ceramics workshops may have employed about five hundred workers (including slaves), in value their products represented only a small part of Athens's exports.[170] In this respect, an assessment of trade in Attic ceramics can legitimately be compared with trade in fine ceramics from the Far East imported to Europe at the end of the eighteenth century: the latter then accounted for less than 3 percent of the sales of the British East India Company.[171] When Athens's star began to dim with its catastrophic defeats in the Lamian War (322 BCE), followed shortly thereafter by the establishment of the regime of Demetrios of Phaleron and Macedon's direct control over the city's destiny, the so-called luxury ceramics workshops suddenly ceased their activity. Thus it is clear that Attic ceramics did not constitute an autonomous export item, but were dependent on a trade network in which they were only an ancillary element.

In the Hellenistic world in general, the types of ceramics produced changed and became more complex, and several specific regional styles developed. Thus in addition to small black-glazed vases of mediocre quality, two types of decorated ceramics merit special attention. Starting at the end of the third century and during the two following centuries, ceramics in relief, but molded, were produced almost everywhere. These ceramics are still sometimes designated by their traditional (modern) name of "Megarian bowls," because the dominant form is a bowl and Megara was supposed to be its production site. In fact, however, everything suggests that around 224–223 BCE (the year of the creation of the Ptolemais tribe in honor of Ptolemy III), Athens was the primary production center, imitating metal vases imported from Alexandria.[172] This was a technique that made standardized production possible, saving time and employing a less skilled work force.[173] Another important type is constituted by the ceramics known as "West Slope," because large numbers of them have been found on the west flank of the acropolis of Athens. These ceramics are also much more mass produced than those of the preceding period. Most of them are small vases, conventional in form (such as cups and paterae), and are no longer comparable with the variety, ambition, and even sometimes exuberance of the preceding period. They have a black glaze (more matte than that of Archaic and Classical Attic ceramics) with very simple painted decorations, such as crowns, flowers, and festoons. This kind of product appears in various centers in continental Greece (including Athens) in the first quarter of the third century, but there are also other production centers such as Pergamon or the "Ivy Platter Workshop," which has not yet been localized, but was probably in southern Asia Minor or in the Levant.[174] The "West Slope" products from Athens, which are rather few in number, were distributed only in continental Greece and in the Kyklades.

This limited distribution contrasts strongly with that of the black-figured and red-figured ceramics of the preceding period, and corresponds to the also limited political and economic role played by Athens throughout the first half of the Hellenistic period. Pergamon's ceramics were more widely distributed: they are found along the west coast of Asia Minor, on the shores of the Black Sea, and sometimes as far away as Cyprus, the Levant, and Alexandria. These ceramics were thus traded along the great axis of circulation that went from Pontos to the Levant and to Alexandria, an axis from which the ports on the west coast of Asia Minor drew their new prosperity and also manifested itself in the distribution of new coins with the image of Alexander on them.

But with regard to "free rider" system, it is the phenomenal expansion of ceramics from Campania in the Hellenistic period that provides the best parallel to Attic ceramics at the end of the Archaic period and in the Classical period.[175] "Campanian A" ceramics were produced mainly in Naples. The production was standardized, with shapes that could be easily stacked. This was a mass production, certainly carried out in the framework of workshops that employed slaves. Production and exportation exploded after the Second Punic War: millions of vases were exported to Gaul, Spain, and Africa, replacing all local products. It is interesting to note that these ceramics exported over long distances were practically unknown in the immediate hinterland of Naples. The cities on the bay of Naples, in Campania, formed the heart of the Roman commercial system during the last two centuries of the Republic (and continued to do so under the early Empire). Naples, which was still a Greek city, and its neighbor Puteoli, a Roman colony established on the site of the ancient Greek port of Dikaiarcheia (itself a neighbor of Kyme-Cumae), served at that time as the gateway for ships coming from all over the Mediterranean and converging on Rome and Italy. That is why these ceramics are also found in the Aegean area, for instance on Delos.[176]

Like Attic ceramics a few centuries earlier, the development of Campanian A ceramics was based on the existence of a trade network onto which the production and exportation of ceramics was grafted. In quantity and in value, most of the cargo of outgoing voyages in fact consisted of oil or wine produced in Campania. That explains why in shipwrecks, Campanian A ceramics usually (there obviously being some exceptions) accompany Greco-Italian amphoras coming from Campania, as in the Grand Congloué A shipwreck, from ca. 200–180 BCE off Marseilles.[177] Attic ceramics could not accompany a specific kind of amphora because Athens did not export its wine or oil.[178] For all that, one must not assume that ceramics production was a negligible activity. Cato the Elder illustrates the mentality of these landowners, who had a very acute sense of profit and who made the most of what they had. Provided that they could take advantage of a pre-established trade flow, the promoters of this activity could realize large profits from it.

Thus one should put the value of fine ceramic products into perspective. In antiquity they did not have the value of art objects that is currently attributed to them. But it cannot be denied that they could yield profits for those who produced them or for those who transported them. Had they not been profitable, even though only in connection with a pre-existing trade network, it would be incomprehensible that these activities persisted over several centuries, whether it is a question of Attic ceramics with figured decoration between the sixth and fourth centuries BCE, West Slope ceramics from the Hellenistic period, or Campanian A ceramics from the late Republican period.

Actors in Trade and Redistribution Centers

The question of the actors involved in trade raises the question of the way in which a city's foreign trade was carried on. One must not imagine that there is a necessary continuity between production and circulation, as if local merchants alone had undertaken all the exports for their own community. In certain cities, foreign trade, whether imports or exports, might be for the most part in the hands of its citizens or metics (resident aliens). In others, it is probable that most or even all of it was carried on by foreigners in transit. In this respect, one can say that every kind of situation could be found. It has been observed that some cities specialized in commerce in a local environment or on a large scale and over long distances. In the first category, we can classify the ferrymen of Tenedos or Anthedon. In the second, merchants from several large cities distinguished themselves by playing a particularly active commercial role. In the late Archaic period, one thinks of Samos, and then especially of Aigina, in the same period and in the fifth century, until it was eliminated as a city by Athens in 431 BCE because the latter thought it too dangerous to its own interests. Chios was also a great city of ship-owners, as Aristotle emphasizes (*Politics* 4.4.1), which leads us to put this city in the same category as Aigina. One could add to it Phaselis, whose merchants traveled all the seas during the Classical period, and which continued to play a prominent role during the Hellenistic period.[179] The difference between Aigina and Phaselis, on the one hand, and between Samos and Chios, on the other hand, was that the former had no specific product, or almost none, to export (even though Phaselis could export its wood). Merchants from these cities transported commodities from all over the Mediterranean. Samos and Chios, on the other hand, were productive cities that lived off their exports, and it is possible that they deliberately favored exports of their products by native merchants. In 545 BCE, the people of Chios disapproved of fugitive Phokaians who had settled in the Oinoussai islands (that is, on their doorstep) because they feared the competition of these formidable merchants.[180]

The sea was a boundless space. It offered opportunities for great profits for someone who was willing to take the financial and physical risk of sailing to a distant port. Here again, of course, one has to expect to see the rule of proximity involved, trade in any given area being for the most part carried on by merchants from that area. But it was permissible for people from more distant lands to participate in it: merchants from Phaselis or from Salamis in Cyprus might be found on the Black Sea, as is clearly shown by fourth-century Attic legal speeches, and during the Hellenistic period merchants from Marseilles traveled as far as Piraeus or even Alexandria.

However, it is necessary to emphasize that in fact the navigator's city of origin mattered little. A commercial voyage usually seems to have implied a loan to finance the cargo and the voyage itself. Whatever the navigator's city of origin, the key point (as already stated) was the place where the commercial contract had been made, which established the identity of the city for the benefit of which the commercial voyage was to be carried out.[181] As already observed, the most frequent kind of commercial contract seems in fact to have been one providing for a round-trip voyage (*amphoteroplous*), which was supposed to give the creditor a guarantee that his debtor would not escape his obligation to repay the loan.

There has been a lively debate as to whether the principal mode of commerce was a kind of short-distance coastal shipping that provided for a distribution of products little by little, or whether there were direct long-distance connections between cities that were related as sellers and consumers. On this point it is certain that there were great maritime trade axes, often involving commerce without intermediaries and over long distances (which does not mean without stopovers), for example between Athens, the Bosporan Kingdom, Egypt, Cyrene, and the Levant. However, not all products delivered to places very far from the Mediterranean arrived there in this way. The tendency (not the general rule) was that the farther a product was from its city of origin, the more likely it was to have been part of a composite cargo. In addition, the quantity of the product in this cargo was very likely to have been inversely proportional to the distance. Concretely, this means that on the Aegean Sea there were complete cargoes of amphoras from Mende, and off Apollonia of Cyrenaica, Alexandria, or Cyprus, there was every chance of finding homogeneous, or nearly homogeneous cargoes of Rhodian amphoras. Out of a total of 404 amphoras, the cargo of the Kyrenia shipwreck included 343 from Rhodes, the rest being from Samos, Paros, Crete, and the Levant. The Serçe Limanı B shipwreck (south of the Rhodian Chersonese), from ca. 300–270 BCE, carried a homogeneous cargo of 600 amphoras of the "Zenon group" produced in Knidos-Datça: the ship thus went down quite near its point of departure.[182]

The situation in the western Mediterranean was symmetrical. For example, at the end of the Archaic period one finds almost homogeneous cargoes of Etruscan amphoras, or mixed cargoes of Etruscan and Punic amphoras, or later on, in the second and third centuries, mixed cargoes of Greco-Italic and Dressel 1 amphoras (two types from Italy or Sicily). On the other hand, amphoras from the Aegean area appear either as minor parts of cargoes that are otherwise very homogeneous or in very composite cargoes. For the first case, one can cite the vessel involved in the previously mentioned Grand Congloué A shipwreck, which was carrying, in addition to more than 400 Greco-Italic amphoras, about thirty Rhodian amphoras and a few amphoras from Knidos, Kos, and other Aegean sources.[183] For the second case, one can cite the El Sec shipwreck. Out of 474 amphoras that were found, there were amphoras from Samos (18.4 percent), Greco-Italic amphoras (14.7 percent), Corinthian-type amphoras (11.3 percent), amphoras from Chios (5.2 percent, it seems), Punic amphoras from Sicily, and a few isolated ones from Mende, Thasos, Sinope, Kos, Rhodes (perhaps), and a certain number that are still not fully identified.[184] The ship probably had a Punic crew. The logical conclusion is that these amphoras from the Aegean area, along with the Attic ceramics and the millstone from Nisyros that accompanied them, had been loaded in at least one intermediate port, in Sicily or in Carthage.

Before being delivered to the final consumer, these goods thus might pass through the hands of several intermediaries. They were pure exchange values. Although at the outset the producer might have an idea of where his products were going, he knew nothing about the final consumer, and in most cases, this had little importance for him so long as his product found a buyer willing to pay a good price. Artisanal products, such as ceramics, might however have been a slightly different case. It seems reasonable to suppose that in a way more or less precise depending on the distance involved, potters might have been able to respond to a specific demand on the basis of information relayed to them by traders. Did the *emporoi* purchase their goods directly in the workshops? Or did the producers have representatives in the *deigma*? This is not yet fully clear. In any case, that Athenian workshops were able to guide their production (decoration or type of vases) in response to the desiderata of foreign buyers in Greece itself, in Pontos, Etruria, or Sicily is a hypothesis that will always be difficult to prove definitively, but remains nonetheless plausible and attractive—after all, to go back to the comparison with trade with the

Far East in early modern Europe, Chinese artisans also made porcelains intended for the Western market and on models provided by Western merchants.[185]

In addition to specific commands, perhaps one should simply imagine that traders setting off in a given direction selected among the products of a workshop the items that seemed to them best adapted to the distant market where they would be sold. After a certain period of time, successive purchases made by various *emporoi* would end up determining the production of the workshops, for or against a certain shape or kind of decoration. In any case, it is clear that these exchanges of economic information do not imply the existence of direct links between producers and consumers. Moreover, the absence of such links cannot be considered a "primitive" trait. In fact, it is commerce characterized by a direct link between producer and customer (ordering without intermediary) that is the less sophisticated of the two types. The breaking of the tie between producer and final consumer, the existence of several intermediaries between producer and consumer, is on the contrary characteristic of an economy dominated by merchandise and belonging to the universe of "exchange value."

Finally, it is clear that while direct lines may have existed between major commercial partners, there were nonetheless places that played the role of warehouses and redistribution centers. This was the case in particular for the Greek or Punic cities of Sicily and for Carthage, which were located at the junction of the two Mediterranean basins, so that a number of merchants from the Aegean area must have limited themselves to transporting their goods there, in order to avoid venturing farther west to cities that were often not Greek and with which they were not familiar, and over seas whose dangers they did not know.

Even in Greece, and for other reasons, cities played the role of redistribution centers. The case of Corinth has already been mentioned. As Thucydides emphasized (1.13.5), this city's commercial calling was virtually imposed by its geography. It was located at the intersection of the overland route between central Greece and the Peloponnese and the maritime route between the Gulf of Corinth and the Saronic Gulf: merchandise arriving in the western port of Lechaion might be re-exported to the Aegean through the port of Kenchreai. Athens was, of course, a center par excellence in which traders could find all sorts of commodities for export (except grain and oil, which it was forbidden to export[186]). It is probable that its role as a redistribution center and a financial center made a major contribution to Athens's wealth during the Classical period: beyond the question of their value, the universal distribution of Attic ceramics shows that Piraeus was then a commercial shipping hub. This role as re-exporter was partially taken over by Rhodes during the Hellenistic period, and there too, beyond their inherent value, the just as universal export of Rhodian amphoras shows the place of this city in trade networks.

The secret of the economic success of the Greek city-states resided in the productivity gains provided by an international division of labor. The latter was founded on differentials in productivity between regions connected through commercial trade. These were at first absolute advantages directly connected with natural privileges.

But the complexity of trade networks and the imagination used in "creating" new products through the exploitation of the natural environment or through artisanal production and commerce made it possible to move beyond the tyranny of natural advantages to produce complex trade networks. The latter were structured around major poles, but "free riders" also benefited greatly from the network, while at the same time adding useful complements to it. In this complex universe, each city played its role. It is these strategies of international trade that should now be explored.

XIV

STRATEGIES OF
INTERNATIONAL TRADE

According to Aristotle, just as a citizen could not by himself be self-sufficient (*au-tarkēs*), and on the contrary, it was only in the framework of the civic collectivity that could hope to achieve this ideal, so a city could not hope to produce by itself all the goods that it required.[1] Just as the division of labor was the foundation of the city-state, so foreign trade was ineluctable and intended to meet city-states' needs through mutual exchange. Plato's or Aristotle's city-state thus could not exist in isolation. The condition of its being is the simultaneous existence of a collectivity of city-states with which it can establish trade that will allow it to achieve its ideal of self-sufficiency. Like domestic trade, foreign trade has to respect the equality of the actors in commerce, so that all the cities involved in foreign trade can benefit from it. Otherwise, commercial disputes would be in danger of growing bitter and degenerating into open warfare.

One might even add that just as in the framework of the civic collectivity generosity rightly understood is indispensable for the maintenance of this collectivity, so in relations among cities generous help must be offered to cities in difficulty. Thus the many decrees thanking other cities for good deeds of all kinds, including those involving direct military, financial or economic aid, were not merely rhetorical. Generally speaking, there was in fact a form of solidarity among city-states, each of them having an interest in maintaining the "society of the city-states." In addition, there were group solidarities among cities that maintained particular relationships with each other. By demonstrating the necessity of trade and equality in trade, Aristotle was simply presenting in a systematic way the institutional system that prevailed in the Greece of the city-states. The details of its organization varied from one city to another. But fundamentally it was everywhere governed by the same principles.

The rules of trade and the distribution of "natural advantages" (which, as already observed, were also largely created by the various actors) thus played the role of a system of constraints within which genuine strategies of foreign trade could be constructed. The objective here is to account for the specificity of these trade strategies, whose particularity is that the cities were not merely "arbiters" in matters of trade but played the role of partners. In this way a complex network not only of "commercial lines" but also trade strategies was formed, which need to be examined in detail. Next will be analyzed the specific case of food supplies, because cities' strategies developed in particular with regard to the question of grain, which was crucial for their population's survival. Finally, a special attention will be devoted to the case of Athens in the Classical period. Athens was, of course, an unusual city, and the strategy of a city like Athens could not be that of a small city. But it had an exceptional weight in the classical world's trade, and as a result it played a structural role that was fundamental for all other trade strategies.

THE LOGIC OF TRADE

Mutual Trade and Nondirectional Trade

Two institutional logics (apparently contradictory, but ultimately complementary) prevailed in the international market. The first, which was favored by Aristotle and conservative thinkers, consisted in setting up a "surpluses for surpluses" trade strategy. For Aristotle (*Politics* 7.5.4), "the import of commodities that they happen not to have in their city and the export of their surplus productions are necessary requirements."[2] A city that had a surplus of grain contracted with another city that had a surplus of wine: in this way, through an exchange of "surpluses," everyone benefited. But this strategy had its limits, one of which was that one of the partners might fail to deliver the goods. Let us take the case of a city exporting its "surplus" wine: it counted on its partner providing it with grain. But if, for one reason or another (an exceptionally bad harvest, a war), this provider did not come through, the city that was counting on the grain delivery was in danger of finding itself in a difficult situation if it had no other partner. That is why even cities that had made mutual import and export agreements could not count exclusively on this system to organize their foreign trade. Moreover, the increasing complexity of trade in a universe of cities with a very large number of potential partners meant that such "exclusive" agreements could not be the sole mode of exchange, as was clear to political leaders of the time.[3] The directions taken by commercial trade and the decisions related to them were far too complex to be managed by a system of agreements to exchange "surpluses for surpluses." Besides, fiscal privileges granted on an individual or collective basis to citizens of a foreign city-state gave an institutional content to privileged trade networks, in the mutual interest of the partners. Such partnership agreements, which already existed in the Classical period, seem to have rapidly superseded agreements for "exchanges of surpluses" in the strict sense of the term.

The second logic, which constituted the dominant tendency in the Classical and Hellenistic periods, was thus to let trade partners act freely. In fact, the great majority of international trade in the world of Greece of the city-states was carried on by private actors acting on their own initiative. For a given product, it was the "invisible hand" of the market that tended to decrease the tension between the two poles of the network mentioned earlier, to equalize quantities and prices between these two poles (which does not mean that at the end of a trade cycle these prices were equal, but only that the difference between them had decreased). In short, it is the merchant's eternal role: buying where prices are low and selling where they are high.[4] The principle of leaving most of international trade to merchants' initiative also held for trade that benefited from framing agreements. Thus merchants who were headed for Athens benefited from a customs privilege to export from Bosporos, but the decision to make the voyage (in general round-trip from Athens) was their own. It was the profit these merchants expected that led them from one port to another on the basis of the information available to them. As already observed, Xenophon (*Economics* 20.27–28) pointed out that merchants go where profit leads them. An example of this is given by an Attic decree from the early second century:[5]

> Gods. Kallimachos son of Kallimachos, of the deme of Paiania, has proposed: whereas [—, from the city of —], who practices the maritime craft and wants to increase as much as he can the city's revenue, in the year (when) Timesianax (was *archōn*) unloaded grain at Piraeus and sold it to the city cheaply; in that (when) Hippakos (was *archōn*), after having purchased in [name of the city or country] one thousand five hundred *metrētai* of oil to import them to Pontos and there to load for the return trip a cargo of grain to be taken to Piraeus, as he was residing temporarily in our cities and saw how great a shortage of oil there was because of the poor harvest that is striking our territory, and because in addition he wanted to do everything in his power to show his devotion to our people, he hastened to import into our *emporion* the oil he had purchased; now, while the oil had been taken out of the *emporion*, the *agoranomoi* approached him and asked him to sell his oil to the city at a price below the one he had declared . . . he was so bold as to sell them.

This merchant, who was supposed to go to the Black Sea with a cargo of oil purchased elsewhere (the name of the place has been lost—it is possible that he came from the Peloponnese) had stopped off in Athens, perhaps to complete his cargo. If he had, for example, reserved the whole space of a ship that could hold 3,000 amphoras, his 1,500 *metrētai* of oil represented roughly only half that amount (one amphora was the equivalent of one *metrētēs*).[6] When he landed in Athens, he found the price of oil there exceptionally high. Was it simply an accident that he came to Athens? In any event, he immediately decided not to continue his voyage and to sell his oil right there—at an advantageous price, because in Athens the olive harvest had been a poor one and the price was high. At first, he planned to sell his cargo on the open market, but then, at the magistrates' request, he sold it to the city. Naturally, this merchant was not acting out of the goodness of his heart, but rather with a sense of his interest rightly understood, since he sold his cargo at a very high price and all at once (it was always in a trader's interest to sell wholesale, as ancient sources emphasize).[7] He also saved himself the trouble of going as far as the Black Sea. It is likely that in doing so he had broken his initial contract, which probably provided for a voyage to the Black Sea: but the opportunity was too good to pass up, and at least, if the loan had not been made in a city on the Black Sea, no one could find anything objectionable in what he did.

On the contrary, in the 320s BCE the Athenians, who were suffering from a severe grain shortage, could legitimately object when a ship with a contract negotiated in Athens to supply the city with grain from Egypt stopped in Rhodes on the way back and sold its cargo. Informed by letter that prices in Rhodes were higher, unscrupulous traders had sold their grain there in violation of the commitment they had made. Thus it is clear that there might have been a genuine information network, with letters exchanged among agents to provide information about prices. Our source is an Athenian legal speech in which the plaintiff explicitly accuses his adversary of belonging to a speculative network organized by Kleomenes of Naukratis, who governed Egypt in Alexander's name after 332.[8] The plaintiff's accusations might suggest that this was an unusual practice. However, the role of price information was so great that it is hard to see how this practice could not have been common in the world of traders. Profits of this kind are related to arbitrage profits, that is, a profit made without risk by taking advantage of the difference in price for a single commodity on two different markets. That said, prices could change rapidly. It must have also happened that before a letter could be delivered and commodities transported, prices at the point of arrival were lower than expected, which would inevitably lead to a decrease in the trader's revenue (if prices were higher, he could, of course, only congratulate himself on his luck). In any case, general economic information, and in particular information concerning price changes, was crucial in the decision to sail for this or that port.[9]

Grain Buyers

Obviously, if the overall supply of grain for sale was sufficient and the supply routes secure, the traders' individual initiative met demand. However, even in the most favorable conditions, insofar as traders made voyages only when they thought they could make a satisfactory profit at a reasonable risk, there was a differential among cities. A large city well situated in a trade network and with plenty of money had a greater chance of being visited by grain traders. A small city off the main trade routes did not attract merchants. It is easy to guess why: small quantities, excess costs connected with transporting commodities to a distant area, uncertainty regarding the conditions on a market that offered few sales alternatives if the city that was the "objective" turned out to have sufficient food supplies or simply lacked good silver money to pay for their imports. In addition to the frequent interruptions of the maritime routes because of chronic political instability, a decline in overall demand led traders to turn first of all to large markets, the ones in which it was possible to find good-quality silver coins or an easily negotiated return cargo, and to neglect small cities off the main routes. If the decline was still more severe, then everyone was affected and tried to find grain at any price.

Whatever the reasons for the market failure, if traders did not make voyages to bring in grain the civic collectivities themselves had to send agents to procure it. This was clearly an effort to correct an imperfection in the market. Grain buyers designated by the city left for foreign lands, provided with a sum of money to make grain purchases. As already observed, these agents were called *sitōnai*, "grain buyers."[10] During the Imperial period, there were analogous agents called *elaiōnai* or "oil buyers."[11] In itself, however, the function of the grain buyer did not necessarily imply foreign travel. Agents who bought grain on site, in their own cities, and on behalf of the city, were also "grain buyers." It was only when the situation became critical and the grain available in the city ran short that "grain buyers" did not hesitate to travel to a foreign market to buy supplies.[12]

In that case, both small and large cities must have made purchases directly in foreign markets. These agents did not arrange for the transportation of the grain on ships belonging to the city. In the *Poroi* (3.14), Xenophon envisages, on the model of a fleet of warships, the creation by Athens of a fleet of trading vessels that belonged to the state and could be rented to shippers. But it does not seem that this project was realized, or that other cities had set up systems of this kind. Xenophon's plan was put into practice only 1,600 years later: the Republic of Venice had a fleet of galleys that it auctioned to its merchants (although the large majority of the Venetian trade remained in fully private hands).[13] In ancient Greece, the transport of goods was operated by private merchants and private ships, who would be hired by grain commissioners if the city decided to undertake to import food directly. The goal was to travel to either a producing country or a place of re-exportation (such as Rhodes or Delos in the Hellenistic period) to buy grain on the market and find shippers to bring this grain back to their city of origin. This is an interesting case in which the city transformed itself into a collective buyer, this time on the international market. This posture is related to the one the city might adopt on the domestic market by negotiating and setting purchase prices with traders, and sometimes also purchasing directly.

An episode in 377 BCE shows concretely under what circumstances a city like Thebes in Boiotia, which under normal conditions, was certainly self-sufficient in grain, might be led to send grain buyers to a foreign market:[14]

> Suffering greatly from a grain shortage, since for the past two years they had not been able to harvest grain on their own territory, the Thebans sent men to Pagasai on two triremes, providing them with ten talents. While the men were buying their grain, the Lakedaimonian Alketas, who was guarding Oreos, secretly fitted out three triremes. When the grain was en route, Alketas seized it, along with the triremes and at least three hundred men. He held them on the acropolis, where he had set up his own camp.

What was at stake is very clear. Thebes sent grain buyers with a large sum of money to a port in southern Thessaly, Pagasai, the region's natural outlet. Thessaly was a rich agricultural region that in normal times had large surpluses. Its wealth in grain and exporting ability were praised by Jason of Pherai.[15] The Lakedaimonians were based at Oreos in northern Euboia, right on the route of the convoy. The interception of the little Theban fleet, despite its escort of two triremes, seemed to have sealed the mission's doom. However, things still turned out well for the Thebans, who finally succeeded in gaining control of the acropolis of Oreos and thus securing access to Thessalian grain.

Another interesting case where particular circumstances must have motivated a city to send "grain buyers" abroad is to be found in a decree from Histiaia, in northern Euboia, in favor of the Rhodian financier Athenodoros. The text is to be dated to about 220 BCE:[16]

> The people of Histiaia [in honor of Athenodoros, son of Peisagoras]. The *archontes* have proposed that the council introduce before the people [the following proposal]: whereas Athenodoros, son of Peisagoras, of Rhodes, constantly shows himself to be devoted to our people and renders services privately to each of our fellow citizens who have asked him to do so and public services to our city, that he has in every way cooperated devotedly with the grain buyers [*sitōnai*] sent by our city to Delos, that he has loaned money without charging interest and that he has seen to it that the grain buyers are able to carry out their task with all dispatch, putting the city's interests before his own; so that everyone might know that the people of Histiaia know how to honor those who bestow upon them benefactions, and that those who want to compete in favor of our interests might be more numerous, seeing that those who deserve it receive honors; let it please the people to praise Athenodoros, son of Peisagoras, of Rhodes, for his devotion to our city and to crown him with a foliage wreath for his valor and his devotion to the people of Histiaia; to proclaim the wreath during the procession of the *Antigoneia*, and let the *agonothētēs* see to this proclamation; to confer citizenship on him and his descendants, in accord with the law, as well as access to the council and the people immediately after religious affairs; to inscribe this decree on a stone stele and to dedicate it here in Histiaia in the sanctuary of Dionysos and in Delos in the sanctuary of Apollo, after having requested the community of Delos to provide a place for it; let the treasurer pay the necessary expenditure for engraving it.

Histiaia came into contact with Athenodoros because it lacked grain. As a result, the city had to send grain buyers to the Delian market to buy it. It seems odd that they should have had to go to Delos. Histiaia was located at the north entrance to the Euboian Channel, and thus on one of the most commonly used maritime routes from the north and from the Black Sea. It was also very close to the grain that might be exported from the ports of southern Thessaly.[17] Because of this favorable geographical position, it seems that the city ought not to have suffered from interruptions in its grain supplies. Therefore there must have been very special circumstances that put the city in such a situation. Should we imagine that traders coming from Pontos did not stop along the way, preferring to go to a redistribution center where they could hope to sell at higher prices? But in doing so they would have taken an additional risk, whereas it would have been easier for them to sell in a city like Histiaia that lay along their route, thereby saving a great deal of time and thus money. Hence one can hypothesize that if the grain the Histiaians bought did not come from the Black Sea, that was simply because that year the grain route from this region that passed through the Euboian Channel was blocked. Didn't this interruption of the grain supply correspond to the war between Rhodes and Byzantion in ca. 220 BCE?

The main lines of the conflict are reported by Polybius (3.2.5 and 4.47–52). We know that at that date Byzantion tried to levy a fee for passage through the Bosporos strait, because it was itself being subjected to extortion by its barbarian neighbors. Called on to help and supported by the cities that had maritime interests, Rhodes had to wage a war against Byzantion, a war that was essentially marked by a blockade of the Straits undertaken in order to get this passage fee abolished.[18] At the same time, central Greece was also going through a very turbulent period. Macedon, which controlled Thessaly, was fighting on several fronts: in 221 BCE, immediately following the Battle of Sellasia (222), Antigonos Doson had to carry out a campaign against Illyrian invaders. The year 220 saw the beginning of fighting in the "Social War," which opposed Aitolia to Achaia and Macedon.[19] Thus it is more than likely that Macedon was keeping its grain to feed its army. Finally, the situation was troubled even on the Aegean: in 220, the Rhodians had to pursue Demetrios of Pharos, who had launched a plundering expedition that continued as far as the Kyklades.[20] The chronological coincidence of these events with Histiaia's decree (which has been independently dated to 230–220) makes the hypothetical dating of Histiaia's grain buyers' voyage to Delos to around 220 plausible, even if it cannot be considered a certainty.[21] The fact that the financier who came to the aid of the Histiaians was a Rhodian was partly a matter of chance (he probably could have been of another origin). Nonetheless, during these years in which, despite the catastrophic earthquake that occurred between 229 and 226 BCE, the political and also financial ascendancy of Rhodes still growing, and it is not surprising that a Rhodian businessman helped grain buyers in Delos. In any case, whatever the date given, there is also every chance that the grain Histiaia bought in Delos came from Egypt (and would thus have passed through Rhodes), or possibly from Cyrene.

As in the case of Thebes in Boiotia in 377, Histiaia's decree is thus probably revealing of the circumstances that might lead to sending grain buyers to foreign markets: a lost harvest or an interruption of the usual supply routes. Regarding the question of grain supplies and grain buyers, no Greek city offers information as rich as that we have for the city of Rome in the fifth century. There we see at work the social tensions that surround the question of food supplies, the stakes involved in sending out grain buyers, and also the difficulties the latter have in carrying out their task. The first episode is situated in 492 BCE (Livy 2.34.1–5):[22]

> The new consuls were T. Geganius and P. Minucius. In this year, whilst all abroad was undisturbed by war and the civic dissensions at home were healed, the commonwealth was attacked by another much more serious evil: first, dearness of food, owing to the fields remaining uncultivated during the secession, and following on this a famine such as visits a besieged city. It would have led to the perishing of the slaves in any case, and probably the plebeians would have died, had not the consuls provided for the emergency by sending men in various directions to buy corn. They penetrated not only along the coast to the right of Ostia into Etruria, but also along the sea to the left past the Volscian country as far as Cumae [Kyme]. Their search extended even as far as Sicily; to such an extent did the hostility of their neighbors compel them to seek distant help. When corn had been bought at Cumae, the ships were detained by the tyrant Aristodemos, in lieu of the property of Tarquin, to whom he was heir. Amongst the Volsci and in the Pontine district it was even impossible to purchase grain, the grain merchants were in danger of being attacked by the population. Some corn came from Etruria up the Tiber; this served for the support of the plebeians. They would have been harassed by a war, doubly unwelcome when provisions were so scarce, if the Volsci, who were already on the march, had not been attacked by a frightful pestilence.

King Tarquin, who had taken refuge in Kyme with the tyrant Aristodemos, who seems to have controlled that city at least between 525 and 474 BCE (the date of the Battle of Kyme in which, allied with Hieron of Syracuse, he defeated the Etruscans). Tarquin died in Kyme in 496 or 495, and Aristodemos thought Rome was indebted to him, so he refused to let the ships leave, even though the grain had already been purchased. For the year 440 BCE, Livy (4.12.6–11) also emphasizes the failure of the grain buyers' missions and the serious famine that resulted from it.[23] Then (4.13–16) he describes at length Spurius Maelius's maneuvers. A very rich member of the equestrian order, Maelius had been able, thanks to his foreign friends and clients, to buy grain in Etruria and to distribute it gratis to the people. According to Livy (4.13.2), that is precisely what thwarted the magistrates' efforts to bring grain prices down. Maelius hoped to constitute thereby a clientele that would allow him to set his sights on the consulate, which was in theory not open to him. But this led him to be accused of aspiring to become king, which was a good way of getting rid of him, since he was very soon assassinated. He was said to be (see *ibid.* 4.15.6) a simple "grain merchant" (*frumentarius*) who had grown wealthy, and we know how the people scorned grain traders.

The reliability of Livy's books on the first centuries of Roman history is an inexhaustible field of controversy. It is clear that his account has been arranged to the benefit of Rome's glory, no doubt from the outset, but also in the course of successive rewritings. However, the narrative core is so rich in perfectly plausible details that it is hard to see how it could be entirely fictitious: *se non è vero è ben trovato*—too *ben trovato*, in fact, to have been simply made up. Thus Livy (2.21.5) provides a chronological reference for the government of the tyrant Aristodemos of Kyme. The reference to southern Italy's exporting capacity corresponds to what one can guess for the exports from Italy and Sicily in the late Archaic and Classical periods.[24] It is the first literary testimony regarding the western potential to which Thucydides refers when he mentions the motives for the Athenian campaign in Sicily in 427.[25]

But Livy's testimony is valuable chiefly for what it tells us about the attitude of a city during a period of shortages and the difficulties it encountered. First, when the crisis arose, grain buyers—*frumentores*, the exact equivalent of Greek *sitōnai*, to be distinguished from *frumentarii*, simple grain merchants—were sent all over. In Rome, they were sent to the Etruscans, other Italic peoples, and the Greeks of southern Italy and Sicily. That is, ethnic considerations were of absolutely no importance. We also know what ties there were between Rome and Carthage. Moreover, it was necessary to send out many buyers in order to obtain even a meager success. Thus in 440 BCE, only one of the potential providers responded positively. As will be shown later, some cities never exported, because a law simply forbade. But that must have been well known, and with particular exceptions (the case of Selymbria, which evaded its own law), grain buyers must have generally avoided them. Then there were cities that might sell, but that in a given year did not authorize exports because they thought the year's harvest, and thus the margin of security, was too slim. Finally, it is very clear that the sellers had their own preferences. That is the situation Isocrates describes in his *Trapeziticus* (17.57): often, when there was not enough grain available for everyone, the dynasts of the Bosporan kingdom forced buyers from cities other than Athens to leave empty-handed. But the Athenians, who were privileged trading partners, always had the right to buy supplies.

In order to be able to find grain on foreign markets, cities had to deploy an intense diplomatic activity. This translated into bestowing privileges and honors to key individuals, private citizens or dynasts, in the cities that were likely providers of grain. The case is particularly well attested for late Classical Athens, but obviously minor cities could not act differently.[26] Indeed, the case of Rome in 492 BCE shows that close neighbors were not necessarily the best partners: quite the contrary, relations between neighboring cities were likely to be tense because of territorial conflicts, so that even in times of peace, there was little chance of finding a warm welcome to a request for grain. Thus Roman grain buyers were not welcome among the Volsci, against whom Rome had fought furious battles and with whom the peace was very fragile (to the point that the Volsci would have been ready to take advantage of the weakness of the Romans by attacking them in times of food shortages). Finally, there were legal and financial conflicts regarding past disputes that might block the export of products that had nonetheless been duly purchased. That was the situation of the Roman grain buyers in Kyme, whose tyrant did not let the ships leave, the goal being to put pressure on the Roman government and force it to recognize him as King Tarquin's heir.

In the first third of the third century BCE, a similar situation can be observed in Delos, where creditors blocked the departure of a cargo of grain because the city (whose identity it has so far proven impossible to determine) that bought it had not yet paid all its debts.[27] This case leads us to raise more broadly the question of how grain purchases by the *sitōnai* were financed:

> [Theo?]doros, son of Theophantos has proposed: Whereas Mnesalkos son of Telesarchides, a Delian, who has been granted hereditary *proxenia*, along with his brothers, has rendered many and eminent services to our people in every circumstance; that during the grain shortage, when our grain had been seized by Delians to whom our city owed a debt, he interceded with those who had taken pledges and was able to send it to our people; that he has often lent money to our city in urgent circumstances and that he has recovered it as the city has been able to pay it back, that he always aids those of our fellow citizens who go to Delos, helping them in conformity with what is just and by doing what each of them might have to ask of him; let it please the people that he receive *proxenia*, he, his sons, and his descendants, and that they be exempted from duties on the commodities they import and export . . . and the right of entering and leaving by sea . . . in war and in peacetime . . .

The first observation should be that the grain purchases in Delos mentioned here are necessarily public purchases made by grain buyers. In fact, not only were these purchases intended for the people of the unknown city (which would be the case even if they were private purchases), but also the loans that had not been repaid (and that justified the seizure) had been taken out by the city (*polis*). The fact that grain buyers came to Delos is not at all surprising, because the city acted as a regional *emporion* for grain.[28] It has been mistakenly thought that the grain was seized at sea: for one thing, the Delians had no fleet, and even if they had, their ships would have had to be on constant patrol to monitor vessels sailing near the island. This scenario is not plausible. Nor could the ships in question have been seized after making an ill-advised stopover in the port. Since the grain buyers from this unknown city could hardly have been unaware of their city's debt to the Delians, it is unlikely that they would be so blind as to allow themselves be caught—twice—in Delos's trap and to allow their grain to be confiscated.[29] One can get out of this impasse if one assumes that these *sitōnai* came to Delos not only to buy grain but first of all to get a loan that would allow them to purchase it. We know from other sources that Mnesalkos, who was one of the most prominent Delian notables of the period, was one of those who had enough capital to be able to make loans to foreigners.[30] It was as both a notable and a major lender that he was able to intercede with the anonymous city's creditors.[31] Were these creditors committing a serious error by agreeing not to be paid immediately? In fact, they knew that in the future also the people of the debtor city would be compelled by necessity to purchase grain in Delos. They had repeatedly contracted loans in the past and must have come there anyway to buy grain, because there was no other nearby market that was both easily accessible to them (limiting transport costs) and that had relatively understanding money lenders. By granting Mnesalkos the title of *proxenos*, which he already held hereditarily, this city was thus providing an institutional framework for the relations of interest that bound it to this notable, or rather, since it already existed, further reinforcing this framework.

Consequently, it is even possible to make a suggestion regarding the origin of the *sitōnai* in question. They obviously did not come from Pontos or any such distant region, a hypothesis that will not stand up to analysis.[32] They must have come from the Kyklades or Euboia, two regions where cities were already borrowing regularly from the Delian sanctuary in the fourth century. It must also have been a city that spoke the Ionian dialect used in this decree. The name Theophantos is rare in the Ionian world of Euboia and the islands. In the period in question, it is attested in Euboia in Eretria and Karystos, in the Kyklades in Ioulis of Keos, Paros, and Tenos.[33] These last three cities had repeatedly borrowed from the Delian sanctuary in the fourth century, and there is every reason to think that loans made to Delian individuals during the Hellenistic period merely continued this pattern.[34] Karystos was Euboian, to be sure, but it was oriented toward the Kyklades, and it is thus not surprising to find it listed among the cities that were in debt to the god of Delos.[35] In addition, a financial record dating from about 350 BCE that was found in Karystos shows that along with its borrowings from the Delian sanctuary, this city had borrowed considerable sums from five notables in Thebes and one in Histiaia.[36] Now, this record shows that at the end of a year, the city had been unable to repay its loans and had an interest balance due amounting to 2,490 drachms, not much less than half a talent. To be sure, this does not constitute a proof for the situation ca. 280 BCE, since it occurred seventy years earlier. However, the document does give us an idea of the city's financial difficulties. In addition, a Theophantos of Karystos is attested in Delos precisely in 279, as one of the entrepreneurs who leased the construction and installation of the roof framework for the "limestone temple" (*pōrinos naos*).[37] It is plausible to maintain that the city of Karystos might have taken advantage of the knowledge of Delian networks enjoyed by some of its members who did business there by appointing them as *sitōnai*. Thus this is a valuable clue regarding the way grain buyers operated. It is the precise period when the Delian notable Mnesalkos was active.[38] And thus there is a good chance that in one way or another the author of the proposed decree was a close relative (son?) of the

Theophantos mentioned in the decree displayed in Delos, and that the decree does in fact come from Karystos.[39]

The common point of all the episodes mentioned here is the cities' need to find money to pay for grain purchases in a foreign market. In Hellenistic Delos and Hellenistic Rhodes, just as in Classical Athens, the role of financial center cannot be disconnected from that of marketplace.[40] In 377, the *sitōnai* of Thebes left for Pagasai with ten talents of silver, while those of Histiaia were able to deal with a Rhodian financier in Delos around 220. One might add that in the case of the grain buyers of the League of the Islanders, with the help provided them by the banker Timon of Syracuse, shortly before 192 BCE they were able to obtain easy terms of money-exchange to buy grain in Delos.[41] On the other hand, Rome's request was not accepted in Kyme in 492 BCE, and its commissioners could not load the grain that they had purchased. Similarly, the *sitōnai* from Karystos in Delos (if indeed, as argued earlier, these commissioners came from that city) saw their grain seized by creditors who had loaned them money they could not repay: they were finally able to load the grain they wanted to buy only through the intercession of a Delian moneylender and notable who made them a bridging loan. In any case, money was the key factor in the grain war. An anecdote reported by Pseudo-Aristotle (*Economics* 2.2.16a) shows how a city that had no money to buy grain could nonetheless acquire some. The episode is situated around 360 BCE:

> Since the Klazomenians were experiencing a food shortage and lacked money, since among them there is an abundance of oil they decreed that individuals who had oil should lend it to the city at interest. Their territory in fact produces abundant quantities of oil. After having borrowed this oil, they loaded it on ships and sent them to trading ports, whence they brought back grain, the value of the oil acting as security for the loan.

Thus it is possible to reconstruct the following schema: in Klazomenai, there was a shortage but the people could not resort either to a direct tax (probably because individuals' finances were exhausted) or to borrowing locally (probably because potential creditors had no confidence in the city). The Klazomenians thus thought up a system based on their ability to produce oil, the city's major source of wealth. Individuals who had oil lent it, in return for interest on its theoretical sales price (though naturally the price of the oil was not yet paid them). Then the *sitōnai* took the oil to ports where they knew they could find grain; there, they sold the oil, and with the proceeds from the sale they were able to buy grain. Thus they could bring grain back to Klazomenai, sell it to individuals, and thereby obtain enough money to repay the debt. It remained only to reimburse (with interest) those who had loaned the oil.[42] Around 243/2 BCE, the Samian notable Boulagoras interceded three times to obtain funds intended for grain purchases by the city, which was suffering from shortages.[43]

Trade Prohibitions and Grain Supplies

The need to send *sitōnai* abroad proves that private initiative had limits in the international market. This situation was connected first of all with the overall insufficient supply of grain, not necessarily every year, but in relation to major climatic vagaries. The causes of these failures were of two kinds: an insufficiency in local production, temporary or chronic, and an insufficiency in the supply spontaneously put on sale by those involved in the international grain trade. It was not fundamentally a matter of a failure in the mercantile circuits, because if grain had been in sufficient supply, it goes without saying that there would have been merchants to transport it, given all the profits expected from this kind of trade. The basic problem was the overall insufficiency of commercial supply, which might in a given region vary considerably from one year to the next depending on uncontrolled variations in the weather. Although there is no doubt that supply may have been insufficient, cautious behaviors, though perfectly justified in the short term, further aggravated this insufficiency. Individual producers who produced more than what was necessary cautiously set aside a reserve of grain in case the next harvest was poor; in this way, part of the grain was spontaneously kept off the market.[44] But collective behaviors also played a role, since some cities had laws prohibiting exports of this or that category of products, and first of all grain. Athens under Solon famously issued a prohibition on exporting foodstuffs, except for oil.[45] But a law of Teos (in Asia Minor) from about 470–460 BCE also strictly forbade exporting grain from the city:[46]

> Anyone who makes poisoned drugs against the city of Teos or against a private individual, let him disappear, along with his family. Anyone who prevents the importation of grain into Teian territory by whatever maneuver or means, whether by sea or by land, or once the importation has been completed, re-exports it, let him die, along with his family.

The style of this law is still archaic, and provides for curses to be made against offenders. The two clauses constitute the first part of a long text that includes a series of dispositions of a constitutional order, in a context in which relations with the barbarians seems to be a genuine concern. Since the text probably goes back to the 470s or 460s, this is hardly surprising. Teos was then part of the Athenian empire, but the war with Persia was still going on. Dangers to the territory of Teos might thus arise at any moment. The first provision may allude to the fabrication of drugs that could be used to poison wells. It is significant that the second provision, the one concerning food supplies, is put on the same level as the provision concerning poisoning: in both cases it is a question of life and death. Thus the law seeks to forestall any maneuver seeking to prevent the importation of grain. How might someone have gone about trying to prevent such imports? The law does not say, perhaps precisely because it sought only to outline a very general framework that would make it possible to initiate legal proceedings on a rather broad basis.

Then one thinks, for example, of the fourth-century Athenian law concerning international trade, which forbade loaning capital for any purpose other than importing grain (and other indispensable products) to Athens.[47] But other inappropriate acts, such as attacking the persons of foreign merchants, might also result in restraints on imports and discourage foreign traders from coming to the city.[48] The prohibition on re-exportation is also significant. First, one can legitimately suppose that a law of Teos initially forbade all exports. Prohibiting re-exportation not only allowed the city to keep all its grain for itself, but forestalled any dispute over the origin of the grain, and thus fraudulent exportation of grain produced on the city's territory. Clearly, the law did not correspond to a temporary situation, but was intended to be permanent. The curses were to be pronounced by the magistrates three times a year (I. B. l. 29–35). Teos imported grain by sea and also from its hinterland. Independently of the periods of tension and war (which were, moreover, so frequent), Teos must certainly have constantly imported grain, and its laws on imports, with the interdiction on re-exporting, might have remained in force for a long time. It is piquant that in a much later document dating from 303–302 BCE, Antigonos's letter concerning the synoecism of Teos and Lebedos, the city still appears to be dependent on imports coming in by sea and from the hinterland.[49]

The most common attitude adopted by cities that did not have enough grain must then have been to prohibit exports. The policy of cities like Athens and Teos must also have been that of many small cities. This law responded to popular pressure. It was in fact the owners of middle-sized and large estates who had grain to export, and even if local prices were high, they might prefer to sell at a still higher price abroad. By contrast, the situation of the early Imperial period, when a form of deregulation had been put in place, helps us to understand what was at stake. By then, accusations against big landowners for creating artificial scarcities by hoarding their grains were obviously common. An episode in Philostratus's *Life of Apollonius of Tyana*, (a largely fictionalized biography of the first-century CE neo-Pythagorean philosopher), sheds light on the social tensions linked to the question of grain export.[50] When Apollonios arrived in Aspendos, the large city of southern Asia Minor (1.15.2–3), he found the chief magistrate of the city clinging to the statues of the emperor in supplication: the furious populace was threatening to burn him alive obviously for having authorized grain exports even though famine was raging in the city. Apollonios persuaded the rich men to open up their granaries, and in this way saved the people from starvation.[51] A similar situation can be observed in the case of Dio Chrysostom speaking in his own defense before the assembly of his home city of Prousa, in Bithynia, in the very early second century CE.[52] Hoarded grain could be sold when local prices were at their peak or exported to foreign markets where prices were higher than the local ones. It was under pressures of this kind that the cities of the Classical and even the Hellenistic period, which were in general much more egalitarian than those of the Imperial period, imposed restrictive measures on exports. This is what bans on grain exports were intended to prevent.

However, permanently prohibiting exports raised difficult problems relating to the under-use of the available surplus and the wasting of resources, or, in other cases, to a loss of revenue for both individuals and the state. An example of this is provided by the city of Selymbria, west of Byzantion, which (around 360 BCE) according to Pseudo-Aristotle's *Economics* prohibited grain exports:[53]

> It happened that the Selymbrians needed money. Since among them there was a law that prohibited exporting grain because a famine had taken place earlier, but they had grain from the preceding year, they decreed that individuals would deliver their grain to the city at a fixed price, each individual keeping for himself only one year's supply. Then they issued an export license for this grain, after having set what seemed to them a suitable price.

Here we touch on the key problem in the system of closed markets: that of a chronic underuse of resources. The city of Selymbria could have abrogated its own law: it preferred to get around it. The city lacked money and therefore organized the sale of old grain, a practice that must not have injured the inhabitants, since on the one hand they could have reserved as usual a certain amount of the year's grain, and on the other hand they could find an additional resource in this reserve. As for the city, the difference between the sale price it set for local producers and the one it set for foreign buyers allowed it to obtain the revenue it lacked.

Laws prohibiting grain exports were obviously not universal, because otherwise no grain would have been available on the international market. Thus there were cities or regions that were regular exporters, even if from time to time they might also have their problems.

The Grain Supply: Free Sale, Forced Sale, and Civic Taxes

Thus we have seen that each city might or might not authorize exports of grain (or other products) from its territory. Since to have the right to export, one had first to obtain an export license, the prohibition on exports simply amounted to a refusal to issue such a license. On the contrary, if the city approved the principle of exportation, the merchants might come to the city to load the available grain, purchasing from intermediaries or landowners who had come themselves to offer their grain for sale. One has to assume that this was the norm, and that in ordinary times the majority of the grain put on the international market was produced by private landowners. If only the circumstances were favorable, they could hope to make large profits. If the price of grain fell, they had to give up growing grain and turn to other activities: that is the situation emphasized by Xenophon in the *Poroi* (4.6). [54]

However, certain special situations might arise. As observed, despite a law prohibiting grain exports the city of Selymbria had to sell the previous year's grain in order to cope with financial problems. It might nonetheless also happen that the demand came from abroad. Thus in the event of a generalized grain shortage, a state might find itself confronted by an exceptional level of demand. In this circumstance, it had to find a solution that allowed it to satisfy the foreign demand as best it could. A characteristic case of this is provided by the city of Cyrene at the beginning of the 320s BCE. Cyrene had been approached by a large number of cities and states that all wanted to buy grain. The details of the text show that as in Selymbria it was the state (*hē polis*), not private individuals, that undertook to provide the grain. It was the state that organized the distribution to foreign buyers, but to supply an exceptional amount, one should suppose that it had collected the grain beforehand by requisitioning it.[55] The details of the procedure employed in Cyrene is not know, but one can suppose that depending on its known productive capacity, each district in the Cyrenean territory was asked to sell the state a certain quantity of grain.

A second-century BCE inscription from Thessaly (unusually restrictive because of the circumstances—namely, Roman demands) shows how requisition procedures might be set up by the state with a view to selling abroad. The situation is exactly similar to that of Cyrene and Selymbria, except that the sale was imposed from outside by a dominant power, in this case Rome. Perhaps in 129 BCE, the Thessalians received a demand formulated by Quintus Caecilius Metellus, who at that time occupied the Roman office of aedile, that is, of the magistrate responsible for food supplies:[56]

> Whereas Quintus Caecilius Metellus, son of Quintus, aedile of Rome, a man who is noble, good, friendly and well-disposed to our *ethnos*, has come before the council and has recalled the benefactions of his ancestors, and gave a speech asking, he who has been elected to the aedileship while their territory presently finds itself confronted by a shortage, that our *ethnos* provide to the senate and the Roman people as much grain as it has to sell,
> —Remembering the good deeds done our people by Quintus and his ancestors, and by the senate and the Roman people, it has been decided by the council to send to Rome, to the senate and the Roman people, in accord with Quintus's speech, four hundred thirty thousand baskets of wheat, and that the distribution among the cities of the quantity of grain previously mentioned shall be carried out by the *stratēgos* Petraios, along with his co-magistrates and the members of the council;
> —That each of the cities shall take responsibility for transferring the required grain to the port, whether it be Demetreion, Phalara, or Demetrias, that is, three hundred twenty thousand baskets, the people of Pelasgiotis and Phthiotis in the month of Aphrios, those of Histiaiotis and Thessaliotis in the month of Thyos, before the twentieth, and one hundred ten thousand baskets in the month of Phyllikos, before the fifteenth, and that the cities pay the expense of loading the grain onto the ships, each one in proportion to the quantity of grain incumbent on it;

—As regards the transport of the grain, given that the Thessalians have no ships, Quintus shall award the shipping contract in whatever way he deems best, and let our envoys sent to Rome pay the freight costs from the proceeds from the sale;

—If Quintus cannot send ships, he shall send charter shippers; Petraios the *stratēgos*, along with those who have been designated, shall see to it that the grain is transported to Rome, and that those who travel with it shall see to it that Petraios participates in the sending of the commodities, and that Petraios the *stratēgos* makes the expenditure for this purpose, and that along with his co-magistrates, Petraios is responsible for the shipment, Petraios being required to note the distribution among the cities;

—Any city who does not deliver the grain to the ports within the prescribed periods, shall pay two staters and nine obols per basket, and Petraios the *stratēgos* and those who are under his command shall exact the amount of the fine on the properties of the city and its inhabitants in whatever way they wish, benefiting from judicial immunity and not liable to be fined for the ways in which they carry this out.

The Thessalian *ethnos*, through the intermediary of its federal magistrates, thus had no choice but to satisfy Rome. It must be clear from the outset that this was not a gift. The Thessalians were forced to put the grain at Rome's disposition. The use of *didonai* to designate the supply must not mislead us. This verb can in fact have many meanings, and not only "to give." Thus it is frequently used to designate financial expenditures: a magistrate "expends" money, he does not "give" it. This notion of putting at disposal is also used to refer to advances of capital. Thus around 306 BCE (or more precisely: shortly before and shortly after this date), a rich benefactor, Malousios of Gargara, on several occasions advanced funds at no interest to the city of Ilion.[57] In no case did Malousios "give" these funds: they were sums of money advanced without demanding interest, which proves that it was a loan, not a gift. It is true that the verb *didonai* could also have the meaning of "give." But then, if one wanted to be explicit, one had to say "give a gift" (*didonai dōrean*), or use the verb *epididonai*.[58]

Quintus Caecilius Metellus belonged to the cream of the Roman elite. His (probably) homonymous grandfather had issued a judgment favorable to Thessaly in a territorial conflict with Macedon. This act and others were the good deeds of which Metellus reminded his audience in his speech to the Thessalians. Besides, Thessaly owed to Rome its "liberation" from the "Macedonian yoke."[59] Now Rome was suffering from a food shortage, and the Thessalians were obligated to come to its aid. Already at this time, Rome's influence in Greece had become crushing, and there could be no question of refusing any demand made by the senate or a Roman magistrate. However, the Thessalians being officially a free people allied with Rome, Metellus could not say in his speech that he required that the grain be donated free of charge.[60] That was not what was asked of the Thessalians. As it is explicitly formulated, what was asked of them was that they deliver all their grain that was available for sale (*en pratōi*). That year, Thessaly's sole customer for their wheat was Rome (no mention is made of the barley produced by the Thessalians, for this now "inferior" grain would not have been acceptable to the Romans), and its usual customers had to wait until the following year.

However, the volume of grain demanded by Rome was not left to the free judgment of individuals. The delivery that the Thessalian cities had to make was mandatory. The enormous fine to be assessed on those who delivered late or resisted was intended to dissuade cities from escaping their obligations. Those that had no reserves preferred to buy grain from their neighbors, if they had any, or even import it from abroad, rather than pay the fine. It was certainly at the express request of Metellus that the Thessalian federal state decided to impose on the cities the provision of 430,000 baskets of wheat. The basket (*kophinos*) seems to have been a unit of measure equivalent to about ten liters. The total of the grain required was thus equivalent to 80,625 Attic *medimnoi*, or about 25,400 quintals. This was a large amount, even for rich Thessaly. The first deliveries, 320,000 baskets representing 75 percent of the total, had to be made in the months of Aphrios and Thyos, which corresponded to February and March. Thus they involved the grain from the previous year's harvest. In other terms, the Thessalians had to sacrifice their own reserves. The balance had to be delivered in the month of Phyllikos— that is, in June, after the harvest, which in Thessaly took place in May and June.

Since the Thessalians had no ships, they could not themselves deliver the grain to Rome. Thus either Metellus had to provide the ships, or he had to find shippers who would find merchants and ships for him. But Metellus and the Roman state paid for none of this. On arrival, Thessalian envoys sent to Rome were to pay the transport costs from the sale price. Thus the sale was not to take place on departure, as one might have thought (in that case it would have been strange that the text did not mention any price). It was the Thessalian envoys who were to be responsible for the sale in Rome itself, and they were to pay the costs of chartering the ships and reimburse themselves from the proceeds of the sale. This represented a genuine financial risk for them, because they could not predict what the price of wheat in Rome would be at the time of delivery. In theory, the price ought to be high, since the city was suffering from a shortage. But the time separating the decision from the actual delivery prevented them from knowing what the grain prices would be on their arrival in Rome. Livy (30.38.5) indicates that at the end of the Second Punic War, the deliveries of grain from Sardinia and Sicily caused prices to fall so low that merchants let shippers keep the grain to pay the cost of shipping. On the other hand, grain prices in Sicily in the time of Verres seem to have been on the order of those that we know for the Aegean in the second century.[61]

The Thessalians therefore in no way "gave" Rome their grain.[62] But in view of the cost of transporting it to Rome, it was only with a comparatively high level of prices that they could hope to make a little profit. Moreover, that was not the goal sought: the Thessalian ethnos must have thought itself lucky if the Roman magistrates and the senate were satisfied with what they did. As for the modalities of requisitioning grain in the cities, we are told nothing about them. One can assume that they were analogous to those in Selymbria: an obligatory sale of grain at a fixed price (in this case, certainly very low) on the basis of an assessment of reserves that was itself based on declarations made by the owners (with heavy penalties, of course, if the declaration proved to be false). The system of forced sale with a view to exportation is documented on this scale only in the framework of Roman domination in Greece, but it is clear that it was frequently employed, was probably used by other dominant powers, in particular Athens during the period of its empire.

The Grain Supply: The Royal Contributions

Outside the civic framework, the kings might contribute large quantities of grain to the cities' markets. If that was the case, it is first because, as already observed, kings had considerable resources at their disposal, either through levies at particularly high rates on agricultural products that were directly under their control, or through the collection of tributes and other taxes on peoples and cities that were dependent on them. The difference between the status of civic land and that of royal land has already been underscored.[63]

If we examine the kings' resources in greater detail, we find that they clearly had large tax revenues, especially from customs duties or *phoroi* levied on the cities or peoples under their control.[64] The kingdom of Bosporos and its massive export of grain toward the Aegean in the mid-fourth century provides already an excellent example of a state mastering by various means the product of the land and the chain of export, as two ports only were open to foreign trade for grain export, Pantikapeion and Theodosia.[65] As is well-known by Demosthenes (*Against Leptines* 20.32), Athens received only 400,000 *medimnoi* (or half of its import) from the kingdom in the mid-fourth century BCE. An inscription also shows that the city of Mytilene enjoyed a privilege of export up to 100,000 *medimnoi*.[66] It should be clear that other Aegean cities also must have had a regular access to the grain from Bosporos.

In the Hellenistic period, the kings also had vast resources in kind. This was the case for the Ptolemies, of course, but also to a large extent for other kingdoms. In addition to grain deliveries, the Ptolemies enjoyed a series of monopolies on (among other items) vegetable oil, linen fabric, salt, and beer.[67] As already mentioned, according to St. Jerome (*In Daniel* 11.5), Ptolemy II received not only 14,800 silver talents from Egypt alone, but also 1.5 million *artabai* of grain, or roughly the equivalent of 45,500 metric tons.[68] According to Strabo (17.1.13), in the middle of the first century Ptolemy XII Auletes had a revenue of 12,500 talents. In reality, as already observed, these figures (including Ptolemy II's 14,800 talents) must be understood in large part as revenues in kind. Similarly, other sovereigns received mainly taxes paid in kind.[69] What did they do with them? To be sure, grain and other commodities were used to feed part of the staff serving the state, particularly the armies, which were a pillar of royal power. But without going into details about the royal economy, which is not the subject of this book, one should point out that this tributary grain had significant consequences for the economy of the cities and in particular for trade.

First, it now seems certain that the kings tended to exploit their cash revenues by putting them into the monetary circuit. In a way, that was the gamble the Ptolemies took by organizing throughout their kingdom a system of taxes payable in cash (de facto, most of the time in bronze coins, the internal money of the Ptolemaic kingdom) that forced the peasants to bring their products into the mercantile circuit. It seems that the same gamble was made by the Seleukids, whose policy of creating cities might well have had as its objective to bring into the monetary economy vast "indigenous" territories that had up to that point remained wholly outside it.[70] But the kings also tried to put their revenues in kind to work in the world of the Aegean cities, from which they knew they could draw monetary resources.[71] Toward the middle of the fourth century (it is not possible to be more precise about the date), the Persian satrap Orontes sold grain to the Athenian army operating in the northern Aegean area.[72] Around 320, grain "from Asia," which came from the province of the satrap (Macedonian, this time) Arrhidaios, arrived in Athens.[73] Around 303–302 BCE, Antigonos I Monophthalmos points out, in a letter to the people of Lebedos concerning the synoecism with Teos, that generally speaking he was not in favor of constituting funds for buying grain, and refused to grant cities under his command the right to import grain, insisting that they get their supplies from the royal land, which was nearby and had abundant grain.[74] In addition to his declared interest in the cities' finances, one may suspect that the king also wanted to make use of his revenues in kind: thus for him it was a question of taking advantage of a "captive market" in the literal sense of the term.

However, it is remarkable that in Teos-Lebedos, by a special privilege, the king had abandoned this project. Was it because in the case of an old Greek city, infringing on its freedom to determine its own import-export policies was too obvious a limitation on its sovereignty, which would have resulted in bad propaganda for him in "Greek public opinion" on the eve of a crucial confrontation with his rivals? However, the rule, along with what it tells us about the mercantile ulterior motives of a king like Antigonos, remains more significant than the exception. For the king, the benefit was evident. As for the city, it could certainly hope to have sources of supply that were nearby, abundant, and even cheap: except that then it was a question of a delivery price, which was arbitrarily defined by the royal authority or its representative, and led to a dangerous relationship of dependency. We know from many examples how jealously cities sought to retain control over their *prosodoi*, their revenues. For the people of Teos-Lebedos, it was clear that it was better to be a wolf, and accept the vagaries of the international market, than to be a dog and forever wear the collar of economic dependence on the king or satrap.

Clearly however, dynasts or kings could be generous donors. But the gifts made by the kings were mainly gifts in kind, grain (especially), oil (for the gymnasium), or wood for construction.[75] In the Classical period, Athens had already benefited from the generosity of foreign sovereigns.[76] In the early Hellenistic period, it also received a series of large gifts of grain, 150,000 *medimnoi* from Antigonos and Demetrios in 307/6 BCE, 10,000 from Lysimachos in 299/8, 100,000 from Demetrios in 295 (to compensate for the destruction caused by his siege of Athens), 15,000 from Spartokos (dynast of the Bosporan kingdom) in 285/4, and 20,000 from Ptolemy II shortly after 285.[77] Other cities benefited from no less magnificent gifts.[78] Rhodes received gifts even larger than those received by Athens. The most important of these are not the ones received after the disastrous earthquake that occurred between 229 and 226.[79] Even though they were very spectacular, these gifts can easily be explained by the desire to help reconstruct a city that was indispensable for the political and economic equilibrium of the Hellenistic world: in sum, it was in the sovereigns' interest rightly understood, and in addition the Rhodians were able to excite emulation and raise the bids. But the Rhodians received still greater amounts of grain in the following century. In the middle of the second century, the Seleukid king Demetrios I (who reigned from 162 to 150) gave them 200,000 *medimnoi* of wheat and 100,000 *medimnoi* of barley.[80] In 162/1 BCE, the Attalid sovereign Eumenes II gave them 280,000 *medimnoi* of grain, which served to finance a school fund:[81] the city must have sold the grain, investing the proceeds and using the revenues on them to pay teachers. According to Klaus Bringmann, they probably realized between 200 and 400 talents from this sale, which, when invested at 10 percent (the usual rate) might have brought in somewhere between 20 and 40 talents a year.[82] In 167, Eumenes II had also made to Miletos a gift of wooden beams for the construction of a gymnasium, along with 160,000 *medimnoi* of grain that were intended for sale and might have brought in between 169 and 266 silver talents.[83] In a sense, the gifts were never so large as in the first half of the second century, but suddenly dried up later on, when, even before they collapsed, the kingdoms began to encounter recurrent difficulties. Around 140 BCE, the city of Priene complained that the kings had suspended their payments for the construction of a gymnasium.[84]

These gifts were motivated by the desire to win indispensable political fidelities and also, of course, by the policy of prestige pursued by sovereigns who wanted to eclipse their rivals on the international scene. But one must inquire into their economic consequences. What impact did these gifts have on the economy of the cities? Obviously, we always have to assess these gifts in proportion to the size of the city: a gift that might satisfy Delos, which had 1,200 citizens, would have been negligible for a city like Athens or Rhodes. As for Athens, the largest gift it received that we know of, 150,000 *medimnoi* of grain given by Antigonos and Demetrios in 307/6 BCE, probably represented more than one-tenth of the city's annual consumption in the age of Demosthenes.[85] Thus it was a considerable amount. Even if it is not possible to exactly assess what was given to the Rhodians, it certainly corresponded to an even greater proportion of the local consumption.

These gifts constituted true godsends, often directly requested by the cities, but in fact rarely granted by the kings.[86] The gifts received by Athens in 307/6 and 295 BCE were intended to allow it to cope with a critical situation after a period of devastation caused by war. They provided a significant relief for the people's misery that free trade could not have provided. On the other hand, one may ask whether, when these gifts were received by a prosperous city living through a period of peace, their impact was really positive. To be sure, since the grain was sold, the city benefited from a fresh influx of money, preserved and increased by means of financial investments. In addition, there is hardly any doubt that a city like Rhodes must not have sold on the domestic market all the grain it received as a gift, but on the contrary distributed it as skillfully as possible among various foreign markets so as to make the most of this capital. Nonetheless, locally these massive deliveries must have helped make the economy still more uncertain, since a year with exceptional deliveries might be followed by one or several years of shortages. The economy of gifts, like that of famines, is an economy of chaos that accentuates uncertainty and can hammer production by artificially depressing prices.

THE GRAIN POLICY OF ATHENS AND THE AEGEAN CITIES' FOOD SUPPLY

The Prohibition of Exports and the Logic of Trade

In the system of importing what one lacks and exporting surpluses, a city claimed the right to forbid exports if the level of local production did not seem capable of ensuring the people's food supply. But as a result, each city had a strategy and laws that it regarded as suitable in this regard. Independent Delos was a small city, but it had an *emporion* that served as a trading hub for the whole of the central Aegean. Naturally, for Delos there was no question of a law prohibiting the re-export of grain. Athens was a great metropolis with a very large population whose production was far from sufficient to feed itself. Its policy was completely different. The reforms introduced when Solon was *archōn*, in 594/3 BCE (if the traditional date is followed), already bear witness to a food crisis.[87] Although unlike so many other city-states, Athens in the Classical age did not undergo a serious economic and social crisis, the same had not been true in the Archaic period—on the contrary. Like many other cities of that time, Athens experienced repeated economic, social, and political crises. At the end of the seventh century and beginning of the sixth, the crisis became particularly acute. Taking advantage of modest peasants' difficulties and the debts they had contracted to survive, wealthy landowners reduced them to dependents on their own land by making them pay one-sixth of their harvest (this was the fate of the *hektēmoroi*). Against the background of what seems to have been a clear increase in population, at the beginning of the sixth century the crisis threatened to become a real civil war. It was to deal with this that the Athenians elected Solon, who, in his elegies, presents himself as a man of the golden mean, a reformer who rejected both the status quo and revolution. The steps he took with regard to foreign trade were thus part of a broader program. In his *Life of Solon* (24.1), Plutarch gives an extended view of the prohibitions on exports:[88]

He permitted only oil to be exported, and those that exported any other fruit, the archon was solemnly to curse, or else pay a fine of an hundred drachms himself; and this law was written in his first table, and, therefore, let none think it incredible, as some affirm, that the exportation of figs was once unlawful, and the informer against the delinquents called a sycophant ["public informer denouncing those exporting figs illegally"].

If in fact, as Plutarch suggests, Solon's first table (*axōn*) bore this law, there is no reason to doubt its authenticity. The curses (*arai*) Solon prescribes against those who break the law are not only characteristic of the religious and judicial practices of the Archaic period and the beginning of the Classical period, but find a close parallel in the law of Teos that targets precisely grain exporters. In addition, it is possible that it was on the first table because Solon considered it particularly important. Finally, this law also takes on meaning in relation to another one. Noting the slenderness of agricultural production and the need to have products to offer in exchange for imports, Solon also provided for the development of the craft trades (*Solon* 22.1):

> Observing the city to be filled with persons that flocked from all parts into Attika for security of living, and that most of the country was barren and unfruitful, and that traders at sea import nothing to those that could give them nothing in exchange, he turned his citizens to craftsmanship, and made a law that no son be obliged to relieve a father who had not bred him up to any craft.

Solon's law regarding foreigners followed the same line: it provided that only foreigners who knew a trade would be admitted (*Solon* 22.2). The goal was to avoid increasing the mass of indigents and, on the contrary, to enhance Athens's ability to import, or at least to see to it that these foreigners produced exportable products that would pay for the food supplies that would have to be imported to feed them. Thus in Solon's time there already existed a threat to the supply of food products that had led the legislator to prohibit exports of foodstuffs. Naturally, as the whole logic of Solon's measures shows, the prohibition on exports affected only agricultural products—except for oil, Plutarch says. Those were the products that had to be reserved for the Athenian people, while craft products were to be exported as much as possible. A passage in Heracleides (1.2 Arenz), confirms this eloquently. For him, in Attika "the products of the earth (*ginomena ek tēs gēs*) are incomparable, but there are too few of them."[89]

It is true that Solon's law seems to contradict what is known about Attic exports during the Classical period. They included ceramics, of course, but also agricultural products such as the famous honey that made Athens's reputation, and figs, since as already mentioned, according to Plutarch himself (*Solon* 24.1) the word "sycophant" was used to designate those who reported fraudulent exports of figs. Thus

Plutarch himself acknowledged that the law on exports had not remained unchanged since Solon. But it is nonetheless clear that honey, figs, and other commodities were not major elements of foreign trade: compared to the cost of grain imports, their value was negligible. Thus it is not possible to put all these kinds of commodities on the same level. On the contrary, the grain law of the Classical period tends toward an Athenian selfishness. We have examined in particular the law regulating the use of capital. On pain of death, it was forbidden to loan money for a voyage whose ultimate objective was not Athens. Thus it is clear that exporting or re-exporting grain that had been imported into Attika was strictly forbidden and inconceivable in the framework of the Attic city between the sixth and the first centuries. Obviously, foreign merchants in transit could not go to the *emporion* (and *a fortiori* to the agora) to re-export grain.[90] On the contrary, the Athenian law's primary goal was to keep grain in Athens, and it forbade any re-exportation. Besides, buying grain at retail in order to re-export it wholesale, with all the associated transport costs and in the most expensive market in Greece, would have been disastrous for merchants. As in Teos, re-exporting grain imported to the *emporion* was inadmissible. No source mentions that it was done, and for good reason. If foreign money lenders passing through the city had been able to make contracts in the *emporion* with foreign merchants who were also in transit, an enormous breach would have been left open in the system of supervision that would have rendered the rest of the legislation meaningless.

Finally, the figures given by Demosthenes (*Against Leptines* 20.32), based on the registers of the *sitophulakes*, do not give us the figures for Attic consumption augmented by those of re-exports, but rather those for Attic consumption alone. Better yet, there is proof that the prohibition on exporting grain and wine, which under Solon did not yet include oil, was later extended to oil as well. This was certainly the case before the end of the sixth century, though we cannot give a more precise date. However, in the seventh century and the early sixth century BCE, Athens was still widely exporting liquid or semi-liquid products in two characteristic types of amphoras: those called "SOS" (because a decoration that looked like these letters was painted on the neck of the amphora) and those known as "à la brosse."[91] There has been much debate about the content of these amphoras. For instance, it has been suggested that amphoras of this kind initially contained oil, and then wine and oil, and then oil only again (after Solon's reforms, which forbade exports of wine and favored exports of oil).[92] Perhaps we should simply consider that initially Attic amphoras could be been used to transport every kind of liquid or semi-liquid product before becoming, after Solon's law (if we accept its historical nature), specialized vessels for oil.[93]

After around 550 BCE, exports of Attic amphoras to destinations all over the Mediterranean gradually came to a stop.[94] It may be that the decline corresponded at first to the increasing consumption of local products by Attika, whose population grew steadily throughout the sixth century. The prohibition on exporting grain and other products might have given official recognition to this situation, in which production was already insufficient for local consumption. In addition, in the Classical and Hellenistic periods, and contrary to the case of Thasos, Chios, or Rhodes (to mention only these three cities), there is (until now) no type of amphora that might indicate large-scale exports of Attic products. After 475 BCE, the local production of Attic amphoras seems to have been very low.[95]

The same is not true of Panathenaic amphoras.[96] These beautiful vessels, decorated with paintings of scenes from the Panathenaic Games, still retained their black-figure decorations even after their time was long since past. Interestingly, they were shaped like the former SOS amphoras, which at least in the last phase contained only oil. The victors in the competitions each received a specific number of them: the winner of the chariot race, the most prestigious contest, received 140; the runner-up, 40. The amphora was a sign of prestige and its decoration a sign of victory. But what counted most for the victor was the oil that these amphoras held: a total of 5,000 liters for the winner, 1,500 for the runner-up. At about twelve drachms per *metrētēs* (a low price in the early fourth century), the oil was worth (in Athens) 1,680 and 480 drachms, respectively.[97] But this oil was naturally intended to be sold on a foreign market, where, in view of the reputation of Attic oil, it would sell at a higher price.

Commenting on one of Pindar's *Nemeans* (10.35–36) that indicates that a winner of the contests in Athens received "the fruit of the olive tree . . . in the belly of richly decorated vases," a scholion mentions: "There are no exports of oil from Athens, except for victors."[98] The same scholion also makes it explicit that the victors received an amphora full of oil and provides an example of export to Argos. The scholion on Pindar implicitly confirms that a special export concession was granted for these amphoras. Literary and archaeological sources thus mutually confirm each other. The contrast between a broad external distribution of Panathenaic amphoras and the silence regarding a possible distribution of "ordinary" Attic amphoras leads to the certainty that in the Classical period Attic oil, except for that in the Panathenaic amphoras, was not exported, any more than wine or grain. It seems that the situation did not change during the Hellenistic period. We know that oil was exported again in the time of Hadrian,[99] but that was a profoundly different world from the one that had prevailed until the end of the Hellenistic age. Athens was thus par excellence a city that did not export its food products, or very few of them.

Concerning the grain production of Athens and its own resources in the fourth century, there exists one exceptional source. This is an inscription from 329/8 BCE (*IG* II² 1672), which identifies the offerings of first fruits (*aparchai*) made at the sanctuary of Eleusis, in honor of Demeter and Kore, the tutelary goddesses of grain. The text lists the offerings made by the various Athenian tribes, thus allowing us to determine Attika's production. But in addition, it lists the first fruits offered by all the territories over which Athens exercised its control, the nearby territories of Drymos, Oropos, and Salamis, and the three islands of the northern Aegean, Skyros, Lemnos, and Imbros, which were populated by Athenian colonists (cleruchs) and over which the city also exercised sovereignty. Of course, the *aparchai* represent only a small part of the harvest. There is good reason for thinking that the first fruits of barley were based on a rate of 1/600th, and those of wheat on a rate of 1/1,200th.[100] On the basis of these data, it is possible to reconstitute the gross production figures and the corresponding percentages (tables 14.1 and 14.2, amounts in *medimnoi* after Garnsey 1988, 98, table 5).

The great question raised by this text is how to interpret the figures it provides. It is well known that for fiscal reasons peasants have generally tended, not only in antiquity but also in modern times, to under-declare the size of their harvests. On the other hand, administrators and political officials are more inclined to inflate their figures. In the present case, various parts of the territory may have competed to see who would make the largest contribution to the first fruits sacrificed to the goddess. All other things being equal, there are thus good reasons to think that these figures give us a reliable picture of the production of Attika and its possessions in 329/8 BCE, and the following analysis will allow us to confirm this.[101]

The crucial issue to be determined is whether these figures reflect a good harvest, an average one, or, on the contrary, a poor or even catastrophic one. We know how much harvests could vary from year to year, especially in view of the irregularity of rainfall. Although these figures are exceptionally precise for the world of Greek and Roman antiquity, they are also a *unicum*, including for Athens. Thus we do not have figures that make comparisons possible, at least for the ancient world. To test their value, scholars have generally attempted to calculate estimated yields per hectare, and also the area of Attika on which cereals could be grown in antiquity. It seems preferable to compare the figures given in our document with the data available for modern Greece. The Office of Statistics in the Minister of the National Economy of the Kingdom of Greece first published an agricultural inventory in 1914, for the year 1911. After a few hesitations, from that time on the same office has published annual statistics. The agricultural inventory for 1911 indicates

TABLE 14.1. Grain Production in Attika and Its External Possessions: Gross

ZONE	BARLEY PRODUC- TION IN MEDIMNOI	WHEAT PRODUC- TION IN MEDIMNOI	TOTAL GRAIN IN MEDIMNOI	BARLEY PRODUC- TION IN QUINTALS	WHEAT PRODUC- TION IN QUINTALS	TOTAL GRAIN IN QUINTALS
Total Attika	339,925	27,062.5	366,987.5	91,779.75	8,389.375	100,169.125
Total external	340,475	120,375	460,850	91,928.25	37,316.25	129,244
Total general	680,400	147,437.5	827,837.5	183,708.00	45,705.625	229,413.125

TABLE 14.2. Grain Production in Attika and Its External Possessions: Percentage

ZONE	BARLEY	WHEAT	BARLEY + WHEAT
Total Attika	50	18	44
Total external	50	82	56
Total general	100	100	100

that the area cultivated in Attika was 49,500 hectares (almost 500 square kilometers), or a little more than one-fifth of the territory (21 percent), on the (ancient) basis of an Attika of 2,400 square kilometers.[102] In that year, Attika's grain production reached a total of ca. 124,000 quintals (91,975 for wheat, 32,154 for barley).[103] The area devoted to grain included 13,000 hectares in wheat and 3,000 hectares in barley, for a total of 16,000 hectares. The average yield would thus have been 7.75 quintals per hectare, which is naturally very low by our present criteria, but perfectly realistic given what is known about Mediterranean agriculture before mechanization. Besides, one must note one difference from antiquity: the proportions of barley and wheat are reversed. In order to be able to make a useful comparison between the 1911 figures and the data available for antiquity, one has to test the former's value.

It should also be observed that a modern hectoliter of grain (wheat) is heavier than that of antiquity: the gradual improvement of varieties by means of a process of selecting seeds has produced this result. Today, a hectoliter of wheat is commonly thought of as weighing 80 to 85 kilos, as compared with only 63 kilos in the fourth century BCE, according to the grain law of Athens.[104] This must be taken into account in comparing harvest figures from antiquity with the corresponding figures from the early twentieth century. For the same volume of grain, the modern harvest is heavier by about one-fifth. On this basis only, it is clear that the figure for 329/8 is entirely comparable to that for 1911, even if we have to consider the fact that wheat now constitutes most of the harvest.

But we still have to assess the figure for 1911, to see whether it was a low, middle, or high figure. This statistical inventory was the first carried out on the scale of the whole kingdom of Greece. In fact, one has reasons to suspect that the figures for 1911 were inflated.[105] But for now let us take them as they are, assuming that, as in the case of antiquity, underdeclaration (by the peasants for fiscal reasons) and overdeclarations (by the administrative authorities, to artificially enhance the image of their region) balanced each other out. It happens that the Greek statistical inventory for 1911 is the only one that provides details about the production of Attika, the statistics for the following years combining data under the rubric "Attika-Boiotia" (that is, the whole formed by Attika, Aigina, Boiotia, and Megaris). But insofar as in the statistics for 1911 Attika represented 26 percent of the wheat production of the combined region of Attika and Boiotia and 25.4 percent of the barley production in this same area, it is possible to generate on this basis a reasonable estimate of the figures of grain production in Attika from 1914 onward.[106] The figure for 1911 is of the same order of that of the following years. On the other hand, a clear fall can be observed in production after 1918. Thus in 1921, on the same bases as before, it is possible to estimate the production of wheat of Attika at 44,091 quintals, and that of barley at 11,652, for a total of only 55,743 quintals.[107] The decline in the early 1920s is obviously to be explained not by climatic reasons (although climate could also impact crops in these years) but by the war between Greece and Turkey, which required the country to make an exceptional effort that strained its resources. Greece mobilized its young men, and it needed draught animals (horses, asses) for the campaign in Asia. The lack of labor and draught animals at home obviously resulted in a very sharp decrease in agricultural production. This phenomenon leads us to consider the consequences of major conflicts on agricultural production in antiquity. Above all, even if wheat (which provides the best yield in calories) accounts for most of the production, it is clear that the harvest in 1921 represented only 55.5 percent of the wheat produced in Attika in 329/8. Table 14.3 summarizes the results.

On this basis, one can conclude that the harvest of 329/8 BCE, about 100,000 quintals, was in no way a bad one. On the contrary, although it may not have been an exceptional harvest, it is very likely to have been about average for a good one. Although no certainty is possible in the matter, it is tempting to believe that, in a context of general insufficient supply, the good crop in Attika and in the islands in 329/8 BCE justified the engraving on stone of the first fruits figures for that year. This would have been a way for the Athenians to show their gratitude to the two goddesses of grain. In any case, it remains that the figure for grain production in 329/8 is a reliable one. *A fortiori*, it is unjustifiable to correct it by multiplying it by two in order to obtain figures that could be assumed to be more in conformity with real production but that are based solely on estimates that the production figures from early twentieth-century Greece show to be unrealistic.[108] The supposed difference between the good harvests in the islands to the north (Imbros and Lemnos) and the catastrophic harvests in Attika does not exist. The hypothesis that there was an exceptional drought in 329/8 evaporates in the same way.

TABLE 14.3. Ancient and Modern Grain Production in Attika

ATTIKA	BARLEY PRODUCTION IN QUINTALS	WHEAT PRODUCTION IN QUINTALS	TOTAL GRAIN IN QUINTALS
329/8 BCE	91,779	8,389	100,169
1911 CE	32,154	91,975	124,129
1921 CE	11,652	44,091	55,743

On this basis, it is possible to attempt to assess Attika's dependency on foreign sources of imported grain. To do so, we have to estimate the population of Attika. Here we will adopt the estimates proposed by Mogens H. Hansen, using as a point of reference a population on the order of 250,000 inhabitants after 350.[109] Attika's population may have been about 330,000 in the fifth century, a third more than in the fourth century. This is a very generous estimate. Indeed, even if we grant that by then there was a citizen population that was larger by a third (that is, 40,000 instead of 30,000) than that of the fourth century, nothing indicates that the number of metics and especially slaves was in proportion to the number of citizens. That is why the figure of 330,000 inhabitants, if it was reached, probably represents a maximum that Athens attained only for a short time. On this point the population figures for modern Greece once again offer a new element for useful comparison.

The end of the nineteenth century and the beginning of the twentieth represented the apogee of early modern rural Greece. It was a full world. In the number of sites occupied and in the density of rural exploitation generally, we see levels of occupation such as Greece had not known since the end of the fourth century (although admittedly in some regions the density of the population in antiquity was even probably higher than at the end of the nineteenth century, but precisely because it could benefit from large scale imports). In 1911, Greece still had not received the flood of refugees from Asia Minor who were to significantly change its demographic landscape in the 1920s. By that time, the city of Athens was no longer the little town of the early nineteenth century. For almost a century, it had been the capital of Greece and it was then the biggest city in the country. In 1911, the population of Attika was 338,000.[110] Although the congruence with the estimates of the population of ancient Attika should be treated with caution, it remains truly striking.[111]

Importers and Suppliers of Grain

It has been assumed that 400,000 *medimnoi* of grain could feed 80,000 persons for a year.[112] Let us accept this figure. Thus the Athenian population's annual consumption of grain between 340 and 330 BCE (ca. 250,000 inhabitants) must have been around 1,250,000 *medimnoi*. On the basis of the preceding data regarding the population and production of Attika in the fourth century, what proportion of its population could be fed by local production? The approximately 340,000 *medimnoi* of grain produced in 329/8 BCE represented enough food for about 68,000 persons.[113] We can therefore conclude that if the harvest was good, as it certainly was in 329/8, Attika's own production could feed 27 percent of its population in the years between 340 and 320. The proportion must have fallen considerably below 25 percent in the event of a bad harvest. In the fifth century, on the basis of a maximum figure of 330,000 inhabitants during a brief period, one has to conclude that Attika could not feed more than 20 percent of its population, this proportion dropping to less than 20 percent in the event of a bad harvest. If the territories of Drymos, Salamis, and Oropos are included, the figures increase a few fractions of a percent, but not significantly. These figures show the extent to which Athens was dependent on outside sources. An episode told by Livy (43.6.3) and dated to 170 BCE is very revealing of the vital necessity of grain import for Athens, and all the more so than this was a time when the local population was lower than in the Classical period. Forced to deliver grain to the Roman troops operating in Greece, the Athenians complained that even (part of) their rural population lived on imported grain (they nevertheless satisfied Roman demands, but obviously by buying grain on the international market). In any case, it is clear that in the fifth century, when Attika was heavily populated, the dependency was at its height. That is why Pericles was able to conceive the policy that he followed on the eve of the Peloponnesian War. We know that this policy foresaw an abandonment of the territory (even if in reality it was not total during the first years) and the withdrawal of the whole rural population behind the fortifications of Athens and Piraeus, which were connected by the Long Walls. This policy was based on the previous level of the city's imports, which provided by far the largest proportion of its food.

By the sixth century at the latest, Athens had entered the cycle of external dependency. Solon's measures show the tension that existed at the beginning of the century. The Athenians' desire to control Eleusis and the island of Salamis, for which they were competing with the Megarians, had certainly already had an agrarian dimension, as is common in border conflicts between cities. Thus after their victory over the Boiotians in 506 BCE, the Athenians seized the territory of Oropos. The desire to take over external territories that produced grain, or to have access to grain trade routes, was certainly a powerful motive for Athens's foreign adventures in the second half of the sixth century. Successes came with the settlement in the Thracian Chersonese, and especially with the conquest of Lemnos and Imbros. These were particularly rich agricultural territories. According to the figures for 329/8, these two territories alone produced 274,525 *medimnoi* of barley and 72,850 *medimnoi* of precious wheat (far more than Attika), for a total of 347,375 *medimnoi*, hardly less than the production of Attika *stricto sensu*. These islands had been settled by Athenian colonists (*klērouchoi*). There is no doubt that the totality of the island's surplus production above and beyond what was needed for its relatively modest population was sent to the Attic market. This is also why, in addition to the fact that these exports were made by private merchants, Athens was able to levy a tax in kind of one-twelfth on the island's products, as is shown by the grain law of 374/3 BCE.[114]

Let us assume that the grain deliveries coming from the foreign possessions (in fact, mainly Imbros and Lemnos) represented 150,000 *medimnoi* (that is, slightly less than half of the local production); those from Pontos 400,000; those that normally came from Cyrene at a little less than 100,000, with about the same amount came from Egypt and the West (Sicily and Italy), the rest being procured by various minor producers. One can thus propose the following estimate for the sources

TABLE 14.4. Estimate of Sources of Grain of Athens in the Mid-Fourth Century BCE

SOURCE OF GRAIN	AMOUNT IN MEDIMNOI	PERCENTAGE
Attika	340,000	27.2
Lemnos and Imbros	150,000	12.0
Pontos	400,000	32.0
Cyrene	90,000	7.2
Egypt	90,000	7.2
West	90,000	7.2
Various other contributors	90,000	7.2
Total	1,250,000	100.0

of grain of Athens, with figures that are those we can directly derive from ancient sources for Attika, Pontos and Cyrene (table 14.4).[115]

We can legitimately assume that Athens must have imported regularly at least 910,000 *medimnoi* per year, of which 150,000 came from its own possessions abroad and 760,000 from foreign territories. But of course each of these figures must have varied from one year to the other, according to the amount of the crops or of political circumstances that could impact exports. If the crop in Attika was poorer than expected, more grain had to be imported, inevitably over one million *medimnoi*. We have seen that we have every reason to believe that the crop of 329/8 was a good or even perhaps a very good one. In the second half of the fourth century BCE, the direct dependency of Athens on grain delivered by sea to its port was of the order of 75 percent (and even more in the fifth century with a higher population level). It is now easy to understand why in Athens every prytany (a civic month of 36 days), at the first assembly (or plenary assembly), it was proposed to put to the agenda of the meeting "the questions of grain and of the defense of the territory," as mentioned by Aristotle in the *Constitution of Athens* (43.4).

It is also easy to understand why grain crises in Athens had to do essentially (although not only) with interruptions affecting imports, even if difficulties with internal production might also cause significant shortfalls. Thus in the early 320s, it was an interruption of supply coming from Egypt following poor harvests in that country that led to major problems in the Aegean markets. Indeed, Egypt was a regular provider of grain for the Aegean, and for large quantities.[116] In 396 BCE, according to Diodorus, the pharaoh Nepherites I had sent "five hundred thousand measures" of grain to the Peloponnesians. It is difficult to determine whether these

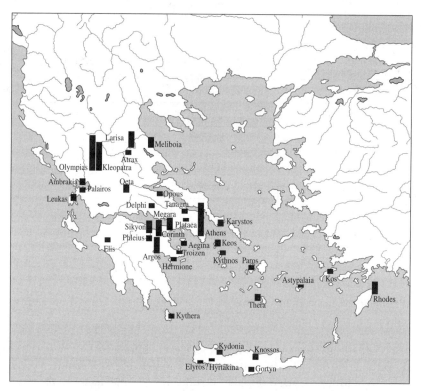

FIGURE 14.1. Map of grain imports from Cyrene in the early 320s BCE.

were *medimnoi* (with a volume of 52.53 liters) or *artabai* (perhaps 39.4 liters). But the figure gives us an idea of Egypt's export capacity, which was on the same order as that of Cyrene.[117] It was against a background of insufficient food supplies that Kleomenes of Naukratis could develop his grain speculation.[118] As for Athens, the policy consisting in trying to obtain export licenses for grain and tax exemptions was not abandoned in the Hellenistic period. Thus, as we know from three decrees of the Thessalian city of Larisa dated to ca. 220–205, ca. 196–192, and ca. 140 BCE, on the request of the Athenians the Larisaeans granted them the right to export grain and then a reduced sales tax rate (1 percent instead of the regular 5 percent).[119]

The other cities of the Aegean world did not have such high proportions of external dependency. But we know that most of these cities were regular importers—Rhodes, Mytilene, or the cities of the Kyklades, but also a large number of cities in continental Greece. The map of grain exports from Cyrene in the early 320s (a huge total of 805,000 *medimnoi*) shows us that the cities in the northern Peloponnese imported large quantities of grain. It is certain that the figures given for these imports corresponded to a single year (figures 14.1 and 14.2).[120]

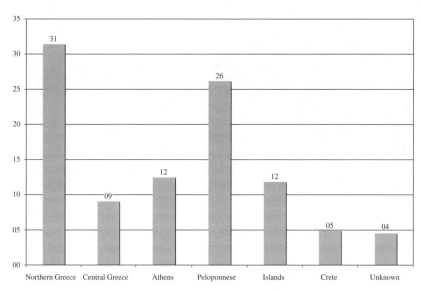

FIGURE 14.2. Distribution of grain imports from Cyrene in the early 320s BCE.

Beyond Athens, this dependency of Aegean cities on imported grain, whether it came from Egypt, Sicily, or Pontos, very largely explains the military strategies adopted during the Peloponnesian War, whether these were the Athenians' determination to conquer Sicily to block grain supplies for the Peloponnesians, or that of the Peloponnesians after 413 BCE to cut all the grain routes to Athens, one after the other.[121] A single route for grain imports to Athens remained open after the crushing defeats of 413 and 412, the one from the Black Sea. This explains why in this period most of the battles took place in the area of the Straits, until the final defeat at Aigos Potamoi in 405, precisely at the Hellespont, sealed the fate of Athens. Thus the cities of the Aegean world had attained a level of population that their own resources did not allow them to feed. But this was not a situation that was harmful to them. On the contrary, to the extent to which a variable but important proportion of their population consumed grain imported at comparatively low prices (despite fluctuations due to crises)—that is, at a price much lower than what it would have been if, hypothetically, they had had to (and been able to) count on their internal production—the result was a considerable gain in productivity. The yields in good years have been estimated at about nine to one (nine grains harvested for one planted) in the Bosporan kingdom and ten to one in Egypt, with the yields in good years in Sicily being of the same order (in the case of adverse climatic conditions, production could fall dramatically: no export was possible and clients had to find other providers). If we compare them with good yields of around seven to one in Attika (at most, and chiefly for barley, which has a lower nutritive value), we see that there is a differential of productivity ranging from 30 to 43 percent, which was perfectly sufficient to create the flow of import from these regions.

Thus significant gains in productivity could be made by connecting through international trade zones where agricultural yields were of very different levels. These policies of importing from distant production zones were combined with logics of security, because people invariably produced as much grain as they could to protect themselves against a market failure that always remained possible. It remains to evaluate the combined effect of these policies on the economic evolution of the ancient Greek world.

XV

THE GREEK CITIES
AND THE MARKET

The time has come to make a general assessment of the extent and the limits of the market in the world of the Greek city-states. The preceding chapters have shown that an analysis in terms of purely local markets that did not communicate with each other cannot provide an adequate description of the reality of trade. At the same time, it should be emphasized that the space of the markets underwent several major reconfigurations between the end of the Archaic period and the first century BCE. In this way, it is possible to bring out the impact of political factors on the establishment of trade networks. But then it is also necessary to show that the political dynamics itself has an economic aspect. In principle, a predatory economy and a market economy contradict each other. However, in fact these two systems are not mutually exclusive. They can also be combined: that was the case in the economy of the world of the Greek city-states. As for prices and their development in the different cities or regions, it would be a mistake to assume that they were not governed by any overall logic. The discontinuity between the general market and the local market explains both the common tendencies and the multiplicity of local economic situations.

In conclusion, it will be possible to analyze the "performance" of the market in the world of the Greek city-states. In this perspective, one will first observe that this market shared numerous common traits with the organization of markets in other periods, in particular those of the medieval and early modern periods. This will provide a way to inquire into the performance of ancient markets. Beyond the similarities, however, one should also stress the specificity of the performance of the ancient Greek markets, which were founded on an optimal utilization of environmental conditions.

Center and Periphery: The Historical Development

The prosperity of the Greek Aegean world in the Archaic and Classical periods was based first on its ability to control a vast, trans-Mediterranean trade network that allowed it to supply itself with massive amounts of grain, metal, slaves, and other unprocessed commodities brought in from peripheral regions, and to which it supplied in return a series of high-value products (oil, fine wines, artisanal products). In the last century of the Archaic period, the cities of western Asia Minor had been the principal centers of development. But they had suffered an initial decline with the Persian takeover in 545 BCE. Their revolt in 499 BCE, which ended in a catastrophic defeat emblematized by the destruction of Miletos in 494 BCE, along with the constant war they waged against Persia until 449 BCE, marked their prolonged disappearance from the scene. In continental Greece, the great mercantile cities at the end of the Archaic period and the beginning of the Classical period, Corinth and Aigina, were rapidly supplanted by Athens. With its silver mines in Laurion, for two centuries Athens was the engine of this economic development. The empire it established in the fifth century tended to establish direct political control over the whole of the trading space of the Aegean world, which extended far beyond the Aegean Sea proper. Thus the Black Sea was also within the political orbit of Athens, and the goal of the great expedition of 415–413 BCE was to take control of Sicily. The collapse of the empire caused fourth-century Greece to return to a balance of powers, but did not change the overall model of the relations between the Aegean world and other centers of development in the Mediterranean world. The center-periphery model thus remains fully pertinent in describing trade during this period, provided that one makes it clear that the development of the periphery proceeded at the same pace as that of the center: development was reciprocal, and cannot be understood without taking both center and periphery into account.[1]

The bases of this model were destroyed at the beginning of the Hellenistic period. Political changes, especially the emergence of Macedon and Alexander's conquests, led to the liquidation of the positions of the great cities of southern Greece. Sparta collapsed in 371 BCE. The destruction of Thebes in 335 BCE and the defeats suffered by Athens in the Lamian War symbolize the establishment of a new power relationship between the city-states and the kingdoms. With certain regional exceptions (for example, the western Peloponnese), in the third century continental Greece entered into an overall economic and demographic decline.[2] New internal equilibria were established, to the advantage of an elite that was more concentrated than it had earlier been. On the broader scene of the eastern Mediterranean, we see the emergence of new centers of development that correspond to the expansion of Hellenism that followed Alexander's conquest. A major commercial axis was established that started on the west coast of the Black Sea, passed along the west and then south coast of Asia Minor, and continued on either to the coasts of the Levant shared between the Seleukids and the Ptolemies, or to the Egypt of the Ptolemies. Having succeeded in retaining its independence despite Demetrios's assault in 305/4 BCE, the city of Rhodes benefited from its central position on this maritime route. The cities of western Asia Minor experienced a new economic boom. Their development was slowed by the political instability of the third century, but resumed in the first half of the second century, after Seleukid control was eliminated: this was the Golden Age of the cities of western Asia Minor, which lasted until the years following 140 BCE.[3]

However, from the end of the third century on, the emergence of a new power gradually shifted the balance of the Hellenistic world as it had been organized after Alexander's death. A new kind of state that was not Greek had arisen in the western Mediterranean. Rome had unified Italy in the second half of the fourth century and the first decades of the third century. Immediately afterward, it collided with Carthage. The final defeat of the Punic forces in 202 BCE gave Rome control over the western Mediterranean, and thus over the Greeks of Italy and Sicily. Rome was responsible for the decline of Macedon's influence (197 BCE) and then the elimination of the Macedonian kingdom (168 BCE). Rome drove the Seleukids out of Asia Minor (188 BCE), and also redrew the borders of the Attalid kingdom (which was expanded considerably toward the interior of Asia Minor) and those of the Rhodian state (which controlled Karia and Lykia between 188 and 166 BCE). At first, Rome's entry onto the scene seemed to have only advantages for the Greek city-states. But following the elimination of Macedon, it appeared that Rome intended, if not to take direct control over all these regions, at least to exercise a power over them that tolerated no opposition. The creation of the province of Macedon after the failure of that country's revolt, the destruction of Carthage, and the destruction of Corinth, the capital of the Achaian League, all of which occurred in 146 BCE, symbolized these new power relationships. The will of the last Attalid king, Attalos III, in which he left his kingdom to Rome, was an opportunity to take direct control over western Asia Minor. After the ferocious war waged against Aristonikos between 133 and 129 BCE, this goal was achieved by creating the Roman province of Asia in 127 BCE. From then on, the theoretical independence of the Greek coastal cities had less and less real content.

A new center was thus established. In spite of its level of development, which was still exceptional in the Mediterranean area, by the middle of the second century the Greek Aegean world was already becoming one of the peripheral regions of an expanded Mediterranean space in which Rome and Roman Italy henceforth played the role of center. The free port of Delos, created by Rome in 166 BCE to thwart Rhodes, was exceptionally prosperous. The tax exemption (*ateleia*) enjoyed by merchants who carried on business there was a very attractive factor, as Strabo emphasizes (10.5.4).[4] It henceforth served as a relay point for goods coming from Asia Minor or Pontos to Rome, and for products from Italy, Sicily, or Africa being sent back to the markets of the eastern Mediterranean.

Predation, Economic Space, and Political Space

This brief outline of the political and economic forces involved in the Aegean world between the end of the Archaic period and the first century CE leads us to reflect on the relationship between political dynamics and economic dynamics. The modern distinction between politics and economics clearly separates systems of power over people from the production and exchange of material or immaterial goods. But as already observed, this distinction is not suitable for the analysis of the ancient world. The Greek city-states were not only political communities but also communities of landowners, because only citizens had the right to own land. In addition, they were defined by their ability to subjugate other people, preferably non-Greeks—but if necessary, Greeks as well. Moreover, in doing so the Greek city-states were only acting like other societies of the Mediterranean world of their time, but with the difference that they gave property rights rigorous legal forms, establishing strict barriers where other cultures drew more flexible borderlines. If our contemporary distinction between politics and economics is not suitable for the ancient world, that is because in that world the inevitable economic role of the state was different from what it is today. War had a predatory aspect. In the short term, it could enable a state to seize its enemy's goods, his harvest, the movable property that constituted his patrimony, and sometimes to enslave his people and transform them into productive chattels. In the longer term, war might also make it possible to establish zones of domination over peoples who would pay tribute.

The existence of predatory actions (in the form of war or piracy) is a defining characteristic of the ancient Greek world.[5] Beyond the sociological approach, it is necessary to inquire into the forms of economic rationality they could assume. Thus one must inquire into the economic rationality of violence. Fundamentally, war could be a profitable economic operation because in the short term acquiring goods by war cost less than producing them. Since land remained the principal factor of production but was not itself a good produced (unlike machines or technological knowledge in our contemporary world), seizing it by war was part of a genuine economic logic. In the traditional model of the Greek city-states, which had an abundant reservoir of young warriors and a long summer season in which people had little to do after the grain was harvested (usually in late spring), war was a good way for a city to try to increase its wealth by using this dead time to the detriment of its neighbors. Thus it is possible to observe why war as a means of winning booty or increasing available agricultural land always remained a "rational" objective for many small city-states, right down to the end of the Hellenistic period.[6] Other states specialized in large-scale piracy, as did the Aitolian League in the third century and especially the Cretan cities until the first century BCE.[7] On the other hand, more ambitious states, such as the Lydian or the Persian monarchies, and later the Hellenistic kingdoms, sought to impose tributes on peoples and cities that would permanently supply receipts in precious metals or in kind. War was also the way cities established their zones of domination, whether these were only regional in ambition or extended over vast areas. Several cities of the Aegean islands set out to create tributary zones, in particular Polycrates's Samos in the second half of the sixth century. But naturally the best example is the Athenian empire of the fifth century, and then again for two decades in the fourth century.[8] In comparison, the "empires" of Sparta or Thebes were very ephemeral. The same was true, in fact, of Rhodes's domination over Karia and Lykia between 188 and 166 BCE, which was, moreover, only a temporary (and poisoned) gift of Rome.

On the economic level, however, we must avoid assuming that political power relationships always structure the economic space. In reality, a series of examples show that there is a complex dynamics between the two terms. It would in any case be incorrect to maintain that politics always took precedence over economics, as if a trade relationship could be established only by the use of force. In this respect, without erecting it into a general law, one must first note that the political domination of a great power like Athens in the fifth century was based on economic foundations: this city's political imperialism was able to develop, starting at the end of the sixth century, only because of the silver from the mines at Laurion, which gave it an enormous advantage over its rivals. Athens took control over the Aegean area, and then tried to subjugate the cities of the Black Sea and later Sicily, because it wanted to have new tributaries. However, the desire to control first maritime routes and then, directly, production zones, was only an extension by political and military means of the desire to ensure secure supplies. If a city had the political means to achieve this aim, it did not hesitate to do so. But this is in no way a peculiarity of ancient states.

In this respect, the policy of Athens speaks volumes. By the end of the sixth century, it consisted first of all of occupying positions in the area of the Straits, and then conquering the grain-producing islands of Lemnos and Imbros.[9] Next it seized Skyros (476 BCE), which provided, in addition to a small amount of grain, an ideal relay base on the route to the north.[10] Then, after the second Persian War, the establishment of the Athenian Empire made possible a genuine policy of control over the grain supplies of all the cities of the Aegean. A decree from the Macedonian city of Methone that goes back to 426 BCE (and thus to the period of the Peloponnesian War), shows that Athens had complete control over the grain coming from Pontos.[11] Athenian magistrates called *Hellespontophulakes*, who were established at Byzantion, monitored the ships. The cities could have grain shipped from the Black Sea in accord with licenses that were granted by Athens and indicated the maximum amount of grain they allowed. This was a way of putting direct pressure on the city-states, because any failure to satisfy Athens's requirements could result in an immediate interruption of grain supplies from the Black Sea. An Attic decree dating from the period 425–410 BCE, which grants an Achaian named Lykon a maritime license to sail and export to all the ports of the empire, is the best concrete illustration of Pseudo-Xenophon's remark that it was impossible to carry on commerce without the authorization of the power that controlled the seas.[12]

Like Athens a few centuries earlier, Rome adopted a policy that centralized supplies to its advantage. When Sicily, Sardinia, and then Africa passed in succession under the Roman yoke, their grain was reserved to supply Rome. The same thing happened later, when in 30 BCE Rome seized control of Egypt. Thus one can understand why, confronted by the supply problems connected with Antiochos IV's campaign against Egypt in 168 BCE, Rhodes had to make a special request to obtain access to Sicilian grain and a license to import a hundred thousand *medimnoi* of it.[13] Generally speaking, the Roman provinces, for example the province of Asia starting in 127 BCE, had to pay, in various ways, a tax in kind intended to supply Rome.[14] As already observed with Athens, even with regard to free and allied cities Rome did not hesitate to make demands for supplies of grain.[15] For instance, as already stated, it required the cities of Thessaly, probably around 130 BCE, to allow it to buy all the grain they had for sale.[16] This was, of course, another form of constraint, but one that had the advantage for Rome of ensuring its food supplies by political means.

One of the most important questions raised by the existence of empires, kingdoms, and other zones of domination is how great a part economic predation played in economic flows, its impact on production, and its long-term influence on economic development. As already observed, in the case of the kingdoms it is clear that tributes in kind and other kinds of obligatory levies represented most of the commodities with which they could engage in the markets. To limit ourselves for the moment to an overall assessment, it is true that some of the commodities traded proceeded from tributes. But if we confine ourselves to trade in the Aegean world, even if no numerical data can be provided, there is every reason to think that most of the goods traded were put on the market by private landowners rather than by kings or dynasts. As for grain imported from other sources—one thinks, of course, of Egypt, a major grain supplier, and of the Bosporan kingdom, with differences depending on the period—the proportion of grain delivered in the form of tributes might have been greater. The same might have been true for wood. But even in the case of grain, nothing allows us to conclude that the proportion of tributary grain was ever more than half. In the case of other commodities, however, private production seems always to have been the rule. In addition, whatever a product's origin (for example, the tributary grain provided by a kingdom or wood from a royal forest), once it was put on the market it was treated by merchants as a commodity like any other: the way in which goods circulated on the international market was not changed by their origin.

This assertion has to be qualified in two ways. First, the way in which commodities proceeding from royal reserves were delivered and their price was not without impact on markets, and thus on the production of the cities involved as well.[17] Second, as the new great power at the center of a vast Mediterranean network, Rome set up a supply system for its markets by making systematic use of tributary commodities in proportions that no Greek state seems to have known. However, analyzing the impact of commodities proceeding from the tributary system on the markets of Greek cities does not oblige us to project onto the latter data that seem to have been valid only for Rome.

Finally, regarding the impact of politics on economics, one must point out that the creation of vast zones of domination accelerated processes of unification that the logic of the international market was already helping to establish. This was the case in particular for zones using the same monetary and weight standards. During the last century of the Archaic period in Asia Minor, the so-called Milesian monetary standard (with a stater of 14.3 grams) was dominant, and it was also used in most of the Lydian kingdom's area of domination, but other cities also accepted it without the reason being that they were subjected to Lydia. The political control exercised by Corinth explains directly why its colonies adopted its standard. The same was not true for the Aiginetan standard (with a stater of 12.6 grams in theory, but in fact often 12 grams), which owed its use in the Aegean, in Crete, and in the Peloponnese only to Aigina's dynamism. But in the fifth century, Athens's policy of suppressing mints in the cities of its empire led in fact to a unification of weights and measures and currencies around the Aegean in accord with Athenian standards. The famous decree imposing the latter's use in all the cities of the empire and the prohibition on minting silver coins (in the mid-420s or perhaps a little before 414 BCE) was certainly the product of a specific political context.[18] But it was also the outcome of a policy of weakening the states of the Athenian alliance pursued for several decades.

It is true that the collapse of the empire prevented this unification from being completed. The cities of continental Greece that had coined money on the standard of Corinth or Aigina continued to do so. After their revolt in 412/1 BCE, the cities of Asia Minor minted new coins on the standard of Chios rather than on that of Athens. This had a considerable impact on the monetary circulation in western Asia Minor and was at the origin of the new Rhodian standard.[19] However, even without the empire, in the fourth century the Attic standard was still the real international standard of Greece, and Attic coins could be described as "Hellenic money."[20] Athens was conquered by Macedon, but the latter did not impose its regional standard: although Philip II continued to mint silver on the Thracian-Macedonian standard, he adopted the Attic standard for his gold coins. As for Alexander, after 333 his gold and silver coins were struck exclusively on the Attic standard. Later, the Attic standard remained the great monetary standard of the Hellenistic world, and it was only in relation to it that pockets of closed currency systems were established in which coins were minted on a different, lighter standard—particularly in Ptolemaic Egypt, in the Attalid monarchy beginning with the reign of Eumenes II, and also in the Rhodian state during the whole period.[21] Finally, the Roman *denarius* was assimilated to the Attic drachm, even though its standard was slightly lower.

The fifth-century Athenian Empire finally gave way to the coalition of the Peloponnesians and the Persians. But it was a powerful unifying factor in the Greek world, in the area of economics as in others. The famous Attic decree imposing the use of the Attic standard of weights and measures, along with the prohibition on minting silver coins, was thus a political measure. In fact, it contributed to the unification of the Greek world in a form that could only favor transactions. Thus, in the second half of the fifth century, a city on the west coast of the Black Sea defined a weight standard that bore the Attic owl and seems to have been a quarter of the Attic commercial mina.[22] Far from Pontos, in Herakleion-Thonis, the Egyptian port situated at the Canopic mouth of the Nile, a weight that seems to date from the early fourth century also bears the image of the Attic owl.[23] It corresponded to ten Attic monetary drachms, which suggests that this port had adopted the Attic system of weights and measures. Whether or not Egypt produced imitations of Attic owls at that time, this weight is thus part of a larger complex that shows that even outside the zone directly controlled by Athens, the Attic standard was increasingly used as a point of reference.[24] It is true that the fact that Egypt was at war with Persia made it all the more tempting to adopt the Attic standard. However, it was a region on which the Athenian standard and Attic models had not been imposed. In Philistian cities (Ashdod, Ashkelon, Gaza), Attic types (Athena or the owl) may be found on local coins struck seemingly apparently as early as the mid-fifth century.[25]

Later, either because of the attraction of established standards or because official state weights and measures were imposed, a certain unification of weights and measures and monetary systems made it possible to decrease transaction costs and thus to facilitate international trade. Hence one cannot consider solely the possible negative effects of the existence of kingdoms and other zones of domination on the constitution and development of markets.

Prices and Market Integration

The question of the level and the development of prices is one of those that has attracted the most attention in defining ancient markets. The divergence of prices from one region to another is often seen as a symptom of a lack of market integration. Admittedly, we are less well informed about prices than about institutional structures. However, despite its inadequacies, our information allows us to determine a few major characteristics. First, the question of prices cannot be separated from that of the structure of markets. It has been shown that markets had a two-level structure, the domestic market being symbolized by the agora, the foreign market by the *emporion* (at least in cities that had one). Both because of high transport costs (especially overland) and prohibitions on engaging in trade (particularly exports or re-exports of grain), there were a multitude of local situations that could lead to very large price differences from one region to another or even from one city to another.[26] If a grain harvest was inadequate in a city that was usually able to meet its own needs, and if its neighbors, little or less affected by the shortage but fearing for the future, prohibited exports, flagrant price disequilibria between these cities rapidly appeared. This is precisely the picture suggested by sources from the

Classical or Hellenistic periods, particularly in the case of grain, but also partly in that of other indispensable commodities such as oil, and less frequently wine or artisanal products. However, at a minimum these variations were directly connected on the one hand with a system of supply through the market, and on the other hand with the discontinuous nature of the supply of certain products.

But these large punctual disparities, which were systemic, do not mean that on the whole prices in various cities did not undergo developments that tended in the same direction throughout the same region, and even over vast areas, at the same time. First, one of the key elements in the establishment of price levels was the monetary material available, which one can for convenience's sake identify with coined currency in circulation, although admittedly the silver "commodity chain" encompasses both coined and uncoined precious metal.[27] In this regard, it is clear that the trend of price evolution is directly connected with the evolution of the overall monetary material available. In the Classical period, our information concerning prices comes chiefly from Athens, but is sometimes corroborated by data from other cities.[28] Even if our information is regrettably inadequate, it is certain that overall price levels, in terms of weight in silver, were higher during the Classical period than in the Archaic period. Within the Classical period, during the fifth century prices first rose, and then declined over the last quarter of the century.[29] This cycle corresponded to activity in the mines of Laurion. Once again, the resumption of mining and the minting of the gold and silver reserves in the sanctuary of Delphi by the Phokians in the fourth century led to an increase in the amount of monetary material and an initial price increase. The latter was followed by a much larger increase that was connected with the minting of the Great King's enormous reserves of gold and silver, which amounted to 180,000 talents, the equivalent of 4,680 tons of silver.[30] Thanks to the accounts of its sanctuary, it is in fact Delos that offers the best observation point for following the evolution of prices in the Aegean world during the Hellenistic period. The work done on this data by Gary Reger provides a basis for fundamental research on the economic history of this period.[31]

The evolution of prices in Delos entirely confirms the analysis according to which price levels tend to follow the evolution of the monetary material available. Traces of this phenomenon are found at both Babylon and Delos, and this convergence is decisive.[32] Observing the graphs of prices in Delos (earlier, pp. 327–28), we see that grain and oil prices fell sharply at the beginning of the century. This decrease has been attributed to purely local factors relating to a reorganization of the sanctuary's finances and to the establishment of a new contractual system, the "sacred contract" (hiera sungraphē).[33] Whatever the reasons for setting up a new system may have been, it is clear that factors of another nature explain the price decrease. With the exhaustion of stocks of precious metals proceeding from the pillaging of the Great King's treasury, at the beginning of the third century the period of massive minting that followed the Macedonian conquest ended. This period was also the one in which the production of the Laurion mines collapsed. The slow erosion of the monetary stock in circulation suffices to explain the price decrease at the beginning of the century, and then the stagnating prices of oil and grain after 270 BCE. As for the following period, the pillaging by Roman troops and the tributes and war indemnities demanded by Rome after its intrusion into the Aegean world in the early second century led to a physical shift of precious metal to the western Mediterranean, where it enabled a massive minting of *denarii*.[34]

These large-scale levies of precious metals explain why there were so few Aegean mints that struck coins during the second and first centuries BCE. Only a few Aegean cities continued to mint large quantities of coins, especially Athens with its *stephanēphoroi* from 164/3 BCE on, and Rhodes with its *plinthophoroi* during the period between the end of the war against Antiochos and 88 BCE.[35] Thus it is not surprising that price levels were not very high: in the Piraeus agoranomic inscription from between 34–33 and 18–17 BCE, which concerns tripe and not luxury foods, prices are given in obols and *chalkoi*.[36] In addition, we have two regulations setting prices: it is surely not insignificant that on the second list, the prices are lower than on the first. One would like to be able to corroborate this observation with other data. If this decrease is significant, which the discovery of new documents might enable us to confirm, the difference in prices between the two lists might testify to the fact that this was a period of continual price decreases.

The second remarkable factor in the graphs of Delian prices is the contrast in the evolution of oil and grain prices (which determines that of farm rents) on the one hand and wood and hog prices on the other hand. This contrast is explained by the difference between prices established on the international market, those for oil and grain, and prices established on a regional market, those for firewood and hogs.[37] In any event, live hogs could not be transported over long distances. Although some large landowners, like the Athenian Phainippos in the fourth century, could also draw considerable revenues from firewood and charcoal, these productions could also be profitable for small producers or small-scale merchants (in Delos, the law forced them to become retailers themselves).[38] On the other hand, all the testimony relative to the grain trade tends to refer to imports from distant sources (the Black Sea, Egypt via Rhodes, and even sometimes Africa in the second century BCE).[39] Whereas prices for oil and grain were tending to decline or stagnate, those for firewood and hogs remained high or rapidly increased during the second half of the third century because of the quick growth of the Delian market and the sanctuary's activity. This increase was all the more remarkable because the general trend was toward declining prices. Thus the existence of regional situations for certain products does not contradict that of broad price trends for products such as grain and oil that were traded internationally and transported over long distances. In turn, the existence of broad price trends does not mean that prices were everywhere the same: it has been observed that because of their superior productivity, in some large productive areas (such as Pontos and Sicily) grain prices were lower than those that could be found in large areas where it was consumed, and playing on this difference was precisely what motivated merchants to transport commodities from one region to another.

Finally, the economic situations of whole regions might be affected by repercussions of events external to them. One can gauge this not by the effect of competition connected with technological innovations, as would be the case today, but by unusual price differences or sudden changes in supply or demand in distant regions (whatever the reason for these changes might be). In the first category, one should probably put the low-priced wine or oil from the great slave-worked *latifundia* in Italy, Sicily, and Africa shipped to regions like the Aegean and the Levant.[40] In the second category, one must first mention the effect of bad harvests like those in Egypt in the early 320s BCE, which caused an abrupt reduction of grain deliveries to the Aegean area and led to a desperate search for other suppliers.[41] But one should also mention the repercussions of political events that might have a direct impact on economic trends.

The best illustration of this phenomenon is the annual rate of production of the Athenian coins known as *stephanēphoroi*. In the second century BCE, Athens minted new coins that modern authors often call "new style coinage" and that ancient texts call *stephanēphoroi*. Whereas up to that point, Athens had for the most part continued to employ the models in use since the end of the Archaic period, it now introduced coins bearing three new images: on the obverse, there still appeared an Athena seen in profile, but with a "modernized" design; on the reverse appeared an owl standing on a recumbent amphora, the whole within a wreath (*stephanos*, whence the name of these coins). The particularity of these coins is that they bear the names of the officials issuing them, usually two in number, which makes it possible to identify annual issues.[42] The first series of these issues ended in 87/6 BCE, since in that year the coins bear the name of Mithridates (in 88, Athens had sided with this king against Rome); thus on the basis of the annual issues it is possible to situate the beginning of the *stephanēphoroi* in 164/3 BCE (figures 15.1 and 15.2).[43]

Margaret Thompson's corpus of the *stephanēphoros* coinage allows to determine the number of dies used each year.[44] If we draw up a table of the issues on an annual basis, we obtain very interesting results. At first, production remained small, only a few dies being used each year. On the other hand, shortly after 146 BCE production increased spectacularly. We know that the year 146 was marked not only by the destruction of Carthage in the West, but also by that of Corinth at the end of the war waged against Rome by the Achaian Confederation. Strabo (10.5.4) already stressed that the destruction of Corinth favored the development of Delos, and this is confirmed by these figures. Thus it is possible to reconstitute a clear schema. The Athenians certainly began the *stephanēphoros* coinage in 164/3 BCE, two years after Delos was entrusted to them and became a "free port" at Rome's command. It served essentially Delian trade. Moreover, discoveries made on the island confirm that after 166 this coinage had a virtual monopoly on monetary circulation on the island. The rest of the series also shows the interconnection of political and economic phenomena over vast geographic zones. After the peak following 146, we observe a marked decline starting in 137/6 BCE, with a real trough

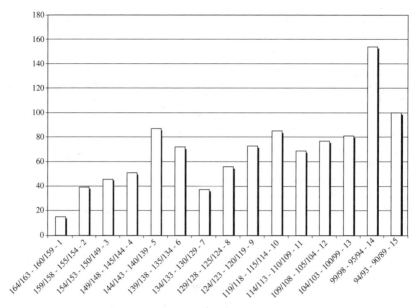

FIGURE 15.1. The production of Attic tetradrachms from 164/3 to 90/89 BCE (number of dies per period of five years).

in the late 130s. The recovery does not start until the mid-120s. This depression must be connected with the war against Aristonikos, which between 133 and 129 ravaged western Asia Minor, where unrest continued during the following years. Trade networks were so disturbed that in Rhodes a decrease in amphora production can be observed precisely in the late 130s.[45] It is logical to suggest that the sharp decrease in trade led in turn to a decrease in monetary coinage.

If this hypothesis is correct, one must nonetheless note that the decline of economic activity on Delos between 137/6 and 133 BCE (thus before the war against Aristonikos) can be explained as an after-effect of the great slave revolt that broke out at this time in Sicily, where a "kingdom" of rebel slaves was set up. The details of the chronology are disputed, some specialists maintaining that the revolt's starting point was anterior to 136, while others situate it only in 135 (though disturbances may have occurred earlier). Nonetheless, to the extent to which, as Strabo indicates (14.5.2), slaves were one of the essential "commodities" of Delos's trade with the West, it seems highly likely that an initial downturn was caused by the events in Sicily. In this unsettled context, it was hardly opportune to send new slaves to the West.[46] It may also be that the increasingly uncertain political situation in the Seleukid East also contributed to a turnabout in the situation. Finally, the revolt of the slaves working at the Laurion mines in 133 BCE might have impacted the production of *stephanēphoroi* more deeply than suspected so far.[47] The development of the Laurion mines in this period might be connected with the new

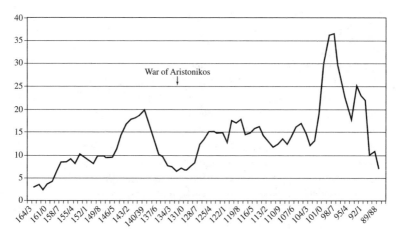

FIGURE 15.2. The production of Attic tetradrachms from 164/3 to 90/89 BCE (moving average of the production of dies on a three-year basis).

ease with which Athens, through Delos, could access the slave market. Moreover, slaves were crucial in the development of the mines. John Kroll might be right in suggesting that the period saw a large-scale new exploitation of the Laurion (and not simply a small-scale reprocessing of Classical period mine waste).[48] New physical analysis of the *stephanēphoroi* coins should make it possible to decide between the two hypotheses. If the bulk of the metal came from the Laurion, that would vindicate the idea of the revival of the Laurion mines. If it did not, that would indicate that the *stephanēphoroi* were minted mainly from other sources of metal—for instance, by melting down coins from various origins.

MARKETS: SUPPLY, DEMAND, AND NASH EQUILIBRIUM

In Perspective: The Medieval and Early Modern European Markets

One must now attempt to assess the overall performance of the market in the world of the Greek city-states.[49] It was not a universe without parallels. In many respects, there are interesting similarities between the structure of the Greek cities' markets and those of the cities of medieval and modern Europe. To turn first to economic theorists, it can be observed that the mercantilists thought a state had to produce all the commodities it could, and import only what was necessary but was not produced domestically. For the mercantilists, imports inevitably represented a kind of cash outlay, which in their view was the worst of errors, since (for them) cash itself was a source of wealth.[50] And they considered exporting unrefined commodities, such as food products, as tantamount to depriving the people of indispensable commodities. Reflecting a form of national selfishness, the mercantilists thus supported a highly protectionist system. But their ideology thus demanded that taxes be levied not only upon importation, in order to prevent the entry of products deemed useless if they could be produced domestically, but also upon exportation, in any case for basic commodities, since exporting goods amounted to depriving national consumers of them. At the same time, according to the mercantilists, the state was supposed to ensure that the people would be fed and in particular to take responsibility for the poor, not permanently, to be sure, but at least in times of shortages. Jean Bodin, in sixteenth-century France, and Thomas Mun, in seventeenth-century England, advocated in the same terms the establishment of public granaries that were supposed to make it possible to control prices and thus ensure subsistence for the poorest people in the event of shortages.[51]

Early modern markets, for their part, were subjected to strict and meticulous controls: prices and profit margins, along with the quantities bought and storage conditions, gave rise to an arsenal of control measures intended to prevent fraud and speculation.[52] The controls went so far as inspections of the homes of producers, intermediaries, and bakers in order to verify that the amount of their stocks corresponded to what had been declared. They helped maintain a state of mistrust among producers and intermediaries. We also know that medieval and modern cities frequently (though not systematically) resorted to the system of public granaries, part of the harvest being bought and deposited in public places. This grain might be used to relieve the people when shortages occurred, and to influence prices during transitional periods. The system of public granaries nonetheless had clear disadvantages. The cost of storage was high. The grain was not always preserved under good conditions and often turned out to be spoiled when it was needed for consumption. Above all, if the harvest was good, this grain served no purpose and had a serious cost for urban finances: this unused capital would have been needed elsewhere. As for prices, covert interventions on the part of public authorities can be observed. They had grain bought with public funds in order to have it resold by proxies who played the role of private merchants, all with the intention of putting pressure on the conditions of sale among other merchants.[53] Given the importance of being the first to announce a price decrease, one can wonder whether in some cases similar techniques were not used in ancient cities.

These control measures seemed indispensable in order to satisfy the poorest strata of the population, which were the most exposed to the impact of interruptions of the food supply, and also the most dangerous socially. At the same time, these measures were one of the main factors of economic stalemate, because they artificially maintained production at a level far below the one it could have reached had these controls been abandoned and prices freely set. The experience of modern Europe is in this respect very eloquent. It became possible to put a definitive end to famines only when the controls, barriers, and taxes of all kinds that prevented the free circulation of grain were abolished—in a universe that was much more peaceful than the earlier one, to be sure.[54] In this domain, as the physiocrats clearly saw, it was the "remedy" that caused the problem. The similarities between the organization of the markets of the Greek city-states and that of the cities of the medieval and early modern worlds are thus obvious, and they can be dealt with using a common conceptual approach.

Uncertainty, Risk Management, and the "Imperfect Market"

An optimal functioning of the market presupposes that supply is able to adjust to demand without encountering obstacles, without individual behaviors or regulations hindering this equilibration. A perfect market ideally corresponds to three conditions. The first is that buyers or sellers are always free to decide to enter or leave the market. The second is that there are also enough of them that it is only the sum of a multitude of individual demands and supplies that can influence the market, and not the demand or supply of a single individual or of a small number of individuals. The third is that goods have a homogeneous value and that the information regarding their performance and price is perfectly known to everyone. One could also add the condition that production factors and goods are mobile, leading to a division of labor, which is itself a source of gains in productivity and thus of growth. One must emphasize that the perfect market is a concept that real societies approach more or less, but that exists no more than the utopias of Thomas More or François Rabelais.

Examining the market of ancient Greece in accord with these criteria, a contradictory situation emerges. Taking into consideration the world of the agora and isolating it from its context, at first sight we might think we are dealing with the ideal of the market. In fact, sellers were not forced to sell. They could bring their merchandise to the agora or take it back as they saw fit. The sole constraint—but an important one—was that for many products, vendors could sell only in the agora (or agoras, if there was more than one of them in the city), which gave real form to the centrality of the city's internal commercial space. Symmetrically, buyers were subject to no obligation. There were also many buyers and sellers. As for information regarding the quality of the products and prices, it was in general guaranteed by the city's laws and by the *agoranomoi*, who were responsible for ensuring transparency. In a way, one might say that the structure of the agora realized the model of the "pure and perfect" market.

As for the international market, our impression seems to be the same. The logic of the market for agricultural products was based on a relationship of complementarity between large areas that had differing levels of productivity. This triggered a very active trade, in which most of the initiative was provided by private merchants. This trade connected very diverse regions. It involved not minimal percentages but very significant quantities of the commodities consumed, since at least in certain cities most of the latter were imported, their equivalent in value being provided by local production. That is how the market system allowed Greece to reach unprecedented levels of need satisfaction that were to be equaled or surpassed only in early modern Europe.

Does this mean that Greece was the country of the perfect market, of a self-regulating market that could have functioned without political institutions? The self-regulating market exists nowhere, and what one can analyze historically is institutions that are adapted to an environment that they themselves help shape. Thus in the domestic market of the cities of ancient Greece, if the "invisible hand of the market" led buyers and sellers to meet, it was the "heavy hand" of the magistrates that was to ensure that the rules were respected, not only regarding economic information but also regarding deliveries or retail profit margins. Furthermore, if sellers and buyers were numerous, that is because through its regulations, the city sought to prevent wholesale purchases of large quantities of goods by a single buyer, or by small groups of buyers, which could have put them in a favorable position for imposing their prices. The anecdote reported by Aristotle, according to which Dionysios of Syracuse forbade the activity of an iron merchant who had grown rich by buying up all the available iron, thus gaining a monopoly on its resale, is very significant.[55] An Imperial period inscription from Pergamon shows a regulation prohibiting coalitions of buyers even in the fish market.[56] True, in this case it was chiefly a question of establishing and supervising the use of small bronze coins, thus ensuring that the city could profit from the currency exchange, but the result is the same. The system tended to prohibit the constitution of what would now be called companies. But as a result, it also prevented the productivity gains connected with economic organization in the form of firms or even of cartels. Here is what can be considered to be a fundamental characteristic of the ancient market: it was a nonliberal market, and its form was decisively structured by the city's intervention.

By examining the way in which the market was supplied, and thus the formation of wholesale prices, one can observe clear distortions. In this sense, the market of ancient Greece was far from being a "perfect market." The achievement of the latter was hindered by the form of risk management adopted by individuals and by cities. Of course, one should not forget that the limitations regarding the quantities imported or exported did not concern all commodities, but only those that might prove to be vital necessities for the city's people, commodities that in many cities must in fact have represented the majority of foreign trade. It was in this domain that the main distortions occurred. In addition to political uncertainties, climatic vicissitudes weighed heavily on agricultural production. It can be estimated that in the Mediterranean system, one harvest out of three was inadequate. In some years, and in an unpredictable way, it could even be catastrophic.[57] The uncertainty concerning this fundamental factor created a logic of chaos and made any rational foresight impossible. In today's developed societies, because of the technological environment of agricultural production and the general level of productivity this logic of chaos no longer plays such a great role, and the impact of climatic variations on production has been considerably lessened. Price fluctuations are connected with the level of supply, of course, but many other factors (the elasticity of demand, currency speculation directly connected with the logic of the market, and so on) also play an important role in price levels. Uncertainty can be transformed into a risk, regarding which the market seeks to build optimal strategies. There is nothing comparable to the sudden, dramatic variations in the level of supply in the traditional world, and in particular in ancient Greece. A series of climatic or political catastrophes was very likely to dislocate the givens of the market, and thus, through a major disequilibrium between supply and demand, to make the result of any market strategy temporarily unpredictable. Confronted by a logic of chaos and abrupt variations in the level of supply, the market struggled to even out these variations, while demand remained the same. Given the technological and institutional inability to increase supply from existing local or regional sources, the sole way to limit uncertainty was to find new sources of supply. In fact, this was a factor that made it possible to lower prices. But because production proved to be chronically insufficient to meet levels of demand, the market was still inadequate to feed the people. State intervention thus became inevitable. The uncertainty connected with the delivery of supplies from abroad corresponding in quantities and prices to the needs of cities and individuals led producers and cities to implement their own strategies for limiting what was put on the market.

In the case of individual producers, security was achieved by retaining much more than what was needed for one year, augmented by the quantity necessary for the next season's sowing. The parallels with modern Greece suggest that if the harvest was sufficient, it was usual for farmers to retain as much as the equivalent of two years' consumption.[58] Storage was also common for the cities. Grain storage from one year to the next is made certain by the references to "old grain" in our sources. [59] In his treaty On Siegecraft, the third-century BCE engineer Philo of Byzantion gave the following advice:"It seems fit that the city store grain at least for one year; it must be bought when it is at the cheapest price, and when the following year has come one should consume it, and store new grain in anticipation of possible sieges and potential shortages."[60] People thus protected themselves against at least one catastrophic harvest, and were sure not to starve for at least one year. Risk management was thus provided both individually and collectively. But at the aggregate level, these behaviors also led inevitably to a limitation of the quantities put on the market.

The experience of famines led many cities to simply prohibit grain exports. This was a kind of transposition of the behavior of the individual producers to the collective level. The prohibition on exports even in the event of a good harvest (the surpluses being put in storage by individuals or by cities) thus kept large quantities of grain from being put on the market that should normally have been available. Such institutional interventions can be understood in the framework of the city, either because in the democratic cities of the Classical period the political influence of the poorest categories of the population partially counterbalanced that of the elites, or because later on the elites in power always had to reckon with popular discontent, which could take violent forms.[61] In fact, it is clear that laws prohibiting exports were not advantageous for large landowners, who had surpluses to export and did not want to count solely on the domestic market to sell their products. Thus these laws kept grain prices at low levels on the domestic market, possibly far below those on the international market. Such prices did not encourage large land-owners to develop the production of grain. Instead, they encouraged them to invest in the production of wine and oil, crops that could produce greater profits and that for the most part were not likely to be subjected to limitations like those imposed on the grain market: that is the logic transmitted to us by the Roman agronomists. Another possibility was to invest outside agriculture, in sectors considered more lucrative, such as "war industries" or other forms of production intended for large-scale trade.

The reasons for which various commodities might be traded internationally varied greatly, ranging from the need to obtain raw materials indispensable for local crafts to satisfying the tastes of elites that had adequate monetary revenues. As for grain, a product that was interchangeable (at least barley for barley or wheat for wheat), we are dealing with a commodity that had to meet a basic need. The demand for grain is nonelastic: once the ordinary need is satisfied, a price decrease will not lead to additional consumption, except among undernourished, low-income groups.[62] However, there too demand rapidly reached a limit. The nonelasticity of the demand for grain explains the wide variations in prices: skyrocketing when supply was insufficient, but also plummeting when it was too large. For Greece, there is Xenophon's key testimony. In his *Poroi* (4.6), written in 355/4 BCE, he considers it obvious that price levels have a direct impact on production and that they are the reason why people turn to one artisanal activity or another or, if they are farmers, decide to develop one kind of production rather than another, or even to seek a different source of income by changing their activity:

> When bronze-makers are too numerous and the prices of their products are low, they give up their trade, and the same goes for blacksmiths; and if grain and wine are abundant and their prices are low, cultivating them is no longer profitable, so that many people give up working the land and turn to large-scale commerce, retail commerce, and lending money at interest.

For handicraft products, and even if a certain portion of the production was commonly exported, it is clear that in a certain state of the trading circuits a sudden and major increase in production would inevitably cause prices to plummet.[63] But it is remarkable that grain also figures in the list of products whose production might be abandoned because of depressed prices. Examples of abrupt price increases are legion. But there are also cases of depression: as we have seen earlier, Livy (30.38.5) reports that at the end of the Second Punic War, in 202 BCE, grain deliveries from Sicily and Sardinia caused prices to fall to such a low level that merchants let ship captains keep the grain to pay the cost of transport. Martial (12.76) emphasizes that an exceptionally abundant harvest was not favorable for the producers' revenues: "An amphora of wine goes for twenty *as*, and a bushel of wheat for four *as*. Drunk and his stomach full, the farmer loses his shirt." This refers not to a permanent situation but to a harvest that is occasionally too abundant. Under similar circumstances, wine prices could also be unstable, but the consequences of an interruption of supply were not as tragic as they might be in the case of grain.[64]

Even if people tended to reserve excess grain for the following year, in a city that had taken the precaution of forbidding exports to prevent occasional shortages an exceptionally good harvest could only depress prices. We recognize here Paul A. Samuelson and William D. Nordhaus's "paradox of the bumper harvest," where what ought in theory to be a favorable factor causes producers' revenues to fall.[65] In the case of ancient Greece, the disequilibrium could be accentuated when exports were prohibited. The paradox is thus that given an insufficiency of supply, the fragmentation of markets and prohibitions on exports limited the area devoted to grain production and thus in turn limited the quantities put on the market. The controls on profits and set profit margins leveled out merchants' activities. The same logic of "official prices" (*kathestēkuiai timai*) in wholesale markets (if one adopts the Athenian definition of a practice that, without bearing this name, was probably the norm, or at least very frequent) was itself counterproductive. In negotiating prices, the city-state's goal was to substitute itself for individual buyers in order to present a common front to sellers, and thus to make prices go down. In economic terms, this situation is called a "monopsony." Economic analysis shows that in this case, although the buyer finds low prices, the quantities put on the market are invariably smaller than they would have been had a free market determined prices, which would be somewhat higher, of course, but would also allow more suppliers to make their goods available. In other words, the city-states' policies of monopsony were counterproductive: they limited the quantities put on the market and thus increased the range of the price variations that they were supposed to reduce.[66]

But one also notes that monopoly situations could be produced either as a result of a city-state's deliberate decision, or as a de facto monopoly, as in the case of grain after a period of unfavorable weather. When, as in Selymbria or Cyrene, the city-state gathered up all the available grain in order to sell it abroad, it was in a situation of monopoly, and was thus able to set its own price. In the case of Cyrene, philanthropy may have played a role in determining the (certainly unusually large) quantities to be sold and the prices set (but the famine seems to have been an exceptional situation). But it certainly played no role in the case of the Selymbrians or in that of Kleomenes of Naukratis and Egyptian grain in the early 320s. In a monopoly situation, selling prices rise. On the other hand, the quantities put on the market are smaller than they would be in a free market situation.[67]

The city-states' willingness to intervene and their desire to regulate trade to profit directly or indirectly from it were not without consequences. The meticulous rules of domestic trade, along with the monitoring of sellers and intermediaries who might be tempted to violate them, inevitably limited the development of production and trade. As for domestic trade, monopolies and monopsonies had the same effect on the level of overall supply.

Institutional Constraints and Nash Equilibrium

The question is how to interpret the impact of this limitation of supply on the functioning of the market: was it a factor that fundamentally paralyzed the market, or a marginal one producing effects that were spectacular but had no serious impact on the logic of the market? The relationship between supply and demand determines the organization of the market. In the ancient world, supply tended to be static, not in volume, but in nature. But when it came to domestic trade, the most serious problem was periodically the inability of supply to meet demand. In ancient Greece, supply and demand were embodied in the framework of the city-state, whether it was a matter of domestic commerce or external commerce. Individually, the concern was to maximize profits, and thus to export if prices abroad were higher than those at home, at least if one could do so without running the risk of social unrest. On the collective level, conquering external markets to make profits was at most a secondary goal. The primary goal was to see to it that supply was locally sufficient—in other terms, that the city-state's market was adequately supplied. In a context in which local supply might prove insufficient, it was therefore important to put on the foreign market only those quantities that exceeded the city-state's needs for its own people's consumption.

But the definition of this level of need was not determined solely by the foreseeable level of one year's consumption. To this amount had to be added the reserve for the following year, in the event that climatic variations (or other factors) made it necessary to draw on the accumulated reserves to meet the people's needs. Thus it was the amount that was considered necessary to ensure the city-state's security that determined the quantity of grain put on the foreign market. Concretely, the only city-states that exported were those that could rationally hope to have a sufficient harvest even in a poor year. On the other hand, in the framework of this policy city-states in which fluctuations in domestic supply were too great had an interest in temporarily allowing only small quantities to be put on the external market or even prohibiting all exports, whereas city-states that regularly had inadequate domestic supplies had to permanently prohibit exports.

This strategy was rational for every city-state taken individually. Of course, city-states could have had more confidence in their peers and been more optimistic about market conditions. But uncertainty related to climatic conditions and politics was too great and the stake too significant: it was a matter of life or death for the people, or at least for the poorest among them. Had the people received no help in securing food supplies, either the city would have imploded because of social conflict or famine would have radically reduced the population and completely changed the city's profile. Because of production conditions in which supply was always potentially unable to meet demand, in the world of the Greek city-states market conditions had all the characteristics of an imperfect market. Civic policies intended to reduce the risk of shortages, which were comprehensible for each city taken individually, nonetheless tended to have the opposite effect on the collective level. This was the paradox of the market in the world of the Greek city-states.

Thus risk aversion was maximal. The basic rule was noncooperation. But in matters of foreign trade, this noncooperation had the well-known defect of preventing larger quantities from being put on the market, which would have made it possible to avoid famines simply by a better distribution of surpluses. Thus the market was a negative non-zero-sum game—that is, one that was unfavorable for everyone.[68] But it was also characterized by a Nash equilibrium—that is, by a stable situation in which no player desires (any longer) to change his strategy. The whole set of strategies, known and predictable, defined a stable institutional environment.

If all the city-states had agreed to cooperate, that is, either to put on the market all their surpluses beyond what was needed for one year's consumption, or even to reject any limitation on exports, leaving the grain market completely open, the quantities of grain put on the general market would have been greater, and it would have been possible to avoid the famines that inevitably struck one city after another. The desire to constitute a grain reserve by prohibiting exports until it had been achieved also artificially isolated price levels on local markets. If the harvest produced surpluses two years out of three, grain prices fell, thus keeping prices at an artificially low level and discouraging farmers from increasing production. Some farmers might even stop growing cereals. If in the third year there was a poor harvest, the risk of shortages was increased by the fact that in the preceding years there had been insufficient investment in grain production. A system of cooperation and opening up the markets would have made it possible to achieve an optimal division of labor that would in turn have made it possible to lower prices and to avoid cultivating marginal lands that were barely profitable in city-states that had chronic shortages: these lands were in fact cultivated only because the average price levels were too high.

But the world of the Greek city-states was not a fairy-tale world in which everyone was willing to cooperate with everyone else by opening up their markets. It was a world of ferocious military, political, and economic competition in which each party seized all the advantages it could. To be sure, there were networks of traditional friendship or alliance (more or less stable), because in the jungle it is better not to hunt alone. But on the whole, there was a classic "lock-in" situation from which no city-state could escape in isolation. Moreover, the opening-up of markets in the early modern period was possible only in the context of an increase in agricultural productivity accompanied by a decrease in political instability and in transportation costs. The result was a rapid disappearance of famines. A comparison of the market of the Greek city-states with that of early modern Europe clearly shows the mutual interaction between the level of technology and productivity on the one hand, and institutions on the other hand. The ancients could dream of open markets, and we find here and there in the sources proof that some actually did think of setting up a system of free trade between cities, as we have seen with

Dio Chrysostom's recommendation to the Nikomedians.[69] But decreeing the "transition to open, liberal market" was not on the agenda. The profit levels that could be drawn from war or simply from pure economic rents made it economically irrational to establish a free-market system. In the short run, these systems of predation, which certainly created maximal insecurity, were much more advantageous than the supplementary profit that could have been made by opening up markets. That is why, even though the system of closed markets had all kinds of defects, it was the one that prevailed in the world of the Greek city-states.

To sum up, three factors directly limited the production of grain to be put on the market: the individual security strategy of the producers (who reserved as much as two year's worth of supplies for themselves), the collective security strategy of the city-states (prohibitions on exports), and the export prohibitions that discouraged major landowners from investing in grain production. Adding to this the effects of policies of monopoly or monopsony, it can be observed that individual behaviors and collective behaviors (civic legislation) clearly reduced the chances of achieving a balance of supply and demand. Over the long term, these factors tended to limit supply. Given prohibitions on exports, in the short term situations might arise in which a city with a surplus of grain practiced a strategy of forced storage, while other cities in the same geographic area suffered catastrophic shortages but could not find on the market the quantities of grain they needed at a satisfactory price. This does not reflect a lack of rationality on the part of the economic actors, but rather a form of rationality in which the logic of security provided individually (by producers on the domestic market, by city-states on the international market) prevailed over that of opening up and confidence in the market, whether domestic or foreign. A perfect market would have required everyone to be virtuous at the same time, both producers and city-states. Extreme political fragmentation, rivalries among city-states, and the frequency of wars made this transformation improbable. It was more advantageous to count on others being open while one retained one's own grain. In other words, those who refused to export found themselves in the role of free riders: they took advantage of the international market system by refusing to contribute to it, even when they could have.

To answer the initial question regarding the impact of supply limitations, it is certain that in the long term this was a factor that did not paralyze the market's functioning but nonetheless weighed on the development of production. However, it is clear that for a city-state, trying to abolish these limitations individually would have been suicidal. The "internal rationality" of the market system in ancient Greece prevented its performance in matters of "external rationality" from being optimized.[70]

Thus the similarities with the organization of markets in medieval and early modern Europe, along with the analysis of the constraints exercised by this kind of structure, show the limits of the performance of the market in the Greek city-states. But one should not forget that these limits are only the other side of the coin and that they did not prevent a remarkable growth (both extensive and intensive growth). The market of the city-states provided commerce with an area of exceptional legal security. At the same time, by making optimal use of a favorable environment, exploiting the possibilities offered by the sea and the winds, the Greek city-states also established a very efficient international market. In this way, they were incomparably better integrated into the networks of foreign markets than their medieval and early modern counterparts (with the exception of maritime cities such as Genoa, Venice, or the Hanseatic cities). The role of long-distance trade in providing the city-states with food supplies—the Aegean cities being connected with partners on the Mediterranean periphery ranging from Pontos to Egypt and from Cyrene to Sicily and Italy—was far greater than it was in German or French cities during the Middle Ages or the early modern period. Here lies one of the paradoxes of the structure of the market of the Greek city-states, where performance and limits on performance are inexorably linked.

The system of today's market-world is based on the sovereignty of territorial states, on the capitalist firm, on permanent innovation and, for the most part, on fossil fuels as sources for the energy to put the system in motion. Some states seek to acquire an economically dominant position by selling more technologically advanced products at a lower price. Others, which have sources of fossil fuels or deposits of raw materials and which can be described as rentier states, can take advantage of their natural resources in various ways and seek to play a dominant role without investing in their domestic economic development. The Greek city-states formed a world-system based on the city and using wind as an energy source. It also had its rentier states, such as those that had silver mines or were located on inevitable transit routes for international trade. Thus if the circumstances were favorable, the latter could hope to play the primary roles. This was the case for Athens, whose rise as an empire was based on its democratic system and its ownership of the mines of Laurion, both of which are necessary to account for its exceptional development in the Classical period. This means also that the awful condition of the slaves in the Laurion mines was a fundamental component of the success of this city.

Thus we are dealing with a market that was highly regulated by the civic authorities on the domestic level, but with forms of self-regulation on the international level. It is certainly not possible to say that the economy of the world of the Greek city-states was merely an "inconsistent aggregate of market elements," as suggested by the evolutionists, according to whom the self-regulating, pure, and perfect market—which does not, moreover, exist anywhere—is the real essence of the market economy. Without acknowledging the existence of this specific market configuration, there is no chance of understanding the underlying structures and trends of the development not only of the economy of the Greek city-states, but also of the whole of the ancient Mediterranean. It would be impossible to reach the inescapable conclusion that thanks to the very particular structure that characterized it, the logic of the market allowed the Greek city-states to attain an unprecedented level of prosperity, but also eventually ended up destroying them.[71]

All societies have to respond to the challenges posed by scarcity and uncertainty. Their impact is at the core of economic theory. Historical analysis has to highlight the institutional forms of the responses to these constraints of scarcity and uncertainty. It is only by combining these analytical principles that it is possible to make sense of the making of the ancient Greek economy.

APPENDIX:
WEIGHTS, MEASURES,
AND CURRENCY UNITS

Liquid Measures

Kotulē	0.27 liter
Chous (12 *kotulai*)	3.28 liters
Metrētēs (12 *choes*)	39.39 liters

Dry Measures

Kotulē	0.27 liter
Choinix (4 *kotulai*)	1.09 liters
Medimnos (48 *choinikes*)	52.53 liters
Weight of one *medimnos* of barley:	ca. 27 kilograms
Weight of one *medimnos* of wheat:	ca. 31 kilograms
(See Stroud 1998, 55.)	

Length Measures

Foot	0.296 meter
Plethron (100 feet)	29.6 meters
Stadion	177.6 meters

Area Measures

Plethron	ca. 0.09 hectare

Currency Units

Drachm, silver	4.33 grams
Obol, silver (6 per drachm)	0.72 gram

(The obol was divided in 8 bronze *chalkoi*.)

Mina (100 drachms)	433 grams
Talent (60 *minai* or 6,000 drachms)	25.980 kilograms

(The mina and the talent are units of account only.)

Weight Units

Drachm (= currency drachm × 1.05)	4.54 grams
Mina (100 drachms)	454 grams
Talent (60 *minai* or 6,000 drachms)	27.279 kilograms

PTOLEMAIC MEASURE UNITS

Dry Measures

Artaba (uncertain value)	39.4 liters

ROMAN MEASURE UNITS (SIMPLIFIED)

Liquid Measures

Amphora	ca. 26 liters

Dry Measures

Modius	ca. 8.75 liters

(There are 6 *modii* in an Attic *medimnos*.)

Weight Units

Uncia	27 grams
Libra	324 grams

(There are 8 *unciae* in a *libra*.)

Length Measures

Mile   1.48 kilometer

Area Measures

Iugerum   0.25 hectare

Currency Units (Silver)

Denarius   ca. 4 grams
  (= 4 *sestertii* = 1 Attic drachm.)

ABBREVIATIONS

AE	*L'Année Épigraphique. 1888–. Paris: E. Leroux, then Presses Universitaires de France.*
Ager, *Arbitrations*	S. L. Ager. 1996. *Interstate Arbitrations in the Greek World, 337–90 B.C.* Berkeley and London: University of California Press.
BL	*Berichtigungsliste der griechischen Papyrusurkunden aus Ägypten.* 1922–. Berlin and Leipzig: Vereinigung Wissenschaftlicher Verleger, then Leiden and Boston: Brill.
BMC Pisidia	G. F. Hill. 1897. *Catalogue of the Greek Coins of Lycia, Pamphylia, and Pisidia.* A Catalogue of the Greek Coins in the British Museum, vol. 19. London: The Trustees of the British Museum.
Brill's New Pauly	H. Cancik and H. Schneider. 2002. *Brill's New Pauly.* Leiden and Boston: Brill.
Bull. amph.	*Bulletin amphorologique* of the *Revue des Études Grecques.*
Bull. ép.	*Bulletin épigraphique* of the *Revue des Études Grecques.*
CH	*Coin Hoards.* 1975–. London: Royal Numismatic Society.
Choix	J. Pouilloux. 2003. *Choix d'inscriptions grecques.* 2nd ed. (1st ed. 1960). Paris: Les Belles Lettres.
Choix Délos	F. Dürrbach. 1921–1922. *Choix d'inscriptions de Délos.* Paris: E. Leroux.
Chr.	L. Mitteis und U. Wilcken. 1912. *Grundzüge und Chrestomathie der Papyruskunde.* Band 1: *Historischer Teil. Zweite Hälfte: Chrestomathie,* by U. Wilcken. Leipzig: Teubner.

CID	*Corpus des inscriptions de Delphes.* 1977–. Paris: De Boccard.
Code of Gortyn	R. F. Willetts. 1967. *The Law Code of Gortyn.* Berlin: de Gruyter.
C.Ptol.Sklav.	R. Scholl. 1990. *Corpus der ptolemäischen Sklaventexte.* 3 vols. Stuttgart: Steiner.
DA	C. Daremberg and E. Saglio. 1873–1919. *Dictionnaire des Antiquités.* 10 vols. Paris: Hachette.
Didyma II	T. Wiegand and A. Rehm. 1958. *Didyma* II: *Die Inschriften.* Berlin: Mann.
FD	*Fouilles de Delphes.* 1902–. Paris: De Boccard.
FGrHist	F. Jacoby. 1923–. *Die Fragmente der griechischen Historiker.* Berlin: Weidmann, then Leiden: Brill.
GHI	P. J. Rhodes and R. Osborne. 2003. *Greek Historical Inscriptions 404–323 BC.* Oxford: Oxford University Press.
Hellmann, *Inscriptions architecturales*	M.-C. Hellmann. 1999. *Choix d'inscriptions architecturales grecques.* Lyon: Maison de l'Orient Méditerranéen.
HTC	P. Debord, and E. Varinlioğlu, eds. 2001. *Les hautes terres de Carie.* Bordeaux: Ausonius.
I.Aeg. Thrace	L. D. Loukopoulou et al., eds. 2005. *Epigraphes tēs Thrakēs tou Aigaiou: metaxy tōn potamōn Nestou kai Hevrou (nomoi Xanthēs, Rhodopēs kai Hevrou).* Athens: Ethnikon Hidryma Ereunōn, Kentron Hellēnikēs kai Rhōmaïkēs Archaiotētos.
IC	M. Guarducci. 1935–1950. *Inscriptiones Creticae.* 4 vols. Rome: Libreria dello Stato.
ID	*Inscriptions de Délos.* 1926–1972. 7 vols. Paris: Champion.
I.Ephesos	H. Wankel et al. 1979–1984. *Die Inschriften von Ephesos.* 8 vols. Inschriften griechischer Städte aus Kleinasien 11–17. Bonn: Habelt.
I.Erythrai	H. Engelmann and R. Merkelbach. 1972–1973. *Die Inschriften von Erythrai und Klazomenai.* 2 vols. Inschriften griechischer Städte aus Kleinasien 1–2. Bonn: Habelt.

IG	*Inscriptiones Graecae.* 1873–. Berlin: De Gruyter.
IGCH	M. Thompson, O. Mørkholm, and C. M. Kraay. 1973. *An Inventory of Greek Coin Hoards.* New York: American Numismatic Society.
IGF	J.-C. Decourt. 2004. *Inscriptions grecques de la France.* Lyon: Maison de l'Orient et de la Méditerranée-Jean Pouilloux.
IGRR	R. Cagnat, ed. 1902–1927. *Inscriptiones Graecae ad res Romanas pertinentes.* 4 vols. Paris: E. Leroux.
I.Iasos	W. Blümel. 1985. *Die Inschriften von Iasos.* 2 vols. Inschriften griechischer Städte aus Kleinasien 28. Bonn: Habelt.
I.Ilion	P. Frisch. 1975. *Die Inschriften von Ilion.* Inschriften griechischer Städte aus Kleinasien 3. Bonn: Habelt.
IJG	R. Dareste, B. Haussoullier, and T. Reinach. 1891–1895. 2 vols. *Recueil des inscriptions juridiques grecques.* Paris: E. Leroux.
I.Kalchedon	R. Merkelbach, F. K. Dörner, and S. Şahin. 1980. *Die Inschriften von Kalchedon.* Inschriften griechischer Städte aus Kleinasien 20. Bonn: Habelt.
I.Keramos	E. Varinlioğlu. 1986. *Die Inschriften von Keramos.* Inschriften griechischer Städte aus Kleinasien 30. Bonn: Habelt.
I.Knidos	W. Blümel. 1992–. *Die Inschriften von Knidos.* Inschriften griechischer Städte aus Kleinasien 41. Bonn: Habelt.
I.Magnesia	O. Kern. 1900. *Die Inschriften von Magnesia am Maeander.* Berlin: Spemann.
I.Mylasa	W. Blümel. 1987–1988. *Die Inschriften von Mylasa.* 2 vols. Inschriften griechischer Städte aus Kleinasien 34–35. Bonn: Habelt.
IOSPE I²	V. Latyshev. 1916. *Inscriptiones antiquae Orae Septentrionalis Ponti Euxini Graecae et Latinae.* 2nd ed. 3 vols. St. Petersburg: Archaeological Society of the Russian Empire.
I.Peraia	W. Blümel. 1991. *Die Inschriften der rhodischen Peraia.* Inschriften griechischer Städte aus Kleinasien 38. Bonn: Habelt.

I.Pérée	A. Bresson. 1991. *Recueil des inscriptions de la Pérée rhodienne*. Besançon and Paris: Les Belles Lettres.
I.Priene²	W. Blümel and R. Merkelbach, in coll. with F. Rumscheid. 2014. *Die Inschriften von Priene*. 2 vols. Inschriften griechischer Städte aus Kleinasien 69. Bonn: Habelt.
ISE	L. Moretti and F. Canali De Rossi. 1967–2002. *Iscrizioni storiche ellenistiche*. 3 vols. Florence: La nuova Italia.
I.SultanDağı	L. Jonnes. 2002. *The Inscriptions of the Sultan Dağı*. Inschriften griechischer Städte aus Kleinasien 62. Bonn: Habelt.
I.Thespies	P. Roesch. 2007 (rev. 2009). *Les inscriptions de Thespies*. Electronic edition. Lyon: www.hisoma.mom.fr.
I.ThessEnipeus	J.-C. Decourt. 1995. *Inscriptions de Thessalie*. Vol. 1. *Les cités de la vallée de l'Énipeus*. Athens: École française d'Athènes.
LGPN	P. M. Fraser and E. Matthews. 1987–. *A Lexicon of Greek Personal Names*. Oxford: Clarendon Press, and New York: Oxford University Press.
LSAG	L. H. Jeffery. 1990. *Local Scripts of Archaic Greece*. 2nd rev. ed. by A. Johnston (1st ed. 1961). Oxford: Clarendon Press, and New York: Oxford University Press.
LSCG	F. Sokolowski. 1969. *Lois sacrées des cités grecques*. Paris: De Boccard.
Magnetto, *Arbitrati*	S. Magnetto. 1977. *Gli arbitrati interstatali greci*. Vol. 2. *Dal 337 al 196 a.C*. Pisa: Marlin.
Meiggs-Lewis	R. Meiggs and D. M. Lewis. 1989. *A Selection of Greek Historical Inscriptions to the End of the Fifth Century*. 2nd ed. Oxford: Clarendon Press.
Migeotte, *Emprunt public*	L. Migeotte. 1984. *L'emprunt public dans les cités grecques*. Québec: Sphinx, and Paris: Les Belles Lettres.
Milet I.3 (*Delphinion*)	G. Kawerau and A. Rehm. 1914. *Das Delphinion in Milet*. Milet Berlin: Reimer.
Milet VI	*Die Inschriften von Milet*. 1996 and 1998. Teil 1A. *Inschriften n. 187–406*, von A. Rehm, mit einem

Beitrag von H. Dessau; B. *Nachträge und Übersetzungen zu den Inschriften n. 1–406*, von P. Herrmann (= *Milet* VI.1). Teil 2. *Inschriften n. 407–1019* (= *Milet* VI.2), von P. Herrmann. Berlin and New York: Walter de Gruyter.

NChoixDélos   C. Prêtre, ed. 2002. *Nouveau choix d'inscriptions de Délos. Lois, comptes et inventaires.* Athens: École française d'Athènes.

Nomima   H. Van Effenterre and F. Ruzé. 1994–1995. *Nomima. Recueil d'inscriptions politiques et juridiques de l'archaïsme grec.* 2 vols. Rome: École française de Rome.

Nouveau Choix   Institut Fernand-Courby. 2005. *Nouveau choix d'inscriptions grecques.* 2nd ed. (1st ed. 1971). Paris: Les Belles Lettres.

NSER   G. Pugliese Carratelli. 1955–1956. "Nuovo supplemento epigrafico rodio." *Annuario della Scuola Archeologica di Atene* 33–34, n.s. 17–18: 157–81.

OGIS   W. Dittenberger. 1903–1905. *Orientis Graeci inscriptiones selectae.* 2 vols. Leipzig: Hirzel.

Oliver, *Greek Constitutions*   J. H. Oliver. 1989. *Greek Constitutions of Early Roman Emperors from Inscriptions to Papyri.* Philadelphia: American Philosophical Society.

OMS   L. Robert. 1969–1990. *Opera Minora Selecta.* 7 vols. Amsterdam: Hakkert.

P.Cairo.Zen.   C. C. Edgar et al. 1925–1951. *Catalogue général des antiquités égyptiennes du Musée du Caire: Zenon Papyri.* 5 vols. Cairo: Imprimerie de l'Institut français d'archéologie orientale.

P.Hib.   B. P. Grenfell, A. S. Hunt, and E. G. Turner. 1906–1955. *The Hibeh Papyri.* 2 vols. London: Egypt Exploration Fund.

P.Oxy.   B. P. Grenfell and A. S. Hunt et al. 1898–. *The Oxyrhynchus Papyri.* London: Egypt Exploration Fund.

Pleket, *Epigraphica*, I   H. W. Pleket. 1964. *Epigraphica.* Vol. 1. *Texts on the Economic History of the Greek World.* Leiden: Brill.

Realencyclopädie   A. F. Pauly and G. Wissowa, eds. 1894–. *Realencyclopädie der Classischen Altertumswissenschaft.* Stuttgart: Metzler.

RC	C. B. Welles. 1934. *Royal Correspondence in the Hellenistic Period.* New Haven, CT: Yale University Press.
Sardis	W. H. Buckler and M. Robinson. 1932. *Greek and Latin Inscriptions.* Publications of the American Society for the Excavation of Sardis VII.1. Leiden: Brill.
SEG	*Supplementum epigraphicum Graecum.* 1923–. Leiden: Sijthoff, then Amsterdam: Gieben, then Leiden: Brill.
SGDI	H. Collitz and F. Bechtel et al. 1884–1915. *Sammlung der griechischen Dialekt-Inschriften.* 4 vols. Göttingen: Vandenhoeck & Ruprecht.
SNG BN Paris	*Sylloge Nummorum Graecorum, France, Bibliothèque Nationale.* 1983–. Paris: Bibliothèque nationale de France.
SNG Cop.	*Sylloge Nummorum Graecorum. The Royal Collection of Coins and Medals, Danish National Museum.* 1942–. Copenhagen: Munksgaard.
SNG von Aulock	*Sylloge Nummorum Graecorum Deutschland: Sammlung von Aulock.* 1957–1968. Berlin: Mann.
Staatsverträge, III	H. H. Schmitt. 1969. *Die Staatsverträge des Altertums.* Vol. 3. *Die Verträge der griechisch-römischen Welt von 338 bis 200 v. Chr.* Munich: Beck.
Syll.[3]	W. Dittenberger. 1915–1924. *Sylloge inscriptionum Graecarum.* 3rd. ed. Leipzig: Hirzel.
TCam	M. Segre and G. Pugliese Carratelli. 1949–1950. "Tituli Camirenses." *Annuario della Scuola Archeologica di Atene* 27–29, n.s. 11–13: 139–318.
Tod	Tod, M. N. 1948. *A Selection of Greek Historical Inscriptions.* Vol. 2. Oxford: Clarendon Press.

NOTES

INTRODUCTION

INTRODUCTION

1. Ober 2010, with Ober 2014.
2. Hoffman 1996.
3. In English: Calhoun 1926; Heichelheim 1938 (translated from the edition in German of the same year); Mitchell 1940; Rostovtzeff 1941 for the Hellenistic world. In French: Glotz 1920; Toutain 1927 (with its translation into English of 1930); Cavaignac 1951.
4. For the geography of Greece, see the general map at the beginning of this volume. For more regional details as well as for a general mapping of the ancient world, see the *Barrington Atlas of the Greek and Roman World* (Talbert et al. 2000).

CHAPTER I: THE ECONOMY OF ANCIENT GREECE

1. Finley 1973, 17–34, with the same views in the "Further Thoughts" of the second (1985) edition, 177–83.
2. The most important texts in the controversy between "primitivists" and "modernists" were republished by Finley 1979.
3. Bücher 1901 [1893]. The second chapter of the work (bearing the same title as that of the book), which concerns historical developments and presents the famous stage development theory, is republished in Finley 1979 (first unpaged part) from the sixth (1906) German edition.
4. Meyer 1895.
5. On the debate between Bücher and Meyer, overdetermined by the ulterior motives of the two protagonists and their contrasting conceptions of the intellectual, social, and economic development of the German Reich, see Schneider 1990 and Wagner-Hasel 2011, 184–221.
6. Bücher 1901 [1893], 89–128 and 142–49. It is striking that Bücher was himself at pains to differentiate his "stage of independent domestic economy" based on "production solely for domestic use" from his "stage of town economy" based on "custom production." As he himself acknowledges apropos "town economy" (ibid., 114), "even in ancient times beginnings of such a development are perceptible."
7. See "Die wirtschaftliche Entwicklung des Altertums" (1895), also in Meyer 1924, 81–168 (republished in Finley 1979, part 2), esp. 88–101.

8. On the German Historical School, Abelshauser 2000 and the essays in Shionoya 2005; on Schmoller, Priddat 1989 and 2004 and Peukert 2001; on Bücher, the essays in Backhaus 2000 and Wagner-Hasel 2004 and 2011. "Nationalökonomie" is often translated into English as "economics," which is clearly mistaken.

9. Schmoller 1881, 35: "Angebot und Nachfrage sind summarische Ausdrücke für Größenverhältnisse, in denen sich Gruppen menschlicher Willen gegenüber treten; die Ursachen, welche diese Größenverhältnisse bedingen, sind theilweise natürliche, überwiegend aber sind es menschliche Beziehungen und Machtverhältnisse, menschliche Überlegungen und Handlungen" (partly quoted by Priddat 1989, 55–56).

10. Schmoller 1920, vol. 1, 5: "Die Volkswirtschaft ist so ein Teilinhalt des gesellschaftlichen Lebens; auf natürlich-technischem Boden erwachsen, ist ihr eigentliches Prinzip die gesellschaftliche Gestaltung der wirtschaftlichen Vorgänge" (partly quoted by Priddat 1989, 56).

11. On Smith and Ricardo, see later, chapters 9, 259, and 13, 343–45.

12. In his various books Hayek is famous above all for insisting on the threat posed to freedom by social and political utopias (see among others his final work Hayek 1973–1979).

13. Here we will adopt the definitions proposed by Samuelson and Nordhaus 2005, 85: "The expression 'marginal' is a key term in economics and always means 'additional' or 'extra.' Marginal utility denotes the additional utility you get from the consumption of an additional unit of a commodity. . . . The diminishing marginal utility results from the fact that your enjoyment of the good drops off as more and more of it is consumed. The law of marginal utility states that, as the amount of a good consumed increases, the marginal utility of a good tends to diminish." To use a food metaphor, as one eats a meal, one's appetite diminishes. Even if there are still many dishes on the table at the end of the meal, their marginal value is zero because appetite is satisfied. Although it is indispensable for life, water long had little commercial value, because supply was superabundant in relation to demand.

14. McKenzie 1987 and Patinkin 1987.

15. On Max Weber's work, see Swedberg 1998, 2004, and 2005. On Max Weber and antiquity, Capogrossi Colognesi 2000.

16. Weber 1968 [1921–1922], vol. 1, 26.

17. Ibid., 25.

18. On economic rationality in Weber and its definition, Swedberg 1998, 33–39.

19. For recent works on Max Weber's thesis, see the references in Conrad 2010, 165, n. 9.

20. Weber 1958 [1920], 155–83.

21. Weber 1958 [1920], 188–89: the most successful component of the population in Baden (his regional example) is the Jewish one, which, against Weber, would seem to vindicate Werner Sombart on the role of the Jews in the development of capitalism (1902, 1911, and 1913; Sombart was Weber's main opponent in the debate on the origins of capitalism). See however Lehmann 1993b, who (rightly) argues for the clear superiority of Weber's analysis to that of Sombart.

22. Weber 1976 [1909].

23. On the alleged sloppy management practices of ancient landlords, see Weber 1976 [1909], 171 and 212–13 for Greece, and 328–29 for Rome.

24. On Weber's analysis of accounting in general, and especially on "capital accounting," see Swedberg 1998, 1518; on Weber's analysis of ancient accounting systems, Bresson and Bresson 2004.

25. Weber 1976 [1909], 208 and 392–93.

26. Ibid., 339–42.

27. Hasebroek 1933 [1928]; see Bresson 2003b.

28. Polanyi 1944, 1957 (with Arensberg and Pearson), 1968 and 1979. On Polanyi's work, see Humphreys 1969, the essay collection edited by Cressier and Rouillard 2005, with the author's contribution, Bresson 2005c.

29. Veblen 1899. For a summary of Veblen's economic thought, McCormick 2006.

30. Commons's article of 1931 is the first effort to define "institutional economics." The book of 1934 (Commons 1934) bearing the same title is a huge synthesis on the history of economics and principles of economic activity. For a kind of rehabilitation of Commons, see Hodgson 2003.

31. Polanyi 1944.

32. See the radical critique of Polanyi's concepts by Cook 1966 and 1968.

33. Robineau 1994, 26–27, on the rhetorical and polemical character of Polanyi's distinction between "substantive" economy, which is supposed to concern reality, and "formal" economy, which is thus by definition incapable of getting to the bottom of things.

34. Finley 1973 (with the new edition of 1985) has eight entries under "Weber" in the index, and each reference receives highly positive comments. On Finley's work and the heritage of Weber and Polanyi, see Nafissi 2005 (with Tompkins' 2008 review), who devotes an extensive study to it (on Weber, 57–123; on Polanyi, 127–88; on Finley, 191–288) and shows the centrality of Weber's influence on Finley's thinking about the basis of the ancient economy. On Finley, see also Bresson 2003c.

35. Polanyi 1957, and 1977, 238–51, on the supposed emergence of the market in Athens in the 320s.

36. See the critique of Finley 1970.

37. On this passage, see in detail chapter 15, 432.

38. Rostovtzeff 1941; see Saller 2005, 223–27, for the modern views on Rostovtzeff.

39. Davies 2001; Reger 2003, with Manning and Morris 2005.

40. See Bresson 2007a.

41. The watermill was an invention of antiquity, and already by the end of the Hellenistic period it had enjoyed great success (see later, chapters 3, 71, and 7, 197–98).

42. Weber 1968 [1921–1922].

43. Weber 2001 [1904–1905], author's introduction, xlii: "When we find again and again that, even in departments of life apparently mutually independent, certain types of rationalization have developed in the Occident, and only there, it would be natural to suspect that the most important reason lay in differences of heredity. The author admits that he is inclined to think the importance of biological heredity very great. But in spite of the notable achievements of anthropological research, I see up to the present no way of exactly or even approximately measuring either the extent or, above all, the form of its influence on the development investigated here. . . . Only then, and when comparative racial neurology and psychology shall have progressed beyond their present and in many ways very promising beginnings, can we hope for even the probability of a satisfactory answer to that problem. In the meantime that condition seems to me not to exist, and an appeal to heredity would therefore involve a premature renunciation of the possibility of knowledge attainable now, and would shift the problem to factors (at present) still unknown." On Weber's prudent handling of the concept of race

(as a last-resort explanation), see Swedberg 1998, 150–51 and 274–75, n. 18–22, and Käsler 1988, 69–70, in the same perspective for the question of "hereditary qualities." It is more problematic to observe that today some interpret the Industrial Revolution as a consequence of a process of genetic selection.

44. Sahlins 1976, 207.
45. Ibid.
46. Bourdieu 2000, 255.
47. See Coase 1987 and Williamson 1985 and 2000. On North's work, see hereafter. The essay collections edited by Ménard and Shirley 2005 and by Brousseau and Glachant 2008 provide a broad survey of the NIE paradigm.
48. Williamson 1998 and 2005.
49. On the concept of institutions, see the clear presentation in Greif 2006, 29–53, where a brief overview of the considerable literature devoted to this question will also be found.
50. On contracting in the NIE paradigm, see chapter 9, 250–54.
51. North 1991.
52. North and Thomas 1973, with the comparison of the cases of France and Spain (120–31) and England (146–56).
53. North 1981, 158–86, as well as North 1990 and 2005.
54. For the literature on collapse, see famously Tainter 1988 and Diamond 2005.
55. For an application of game theory to the genesis of institutions in the medieval world, see Greif 2006. For the interaction between economic and political constraints, and the role of pooling and sharing information in the development of democratic institutions that were key to the success of Athens in the Classical period, see Ober 2008 and Lyttkens 2013 (with final synthesis 135–42).
56. On this aspect of Polanyi's work, see Bresson 2005c.
57. See Bresson 2005c. This quadripartite model is inevitably close to that of Michael Mann, who famously considers that (Western) power structures are based on four "overlapping and intersecting socio-spatial networks of power" (Mann 1986, 1). The four networks are ideological, economic, military, and political (ibid., 22–32)—this is the so-called IEMP model. Our focus is here not on the "structures of power" but on institutions in general. Even if institutions are inevitably also structures of power, their role in the "production of society" goes far beyond their political aspect.
58. J. K. Davies (2001 and 2005) emphasizes the construction of integral models of flows in the ancient economy. The present work sees things, as it were, in terms of the way in which flows could come into being.

CHAPTER II: PEOPLE IN THEIR ENVIRONMENT

1. Popper 1976, 199.
2. Grove and Rackham 2001, 26. See also Rackham 1990 for a short introduction to the ancient Greek landscape and environment.
3. Horden and Purcell 2000, 172–73.
4. Broodbank 2013, 63–71.
5. Higgins and Higgins 1996 on the geology of Greece in general, especially 16–25, with the regional studies in the rest of the book; Broodbank 2013, 63–65.

6. For a geological approach, Higgins and Higgins 1996, 210–14. On earthquakes and their consequences in the Classical world, see the essay collection edited by Guidoboni 1989, especially the pages devoted to Greece by Helly 1989.
7. Plutarch *Cimon* 16.4–5, with Thucydides 1.128.1; see Higgins and Higgins 1996, 52–54, for the geological explanation (a fault line at the base of Mount Taygetos, near Sparta) and Hodkinson 2000, 417–20, on the political consequences.
8. Lafond 1998 (analysis of the ancient tradition); Katsonopoulou 2002 (localization of the site according to surveys).
9. Polybius 5.88–90. See Cataudella 1998.
10. See Adam 1989, who shows the effects of earthquakes on structures constructed in the traditional Mediterranean way, and also the influence of the terrain on the transmission of vibrations (easier, and thus more destructive, in schistose terrains), as well as Stiros and Dakoronia 1989 and Soren and Leonard 1989 (direct reconstitution of the effects of an earthquake on the settlement at Kourion in Cyprus).
11. Grove and Rackham 2001, 245–46.
12. Higgins and Higgins 1996, 74–78.
13. On the question of marshes in general, as well as the project of draining Lake Ptechai, see chapter 6.
14. Grove and Rackham 2001, 224–36.
15. Source for Greece: Isager and Skydsgaard 1993, 13, and maps in Kayser and Thompson 1964, 1/03 (average annual precipitation) and 1/04 (temperatures); for Turkey: *Yeni Türkiye Atlası* 1977, (unnumbered) page "Yıllık ortalama yağış dağılışı haritası" (average annual rainfall distribution map).
16. On the system of winds and its importance, see chapter 3.
17. Grove and Rackham 2001, 288, on the role of the floods in Plato's schema.
18. Grove and Rackham 2001, 241–311, who provide a series of regional examples of both the destructive and the constructive role of erosion in the Greek landscape.
19. On this point, see chapter 3, 72–75. See Harris 2011b, who is justified in his correction of the overoptimistic view of Grove and Rackham that the impact of human societies on the landscape remains very limited.
20. Le Roy Ladurie 1971 and 2004–2006.
21. Grove and Rackham 2001, 141–42.
22. See the data in Hin 2013, 63–97, and Manning 2013 (mainly for the Roman period, but with most useful methodological analyses for the analysis of the ancient climate), as well as in Bresson 2014b for the long-term evolution starting from the late Classical period.
23. Ortolani and Pagliuca 2003.
24. Fouache 1999, 126–30.
25. See Bresson 2014b and the parallel presentation of ancient authors and of modern climatic data.
26. Here we need not take into account the possible reasons for these climatic changes, on which there is no unanimous agreement (cycles of solar activity, according to Ortolani and Pagliuca 2003).
27. Beloch 1886; Gomme 1933.
28. Hansen 1986 and 2006; Scheidel 2001.
29. Bibliography in Corvisier and Suder 1996; methodological clarification in Corvisier 2001, with Brun (P.) 1999 for a presentation of the method; Scheidel 2007, who

presents, however, a model of necessarily slow growth that differs significantly from the one defended here.

30. On the notion of a model in the demography of antiquity, see Bresson 1985.

31. See in this perspective, Scheidel 2003.

32. Hassan 1981, 125–42.

33. Benedict 1972.

34. Amundsen and Diers 1969.

35. *Code of Gortyn* XII, ll. 17–19.

36. Ephorus *FGrHist* 70 F149, quoted by Strabo 10.4.20.

37. See the ritual regulation of ca. 350 BCE regarding the deceased, Pouilloux 1954, 371, no. 141, and *Nouveau choix* 19, ll. 21–22.

38. The detailed references to Marseilles in the passage suggest that the anecdote may have reflected a real situation that went back to a time preceding the Imperial period.

39. Regarding the age of marriage in Greece, see Golden 1981 and Vérilhac and Vial 1998, 215–18.

40. On divorces, widowhoods, and remarriages, Thompson 1972.

41. Pomeroy 1975, 66–67.

42. This is the basic idea found in Engels 1980, Hopkins 1966, and Ingalls 2002.

43. Braudel and Labrousse 1970, table p. 71 (see in general 9–84 on French demography at the end of the seventeenth century and the end of the eighteenth century). On the case of Saint-Trivier-en-Dombes (a town near Lyons), see Bideau et al. 1978.

44. On Crulai, see Gauthier and Henry 1958, 162 ff.

45. On the variation of demographic behaviors from one region to another, see Goubert 1965 and Chaunu 1966, 205.

46. See Martin 1974 and Höpfner and Schwandner 1994.

47. Vitruvius *On Architecture* 1.4.1. See Martin 1974, 27, for the quotation.

48. See for example Hippocrates, *Airs, Waters, Places* 5–6. In this treatise Hippocrates proposes, among other things, a typology of peoples in relation to climate.

49. On Priene, Wiegand and Schrader 1904; Martin 1974, 112–13; Crouch 1993, 158–65 (the water system of the town being compared with that of Selinous).

50. Heracleides Criticus fr. 1.1 Arenz. (Arenz 2006 reproduces the text and provides an exhaustive commentary; see also Perrin 1994, who however would prefer a dating in the second half of the third century.)

51. On Argos, Plutarch *Pyrrhus* 32–33, and on Argos and Athens, the commentary in Martin 1974, 76.

52. See chapter 7, 190.

53. Martin 1974, 46.

54. Aristotle *Constitution of Athens* 54.1. On the municipal road service in Athens in the fifth and fourth centuries, with its prescribed deposits of trash and its team of trashmen who were to carry this trash out of the city, see Vatin 1976, 555–58.

55. On Paros, see the law on garbage *IG* XII.5 107 and *IG* XII.Suppl. p. 105 (*LSAG*, 305, no. 37): it was forbidden to throw trash into the streets. On Thasos, Vatin 1976, 559–64: in this city, an individual was supposed to clean up in exchange for the use of a garden.

56. Regulation regarding the *astunomoi* of Pergamon: *OGIS* 483; Klaffenbach 1954; Martin 1974, 57 ff.; on the roads in Pergamon, see Vatin 1976, 558–59

(the responsibility for cleaning fell not to the city's magistrates but to property owners organized into associations).

57. On sewers in Greek cities in general, see Martin 1974, 209–11; Crouch 1993, especially on the integrated water systems at Olynthos (171–76), Akragas (205–13), and Morgantina (213–18).

58. See Diodorus 19.45.1–8 on sewers in Rhodes, , where they failed to perform their intended role of evacuating water when a catastrophic rainstorm occurred in 316 BCE, because their outlets had been closed.

59. Tölle-Kastenbein 1990.

60. Aristotle *Politics* 7.10.3.

61. Pausanias 7.27.4; see Martin 1974, 22 and 65.

62. See Martin 1974, 213.

63. Corinth and its fountain Peirene: Herodotus 5.92.b3; Pausanias 2.3.2–3; other literary sources are cited by Robinson 2011, 28–32, with a full history and archaeological description of the monument. Megara: Pausanias 1.40.1, with Muller 1981, 203–18, who emphasizes the importance of the works that Pausanias attributes to Theagenes, and dates them to the beginning of the sixth century; an upgrading and a renovation took place in the early fifth century. Athens: Herodotus 6.137.3; Thucydides 2.15.5; Pausanias 1.14.1, with Camp 1986, 42–43 (on the location of the famous "Nine-Spouts" fountain [*Enneakrounos*] in the agora), and Tölle-Kastenbein 1994. Samos and the famous tunnel built by Eupalinos of Megara: Herodotus 3.60.1–3, with Kienast 1995, Jantzen 2004, and Grewe 2008, 324–25 (discussion of the building strategy).

64. See Inglieri 1936, *Carta archeologica di Rodi e dintorni, foglio città*, and briefly Crouch 1993, 90–91.

65. Debord and Varinlioğlu 2010, 124, with 121, fig. 204.

66. Martin 1974, 63–65.

67. Vitruvius *On Architecture* 2.1.5.

68. On Olynthos, Martin 1974, 227–31, and Cahill 2002, 74–193.

69. Aylward 2005.

70. Tsakirgis 2005 and Ault 2005.

71. Trümper 1998 (for the types of houses) and 2005, and Karvonis and Malmary 2009 for examples of multifunctional spaces.

72. Habicht 1972, 210–25, no. 9; *IG* XII.6.1 169.

73. Ginouvès 1962, 176–77; it is remarkable that the bathrooms in Olynthos were provided for in the initial construction plan.

74. Ginouvès 1962, 181. Regarding new cities other than Olynthos (for example, Priene), we can nonetheless wonder whether the fact that we have not found more installations of private bathrooms like the one published by Wiegand and Schrader 1904, 292, is not connected with the site's state of preservation, which is necessarily poorer than that of Olynthos, which was destroyed and then abandoned (or saw limited reoccupation).

75. Crouch 1993, 246–51.

76. See Ginouvès 1962 on this question.

77. Hippocrates *On Airs, Waters, and Places* 10: if a hot summer follows a rainy spring, women and children will succumb to fevers and dysentery.

78. On infant mortality during the summer as a result of the development of enterocolitis in early modern Europe, see Chaunu 1966, 205–8 and 210.

79. See Joly 1978, 535: "Though the physicians of Knidos distinguished several varieties of a disease, they did so not in the name of scientific observation, but in order to fulfill the etiological role of a plurality of humors"; as for bile, which plays a major role in medical theory, it "has only a very mythical reality and a myth is not observed." The same objection could be made to the theory of the medical school of Kos, which did not really differ from that of the school of Knidos (see in general Thivel 1981, particularly on the theory of humors and its inability to satisfy the requirement of measure, which was nonetheless felt, ibid., 382–83). See also Jouanna 1992 on Hippocrates, particularly 202–53, who shows the limits of medical knowledge at the time.

80. Woodhead 1977 and Samama 2003.

81. Samama 2003, 29–58.

82. Bourgey 1975.

83. See the corpus assembled in Samama 2003.

84. On the absence of cholera and (possibly) of smallpox, Scheidel 2001, 216–17, and 2012; on the absence of syphilis, Grmek 1989, 133–51. For malaria, Grmek 1989, 284–305 (case study of Philiskos); Sallares 1991, 271–81; Scheidel 2001, 75–91; Sallares 2002, 16–22 (for malaria in Greece and in the Hippocratic corpus). For tuberculosis, Grmek 1989, 177–97, and Scheidel 2012; for leprosy, Grmek 1989, 152–76. The broad spectrum of diseases observed in Ptolemaic and Roman Egypt (for which see Lang 2013, 10–18) was in general already present in Classical Greece.

85. See Thucydides 2.47–54 (the allusion to the fetid breath of the infected people is a good indication of typhus). On this "plague," see Gomme et al. 1945–1981, vol. 2, 145–62 and 388–89.

86. [Hippocrates] *Epidemics* 6.7. See also [Hippocrates] *Dentition* 24 and 31. See Grmek 1989, 337–38, and Lang 2013, 12.

87. On malnutrition and its consequences, Garnsey 1999, 43–61.

88. The interdictions in the inscription in Piraeus *IG* II² 380, ll. 37 ff. (320/19; translation Oliver 2012, 91, but for the end of the text see Vatin and Owens later), allow us to guess the state of filthiness to which the agora in Piraeus had been reduced by the negligence of those who went there (if the restoration of the text is correct) to defecate despite the interdictions; see in general Martin 1951, 367–68, and Garland 2001, 77, 233 III no. 52, 195–96, with detailed comment by Vatin 1976 and by Owens 1983 (arguing that the prohibitions were motivated by a religious agenda rather than by a general concern for public hygiene).

89. Chaunu 1966, 203.

90. Ibid., 198.

91. Wrigley and Schofield 1981, 254.

92. Ibid., 257–65.

93. Ibid., 230–36.

94. See Henry 1972, 122; Clark 2007, 72–73.

95. Plato *Laws* 784be (cf. 740d); see Vilquin 1982, 15–16 (Mulhern 1975 cannot be followed on the supposed absence of real demographic concern in Plato).

96. See Moreau 1949.

97. Chaunu 1966, 198.

98. Engels 1980, 119–20.

99. On abortion and contraception, see Fontanille 1977; Eyben 1982–1983, which also deals with infanticide; Prioreschi 1998, 643–61. Specifically on abortion, see the frag-

ments of Lysias' *Against Antigenes*, in *Lysias* ed. C.U.F., vol. 2, Paris, 1926, fr. X.1–2 p. 261, with comm. pp. 238–40; this is probably an indictment for abortion by a relative of the husband of a widow defended by her son, see Harrison 1968–1971, vol. 1, 72, and Todd 2003; an accusation of the same sort in a partially similar situation is described by Cicero *Pro Cluentio* 11.32. In a passage in Plato's *Theaetetus* (149cd), Socrates indicates that midwives commonly performed abortions; shortly before, he had pointed out that he was himself the son of a midwife (149a), thus guaranteeing the value of his statement.

100. Pomeroy 1997, 120–21 and 226–29.

101. Sallares 1991, 151–57, notes in passing the question of the increase in potential fertility connected with early marriage, but does not include it in his model. He also does not discuss the mortality rate, which was certainly lower than in late medieval and early modern Europe. These are, however, fundamental questions that must be answered. In the same way, the testimony of authors of the Classical period regarding the threat of overpopulation is not taken into account by Sallares.

102. Germain 1975 granted that infanticide might have been widely practiced in Greece, but not in Athens.

103. On this text, see later, 61–62.

104. Pomeroy 1983 and Brulé 1990 for the Cretans in Miletos; Clarysse and Thompson 2006, 307–14 for the situation in the Fayum.

105. Scheidel 2010 rightly underscores the common concealment of females in ancient funerary or votive documents and suggests that the tax documents relating to the Cretans in Miletos or to the Fayum villages might also conceal the presence of females. Indeed, massive concealment of women in tax documents is not without parallel, as in England in 1381 (see Oman 1906, 26–28). But this was quite an exceptional situation, of which there is no hint in third-century BCE Egypt. In the end Scheidel admits that our documentation might "reflect femicidal practices," although according to him it does not constitute conclusive proof.

106. Theopompus *FGrHist* 115 F204 (= Athenaeus 12 517e); Aristotle *Zoika* fr. 283 Rose.

107. Diodorus 1.80.3; Strabo 17.2.5.

108. Golden 1990, 89–92, and 2003; Beaumont 2012, 104–52 for iconographic sources concerning the life of children in Athens, and 186–205 for the funerary monuments and the parents' sorrow, on which see also Oakley 2003; Vérilhac 1978–1982 for funerary poems in memory of youngsters.

109. Bodin 1955 [1576], 159 (excerpt from book 5, chap. 2).

110. Malthus 1998 [1798].

111. Beloch 1886, Attika: 99; Lakonia and Messenia: 112: 149–50; Macedon and Chalkidike: 212.

112. Beloch 1886, 494.

113. Hansen 2006b, 32. The book is stimulating, even if the estimates provided seem too high.

114. Price 2011.

115. Egypt: Scheidel 2001.

116. Manning 2003, 47–49.

117. The East and the Seleukid kingdom: Aperghis 2004, 56–58, who emphasizes that he favors low estimates and refers to the figures of previous estimates, which are generally higher.

118. Augustus *Res Gestae* 8.2.
119. "Low count:" Beloch 1886, 370–78 and 507; Brunt 1987, 54–112. "High count:" Lo Cascio 1994 and Lo Cascio and Malanima 2005. See full presentation of the debate in Hin 2013, 20–22 and 275–78.
120. Hin 2013, 292–96.
121. Beloch 1886; Corvisier and Suder 2000, 34, table by region, and 36, a map of densities.
122. A complete regional and chronological survey up to 1993 is to be found in Alcock 1993a, 35. Messenia: McDonald and Rapp 1972; Lakonia: Cavanagh et al. 1996; Melos: Renfrew and Wagstaff 1982; Keos: Cherry 1991; Boiotia: Bintliff and Snodgrass 1985 and 1988; southern Argolis: Jameson et al. 1994; Methana: Mee and Forbes 1997; Phaistos and the Mesara: Watrous et al. 2004 and Alcock and Cherry 2004. See also Shipley and Salmon 1996 and van Andel and Runnels 1987.
123. Kolb 1993–2000; Kolb and Thomsen 2004.
124. Saprykin 2001 and 2006. The literature on the territories of the cities of the Black Sea is immense. The synthesis by Grammenos and Petropoulos 2003 allows a detailed regional approach. See also the contributions collected in Bresson and Ivantchik 2007 on northern Pontos, and now the synthesis in Müller 2010.
125. Alcock 1993a. See also Alcock et al. 1994, Alcock 2002.
126. Étienne et al. 2000, 105–8 and 319–26; Brunet 2001 (who emphasizes in particular the limits of the method); Shipley 2002; Corvisier 2004; Rousset 2004 (who presents a strongly critical survey of Alcock's thesis on the "Romanization" of the countryside starting in the second century and of the survey method in general); Müller 2007 (regional surveys not being incompatible with the concept of the city and the civic territory).
127. See Morris 1987, 99–101, and the presentation of the problem in Whitley 2001, 185–87 and 234–38 (although Whitley's discussion [p. 236] of the data relating to the population of Attika in the sixth and fifth centuries is not to be followed).
128. Data excerpted from the more exhaustive array in Corvisier 2004, 27, corrected for the southern Argolid by the data of Jameson et al. 1994, 229. Despite the remaining uncertainties with regard to the identification of sites and their chronology, the results remain quite revealing.
129. See Lohmann 1993 and 1994. See chapter 6, 145, and chapter 8, 202–3.
130. See Alcock 1993a, 33–48, with histograms and maps.
131. Ibid., 53–55, and 89–91.
132. That is the significance of Rousset's criticism (2004, 370–72).
133. Morris 2004 and 2005. For house architecture (and its sophistication) in the Classical period, see Nevett 1999, 53–79, with the case of Olynthos. Even if Olynthos (destroyed in 348 BCE) was certainly one of the most advanced and richest towns of its time, it was not "exceptional" in the sense that there were no others like it in the world of the time.
134. On these questions, see later, chapter 14.
135. Cohen 2002.
136. The population figure for Athens is hotly debated, and depends on the interpretation of two contradictory sources. It will suffice to refer to Ruschenbusch 1981a and 1981b and 1999, who claims that the population was no more than 21,000 citizens, and Hansen 2006a, 19–60, who thinks it was at least 30,000. The higher figure is accepted here (see chapter 14 for the issue of feeding the population).

137. Gallo 1980.
138. See Habicht 2006, 101–5 and 161–67.
139. Bresson 2000, 283.
140. Tr. W. R. Paton.
141. Strabo 7.7.3: decline of the population of western Greece, explicitly related to the destruction wrought by Roman armies; 8.4.11: depopulation of Messenia and Lakonia; 8.8.1: the desertification of Megalopolis in the Peloponnese.
142. Plutarch *On the Cessation of Oracles* 413f–414a.
143. Even Alcock (1993a, 24–29) seems to be reluctant to admit this reality, which is, however, fundamental for Hellenistic and Roman Greece.
144. Figures provided for Athens by Athenaeus (6 272cd) have puzzled researchers. Athenaeus quotes Ctesicles (*FGrHist* 245 F1), who referred to a census carried out at Athens by Demetrios of Phaleron perhaps between 311 and 307. At that date, Athens is supposed to have had 21,000 citizens, 10,000 metics, and 400,000 *oiketai*. The usual meaning of *oiketēs* is "slave." Given that the passage as a whole discusses slaves and especially their number, it is beyond doubt that Athenaeus thought that Athens counted 400,000 slaves at that time. However, Andreau and Descat (2011, 44–46) want to see in the *oiketai* a reference to "people in the households," which is claimed to be the original meaning of the word in Ctesicles's text. Thus they conclude that the whole population of Attika at that time was 431,000 inhabitants. Accepting with Hansen (2006a, 56) the higher figure of 140,000 free persons in Athens, we would have a total of 291,000 slaves, or 66 percent of the total. The slave population would thus have represented two-thirds of the city's population, and free persons, both citizens and noncitizens, only one-third. But this figure of 431,000 inhabitants for Athens at the end of the fourth century, even after considerable demographic losses, goes beyond all the ceilings proposed so far for the maximal population of the city (200,000–250,000 in the fourth century and 300,000 or more in the Periclean period for Hansen 1988, 12, see 2006, ibid.; 250,000–300,000 for Whitby 1998, 109–14). This figure should also be weighed against what we know about the city's production and importation of grain. The population density of Attika is said to have been around 200 inhabitants per square kilometer and to constitute an absolute record before the contemporary period. What is more, even if we do not have the original text of Ctesicles, the sequence "citizens, metics, *oiketai*" can only make sense if the final term of the series means "slaves." While in the whole passage Athenaeus switches constantly between *douloi* and *oiketai* to refer to the slaves, in the same lines he mentions 460,000 slaves (*douloi*) for Corinth and 470,000 more for Aigina, figures that are just as improbable (see explicitly on this point Hansen 2006a, 6–7 and 20). The conclusion is clear. The figures put forward by Athenaeus or his sources are only metaphorical. Strabo (14.5.2) also counts slaves by "myriads"—that is, by tens of thousands—and claims that 10,000 a day were sold on Delos: this figure is just as unrealistic. When people spoke of "myriads" they meant "many." With regard to the series of numbers of slaves for Corinth, Aigina, or Athens, Athenaeus's precision is therefore misleading, and unfortunately we cannot conclude anything from it concerning the real numbers of slaves in these three cities. We are left with a rough estimate for the slave population of Athens at 40 percent to 50 percent of the total population, which remains a very high percentage and suffices to illustrate how crucial the issue of slavery was for the economic development of Athens and other

Greek cities. On the difficulty of providing estimates for the population of Classical Athens, see also Akrigg 2011.

145. This model is thus different from that of the "low-equilibrium trap" described in Walter Scheidel's fundamental analysis of the relationship between ancient demography and economic growth (Scheidel 2004, 753). Among other things, it admits the existence of a massive infanticide when the economic situation deteriorated.

146. See earlier, n. 123, with the case of Kyaneai.

147. On the variations in prosperity that can be observed in Rhodes, see as a first approach Bresson 1988 and 2004b.

148. See chapter 6, 149.

149. *OGIS* 233 (tr. in Burstein 1985, 41–43, no. 32, and Austin 2006, 342–44, no. 190), ll. 10–17.

150. See Brulé 1990.

151. Corvisier 1991.

152. Jacob 1991, 49–72, especially 52–54.

153. Reger 1994, 102–3.

154. Figures cited by Amouretti 1986, 24.

155. Gallant 1989, 396.

156. Garnsey 1988, 17–39.

157. Kuniholm 1990.

158. Wiemer 1997.

159. For these data, see Wiemer 1997, 208–9, with references.

160. Meiggs-Lewis 5; see Chamoux 1953, 104–11, and Graham 1983, 226. On the question of the authenticity of the oath, see Graham 1960, who supports the thesis of authenticity (with reservations, however), and Dušanić 1978, who maintains that it is a fourth-century reconstruction reflecting the internal political conflicts in Cyrene and bearing the mark of the philosophical schools of the time (he suggests a date for the text of between 363 and 361).

161. The text is uncertain in these lines.

162. Syriac *Chronicle* of Pseudo-Joshua the Stylite (ed. Trombley and Watt), 38–44 (see Garnsey 1988, 3–7; and Pollard 2000, 224, who, however, also underscores the burden of the army on the local populations).

163. On these questions, see chapter 14.

164. On the episode, see also later, chapters 12, 336, and 14, 388.

165. For Rome, see the situation in 492 BCE, Livy 2.34.3.

CHAPTER III: ENERGY, ECONOMY, AND TRANSPORT COST

1. On the rotary mill and the watermill, see chapter 7.

2. See chapter 2, 46.

3. See chapter 6, 145.

4. Meigg's synthesis (1982) remains essential, even if it has to be revised on certain points.

5. Aristophanes *Ploutos* 535 and 951–54.

6. Conophagos 1980, 352, see 275–76. Laurion probably consumed 600 tons of wood and 6,500 tons of charcoal annually. On the basis of modern parallels, Picard 2001

carefully suggests that 10,000 tons of wood for charcoal might have been necessary to produce one ton of silver.

7. Ps.-Demosthenes 42.7 (*Against Phaenippus*). On this passage, see chapter 6, 146–48.
8. See earlier, chapter 2, 38, the analysis of Plato's *Critias* (110d–111e) and the question of the deforestation of Attika.
9. See Harris 2011a and 2013b.
10. *IG* II² 1362, ll. 5–7 (it should be clear that with *xula*, here translated "logs," it is not construction wood that is at stake but fuel wood); see also parallel regulations in the deme of Piraeus *IG* II² 1177, ll. 17–21, with Papazarkadas 2011, 127 and 138, for the institutional context.
11. *I.Pérée* 49b, l. 2, and 51b, l. 12 = *I.Peraia* 352B, l. 2, and 354B, l. 11.
12. Asia Minor: Robert 1961, 115–37 (= *OMS* VII 19–41), and 1980, 276; Egypt: Meyer 1989.
13. Meiggs 1982, 203–10, on the source of fuel of Attika.
14. On charcoal in Athens, see Olson 1991.
15. FAO Forestry Paper 1983, 4, table 2.
16. FAO Forestry Paper 1983, 6.
17. Theophrastus *Enquiry into Plants* 5.9.4. As observed by Harris 2013b, 190, the careful attention devoted by Theophrastus (ibid., 5.9.1–8) to the "merits and demerits" of various kinds of species of wood for charcoal-making reveals the existence of a sophisticated charcoal market in the world of his time (late fourth century BCE).
18. Veal 2013.
19. Robert and Robert 1976, 175–87, esp. 185–86 on wood.
20. Tr. H. Rackham, modified (*xulon* is translated here by "wood," not timber, to avoid any possible ambiguity).
21. *ID* 509 (*NChoixDélos*, 195–98), ll. 2, 33–34 and 39–40. The text mentions the weights and scales for weighing wood and the measures for charcoal. See chapter 12, 329–30.
22. Reger 1994, 290–94, table of the data and critical apparatus (with 171–76 on the development of prices), which differs from Meiggs's data (1982, 441–57, esp. tables 450–51), with a higher maximum of 2 dr. 4 ob.
23. On salaries in Athens, Loomis 1998, 120, for the amount used here (1 1/2 dr. per day for an unskilled worker), with 232–39 on the variability of salaries.
24. Reger 1994, 127 and n. 2, according to *IG* XI.2 203A l. 59, from 269, the only figure in which the measure is specified, but it is a significant order of prices (see Glotz 1913, 24).
25. Pomeranz 2000, 60–61; for details see Bresson 2006e, 64.
26. Standard edition: W. Schmidt, *Heronis Alexandrini opera quae supersunt omnia*, vol. 1, 1899, with German tr.; English tr. by B. Woodcroft 1851; Greek text and French tr. Argoud and Guillaumin 1997; see Fleury 1994 and Argoud 1998. On Hero, Argoud 1994b.
27. Drachmann 1963, 206; Landels 2000, 28–31.
28. The actual use of a steam turbine to propel ships goes back only to 1897, and to 1922 for locomotives (Needham 1965, 4.2, 226). Historically, the industrial development of the turbine is thus two centuries later than the steam piston engine. Could the technology of the Greeks have bypassed this "detour"? We can only note that history turned out quite differently.

29. Gille 1980, 193.
30. Wilson 2002, 16; Wilson 2008a.
31. Ritti et al. 2007 for the water-powered stone saw mill figured on a sarcophagus at Hierapolis, third century CE (see later, chapter 8); for the old orthodoxy, see Gille 1980, 192–93 (the technology would have been imported from China in the Middle Ages only, which is now proved wrong).
32. That is the meaning of the study by Krischer 1997, who emphasizes how little interest in the kinematic was shown by the Greek tradition—including the Platonic tradition.
33. Keyser 1992.
34. From the same point of view, see Wilson 2002, 3 and n. 9.
35. Beaune 1980 on interest in automatons in modern Europe. Mokyr 1992, 85 and 103–104, as well as Pomeranz 2000, 67, for the economic consequences.
36. Nef 1932, vol. 1, 19–20 (for more details, 19–77 and vol. 2, 353–66; Burt 2004, 420–21).
37. It is noteworthy that the conditions allowing the expansion of the steam engine were directly dependent on access to a source of coal (see in particular Robinson 1974, 101–2). Thus the first machines installed at Saint Petersburg in the eighteenth century operated using the coal that served as ballast in ships engaged in commerce with Russia. Similarly, Watt's steam engine, which required less energy, was much more quickly adopted in the tin mines of Cornwall (where coal had to be brought in) than on sites with mine shafts, where Newcomen's engine sometimes continued to be used until the beginning of the nineteenth century.
38. Robinson 1974; Pomeranz 2000, 61.
39. Wrigley 1988, 102–3, 127.
40. English tr. in the 1952 Thompson ed. Detailed commentary in the Giardina ed. 1989, 96–99 (see especially the parallel with Vitruvius). The text is cited by Humphrey et al. 1998, 34–35. The best analysis of the development of the steam paddleboat is found in Needham 1965, 4.2, 413–35. The authenticity of the ms. of *De rebus bellicis* is not in question, but the project found no application in Europe before the Middle Ages. On the other hand, in the Chinese world, a type of boat with a paddle wheel turned by manpower was developed, perhaps as early as the fifth century. This tradition was preserved until the twentieth century.
41. Schiavone 2000, 145–46.
42. See the following and chapters 7, 197–98, and 8, 208–11.
43. Horden and Purcell 2000. See for example the rather favorable reception in Shaw 2001 and the more critical viewpoint of Harris 2005b. See also Bresson 2005b on the importance of "connectivity" in the development of ancient Mediterranean civilizations. On transportation, Casson 1994a and, in general, Meijer and van Nijf 1992. On connectivity, see earlier, chapter 2, 31–2.
44. Braudel 1972, vol. 1, 441–45 for long-distance trade and capitalism.
45. Horden and Purcell 2000, 123–72.
46. The relationship is not linear. We have $C_{tu} = a/V_u$, where a is defined by the mode of transportation, and V_u is the value per unit of weight or volume. On a graph, the values of the unit cost of transportation follow a hyperbolic curve.
47. Chankowski 1997, 80.
48. Duncan-Jones 1982, 366–69.

49. See the critique in Arnaud 2005, 11–14, and 2007 (the real itineraries followed by ships were not straight lines) and 139–45 (bureaucratic accounting of rates in the Edict on Maximum Prices).

50. Lohmann 2002; Mitchell 1993, vol. 1, 246–48.

51. Rackham 1990, 105–6.

52. Raepsaet 2002 is now fundamental for the question of the technological aspects of overland transportation in antiquity (particularly in Greece). In addition, it provides many anthropological parallels, with photographs. See also more briefly Raepsaet 2008.

53. Burford 1960; Raepsaet 2002, 191–202; Feyel 2006, 358–63.

54. See Steinhauer 2001a, 81–107.

55. Maiuri 1916, 285–88; Inglieri 1936, *Foglio Sud*, 54, no. 5.

56. *Milet* I.3 (*Delphinion*) 149, ll. 44–45, see chapter 6, 173, for a detailed analysis.

57. Chaniotis 1996, 358–83, no. 61, A ll. 36–38 = B ll. 61–66; see chapter 11, 302.

58. Velkov and Domaradzka 1994 (*SEG* 43 486), ll. 21–25, with new edition Chankowski and Domaradzka 1999. See von Bredow 2002 (but the material form taken by these routes remains undetermined). On this text see also chapter 11, 301–2.

59. Cuinet 1890–1894, vol. 4, 431, to which Mitchell 1993, vol. 1, 246, n. 24, has drawn attention.

60. Cuinet 1890–1894, vol. 4, 256–59.

61. See Cuinet 1890–1894, vol. 1, 635–37.

62. Bulliet 1990, 28–140, on the domestication of the dromedary and its widespread use first in the Middle East in the first millennium, then in Roman Africa.

63. Cuinet 1890–1894, vol. 1, 644.

64. Raepsaet 2002, 33 and 69.

65. On the *cursus publicus*, see Kolb 2000, and on the particular case of the *frumentarii* with respect to the circulation of information, Rankov 2006.

66. Here we follow the thesis of Chandler 1977, according to which it is the particular nature of the technology used that explains the constitution of among others large railway companies in the nineteenth century (see ibid., 79–205), when at the same time traditional forms of organization continued in other sectors. See also Williamson 1985, 274–79.

67. See Mitchell 1993, vol. 1, 247–48.

68. On Aquilius's road policy at the time of the creation of the province of Asia between 129 and 126 BCE, see Mitchell 1999 (see *AE* 1999, 1507).

69. Le Goff 1972, 15.

70. Strabo 13.4.17.

71. DeVries 1997.

72. *Emporion* of inland Thrace: Velkov and Domaradzka 1994; Avram 1997/98; see the dossier in *Bulletin de Correspondance Hellénique* 123 (1999): 245–371. The *emporion* was on the river Hebros, but it seems that in this case the waterway was of little use for the transport of goods.

73. See chapter 5, 125–27.

74. Rhodian amphoras are ubiquitous in the coastal sites around the Mediterranean area in the middle and late Hellenistic period and their bibliography is huge. On Rhodian amphoras and their trade in the eastern Mediterranean, see Rauh 1999; Lund 1999;

Finkielsztejn 2001a, 166–178. For Failaka: Hannestad 1983, 71–72; for Vieille-Toulouse, Labrousse 1971.

75. Dupont and Lungu in press, Apameia being compared with Sardis.
76. Pliny the Younger *Letters* 10.41.2, with Trajan's reply, letter 42; see also letters 10.61 and 62.
77. See the detail in the inscriptions *Didyma* II, no. 39–41, with A. Rehms's commentary, pp. 39–59.
78. Mulliez 1982; Borza 1987, 37.
79. Aliki marble quarries: Grandjean and Salviat 2000, 165–67.
80. On the questions regarding the conditions of maritime shipping, see now the magisterial synthesis of Arnaud 2005, especially 7–148, whose main conclusions are adopted here. Regarding ships and equipment, Casson 1995 remains an unequaled general account (see also Casson 1991 and 1994b).
81. See Pomey 1981, 1995, and 2011. Ancient ships were constructed "shell first." For an overview of ancient seafaring and ancient shipbuilding techniques and their evolution, see Polzer 2011 (which covers also the Phoenician world and gives a detailed survey from the end of the Bronze Age to the beginning of the Classical period) and Carlson 2011.
82. See Wilson 2011a and 2011b.
83. Kapitän 1984.
84. Gibbins 2001.
85. Concerning the Kyrenia ship, see Swiny and Katzev 1973 and Steffy 1985 on the techniques of the ship's construction. On the size of ships, see also chapter 13, 377–78. See Wilson 2011b, 214–15, for a (chronologically sorted) list of the cargo weights represented by shipwrecks in the Mediterranean, which (unsurprisingly) proves the existence of many small-size ships even in the late Hellenistic and Roman period.
86. See the table in Casson 1995, 183–84, and the more developed one in Arnaud 2005, 37, where all the weights based on *medimnoi* must be reduced by one-quarter.
87. Here we have rounded the figure to 30 kilograms. For the respective weights of a *medimnos* of barley and a *medimnos* of wheat, see the appendix on weights, measures, and currency units.
88. IG XII.Suppl. 348 (Pleket, *Epigraphica*, 1, no. 9; Engl. tr. Austin 2006, 235, no. 126). On the port of Thasos, see Grandjean and Salviat 2000, 52–57.
89. Ashkelon: Ballard et al. 2002, 400-plus amphoras, each with a capacity of ca. 18 liters, to which should be added the weight of the amphora. Grand Ribaud F: Long et al. 2006, 800–1,000 amphoras. Alonnisos: Hadjidaki 1996 and Hatzidake 1997, over 4,000 amphoras. Mahdia: Pomey and Tchernia 1978, 234; Parker 1992, 252–53, no. 621 (marble transport); Albenga: Pomey and Tchernia 1978, 235; Parker 1992, 49–51, no. 28, probably over 10,000 amphoras. La Madrague de Giens: Pomey and Tchernia 1978, 234; Parker 1992, 249–50, no. 616, 6,000–7,000 amphoras. On the Ashkelon and Alonnisos wrecks, see also chapter 13, nn. 20, 28 and 153.
90. On the Uluburun ship, see chapter 4, 98–9.
91. See full discussion in Wilson 2011b, 211–17.
92. Athenaeus quoted Moschion (*FGrHist* 575 F 1), an author of the third or second century BCE. See the new translation proposed by Casson 1995, 191–99, with the commentary pp. 184–86, as well as Pomey and Tchernia 2006. See also chapter 7, 193.

93. Pomey and Tchernia 2006.

94. Casson 1995, 157–269, on commercial ships (with their different types adapted to various uses) and on naval construction in general; Arnaud 2005, 38–42; Whitewright 2011.

95. For the introduction of the lateen sail in late antiquity, see Whitewright 2009 and 2011.

96. Arnaud 2011b.

97. Arnaud 2005, 42–45.

98. Ibid., 45–60.

99. Gould 1923, 1–15, on the issues involved, and 40–70, on John Harrison's (1693–1776) chronometer.

100. Horden and Purcell 2000, 143–52.

101. Arnaud 2005, 107–26.

102. Arnaud 2007 and 2011a.

103. See the data collected by Casson 1995, 281–96, and the table in Arnaud 2005, 128–31.

104. See Parker 1992. The list is considerably longer today.

105. On these estimates, see Gibbins 2001, 277.

106. Garland 2001, 151–54, with 218–19.

107. Garland 2001, 8, map fig. 9, 14–32, and 43–45, and Sanidas 2013, 31, map pl. II. See Thucydides 1.93.3–7 on the initial role of Themistokles.

108. Blackman 1999; Philimonos-Tsopotou 2004, 35, fig. 9.

109. Aristides *Orations* 25.3 Behr. The text dates from the Imperial period, but describes the situation that generally prevailed before the great earthquake of the second century; thus the system could go back all the way to the Hellenistic period.

110. von Gerkan 1924, 117, with Bresson 2011b for the detail of the topography of the site.

111. Aupert 1996, 164–68 (preface by J.-Y. Empereur).

112. Duchêne and Fraisse 2001.

113. Lighthouses hypothesized at Thasos: Kozelj and Wurch-Kozelj 1989 (Giardina 2010, 76–77, no. 28); at Delos: Bruneau 1979, 99–104 ("32. Le problème des phares"; the case of Delos has been apparently skipped by Giardina 2010), with a slight nuance of doubt. Doubts on the existence of lighthouses in Thasos: Young 1956, 132. One of the monuments interpreted as a lighthouse at Thasos bears a metric inscription of the late sixth century BCE (*IG* XII.8 683, p. x) that states the following: "I am the memorial of Akeratos, the son of Phrasierides. I lie down at the tip of the port as a safety for ships and sailors." The monument was clearly a beacon. To grant that it was also a lighthouse one must suppose the existence of a financial support and permanent organization to pay for a lighthouse keeper and for the fuel. In other words, the institutional aspect of the question should also be examined. Obviously, the question needs further study.

114. Giardina 2010, 12–23.

115. Pliny the Younger *Letters* 10.41. See the good commentary in Sherwin-White 1966, 622–25 on letters 41 and 42, and 646–48 on letters 61 and 62.

116. This question should be reconsidered, but that cannot be done here. Finkel and Barka 1997 provide interesting testimonies on canal-building projects in the Ottoman period. Using aerial photos, they have identified west of the lake the remains of a first leg of the canal, 2 kilometers long and 20 meters wide (interpreted as the canal of the Hellenistic period), and west of it, another relatively advanced section 6 kilometers long

and 40 meters wide (interpreted as an Ottoman canal), but apparently nothing in the Roman period. Besides, they did not know any of the Byzantine texts on the region. See the debate regarding Justinian's bridge and the topography of the area of the lower Sangarios (and later its defensive function against the Turks) in Whitby 1985, Froriep 1986 and 1991, and Leiner 1991, who appropriately cites a series of Byzantine texts, to which must be added the testimony of Anna Comnena *Alexiad* 10.5.1–3, which so far does not seem to have been brought into the debate. Anna Comnena mentions that her father Alexis I had had dredged out a "very long" ditch, the function of which was no longer known. The use of the formula "below the lake of Baane" to locate the canal translates the Greek *katōterō tēs Baanēs limnēs*. The ditch thus reached the lake, on the east or on the west. If it was intended to provide a continuous barrier by connecting with the Sangarios, the canal must have been to the east of the lake. Alexis's investigation is supposed to have shown that the canal went back to Anastasios II, emperor from 713 to 715. This information cannot be verified. In any case, the works of Justinian in the same sector (see the important Byzantine literature cited by Leiner 1991) must also be taken in to account. Anna Comnena's testimony fits perfectly into the series of Byzantine testimonies regarding the region. Thus it is tempting to conclude that the same or a partially identical canal between the lake and the Sangarios was periodically dredged after being initially put in service under a king of Bithynia.

117. See later and the following note.
118. See Herodotus 4.42.2–4 on Necho's use of the canal and 4.39.1 for its reconstruction under Darius I; see Bresciani 1998 on Darius's canal. Later abandoned (see Aristotle *Meteorologics* 1.14.27 352b), the canal was put back in service under Ptolemy II (see Diodorus 1.33.9–12 and Strabo 17.1.25), and still later under the empire, in the second century CE (see in detail Aubert 2004).
119. Herodotus 7.22–24, with 7.37, 116–17 and 122.
120. Müller 1987–1997, vol. 1, 156–61, with a series of photographs of the current site.
121. While Molkenthin 2006, 54–81, maintains that the canal was completed, this still remains uncertain: see Leitholdt et al. 2012, who also show that the canal might actually have been rather a chain of ponds rather than a continuous canal.
122. Finkel and Barka 1997, 435.
123. In Sicily, after the battle of Himera, Akragas used the Carthaginian prisoners to build impressive sewers and a large fishpond: Diodorus 11.25.3–4, and see earlier, chapter 2, 45, and chapter 7, 185.
124. On the *diolkos*, see Raepsaet 1993 and 2002, 206–12, and Werner 1997.
125. Thucydides 3.15.1, see 8.7 and 8.8.3–4.
126. Salmon 1984, 132–54.
127. See M. Tolley's calculations in Raepsaet 1993, 257–61.
128. The ship travels from Athens to Syracuse (32.4 and 18), after calling in at Kephallenia 32.8–9, 14 and 23. Whether or not the speech was written by Demosthenes himself, who was the uncle by marriage of the defendant Demo (32.31–32), remains, however, uncertain.
129. Strabo 10.5.4 and Bresson 2006b. See in detail chapter 15, 425–27. On the *diolkos*, see also Pettegrew 2011, who has missed my contribution in Bresson 2007–2008, vol. 1, 100–102, but who has reached conclusions parallel to mine, although downplaying the economic role.

130. See also chapters 7 and 15.

131. Scheidel 2011 and Wilson 2011b.

CHAPTER IV: THE *POLIS* AND THE ECONOMY

1. See Broodbank 2013, 345–444, for a trans-Mediterranean overview.

2. For a synthetic account of the Aegean Bronze Age, see Dickinson 1994, especially 45–94 on the economy and 234–56 on trade; Treuil et al. 1989; Bennet 2007; Shelmerdine 2008 and particularly Shelmerdine and Bennet 2008 on the economy and administration of the Mycenaean states; Burns 2010b (for trade); Bintliff 2012, 181–205, for the archaeological broad view.

3. Perna 2004; Shelmerdine and Bennet 2008, 299–303.

4. Halstead 2007.

5. Nakassis 2010.

6. Joannès 2001, 407, and Perna 2004, 290–95.

7. Nakassis 2013, 173–86.

8. Shelmerdine 2013; Pullen 2013; Feinman 2013.

9. Shelmerdine and Bennet 2008, 305; Halstead 1996, 33, on the composition of these flocks.

10. Uluburun: Pulak 1998, with Broodbank 2013, 399–402; Cape Gelidonya: Bass 1967 and 2010; Point Iria: Phelps et al. 1999, and esp. Lolos 1999. See also Sauvage 2012, 86–90 (overview of the goods transported) and 270–73 (navigation routes).

11. On the interconnections within the Mycenaean world and their role in the formation of a common identity, see Burns 2010a.

12. Broodbank 2013, 460–82, for the attractive "revisionist explanation;" Demand 2011, 200–14 on the origin of the Sea Peoples.

13. On the question of the collapse at the end of the Bronze Age, see most recently the careful discussions of Dickinson 2006, 41–57, and Deger-Jalkotzy 2008, although the former rejects the Sea Peoples hypothesis and the latter lays less weight on the role of the Sea Peoples. But as well observed by Bintliff 2012 (209–11), the simultaneous collapses of the Mycenaean world and of several states of the Eastern Mediterranean suggests that the Sea Peoples hypothesis remains the best solution (although admittedly there remains much to do to reach a better understanding of what really took place). The exceptional dynamism of the Western Mediterranean in the Bronze Age might well justify the emergence of the Sea Peoples. What is perhaps still lacking is a combined study of the two basins of the Mediterranean in that period.

14. The classical picture is that of Snodgrass 2000 (first edition 1971), with a systematic archaeological and regional analysis, with 360–86 on the economic and demographic decline,

15. Homer *Il.* 2.649 (in the *Odyssey* 19.174, the figure is ninety). See Perlman 1992.

16. Shelmerdine and Bennet 2008, 299, for the size of Knossos and other Mycenaean states.

17. Morgan 2009.

18. Morris 1986 favors a date of ca. 700 BCE. Admittedly the date of Homer is still controversial.

19. White 1984, 122–24, on the technical aspects.

20. Shelmerdine and Bennet 2008, 299–301.
21. Tr. A. T. Murray.
22. Morgan 2009, with Bintliff 2012, 209–33.
23. Waldbaum 1978.
24. Morris 2009a.
25. Stein-Hölkeskamp 2009.
26. Vargyas 1997 and 2001; van der Spek 2006.
27. Jursa 2010, 754–816.
28. See Moreno García 2014.
29. Descat 1985; Briant 2002, 419–21 and 946–47 for the *tagē*, 69–69 and 491–92 for the *phoros*. The difference between payments in kind and payments in silver was how- ever probably less clearcut than has been assumed so far.
30. Aperghis 2004, 78.
31. Préaux 1978, vol. 1, 366; Manning 2003, 57 and 123, for the figures used here for the tax on grain and on vineyard or orchard production.
32. Migeotte 1995 and Migeotte 2014, 230–44.
33. See also Diogenes Laertius 1.53. On this point, see the literature collected by Stroud 1998, 27, n. 44, and Migeotte 2014, 504–5.
34. Stroud 1998, 27–30, who brings together various amounts of taxes levied in Athens, all of them lower than the tax rate on the islands with cleruchs.
35. Ed. princeps Wiegand and Wilamowitz 1904 (*Syll.*[3] 976; *Choix* 34). See the comple- mentary bibliography in Bresson 2000, 254, n. 60, and commentary 253–57.
36. Shipley 1987, 34–36, emphasizes that originally the population of Anaia consisted of Karians, but that Samian immigration came early. Anaia had served as a base for the Samians who fought against Athens in the Peloponnesian War (ibid., 122–23 and 125–26). We do not know for certain whether the territory had remained in the hands of the Samians during the period of the Athenian cleruchy in the fourth century, be- tween 365 and 322 (ibid., 167); however, it will be noted that the decree for Antileon of Chalkis (*IG* XII.6 42, ll. 5–6) does not prevent us from thinking so. Whatever the eth- nic origin of the people working on the properties of Anaia at the beginning of the Hel- lenistic period, in the third century it was in fact Samian citizens who paid the *eikostē* in grain to the city.
37. Salomon 1997 (but on cleruchies see also later, 115–17).
38. *SEG* 41 929, ll. 4–5.
39. Stroud 1998, 27, n. 39.
40. *I.Ephesos* 4 (*Syll.*[3] 364), ca. 300/299 BCE, with the new edition and detailed commen- tary by Walser 2008 (*SEG* 58 1302) l. 74 (limitation of the interest to a rate of 1/12).
41. Osborne 1988, 285; Walbank 1983, 217; see Stroud 1998, 32.
42. Tyrtaeus *Elegy* fr. 6, tr. D. E. Gerber, quoted in Pausanias 4.14.4–5, also interpreted by Aelian *Varia Historica* 6.1.
43. See Luther 2004, 59–79, who is tempted to follow the judgment of W. Jaeger in admit- ting that part of what would be a composite work might date back to the Archaic pe- riod, but who finally dates Tyrtaeus to the fifth century BCE.
44. Meier 1998, 266–69.
45. Hodkinson 2000, 126–28; Alcock 2002 on the archaeological aspects, as well as on the "helot danger" and on the notion of sharecropping.

46. Lévy 2003, 120.

47. Theopompus *FGrHist* 115 F 13 (= Athenaeus 6 272a).

48. Zaccagnini 1994 and 1995. When in Aristophanes' *Acharnians* (759–817) the Megarian offers to sell his two daughters under the guise of piglets, the comic scene hardly conceals the despair of a starving family. But the scene takes place in a context of war and, despite the frequency of wars, cannot be taken to be representative of an ordinary situation in Greece.

49. Stahl and Walter 2009. That we have every reason to believe in the historical validity of Solon's law is shown convincingly by Rhodes 2006. It should be stressed however that Solon did not abolish debt-bondage, as shown convincingly by Harris 2002b.

50. Plato's argument is analyzed in detail by Harris 2002a, 71–75. See also chapter 7, 187–88, where the text is quoted in full.

51. On self-consumption, see chapter 8.

52. Aristotle *Politics* 5.4.1–5.

53. One of the indices of the efficiency of Hellenic military organization is the use of Greek mercenaries, as early as the end of the seventh or the beginning of the sixth century, in Egypt and in the Mesopotamian kingdoms.

54. Grunauer von Hoerschelmann 1978, 1–6: coins of King Areus, probably minted during the Chremonidean War (268–262 BCE).

55. Cartledge and Spawforth 1992, 35.

56. See earlier, 107, and later chapter 7, 187–88, for the details of Plato's argument.

57. Finley 1970, 4, and 1981, 186–87. In his *Ancient Economy* (1973, 135) Finley also refers in parallel to Xenophon's *Poroi* 4.4–6, not to Plato's *Republic*.

58. De Callataÿ 2000.

59. Chaniotis 2005 for the Hellenistic world: 44–56 on the maintained citizen armies, and 115–21 on the massive cost of war.

60. Phocylides of Miletos fr. 5 Edmonds (= Dio Chrysostom 36.13), quoted by Cahill 2002, vii, from whom this translation is borrowed.

61. Phocylides of Miletos fr. 12 Edmonds (= Aristotle *Politics* 4.9.7), tr. J. M. Edmonds.

62. Kim 2001; Bresson 2001a.

63. On this text, see chapter 15, 432.

64. An outline is provided by the studies of Papazoglou 1997, 105–12 (with discussion of the text of Kassandros's donation mentioned later), Schuler 1998 (160–80), Corsaro 2001, Boffo 2001 (overall historiographical survey), and Mileta 2002 (who proposes to replace the concept of "royal land" by that of "royal area" for the *chōra basilikē*, to show that it is not only a matter of lands but also of rights); see also the synthetic update by Capdetrey 2007, 135–66, and the analyses later, chapter 14, 400–1.

65. *I.Priene*² 1, ll. 10–13, with the comment of Thonemann 2012.

66. *I.SultanDağı* 393, with *SEG* 47 1745.

67. *RC* 10–13; *I.Ilion* 33; English tr. Bagnall and Derow 2004, 36–38, no. 18; Aperghis 2004, 101–2 and text and translation 312–15; Bencivenni 2004 for detailed historiographical comment; Austin 2006, 301–3, no. 164. The actual size of Aristodikides's estate has been much discussed (6,000 or even 8,000 *plethra* for Bagnall and Derow, 5,500 *plethra* for Aperghis, which is more likely; however if the estate mentioned in *RC* 10 was only part of the further donations mentioned, the amount would be only 3,500 *plethra*. See also later, chapter 6, 150–51, on the question of the annexation of a large estate to a city.

68. *I.Priene*² 29–31, with Gauthier 1980.

69. *Didyma* II 492ac; *RC* 19, 18, 20; English tr. Austin 2006, 312–14, no. 173. See Aperghis 2004, 102–3 and text and translation 315–18.

70. *IJG* vol. 2, 116–18, no. XXVA; Hatzopoulos 1988, 22–26; Hatzopoulos 1996, vol. 2, 43–45, no. 20.

71. The solution that had been proposed by the present writer in the original French edition, that of two domains only and given to the grandfather, is thus abandoned.

72. Hatzopoulos 1988, 17–54 (*SEG* 38 619); Hatzopoulos 1996, vol. 2, 45–46. For the date of the second document, Hatzopoulos 1988, 21 and 38.

73. For the details, see chapter 6, 150–51.

74. On Koinos, Hatzopoulos 1996, vol. 1, 333, 336, 345–46 and 435.

75. Hatzopoulos 1988, 38.

76. Ibid.

77. Diodorus 19.52.2–3; Marble of Paros *FGrHist* 239 F B 14 (these two sources allow us to date the foundation exactly to 316/5); Livy 44.11.2; Strabo 7 fr. 25; Pausanias 5.23.3; Athenaeus 11 784c; Stephanus of Byzantion *s.v.* Kassandreia; on the foundation of the city, see Hatzopoulos 1988, 45–48, and 1996, vol. 1, 160–63 and 199–202; Landucci Gattinoni 2003, 96–103, with the earlier bibliography.

78. Hatzopoulos 1988, 48–49.

79. This crucial point has been made by Criscuolo 2011, who gives also a new translation and analysis of the Hefzibah inscription *SEG* 29 1613, with 29 1808 (Austin 2006, 347–50, no. 193), ll. 22–27, to be dated between 199 and 195 BCE. This proves that the villages attributed to Ptolemaios, the Seleukid governor of Syria, had been given to him *en ktēsei kai eis to patrikon*, "in ownership and as a patrimony." The interpretation of the donation to Perdikkas, many times commented upon, has been the object of a famous debate, starting with Rostovtzeff 1910, 251–52 (who noted that in this document it was not a question of attributing land to a city), Welles 1938, 248, and Behrend 1973, 148–53, who argued for the limited property of the holder, meaning that the superior rights of the king never disappeared. Corsaro 2001 (particularly 242–43), Schuler 1998, 166–67, and, although with different arguments, Capdetrey 2007, 153–55, also basing themselves explicitly on this text, considered that donations of land in the *chōra basilikē* became *ipso facto* the private property of the holder. Acknowledging that the land in donation was a *klērouchia* means that the thesis of the former is vindicated, with the important correction that validation of the new ownership did not intervene when the sovereign changed, but when the *klērouchos* died.

80. Scheuble-Reiter 2012, 11–55, for the cleruch cavalrymen.

81. The literature on cleruchs is extensive. See recently Manning 2003, 38, 56, 70, 110–15, and 178–80, who insists on the military character of the cleruchy; Kehoe 2010, 314–20, who shows the diversity and complexity of the landholding system; Pollard 2010, 450–52, for the military aspects; Monson 2012, 76–79, 88–90, 94–95; Thompson 2012, who announces a new article on the topic; Fischer-Bovet 2014, 210–37.

82. Scheuble-Reiter 2012, 178–94, for the cleruch cavalrymen.

83. See *P.Hib.* 81, Egypt, Arsinoite nome, 238/7 BCE.

84. See *P.Lille* I 4, Egypt, 217 BCE, which is crucial for the definition of status of the cleruchs, with other documents quoted by Criscuolo 2011, 476–77. For the evolution of the system in the second century BCE, see Scheuble-Reiter 2012, 171–78 (land

inherited by daughters), and 323. In 61/60 BCE (*BGU* IV 1185, ll. 12–20), Ptolemy XII's confirmed that when a cleruch died intestate, his land could be inherited by his closest relative, including a female relative (see Fischer-Bovet 2014, 231–34).

85. This is Criscuolo's hypothesis (2011, 484–85).

86. See Bencivenni 2004.

87. On the status of the lands *en dōreai* in general, see the synthetic presentation in Papazoglou 1997, 100–104, and also Bresson 1998 regarding Karia and Lykia given *en dōreai* to the Rhodians.

88. Tr. H. Rackham. On this passage, see Nielsen 2013.

89. This conclusion is thus the opposite of that of Hatzopoulos *Bull. ép.*, no 2008, 340; 2011, 399; and 2012, 264; and of Criscuolo 2011.

90. Foundation of Lysimacheia and its role as capital: Lund 1992, 64 and 175.

91. Inscription from Kassandreia: Vokotopoulou 1997; see *Bull. ép.* 1998, no. 269, and *SEG* 47 940. For the identity with the homonymous of the Eretria document, see Knoepfler 2001b, 60 and 67. On the privileges granted to Chairephanes, see also chapter 6, 165–66.

92. Borza 1987.

93. *Pace* Thonemann 2009, the status of the land in Macedonian Asia Minor was not different from that of the status of the land in Macedon proper, which itself bore close resemblance to that of pre-Macedonian times (see ibid., 380, on the status of land in early Achaemenid Egypt).

94. See chapter 6, 166–67.

95. *Pace* Salomon 1997, 162–71; see rather Moreno 2007, 83–90, 103, and 106.

CHAPTER V: AGRICULTURAL PRODUCTION

1. *GHI* 88. See Habicht 2006, 35–41, for the context, and for the religious aspects, Mikalson 1998, 161 and 164, with a detailed commentary on the oath and the inscription *SEG* 33 115, from 246/45 BCE (thus from the period of Macedonian domination), where one can see the priestess of Aglauros, Timokrite, honored for having made sacrifices to Aglauros, Ares, Helios, the Horai, Apollo, and the other gods for the "health and salvation of the Council and the people of the Athenians, their children and their spouses, in the name of King Antigonos, his consort Phile and their children." See also Habicht 2006, 186–87.

2. Brun 2004, 83.

3. Halstead 2014.

4. Vidal-Naquet 1986, 15–38 ("Land and sacrifice in the Odyssey").

5. See *Odyssey* 9.191.

6. On this point, see the discussion later, 132–33.

7. For cereals in the ancient world in general, see Zohary et al. 2012, 19–88; for a detailed discussion of the (complex) history of *Triticum*, see also Sallares 1991, 313–68. For the taxonomy and ecology of wheat in general, McCorriston 2000b, and for barley, McCorriston 2000a.

8. Crawford 1979, 140, and Sallares 1991, 368–72, who considers however that the cultivation of naked wheats only increased in Hellenistic Egypt, but that these wheats were already known before.

9. On the wheat from the northern Black Sea, see Sallares 1991, 331–32.
10. Amouretti 1986, 57–58 and 77, for this description.
11. For a description of plowing and cultivation and the need to fight parasitic weeds, see Xenophon *Economics* 16.9–15 and 17.12–15.
12. For the many plowings in modern Greece, Halstead 2014, 34–35.
13. Halstead 1987, 84, refers to a maximum of 3.5 hectares for land cultivated by hand, a figure that seems too high, however—the norm probably being about 2 hectares. The figure of 10 to 12 hectares of pasture to feed a single ox seems exaggerated. The amount of pasture necessary to feed an ox depends on the size of the animal and the quality of pasture. As a point of reference, today it is often assumed that 1 hectare of good pasture suffices for one ox (more than double that amount for a lactating cow).
14. Amouretti 1986, 107–8.
15. For threshing and winnowing in modern Greece, see Halstead 2014, 166–73, who insists on the labor constraints linked to these operations.
16. Hesiod *Works and Days* 405–6, 459, 470, 502, 573, 597, 766.
17. Tchernia 1986, 21–27; Brun 2003, 120.
18. Moretti 1980, 36–47, ll. 40–41; see Reger 1994, 182.
19. Grace 1963 (the date of these amphoras, which must certainly go back to the period of the war, must now be revised in view of the new chronology proposed by Finkielsztejn 2001a, 184).
20. On the production of wine in Rome, and by extension in the Greek world as well, see the synthetic presentation in Tchernia 1986.
21. On the technology of producing wine grapes and wine, see now the fundamental works of J.-P. Brun, 2003; 2004a, 82–129; 2004b; and 2005. On the production of and trade in Italian wine, with many consequences for Greece, see also Tchernia 1986. However, Billiard 1913 still remains useful for certain economic aspects.
22. Amos leases: Salviat 1993.
23. See the following on the grape stakes used in Kerkyra.
24. Plutarch *Lycurgus* 12.2; Dicearchus 87 Mirhady = Athenaeus 4 141ac. See Hodkinson 2000, 190–94.
25. Robertson 1993. Parker 2005, 290–326, esp. 206. The connection between the festival of the *Lēnaia* and the wine press (*lēnos*) is less obvious, see Parker, ibid., 206, n. 62.
26. Ehrenberg 1962, 74, 92 and passim; Bowie 1995.
27. *IG* I³ 426. On the basis of figures given by Pritchett and Pippin 1956, 182, with 1 *metrētēs* = 39.39 liters and 1 *chous* = 3.27 l, or a total of 4,119.5 liters. The price of this wine is mutilated on the stone. The figure ends in [—]20, and Pritchett and Pippin, ibid., 199–203, offers good arguments for a price of 520 dr.: thus we have the figure of about 5 dr. the *metrētēs* if we leave aside the seven additional *choes*, which introduces a negligible difference of 5/1,000 of the total amount. On wine production in Attika, see also Pernin 2012 (but for the quantities of wine referred to, see Pritchett and Pippin 1956, 195–96 and 199–203; for the most part, this wine was certainly sold and did not represent the consumption of the farms, as implied in the article).
28. Osborne 1987, 42–43.
29. Brunet 1993.
30. Salviat 1990, 475.
31. On early Archaic wine (and oil) exports, see chapter 14, 404–5.

32. Johnston 1984.

33. On the meaning of this standardization of the products of each city, see chapter 9, 243.

34. Salviat 1990.

35. Doulgeri-Intzessiloglou and Garlan 1990; Sarris et al. 2002.

36. Mende: Salviat 1990; Thasos: Salviat 1986.

37. Salviat 1993.

38. See Boulay 2012, 104–5.

39. Theopompus *Histories* 15, *FGrHist* 115 F122, quoted by Athenaeus 6 265b. See Descat 2006a.

40. Theopompus *Histories sine loc.*, *FGrHist* 115 F276, quoted by Athenaeus 1 26bc.

41. L. Rubinstein, in Hansen and Nielsen 2004, 1069.

42. As is noted by Gomme et al. 1945–1981, vol. 5, 86–87.

43. On long-standing slave revolts in Chios, the role of the slave leader Drimakos and transhistorical parallels, see Urbainczyk 2008, 29–31, 37–38, 53–54, and 91; for the imaginary aspects, Forsdyke 2012, 37–42 and 78–89.

44. Ps.-Aristotle *On Marvellous Things Heard* 104, which might be a treatise of the Peripatetic school, and thus date from the early Hellenistic period.

45. Wilson 2006a.

46. On olive cultivation, see in general Foxhall 2007.

47. Foxhall 2007, 85–95.

48. Foxhall 2007, 5–9.

49. Pébarthe in press. On perfumes see also Reger 2005.

50. Hellenistic and Roman inland Asia Minor provides cases where the olive tree was indeed cultivated slightly above 1000 meters. It is thus clear that the development of olive cultivation was linked to the spreading of Hellenic culture and a specific market demand (see Mitchell 2005 and 2009, and discussion in Thonemann 2011, 53–56).

51. On mixed farming in more detail, see chapter 6, 157–61.

52. For details on growing and processing olives, see Brun 2003 and 2004a, as well as Foxhall 2007, 97–129.

53. Foxhall 2007, 124–29, with fig. 5.5 reproduction of the Attic black-figure amphora London BM B226 (ca. 520 BCE) illustrating the harvesting of olives by knocking them from the tree.

54. Robert 1984, 516–17. Kamiros and Idyma advertised a fig leaf on their coins.

55. Polybius 16.24.5 and 9.

56. Salviat 1993.

57. See Harris 2002a, 98, on the names of the sellers of several of these products in the Athenian agora.

58. Pritchett and Pippin 1956, 180–92.

59. *GHI* 4, back, col. vi, l. 6 (gardener); the list also includes twelve *geōrgoi* or "farm-workers" (tr. Rhodes-Osborne): front, cols. iv, ll. 1 and 15; back, cols. v, ll. 40, 63 (?), and 81; vi, ll. 1, 9, 11, and 55; col. vii, ll. 2 and 5 (numbering to be used in connection with Osborne 1981–1983, vol. 1, pp. 37–41, D6).

60. Pliny 21.10 [19].

61. On honey production in antiquity, Crane 1983 and Balandier 2004.

62. *P.Cairo.Zen.* 59012, from 259 BCE, on Patron's ship. On luxury goods and their taxation in this document, see Bresson 2012c.

63. Attika, Vari: Jones et al. 1973, 397–448; Trachones (5 kilometers south of Athens), M. I. Geroulanos in Jones et al. 1973, 443–48; "the Princess's Tower" near Sounion, Jones ibid., 448–52. Isthmia: Anderson-Stojanovic and Jones 2002.

64. Tr. E. S. Forster and E. H. Heffner.

65. Three cities in Sicily bore the name "Hybla," and there have been hesitations as to which one this is. Is it the Hybla located west of Syracuse in the area of the Hyblean Mountains?

66. Dioscorides was a Greek physician of the first century CE. On the honey produced in the islands, in particular on Keos, see Brun 1996, 104–6.

67. See earlier, chapter 4, 98.

68. Snodgrass 1980, 35–36, and 1987, 193–209.

69. Isager and Skydsgaard 1992, 99; Chandezon 2003, 406.

70. Morgan 2009, 52.

71. Vidal-Naquet 1986, 15–38, and see earlier, 119.

72. See now in detail McInerney 2010, 74–145, on heroic consumptions and the social role of cattle in Homer's world, and 167–71, on a nuanced evaluation of the role of animal husbandry. Howe 2008, 27–42, is right in considering that animal husbandry always played a major role in defining the values of the Greek aristocracy, both in the Homeric period and later. But its exceptional role in the Homeric world is not an illusion: it simply reveals a relative weight in the hierarchy of forms of wealth that was much greater in the Early Iron Age than in the later period.

73. Becker 1986, 294.

74. For Thesprotia, see Niskanen 2009.

75. Logically Morgan 2009, 52, also links demography and animal husbandry but with different premises: she considers that after the collapse of the palaces, "the eleventh to ninth centuries saw neither extensive depopulation nor a wholesale shift to specialist pastoralism."

76. Britnell 2008 for the case of England.

77. Lazenby 1947; Pollard 1977, 135–40.

78. See Howe 2008, 1–26, for an excellent overview of the recent historiography of animal husbandry in Archaic and Classical Greece.

79. Brun 1996, 89, cites figures of a few hundred heads for some islands (in 1971, 100 in Melos, 1,300 in Keos, under conditions far more favorable than in antiquity because of the possibility of importing fodder and the existence of pumps that can reach deep-lying aquifers). But even these figures remain very low if we consider just the number of agricultural operations needing a pair of oxen. The exportation of 1,100—and calves—from Andros in 1878 could be explained precisely by the seasonal exportation of animals—in particular, for slaughter. What is most likely is that more or less everywhere, many peasants had to rent a pair of oxen for agricultural work (with pairs of oxen plowing several small properties, and not just one), because each farm could not have its own.

80. Leguilloux 2000, 75.

81. Chandezon 2003, 402–3.

82. Chandezon 2003, 401–2.

83. *IG* I^3 426; Chandezon 2003, 17–21, no. 1.

84. *Pace* Amouretti 1986, 62–63.

85. On the debate over transhumance in Ancient Greece, see Howe 2008, 14–26. On the variable conditions of stock raising on the islands, Brun 1996, 88–104.

86. Migeotte, *Emprunt public*, 48–53, no. 12 (beginning with two forms for the reimbursement of the city of Elateia's debt); Chandezon 2003, 41–45, no. 7.
87. Chandezon 2003, 403–4.
88. Campbell 1964 on the Sarakatsani.
89. Varro *On Agriculture* 2.2.18–19, who emphasizes the special care taken in producing the fine woolens of Taras or Attika (among others, the sheep were "jacketed" with skin, to preserve the quality of the wool).
90. On the export of products from Kerkyra into the interior, see earlier, 127.
91. Howe 2008, 49–76, for the various strategies.
92. See Georgoudi 1974; Hodkinson 1988; Skydsgaard 1988; Isager and Skydsgaard 1992, 99–101.
93. That is clearly what emerges from the information in the bibliography assembled by Horden and Purcell 2000, 80–87 and 550–51.
94. See the discussion in Chandezon 2003, 351–89.
95. See the convention between Hierapytna and Priansos in the second century BCE, Chandezon 2003, 171–73, no. 45, where, however, the word *ennomion* does not appear.
96. IG XII.7 509; Robert 1949, "Les chèvres d'Hérakleia," 161–70; Brun 1996, 101–2; Chandezon 2003, 147–49, no. 35.
97. Robert 1949, 155–57 (in "Bergers grecs," 152–60).
98. The point is well made by Howe 2008, 77–97, for the Archaic and Classical periods, and his observations would still be largely valid for the Hellenistic period.
99. *Hellenica Oxyrhynchia* 21.2–3 (col. 14); see also Xenophon *Hellenica* 3.5.3 and Pausanias 3.9.9. Thus a war broke out in 395 BCE.
100. Chandezon 2003, 173–81, no. 46.
101. Tr. R. Fagles.
102. On the "common territories," see Daverio-Rocchi 1988, 37–40.
103. *TCam* 110, II. 39–40. The case should be added to the list provided by Daverio-Rocchi (see previous note).
104. Chaniotis 1996, 114–20 and 191–92.
105. Agreement between Hierapytna and Praisos: Chaniotis 1996, 185–90, no. 5 = Chandezon 2003, 170–71, no. 44; with Priansos, Chaniotis 1996, 255–64, no. 28 = Chandezon 2003, 171–73, no. 45; arbitration with Itanos: *Syll.*[3] 685 = Chaniotis 1996, 307–10, no. 49 and 333–37, no. 57 = Chandezon 2003, 173–81, no. 46 (literature on frontiers and cattle raising; on this text see other literature, chapter 7, n. 59). Expansion of Hierapytna: Guizzi 2001, 304–22, with discussion of the localization of the communities, and 366–82, with Strabo 10.4.12 for the destruction of Praisos. For the question of Stalai and Leuke, see chapter 7, 183–84.
106. Saller 2005, 233.

CHAPTER VI: THE ECONOMY OF THE AGRICULTURAL WORLD

1. On cadastral land registration, see chapter 9, 227, and n. 9. For the exceptional case of Larisa in Thessaly, see later, 150 and 154.
2. See chapter 2, 61.
3. Burford Cooper 1977, 171. In the table the figures for percentages are rounded off.

4. Jones et al. 1962.
5. Jones et al. 1973.
6. Lohmann 1993 and 1994.
7. Morris 2009b, 120. Gini's index measures the difference between what would be a completely egalitarian distribution of land and a completely inegalitarian one. In the former the coefficient would be zero, in the latter it would be one. Indeed in ancient Greece the distribution of wealth between citizens was unusually egalitarian. But the citizen body exploited a very large slave population, which is extremely difficult to quantify (see chapter 2, n. 144) but lived in the poorest conditions. Thus the Gini coefficient applied to property ownership of the citizens only does not allow a direct comparison between ancient and modern societies in terms of overall distribution of wealth.
8. IG IX.2 234 (= *I. ThessEnipeus* 61–63, no. 50, ll. 1–4); the new citizens were probably *penestai* (unfree population tilling the land for their Thessalian masters), as proposed by *Bull. ép.* 2013, no. 227, rather than soldiers having fought in the Macedonian army, as suggested by Oetjen 2010.
9. Mendoni 1994.
10. For these estimates and the following ones, see Hodkinson 2000, 382–85.
11. Demosthenes *Against Leptines* 20.115; see Plutarch *Aristides* 27.1, who adopts the figure of 100 *plethra* only, simplifying the data at his disposal. The reality of the gift has been disputed and it has been suggested that the decree on which Demosthenes based his argument was a characteristic forgery of the fourth century (on the passage, see the discussion in Kremmydas 2012, 385–87). The Alkibiades who is the author of the decree establishing the donation cannot be the famous Alkibiades of the end of the fifth century. Given the chronology, it must be the grandfather of his famous namesake.
12. Langdon and Watrous 1977, 175.
13. Plato *Alcibiades I* 123c.
14. Lysias *On the Property of Aristophanes* 19.29. The trial took place in 387 BCE. Nikophemos and his son Aristophanes were sentenced to death after the failure of an expedition to help King Evagoras of Salamis in 390. Prosopographic references on Alkibiades, Aristophanes, and Phainippos in Jones 2004, 71.
15. On the deme of Kytheros, see Lohmann 2004a.
16. On the deme of Erchia, its location, and the main characters who originated from them, see Lohmann 2004b; on its economy and cultic activity (which is linked to its economy), see also Mikalson 1998, 127–28.
17. Jardé 1925, 48, 78, 121 and 157; Finley 1981, 64, depending on the contour of the land.
18. De Ste. Croix 1966.
19. The warning is that of Hatzopoulos 1988, 49, n. 3; see 49–54 on the size of properties in Classical and Hellenistic Greece. For the impact of de Ste. Croix's figure, see the author's previously cited regarding the distribution of property in Attika, along with Langdon 1977, 175, n. 2.
20. See Harrison 1968–1971, vol. 2, 236–38, and Todd 1993, 120 and 361 (legal aspects); Christ 1990 (social context).
21. Christ 1990.
22. On grain production in Attika, see chapter 14.

23. For the productivity of the vineyards, see Tchernia 1986, appendix VII, 359–60.
24. Ps.-Demosthenes 34.6 (*Against Phormio*) and 35.18 (*Against Lacritus*), with Amemiya 2007, 34.
25. See also Plutarch *Cimon* 10.1–2.
26. Holleaux 1897, 41–44 [= 1938, 112–16].
27. See chapter 5, 136–37.
28. Finley 1981, 62–67; see also Hanson 1998, 169 and n. 83.
29. Davies 1977, 113.
30. Diodorus 18.18.1–6. Hansen 2006a, 38–43: the precise number of those who left for Thrace cannot be determined, but it may have been several thousand (perhaps more than 10,000, according to M. H. Hansen, who nonetheless grants that the real figure remains unknown).
31. Habicht 2006, 59, on the poll tax under Phokion, and 71, under Demetrios of Phaleron.
32. See Steinhauer 2000b, 140–42.
33. *IG* IX.2 517, esp. ll. 8–9 and 30 for the situation of the territory, with Helly 1984, 230, and *Bull. ép.* 2013, no. 227.
34. Hatzopoulos 1988, esp. 29–54. On this donation and another similar one in the same region under Kassandros, see chapter 4, 112–15.
35. See chapter 4, 112, and n. 67.
36. *RC* 12.
37. For new proposals regarding the history of Alexandria Troas, see Bresson 2007b.
38. See chapter 4, 112, and n. 69.
39. Strabo 13.1.5 on the geography of the region.
40. Adam-Veleni et al. 2003.
41. On the farm of Komboloi, Adam-Veleni et al. 2003, 63–70.
42. On the farm of Tria Platania, Adam-Veleni et al. 2003, 56–60.
43. Adam-Veleni et al. 2003, 101–7.
44. See also chapter 4 for the lands *en dōreai*.
45. Adam-Veleni et al. 2003, 252–58, no. 417–24.
46. Touratsoglou 2010, 102–3 and maps: 15 hoards of gold staters and 16 hoards of Alexander tetradrachms for the period 325–280 BCE in Macedon.
47. Kallet-Marx 1996, 62.
48. See chapter 8, 212 and 214.
49. Eleusis: *GHI* 58. Delphi: Rousset 2002, 183–92.
50. For a general presentation of these leases, see Osborne 1987, 37–44, and 1988; Brunet et al. 1998. Pernin 2014 was not available when the final version of this chapter was completed.
51. Athens: see previous note; Amos leases: *I.Pérée* 49–51 and *I.Peraia* 352–54 with *SEG* 52 1029–30 and 53 1189–90, with Salviat 1993 for an analysis of the vineyards leases.
52. For these figures, see Pernin 2004, who estimates the surface of the land corresponding to the lease at 1,451 drachms to 50 hectares.
53. Foxhall 2006, 250–54, on fragmentation into parcels.
54. Mieza: Lilimbaki-Akamati and Stephani 2003; see *Bull. ép.* 2006, no. 252.
55. For Athens, see earlier. For Macedon, see chapter 4, 112–115. For Chalkidike and Amphipolis, see the bills of sale published by M. Hatzopoulos, in 1988 and 1991,

respectively. These bills of sale date from the period immediately preceding the Macedonian conquest (348 BCE) in the case of Olynthos, and shortly before and shortly after the Macedonian conquest (357 BCE) in the case of Amphipolis (ten documents out of twelve, the two other documents dating from the third century). Circumstances may have played a role in the practice of displaying these documents on stone, but certainly not in the purchase and sale of real estate, which was very common.

56. Despite Hodkinson 2000, 90–94. It is not possible to debate this question in detail here.

57. Burford Cooper 1977, 168–70, provides information that shows to what extent the uncertainty of our sources does not allow us to draw reliable conclusions.

58. For these exceptions, Foxhall 1989, 33–34, and Vérilhac and Vial 1998, 186.

59. Aristotle *Politics* 2.6.11; Plutarch *Agis* 7.3–4. In a forthcoming study I will show that the question of property held by women in Sparta can be answered only in the framework of a system of parallel descent—that is, one in which girls inherited essentially from their mothers and sons from their fathers.

60. Code of Gortyn IV, ll. 23–51; see Ephorus *FGrHist* 70 F149, ap. Strabo 10.4.20, for the rule of two-thirds versus one-third in Crete in general.

61. Habicht 1976, with van Bremen 1983 and 1996, 237–72.

62. *IG* XII.5 872, with the commentaries of Étienne 1990, 51–83, and van Bremen 1996, 263–66.

63. See the dossier commented on by Schaps 1979, 48–60.

64. Plutarch *Pericles* 16.5.

65. Plutarch *On the Education of Children, Moralia* 10d.

66. Osborne 1983 has maintained that for Athens the habitat was grouped into villages that served as administrative centers for the demes. Lohmann 1992 and 1993 on the contrary maintained that the habitat was scattered. Langdon 1991 argues for a mixed habitat. Survey of the question in Whitley 2001, 377–82.

67. Jones 2004, 34–47.

68. Andreou 1994; Nevett 2005.

69. Diodorus 20.83.4, with Bresson 2010b.

70. See Debord in *HTC*, 11–19, and Brun et al., ibid. 23–75.

71. Kolb and Thomsen 2004.

72. Estimates respectively of Price 2011, 22–23 (low count), and Thonemann 2009b, 233 (high count).

73. Morris and Papadopoulos 2005, 155.

74. Morris and Papadopoulos 2005.

75. On these aspects, see the chapter that Osborne 1987 has devoted to the occupation of the land ("A Settled Country," 53–74).

76. Chandezon 2003, 400, n. 4.

77. Brun 2003, 63–71.

78. See an Egyptian document from the second century CE (*P.Oxy.* 14.1673), quoted by Brun 2003, 71.

79. See earlier, chapter 2. On Greek agriculture's management of climatic risks, see above all Gallant 1991, particularly 34–59 and 113–42.

80. See chapters 2 and 15.

81. For similar attitudes in modern Greek peasantry, see Halstead 2014, 210–11.

82. Halstead and Jones 1989.

83. Krasilnikoff 2002. On the question of drainage, see later, 165–66.
84. On the question of water in ancient Greece, Argoud 1987; Wilson 2008a, esp. 285–90, on wells and cisterns.
85. Brunet 1999.
86. Krasilnikoff 2002, whose conclusions we adopt here.
87. Ps.-Aristotle *Economics* 2.2.17, accumulation and sale of old grain in Selymbria (see chapter 14, 395).
88. See the case of Selymbria mentioned in the preceding note.
89. Langdon 1976, 79–86, on the sites all over Greece where *Zeus Ombrios* or *Zeus Hyetios* were worshiped; *TCam* 154, on the altar of Kamiros (Hellenistic period).
90. On the selling of children into slavery in the ancient Mesopotamian world and on Solon, see earlier, chapter 4, 106.
91. See chapters 13 and 14 on loans taken out from other cities and to the possibilities of exporting a product in order to be able to buy grain.
92. See chapter 5, 122.
93. See chapter 7, 195–98.
94. See the references quoted in chapter 5, 120.
95. *P.Cairo.Zen.* 59033, 257 BCE (quoted by Salviat 1990, 460). Zenon is not exceptional on this subject; it seems so only because of the preservation of papyri in Egypt. We would see the same thing if we had similar documentation on Chalkidike or on the Troad.
96. For these figures and the problem of improving livestock, see Leguilloux 2000, 77–78, with figs. 15–17, pp. 94–95.
97. See earlier, chapter 4.
98. *SEG* 45 1508, ll. 4–9.
99. Tr. E. C. Marchant.
100. Delos: Brunet 1999.
101. Keos: Doukellis 1998, with rich illustrative material and aerial view p. 321.
102. Kolb and Thomsen 2004: 8–12.
103. *IJG* vol. 1,143–57, no. IX; *IG* XII.9 191. On this document see Knœpfler 2001b, as well as that of Chatelain 2001; see *SEG* 51 1109. On questions of drainage in general, see Traina 1988, who emphasizes that the Greeks were not in principle against marshes, and the detailed study by Fantasia 1999.
104. Knœpfler 2001b, 49.
105. See the hypothesis of Knœpfler 2001b, 60 and 67. The inscription from Kassandreia was published by Vokotopoulou 1997; see *Bull. ép.* 1998, no. 269, and *SEG* 47 940 (and see earlier, chapter 4, n. 91).
106. *HTC*, 157–59, no. 47.
107. This point is strongly emphasized by Knœpfler 2001b, 53 and 73; see also Fantasia 1999, 76–77.
108. Theophrastus *On Plant Physiology* 5.14.2 refers to a climate change caused by humans: the drying up of the marshes of Larisa in Thessaly led to a cooler climate (see the allusion of Strabo 9.5.19 to the floods of the Peneios River before the people of Larisa decided to build levees to check them). He also mentions (ibid., 5.14.5) the climate changes that occurred after the land was cleared and dried out in Philippoi, but in less explicit terms (see Lespez and Tirologos 2004).

109. Orrieux 1983, 88–92.

110. *P.Cairo.Zen* 59195, see Orrieux 1983, 91, and 1985, 207; Chandezon 2004, 489.

111. Rathbone 1991.

112. For Weber, see earlier, chapter 1, 10–1; see Finley 1973, 113–14.

113. The point is well made by Hanson 1995, 127–77.

114. See Lhôte 2006 and Eidinow 2007.

115. See also Eidinow 2007, 96, no. 4.

116. The parallel between Demeter and Dionysos makes sense, and here these are not top-onyms. In Athens a lease from the deme of Aixone from the second half of the fourth century (*IG* II² 2492, ll. 18–20) similarly opposes *Dēmētrios karpos*, cereals, to *xulinos karpos*, the fruit-tree harvest.

117. See Allen 2004 on the take-off of English agriculture, and particularly 98 on the productivity of agricultural work.

118. On lack of manure in modern Greek agriculture in the cases of the islands of Amorgos and Karpathos, Halstead and Jones 1989, 43.

119. On the various and complex strategies of manuring used by modern Greek peasants, see Halstead 2014, 212–30. The tendency was to favor manure for gardens and cash-crops, grain fields receiving far less.

120. Ruschenbusch 1988, 150.

121. Amouretti 1986, 62–63.

122. These data are analyzed in detail by Halstead 1987.

123. *IG* II² 2493, ll. 6–10. Other examples in Osborne 1987, 42–43. See Amouretti 1986, 52–56, on legumes in ancient Greece and the adjustments made to biennial crop rotation. See also Brun 1996, 95–97, on the use of *cytisus* ("common broom") as fodder, particularly in the Kyklades, where pastures were notoriously insufficient. Crop rotation was clearly known to traditional modern Greek peasants even before the transformations introduced after World War I; see Halstead 2014, 201–6.

124. See Halstead 2014, 32–33, 200, 236, 240.

125. Harrow: Amouretti 1986, 107–8 (see earlier); plows, chiefly on the plains of the Po Valley: Forni 2006; harvester: Zelener 2006, 312; scythe and harvester: Shaw 2013, 93–149, who insists on the specific social and ecological conditions for the innovation and its lack of diffusion.

126. On the profitability of Phainippos's estate (the cash revenue certainly being well above the running cost of the estate), see Osborne 1991.

127. Pritchett and Pippin 1956, 199–203, on wine prices in Athens in the fifth and fourth centuries.

128. Johnston 1991 [1996] and Lawall 2000.

129. *P.Cairo.Zen.* 59012, ll. 17–24, with Salviat's commentary1986, 155–56 and 180–81, fundamental for the question of wine prices outside Athens. Pritchett and Pippin 1956, 202–3, on the basis of figures that were unfortunately mutilated in the inscriptions of the Hermokopids, shows that the wines from Thasos and Chios could not have been sold for less than 9 to 11 drachms, and the real figures may have been higher. These amounts are compatible with the indications on the Pelousion papyrus (on which see also Bresson 2012c).

130. See chapter 15, 423–24.

131. Wallace 1986, 88.

132. *ID* 440, ll. 60–68.

133. For freight costs, see the estimates in chapter 3, 80, and chapter 13, 364–68.

134. See chapter 5, 125.

135. *IG* I³ 426, ll. 43–50; see Salviat 1986, 151–52.

136. *IG* I³ 426, ll. 144–50; see Salviat 1986, ibid.

137. See Brunet 2007, although with slightly different conclusions.

138. *Milet* I.3 (*Delphinion*) 149, ll. 39–47. The financial clauses in the document have been commented upon by Migeotte 2001a (but whose analysis on the wine from Euromos cannot be accepted).

139. See the index to *I.Mylasa*.

140. Peschlow-Bindokat 1996, 5 (map of the network, including a road coming from the east and leading to Ioniapolis) and 43–48 (paved roads).

141. On these questions, see detail in chapter 8.

CHAPTER VII: NONAGRICULTURAL PRODUCTION, CAPITAL, AND INNOVATION

1. Braudel 1981, 214–19.

2. Jameson et al. 1994, 311.

3. Gallant 1985.

4. For the salt marshes at Tuzla (Hamaxitos), in the Troad, 1,558 tons annually according to Cuinet 1890–1894, vol. 3, 708–9. The salt marshes of the vilayet of Sivas (salt springs, as at Hamaxitos-Tuzla) produced 8,500 tons per year (Cuinet, vol. 1, 632–33), those of the Gulf of Mandalya (in the sector of the Gulf of Bargylia in the mouth of the Sarı Çay) 2,000 tons per year (Cuinet, vol. 3, 650 and 669). See later on salt marshes in general.

5. Plutarch *Table Talk* 5.4 = *Moralia* 685d, see Davies 2001, 24–25.

6. Bintliff 1977, 117–22, 216–18, and 240–44; Bekker-Nielsen 2005a, with the various essays collected in the volume.

7. See particularly Matthew 13.47. On the milieu of Galilean fishermen, which is that of Jesus, see Hanson 1997.

8. Jameson et al. 1994, 311–16.

9. Brun 1996, 131–36.

10. Ehrenberg 1962, 130–32.

11. Museum of Cefalù, Italiote krater from the fourth century, see Jameson et al., 312.

12. Aristotle *History of Animals* 6.17 571a and 8.13 598a–b, for the habits and migrations of tuna, and also in addition, on fishing, Pliny 9.19–20 [49–53] (whose source was certainly Aristotle on many points). On tuna fishing in general, see García Vargas and Florido del Corral 2010 and Lytle 2012a, 24–36. For the case of Byzantion, see details in Dumont 1976–77. See also Étienne and Mayet 2002, 24–35.

13. Athenaeus 3 116b, citing Euthydemus of Athens (early to mid-Hellenistic period, see Dalby 2003, 136).

14. Athenaeus 6 297e, citing Antigonus of Karystos (third century BCE), with remarks by Jameson et al., 314, n. 7.

15. Brun 1996, 133.

16. See earlier, the case of the Kerkyrians' miraculous fishing. Lookout towers: Bintliff 1977, 240, and Gallant 1985, pl. 14 (the modern system).
17. Vreeken 1953, 71–72.
18. Jameson et al. 1994, 314.
19. For fishing at Byzantion and Kyzikos, see Schlosser 2008.
20. Athenaeus 3 116c, citing Euthydemus.
21. On Iasos, see Hicks 1887 and Delrieux 2008. On the Little Sea, see later, 180 and 183.
22. On the *dalyan* (fish dam) of Kaunos, see Robert 1984, 521–25.
23. See Dumont 1976–77, 107–9, with the details of ancient sources.
24. Leguilloux 2000, 72–73.
25. Dumont 1976–77, 112–13.
26. See Traina 1988 for the ancient world's attitude toward marshes, which was not at all hostile, and Fantasia 1999 for the details of the Greek sources.
27. *I.Erythrai* 17, with the editors' detailed commentary on the inscription.
28. *SEG* 22 508, A l. 36.
29. Lhôte 2006, 238, no. 109, beginning of the fourth century BCE.
30. On a possible fish-smoking plant at Elizavetovskoie/Elizavetovka, see Højte 2005, 142 (on the site of Elizavetovskoie at the mouth of the Don, see the presentation in Bresson 2002b).
31. Dumont 1976–77, 110, for the details of the techniques used. Garum, a sauce based on fish entrails, seems to have been more a taste of the Roman period. On salt in the Greek world in general, see now the detailed study of Carusi 2008.
32. On salted foods and garum in Greek sources, see Counillon and Étienne 1997 and Étienne and Mayet 2002, 37–53.
33. Carusi 2008, 149–53.
34. On the production of salt in Greece and Rome, which was frequently a state monopoly, see now Carusi 2008, 189–235, and in addition Étienne 2002, 15–23; for the Seleukid monopoly in particular, Aperghis 2004, 154–56, on the basis of documents from Judea and Mesopotamia. For Lysimachos's attempt to take control of the salt production of Hamaxitos, see Phylarchus *FGrHist* 81 F65 (*apud* Ath. 3.3 73d), with Bresson 2007b (and see later for Hamaxitos).
35. See Bresson 2007b.
36. See earlier and n. 4.
37. See *I.Priene*² 67, ll. 112–15, with the conflict between the city of Priene and the Roman *publicani* about which saltpans had been the property of the former kings (whose property was inherited by Rome) and which were the property of Athena Polias and the city of Priene; detailed comment in Carusi 2008, 81–83, 192–95, and 236–37, and Thonemann 2011, 227–32, with Byzantine and Ottoman testimonies for the exploitation of the lower Maeander valley saltpans, and estimates on the amount produced with a potentially considerable revenue of 70–90,000 *denarii*, or Attic drachms.
38. See later 183 and n. 57.
39. Pliny 31.45 [99]. See Robert 1984, 525; *I.Kaunos* 179, no. 35 B, l. 8.
40. The salt marshes of Argolis, which all the evidence proves already existed in antiquity and on which there is abundant documentation from the medieval and modern periods, see Jameson et al. 1994, 310–11, and Carusi 2008, 59–62.

41. Lambert 1997 (new edition of Ferguson 1938) = *GHI* 37, document of the Salaminians, stele from 363/2 BCE, ll. 17, 38, 54. On salt production of Attika in general, see Carusi 2008, 49–56.

42. *IG* IV².1 76 (with Ager, *Arbitrations*, 381–85, no. 138, and Carusi 2005 for the combined text of the various versions of the arbitration between the two cities), ll. 29–32. See also Carusi 2008, 59–61. On Troizen's revenues from tuna fishing see later, 183.

43. On fishing rights, Dumont 1977.

44. Purpura 2008 (mainly on the Roman world); Lytle 2012a (mainly on the Greek world), with Lytle 2012b.

45. Sea in common access to all: *Digest* 1.8.2.1; 47.10.13.7; fishing rights everywhere: *Digest* 1.8.5; 41.1.1–3; definition of the shore as the extreme point reached by the sea: *Digest* 50.16.96. Full references in Lytle 2012a, 3–4.

46. O'Connell 1982–84, vol. 1, 1–20, and Anand 1983, 72–123, and on the context of rivalries between the Portuguese, Dutch, English, French and other European powers of the time.

47. Plato *Laws* 822d–824c.

48. Plato *Laws* 823e–824a.

49. On leases and loans in a local framework, see chapters 6, 153; 9, 227; 10, 279.

50. In Alciphron's *Letters of Fishermen* (1.2), a slave fisherman working for an Athenian master embarks on a Rhodian ship and, as a runaway slave, will not come back to Athens.

51. From the early modern to the contemporary period, the question of fishing rights in coastal waters has been endlessly disputed. Over time, the zone where exclusive fishing rights have been guaranteed to (or claimed by) the littoral states has grown considerably: from the traditional three-mile zone, representing the approximate range of guns at the time, to 200 miles and more today see Anand 1983, 145–49, 182–84, and 215–16. It should be noticed that even at the time when "Britannia ruled the waves" and when the principle of the "freedom of the seas" was at the peak of its success, an exclusive fishing right was still recognized within the three-mile limit of the territorial waters (O'Connell 1982–1984, vol. 1, 19–20). On the techniques of measurement, O'Connell 1982–84, vol. 2, 635–57.

52. Xenophon *Poroi* 1.3.

53. Diogenes Laertius 1.27 and 31 (for a different conclusion, Lytle 2012a, 7).

54. *Digest* 1.8.4. As noted by Lytle 2012a, 4 n. 7, the law prevailed in favor of the fishermen of Formiae and Capena even (probably) against the powerful local owners of villas. But this is not international law and the same rule could have prevailed within any Greek city-state in the Classical or Hellenistic period.

55. See the preliminary discussion in Bekker-Nielsen 2010, 194–97.

56. *IG* IV².1 76, ll. 8 and 12–13, with Ager, *Arbitrations*, 381–85, no. 138, and Carusi 2005 for the combined text, ll. 39 and 43–44; detailed comment of the passage and translation in Lytle 2012a, 28–30.

57. *SEG* 57 1085 (*I.Iasos* 24 + 30 = *GHI* 90A), ll. 5–6; for the other elements of the dossier of Gorgos and Minnion, see Ephippus of Olynthos *FGrHist* 126 F5 (see 2B Komm. p. 439) ap. Ath. 12 537e–538b; *IG* XII.6 17 = *GHI* 90B; *I.Iasos* T 51 and 52. For the topography and economic role of the "Little Sea," see Delrieux 2001 and 2008, and Bresson 2010a, 450–51. Lytle 2012a, 17–19, discusses in detail the question of the revenues drawn by the people of Iasos from the Little Sea. He considers that the Iasians

might have been also interested in the exploitation of the coastal wetland of this inland gulf (for the suggestion that the Iasians could also exploit saltpans in the marshy zones of the Little Sea, see Pierrobon Benoit 2013), and also on the exploitation of transit fees exacted from the cities of the hinterland (which however are not mentioned by Strabo).

58. Chaniotis 1996, 383–93, no. 64 (*Syll.*[3] 524), A ll. 18–19.

59. *Syll.*[3] 685 = Ager, *Arbitrations*, 431–46, no. 158 = Camia 2009, 112–32, no. 10 (on this text, see already the literature specific to frontiers and cattle-raising issues in chapter 5, n. 105). See Viviers 1999, 222–26, on the identification of Leuke (today Koufonissi), its economic importance, and its very likely identity with one of the islands exploited by the Stalitai. The settlement imposed by Praisos on Stalai referred to the 10 percent rates (*dekata*) of harbor duties and of the tax on purple shell and fish levied in these islands (earlier, n. 58, ll. 4–9). The Stalitai were able to keep half of the product of these taxes. On the conflict between Hierapytna and Itanos, see earlier, chapter 5, 140–41.

60. *Syll.*[3] 1000, respectively, ll. 10–11 and 18, 15, 21, with Vreeken's commentary 1953, respectively, 70–73, 66–68 and 83–84.

61. The *modern* concept of "territorial waters" did not exist in antiquity. But, *pace* Migeotte 2014, 132–33, the current analysis, with the analysis of the text of Plato, now made explicit, fully vindicates the core of the argument that was developed in the original edition (Bresson 2007–2008, vol. 1, 190).

62. Lhôte 2006, 170–80, no. 83.

63. The status of fishermen: see for example the letters of fishermen from Alciphron and the milieu of Galilean fishermen (see n. 7).

64. On *opsophagia* and its negative connotations, see Davidson 2011, 3–35 and 144–47.

65. See now the new edition and full comment by Lytle 2010, which replaces Salviat and Vatin 1971, 100–105.

66. Lytle 2013a, who also shows convincingly that the Delian tax was not a right to fish exploitation (catching fish?) but a tax on fish sales. See also Lytle 2012b on the tax on fish at Ephesos in the Imperial period, but with Classical and Hellenistic parallels.

67. Athenaeus 1 27e, citing Hermippus (fifth century BCE), *PCG* fr. 63.

68. Athenaeus 3 116f–117b, citing Archestratus (fourth century BCE), fr. 39 Olson-Sens.

69. Koehler 1981; Zimmerman Munn 2003; Carlson 2003, 589, on Punic preservation of meat.

70. On the fisheries of the Black Sea, see Stolba 2005 (fish, particularly sturgeon, as a monetary type) and Højte 2005 (archaeological aspects).

71. On Sinope's productions, see Doonan 2004, 69–117; on its trade network Barat 2009.

72. Lund and Gabrielsen 2005.

73. Carlson 2003, 589–90. One must be skeptical regarding the hypothesis that here we are dealing with an amphora full of "meat for the crew," which remains an ad hoc explanation, given in addition that probably only a rather small part of the cargo was recovered.

74. See also Wilkins 2005 for an analysis of literary sources.

75. Bats 1988.

76. Bekker-Nielsen 2002 and 2005b.

77. Zenobius 1.84. On the consumption of fish, see also for Athens Ehrenberg 1962, 130–32, and in general Garnsey 1999, 116–18.

78. Acton 2014 was not available when the final version of this chapter was completed.

79. Tr. P. Shorey in Hamilton and Cairns 1971, 616.

80. On this text and on division of labor, see earlier, chapter 4, 108.

81. Harris 2002a. For an illustration of artisanal scenes in ceramics (especially Attic), see Villanueva-Puig 1992, 76–81.

82. Feyel 2006, 31–37, for the columns of the Erechtheion in Athens (*IG* I^3 474–79, last decade of the fifth century BCE, and *IG* I^2 1654, beginning of the fourth century).

83. Feyel 1998 (for Eleusis) and 2006, 442–55.

84. Harris 2002a, 70–71.

85. Steinhauer 2001a, 97–99, workshops near Vathy Pighadi.

86. Steinhauer 2001a, ibid.

87. For Thasos, see Picon and Garlan 1986 and Garlan 2000, 39, fig. 17, map of the amphora workshops in Thasos (sixteen of which are certainly identified as such; four others are possible workshops): all are close to the coast, generally at a distance less than two kilometers, or directly on the coast.

88. See earlier, chapter 2, 45.

89. Huguenot 2012 and Lentini 2012; Sanidas 2013, 222–27 and 232–39.

90. Monaco 2012 and Stissi 2012.

91. Monaco 2012.

92. Bentz et al. 2013.

93. Meirano 2012.

94. Pichot 2012. The zone developed even more in the Imperial period.

95. See later, 195, on this point.

96. On these operations, see also chapter 13, 354–55.

97. Cahill 2002, 169–79 and 250–52.

98. Rosivach 1989. Contra Labarre 1998, which is the basic study on this question; see the catalogue of sources he draws up, pp. 809–13.

99. On this effect of substitution, see the following. On women's work in Athens, Brock 1994.

100. On the notion of start-up capital (*aphormē*) and also on this anecdote, see chapter 10, 280.

101. Rosivach 1989.

102. On animal husbandry and its constraints, see chapter 5, 133–41.

103. Purchase of tunics: Plutarch *Tranquility of Mind* 470 f (see Bresson 2000, 180). Importation of crates of cloaks: Aeneas Tacticus *Poliorcetics* 29.4–7. See also infra for Megarian products, which were ready-made clothes.

104. See earlier and chapter 3, 88.

105. Xenophon *Memorabilia* 2.7.6. See earlier Aristophanes's *Acharnians* 519, with Legon 1981, 280–82, and Smith 2006, 78.

106. Salmon 1984, 87–89.

107. Labarre and Le Dinahet 1996; Arnaoutoglou 2011.

108. On the question of transportation costs, see details in chapter 3, 79–81.

109. On the perfume industry, see Reger 2005 and 2010.

110. See chapter 6, 151–52.

111. On the technological aspects of machines and engineering in the ancient world (Greece and Rome), see the survey provided by Wilson 2008b.

112. Aristotle *History of Animals* 5.19 551b; Pliny 11.26 [76].

113. On these points and on the reputation of textiles from Kos, see Labarre and Le Dinahet 1996, 50–52.

114. On flour milling and the evolution of its technology, see Moritz 1958 and Curtis 2008, 374–76. See in addition Takaoğlu 2008 for the Troad, which provides a good regional case of the transition from hopper-rubber to rotary mill in the Hellenistic period). For the case of Delos in the Hellenistic period, see Chamonard 1922, 214–15, with fig. 108–9, p. 229; Deonna 1938, 123–35, on the grinders (with figs. 362–97, pls. XLVIII–LII), particularly 131–35 on rotary mills; Curtis 2008, 375, for seemingly the first attempt to develop a grain rotary mill based on the olive-crusher *trapetum*.

115. Frankel 2003.

116. See Morel 2001 for a possible Punic origin, but Jaccottey et al. 2013, on the basis of systematic database, argue convincingly in favor of an origin in today's Catalonia and the Iberian culture context.

117. In the case of Olynthos, see the discussion in Cahill 2002, 246–47 on the *trapetum*, and 45–61 on the provisional reoccupation of one part of the city (on the northwest) pending the foundation of Kassandreia.

118. Sanidas 2013, 206.

119. Samuel 2006, 63–64, with several illustrations for the use of the technology of the saddle quern in Egypt.

120. Halstead 2014, 182–83.

121. Ersoy 2003 and Ersoy et al. 2004. On wine press technology and the spread of the innovation, see Brun 1993 and this author's other references, chapter 5, n. 21.

122. Russo 2004, 96–98.

123. See Gow and Page 1968, vol. 2, 18–20, on Antipater of Thessalonike and "the difficulty, indeed the impossibility, of distributing with certainty the epigrams ascribed to Antipater between the Sidonian and the Thessalonician namesake." See also the comment on the epigram, ibid. 84–85.

124. Mills of Kabeira, Roos 1996; hydraulic energy in general, Wikander 2008.

CHAPTER VIII: THE LOGIC OF GROWTH

1. Ovid *Metamorphoses* 8.620–724.

2. Aristophanes *Acharnians* 33–36.

3. For Athens, this particular rural sociability has been recently studied by Schmitz 2004, who shows, however, the transformations that occurred in the fourth century. See in general Gallant 1991, 143–69.

4. Wagner-Hasel 2004, 172–73, and 2011, 26–31. It is worth noticing that Bücher's father managed a small enterprise that produced and sold brushes in northern Germany, and through intermediaries, even in Spain and South America (Wagner-Hasel 2004, 26–28).

5. Attitude of Pericles: Plutarch *Pericles* 16.4.

6. Pearson 1957, 331.

7. Lohmann 1992 and 1993.

8. Jones et al. 1973, 414–45.

9. See chapter 6, 149–50.
10. Jones 1978, 56–64; Bertrand 1992.
11. Cahill 2002, 223–81, for a detailed archaeological analysis, and 281–88, for historical conclusions, with the analysis of Plutarch *Pericles* 16.3–5 and Ps.-Aristotle *Economics* 1.6.2–3 on the various management strategies that could be followed, the Attic one (corresponding frequently to smaller estates) consisting in buying the product of the sales immediately so that no deposit was kept idle in store, and the Lakonian and Persian ones, which apparently corresponded to strategy of longer-term storage.
12. Ober 2010.
13. See chapter 3, 85–88.
14. Berggren and Jones 2000, 31–40.
15. Saller 2005.
16. De Vries and van der Woude 1997, 665–87; see 618–19 and 627 on the curve of the development of real salaries and 707 on the curve of this development compared with England in terms of purchasing power.
17. Morris 2004, 720–23, and 2005, 108.
18. See De Vries and van der Woude 1997.
19. Ober 2010, 251.
20. Agricultural production: see chapter 6, 170–71. Mines and metallurgy: Domergue and Bordes 2006.
21. For the role of the exogenous shocks, see Jongman 2014.
22. Brun 2006, 122–23. On innovation, see Zelener 2006, Greene 2000 and his qualifications in 2008a and 2008b, and Wilson 2002.
23. On the introduction of the steam engine and its constraints, see earlier, chapter 3, 75–78.
24. See Shaw 2013, 96, on the contradictions of the orthodox model.
25. Brun 2005, 164–65, and 2006, 122–23.
26. See also Bresson 2006e, 74–75.
27. Wilson 2002 is fundamental on the matter.
28. On the application of hydraulic force to a saw in Hierapolis in Phrygia in the third century CE, see Ritti et al. 2007, who also mention the other sites where installations of the same kind have been found.
29. Ausonius *Mosella* vv. 361–64, with a translation of vv. 363–64: *stridensque trahens per levia marmora serras / audit perpetuos ripa ex utraque tumultus*; see the commentary by Green 1991, 501–2 (and also White 1984, 56).
30. Wilson 2002, 15–17.
31. Mayer 2012.
32. Brown 2012, 190–1 for the case of Ausonius, and 210–11 and 216–18 for that of Paulinus of Nola.
33. Bresson 2005a, 51 and 63 on the financial causes.
34. Brun 2006, 125–26.
35. Plutarch *Pericles* 12.5 (and see also later the analysis of this case).
36. Salmon 1999 for the case of Athens.
37. De Vries and van der Woude 1997, 520–21, with the case of the growth (and shrinking) of Delft.
38. Brun 2006, 123–24.

39. Hennig 1994.

40. Danzig 2000; Morrison 2013 (especially p. 194); Gallagher 2013.

41. Pirenne-Delforge 1994, 446–50, on Aphrodite and the constellation of deities around her, with Pirenne-Delforge 1991 on Peitho; for the specific link with the agora, see Sokolowski 1964 and (for Macedon) Archibald 2012, 115.

42. Aristotle *Politics* 1.4.7–8.

43. *IG* I³ 426, *c* ll. 43–50, among Adeimantos's properties, a wine-producing farm in Thasos with its manager (see earlier, chapter 6, 172–73); properties in Thasos (*l*l. 144) and Eretria (*n* l. 162) are also mentioned in a context that cannot be restored.

44. *IG* II² 43 = *GHI* 22, ll. 25–46.

45. Polybius 21.42.16–17: after the Seleukid defeat in 189 BCE, the Rhodians ask from Rome the recovery of the properties they had in Seleukid territories and the payment of the debts owed to them in the same territories; 31.4.3: in 164/3 BCE, they "ask the senate to allow those of their citizens who owned property in Lykia and Karia [lost by decision of Rome] to hold possession of it as before" (tr. W. R. Paton, F. W. Walbank, C. Habicht, and S. D. Olson); for a rich Rhodian family probably still holding land in the town of Kys (central Karia) in 52/3 CE, see Cousin and Deschamps 1887, 306–8, no. 1 (tr. Lewis 1974, 84–85, no. 26).

46. For a possible case in Asia Minor in the late Hellenistic period, see *HTC*, 240–41, no. 2.

47. Gauthier 1974 and 1981a; Bresson 2006a on the preference for close kin marriage in the Greek cities, which forms the background of their political system.

48. For Athens, see now Pébarthe 2006, 33–67 on the forms of literate education, and 69–110 on the usage of written documents in social life.

49. Aeschines 1.9–11 (*Against Timarchus*), who refers to an established law regulating schools in Athens (see Pébarthe 2006, 44–45).

50. Millender 2001.

51. Sickinger 1999 (which analyzes the various aspects mentioned here); Pébarthe 2006, 291–343; Missiou 2011, 109–49.

52. On Hellenistic schools, Nilsson 1955, 57–61 on the institution of *paidonomoi* in the Hellenistic period.

53. Miletos: *Syll.*³ 577, foundation of Eudemos, capital 10 talents (see tr. in Austin 2006, 257–60, no. 138, and commentary by Migeotte 2012); Teos: *Syll.*³ 578: foundation of Polythrous, capital 5 talents 4,000 drachms; Delphi, *Syll.*³ 672: foundation of King Attalos II, capital 3 talents. On these school foundations, see Bringmann 2001, 157–59.

54. Mokyr 2009, 30–144, with explicit comparison with the ancient world, p. 57.

55. See fundamentally Russo 2004, especially 171–202 on the Hellenistic scientific method and 231–41 on the decadence of Greek science in a Roman context.

56. For the concept of "competitive critical community" and the emergence of history in the Classical period, see Dewald 2006, 131.

57. On this topic, see fundamentally Ober 2008, although social and political innovation, rather than technological innovation strictly speaking, is the main focus of the book.

58. The parallel with Newcomen's engine is striking (see chapter 3, 77–78).

59. Keyser in press.

60. Deakin 2007.

61. De Vries and van der Woude 1997, 700.

62. Morris 2006.

1. See M. Hatzopoulos, "An Old and New Inscription from Mieza: The Constitution of Extensive Landed Properties in the Central Macedonian Plain and the Question of *laoi* in Hellenistic Macedonia," paper presented at the 13th International Congress of Greek and Latin epigraphy, held at Oxford (6 September 2007): a new unpublished decree from Kyrrhos (between Aigai and Pella, in central Macedon) mentions *laoi* in a context from the beginning of the third century BCE.
2. Aristotle *Politics* 2.2–5, particularly 2.2.4–6, with the radical criticism of the Platonic theses regarding property.
3. See chapter 4, 106–7.
4. On ancient Greek slavery in general, see Westermann 1955, 1–57, and Garlan 1988.
5. Manumission documents have been found all over the Greek world. See the famous cases of Delphi (Hopkins 1978, 133–71, and Mulliez 1992) and Boiotia (Darmezin 1999). For clauses of *paramonē*, see Westermann 1955, 55–56, and Garlan 1988, 78–80.
6. Eidinow 2012.
7. See Robert 1980, 311–18 ("Un jardin du dieu Men en Pisidie": parallel between the situation in ancient Asia Minor and that in present-day Turkey).
8. On the *horophulakes* of Chios, Faraguna 2005b.
9. Faraguna 1997, 2000, 2003, and 2005a.
10. For the management of sacred property in Athens, see Papazarkadas 2011. See also chapter 6, 153.
11. This point has been properly emphasized by Rousset 2002, 192–211.
12. On loans made by sanctuaries, see chapter 10, 279.
13. See Hodkinson 2000, 66–68.
14. Asheri 1969.
15. Fuks 1984, especially 9–39; Gehrke 1985 (systematic analysis); Cartledge 2000, 18–20 (overview).
16. Hübsch 1968; Scholl 1990.
17. *Milet* I.3 (*Delphinion*) 150, ll. 87–99.
18. On Antimenes and slaves, Ps.-Aristotle *Economics* 2.2.34 (with 38 for other financial activity). On Antimenes, see Le Rider 1998 and Müller 2005, 362–64: bearing the title *hēmiolios*, Antimenes was King Alexander's director of finance.
19. See chapter 5, 126–27.
20. Thucydides 7.27.5 (most of them were *cheirotechnai*, employed in "industry" rather than in agriculture; a significant part of them were probably employed in the mines of Laurion; see Xenophon *Poroi* 4.25, for the escape of slaves employed in the mines during the last phase of the Peloponnesian War).
21. Diodorus 34.2.19; Orosius 5.9.4–8.
22. On the slave revolts in Sicily, see detail in Bradley 1989, 46–65, with Bresson 2006b, 71–73, for additional bibliography.
23. Aristotle *Nicomachean Ethics* 1.7.11 and 5.5.12–13, with *Politics* 7.4.7.
24. Aristotle *Politics* 3.5.13.
25. On the *chorēgia* in Athens, see Wilson 2000; on the trierarchy in the same city, Gabrielsen 1994.

26. See Migeotte 1992, 327–45.
27. See Aristotle *Politics* 1.3.16.
28. Gagarin 2005, who shows the diversity of Greek law, while at the same time emphasizing a common tendency in the law of the city states to allow the development of an open and contradictory debate between the parties and the judges.
29. See Todd 1993, 10–13, on the relationship between Roman law and Greek law, as well as on the fate of Roman law in medieval and modern European law after Justinian.
30. See Cohen 1993, especially 312 and n. 58.
31. See Mirhady 2006, especially 11–13, and Sadler 2012, especially 120–23.
32. The theme of the "inferiority" of the concept of property and of Greek law in general with respect to the situation that prevailed in Rome is a commonplace of legal literature. See Pringsheim 1950, particularly 509–11, for legislation on sales; for property, Harrison 1968–1971, vol. 1, 200–205.
33. Demosthenes 43.71 (*Against Macartatus*), see Foxhall 2007, 104–9. The law is cited in the polemical context of the "Legacy of Hagnias," to prove that the defendant had made poor use of the ancestral property. Did this involve a religious vow, left over from the period of Solon, or rather a law with a real application? It is difficult to say.
34. The case of *antidosis* on which we have the most information is that of Demosthenes' *Against Phaenippus*.
35. The formula is often attributed to Accursius, a professor of law at the University of Bologna, in the thirteenth century, although in fact no clear conclusion can be drawn; see detailed discussion in Abramovitch 1961–1962, 250–53.
36. Tr. J. H. Freese.
37. This point was well brought out by Cohen 2006.
38. Tr. J. H. Freese (modified: *kurion* is rendered by "binding" instead of "authoritative").
39. Pringsheim 1950, 34–54, with ref. For Pringsheim, the analogy developed by Plato's Socrates (*Crito* 52d and 54c), who denounces the violations of the contract between him and the city, has allowed one lexicographer to imagine a law of this kind. But how could Socrates, even in analogy, develop such an argument if, as Pringsheim thought, the law never granted a trial in the case of a violation of a consensual obligation? The argument thus counts against Pringsheim's supposed "Greek law of sale."
40. *IGF*, 179–84, no. 135 (though we cannot fully endorse the commentary).
41. The word (in the accusative) *[arab]ōna* had been wrongly restituted on a mortgage stone, see Harris 1992 and Harris and Tuite 2000.
42. Guéraud 1931, 6–8, no. 2.
43. *IG* XII.Suppl. 347 I and II, with Salviat 1986, 147–50 (commentary on "perfect sales" of wines), and full translation Arnaoutoglou 1998, 29, no. 36. On wine sales in general, Tchernia 2000.
44. *Digest* 18.6.1.2: *Si dolium signatum sit ab emptore, Trebatius ait id traditum videri.* C. Trebatius Testa was a legal expert of the first century BCE and a friend of Cicero.
45. Tr. A. D. Godley.
46. On this anecdote and the reference to Anacharsis, see details in the commentary by Kurke 1999, 68–80.
47. Cicero *De officiis* 1.150: "Vulgar we must consider those also who buy from wholesale merchants to retail immediately; for they would get no profits without a great deal of downright lying."

48. See in detail Dixon 295, 241–43.

49. Van Alfen 2010 on this point.

50. Demosthenes 20.9 (*Against Leptines*).

51. Hyperides 3.14 (*Against Athenogenes*).

52. On this point, see later, 250–54.

53. On the law of Erythrai, see later, 239–40, 242, and 250.

54. On the Delian law on wood and charcoal *ID* 509, see chapter 12, 329–32. On the chronology of the law of Andania, see Gawlinski 2012, 3–11. On the law itself, see also later, 240–41.

55. Boston, Museum of Fine Arts, H. L. Pierce Fund inv. 01.8035 (Villanueva-Puig 1992, 80).

56. Aristophanes *Knights* 1245–47.

57. Aristophanes *Knights* 1397–401.

58. Xenophon *Economics* 8.22, for the specialization by product.

59. Akamatis 2012.

60. Moretti et al. 2012.

61. Whitehead 1986; Kakavogianni and Anetakis 2012 for the archaeological side (agoras in the Mesogaia and in the region of Laurion—respectively the southeast and south of Attika).

62. *SEG* 41 75, l. 12 (236/5 BCE).

63. Lambert 1997 = *GHI* 37, decree of 363/2 BCE, ll. 16–18; Kakavogianni and Anetakis 2012, 195–97, for the site of Limani Passa that the authors identify with this agora.

64. See the two dedications found in Lindos, *NSER* 21 (which was made by an *agoranomos*) and *Lindos* 221, both from the second century BCE. We will show elsewhere that the worship of the Zeus Agoraios of these two dedications corresponds to a local cult in Lindos and that here is a question of the agora of Lindos, not that of Rhodes.

65. See Demosthenes 23.39 (*Against Aristocrates*), with Fachard 2013 for the convincing hypothesis that the fortress of Eleutherai, on the northern border of Attika (but in Boiotian territory), was one of these "frontier markets" (*agorai ephoriai*).

66. On religious festivals and fairs, see (although its main concern is the Imperial period) de Ligt 1993, especially 1–55 on the concept of fairs and on the relationship with the agoras and festivals, and Chandezon 2000.

67. *LSCG* 92, l. 32; see Chandezon 2000, 87 and n. 73–74.

68. Habicht 1957, ll. 31–34, with commentary pp. 106–7; see also Debord 1982, 25, and Chandezon 2000, 91, n. 91.

69. On retail sales in the agora, see Dixon 1995, which provides also many illustrations.

70. Boerner 1907; Schwahn 1934, 244–45; Stroud 1998, 61–64.

71. On this law, see chapter 2, n. 88.

72. On the law of Andania, see the text later.

73. On the *agoranomoi*, see Couilloud-Le Dinahet 1988, Migeotte 1997 and 2005, as well as the various contributions in Capdetrey and Hasenohr 2012a, especially Capdetrey and Hasenohr 2012b (general presentation), Oliver 2012 (Athens), Fantasia 2012a (*agoranomoi* and grain provisioning) and 2012b (general survey of the magistrates of the *agorai* of Classical and Hellenistic Greek cities).

74. Tr. H. Rackham.

75. The translation by Arnaoutoglou 1998, 40–41, no. 38, who considers that the final prohibition bears on the sale of wool produced by someone else (a prohibition on selling "from any other source but their own; whoever sells wool from another flock shall be deprived of the wool"), is not appropriate: the law prohibits the sale from anyplace other than the woolen market. On the preparation of wool before sale (washing the sheep before shearing in order to improve the quality of the wool), see Chandezon 2003, 73–74.

76. *Syll.*[3] 736; Deshours 2006, 38–39; Gawlinski 2012, 86–87, ll. 100–103.

77. On the *sitophulakes*, see chapter 12, 314–15 and 331.

78. Athens: *Scholia* on Homer *Il.* 21.203. Miletos: a *nomos agoranomikos* is mentioned in the Milesian decree organizing the school foundation of Eudemos *Milet* I.3 (*Delphinion*) 145, l. 64, from the mid-Hellenistic period.

79. On the boundary stones of the agora, see Camp 2001, 45–46.

80. On this law, also later, 242–50.

81. On the *agoranomion*, see Bresson 2000, 166, and Capdetrey and Hasenohr 2012b, 21–23. Scales in the *agoranomion* of Delos, clearly including a precision scale for precious objects: *IG* XI.2 287B, ll. 142–43 (see Bresson 2000, 229). In Egypt, planned sales of slaves were displayed in front of the *agoranomion* according to the regulation of 265 BCE (*P.Hib.* 29 = *C.Ptol.Sklav.* 6, ll. 9–10, see Bresson 2000, 178). See also the dedication made in the *agoranomoi* office mentioned in the decree from Paros for the *agoranomos* Killos from the beginning of the second century BCE *IG* XII.5 129, ll. 44–45 (see also later for this decree).

82. *P.Oxy.* 8.1124, 26 CE, l. 11.

83. *IG* XII Suppl. 347, II, ll. 10–11 (Salviat 1986, 147–48), and see earlier, n. 43.

84. See later, 253 and n. 145, on the technical aspects of the monitoring.

85. The comic poet Xenarchus (*Porphyra* 7 Kock and Kassel-Austin) imagines a brawl contrived as a pretext for throwing a pail of water on the fish that will providentially cool them. Many other stories show the mistrust with regard to fish merchants.

86. Aristophanes *Frogs* 1386–87.

87. On the frauds committed by drug merchants, see details in Samama 2006, 20.

88. For Athens, see *IG* II[2] 1013, with Bresson 2000, 230–31.

89. For the weights of the Hellenistic cities of the Levant, see Finkielsztejn 2012a and 2012b.

90. Aristotle *Mechanics* 1 849b 34–39.

91. Merriam-Webster's Dictionary defines the steelyard as "a balance in which an object to be weighed is suspended from the shorter arm of a lever and the weight determined by moving a counterpoise along a graduated scale on the longer arm until equilibrium is attained."

92. Deonna 1938, 139–49 and Hasenohr 2012 for Delos; Fritzilas 2012 for Megalopolis and for a survey of the question of *sēkōmata*; Finkielsztejn 2010 for Maresha.

93. Deonna 1938, 167–85. For liquids, Deonna (ibid., 169) suggested (with good likelihood) that in order to prevent fraud and for reasons of convenience (if only for cleaning), a metal container must have been devised and attached to the *sēkōma*.

94. Deonna 1938, 139 and 171–72.

95. Deonna knew of 58, including five large ones with a single measure, the others with the series of cavities for various measures of capacity.

96. Deonna 1938, 175, Ia, no. 5.
97. Deonna 1938, 184–85, IIIb, no. 57.
98. Large scales served to weigh heavy loads. The municipal authority was responsible for it. On the *stathma xulēra*, the specific weights for weighing wood, see the Delian law *ID* 509, ll. 2 and 33–34; on this document and the sales of wood and charcoal, see later chapter 12, 329–32.
99. "Small-scale": *IG* XI.2, 287B, ll. 142–43 (the small scale has been preserved in the *agoranomion*); *ID*, 442B, l. 27 and 455Ba, l. 27 (see Bresson 2000, 217, on the context in which the scales were used).
100. See chapter 10, 271.
101. Standard for tiles in the agora of Athens: Stevens 1950. Standardized tiles: Billot 2000, 204 (short presentation of the question). Calibrated spring balances: Finkielsztejn 2006.
102. Finkielsztejn 2006.
103. Garlan 2004b and 2006 for the case of the amphoras from Akanthos.
104. On amphoras and amphora stamps, Garlan 2000, 167–71, who rightly insists on the absence of institutional link between amphora stamp and capacity of the amphora. But (despite Garlan 2000, 76–82), Finkielsztejn 2006 is right that the city's priority was to standardize the amphora capacity.
105. The passage raises a problem. Like the other translations, the French one in the CUF edition of the *Politics* (see the translation and the notes of volume II.2, and notes pp. 290–91) interprets this passage as alluding to small contracts made in the agora for the mutual satisfaction of citizens. The Greek does not seem to authorize this interpretation: consider particularly the meaning of *schedon*, which seems to allude to the fact that the necessity of importing applies to "almost" all the city-states since none of them was self-sufficient without foreign trade: it is hard to see why the word would be used if only small contracts were concerned, since everyone regarded them as indispensable anyway; and then the Greek does not indicate the necessity "in" all the city-states (as if there was one), but "for" all the city-states (simple dative). The contracts that were made in the agora that are alluded to here include those contracts for large-scale commerce which provided for the city's self-sufficiency.
106. On the novel *Chaereas and Callirhoe*, see later, chapter 12, 306–7.
107. On *sumbolaion* and *sunthēkē*, see Mirhady 2004. On oral and written contracts, see further chapters 10 and 12.
108. On the magistrates of the agora and contracts, see Erdas 2012.
109. *IG* XII.5 129, ll. 16–20 (see earlier, n. 81, for this decree).
110. *I.Magnesia* 239a.
111. Rochefort 1961, 177–81, with Schneider and Schneider 1976, 209–10. A similar system could be observed at Kolindros in Macedon in the early twentieth century (see Halstead 2014, 16), and this must have been common practice in many other places in the ancient and in the modern world.
112. *Milet* VI.2, 935; Hellmann, *Inscriptions architecturales*, 111–12, no. 47.
113. *Sardis* VII.1, no. 18. On the subject of labor conflicts, see Buckler 1923, which remains fundamental.
114. Andocides *Against Alcibiades* 4.17 (see Plutarch *Alcibiades* 16.4). On craftsmen's contracts, Feyel 2006, 485–509.

115. Brélaz 2005, 174–82, for the Imperial period.

116. Depending on the Gospel, the scene has different emphases. In Matthew (21:12–17), Jesus drives out sellers and buyers before overturning tables and chairs. In Mark (11:15–19), Jesus prevents people from bringing objects into the temple. In Luke (19: 45–48), Jesus limits himself to driving out the sellers. In John (2:13–22), the detail of the whip adds to the realism. On the disciplinary role of the *agoranomos*, see Roubineau 2012.

117. Apuleius *Metamorphoses* 1.24–25. See further details on this text later.

118. On the procedure of preparing a legal case for trial (*anakrisis*) in Greek law, see Bertrand 2006.

119. See Aristotle *Constitution of Athens* 53.3, for the principles of variable number of members of the tribunal and 48.4 and 53.2 (with 69.2 for the final decision of the tribunal) for the *timēma*, or the estimated amount of the fine; see Harrison 1968–1971, vol. 2, 47, and Makarov 2007, 327, for the maintenance of this principle in the cities of the Imperial period (in this case, Tauric Chersonesos).

120. This point has been well brought out by Harrison 1968–1971, vol. 2, 4–7, especially 5, n. 2.

121. Tr. H. Rackham.

122. Tr. H. Rackham, modified.

123. Stroud 1974, ll. 18–28.

124. *ID* 509. On this law, see detail in chapter 12, 329–32.

125. On the judicial system in Delos, see the synthetic account by Vial 1984, 147–62.

126. *Syll.*³ 736; Deshours 2006, 38–39; Gawlinski 2012, 86–87, ll. 101–2, 105–6, 110–11.

127. *CID* IV 127. On this document see also the analyses in chapters 10, 273, and 15, 425–27.

128. *Syll.*³ 546 B; *IG* IX.1² 188; Migeotte, *Emprunt public*, 111–13, no. 31; Ager, *Arbitrations*, 153–57, no. 56; Magnetto, *Arbitrati*, 339–48, no. 55.

129. Aristophanes *Acharnians* 522.

130. Stroud 1974, ll. 16–18.

131. *I.Erythrai* 15, ll. 20–24.

132. On this law and its clause 4, see the analyses in chapter 12, 329–32.

133. Theophrastus, *On the Laws*, cited by Harpocration *Lexicon of the Ten Orators* s.v. *kata tēn agoran apseudein* ("do not deceive in the agora").

134. The comic character of the scene from the *Wasps* does not reside in the invention of an impossible procedure, because the sum in question would be too small, but, on the contrary, in the discredit into which Philocleon is cast by letting himself be drawn into trials of this kind. For the jurisdiction competent in a case of as little importance as this one, see earlier, Aristotle's considerations in the *Politics* (4.13.2) and our remarks on the possible jurisdictional competencies of the Athenian *agoranomoi*.

135. Aristotle *Nicomachean Ethics* 5.5.10–13.

136. See earlier, 239–46.

137. Arrow 1963.

138. Akerlof 1970.

139. Following the works of Akerlof, Joseph E. Stiglitz (1987) has emphasized that prices were not solely the resultant of supply and demand but in themselves provided information regarding the quality of products: thus for example, a decrease in the price of a

product might be considered a sign of a decrease in its quality and thus lead to a decrease in demand for it.

140. Akerlof 1970.

141. See Stewart 2012, 37–47.

142. On *mancipium* and its use by Plautus, see Stewart 2012, 76–77.

143. Brun 1997. See detail in chapter 13, 359–60.

144. See earlier, 243.

145. Billiard 1913, 188 on the practice of wine tasting, and 512–14 on the difficulties inherent in monitoring the quality of wine. See earlier, 241, on these questions.

146. Delos, *ID* 1648, 124/3 BCE, dedication for the *agoranomos* Kalliphon. Athens, *IG* II² 3493, probably from the late 30s or early 20s BCE, dedication for the *agoranomos* Pammenes, with Bresson 2000, 163; Oliver 2012, 93; and Schmalz 2009, 297, for the date.

147. Tr. W. D. Hooper.

148. Jakab 1997, 90–94; Chandezon 2003, 106.

149. Chandezon 2003, 105–8, no. 23.

150. Chandezon 2003, 167–69, no. 43.

151. On these options see, see later, chapters 12, 332–38, and 14, 384–92, as well as Fantasia 2012a.

152. See the commentary by Migeotte 1997, 36.

153. See the commentary in Bresson 2000, 186.

154. *Pace* Figueira 1986 and Bissa 2009, 180, the sense of *sunōneisthai* and of *sumpriasthai* in the passage of Lysias (22.5–11) is "to buy cumulatively," not "to buy together," which would make the limit of 50 *phormoi* meaningless. Figueira himself provides a wealth of parallels of *sunōneisthai* in the sense of speculative purchase. For the question of the value of the *phormos*, see mainly Pritchett and Pippin 1956, 194–95; Bissa 2009, 180–82; Johnstone 2011, 95–109, each providing further literature. Everyone agrees that a *phormos* was a kind of sack to transport the grain (but also several other stuffs, as is made clear by Pritchett and Pippin: wheat, barley, almonds, vetch, coriander, figs; see index Pritchett 1953, 296). Pritchett and Pippin, although obviously not happy with the solution, followed Boeckh (1886, vol. 1, 104, n. c) in concluding that the *phormos* was the equivalent of a *medimnos*. Basing herself on Lysias, *Against the grain dealers* 22.12, who refers to an increase of one drachm—assumed to be for one *phormos*—in a single day, corresponding to an—also assumed—increase of 1 obol per *medimnos*, Bissa makes the *phormos* the equivalent of six *medimnoi*. Johnstone sees in it a pure container, not standardized into a system of measures. But the latter's view directly contradicts our sources, which every time associate a *phormos* with a price (see the references corresponding to the index in Pritchett 1953, 296, as well as Lysias 22.5–6, 12). A *phormos*, viz. "a load," which physically must have corresponded to a sack rather than to a basket, was thus also a measure. A "load" was in every case notionally associated with a volume, which was not the same for every type of good: the "*phormos* of grain" did not have the same weight as the "*phormos* of coriander." Parallels can easily be found in early modern Europe, where "sacks" corresponded to different volumes according to the good concerned (see Savary des Bruslons, *Dictionnaire universel du commerce*, 1748, vol. 3, Letter S, pp. 2–3, s.v. "Sac," for charcoal, gypsum, and grain). Although certainly not reserved to that type of sale, the *phormos* (especially for grain) was

well adapted to wholesale trade. For dry grain, traders knew the correspondence that could be established between weight and volume: see the Athenian grain law of 374/3 BCE *apud* Stroud 1998, ll. 21–25 and commentary pp. 53–56: one talent corresponded to 5 *hektai* ("sixths") of wheat, and to 1 *medimnos* (= 6 *hektai*) of barley, the two volumes thus being in a proportion of 5 to 6. The question of the volume and thus of the weight of a *phormos* remains open. The six *medimnoi* per *phormos* of grain assumed by Bissa, viz. ca. 180 kilograms, may seem very heavy, but it happens that in eighteenth-century France, the standard Paris "sac" had a weight of 345 pounds, viz. 169 kilograms (see Kaplan 1984, 366, and 1996, 441), close to the approximate weight of 6 *medimnoi*. In other words Bissa's attractive hypothesis is also plausible. On the system of the 50 *phormoi*, see also chapter 12, 315 and n. 50.

155. *ID* 509.
156. See in detail Bresson 2000, 183–206. Ampolo 2010 develops a detailed argument on the relationship between the price of the grain sold by the city and the price of the grain sold on the free market; however, among other things, it remains very difficult to believe (57) that it was the price of the grain *sold* by the city (which supposedly underwent minimal variations only) that attracted the merchants, and not the prices on the market at the *emporion* (whether the grain was *bought* by the city or by private dealers).
157. See chapters 12 and 15.
158. Vatin 1966, with *SEG* 23 326 and Lytle 2010, 268.
159. Feyel 1936; Salviat and Vatin 1971, 95–109; the discussion in Migeotte 1997, 49, n. 37; Bresson 2000, 174; with the new edition with detailed comment of Lytle 2010, which replaces the previous editions.
160. Wörrle 1988, text pp. 1–16, ll. 60–61 (*SEG* 38 1462), and comment 209–15 on the panegyriarchs.
161. Oliver, *Greek Constitutions*, 208–15, no. 84, ll. 16–17.
162. Garnsey and van Nijf 1998.
163. On the regulation from Andania, see earlier, 240–41.
164. Steinhauer 1994; Bresson 2000, 151–82. For the date, see Schmalz 2009, 9 (but he missed the debate on the chronology of the two faces of the inscription), and 297–98 (for the chronology of the archon Pammenes).
165. *Pace* Descat 1997, it must be emphasized that here the point was not the amount of taxes, but the price of products. Indeed there were taxes in the agora, but that is not the subject of this text (see in detail Bresson 2000, 168).
166. Five *metronomoi* of the city, with their secretaries, Vanderpool 1968 (*SEG* 24 157), which assumes that there were five others for Piraeus. The second secretary had been appointed and not chosen by lot. This structure suggests that there might have been a board of the same composition in Piraeus at a time when the number of tribes was 13, with the addition of the Ptolemaïs (Traill 1975, 33, and 61–63; see Habicht 2006, 202, on the date in the context of the creation of the new tribe). We have two similar lists, from Piraeus this time, without a heading, which gives the names of five magistrates and their two secretaries, one of them chosen by lot and the other appointed (with an assistant as well), *IG* II² 1710, beginning of the second century BCE and 1711, middle of the second century BCE.
167. Therefore it is necessary to modify the translation given in Bresson 2000, 172, and, of the two choices suggested, ibid., 171, adopt the first one, amended.

168. Stroud 1998.
169. Among a large body of evidence, see for instance the case of Toulouse, with a poster for the tax on fish from the sea and from freshwater during Lent (year 1724), Archives municipales, no. BB 285, and that of the town of Avallon in Burgundy in the eighteenth century, Tartat 1946. In a striking parallel with the ancient world, in one case the tariff was even written on stone: see the inscription of 1661 set in the Porte Cabirole, at the entrance of the town of Saint-Bertrand-de-Comminges, referred to by Pottier 1892, 171, and still visible today.
170. Source: Lazare 1855, cited by Leteux 2005, n. 1506.
171. See in the same vein Morley 2007, 55–78.
172. See Foster 1970; Constable 1994, 116–17; Glick 2005, 127–30 (with even the clear continuity between the situation of Moslem and Christian, post-Reconquista Spain).
173. See Davis 2011 and 2012 for England.

CHAPTER X: MONEY AND CREDIT

1. On the monetary history of the Greek world, see Kraay 1976; Howgego 1990 and 1995; Nicolet-Pierre 2002; Le Rider 2001b, 2003; and Le Rider and de Callataÿ 2006; as well as von Reden 2002 and 2010.
2. See the data provided by Kletter 2003 and 2004 and by Gitin and Golani 2004, the former stressing convincingly the difference between uncoined and coined silver.
3. Jursa 2010, 469–753 and 773–83 (conclusions).
4. Treister 1995 provides a valuable synthesis on the role of metals in the ancient Greek world. For the price of the talent of bronze (see ibid. 249–50), we keep the amount of 60 drachms 1.5 obols, the only one which is realistic.
5. King 2005.
6. See chapter 13, 353.
7. Domergue et al. 2003 for the technical aspects of the bloomeries on the Martys site; Domergue and Bordes 2006 puts this operation in context. Healy 1978, 196, proposed a figure of 82,500 tons per year for the production of iron in the whole Roman Empire, which included many provinces much richer in wood than Greece; see for the production of iron in Britain estimates between 2,250 and 5,400 tons per year, Sim and Ridge 2002, 22–24.
8. Gill 1994, 102.
9. See later, 277–78.
10. De Callataÿ 2006a.
11. See the various contributions in the proceedings of the White Gold conference (Konuk et al., in press).
12. Bresson 2009 for a first analysis of this monometallism.
13. On cyzicenes, see Mildenberg 1993–1994; on the electrum from Phokaia and Mytilene, Bodenstedt 1981, Heisserer 1984, and de Callataÿ 2003, 179–83. On the role of these coins in Athens and the fifth-century Athenian empire, see Figueira 1998, 92–109.
14. Sidon: Elayi and Elayi 2004: 617–25 (shortly after 450); Tyre: Elayi and Elayi 2009, 328–36; cities of Philistia: Gitler and Tal 2006: 63–68 and 335–37.
15. Karia: Konuk 2003. Lykia: Vismara 1989–1996.

16. *SEG* 40 991–92 (*HTC*, 216–22, no. 90–91; see van Bremen 2013).

17. Mylasa: see *I.Mylasa* 1–5. Bilingual decree from Kaunos, *I.Kaunos* 119–21, no. K1. Trilingual decree from Xanthos: Metzger et al. 1979. Both documents predate the conquest of Alexander. Carian coins: Konuk 2007.

18. De Callataÿ 1989.

19. On the difference between the rates of the levies in the Eastern Mediterranean kingdoms and those in the Greek city-states, see chapter 4, 102–10.

20. See Bresson 2001a, 60–61.

21. Henkelman 2013, on the basis of the tablets from Persepolis.

22. Herodotus 1.206–7.

23. Herodotus 4.136–39 and 143.

24. See Jursa 2010 for sixth-century Mesopotamia, as well as Joannès 1994 and 1997, Vargyas 1997 and 2001, van der Spek 2000 and 2006 both for the Achaemenid and Hellenistic periods.

25. Lewis 1990.

26. For the commercial aspects, see Bresson 2000, 264–65, on this point against the background of the reference to Polanyi's schema of separate circulations for different products depending on the social level.

27. Jursa 2010, 474.

28. Thompson 2003.

29. Jursa 2010, 474–90

30. Price and Waggoner 1975 (see the chronological qualification in Flament 2007a, 165–67).

31. Herodotus 1.153. See chapter 9, 234–35.

32. See Bresson 2000, 243–61.

33. Von Reden 1997.

34. See earlier, chapter 9, ibid.

35. Bresson 2005e.

36. On capital accumulation in the city-states (first of all in Athens), see Kallet-Marx 1993 and Kallet 2001, and Samons 2000.

37. Picard 1984, 679–682

38. Viviers 1994; *Nomima*, vol. 1, 102–7, no. 22.

39. Samama 2003, 456–59, no. 367 (but it is noteworthy that the lands given replace a certain sum of money, which amounted to estimating the price of the land in monetary terms).

40. See Bresson 2000, 291, and later the difference from the case of Sparta.

41. See details in Figueira 2003.

42. On silver coinage in Sparta, which began only with King Areus I (309–265), see Grunauer von Hoerschelmann 1978 (see earlier, chapter 4 and n. 54).

43. Xenophon *Constitution of the Lacedaemonians* 7.5–6; Plutarch *Lysander* 17.1–6, with Plutarch *Lycurgus* 9.1–2; see Bresson 2001a and Christien 2002.

44. The convention between Mytilene and Phokaia called for capital punishment for counterfeiting electrum coins: *IG* XII.2 1 (Pleket, *Epigraphica*, I, no. 6). Sentence of Dyme of Achaia (end of the third century or beginning of the second century) for having counterfeited bronze coins: *SGDI* 1613; *Syll.*[3] 530 (Pleket, *Epigraphica*, I, no. 11, see *SEG* 13 274).

45. *IG* XII.9 1273–74, p. viii–ix. See Ducrey 2004, 146–47.
46. *IOSPE* I² 24 and IV, p. 264–65; *I.Kalchedon* 16; Dubois 1996, 28–39, no. 14 (for this decree, see also chapter 11, 300–1, and n. 81, and chapter 12, n. 73.
47. Bresson 1993a; Apostolou 2002.
48. Stroud 1974, with the analysis of Ober 2008, 211–40.
49. Stroud 1974, 157–58, ll. 16–18.
50. *IC* IV 162 (Melville-Jones 1993, 334).
51. See chapter 13, 356 and 367. For Egypt, see the Asyut hoard mentioned earlier, 268.
52. Price 1991.
53. See Marcellesi 2000.
54. Le Rider 2001a.
55. On this coinage and the phases of its issuance, see more details in chapter 15, 425–27.
56. *CID* IV 127, with Lefèvre's commentary, and Bresson 2006b.
57. De Callataÿ 1997 and 2000.
58. Ashton 2001.
59. On these policies of a closed currency system, see also chapter 15, 421.
60. On mercantilism and the interest in increasing the amount of currency in modern Europe, Michel Foucault (1970, 174–80) showed how little we can limit ourselves to negative value judgments from an evolutionary point of view regarding mercantilist theses. Mercantilism was not a clumsy prehistory of contemporary economic science. It constituted a coherent epistemological system that was rooted in institutional practices of the time and as such must be taken into account. See a similar view in Deyon 1969, 57–61, on the policy of abundant currency.
61. Kim 2002 and 2004; Lazzarini 2004.
62. Bresson 2006d.
63. Rutter 1997, 65–68 (southern Italy) and 139–43 (Sicily); Brousseau 2010 and 2013; as well as the several papers in Grandjean and Moustaka 2013 on the spread of bronze coins in the Aegean in the fifth and fourth centuries.
64. See the case of the bronze coinage of Sestos in the second century: *OGIS* 339; *I.Sestos* 1, ll. 44 and 49, with Robert 1973 and Le Rider 2001b, 242–44.
65. Regarding the fate of bronze coinage from the fourth century on, see de Callataÿ 2006b.
66. For the case of Olynthos, see Cahill 2002, 266–73.
67. Flament 2007a, 9–23.
68. However, some still think that it was in 508, at the time when the regime changed.
69. On this point, see Picard 2001, and Flament 2007a, 26–28.
70. These figures are the translation of the data in Starr 1970 into the equivalents in drachms and then into talents. See Flament 2007a, 47–54.
71. Flament, 2007b, 245–47.
72. On this question, see also Pébarthe 2008.
73. For the connection between money, money supply, and prices, see chapter 7 as well as Bresson 2005a.
74. Finley 1952 (1985).
75. Cohen 1992, 171–83. On bankers in general, Bogaert 1968 remains fundamental.
76. Cohen 1992, 209–15.
77. Millett 1991, 145 and 153–59.
78. *IG* I³ 248; see Millett 1991, 173–76, and Shipton 2000, 74, n. 56.

79. Millett 1991, 171–77; Shipton 2000, 73–74 and 84–86.
80. On this point, see the clear and convincing answer provided by Shipton 2000. See chapter 7, 192, and the dialogue between Aristarchos and Socrates as told by Xenophon, *Memorabilia* 2.7.2–12. *Pace* Millett 1991, 73–74, the anecdote does not prove a reluctance to borrow money for productive investment. First, the discussion is not focused on whether or one should borrow or not, but on how to put free women from (under normal conditions) wealthy families to productive work, just like slaves. When Aristarchos is convinced by Socrates to put his women to work, he immediately decides to borrow the money that will allow him to buy wool to start a business, no doubt just as everyone did when it came to putting slaves to work. Although initially, before deciding to put the women of his household to work, Aristarchos stated that it was difficult to find money lenders—for a nonproductive loan, this was quite understandable: lenders would not easily lend to him knowing that he would not be able to reimburse the loan—he does not seem to doubt that he will immediately find a loan for a productive investment.
81. Bogaert 1986, 26,
82. On the profits the Delians made by using their sanctuary's money, see Chankowski 2005 and Gabrielsen 2005.
83. Cohen 1992, 121–29 and 171–72.
84. Harrauer and Sijpestein 1985. For another Alexandrine contract that dates from the Hellenistic period but is very mutilated, see Vélissaropoulos 1980, 356–57.
85. In fact, this specific form of credit transaction where the merchandise is the pledge was at the heart of the system of the letter of credit in medieval times. It has been used again in modern international trade, particularly for oil, from the 1970s on.
86. On this translation, see chapter 14, n. 42.
87. On the *dikai emporikai*, see chapter 12, 322–24.
88. For a detailed demonstration of the notion of insurance and the leverage effect, see Bresson and Bresson 2004, where the question of account management in entrepreneurial life is also taken up.
89. On the connection between Athens and Phaselis, see chapter 12, 315–16. On the agreement between the two cities, ibid., 319–21.

CHAPTER XI: CITY-STATES, TAXES, AND TRADE

1. See Bresson 2007e.
2. Tr. J. Henderson.
3. On the rivalry between Nikomedia and its neighbor Nikaia, see Robert 1977; Jones 1978, 83–94; other relations between Nikomedia, its neighbor Nikaia, and the cities of the interior, Heller 2006, 100–104.
4. On the interpretation of this difficult passage, see Cuvigny 1994, 36, n. 18.
5. Miletos and Sardis: *Milet* I.3 (*Delphinion*) 135; Magnesia on the Meander, and Phokaia: *I.Magnesia* 7b. Both texts are reproduced with French translation in Bresson 2007e, 64–66, no. 6, and 68, no. 8, respectively.
6. See later for the example of the agreement between Lato and Olous.
7. On the practices of the right of seizure, see later.

8. *I.Ephesos* 2, reproduced with French translation in Bresson 2007e, 66–68, no. 7.

9. *IG* XII.4.1 15.

10. *IG* IX.1².2 390.

11. The *pronomia* might have corresponded to what was elsewhere the privilege of access to the council and to the people (see commentary *ad IG*), and the *propraxia* to the privilege of benefiting from an immediate judicial enforcement (see Francotte 1903, 19, with reference to *I.Iasos* 23) or perhaps of a privilege of guarantee for a seizure of property at the expense of a citizen of Stratos (see Gauthier 1972, 55–56). Phoitiai was a municipal subdivision or dependent polis of Stratos (on Stratos, see Hansen and Nielsen 2004, 372, and on Phoitiai, ibid. 370).

12. Knœpfler 2001a, 55–60.

13. Ibid., 55–56.

14. *I.Ilion* 40, ll. 12–13 (third century BCE) and 53, ll. 12–13 (second century BCE).

15. *Syll.*³ 481AB.

16. *SEG* 36 982–83 and 38 1059.

17. *SEG* 36 982A.

18. Knœpfler 2001a, 57–60, with a detailed discussion.

19. *I.Aeg.Thrace* 8, ll. 27–30.

20. Chaniotis 1996, 358–83, no. 61A, ll. 15–17 (see B, p. 362). We find something similar in a series of other conventions from Crete, which shows the importance that the right to export assumed.

21. Vokotopoulou 1997 (*SEG* 47 940), see *Bull. ép.*, 1998, no. 269. The Hippotadai must have been a subdivision of Kassandreia, deme, tribe, phratry, or something else. For this Chairephanes and the (very plausible) hypothesis that this was the same person as the Chairephanes who leased the drainage of the lake of Ptechai in Eretria, see chapter 4, 115, and chapter 6, 165–66.

22. *I.Ilion* 24, with commentary *apud* Wilhelm 1942, 72–76; see Knœpfler 2001a, 56, n. 179, for a parallel at Krannon of Thessaly (Mastrokostas 1964, 312–15, see *SEG* 23 437: exemption from all the *phoroi* and all the other taxes, with the privilege of security in peacetime and wartime).

23. On this law, see chapter 12.

24. Demosthenes 20.31–32.

25. *IG* XII.2 3 (Tod 163). Unfortunately the inscription is mutilated. It appears that the fee demanded from foreign merchants was 3.33 percent, of which Mytileneans had to pay only half. The reference to 100,000 *medimnoi* suggests a system of fixed quotas for exported quantities, such as we see in the inscription regarding grain exports from Cyrene (see chapter 14). The fixed quota makes sense in correlation with the Cyrene inscription. We may suppose that grain corresponding to this quota aimed at providing food for the local population. Beyond that limit, the kingdom of Bosporos must have considered that the grain could have been sold abroad by the Mytileneans.

26. Porten and Yardeni 1993; Yardeni 1994; Briant and Descat 1998; Bresson 2000, 67–73; Cottier 2012, 53, considers that the chronology of the document is not decided, but see Bresson 2007e, 42–43 (missed by Cottier). On the usage of natron, see chapter 13, 353–55.

27. *P.Cairo.Zen* 59012; see Orrieux 1983, 56–58 and Bresson 2012c.

28. Gauthier 1982.

29. See Bresson 2000, 101–8.
30. Van Bremen 2013.
31. Brulé 1978, 148–56. See also the case of the island of Tenos, in the Kyklades, Étienne 1990, 15–24.
32. See chapters 3, 81, and 6, 173.
33. See *HTC*, 159–71, ad no. 48. On Rhodian interests in Karia, see Bresson 2003a.
34. *I.Keramos* 6, l. 4, usually dated to the second century BCE, with the interpretation by Robert, 1962, 61, n. 3. Gary Reger (1999, 84, and 2004, 169–70, n. 87) dates the text to 240–50 BCE and maintains that Stratonikeia is not the best candidate. If indeed the attempt at absorption did not come from Stratonikeia, there would be only one other possible candidate: Halikarnassos, to the west. It is difficult to make a definitive decision. However we can note that everything that can be guessed about Stratonikeia's expansionist efforts at this time, its monetary history, its conflicts with Rhodes, and also its landlocked position in the interior of Asia Minor, seems to encourage us to suspect this was this city that was involved.
35. See the case referred to in Demosthenes 52.5–6 (*Against Callippus*). See also, even if it took place in the Imperial period, the case of the trial concerning the liquidation of a wine-trading business brought against a woman named Berenike in Roman Egypt, in 102 CE; see *P.Oxy.* 22.234, with Jakab 2001. Such documents are rare but they can give us an idea of the procedures in force as early as the Classical and Hellenistic periods.
36. On forms of taxation, see for example the inscription regarding the grain from the islands, from 374/3 BCE (Stroud 1998); the inscription of Olamış from the end of the fourth century BCE (Robert and Robert 1976, 175–87; see chapter 3, 75 and n. 19); the treaty between Miletos and Pidasa from the beginning of the second century BCE, *Milet* I.3 (*Delphinion*), 149, ll. 18–25, 28–37, and 39–47 (see Migeotte 2001a and chapter 6, 173–74), or again the decree concerning the tax levied on the city of Telmessos, in Lykia, in 240 BCE (*OGIS* 55). On taxation in general, see Gabrielsen 2013b, Migeotte 2003 (direct taxation) and 2014 (synthesis on Greek finances).
37. Thucydides 7.28.4; see Blamire 2001, 114, n. 106.
38. Ps.-Aristotle *Economics* 2.2.22. The king whom Kallistratos served was Philip II for Picard 1994, and Hatzopoulos 1996, vol. 1, 434 and n. 11, and Perdikkas III for Lane Fox 2011, 266–67.
39. The identity of these *emporia* is debated. Loukopoulou 2002 grants that these may be Greek cities on the coasts of Aegean Thrace whose revenues were traditionally shared among themselves, Athens, and the Odrysian kingdom; Veligianni-Terzi 2004, 241–42 and n. 759, argues that they were in the Chersonese. Thucydides (2.97.3) already pointed out that the Odrysian kingdom received tax revenues in gold and silver in the amount of 400 talents (1,000, according to Diodorus 12.50.2). See the discussion of Veligianni-Terzi's theses by P. Danev *BMCR*, 2005.07.84.
40. Livy 39.24.2. See Hatzopoulos 1996, vol. 1, 439.
41. Polybius 30.31.12.
42. Polybius 30.31.5–8.
43. See Bresson 2002a, 156–62, and the customs inscription from Kaunos, *I.Kaunos*, 171–221, no. 34, which Christian Marek dates to the beginning of the reign of Hadrian.
44. Engelmann and Knibbe 1989; see Nicolet 1991, 1993 and 1999. New edition Cottier et al. 2008, 16–164.

45. Livy 38.44.4.

46. Daverio-Rocchi 1988, 103–6, no. 2; Lucas 1997, 88–89, no. 40, ll. 5–18 (see ibid., 191–99 on the localization of Askyris).

47. Purcell 2005.

48. Dio Chrysostom 40.33; see Robert 1977; Heller 2006, 100–114; Bresson 2007e, 53–54 and map p. 61.

49. See Gomme et al. 1945–1981, vol. 1, 415, which mentions the Arcadian cities, Tegeia, Mantineia, among others, and even Elis.

50. On wine from Phleious, see Athenaeus 1 27d, who cites Antiphanes (fr. 236 Kock = 233 Kassel-Austin), a poet of the Middle Comedy, with commentary by Baladié 1980, 181 and n. 51, who shows the importance of wine in the region of Phleious. On Phleious and its prosperity starting in the Archaic period and maintained until the Imperial period, see Alcock 1991 for the results of an urban archaeological survey.

51. Apuleius *Apologia* 10.24, certainly dependent on an author from the Classical period. See also chapter 5, 130, on the products of Phleious. When he says that all of Greece or almost all is on the sea (and corrupted by it), Cicero (*De re publica* 2.4 [8]) does not fail to mention that Phleious was an exception in the Peloponnese. His original source was the Greek geographer Dicearchus, who maintained that even in the Peloponnese all states had a connection to the sea; Cicero had to correct him on this point as becomes clear in his erudite conversation with his friend Atticus *Att.* 6.2.3.

52. Manganaro 2000 (*SEG* 50 1195; see *Bull. ép.* 2001, no. 54 and 373), l. 9.

53. *Diagōgion* in Polybius 4.52.5.

54. On this episode, see Polybius 3.2.5 and 4.47–52; on the possible consequences, see also later, chapter 14, 387.

55. Hopkins 1995–1996.

56. *I.Kaunos*, 171–221, no. 34.

57. On these questions, see Robert 1987, 487–520.

58. Bresson 2002a.

59. See *I.Kaunos*, 171–221, no. 34, with Marek 2006 (and Takmer 2007 for the customs text of Andriake).

60. *IGRR* IV 146; *Syll.*³ 799 (38 CE); see Migeotte 1997, 41–42, and Bresson 2000, 175–76.

61. Bousquet 1986.

62. Arnaud 2011a, 71–73.

63. On this episode, Xenophon *Hellenica* 3.4.1; see Lewis 1996, 1–2 and 31–32; Bresson 2000, 70 and n. 38, where the importance of neutrality is emphasized (in a different way Descat 2002, 265–66); Buckler 2003, 58–59.

64. Ps.-Demosthenes 56.7–10 (*Against Dionysodorus*), see Bresson 2000, 187–88.

65. See the detailed commentary of Schofield 1999, 140–54.

66. Dubois 1996, 31, n. 80 (*I.Kalchedon* 16, and p. 98 for the *testimonia* on Hieron).

67. *GGM* I 402 ff. (see *I.Kalchedon*, *testimonia*, pp. 123–24).

68. Bresson 2000, 131–49.

69. Dubois 1996, 28–31, no. 14. See earlier, chapter 10, 271.

70. See earlier, 292.

71. Velkov and Domaradzka 1994 with new edition Chankowski and Domaradzka 1999; on this text see earlier, chapter 3, 84 and n. 72.

72. Plutarch *Cimon* 8.3–4. On the next phase of the dispute, see later.

73. *I. Ephesos* 2, see Bresson 2007e, 55–66 and 64–66, no. 7.

74. Chaniotis 1996, 358–83, no. 61A, ll. 36–38 = B, ll. 61–66.

75. Velkov and Domaradzka 1994 with Chankowski and Domaradzka 1999, ll. 20–25 .

76. On the ambiguous character of piracy, see the (somewhat challenging) views of Gabrielsen 2001, 2003, and 2013a (for the Hellenistic world). On piracy in the Greek world in general, see De Souza 1999, 17–178 (from the late Archaic period to the end of the Hellenistic period).

77. Şahin 1994, see *Bull. ép.* 1996, no. 353; Merkelbach 2000; De Souza 1999, 67–70.

78. See already earlier for the starting point of the episode. Source: Plutarch *Cimon* 8.3–5, with Thucydides 1.98.2 and Diodorus 11.60.2; see Podlecki 1971 for the date of the campaign.

79. The pessimistic view of De Souza 1999, 26–30, on the Athenian policy of suppressing piracy in the fifth century does not seem to be justified.

80. Flament 2007b, 138–60, for the pay of the rowers in the fleet and estimates of the costs of naval campaigns during the first part of the Peloponnesian War.

81. For the Attic decree of 324 BCE providing for the creation of a naval base on the Adriatic, see *IG* II³ 370 (*GHI* 100, with Bresson 1993b, 171–77). On Etruscan pirate activity, see Ientile 1983.

82. On convoys in the fourth century, Vélissaropoulos 1980, 135, and Rutishauser 2012, 160 and 225–29.

83. For an analysis of the case of the "attack on Hieron," see Bresson 2000, 131–49.

84. Polybius 30.5.6–8. See Bresson 2007d for the epigraphic dossier, with Badoud 2011b for a down-dating of the dossier by a few years (but the Rhodians were already active against the Tyrrhenians even before the great siege of 305/4 BCE, as explicitly stated by Diodorus 20.81.3.).

85. *IG* XI.2 148, ll. 73–74; see Gabrielsen 1997, 43.

86. On this point see the remarks by Wiemer 2002, 111–42.

87. See details in Gabrielsen 1997, 42–44, 53–60, and 108–11, as well as the point of view defended in Gabrielsen 2001.

88. Polybius 4.46–52; see Gabrielsen 1997, 44–46.

89. See the demonstration of Yntema 2009 on the long-term negative impact of internal tariffs between provinces of the Dutch Republic in the seventeenth and eighteenth century on beer production, trade, and consumption, and on individual income. For the well-known cases of internal tariffs in early modern France and Germany and their negative consequences, see the bibliography quoted in Yntema 2009, 258.

CHAPTER XII: THE *EMPORION* AND THE MARKETS

1. On the *emporion*, see Vélissaropoulos 1980, and on these basic definitions particularly 29–33.

2. *IG* I² 887B.

3. On Chariton's date, see Tilg 2010, 36–79, who suggests "a likely period of composition from AD 41 to AD 62."

4. See Vélissaropoulos 1980, 218–19, Vial 1984, 231 and 344–46, and Chankowski 2008, 299–300 (whose conclusions are followed here).

5. *SEG* 10 10 and add. corr. p. 156, ad ll. 15–24; Vélissaropoulos 1980, 221 and n. 106.

6. See chapter 3, 86.

7. Both harbor taxes and customs duties could be defined as *ellimenion* (or *ellimenia*); see Carrara 2014.

8. *IJG* vol. 2, 340–43, no. XXXIV; *Syll.*[3] 952; Pleket, *Epigraphica*, I, no. 8; see Migeotte 2001b.

9. Minaud 2004 for the dossier; see ibid. for the earlier literature and for photographs of these documents. Relief of the *Tabularii*: Rome, Museo Torlonia, no. 338; painting of Isis Giminiana: Rome, Musei Vaticani, no. 79638. See also the mosaic in the *aula dei mensores*, the Hall of the Grain Measurers, in Ostia (I.XIX.3), which depicts the same object (same period as the other two documents).

10. Kuchenbuch 2006, 122–23.

11. On this point, see chapter 6, 171–72.

12. Aeneas Tacticus 29.3–7. See however later, n. 33, for the possible complete unloading of a cargo on the order of a tax official.

13. Translation J. Dryden in *Plutarch's Lives*.

14. Euripides *Cyclops* 135–61, quotation of v. 150. Translation E. P. Coleridge.

15. Aeneas Tacticus 30.2.

16. Hyperides, fr. 186 J. (Pollux 9.34). The reference is to the speeches *For Chairephilos, On Salt Fish* (see ed. Jensen, Teubner 1963, pp. 145–46, fr. 181–91, ad fr. 186).

17. Harpocration *Lexicon of the Ten Orators* s. v. *deigma*. The title of the speech of Demosthenes (24.8) is simplified and should read in full: *Against Polycles in the Matter of a Period of Supplementary Service as Trierarch.*

18. Xenophon *Hellenica* 5.21.

19. Ps.-Demosthenes 35.29 (*Against Lacritus*). Allusion also in Demosthenes 50.24 (*Against Polycles*). See as well Schol. Aristophanes *Knights* 979; Lysias fr. 17.6 C.U.F.; Polyaenus 6.2.2.

20. Stanley 1976, 157–58; see Pausanias 1.1.3.

21. Judeich 1931, 448; Heichelheim 1964–1970, vol. 2, 62–63, and 189, n. 26; Gofas 1982.

22. *IG* II[2] 1035, l. 47. On this identification, see Garland 2001, 219. For the date, ca. 10/9–2/1 BCE, see Schmalz 2009, 10–11.

23. *IG* II[2] 1103. See Garland 2001, 154 and 219, and above all Lytle 2007.

24. Vallois 1944–1966, vol. 1, 65–66.

25. Fraisse 1983, 307.

26. *Syll.*[3] 495, and Latyschew, *IOSPE* I[2] 32B, ll. 48–49: the benefactor Protogenes of Olbia had a *pulōn* (a porch or gateway) repaired "on the *deigma*" (on Protogenes, see Gauthier 1985, chiefly 31 and 70–72; dates from not earlier than 200 BCE, according to Gauthier; for a translation of the text, see Austin 2006, 217–22, no. 115).

27. Diodorus 19.45.4

28. Polybius 5.88.8.

29. Étienne 2004, 107–8.

30. See later, the analysis of the Delian law on wood and charcoal, which for the specific case of wood and charcoal prohibits this practice, which however must have been a common practice.

31. Étienne 2004, 107, with reference to Gofas 1982, who does not specifically inquire into the unloading of cargoes and remains vague on this point.

32. Demosthenes 20.33 (*Against Leptines*), with Bresson 1993b, 166.
33. *P.Oxy.* 1.36 (= *Chr.* 273), col. 2, ll. 6–15 (with *BL* 2.2.92), second to third century CE, which details the conditions of the *ekphortismos* (unloading): if a customs officer searches a ship to check a customs declaration and finds no infraction, he has to repay the cost of unloading to the merchant.
34. Isocrates *Antidosis* 15.54.
35. See Ziebarth 1940a.
36. See Ziebarth 1940b.
37. Gofas 1982 on these two points.
38. See Brunet 2007.
39. In the city of Chersonesos (in Pontos), might the amphora marked "for the *emporion*" (Garlan 1993, apparently from the beginning of the third century BCE), have been one of these sample amphoras?
40. Stroud 1974, ll. 20–22, with commentary 181–83.
41. On the notion of *emporion nomimon* in general, see Bresson 1993b, 191–93.
42. For the sectors of the port, see chapter 3, 90; for the sectors of the agora, see chapter 9, 235–37.
43. See later, the analysis of the Delian law concerning wood and charcoal.
44. See chapter 9, 239–40 and 247–48.
45. Gauthier's fundamental analysis (1981b) fits well with the ban on exporting grain from Athens (on this point *pace* Oliver 2007, 26) and with the literal interpretation of the text. Thus one should notice that Athens had two *poleis* (towns), just as Rhodes had three.
46. Transportation from the port was certainly carried out preferably by wagons rather than by donkeys or mules (*pace* Gauthier 1981b, 22, on this detail). Not all streets of Athens were open to wheeled vehicles, but "Piraeus Street" (see Young 1951, map p. 246), from the southwest district of the agora, to the Piraeus gate, definitely was, as proved by many wheel ruts found there (see Young 1951, 150–51, 155, on questions of circulation in Athens). This is an indication that there existed a road used by wagons between Athens and Piraeus. On transport wagons and their use, see Raepsaet 2008, 588–98, with Raepsaet 1988 for the type of vehicles (two or four wheels) and Mulliez 1982, 111, for the transport of wood in wagons. See chapter 3, 81–84, for the reevaluation of roads and land transportation in ancient Greece.
47. On this point, Descat 2004, 598, must be preferred to Gauthier 1981b, 23.
48. The *sitos*, or grain market, of the Attic law of 375/4 BCE (Stroud 1974, ll. 18–19 and 22–23, with commentary p. 180), where the *sitophulakes* operate, must apparently have referred both to the *sitikon emporion* and to the grain markets of Athens and Piraeus.
49. This time, it is Gauthier's view (1981b, 24) that must be preferred to that of Descat (2004, 598).
50. On the question of the *phormos*, see earlier, chapter 9, 255–56 and n. 154. If a *phormos* corresponded to six *medimnoi*, this would mean that, per day (?), middlemen could not buy more that 300 *medimnoi*.
51. On the Delian law *ID* 509 regarding trade in wood and charcoal, see later.
52. See chapter 9, 247–48, on this point.
53. On this point, see later.
54. *IG* XII.Suppl. 347, II, ll. 8–11. Salviat 1986, 147–50 and 183–85 (with a map of the region). For this text, see earlier, chapter 9, 241 and n. 83.

55. For these analyses of the Thasian law, see Descat in Brulé et al. 2004, 408–9. On the date of the beginning of stamping in Thasos, see Garlan 1999a, 48–54.

56. See Garlan et al., in *Bull. amph.* 2012, 211, no. 245.

57. Heracleides fr. 1.14–16 ed. Arenz 2006, with German translation 122, and commentary 150–51 and 204–5.

58. On justice in Boiotia, which would not have corresponded to the descriptions of ancient authors, see Roesch 1985 and Müller 2013.

59. Gauthier 1972, 210–19; Bravo 1980.

60. For this hypothesis, see Laronde 1987, 149–61, with text and detailed commentary.

61. See Bresson 2011a and chapter 14, 412–13.

62. On *silphion*, see chapter 13, 358.

63. Chaniotis 1996, 358–83, no. 61A, ll. 39–42 = B, ll. 68–77 (110/9–109/8 BCE).

64. Polybius 3.22–26; see Aristotle *Politics* 3.5.10. The commercial clauses of the treaties are analyzed in Bresson 2004a.

65. Polybius 3.22.8–10; see Bresson 2004a, 667–71.

66. Bresson 2004a, 670–73, with an analysis of transactions between Rome and Carthage in Sicily.

67. Gauthier 1972, 157–205.

68. *IG* I³ 10. On this inscription, which has been frequently commented upon, see chiefly Hopper 1943; Wade-Gery 1958, 180–200; de Ste. Croix 1961; Meiggs 1972, 231–32; Gauthier 1972, 158–61 and 174–81; Fornara 1979; Cataldi 1983, 99–143 (complete bibliography up to that time). These studies have considerably advanced the debate on this agreement, but all of them accept the idea that here we are dealing with the regulation of "business conflicts" (see *xumbolaion* ll. 6–7). Here we propose a different analysis in translation of several points in the text. A date around 460 was commonly accepted until Jameson 2000–2003, on the basis of both script and language, suggested a date in the 420s. Even if the decree dated from the 420s, it remains that it refers to previous conventions with the Phaselitans, which must have been concluded when they joined the Athenian empire in the 460s.

69. This point has been well brought out by Cataldi 1983.

70. Herodotus 2.178; on Naukratis, see Bresson 2000, 13–84, and 2005d, and Malkin 2011, 65–95.

71. Bresson 2000, 68–73.

72. On the *nautodikai*, Gauthier 1972, 153–55; Vélissaropoulos 1980, 251–58.

73. In the currency decree from Olbia (*IOSPE* I², 24; *I.Kalchedon* 16; Dubois 1996, 28–39, no. 14, ll. 9–10), it is noted that currency exchanges must take place on the stone of the *ekklēsiastērion*. But it is also noted that exchange must not take place anywhere else: anyone who sells or buys elsewhere (*allothi*) will be punished. The "elsewhere" (*allothi*) in the decree from Phaselis is not aimed at trials that might take place "outside Athens," because this point is settled by the initial stipulation that trials must take place in Athens (which makes unacceptable the "imperialist" interpretations to which this text has given rise, supposing that Athens imposed a kind of judicial centralization). It refers to the following part of the text, which explains that no magistrate other than the polemarch shall have the right to institute a legal proceeding.

74. *Milet* I.3 136 (*Syll.*³ 286; *Staatsverträge*, III, 408; *Milet* VI.1, pp. 170–71); German translation Brodersen et al. 1992–1999, vol. 2, 61–62, no. 269; see Gauthier 1972, 358–61.

75. On this kind of exemptions, see earlier, chapter 11, 288–93.
76. See Ps.-Demosthenes 34.42 (*Against Phormio*): in the framework of the procedure of the *dikai emporikai* (see later), Attic law allowed the institution of a judicial procedure not only for contracts that had been made in Athens, but for "those that have been made with a view to a sea voyage to Athens" (*hosa an genētai heneka tou plou tou Athēnaze*); similarly, ibid., 43: the plaintiff emphasizes before the jury that it would be absurd for the tribunal to declare itself incompetent, "since the contract had been made in your *emporion*" (*en tōi humeterōi emporiōi gegone*). See also Aristotle *Rhetoric* 1.4.11, with commentary Bresson 2000, 119–20.
77. On this point, we just take a position opposed to that of our predecessors, who have all chosen the inverse option.
78. The absence of the Athenian banker Pasion is only a supplementary reason for not holding a trial, not the main one. On Satyros and Athens, see Tuplin 1982.
79. Dionysius of Halicarnassus *Roman Antiquities* 6.95.2. Fornara 1979, 51, n. 1, a firm supporter of the *forum rei*, has to admit that this passage can have no meaning other than that of allowing a trial to be held at the place where the contract was made.
80. *Code of Gortyn* IX, 1. 43–X, l. 1 ff. = *Nomima*, vol. 2, 276–78, no. 76.
81. See chapter 10, 281–84, and the contract in the Demosthenic speech *Against Lacritus* 35.10–14.
82. Law of Paros: Lambrinoudakis and Wörrle 1983.
83. From a methodological viewpoint, the interest of the hypothesis presented is that it always translates and explains the syntagm *sumbolaion gignetai* in the same way, whereas the alternative theories are forced to produce ad hoc solutions that differ in each case. In the agreement between Athens and Phaselis, a mutilation of the stone requires a restoration. Up to this point it has been granted that trials could be instituted if the contract had been made "in Athens" (*Athēnēsi*). Could one grant that it concerned contracts made "toward Athens" (*Athēnaze*)? That does not seem likely. The question is how to determine whether the modifying clause bears on the establishment of a basic privilege, that of commercial contracts (in this case we will read *Athēnēsi*), or whether it is a question of adding one commercial privilege to another that has already been granted (in that case one would add "toward Athens," *Athēnaze*, since "to Athens" would have already been granted in the main agreement). In fact, there would have been a direct reference to the agreement previously made with the Phaselites, which would necessarily have had to mention this privilege already: since there is a reference to the agreement with the Chiotes, therefore the commercial privilege had not been granted, and only the first solution is admissible, in conformity with the other testimonies relating to the opening of trials until, in the second half of the fourth century, the *dikai emporikai* came to add the clause concerning the direction. As for the repetition "if the contract is made in Athens, the trials take place in Athens before the polemarch," it establishes a basic principle for avoiding any possible challenge. The agreement between Rome and the Latins, which stipulates that trials would systematically take place in the city where the contract was made, in fact presupposes that challenges might be made on this subject.
84. On the *dikai emporikai*, Gauthier 1972, 198–201; Cohen 1973; Vélissaropoulos 1980, 235–48.

85. *Pace* Vélissaropoulos 1980, 236–41. It may be that certain procedures were assimilated to those having to do with large-scale commerce, but that does not affect the definition of the latter.

86. See along these lines Vélissaropoulos 1980, 245–47.

87. Cohen 1973, 42–59, with all the necessary parallels.

88. On the contract in the speech *Against Lacritus*, see chapter 10, 281–84.

89. Here again, one must follow the whole demonstration in Cohen 1973, 23–42 (despite Vélissaropoulos 1980, 241–45).

90. The good reputation of the Athenian port and currency in the mid-fourth century is famously described by Xenophon, *Poroi* 3.1–2.

91. Hansen and Nielsen 2004 have 1,035 entries in their catalogue of Archaic and Classical *poleis*.

92. Bresson 2000, 245–47.

93. Bresson 2000, 109–30, on the care taken with exports and imports.

94. *Syll.*³ 354 (*I.Ephesos* 1455). On Agathokles and his family, Bresson 2000, 95–99.

95. On this point, see chapter 11, 288–92.

96. Xenophon *Poroi* 3.4, with the commentary in Gauthier 1976, 84–86. Along the same lines as Xenophon, see Aeneas Tacticus *Poliorcetics* 10.12 (premium depending on the size of the cargo imported by foreign merchants and gold crown).

97. On this type of sale, see also later, 329–30.

98. See the detailed demonstration and explanation of the notion of "official price" (*kathestēkuia timē*) in Bresson 2000, 183–210, and earlier, chapter 9, 254–57.

99. Lysias 22.8–9 (*Against the grain dealers*).

100. On this point, see chapter 15.

101. Thus Andreau 1997.

102. See chapter 3, 74–76.

103. Pliny 34.4 [9], with also 33.51 [144] for silver-plated bronze bedsteads.

104. Chamonard 1922, 213–15, on these aspects of artisanal archaeology in Delos; for the remains of a bronze-working shop, ibid. (see p. 60), house VI L in the theater quarter, room g.

105. Kent 1948 (see p. 306, one of the estates is called Kerameion) and Vial 1984, 348–55.

106. I owe this suggestion to Christophe Pébarthe. On the production of perfumes in Delos, see Brun (P.) 1999 and 2000, and briefly chapter 13.

107. Chamonard 1922, ibid., house B of insula 1 in the stadium quarter, at the back of room f, see Plassart 1916, 170. Chamonard also mentions (in the theater district) house III N, which has six rectangular vats lined up on each side of room e, perhaps to be used for fulling (see pp. 43–45).

108. On the production of purple in Delos, see chapter 13, 357 and n. 80.

109. On this point, see chapter 15.

110. *ID* 509 (*NChoixDélos* pp. 195–98). This translation is based on the new edition of Chankowski 2012, which supersedes all previous ones. Gauthier 1977 has provided a detailed institutional analysis of the public auction sales of wood and charcoal. Reger 1994, 171–76, has suggested that the rise in the price of charcoal and wood was the result of a deliberate policy adopted by the city to maximize its fiscal revenues. For Descat 2001, 129, the increase was the result of an expansion of transit commerce, an

expansion that was both encouraged and supervised by the city; the rise in prices is supposed to have been only a secondary objective of the law, but the city would nonetheless have seen the rise in a very favorable light. For an opposite view and a detailed economic commentary, see Bresson 2006c and a new study in preparation.

111. On this point, see chapter 15.
112. This analysis and its implications will be developed in the study announced earlier, n. 110.
113. Reger 1994, 142.
114. *IG* XII.5 129, ll. 11–14, first half of the second century; see Lambrinudakis and Wörrle 1983, 290, n. 16, with pl. 9.
115. *IG* XII.3 Suppl. 169 and 170, from the second century.
116. *IG* XII.5 714, with *IG* XII Suppl., p. 119, ca. 350–336.
117. *ID* 647, ll. 4–10 = *Choix Délos*, 57–58, no. 46; see Vial 1984, 139.
118. Andocides 1.137; Lysias 6.19 (with negative comments); see Bresson 2003b, 154.
119. On monthly changes in grain prices in Delos, Reger 1993, 304–310, who mentions the harvest calendar, but notes the erratic developments. The harvest calendar certainly ultimately played a role, but it seems that the accent should be put instead on the erratic character of supply.
120. See chapter 15.
121. See earlier, 325–30.
122. *ISE* 64, ll. 1–8.
123. *IG* II³ 1315. On this inscription, see chapter 14, 383.
124. See later, the cases of Rome in 440 BCE and Antioch in Pisidia in 92 or 93 CE, 337–38.
125. On the question of public funds for public grain distribution or sale at reduced price, see Migeotte 1989–1990, 1990, 1991, 1993, and 1998 (and succinctly, 2002, 138–39); Fantasia 1989; and Couilloud-Le Dinahet 1988. For the grain funds in the Greek cities in the Roman period, see Erdkamp 2008 and Zuiderhoek 2008.
126. Ps.-Plutarch *Lives of the Ten Orators* 851b.
127. *IG* II³ 367, ll. 10–12 and 70–72.
128. Demosthenes 18.248 (*On the crown*).
129. Oliver 2007, 215–22, and 255–59.
130. On the Delian *sitōnai*, see Vial 1984, 237–39, and later, 335.
131. On this point, see chapter 14.
132. Gift of Eumenes II to Delphi in 159/8, *Syll.*³ 671B, ll. 2–7; *FD* III.3 237.4–7 (Bringmann and von Steuben 1995–2000, vol. 1, 148–49, no. 93 [E1]). See Sosin 2004, 195 and n. 18. Gift of Masinissa: 2,796.5 *medimnoi* of grain, *ID* 442A, ll. 100–106, see Vial 1984, 138–39 (with Gauthier 1988 on the ambassador Rhodon). For other examples of princely or royal generosity, Bresson 2000, 208–10, and more generally Bringmann and von Steuben 1995–2000 and Bringmann 2001.
133. Migeotte, *Emprunt public*, 361, 367, 370.
134. Migeotte 1992, 341–43 and 347.
135. Law of Samos: *Syll.*³ 976, and *Choix* 34. See analysis and bibliography in Bresson 2000, 253–57.
136. Attic law on grain from the islands: see fundamentally Stroud 1998 (with a brief commentary in Bresson 2000, 207–10).
137. *I. Thespies*, vol. 2, 42–45, no. 84, ll. 31–37.

138. *I. Thespies*, vol. 1, 53–58, no. 41A, ll. 9–11, with commentary pp. 56 and 58.

139. See details in Vial 1984, 236–239, and Fantasia 1989, 49–54.

140. Migeotte 1989–1990, 1991 and 1992.

141. *IG* XI.4 627. Different point of view in Duchêne and Fraisse 2001, 161–62.

142. On the climatic conditions prevailing in the interior of Asia Minor, see chapter 2, 66–67.

143. The *duumviri* and decurions were respectively the two chief magistrates and the members of the city senate of a Roman provincial town.

144. Another parallel can be found, this time in the Roman period, with the Athenian law of the age of Hadrian that requires producers to sell the city one-third of their oil production (see *IG* II² 1100; on this text, see chapter 14, 405 with n. 99). The inscription from Antioch in Pisidia (*AE* 1925 126b) gave rise to the famous debate among specialists at the time of its discovery (on this point, see Wiemer 1997, 195). Since that time, the inscription has often been republished and commented upon. The most recent clarifications will be found in Garnsey 1988, 19, 32, 77, and 258; Wiemer 1997; Erdkamp 2005, 286–288, and 293; Andreau 2007. Here we follow the text of Wiemer 1997. Depending on the translation chosen, one can arrive at very different logics. The first point in debate is that of the nature of the "buyers." Robinson 1924, 10 and 19, had identified them with the *sitōnai*, but without offering any particular commentary on this point. Among the authors cited (for the earlier literature, see the references they cite), only Garnsey has pursued the point of view according to which the "buyers" were not other than the grain commissioners of the city of Antioch. Indeed trying to make them private buyers leads inevitably to a dead end. How could these private buyers have been able to buy the grain in question all at once (the first day of the calends)? If the private purchases took place on that day or starting on that day, as some commentators have suggested (which is moreover an interpretation that the Latin text does not authorize), and if the measure was intended to prevent speculation, how could massive purchases and monopolization by a few buyers have been prevented? If it had been a question of private buyers—all of them supposed to come to buy in a single day all the available brain to store it in their own granaries (assuming that each buyer had individual granary), it would have been necessary to set an upper limit on the quantity of grain that each buyer was allowed to acquire. The edict says nothing about this. Since its goal was not to permit and accentuate speculation, but rather to prevent it, the solution of public buyers is the only one acceptable. Wiemer's analysis is valuable for the general context of the edict. Erdkamp has clearly seen the importance of the maximum price. The arguments put forth by Andreau (who has not recognized the existence of grain funds and leans toward private buyers) are refuted by the objections mentioned earlier.

145. That is the objection made in Wiemer 1997, 203–4.

146. On the question of transportation and the risks of famine in the interior of Anatolia, see chapter 2, 66–67, and chapter 3, 82–83.

CHAPTER XIII: INTERNATIONAL TRADE NETWORKS

1. Tr. H. Rackham.

2. On Polybius's view on the economy, see Bresson 2013 and Davies 2013.

3. See chapter 6.

4. Zolotarev 2003.

5. Montchrestien 1999 [1615], 55.

6. Montchrestien 1999 [1615], 280. A major part of the work is constituted by reflections on the forms taken by foreign trade in the Europe of his time. This was the case (see ibid., pp. 338–45) with a critique of the monopoly that the English exercise over their foreign trade to the benefit of their businessmen and their products. This policy anticipated that of the Navigation Acts of 1651, which systematized these practices.

7. On Montchrestien's appreciative judgment on antiquity and ancient authors, see, however, Andreau 2011.

8. Plato *Republic* 369b–70e. The passage is analyzed later.

9. In a complex economy of the contemporary period, the value of a currency is certainly not dependent solely on external balances (commercial and financial), even though the "true prices" always finally emerge.

10. Translation J. Dryden. On this passage, see also later chapter 14, 403.

11. On this point, see chapter 14, 390–92.

12. On Aristotle's views on money and coinage, see Bresson 2012b, with the discussion of the role of Aegina and the link established in the conception of the time between long-distance trade and development of coined money.

13. On all these points, see chapter 2, 49–51.

14. Translation P. Shorey in Hamilton and Cairns 1971.

15. On Smith and Ricardo, see briefly chapter 1, 5.

16. Smith 1976 [1776], vol.1, 7–25 [= Vol. 1, Book 1, chapters 1–3 of the first edition].

17. Ricardo 1948 [1817], chapter 7, "On Foreign Trade," 77–93, particularly 81–83.

18. On the development of the theory of international trade, see Samuelson and Nordhaus 2005, 293–317; Krugman et al. 2010, 24–49 (analysis of the Ricardian model).

19. On the "HOS model," see Krugman et al. 2010, 80–110.

20. Pithekoussai: Buchner and Ridgway 1993; Nizzo 2007, 140–44 for a catalogue of transport amphoras (from Euboia, Corinth, Athens and Chios); short presentation by Broodbank 2013, 512–13; see also Sourisseau 2011 and 2012, who stresses the role of amphoras from Corinth and Athens in the west in the earlier period. Methone: see Tzifopoulos 2012, for the imports of amphoras from Athens and of the cities of Asia Minor (Lesbos, Chios, Samos, Miletos). In Pithekoussai and Methone have been found not only local productions but also imports both of amphoras and some fine ware coming from distant production centers. In the eastern Mediterranean, the two mid-eighth century Phoenician wrecks found off Ashkelon (Ballard et al. 2002, with Broodbank 2013, 513–14), which together represent a total of almost 800 amphoras, prove that this form of development was not limited to the Greek world (see Sourisseau 2012, 192, for a nuanced approach of the comparative phases of development of the Greek and Phoenician networks).

21. For the eastern Mediterranean, see the Kekova wreck (to the south of Lykia), of perhaps the mid-seventh century BCE, and Kepçe Burnu wreck (to the north of the Keramic Gulf), of the end of the seventh or perhaps the beginning of the sixth century. Both wrecks have basket-handle amphoras that suggest transport of olive oil, or perhaps wine (Greene 2011). For the western Mediterranean, see the Giglio wreck of ca. 600 BCE (later, n. 28).

22. See Osborne 1996.

23. See Whitbread 1995 (see 4–7 for a short overview of the chronological evolution).

24. On productivity differences in production of grain, see chapter 6.

25. Jongman 2007 and 2014, 94.
26. For the concomitant development of slavery and wine trade in late Archaic Chios, see earlier, chapter 5, 126–27.
27. On artisanal products, see the volume *Topoi*, 8.2, 1998, which abundantly illustrates the range of products in the various cities.
28. For a series of these products, see the cargoes of the shipwrecks of Giglio (island of Giglio, off the coast of Tuscany, probably an Etruscan ship but transporting also Greek goods; around 600 BCE; see Bound 1991 and Parker 1992, 192, no. 451); Porticello (in the straits of Messina; around 425–400 BCE; see Eiseman and Ridgway 1987 and Parker 1992, 332–34, no. 879); El Sec (Balearic Islands; around 350 BCE; see later, n. 142); Kyra Panagia and Alonnisos (northern Sporades; mid-fifth century and end of the fifth century BCE; see later, n. 153). Thus the ship that sank at Porticello was carrying a bronze statue, significant parts of which have been recovered (Eiseman and Ridgway 1987, 63–113). One might also mention among others the famous late Archaic Vix crater, imported from Southern Italy into Gaul probably by way of Marseilles together with Attic ceramics, or the mid-fifth century Riace bronzes, found in the sea off Calabria at the tip of the Italian peninsula.
29. See chapter 6, 171–72, which indicates the relationship of 1 to 8 between the price of ordinary wine and that of a quality wine, which gives an idea of the price ranges for this kind of product and, at the same time, the profits that could be made on large estates.
30. On textile prices, see later, 356–57.
31. That is exactly the mechanism described by Adam Smith (1995 [1776], vol. 2, 159–209 [= Vol. 2, Book 4, chapters 8 and 9 of the first edition]) reflecting on the experience of Holland and England in modern times.
32. See chapter 15. Analogous developments can be observed in other historical periods, thus with the depression that struck Europe after 1630–1650 had serious consequences in the "semi-peripheral areas," see Wallerstein 1979–1984, vol. 2, 129–241, and especially 130–43 for the case of the countries of the Baltic Sea (particularly Poland) and Hungary.
33. Alcock 1993b.
34. See Porten and Yardeni 1993, synthesis xx–xxi.
35. For fundamental definitions on the notion of network in ancient history, see Rutherford 2009 and Malkin 2011, 3–64.
36. See chapter 3.
37. For Ephesos, see the amphoras from the "tetragonal" agora, Bezeczky 2002, 2004 and 2013, 35–119, for the late Republican and early Imperial period; on the Italians in Ephesos, Kirbihler 2007. For Maresha, see the general political and economic context in Finkielsztejn 1998; besides the imports of Rhodian wine, see the imports of oil amphoras of the Brindisi type, ovoid republican, African, and perhaps Sicilian amphoras ("tubular amphoras"), Finkielsztejn 2000, 213–14, and 2002a, 230–32, with 2002b, 139–40 on the characteristics of amphoras from Brindisi, and more generally 2012b.
38. On the use of perfumes, their prices and the way in which they were sold (with the question of the *unguentaria*), see Reger 2005. On the production of perfumes, with data from Delos and Paestum, see Brun 1999 and 2000.
39. Badinou 2003, 51–125, on alabasters and perfumes, and particularly 59–61 for vases representing scenes of the purchase of alabasters for perfumes.

40. Reger 2005, 279. If, for the same product, the other Delian prices that we know about, but without any indication of quality, had also been calculated on the same basis, the prices in drachms in Delos are supposed to have fluctuated between 2 2/3 and 5 1/3 in the third century and at the beginning of the second century. But we have to acknowledge that the quantity bought by the sanctuary was always the same, that is 1.5 *kotulai*, which is possible but far from certain. We will note that even if, as in the case of purchases made by the sanctuary in Delos, we cannot determine precisely the number of users, perfumes were evidently sold by the *kotulē*, that is a unit of 0.27 liter, a rather surprising quantity for perfumes today. That is because contemporary perfumes are based on processes of distillation that concentrate the fragrances. But distillation was not known in antiquity (see chapter 7, 180).

41. Dioscorides 1.55.1–2.

42. Teles 2.2.106–109 (*On Self-Sufficiency*), p. 12 O'Neil 1977 (13 Hense).

43. See chapter 4, 98–101.

44. On the tin supply, see Forbes 1964–1972, vol. 9, 140–48 (and more generally 134–86 on tin production and processing) and Kaptan 1983.

45. See Aronis 1952 and the convenient map in Bakhuizen 1977, 225 (after Aronis). On an iron mine near Chalkidike, see chapter 6, 151–52.

46. For the Kyklades, Brun 1996, 130–31.

47. On this point, see the demonstration in Robert 1969.

48. Neppi Modona 1981 and Camporeale 1985.

49. General views on the production of ancient textiles in Schneider 1992, 120–29.

50. On textile processing (washing the fibers or finishing the fabrics by fulling, spinning, dyeing, weaving), Forbes 1964–1972, vol. 4: linen, 27–43 (with heating the flax for bleaching); for wool, 20–22 on the operations of washing and preparing the wool, and 99–150 on dyes and dyeing.

51. For natron and its uses in antiquity (Egypt, Orient and Classical world), see Forbes 1964–1972, vol. 3, 181–87.

52. See Doumet 2007.

53. Allgrove-McDowell 2003, 36, and Forbes 1964–1972, earlier, n. 50.

54. *P.Cairo.Zen.* 3 59304, a letter from Protarchos to Zenon asking to send him the promised natron, so that the linen bleachers may not remain inactive (literally the linen bleachers were known as "linen boilers," for flax had to be boiled to be processed). On the monopoly on natron in Ptolemaic Egypt, see Forbes 1964–1972, earlier, n. 50.

55. Institut d'Égypte 1800, 262–68.

56. See later and n. 67.

57. For alum, see Forbes 1964–1972, vol. 3, 189–91. On "alum in the Mediterranean area" see Borgard et al. 2005 (but this is especially true for the Imperial and medieval periods).

58. See Halleux 2005 and Picon 2005.

59. Borgard 2005.

60. Borgard 2005, 161, with a very useful presentation.

61. *I.Priene*[2] 417 (see Debord 1982, 342, n. 166). The text refers either to a monopoly on the sale of alum or to the revenue of a tax on the sale of alum.

62. Aulus Gellius 15.1.

63. See earlier, 339–40.

64. Pausanias 6.26.6.

65. Baumann 2000, 34–35, and de Callataÿ 2004 (study of the first series of Amastris bearing on its reverse the related type of the flax flower).

66. See later on this point, concerning the case of Hermione.

67. Wool: references in Tal 2009, 7, n. 36. Natron: references in Porten and Yardeni 1993, index p. xlv; see comment in Briant and Descat 1998, 95, who do not take into account the use of natron for bleaching linen, but who are right to note that all the natron did not necessarily go to Greece. However, even at this date and (475 BCE) and despite the context of war between the Persian Empire and the Athenian alliance, the Phaselitans may well have found a way to send part of their natron toward the Greek cities of the Aegean (on the context, see earlier, chapter 11, 293).

68. Pliny 31.46 [111], with Strabo 17.1.23, who mentions two large natron beds above Memphis and stresses the proximity to Naukratis. See the detailed discussion of ancient sources and modern investigations in Lucas 1962, 263–67.

69. Oppenheim 1967, 242–43, 246, and 248. On producing and selling purple in Phoenicia, see Doumet in 2007, and Gratton 2007 for the Imperial period.

70. On this passage see the detailed commentary and references in Rizakis 1995, 185, no. 274. It is tempting to explain the allusions made by Pausanias, who also connects the women of Patras with Aphrodite, by certain women's concern to find additional resources. On textile production, see chapter 7, 190–94, chapter 8, 210–11, and chapter 10, 280.

71. On the transportation of wool and the hypothesis that the cities of the Corinthian isthmus were supplied by wool coming from western Greece, see chapter 7, 192.

72. See earlier, chapter 11, 289.

73. *IG* VII 12.

74. Gjongecaj and Nicolet-Pierre 1991.

75. See later for Pliny and fashions in purple clothes. For the existence of fashions in perfumes, see Reger 2010.

76. On these aspects of innovation, see chapter 8, 208–10.

77. Jameson et al. 1994, 317, with references. It will be recalled that the giant *Syracusan* ship designed by Archimedes was supposed to have transported, among other things, 520 tons of wool (see chapter 3, 88, and chapter 7, 193).

78. On dye production, Monaghan 2000.

79. On the existence of Boulis at least as early as the Classical period, see Ouhlen, in Hansen and Nielsen 2004, 410–11. In the small Boiotian city of Chorsiai, east of Boulis but inland, excavations have revealed cisterns corresponding to the site of a small textile production area (see Fossey and Gauvin 1992, 339–59, and McInerney 1999, 329–32). The area, the "south industrial zone," was situated outside the city about 40 meters south of the wall. It had a system of water conveyance that ran through the city before descending to this production area. The unpleasant odors might explain why the site was chosen (for the siting of the Delian production facilities, see chapter 12, 328, and following note).

80. Euboia: see Dio Chrysostom 7.2. Delos: Bruneau 1969, who brings together the textual and archaeological documentation (vat) and shows that, *ceteris paribus*, murex was harvested in Delos, Rheneia, and Mykonos, and purple was made in Delos, with Bruneau 1978, 110–14 ("La fabrication de la pourpre à Délos," new installation); see

also Hellmann 1992, 191, with reference to Chamonard 1922, 43–45 and 214–15, for a hypothetical localization of these workshops. Miletos: Herrmann 1975. Aperlai: Hohlfelder and Vann 2000. Euhesperides: Wilson 2006a and Wilson and Tébar Megías 2008.

81. Boulis: Pausanias 10.37.2–3; see Rousset 2002, 38 and 61, no. 42.

82. Thucydides 1.67.4 and 139.1–2; Aristophanes *Acharnians* 532–34; Diodorus 12.39.4; Plutarch *Pericles* 29.4. See Legon 1981, 200–27 and Smith 2008, 103–4, with other ancient sources and the most recent bibliography.

83. Amigues 2004.

84. See Robert 1936, 77–79 (= Robert 2007, 444–46). On honey from Theangela, see chapter 5, 130–31.

85. On other saltworks, see chapter 7, 180–81.

86. Lytle 2013b.

87. Strabo 12.2.10, with Doonan 2002, 194–95, and Barat 2009 for a global view of Sinope's trade networks.

88. Brun 1997, other reputation of the cheese from Kythnos and exports.

89. Stone from Siphnos: Pliny 36.44 [159]. Pliny probably referred to a soapstone (steatite) deposit.

90. Athenaeus 8 349ef, Hesychius s.v. *sikuōnia*. See Griffin 1982, 32 and n. 21 (with the other references).

91. *Tarantina*: Cleland et al. 2007, 187; *amorgina*: Cleland et al. 2007, 5 (with the reference to *amorgis* as a type of fabric. *Tarantina* and *amorgina* were commonly worn by *hetaireiai* and prostitutes (see Dalby 2002, 115–21). On the *exōmis*, see Cleland et al. 2007, 64, and for Megara, see chapter 7, 193.

92. On the activities of the ferrymen of Tenedos, see Rutishauser 2001 and Barnes 2006.

93. Heracleides fr. 1.23–24 Arenz (2006, with German translation 123–24 and commentary 151–52 and 208–9; see also Barnes 2006, n. 45, pp. 175–76). On the chronology of Heracleides, see chapter 2, 45, and n. 50. On *phukos*, see Theophrastus *Enquiry into Plants* [*Historia Plantarum*] 4.6.5; Pliny. 13.48 [136]. The suggestion of the present writer (Bresson 2007–2008, vol. 2, 155, the French edition of this volume) that the text referred to the collection of seaweed (assimilated to orchil, which however was not correct) for tinctorial usage has been challenged by Lytle 2010, 278–79, n. 95; but for a detailed analysis of the logic of the passage and for the role of this seaweed, *Rytiphloea tinctoria*, see Bresson 2015. According to Plutarch (*Greek Questions* 19 = *Moralia* 295de), Anthedon produced little wine, which seems to contradict Heracleides (Arenz 2006, 209). But perhaps we should assume that the city's wine was good, which is why Heracleides described it as *euoinos*, but not abundant, which is why Plutarch described it as *ou poluoinos*. On the economy of Anthedon, see also Lytle 2010, 277–80.

94. Beopoulou 1987 and 1989.

95. Ephorus, *apud* Strabo 8.6.16 = FGrHist 70 F176.

96. Late Hellenistic coins from Selge featuring the *sturax* (silver): Baumann 2000 and *BMC Pisidia* 37, *SNG BN Paris* (France 3) 1959, *SNG Cop.* (32 Pisidia) 256, *SNG von Aulock* 5284.

97. On the concept of niche, see Levick 2004, 194, who quotes among other examples precisely that of fabrics made of goat hair. Varro (*On Agriculture* 2.11.12) explains the origin of the name; see also Sisenna *Hist.* 107: usage around 70 BCE; Cicero *Verrines*

2.1.95; Strabo 2.5.32 (for Scenite Arabs) and 11.2.1 (for barbarian tribes in the Caucasus area); Pliny 6.30 [125] and 6.32 [143]: Scenite Arabs; Solin 34: use by the Scenite Arabs, who "lived under tents" (*skēnē* = tent), of these fabrics made of goat hair.

98. Brun 1997 clearly demonstrates this.

99. This is the complex question of "imitations" of amphora shapes, which cannot be reduced to the simplistic desire to benefit from the "branded" shape of another city; see in detail Lawall 2010, especially 47–49.

100. *P.Cairo.Zen.* 59012; see Bresson 2012c.

101. On the question of amphora stamps, see earlier, chapter 9, 243.

102. Horden and Purcell 2000, 352–64, who situate, in a very suggestive way, developments of this kind in a transhistorical perspective and show that in this respect the Western Middle Ages was for a long time much closer to antiquity and less "industrial" than has been assumed until recently.

103. On milling techniques, see chapter 7, 195–98.

104. Presentation of Hermione: Jameson 1994, particularly 37–39 and 581–95 on the city, with map 4 on the territory immediately adjacent to the city; Baladié 1980, 190–91, for the geography. On the political aspects of the Classical period, see Piérart in Hansen and Nielsen 2004, 609–10.

105. Jameson 994, 596–606 (who retains the traditional date in the middle of the second century established on the basis of prosopographic cross-checking); Chandezon 2003, 28–33, no. 5 (who accepts the earlier dating to the end of the third century).

106. Jameson et al. 1994, 262–67.

107. Grandjean 1990.

108. Ault 1999; Jameson et al. 1994, 268–76.

109. van Andel and Runnels 1987, 105–109.

110. Ibid., 115.

111. Hood 1961–1962, 5 (see Parker 1992, 309–10, no. 808, shipwreck of Petrokaravo). The specifications "Laconian" or "Corinthian" do not designate a provenance but a type of fabrication: "Laconian roofs are characterized by large, concave pan tiles which drain rain- water from the slopes and narrower, convex cover tiles, so called because they cover the spaces between pan tiles. Corinthian roofs have relatively flat pan tiles and pitched cover tiles" (Winter 1990, 13; see Ginouvès et al. 1985–1998, vol. 2, 186–88, and pl. 82–83). In the framework of this broad distinction, there existed however specific regional styles of tile productions, as shown by Winter 1990. The two types of tiles could be used locally for the roofs of two building standing side by side (thus at Halieis, see Cooper 1990). Numerous tiles of the Corinthian type have been discovered in Halieis, see Ault 1999, with figs. 7 and 8, p. 553. For a workshop producing Laconian tiles in Thasos at the end of the archaic period or at the very beginning of the Classical period, see Perreault 1990. For production and trade in tiles in the Greek world, Billot 2000.

112. On purple from Hermione, see Jameson et al. 1994, 316–19.

113. The restaurant of Pithaknion (the name means literally "Little Jar") is supposedly a place where it is possible to get food in large quantity. On the ideology of the parasites and the undermining of the conventions of elite aspirations it reveals, see König 2013, especially 203.

114. On white oil and its preparation, see Dioscorides 1.30.3–4, with Bresson 2012a, 76–77.

115. Thus finally Jameson et al. 1994, 316.

116. Oppenheim 1967, 237–38 and 242–43.

117. For use in the Achaemenid world, see the paintings on the tomb of Tatarlı (see Summerer 2007 and Emmerling 2010).

118. Bruneau 1969, 763.

119. Ibid.

120. Salamis: Herodotus 8.43; Plataiai: Herodotus 9.28.4; see Jameson et al. 1994, 556–59.

121. See chapter 7, 178, 181 and 183.

122. *GHI* 96, l. 40. Analysis by Jameson et al. 1994, 559–61.

123. On this question, see chapter 15.

124. Hermione borrowing from Delos: Migeotte, *Emprunt public*, 147–50, no. 45, VII, IX, XI, XII.

125. Ault 1999, n. 69, p. 566.

126. See Grandjean 1990.

127. Krugman and Obstfeld 2010, 14–15. On the question of energy and transportation costs, see chapter 3.

128. Burford 1960 and 1969.

129. Hermippus fr. 63 Kock and Kassel-Austin, l. 14 (*apud* Athenaeus 1 27e–28a).

130. See later.

131. On this wreck, see earlier, 361.

132. *I.Pérée* 86–87 (with references), complemented by *I.Knidos* 672, for Knidos-Datça.

133. See chapter 3, 80.

134. Aischylides, cited by Aelian *On Animals* 16.32.

135. For similar observations for the western Mediterranean contexts, see Sourisseau 2011, 224–25.

136. The circulation of coins was also strongly influenced by financial and political considerations, like the overvaluation of local coins and the creation of closed currency systems. See Bresson 1993a for the case of the limited circulation of Rhodian coins in the Hellenistic period, at a time when the city was the hub of international trade.

137. Arnold-Biucchi 1988.

138. See Garlan 1999c and 2000, 173–92, and Lund and Gabrielsen 2005.

139. Heilporn 2000.

140. Tomber 1987; Wilson 2006b, 228–28.

141. See chapter 7, 196–97.

142. Kyrenia shipwreck: Swiny and Katzev 1973; see Parker 1992, 231–32, no. 563. El Sec shipwreck: Arribas et al. 1987a, 563–73, and 1987b; Parker 1992, 392–94, no. 1058, Williams-Thorpe and Thorpe 1990 for the analysis of the millstones from El Sec: out of 42 mills with funnels, 27 are made of lava from Pantelleria (and 10 others that may be of the same origin), one from Nisyros; of the rotary mills, one comes from Mulargia in Sardinia.

143. On the existence of routes and regular commercial partnerships as early as the archaic period, see Osborne 1996, who bases his demonstration on the distribution of Attic ceramics as a commercial marker.

144. British Admiralty, *The Mediterranean Pilot*, 1941, 191.

145. On Cape Kaphereus, see Geisau 1919.

146. Coleman et al. 1992; O'Neill et al. 1999; Whitley 2003–2004.

147. On Anthedon, see earlier. On fishing in Halai, see the anecdote reported by Plutarch *Sylla* 26.3–4 (in 86 BCE, the Roman general destroyed the three neighboring cities

Halai, Larymna, and Anthedon, but he is supposed to have spared the survivors from Halai because of the quality of the fish that the local fishermen had brought him).

148. Lesbos: see Bresson 2000, 101–8, with map p. 103. See also Bresson 2011b for the case of the Knidian peninsula in Asia Minor, with the contrast between the northern coast open to the northern winds and sparsely occupied and the southern coast on the route protected form the northern winds and densely occupied.

149. See chapter 10.

150. On the amphoras and the wine from Peparethos and Ikos, Doulgeri-Intzessiloglou and Garlan 1990; for Akanthos, Garlan 2004b and 2006, and Filis 2013.

151. Salviat 1990 and Papadopoulos and Paspalas 1999.

152. Three amphoras from Mende at El Sec: Arribas et al. 1987, 468–70.

153. Kyra Panagia: Blackman 2001–2002, 59, with fig. 94-97. Alonnisos: Hadjidaki 1996 and Hatzidake 1997. See also earlier, chapter 3, n. 89.

154. Flensted-Jensen 1999; Badoud 2013.

155. Stamatopoulou 2011, 80–81. On Peparethos, see earlier, n. 150, and chapter 5, 126.

156. Garlan 2004a; Badoud 2013.

157. On Kassandreia, see chapter 4, 113–15.

158. Papadopoulos and Paspalas 1999, 173.

159. For Thasos, see Garlan in Grandjean and Salviat 2000, 185–91.

160. Similarly, on Alciphron and the purple from Hermione, see earlier, 361–62.

161. Coase 1960; Margolis 1991.

162. Gill 1991 and 1994; see also Vickers and Gill 1996, 85–92.

163. Arafat and Morgan 1994, 117, with table fig. 7.4.

164. On the other hand, it is not possible to agree with Gill 1994, 102, in his estimates of the quantity of ceramics that arrived in Etruria or other sites, as if archaeological discoveries corresponded to the quantities that objectively arrived at their destination: although we can rely on discoveries in estimating the chronological development of these arrivals, we cannot in any way maintain that these discoveries directly reflect the volume of the quantities that arrived— as if all the sites had been excavated, and in addition excavated exhaustively. Obviously, there is every chance that they represent only a tiny portion of the quantities that actually arrived, in a proportion that must be estimated using entirely different methods.

165. Gill 1991, 35–37.

166. See the information collected by Sabattini 2000.

167. In the same vein (the Piraeus as a market at the center of Greece where it is possible to buy every possible good), see Isocrates *Panegyric* 4.42.

168. On this question, the point of view of Gill 1991, 37–38, according to which the prices of ceramics were as low on arrival as they were on departure cannot be adopted. Gill can mention only a single case of a graffito put on a ceramic in Cyprus where in fact the mention of the number 3 is more likely to correspond to three shekels than to three obols. At a minimum, the case should have been left open. The claim that pottery makers must necessarily have been poor (Vickers and Gill 1996, 92–95) is no more convincing.

169. In the same vein but with a different argument, Salmon 2000.

170. For the figure of 500 people, see Cook 1959, 118–21, and Arafat and Morgan, 326–27, who emphasize, however, the uncertainties of this estimate.

171. Vickers and Gill 1996, 91–92.

172. Rotroff 2006.
173. On the workshops in the Peloponnese, see Siebert 1978; on Athens, see a quick presentation in Rotroff 1984.
174. On ceramics from the West Slope of Athens, see Rotroff 1997; on the distribution of various productive centers, Rotroff 2002.
175. See the fundamental works of Morel 1981 and 2002–2003, on which the analysis presented here is based.
176. Morel 1986, 463–69.
177. Grand Congloué A shipwreck: Parker 1992, 200–201, no. 472. Similarly on the later Grand Congloué B shipwreck (Parker 1992, 201, no. 473) from the late second century or early first century BCE, Campanian B ceramics probably from Etruria accompanied Dressel 1A amphoras from the same provenance; see Wilson 2009, 227, on wrecks of this period where table pottery also accompanied amphoras.
178. On this point, see the following chapter.
179. Hellenistic period: see briefly Bresson 1998.
180. Herodotus 1.165.1.
181. On this point, see chapter 12, 322–25.
182. Pulak et al. 1987; Empereur and Tuna 1988 (for the provenance of the amphoras); see Parker 1992, 399–400, no. 1071.
183. Parker 1992, 200–201, no. 472.
184. Arribas et al. 1987, with synthetic table 410–11.
185. See de La Genière 1999 and 2006b, who gives various examples of vases that might correspond to orders made by distant purchasers; see in particular 2006, 12, on items ordered by Westerners from Chinese craftsmen.
186. On this point, see chapter 14, 393–94.

CHAPTER XIV: STRATEGIES OF INTERNATIONAL TRADE

1. On the notion of *autarkeia* for individuals and for the city, see earlier, chapters 9, 229 and 244, and 13, 339–41. For the attitude of the city toward foreign exchange, see mainly Aristotle *Politics* 1.3.12–13; 7.5.4; *Rhetoric* 1.4.11; *Nicomachean Ethics* 5.5.13; with other references and detailed comment in Bresson 2000, 111–30.
2. In the same vein, see also Isocrates 4.42 (*Panegyricus*); Polybius 4.38.8–9.
3. See on this point the speech by Ps.-Demosthenes 7.11–13 (*On Halonnesus*), with the detailed commentary in Bresson 2000, 292–93.
4. For the same logic in the imperial period, see Arnaud 2011a, 71–73.
5. *IG* II³ 1315 (shortly after 176/5 BCE). See Gauthier 1982.
6. For the sake of convenience, one posits an equivalence between one amphora and one Attic *metrētēs*, which indeed is correct for Athens but not for most other cities, where the amphora had a capacity lower than that of the Attic *metrētēs*).
7. Ps.-Aristotle *Economics* 2.2.8 (see Bresson 2000, 197–98).
8. Ps.-Demosthenes 56.9–10 *Against Dionysodorus*. See Le Rider 1997.
9. On information relating to trade, see details in chapter 11, 299–301.
10. On the *sitōnai* in general, Fantasia 1984. On *sitōnia* in Athens at the end of the fourth century and in the third century, see details in Oliver 2007, 215–22 and 255–59: it is

clear that even after the catastrophic defeats against Macedon and the decrease of the Athenian population, the state still had to care of the food supply. See also chapter 12, 333–38, on the role of the *sitōnai* as grain buyers for the cities' public funds.

11. *Digest* 50.4.18.5 on the existence of *curatores emendi frumenti olei*. For Athens, see the Athenian law concerning oil in force in the age of Hadrian, *IG* II² 1100 (on this law, see later, n. 99).

12. On the public grain funds, see earlier, chapter 12, 332–35.

13. Lane 1973, 119–32 and 337–52.

14. Xenophon *Hellenica* 4.56; see 57 for the end of the episode. Erdkamp 2005, 185–86, thinks that here the reference is to Phthiotic Thebai, which is hardly possible as the episode takes place in the context of the war between Boiotian Thebes and Sparta and as the route taken by the grain obviously passed through the Euboian Channel, whence the ambush set up by the Spartans at Oreos.

15. Xenophon *Hellenica* 6.1.11. On precipitation in Thessaly, see chapter 2, 37 (with 35); modern *comparanda*: Garnsey et al. 1984.

16. *IG* XI.4 1055 + 1025 (*Syll.*³ 493; *Choix* 7); on the same stone there follows a decree from Delos granting the Histaeians a location to set up the stele bearing the decree in honor of Athenodoros.

17. On Thessalian grain, see later, 396–99 and 412.

18. On this war, Will 1979–1982, vol. 2, 45–46; Gabrielsen 1997, 44–46.

19. Will 1979–1982, vol. 1, 396–401; vol. 2, 69–75; Walbank 1984, 473–78.

20. Polybius 4.16.6–8 and 19.7–8, see Wiemer 2002, 125.

21. Between 239 and 229 BCE, an envoy of the King of Macedon Demetrios II had come to Delos to purchase grain (see *IG* XI.4 666; *Choix Délos* 48), in a context of war, according to Reger 1994, 119–22.

22. Tr. W. M. Roberts.

23. On this crisis, see details in chapter 12, 336.

24. See Pazdera 2006, 165–72.

25. See later, n. 121.

26. For Athens, see Engen 2010; his chart pp. 225–29 provides a list of 34 cases for the period 415–307, most of them being related to grain trade.

27. *IG* XI.4 1049; Migeotte, *Emprunt public*, 345–47, no. 117; Duchêne and Fraisse 2001, 162–63; Gabrielsen 2005, 154.

28. *Pace* Duchêne and Fraisse 2001, ibid.; see for the opposite point of view, Vial 1984, 341–42, and Bresson 2000, 281–83.

29. *Pace* respectively Duchêne and Fraisse 2001, earlier n. 27 (seizures at sea), and Migeotte, earlier n. 27 (seizures in transit at Delos). The maritime contract in the speech *Against Lacritus* (see chapter 10, 281–84) stipulates explicitly that the ship may not stop at any port in which a seizure from the Athenians might be carried out.

30. Vial 1984, stemma XVI, p. 136 and passim.

31. These creditors are necessarily private creditors (the text does not say that the city went into debt to *the* Delians, but to *some* Delians). On the cycle of capital in Delos, see Gabrielsen 2005, 154.

32. This point was made by Migeotte, earlier n. 27.

33. *LGPN* I s.v.

34. See Migeotte, *Emprunt public*, 151–56, and no. 45.

35. See Brun 1996, 10.

36. Migeotte, *Emprunt public*, 248–52, no. 73.

37. *IG* XI.2 161A, l. 52 (*NChoixDélos* pp. 59–86, part. p. 61, Greek text, and 67, transl.).

38. Migeotte, earlier n. 27, has drawn up a list of the series of inscriptions in which Mnesalkos is mentioned. It just happens that he appears precisely in the same inscription, *IG* XI.2 161A, ll. 29–30, as remitting a sum of 60 dr. as payment of interest on a mortgage. These people belong to the same milieu and had all kinds of opportunities to meet one another.

39. For cases of food shortages in Boiotia and Euboia, see Reger 1994, 278–79.

40. See Bresson 1996, 75–77.

41. See details in Bresson 2001b.

42. In this reconstruction, we follow the commentary of van Groningen 1933, 111–15, modified and completed by Migeotte, *Emprunt public*, 271–72, no. 82, which offers the most plausible reconstruction. The word *hupothēkē* must certainly be understood as a "fund," see Migeotte, ibid., 234, n. 358; see also Gauthier 1989, 89–90 and n. 23. Vélissaropoulos 1980, 197, n. 156, understood that it was a "capital" and Fantasia 1984, 292–300, adopted that of "foundation capital." But this "foundation," or rather this "sum of money," was allocated for a reimbursement. Thus it is indeed a sum of money reserved for a specific use, in the context of a loan. Thus in the contract in *Against Lacritus* (see chapter 2), the 3,000 amphoras, or the proceeds from their sale, served as security for the loan. These thus played the role of a "reserved security" in the specific context of a loan. The translation must be the same in both occurrences of the word.

43. *Choix* 3; Migeotte, *Emprunt public*, 232–35, no. 67.

44. See chapter 6, 159–60.

45. See later.

46. Meiggs-Lewis 30 A, ll. 1–12; see *SEG* 31 984–85, and Brodersen et al., 1992–1999, I, 26–28, German translation and lemma; *Nomima*, vol. 1, 366–70, no. 104. The Greek words must be understood as having a practical and concrete sense. Thus the *pharmaka dēlētēria* are "poisoned drugs," rather than "acts of magic" (*Nomima*): hence the suggestion that here the matter was about substances that might contaminate wells, or in any other way might poison large numbers of people.

47. See chapter 12, 315–16.

48. On physical attacks on foreigners, see earlier, chapter 11, 302.

49. Teos-Lebedos: *RC* 3, § 10, ll. 72–94 (= Ager, *Arbitrations*, 61–64, no. 13). On the question of imports and exports and the problems raised by Antigonos's letter, see Bresson 1993b, 168–69 and n. 23.

50. Philostratus lived at the end of the second century and in the first half of the third century CE. See Jones 2005, 1–21, and Erdkamp 2002 for the questions of the food riots in the Late Hellenistic and Imperial periods.

51. Garnsey 1988, 76–77, for a short commentary on the episode.

52. Dio Chrysostom 46.8–11 (in self-defense, in his hometown of Prousa). See Sheppard 1984, 169–70; the speech is to be dated to the year of the proconsulship of Varenus Rufus, that is, probably 105/6 CE.

53. Ps.-Aristotle *Economics* 2.2.17. On the text see Bresson 2000, 202, and 2011a, 80–82. On old grain, see Gauthier 1987.

54. On the passage, see later, chapter 15, 432.

55. See Bresson 2011a. The case is also discussed later.
56. Garnsey et al. 1984 provide this text with a detailed and important commentary, among others on the ecology of Thessaly and its export capacities; see also Garnsey and Rathbone 1985, 25 (appendix) for the revised date of perhaps 129 BCE. See moreover *SEG* 34 558, *SEG* 45 614 (alternative chronological hypothesis); Bagnall and Derow 2004, 140–41, no. 81 (with an English translation and a short discussion of the dates that have been proposed for the text); as well as Graninger 2011, 28–33, for the structure of the Thessalian league and the role of the *stratēgos* (general). The translation given by Garnsey et al. 1984, of ll. 8–9, "that the *koinon* give as much grain as it has available," might lead to an inappropriate interpretation regarding what was actually a sale of grain to Rome. The authors claim that it was the aediles who profited from the sale of grain (p. 44). In fact it is clear that the sale referred to was made by the envoys of the Thessalian *ethnos* (they must have sold the grain to the aediles, who themselves would sell it in Rome, but this is another story). The authors correctly emphasize that Rome rejected the gifts (examples on p. 44). The supply procured by the Thessalians did not fall into this category, and the Thessalian case only further strengthens their argument. Indeed, in the end the authors admit that this "gift" must have been a sale.
57. *I.Ilion* 1; Migeotte, *Emprunt public*, 262–67, no. 79, before and after 306, l. 7 (*dous*), 9 (*edōke*), 10 (*edōke*), l. 26 (*edōke*), see l. 27 (*pareskeuase*, "he has procured"), l. 42 (*dounai*). It was a matter of money advanced at no interest (*chrēmata atoka*), but whose reimbursement was therefore foreseen.
58. For the remark on *epididonai*, see Gauthier, *Bull. ép.* 2006, no. 332.
59. Graninger 2011, 27–28.
60. On the situation of Thessaly in this period, see Pounder and Dimitrova 2003.
61. For the price of wheat in Sicily ca. 70, see Cicero *Verrines* 2.3.189–91: ordinarily 2 to 3 sesterces the *modius*, or 3 to 4.5 drachms the *medimnos*.
62. See earlier.
63. See chapter 4, 110–17.
64. See the case of Seleukid taxation, Capdetrey 2007, 395–422.
65. See Bresson 2007c and Müller 2010, 169–81 and 204–206. Tsetskhladze 2008 cannot provide a positive argument in favor of his view that Demosthenes's figure for Athenian imports was exaggerated.
66. See *IG* XII.2 3 (Tod 163). On the meaning of the grain quota for Mytilene, see chapter 11, n. 25.
67. Préaux 1939, 61–435 (chapters on the revenues of the Ptolemies); Manning 2010, 11–12, 45–49, and 152–57, for a nuanced new approach of the economy of Ptolemaic Egypt.
68. See Aperghis 2001, 78.
69. On the sources of revenue of the Seleukid king Demetrios I in 152, see chapter 4, 104.
70. That is the central thesis of Aperghis 2004.
71. Briant 1994.
72. *IG* II³ 295, with Briant 1994, 72–73, and Debord 1999, 350–52, who is thinking of an Orontes II, the grandson of the Orontes of the revolt of the satraps.
73. *IG* II² 401.
74. *RC* 3, ll. 72–75.

75. For the generous gifts made by the Seleukids, grain and oil, see Capdetrey 2007, 422–25.
76. See Bresson 2000, 208–10.
77. Oliver 2007, 228–59, and table pp. 285–89, with the complete table of the gifts received by the Athenians
78. On royal gifts in the Hellenistic period, Bringmann and von Steuben 1995–2000 and Bringmann 2001.
79. Polybius 5.88–90, with Bringmann and von Steuben 1995–2000, vol. 1, 238–40.
80. Diodorus 31.36, with Bringmann and von Steuben 1995–2000, vol. 1, 242.
81. Polybius 31.31.1–3, with Bringmann and von Steuben 1995–2000, vol. 1, 242–44.
82. Bringmann 2001, 208–9.
83. *I.Milet* 1039 I.6–7, with Bringmann and von Steuben 1995–2000, vol. 1, 242–44, and Bringmann 2001, 208–9.
84. *I.Priene*[2] 64, ll. 111–17; see Gauthier 1985, 55–56, on the phenomenon.
85. On this figure, see later.
86. On royal gifts and their significance for the grain supply in Athens at the beginning of the Hellenistic period, see Oliver 2007, 233–36.
87. On the context of Solon's reforms, see Foxhall 1997.
88. For this excerpt and the following, translations J. Dryden in *Plutarch's Lives*. See fragment F 65 in Ruschenbusch 1966 and Ruschenbusch 2010, 130–31.
89. It is almost unanimously thought (see L'Homme-Wéry 2004, 151, n. 52) that Solon was thinking of food products. However, it has been proposed (Descat 1993) to see in these *ginomena* an allusion to all the products of Attika, including those of craft activity and mines. As a result it has been concluded that Solon's law sought not to prohibit exports but to concentrate the sale of Attic products in the agora, where foreigners were supposed to be admitted only by express permission of the city. As L'Homme-Wéry notes (2004, 151, n. 52; see also the doubts expressed by Garlan 2000, 90, n. 93), this point of view is not convincing: why would Solon have urged the Athenians to have a trade? On this hypothesis, the overall logic of Solon's law disappears.
90. The whole point of the Athenian legislation was to keep the grain in Athens (*pace* Descat 2004, 599). On the process of selling the grain in Athens, see earlier, chapter 12.
91. Johnston and Jones 1978; Dupont 1995–1996 (low level of imports in the Black Sea).
92. Docter 1991.
93. The question of the link between amphora shape and content is not only a technical one. It has to do with the social and economic conditions of production of agricultural products and amphoras, as is shown by Lawall 2011.
94. See Johnston and Jones 1978 (typology, clay analysis, geographical distribution, and chronology). Their conclusion is worth quoting: "With regard to Attic exports, we must conclude from the distribution of SOS amphorae that good quantities of olive oil were shipped from Attika during the seventh century; judging solely from the evidence of the amphorae this trade tailed off in the sixth century, at just the time when Solon is supposed to have stimulated it rather than other exports." Lawall 2002, 202 and 223, no. 75–76, for the presence of a few amphoras "à la brosse" down to the last quarter of the sixth century in Troad.
95. Lawall 2000, 77, n. 118. Thus one cannot follow the interpretation of Gauthier (1982, 290), according to which at least in the Hellenistic period, "Attika ordinarily produced

sufficient quantity of oil and even exported it." At best, the city was self-sufficient: if the harvest was bad, it had to import, which is the situation described in the inscription *IG* II³ 1315, analyzed earlier, 383–84.

96. Valavanis 1986; Bentz 1998 provides a complete study (technique, décor, fabrication of the oil, and so on): see particularly 31–40 on the capacity of the amphoras, 89–95 on sale of oil and 111–15 the map of distribution of the amphoras; Tiverios 2007 on the continuity of the shape between SOS and Panathenaic amphoras and on the various systems (over time) by which the Athenian state procured the "sacred oil."

97. Price of oil: *IG* II² 1356, ll. 7–8 and 13–14, with Markle 1985, 280–81. For the prices of oil and their variations, see Pritchett and Pippin 1956, 184.

98. Drachmann 1903–1927, vol. 3, 174, 64b.

99. *IG* II² 1100 (Abbott and Johnson, 1926, 411–13, no. 90; Oliver, *Greek Constitutions*, 208–15, no. 84); see Graindor 1934, 74–79; Boatwright 2000, 91–92: Hadrian as a new *nomothētēs* (lawgiver) for Athens; Harter-Uibopuu 2008, with full text and detailed institutional comments; for her, the law was based on a Roman model of economic management but with a high degree of traditionalism in terms of Athenian institutions.

100. See in detail Garnsey 1988, 98–106, and 1998c, 201–13.

101. Moreno 2007, 3–33, devotes a detailed analysis to the production of grain in Attika. He denies any value to the Eleusis inscription (13–14) and calculates on a speculative basis (see chart p. 10) a total production for Attika of 700,000 *medimnoi*, which he equates to roughly 20,000 tons or 200,000 quintals. This is exactly 100 percent above the figures that can be derived from the inscription from Eleusis. As is shown later, we have every reason to think both that the figures from the Eleusis inscription provide valid information on the grain production of Attika and that ancient (or early modern Attika) was—by very far—never able to produce the quantity of grain he calculates. For a historiographical presentation of the question of grain production and consumption in Attika, see Pazdera 2006, 84–96. See also Oliver 2007, 15–40 and 228–59, and Bissa 2009, 169–76, who also insist on the dependency of Athens on imported grain.

102. *Recensement* 1914, p. VII.

103. *Recensement* 1914, table IV, p. 372.

104. See the appendix on weights, measures and currency units.

105. The average grain yield of 7.75 quintal per hectare is superior to the average yield for Attika and Boiotia for the period 1921–1932 (4.9 for wheat and 6.3 for barley) and rather on the order of those of the period 1933–1939 (7.9 for wheat and 9.2 for barley), at a time when the "agricultural revolution" was beginning to take effect in Greece (for the figures of yields from 1921 onward, see Ruschenbusch 1988).

106. A detailed study will have be devoted to the question, of which only a first sketch can be provided here.

107. *Recensement* 1923, summary table no. V, pp. 24–25.

108. Garnsey 1988, 96–106, multiplies the figure of 329/8 by two (or more than two), maintaining that it reflected a bad harvest.

109. Hansen 1988, 12, and 2006, 56.

110. *Recensement* 1914, p. VII.

111. As mentioned in chapter 2, 63 and n. 144, an estimate of a level of population of as much as 431,000 inhabitants in 316, moreover at a time of demographic depression following military losses in the Lamian War and the emigration of poor citizens,

cannot be adopted. One would have to reckon with a population of as many as 575,000 inhabitants (or considerably more) in the fifth century, because the figures for 316 are necessarily lower than those of the years of prosperity 330–320. On this basis, population figures going far beyond 600,000 inhabitants would inevitably have to be adopted for the fifth century: they are completely unrealistic if we take into account not only modern *comparanda*, but also the grain import figures that are known to us from ancient sources.

112. Garnsey 1988, 97.
113. The figure would be about 387,000 *medimnoi* if are included the 46,975 *medimnoi* of the territories of the nearby possessions of Drymos, Salamis and Oropos. On the conquest of these territories, see later.
114. Stroud 1998.
115. The figures proposed here are slightly lower than those presented in Bresson 2007c, 65. The list of grain exporters should of course include Thessaly, a region that was a large grain producer, while many smaller partners certainly also exported some grain to Athens. For an overview of the grain exporters, see Pazdera 2006, 101–72 (Black Sea, Egypt, Cyrene, Cyprus, and the West).
116. For grain export from Egypt, both for both the Classical and Hellenistic (Ptolemaic) periods, see Buraselis 2013, who concludes that until the end of the dynasty grain exports remained a fundamental asset for the Ptolemies.
117. Diodorus 14.79.4; *Hell. Oxy.* 10.3; Justin, 6.2.1–3 indicates that the Pharaoh sent them "100 triremes and 600,000 bushels of wheat." The figure for the exports of Cyrene in the early 320s, that is, more than 800,000 *medimnoi*, is certainly an exceptional amount, commensurate with the famine that was then raging in Greece. Normal export figures must have been lower.
118. The speculation consisted in setting up a monopoly on exportation, which put it in a favorable position to set its prices. On the notions of monopoly and monopsony, see later, chapter 15.
119. Helly 2008 (*SEG* 58 525).
120. *SEG* 9 2; Laronde 1987, 30–34; Marasco 1992; *GHI* 96; see detailed analysis in Bresson 2011a.
121. Thucydides 3.86.4 for the export of Sicilian grain toward the Peloponnese and the will of the Athenians to cut that supply route (with 6.20.4 for the grain production of Syracuse and Selinous).

CHAPTER XV: THE GREEK CITIES AND THE MARKET

1. See chapter 13, 346–49.
2. On this point, see chapter 2, 56–64.
3. See Bresson 2001c and the information collected in Bresson and Descat 2001.
4. See Roussel 1916, 1–18, on the conditions of creation of the "free port" of Delos.
5. See already chapter 4, 109.
6. On booty, the sharing of war profits, the importance of piracy, and more generally the connection between war and economics, see Garlan 1989 and Couvenhes and Fernoux 2004 for Asia Minor, with the survey drawn up by Gabrielsen 2007 on the relationship

between the state and war (the traditional model was that of a direct appropriation by individuals; the state increasingly tended to control the war profits); Chaniotis 2005, 129–37, specifically for the Hellenistic period.

7. Scholten 2000 on Aitolian piracy; Brulé 1978 on Cretan piracy.

8. See in particular Meiggs 1972 and Cargill 1981, where one will find the basics of a considerable literature.

9. Salomon 1997, 31–37.

10. Salomon 1997, 37–38.

11. IG I³ 61, ll. 34–41; see Pébarthe 2000, 63–64. On the political controls exercised by various powers at different periods along the route to the Bosporos, see Bresson 2007c and Pébarthe 2000.

12. IG I³ 174; see Pébarthe 2000, 63 (but the origin of this Achaian—from Phthiotic Achaia or the Peloponnese—still seems not established). For the passage from the *Constitution of Athenians* (2.11–13), see chapter 13, 339–40.

13. Polybius 28.2.1–6.

14. On an aspect of this tax in kind in Asia, see earlier, chapter 3, 83.

15. For Athens, see Livy (43.6.3) with earlier, chapter 14, 410.

16. On this point, see chapter 14, 396–98.

17. On this point, see later.

18. IG I³ 1453; new fragment Hatzopoulos 2000–2003; on the complex history of this text (through its various local copies), see Papazarkadas 2009, 72, and Scafuro 2013, 409, who would not exclude the possible existence of several decrees.

19. Meadows 2011; for the Rhodian standard, Ashton 2001, 79–82 (tetradrachm originally at 15.30 grams, as against 17.30 grams for the Attic tetradrachm at this time).

20. Picard 1980 and 2007.

21. Attalids and Ptolemies: Le Rider 1986, 1989 and 1998b; Le Rider and de Callataÿ 2006; Rhodes: Bresson 1993a.

22. Meyer and Moreno 2004.

23. Goddio 2007, 208, and 310, no. 422 (weight 416 grams, hardly less than that of 10 Attic drachms: wear and loss of weight easily explain the difference). Coins with Attic types at Herakleion, 208, and 310, no. 423 and 424.

24. On the question of the production of Attic owls in Egypt at the end of the fifth or the beginning of the fourth century, see briefly Picard 2007.

25. Gitler and Tal 2006, 63–68 and 335–37 (with 315 on the weight standard, lower than the Attic standard, but with denomination following the Attic system) and 2009.

26. On transportation costs, see chapter 3, 79–88; on prohibitions on exports, chapter 14, 402–5.

27. On this notion of silver "commodity chain," see the convincing analyses of Panagopoulou 2007.

28. On grain prices and their evolution Greece and Rome, see now von Reden and Rathbone 2014.

29. Loomis 1998.

30. See de Callataÿ 1989. On the relations between prices and money supply, see Bresson 2005a and earlier, chapter 2.

31. Reger 1994 (synthesis) and 1997 (on the difficulties of building a price history from the Delian data).

32. For prices on the Babylonian market, see Joannès 1997; van der Spek 2000 and 2006; Vargyas 1997 and 2001.

33. Reger 1994, 226–31.

34. See de Callataÿ 2006a.

35. Bresson 2006b.

36. See earlier, chapter 9, 257–58.

37. If some of the grain sold in Delos could come from other Kykladic islands, there is no doubt that (on this point *pace* von Reden in von Reden and Rathbone 2014, 167) that grain produced in distant regions represented the large majority of the grain sold on this market. See Bresson 2000, 279–82, and 2006c (and also 2011a for the grain imported from Cyrene by the Kykladic cities). When in the first years of the second century BCE we see the grain commissioners (*sitōnai*) of the confederation (*koinon*) of the islanders coming to Delos to buy grain, it is hard to believe that they bought grain produced on their islands: clearly they came to Delos to buy grain provided by distant suppliers (see in detail Bresson 2001b). Besides, if there is no doubt that some grain produced in the Kyklades might have been be sold on the Delian market, it remains that we still have no testimony proving that grain was sold in Delos by islanders, and that for now all our data point directly or indirectly toward distant suppliers.

38. On Phainippos, see chapter 6, 146–48.

39. See chapter 14.

40. On this hypothesis, see chapter 13, 350.

41. See earlier, chapter 14, 411–12.

42. On *stephanēphoros* coinage in Athens, see Thompson 1961.

43. Other chronologies have been proposed for the beginning of the *stephanēphoros* on the assumption that during the first years, magistrates were not changed annually. For a summary of the chronological debate, see Grierson in Mørkholm 1991, 170–71; Sosin 2004, 197–98; and Bresson 2006b, 61–62; with Boehringer quoted in Picard 2000, 154, n. 15. On the basis of the Bakërr hoard *IGCH* 559, which contains four early Athenian *stephanēphoroi* (years 2 and 7 Thompson), Picard (2010a, 169–74, and 2011, 99, with 2010b, 53, for the chronological consequence for the coinage of Thasos; see Picard and Gjongecaj 2000, 154, and 2001, 243–49) has however recently reargued in favor of a beginning of the *stephanēphoroi* around 185–180 BCE (chronology Mørkholm 1984; see Grierson in Mørkholm 1991, 170–71, for a presentation of the debate) or rather 172–74 BCE (in order to "prepare the war" against Macedon). According to Picard, given that the Bakërr hoard contains coins of the Epirote confederation minted immediately before 167, this hoard must have buried in that year, right after these coins had been minted. But there is no compelling reason to accept this view. Apollonia was on the Roman side and besides the hoard may perfectly well have been buried later, even though the Epirote confederation had disappeared in 168. The Larissa ("Sitichoro") hoard *IGCH* 237 = *CH* 9 247 buried ca. 165 BCE (see Price 1989, 238–39 and 243; de Callataÿ 2009, 86), which contains both various series of coins back to the time of Alexander III and coins corresponding to the period of the third Macedonian war, has twenty-two Athenian coins, all pre-*stephanēphoroi* obviously struck immediately before the beginning of the *stephanēphoroi*, but not a single *stephanēphoros* tetradrachm. This would be unexpected if the *stephanēphoroi* had really

been circulated for one or two decades. An annual minting and a beginning of the *stephanēphoroi* in 164/3 BCE remains by far the best hypothesis.

44. Thompson 1961.
45. Finkielsztejn 2001b, with chart p. 186, fig. 1b, for the decline in production revealed by the collection of amphora stamps from Lindos. It is likely that the way in which the collection was made accentuated these developments but one cannot doubt the validity of the schema as a whole.
46. For the details of the analysis of the Delian economic situation in the second century and at the beginning of the first century, and for the analysis of the amphictionic decree *CID* IV 127, see Bresson 2006b. On the decree see also Psoma 2006, and for the *stephanēphoroi* Picard 2010a, 169–74, but with a different presentation of the chronology (see earlier).
47. On the slave revolt of 133 BCE, see Orosius 5.9.4–8. For a second slave revolt at Laurion at the end of the century, see Poseidonius *FGrHist* 87 F35 *apud* Athenaeus 6 272ef (Tracy 1979 thought that the likeliest date was 100–99 BCE, but Habicht 2006, 322, has insisted that one should not exclude the years 104–103 BCE).
48. Private communication from John Kroll.
49. For an overall assessment, see now the chapters in van der Spek et al. 2014.
50. See earlier, chapter 10, 275, and 13, 341.
51. On the views of the mercantilists on the subject of external trade, see Clément 2001, 44–50.
52. See fundamentally the work of Miller 1999 (especially 27–92) on the way markets functioned in Old Regime France,
53. Miller 1999, 56–57.
54. Persson 1999.
55. Aristotle *Politics* 1.4.7–8. See chapter 8, 215–16.
56. *OGIS*, vol. 1, pp. 105–12, no. 484, and vol. 2, p. 552 (Oliver, *Greek Constitutions*, 208–15, no. 84), with Macro 1976.
57. Persson 2014 is absolutely right in insisting on the disruptive impact of bad crops: shortages and famines in preindustrial societies were not caused only or mainly by poor institutional management but chiefly by currently insufficient supplies. It remains that, in both the short term and the long term, good or bad institutions could also contribute to the management of food crises in an uncertain environment.
58. Halstead and Jones 1989, 54; Halstead 1990; Reger 1994, 92. See Halstead and O'Shea 1989b for the four types of traditional responses to uncertainty, viz. mobility, diversification, storage and exchange.
59. Ps.-Aristotle *Economics* 2.2.17 (Selymbria; see earlier, chapter 14, 395).
60. Philo of Byzantion *On Siegecraft* (*Poliorcetica*) 2.30, with Gauthier 1987, 417.
61. On popular pressure, see chapter 14, 394.
62. See in detail Persson 2014.
63. *Pace* Gauthier 1976, 129, on this point, there is no need to exclude exports from Xenophon's reasoning.
64. For the instability of wine prices, see Tchernia 1986, 223.
65. See Samuelson and Nordhaus 2005, 71–72, and Persson 2014, on the negative impact on investments both of very bad and very good harvests.

66. See Samuelson and Nordhaus 2005, 745 and 198–99.
67. Ibid., 168–81 on the logic of monopoly.
68. See chapter 1, 26.
69. See earlier, chapter 11, 287–88 and 296.
70. On these concepts, see chapter 1, 22–25.
71. See chapter 8, 214–19.

SOURCES

The reader will find here not a comprehensive catalogue of the literary sources that have been cited in this book but a list of the editions and translations that have been referred to. For the epigraphic, papyrological, and numismatics sources, see the list of abbreviations.

Anonymous, *De rebus bellicis*
>> *A Roman Reformer and Inventor, Being a New Text of the Treatise* De rebus bellicis. 1952. Ed. and tr. E. A. Thompson. Oxford: Clarendon Press.
>> *Anonimo. Le cose della guerra.* 1989. Ed. and tr. A. Giardina. Milan: Mondadori.

Antipater of Thessalonike
>> See Greek Anthology.

Archestratus
>> *Archestratos of Gela: Greek Culture and Cuisine in the Fourth Century BCE: Text, Translation, and Commentary.* 2000. By S. D. Olson and A. Sens. New York: Oxford University Press.

Aristophanes
>> *Aristophanes.* 1998–2007. Ed. and tr. by J. Henderson. 5 vols. Loeb Classical Library. Cambridge, MA: Harvard University Press.

Aristotle
>> *Aristotelis qui ferebantur librorum fragmenta.* 1886. Ed. V. Rose. Leipzig: Teubner.
>> *The Athenian Constitution: The Eudemian Ethics. On Virtues and Vices.* 1952. Tr. H. Rackham. Loeb Classical Library. Cambridge, MA: Harvard University Press.
>> *Politics.* 1972. Tr. H. Rackham. Loeb Classical Library. Cambridge, MA: Harvard University Press.
>> *Rhetoric.* 1926. Tr. J. H. Freese. Loeb Classical Library. Cambridge, MA: Harvard University Press.

Cato
>> *Marcus Porcius Cato. On Agriculture. Marcus Terentius Varro. On Agriculture.* 1933. Tr. W. D. Hooper, revised by H. B. Ash. Loeb Classical Library. Cambridge, MA: Harvard University Press.

Columella
>   *On Agriculture.* 1941–1955. Tr. E. S. Forster and E. H. Heffner. 3 vols. Loeb Classi-
>   cal Library. Cambridge, MA: Harvard University Press.

Comicorum Atticorum Fragmenta
>   *Comicorum Atticorum Fragmenta.* 1880–1888. Ed. T. Kock. 3 vols. Leipzig: Teubner.

Dicaearchus of Messana
>   *Dicaearchus of Messana: Text, Translation, and Discussion.* 2001. Ed. by W. Forten-
>   baugh and E. Schütrumpf. New Brunswick, NJ: Transaction Pub.
>   [Mirhady, D. C. 2001. "Dicaearchus of Messana: The Sources, Texts, and Transla-
>   tions." In Fortenbaugh and Schütrumpf 2001: 1–142.]

Elegy and Iambus
>   *Elegy and Iambus with the Anacreontica.* 1931. Tr. J. M. Edmonds. 2 vols. Loeb Clas-
>   sical Library. Cambridge, MA: Harvard University Press.

Euripides
>   *The Plays of Euripides.* 1907–1910. Tr. E. P. Coleridge. 3 vols. London: Bell.

Greek Anthology
>   *The Greek Anthology.* 1916–1918. Tr. W. R. Paton. 5 vols. Loeb Classical Library.
>   Cambridge, MA: Harvard University Press.
>   *The Greek Anthology: The Garland of Philip.* 1968. Ed. by A.S.F. Gow and D. L. Page.
>   2 vols. London: Cambridge University Press.

Greek Elegiac Poetry
>   *Greek Elegiac Poetry: From the Seventh to the Fifth Centuries B.C.* 1999. Ed. and tr. by
>   D. E. Gerber. Loeb Classical Library. Cambridge, MA: Harvard University
>   Press.

Hellenica Oxyrhynchia
>   *Hellenica Oxyrhynchia.* 1993. Ed. M. Chambers, Stuttgart and Leipzig: Teubner.

Heracleides Criticus
>   *Herakleides Kritikos "Über die Städte in Hellas" Eine Periegese Griechenlands am Vor-
>   abend des Chremonideischen Krieges.* 2006. Ed. and German tr. by A. Arenz.
>   Munich: Utz.

Hermippus
>   See Poetae Comici Graeci.

Hero of Alexandria, *Pneumatics*
>   *The Pneumatics of Hero of Alexandria, from the Original Greek.* 1851. Tr. and ed. B.
>   Woodcroft. London: Charles Whittingham.
>   *Heronis Alexandrini opera quae supersunt Omnia.* 1899. Vol. 1. Ed. W. Schmidt. Text
>   with German tr. Berlin: Teubner.

Les Pneumatiques d'Héron d'Alexandrie. 1997. Ed. by G. Argoud and J.-Y. Guillaumin, with the collaboration of A. Cachard. Saint-Étienne: Publications de l'Université de Saint-Étienne.

Herodotus

Herodotus. 1921–1924. Tr. by A. D. Godley. 4 vols. Loeb Classical Library. Cambridge, MA: Harvard University Press.

Hippocrates

Hippocrates Vol. 1. *Ancient Medicine. Airs, Waters, Places. Epidemics 1 and 3. The Oath. Precepts. Nutriment*. 1923. Tr. by W. H. S. Jones. Loeb Classical Library. Cambridge, MA: Harvard University Press.

Hippocrates Vol. 2. *Prognostic. Regimen in Acute Diseases. The Sacred Disease. The Art. Breaths. Law. Decorum. Physician (Ch 1). Dentition*. 1923. Tr. by W. H. S. Jones. Loeb Classical Library. Cambridge, MA: Harvard University Press.

Hippocrates Vol. 7. *Epidemics 2, 4–7*. 1994. Ed. and tr. by W. D. Smith. Loeb Classical Library. Cambridge, MA: Harvard University Press.

Homer

Odyssey. 1919. Tr. by A. T. Murray. 2 vols. Loeb Classical Library. Cambridge, MA: Harvard University Press.

Hyperides

Orationes. 1963. Ed. C. Jensen. Stuttgart: Teubner.

Joshua the Stylite, *Chronicle*

The Chronicle of Pseudo-Joshua the Stylite. 2000. Tr. into English and notes by F. R. Trombley and J. W. Watt. Liverpool: Liverpool University Press.

Livy

The History of Rome by Titus Livius. 1912–1924. Tr. with intro. by W. M. Roberts. 6 vols. London and Toronto: Dent, and New York: Dutton.

Philostratus

The Life of Apollonius of Tyana. Books I–IV. 2005. Ed. and tr. by C. P. Jones. Loeb Classical Library. Cambridge, MA: Harvard University Press.

Phocylides

See Elegy and Iambus.

Plato

The Collected Dialogues of Plato, Including the Letters. 1971. Eds. E. Hamilton and H. Cairns. Tr. L. Cooper et al. Princeton, NJ: Princeton University Press.

Plutarch
> Plutarch's Lives, the "Dryden's Plutarch." 1910. Tr. corrected from the Greek and re-
> vised by A. H. Clough. 3 vols. London: Dent and Sons, and New York:
> Dutton.

Poetae Comici Graeci
> Poetae Comici Graeci. 1983–2001. Ed. and tr. by C. Austin and R. Kassel. 8 vols.
> Berlin and New York: de Gruyter.

Polybius
> The Histories. 2012. Tr. by W. R. Paton, revised by F. W. Walbank and C. Habicht.
> 6 vols. Loeb Classical Library. Cambridge, MA: Harvard University Press.

Poseidippus
> See Comicorum Atticorum Fragmenta and Poetae Comici Graeci.

Pseudo-Skylax
> Pseudo-Skylax's Periplous: the Circumnavigation of the Inhabited World. 2011. Text, tr.
> and comment by G. Shipley: Exeter: Bristol Phoenix Press.

Solon
> Solōnos Nomoi. Die Fragmente des Solonischen Gesetzeswerkes, mit einer Text- und
> Überlieferungsgeschichte. 1966. Ed. E. Ruschenbusch. Wiesbaden: Steiner.
> Solon: Das Gesetzeswerk-Fragmente. Übersetzung und Kommentar. 2010. German tr.
> and comment by E. Ruschenbusch. Wiesbaden: Steiner.

Sophocles
> Sophocles: The Three Theban Plays. 1984. Tr. by R. Fagles, intro. and notes by B. Knox.
> Harmondsworth and New York: Penguin Books.

Teles
> Teletis reliquiae. 1909. Ed. O. Hense (2nd ed.) Tübingen: Mohr.
> Teles (the Cynic Teacher). Ed. tr. E. D. O'Neil. Missoula, MT: Scholars Press for the
> Society of Biblical Literature.

Tyrtaeus
> See Greek Elegiac Poetry.

Varro
> See Cato.

Xenophon
> Xenophon in Seven Volumes. VII. Scripta minora. 1968. Tr. by E. C. Marchant and
> G. W. Bowersock. Loeb Classical Library. Cambridge, MA: Harvard Uni-
> versity Press.

BIBLIOGRAPHY

Abbott, F. F., and A. C. Johnson. 1926. *Municipal Administration in the Roman Empire.* Princeton, NJ: Princeton University Press.

Abelshauser, W. 2000. "Die Historische Schule und die Probleme von heute." In Becker and Lademacher 2000: 39–55.

Abramovitch, Y. 1961–1962. "The Maxim 'cujus est solum ejus usque ad coelum' as applied in Aviation." *McGill Law Journal* 8: 247–69.

Acton, P. 2014. *Poiesis: Manufacturing in Classical Athens.* Oxford: Oxford University Press.

Adam, J.-P. 1989. "Gli antichi paesi: effetti sismici nell'edilizia storica." In Guidoboni 1989: 388–97.

Adam-Veleni, P., E. Poulaki, and K. Tsakalou-Tzanavari. 2003. *Ancient Country Houses on Modern Roads, Central Macedonia.* Athens: Archaeological Receipts Fund.

Adiego, I. J. 2007. *The Carian Language.* Leiden: Brill.

Ager, A., and R. Faber, eds. 2013. *Belonging and Isolation in the Hellenistic World.* Toronto: University of Toronto Press.

Aikaterinidis, G. N. ed. 2001. *Mesogaia: History and Culture of Mesogeia.* Athens: Athens International Airport.

Akamatis, G. 2012. "L'agora de Pella." In Chankowski and Karvonis 2012: 49–59.

Akerlof, G. 1970. "The Market for 'Lemons': Quality Uncertainty and the Market Mechanism." *Quarterly Journal of Economics* 84.3: 488–500.

Akrigg, B. 2011. "Demography and Classical Athens." In Holleran and Pudsey 2011: 37–59.

Akten des VI. Kongresses. 1973. *Akten des VI. Internationalen Kongresses für griechische und lateinische Epigraphik. München 1972.* Munich: Beck.

Alcock, S. 1991. "Urban Survey and the *Polis* of Phlius." *Hesperia* 60: 421–63.

———. 1993a. *Graecia Capta: The Landscapes of Roman Greece.* Cambridge and New York: Cambridge University Press.

———. 1993b. "Surveying the Peripheries of the Hellenistic World." In Bilde et al. 1993: 162–75.

———. 2002. *Archaeologies of the Greek Past: Landscape, Monuments, and Memories.* New York: Cambridge University Press.

Alcock, S. E., J. F. Cherry, and J. L. Davis. 1994. "Intensive Survey, Agricultural Practice, and the Classical Landscape of Greece." In Morris 1994: 137–70.

Alcock, S., and J. F. Cherry, eds. 2004. *Side-by-Side Survey: Comparative Regional Studies in the Mediterranean World.* Oxford: Oxbow.

Allen, R. C. 2004. "Agriculture during the Industrial Revolution." In Floud and Johnson, vol. 1: 96–116.

Allgrove-McDowell, J. 2003. "Industries of the Near-East and Europe in Prehistory. Ancient Egypt, 5000–332 BC." In Jenkins 2003, vol. 1: 30–39.

Alston, R., and O. van Nijf, eds. 2008. *Feeding the Ancient Greek City*. Leuven: Peeters.

Ameling, W. 1993. *Karthago. Studien zu Militär, Staat und Gesellschaft*. Munich: Beck.

Amemiya, T. 2007. *Economy and Economics of Ancient Greece*. London and New York: Routledge.

Amigues, S. 2004. "Le silphium. État de la question." *Journal des Savants* 2004: 191–226.

Amouretti, M.-C. 1986. *Le pain et l'huile dans la Grèce antique*. Paris: Les Belles Lettres.

Amouretti, M.-C., and J.-P. Brun. 1993. *La production du vin et de l'huile en Méditerranée*. Athens: École française d'Athènes, and Paris: De Boccard.

Ampolo, C. 2010. "Le motivazioni della legge sulla tassazione del grano di Lemno, Imbro e Sciro e il prezzo di grano e pane." In Magnetto et al. 2010: 39–66.

Ampolo, C., ed. 2012. *Agora greca, agorai di Sicilia*. Pisa: Edizioni della Normale.

Amundsen, D. W., and C. J. Diers. 1969. "The Age of Menarche in Classical Greece and Rome." *Human Biology* 41: 125–32.

Anand, R. P. 1983. *Origin and Development of the Law of the Sea: History of International Law Revisited*. The Hague and Boston: Martinus Nijhoff.

Anderson-Stojanovic, V. R., and J. Ellis Jones. 2002. "Ancient Beehives from Isthmia." *Hesperia* 71: 345–76.

Andreau, J. 1997. "Deux études sur les prix à Rome: les 'mercuriales' et le taux d'intérêt." In Andreau et al. 1997: 105–20.

———. 2007. "Le prix du blé en Sicile et à Antioche de Pisidie (*AE*, 1925, 126b)." In Dubouloz and Pittia 2007: 111–25.

———. 2011. "Les allusions à l'Antiquité dans le Traité de Montchrestien." In Guéry 2011: 83–99.

Andreau, J., and R. Descat. 2011. *The Slave in Greece and Rome*. Tr. from the French ed. 2006. Madison: University of Wisconsin Press.

Andreau, J., P. Briant, and R. Descat, eds. 1994. *Économie antique. Les échanges dans l'Antiquité: le rôle de l'État*. Saint-Bertrand-de-Comminges: Musée archéologique départemental de Saint-Bertrand-de-Comminges.

———. 1997. *Économie antique. Prix et formation des prix dans les économies antiques*. Saint-Bertrand-de-Comminges: Musée archéologique départemental de Saint-Bertrand-de-Comminges.

———. 2000. *Économie antique. La guerre dans les économies antiques*. Saint-Bertrand-de-Comminges: Musée archéologique départemental de Saint-Bertrand-de-Comminges.

Andreau, J., and C. Virlouvet, eds. 2002. *L'information et la mer dans le monde antique*. Rome: École française de Rome.

Andreou, I. 1994. "O dēmos tōn Aixōnidōn Alōn." In Coulson et al. 1994: 191–209.

Aperghis, G. G. (M.) 2001. "Population–Production–Taxation–Coinage—A Model for the Seleukid Economy." In Archibald et al. 2001: 69–102.

———. 2004. *The Seleukid Royal Economy: The Finances and Financial Administration of the Seleukid Empire*. Cambridge: Cambridge University Press.

Apostolou, E. 2002. "Rhodes hellénistique. Les trésors et la circulation monétaire." *Eulimene* 3: 117–82.

Arafat, K., and C. Morgan. 1994. "Athens, Etruria, and the Heuneburg: Mutual Misconceptions in the Study of Greek-Barbarian Relations." In Morris 1994: 108–34.

Archibald, Z. H. 2012. "*Agoranomoi* in Macedonia." In Capdetrey and Hasenohr 2012: 109–19.

Archibald, Z. H., J. K. Davies, and V. Gabrielsen, eds. 2005. *Making, Moving and Managing: The New World of Ancient Economies, 323–31 BC*. Oxford: Oxbow Books.

———. 2011. *The Economies of Hellenistic Societies, Third to First Centuries BC*. Oxford: Oxford University Press.

Archibald, Z. H., J. K. Davies, V. Gabrielsen, and G. J. Oliver, eds. 2001. *Hellenistic Economies*. London and New York: Routledge.

Argoud, G. 1987. "Le problème de l'eau dans la Grèce antique." In Réparaz 1987: 205–19.

———. 1994b. "Héron d'Alexandrie, mathématicien et inventeur." In Argoud 1994a: 53–65.

———. 1998. "Héron d'Alexandrie et les *Pneumatiques*." In Argoud and Guillaumin 1998: 127–45.

Argoud, G., ed. 1994a. *Science et vie intellectuelle à Alexandrie (Ier–IIIe siècle après J.-C.)*. Saint-Étienne: Publications de l'Université de Saint-Étienne.

Argoud, G., and J.-Y. Guillaumin, eds. 1998. *Sciences exactes et sciences appliquées à Alexandrie*. Saint-Étienne: Publications de l'Université de Saint-Étienne.

Argoud, G., L. I. Marangou, V. Panayotopoulos, and C. Villain-Gandossi, eds. 1992. *L'eau et les hommes en Méditerranée et en mer Noire dans l'Antiquité de l'époque mycénienne au règne de Justinien*. Athens: Centre National de Recherches Sociales.

Arnaoutoglou, I. 1998. *Ancient Greek Laws: A Sourcebook*. London and New York: Routledge.

———. 2011. "Craftsmen Associations in Roman Lydia—A Tale of Two Cities?" *Ancient Society* 41: 257–90.

Arnaud, P. 2005. *Les routes de la navigation antique. Itinéraires en Méditerranée*. Paris: Errance.

———. 2007. "Diocletian's Prices Edict: The Prices of Seaborne Transport and the Average Duration of Maritime Travel." *Journal of Roman Archaeology* 20: 321–35.

———. 2011a. "Ancient Maritime Trade and Sailing Routes in Their Administrative, Legal, and Economic Contexts." In Robinson and Wilson 2011: 59–78.

———. 2011b. "Sailing 90 Degrees from the Wind: Norm or Exception?" In Harris and Iara 2011: 147–60.

Arnold-Biucchi, C., L. Beer-Tobey, and N. M. Waggoner. 1988. "A Greek Archaic Silver Hoard from Selinus." *American Numismatic Society Museum Notes* 33: 1–35.

Aronis, G. 1952. "Les minerais de fer de Grèce." In Blondel and Marvier 1952, vol. 2: 223–26.

Arribas, A., G. Trias, D. Cerdá and J. de Hoz. 1987a. *El barco de El Sec (Costa de Calviá, Mallorca). Estudio de los materiales*. Majorca: Gráficas Miramar.

———. 1987b. "L'épave d'El Sec (Mallorca)." *Revue des Études Anciennes* 89 (= Rouillard and Villanueva-Puig 1987): 13–146.

Arrow, K. 1963. "Uncertainty and the Welfare Economics of Medical Care." *American Economic Review* 53.5: 941–73.

Ascani, K., V. Gabrielsen, K. Kvist, and A. H. Rasmussen. 2002. *Ancient History Matters: Studies Presented to Jens Erik Skydsgaard on His Seventieth Birthday*. Rome: L'Erma di Bretschneider.

Asheri, D. 1969. *Leggi greche sul problema dei debiti*. Pisa (= *Studi Classici e Orientali* 18).

Ashton, R.H.J. 2001. "The Coinage of Rhodes 408–ca.190 B.C." In Meadows and Shipton 2001: 79–115.

Aspects. 1996: *Aspects de l'artisanat du textile dans le monde méditerranéen (Égypte, Grèce, monde romain).* Lyon: Université Lumière-Lyon 2, Institut d'archéologie et d'histoire de l'Antiquité, and Paris: De Boccard.

Association Guillaume Budé. 1970. *Actes du VIIIe congrès, Paris, 5–10 avril 1968.* Paris: Les Belles Lettres.

Aubert, J.-J. 2004. "Aux origines du canal de Suez? Le canal du Nil à la mer Rouge revisité." In Clavel-Lévêque and Hermon 2004: 219–52.

Ault, B. A. 1999. "Koprones and Oil Presses at Halieis: Interactions of Town and Country and the Integration of Domestic and Regional Economies." *Hesperia* 68: 549–73.

———. 2005. "Housing the Poor and the Homeless in Ancient Greece." In Ault and Nevett 2005: 140–59.

Ault, B. A., and L. C. Nevett, eds. 2005. *Ancient Greek Houses and Households: Chronological, Regional, and Social Diversity.* Philadelphia: University of Pennsylvania Press.

Aupert, P. 1996. *Guide d'Amathonte.* Athens. École française d'Athènes and Fondation A. G. Leventis.

Austin, M. M. 1994. "Society and Economy." In Lewis et al. 1994: 527–64.

———. 2006. *The Hellenistic World from Alexander to the Roman Conquest: A Selection of Ancient Sources in Translation.* 2nd augmented ed. Cambridge: Cambridge University Press.

Austin, M. M., and P. Vidal-Naquet. 1977. *The Economic and Social History of Ancient Greece: An Introduction.* Tr. from the French ed. 1972. Berkeley: University of California Press.

Avram, A. 1997–1998. "Notes sur l'inscription de l'emporion de Pistiros en Thrace." *Il Mar Nero* 3: 37–46.

Aylward, W. 2005. "Security, Synoikismos, and Koinon as Determinants for Troad Housing in Classical and Hellenistic Times." In Ault and Nevett 2005: 36–53.

Backhaus, J. G., ed. 2000. *Karl Bücher: Theory–History–Anthropology–Nonmarket Economies.* Marburg: Metropolis.

Badian, E., ed. 1966. *Ancient Society and Institutions: Studies Presented to Victor Ehrenberg on His 75th Birthday.* Oxford: Blackwell.

Badinou, P. 2003. *La laine et le parfum. Épinetra et alabastres. Forme, iconographie et fonction.* Louvain and Dudley, MA: Peeters.

Badoud, N. 2011b. "L'intégration de la Pérée au territoire de Rhodes." In Badoud 2011a: 533–65.

———. 2013. "Timbres amphoriques de Mendée et de Cassandreia." In Buzoianu et al. 2013: 89–103.

Badoud, N., ed. 2011a. *Philologos Dionysios. Mélanges offerts au professeur Denis Knœpfler.* Geneva: Droz.

Bagnall, R. S., and P. Derow. 2004. *The Hellenistic Period: Historical Sources in Translation.* 2nd ed. Malden, MA, and Oxford: Blackwell.

Bagnall, R. S., K. Brodersen, C. B. Champion, A. Erskine, and S. R. Huebner, eds. 2012. *The Encyclopedia of Ancient History.* Malden, MA: Wiley-Blackwell.

Bakhuizen, S. C. 1977. "Greek Steel." *World Archaeology* 9.2 (Architecture and Archaeology, Oct. 1977): 220–34.

Baladié, R. 1980. *Le Péloponnèse de Strabon.* Paris: Les Belles Lettres.

Balandier, C. 2004. "L'importance de la production du miel dans l'économie gréco-romaine." *Pallas* 64: 183–96.

Baldoni, D., F. Berti, and M. Giuman, eds. 2013. *Iasos e il suo territorio.* Rome: L'Erma di Bretschneider.

Ballard, R. D., D. Master, D. Yoerger, D. Mindell, L. L. Whitcomb, H. Singh, and D. Piechota. 2002. "Iron Age Shipwrecks in Deep Water off Ashkelon, Israel." *American Journal of Archaeology* 106: 151–68.

Barat, C. 2009. "Sinope et ses relations avec la péninsule anatolienne: réseaux, échanges des biens et des hommes." In Bru et al. 2009: 351–61.

Barnes, C.L.H. 2006. "The Ferries of Tenedos." *Historia* 55: 167–77.

Baslez, M.-F., P. Hoffman, and M. Treddé, eds. 1992. *Le monde du roman grec.* Paris: Presses de l'École normale supérieure.

Bass, G. F. 1967. *Cape Gelidonya: A Bronze Age Shipwreck.* Philadephia: American Philosophical Society.

———. 2010. "Cape Gelidonya Shipwreck." In Cline 2010: 797–803.

Bats, M. 1988. *Vaisselle et alimentation à Olbia de Provence, v. 350–v. 50 av. J.-C.: modèles culturels et catégories céramiques.* Paris: Éditions du Centre National de la Recherche Scientifique.

Baumann, H. 2000. *Pflanzenbilder auf griechischen Münzen.* Munich: Hirmer.

Beaumont, L. A. 2012. *Childhood in Ancient Athens: Iconography and Social History.* New York: Routledge.

Beaune, J.-C. 1980. *L'automate et ses mobiles.* Paris: Flammarion.

Beck, H., ed. 2013. *A Companion to Ancient Greek Government.* Chichester, UK: Wiley-Blackwell.

Becker, B., and H. Lademacher, eds. 2000. *Geist und Gestalt im historischen Wandel. Facetten deutscher und europäischer Geschichte.* Festschrift für Siegfried Bahne zum 72. Geburtstag. Münster, Berlin, and New York: Waxmann.

Becker, C. 1986. *Kastanas. Die Tierknochenfunde. Ausgrabungen in einem Siedlungshügel der Bronze- und Eisenzeit Makedoniens 1975–1979.* Kastanas, vol. 4, Prähistorische Archäologie in Südosteuropa. Berlin: Spiess.

Behrend, D. 1973. "Rechtshistorische Betrachtungen zu den Pachtdokumenten aus Mylasa und Olymos." In *Akten des VI. Kongresses:* 145–68.

Bekker-Nielsen, T. 2002. "Fish in the Ancient Economy." In Ascani et al. 2002: 29–37.

———. 2005b. "The Technology and Productivity of Ancient Sea Fishing." In Bekker-Nielsen 2005a: 83–96.

———. 2010. "Fishing in the Roman World." In Bekker-Nielsen and Bernal Casasola 2010: 187–203.

Bekker-Nielsen, T., ed. 2005a. *Ancient Fishing and Fish Processing in the Black Sea Region.* Aarhus: Aarhus University Press.

Bekker-Nielsen, T., and D. Bernal Casasola, eds. 2010. *Ancient Nets and Fishing Gear: Proceedings of the International Workshop on "Nets and Fishing Gear in Classical Antiquity: A First Approach," Cádiz, November 15–17, 2007.* Cadiz: Universidad De Cádiz, Servicio De Publicaciones, and Aarhus: Aarhus University Press.

Bellancourt-Valdher, M., and J.-N. Corvisier, eds. 1999. *La démographie historique antique.* Arras: Artois Presses Université.

Beloch, J. 1886. *Die Bevölkerung der griechisch-römischen Welt.* Leipzig: Duncker und Humblot.

Bencivenni, A. 2004. "Aristodikides di Asso, Antioco I e la scelta di Ilio." *Simblos* 4: 159–85.

Benedict, B. 1972. "Social Regulation of Fertility." In Harrison and Boyce 1972: 73–89.

Bennet, J. 2007. "The Aegean Bronze Age." In Scheidel et al. 2007: 175–210.

Bentz, M. 1998. *Panathenäische Preisamphoren. Eine athenische Vasengattung und ihre Funktion vom 6.–4. Jahrhundert v. Chr.* Basel: Archäologisches Seminar der Universität.

Bentz, M., L. Adorno, J. Albers, J. M. Müller, and G. Zuchtriegel. 2013. "Das Handwerkerviertel von Selinunt. Die Töpferwerkstatt in der Insula S 16/17–E. Vorbericht zu den Kampagnen 2010–2012." *Mitteilungen des Deutschen Archäologischen Instituts, Römische Abteilung* 119: 69–98.

Beopoulou, I. 1987. "Trajets du patrimoine dans une société maritime grecque: lieux masculins et féminins dans l'acquisition et la circulation des biens." In Ravis-Giordanni 1987: 307–25.

———. 1989. "Dot, propriété et économie marchande dans un village grec." In Peristiany and Handman 1989: 335–53.

Berggren, J. L., and A. Jones. 2000: *Ptolemy's Geography: An Annotated Translation of the Theoretical Chapters.* Princeton, NJ: Princeton University Press.

Bertrand, J.-M. 1992. "Le chasseur dans la ville." In Baslez et al. 1992: 85–92.

———. 2006. "À propos de la *Rhétorique* d'Aristote (I, 1373b1–1374b23), analyse du processus judiciaire II. *anakrisis/erôtèsis*." In *Symposion 2003* 2006: 191–202.

Bezeczky, T. 2002. "Brindisian Olive Oil and Wine in Ephesos." In Rivet and Sciallano 2002: 355–58.

———. 2004. "Early Roman Food Import from Ephesus: Amphorae from the Tetragonos Agora." In Eiring and Lund 2004: 85–97.

———. 2013. *The Amphorae of Roman Ephesus.* Vienna: Verlag der Österreichischen Akademie der Wissenschaften.

Bideau, A., G. Brunet, and R. Desbos. 1978. "Variations locales de la mortalité des enfants: l'exemple de la châtellenie de Saint-Trivier-en-Dombes (1730–1869)." *Annales de démographie historique*: 7–29.

Bilde, P., T. Engberg-Pedersen, L. Hannestad, J. Zahle, and R. Klaus, eds. 1993. *Centre and Periphery in the Hellenistic World.* Aarhus: Aarhus University Press.

Bilde, P. G., and V. F. Stolba, eds. 2006. *Surveying the Greek Chora: The Black Sea Region in a Comparative Perspective.* Aarhus: Aarhus University Press.

Billiard, R. 1913. *La vigne dans l'antiquité.* Lyon: H. Lardanchet.

Billot, M.-F. 2000. "Centres de production et diffusion des tuiles dans le monde grec." In Blondé and Muller 2000: 193–240.

Bintliff, J. L. 1977. *Natural Environment and Human Settlement in Prehistoric Greece.* BAR International Series 28. Oxford: British Archaeological Reports.

———. 2012. *The Complete Archaeology of Greece: From Hunter-Gatherers to the 20th Century AD.* Malden, MA: Wiley-Blackwell.

Bintliff, J. L., and A. M. Snodgrass. 1985. "The Cambridge/Bradford Boeotian Expedition: The First Four Years." *Journal of Field Archaeology* 12: 123–61.

———. 1988. "Mediterranean Survey and the City." *Antiquity* 62: 57–71.

Bissa, E. 2009. *Governmental Intervention in Foreign Trade in Archaic and Classical Greece.* Leiden: Brill.

Blackman, D. J. 1999. "*Oi limenes tēs archaias Rhodou.*" In Kypraiou and Zapheiropoulou 1999: 41–50.

———. 2001–2002. "Archaeology in Greece, 2001–2002." *Archaeological Reports* 48: 1–115.

Blackman, D. J., ed. 1973. *Marine Archaeology*. London: Butterworth.

Blamire, A. 2001. "Athenian Finance, 454–404 B.C." *Hesperia* 70: 99–126.

Blok, J. H., and A.P.M.H. Lardinois, eds. 2006. *Solon of Athens: New Historical and Philological Approaches*. Leiden: Brill.

Blondé, F., and A. Muller, eds. 2000. *L'artisanat en Grèce ancienne. Les productions, les diffusions*. Villeneuve-d'Ascq: Université Charles-de-Gaulle—Lille 3.

Blondé, F., P. Ballet, and J.-F. Salles, eds. 2002. *Céramiques hellénistiques et romaines: productions et diffusion en Méditerranée orientale (Chypre, Égypte et côte syro-palestinienne)*. Lyon: Maison de l'Orient méditerranéen, and Paris: De Boccard.

Blondel, F., and L. Marvier, eds. 1952. *Symposium sur les gisements de fer du monde*. 3 vols. Mesnil: Typographie Firmin-Didot.

Boatwright, M. T. 2000. *Hadrian and the Cities of the Roman Empire*. Princeton, NJ: Princeton University Press.

Bodenstedt, F. 1981. *Die Elektronmünzen von Phokaia und Mytilene*. Tübingen: Wasmuth.

Bodin, J. 1955 [1576]. *Six Books of the Commonwealth*. First French ed. 1576, abridged and tr. by M. J. Tooley. Oxford: Blackwell.

Boeckh, A. 1886. *Die Staatshaushaltung der Athener*. 2 vols. 3rd ed. Berlin: Reimer.

Boerner, A. 1907. "Epōnion." *Realencyclopädie* VI.1: col. 243.

Boffo, L. 2001. "Lo statuto di terre, insediamente e persone nell'Anatolia ellenistica." *Dike* 4: 233–55.

Bogaert, R. 1968. *Banques et banquiers dans les cités grecques*. Leiden: Sijthof.

———. 1986. "La banque à Athènes au IVᵉ siècle avant J.-C.: état de la question." *Museum Helveticum* 43: 19–49.

Bolkestein, H. 1922. "The Exposure of Children at Athens and the *Enchitristriai*." *Classical Philology* 17: 222–39.

Borgard, P. 2005. "Les amphores à alun (Iᵉʳ siècle avant J.-C.–IVᵉ siècle après J.-C.)." In Borgard 2005: 157–69.

Borgard, P., J.-P. Brun, and M. Picon, eds. 2005. *L'alun de Méditerranée*. Naples and Aix-en-Provence: Centre Jean Bérard.

Borza, E. N. 1987. "Timber and Politics in the Ancient World: Macedon and the Greeks." *Proceedings of the American Philosophical Society* 131: 32–52.

Boulay, T. 2012. "Les techniques vinicoles grecques, des vendanges aux Anthestéries: nouvelles perspectives." In *Dialogues d'histoire ancienne*. Supplément 7: 95–115.

Bound, M. 1991. *The Giglio Wreck: A Wreck of the Archaic Period (ca. 600 BC) off the Tuscan Island of Giglio*. Athens: Hellenic Institute of Marine Archaeology.

Bourdieu, P. 2000. *Distinction: A Social Critique of the Judgement of Taste*. Tr. from the French ed. 1979. Cambridge, MA: Harvard University Press.

Bourgey, L. 1975. "La relation du médecin au malade dans les écrits de l'école de Cos." In Bourgey and Jouanna 1975: 209–27.

Bourgey, L., and J. Jouanna, eds. 1975. *La collection hippocratique et son rôle dans l'histoire de la médecine*. Leiden: Brill.

Bousquet, J. 1986. "Une nouvelle inscription trilingue à Xanthos?" *Revue Archéologique*: 101–6.

Bowie, E. L. 1995. "Wine in Old Comedy." In Murray and Tecusan 1995: 113–25.

Bowman, A., and A. Wilson, eds. 2011. *Settlement, Urbanization, and Population*. Oxford and New York: Oxford University Press.

Bradley, K. R. 1989. *Slavery and Rebellion in the Roman World 140 B.C.–70 B.C.* Bloomington: Indiana University Press, and London: B.T. Batsford.

Braudel, F. 1972. *The Mediterranean and the Mediterranean World in the Age of Philip II.* 2 vols. Tr. from the French ed. 1966 (1st ed. 1949). New York: Harper & Row.

———. 1981. *Civilization and Capitalism 15th–18th Century.* Vol. 1. *The Structures of Everyday Life.* Tr. from the French ed. 1979. London: William Collins Sons & Co, and New York: Harper & Row.

Braudel, F., and E. Labrousse, eds. 1970. *Histoire économique et sociale de la France.* Vol. 2. *Des derniers temps de l'âge seigneurial aux préludes de l'âge industriel (1660–1789).* Paris: Presses Universitaires de France.

Bravo, B. 1980. "Sulân." *Annali della Scuola Normale Superiore di Pisa, classe di lettere e filosofia* s. 3, 10.3: 675–987.

Bredow, I. von. 2002. "Handelsverbindungen zwischen Pontos und Ägäis zur Zeit der Odrysenreiches." In Olshausen and Sonnabend 2002: 445–51.

Brélaz, C. 2005. *La sécurité publique en Asie mineure sous le principat (Iᵉʳ– IIIᵉᵐᵉ s. ap. J.-C.): institutions municipales et institutions impériales dans l'Orient romain.* Basel: Schwabe.

Bresciani, E. 1998. "L'Egitto achemenide: Dario I e il canale del mar Rosso." *Transeuphratène* 14: 103–11.

Bresson, A. 1985. "Démographie grecque antique et modèle statistique." *Revue, Informatique et Statistique dans les Sciences Humaines* 21: 7–34.

———. 1988. "Richesse et pouvoir à Lindos (époque hellénistique)." In Dietz and Papachristodoulou 1988: 145–54.

———. 1993a. "La circulation monétaire rhodienne jusqu'en 166." *Dialogues d'Histoire Ancienne* 19: 119–69.

———. 1993b. "Les cités grecques et leurs *emporia*." In Bresson and Rouillard 1993: 163–226.

———. 1996. "Drachmes rhodiennes et imitations: une politique économique de Rhodes?" *Revue des Études Anciennes* 98: 65–77.

———. 1998. "Rhodes, Cnide et les Lyciens au début du IIᵉ siècle av. J.-C." *Revue des Études Anciennes* 100: 65–88.

———. 2000. *La cité marchande.* Bordeaux: Ausonius.

———. 2001a. "Monnayage et société dans les mondes antiques." *Revue Numismatique* 157: 51–68.

———. 2001b. "Timon de Syracuse et les drachmes rhodiennes à Délos." *Revue des Études Anciennes* 103: 131–56.

———. 2001c. "La conjoncture du IIᵉ siècle a.C." In Bresson and Descat 2001: 11–15.

———. 2002a. "Italiens et Romains à Rhodes et à Caunos." In Müller and Hasenohr 2002: 147–62.

———. 2002b. "Quatre *emporia* antiques: Abul, La Picola, Elizavetovskoie, Naucratis." *Revue des Études Anciennes* 104: 475–505.

———. 2003a. "Les intérêts rhodiens en Carie à l'époque hellénistique jusqu'en 167 a.C." In Prost 2003: 169–92.

———. 2003b. "Merchants and Politics in Ancient Greece: Economic Aspects." In Zaccagnini 2003: 139–63.

———. 2003c. "Moses Finley." In Sales 2003: 178–92.

———. 2004a. "Les accords romano-carthaginois." In Moatti 2004: 649–76.

———. 2004b. "Dédicaces de Lindos et de Rhodes pour Titus Flavius Aglôchartos." In Follet 2004: 178–92.

———. 2005a. "Coinage and Money Supply in the Hellenistic World." In Archibald et al. 2005: 44–72.

———. 2005b. "Ecology and Beyond." In Harris 2005a: 94–114.

———. 2005c. "Économie et institution. Bilan critique des thèses polanyiennes et propositions nouvelles." In Cressier and Rouillard 2005: 97–111.

———. 2005d. "Naucratis: de l'emporion à la cité." *Topoi* 12–13: 133–55.

———. 2005e. "Avant-propos" and "Les cités grecques et leurs inscriptions." In Bresson et al. 2005: 11–16 and 153–68.

———. 2006a. "La parenté grecque en palindrome." In Bresson et al. 2006: 13–22.

———. 2006b. "The Athenian Mint in the 2nd Century BC and the Amphictionic Decree." *Annali dell' Istituto Italiano di Numismatica* 52: 45–85.

———. 2006c. "Marché et prix à Délos: charbon, bois, porcs, huile et grains." In Descat 2006b: 311–39.

———. 2006d. "The Origin of Lydian and Greek Coinage: Cost and Quantity." 3rd International Conference of Ancient History, Fudan University, Shanghai, 17–21.08.2005. *Historical Research* 5: 149–65 [in Chinese].

———. 2006e. "La machine d'Héron et le coût de l'énergie dans le monde antique." In Lo Cascio 2006: 55–80.

———. 2007a. "Au delà du modernisme et du primitivisme: Max Weber ou John Nash?" *Pallas* 74: 15–28.

———. 2007b. "Hamaxitos en Troade." In Dalaison 2007: 139–58.

———. 2007c. "La construction d'un espace d'approvisionnement: les cités égéennes et le grain de mer Noire." In Bresson and Ivantchik 2007: 49–68.

———. 2007d. "Rhodes, Rome et les pirates tyrrhéniens." In Brun 2007: 145–64.

———. 2007e. "L'entrée dans les ports en Grèce ancienne." In Moatti and Kaiser 2007: 37–78.

———. 2007–2008 *L'économie de la Grèce des cités*. Vol. 1, *Les structures et la production*. Vol. 2, *Les espaces de l'échange*. Paris: Colin.

———. 2009. "Electrum Coins, Currency Exchange, and Transaction Costs in Archaic and Classical Greece." *Revue Belge de Numismatique* 140: 71–80.

———. 2010a. "Knidos: Topography for a Battle." In van Bremen and Carbon 2010: 435–51.

———. 2010b "The Siege of Rhodes of 305–304 BC: Population, Territory and Defense Strategy." In Faucherre and Pimouguet-Pédarros 2010: 103–33.

———. 2011a. "Grain from Cyrene." In Archibald et al. 2011: 66–95.

———. 2011b. "Naviguer au large du cap Triopion." *Anatolia Antiqua* 19: 395–409.

———. 2012a. "Greek Epigraphy and Ancient Economics." In Davies and Wilkes 2012: 223–47.

———. 2012b. "Le marché des philosophes: Platon, Aristote et la monnaie." In Chankowski and Karvonis 2012: 365–84.

———. 2012c. "Wine, Oil and Delicacies at the Pelousion Customs." In Günther and Grieb 2012: 69–88.

———. 2013. "Polybius and the Economy." In Grieb and Koehn 2013: 269–84.

Bresson, A. 2014a. "Capitalism and the Ancient Greek Economy." In Neal and Williamson 2014, vol. 1: 43–74.

———. 2014b. "The Ancient World: a Climatic Challenge." In de Callataÿ 2014: 43–62.

———. 2015. "Red Fishermen from Anthedon." In Panzram et al. 2015: 69–83.

———. In press. "Women and Inheritance in Ancient Sparta: The Gortynian Connection." *Studi Ellenistici*. In press.

Bresson, A., and F. Bresson. 2004. "Max Weber, la comptabilité rationnelle et l'économie du monde gréco-romain." In Bruhns and Andreau 2004: 91–114.

Bresson, A., A.-M. Cocula, and C. Pébarthe, eds. 2005. *L'écriture publique du pouvoir*. Bordeaux: Ausonius.

Bresson, A., and R. Descat, eds. 2001. *Les cités d'Asie Mineure occidentale au IIᵉ siècle a.C.* Bordeaux: Ausonius.

Bresson, A., and A. Ivantchik, eds. 2007. *Une koinè nord-pontique*. Bordeaux: Ausonius.

Bresson, A., M.-P. Masson, S. Perentidis, and J. Wilgaux, eds. 2006. *Parenté et société dans le monde grec de l'Antiquité à l'âge moderne*. Bordeaux: Ausonius.

Bresson, A., and P. Rouillard, eds. 1993. *L'emporion*. Paris: De Boccard.

Briant, P. 1994. "Prélèvements tributaires et échanges en Asie Mineure achéménide et hellénistique." In Andreau et al. 1994: 69–81.

———. 2002. *From Cyrus to Alexander: A History of the Persian Empire*. Tr. from the French ed. 1996. Winona Lake, IN: Eisenbrauns.

Briant, P., ed. 2001. *Irrigation et drainage dans l'Antiquité, qanāts et canalisations souterraines en Iran, en Égypte et en Grèce*. Paris: Thotm.

Briant, P., and R. Descat. 1998. "Un registre douanier de la satrapie d'Égypte à l'époque achéménide." *Bulletin d'Égyptologie* 121 (= Grimal and Menu 1998): 59–104.

Brijder, H.A.G., ed. 1984. *Ancient Greek and Related Pottery: Proceedings of the International Vase Symposium Amsterdam, 12–15 April 1984*. Amsterdam: Allard Pierson Museum.

Bringmann, K. 2001. "Grain, Timber and Money: Hellenistic Kings, Finance, Buildings and Foundations in Greek Cities." In Archibald et al. 2001: 205–14.

Bringmann, K., and H. von Steuben. 1995–2000. *Schenkungen hellenistischer Herrscher an griechische Städte und Heiligtümer*. 2 vols. Berlin: Akademie Verlag.

British Admiralty. 1941. *Mediterranean Pilot. Vol. IV. Comprising the Islands of the Grecian Archipelago, with the Adjacent Coasts of Greece and Turkey from Cape Tainaron on the West to Kara Burun on the East, Including also the Island of Kriti*. 7th ed. London: Admiralty Hydrographic Office.

Britnell, R. H. 2008. "English Agricultural Output and Prices, 1350–1450: National Trends and Regional Divergences." In Dodds and Britnell 2008: 20–39.

Brock, R. 1994. "The Labour of Women in Classical Athens." *Classical Quarterly* 44: 336–46.

Brodersen, K., W. Günther, and H. H. Schmitt. 1992–1999. *Historische griechische Inschriften in Übersetzung*. 3 vols. Darmstadt: Wissenschaftliche Buchgesellschaft.

Broodbank, C. 2013. *The Making of the Middle Sea: A History of the Mediterranean from the Beginning to the Emergence of the Classical World*. Oxford: Oxford University Press.

Brousseau, E., and J.-M. Glachant, eds. 2008. *New Institutional Economics: A Guidebook*. Cambridge: Cambridge University Press.

Brousseau, L. 2010. "Sybaris et l'origine de la monnaie de bronze." *Revue Belge de Numismatique* 96: 23–34.

Brousseau, L. 2013. "La naissance de la monnaie de bronze en Grande Grèce et en Sicile." In Grandjean and Moustaka 2013: 81–96.

Brown, P. 2012. *Through the Eye of a Needle*. Princeton, NJ: Princeton University Press.

Bru, H., F. Kirbihler, and S. Lebreton, eds. 2009. *L'Asie Mineure dans l'Antiquité: échanges, populations et territoires*. Rennes: Presses Universitaires de Rennes.

Bruhns, H., and J. Andreau, eds. 2004. *Sociologie économique et économie de l'Antiquité. À propos de Max Weber = Cahiers du Centre de Recherches historiques (EHESS)* 34, Oct. 2004. Paris: CRH.

Bruhns, H., ed. 2004. *Histoire et économie politique en Allemagne de Gustav Schmoller à Max Weber*. Paris: Maison des Sciences de l'Homme.

Brulé, P. 1978. *La piraterie crétoise hellénistique*. Besançon and Paris: Les Belles Lettres.

———. 1990. "Enquête démographique sur la famille grecque antique. Étude de listes de politographie d'Asie Mineure d'époque hellénistique (Milet et Ilion)." *Revue des Études Anciennes* 92: 234–58.

Brulé, P., R. Descat, P. Brun, J.-L. Lamboley, S. Le Bohec, and J. Ouhlen. 2004. *Le monde grec aux temps classiques*. Vol. 2. *Le IVᵉ siècle*. Paris: Presses Universitaires de France.

Brun, J.-P. 1993. "Les innovations techniques et leur diffusion dans les pressoirs." In Amouretti and Brun 1993: 539–50.

———. 1999. "*Laudatissimum fuit antiquitus in Delo insula*. La maison IB du Quartier du Stade et la production des parfums à Délos." *Bulletin de Correspondance Hellénique* 123: 87–155.

———. 2000. "The Production of Perfume in Antiquity: The Cases of Delos and Paestum." *American Journal of Archaeology* 104: 277–308.

———. 2003. *Le vin et l'huile dans la Méditerranée antique: viticulture, oléiculture et procédés de transformation*. Paris: Errance.

———. 2004a. *Archéologie du vin et de l'huile de la préhistoire à l'époque hellénistique*. Paris: Errance.

———. 2004b. *Archéologie du vin et de l'huile dans l'empire romain*. Paris: Errance.

———. 2005. *Archéologie du vin et de l'huile en Gaule romaine*. Paris: Errance.

———. 2006. "L'énergie hydraulique durant l'Empire romain: quel impact sur l'économie agricole?" In Lo Cascio 2006: 101–30.

Brun, J.-P., and P. Jockey, eds. 2001. *Techniques et sociétés en Méditerranée*. Paris: Maisonneuve et Larose, and Maison Méditerranéenne des Sciences de l'Homme.

Brun, P. 1996. *Les archipels égéens dans l'Antiquité grecque (Vᵉ–IIᵉ siècles av. notre ère)*. Besançon and Paris: Les Belles Lettres.

———. 1997. "Du fromage de Kythnos au marbre de Paros: La question des appellations contrôlées (?) dans l'Antiquité grecque." *Revue des Études Anciennes* 99: 401–9.

———. 1999. "Les nouvelles perspectives de l'étude démographique des cités grecques." In Bellancourt-Valdher and Corvisier 1999: 13–25.

Brun, P., ed. 2007. *Scripta Anatolica. Mélanges Pierre Debord*. Bordeaux: Ausonius.

Bruneau, P. 1969. "Documents sur l'industrie délienne de la pourpre." *Bulletin de Correspondance Hellénique* 93: 759–91 (= Bruneau 2006: 189–221).

———. 1978. "Deliaca (II)." *Bulletin de Correspondance Hellénique* 102: 109–71 (= Bruneau 2006: 375–437).

———. 1979. "Deliaca (III)." *Bulletin de Correspondance Hellénique* 103: 83–107 (= Bruneau 2006: 473–97).

Bruneau, P. 2006. *Études d'archéologie délienne*. Ed. by J.-C. Moretti. Athens: École française d'Athènes.

Bruneau, P., et al., eds. 1970. *L'îlot de la Maison des Comédiens. Exploration archéologique de Délos 27*. Paris: De Boccard.

Brunet, M. 1993. "Vin local et vin de cru. Les exemples de Délos et de Thasos." In Amouretti and Brun 1993: 201–11.

———. 1999. "Le paysage agraire de Délos dans l'Antiquité." *Journal des Savants*: 1–50.

———. 2001. "À propos des recherches sur les territoires ruraux en Grèce égéenne: un bilan critique." In Stazio and Ceccoli 2001: 27–46.

———. 2007. "L'économie d'une cité à l'époque classique: Thasos." In Debidour 2007: 211–31.

Brunet, M., G. Rougemont, and D. Rousset. 1998. "Les contrats agraires dans la Grèce antique. Bilan historiographique illustré par quatre exemples." *Histoire et Sociétés Rurales* 9: 211–45.

Brunt, P. A. 1987. *Italian Manpower*. 2nd ed. (1st ed. 1971). Oxford: Oxford University Press.

Bücher, K. 1901. *Industrial Evolution*. New York: H. Holt and Company (first German ed. 1893, *Die Entstehung der Volkswirtschaft. Sechs Vorträge*. Tübingen: Laupp. Tr. from the 3rd German ed. 1901).

Buchner, G., and D. Ridgway. 1993 *Pithekoussai I*. Rome: L'Erma di Bretschneider.

Buckler, J. 2003. *Aegean Greece in the Fourth Century BC*. Leiden and Boston: Brill.

Buckler, W. H. 1923. "Labour Disputes in the Province of Asia." In Buckler and Calder 1923: 27–50.

Buckler, W. H., and W. M. Calder. 1923. *Anatolian Studies Presented to Sir William Mitchell Ramsay*. Manchester: University Press, and London and New York: Longmans, Green.

Bulliet, R.W. 1990. *The Camel and the Wheel*. New York: Columbia University Press.

Buraselis, K. 2013. "Ptolemaic Grain, Seaways, and Power." In Buraselis et al. 2013: 97–107.

Buraselis, K., M. Stefanou, and D. J. Thomson, eds. 2013. *The Ptolemies, the Sea and the Nile: Studies in Waterborne Power*. Cambridge: Cambridge University Press.

Burford, A. 1960. "Heavy Transport in Classical Antiquity." *Economic History Review* 13: 1–18.

———. 1969. *The Greek Temple Builders at Epidauros, a Social and Economic Study of Building in the Asklepian Sanctuary during the Fourth and Early Third Centuries B.C.* Liverpool: Liverpool University Press.

Burford Cooper, A. 1977. "The Family Farm in Greece." *Classical Journal* 73: 162–75.

Burns, B. E. 2010a. *Mycenaean Greece, Mediterranean Commerce, and the Formation of Identity*. Cambridge: Cambridge University Press.

———. 2010b. "Trade." In Cline 2010: 291–304.

Burstein, S. M. 1985. *The Hellenistic Age from the Battle of Ipsos to the Death of Kleopatra VII*. Cambridge: Cambridge University Press.

Burt, R. 2004. "The Extractive Industries." In Floud and Johnson 2004: 417–50.

Buzoianu, L., P. Dupont, and V. Lungu, eds. 2013. *Production and Trade of Amphorae in the Black Sea (PATABS III)*. Constanţa: Natural History and Archaeology Museum.

Cahill, N. 2002. *Household and City Organization at Olynthus*. New Haven, CT: Yale University Press.

Cairns, D. L., and R. A. Knox, eds. 2004. *Law, Rhetoric and Comedy in Classical Athens.* Swansea: Classical Press of Wales.

Calder, W. M., III, and Demandt, A. 1990. *Eduard Meyer. Leben und Leistung eines Universalhistorikers*. Leiden and New York: Brill.

Calhoun, B.G.M. 1926. *The Business Life of Ancient Athens*. Chicago: University of Chicago Press.

Callataÿ, F. de. 1989. "Les trésors achéménides et les monnayages d'Alexandre: espèces immobilisées et espèces circulantes." *Revue des Études Anciennes* 91: 259–74.

———. 1997. *L'histoire des guerres mithridatiques vue par les monnaies*. Louvain-la-Neuve: Département d'archéologie et d'histoire de l'art, séminaire de numismatique Marcel Hoc.

———. 2000. "Guerres et monnayages à l'époque hellénistique. Essai de mise en perspective suivi d'une étude sur le monnayage de Mithridate VI Eupator." In Andreau et al. 2000: 337–64.

———. 2003. *Recueil quantitatif des émissions monétaires archaïques et classiques*. Wetteren: Éditions Numismatique romaine.

———. 2004. "Le premier monnayage de la cité d'Amastris." *Schweizerische Numismatische Rundschau* 83: 57–80.

———. 2006a. "Réflexions quantitatives sur l'or et l'argent non monnayés à l'époque hellénistique." In Descat 2006b: 37–84.

———. 2006b. "Greek Coins from Archaeological Excavations: A Conspectus and a Call for Chronological Tables." In van Alfen 2006: 177–200.

———. 2006c. *Quantifications et numismatique antique: choix d'articles (1984–2004)*. Wetteren: Moneta.

———. 2009. "The First Royal Coinages of Pontos (from Mithridates III to Mithridates V)." In Højte 2009: 63–94.

———, ed. 2014. *Quantifying the Graeco-Roman Economy and Beyond*. Bari: Pragmateia.

Cameron, A. 1932. "The Exposure of Children and Greek Ethics." *Classical Review* 46: 105–14.

Cameron, A., and A. Kuhrt, eds. 1983. *Images of Women in Antiquity*. London and Canberra: Croom Helm.

Camia, F. 2009. *Roma e le poleis: l'intervento di Roma nelle controversie territoriali tra le comunità greche di Grecia e d'Asia Minore nel secondo secolo a.C.: le testimonianze epigrafiche*. Athens: Scuola archeologica italiana di Atene.

Camp, J. M., II. 1986. *The Athenian Agora: Excavations in the Heart of Classical Athens*. New York: Thames and Hudson.

———. 2001. *The Archaeology of Athens*. New Haven, CT: Yale University Press.

Campbell, J. K. 1964. *Honour, Family and Patronage: A Study of Institutions and Moral Values in a Greek Mountain Community*. Oxford: Clarendon Press.

Camporeale, G. 1985. *L'Etruria mineraria*. Catalog of an exhibition held in Portoferraio, Massa Marittima and Populonia in 1985. Milan: Electa.

Cantat, O., and J.-O. Gires, eds. 2004. *Actes du XVIIe colloque international de climatologie: Climat, Mémoires du temps, Caen, 8–10 septembre 2004*. Caen: Université de Caen.

Capdetrey, L. 2007. *Le pouvoir séleucide. Territoire, administration, finances d'un royaume hellénistique (312–129 avant J.-C.)*. Rennes: Presses Universitaires de Rennes.

Capdetrey, L., and C. Hasenohr. 2012b. "Surveiller, organiser, financer: fonctionnement de l'*agoranomia* et statut des agoranomes dans le monde égéen." In Capdetrey and Hasenohr 2012a: 13–34.

Capdetrey, L., and C. Hasenohr, eds. 2012a. *Agoranomes et édiles. Institutions des marchés antiques*. Bordeaux: Ausonius.

Capdetrey, L., and J. Nelis-Clément, eds. 2006. *La circulation de l'information dans les États antiques*. Bordeaux: Ausonius.

Capdetrey, L., and J. Zurbach, eds. 2012. *Mouvements, réseaux, contacts en Méditerrannée, de l'époque archaïque à l'époque hellénistique*. Bordeaux: Ausonius.

Capogrossi Colognesi, L. 2000. *Max Weber e le economie del mondo antico*. Rome: Laterza.

Cardon, D., and M. Feugère, eds. 2000. *Archéologie des textiles des origines au Ve siècle. Actes du colloque de Lattes, octobre 1999*. Montagnac: Éditions Monique Mergoil.

Cargill, J. 1981. *The Second Athenian League: Empire or Free Alliance?* Berkeley: University of California Press.

Carlson, D. N. 2003. "The Classical Greek Shipwreck at Tektaş Burnu, Turkey." *American Journal of Archaeology* 107: 581–600.

———. 2011. "The Seafarer and Shipwrecks of Ancient Greece and Rome." In Catsambis et al. 2011: 379–405.

Carrara, A. 2014. "Tax and Trade in Ancient Greece: About the *Ellimenion* and the Harbour Duties." *Revue des Études Anciennes* 116: 441–64.

Cartledge, P. 2000. "Greek Political Thought: The Historical Context." In Rowe and Schofield 2000: 7–22.

Cartledge, P., and A. Spawforth. 1992. *Hellenistic and Roman Sparta: A Tale of Two Cities*. 2nd ed. London: Routledge.

Cartledge, P., and F. D. Harvey, eds. 1985. *Crux: Essays in Greek History Presented to G.E.M. de Ste. Croix on His 75th Birthday*. London: Duckworth and Imprint Academic.

Cartledge, P., E. E. Cohen, and L. Foxhall, eds. 2002. *Money, Labour and Land: Approaches to the Economies of Ancient Greece*. London and New York: Routledge.

Carusi, C. 2005. "Nuova edizione della homologia fra Trezene e Arsinoe (*IG* IV 752, *IG* IV² 76+77)." *Studi Ellenistici* 16: 79–140.

———. 2008. *Il sale nel mondo greco (VI a.C.–III d.C.): luoghi di produzione, circolazione commerciale, regimi di sfruttamento nel contesto del Mediterraneo antico*. Bari: Edipuglia.

Casson, L. 1991. *The Ancient Mariners: Seafarers and Sea Fighters of the Mediterranean in Ancient Times*. 2nd ed. Princeton, NJ: Princeton University Press.

———. 1994a. "Mediterranean Communications." In Lewis et al. 1994: 512–26.

———. 1994b. *Ships and Seafaring in Ancient Times*. Austin: University of Texas Press.

———. 1995. *Ships and Seamanship in the Ancient World*. 2nd ed. Baltimore: Johns Hopkins University Press (1st ed. 1971, Princeton University Press).

Cataldi, S. 1983. *Symbolai e relazioni tra le città greche nel v secolo a.C.* Pisa: Scuola normale superiore.

Cataudella, M. 1998. "Polibio (5.88–90) e il terremoto di Rodi." In Olshausen and Sonnabend 1998: 190–97.

Catsambis, A., N. Ford, and D. L. Hamilton, eds. 2011. *The Oxford Handbook of Maritime Archaeology*. Oxford and New York: Oxford University Press.

Cavanagh, W. G., J. Crouwel, R.W.V. Catling, and G. Shipley. 1996. *Continuity and Change in a Greek Rural Landscape: The Laconia Survey: Volume II: Archaeological Data*, London: British School at Athens.

Cavaignac, E. 1951. *L'économie grecque*. Paris: Plon.

Chamonard, J. 1922. *Le quartier du théâtre. Exploration archéologique de Délos 8.1.* Paris: De Boccard.

Chamoux, F. 1953. *Cyrène sous la monarchie des Battiades.* Paris: De Boccard.

Chandezon, C. 1999. "L'économie rurale et la guerre." In Prost 1999: 195–208.

———. 2000. "Foires et panégyries dans le monde grec classique et hellénistique." *Revue des Études Grecques* 113: 70–100.

———. 2003. *L'élevage en Grèce (fin V^e–fin Ier s. a.C.).* Bordeaux: Ausonius.

———. 2004. "Pratiques zootechniques dans l'Antiquité grecque." *Revue des Études Anciennes* 106: 477–97.

Chandler, A. D., Jr. 1977. *The Visible Hand: The Managerial Revolution in American Business.* Cambridge, MA: Belknap Press.

Chaniotis, A. 1996. *Die Verträge zwischen kretischen Poleis in der hellenistischen Zeit.* Stuttgart: Steiner.

———. 2005. *War in the Hellenistic World.* Malden, MA, and Oxford: Blackwell.

Chaniotis, A., ed. 1999. *From Minoan to Roman Traders: Sidelights on the Economy of Ancient Greece.* Stuttgart: Steiner.

Chankowski, V. 1997. "Le sanctuaire d'Apollon et le marché délien." In Andreau et al. 1997: 73–89.

———. 2005. "Techniques financières, influences, performance dans les activités bancaires des sanctuaires grecs." *Topoi* 12–13: 69–93.

———. 2008. *Athènes et Délos à l'époque classique: recherches sur l'administration du sanctuaire d'Apollon délien.* Athens: École française d'Athènes.

———. 2012. "Délos et les matériaux stratégiques. Une nouvelle lecture de la loi délienne sur la vente du bois et du charbon (*ID* 509)." In Konuk 2012: 31–51.

Chankowski, V., and L. Domaradzka, 1999. "Réédition de l'inscription de Pistiros et problèmes d'interprétation." *Bulletin de Correspondance Hellénique* 123: 246–58.

Chankowski, V., and P. Karvonis, eds. 2012. *Tout vendre, tout acheter. Structures et équipements des marchés antiques.* Bordeaux: Ausonius.

Chatelain, T. 2001. "Assèchement et bonification des terres dans l'Antiquité grecque. L'exemple du lac de Ptéchai à Érétrie; aspects terminologiques et techniques." In Briant 2001: 81–108.

Chaunu, P. 1966. *La civilisation de l'Europe classique.* Paris: Arthaud.

Cherry, J. F., J. L. Davis, and E. Mantzourani. 1991. *Landscape Archaeology as Long-Term History: Northern Keos in the Cycladic Islands from Earliest Settlement until Modern Times.* Los Angeles: UCLA Institute of Archaeology.

Christ, M. R. 1990. "Liturgy Avoidance and Antidosis in Classical Athens." *Transactions of the American Philological Association* 120: 147–69.

Christien, J. 2002. "Iron Money in Sparta: Myth and History." In Powell and Hodkinson 2002: 171–90.

Clark, G. 2007. *A Farewell to Alms: A Brief Economic History of the World.* Princeton, NJ: Princeton University Press.

Clarysse, W., and D. J. Thompson. 2006. *Counting the People in Hellenistic Egypt.* Vol. 2. *Historical Studies.* Cambridge: Cambridge University Press.

Clavel-Lévêque, M., and E. Hermon, eds. 2004. *Espaces intégrés et ressources naturelles dans le monde romain.* Besançon: Presses Universitaires de Franche-Comté.

Cleland, L., G. Davies, and L. Llewellyn-Jones. 2007. *Greek and Roman Dress from A to Z.* Abingdon, UK, and New York: Routledge.

Clément, A. 2001. "Les deux mercantilismes et la question alimentaire (XVIᵉ–XVIIᵉ siècle)." In *Mercantilisme* 2001: 43–65.

Cline, E. H., ed. 2010. *The Oxford Handbook of the Bronze Age Aegean (ca. 3000–1000 BCE).* Oxford: Oxford University Press.

Coase, R. 1987. *The Firm, the Market, and the Law.* Chicago: University of Chicago Press.

Cohen, D. 1993. "Law, Autonomy, and Political Community in Plato's Laws." *Classical Philology* 88: 301–17.

Cohen, E. E. 1973. *Ancient Athenian Maritime Courts.* Princeton, NJ: Princeton University Press.

———. 1992. *Athenian Economy and Society: A Banking Perspective.* Princeton, NJ: Princeton University Press.

———. 2002. *The Athenian Nation.* Princeton, NJ: Princeton University Press.

———. 2006. "A Legal Fiction: The Athenian Law of Sale." In van Alfen 2006: 87–98.

Coleman, J. E., K. O'Neill, M. Pomeroy, K. E. Carr, and A. Heafitz. 1992. "Excavations at Halai, 1990–1991." *Hesperia* 61: 265–89.

Collard, F., and É. Samama, eds. 2006. *Pharmacopoles et apothicaires. Les "pharmaciens" de l'Antiquité au Grand Siècle.* Paris: L'Harmattan.

Colvin, S., ed. 2004. *The Graeco-Roman East, Politics, Cultures, Society.* Cambridge and New York: Cambridge University Press.

Commons, J. R. 1931. "Institutional Economics." *American Economic Review* 21: 648–57.

———. 1934. *Institutional Economics: Its Place in Political Economy.* New York: Macmillan.

Conophagos, C. 1980. *Le Laurium antique et la technique grecque de la production de l'argent.* Athens: Ekdotike Hellados.

Conrad, S. 2010. "Work, Max Weber, Confucianism: The Confucian Ethic and the Spirit of Japanese Capitalism." In Kocka 2010: 153–68.

Constable, O. R. 1994. *Trade and Traders in Muslim Spain: The Commercial Realignment of the Iberian Peninsula, 900–1500.* Cambridge and New York: Cambridge University Press.

Convegno. 2011. *La vigna di Dioniso: vite, vino e culti in Magna Grecia: Atti del quarantanovesimo convegno di studi sulla Magna Grecia, Taranto 24–28 settembre 2009.* Taranto: Istituto per la storia e l'archeologia della Magna Grecia.

Cook, R. M. 1959. "Die Bedeutung der bemalten Keramik für den griechischen Handel." *Jahrbuch des Deutschen Archäologischen Instituts* 74: 114–23.

Cook, S. 1966. "The Obsolete 'Anti-Market' Mentality: A Critique of the Substantive Approach to Economic Anthropology." *American Anthropologist* 68: 323–45.

———. 1968. Review of Polanyi 1968. *American Anthropologist* 70: 966–69.

Cooper, N. K. 1990. "Archaic Architectural Terracottas from Halieis and Bassai." *Hesperia* 59: 65–93.

Coquery, N., F. Menant, F. Weber, eds. 2006. *Écrire, compter et mesurer. Vers une histoire des rationalités pratiques* Paris: Ed. Rue d'Ulm.

Corsaro, M. 2001. "Doni di terra ed essenzioni dai tributi: un riflessione sulla natura dello stato ellenistico in Asie Minore." *Simblos* 3: 227–61.

Corvisier, J.-N. 1991. *Aux origines du miracle grec: population et peuplement en Grèce du Nord.* Paris: Presses Universitaires de France.

————. 2001. "L'état présent de la démographie historique antique: tentative de bilan." *Annales de démographie historique* 102: 101–40.

————. 2004. "Le bilan des land surveys pour la Grèce." *Pallas* 64: 15–33.

Corvisier, J.-N., and W. Suder. 2000. *La population de l'Antiquité classique*. Paris: Presses Universitaires de France.

Corvisier, J.-N., and W. Suder, with the collaboration of C. Didier. 1996. *Polyanthropia/ Oliganthropia, Bibliographies de la démographie du monde grec*. Wroclaw: Arboretum.

Cottier, M. 2012. "*Retour à la source*: A Fresh Overview of the Persian Customs Register *TAD* C.3.7." In Konuk 2012: 53–61.

Cottier, M., M. H. Crawford, C. V. Crowther, J.-L. Ferrary, B. M. Levick, O. Salomies, and M. Wörrle. 2008. *The Customs Law of Asia*. Oxford: Oxford University Press.

Couilloud-Le Dinahet, M.-T. 1988. "Les magistrats grecs et l'approvisionnement des cités." *Cahiers d'Histoire* 33: 321–32.

Coulson, D. E., O. Palagia, T. L. Shear, H. A. Shapiro, and H. J. Frost, eds. 1994. *The Archaeology of Athens and Attica under the Democracy*. Oxford: Oxbow Books.

Counillon, P., and R. Étienne. 1997. "Les *taricheiai* d'après les sources grecques." In Étienne 1997: 181–93.

Cousin, G., and G. Deschamps 1887. "Emplacement et ruines de la ville de Kys en Carie." *Bulletin de Correspondance Hellénique* 11: 305–11.

Couvenhes, J.-C., and H.-L. Fernoux, eds. 2004. *Les cités grecques et la guerre en Asie Mineure à l'époque hellénistique*. Tours: Presses Universitaires François-Rabelais.

Crane, E. 1983. *The Archaeology of Beekeeping*. London: Cornell University Press.

Crawford, D. J. 1979. "Food: Tradition and Change in Hellenistic Egypt." *World Archaeology* 11: 136–46.

Cressier, P., and P. Rouillard, eds. 2005. *Autour de Polanyi*. Paris: De Boccard.

Criscuolo, L. 2011. "La formula *en patrikois* nelle iscrizioni di Cassandrea." *Chiron* 41: 461–85.

Criscuolo, L., and G. Geraci, eds. 1989. *Egitto e storia antica dall'ellenismo all'età araba. Bilancio di un confronto*. Bologna: CLUEB.

Crouch, D. P. 1993. *Water Management in Ancient Greek Cities*. New York and Oxford: Oxford University Press.

Cuinet, V. 1890–1894. *La Turquie d'Asie*. 4 vols. Paris: Leroux.

Curtis, R. I. 2008. "Food Processing and Preparation." In Oleson 2008: 369–92.

Cuvigny, M. 1994. *Dion de Pruse. Discours bithyniens: discours 38–51*. Besançon and Paris: Les Belles Lettres.

Dalaison, J., ed. 2007. *Espaces et pouvoirs dans l'Antiquité. De l'Anatolie à la Gaule, Mélanges Bernard Rémy*. Grenoble: Centre de recherche en histoire et histoire de l'art Italie-Pays alpins.

Dalby, A. 2002. "Levels of Concealment: The Dress of Hetairai and Pornai in Greek Texts." In Llewellyn-Jones 2002: 111–24.

————. 2003. *Food in the Ancient World from A to Z*. London and New York: Routledge.

Danzig, G. 2000. "The Political Character of Aristotelian Reciprocity." *Classical Philology* 95: 399–424.

Darmezin, L. 1999. *Les affranchissements par consécration en Béotie et dans le monde grec hellénistique*. Nancy: Association pour la diffusion de la recherche sur l'Antiquité.

Daverio Rocchi, G. 1988. *Frontiera e confini nella Grecia antica*. Rome: L'Erma di Bretschneider.

Davidson, J. N. 2011. *Courtesans and Fishcakes: The Consuming Passions of Classical Athens.* Chicago: University of Chicago Press.

Davies, J. K. 1977. "Athenian Citizenship: The Descent Group and the Alternatives." *Classical Journal* 73: 105–21.

———. 2001. "Hellenistic Economies in the Post-Finley Era." In Archibald et al. 2001: 11–62.

———. 2005. "Linear and Nonlinear Flow Models for Ancient Economy." In Manning and Morris 2005: 127–56.

———. 2013. "Mediterranean Economies through the Text of Polybius." In Gibson and Harrison 2013: 319–35.

Davies, J. K., and J. Wilkes, eds. 2012. *Epigraphy and the Historical Sciences.* Oxford: British Academy and Oxford University Press.

Davis, J. 2011. "Market Regulation in Fifteenth-Century England." In Dodds and Liddy 2011: 81–106.

———. 2012. *Medieval Market Morality: Life, Law and Ethics in the English Marketplace, 1200–1500.* Cambridge: Cambridge University Press.

Deakin, M.A.B. 2007. *Hypatia of Alexandria: Mathematician and Martyr.* Amherst, MA: Prometheus Books.

Debidour, M., ed. 2007. *Économies et sociétés dans la Grèce égéenne 478–88 av. J.-C.* Nantes: Éditions du Temps.

De Blois, L., and J. Rich, eds. 2002. *The Transformation of Economic Life under the Roman Empire.* Amsterdam: Gieben.

Debord, P. 1982. *Aspects sociaux et économiques de la vie religieuse dans l'Anatolie gréco-romaine.* Leiden: Brill.

———. 1999. *L'Asie Mineure au IVe siècle (412–323 a.C.).* Bordeaux: Ausonius.

Debord, P., and E. Varinlioğlu, eds. 2010. *Cités de Carie: Harpasa, Bargasa, Orthosia dans l'Antiquité.* Rennes: Presses Universitaires de Rennes.

Deger-Jalkotzy, S. 2008. "Decline, Destruction, Aftermath." In Shelmerdine 2008: 387–415.

Delemen, İ., ed. 2007. *The Achaemenid Impact on Local Population and Cultures in Anatolia (6th–4th B.C.).* Istanbul: Turkish Institute of Archaeology.

De Ligt, L. 1993. *Fairs and Markets in the Roman Empire: Economic and Social Aspects of Periodic Trade in a Preindustrial Society.* Amsterdam: Gieben.

Delrieux, F. 2001. "Iasos à la fin du IVe siècle. Les monnaies aux fruits de mer, des fils de Théodotos au versement de l'*ekklesiastikon*." *Revue des Études Grecques* 114: 160–89.

———. 2008. "L'exploitation de la mer et ses implications économiques, politiques et militaires dans le golfe de Bargylia en Carie à l'époque gréco-romaine." In Napoli 2008: 273–93.

Demand, N. H. 2011. *The Mediterranean Context of Early Greek History.* Chichester, UK, and Malden, MA: Wiley-Blackwell.

Dentzer, J. M., P. Gauthier, and T. Hackens, eds. 1975. *Numismatique antique, Problèmes et méthodes.* Nancy: Université de Nancy II, and Louvain: Peeters.

Deonna, W. 1938. *Le mobilier délien. Exploration archéologique de Délos 18.* Paris: De Boccard.

Descat, R. 1985. "Mnésimachos, Hérodote et le système tributaire achéménide." *Revue des Études Anciennes* 87: 97–112.

———. 1993. "La loi de Solon sur l'interdiction d'exporter les produits attiques." In Bresson and Rouillard 1993: 145–61.

————. 1997. "Les prix dans l'inscription agoranomique du Pirée." In Andreau et al. 1997: 13–20.

————. 2001. "La loi délienne sur les bois et charbons et le rôle de Délos comme marché." *Revue des Études Anciennes* 103: 125–30.

————. 2002. "La mer et l'information économique dans le monde antique." In Andreau and Virlouvet 2002: 263–78.

————. 2004. "L'approvisionnement en grains dans le monde grec des cités: histoire d'une politique." In Virlouvet and Marin 2004: 589–612.

————. 2006a. "Argyrônètos: Les transformations de l'échange dans la Grèce archaïque." In van Alfen 2006: 21–36.

Descat, R., ed. 2006b. *Approches de l'économie hellénistique*. Saint-Bertrand-de-Comminges: Musée archéologique de Saint-Bertrand-de-Comminges, and Paris: de Boccard.

Deshours, N. 2006. *Les mystères d'Andania. Étude d'épigraphie et d'histoire religieuse.* Bordeaux: Ausonius.

Deslauriers, M., and P. Destrée, eds. 2013: *The Cambridge Companion to Aristotle's Politics.* Cambridge: Cambridge University Press.

De Souza, P. 1999. *Piracy in the Graeco-Roman World.* Cambridge: Cambridge University Press.

De Vries, J., and A. van der Woude. 1997. *The First Modern Economy: Success, Failure, and Perseverance of the Dutch Economy, 1500–1815.* Cambridge: Cambridge University Press.

DeVries, K. 1997. "The Attic Pottery from Gordion." In Oakley et al. 1997: 447–55.

Dewald, C. 2006. "Paying Attention: History as the Development of a Secular Narrative." In Goldhill and Osborne 2006: 164–82.

Deyon, P. 1969. *Le mercantilisme.* Paris: Flammarion.

Diamond, J. M. 2005. *Collapse: How Societies Choose to Fail or Succeed.* New York: Viking Press.

Dickinson, O.T.P.K. 1994. *The Aegean Bronze Age.* Cambridge and New York: Cambridge University Press.

————. 2006. *The Aegean from Bronze Age to Iron Age: Continuity and Change between the Twelfth and Eighth Centuries B.C.* London and New York: Routledge.

Dietz, S., and I. Papachristodoulou, eds. 1988. *Archaeology in the Dodecanese.* Copenhagen: National Museum of Denmark, Department of Near Eastern and Classical Antiquities.

Dixon, D. F. 1995. "Retailing in Classical Athens: Gleanings from Contemporary Literature and Art." *Journal of Macromarketing* 16.1: 74–85.

Docter, R. F. 1991. "Athena vs Dionysos: Reconsidering the Contents of SOS Amphorae." *BABesch* 66: 45–49.

Dodds, B., and R. H. Britnell, eds. 2008. *Agriculture and Rural Society after the Black Death: Common Themes and Regional Variations.* Hatfield, UK: University of Hertfordshire Press.

Dodds, B., and C. D. Liddy, eds. 2011. *Commercial Activity, Markets and Entrepreneurs in the Middle Ages: Essays in Honour of Richard Britnell.* Woodbridge, UK, and Rochester, NY: Boydell Press.

Domergue, A. Beyrie, C. Jacquet, C. Jarrier, and F. Tollon. 2003. "Un bas fourneau de petit module sur le site sidérurgique romain du domaine des Forges (Les Martys, Aude, France)." In Stöllner et al. 2003: 127–36.

Domergue, C., and J.-L. Bordes. 2006. "Quelques nouveautés techniques dans les mines et la métallurgie à l'époque romaine: leur efficacité et leurs effets sur la production." In Lo Cascio 2006: 197–223.

Doonan, O. P. 2002. "Production in a Pontic Landscape: The Hinterland of Greek and Roman Sinope," In Faudot et al. 2002: 185–98.

———. 2004. *Sinop Landscapes: Exploring Connection in a Black Sea Hinterland*. Philadelphia: University of Pennsylvania Museum of Archaeology and Anthropology.

Doukellis, P. 1998. "Versants pierreux et champs de culture à Céos." In Mendoni and Mazarakis 1998: 309–30.

Doukellis, P., and L. Mendoni, eds. 1994. *Structures rurales et sociétés antiques*. Besançon and Paris: Les Belles Lettres.

Doulgeri-Intzessiloglou, A., and Y. Garlan. 1990. "Vin et amphores de Péparéthos et d'Ikos," with Annex by M. Picon, "Origine du groupe d'amphores dit Solocha II, trouvées en Russie." *Bulletin de Correspondance Hellénique* 114: 361–93.

Doumet, J. E. 2007. "La pourpre." In Fontan and Le Meaux 2007: 87–91.

Drachmann, A. B. 1903–1927. *Scholia Vetera in Pindari Carmina*. Leipzig: Teubner.

Drachmann, A. G. 1963. *The Mechanical Technology of Greek and Roman Antiquity*. Copenhagen: Munksgaard, and Madison: University of Wisconsin Press.

Dubois, L. 1996. *Inscriptions dialectales d'Olbia du Pont*. Geneva: Droz.

Dubouloz, J., and S. Pittia, eds. 2007. *La Sicile de Cicéron. Lecture des* Verrines. Besançon: Presses Universitaires de Franche-Comté.

Duchêne, H., and P. Fraisse. 2001. *Le paysage portuaire de la Délos antique. Recherches sur les installations maritimes, commerciales et urbaines du littoral délien. Exploration archéologique de Délos 39*. Athens: École française d'Athènes.

Ducrey, P., ed. 2004. *Eretria: A Guide to the Ancient City*. Gollion: Infolio.

Dumont, J. 1976–1977. "La pêche du thon à Byzance à l'époque hellénistique." *Revue des Études Anciennes* 78–79: 96–119.

———. 1977. "Liberté des mers et territoire de pêche en droit grec." *Revue Historique de Droit Français et Étranger* 5: 53–57.

Duncan, C.A.M., and D. W. Tandy, eds. 1993. *From Political Economy to Anthropology*. Montreal, New York, and London: Black Rose Books.

Duncan-Jones, R. P. 1982. *The Economy of the Roman Empire*. 2nd ed. (1st ed. 1974). Cambridge and New York: Cambridge University Press.

Dupont, P. 1995–1996. "Amphores archaïques de Grèce propre en mer Noire: état de la question." *Il Mar Nero* 2: 85–98.

Dupont, P., and V. Lungu. In press. "Kelainai–Apamée Kibôtos. Un faciès céramique centre-anatolien: traits saillants." In Summerer et al.: In press.

Dušanić, S. 1978. "The *horkion tōn oikistērōn* and Fourth Century Cyrene." *Chiron* 8: 55–76.

E' epistēmonikē synantēsē gia tēn hellēnikē keramikē. 2000. Athens: Hypourgeio Politismou. Tameio Archaiologikōn Porōn kai Apallotriōseōn.

Eatwell, J., M. Milgate, and P. Newman, eds. 1987. *The New Palgrave: A Dictionary of Economics*. 4 vols. London and New York: Macmillan and Stockton.

Eck, W., ed. 1999. *Lokale Autonomie und römische Ordnungsmacht in den kaiserzeitlichen Provinzen vom 1. bis 3. Jahrhundert*. Munich: R. Oldenbourg Verlag.

Ehrenberg, V. 1962: *The People of Aristophanes*. 3rd rev. ed. New York: Schocken Books.

Eidinow, E. 2007. *Oracles, Curses, and Risk among the Ancient Greeks*. Oxford: Oxford University Press.

———. 2012. "'What Will Happen to Me if I Leave?' Ancient Greek Oracles, Slaves and Slave Owners." In Hodkinson and Geary 2012: 244–78.

Eiring, J., and J. Lund, eds. 2004. *Transport Amphorae and Trade in the Eastern Mediterranean*. Aarhus: Aarhus University Press.

Eiseman, C. J., and B. S. Ridgway. 1987. *The Porticello Shipwreck: A Mediterranean Merchant Vessel of 415–385 B. C.* College Station, Texas: Published with the cooperation of the Institute of Nautical Archaeology by Texas A&M University Press.

Elayi, J., and A. G. Elayi. 2004. *Le monnayage de la cité phénicienne de Sidon à l'époque perse (V^e–IVe s. av. J.-C.)*. Paris: Gabalda.

———. 2009. *The Coinage of the Phoenician City of Tyre in the Persian Period (5th–4th cent. BCE)*. Leuven and Walpole, MA: Peeters.

Emmerling, E., K. Adelfinger, and J. Reischl. 2010. "On the Painting Technique of the Tomb Chamber." In Summerer and von Kienlin 2010: 204–33.

Empereur, J.-Y., and N. Tuna. 1988. "Zénon de Caunos et l'épave de Serçe Limanı." *Bulletin de Correspondance Hellénique* 112: 341–47.

Empereur, J.-Y., and Y. Garlan, eds. 1986. *Recherches sur les amphores grecques*. Athens and Paris: De Boccard.

Engelmann, H., and D. Knibbe. 1989. "Das Zollgessetz der Provinz Asia." *Epigraphica Anatolica* 14: 1989.

Engels, D. 1980. "The Problem of Female Infanticide in the Greco-Roman World." *Classical Philology* 75: 112–20.

Engen, D. T. 2010. *Honor and Profit: Athenian Trade Policy and the Economy and Society of Greece, 415–307 B.C.E.* Ann Arbor: University of Michigan Press.

Erdas, D. 2012. "Aspetti giuridici dell'agora greca." In Ampolo 2012: 57–69.

Erdkamp, P. 2002. "Urban Markets and Food Riots in the Roman World, 100 BC – 400 AD." In de Blois and Rich 2002: 93–115.

———. 2005. *The Grain Market in the Roman Empire: A Social, Political and Economic Study*. Cambridge and New York: Cambridge University Press.

———. 2008. "Grain Funds and Market Intervention in the Roman World." In Alston and van Nijf 2008: 109–26.

Erskine, A., ed. 2003. *A Companion to the Hellenistic World*. Malden, MA: Blackwell.

———. 2009. *A Companion to Ancient History*. Chichester, UK, and Malden, MA: Wiley-Blackwell.

Ersoy, Y. 2003. "Pottery Production and Mechanism of Workshops in Archaic Clazomenae." In Schmaltz and Söldner 2003: 254–57.

Ersoy, Y., A. Moustaka, and E. Skarlatidou, eds. 2004. *Klazomenai, Teos and Abdera: Mother City and Colonies. Proceedings of the Symposium, Abdera 20–21 October 2001*. Thessaloniki: 19th Ephorate of Prehistoric and Classical Antiquities of Komotini, and University Studio Press.

Esposito, A., and G. M. Sanidas, eds. 2012. *Quartiers artisanaux en Grèce ancienne: une perspective méditerranéenne*. Lille: Presses Universitaires du Septentrion.

Étienne, R. 1990. *Ténos*. Vol. 2. *Ténos et les Cyclades: du milieu du IVe siècle av. J.-C. au milieu du IIIe siècle ap. J.-C.* Athens: École française d'Athènes, and Paris: De Boccard.

Étienne, R. 2004. *Athènes, espaces urbains et histoire. Des origines à la fin du III* siècle ap. J.-C.* Paris: Hachette.

Étienne, R., and F. Mayet. 2002. *Salaisons et sauces de poisson hispaniques.* Paris: De Boccard.

Étienne, R., C. Müller, and F. Prost. 2000. *Archéologie historique de la Grèce antique.* Paris: Ellipses.

Eyben, E. 1982–1983. "Family Planning in Graeco-Roman Antiquity." *Ancient Society* 11–12: 5–82.

Fabbricotti, E., and O. Menozzi, eds. 2006. *Cirenaica: studi, scavi e scoperte. Atti del X Convegno di Archeologia Cirenaica Chieti 24–26 Novembre 2003. Nuovi dati da città e territorio.* BAR International Series 1488. Oxford: John & Erica Hedges.

Fachard, S. 2013. "Eleutherai as the Gates to Boeotia." *Revue des Études Militaires Anciennes* 6: 81–106.

Fantasia, U. 1984. "Mercanti e 'sitonai' nelle città greche. In margine a tre documenti epigrafici della prima età ellenistica." *Civiltà classica e cristiana* 5: 283–311.

———. 1989. "Finanze cittadine, liberalità private e sitos demosios: considerazioni su alcuni documenti epigrafici." *Serta Historica Antiqua* 2: 47–84.

———. 1999. "Aree marginali nella Grecia antica: paludi e bonifiche." In Vera 1999: 65–116.

———. 2012a. "Gli agoranomi e l'approvvigionamento granario delle città greche in età ellenistica." In Capdetrey and Hasenohr 2012a: 35–45.

———. 2012b. "I magistrati dell'agora nelle città greche di età classica ed ellenistica." In Ampolo 2012: 31–56.

FAO Forestry Paper 41. 1983. *Simple Technologies for Charcoal Making.* FAO Forestry Paper 41 (reprint 1987). Rome Food and Agricultural Organization of the United Nations.

Faraguna, M. 1997. "Registrazioni catastali nel mondo greco: il caso di Atene." *Athenaeum* 85: 7–33.

———. 2000. "A proposito degli archivi nel mondo greco: terra e registrazioni fondiarie." *Chiron* 30: 65–115

———. 2003. "Vendite di immobili e registrazione pubblica nelle città greche." In *Symposion 1999* 2003: 97–122.

———. 2005a. "Scrittura e amministrazione nelle città greche: gli archivi pubblici." *Quaderni Urbinati di Cultura Classica* 79: 61–86.

———. 2005b. "Terra pubblica e vendite di immobili confiscati a Chio nel V secolo a.C." *Dike* 8: 89–99.

Faucher, T., M.-C. Marcellesi, and O. Picard, eds. 2011. *Nomisma: La circulation monétaire dans le monde grec.* Athens: École française d'Athènes, and Paris: De Boccard.

Faucherre, N., and I. Pimouguet-Pédarros, eds. 2010. *Les sièges de Rhodes de l'Antiquité à la période moderne.* Rennes: Presses Universitaires de Rennes.

Faudot, M., A. Fraysse, and É. Geny, eds. 1999. *Pont-Euxin et commerce: la genèse de la "route de la soie."* Besançon: Presses Universitaires franc-comtoises.

Feinman, G. M. 2013 "Reenvisioning Ancient Economies: Beyond Typological Constructs." *American Journal of Archaeology* 117: 453–59.

Ferguson, W. S. 1938. "The Salaminioi of Heptaphylai and Sounion." *Hesperia* 7: 1–74.

Feyel, C. 1998. "La structure d'un groupe socio-économique: les artisans dans les grands sanctuaires grecs du IV* siècle." *Topoi* 8: 561–79.

————. 2006. *Les artisans dans les sanctuaires grecs à travers la documentation financière en Grèce*. Athens: École française d'Athènes.

Feyel, M. 1936. "Nouvelles inscriptions d'Akraiphia." *Bulletin de Correspondance Hellénique* 60: 27–36.

Figueira, T. J. 1986. "*Sitopolai* and *Sitophylakes* in Lysias' '*Against the Graindealers*': Governmental Intervention in the Athenian Economy." *Phoenix* 40: 149–71.

————. 1998. *The Power of Money. Coinage and Politics in the Athenian Empire*. Philadelphia: University of Pennsylvania Press.

————. 2003. "*Xenelasia* and Social Control in Classical Sparta." *Classical Quarterly* 53: 44–74.

Filis, K. 2013. "Transport Amphorae From Akanthos." In Buzoianu 2013: 67–87.

Finkel, C., and A. Barka. 1997. "The Sakarya River–Lake Sapanca–İzmit Bay Canal Project." *Istanbuler Mitteilungen* 47: 429–42.

Finkielsztejn, G. 1998. "More Evidence on John Hyrcanus I's Conquests: Lead Weights and Amphora Stamps." *Bulletin of the Anglo-Israel Archaeological Society* 16: 33–63.

————. 2000. "Amphores importées au Levant Sud à l'époque hellénistique." In *E' epistēmonikē synantēsē gia tēn ellēnikē keramikē* 2000: Keimena 207–20; Pinakes 105–12.

————. 2001a. *Chronologie détaillée et révisée des éponymes rhodiens, de 270 à 108 av. J.-C. environ*. BAR International Series 990. Oxford: Archeopress.

————. 2001b. "Politique et commerce à Rhodes au IIe siècle a.C.: le témoignage des exportations d'amphores." In Bresson and Descat 2001: 181–96.

————. 2002a. "Du bon usage des amphores hellénistiques en contextes archéologiques." In Blondé et al. 2002: 227–33.

————. 2002b. "Les amphores hellénistiques de Crète et les questions des imitations d'amphores et des timbres amphoriques à types monétaires." In *Oinos palaios* 2002: 137–45.

————. 2006. "Production et commerce des amphores hellénistiques: récipients, timbrage et métrologie." In Descat 2006b: 17–34.

————. 2010. "The *Sekoma*: A Volume Standard for Liquids." In Kloner et al. 2010: 193–203.

————. 2012a. "Témoignages sur les agoranomes du Levant à l'époque hellénistique." In Capdetrey and Hasenohr 2012: 131–54.

————. 2012b. "Agora. Instruments inscrits, boutiques, agora et cités au Levant sud hellénistique." In Chankowski and Karvounis 2012: 303–18.

Finley, M. I. 1952. *Studies in Land and Credit in Ancient Athens, 500–200 B.C. The Horos-Inscriptions*. New Brunswick, NJ: Rutgers University Press (with new ed. 1985 completed by P. Millett, New Brunswick: Transaction Books).

————. 1970. "Aristotle and Economic Analysis." *Past and Present* 47 (= Finley 1974: 26–52).

————. 1973. *The Ancient Economy*. Berkeley: University of California Press (with 2nd ed. 1985, and new updated version 1999).

————. 1981. *Economy and Society in Ancient Greece*. Ed. with an introduction by B. D. Shaw and R. P. Saller. London: Penguin Books.

Finley, M. I., ed. 1974. *Studies in Ancient Society*. London: Routledge.

————. 1979. *The Bücher-Meyer Controversy*. New York: Arno Press.

Fischer-Bovet, C. 2014. *Army and Society in Ptolemaic Egypt*. Cambridge: Cambridge University Press.

Fisher, N., and H. van Wees, eds. 1998. *Archaic Greece: New Approaches and New Evidence.* London: Duckworth; Swansea: Classical Press of Wales; and Oakville, CT: D. Brown Book.

Flament, C. 2007a. *Le monnayage en argent d'Athènes. De l'époque archaïque à l'époque hellénistique (ca. 550–ca. 40 av. J.-C.).* Louvain-la-Neuve: Association Professeur Marcel Hoc.

———. 2007b. *Une économie monétarisée: Athènes à l'époque classique (440–338). Contribution à l'étude du phénomène monétaire en Grèce ancienne.* Louvain-la-Neuve: Peeters.

Flensted-Jensen, P. 1999. "Mende, a City-State in Northern Greece." *Classica et Mediaevalia* 50: 221–26.

Fleury, P. 1994. "Héron d'Alexandrie et Vitruve. À propos des techniques dites 'pneumatiques.'" In Argoud 1994: 67–81.

Floud, R., and P. Johnson, eds. 2004. *The Cambridge Economic History of Modern Britain.* Vol. 1: *Industrialisation, 1700–1860.* Cambridge and New York: Cambridge University Press.

Fol, A., ed. 2002. *Thrace and the Aegean.* 2 vols. Sofia: International Foundation Europa Antiqua, and Institute of Thracology, Bulgarian Academy of Sciences Press.

Follet, S., ed. 2004. *L'hellénisme d'époque romaine. Nouveaux documents et nouvelles approches (Ier s. a. C. – IIIe s. p. C.).* Paris: De Boccard.

Fontan, É., and H. Le Meaux, eds. 2007. *La Méditerranée des Phéniciens: De Tyr à Carthage.* Paris: Somogy and Institut du monde arabe.

Fontanille, M.-T. 1977. *Avortement et contraception dans la médecine gréco-romaine.* Montrouge: Laboratoires Searle.

Forbes, R. J. 1964–1972. *Studies in Ancient Technology.* 2nd ed. 9 vols. Leiden: Brill.

Fornara, C. W. 1979. "The Phaselis Decree." *Classical Quarterly* 29: 49–52.

Forni, G. 2006. "Innovazione e progresso nel mondo romano. Il caso dell'agricoltura." In Lo Cascio 2006: 145–79.

Forsdyke, S. 2012. *Slaves Tell Tales.* Princeton, NJ: Princeton University Press.

Forsén, B., ed. 2009. *Thesprotia Expedition I: Towards a Regional History.* Helsinki: Finnish Institute at Athens.

Fossey, J. M., ed. 1993. *Boeotia Antiqua III. Papers in Boiotian History, Institutions and Epigraphy in Memory of Paul Roesch.* Amsterdam: Gieben.

Fossey, J. M., and G. Gauvin. 1992. "Aspect of the Water Supply at Khostia, Boiotia, in Classical-Roman Times." In Argoud et al. 1992: 339–59.

Fossey, J. M., and H. Giroux, eds. 1985. *Actes du Troisième congrès international sur la Béotie antique.* Amsterdam: Gieben.

Foster, B. R. 1970. "Agoranomos and Muḥtasib." *Journal of the Economic and Social History of the Orient* 13: 128–44.

Fouache, É. 1999. *L'alluvionnement historique en Grèce Occidentale et au Péloponnèse: géomorphologie, archéologie, histoire.* Athens: École française d'Athènes.

Foucault, M. 1970. *The Order of Things: An Archaeology of the Human Sciences.* Tr. from the French ed. 1966. New York. Pantheon Books.

Foxhall, L. 1989. "Household, Gender and Property in Classical Athens." *Classical Quarterly* 39: 22–44.

———. 1997. "A View from the Top: Evaluating the Solonian Property Classes." In Mitchell and Rhodes 1997: 113–36.

———. 1998. "Cargoes of the Heart's Desire." In Fisher and van Wees 1998: 295–309.

———. 2006. "Environments and Landscapes in Greek Culture." In Kinzl 2006: 245–80.

———. 2007. *Olive Cultivation in Ancient Greece. Seeking the Ancient Economy*. Oxford: Oxford University Press.

Fraisse, P. 1983. "Analyse d'espace urbain: Les 'places' à Délos." *Bulletin de Correspondance Hellénique* 107: 301–13.

Francotte, H. 1903. *De la condition des étrangers dans les cités grecques*. Louvain: Peeters, and Paris: Bouillon.

Frankel, R. 2003. "The Olynthus Mill, Its Origin, and Diffusion: Typology and Distribution." *American Journal of Archaeology* 107: 1–21.

Fritzilas, S. 2012. "*Amphoreus Magalopolitōn*. Un *sékôma* en marbre de Mégalopolis." In Chankowski and Karvonis 2012: 319–32.

Froriep, S. 1986. "Ein Wasserweg in Bithynien. Bemühungen der Römer, Byzantiner und Osmanen." *Antike Welt*. 2nd Special Edition. *Antiker Wasserbau*: 39–50.

———. 1991. "Über eine mögliche Flußlaufveränderung am Sangarios in Bithynien." In Olshausen and Sonnabend 1991: 53–65.

Fuks, A. 1984. *Social Conflict in Ancient Greece*. Jerusalem: Magness Press, The Hebrew University, and Leiden: Brill.

Gabrielsen, V. 1994. *Financing the Athenian Fleet. Public Taxation and Social Relations*. Baltimore: Johns Hopkins University Press.

———. 1997. *The Naval Aristocracy of Hellenistic Rhodes*. Aarhus: Aarhus University Press.

———. 2001. "Economic Activity, Maritime Trade and Piracy in the Hellenistic Aegean." *Revue des Études Anciennes* 103: 219–40.

———. 2003. "Piracy and the Slave-Trade." In Erskine 2003: 389–404.

———. 2005. "Banking and Credit Operations in Hellenistic Times." In Archibald et al. 2005: 136–64.

———. 2007. "Warfare and the State." In Sabin et al. 2007: 248–72.

———. 2013a. "Warfare, Statehood and Piracy in the Greek World." In Jaspert and Kolditz 2013: 133–53.

———. 2013b. "Finance and Taxes." In Beck 2013: 332–48.

Gabrielsen, V., Bilde, P., T. Engberg-Pedersen, L. Hannestad, and J. Zahle, eds. 1999. *Hellenistic Rhodes: Politics, Culture and Society*. Aarhus: Aarhus University Press.

Gagarin, M. 2005. "The Unity of Greek Law." In Gagarin and Cohen 2005: 29–40.

Gagarin, M., and D. Cohen, eds. 2005. *The Cambridge Companion to Ancient Greek Law*. Cambridge and New York: Cambridge University Press.

Galaty, M. L., and W. A. Parkinson. 2007. *Rethinking Mycenaean Palaces II*. Revised and expanded 2nd ed. Los Angeles: Cotsen Institute of Archaeology, University of California.

Gallagher, R. L. 2013. "The Role of Grace in Aristotle's Theory of Exchange." *Méthexis*. 27: 143–62.

Gallant, T. W. 1985. *A Fisherman's Tale*. Gent: Belgian Archaeological Mission in Greece.

———. 1989. "Crisis and Response: Risk-Buffering Behavior in Hellenistic Greek Communities." *Journal of Interdisciplinary History* 19: 393–413.

———. 1991. *Risk and Survival in Ancient Greece*. Stanford, CA: Stanford University Press.

Gallo, L. 1980. "Popolosità e scarsità di popolazione. Contributo allo studio di un topos." *Annali della Scuola normale superiore di Pisa* 10: 1233–70.

García Vargas, E., and D. Florido del Corral. 2010. "The Origin and Development of Tuna Fishing Nets (Almadrabas)." In Bekker-Nielsen and Bernal Casasola 2010: 205–27.

Garlan, Y. 1988. *Slavery in Ancient Greece*. Tr. from the French ed. 1982. Ithaca, NY: Cornell University Press.

———. 1989. *Guerre et économie en Grèce ancienne*. Paris: Éditions La Découverte.

———. 1993. "*Eis emporion* dans le timbrage amphorique de Chersonèse." In Bresson and Rouillard 1993: 99–102.

———. 1999a. *Les timbres amphoriques de Thasos*. Vol. 1. *Timbres protothasiens et thasiens anciens*. Athens: École française d'Athènes.

———. 1999c. "Réflexions sur le commerce des amphores grecques en mer Noire." In Garlan 1999b: 131–42.

———. 2000. *Amphores et timbres amphoriques grecs. Entre érudition et idéologie*. Paris: Académie des Inscriptions et Belles-Lettres.

———. 2004a. "Ē proeleusē 'tēs omadas Parmeniskou' apo tē Mendē." *Archaiologiko Ergo stē Makedonia kai Thrakē* 18: 141–48.

———. 2004b. "Ē anagnōsē tōn sphragismatōn amphoreōn 'me trocho' apo tēs Akantho." *Archaiologiko Ergo stē Makedonia kai Thrakē* 18: 181–90.

———. 2006. "Interprétation des timbres amphoriques 'à la roue' d'Akanthos." *Bulletin de Correspondance Hellénique* 130: 263–91.

Garlan, Y., ed. 1999b. *Production et commerce des amphores anciennes en mer Noire*. Aix-en-Provence: Publications de l'Université de Provence.

Garland, R. 2001. *The Piraeus*. 2nd ed. London: Duckworth.

Garnsey, P. 1988. *Famine and Food Supply in the Graeco-Roman World: Responses to Risk and Crisis*. Cambridge and New York: Cambridge University Press.

———. 1998a. *Cities, Peasants and Food*. Cambridge: Cambridge and New York: Cambridge University Press.

———. 1998b. "Grain for Athens." In Garnsey 1998: 183–200 (reprinted from Cartledge and Harvey 1985: 62–75, augmented ed.).

———. 1998c. "The Yield of the Land in Ancient Greece." In Garnsey 1998: 201–13 (reprinted from Wells 1992: 62–75).

———. 1999. *Food and Society in Classical Antiquity*. Cambridge and New York: Cambridge University Press.

Garnsey, P., T. Gallant, and D. Rathbone. 1984. "Thessaly and the Grain Supply of Rome during the Second Century B.C." *Journal of Roman Studies* 74: 30–44.

Garnsey, P., K. Hopkins, and C. R. Whittaker, eds. 1983. *Trade in the Ancient Economy*. Berkeley: University of California Press.

Garnsey, P., and D. Rathbone. 1985. "The Background to the Grain Law of Gaius Gracchus." *Journal of Roman Studies* 75: 20–25.

Garnsey, P., and O. Van Nijf. 1998. "Contrôle des prix du grain à Rome et dans les cités de l'Empire." In *Mémoire perdue* 1998: 303–15.

Gauthier, E., and L. Henry. 1958. *La population de Crulai, paroisse normande*. Paris: Presses Universitaires de France.

Gauthier, P. 1972. *Symbola: Les étrangers et la justice dans les cités grecques*. Nancy: Université de Nancy II.

———. 1974. "'Générosité' romaine et 'avarice' grecque: Sur l'octroi du droit de cité." In *Mélanges Seston*: 207–15 (= Gauthier 2011: 3–12).

———. 1976. *Un commentaire historique des Poroi de Xénophon*. Geneva and Paris: Droz.

———. 1977. "Les ventes publiques de bois et de charbon: à propos d'une inscription de Délos." *Bulletin de Correspondance Hellénique* 101: 203–8.

———. 1980. "Les honneurs de l'officier séleucide Larichos à Priène." *Journal des Savants*: 35–50.

———. 1981a. "La citoyenneté en Grèce et à Rome: participation et intégration." *Ktèma* 6: 167–79 (= Gauthier 2011: 13–33).

———. 1981b. "De Lysias à Aristote (*Ath. pol.*, 51, 4): le commerce du grain à Athènes et les fonctions des sitophylaques." *Revue Historique de Droit Français et Étranger* 59: 5–28 (= Gauthier 2011: 193–219).

———. 1982. "Les villes athéniennes et un décret pour un commerçant (*IG*, II², 903)." *Revue des Études Grecques* 95: 275–90.

———. 1985. *Les cités grecques et leurs bienfaiteurs*. Athens: École française d'Athènes.

———. 1987. "Nouvelles récoltes et grain nouveau: À propos d'une inscription de Gazoros." *Bulletin de Correspondance Hellénique* 111: 413–18.

———. 1988. "Sur le don de grain numide à Délos: un pseudo-Rhodien dans les comptes des hiéropes." In Knœpfler 1988: 61–69.

———. 1989. *Nouvelles inscriptions de Sardes*. Vol. 2. Geneva: Droz.

———. 2011. *Études d'histoire et d'institutions grecques: choix d'écrits*. Ed. and index by D. Rousset. Geneva: Droz.

Gawlinski, L. 2012. *The Sacred Law of Andania: A New Text with Commentary*. Berlin and Boston: De Gruyter.

Geerard, M., ed. 1990. *Opes Atticae. Miscellanea philologica et historica Raymondo Bogaert et Hermanno Van Looy oblata* (= *Sacris erudiri* 31, 1989–1990). Steenbrugge: Uitgave van de Sint-Pietersabdij, and The Hague: M. Nijhoff.

Gehrke, H.-J. 1985. *Stasis: Untersuchungen zu den inneren Kriegen in den griechischen Staaten des 5. und 4. Jahrhunderts v. Chr.* Munich: Beck.

Geisau, H. von. 1919. "Kaphereus." In *Realencyclopädie* X.2: cols. 1893–94.

Gelderblom, O., ed. 2009. *The Political Economy of the Dutch Republic*. Farnham, UK, and Burlington, VT: Ashgate.

Georgoudi, S. 1974. "Quelques problèmes de la transhumance dans la Grèce ancienne." *Revue des Études Grecques* 87: 153–85.

Gerkan, A. von. 1924. *Griechische Städteanlagen*. Berlin: De Gruyter.

Germain, L.R.F. 1975. "L'exposition des enfants nouveau-nés dans la Grèce ancienne. Aspects sociologiques." *Recueils Jean Bodin* 35: 211–46.

Giardina, B. 2010. Navigare necesse est: *Lighthouses from Antiquity to the Middle Ages: History, Architecture, Iconography and Archaeological Remains*. BAR International Series 2096. Oxford: Archaeopress.

Gibbins, D. 2001. "Shipwrecks and Hellenistic Trade." In Archibald et al. 2001: 273–312.

Gibson, B., and T. Harrison. 2013. *Polybius and His World: Essays in Memory of F. W. Walbank*. Oxford: Oxford University Press.

Gill, D.W.J. 1991. "Pots and Trade: Spacefillers or Objets d'Art?" *Journal of Hellenic Studies* 111: 29–47.

———. 1994. "Positivism, Pots and Long-Distance Trade." In Morris 1994: 99–107.

Gille, B. 1980. *Les mécaniciens grecs. La naissance de la technologie*. Paris: Éditions du Seuil.

Ginouvès, R. 1962. *Balaneutikè. Recherches sur le bain dans l'Antiquité grecque*. Paris: De Boccard.

Ginouvès, R., et al. 1985–1998. *Dictionnaire méthodique de l'architecture grecque et romaine*. 3 vols. Athens: École française d'Athènes, and Rome: École française de Rome.

Gitin, S., and A. Golani. 2004. "A Silver-Based Monetary Economy in the Seventh Century BCE: A Response to Raz Klettner." *Levant* 36: 203–5.

Gitler, H., and O. Tal. 2006. *The Coinage of Philistia of the Fifth and Fourth Centuries BC: A Study of the Earliest Coins of Palestine*. Milan: Ennerre, and New York: Amphora Books: B & H Kreindler.

———. 2009. "More Evidence on the Collective Mint of Philistia." *Israel Numismatic Research* 4: 21–37.

Gjongecaj, S., and H. Nicolet-Pierre. 1991. "Le monnayage d'argent d'Égine et le trésor de Hollm (Albanie)." *Bulletin de Correspondance Hellénique* 119: 283–332.

Glass, D. V., and D.E.C. Eversley, eds. 1965. *Population in History: Essays in Historical Demography*. London: Arnold.

Glick, T. F. 2005. *Islamic and Christian Spain in the Early Middle Ages*. 2nd ed. Leiden and Boston: Brill.

Glotz, G. 1892. "*Expositio. Grèce*." In *DA* 2: 930–39.

———. 1900. "*Infanticidium. Grèce*." In *DA* 6: 488–90.

———. 1913. "Le prix des denrées à Délos." *Journal des Savants*: 16–29.

———. 1920. *Le travail dans la Grèce ancienne, histoire économique de la Grèce depuis la période homérique jusqu'à la conquête romaine*. Paris: Alcan.

Goddio, F. 2007. *Trésors engloutis d'Égypte*. Catalogue de l'exposition. Paris: Seuil, and Milan: 5 Continents.

Goette, H. R., ed. 2002. *Ancient Roads in Greece*. Hamburg: Kovac.

Gofas, D. C. 1982. "La vente sur échantillon à Athènes d'après un texte d'Hypéride." In *Symposion 1977* 1982: 121–29 (= Gofas 1993: 79–85).

———. 1993. *Meletes historias tou Hellēnikou dikaiou tōn synallagōn, archaiou, byzantinou, metabyzantinou*. Athens: Archaiologikē Hetaireia.

Golden, M. 1981. "Demography and the Exposure of Girls at Athens." *Phoenix* 35: 316–31.

———. 1990. *Children and Childhood in Classical Athens*. Baltimore: Johns Hopkins University Press.

———. 2003. "Childhood in Ancient Greece." In Neils and Oakley 2003: 13–30.

Goldhill, S., and R. Osborne, eds. 2006. *Rethinking Revolutions through Ancient Greece*. Cambridge: Cambridge University Press.

Gomme, A. W. 1933. *The Population of Athens*. Oxford: Blackwell.

———. 1945–1981. *A Historical Commentary on Thucydides*. 5 vols. Oxford: Clarendon Press.

Gori, S., and M. C. Bettini, eds. 2006. *Gli Etruschi da Genova ad Ampurias*. 2 vols. Pisa: Istituti Editoriali e Poligrafici Internazionali.

Goubert, P. 1965. "Recent Theories and Research in French Population between 1500 and 1700." In Glass and Eversley 1965: 457–73.

Gould, R. T. 1923. *The Marine Chronometer: Its History and Development*. London: J. D. Potter.

Gow, A.S.F., and D. L. Page, eds. 1968. *The Greek Anthology: The Garland of Philip*. 2 vols. London: Cambridge University Press.

Grace, V. 1963. "Notes on the Amphoras from the Koroni Peninsula." *Hesperia* 32: 319–34.

Graham, A. J. 1960. "The Authenticity of the *Horkion Tōn Oikistērōn*." *Journal of Hellenic Studies* 80: 95–111.

—. 1983. *Colony and Mother City in Ancient Greece*. 2nd ed. Manchester: Manchester University Press.

Graindor, P. 1934. *Athènes sous Hadrien*. Cairo: Imprimerie nationale.

Grammenos, D. V., and E. K. Petropoulos, eds. 2003. *Ancient Greek Colonies in the Black Sea*. 2 vols. Thessaloniki: Archaeological Institute of Northern Greece.

Grandjean, C. 1990. "Le monnayage d'argent et de bronze d'Hermioné, Argolide." *Revue Numismatique* 6.32: 28–55, pl. 8–11.

Grandjean, C., and A. Moustaka, eds. 2013. *Aux origines de la monnaie fiduciaire: traditions métallurgiques et innovations numismatiques*. Bordeaux: Ausonius.

Grandjean, Y., and F. Salviat. 2000. *Guide de Thasos*. Athens: École française d'Athènes.

Graninger, D. 2011. *Cult and Koinon in Hellenistic Thessaly*. Leiden and Boston: Brill.

Gratton, K. 2007. "Production et échange de la pourpre au Proche-Orient aux époques grecque et romaine." In Sartre 2007: 151–72.

Green, P. 1961. "The First Sicilian Slave War." *Past and Present* 20: 10–29.

Green, R.P.H. 1991. *The Works of Ausonius*. Oxford: Clarendon Press, and New York: Oxford University Press.

Greene, E. S., J. Leidwanger, and H. Özdaş. 2011. "Two Early Archaic Shipwrecks at Kekova Adası and Kepçe Burnu, Turkey." *International Journal of Nautical Archaeology* 40.1: 60–68.

Greene, K. 2000. "Technological Innovation and Economic Progress in the Ancient World: M. I. Finley Re-Considered." *Economic History Review* 53: 29–59.

—. 2008a. "Historiography and Theoretical Approaches." In Oleson 2008: 62–90.

—. 2008b. "Inventors, Invention, and Attitudes toward Innovation." In Oleson 2008: 800–818.

Greif, A. 2006. *Institutions and the Path to the Modern Economy: Lessons from Medieval Trade*. Cambridge and New York: Cambridge University Press.

Grewe, K. 2008. "Tunnels and Canals." In Oleson 2008: 319–36.

Grieb, V., and C. Koehn, eds. 2013. *Polybios und seine Historien*. Stuttgart: Steiner.

Griffin, A. 1982. *Sikyon*. Oxford: Clarendon Press, and New York: Oxford University Press.

Grimal, N., and B. Menu, eds. 1998. *Le commerce en Égypte ancienne*. Cairo: Institut français d'Archéologie Orientale.

Grmek, M. D. 1989. *Diseases in the Ancient Greek World*. Baltimore: Johns Hopkins University Press.

Grove, A. T., and O. Rackham. 2001. *The Nature of Mediterranean Europe: An Ecological History*. New Haven, CT: Yale University Press.

Grunauer von Hoerschelmann, S. 1978. *Die Münzprägung der Lakedaimonier*. Berlin: De Gruyter.

Guéraud, O. 1931. *Enteuxeis. Requêtes et plaintes adressées au roi d'Égypte au IIIᵉ siècle avant J.-C.* Cairo: Imprimerie de l'Institut français d'Archéologie Orientale.

Guéry, A. ed. 2011. *Montchrestien et Cantillon: Le commerce et l'émergence d'une pensée économique*. Lyon: ENS Éditions.

Guidoboni, E., ed. 1989. *I terremoti prima del Mille in Italia e nell'area mediterranea. Storia Archeologia Sismologia*. Bologna: Istituto Nazionale di Geofisica.

Guizzi, F. 2001. *Hierapytna. Storia di una polis cretese dalla fondazione alla conquista romana*. Atti della Accademia Nazionale dei Lincei, Classe di Scienze morali, storiche e filologiche, Memorie IX.xiii.3. Roma: Accademia Nazionale dei Lincei.

Günther, L.-M., and V. Grieb, eds. 2012. *Das imperiale Rom und der hellenistische Osten. Festschrift für Jürgen Deininger zum 75. Geburtstag.* Stuttgart: Steiner.

Habicht, C. 1957. "Eine Urkunde des Akarnanischen Bundes." *Hermes* 85: 86–122.

———. 1972. "Hellenistische Inschriften aus dem Heraion von Samos." *Mitteilungen des Deutschen Archäologischen Instituts, Athenische Abteilung* 87: 191–228.

———. 1976. "Eine hellenistische Urkunde aus Larisa." In *Demetrias*, vol. 1. Bonn: 157–73.

———. 2002. "Die Ehren der Proxenoi." *Museum Helveticum* 59: 13–30.

———. 2006. *Athènes hellénistique. Histoire de la cité d'Alexandre le Grand à Marc-Antoine.* Paris: De Boccard (new updated and augmented ed. by D. Knœpfler, tr. by M. and D. Knœpfler from the German ed., *Athen. Die Geschichte der Stadt in hellenistischer Zeit*, Munich, 1995, and the English ed., *Athens from Alexander to Antony*, Cambridge, MA, 1997).

Hadjidaki, E. 1996. "Underwater Excavations of a Late Fifth Century Merchant Ship at Alonnesos, Greece." *Bulletin de Correspondance Hellénique* 120: 561–93.

Halleux, R. 2005. "L'alun dans la littérature des recettes du Ier au XIIe siècle." In Borgard et al. 2005: 9–12.

Halstead, P. 1987. "Traditional and Ancient Rural Economy in Mediterranean Europe: plus ça change?" *Journal of Hellenic Studies* 107: 77–87 (= *Id.*, in Scheidel and von Reden 2002: 53–70).

———. 1990. "Waste Not, Want Not: Traditional Responses to Crop Failure in Greece." *Rural History* 1: 147–64.

———. 1996. "Pastoralism or Household Herding? Problems of Scale and Specialization in Early Greek Animal Husbandry." *World Archaeology* 28: 20–42.

———. 2007. "Towards a Model of Mycenaean Palatial Mobilization." In Galaty and Parkinson 2007: 66–73.

———. 2014. *Two Oxen Ahead: Pre-Mechanized Farming in the Mediterranean.* Chichester, UK: Wiley-Blackwell.

Halstead, P., and G. Jones. 1989. "Agrarian Ecology in Greek Islands: Time Stress, Scale and Risk." *Journal of Hellenic Studies* 109: 41–55.

Halstead, P., and J. O'Shea, eds. 1989a. *Bad Years Economics: Cultural Responses to Risk and Uncertainty.* Cambridge and New York: Cambridge University Press.

Halstead, P., and J. O'Shea. 1989b. "Introduction: Cultural Responses to Risk and Uncertainty." In Halstead and O'Shea 1989a: 1–7.

Hamilton, Edith, and Huntingdon Cairns, eds. 1971. *The Collected Dialogues of Plato.* Princeton, NJ: Princeton University Press.

Hannestad, L. 1983. *Ikaros: The Hellenistic Settlements: The Hellenistic Pottery from Failaka: with a Survey of Hellenistic Pottery in the Near East.* Vol. 2.1. Copenhagen: In Commission at Gyldendalske Boghandel, Nordisk Forlag.

Hansen, M. H. 1986. *Demography and Democracy: The Number of Athenian Citizens in the Fourth Century B.C.* Herning: Systime.

———. 1988. *Three Studies in Athenian Demography.* Copenhagen: Det Kongelige Danske Videnskabernes Selskab, Munksgaard.

———. 2006a. *Studies in the Population of Aigina, Athens and Eretria.* Copenhagen: Det Kongelige Danske Videnskabernes Selskab.

———. 2006b. *The Shotgun Method: the Demography of the Ancient Greek City-State Culture.* Columbia: University of Missouri Press.

Hansen, M. H., and T. H. Nielsen, eds. 2004. *An Inventory of Archaic and Classical Poleis.* Oxford and New York: Oxford University Press.

Hanson, K. C. 1997. "The Galilean Fishing Economy and the Jesus Tradition." *Biblical Theology Bulletin* 27: 99–111.

Hanson, V. D. 1995. *The Other Greeks: The Family Farm and the Agrarian Roots of Western Civilization.* New York.

———. 1998. *Warfare and Agriculture in Ancient Greece.* 2nd revised ed. Berkeley: University of California Press.

Harrauer, H., and P. Sijpestein. 1985. "Ein neues Dokument zu Roms Indienhandel, P. Vindob. G 40822." *Anzeiger der Österreichischen Akademie der Wissenschaften, phil.-hist. Kl.* 122: 124–55.

Harris, E. M. 1992. "Women and Lending in Athenian Society: A Horos Re-examined." *Phoenix* 46: 309–21 (= Harris 2006: 333–46).

———. 2002a. "Workshop, Marketplace and Household: The Nature of Technical Specialization in Classical Athens and Its Influence on Economy and Society." In Cartledge et al. 2002: 67–99.

———. 2002b. "Did Solon Abolish Debt-Bondage?" *Classical Quarterly* 52: 415–30 (= Harris 2006: 249–69).

———. 2006. *Democracy and the Rule of Law in Classical Athens: Essays on Law, Society, and Politics.* Cambridge and New York: Cambridge University Press.

Harris, E. M., and K. Tuite. 2000. "Notes on a Horos from the Athenian Agora." *Zeitschrift für Papyrologie und Epigraphik* 131: 101–105 (= Harris 2006: 347–54).

Harris, W. V. 1982. "The Theoretical Possibility of Extensive Infanticide in the Greco-Roman World." *Classical Quarterly* 32: 114–16.

———. 1994. "Child-Exposure in the Roman Empire." *Journal of Roman Studies* 84: 1–22.

———. 2005b. "The Mediterranean and Ancient History." In Harris 2005a: 1–42.

———. 2011a. "Bois et déboisement dans la Méditerranée antique." *Annales. Histoire, Sciences Sociales* 66: 105–40.

———. 2011b. "Plato and the Deforestation of Attica." *Athenaeum* 99: 479–82.

———. 2013b. "Defining and Detecting Mediterranean Deforestation 800 BCE to 700 CE." In Harris 2013a: 173–94.

Harris, W. V., ed. 2005a. *Rethinking the Mediterranean,* Oxford: Oxford University Press

———. 2013a. *The Ancient Mediterranean Environment between Science and History.* Leiden and Boston: Brill.

Harris, W. V., and K. Iara, eds. 2011. *Maritime Technology in the Ancient Economy.* Portsmouth, RI: Journal of Roman Archaeology Supplements 84.

Harrison, A.R.W. 1968–1971. *The Law of Athens.* Vol. 1. *The Family and Property* (1968). Vol. 2. *Procedure* (1971). Oxford: Oxford University Press.

Harrison, G. A., and A. J. Boyce, eds. 1972. *The Structure of Human Population.* Oxford: Clarendon Press.

Harter-Uibopuu, K. 2008. "Hadrian and the Athenian Oil Law." In Alston and van Nijf 2008: 127–41.

Hasebroek, J. 1933. *Trade and Politics in Ancient Greece.* Tr. from the German ed. (*Staat und Handel im alten Griechenland,* Tübingen, 1928). London: G. Bell and Sons.

Hasenohr, C. 2012. "Ariarathès, épimélète de l'*emporion* et les magasins du Front de mer à Delos." In Chankowski and Karvonis 2012: 247–76.

Hassan, F. A. 1981. *Demographic Archaeology*. New York: Academic Press.

Hatzidake, E. 1997. "The Classical Shipwreck at Alonnesos." In Swiny et al. 1997: 125–34.

Hatzopoulos, M. B. 1988. *Actes de vente de la Chalcidique centrale*. Meletemata 6. Athens: Centre de Recherches de l'Antiquité grecque et romaine, and Paris: De Boccard.

———. 1991. *Actes de vente de Chalcidique*. Meletemata 14. Athens: Centre de Recherches de l'Antiquité grecque et romaine, and Paris: De Boccard.

———. 1996. *Macedonian Institutions under the Kings*. 2 vols. Meletemata 22. Athens: Centre de Recherches de l'Antiquité grecque et romaine, and Paris: De Boccard.

———. 2000–2003. "Neo apotmēma apo tēn Aphyti tou Attikou psēphismatos peri nomismatos, stathmōn kai metrōn." *Horos* 14–16: 31–43.

Hayek, F. A. 1973–1979. *Law, Legislation and Liberty*. 3 vols. Chicago: University of Chicago Press.

Healy, J. F. 1978. *Mining and Metallurgy in the Greek and Roman World*. London: Thames and Hudson.

Heichelheim, F. M. 1964–1970 [1938]. *An Ancient Economic History: From the Palaeolithic Age to the Migrations of the Germanic, Slavic, and Arabic Nations*. Tr. with supplements of the German ed. (*Wirtschaftsgeschichte des Altertums*, Leiden, 1938). 3 vols. Leiden: A. W. Sijthoff.

Heilporn, P. 2000. "Registre de navires marchands." In Melaerts 2000: 339–59.

Heisserer, A. J. 1984. "IG XII, 2, 1. (The Monetary Pact between Mytilene and Phokaia)." *Zeitschrift für Papyrologie und Epigraphik* 55: 115–32.

Heller, A. 2006. *"Les bêtises des Grecs." Conflits et rivalités entre cités d'Asie et de Bithynie à l'époque romaine (129 a.C.–235 p.C.)*. Bordeaux: Ausonius.

Hellmann, M.-C. 1992. "Le vocabulaire de l'eau dans les inscriptions de Délos." In Argoud et al. 1992: 181–96.

Helly, B. 1984. "Le territoire de Larisa: ses limites, son extension, son organisation." *Ktèma* 9: 213–34.

———. 1989. "La Grecia antica e i terremoti." In Guidoboni 1989: 75–91.

———. 2008. "Encore le blé thessalien. Trois décrets de Larisa (*IG* IX 2, 506) accordant aux Athéniens licence d'exportation et réduction des droits de douane sur leurs achats de blé." *Studi ellenistici* 20: 25–108.

Henkelman, W.F.M. 2013. "Administrative Realities: The Persepolis Archives and the Archaeology of the Achaemenid Heartland." In Potts 2013: 528–46.

Hennig, D. 1994. "Immobilienerwerb durch Nichtbürger in der klassischen und hellenistischen Polis." *Chiron* 24: 305–44.

Henry, L. 1972. *Démographie. Analyse et modèles*. Paris: Larousse.

Herrmann, P. 1975. "Milesischer Purpur." *Istanbuler Mitteilungen* 25: 141–47 and pl. 31.1.

Hicks, E. L. 1887. "Iasos." *Journal of Hellenic Studies* 8: 83–118.

Higgins, M. D., and R. Higgins. 1996. *A Geological Companion to Greece and the Aegean*. Ithaca, NY: Cornell University Press.

Hin, S. 2013. *The Demography of Roman Italy*. Cambridge and New York: Cambridge University Press.

Hodgson, G. M. 2003. "John R. Commons and the Foundations of Institutional Economics." *Journal of Economic Issues* 37.3: 547–76.

Hodkinson, O., P. Rosenmeyer, and E. Bracke, eds. 2013. *Epistolary Narratives in Ancient Greek Literature*. Leiden and Boston: Brill.

Hodkinson, S. 1988. "Animal Husbandry in the Greek *Polis*." In Whittaker 1988: 35–74.

———. 2000. *Property and Wealth in Classical Sparta.* London: Duckworth, and Swansea: Classical Press of Wales.

Hodkinson, S., and D. Geary, eds. 2012. *Slaves and Religions in Graeco-Roman Antiquity and Modern Brazil.* Cambridge: Cambridge Scholars Publishing.

Hoffman, P. T. 1996. *Growth in a Traditional Society: The French Countryside, 1450–1815.* Princeton, NJ: Princeton University Press.

Hohlfelder, R. L., and R. L. Vann. 2000. "Cabotage at Aperlae in Ancient Lycia." *International Journal of Nautical Archaeology* 29: 126–35.

Højte, J. M. 2005. "The Archaeological Evidence for Fish Processing in the Black Sea Region." In Bekker-Nielsen 2005a: 133–60.

Højte, J. M., ed. 2009. *Mithridates VI and the Pontic Kingdom.* Aarhus: Aarhus University Press.

Holleaux, M. 1897. "Questions épigraphiques II." *Revue des Études Grecques* 10: 26–49 (= Holleaux 1938: 99–120).

———. 1938. *Études d'épigraphie et d'histoire grecques.* Vol. 1. Paris: Librairie d'Amérique et d'Orient, Adrien-Maisonneuve.

Holleran, C., and A. Pudsey, eds. 2011. *Demography and the Graeco-Roman World: New Insights and Approaches.* Cambridge: Cambridge University Press.

Hommages Lerat. 1984. *Hommages à Lucien Lerat.* Vol. 2. Paris: Les Belles Lettres.

Hood, M.S.F. 1961–1962. "Archaeology in Greece, 1961–62." *Archaeological Reports* 8: 3–31.

Höpfner, W., and E. L. Schwandner. 1994. *Haus und Stadt im klassischen Griechenland.* 2nd ed. Munich: Deutscher Kunstverlag.

Hopkins, K. 1966. "On the Probable Age Structure of the Roman Population." *Population Studies* 19: 245–64.

———. 1978. *Conquerors and Slaves.* Cambridge: Cambridge University Press.

———. 1995–1996. "Rome, Taxes, Rents and Trade." *Kodai, Journal of Ancient History* 6–7: 41–75 (reprinted abridged format in Lo Cascio 2000: 253–67).

Hopper, R. J. 1943. "Interstate Juridical Agreements in the Athenian Empire." *Journal of Hellenic Studies* 63: 35–51.

Horden, P., and N. Purcell. 2000. *The Corrupting Sea: A Study of Mediterranean History.* Oxford: Oxford University Press.

Howe, T. 2008. *Pastoral Politics: Animals, Agriculture and Society in Ancient Greece.* Claremont: Regina Books.

Howgego, C. 1990. "Why Did Ancient States Strike Coins?" *Numismatic Chronicle* 150: 1–25.

———. 1995. *Ancient History from Coins.* London and New York: Routledge.

Hübsch, G. 1968. *Die Personalangaben als Identifizierungsvermerke im Recht der gräko-ägyptischen Papyri.* Berlin: Duncker & Humblot.

Huguenot, C. 2012. "Production et commerce dans la cité hellénistique d'Érétrie." In Esposito and Sanidas 2012: 175–99.

Humphrey, J. W., J. P. Oleson, and A. N. Sherwood. 1998. *Greek and Roman Technology: A Sourcebook.* London and New York: Routledge.

Humphreys, S. C. 1969. "History, Economics and Anthropology: The Work of Karl Polanyi." *History and Theory* 8: 172–96 (= Humphreys 1978: 31–75).

Humphreys, S. C. 1978. *Anthropology and the Greeks*. London and Boston: Routledge & K. Paul.

Ientile, M. G. 1983. *La pirateria tirrenica*. Rome: L'Erma di Bretschneider.

Ikram, S., and A. Dodson, eds. 2009. *Beyond the Horizon: Studies in Egyptian Art, Archaeology and History in Honour of Barry J. Kemp*. Cairo: Publications of the Supreme Council of Antiquities.

Ingalls, W. 2002. "Demography and Dowries: Perspectives on Female Infanticide in Classical Greece." *Phoenix* 56: 246–54.

Inglieri, R. U. 1936. *Carta archeologica dell'isola di Rodi*. Florence: Istituto geografico militare.

Institut d'Égypte. 1800. *Memoirs Relative to Egypt, Written in that Country during the Campaigns of General Bonaparte, in the Years 1798 and 1799, by the Learned and Scientific Men who Accompanied the French Expedition*. Tr. from the French ed. London: printed by T. Gillet, for R. Phillips.

Isager, S., and J. E. Skydsgaard. 1992. *Ancient Greek Agriculture: An Introduction*. London and New York: Routledge.

Jaccottey, L., N. Alonso, S. Defressigne, C. Hamon, S. Lepareux-Couturier, V. Brisotto, S. Galland-Crety, F. Jodry, J.-P. Lagadec, H. Lepaumier, S. Longepierre, B. Robin, and N. Zaour. 2013 "Le passage des meules va-et-vient aux meules rotatives en France." In Krausz et al. 2013: 405–20.

Jacob, C. 1991. *Géographie et ethnographie en Grèce ancienne*. Paris: Colin.

Jakab, E. 1997. *Praedicere und cavere beim Marktlauf. Sachmängel im griechischen und römischen Recht*. Munich: Beck.

———. 2001. "Berenike vor Gericht. Apokeryxis, Gesellschaft und Buchführung in P. Oxy. XXII 2342." *Tyche* 16: 63–86.

Jameson, M. H., C. N. Runnels, and T. H. van Andel. 1994. *A Greek Countryside: the Southern Argolid from Prehistory to the Present Day*. Stanford, CA: Stanford University Press.

Jameson, M. J. 2000–2003. "Athens and Phaselis, IG I³ 10 (EM 6918)." *Horos* 14–16: 23–29.

Jantzen, U. 2004. *Samos XX. Die Wasserleitung des Eupalinos auf Samos: die Funde*. Bonn: In Kommission bei Habelt.

Jardé, A. 1925. *Les céréales dans l'Antiquité grecque*. Paris: De Boccard.

Jaspert, N., and S. Kolditz, eds. 2013. *Seeraub im Mittelmeerraum. Piraterie, Korsarentum und maritime Gewalt von der Antike bis zur Neuzeit*. Paderborn: Ferdinand Schöningh.

Jenkins, D., ed. 2003. *The Cambridge History of Western Textiles*. 2 vols. New York: Cambridge University Press.

Jentel, M.-O., and G. Deschênes-Wagner, ed. 1994. *Tranquillitas: Mélanges en l'honneur de Tran Tam Tinh*. Québec: Université Laval.

Joannès, F. 1994. "Métaux précieux et moyens de paiement en Babylonie achéménide et hellénistique." *Transeuphratène* 8: 137–44.

———. 1997. "Prix et salaires en Babylonie du VIIᵉ au IIIᵉ siècle avant notre ère." In Andreau et al. 1997: 313–33.

———. 2001. *Dictionnaire de la civilisation mésopotamienne*. Paris: Laffont.

Johnston, A. W. 1979. *Trademarks on Greek Vases*. Warminster: Aris & Philips.

———. 1984. "The Development of Amphora Shapes, Symposium, and Shipping." In Brijder 1984: 208–11.

———. 1991 [1996]. "Fifth Century Prices." In *Vasi attici* 1991 [1996], vol. 2: 80–87.

Johnston, A. W., and R. E. Jones. 1978. "The 'SOS' Amphora." *Annual of the British School at Athens* 73: 103–41.

Johnstone, S. 2011. *A History of Trust in Ancient Greece*. Chicago: University of Chicago Press.

Joly, R. 1978. "L'école médicale de Cnide et son évolution." *L'Antiquité Classique* 47: 528–37.

Jones, C. 1978. *The Roman World of Dio Chrysostom*. Cambridge, MA: Harvard University Press.

Jones, J. E., A. J. Graham, and L. H. Sackett. 1973. "An Attic Country House below the Cave of Pan at Vari." *Annual of the British School at Athens* 68: 355–452.

Jones, J. E., L. H. Sackett, and A. J. Graham. 1962. "The Dema House in Attica." *Annual of the British School at Athens* 57: 75–114.

Jones, N. F. 2004. *Rural Athens under Democracy*. Philadelphia: University of Pennsylvania Press.

Jongman, W. M. 2007. "The Early Roman Empire: Consumption." In Scheidel et al. 2007: 592–618.

———. 2014. "Re-Constructing the Roman Economy." In Neal and Williamson 2014, vol. 1: 75–100.

Jouanna, J. 1992. *Hippocrate*. Paris: Fayard.

Judeich, W. 1931. *Topographie von Athen*. 2nd ed. Munich: Beck.

Jursa, M. 2010. *Aspects of the Economic History of Babylonia in the First Millennium BC: Economic Geography, Economic Mentalities, Agriculture, the Use of Money and the Problem of Economic Growth*. Münster: Ugarit-Verlag.

Kakavogianni, O., and M. Anetakis. 2012. "Les agoras commerciales des dèmes antiques de la Mésogée et de la région du Laurion." In Chankowski and Karvonis 2012: 185–99.

Kallet, L. 2001. *Money and the Corrosion of Power in Thucydides: The Sicilian Expedition and Its Aftermath*. Berkeley: University of California Press.

Kallet-Marx, L. 1993. *Money, Expense, and Naval Power in Thucydides' History 1–5.24*. Berkeley: University of California Press.

Kallet-Marx, R. M. 1996. *Hegemony to Empire: The Development of the Roman Imperium in the East from 148 to 62 B.C.* Berkeley: University of California Press.

Kapitän, G. 1984. "Ancient Anchors-Technology and Classification." *International Journal of Nautical Archaeology* 13: 33–44.

Kaplan, S. L. 1984. *Provisioning Paris: Merchants and Millers in the Grain and Flour Trade*. Ithaca, NY: Cornell University Press.

———. 1996. *The Bakers of Paris and the Bread Question, 1700–1775*. Durham, NC: Duke University Press.

Kaptan, E. 1983. "The Significance of Tin in Turkish Mining History and Its Origin." *Bulletin of the Mineral Research and Exploration Institute of Turkey* 95–96: 106–14.

Karvonis, P., and J.-J. Malmary. 2009. "Étude architecturale de quatre pièces polyvalentes du Quartier du Théâtre à Délos." *Bulletin de Correspondance Hellénique* 133: 195–26.

Käsler, D. 1988. *Max Weber: An Introduction to His Life and Work*. Tr. from the German ed. 1979. Chicago. University of Chicago Press.

Katsonopoulou, D. 2002. "Helike and Her Territory in Historical Times." *Pallas* 58: 175–82.

Kayser, B., and K. Thompson. 1964. *Oikonomikos kai koinōnikos atlas tēs Hellados (Economic and Social Atlas of Greece)*. Athens: Ethnikē Statistikē Hypēresia tēs Hellados.

Kehoe, D. 2010. "The Economy, Graeco-Roman." In Lloyd 2010: 309–25.

Kent, J. H. 1948. "The Temple Estates of Delos, Rheneia and Mykonos." *Hesperia* 17: 243–338.

Keyser, P. T. 1992. "A New Look at Heron's 'Steam Engine.'" *Archive for History of Exact Sciences* 44: 107–24.

———. In press. "Economics of Science": In press.

Kienast, H. J. 1995. *Samos XIX. Die Wasserleitung des Eupalinos auf Samos.* Bonn: In Kommission bei R. Habelt.

Kim, H. 2001. "Archaic Coinage as Evidence for the Use of Money." In Meadows and Shipton 2001: 7–21.

———. 2002. "Small Change and the Moneyed Economy." In Cartledge et al. 2002: 44–51.

King, A. 2004. *The Structure of Social Theory.* London and New York: Routledge.

King, P. W. 2005. "The Production and Consumption of Iron in Early Modern England and Wales." *Economic History Review* 58: 1–33.

Kinzl, K. H., ed. 2006. *A Companion to the Classical Greek World.* Malden, MA: Blackwell.

Kiple, K. F., and K. C. Ornelas, eds. 2000. *The Cambridge World History of Food.* Part 1. Cambridge: Cambridge University Press.

Kirbihler, F. 2007. "Die Italiker in Kleinasien, mit besonderer Berücksichtigung von Ephesos (133 v. Chr.–1. Jh. n. Chr.)" In Meyer 2007: 19–35.

Klaffenbach, G. 1954. *Die Astynomeninschrift von Pergamon.* Berlin: Akademie Verlag.

Kletter, R. 2003. "Iron Age Hoards of Precious Metals in Palestine—an 'Underground' Economy?" *Levant* 5: 139–52.

———. 2004. "Coinage before Coins? A Response." *Levant* 36: 207–10.

Kloner, A., E. Eshel, G. Finkielsztejn, and H. B. Korzakova, eds. 2010. *Maresha Excavations Final Report. III, Epigraphic Finds from the 1989–2000 Seasons.* Jerusalem: Israel Antiquities Authority.

Knœpfler, D. 2001a. *Eretria. XI. Décrets érétriens de proxénie et de citoyenneté.* Lausanne: Éditions Payot.

———. 2001b. "Le contrat d'Érétrie en Eubée pour le drainage de l'étang de Ptéchai." In Briant 2001: 41–80.

Knœpfler, D., ed. 1988. *Comptes et inventaires dans la cité grecque. Actes du colloque en l'honneur de J. Tréheux.* Neuchâtel: Université de Neuchâtel, Faculté des lettres, and Geneva: Droz.

Kocka, J., ed. 2010. *Work in a Modern Society: The German Historical Experience in Comparative Perspective.* New York: Berghahn Books.

Koehler, C. 1981. "Corinthian Developments in the Study of Trade in the Fifth Century." *Hesperia* 50: 449–58.

Kolb, A. 2000. *Transport und Nachrichtentransfer im römischen Reich.* Berlin: Akademie Verlag.

Kolb, F., and A. Thomsen. 2004. "Forschungen zu Zentralorte und Chora auf dem Gebiet von Kyaneai (Zentrallykien): Methoden, Ergebnisse, Probleme." In Kolb 2004: 1–42.

Kolb, F., ed. 1993–2000. *Lykische Studien.* Vol. 1–5. Bonn. Habelt.

———. 2004. *Chora und Polis.* Munich: Oldenburg Verlag.

König, J. 2013. "Alciphron and the Sympotic Letter Tradition." In Hodkinson et al. 2013: 187–206.

Konuk, K. 2003. *Karun'dan Karia'ya—From Kroisos to Karia, Early Anatolian Coins from the Muharrem Kayhan Collection.* Istanbul: Ege Yayınları.

————. 2007. "Coin Legends in Carian." In Adiego 2007: 71–92.

Konuk, K., ed. 2012. *Stephanèphoros: de l'économie antique à l'Asie Mineure. Hommages à Raymond Descat.* Bordeaux: Ausonius.

Konuk, K., C. Lorber, and H. Gitler, eds. In press. *White Gold: Studies in Electrum Coinage.* Proceedings of the International Congress, Israel Museum, Jerusalem, 25–26 June 2012, New York.

Kozelj, T., and M. Wurch-Kozelj. 1989. "Phares de Thasos." *Bulletin de Correspondance Hellénique* 113: 161–81.

Kraay, C. M. 1976. *Archaic and Classical Greek Coins.* Berkeley: University of California Press.

Krasilnikoff, J. A. 2002. "Water and Farming in Classical Greece: Evidence, Method and Perspectives." In Ascani et al. 2002: 47–62.

Krausz, S., A. Colin, K. Gruel, I. Ralston, and T. Dechezleprêtre, eds. 2013. *L'âge du Fer en Europe. Mélanges offerts à Olivier Buchsenchutz.* Bordeaux: Ausonius.

Kremmydas, C. 2012. *Commentary on Demosthenes* Against Leptines, *with Introduction, Text, and Translation.* Oxford: Oxford University Press.

Krischer, T. 1997. "Die Genealogie der Dampfmaschine. Über den Zusammenhang von klassischer Tradition und Industrialisierung." *Klio* 79: 194–206.

Krugman, P. R., M. Obstfeld, and M. Melitz. 2010. *International Economics: Theory and Policy.* 9th ed. Boston: Pearson Addison-Wesley.

Kuchenbuch, L. 2006. "Les baguettes de taille au Moyen Âge: un moyen de calcul sans écriture." In Coquery et al. 2006: 113–42.

Kuniholm, P. I. 1990. "Archaeological Evidence and Non-Evidence for Climatic Change." In Runcorn and Pecker 1990: 645–55.

Kurke, L. 1999. *Coins, Bodies, Games and Gold: The Politics of Meaning in Archaic Greece.* Princeton, NJ: Princeton University Press.

Kypraiou, E., and D. Zapheiropoulou, eds. 1999. *Rodos 2,400 chronia: hē polē tēs Rodou apo tēn hidrysē tēs mechri tēn katalēpsē apo tous Tourkous (1523): diethnes epistēmoniko synedrio, Rodos, 24–29 Oktovriou 1993: praktika.* Athens: Hypourgeio Politismou, 22. Ephoreia Proistorikōn kai Klasikōn Archaiotētōn, 4ē Ephoreia Vyzantinōn Archaiotētōn.

Labarre, G. 1998. "Les métiers du textile en Grèce ancienne." *Topoi* 8: 791–814.

Labarre, G., and M.-T. Le Dinahet. 1996. "Les métiers du textile en Asie Mineure de l'époque hellénistique à l'époque impériale." In *Aspects* 1996: 49–115.

Labrousse, M. 1971. "Amphores rhodiennes trouvées à Toulouse et Vieille-Toulouse." *Revue Archéologique de Narbonnaise* 4: 35–46.

Laffont, P.-Y., ed. 2006. *Transhumance et estivage en Occident des origines aux enjeux actuels.* Toulouse: Presses Universitaires du Mirail.

Lafond, Y. 1998. "Die Katastrophe von 373 v. Chr. und das Verschwinden der Stadt Helike in Achaia." In Olshausen and Sonnabend 1998: 118–23.

La Genière, J. de. 1999. "Quelques réflexions sur les clients de la céramique attique." In Villanueva-Puig et al. 1999: 411–23.

La Genière, J. de, ed. 2006a. *Les clients de la céramique grecque.* Paris: Académie des Inscriptions et Belles-Lettres.

————. 2006b. "Clients, potiers et peintres." In La Genière 2006a: 9–16.

Lambert, S. D. 1997. "The Attic Genos Salaminioi and the Island of Salamis." *Zeitschrift für Papyrologie und Epigraphik* 119: 85–106.

Lambrinudakis, W., and M. Wörrle. 1983. "Ein hellenistisches Reformgesetz über das öffentliche Urkundenwesen von Paros." *Chiron* 13: 283–368.

Landels, J. G. 2000. *Engineering in the Ancient World*. Rev. ed. of 1st ed. 1978. Berkeley: University of California Press.

Landucci Gattinoni, F. 2003. *L'arte del potere. Vita e opere di Casandro di Macedonia*. Stuttgart: Steiner.

Lane, F. C. 1973. *Venice: A Maritime Republic*. Baltimore: Johns Hopkins University Press.

Lane Fox, R. J. 2011b. "The 360's." In Lane Fox 2011a: 257–69.

Lane Fox, R. J., ed. 2011a. *Brill's Companion to Ancient Macedon: Studies in the Archaeology and History of Macedon, 650 BC–300 AD*. Leiden and Boston: Brill.

Lang, P. 2013. *Medicine and Society in Ptolemaic Egypt*. Leiden and Boston: Brill.

Langdon, M. K. 1976. *A Sanctuary of Zeus on Mount Hymettos*. Hesperia Suppl. 16. Princeton: American School of Classical Studies at Athens.

———. 1991. "On the Farm in Classical Attica." *Classical Journal* 86: 209–13.

Langdon, M. K., and L. V. Watrous. 1977. "The Farm of Timesios: Rock-Cut Inscriptions in South Attica." *Hesperia* 46: 162–77.

Laronde, A. 1987. *Cyrène et la Libye hellénistique. Libykai Historiai. De l'époque républicaine au principat d'Auguste*. Paris: Éditions du Centre de la Recherche Scientifique.

Lawall, M. L. 1998. "Bolsals, Mendean Amphoras, and the Date of the Porticello Shipwreck." *International Journal of Nautical Archaeology* 27: 16–23.

———. 2000. "Graffiti, Wine Selling, and the Reuse of Amphoras in the Athenian Agora, ca. 430 to 400 B.C." *Hesperia* 69: 3–90.

———. 2002. "Ilion before Alexander: Amphoras and Economic Archaeology." *Studia Troica* 12: 197–244.

———. 2010. "Imitative Amphoras in the Greek World." *Marburger Beiträge zur antiken Handels-, Wirtschafts- und Sozialgeschichte* 28: 45–88.

———. 2011. "Socio-Economic Conditions and the Contents of Amphorae." In Tzochev et al. 2011: 23–33.

Lazare, L. 1855. "De la boucherie parisienne." *La Revue Municipale* 176 (1 August 1855): 1517–19.

Lazenby. F. D. 1947. "Greek and Roman Household Pets." *Classical Journal* 44: 245–52 and 299–307.

Lazzarini, L. 2004. "I primi oboli di Selinunte arcaica." *Schweizerische Numismatische Rundschau* 83: 17–26.

Le Goff, J. 1972. *Marchands et banquiers du Moyen Age*. 5th ed. Paris: Presses Universitaires de France.

Legon, R. P. 1981. *Megara: The Political History of a Greek City-State to 336 B.C.* Ithaca, NY: Cornell University Press.

Leguilloux, M. 2000. "L'alimentation carnée au Ier millénaire avant J.-C. en Grèce continentale et dans les Cyclades: premiers résultats archéozoologiques." *Pallas* 52: 69–95.

Lehmann, H. 1993b. "The Rise of Capitalism: Weber versus Sombart." In Lehmann 1993a: 195–208.

Lehmann, H., ed. 1993a. *Weber's Protestant Ethic. Origins, Evidence, Contexts*. Cambridge: Cambridge University Press.

Leiner, W. 1991. "Justinians Brücke über den Sangarios." In Olshausen and Sonnabend 1991: 67–82.

Leitholdt, E., C. Zielhofer, S. Berg-Hobohm, K. Schnabl, B. Kopecky-Hermanns, J. Bussmann, J. W. Härtling, K. Reicherter, and K. Unger. 2012. "Fossa Carolina: The First Attempt to Bridge the Central European Watershed—A Review, New Findings, and Geoarchaeological Challenges." *Geoarcheology* 27: 88–104.

Lentini, M C. 2012. "Fours et quartiers de potiers à Naxos de Sicile (VIIe–Ve siècles av. J.-C.)." In Esposito and Sanidas 2012: 281–300.

Le Rider, G. 1986. "Les alexandres d'argent en Asie Mineure et dans l'Orient séleucide au IIIe siècle av. J.-C. (ca. 275–ca. 225). Remarques sur le système monétaire des Séleucides et des Ptolémées." *Journal des Savants*: 3–51 (= Le Rider 1999: 1183–1237).

———. 1989. "La politique monétaire du royaume de Pergame après 188." *Journal des Savants*: 163–89 (= Le Rider 1999: 1287–1314).

———. 1997. "Cléomène de Naucratis." *Bulletin de Correspondance Hellénique* 121: 71–93 (= Le Rider 1999: 1135–57).

———. 1998a. "Antimène de Rhodes à Babylone." *Bulletin of the Asia Institute* 12: 121–40.

———. 1998b. "Histoire économique et monétaire de l'Orient hellénistique (le monnayage des Ptolémées)." *Annuaire du Collège de France 1997–1998. Résumé des cours*, 98: 783–809 (= Le Rider 1999: 1107–33).

———. 1999. *Études d'histoire monétaire et financière du monde grec. Écrits 1958–1998.* Ed. by E. Papaefthymiou, F. de Callataÿ, and F. Queyrel. Athens: Société Hellénique de Numismatique.

———. "Sur un aspect du comportement monétaire des villes libres d'Asie Mineure occidentale au IIe siècle." In Bresson and Descat 2001: 37–59 (= Le Rider 1999: 1315–41).

———. 2001b. *La naissance de la monnaie. Pratiques monétaires de l'Orient ancien.* Paris: Presses Universitaires de France.

———. 2003. *Alexandre le Grand. Monnaie, finances et politique.* Paris: Presses Universitaires de France.

Le Rider, G., and F. de Callataÿ. 2006. *Les Séleucides et les Ptolémées. L'héritage monétaire et financier d'Alexandre le Grand.* Monaco: Éditions du Rocher.

Le Rider, G., N. Waggoner, G. K. Jenkins, and U. Westermark, eds. 1989. *Kraay-Mørkholm Essays. Numismatic Studies in the Memory of C. M. Kraay and O. Mørkholm.* Louvain-la-Neuve: Institut Supérieur d'Archéologie et d'Histoire de l'Art, Séminaire de Numismatique Marcel Hoc.

Le Roy Ladurie, E. 1971. *Times of Feast, Times of Famine: A History of Climate since the Year 1000.* Tr. from the French ed. 1967. Garden City, NY: Doubleday.

———, E. 2004–2006. *Histoire humaine et comparée du climat.* Vol. 1. *Canicules et glaciers (XIIIe–XVIIIe siècle).* Vol. 2. *Disettes et révolutions, 1740–1860.* Paris: Fayard.

Lespez, L., and G. Tirologos. 2004. "Changements climatiques, transformations des paysages et sources anciennes: l'exemple du témoignage de Théophraste à propos de Philippes (Grèce)." In Cantat and Gires 2004: 59–62.

Leteux, S. 2005. *Libéralisme et corporatisme chez les bouchers parisiens (1776–1944)*, thèse Lille 3. Lille: ANRT.

Levick, B. 2004. "The Roman Economy: Trade in Asia Minor and the Niche Market." *Greece and Rome* 51: 180–98.

Lévy, E. 2003. *Sparte. Histoire politique et sociale jusqu'à la conquête romaine.* Paris: Seuil.

Lewis, D. M. 1962. "The Chronology of the Athenian New Style Coinage." *Numismatic Chronicle* 275–300 (= Lewis 1997: 294–320).

Lewis, D. M. 1990. "Persepolis Fortification Texts." In Sancisi-Weerdenburg and Kuhrt 1990: 2–6.

———. 1997. *Selected Papers in Greek and Near Eastern History*. Ed. P. J. Rhodes. Cambridge and New York: Cambridge University Press.

Lewis, D. M., J. Boardman, S. Hornblower, and M. Ostwald, eds. 1994. *The Cambridge Ancient History*. Vol. 6. *The Fourth Century BC*. 2nd ed. Cambridge and New York: Cambridge University Press.

Lewis, N. 1974. *Greek Historical Documents. The Roman Principate: 27 B.C.–285 A.D.* Toronto: Hakkert.

Lewis, S. 1996. *News and Society in the Greek Polis*. Chapel Hill: University of North Carolina Press.

L'Homme-Wéry, L.-M. 2004. "La législation de Solon: une solution à la crise agraire d'Athènes?" *Pallas* 64: 145–55.

Lhôte, É. 2006. *Les lamelles oraculaires de Dodone*. Geneva: Droz.

Lilimbaki-Akamati, M., and L. Stephani. 2003. "Hōnai ek tēs Ēmatias." *Archaiologikē ephēmeris* 142: 156–96.

Link, S. 1991. *Landverteilung und sozialer Frieden im archaischen Griechenland*. Stuttgart: Steiner.

Llewellyn-Jones, L. ed. 2002. *Women's Dress in the Ancient Greek World*. London: Duckworth Publishing.

Lloyd, A. B., ed. 2010. *A Companion to Ancient Egypt*. Vol. 1. Chichester, UK, and Malden, MA: Wiley-Blackwell.

Lo Cascio, E. 1994. "The Size of the Roman Population: Beloch and the Meaning of the Augustan Census Figures." *Journal of Roman Studies* 84: 23–40.

———, E., ed. 2000. *Mercati permanenti e mercati periodici nel mondo romano. Atti degli Incontri capresi di storia dell' economia antica, Capri 13–15 ottobre 1997*. Bari: Edipuglia.

Lo Cascio, E., and P. Malanima. 2005. "Cycles and Stability: Italian Population before the Demographic Transition (225 BC–AD 1900)." *Rivista di Storia Economica* 21.3: 5–40.

Lo Cascio, E., ed. 2006. *Innovazione tecnica e progresso economico nel mondo romano*. Bari: Edipuglia.

Lohmann, H. 1992. "Agriculture and Country Life in Classical Athens." In Wells 1992: 29–60.

———. 1993. *Atene: Forschungen zu Siedlungs- und Wirtschaftsstruktur des klassischen Attika*. 2 vols. Cologne and Weimar: Böhlau.

———. 1994. "Ein 'alter Schafstall' in neuem Licht: die Ruinen von Palaia Kopraisia bei Legrena (Attika)." In Doukellis and Mendoni 1994: 81–132.

———. 2002. "Ancient Roads in Attica and the Megaris." In Goette 2002: 73–91, pl. 20–30.

———. 2004a. "Cytherus." In *Brill's New Pauly* 4: col. 25.

———. 2004b. "Erchia." In *Brill's New Pauly* 5: col. 20.

Lolos, Y. G. 1999. "The Cargo of Pottery from the Point Iria Wreck: Character and Implications." In Phelps et al. 1999: 43–58.

Long, L., L.-F. Gantès, and M. Rival. 2006. "L'épave Grand Ribaud F. Un chargement de produits étrusques du début du Vᵉ siècle avant J.-C." In Gori 2006: 455–95.

Loomis, W. T. 1998. *Wages, Welfare Costs and Inflation in Classical Athens*. Ann Arbor: University of Michigan Press.

Loukopoulou, L. 2002. "The 'Prosodos' of the Thracian Kings." In FoI 2002, vol. 1: 345–53.

Lucas, A. 1962. *Ancient Egyptian Materials and Industries*. 4th ed. London: E. Arnold.

Lucas, G. 1997. *Les cités antiques de la haute vallée du Titarèse*. Lyon: Maison de l'Orient méditerranéen.

Lund, H. S. 1992. *Lysimachus. A Study in Early Hellenistic Kingship*. London and New York: Routledge.

Lund, J. 1999. "Rhodian Amphorae in Rhodes and Alexandria as Evidence of Trade." In Gabrielsen et al. 1999: 187–204.

Lund, J., and V. Gabrielsen. 2005. "A Fishy Business: Transport Amphorae of the Black Sea Region as a Source for the Trade in Fish and Fish Products in the Classical and Hellenistic Periods." In Bekker-Nielsen 2005a: 161–70.

Luther, A. 2004. *Könige und Ephoren: Untersuchungen zur spartanischen Verfassungsgeschichte*. Frankfurt am Main: Verlag Antike.

Lytle, E. 2007. "Fishless Mysteries or High Prices at Athens?" *Museum Helveticum* 64: 100–111.

———. 2010. "Fish Lists in the Wilderness: The Social and Economic History of a Boiotian Price Decree." *Hesperia* 79: 253–303.

———. 2012a. "*Hē thalassa koinē*: Fishermen, the Sea, and the Limits of Ancient Greek Regulatory Reach." *Classical Antiquity* 31: 1–55.

———. 2012b. "A Customs House of Our Own: Infrastructure, Duties and a Joint Association of Fishermen and Fishmongers (*IK*, 11.1a–Ephesos, 20)." In Chankowski and Karvonis 2012: 213–24.

———. 2013a. "Entirely Ignorant of the Agora" (Alkiphron 1.14.3): Fishermen and the Economy of Hellenistic Delos." In Ager and Faber 2013: 295–315.

———. 2013b. "Farmers into Sailors: Ship Maintenance, Greek Agriculture, and the Athenian Monopoly on Kean Ruddle (*IG* II² 1128)." *Greek, Roman and Byzantine Studies* 53: 520–50.

Lyttkens, C. H. 2013. *Economic Analysis of Institutional Change in Ancient Greece. Politics, Taxation and Rational Behaviour*. New York: Routledge.

Ma, J., N. Papazarkadas, and R. Parker, eds. 2009. *Interpreting the Athenian Empire*. London: Duckworth.

MacDowell, D. 1978. *The Law in Classical Athens*. Ithaca, NY: Cornell University Press.

Macro, A. D. 1976. "Imperial Provisions for Pergamum: *OGIS* 484." *Greek, Roman, and Byzantine Studies* 17: 169–79.

Magnetto, A., D. Erdas, and C. Carusi, eds. 2010. *Nuove ricerche sulla legge granaria ateniese del 374/3 a.C.* Pisa: ETS.

Maiuri, A. 1916. "Ricerche archeologiche nell'isola di Rodi (1915)." *Annuario della Scuola Archeologica di Atene* 2: 285–302.

Makarov, I. 2007. "La ville libre grecque et l'administration romaine: le cas de Chersonèse Taurique." In Bresson and Ivantchik 2007: 327–42.

Malkin, I. 2011. *A Small Greek World: Networks in the Ancient Mediterranean*. Oxford: Oxford University Press.

Malkin, I., C. Constantakopoulou, and K. Panagopoulou, eds. 2009. *Greek and Roman Networks in the Mediterranean*. London: Routledge.

Malthus, T. R. 1998 [1798]. *An Essay on the Principle of Population, as It Affects the Future Improvements of Society, with Remarks on the Speculations of Mr. Godwin, Mr. Condorcet and Other Writers*. First ed. London 1798. Amherst: Prometheus Books.

Manganaro, G. 2000. "Kyme e il dinasta Philetairos." *Chiron* 30: 403–14.

Mann, M. 1986. *The Sources of Social Power*. Vol. 1. Cambridge: Cambridge University Press.

Manning, J. G. 2003. *Land and Power in Ptolemaic Egypt: The Structure of Land Tenure*. Cambridge: Cambridge University Press.

———. 2010. *The Last Pharaohs: Egypt under the Ptolemies 303–30 B. C.* Princeton, NJ: Princeton University Press.

Manning, J. G., and I. Morris, eds. 2005. *The Ancient Economy: Evidence and Models*. Stanford, CA: Stanford University Press.

Manning, S. W. 2013. "The Roman World and Climate: Context, Relevance of Climate Change, and Some Issues." In Harris 2013a: 103–70.

Marasco, G. 1992. *Economia e storia*. Viterbo: Università degli studi della Tuscia.

Marcellesi, M.-C. 2000. "Commerce, monnaies locales et monnaies communes dans les États hellénistiques." *Revue des Études Grecques* 113: 326–58.

Marek, C. 2006. "Stadt, Bund und Reich in der Zollorganisation des kaiserzeitlichen Lykien. Eine neue Interpretation der Zollinschrift von Kaunos." In Wiemer 2006: 107–22.

Margolis, H. 1991. "Free Riding versus Cooperation." In Zeckhauser 1991: 83–105.

Markle, M. M. 1985. "Jury Pay and Assembly Pay at Athens." In Cartledge and Harvey 1985: 265–97.

Martin, R. 1951. *Recherches sur l'agora grecque*. Paris: De Boccard.

———. 1974. *L'urbanisme dans la Grèce antique*. 2nd ed. Paris: Picard.

Martzavou, P., and N. Papazarkadas, eds. 2012. *Epigraphical Approaches to the Post-Classical Polis*. Oxford: Oxford University Press.

Mastrokostas. 1964. "Inscriptions de Locride et de Thessalie." *Revue des Études Anciennes* 66: 291–319.

Mayer, E. 2012. *The Ancient Middle Classes: Urban Life and Aesthetics in the Roman Empire, 100 BCE–250 CE*. Cambridge, MA: Harvard University Press.

McCormick, K. 2006. *Veblen in Plain English: A Complete Introduction to Thorstein Veblen's Economics*. Youngstown, NY: Cambria Press.

McCorriston, J. 2000a. "Barley." In Kiple and Ornelas 2000: 81–89.

———. 2000b. "Wheat." In Kiple and Ornelas 2000: 158–74.

McDonald, W. A., and G. R. Rapp, Jr., eds. 1972. *The Minnesota Messenia Expedition: Reconstructing a Bronze Age Regional Environment*. Minneapolis: University of Minnesota Press.

McInerney, J. 1999. *The Folds of Parnassos: Land and Ethnicity in Ancient Phokis*. Austin: University of Texas Press.

———. 2010. *The Cattle of the Sun: Cows and Culture in the World of the Ancient Greeks*. Princeton, NJ: Princeton University Press.

McKenzie, L. D. 1987. "General Equilibrium." In Eatwell et al. 1987, vol. 2: 498–512.

Meadows, A. 2011. "Changing Patterns of Hoarding in 4th Century BC Western Asia Minor." In Faucher et al. 2011: 397–416.

Meadows, A., and K. Shipton, eds. 2001. *Money and Its Uses in the Ancient Greek World*. Oxford: Oxford University Press.

Mee, C. B., and H. A. Forbes, eds. 1997. *A Rough and Rocky Place: The Landscape and Settlement History of the Methana Peninsula, Greece. Results of the Methana Survey Project*

Sponsored by the British School at Athens and the University of Liverpool. Liverpool: Liverpool University Press.

Meier, M. 1998. *Aristokraten und Damoden. Untersuchungen zur inneren Entwicklung Spartas im 7. Jahrhundert v. Chr. und zur politischen Funktion der Dichtung des Tyrtaios.* Stuttgart: Steiner.

Meiggs, R. 1972. *The Athenian Empire.* Oxford: Clarendon Press.

———. 1982. *Trees and Timber in the Ancient Mediterranean World.* Oxford: Clarendon Press.

Meijer, F., and O. van Nijf, eds. 1992. *Trade, Transport, and Society in the Ancient World: a Sourcebook.* London and New York: Routledge.

Meikle, S. 1995. *Aristotle's Economic Thought.* Oxford: Clarendon Press, and Oxford and New York: Oxford Unitersity Press.

Meirano, V. 2012. "Productions et espaces artisanaux à Locres Épizéphyrienne." In Esposito and Sanidas 2012: 257–79.

Melaerts, H., ed. 2000. *Papyri in honorem Johannis Bingen octogenarii (P.Bingen).* Leuven: Peeters.

Mélanges Seston. 1974. *Mélanges d'Histoire Ancienne offerts à William Seston.* Paris: De Boccard.

Melville-Jones, J. R. 1993. Testimonia Numaria: *Greek and Latin Texts Concerning Ancient Greek Coinage.* Vol. 1. London: Spink.

Mémoire perdue. 1998. *La mémoire perdue. Recherches sur l'administration romaine.* Rome: École française de Rome.

Ménard, C., and M. M. Shirley. 2005. *Handbook of New Institutional Economics.* Dordrecht: Springer.

Mendoni, L. 1994. "The Organisation of the Countryside in Kea." In Doukellis and Mendoni 1994: 147–62.

Mendoni, L., and A. Mazarakis Ainian, eds. 1998. *Kea–Kythnos: History and Archaeology.* Athens: Centre de Recherches de l'Antiquité grecque et romaine, and Paris: De Boccard.

Mercantilisme. 2001. *Le mercantilisme en Europe—Un éclairage contemporain.* 2nd ed. Tours: Publications de l'Université François-Rabelais.

Merkelbach, R. 2000. "Der Überfall der Piraten auf Teos." *Epigraphica Anatolica* 32: 2000: 101–14.

Metzger, H., E. Laroche, A. Dupont-Sommer, and M. Mayrhofer. 1979. *Fouilles de Xanthos.* VI. *La stèle trilingue du Létôon.* Paris: Klincksieck.

Meyer, B. 1989. "Problèmes du combustible dans les bains publics de l'Égypte grecque et romaine." In Criscuolo and Geraci 1989: 565–71.

Meyer, E. 1895. "Die wirtschaftliche Entwicklung des Altertums." *Jahrbücher für Nationalökonomie und Statistik* 9: 696–750 (= Meyer 1924: 79–168).

———. 1924. *Kleine Schriften zur Geschichtstheorie und zur wirtschaftlichen und politischen Geschichte des Altertums.* 2 vols. Halle: Niemeyer.

Meyer, H.-C., and A. Moreno. 2004. "A Greek Metrological *Koine*: A Lead Weight from the Western Black Sea Region in the Ashmolean Museum, Oxford." *Oxford Journal of Archaeology* 23: 209–16.

Meyer, M., ed. 2007. *Neue Zeiten—Neue Sitten. Zu Rezeption und Integration römischen und italischen Kulturguts in Kleinasien.* Vienna: Phoibos Verlag.

Migeotte, L. 1989–1990. "Distributions de grain à Samos à la période hellénistique: le 'pain gratuit' pour tous?" In Geerard 1990: 297–308 (= Migeotte 2010: 295–304).

———. 1990. "Le pain quotidien dans les cités hellénistiques: Une 'affaire d'État'?" *Hommages à la mémoire d'Ernest Pascal* (= *Cahiers des Études Anciennes* 23–24): 291–300.

———. 1991. "Le pain quotidien dans les cités hellénistiques. À propos des fonds permanents pour l'approvisionnement en grain." *Cahiers du Centre Gustave Glotz* 2: 19–41 (= Migeotte 2010: 305–29).

———. 1992. *Les souscriptions publiques dans les cités grecques.* Geneva: Droz, and Quebec: Sphinx.

———. 1993. "Un fonds d'achat de grain à Coronée." In Fossey 1993: 11–23 (= Migeotte 2010: 331–41).

———. 1995. "Les finances publiques des cités grecques au delà du primitivisme et du modernisme." *Topoi* 5: 7–32 (= Migeotte 2010: 455–76).

———. 1997. "Le contrôle des prix dans les cités grecques." In Andreau et al. 1997: 33–52 (= Migeotte 2010: 419–38).

———. 1998. "Les ventes de grain public dans les cités grecques aux périodes classique et hellénistique." In *Mémoire perdue* 1998: 247–70 (= Migeotte 2010: 343–58).

———. 2001a. "Le traité entre Milet et Pidasa (*Delphinion* 149). Les clauses financières." In Bresson and Descat 2001: 129–35 (= Migeotte 2010: 401–8).

———. 2001b. "Les concours d'Aktion en Acarnanie: organisation financière et fiscale." *Ancient World* 32: 164–170 (= Migeotte 2010: 393–400).

———. 2003. "Taxation directe en Grèce ancienne." In *Symposion 1999* 2003: 297–314.

———. 2005. "Les pouvoirs des agoranomes dans les cités grecques." In *Symposion 2001* 2005: 287–301.

———. 2010. *Économie et finances publiques des cités grecques.* Vol. 1. Lyon: Maison de l'Orient et de la Méditerranée-Jean Pouilloux.

———. 2012. "A propos de la fondation d'Eudèmos à Milet. Questions administratives et numismatiques." *Phoenix* 66: 1–10.

———. 2014. *Les finances des cités grecques aux périodes classique et hellénistique.* Paris: Les Belles Lettres.

Mikalson, J. D. 1998. *Religion in Hellenistic Athens.* Berkeley: University of California Press.

Mildenberg, L. 1993–1994. "The Cyzicenes: A Reappraisal." *American Journal of Numismatics* 5–6: 1–14.

Mileta, C. 2002. "The King and His Land: Some Remarks on the Royal Area (*basilikē chōra*) of Hellenistic Asia Minor." In Ogden 2002: 157–76.

Millender, E. 2001. "Spartan Literacy Revisited." *Classical Antiquity* 20: 121–64.

Miller, J. A. 1999. *Mastering the Market: The State and the Grain Trade in Northern France, 1700–1860.* Cambridge: Cambridge University Press.

Millett, P. 1991. *Lending and Borrowing in Ancient Athens.* Cambridge and New York: Cambridge University Press.

Minaud, G. 2004. "Regard sur la comptabilité antique romaine: la mosaïque de l'aula des mensores à Ostie, des doigts et des comptes." *Mélanges de l'École française de Rome. Antiquité* 116: 437–68.

Mirhady, D. C. 2004. "Contracts in Athens." In Cairns and Knox 2004: 51–63.

———. 2006. "Aristotle and the Law Courts." *Polis* 23.2: 302–18.

Missiou, A. 2011. *Literacy and Democracy in Fifth-Century Athens*. Cambridge and New York: Cambridge University Press.

Mitchell, H. 1940. *The Economics of Ancient Greece* (2nd ed. 1957). Cambridge: Cambridge University Press.

Mitchell, L. G., and P. J. Rhodes, eds. 1997. *The Development of the Polis in Archaic Greece*. London and New York: Routledge.

Mitchell, S. 1993. *Anatolia: Land, Men, and Gods in Asia Minor*. 2 vols. Oxford: Clarendon Press, and New York: Oxford University Press.

———. 1999. "The Administration of Roman Asia from 133 BC to AD 250." In Eck 1999: 17–46.

———. 2005. "Olive Cultivation in the Economy of Roman Asia Minor." In Mitchell and Katsari 2005: 83–113.

———. 2009. "L'olive, Louis Robert et la répartition de la culture hellénique en Anatolie." In Bru et al. 2009: 439–46.

Mitchell, S., and C. Katsari, eds. 2005. *Patterns in the Economy of Roman Asia Minor*. Swansea: Classical Press of Wales.

Mnēmē Andronikou. 1997: *Mnēmē Manolē Andronikou*. Thessaloniki: Hetaireia Makedonikōn Spoudōn.

Mnēmē Lazaridē. 1990. *Mnēmē D. Lazaridē: polis kai chōra stēn archaia Makedonia kai Thrakē: Praktika Archaiologikou Synedriou, Kavala, 9–11 Maiou 1986*. Thessaloniki: Hypourgeio Politismou, Archaiologiko Mouseio Kavalas, and Athens: École française d'Athènes.

Moatti, C., ed. 2004. *La mobilité des personnes en Méditerranée de l'Antiquité à l'époque moderne II, La mobilité négociée*. Rome: École française de Rome.

Moatti, C., and W. Kaiser, eds. 2007. *Gens de passage en Méditerranée de l'Antiquité à l'époque moderne. Procédures de contrôle et d'identification*, Paris: Maisonneuve & Larose.

Mokyr, J. 1992. *The Lever of Riches*. New York and Oxford: Oxford University Press.

———. 2009. *The Enlightened Economy: An Economic History of Britain 1700–1850*. New Haven, CT: Yale University Press.

Molkenthin, R. 2006. *Straßen aus Wasser. Technische, wirtschaftliche und militärische Aspekte der Binnenschiffahrt im Mitteleuropa des frühen und hohen Mittelalters*. Münster: LIT Verlag.

Monaco, M. C. 2012. "Dix ans après: nouvelles données et considérations à propos du Céramique d'Athènes." In Esposito and Sanidas 2012: 155–74.

Monaghan, M. 2000. "Dyeing Establishments in Classical and Hellenistic Greece." In Cardon and Feugère 2000: 167–72.

Monson, A. 2012. *From the Ptolemies to the Romans: Political and Economic Change in Egypt*. Cambridge: Cambridge University Press.

Montchrestien, A. de. 1999 [1615]. *Traicté de l'œconomie politique*. Geneva: Droz.

Moreau, J. 1949. "Les théories démographiques dans l'Antiquité grecque." *Population* 4: 597–614.

Morel, J.-P. 1981. *Céramique campanienne: les formes*. 2 vols. Rome: École française de Rome.

———. 1986. "Céramiques à vernis noir d'Italie trouvées à Délos." *Bulletin de Correspondance Hellénique* 110: 461–93.

———. 2001. "Aux origines du moulin rotatif? Une meule circulaire de la fin du VIe siècle avant notre ère à Carthage." In Brun and Jockey 2001: 241–50.

Morel, J.-P. 2002–2003. "Les céramiques dans l'Afrique antique: quelques problèmes de 'marché.'" *Antiquités Africaines* 38–39: 331–43.

Moreno, A. 2007. *Feeding the Democracy: The Athenian Grain Supply in the Fifth and Fourth Century BC.* Oxford: Oxford University Press.

Moreno García, J. C. 2014. "Penser l'économie pharaonique." *Annales. Histoire, Sciences sociales* 69: 7–38.

Moretti, J.-C., M. Fincker, and V. Chankowski. 2012. "Les cercles de Sôkratès: un édifice commercial sur l'agora de Théophrastos à Délos." In Chankowski and Karvonis 2012: 225–46.

Moretti, L. 1980. "Chio e la lupa Capitolina." *Rivista di Filologia e di Istruzione Classica* 108: 33–54.

Morgan, C. 2009. "The Early Iron Age." In Raaflaub and van Wees 2009: 43–63.

Moritz, L. A. 1958. *Grain-Mills and Flour in Classical Antiquity.* Oxford: Clarendon Press.

Mørkholm, O. 1984. "The Chronology of the New Style Coinage of Athens." *American Numismatic Society Museum Notes* 29: 29–42.

———. 1991. *Early Hellenistic Coinage from the Accession of Alexander to the Peace of Apamea (336–188 B.C.).* Ed. by P. Grierson and U. Westermark. Cambridge and New York: Cambridge University Press.

Morley, N. 2007. *Trade in Classical Antiquity.* Cambridge and New York: Cambridge University Press.

Morris, I. 1986. "The Use and Abuse of Homer." *Classical Antiquity* 5: 81–138.

———. 1987. *Burial and Ancient Society: The Rise of the Greek City-State.* Cambridge and New York: Cambridge University Press.

———. 2004. "Economic Growth in Ancient Greece." *Journal of Institutional and Theoretical Economics* 160: 709–42.

———. 2005. "Archaeology, Standards of Living, and Greek Economic History." In Manning and Morris 2005: 91–126.

———. 2006. "The Collapse and Regeneration of Complex Society in Greece, 1500–500 BC." In Schwartz and Nichols 2006: 72–85.

———. 2009a. "The Eighth-Century Revolution." In Raaflaub and van Wees 2009: 64–80.

———. 2009b. "The Greater Athenian State." In Morris and Scheidel 2009: 99–177.

Morris, I., ed. 1994. *Classical Greece: Ancient Histories and Modern Archaeologies.* Cambridge and New York: Cambridge University Press.

Morris, I., and W. Scheidel, eds. 2009. *The Dynamics of Ancient Empires: State Power from Assyria to Byzantium.* Oxford and New York: Oxford University Press.

Morris, S. P., and J. K. Papadopoulos. 2005. "Greek Towers and Slaves: An Archaeology of Exploitation." *American Journal of Archaeology* 109: 155–225.

Morrison, D. 2013. "The Common Good." In Deslauriers and Destrée 2013: 176–98.

Mulhern, J. J. 1975. "Population and Plato's Republic." *Arethusa* 8: 265–81.

Muller, A. 1981. "Megarika III–VII." *Bulletin de Correspondance Hellénique* 105: 203–18.

Müller, C. 2007. "Quelques réflexions à propos de la chôra d'Hermonassa dans le Bosphore Cimmérien." In Bresson and Ivantchik 2007: 69–78.

———. 2010. *D'Olbia à Tanaïs. Territoires et réseaux d'échanges dans la mer Noire septentrionale aux époques classique et hellénistique.* Bordeaux: Ausonius.

———. 2013. "The Rise and Fall of the Boeotians: Polybius 20.4–7 as a Literary Topos." In Gibson and Harrison 2013: 267–78.

Müller, C., and C. Hasenohr. 2002. *Les Italiens dans le monde grec (IIe s. av. J.-C.–Ier s. ap. J.-C.* Paris: École française d'Athènes.

Müller, D. 1987–1997. *Topographischer Bildkommentar zu den Historien Herodots.* 2 vols. Tübingen: Wasmuth.

Müller, H. 2005. "Hemiolios. Eumenes II., Toriaion und die Finanzorganisation des Alexanderreiches." *Chiron* 35: 355–84.

Mulliez, D. 1982. "Notes sur le transport du bois." *Bulletin de Correspondance Hellénique* 107: 107–18.

———. 1992. "Les actes d'affranchissement delphiques." *Cahiers du Centre Gustave Glotz* 3: 31–44.

Murray, O., and S. Price. 1990. *The Greek City from Homer to Alexander.* Oxford: Clarendon Press.

Murray, O., and M. Tecusan, eds. 1995. *In Vino Veritas.* London: British School at Rome in association with American Academy at Rome.

Nafissi, M. 2005. *Ancient Athens and Modern Ideology: Value, Theory and Evidence in Historical Sciences. Max Weber, Karl Polanyi and Moses Finley.* London: Institute of Classical Studies, School of Advanced Study, University of London.

Nakassis, D. 2010. "Reevaluating Staple and Wealth Finance at Mycenaean Pylos." In Pullen 2010: 127–48.

———. 2013. *Individuals and Society in Mycenaean Pylos.* Leiden: Brill.

Napoli, J. ed. 2008. *Ressources et activités maritimes des Peuples de l'Antiquité, Actes du Colloque international de Boulogne-sur-Mer, 12, 13 et 14 mai 2005.* Boulogne-sur-Mer: Maison de la Recherche de l'Université du Littoral (= *Les cahiers du littoral* 6).

Neal, L., and J. G. Williamson, eds. 2014. *The Cambridge History of Capitalism.* 2 vols. Cambridge: Cambridge University Press.

Needham, J., et al. 1965. *Science and Civilisation in China, Volume 4: Physics and Physical Technology, Part 2, Mechanical Engineering.* Cambridge: Cambridge University Press.

Nef, J. 1932. *The Rise of the British Coal Industry.* 2 vols. London: Routledge.

Neils, J., and J. H. Oakley, eds. 2003. *Coming of Age in Ancient Greece: Images of Childhood from the Classical Past.* New Haven, CT: Yale University Press, and Hanover, NH: Hood Museum of Art, Dartmouth College.

Neppi Modona, A. 1981. *L'Etruria mineraria: atti del XII Convegno di studi etruschi e italici.* Florence: Olschki.

Nevett, L. C. 1999. *House and Society in the Ancient Greek World.* Cambridge and New York: Cambridge University Press.

———. 2005. "Between Urban and Rural: House-Form and Social Relations in Attic Villages and Deme Centers." In Ault and Nevett 2005: 83–98.

Nicolet, C. 1991. "Le *monumentum Ephesenum* et les dîmes d'Asie." *Bulletin de Correspondance Hellénique* 115: 465–80.

———. 1993. "Le *monumentum Ephesenum* et la délimitation du *portorium* d'Asie." *Mélanges de l'École française de Rome. Antiquité* 105: 929–59.

———. 1999. "Le *monumentum Ephesenum*, la loi Terentia-Cassia et les dîmes d'Asie." *Mélanges de l'École française de Rome. Antiquité* 111: 191–215.

Nicolet-Pierre, H. 2002. *Numismatique grecque.* Paris: Colin.

Nielsen, K. M. 2013, "Economy and Private Property." In Deslauriers and Destrée 2013: 67–91.

Nilsson, M. P. 1955. *Die hellenistische Schule*. Munich. Beck.

Niskanen, M. 2009. "A Shift in Animal Species Used for Food from the Early Iron Age to the Roman Period." In Forsén 2009: 145–54.

Nizzo, V. 2007. *Ritorno ad Ischia: dalla stratigrafia della necropoli di Pithekoussai alla tipologia dei materiali*. Naples: Centre Jean Bérard.

North, D. C. 1981. *Structure and Change in Economic History*. New York: Norton.

———. 1990. *Institutions, Institutional Change, and Economic Performance*. Cambridge and New York: Cambridge University Press.

———. 1991. "Institutions." *Journal of Economic Perspectives* 5: 97–112.

———. 2005. *Understanding the Process of Economic Change*. Princeton, NJ: Princeton University Press.

North, D. C., and R. P. Thomas. 1973. *The Rise of the Western World: A New Economic History*. Cambridge: Cambridge University Press.

Oakley, J. H. 2003 "Death and the Child." In Neils and Oakley 2003: 163–94.

Oakley, J. H., W.U.E. Coulson, and O. Palagia, eds. 1997. *Athenian Potters and Painters: The Conference Proceedings*. Oxford: Oxbow Books.

Ober, J. 2008. *Democracy and Knowledge: Innovation and Learning in Classical Athens*. Princeton, NJ: Princeton University Press.

———. 2010. "Wealthy Hellas." *Transactions of the American Philological Association* 140: 241–86.

———. 2014. "Greek Economic Performance, 800–300 BCE: A Comparison Case." In de Callataÿ 2014: 103–22.

O'Connell, D. P. 1982–1984. *The International Law of the Sea*. 2 vols. Oxford: Clarendon Press.

Oetjen, R. 2010. "Antigonid Cleruchs in Thessaly and Greece: Philip V and Larisa." In Reger et al. 2010: 237–54.

Ogden, D., ed. 2002. *The Hellenistic World: New Perspectives*. London: Classical Press of Wales and Duckworth.

Oinos palaios. 2002. *Oinos palaios hēdypotos To Krētiko krasi apo ta prohistorika hos ta neōtera chronia*. Athens: Hypourgeio Politismou. Tameio Archaiologikōn Porōn kai Apallotriōseōn.

Oleson. J. P., ed. 2008. *The Oxford Handbook of Engineering and Technology in the Classical World*. Oxford: Oxford University Press.

Oliver, G. J. 2007. *War, Food and Politics in Early Hellenistic Athens*. Oxford: Oxford University Press.

———. 2012. "The *Agoranomoi* at Athens." In Capdetrey and Hasenohr 2012a: 81–100.

Olshausen, E., and H. Sonnabend, eds. 1991. *Stuttgarter Kolloquium zur historischen Geographie des Altertums 2, 1984 und 3,1987*. Geographica historica 5. Stuttgart: Habelt.

———. 1998. *Naturkatastrophen in der antiken Welt, Stuttgarter Kolloquium zur historischen Geographie des Altertums 6,1996*. Geographica historica 10. Stuttgart: Steiner.

———. 2002. *Zu Wasser und zu Land. Verkehrswege in der antiken Welt, Stuttgarter Kolloquium zur historischen Geographie des Altertums 7, 1999*. Geographica historica 17. Stuttgart: Steiner.

Olson, D. S. 1991. "Firewood and Charcoal in Classical Athens." *Hesperia* 60: 411–20.

Oman, C. 1906. *The Great Revolt of 1381*. Oxford: Clarendon Press.

O'Neill, K., W. Yielding, J. Near, J. E. Coleman, P. S. Wren, and K. M. Quinn. 1999. "Halai the 1992–1994 Field Seasons." *Hesperia* 68: 285–341.

Oppenheim, A. L. 1967. "Essay on Overland Trade in the First Millennium B.C." *Journal of Cuneiform Studies* 21: 236–54.

Orrieux, C. 1983. *Les papyrus de Zénon*. Paris: Macula.

———. 1985. *Zénon de Caunos, parépidèmos et le destin grec*. Paris and Besançon: Les Belles Lettres.

Ortolani, F., and S. Pagliuca. 2003. "Cyclical Climatic-Environmental Changes in the Mediterranean Area (2500 BP–Present Day)." *Pages News* 11.1: 15–17.

Osborne, R. 1983. "Buildings and Residence on the Land in Classical and Hellenistic Greece." *Annual of the British School at Athens* 80: 119–28.

———. 1987. *Classical Landscape with Figures*. Dobbs Ferry, NY: Sheridan House.

———. 1988. "Social and Economic Implications of the Leasing of Land and Property in Classical and Hellenistic Greece." *Chiron* 18: 279–323.

———. 1991. "Pride and Prejudice, Sense and Subsistence: Exchange and Society in the Greek city." In Rich and Wallace-Hadrill 1991: 119–45 (= Osborne 2010: 104–26).

———. 1996. "Pots, Trade and the Archaic Greek Economy." *Antiquity* 70: 31–44.

———. 2010. *Athens and Athenian Democracy*. Cambridge and New York: Cambridge University Press.

Osborne, R. 1981–1983. *Naturalization in Athens*. 4 vols. Brussels: AWLSK.

Owens, E. J. 1983. "The Koprologoi at Athens in the Fifth and Fourth Centuries B.C." *Classical Quarterly* n.s. 33: 44–50.

Palagia, O., and A. Choremi-Spetsieri, eds. 2007. *The Panathenaic Games*. Oxford: Oxbow.

Panagopoulou, K. 2007. "Between Necessity and Extravagance: Silver as a Commodity in the Hellenistic Period." *Annual of the British School at Athens* 102: 315–43.

Panzram, S., W. Riess, and C. Schäfer, eds. 2015. *Menschen und Orte der Antike. Festschrift für Helmut Halfmann zum 65. Geburtstag*. Rahden: Verlag Marie Leidorf.

Papadopoulos, J. K., and S. A. Paspalas. 1999. "Mendaian as Chalkidian Wine." *Hesperia*, 68: 161–88.

Papazarkadas, N. 2009. "Epigraphy and the Athenian Empire: Reshuffling the Chronological Cards." In Ma et al. 2009: 67–88.

———. 2011. *Sacred and Public Land in Ancient Athens*. Oxford: Oxford University Press.

Papazoglou, F. 1997. *Laoi et paroikoi. Recherches sur la structure de la société hellénistique*. Beograd: Université de Belgrade.

Parker, A. J. 1992. *Ancient Shipwrecks of the Mediterranean and the Roman Provinces*. BAR International Series 580. Oxford: Tempus Reparatum.

Parker, R. 2005. *Polytheism and Society at Athens*. Oxford: Oxford University Press.

Parkins, H., and C. Smith, eds. 1998. *Trade, Traders, and the Ancient City*. London and New York: Routledge.

Patinkin, D. 1987. "Walras's Law" In Eatwell et al., vol. 4: 863–68.

Patterson, C. 1985. "'Not Worth the Rearing': The Causes of Infant Exposure in Ancient Greece." *Transactions of the American Philological Association* 115: 103–23.

Pazdera, M. 2006. *Getreide für Griechenland: Untersuchungen zu den Ursachen der Versorgungskrisen im Zeitalter Alexanders des Grossen und der Diadochen*. Berlin: Lit Verlag.

Pearson, H. W. 1957 "The Economy Has No Surplus." In Polanyi et al. 1957: 320–41.

Pébarthe, C. 2000. "Fiscalité, empire d'Athènes et écriture: retour sur les causes de la guerre du Péloponnèse." *Zeitschrift für Papyrologie und Epigraphik* 129: 47–96.

———. 2006. *Cité, démocratie et écriture: histoire de l'alphabétisation d'Athènes à l'époque classique*. Paris: De Boccard.

———. 2008. *Monnaie et marché à Athènes à l'époque classique*. Paris: Belin.

———. In press. "L'huile, le charbon et le parfum à Délos. Localisation des activités artisanales et économie des cités." In press.

Peristiany, J., and M. E. Handman, ed. 1989. *Le prix de l'alliance en Méditerranée*. Paris: Editions du Centre National de la Recherche Scientifique.

Perlman, P. 1992. "One Hundred-Citied Crete and the Cretan ΠΟΛΙΤΕΙΑ." *Classical Philology* 87: 193–205.

Perna, M. 2004. *Recherches sur la fiscalité mycénienne*. Nancy: A.D.R.A., and Paris: De Boccard.

Pernin, I. 2004. "Les baux de Thespies (Béotie). Essai d'analyse économique." *Pallas* 64: 221–32.

———. 2012. "La culture de la vigne en Attique à l'époque classique d'après les inscriptions." In Konuk 2012: 139–44.

———. 2014. *Les baux ruraux en Grèce ancienne. Corpus épigraphique et étude*. Lyon: Maison de l'Orient et de la Méditerranée-Jean Pouilloux.

Perreault, J.-Y. 1990. "L'atelier de potier archaïque de Phari (Thasos). La production de tuiles." *Hesperia* 59: 201–9.

Perrin, É. 1994. "Héracleidès le Crétois à Athènes: les plaisirs du tourisme." *Revue des Études Grecques* 104: 192–202.

Persson, K. G. 1999. *Grain Markets in Europe 1500–1900*. Cambridge and New York: Cambridge University Press.

———. 2010. *An Economic History of Europe: Knowledge, Institutions and Growth, 600 to the Present*. New York: Cambridge University Press.

———. 2014. "Market Performance and Welfare: Why Price Instability Hurts." In van der Spek et al. 2014: 68–80.

Peschlow-Bindokat, A. 1996. *Der Latmos: eine unbekannte Gebirgslandschaft an der türkischen Westküste*. Mayence: von Zabern.

Pettegrew, D. K. 2011. "The Diolkos of Corinth." *American Journal of Archaeology* 115: 549–74.

Peukert, H. 2001. "The Schmoller Renaissance." *History of Political Economy* 33: 71–116.

Pfohl, G., ed. 1977. *Inschriften der Griechen. Epigraphische Quellen zur Geschichte der antiken Medizin*. Darmstadt: Wissenschaftliche Buchgesellschaft.

Phelps, W., Y. Lolos, and Y. Vichos, eds. 1999. *The Point Iria Wreck: Interconnections in the Mediterranean ca. 1200 B.C.* Athens: Hellenic Institute of Marine Archaeology.

Philimonos-Tsopotou, M. 2004. *Hē hellinistikē ochyrosē tēs Rhodou*. Athens: Hypourgeio Politismou. Tameio Archaiologikōn Porōn kai Apallotriōseōn.

Picard, O. 1980. "Aristote et la monnaie." *Ktèma* 5: 267–76.

———. 1984. "Sur deux termes des inscriptions de la trésorerie d'Aï Khanoum." In *Hommages Lerat* 1984, vol. 2: 679–90.

———. 1994. "Les Thasiens du Continent et la fondation de Philippes." In Jentel and Deschênes-Wagner 1994: 468–71.

———. 2000. "Le contre-exemple du monnayage stéphanéphore d'Athènes." *Revue Numismatique* 155: 79–85.

———. 2001. "La découverte des gisements du Laurion et les débuts de la chouette." *Revue Belge de Numismatique* 147: 1–10.

———. 2007. "Monnaie et circulation monétaire à l'époque classique." *Pallas* 74: 113–28.

———. 2010a. "Rome et la Grèce à la basse période hellénistique: monnaies et impérialisme." *Journal des Savants* 2010: 161–92.

———. 2010b. "Iconographie et mémoire monétaires: l'exemple de Thasos." *Obolos* 9: 45–57.

———. 2011. "La circulation monétaire dans le monde grec: le cas de Thasos." In Faucher et al. 2011: 79–109.

Picard, O., and S. Gjongecaj. 2000. "Les drachmes d'Apollonia à la vache allaitant." *Revue numismatique* 155: 137–60.

———. 2001. "Apollonia et le monnayage épirote: le trésor de Bakërr." *Revue numismatique* 157: 223–49.

Pichot, V. 2012. "La Maréotide: région fertile de la chôra d'Alexandrie, carrefour du commerce à l'époque gréco-romaine." In Esposito and Sanidas 2012: 81–104.

Picon, M. 2005. "Des aluns naturels aux aluns artificiels et aux aluns de synthèse: matières premières, gisements et procédés." In Borgard et al. 2005: 13–38.

Picon, M., and Y. Garlan. 1986. "Recherches sur l'implantation des ateliers amphoriques à Thasos et analyse de la pâte des amphores thasiennes." In Empereur and Garlan 1986: 287–309.

Pierrobon Benoit, R. 2013. "Archestrato e Iasos: note a margine." In Baldoni et al. 2013: 193–200.

Pirenne-Delforge, V. 1991. "Le culte de la persuasion. Peithô en Grèce ancienne." *Revue de l'Histoire des Religions* 208: 395–413.

———. 1994. *L'Aphrodite grecque*. Liège: Centre International d'Étude de la Religion Grecque Antique.

Plassart, A. 1916. "Fouilles de Délos, exécutées aux frais de M. le duc de Loubat (1912–1913). Quartier d'habitations privées à l'est du stade (pl. V–VII)." *Bulletin de Correspondance Hellénique* 40: 145–256.

Podlecki, A. J. 1971. "Cimon, Skyros and 'Theseus' Bones.'" *Journal of Hellenic Studies* 91: 141–43.

Polanyi, K. 1944. *The Great Transformation*. New York: Farrar & Rinehart.

———. 1957. "Aristotle Discovers the Economy." In Polanyi and Arensberg 1957: 64–94 (= Polanyi 1968: 78–115).

———. 1968. *Primitive, Archaic and Modern Economies. Essays of Karl Polanyi Edited by George Dalton*. Garden City, NY: Anchor Books.

———. 1977. *The Livelihood of Man*. Essays edited by H. W. Pearson. New York, San Francisco, and London: Academic Press.

Polanyi, K., C. M. Arensberg, and H. W. Pearson, eds. 1957. *Trade and Market in the Early Empires: Economies in History and Theory*. Glencoe, IL: Free Press, and Falcon's Wing Press.

Pollard, J. 1977. *Birds in Greek Life and Myth*. London: Thames and Hudson.

Pollard, N. 2000. *Soldiers, Cities, and Civilians in Roman Syria*. Ann Arbor: University of Michigan Press.

———. 2010. "Military Institutions and Warfare: Graeco-Roman." In Lloyd 2010: 446–65.

Polzer, M. E. 2011. "Early Shipbuilding in the Eastern Mediterranean." In Catsambis et al. 2011: 349–78.

Pomeranz, K. 2000. *The Great Divergence: Europe, China and the Making of the Modern World Economy*. Princeton, NJ: Princeton University Press.

Pomeroy, S. B. 1975. *Goddesses, Whores, Wives, and Slaves*. New York: Schocken Books.

———. 1983. "Infanticide in Hellenistic Greece." In Cameron and Kuhrt 1983: 207–22.

———. 1997. *Families in Classical and Hellenistic Greece: Representations and Realities*. Oxford: Clarendon Press.

Pomey, P. 1981. "L'épave de Bon-Porté et les bateaux cousus de Méditerranée." *The Mariner's Mirror* 67.3: 225–43.

———. 1995. "Les épaves grecques et romaines de la Place Jules Verne à Marseille." *Comptes Rendus des Séances de l'Académie des Inscriptions et Belles-Lettres*: 459–84.

———. 2011. "Les conséquences de l'évolution des techniques de construction navale sur l'économie maritime antique." In Harris and Iara 2011: 39–55.

Pomey, P., and A. Tchernia. 1978. "Le tonnage maximum des navires de commerce romains." *Archaeonautica* 2: 233–51.

———. 2006. "Les inventions entre l'anonymat et l'exploit: le pressoir à vis et la *Syracusia*." In Lo Cascio 2006: 81–99.

Popper, K. 1976. *Unended Quest: An Intellectual Autobiography*. London: Routledge.

Porten, B., and A. Yardeni. 1993. *Textbook of Aramaic Documents from Ancient Egypt III: Literature, Accounts, Lists*. Jerusalem: Hebrew University, Department of the History of the Jewish People.

Pottier, F. 1892. "Excursion en Comminges." *Revue de Comminges* 7: 167–76.

Potts, D. T. 2013. *The Oxford Handbook of Ancient Iran*. Oxford: Oxford University Press.

Pouilloux, J. 1954. *Recherches sur l'histoire et les cultes de Thasos*. Vol. 1. Paris: De Boccard.

Pounder, R. L., and N. Dimitrova. 2003. "Dedication by the Thessalian League to the Great Gods in Samothrace." *Hesperia* 72: 31–39.

Powell, A., and S. Hodkinson, eds. 2002. *Sparta beyond the Mirage*. London: Classical Press of Wales and Duckworth.

Préaux, C. 1939. *L'économie royale des Lagides*. Brussels: Éditions de la Fondation égyptologique reine Élisabeth.

———. 1978. *Le monde hellénistique, la Grèce et l'Orient*. 2 vols. Paris: Presses Universitaires de France (6th ed. with suppl. bibliography 2002).

Price, M. J. 1989. "The Larissa 1968 Hoard (*IGCH* 237)." In Le Rider et al. 1989: 233–43.

———. 1991. *The Coinage in the Name of Alexander the Great and Philip Arrhideus*. 2 vols. Zurich and London: The Swiss Numismatic Society in association with British Museum Press.

Price, M. J., and N. Waggoner. 1975. *Archaic Greek Coinage: The 'Asyut' Hoard*. London: V. C. Vecchi.

Price, S. 2011. "Estimating Ancient Greek Populations. The Evidence of Field Survey." In Bowman and Wilson 2011: 17–35.

Priddat, B. P. 1989. "Schmoller on Ethics and Economics." *International Journal of Social Economics* 16, 9–10–11: 47–68.

———. 2004. "Gustav Schmoller: L'économie comme moralité institutionnalisée." In Bruhns 2004: 53–74.

Pringsheim, F. 1950. *The Greek Law of Sale*. Weimar: H. Böhlaus Nachfolger.

Prioreschi, P. A. 1998. *A History of Medicine*. Lewiston, NY: Edwin Mellen Press.

Pritchett, W. K. 1953. "The Attic Stelai, Part I." *Hesperia* 22: 225–99.

Pritchett, W. K., and A. Pippin. 1956. "The Attic Stelai, Part II." *Hesperia* 25: 178–328.

Prost, F., ed. 1999. *Armées et sociétés de la Grèce classique. Aspects sociaux et politiques de la guerre aux Ve et IVe s. av. J.-C.* Paris: Errance.

———. 2003. *L'Orient méditerranéen de la mort d'Alexandre aux campagnes de Pompée. Cités et royaumes à l'époque hellénistique.* Actes du colloque international de la SOPHAU Rennes, avril 2003 (= *Pallas* 62): Rennes: Presses Universitaires de Rennes, and Toulouse: Presses Universitaires du Mirail.

Psoma, S. 2006. "À propos de drachmes d'argent du décret amphictyonique *CID* IV 127." *Zeitschrift für Papyrologie und Epigraphik* 160: 79–88.

Pulak, C. 1998. "The *Uluburun* Shipwreck: An Overview." *International Journal of Nautical Archaeology* 27: 188–224.

Pulak, C., R. F. Townsend, C. G. Koehler, and B. Wallace. 1987. "The Hellenistic Shipwreck at Serçe Limanı, Turkey: Preliminary Report." *American Journal of Archaeology* 91: 31–57.

Pullen, D. J. 2013. "Crafts, Specialists, and Markets in Mycenaean Greece: Exchanging the Mycenaean Economy." *American Journal of Archaeology* 117: 437–45.

Pullen, D. J., ed. 2010. *Political Economies of the Aegean Bronze Age.* Oxford and Oakville, CT: Oxford Books.

Purcell, N. 2005. "The Ancient Mediterranean: The View from the Customs House." In Harris 2005a: 200–232.

Purpura, G. 2008. "'Liberum Mare,' Acque territoriali e riserve di pesca nel mondo antico." In Napoli 2008: 533–54.

Raaflaub, K. A., and H. van Wees, eds. 2009. *A Companion to Archaic Greece.* Chichester, UK, and Malden, MA: Wiley-Blackwell.

Rackham, O. 1990. "Ancient Landscapes." In Murray and Price 1990: 85–111.

Raepsaet, G. 1988. "Charrettes en terre cuite de l'époque archaïque à Corinthe." *L'Antiquité Classique* 57: 56–88.

———. 1993. "Le diolkos de l'Isthme à Corinthe: son tracé, son fonctionnement." *Bulletin de Correspondance Hellénique* 117: 233–61.

———. 2002. *Attelages et techniques de transport dans le monde gréco-romain.* Brussels: Livre Timperman.

———. 2008. "Land Transport, Part 2: Riding, Harnesses, and Vehicles." In Oleson 2008: 580–605.

Rankov, B. 2006. "Les *frumentarii* et la circulation de l'information entre les empereurs romains et les provinces." In Capdetrey and Nelis-Clément 2006: 129–40.

Rathbone, D. 1991. *Economic Rationalism and Rural Society in Third-Century A.D. Egypt.* Cambridge and New York: Cambridge University Press.

Rauh, N. K. "Rhodes, Rome, and the Eastern Mediterranean Wine Trade, 166–88 BC." In Gabrielsen et al. 1999: 187–204.

Ravis-Giordanni, G., ed. 1987. *Femmes et patrimoine dans les sociétés rurales de l'Europe méditerranéenne.* Paris: Éditions du Centre National de la Recherche Scientifique.

Recensement. 1914. *Recensement agricole de 1911. Superficie, rendement agricole et valeur du rendement.* Athens: Ministère de l'économie nationale.

———. 1923. *Recensement agricole de 1921. Superficie, rendement agricole et valeur du rendement.* Athens: Ministère de l'économie nationale.

Reden, S. von. 1995. *Exchange in Ancient Greece,* London.

Reden, S. von. 1997. "Money, Law and Exchange: Coinage in the Greek *Polis*." *Journal of Hellenic Studies* 117: 154–76.

———. 2002. "Money in the Ancient Economy: A Survey of Recent Research." *Klio* 84: 141–74.

———. 2010. *Money in Classical Antiquity*. New York: Cambridge University Press.

Reden, S. von, and D. Rathbone. 2014. "Mediterranean Grain Prices in Classical Antiquity." In van der Spek et al. 2014: 148–234.

Reger, G. 1993. "The Purchase of Grain on Independent Delos." *Classical Antiquity* 12: 300–334.

———. 1994. *Regionalism and Change in the Economy of Independent Delos*. Berkeley: University of California Press.

———. 1997. "The Price Histories of Some Imported Goods on Independent Delos." In Andreau et al. 1997: 53–72 (= *Id.*, in Scheidel and von Reden 2002: 133–54).

———. 1999. "The Relations between Rhodes and Caria from 246 to 167 BC." In Gabrielsen 1999: 76–97.

———. 2003. "Aspects of the Role of Merchants in the Political Life of the Hellenistic World." In Zaccagnini 2003: 165–97.

———. 2003. "The Economy." In Erskine 2003: 331–53.

———. 2004. "Sympoliteiai in Hellenistic Asia Minor." In Colvin 2004: 144–80.

———. 2005. "The Manufacture and Distribution of Perfume." In Archibald 2005: 252–97.

———. 2010. "Formation of Taste and Fashion Perfumes and Imitations in the Hellenistic and Early Imperial World." *Marburger Beiträge zur antiken Handels-, Wirtschafts- und Sozialgeschichte* 28: 21–44.

Reger, G., F. X. Ryan, and T. F. Winters, eds. 2010. *Studies in Greek Epigraphy and History in Honor of Stephen V. Tracy*. Bordeaux: Ausonius.

Renfrew, C., and M. Wagstaff, eds. 1982. *An Island Polity: The Archaeology of Exploitation in Melos*. Cambridge and New York: Cambridge University Press.

Réparaz, A. de, ed. 1987. *L'eau et les hommes en Méditerranée*. Paris: Éditions du Centre National de la Recherche Scientifique.

Rhodes, P. J. 2006. "The Reform and Laws of Solon: An Optimistic View." In Blok and Lardinois 2006: 248–60.

Ricardo, D. 1948 [1817]. *On the Principles of Political Economy and Taxation*. London: Dent and New York: Putton.

Rich, J., and A. Wallace-Hadrill, eds. 1991. *City and Country in the Ancient World*. London and New York: Routledge.

Riggs, C. ed. 2012. *The Oxford Handbook of Roman Egypt*. Oxford: Oxford University Press.

Ritti, T., K. Grewe, and P. Kessener. 2007. "A Relief of a Water-Powered Stone Saw Mill on a Sarcophagus at Hierapolis and Its Implications." *Journal of Roman Archaeology* 20: 138–63.

Rivet, L., and M. Sciallano, eds. 2002. *Vivre, produire et échanger: reflets méditerranéens. Mélanges offerts à Bernard Liou*. Montagnac: Mergoil.

Rizakis, A. D. 1995. *Achaïe I. Sources textuelles et histoire régionale*. Meletemata 20. Athens: Centre de Recherches de l'Antiquité grecque et romaine, and Paris: De Boccard.

Robert, L. 1936. *Collection Froehner*. Vol. 1. *Inscriptions grecques*. Paris: Éditions des Bibliothèques Nationales.

———. 1949. *Hellenica*. VII. Paris: Librairie d'Amérique et d'Orient Adrien-Maisonneuve.

————. 1961. "Les Kordakia de Nicée, le combustible de Synnada et les poissons-scies. Sur des lettres d'un métropolite de Phrygie au Xe siècle. Philologie et réalités" (part 1). *Journal des Savants*: 97–166 (= *OMS* VII: 1–70).

————. 1962. *Villes d'Asie Mineure*. 2nd ed. Paris: De Boccard.

————. 1969. "Apollonios de Rhodes et le fer de Bithynie." In Association Guillaume Budé 1970: 67–86 (= *OMS* IV: 383–403 = *Choix d'écrits*, 157–71).

————. 1973: "Les monétaires et un décret hellénistique de Sestos." *Revue Numismatique* 6.15: 43–53 (= *OMS* VI: 125–35).

————. 1977. "La titulature de Nicée et de Nicomédie: la gloire et la haine." *Harvard Studies in Classical Philology* 81: 1–39 (= *OMS* VI: 211–49 = Robert 2007: 673–703).

————. 1980. *À travers l'Asie Mineure*. Paris: De Boccard.

————. 1984. "Documents d'Asie Mineure. XXXIII. À Caunos avec Quintus de Smyrne." *Bulletin de Correspondance Hellénique* 108: 499–532 (= Robert 1987: 487–520).

————. 1987. *Documents d'Asie Mineure*. Paris: De Boccard.

————. 2007. *Choix d'écrits*. Ed. by D. Rousset in collaboration with P. Gauthier and I. Savalli-Lestrade. Paris: Les Belles Lettres.

Robert, L., and J. Robert. 1976. "Une inscription grecque de Téos en Ionie: l'union de Téos et de Kyrbissos." *Journal des Savants*: 154–235 (= *OMS* VII: 297–379).

Robertson, N. 1993. "Athens' Festival of the New Wine." *Harvard Studies in Classical Philology* 95: 197–250.

Robineau, C. 1994. "Anthropologie économique et marché." *Cahiers des Sciences Humaines* 30.1–2: 23–33.

Robinson, B. A. 2001. *Histories of Peirene: A Corinthian Fountain in Three Millennia*. Princeton, NJ: American School of Classical Studies at Athens.

Robinson, D. M. 1924. "A New Latin Economic Edict from Pisidian Antioch." *Transactions of the American Philological Association* 55: 5–20.

Robinson, D. M., and A. I. Wilson, eds. 2011. *Maritime Archaeology and Ancient Trade in the Mediterranean*. Oxford: Oxford Centre for Maritime Archaeology, Institute of Archaeology.

Robinson, E. H. 1974. "The Early Diffusion of Steam Power." *Journal of Economic History* 34: 91–107.

Rochefort, R. 1961. *Le travail en Sicile: Étude de géographie sociale*. Paris: Presses Universitaires de France.

Roesch, P. 1985. "La justice en Béotie à l'époque hellénistique." In Fossey and Giroux 1985: 127–34.

Roos, P. 1996. "Strabo and the Water-Mill at Cabeira." *Opuscula Romana* 20: 99–103.

Rosivach, V. J. 1989. "*Talasiourgoi* and *paidia* in IG 2^2 1553–1578: A Note on Athenian Social History." *Historia* 38: 365–70.

Rostovtzeff [Rostowzew], M. 1910. *Studien zur Geschichte des römischen Kolonates*. Erstes Beiheft zum Archiv für Papyrusforschung und Verwandte Gebiete. Leipzig: Teubner.

————. 1941. *A Social and Economic History of the Hellenistic World*. 3 vols. Oxford: Clarendon Press.

Rotroff, S. I. 1984. "Ceramic Workshops in Hellenistic Athens." In Brijder 1984: 173–77.

————. 1997. *Hellenistic Pottery: Athenian and Imported Wheelmade Table Ware and Related Material*. 2 vols. Princeton, NJ: American School of Classical Studies at Athens.

————. 2002. "West Slope in the East." In Blondé et al. 2002: 97–115.

—. 2006. "The Introduction of the Moldmade Bowl Revisited: Tracking a Hellenistic Innovation." *Hesperia* 75: 357–78.

Roubineau, J.-M. 2012. "La main cruelle de l'agoranome." In Capdetrey and Hasenohr 2012a: 47–59.

Rouillard, P., and M.-C. Villanueva-Puig, eds. 1987. *Grecs et Ibères au IVᵉ siècle avant Jésus-Christ. Commerce et iconographie* (= *Revue des Études Anciennes* 89, 1987).

Roussel, P. 1916. *Délos colonie athénienne*. Paris: De Boccard (new ed. with biblio. suppl., Paris 1987).

Rousset, D. 2002. *Le territoire de Delphes et la terre d'Apollon*. Athens: École française d'Athènes, and Paris: De Boccard.

—. 2004. "La cité et son territoire dans la province d'Achaïe et la notion de 'Grèce romaine.'" *Annales Histoire, Sciences sociales* 59.2: 363–83.

Rowe, C. J., and M. Schofield, eds. 2000. *The Cambridge History of Greek and Roman Political Thought*. Cambridge: Cambridge University Press.

Runcorn, S. J., and J.-C. Pecker, eds. 1990. *The Earth's Climate and Variability of the Sun over Recent Millennia*. London: Royal Society.

Ruschenbusch, E. 1966. *Solōnos Nomoi. Die Fragmente des Solonischen Gesetzeswerkes, mit einer Text- und Überlieferungsgeschichte*. Wiesbaden: Steiner.

—. 1981a. "Epheben, Buleuten und die Bürgerzahl von Athen um 330 v. Chr." *Zeitschrift für Papyrologie und Epigraphik* 41: 103–5.

—. 1981b. "Noch einmal die Bürgerzahl Athens um 330 v. Chr." *Zeitschrift für Papyrologie und Epigraphik* 44: 110–12.

—. 1988. "Getreideerträge in Griechenland in der Zeit von 1921 bis 1938 n. Chr. als Maßstab für die Antike." *Zeitschrift für Papyrologie und Epigraphik* 72: 141–53.

—. 1999. "La démographie d'Athènes au IVᵉ siècle." In Bellancourt-Valdher and Corvisier 1999: 91–95.

—. 2010. *Solon: Das Gesetzeswerk-Fragmente. Übersetzung und Kommentar*. Wiesbaden: Steiner.

Russo, L. 2004. *The Forgotten Revolution: How Science Was Born in 300 BC and Why It Had to Be Reborn*. Tr. from the Italian ed. 1996. Berlin and New York: Springer.

Rutherford, I. 2009. "Network Theory and Theoric Networks." In Malkin et al. 2009: 24–38.

Rutishauser, B. 2001. "Island Strategies: The Case of Tenedos." *Revue des Études Anciennes* 103: 197–204.

—. 2012. *Athens and the Cyclades: Economic Strategies 540–314 BC*. Oxford: Oxford University Press.

Rutter, N. K. 1997. *The Greek Coinages of Southern Italy and Sicily*. London: Spink.

Sabbatini, B., ed. 2000. *La céramique attique du IVᵉ siècle en Méditerranée occidentale*. Naples: Centre Jean Bérard.

Sabin, P., H. van Wees, and M. Whitby, eds. 2007. *The Cambridge History of Greek and Roman Warfare*. Vol. 1. *Greece, The Hellenistic World and the Rise of Rome*. Cambridge and New York: Cambridge University Press.

Sadler, G. 2012. "*Aneu Orexeos Nous*: Virtue Affectivity and Aristotelian Rule of Law." *Studia Neoaristotelica* 9: 105–32.

Şahin, S. 1994. "Piratenüberfall auf Teos. Volksbeschluß über die Finanzierung der Erpressungsgelder." *Epigraphica Anatolica* 23: 1–40.

Sahlins, M. D. 1976. *Culture and Practical Reason.* Chicago: University of Chicago Press.

Sales, V., ed. 2003. *Les historiens.* Paris: Colin.

Sallares, R. 1991. *The Ecology of the Ancient Greek World.* Ithaca, NY: Cornell University Press.

———. 2002. *Malaria and Rome: A History of Malaria in Ancient Italy.* Oxford: Oxford University Press.

Saller, R. 2005. "Framing the Debate over Growth in the Ancient Economy." In Manning and Morris 2005: 223–38.

Salmon, J. B. 1984. *Wealthy Corinth: A History of the City to 338 B.C.* Oxford: Clarendon Press, and New York: Oxford University Press.

———. 1999. "The Economic Role of the Greek City." *Greece & Rome* 46: 147–67.

———. 2000. "Pots and Profits." In Tsetskhladze et al. 2000: 245–52.

Salomon, N. 1997. *Le cleruchie di Atene. Caratteri e funzione.* Pisa: ETS.

Salviat, F. 1986. "Le vin de Thasos: Amphores, vin et sources écrites." In Empereur and Garlan 1986: 145–95.

———. 1990. "Vignes et vins anciens de Maronée à Mendè." In *Mnēmē Lazaridē* 1990: 457–76.

———. 1993. "Le vin de Rhodes et les plantations du dème d'Amos." In Amouretti and Brun 1993: 201–11.

Salviat, F., and C. Vatin. 1971. *Inscriptions de Grèce centrale.* Paris: De Boccard.

Samama, É. 2003. *Les médecins dans le monde grec. Sources épigraphiques sur la naissance d'un corps médical.* Geneva: Droz.

———. 2006. "Thaumatopoloi pharmakopôlai. La singulière image des préparateurs et vendeurs de remèdes dans les textes grecs." In Collard and Samama 2006: 7–27.

Samons, L. J. 2000. *Empire of the Owl.* Stuttgart: Steiner.

Samuel, D. 2009. "Experimental Grinding and Ancient Egyptian Flour Production." In Ikram and Dodson: 456–77.

Samuelson, P. A., and W. D. Nordhaus. 2005. *Economics.* 18th ed. Boston: McGraw-Hill.

Sancisi-Weerdenburg, H., and A. Kuhrt, eds. 1990. *Achaemenid History IV: Centre and Periphery, Proceedings of the Groningen 1986 Achaemenid History Workshop.* Leiden: Nederlands Instituut voor het Nabije Oosten.

Sanidas, G. M. 2013. *La production artisanale en Grèce.* Paris: Comité des travaux historiques et scientifiques.

Saprykin, S. J. 2001. "Polis *Chora* in the Kingdom of Bosporus." In Stazio and Ceccoli 2001: 635–65.

———. 2006. "The Chora in the Bosporan Kingdom." In Bilde and Stolba 2006: 273–88.

Sarris, A., E. Athanassopoulou, A. Doulgeri-Intzessiloglou, E. Skafida, and J. Weymouth. 2002. "Geophysical Prospection Survey of an Ancient Amphorae Workshop at Tsoukalia, Alonnisos (Greece)." *Archaeological Prospection* 9: 183–95.

Sartre, M., ed. 2007. *Productions et échanges dans la Syrie grecque et romaine.* Lyon: Maison de l'Orient méditerranéen.

Sauvage, C. 2012. *Routes maritimes et systèmes d'échanges internationaux au Bronze récent en Méditerranée orientale.* Lyon: Maison de l'Orient et de la Méditerranée-Jean Pouilloux.

Savary des Bruslons, J. 1748. *Dictionnaire universel du commerce.* New ed. 3 vols. Paris: Veuve Estienne.

Scafuro, A. C. 2013. "Keeping Record, Making Public: The Epigraphy of Government." In Beck 2013: 400–416.

Schaps, D. M. 1979. *Economic Rights of Women in Ancient Greece*. Edinburgh: Edinburgh University Press.

Scheidel, W. 2001. *Death on the Nile: Disease and the Demography of Roman Egypt*. Leiden: Brill.

———. 2003. "The Greek Demographic Expansion." *Journal of Hellenic Studies* 123: 120–40.

———. 2004. "Demographic and Economic Development in the Ancient Mediterranean World." *Journal of Institutional and Theoretical Economics* 160: 743–57.

———. 2007. "Demography." In Scheidel et al. 2007: 38–86.

———. 2010. "Ancient Sex Ratios and Femicide in Comparative Perspective." In *Sex, Death and Bones: Paleodemography and Gender Differentials in the Mediterranean World, Conference at the American School of Classical Studies at Athens, Athens (Greece), March 16, 2010*. Princeton, NJ, and Stanford, CA: Working Papers in Classics.

———. 2011. "A Comparative Perspective on the Determinants of the Scale and Productivity of Maritime Trade in the Roman Mediterranean." In Harris and Iara 2011: 21–37.

———. 2012. "Age and Health." In Riggs 2012: 305–16.

Scheidel, W., I. Morris, and R. Saller, eds. 2007. *The Cambridge Econonomic History of the Greco-Roman World*. Cambridge and New York: Cambridge University Press.

Scheidel, W., and S. von Reden, eds. 2002. *The Ancient Economy*. New York: Routledge.

Scheuble-Reiter, S. 2012. *Die Katökenreiter im ptolemäischen Ägypten*. Munich: Beck.

Schiavone, A. 2000. *The End of the Past: Ancient Rome and the Modern West*. Tr. from the Italian ed. 1996. Cambridge, MA: Harvard University Press.

Schlosser, P. 2008. "Pêche et ressources maritimes de la région des Détroits aux époques grecque et romaine." In Napoli 2008: 375–84.

Schmaltz, B., and M. Söldner, eds. 2003. *Griechische Keramik im kulturellen Kontext*. Münster: Scriptorium.

Schmalz, G.C.R. 2009. *Augustan and Julio-Claudian Athens: A New Epigraphy and Prosopography*. Leiden and Boston: Brill.

Schmitz, W. 2004. *Nachbarschaft und Dorfgemeinschaft im archaischen und klassischen Griechenland*. Berlin: Akademie Verlag.

Schmoller, G. 1881. "Die Gerechtigkeit in der Volkswirtschaft." *Jahrbuch für Gesetzgebung, Verwaltung und Volkswirtschaft im Deutschen Reich* 5: 19–54.

———. 1920. *Grundriß der allgemeinen Volkswirtschaftslehre*. 2 vols. Leipzig: Duncker & Humblot.

Schneider, H. 1990. "Die Bücher–Meyer Kontroverse." In Calder and Demandt 1990: 417–45.

———. 1992. *Einführung in die antike Technikgeschichte*. Darmstadt: Wissenschaftliche Buchgesellschaft.

Schneider, J., and P. Schneider. 1976. *Culture and Political Economy in Western Sicily*. New York: Academic Press.

Schofield, M. 1999. *Saving the City: Philosopher-Kings and Other Classical Paradigms*. London and New York: Routledge.

Scholl, R. 1990. *Corpus der Ptolemäischen Sklaventexte*. 3 vols. Stuttgart. Steiner.

Scholten, J. B. 2000. *The Politics of Plunder: Aitolians and Their Koinon in the Early Hellenistic Era, 279–217 B.C.* Berkeley: University of California Press.

Schuler, C. 1998. *Ländliche Siedlungen und Gemeinden im hellenistischen und römischen Kleinasien.* Munich: C. H. Beck.

Schwahn, W. 1934. "*Telē.*" *Realencyclopädie* II 5.1: cols. 226–310.

Schwartz, G. M., and J. J. Nichols. 2006. *After Collapse: The Regeneration of Complex Societies.* Tucson: University of Arizona Press.

Shaw, B. D. 2001. "Review of Horden and Purcell 2000." *Journal of Roman Archaeology* 14: 419–53.

———. 2013. *Bringing in the Sheaves: Economy and Metaphor in the Roman World.* Toronto: University of Toronto Press.

Shelmerdine, C. W. 2013. "Economic Interplay among Households and States." *American Journal of Archaeology* 117: 447–52.

Shelmerdine, C. W., ed. 2008. *The Cambridge Companion to the Aegean Bronze Age.* Cambridge: Cambridge University Press.

Shelmerdine, C. W., J. Bennet, and L. Preston. 2008. "Mycenaean States: Economy and Administration." In Shelmerdine 2008: 289–309.

Sheppard, R. R. 1984. "Dio Chrysostom: The Bithynian Years." *L'Antiquité classique* 53: 157–73.

Sherwin-White, A. N. 1966. *The Letters of Pliny: A Historical and Social Commentary.* Oxford: Clarendon Press.

Shionoya, Y. 2005. *The Soul of the German Historical School: Methodological Essays on Schmoller, Weber, and Schumpeter.* New York: Springer.

Shipley, G. 1987. *A History of Samos, 800–188 BC.* Oxford: Clarendon Press, and New York: Oxford University Press.

———. 2002. "Hidden Landscapes: Greek Field Survey Data and Hellenistic History." In Ogden 2002: 177–98.

Shipley, G., and J. Salmon, eds. 1996. *Human Landscapes in Classical Antiquity: Environment and Culture.* London and New York: Routledge.

Shipton, K. 2000. *Leasing and Lending: The Cash Economy in Fourth-Century BC Athens.* London: Institute of Classical Studies, School of Advanced Study, University of London.

Sickinger, J. P. 1999. *Public Records and Archives in Classical Athens.* Chapel Hill: University of North Carolina Press.

Siebert, G. 1978. *Recherches sur les ateliers de bols à reliefs du Péloponnèse à l'époque hellénistique.* Athens: École française d'Athènes, and Paris: De Boccard.

Sim, D., and I. Ridge. 2002. *Iron for the Eagles: The Iron Industry of Roman Britain.* Stroud: Tempus.

Skydsgaard, J. E. 1988. "Transhumance in Ancient Greece." In Whittaker 1988: 75–86.

Smith, A. 1976 [1776]. *An Inquiry into the Nature and Causes of the Wealth of Nations.* Chicago: University of Chicago Press.

Smith, P. J. 2006. "Megara and Her Colonies: What Could the Metropolis Have Exported to Her Colonies?" *Ancient World* 37 (= P. J. Smith, ed. *Cults, Coins, History and Inscriptions V: Studies in Honor of John M. Fossey III*): 54–59.

———. 2008. *The Archaeology and Epigraphy of Hellenistic and Roman Megaris, Greece.* BAR International Series 1762. Oxford: John & Erica Hedges.

Snodgrass, A. M. 1980. *Archaic Greece: The Age of Experiment*. London: J. M. Dent.

———. 1987. *An Archaeology of Greece: The Present State and Future Scope of a Discipline*. Berkeley: University of California Press.

———. 2000. *The Dark Age of Greece: An Archaeological Survey of the Eleventh to the Eighth Centuries BC*. Edinburgh: Edinburgh University Press.

Sokolowski, F. 1964. "Aphrodite as Guardian of Greek Magistrates." *Harvard Theological Review* 57: 1–8.

Sombart, W. 1902. *Der moderne Kapitalismus*. 2 vols. Leipzig: Duncker & Humblot.

———. 1911: *Die Juden und das Wirtschaftsleben*. Leipzig: Duncker & Humblot.

———. 1913. *Studien zur Entwicklungsgeschichte des modernen Kapitalismus*. 2 vols. Munich and Leipzig: Duncker & Humblot.

Soren, D., and J. R. Leonard. 1989. "Archeologia sismica a Kourion: un approccio multidisciplinare in azione per un terremoto del IV secolo d.C." In Guidoboni 1989: 438–48.

Sosin, J. D. 2004. "Alexanders and Stephanephoroi at Delphi." *Classical Philology* 99: 192–208.

Sourisseau, J.-C. 2011. "La diffusion des vins grecs d'Occident du VIIIᵉ au IVᵉ s. av. J.-C., sources écrites et documents archéologiques." In Convegno 2011: 145–252.

———. 2012. "Documents archéologiques et réseaux d'échanges en Méditerranée centrale (VIIIᵉ–VIIIᵉ s. a.C.)." In Capdetrey and Zurbach 2012: 179–97.

Stahl, M., and U. Walter. 2009 "Solon." In Raaflaub and van Wees 2009: 130–61.

Stamatopoulou, M. 2011. "Thessaly (Archaic to Roman)." *Archaeological Reports* 57: 73–84.

Stanley, P. V. 1976. *Ancient Greek Market Regulations and Controls*. Dissertation, Berkeley.

Starr, C. G. 1970. *Athenian Coinage 480–449 B.C.* Oxford: Clarendon Press.

Stazio, A., and S. Ceccoli, eds. 2001. *Problemi della chora coloniale dall'Occidente al mar Nero. Atti del quarantesimo convegno di studi sulla Magna Grecia, Taranto 29 sept.–3 oct. 2000.* Taranto: Istituto per la storia e l'archeologia della Magna Grecia.

Ste. Croix, G.E.M. de. 1961. "Notes on Jurisdiction in the Athenian Empire." *Classical Quarterly* 55: 94–112.

———. 1966. "The Estate of Phainippos (Ps.-Dem., xlii)." In Badian 1966: 109–14.

Steffy, J. R. 1985. "The Kyrenia Ship: An Interim Report on Its Hull Construction." *American Journal of Archaeology* 89: 71–101.

Stein-Hölkeskamp, E. 2009. "The Tyrants." In Raaflaub and van Wees 2009: 100–116.

Steinhauer, G. 1994. "Inscription agoranomique du Pirée." *Bulletin de Correspondance Hellénique* 118: 51–68.

———. 2001a. "The Classical Mesogaia." In Aikaterinidis 2001: 81–139.

———. 2001b. "The Hellenistic Mesogaia." In Aikaterinidis 2001: 141–42.

Stevens, G. P. 1950. "A Tile Standard in the Agora of Ancient Athens." *Hesperia* 19: 174–88.

Stewart. R. 2012. *Plautus and Roman Slavery*. Malden, MA: Wiley-Blackwell.

Stiglitz, J. E. 1987. "The Causes and Consequences of the Dependence of Quality on Price." *Journal of Economic Literature* 25: 1–48.

Stiros, S. C., and P. Dakoronia. 1989. "Ruolo storico e identificazione di antichi terremoti nei siti della Grecia." In Guidoboni 1989: 422–37.

Stissi, V. 2012: "Giving the *Kerameikos* a Context: Ancient Greek Potters' Quarters as Part of the *Polis* Space, Economy and Society." In Esposito and Sanidas 2012: 201–30.

Stolba, V. F. 2005. "Fish and Money: Numismatic Evidence for Black Sea Fishing." In Bekker-Nielsen 2005: 115–32.

Stöllner, T., G. Körlin, G. Steffens, and J. Cierny, eds. 2003. *Man and Mining—Mensch und Bergbau: Studies in Honour of Gerd Weisgerber on Occasion of His 65th Birthday*. Bochum: Deutsches Bergbau-Museum.

Stroud, R. S. 1974. "An Athenian Law on Silver Coinage." *Hesperia* 43: 145–88.

———. 1998. *The Athenian Grain-Tax Law of 374/3 B.C.* Princeton, NJ: American School of Classical Studies at Athens.

Summerer, L. 2007. "From Tatarlı to Munich: The Recovery of a Painted Wooden Tomb Chamber in Phrygia." In Delemen 2007: 131–58.

Summerer, L., A. Ivantchik, and A. von Kienlin, eds. In press. *Kelainai—Apameia Kibotos II*. Bordeaux: Ausonius.

Summerer, L., and A. von Kienlin, eds. 2010. *Tatarlı: Renklerin dönüşü. The Return of Colour*. Istanbul: T. C. Kültür ve Turizm Bakanlığı and Yapı Kredi Yayınları.

Swedberg, R. 1998. *Max Weber and the Idea of Economic Sociology*. Princeton, NJ: Princeton University Press.

———. 2004. "La sociologie économique de Max Weber: une introduction." In Bruhns 2004: 211–28.

———. 2005. *The Max Weber Dictionary: Key Words and Central Concepts*. Stanford, CA: Stanford Social Sciences.

Swiny, H. W., and M. L. Katzev. 1973. "The *Kyrenia* Shipwreck: A Fourth-Century B.C. Greek Merchant Ship." In Blackman 1973: 339–59.

Swiny, S., R. L. Hohlfelder, and H. W. Swiny, eds. 1997. *Res Maritimae: Cyprus and the Eastern Mediterranean from Prehistory to Late Antiquity*. Atlanta: Scholars Press.

Symposion 1977. 1982. *Symposion 1977. Vorträge zur griechischen und hellenistischen Rechtsgeschichte (Chantilly, 1.–4. Juni 1977)*. Ed. J. Modrzejewski and D. Liebs. Cologne and Vienna: Böhlau Verlag.

Symposion 1999. 2003. *Symposion 1999. Vorträge zur griechischen und hellenistischen Rechtsgeschichte (Pazo de Mariñán, La Coruña, 6.–9. September 1999)*. Ed. G. Thür and F.J.F. Nieto. Cologne, Weimar, and Vienna: Böhlau Verlag.

Symposion 2001. 2005. *Symposion 2001. Vorträge zur griechischen und hellenistischen Rechtsgeschichte (Evanston, Illinois, 5.–8. September 2001)*. Ed. R. W. Wallace and M. Gagarin. Vienna: Verlag der Österreichischen Akademie der Wissenschaften.

Symposion 2003. 2006. *Symposion 2003. Vorträge zur griechischen und hellenistischen Rechtsgeschichte (Rauischholzhausen, 30. September–3. Oktober 2003)*. Ed. H.-A. Rupprecht. Vienna: Verlag der Österreichischen Akademie der Wissenschaften.

Szanto, E. 1904. "Deigma." *Realencyclopädie*. IV.2: cols. 2383–84.

Tainter, J. A. 1988. *The Collapse of Complex Societies*. Cambridge: Cambridge University Press.

Takaoğlu, T. 2008. "Archaeological Evidence for Grain Mills in the Greek and Roman Troad." In Winter 2008: 673–79.

Takmer, B. 2007. "Lex Portorii Provinciae Lyciae. Ein Vorbericht über die Zollinschrift aus Andriake aus neronischer Zeit." *Gephyra* 4: 165–88.

Tal, O. 2009. "On the Identification of the Ships of KZD/RY in the Erased Customs Account from Elephantine." *Journal of Near Eastern Studies* 68: 1–8.

Talbert, R., et al., eds. 2000. *Barrington Atlas of the Greek and Roman World*. Princeton, NJ: Princeton University Press.

Tarn, W. W. 1952. *Hellenistic Civilisation*. 3rd ed. London.

Tartat, P. 1946. "Municipalité et ravitaillement dans une petite ville. Viande et poisson à Avallon au XVIIIᵉ siècle." *Annales de Bourgogne* 18: 131–32.

Tchernia, A. 1986. *Le vin de l'Italie romaine*. Rome: École française de Rome.

———. 2000. "La vente du vin." In Lo Cascio 2000: 199–209.

Thivel, A. 1981. *Cnide et Cos? Essai sur les doctrines médicales dans la collection hippocratique*. Paris: Les Belles lettres.

Thompson, C. M. 2003. "Sealed Silver in Iron Age Cisjordan and the 'Invention' of Coinage." *Oxford Journal of Archaeology* 22: 67–107.

Thompson, D. J. 2012. "Cleruchs, Egypt." in Bagnall et al. 2012: 1574–75.

Thompson, M. 1961. *The New Style Silver Coinage of Athens*. New York: American Numismatic Society.

Thompson, W. E. 1972. "Athenian Marriage Patterns: Remarriage." *California Studies in Classical Antiquity* 5: 211–25.

———. 1976. *De Hagniae Hereditate: An Athenian Inheritance Case*. Leiden: Brill.

Thonemann, P. 2009a. "Estates and the Land in Early Hellenistic Asia Minor: The Estate of Krateuas." *Chiron* 39: 363–93.

———. 2009b. "Asia Minor." In Erskine 2009: 222–35.

———. 2011. *The Maeander Valley: A Historical Geography from Antiquity to Byzantium*. Cambridge: Cambridge University Press.

———. 2012. "Alexander, Priene, and Naulochon." In Martzavou and Papazarkadas 2012: 23–36.

Tilg, S. 2010. *Chariton of Aphrodisias and the Invention of the Greek Love Novel*. Oxford: Oxford University Press.

Tiverios, M. 2007. "Panathenaic Amphoras." In Palagia and Choremi-Spetsieri 2007: 1–19.

Todd, S. C. 1993. *The Shape of Athenian Law*. Oxford: Clarendon Press.

———. 2003. "Lysias on Abortion." In *Symposion 1999* 2003: 235–56.

Tölle-Kastenbein, R. 1990. *Antike Wasserkultur*. Munich: Beck.

———. 1994. *Das archaische Wasserleitungsnetz für Athen und seine späteren Bauphasen*. Mainz an Rhein: Philipp von Zabern.

Tolles, R. 1941. *Untersuchungen zur Kindesaussetzung bei den Griechen*. Dissertation, Breslau: Bernhard Sporn.

Tomber, R. 1987. "Evidence for Long-Distance Commerce : Imported Bricks and Tiles at Carthage." *Rei Cretariae Romanae Fautorum Acta* 25–26: 161–74.

Tompkins, D. P. 2008. "Weber, Polanyi and Finley." *History and Theory* 47: 123–36.

Touratsoglou, I. 2010. *A Contribution to the Economic History of the Ancient Kingdom of Macedonia (6th–3rd century BC)*. Athens: Society for the Study of Numismatics and Economic History.

Toutain, J. 1930. *The Economic Life of the Ancient World*. Tr. from the French ed. 1927. New York: Knopf.

Tracy, S. 1979. "Athens in 100 B.C." *Harvard Studies in Classical Philology* 83: 213–35.

Traill, J. 1975. *The Political Organization of Attica: A Study of the Demes, Trittyes, and Phylai, and Their Representation in the Athenian Council*. Princeton, NJ: American School of Classical Studies at Athens.

Traina, G. 1988. *Paludi e bonifiche del mondo antico. Saggio di archeologia geografica.* Rome: L'Erma di Bretschneider.

———. 1994. *La tecnica in Grecia e a Roma.* Rome: Laterza.

Treister, M. Y. 1995. *The Role of Metal in the Ancient Greek History.* Leiden and New York: Brill.

Treuil, R., P. Darcque, J.-C. Poursat, and G. Touchais, eds. 1989. *Les civilisations égéennes du Néolithique et de l'Âge du bronze.* Paris: Presses Universitaires de France.

Trümper, M. 1998. *Wohnen in Delos. Eine baugeschichtliche Untersuchung zum Wandel der Wohnkultur in hellenistischer Zeit.* Rahden: Verlag Marie Leidorf.

———. 2005. "Modest Housing in Late Hellenistic Delos." In Ault and Nevett 2005: 119–39.

Tsakirgis, B. 2005. "Living and Working around the Athenian Agora: A Preliminary Case Study of Three Houses." In Ault and Nevett 2005: 67–82.

Tsetskhladze, G. R. 2008. "'Grain for Athens.' The View from the Black Sea." In Alston and van Nijf 2008: 47–62.

Tsetskhladze, G. R., A.J.N.W. Prag, and A. M. Snodgrass, eds. 2000. *Periplous: Papers on Classical Art and Archaeology presented to Sir John Boardman.* London and New York: Thames & Hudson.

Tuplin, C. 1982. "Satyros and Athens: IG II^2 212 and Isokrates 17.57." *Zeitschrift für Papyrologie und Epigraphik* 49: 121–28.

Tzifopoulos, G. A. ed. 2012. *Methōnē Pierias I. Epigraphes, charagmata kai emporika symbola stē geōmetrika kai archaïkē keramikē apo to "Hypogeio" tēs Methōnēs Pierias stē Makedonia.* Thessaloniki: Center for the Greek Language.

Tzochev, C., T. Stoyanov, and A. Bozkova, eds. 2011. *Production and Trade of Amphorae in the Black Sea (PATABS II).* Sofia: Bulgarian Academy of Sciences, National Archaeological Institute.

Urbainczyk, T. 2008. *Slave Revolts in Antiquity.* Berkeley: University of California Press.

Valavanis, P. 1986. "Les amphores panathénaïques et le commerce athénien de l'huile." In Empereur and Garlan 1986: 453–60.

Vallois, R. 1944–1966. *L'architecture hellénique et hellénistique à Délos jusqu'à l'éviction des Déliens (166 av. J.-C.).* 2 vols. Paris: De Boccard.

Van Alfen, P. G. 2010. "Social Controls, Institutions and the Regulation of Commodities in Classical Aegean Markets." *Marburger Beiträge zur antiken Handels-, Wirtschafts- und Sozialgeschichte* 28: 197–229.

Van Alfen, P. G., ed. 2006. *Agoranomia: Studies in Money and Exchange Presented to John H. Kroll.* New York: American Numismatic Society.

Van Andel, T. H., and C. N. Runnels. 1987. *Beyond the Acropolis: A Rural Greek Past.* Stanford, CA: Stanford University Press.

Van Bremen, R. 1983. "Women and Wealth." In Cameron and Kuhrt 1983: 223–42.

———. 1996. *The Limits of Participation.* Amsterdam: Gieben.

———. 2013. "A Property Transaction between Kindye and Mylasa. *I.Mylasa* 11 Reconsidered." *Epigraphica Anatolica* 46: 1–26.

Van Bremen, R., and J.-M. Carbon, eds. 2010. *Hellenistic Karia.* Bordeaux: Ausonius.

Vanderpool, E. 1968. "Metronomoi." *Hesperia* 37: 73–76.

Van der Spek, R. J. 2000. "The Effect of War on the Prices of Barley and Agricultural Land in Hellenistic Babylonia." In Andreau et al. 2000: 293–313.

Van der Spek, R. J. 2006. "How to Measure Prosperity? The Case of Hellenistic Babylonia." In Descat 2006: 287–310.

Van der Spek, R. J., J. Luiten, J. L. van Zanden, and B. van Leeuwen, eds. 2014. *A History of Market Performance: From Ancient Babylonia to the Modern World*. London and New York: Routledge.

Van Groningen, B. A. 1933: *Aristote. Le second livre de l'Économique*. Leiden: Sijthoff.

Van Hook, L. 1920. "The Exposure of Infants at Athens." *Transactions of the American Philological Association* 51: 134–45.

Vargyas, P. 1997. "Le prix des denrées alimentaires de première nécessité en Babylonie à l'époque achéménide et hellénistique." In Andreau et al. 1997: 335–54.

——. 2001. *A History of Babylonian Prices in the First Millennium BC. 1. Prices of the Basic Commodities*. Heidelberg: Heidelberger Orientverlag.

Vasi attici. 1991 [1996]. *I vasi attici ed altre ceramiche coevi in Sicilia. Atti del convegno internazionale, Catania, Camarina, Gela, Vittoria, 22 marzo–1 aprile 1990*. 2 vols., Cronache di Archeologia 30, 1991 [published in1996]. Palermo: Nuova Graphicadue.

Vatin, C. 1966. "Un tarif des poissons à Delphes." *Bulletin de Correspondance Hellénique* 90: 274–80.

——. 1976. "Jardins et services de voirie." *Bulletin de Correspondance Hellénique* 100: 555–64.

Veal, R. J. 2013. "Fuelling Ancient Mediterranean Cities: A Framework for Charcoal Research." In Harris 2013a: 37–58.

Veblen, T. 1899. *The Theory of the Leisure Class: An Economic Study of Institutions*. New York and London: Macmillan.

Veligianni-Terzi, C. 2004. *Oi Hellēnides poleis kai to basileio tōn Odrysōn apo Abdērōn poleōs mechri Istrou potamou*. Thessaloniki: Ekdotikos Oikos Adelphōn Kuriakidē.

Vélissaropoulos, J. 1980. *Les nauclères grecs. Recherches sur les institutions maritimes en Grèce et dans l'Orient hellénisé*. Geneva: Droz, and Paris: Minard.

Velkov, V., and L. Domaradzka. 1994. "Kotys I (383/2–359) et l'emporion de Pistiros en Thrace." *Bulletin de Correspondance Hellénique* 118: 1–15.

Vera, D., ed. 1999. *Demografia, sistemi agrari, regimi alimentari nel mondo antico*. Bari: Edipuglia.

Vérilhac, A.-M. 1978–1982. *Paides aōroi—Poésie funéraire*. 2 vols. Athens: Grapheion Dēmosiegmatōn tēs Akadēmias Athēnōn.

Vérilhac, A.-M., and C. Vial. 1998. *Le mariage grec du VIᵉ siècle av. J.-C. à l'époque d'Auguste*. Athens: École française d'Athènes, and Paris: De Boccard.

Vial, C. 1984. *Délos indépendante*. Athens: École française d'Athènes, and Paris: De Boccard.

Vickers, M., and D.W.J. Gill. 1996. *Artful Crafts: Ancient Greek Silverware and Pottery*. Oxford: Clarendon Press, and Oxford and New York: Oxford University Press.

Vidal-Naquet, P. 1986. *The Black Hunter: Forms of Thought and Forms of Society in the Greek World*. Tr. from the French ed. 1981. Baltimore: Johns Hopkins University Press.

Villanueva, M.-C. 1992. *Images de la vie quotidienne en Grèce dans l'Antiquité*. Paris. Hachette.

Villanueva-Puig, M.-C., F. Lissarrague, P. Rouillard, and A. Rouveret, eds. 1999. *Céramique et peinture grecques. Modes d'emploi*. Paris: Documentation française.

Vilquin, E. 1982. "La doctrine démographique de Platon." *European Demographic Information Bulletin*. 13.1: 1–18.

Virlouvet, C., and B. Marin. 2004. *Nourrir les cités de Méditerranée: Antiquité–Temps Moderne*. Paris: Maisonneuve & Larose, Aix-en-Provence: Maison méditerranéenne des Sciences de l'Homme, and Madrid: Universidad Nacional de Educación a Distancia.

Vismara, N. 1989–1996. *Monetazione arcaica della Lycia*. 3 vols. Milan: Ennerre.

Viviers, D. 1994. "La cité de Datalla et l'expansion territoriale de Lyktos en Crète centrale." *Bulletin de Correspondance Hellénique* 118: 229–59.

———. 1999. "Economy and Territorial Dynamics in Crete from the Archaic to the Hellenistic Period." In Chaniotis 1999: 221–34.

Vokotopoulou, J. 1997. "Ho Kassandros, hē Kassandreia kai hē Thessalonikē." In *Mnēmē Andronikou*: 39–50.

Vreeken, W.A.L. 1953. *De lege quadam sacra Coorum*. Groningen: de Waal.

Wade-Gery, H. T. 1958. *Essays in Greek History*. Oxford: Blackwell.

Wagner-Hasel, B. 2004. "Le regard de Karl Bücher sur l'économie antique." In Bruhns 2004: 159–82.

———, B. 2011. *Die Arbeit des Gelehrten. Der Nationalökonom Karl Bücher (1847–1930)*. Frankfurt am Main: Campus Verlag.

Walbank, F. W. 1984. "Macedonia and the Greek Leagues." In Walbank et al. 1984: 446–81.

Walbank, F. W., A. E. Astin, M. W. Frederiksen, and R. M. Ogilvie, eds. 1984. *The Cambridge Ancient History*. Vol. 7.1. *The Hellenistic World*. 2nd ed. Cambridge and New York: Cambridge University Press.

Walbank, M. B. 1983. "Leases of Sacred Property in Attica, Part IV." *Hesperia* 52: 207–31.

Waldbaum, J. C. 1978. *From Bronze to Iron: The Transition from the Bronze Age to the Iron Age in the Eastern Mediterranean*. Göteborg: P. Aström.

Wallace, M. B. 1986. "Progress in Measuring Amphora Capacities." In Empereur and Garlan 1986: 87–94.

Wallerstein, I. M. 1979–1989. *The Modern World-System*. 3 vols. New York: Academic Press.

Walser, A. V. 2008. *Bauern und Zinsnehmer*. Munich: Beck.

Watrous, L. V., D. Hadzi-Vallianou, and H. Blitzer, eds. 2004. *The Plain of Phaistos: Cycles of Social Complexity in the Mesara Region of Crete*. Los Angeles: Cotsen Institute of Archaeology, and University of California, Los Angeles.

Weber, M. 1968 [1921–1922]. *Economy and Society. An Outline of Interpretative Sociology*. Ed. G. Roth and C. Wittich (from *Wirtschaft und Gesellschaft: Grundriß der verstehenden Soziologie*, Tübingen, 1921–1922: Mohr-Siebeck; tr. from the 4th German ed., Tübingen 1956: Mohr-Siebeck and revised ed. Cologne and Berlin 1964: Kiepenheuer & Witsch). New York: Bedminster Press.

———. 1976 [1909]. *The Agrarian Sociology of Ancient Civilizations*. Tr. from the German ed. (*Agrarverhältnisse im Altertum*, in *Handwörterbuch der Staatswissenschaften*, 3rd ed., I, Jena 1909: Fischer; new ed. by J. Deininger, *Max Weber. Zur Sozial- und Wirtschaftsgeschichte des Altertums, Schriften und Reden 1893–1908*, Tübingen 2006: Mohr-Siebeck, with the three versions of the *Agrarverhältnisse*, and among others the essays *Die sozialen Gründe des Untergangs der antiken Kultur, Kapitalismus im Altertum*, and *Agrargeschichte. Altertum*). London: NLB, and Atlantic Highlands, NJ: Humanities Press.

———. 2001 [1920]. *The Protestant Ethic and the Spirit of Capitalism*. Tr. by T. Parsons and A. Giddens (first ed. of the translation 1930, from *Die protestantische Ethik und der*

Geist des Kapitalismus. In *Gesammelte Aufsätze zur Religionssoziologie.* Vol. 1, pp. 1–206, Tübingen 1920: Mohr). London and New York: Routledge.

Welles, C. B. 1938. "New Texts from the Chancery of Philip V of Macedonia and the Problem of the 'Diagramma.'" *American Journal of Archaeology* 42: 245–60.

Wells, B., ed. 1992. *Agriculture in Ancient Greece: Proceedings of the Seventh International Symposium at the Swedish Institute at Athens, 16–17 May 1990.* Stockholm: The Institute, and Göteborg: Åströms.

Werner, W. 1997. "The Largest Ship Trackway in Ancient Times: The Diolkos of the Isthmus of Corinth, Greece, and Early Attempts to Build a Canal." *International Journal of Nautical Archaeology* 26.2: 98–119.

Westermann, W. L. 1955. *The Slave Systems of Greek and Roman Antiquity.* Philadelphia: American Philosophical Society.

Whitbread, I. 1995. *Greek Transport Amphorae: A Petrological and Archaeological Study.* Athens: British School at Athens.

Whitby, M. 1985. "Justinian's Bridge over the Sangarius and the Date of Procopius' *De aedificiis.*" *Journal of Hellenic Studies* 105: 129–48.

———. 1998. "The Grain Trade of Athens in the Fourth Century BC." In Parkins and Smith 1998: 102–28.

White, K. D. 1984. *Greek and Roman Technology.* London: Thames and Hudson.

Whitehead, D. 1986. *The Demes of Attica, 508/507–ca. 250 B.C.: A Political and Social Study.* Princeton, NJ: Princeton University Press.

Whitewright, J. 2009. "The Mediterranean Lateen Sail in Late Antiquity." *International Journal of Nautical Archaeology* 38: 97–104.

———. 2011. "Efficiency or Economics? Sail Development in the Ancient Mediterranean." In Harris and Iara 2011: 89–102.

Whitley, J. 2001. *The Archaeology of Ancient Greece.* New York: Cambridge University Press.

———. 2003–2004. "Archaeology in Greece 2003–2004." *Archaeological Reports* 50: 1–92.

Whittaker, C. R., ed. 1988. *Pastoral Economies in Classical Antiquity.* Cambridge: Cambridge Philological Society.

Wiegand, T., and H. Schrader. 1904. *Priene: Ergebnisse der Ausgrabungen und Untersuchungen in den Jahren 1895–1898.* Berlin: Reimer.

Wiegand, T., and U. von Wilamowitz. 1904. "Ein Gesetz von Samos über die Beschaffung von Brotkorn aus öffentlichen Mitteln." *Sitzungsberichte der Königlich Preussischen Akademie der Wissenschaften zu Berlin* 27: 917–31.

Wiemer, H. U. 1997. "Das Edikt des L. Antistius Rusticus: eine Preisregulierung als Antwort auf eine überregionale Versorgungskrise?" *Anatolian Studies* 47: 195–215.

———. 2002. *Krieg, Handel und Piraterie: Untersuchungen zur Geschichte des hellenistischen Rhodos.* Berlin: Akademie Verlag.

Wikander, Ö. 2008. "Sources of Energy and Exploitation of Water Power." In Oleson 2008: 136–57.

Wilhelm, A. 1942. "Proxenie und Euergesie." In *Attische Urkunden.* V. *Sitzungsberichte der Akademie der Wissenschaften in Wien* 220.5: 11–86 (= Wilhelm 1974. I.1: 627–702).

———. 1974. *Akademieschriften zur griechischen Inschriftenkunde (1895–1951).* Leipzig: Zentralantiquariat der Deutschen Demokratischen Republik.

Wilkins, J. 2005. "Fish a Source of Food in Antiquity." In Bekker-Nielsen 2005a: 21–30.

Will, É. 1979–1982. *Histoire politique du monde hellénistique (323–30 av. J.-C.)*. 2 vols. 2nd ed. Nancy: Berger-Levrault.

Williams, C. K., and N. Bookidis, eds. 2003. *Corinth*. Vol. 20. *Corinth, the Centenary, 1896–1996*. Princeton, NJ: American School of Classical Studies at Athens.

Williamson, O. E. 1985. *The Economic Institutions of Capitalism*. New York: Free Press, and London: Collier Macmillan.

———. 1998. "Transaction Costs Economics: How It Works; Where It Is Headed." *Economist* 146: 23–58.

———. 2000. "The New Institutional Economics: Taking Stock, Looking Ahead." *Journal of Economic Literature* 38: 595–613.

———. 2005. "Transaction Cost Economics." In Ménard and Shirley 2005: 41–65.

Williams-Thorpe, O., and R. S. Thorpe. 1990. "Millstone Provenancing Used in Tracing the Route of a Fourth-Century BC Greek Merchant Ship." *Archaeometry* 32: 115–37.

Wilson, A. I. 2002. "Machines, Power and the Ancient Economy." *Journal of Roman Studies* 92: 1–32.

———. 2006a. "New Light on a Greek City: Archaeology and History at Euesperides." In Fabbricotti and Menozzi 2006: 141–49.

———. 2006b. "The Economic Impact of Technological Advances in the Roman Construction Industry." In Lo Cascio 2006: 225–36.

———. 2008a. "Hydraulic Engineering and Water Supply." In Oleson 2008: 285–318.

———. 2008b. "Machines in Greek and Roman Technology." In Oleson 2008: 337–66.

———. 2009. "Approaches to Quantifying Roman Trade." In Wilson and Bowman 2009: 213–49.

———. 2011a. "Developments in Mediterranean Shipping and Maritime Trade from the Hellenistic Period to AD 1000." In Robinson and Wilson 2011: 33–59.

———. 2011b. "The Economic Influence of Developments in Maritime Technology in Antiquity." In Harris and Iara 2011: 211–33.

Wilson, A. I., and A. K. Bowman, eds. 2009. *Quantifying the Roman Economy: Methods and Problems*. Oxford: Oxford University Press.

Wilson, A. I., and E. Tébar Megías. 2008. "Purple Dye Production at Hellenistic Euesperides (Benghazi, Libya)." In Napoli 2008: 231–38.

Wilson, P. 2000. *The Athenian Institution of the Khoregia: The Chorus, the City and the Stage*. Cambridge and New York: Cambridge University Press.

Winter, E., ed. 2008. *Vom Euphrat bis zum Bosporus: Kleinasien in der Antike. Festschrift für Elmar Schwertheim zum 65. Geburtstag*. Bonn: Habelt.

Winter, N. A. 1990. "Defining Regional Styles in Archaic Greek Architectural Terracottas." *Hesperia* 59: 13–32.

Woodhead, A. G. 1977. "Der Staatliche Gesundheitsdienst im antiken Griechenland." In Pfohl 1977.

Wörrle, M. 1988. *Stadt und Fest im kaiserzeitlichen Kleinasien. Studien zu einer agonistischen Stiftung aus Oinoanda*. Munich: Beck.

Wrigley, E. A. 1988. *Continuity, Chance, and Change: The Character of the Industrial Revolution in England*. Cambridge and New York: Cambridge University Press.

Wrigley, E. A., and R. Schofield. 1981. *The Population History of England, 1541–1871: A Reconstruction*. Cambridge, MA: Harvard University Press.

Yardeni, A. 1994. "Maritime Trade and Royal Accountancy in an Erased Customs Account from 475 B.C.E. on the Ahiqar Scroll from Elephantine." *Bulletin of the American Schools of Oriental Research* 293: 67–78.

Yeni Türkiye Atlası. 1977. *Yeni Türkiye Atlası.* Ankara: M.S.B. Harita Genel Müdürlüğü.

Yntema, R. 2009. "The Union of Utrecht, Tariff Barriers, and the Interprovincial Beer Trade in the Dutch Republic." In Gelderblom 2009: 255–89.

Young, J. H. 1956. "Studies in South Attica: Country Estates at Sounion." *Hesperia* 25: 122–46.

Young, R. S. 1951. "An Industrial District of Ancient Athens." *Hesperia* 20: 135–288.

Zaccagnini, C. 1994. "Feet of Clay at Emar and Elsewhere." *Orientalia* 63: 1–4.

———. 1995. "War and Famine at Emar." *Orientalia* 64: 92–109.

Zaccagnini, C., ed. 2003. *Mercanti e politica nel mondo antico.* Rome: L'Erma di Bretschneider.

Zeckhauser, R., ed. 1991. *Strategy and Choice.* Cambridge, MA: MIT Press.

Zelener, Y. 2006. "Between Technology and Productivity." In Lo Cascio 2006: 303–18.

Ziebarth, E. 1940a. "*Deigma.*" *Realencyclopädie.* Supplement VII: col. 116.

———. 1940b. "*Deigmatokatagōgos.*" *Realencyclopädie.* Supplement VII: col. 116.

Ziegler, T. 1914. "Hybla." *Realencyclopädie* IX.1: cols. 25–29.

Zimmerman Munn, M. L. 2003. "Corinthian Trade with the Punic West in the Classical Period." In Williams and Bookidis 2003: 195–217.

Zohary, D., M. Hopf, and E. Weiss. 2012. *Domestication of Plants in the Old World: The Origin and Spread of Domesticated Plants in Southwest Asia, Europe, and the Mediterranean Basin.* 4th ed. Oxford: Oxford University Press.

Zolotarev, M. I. 2003. "Chersonesus Tauricus: The Foundation and the Development of the Polis." In Grammenos and Petropoulos 2003: 603–44.

Zuiderhoek, A. 2008. "Feeding the Citizens: Municipal Grain Funds and Civic Benefactors in the Roman East." In Alston and van Nijf 2008: 159–80.

INDEX

Note: Page numbers in *italics* indicate illustrations; those with a *t* indicate tables.

Abdera, 254, 291, 367

abortion, 42, 51–52, 457n99

accounting techniques, 155, 218; Linear B mentions of, 97–98; Persian, 267; tally sticks for, 309

Achaemenids. *See* Persian Empire

Aeneas Tacticus, 73, 193, 309, 485n103, 509n96

Aeschylus, 86, 119, 278

agora, 107–8, 225, 235–46; Aphrodite's association with, 215, 488n41; boundary stones of, 306–7; *emporion* and, 238, 307; on frontiers, 491n65; monetization of, 276; Plutarch on, 240; regulation of, 234–46, 252, 259, 307, 332–38; taxation of, 236–38; transaction costs of, 238, 259; Xenophon on, 236

agoranomoi (magistrates), 225, 237–50, 253, 307; contracts and, 244–46, 259; of *emporion*, 313; price control by, 257–58, 326–31; whips of, 246

agricultural production, 118–31, 132–33, 141; diversified approach to, 159; increased cultivated areas for, 164–66; increased yields in, 166–70; innovations in, 161–62, 166–67, 170–71, 195–98; loans for, 280; manure for, 121, 129–30, 133, 147, 169, 480n119; market system of, 171–74, 199–206; taxation of, 294. *See also* animal husbandry

Aigina, coins and currency standard of, 264, 272, 277, 356, 367, 421; imports of grain to, *412*; merchants from, 193, 320, 359, 367, 377; prosperity and decline of, 61; slaves at, 459

Aitolian League, 249, 304, 418

Akarnania, 137, 151, decree of Stratos of, 289, 356

Akerlof, George, 251–53

Akragas, fishpond at, 185

Alciphron, 182, 279–80, 361–63, 371

Alcock, Susan, 57–60

Alexander the Great, 56, 96–97, 149, 207; coins of, 273–74; Greek conquests of, 416–17; Persian conquests of, 347; royal/civic lands of, 111

Alexandria Troas, 150, 477n37

Alexandria, 55, 88, 171, 190, 197, 281, 300, 312, 367, 372, 375, lighthouse of, 91

alfalfa, 162, 168, 204

Alkibiades (grandfather), 476n11

Alkibiades (grandson), 145–46, 246

alum, 349, 353–55, 357, 358; tax on, 514n62; transport cost of, 84

Amastris, 355

Amathous, port of, 90

Ambrakia, 295, import of grain to, *412*

Amisos, 82, 353

Amorgos, Battle of, 63, 202, 304, fabrics from, 191, 358, 360

Amos land leases, 123, 129

amphoras, 125–27, 152, 180, 186, 362, 367, 370–71; from Athens, 404–5; from Campania, 376; from Carthage, 186; from Kerkyra, 127; from Mende, 370–71, 378; from Rhodes, 84, 86, 126, 360, 378, 463n74; size variation in, 171, 243, 520n6; stamps on, 243, 253, 316–17, 360, 493n104; workshops for, 152, 190, 360. *See also* ceramics

Amyntas III, king of Macedon, 115

Anaktorion, fairs at, 237

Andania, festival and market at, 236, 238, 240–41, 249, 257

animal husbandry, 131–41, 147; cattle raising and, 132–34, 136–38, 257, 258; constraints

animal husbandry (*continued*)
in, 133–35, 159; dairy products and, 132–35, 138, 163, 176, 358, 360, 366; dogs and, 133–34; fallow ground and, 169; grain production versus, 120–21, 132, 141; in Homer, 132, 139, 474n72; horses and, 134, 138, 163; innovations in, 162–64, 167, 170; oxen and, 81, 93, 121, 134–36, 147, 163–64, 254; pigs and, 133, 162–63, 257, 258, *327*, 329; regional types of, 135–38; risks with, 157; sheep, 132–41, 147, 162–63, 166, 257. *See also* agricultural production

Anthedon, sea-activities at, 359, 369, 376

Anthestēria festival, 124–25

antidosis (exchange of property), 146, 231

Antigonos I Monophthalmos, 150, 394, 400

Antigonos II Gonatas, 152

Antigonos III Doson, 387

Antimenes of Rhodes, insurance system devised by, 228

Antioch in Persis, colonists to, 63

Antioch in Pisidia, grain shortage at, 66–67, 336–38

Antiochos I, Seleukid king, 112, 150

Antiochos II, Seleukid king, 150

Antiochos IV, Seleukid king, 420

Antipater of Sidon, 197

Antipater of Thessalonike, 197, 486n123

Antistius Rusticus, 66, 336–37

Anytos (Athenian politician), and grain sales, 256, 327

Apameia in Bithynia, 296

Apameia in Phrygia, amphoras at, 84

Aperghis, Makis, 56

Aperlai, murex fishing at, 357

aphormē (start-up capital), 192, 280

Aphrodite (deity), 215, 488n41, 515n70

Apollo (deity), 73–74, 300

Apollonios of Tyana, 394

Apollonius of Rhodes, 353

Apuleius, Lucius, 130, 253, 503n51

Archimedes, 88, 218–19

Archytas of Taras, 155

Aristodemos of Kyme, 389

Aristodikides of Assos, 112, 150

Aristonikos, War of, 417, 426–27

Aristophanes, works of: *Acharnians*, 74, 179, 200, 240, 241, 326, 373, 469n48; *Assembly-women*, 276; *Birds*, 287, 295; *Knights*, 178, 236; *Wasps*, 129, 250, 494n134

Aristotle, 5, 234; on *agoranomoi*, 240–41, 247, 258; on Athenian constitution, 148, 239, 247–48, 258, 280, 313, 322, 331; on birth control, 50–51, 53; on Chios, 377; on city-states, 109; on contracts, 232, 244; on division of labor, 229; on *epimelētai*, 313–14; on ethics, 215; on "fair prices," 331; on hygiene, 44, 45; on money, 340, 342; on monopolies, 215–16; on property rights, 114, 226, 231, 489n2; on rule of law, 227, 231; on self-sufficiency, 229, 244, 381; on taxation, 104, 107; on trade, 251, 382; on weights and measures, 75; on women landowners, 154. *See also* Pseudo-Aristotle

Arrow, Kenneth, 251

Artemis (deity), 163, 237

artisanal trades, 175, 187–98, 203, 348; export trade and, 378–79; imported materials for, 352, 358; Pericles and, 214; Solon on, 403; strikes among, 246

Astakos (Akarnania), *proxenos* of Megara at, 356

astunomoi (urban policemen), 45, 227, 243, 246–47

Astypalaia, 331, import of grain to, *412*

Athena (deity), 118; on coins, 272, 277, 422, 425

Athenaeus, 88, 125, 179, 185, 370, 459n144

Athenodoros of Rhodes, 386–87

Athens, ceramics production and sales in, 190, 364–65, 371–75, 378–79, 404–5; city grain fund of, 333–34; cleruchies of, 105, 116; climate of, 35–37, 65t; coinage, 264, 271–78, 367, 422, 424; dairy or meat production and consumption in, 135–36, 138; division of labor in, 188; empire of, 216–17, 303–5, 320, 416, 419, 421–22, 437; *emporion* of, 306–7, 309–10, 312–16, 320; ephebes' military service oath in, 118; farms in, 143–50, 154, 202; fishing and fish sales in, 177, 179, 185; foreign trade of, 287, 290, 292–94, 300–1, 315–16, 318–21, 327, 339–40, 351, 358, 368–76, 379, 383–85, 389, 394, 399–405, 409–13; gardening in, 130; grain production in, 158, 405–9; import of grain to, 402–11, *412*; land occupation in, 155–56, 182; law of, 231, 235, 321–24, 394–405; loans in, 279–85; market of, 235, 237–41, 243–50, 252, 255–58, 331; oil production and commerce in, 333, 383–84, 405; "plague" in, 48; population of, 41, 51–52, 54, 60–61, 63–64, 68, 143–44, 459–60n144; prices in, 255–58, 262t, 352, 365t, 424–27, 433; rents and taxes in, 104–6; roads in, 81; salaries in, 275; textile production in, 191–93; wine production and sales in, 124–25, 171, 173, 349; women's property in, 154. *See also* Laurion mines, Megarian Decree, Pericles, Piraeus, Solon

Attalos III ((king of Pergamon), 417

Attika. *See* Athens

Augustus (Roman emperor), 56, 219

Ausonius, 211

Austin, Michael M., xxiii

autarkeia. See self-sufficiency

Babylon, 102, 228, 261, 266–67, 362, 423

Bargasa, water supply at, 46

Bargylia, 163, 180

barley, 120–21, 374, 406; production of, 147, 169, 201; transport costs of, 364–67, 365t; wheat mixed with, 241. *See also* grain production

basileis (kings), 101, 110

baths, public, 47, 72, 74

beekeeping, 130–31, 157, 159, 341. *See also* honey

Bekker-Nielsen, Tønnes, 177, 187

Beloch, Karl J., 41, 54–56

Bintliff, John L., 177, 467n13

birth control, 42, 49–53

Bismarck, Otto von, 4

Bissa, Errietta, 495n154

Bodin, Jean, 54

Bogaert, Raymond, 280

Boiotia, cattle raising in, 148; ecology of, 33, 35, 47, 164–65; fishing and fish sales in 179, 185, 359, 369; justice in, 317; land leases in, 153; land occupation in, 56, 58–59; sites and population of, 59t, 64. *See also* Anthedon, Lake Kopais, Orchomenos, Thebes, Thespiai

Bosporos (Kimmerian), 57, 368–70, 399; archaeological survey in, 57; *emporia* of, 311; exports of grain from, 350, 368, 399, 401, 413–14, 420, 501n25; fish from, 186; justice on trade conflict in, 322; navigation to, and from, 89, 281–84; tax exemption and privileges for grain bound to Athens, 292, 301, 383, 389. *See also* Pantikapeion, Theodosia

Bosporos (Straits), *34*; fishing at the, 177–79; transit fees at the, 297, 305, 387. *See also* Byzantion

Boulis, murex fishing at, 357

Boura, earthquake at, 33

Bourdieu, Pierre, 18

Braudel, Fernand, 79–80, 89, 175–76, 184

bricks, 80, 243, 364, 368. *See also* ceramics

Bringmann, Klaus, 401

Britain, coal mining in, 76–78; early iron production in, 263, 497n7; East India Company of, 374; economic growth in, 205; Portuguese trade with, 344t

Bronze Age, xxiv, 97–99; animal husbandry in, 132–33, 162–63; crisis of, 99–100, 467n13

bronze, 220, 262t

Broodbank, Cyprian, 32

Brunt, Peter A., 56

Bücher, Karl, 2–5, 14, 200, 486n4

Burford Cooper, Alison, 81, 143, 478n57

Byzantion, 179, 183, 185–86; transit fees of, 297, 305, 387

camels, 82

canals, 85, 92–93.

Cape Kaphereus, 369

capital, 215, 348; start-up, 192, 280; trade and, 212–13, 345, 373–74, 404

Carthage, agronomists of, 119, 131; amphoras from, 186; flax products from, 355; imperial period imports of bricks to, 368; late adoption of coinage by, 264; prisoners used to dig a fishpond at Akragas, 45; role of trade hub of, 378–79; salt meat and fish from, 186; treaties between Rome and, 318–19. *See also* Punic Wars

Cato the Elder, 119, 122, 129, 253, 376

Celsus, Aulus Cornelius, 131

center-periphery model, 348–51, 416–17

ceramics, 84, 186–90, 193, 348; bricks and, 80, 243, 364, 368; British East India Company and, 374; decorative techniques of, 211, 372, 375, 378; fuel needed for, 328; imported materials for, 352; of Naples, 375–76; tiles and, 80, 243, 364–66, 365t, *366*, 517n111; trade flow of, 371–76, 372t, 519n168; transport costs of, 364, 365t. *See also* amphoras

cereals. *See* grain production

Chaereas and Callirhoe, 306–7

Chairephanes, 165–66, 501n21

Chalkidian League, 112–13

Chalkidike, colonization of, 101; iron deposits in, 353; Macedonian control of, 112–13; population of 55; wines from, 126, 369–71, 373. *See also* Kassandreia, Mende, Olynthos, Skione, Torone

Chandezon, Christophe, 138

Chandler, A. D., Jr., 463n66

Chaniotis, Angelos, 140–41

charcoal, 73–75, 353; sale of, 235–36, 242, 250, 315, 327–31, *327*, 509n110. *See also* wood

Chariton of Aphrodisias, 244, 306–7

Charlemagne, 92

Chaunu, Pierre, 50

Chersonesos (Tauric), vineyards at, 341, 371

Chios, Athens and, 319–20; boundary stones in, 227; coinage standard of, 421; foreign trade of, 304, 377; school in, 217; slavery and slave revolts in, 110, 126–27, 228, 347; wine from, 122, 126–27, 171–72, 179, 360, 365t, 378

chōrion estates of Attika, 155–56

Chremonidean War, 61

Christianity, 177, 246, 494n116

Cicero, *De officiis*, 235, 300, 490n47; *De re publica*, 503n51; *Pro Cluentio* 11.32, 457n99; *Verrines*, 83

cisterns, 46, 49, 134–35, 159–60

city-states, 96–97, 105–10; Aristotle on, 109; center-periphery model of, 145, 270, 348–51; collapse of, 215, 221–22, 416–17; division of labor in, 381; estates and, 170; legal systems of, 214–15, 221, 230–32; origins of, xxiv, 116–17; Plato on, 107; property rights in, xxv, 116, 216, 418; society of, 217, 381; taxation by, 104–5, 111, 286–93, 296–99

climate, 47; constraints of, 35–38, *36–38*, 36t, 64–70; global warming of, 39–40; variability of, 39–41, 80, 158–61, 325; wind patterns and, 85. *See also* drought, Medieval Climate Anomaly, precipitation

cliometrics, 21

coal, 72, 76–78, 95, 221

Coase, Ronald H., 19, 20

coastal waters, 181–84, 286. *See also* fishing

Cohen, Edward E., 323

coin hoards, 152, 261, 271, 347, 363; specific: Asyut, 268; Hollm, 272, 356; Selinous, 272, 367; Taranto, 367

coinage, 61, 151–52; of Athens, 271–73, 277–78, 373, 422, 425; bronze coinage,

151, 236, 243, 266, 271–72, 276, 363, 400, 430; circulation of, 274–75; costs of, 269; counterfeiting of, 243, 271–72; development of, xxv, 96, 260–61, 264–65, *265*; economic growth and, 276–78; in Egypt, 267, 272; functions of, 265–70; of Hermione, 363–64; for market transactions, 242–43; minting of, 108, 243–44, 260–61, 264, 272–76, 363–64, 421–24; Persian, 264, 266; Zeus on, 273. *See also* coin hoards, electrum, gold, money, silver

Columella, 119, 123, 124; on animal husbandry, 163; on beekeeping, 131, 157; on wine production, 167; on yield ratios, 168

Commons, John, 12, 19

Comnena, Anna, 466n116

Constitution of Athens (Aristotle), 104, 148, 239, 247–48, 258, 280, 313, 322, 411

Constitution of the Athenians (Pseudo-Xenophon), 339–40, 352–54, 419

"consumer city," 193

contracts, 19, 102–3, 231–34, 307; Aristotle on, 232, 244; court system for, 247–48, 316–25; Isocrates on, 313; for maritime loans, 281–85, 316; *sumbolaion*, 244, 245, 313, 319–22, 508n83

copper, 98–100, 262t, 353

Corinth, 296–97, 379, 416; ceramics of, 372, 378; destruction of, 95, 417; isthmus of, 93–94, 466n129; textiles of, 193, 355, 357. *See also diolkos*

Corvisier, Jean-Nicolas, 56

credit, 217, 247, 261; forms of, 278–80; during Middle Ages, 500n85. *See also* loans

Crete, *34*, 132, 183–84, 270, 294; during Bronze Age, 97; gender norms in, 51, 53; Homer's description of, 100; Miletos emigrants from, 64; palace economy of, 98–100; property rights in, 226; security concerns in, 302; trade agreements in, 288, 318. *See also* Datalla, Gortyn, Hierapytna, Knossos, Lato, Olous, Praisos, Priansos, Stalai

Croesus (king of Lydia), 264

Ctesicles (historian), 459n144

Cuinet, Vital, 82

customs duties, 286–95, 307–9, 311; exemption from, 298–99, 301, 329–30, 390. *See also* taxation

Cyprus, contract with payment in land, 269; copper from, 98–99, 353. *See also* Amathous, Salamis, shipwrecks/Kyrenia

Cyrene, 89, agricultural products from, 358; export of grain from, 363, 387, 396, 410–13, 433, 501n25, 526n117; financial compensations paid by, 318; political conflicts in, 318, 460n160; roses of, 130; Thera and, 67–68
Cyrus (king of Persia), 234–35, 268

Danube, 92, 186, 362
Darius (king of Persia), 264
Dark Ages of Greece, 14, 99, 132, 207, 220
Datalla, contract at, 269
Davies, John K., 176, 452n58
deforestation, 38. *See also* ecological environment
deigma, 309–13
Delos, 315; agora of, 235–36, 242; city grain fund of, 333–35, 338; economic growth of, 305; fish consumption in, 185; grain market of, 390–91, 528n37; imports of tiles to, 366; perfumes of, 348, 352, 514n40; port facilities at, 90–91, 295; price controls in, 327–31, *327*, *328*; rise of, 95, 417
Delphi, 334; amphictiony of, 249, 273, 302–3; land leases of, 153
Demeter (deity), 361, 405
Demetrios I (Seleukid king), 401
Demetrios of Phaleron, 149, 374
Demetrios of Pharos, 387
Demetrios Poliorketes, 156, 304, 317
demography, economic growth and, 102, 133, 204–206, 208, 416; food shortage and, 67–69; Greek model of, 41–64, 70. *See also* abortion, fertility rates, infant mortality, infanticide, marriage
Demosthenes, Aeschines and, 156; on contracts, 232; on fraud, 235; Plutarch on, 309; on shipping, 91, 295, 304; on taxation, 105, 146; works of (*See also* Pseudo-Demosthenes): *Against Apaturius*, 323; *Against Aphobus*, 189; *Against Aristocrates*, 295; *Against Callippus*, 502n35; *Against Eratosthenes*, 189; *Against Leptines*, 301, 314, 399, 404; *On the Affairs of the Chersonese*, 304
Didyma, 85
Dikaiarcheia, 376
Dio Chrysostom, 203, 369, 394; on depopulation, 62; on Nikomedia, 287–88, 296–97, 436

Diodorus, 45, 53, 113, 130, 185; on the *deigma* in Rhodes, 310; on Egyptian grain exports, 411–12
Diogenes Laertius, 235
Diogenes of Babylon, 300
diolkos (portage route), 93–94, 466n129
Dionysian festivals, 124–25
Dionysios of Syracuse, measure against iron monopoly, 215–16
Dionysius of Halicarnassus, 69, 322, 508n79
Dioscorides, 131, 241, 351, 474n66
diphtheria, 48
division of labor, 2, 107–8, 110, 187–88; Aristotle on, 229; as basis of city-state, 381; international trade and, 343–47, 344t; 379–80; interregional, 218; Plato on, 108, 228; Weber on, 189
divorce, 42–43
Dodona, oracular tablets from, 167–68, 179, 185
dogs, 133–34
Domitian (Roman emperor), 337
dowries, 154, 159, 247. *See also* marriage
Drachmann, Aage G., 76
drought, 65–67, 159–61. *See also* precipitation
Dumont, Jacques, 181–82
Durkheim, Émile, 8
dyes, 191, 328, 343; natron for, 354; preservatives for, 362; price of, 356, 363; purple, 182, 184, 194, 242, 356–58, 361–63; saffron, 356; seaweed for, 359, 516n93

earthquakes, 32–33, 387
ecological environment, 31–41, 120, 138–41; deforestation of, 38; population and, 64–70; technological innovation and, 78–79; tuna fishing and, 185
economic growth, xxi–xxii; education and, 217–18, 222; energy costs and, 71–72, 78–79; increased population and, 41–42; market system and, 203–6
Edessa (Syria), famine at, 68
Edict on Maximum Prices (Diocletian's), 80
education, 217–18, 222, 401
Egypt, 53, 312, 417; coins in, 267, 272; grain exports of, 410–12, 411t; grain production in, 120, 162, 300; international trade of, 99, 349; market regulations in, 241; natron of, 354–55, 357; population of, 55–56; price controls in, 255; Red Sea canal of, 92; Roman conquest of, 207; "Sea Peoples"

Egypt (*continued*)
 and, 99; taxation in, 104; wool contract
 from, 233
Elateia, cattle raising at, 136–37, 148
Elba, 263, 353
electrum, 186, 261, 264, 269, 301. *See also*
 coinage
Eleusis, 93, 153, 155, 189, 310, 364, first fruits
 inscription from, 405–9
emporion, 238, 242–43, 306–38, 379; agora
 and, 238, 307; customs duties at, 286–95,
 307–9, 311; *deigma* in, 309–13; in Piraeus,
 248; price controls of, 325–26, 338; rules
 of, 284, 313–17, 404; supervision of, 248,
 307–9, 313, 314, 316, 320
energy, 71–75, 78, 95, 133, 437; cost of, 75, 79.
 See also charcoal
Engels, Donald, 51–53
Epeiros, cattle raising in, 133, 137–38; ecology
 of, 34–37
Ephesos, 45, 83; import of grain to, 325–27;
 import of oil and wine to, 350; price of
 bread at, 257; security of religious envoys
 from, 289, 302; trade networks of, 358
Epidamnos, 138
Epidauros, 189, 262t, 361, 364
epidemics, 48, 157, 208
epilepsy, 254
epimelētai (*emporion* inspectors), 248, 307,
 313–14, 316, 320
Epitadeus's law, 154
epōnion (market tax), 238
Erdkamp, Paul, 511n144, 521n14
Eretria, fairs at, 237
Etruria (*Tūrrhēnia*), children raising in, 53;
 defeat against the Greeks at Kyme, 388;
 late beginning of coinage in, 265; pirates
 from, 304; Roman *sitōnai* in, 389; traders
 from, 233
Eubolos of Elateia, 137, 148
Euhesperides, amphora imports to 127; murex
 fishing at, 357
Eumenes II (king of Pergamon), 111, 334, 401
Eupalinos of Megara, 46
Euripides, 309, 369
Euromos, vineyards in, 173

famine, 80, 333, 337, 435, 529n57; drought
 and, 65–67; malnutrition and, 49; in
 Rome, 336, 388
fertility rates, 42–43, 49–50, 70

figs, 129, 160, 341, 403
Finley, Moses I., 13–15, 146; on absentee
 landlords, 167; on consumer loans, 280;
 on division of labor, 108; on Peloponnesian War aftermath, 149; Polanyi and, 8,
 14–15; Weber and, 8, 13–14, 27, 167, 206
fishing and fish, 175–87; Braudel on, 175–76,
 184; markets for, 177, 184–87; rights to,
 181–84, 484n51; salt for, 176, 179–81;
 smoking of, 180. *See also* coastal waters,
 herring, ships, tuna,
fishmongers, 241, 310, 492n85
Flament, Christophe, 278
flax. *See* linen manufacturing
flour mills, 195–98, 208–11; grinding stones
 for, 196–97, 368, 378
flower cultivation, 130
Fordism, 213
Foucault, Michel, 499n60
fraud, 253, 316; Demosthenes on, 235; fines
 for, 249, 256; profiteering from, 255; with
 weights and measures, 240–42
"free rider" system, 371, 374–75, 380
Friedman, Milton, 276–77

Gallant, Thomas W., 176–77, 179
game theory, 6–7, 25–26, 435
Garnsey, Peter, 66, 511n144, 523n56
garum (fish sauce), 180, 482nn31–32
Gauthier, Philippe, 112, 314
gender norms, 154; sex ratio and, 53, 153. *See
 also* women
German Historical School of Political Economy, 4–5, 7–9, 12
Gill, David W. J., 371–72, 519n164
Gini coefficient, 108, 145, 476n7
glassmaking, 220–21, 354
Glotz, Gustave, 52
goats, 38, 73, 133–37, 139; hair of, 360,
 516n97; prices for, 136, 257–58; wineskins
 from, 173
gold, 262t, 275; coinage of, 261–62, 265; electrum and, 186, 261, 264, 269, 301
Gomme, Arnold W., 41
Gordion, imports of Attic pottery to, 84
Gortyn, 100; code, 43, 154, 230, 322; imports of
 grain to, *412*; law on bronze coinage of, 272
grain commissioners (*sitōnai*), 333–34, 337,
 385–86, 389–92
grain and grain production, 119–22; Athenian, 158, 202, 405–12; climate and, 120,

158, 341, 393; Egyptian, 120, 162, 300; livestock-raising versus, 120–21, 132, 141, 170; olive cultivation and, 159, 347; requisition of, 396–99; for self-consumption, 200–201; stockpiling of, 160, 331–38; transit fees of, 297; transport costs and, 365t, 366–67, 397–99; yield ratios of, 168–69. *See also* barley, wheat

grain sales, 253, 300, 358; city purchase funds for, 306, 333–35, 338; inspectors of, 239–41, 247–48, 314–15, 331, 404; price controls for, 254–56, 258, 306, 325–27, 394–95; regulation of, 315, 331–38, 393–99; royal contributions to, 399–402; samples for, 309; taxation of, 395–97; trade strategies for, 384–414

grapes. *See* wine production

Gresham's law , 21, 252

Grotius, Hugo, 181–82

Grove, Alfred T., 31–32

growth, division of labor and, 110; economic analysis and, xxi–xxv; finance and, 285; growth rates, 199–208; institutions, technology and 95; market and, 429, 436–37; phases of, 60–63, 99, 214–20; taxes and, 305; the city-state and, 96–97, 101–3; trade and, 346

gymnasiums, 47, 74, 111, 333

Hadrian (Roman emperor), 257, 298, 310, 405, 502n43

Halai (Boiotia), sea-activities at, 369

Halieis (Argolis), ceramic imports to, 363; oil production at, 361; sea-activities at, 178, 361

Halstead, Paul, 119, 196, 472n13

Hamaxitos, salt from, 180

Hansen, Mogens H., 41, 55, 477n30

Harpocration, 310

Harris, Edward, 189

Harris, William V., 52

Hasebroek, Johannes, 11

Hayek, Friedrich, 5, 450n12

Heckscher, Ohlin, and Samuelson (HOS) model, 345

Hekaton of Rhodes, 300

Helike, tsunami at, 373

Hellespont, *34*, 67, 179, 186, 359

Heracleides Criticus, 45, 317, 324, 359, 403, 516n93

Heraklean Way, 302

Herakleia (island), ban on goat raising in, 139

Herakleia Pontika, amphoras from, 186, 367; mines in the hinterland of, 353

Herakleides of Salamis, 333

Herakleion-Thonis (Egypt), 422

Hermione, 355, 361–64

Hermokopid scandal, 125, 130, 172, 216, 480n129

Hero of Alexandria, 76–79, 95

Herodotus, 92–93, 217; on agriculture, 119; on climate, 47, 64–65; on Cyrus of Persia, 234–35; on exchange, 268; on flax, 355; on Spartan population, 145; on Theran emigration, 67–68; on Xerxes of Persia, 369

Heroninos, 167

herring, 175, 184–85. *See also* fishing

Hesiod, 110, 119, 155, 161

Hierapolis (Phrygia), sawmill relief, 77; textile production at, 84, 193, 354

Hierapytna, cattle raising and expansion of, 140–41, 184; dispute over the island of Leuke, 141, 184

Hieron II of Syracuse, 88, 185, 193, 310

Hieron (town and sanctuary), role of navigation hub of, 281, 300–1, 304

Himera, Battle of, 185

Hin, Saskia, 56

Hippocrates, 44, 47–48

Hippodamian city layout, 45–46

Histiaia, 369, creditor from, 391; import of grain to, 386–87, 392

Historical School. *See* German Historical School of Political Economy

Hodkinson, Stephen, 106

Hoffman, Philip, xxii

Holland, 47, 504n89; economic development of, 205, 214, 219, 305

Homer, 119; animal husbandry in, 132, 139, 474n72; description of Crete by, 100; works of: *Iliad*, 97, 100, 139; *Odyssey*, 100–101, 132, 191, 317

homo economicus, 6, 11, 16–28

homo politicus, 11, 24

homosexuality, 51, 70

honey, 130–31, 157, 341, 403; as preservative for dyes, 362; prices of, 135, 171

Hopkins, Keith, "tax and trade" model, 297

hoplites, 102, 363; costs incurred by, 109; estates owned by, 143

Horden, Peregrine, 31–32, 79–80, 89, 293, 517n102

horses, 134, 138, 163

Hypaipa, textile production at, 193
Hypatia of Alexandria, 219
Hyperides, 235, 244, 254, 309–10

Ialysos, farms in, 156
Iberia, exports to, 368, 373; mines from, 265; road to, 302; salted food from, 186; trade with Greeks and Etruscans, 233
Imbros, Athenian control of and grain production at, 105, 334, 405, 408, 410–11, 419
India, ancient trade with, 281, 352, 366; sugarcane in, 130
Industrial Revolution, 12, 20, 206, 211; steam engine and, 17, 77–79, 209
infant mortality, 44, 49–51
infanticide, 42, 51–52
innovation. *See* technological innovation
institutionalism, 16–18; evolution of, 3, 16–17, 25–27; New Institutional Economics and, 19–25; of Polanyi, 11–13
insurance, 90, 228
international trade, 339–43, 402–9; commercial networks of, 339, 345–47, 351–53, 364–80; division of labor and, 343–47, 344t, 379–80; information networks of, 235, 239, 250–54, 299–301, 384; licenses for, 287–90, 395, 412, 419–20; niches for, 358–61; redistribution of, 376–79, 394, 404; regional supply and, 364–68; security of, 302–5, 318; strategies of, 381–414; textiles and, 353–58
Iron Age, 96, 99–101, 220; animal husbandry during, 132–33; silver hoards from, 261
iron, 100–101, 150, 263, 353; production of, 262–63, 497n7; transport costs of, 367; value of, 262t
Isocrates, 164, 340; on business contracts, 322; on *emporion*, 312–13, 317; deme of, 146
Itanos, 184; economic conflicts with neighbors, 140–41, 184

Jardé, Auguste, 146
Jason of Pherai, 163, 386
Jerome (saint), 104, 399
Jesus, the Temple money changers and, 246
Jones, Nicholas, 155–56
Jongman, Willem M., 347
Justinian the Great, Byzantine emperor, 230

Kallistratos of Athens, reorganizes the finances of Macedon, 295

Kalynda, 298
Kamiros, common territory with Lindos, 140; figs from, 129; road network at, 81; sacrifice for rain at, 161
Karia, 38; coinage in, 264; controlled by Rhodes between 188 and 166 BCE, 417, 419; figs from, 129; form of settlement in, 157; octopus from, 179. *See also* Kalynda, Keramos, Mylasa, Pidasa, Pisye, Pladasa, Stratonikeia, Theangela
karpos ("fruits of the earth"), 312
Karystos, 281–84, 369; monies borrowed by, 391–92, import of grain to, *412*
Kassandreia, 113–15, 150, 165, 291, 370–71
Kassandros (king of Macedon), 112–15, 151, 165, 291
Kassiterides islands ("Tin Islands"), 98, 353
Kassope, meat and seafood consumption at, 133
Kastanas, meat consumption at, 132–33
kathestēkuia timē (official price), 256, 326, 433, 496n56
Kaunos, figs from, 129; fishing and salt at, 179–80; imports of tiles to, *366*; political life at, 265; tax and trade at, 298–99, 311; tribute to Rhodes, 295. *See also* Zenon of Kaunos
Kelts, 151–52, 302, 305
Keos, sites and population of, 56, 58, 59t, 145, 164; circulation of coins from, 61; ochre from, 352, 358; import of grain to, *412*
Keramic Gulf, 32, *34*, 37–38, 156, 294
Keramos, 294
Kerkyra, slave revolts in, 228; trade in, 138; tuna fishing in, 178; wine production in, 123, 127
Kersobleptes (king of Thrace), revenues of, 295
Keynesian economics, 7, 276–77
Kibyra, trade relations of, 298; worked iron from, 84
Klazomenai, oil production in, 197; requisitions to finance grain import in, 333, 392
Kleomenes of Naukratis, 300, 384, 412, 433
klērouchoi (land-lot-holders), 114–17, 470n79
Knidos, 392, amphoras of, 126; 243, 378; imports of tiles to, *366*; ports of, 90; wine production and sales of, 126, 172, 371
Knoepfler, Denis, 290
Knossos, imports of grain to, *412*; law on redhibition, 254; Mycenaean kingdom of, 97–98, 100, 132

Kolb, Frank, 57
Kolchis, flax from, 355
Kondaia (Thessaly), transit fee (*paragōgion*) at, 295–96
Kos, amphoras from, 378; decree for a Tyrian, 289; fishing in, 183–84; harvest festival in, 121; import of grain to, *412*; iron deposits in, 353; silk production in, 190, 193, 195; wine production and sales in, 126, 172, 351, 371
Kotys I (king of Thrace), 301
Krates of Chalkis, 165
Kyaneai, land occupation in, 57, 157, 164
Kyklades, cattle raising in the, 135, 139; climate of the, 40; coins from the Kykladic cities in the Taranto hoard, 367; fishing in the, 177; honey production in the, 131; import of grain to, *412–413*; iron deposits in the, 353; monies borrowed by the cities of the, 391; pirates in the, 387; population of the, 63; wood resources of the, 74
Kyme (Aeolis), transit fees in, 297
Kyme (Italy), trade conflict at, 388–90, 392
Kyparissia, customs law, 308–9
Kythera, imports of grain to, *412*; murex fishing at, 357
Kythnos, cheese from, 358, 360, 366; import of grain to, *413*
Kyzikos, 112, 150; electrum coinage of, 264; fishing at, 186; religious festival and fair at, 299

Lake Kopais, ecology of, 35, 135, 164–6; fishes from, 185
Lakonia. *See* Sparta
Lamian War, 374, 416, 525n111
Landels, John G., 76–77
Laodikeia (Phrygia), textile production at, 193
laoi (dependent peasants), 150, 155, 226, 489n1
Larisa (Thessaly), exports of grain to Athens from, 412; import of grain to, *412*; internal land colonization in, 150, 166; land register in, 154
latifundian system, 148–49
Lato, treaty with Olous, 81, 291, 302, 318
Laurion mines, 60–61, 73–74, 194, 202, 263, 265, 272–74, 276–78, 371–72, 416, 419, 423, 426–27, 437
Le Goff, Jacques, 84
Le Roy Ladurie, Emmanuel, 39

leather goods, 133, 191, 193, 358
Lebedos, synoecism with Teos, 333–34, 394, 400
Lemnos, Athenian control of and grain production at, 105, 334, 405, 408, 410–11, 419; fishing in, 178; salt pans at, 358; volcanic soils of, 35
leprosy, 48
Lesbos, iron deposits in, 353; unequal development of the cities of, 293–94, 369; wines from, 126–27. *See also* Methymna, Mytilene
Leuke (island), fishing rights in, 141, 184, 484n59
Leuktra, Battle of, 145, 148
Lévy, Edmond, 106
lighthouses, 91, 465n113
Lindos, *agoranomos* in, 237; common territory with Kamiros, 140
Linear B writing, 97–98, 100, 220
linen manufacturing, 190, 353–55, 358
Lipari islands, alum and alum amphoras from, 354, 357
List, Friedrich, 4
livestock. *See* animal husbandry
Livy, 68–69; on grain supplies, 335–36, 367, 387–89, 398, 410, 432
Lo Cascio, Elio, 56
loans, 217, 247, 261, 363, 397; collateral for, 270, 279–80, 283; "consumer," 280; for grain shipments, 316; interest rates on, 217, 247, 279–83, 303; maritime, 280–85, 315–16, 373–74, 377, 404; for ransom, 303; by religious sanctuaries, 279, 291; for starting workshops, 192, 280; types of, 278–81. *See also* credit
Lohmann, Hans, 81
Lucian, 43
Luristan, tin from, 98, 353
Lykia, archaeological survey in, 56–57; coinage of, 264; controlled by Rhodes between 188 and 166 BCE, 417, 419; growth in, 63. *See also* Aperlai, Kaunos, Kyaneai, Lykian League, Myra, Oinoanda, Xanthos
Lykian League, 298
Lysias, 189, 310; works of: *Against the Grain Dealers*, 256–57, 315, 495n154; *On the Property of Aristophanes*, 476n14
Lysimachos (king of Macedon), 113, 115, 150
Lysippus, 370

Lytle, Ephraim, 181–82, 481n12, 483n57, 484n65–66, 496n158–59, 505n23, 516n86, 516n93

Maccabean revolt, 104
Macedon (kingdom of), conquers the Persian Empire, 54; 96–97; controls Greece, 61, 149, 222, 304, 309, 374, 387, 416–17; defeated by Rome and under its control, 207, 397; notables of, 166–67; royal coinage of, 151, 273, 421; royal land in, 111–16. *See also* Kallistratos of Athens, Amyntas III, Philip II, Alexander the Great, Kassandros, Lysimachos, Antigonos I, Antigonos II, Antigonos III, Philip V
Macedon (region), alum from, 354; cattle raising in, 137; climate of, 36–37; farms in 151–52, 194; iron deposits in, 353; *laoi* in, 226; population of, 55, 64; relief of, 34; timber from, 74, 91. *See also* Methone, Kassandreia, Kastanas, Mieza, Pella
Macedonian kingdoms, 111, 114, 199, 207, 228, 273, 400
Magnesia on the Maeander, arbitration by judges from, 141, 184; coins of, 273; colonists from, 63; market at, 236–37, 245; treaty with Miletos, 228; treaty with Phokaia, 288
Malanima, Paolo, 56
malaria, 48
Malthus, Thomas, 16, 54
Mann, Michael, 452n57
Manning, Joseph G., 56
manure, 121, 129–30, 133, 147, 169, 480n119. *See also* agricultural production
marble, 358, 364; sawing of, 211; transport of, 81, 84–85
Marek, Christian, 298
Maresha, imports of oil and wine to, 350; *sēkōma* at, 242
market system, xxiv–xxv, 306, 415–38; accounting techniques and, 97–98, 155, 218, 267, 309; of agricultural products, 171–74; commercial courts and, 317–25; competition in, 6, 16, 295, 345; economic growth and, 203–6; "fair price" in, 331–32; for fish, 177, 184–87; "invisible hand" of, 5, 383, 430; mutual trade in, 382–84; opportunity costs in, 124; Polanyi on, 14–15; predation and, 415, 418–19; price fluctuations in, 171–72, 331–32, 432–33,

494n139; risk management and, 429–38; self-consumption and, 199–203, 350
Maroneia, inland roads from, 81; wine of, 126, 162
marriage, 19, 42; age of, 42–43, 49–50, 70; divorce and, 42–43; loans for, 280; widowhood and, 42–43. *See also* dowries
Martial (Marcus Valerius Martialis), 432–33
Marx, Karl, 4–5, 17–18
Masinissa (king of Numidia), 334
Massalia (Marseilles), coins of, 264, 367; merchants from, 377; roofs in, 46; ships found at, 86; shipwreck near 376
medicine, 43–49, 130, 358, 456n79
Medieval Climate Anomaly (MCA), 39–40
Megara, 250, 358; textile workshops of, 193, 355–56, 358
Megarian Decree, 250, 286–287, 358
Meier, Mischa, 105–6
Melitaia (Achaia Phthiotis), *agoranomoi* of, 249
Melos, alum from, 354; archaeological survey at, 56, 58; climate of, 65; financial compensation paid by Cyrene, 318; fishing at, 178; sites and population of, 59t; volcanic relief of, 32
Menander, 75
Mende, amphoras from, 152, 186, 281, 378; wine from, 126, 162, 281–82, 369–71
Menger, Carl, 5
mercantilism, 343, 512n6; Foucault on, 499n60
mercenaries, 109, 469n53
merchant's dilemma, 300
Mesopotamia, economic structures of, 98, 102–3, 106–8, 221, 226, 261, 266–67; imports of natron and alum from Egypt, 355
Messenia, population of, 55, 63, archaeological survey in, 56; helots of, 105–6; lost by Sparta, 148. *See also* Andania, Kyparissia, Pylos
metallurgy, 73–76, 204, 220, 352–53; bronze, 220; comparative values of metals in, 262t; copper, 98–100, 353; iron, 100–101, 150, 262–63, 353, 367; tin, 98–100, 353; water power for, 211. *See also* silver
Metellus, Quintus Caecilius, 396–98
Methana-Arsinoe (Argolis), exploitation of coastal resources, 181, 183; volcano of, 32
Methone (Macedon), early-Archaic excavations at, 346; decree on grain imports of, 419
Methymna, 293, 369

metics, 61, 143, 459n144; property rights of, 226–27, 229

metronomoi (controllers of measures), 239, 241, 496n166

Meyer, Eduard, 2–4

microeconomics, 6, 20, 208–9

Midas, 229

midwives, 48, 457n99

Mieza (Bottiaia), land sales at, 153

Miletos, 321; market law of, 240; textiles of, 193, 356, 357; treaty with Olbia, 321

millet cultivation, 120

millstones, 196–97, 368, 378

Mises, Ludwig von, 5

Mitchell, Stephen, 81

Mithridates VI (king of Pontos), 274

"model life tables," 41

modernists, primitivists versus, 2–4, 11, 13–15, 27, 207

modernity, 219–21

Mokyr, Joel, 218

money, 340, 342; functions of, 260, 274–76; as institution, 271–74; "veil" of, 276. *See also* coinage

monopoly, 6, 433, 436, 514n62; Aristotle on, 215–16

monopsony, 6, 327, 338, 433, 436

Montchrestien, Antoine de, 341, 512n6

Montesquieu, 234–35

Morris, Ian, 57, 145, 205

mortality rates, 41–51, 70

murex, 182, 184, 194, 242, 356–58, 361–63. *See also* dyes

Mycenaean kingdoms, 97–102

Mykenai, Mycenaean kingdom of, 97, 99

Mylasa, land leases of, 173; decrees from, 265; buys track of land from Kindye, 294

Myra, tax document from, 298

Mytilene, import of grain to, 292, 399, *412*; joint coinage with Phokaia, 264; prosperity of, 293, 358, 369

Naples, ceramic production and trade at, 375–76

Naples (kingdom of), 138

Nash, John, 25, 435

natron, 293, 349, 353–55, 357

"natural advantages," 296, 339–41, 344, 358, 380–81

Naukratis, Hellenion of, 320; natron production near, 355

navigational techniques, 88–91, 220

Naxos (Kyklades), climate in, 65; fishing in, 178

Naxos (Sicily), ceramic workshops at, 190

Netherlands. *See* Holland

New Institutional Economics (NIE), 19–22

Newcomen, Thomas, 77–78, 95, 462n37

Nikaia, rivalry with Nikomedia, 287–88

Nikomedia, Dio Chrysostom on, 206, 287–88, 297, 436; marble from, 358; Pliny the Younger on, 84–85, 91–92; rivalry with Nikaia, 287–88

Nile, canal to the Red Sea, 92; Canopic mouth of the, 422; symbolic value of the water of the, 362

Nisyros, *aspalathos* from 352; imports of tiles to, *366*; millstones from, 196–97, 368, 378; volcano of, 32

Nordhaus, William D., 433, 450n13

Norfolk agricultural revolution, 169–70

North, Douglass C., 19–22

Ober, Josiah, xxii, 204

ochre, 352, 358

Odrysian kings (Thrace), 81, 295. *See also* Kotys I, Kersobleptes

Oinoanda, festival and fair at, 257

Olbia (Black Sea), currency decree of, 271, 301; *deigma* at, 310, treaty with Miletos, 321

Olbia (Gaul), seafood at, 186–87

olive oil, 127–29, 333, 341; as athletic prize, 405; grain cultivation and, 159, 347; preservative for dyes with, 362; press for, 195–98, 220, 361; sale of, 253, *328*, 348, 511n144; Solon's law on, 403–4; transport costs of, 365t

Olous, treaty with Lato, 81, 291, 302, 318

Olynthos, Chalkidian League and, 112; destruction of, 112, 204; grain and olive crushers at, 195–196; role of the market at, 203; textile production at, 191, 195–96; urbanism of, 46–47, 72; wealth of, 204

Orchomenos, agreement with Eubolos of Elateia, 136–37, 139; Battle of, 152; drainage at, 165

Oropos, grain import to, 332–33; control by Athens and grain production at, 405, 410

Ostia, 308, 367, 388

Ovid, 199–200

oxen, 81, 93, 121; during Bronze Age, 162–63; estate size and, 147; renting of, 474n79; for sacrifice, 163–64; sale of, 135–36, 254; water for, 134–35

palace economies, xxv, 97–101, 226
Panaitios, 125, 135–36
panēguris (religious festival), 236–38, 249; tax exemption during, 299
Pangaion (Mount), mines of, 265
Pantikapeion, emporion of, 311, 399; salt fish from, 187
Paoli, Ugo Enrico, 323
paper-making, 221
paramonē clause, 227
Pareto, Vilfredo, 6
Paros, *agoranomoi* of, 245–46, 248, 331; amphoras from, 378; grain imports to, *412*; marble from, 85, 358; public archives at, 322; refuse service at, 45
Patras, textile production at, 355
Pausanias, 178, 310, 355, 357
Pearson, Harry W., 202
Peisistratos, tyrant of Athens, 46, 104
Pella, agora of, 236
Pellene, water management at, 45
Peloponnesian War, 2, 43, 217, 410, 419; military spending during, 109; origins of, 296, 358; "plague" of Athens during, 48; poverty after, 149; slave revolt during, 228
Pelousion, customs document from, 131, 171, 293, 360
pentēkostē tax, 291, 308–9, 330
Peparethos, wine production of, 126, 351, 370
Peraia (Achaia Phthiotis), management of the agora at, 249
perfume, 193, 328, 348, 352, 366; containers for, 514n40; flowers for, 130; oleaster for, 128; *sturax* for, 359–60
Pergamon, 295, 375
Pericles, 200, 203, 410; public works policies of, 214; on Spartan trade rules, 286–87. *See also* Megarian Decree
perioikoi (peripheral cities), 145, 270
periphery-center model, 348–51, 416–17
Persepolis, Achaemenid accounting systems at, 267
Persian Empire, 299–300; coins of, 264, 266–68; property rights in, 225–26. *See also* Cyrus, Darius, Persepolis, Xerxes
Persian Wars, 96, 268, 277, 419

Persson, Karl G., 529n57
Phainippos, estate of, 146–48, 171
Phaistos, archaeological survey at, 56
Pharsalos, grant of land at, 145
Phaselis, merchants from, 281–82, 284–85, 315, 377; treaty with Athens, 319–21; ships in Egypt in 475 BCE, 293
Philadelphia (Phrygia), textile production at, 193
Philemon and Baucis, 199–200
Philip II (king of Macedon), 204, 295; destruction of Chalkidian League by, 112; destruction of Olynthos by, 46
Philip V (king of Macedon), 129, 150–51, 295
Philippoi, 166
Philomelion, Roman tax in grain at, 83
Philostratus, 394, 522n50
Phleious, agricultural products from, 130, 297
Phocylides of Miletos, 109
Phoenicians, 349; coins of, 264–65; during Iron Age, 101; during Persian Wars, 299–300. *See also* shipwrecks/Ashkelon
Phokaia, joint coinage with Mytilene, 264; traders feared by Chios, 377; treaty with Magnesia on the Maeander, 288
Phokion, 149
Phokis, sites and population in, 58, 59t. *See also* Elateia, Boulis
phormos, 315, 495n154, 506n50
Physiocrats, 202
Pidasa, wants to be connected to the sea, 81, 294; exports from, 173
pigs, 133, 162–63; price of, 257–58, *327*, 329. *See also* animal husbandry
Pindar, 159, 405
Pindos mountains, *34*, 36, 65; livestock-raising in, 137–38
piracy, 182–83, 281, 283, 302–4, 415, 504n76
Piraeus, 46, 90; *deigma* of, 310; development of, 293–94; grain sales in, 315
Pistiros, 81
Pisye, expansion of, 294
Pithekoussai, 346
Pladasa, absorbed by Pisye, 294; loan to, 165–66
plague, 48, 133
Plataiai, Battle of, 62
Plato, on division of labor, 107–8, 187–88, 228; on fishing rights, 181–83; on international trade, 342, 343; on police, 246–47; on population growth, 50, 51; works of: *Critias,*

38; *Crito*, 38; *The Laws*, 50, 181–83, 231, 246–47, 343; *The Republic*, 50, 107, 108, 187–88, 228, 343

Plautus, 52, 252

Pliny the Elder, 123, 180, 195, 328, 354–58

Pliny the Younger, canal project of, 84–85, 91–92

Plutarch, 105, 106, 214; on agoras, 240; on Cato the Elder, 253; on Demosthenes, 309; on depopulation, 62; on dyes, 362; on international trade, 342; on land purchases, 154; on livestock-raising, 137; on salt production, 176–77; on Solon, 402–4; on Sulla, 152, 518n147; on wine production, 124, 171

Polanyi, Karl, 11–13, 26; Finley and, 8, 14–15; Weber and, 12–13, 15

polemarch (court official), 319–21, 332, 507n73

police, 308; urban, 45, 227, 243, 246–47

polis. See city-states

Pollux (lexicographer), 232, 309, 312, 355

Polybius, 53, 61–62, 186; on Black Sea trade, 351; on Bosporos transit fees, 298, 305; on Carthage treaties, 318–19; on educational funding, 218; on international trade, 340; on Rhodes earthquake, 310; on Theban judicial system, 317–18, 324

polygamy, 42–43. *See also* marriage

Pomeroy, Sarah B., 52

Pompeii, 204

Pontos, 304, 351, 368; grain exports of, 410–11, 411t, 419; transit fees to, 297; tuna from, 185–86; wine from, 371

Popper, Karl, 31

port facilities, 90–91

portage systems, 93–94, 466n129

Poseidippus, 53

Poseidon (deity), 33, 178

Posideia festival, 172

Praisos, relations with neighbors and destruction of, 141; rights granted to Stalai, 183–84

precipitation, 64–67, 65t, 406; constraints of, 35–38, *36–38*, 36t; drought and, 65–67, 159–61; grain cultivation and, 120, 158, 341; livestock-raising and, 135; olive cultivation and, 128

press, screw, 195–98, 200, 361

Priansos, agreement with Hierapytna, 141

price fluctuations, 6, 185; control of, 254–59, 306, 325–32, 338, 394–95; information networks on, 384; in market system,

171–72, 331–32, 432–33, 494n139; Polanyi on, 13–14; Xenophon on, 14–15, 110

Price, Simon, 55

Priene, end of the royal gifts at, 401; privileges of Larichos, 112; saltpans at, 180; *sitophulakes* at, 240; urbanism at, 45; villages near, 111

primitivists. *See* modernists

Pringsheim, Fritz, 231–32, 490n39

Prokonnesos, marble from, 358

property rights, 98; Aristotle on, 114, 226, 231, 489n2; in city-states, xxv, 116, 216, 418; of foreigners, 215; of metics, 226–27, 229; Persian, 225–26; trade and, 225–30; of women, 154

property, boundary stones of, 227; distribution of, 142–49; land grants of, 150; land leases of, 123, 129, 153, 182, 227, 269; real estate market for, 153–54, 216; in Roman law, 252; sizes of, 144t, 145–52; stewards of, 155, 157, 166, 167

propraxia, 501n11

prostitution, 236, 352

Prousa, difficult access to the sea of, 296; grain hoarding at, 394

Pseudo-Aeschines, 156

Pseudo-Aristotle, 160, 183, 302, 395

Pseudo-Demosthenes, works of: *Against Lacritus*, 187, 193, 281, 300–301, 306, 310, 315, 318, 323, 351, 369–70; *Against Phaenippus*, 146–48, 171; *Against Phormio*, 333, 508n76; *Against Zenothemis*, 94, 322–23; *On Halonnesus*, 520n3

Pseudo-Skylax, 300

Pseudo-Xenophon, 114, 339–40, 352–54, 411, 419

Ptolemy (geographer), 205

Ptolemy II, 122, 399, 401, 466n118

Ptolemy III, 375

Ptolemy IV, 233

Ptolemy XII Auletes, 399

Punic Wars, 367, 375, 398, 417, 432

Purcell, Nicholas, 31–32, 79–80, 89, 293, 517n102

Purpura, Gianfranco, 181–82

Puteoli, 376

Pylos, Mycenean kingdom of, 97–98; Nestor of, 139; sites and population of, 59t, 63

race and ethnicity, 157, 451n43

Rackham, Oliver, 31–32, 81

Raepsaet, Georges, 81–82
ransom, 281, 283, 303
Reden, Sitta von, 268
Reger, Gary, 327–28, 423, 502n34
rentier states, 437
reprisal, right of (*sulān*), 318
Rhodes, 156; agoras of, 225, 237; amphoras
    from, 84, 86, 126, 360, 378, 463n74; coins
    of, 271; customs duties of, 297–98, 305;
    earthquakes on, 33, 387, 401; education at,
    218, 401; grain trade of, 240, 386–87, 412;
    imports of grain to, *412*, 420; influence of,
    293, 294; port of, 90, 310–12; precipitation
    on, 68; security concerns of, 304–5; Ptol-
    emaic and Seleukid kingdoms and, 417,
    488n45; trade networks of, *366*; tribute
    paid to, 295; water system of, 46. *See also*
    Ialysos, Kamiros, Lindos, Rhodian Peraia
Rhodian Peraia, land leases from the, 123, 153;
    Pseudo-Aischines's estate in the, 156; tile
    production in the, 364, *366*. *See also* Amos
Ricardo, David, 5, 16, 259, 343–47, 344t
Robert, Louis, 179, 298
Robinson, D. M., 511n144
Rodbertus, Johann Karl, 4
Roman conquest and Roman Empire, 222,
    417; Athenian Empire versus, 217; decline
    of, 219; economic growth in, 205; epidem-
    ics in, 208; grain delivery by Athens to
    the Roman army, 410; Italian population
    of, 56; rise of, 207–8; tax exemptions and,
    295, 417. *See also* Augustus, Domitian,
    Trajan, Hadrian
Roman law, 230, 234; on fishing rights, 181;
    property in, 252; Todd on, 490n29
Rome (city), food shortage in, 68–9, 335–36,
    338, 387–90, 392; imports of grain from
    Italy and Sicily, 336; imports of grain from
    Sardinia, 367, 398; imports of grain from
    Thessaly, 396–99; in control of the grain
    of Sicily, 420; treaties between Carthage
    and, 318–19
Rosivach, Vincent J., 192
Rostovtzeff, Mikhail I., 15
Rousseau, Jean-Jacques, 203
royal land, civic land versus, 110–17
rule of law, 231
Russo, Lucio, 218

sacrifices, 138, 160–61, 163–64, 328
Sahlins, Marshall, 18

Saittai, textile production at, 193
Salamis (Cyprus), merchants from, 333, 377
Salamis, Battle of, 60, 277, 363
Sallares, R., 457n101
Saller, Richard, 205
salt production, 176, 179–81
salted foods, 180, 185–86, 236, 351
Samos, amphoras from, 86, 378; dependence
    on imports of, 68; fishing in 178; grain
    fund in, 333; outcasts at the Heraion of,
    47; five percent tax in kind on continen-
    tal territory of, 105, 334; prisoners put
    to work to build a moat, 92–93; trade of
    Samos, 376–77; tyranny at, 102; water
    supply at, 46
Samuelson, Paul A., 345, 433, 450n13
Sardinia, Sea Peoples and, 99; in the Treaties
    between Rome and Carthage, 319; grain
    from, 367, 398, 420, 432
Sardis, agreements between Miletos and, 288;
    masons' contract at, 246; security of reli-
    gious envoys from Ephesos at, 289, 302
sawmills, 77, 211, 213, 487n28
Scheidel, Walter, 41, 95; on "low-equilibrium
    trap," 460n145; on population growth,
    50–51; on sex ratios, 457n105
Schmoller, Gustav von, 4
Schumpeter, Joseph A., 78
science, economic growth and, 76–79, 197–98,
    218–19
"Sea Peoples" of late Bronze Age, 99, 467n13
sēkōma tables, 242
Selden, John, 181–82
Seleukid kingdom, 417; population of, 56;
    Rhodes and, 488n45; Roman conquest
    of, 207; salt monopoly in, 180; taxes in,
    104. *See also* Antiochos I, Antiochos II,
    Antiochos IV, Demetrios I
self-sufficiency, xxii, 80; Aristotle on, 229, 244,
    381; Isocrates on, 340; market system and,
    199–203, 350
Selinous, soil analysis and climate at, 40;
    "industrial district" at, 190; Selinous
    hoard, 272
Sellasia, Battle of, 387
Selymbria, grain shortage at, 160, 337, 389,
    395–96, 399, 433
sewers, hygiene and, 45
Shakespeare, William, 18
sheep, 132–38, 166; during Bronze Age,
    162–63; "covered," 135; manure of, 147;

prices for, 257; transhumance of, 138–41. *See also* wool

shellfish. *See* murex

shipping, 302–5; costs of, 80–81, 84, 91, 293, 307–8; loans for, 280–85, 315–16; protection of, 302–5, 318.

ships, 79–81, 84–88; ballast for, 196, 368, 374, 462n37; construction of, xxiv, 85–88, 204, 303; medieval, 220; navigational techniques of, 88–91, 220; paddlewheel, 79, 462n40; sails of, 88; sizes of, 86–88, 87t, 326; speeds of, 89; taxation of, 307–8. *See also* fishing, shipwrecks

shipwrecks, 86, 87t, 90, 282–84, 346, 348, 351, 369; 464n89; 513n28; specific: Alonnisos, 87t, 370; Ashkelon, 87t, 512n20; Cape Gelidonya, 98–99; El Sec, 368, 370, 378; Giglio, 513n28, Grand Congloué, 376, 378, 520n177; Kyra Panagia, 370, Kyrenia, 86, 94, 368, 378; Petrokaravo, 361, 364; Point Iria, 99; Porticello, 370; Serçe Limanı B, 378; Tektaş Burnu, 186; Uluburun, 87, 98–99; Varna, 186

Sicily, 40, 102; Carthaginian, 319, 417; ceramic workshops of, 190; coins of, 367; grain trade of, 83, 336, 389, 398, 420; slave revolt in, 228–29, 426; tuna from, 184–85

Sidon, coinage from, 264; grain merchants from, 332–33

Sikyon, imports of grain to, *412*; leather shoes from, 358; tyranny at, 102

silk, 84, 190, 195

silphion plant, 318, 358

silver, 263–64, 274–75, 277–78, 437; charcoal for, 461n6; coinage of, 261–62, 264–68, *265*, 373–74; value of, 262t, 275

Siphnos, silver mines of, 265; alum of, 358; soapstone of, 358, 516n89

sitophulakes (grain wardens), 239–40, 247–48, 314–15, 331, 404

Skione, amphoras from, 281; wine from, 370

Skyros, Athenian control of and grain production at, 105, 334, 405, 419; Dolopian pirates at, 302–3; honey production at, 131

slavery, 11, 226, 347, 348; in Athens, 61; of debtors, 106–7, 161, 469n48; democracy and, 218, 222; foundlings and, 52; in Roman Italy, 56; taxation of, 105; wealth inequality and, 214

slaves, 155, 182, 188; demographics of, 459n144; diet of, 121; fugitive, 228;

illnesses among, 253–54; literacy among, 217; manumission of, 191, 226–27, 489n5; piracy as source of, 302–3; revolts of, 127, 228–29, 426, 473n43, 529n47; sale of, 244–45, 253–54, 280, 307; supervision of, 157. *See also* Sparta/helots

Smith, Adam, 16, 259; on invisible hand, 5, 383, 430; on pin factory, 343–44

smuggling, 182–83, 288

Snodgrass, Anthony, 132

Socrates, 187–88, 192, 280, 457n99, 500n80

Solon, ban on foodstuffs exports except oil, 393, 403–4; economic reforms of, 106–7, 161, 226, 402, 410, 524n89; law on access to water, 159; law on apiaries, 130; law on the development of craft trades, 403

Sombart, Werner, 450n21

Sophocles, 140

Sparta, arable land at, 145; collapse of, 416; earthquake at, 33; elite consumption at, 138; "empire" of, 419; helots at, 105–6, 155, 226; inegalitarian character of the city of, 270; late minting of coinage at, 242–43; land ownership at, 148–49, 153–4, 228; law at Sparta, 230; literacy at, 217; market at, 108, 234; population of, 148; Spartan conservatism, 194; sport for female citizens at, 47; strict control of foreigners at, 286; wine at, 124. *See also* Messenia, *sussition*, Tyrtaeus

sponges, 182, 184, 359

Stalai, 141, 184–84

Starr, Chester G., 278

Ste. Croix, Geoffrey de, 146–48

steam engine, 17, 77–79; prototype of, xxiv, 76–79, 95; watermill and, 209

Stiglitz, Joseph E., 494n139

Strabo, 45, 53, 196, 353, 399; on Delos, 95, 417; on drainage projects, 165; on Iasos, 179; on slave population, 459n144; on Susa, 362; on *taricheiai* factories, 185; on watermill, 197

Stratonikeia, tries to control Keramos, 294; tribute to Rhodes, 295

Stroud, Ronald S., 105

sturax plant, 359–60, 516n96

Suder, Wiesław, 56

Sulla, 152, 310, 354, 518n147

sumbolaion, 244–45, 313, 319–22, 508n83. *See also* contracts

suntaxis, 111–12

Susa, Achaemenid treasures accumulated at, 331, 362–63

sussition (Spartan banquet), 124

Syracusan (ship), 88, 193

Syracuse, in the novel *Chaereas and Callirhoe*, 306–7; ship coming from, 322; Syracusan in Phoenicia, 299–300. *See also* Dionysios of Syracuse, Hieron II

Syros, freight cost of tiles to Delos, 80

Taras (Tarentum), murex fishing at, 357; fine textiles from, 358, 360. *See also* Archytas

taricheiai (salted foods), 180, 185–86, 236, 351

Tarn, William W., 52

taxation, 104–6, 253, 294–95, 334, 399–400, 410; of agoras, 236–38; of agricultural products, 294; of alum, 514n62; Aristotle on, 104, 107; for city grain funds, 334; customs duties and, 286–95, 307–9, 311; exemptions from, 287, 289, 292–95, 298–99, 301, 326, 329–30, 390, 417; *pentēkostē*, 291, 308–9, 330; rates of, 102–5; of royal cities, 111; Seleukid, 104; of ships, 307–8; smuggling and, 182–83, 288; of trade, 286–88, 293–99, 360; transit fees and, 295–99, 302, 387, 484n57

technological innovation, 11, 17, 76–79, 222; in agriculture, 161–64, 166–67, 170–71, 195–98; by artisans, 194–98; democracy and, 218–19; institutional change and, 95, 163–64, 194; pace of, 208–11; productivity gains from, 203, 208–11, 437; in ship building, 87–88, 204; supply and demand of, 211–19; in textile manufacturing, 194–95, 360–61; Thucydides on, 194

Teles, Cynic philosopher, 352

Teleutias, 177, 310

Telos, imports of tiles to, *366*

Tenedos, benefactors from T. at Ilion, 292; ferrymen from, 359, 376

Tenos, 153–54, female property at, 154; land market at, 153

Teos, grain exports banned at, 393–94, 404; grain fund at, 333–34, 400, 403; pirate attack against, 303; schools at, 218; synoecism with Lebedos, 333–34, 394, 400; wood and charcoal production in the hinterland of, 75

Terence (Roman playwright), 52

textile manufacturing, 190–95, 348, 353–58; goat hair for, 360, 516n97; linen and, 190,

353–55, 358; loans for, 192, 280; looms for, 78, 243; silk and, 84, 190, 195; women and, 192, 195, 196, 210–11, 280, 355, 360–61. *See also* alum, dyes, linen manufacturing, natron, wool

Thasos, amphoras from, 127, 172–73, 190, 360, 378; beacons or lighthouses at, 91; iron deposits in, 353; marble from, 85, 358; octopus from, 179; port regulation at, 86, 90, 308; refuse service at, 45; saltpans at, 181; wine from, 126, 130, 171–73, 233–34, 241, 297, 311–12, 316–17, 351, 360, 365t, 370–71; women's age at marriage at, 43

Theangela, honey from, 130–31, 358

Thebai at Mykale, alum from, 354

Thebes (Boiotia), creditors from, 391; empire of, 419; destruction of, 416; justice in, 317–18; shepherds from in Sophocles, 140; *sitōnai* from, 385–86, 392

Themistokles, 90

Theocritus, 121, 193

Theodosia, *emporion* of, 311, 399; salt fish for workers at, 187

Theophrastus, 350, 354; on charcoal production, 75, 461n17; on climate change, 479n108; on lignite mining, 72; works of: *Characters*, 250; *Enquiry into Plants*, 119, 461n17; *On Plant Physiology*, 119, 479n108; *On the Laws*, 250

Theopompus, 53, 106, 126

Theopropos of Aigina, 178

Thera, climate of, 65t, 67–68; colonization of Cyrene, 67–68; fishing at, 178; imports of grain to, *412*; volcano of, 32

Thespiai, estates in, 148; grain fund at, 333–5; land leases at, 153

Thessaly, cattle raising in, 136, 138; coins from Thessaly; exports of grain from, 386–87, 396–99, 420; murex fishing in, 357; relief of, 32–35. *See also* Kondaia, Larisa, Melitaia, Peraia, Pharsalos

Thonis. *See* Herakleion

Thrace, Athenian colonists in, 63, 149; controlled by Macedon, 152; *emporion* in central Thrace, 81, 84, 301–2; silver mines in, 263, 265; wines from, 162. *See also* Abdera, Maroneia, Odrysian kings, Pangaion (Mount), Philippoi, Pistiros

Thucydides, 217; on Athenian trade, 296–97; on Chios's slaves, 126–27; on Corinth, 379;

on innovation, 194; on Odrysian kingdom, 502n39; on portage of ships, 93; on Spartan trade, 286–87; on taxation, 104–5

Thyateira, textile production at, 193

tiles, 80, 243, 364–66, 365t, *366*, 517n111. *See also* ceramics

Timon of Syracuse, 392

tin, 98–100, 262t, 353

Tiryns, Mycenaean kingdom of, 97; size of sheep at, 162

Tmolos (Mount), crocuses from, 356

Toriaion/Tyriaion, 356

Torone, coins of, 370; decline in the Hellenistic period, 370

trades. *See* artisanal trades

Trajan (Roman emperor), 84–85

transaction costs, 19–22, 344; of agoras, 238, 259

transit fees, 295–99, 302, 387, 484n57

transportation, 74; costs of, 80–81, 84, 91, 293, 344, 364–67, 365t; maritime, 79–81, 84–88, 297, 368; overland, 80–84, 93–94

trapetum (olive press), 195–98, 220, 361

tribute, xxv, 111–12, 116, 266–68, 400; to Athens, 294, 303, 370; to Rhodes, 295

Troizen, exploitation of coastal resources, 181, 183; imports of grain to, 412t

tuberculosis, 48

tuna, 177–79, 184–86. *See also* fishing

typhus, 48

Tyre, coinage of, 264; decree of Kos for a Tyrian, 289

Tūrrhēnia. See Etruria

Tyrtaeus, on Spartan helots, 105–6

urban planning, 44–47

Varro, Marcus Terentius, 119, 128, 171

vault construction, 33, 205, 220

Veblen, Thorstein, 12, 19

Venice, public fleet of galleys, 385; trade networks of, 437; Venetian insurance rates, 90

Vidal-Naquet, Pierre, xxiii

Virgil, 356

viticulture. *See* wine production

Vitruvius, 44–45, 198

Volsci, 389–90

Walras, Léon, 6

water management, 164–65; cisterns and, 46, 49, 134–35, 159–60. *See also* precipitation, wells

watermill, 71, 197–98, 451n41; economics of, 208–11; endurance of, 203, 220; feudalism and, 17

Watt, James, 77, 462n37

wealth inequality, 215–16; gender norms and, 154; slavery and, 214

Weber, Max, 8–17, 219; on absentee landlords, 167; critics of, 450n21; on division of labor, 189; on economic rationality, 9–11, 19–22; on elites' incapacity, 213–14; Finley and, 8, 13–14, 27, 167, 206; on ideal types, 9; on institutions, 17–18, 21; Polanyi and, 12–13, 15; on race, 451n43; sociology of, 8–10, 12, 206–7

weights and measures, 75; in palace economy, 98; and *phormos*, 495n154, 506n50; supervision of, 239–42, 496n166

wells, 159–60

wheat, 120, 162, 406; precipitation and, 158; production of, 120–21, 169; sale of, 241, 300, 374; transport costs of, 82, 364–67, 365t. *See also* grain production

Williamson, Oliver E., 19–20

Wilson, Andrew, 95

wind, as a source of energy, xxiv, 79, 122, 180, 437; winds in the Aegean, 37–38, 85; navigation and, 86, 88–90, 359, 368–69

wine production, 170–74, 341, 348–49; Columella on, 167; estates for, 147, 151, 167; Plutarch on, 124, 171; press for, 195–98, 200; risks with, 158, 234; Theopompus on, 126

wine, 122–27, 347, 350–51; amphoras for, 125–27, 152, 370–71; contracts for, 233–34, 370; goatskins for, 173; prices of, 135, 172–73; quality of, 241, 253, 309; special varieties of, 125, 162; transport costs of, 365t

women, 195–97; divorced, 42–43; education of, 217; property rights of, 154; sex ratio, 53, 153; textile production by, 192, 195–96, 210–11, 280, 355, 360–61; widowed, 42–43

wood, 180; price of, 327–31, *327*; sale of, 147, 235–36, 242, 250, 315, 364, 509n110. *See also* charcoal

wool, 132–35, 138, 166; contracts for, 233; dyeing of, 354, 356–57; manufacturing of, 190–94, 353–55; sale of, 235, 239–42, 356, 492n75; transportation of, 84, 193. *See also* sheep; textile manufacturing workshops, Delian, 46, 328; metal, 74, 152; organization of, 187–92, 236, 352, 361, 374–79. *See also* amphora workshops and textile manufacturing

Wrigley, Edward A., 78

Xanthos, decrees from, 265; commercial taxes in, 299

Xenarchos, 492n85

Xenophon, 146, 236, 339; works of: *Cyropaedia*, 108; *Economics*, 119, 146, 154, 191, 300, 383; *Hellenica*, 108, 163, 177, 310; *Hieron*, 163–64; *Memorabilia*, 192; *On Hunting*, 355; *Poroi*, 14–15, 110, 373, 385, 395, 432. *See also* Pseudo-Xenophon

Xerxes I (king of Persia), 92, 369

Zenon of Kaunos, 116, 125, 162, 166–67, 312, 479n95

zero-sum game, 26, 435

Zeus (deity), 118, 200, 491n64; on coins, 273; as rain god, 160–61